KEY TO MAP PAGES OCEANIA, ASIA, EUROPE

(see back endpapers for Africa, North America and South America)

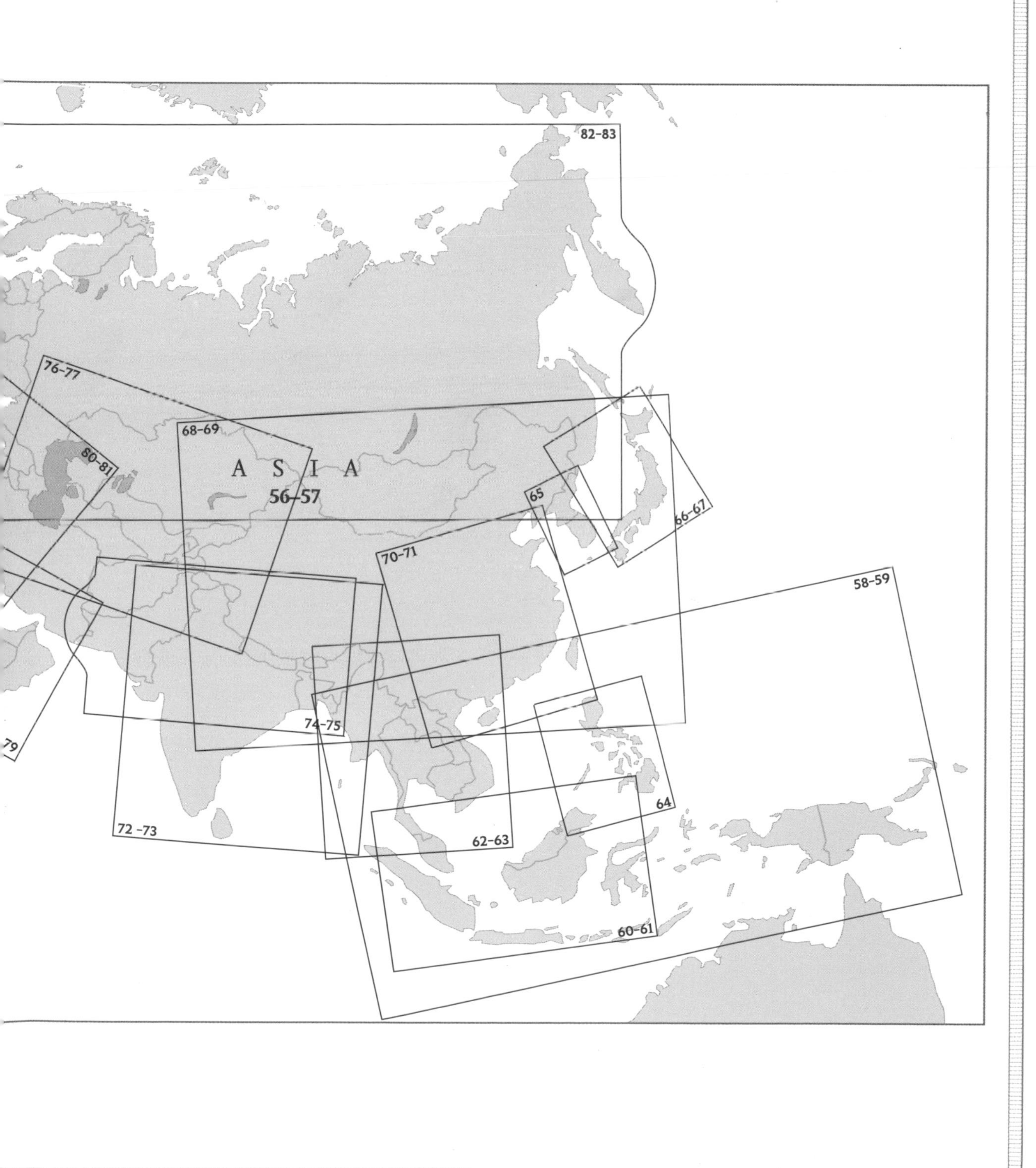

ATLAS OF THE WORLD

This 2010 edition published by Metro Books,
by arrangement with HarperCollins Publishers

Metro Books
122 Fifth Avenue
New York, NY 10011

ISBN 978-1-4351-1817-1

Printed and bound in Singapore

1 3 5 7 9 10 8 6 4 2

All mapping in this atlas is generated from Collins Bartholomew digital databases. Collins Bartholomew, the UK's leading independent geographical information supplier, can provide a digital, custom, and premium mapping service to a variety of markets.

For further information:
tel: +44 (0) 141 306 3752
e-mail: collinsbartholomew@harpercollins.co.uk
or visit our website at: www.collinsbartholomew.com

www.timesatlas.com
The world's most authoritative and prestigious world atlases.

THE TIMES DESKTOP ATLAS OF THE WORLD

METRO BOOKS
NEW YORK

CONTENTS

Pages	Title	Scale
	THE WORLD TODAY	
6–29	States and Territories of the World	
30–33	Continents and Oceans	
34–35	Climate	
36–37	Environment	
38–39	Population and Cities	
40–41	Telecommunications	
	ATLAS OF THE WORLD	
42–43	Introduction to Atlas of the World	
44–45	World Physical Features	
46–47	World Countries	
48–49	OCEANIA	1:40 000 000
50–51	Australia	1:16 000 000
52–53	Australia Southeast	1:6 000 000
54	New Zealand	1:6 000 000
55	Antarctica	1:36 000 000
56–57	ASIA	1:44 000 000
58–59	Southeast Asia	1:20 000 000
60–61	Malaysia and Indonesia West	1:9 600 000
62–63	Continental Southeast Asia	1:9 600 000
64	Philippines	1:9 600 000
65	North Korea and South Korea	1:5 200 000
66–67	Japan	1:6 000 000
68–69	China and Mongolia	1:20 000 000
70–71	China Central	1:9 600 000
72–73	South Asia	1:12 000 000
74–75	Pakistan, India North and Bangladesh	1:9 600 000
76–77	Central Asia	1:12 000 000
78–79	Arabian Peninsula	1:9 600 000
80–81	East Mediterranean	1:9 600 000
82–83	Russian Federation	1:24 000 000
84–85	EUROPE	1:20 000 000
86–87	European Russian Federation	1:12 000 000
88–89	Northeast Europe	1:4 800 000
90–91	Ukraine and Moldova	1:4 800 000
92–93	Scandinavia and Iceland	1:6 000 000
94–95	British Isles	1:4 800 000
96	Scotland	1:2 400 000
97	Ireland	1:2 400 000
98–99	England and Wales	1:2 400 000
100–101	Northwest Europe	1:2 400 000

Pages	Title	Scale
102–103	Central Europe	1:4 800 000
104–105	France and Switzerland	1:4 800 000
106–107	Spain and Portugal	1:4 800 000
108–109	Italy and The Balkans	1:4 800 000
110–111	Southeast Europe	1:4 800 000
112–113	AFRICA	1:36 000 000
114–115	Northwest Africa	1:16 000 000
116–117	Northeast Africa	1:16 000 000
118–119	Central Africa	1:12 000 000
120–121	Southern Africa	1:12 000 000
122–123	Republic of South Africa	1:6 000 000
124–125	NORTH AMERICA	1:32 000 000
126–127	Canada	1:20 000 000
128–129	Canada West	1:9 600 000
130–131	Canada East	1:9 600 000
132–133	United States of America	1:16 000 000
134–135	USA West	1:6 400 000
136–137	USA North Central	1:6 400 000
138–139	USA Northeast	1:6 400 000
140–141	USA Southeast	1:6 400 000
142–143	USA South Central	1:6 400 000
144–145	Mexico	1:9 600 000
146–147	Central America and the Caribbean	1:12 000 000
148–149	SOUTH AMERICA	1:28 000 000
150–151	South America North	1:16 000 000
152–153	South America South	1:16 000 000
154–155	Brazil Southeast	1:6 000 000
	OCEANS	
156–157	Pacific Ocean	1:72 000 000
158	Atlantic Ocean	1:72 000 000
159	Indian Ocean	1:72 000 000
160	Arctic Ocean	1:36 000 000
	WORLD FACTS AND FIGURES	
161	Contents	
162–167	World Statistics	
168–169	World Time Zones	
170–171	Geographical Tables	
172–173	Climate Around the World	
174–175	Useful Facts and Web Links	
176	Distance and Conversion Charts	
177–240	INDEX AND ACKNOWLEDGEMENTS	

All independent countries and populated dependent and disputed territories are included in this list of the states and territories of the world; the list is arranged in alphabetical order by the conventional name form. For independent states, the full name is given below the conventional name, if this is different; for territories, the status is given. The capital city name is the same form as shown on the reference maps.

The statistics used for the area and population are the latest available and include estimates. The information on languages and religions is based on the latest information on 'de facto' speakers of the language or 'de facto' adherents to the religion. The information available on languages and religions varies greatly from country to country. Some countries include questions in censuses, others do not, in which case best estimates are used. The order of the languages and religions reflect their relative importance within the country; generally, languages or religions are included when more than one per cent of the population are estimated to be speakers or adherents.

Membership of selected international organizations is shown for each independent country. Territories are not shown as having separate memberships of these organizations.

ABBREVIATIONS

CURRENCIES

CFA	Communauté Financière Africaine
CFP	Comptoirs Français du Pacifique

ORGANIZATIONS

APEC	Asia-Pacific Economic Cooperation
ASEAN	Association of Southeast Asian Nations
CARICOM	Caribbean Community
CIS	Commonwealth of Independent States
COMM.	The Commonwealth
EU	European Union
OECD	Organization of Economic Co-operation and Development
OPEC	Organization of Petroleum Exporting Countries
SADC	Southern African Development Community
UN	United Nations

AFGHANISTAN
Islamic State of Afghanistan

Area Sq Km	652 225	**Religions**	Sunni Muslim, Shi'a Muslim
Area Sq Miles	251 825	**Currency**	Afghani
Population	27 145 000	**Organizations**	UN
Capital	Kābul	**Map page**	76–77
Languages	Dari, Pushtu, Uzbek,Turkmen		

ALBANIA
Republic of Albania

Area Sq Km	28 748	**Religions**	Sunni Muslim, Albanian Orthodox, Roman Catholic
Area Sq Miles	11 100	**Currency**	Lek
Population	3 190 000	**Organizations**	UN
Capital	Tirana (Tiranë)	**Map page**	109
Languages	Albanian, Greek		

ALGERIA
People's Democratic Republic of Algeria

Area Sq Km	2 381 741	**Religions**	Sunni Muslim
Area Sq Miles	919 595	**Currency**	Algerian dinar
Population	33 858 000	**Organizations**	OPEC, UN
Capital	Algiers (Alger)	**Map page**	114–115
Languages	Arabic, French, Berber		

American Samoa
United States Unincorporated Territory

Area Sq Km	197	**Religions**	Protestant, Roman Catholic
Area Sq Miles	76	**Currency**	United States dollar
Population	67 000	**Map page**	49
Capital	Fagatogo		
Languages	Samoan, English		

ANDORRA
Principality of Andorra

Area Sq Km	465	**Religions**	Roman Catholic
Area Sq Miles	180	**Currency**	Euro
Population	75 000	**Organizations**	UN
Capital	Andorra la Vella	**Map page**	104
Languages	Spanish, Catalan, French		

ANGOLA
Republic of Angola

Area Sq Km	1 246 700	**Religions**	Roman Catholic, Protestant, traditional beliefs
Area Sq Miles	481 354	**Currency**	Kwanza
Population	17 024 000	**Organizations**	OPEC, SADC, UN
Capital	Luanda	**Map page**	120
Languages	Portuguese, Bantu, local languages		

Anguilla
United Kingdom Overseas Territory

Area Sq Km	155	**Religions**	Protestant, Roman Catholic
Area Sq Miles	60		
Population	13 000	**Currency**	East Caribbean dollar
Capital	The Valley	**Map page**	147
Languages	English		

ANTIGUA AND BARBUDA

Area Sq Km	442	**Religions**	Protestant, Roman Catholic
Area Sq Miles	171		
Population	85 000	**Currency**	East Caribbean dollar
Capital	St John's	**Organizations**	CARICOM, Comm., UN
Languages	English, creole	**Map page**	147

ARGENTINA
Argentine Republic

Area Sq Km	2 766 889	**Religions**	Roman Catholic, Protestant
Area Sq Miles	1 068 302		
Population	39 531 000	**Currency**	Argentinian peso
Capital	Buenos Aires	**Organizations**	UN
Languages	Spanish, Italian, Amerindian languages	**Map page**	152–153

ARMENIA
Republic of Armenia

Area Sq Km	29 800	**Religions**	Armenian Orthodox
Area Sq Miles	11 506	**Currency**	Dram
Population	3 002 000	**Organizations**	CIS, UN
Capital	Yerevan (Erevan)	**Map page**	81
Languages	Armenian, Azeri		

Aruba
Self-governing Netherlands Territory

Area Sq Km	193	**Religions**	Roman Catholic, Protestant
Area Sq Miles	75		
Population	104 000	**Currency**	Aruban florin
Capital	Oranjestad	**Map page**	147
Languages	Papiamento, Dutch, English		

Ascension
Dependency of St Helena

Area Sq Km	88	**Religions**	Protestant, Roman Catholic
Area Sq Miles	34		
Population	1 122	**Currency**	Pound sterling
Capital	Georgetown	**Map page**	113
Languages	English		

AUSTRALIA
Commonwealth of Australia

Area Sq Km	7 692 024	**Religions**	Protestant, Roman Catholic, Orthodox
Area Sq Miles	2 969 907		
Population	20 743 000	**Currency**	Australian dollar
Capital	Canberra	**Organizations**	APEC, Comm., OECD, UN
Languages	English, Italian, Greek	**Map page**	50–51

Australian Capital Territory (Federal Territory)

Area Sq Km	2 358	**Population**	329 500
Area Sq Miles	910	**Capital**	Canberra

Jervis Bay Territory (Territory)

Area Sq Km	73	**Population**	611
Area Sq Miles	28		

New South Wales (State)

Area Sq Km	800 642	**Population**	6 844 200
Area Sq Miles	309 130	**Capital**	Sydney

Northern Territory (Territory)

Area Sq Km	1 349 129	**Population**	207 700
Area Sq Miles	520 902	**Capital**	Darwin

Queensland (State)

Area Sq Km	1 730 648	**Population**	4 070 400
Area Sq Miles	668 207	**Capital**	Brisbane

South Australia (State)

Area Sq Km	983 482	**Population**	1 558 200
Area Sq Miles	379 725	**Capital**	Adelaide

Tasmania (State)

Area Sq Km	68 401	**Population**	489 600
Area Sq Miles	26 410	**Capital**	Hobart

Victoria (State)

Area Sq Km	227 416	**Population**	5 110 500
Area Sq Miles	87 806	**Capital**	Melbourne

Western Australia (State)

Area Sq Km	2 529 875	**Population**	2 061 500
Area Sq Miles	976 790	**Capital**	Perth

AUSTRIA
Republic of Austria

Area Sq Km	83 855	**Religions**	Roman Catholic, Protestant
Area Sq Miles	32 377		
Population	8 361 000	**Currency**	Euro
Capital	Vienna (Wien)	**Organizations**	EU, OECD, UN
Languages	German, Croatian, Turkish	**Map page**	102–103

AZERBAIJAN
Azerbaijani Republic

Area Sq Km	86 600	**Religions**	Shi'a Muslim, Sunni Muslim, Russian and Armenian Orthodox
Area Sq Miles	33 436		
Population	8 467 000		
Capital	Baku (Bakı)	**Currency**	Azerbaijani manat
Languages	Azeri, Armenian, Russian, Lezgian	**Organizations**	CIS, UN
		Map page	81

Azores (Arquipélago dos Açores)
Autonomous Region of Portugal

Area Sq Km 2 300
Area Sq Miles 888
Population 242 712
Capital Ponta Delgada
Languages Portuguese
Religions Roman Catholic, Protestant
Currency Euro
Map page 112

THE BAHAMAS
Commonwealth of The Bahamas

Area Sq Km 13 939
Area Sq Miles 5 382
Population 331 000
Capital Nassau
Languages English, creole
Religions Protestant, Roman Catholic
Currency Bahamian dollar
Organizations CARICOM, Comm., UN
Map page 146–147

BAHRAIN
Kingdom of Bahrain

Area Sq Km 691
Area Sq Miles 267
Population 753 000
Capital Manama (Al Manāmah)
Languages Arabic, English
Religions Shi'a Muslim, Sunni Muslim, Christian
Currency Bahraini dinar
Organizations UN
Map page 79

BANGLADESH
People's Republic of Bangladesh

Area Sq Km 143 998
Area Sq Miles 55 598
Population 158 665 000
Capital Dhaka (Dacca)
Languages Bengali, English
Religions Sunni Muslim, Hindu
Currency Taka
Organizations Comm., UN
Map page 75

BARBADOS

Area Sq Km 430
Area Sq Miles 166
Population 294 000
Capital Bridgetown
Languages English, creole
Religions Protestant, Roman Catholic
Currency Barbados dollar
Organizations CARICOM, Comm., UN
Map page 147

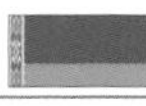

BELARUS
Republic of Belarus

Area Sq Km 207 600
Area Sq Miles 80 155
Population 9 689 000
Capital Minsk
Languages Belorussian, Russian
Religions Belorussian Orthodox, Roman Catholic
Currency Belarus rouble
Organizations CIS, UN
Map page 88–89

BELGIUM
Kingdom of Belgium

Area Sq Km 30 520
Area Sq Miles 11 784
Population 10 457 000
Capital Brussels (Bruxelles)
Languages Dutch (Flemish), French (Walloon), German
Religions Roman Catholic, Protestant
Currency Euro
Organizations EU, OECD, UN
Map page 100

BELIZE

Area Sq Km 22 965
Area Sq Miles 8 867
Population 288 000
Capital Belmopan
Languages English, Spanish, Mayan, creole
Religions Roman Catholic, Protestant
Currency Belize dollar
Organizations CARICOM, Comm., UN
Map page 147

BENIN
Republic of Benin

Area Sq Km 112 620
Area Sq Miles 43 483
Population 9 033 000
Capital Porto-Novo
Languages French, Fon, Yoruba, Adja, local languages
Religions Traditional beliefs, Roman Catholic, Sunni Muslim
Currency CFA franc
Organization UN
Map page 114

Bermuda
United Kingdom Overseas Territory

Area Sq Km 54
Area Sq Miles 21
Population 65 000
Capital Hamilton
Languages English
Religions Protestant, Roman Catholic
Currency Bermuda dollar
Map page 125

BHUTAN
Kingdom of Bhutan

Area Sq Km 46 620
Area Sq Miles 18 000
Population 658 000
Capital Thimphu
Languages Dzongkha, Nepali, Assamese
Religions Buddhist, Hindu
Currency Ngultrum, Indian rupee
Organizations UN
Map page 75

BOLIVIA
Republic of Bolivia

Area Sq Km 1 098 581
Area Sq Miles 424 164
Population 9 525 000
Capital La Paz/Sucre
Languages Spanish, Quechua, Aymara
Religions Roman Catholic, Protestant, Baha'i
Currency Boliviano
Organizations UN
Map page 152

Bonaire
part of Netherlands Antilles

Area Sq Km 288
Area Sq Miles 111
Population 10 638
Capital Kralendijk
Languages Dutch, Papiamento
Religions Roman Catholic, Protestant
Currency Netherlands Antilles guilder
Map page 147

Bonin Islands (Ogasawara-shotō)
part of Japan

Area Sq Km 104
Area Sq Miles 40
Population 2 300
Capital Ōmura
Languages Japanese
Religions Shintoist, Buddhist, Christian
Currency Yen
Map page 69

BOSNIA-HERZEGOVINA
Republic of Bosnia and Herzegovina

Area Sq Km 51 130
Area Sq Miles 19 741
Population 3 935 000
Capital Sarajevo
Languages Bosnian, Serbian, Croatian
Religions Sunni Muslim, Serbian Orthodox, Roman Catholic, Protestant
Currency Marka
Organizations UN
Map page 109

BOTSWANA
Republic of Botswana

Area Sq Km 581 370
Area Sq Miles 224 468
Population 1 882 000
Capital Gaborone
Languages English, Setswana, Shona, local languages
Religions Traditional beliefs, Protestant, Roman Catholic
Currency Pula
Organizations Comm., SADC, UN
Map page 120

BRAZIL
Federative Republic of Brazil

Area Sq Km 8 514 879
Area Sq Miles 3 287 613
Population 191 791 000
Capital Brasília
Languages Portuguese
Religions Roman Catholic, Protestant
Currency Real
Organizations UN
Map page 150–151

BRUNEI
State of Brunei Darussalam

Area Sq Km 5 765
Area Sq Miles 2 226
Population 390 000
Capital Bandar Seri Begawan
Languages Malay, English, Chinese
Religions Sunni Muslim, Buddhist, Christian
Currency Brunei dollar
Organizations APEC, ASEAN, Comm., UN
Map page 61

BULGARIA
Republic of Bulgaria

Area Sq Km 110 994
Area Sq Miles 42 855
Population 7 639 000
Capital Sofia (Sofiya)
Languages Bulgarian, Turkish, Romany, Macedonian
Religions Bulgarian Orthodox, Sunni Muslim
Currency Lev
Organizations EU, UN
Map page 110

BURKINA
Democratic Republic of Burkina Faso

Area Sq Km 274 200
Area Sq Miles 105 869
Population 14 784 000
Capital Ouagadougou
Languages French, Moore (Mossi), Fulani, local languages
Religions Sunni Muslim, traditional beliefs, Roman Catholic
Currency CFA franc
Organizations UN
Map page 114

BURUNDI
Republic of Burundi

Area Sq Km 27 835
Area Sq Miles 10 747
Population 8 508 000
Capital Bujumbura
Languages Kirundi (Hutu, Tutsi), French
Religions Roman Catholic, traditional beliefs, Protestant
Currency Burundian franc
Organizations UN
Map page 119

CAMBODIA
Kingdom of Cambodia

Area Sq Km 181 000
Area Sq Miles 69 884
Population 14 444 000
Capital Phnom Penh
Languages Khmer, Vietnamese
Religions Buddhist, Roman Catholic, Sunni Muslim
Currency Riel
Organizations ASEAN, UN
Map page 63

CAMEROON
Republic of Cameroon

Area Sq Km 475 442
Area Sq Miles 183 569
Population 18 549 000
Capital Yaoundé
Languages French, English, Fang, Bamileke, local languages
Religions Roman Catholic, traditional beliefs, Sunni Muslim, Protestant
Currency CFA franc
Organizations Comm., UN
Map page 118

CANADA

Area Sq Km 9 984 670
Area Sq Miles 3 855 103
Population 32 876 000
Capital Ottawa
Languages English, French, local languages
Religions Roman Catholic, Protestant, Eastern Orthodox, Jewish
Currency Canadian dollar
Organizations APEC, Comm., OECD, UN
Map page 126–127

Alberta (Province)
Area Sq Km 661 848
Area Sq Miles 255 541
Population 3 435 511
Capital Edmonton

British Columbia (Province)
Area Sq Km 944 735
Area Sq Miles 364 764
Population 4 338 106
Capital Victoria

Manitoba (Province)
Area Sq Km 647 797
Area Sq Miles 250 116
Population 1 180 004
Capital Winnipeg

New Brunswick (Province)
Area Sq Km 72 908
Area Sq Miles 28 150
Population 748 582
Capital Fredericton

Newfoundland and Labrador (Province)
Area Sq Km 405 212
Area Sq Miles 156 453
Population 508 548
Capital St John's

Northwest Territories (Territory)
Area Sq Km 1 346 106
Area Sq Miles 519 734
Population 41 777
Capital Yellowknife

CANADA

Nova Scotia (Province)

Area Sq Km	55 284	**Population**	933 793
Area Sq Miles	21 345	**Capital**	Halifax

Nunavut (Territory)

Area Sq Km	2 093 190	**Population**	30 947
Area Sq Miles	808 185	**Capital**	Iqaluit (Frobisher Bay)

Ontario (Province)

Area Sq Km	1 076 395	**Population**	12 726 336
Area Sq Miles	415 598	**Capital**	Toronto

Prince Edward Island (Province)

Area Sq Km	5 660	**Population**	138 632
Area Sq Miles	2 185	**Capital**	Charlottetown

Québec (Province)

Area Sq Km	1 542 056	**Population**	7 676 097
Area Sq Miles	595 391	**Capital**	Québec

Saskatchewan (Province)

Area Sq Km	651 036	**Population**	987 939
Area Sq Miles	251 366	**Capital**	Regina

Yukon (Territory)

Area Sq Km	482 443	**Population**	31 032
Area Sq Miles	186 272	**Capital**	Whitehorse

Canary Islands (Islas Canarias)

Autonomous Community of Spain

Area Sq Km	7 447	**Languages**	Spanish
Area Sq Miles	2 875	**Religions**	Roman Catholic
Population	1 995 833	**Currency**	Euro
Capital	Santa Cruz de Tenerife/Las Palmas	**Map page**	114

CAPE VERDE

Republic of Cape Verde

Area Sq Km	4 033	**Religions**	Roman Catholic, Protestant
Area Sq Miles	1 557		
Population	530 000	**Currency**	Cape Verde escudo
Capital	Praia	**Organizations**	UN
Languages	Portuguese, creole	**Map page**	46

Cayman Islands

United Kingdom Overseas Territory

Area Sq Km	259	**Religions**	Protestant, Roman Catholic
Area Sq Miles	100		
Population	47 000	**Currency**	Cayman Islands dollar
Capital	George Town	**Map page**	146
Languages	English		

CENTRAL AFRICAN REPUBLIC

Area Sq Km	622 436	**Religions**	Protestant, Roman Catholic, traditional beliefs, Sunni Muslim
Area Sq Miles	240 324		
Population	4 343 000		
Capital	Bangui	**Currency**	CFA franc
Languages	French, Sango, Banda, Baya, local languages	**Organizations**	UN
		Map page	118

Ceuta

Autonomous Community of Spain

Area Sq Km	19	**Religions**	Roman Catholic, Muslim
Area Sq Miles	7		
Population	75 861	**Currency**	Euro
Capital	Ceuta	**Map page**	106
Languages	Spanish, Arabic		

CHAD

Republic of Chad

Area Sq Km	1 284 000	**Religions**	Sunni Muslim, Roman Catholic, Protestant, traditional beliefs
Area Sq Miles	495 755		
Population	10 781 000		
Capital	Ndjamena	**Currency**	CFA franc
Languages	Arabic, French,Sara, local languages	**Organizations**	UN
		Map page	115

Chatham Islands

part of New Zealand

Area Sq Km	963	**Religions**	Protestant
Area Sq Miles	372	**Currency**	New Zealand dollar
Population	612	**Map page**	49
Capital	Waitangi		
Languages	English		

CHILE

Republic of Chile

Area Sq Km	756 945	**Religions**	Roman Catholic, Protestant
Area Sq Miles	292 258		
Population	16 635 000	**Currency**	Chilean peso
Capital	Santiago	**Organizations**	APEC, UN
Languages	Spanish, Amerindian languages	**Map page**	152–153

CHINA

People's Republic of China

Area Sq Km	9 584 492	**Religions**	Confucian, Taoist, Buddhist, Christian, Sunni Muslim
Area Sq Miles	3 700 593		
Population	1 313 437 000		
Capital	Beijing (Peking)	**Currency**	Yuan, Hong Kong dollar, Macao pataca
Languages	Mandarin, Wu, Cantonese, Hsiang, regional languages	**Organizations**	APEC, UN
		Map page	68–69

Anhui (Province)

Area Sq Km	139 000	**Population**	61 140 000
Area Sq Miles	53 668	**Capital**	Hefei

Bejing (Municipality)

Area Sq Km	16 800	**Population**	15 360 000
Area Sq Miles	6 487	**Capital**	Beijing (Peking)

Chongqing (Municipality)

Area Sq Km	23 000	**Population**	27 970 000
Area Sq Miles	8 880	**Capital**	Chongqing

Fujian (Province)

Area Sq Km	121 400	**Population**	35 320 000
Area Sq Miles	46 873	**Capital**	Fuzhou

Gansu (Province)

Area Sq Km	453 700	**Population**	25 920 000
Area Sq Miles	175 175	**Capital**	Lanzhou

Guangdong (Province)

Area Sq Km	178 000	**Population**	91 850 000
Area Sq Miles	68 726	**Capital**	Guangzhou (Canton)

Guangxi Zhuangzu Zizhiqu (Autonomous Region)

Area Sq Km	236 000	**Population**	46 550 000
Area Sq Miles	91 120	**Capital**	Nanning

Guizhou (Province)

Area Sq Km	176 000	**Population**	37 250 000
Area Sq Miles	67 954	**Capital**	Guiyang

Hainan (Province)

Area Sq Km	34 000	**Population**	8 260 000
Area Sq Miles	13 127	**Capital**	Haikou

Hebei (Province)

Area Sq Km	187 700	**Population**	68 440 000
Area Sq Miles	72 471	**Capital**	Shijiazhuang

Heilongjiang (Province)

Area Sq Km	454 600	**Population**	38 180 000
Area Sq Miles	175 522	**Capital**	Harbin

Henan (Province)

Area Sq Km	167 000	**Population**	93 710 000
Area Sq Miles	64 479	**Capital**	Zhengzhou

Hong Kong (Special Administrative Region)

Area Sq Km	1 075	**Population**	6 936 000
Area Sq Miles	415	**Capital**	Hong Kong

Hubei (Province)

Area Sq Km	185 900	**Population**	57 070 000
Area Sq Miles	71 776	**Capital**	Wuhan

Hunan (Province)

Area Sq Km	210 000	**Population**	63 200 000
Area Sq Miles	81 081	**Capital**	Changsha

Jiangsu (Province)

Area Sq Km	102 600	**Population**	74 680 000
Area Sq Miles	39 614	**Capital**	Nanjing

Jiangxi (Province)

Area Sq Km	166 900	**Population**	43 070 000
Area Sq Miles	64 440	**Capital**	Nanchang

Jilin (Province)

Area Sq Km	187 000	**Population**	27 150 000
Area Sq Miles	72 201	**Capital**	Changchun

Liaoning (Province)

Area Sq Km	147 400	**Population**	42 200 000
Area Sq Miles	56 911	**Capital**	Shenyang

Macao (Special Administrative Region)

Area Sq Km	17	**Population**	477 000
Area Sq Mile	7		

Nei Mongol Zizhiqu (Inner Mongolia) (Autonomous Region)

Area Sq Km	1 183 000	**Population**	23 860 000
Area Sq Miles	456 759	**Capital**	Hohhot

Ningxia Huizu Zizhiqu (Autonomous Region)

Area Sq Km	66 400	**Population**	5 950 000
Area Sq Miles	25 637	**Capital**	Yinchuan

Qinghai (Province)

Area Sq Km	721 000	**Population**	5 430 000
Area Sq Miles	278 380	**Capital**	Xining

Shaanxi (Province)

Area Sq Km	205 600	**Population**	37 180 000
Area Sq Miles	79 383	**Capital**	Xi'an

Shandong (Province)

Area Sq Km	153 300	**Population**	92 390 000
Area Sq Miles	59 189	**Capital**	Jinan

Shanghai (Municipality)

Area Sq Km	6 300	**Population**	17 780 000
Area Sq Miles	2 432	**Capital**	Shanghai

Shanxi (Province)

Area Sq Km	156 300	**Population**	33 520 000
Area Sq Miles	60 348	**Capital**	Taiyuan

Sichuan (Province)

Area Sq Km	569 000	**Population**	82 080 000
Area Sq Miles	219 692	**Capital**	Chengdu

Tianjin (Municipality)

Area Sq Km	11 300	**Population**	10 430 000
Area Sq Miles	4 363	**Capital**	Tianjin

Xinjiang Uygur Zizhiqu (Sinkiang) (Autonomous Region)

Area Sq Km	1 600 000	**Population**	20 080 000
Area Sq Miles	617 763	**Capital**	Ürümqi

Xizang Zizhiqu (Tibet) (Autonomous Region)

Area Sq Km	1 228 400	**Population**	2 760 000
Area Sq Miles	474 288	**Capital**	Lhasa

Yunnan (Province)

Area Sq Km	394 000	**Population**	44 420 000
Area Sq Miles	152 124	**Capital**	Kunming

Zhejiang (Province)

Area Sq Km	101 800	**Population**	48 940 000
Area Sq Miles	39 305	**Capital**	Hangzhou

Christmas Island
Australian External Territory

Area Sq Km 135
Area Sq Miles 52
Population 1 508
Capital The Settlement
Languages English
Religions Buddhist, Sunni Muslim, Protestant, Roman Catholic
Currency Australian dollar
Map page 58

Cocos Islands (Keeling Islands)
Australian External Territory

Area Sq Km 14
Area Sq Miles 5
Population 621
Capital West Island
Languages English
Religions Sunni Muslim, Christian
Currency Australian dollar
Map page 58

COLOMBIA
Republic of Colombia

Area Sq Km 1 141 748
Area Sq Miles 440 831
Population 46 156 000
Capital Bogotá
Languages Spanish, Amerindian languages
Religions Roman Catholic, Protestant
Currency Colombian peso
Organizations UN
Map page 150

COMOROS
Union of the Comoros

Area Sq Km 1 862
Area Sq Miles 719
Population 839 000
Capital Moroni
Languages Comorian, French, Arabic
Religions Sunni Muslim, Roman Catholic
Currency Comoros franc
Organizations UN
Map page 121

CONGO
Republic of the Congo

Area Sq Km 342 000
Area Sq Miles 132 047
Population 3 768 000
Capital Brazzaville
Languages French, Kongo, Monokutuba, local languages
Religions Roman Catholic, Protestant, traditional beliefs, Sunni Muslim
Currency CFA franc
Organizations UN
Map page 118

CONGO, DEMOCRATIC REPUBLIC OF THE

Area Sq Km 2 345 410
Area Sq Miles 905 568
Population 62 636 000
Capital Kinshasa
Languages French, Lingala, Swahili, Kongo, local languages
Religions Christian, Sunni Muslim
Currency Congolese franc
Organizations SADC, UN
Map page 118–119

Cook Islands
Self-governing New Zealand Overseas Territory

Area Sq Km 293
Area Sq Miles 113
Population 13 000
Capital Avarua
Languages English, Maori
Religions Protestant, Roman Catholic
Currency New Zealand dollar
Map page 49

COSTA RICA
Republic of Costa Rica

Area Sq Km 51 100
Area Sq Miles 19 730
Population 4 468 000
Capital San José
Languages Spanish
Religions Roman Catholic, Protestant
Currency Costa Rican colón
Organizations UN
Map page 146

CÔTE D'IVOIRE
Republic of Côte d'Ivoire

Area Sq Km 322 463
Area Sq Miles 124 504
Population 19 262 000
Capital Yamoussoukro
Languages French, creole, Akan, local languages
Religions Sunni Muslim, Roman Catholic, traditonal beliefs, Protestant
Currency CFA franc
Organizations UN
Map page 114

CROATIA
Republic of Croatia

Area Sq Km 56 538
Area Sq Miles 21 829
Population 4 555 000
Capital Zagreb
Languages Croatian, Serbian
Religions Roman Catholic, Serbian Orthodox, Sunni Muslim
Currency Kuna
Organizations UN
Map page 109

CUBA
Republic of Cuba

Area Sq Km 110 860
Area Sq Miles 42 803
Population 11 268 000
Capital Havana (La Habana)
Languages Spanish
Religions Roman Catholic, Protestant
Currency Cuban peso
Organizations UN
Map page 146

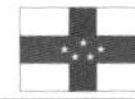

Curaçao
part of Netherlands Antilles

Area Sq Km 444
Area Sq Miles 171
Population 135 822
Capital Willemstad
Languages Dutch, Papiamento
Religions Roman Catholic, Protestant
Currency Netherlands Antilles guilder
Map page 147

CYPRUS
Republic of Cyprus

Area Sq Km 9 251
Area Sq Miles 3 572
Population 855 000
Capital Nicosia (Lefkosia)
Languages Greek, Turkish, English
Religions Greek Orthodox, Sunni Muslim
Currency Euro
Organizations Comm., EU, UN
Map page 80

CZECH REPUBLIC

Area Sq Km 78 864
Area Sq Miles 30 450
Population 10 186 000
Capital Prague (Praha)
Languages Czech, Moravian, Slovakian
Religions Roman Catholic, Protestant
Currency Czech koruna
Organizations EU, OECD, UN
Map page 102–103

DENMARK
Kingdom of Denmark

Area Sq Km 43 075
Area Sq Miles 16 631
Population 5 442 000
Capital Copenhagen (København)
Languages Danish
Religions Protestant
Currency Danish krone
Organizations EU, OECD, UN
Map page 93

DJIBOUTI
Republic of Djibouti

Area Sq Km 23 200
Area Sq Miles 8 958
Population 833 000
Capital Djibouti
Languages Somali, Afar, French, Arabic
Religions Sunni Muslim, Christian
Currency Djibouti franc
Organizations UN
Map page 117

DOMINICA
Commonwealth of Dominica

Area Sq Km 750
Area Sq Miles 290
Population 67 000
Capital Roseau
Languages English, creole
Religions Roman Catholic, Protestant
Currency East Caribbean dollar
Organizations CARICOM, Comm., UN
Map page 147

DOMINICAN REPUBLIC

Area Sq Km 48 442
Area Sq Miles 18 704
Population 9 760 000
Capital Santo Domingo
Languages Spanish, creole
Religions Roman Catholic, Protestant
Currency Dominican peso
Organizations UN
Map page 147

Easter Island (Isla de Pascua)
part of Chile

Area Sq Km 171
Area Sq Miles 66
Population 3 791
Capital Hanga Roa
Languages Spanish
Religions Roman Catholic
Currency Chilean peso
Map page 157

EAST TIMOR
Democratic Republic of Timor-Leste

Area Sq Km 14 874
Area Sq Miles 5 743
Population 1 155 000
Capital Dili
Languages Portuguese, Tetun, English
Religions Roman Catholic
Currency United States dollar
Organisations UN
Map page 59

ECUADOR
Republic of Ecuador

Area Sq Km 272 045
Area Sq Miles 105 037
Population 13 341 000
Capital Quito
Languages Spanish, Quechua, Amerindian languages
Religions Roman Catholic
Currency United States dollar
Organizations APEC, OPEC, UN
Map page 150

EGYPT
Arab Republic of Egypt

Area Sq Km 1 000 250
Area Sq Miles 386 199
Population 75 498 000
Capital Cairo (Al Qāhirah)
Languages Arabic
Religions Sunni Muslim, Coptic Christian
Currency Egyptian pound
Organizations UN
Map page 116

EL SALVADOR
Republic of El Salvador

Area Sq Km 21 041
Area Sq Miles 8 124
Population 6 857 000
Capital San Salvador
Languages Spanish
Religions Roman Catholic, Protestant
Currency El Salvador colón, United States dollar
Organizations UN
Map page 146

EQUATORIAL GUINEA
Republic of Equatorial Guinea

Area Sq Km 28 051
Area Sq Miles 10 831
Population 507 000
Capital Malabo
Languages Spanish, French, Fang
Religions Roman Catholic, traditional beliefs
Currency CFA franc
Organizations UN
Map page 118

ERITREA
State of Eritrea

Area Sq Km 117 400
Area Sq Miles 45 328
Population 4 851 000
Capital Asmara
Languages Tigrinya, Tigre
Religions Sunni Muslim, Coptic Christian
Currency Nakfa
Organizations UN
Map page 116

ESTONIA
Republic of Estonia

Area Sq Km 45 200
Area Sq Miles 17 452
Population 1 335 000
Capital Tallinn
Languages Estonian, Russian
Religions Protestant, Estonian and Russian Orthodox
Currency Kroon
Organizations EU, UN
Map page 88

ETHIOPIA
Federal Democratic Republic of Ethiopia

Area Sq Km 1 133 880
Area Sq Miles 437 794
Population 83 099 000
Capital Addis Ababa (Ādīs Ābeba)
Languages Oromo, Amharic, Tigrinya, local languages
Religions Ethiopian Orthodox, Sunni Muslim, traditional beliefs
Currency Birr
Organizations UN
Map page 117

Falkland Islands
United Kingdom Overseas Territory

Area Sq Km 12 170
Area Sq Miles 4 699
Population 3 000
Capital Stanley
Languages English
Religions Protestant, Roman Catholic
Currency Falkland Islands pound
Map page 153

Faroe Islands
Self-governing Danish Territory

Area Sq Km 1 399
Area Sq Miles 540
Population 49 000
Capital Tórshavn
Languages Faroese, Danish
Religions Protestant
Currency Danish krone
Map page 94

FIJI
Sovereign Democratic Republic of Fiji

Area Sq Km 18 330
Area Sq Miles 7 077
Population 839 000
Capital Suva
Languages English, Fijian, Hindi
Religions Christian, Hindu, Sunni Muslim
Currency Fiji dollar
Organizations UN, Comm.
Map page 49

FINLAND
Republic of Finland

Area Sq Km 338 145
Area Sq Miles 130 559
Population 5 277 000
Capital Helsinki (Helsingfors)
Languages Finnish, Swedish
Religions Protestant, Greek Orthodox
Currency Euro
Organizations EU, OECD, UN
Map page 92–93

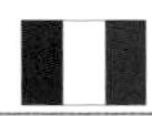

FRANCE
French Republic

Area Sq Km 543 965
Area Sq Miles 210 026
Population 61 647 000
Capital Paris
Languages French, Arabic
Religions Roman Catholic, Protestant, Sunni Muslim
Currency Euro
Organizations EU, OECD, UN
Map page 104–105

French Guiana
French Overseas Department

Area Sq Km 90 000
Area Sq Miles 34 749
Population 202 000
Capital Cayenne
Languages French, creole
Religions Roman Catholic
Currency Euro
Map page 151

French Polynesia
French Overseas Territory

Area Sq Km 3 265
Area Sq Miles 1 261
Population 263 000
Capital Papeete
Languages French, Tahitian, Polynesian languages
Religions Protestant, Roman Catholic
Currency CFP franc
Map page 49

GABON
Gabonese Republic

Area Sq Km 267 667
Area Sq Miles 103 347
Population 1 331 000
Capital Libreville
Languages French, Fang, local languages
Religions Roman Catholic, Protestant, traditonal beliefs
Currency CFA franc
Organizations UN
Map page 118

Galapagos Islands (Islas Galápagos)
part of Ecuador

Area Sq Km 8 010
Area Sq Miles 3 093
Population 18 640
Capital Puerto Baquerizo Moreno
Languages Spanish
Religions Roman Catholic
Currency United States dollar
Map page 125

THE GAMBIA
Republic of The Gambia

Area Sq Km 11 295
Area Sq Miles 4 361
Population 1 709 000
Capital Banjul
Languages English, Malinke, Fulani, Wolof
Religions Sunni Muslim, Protestant
Currency Dalasi
Organizations Comm., UN
Map page 114

Gaza
Semi-autonomous region

Area Sq Km 363
Area Sq Miles 140
Population 1 586 008
Capital Gaza
Languages Arabic
Religions Sunni Muslim, Shi'a Muslim
Currency Israeli shekel
Map page 80

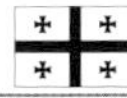

GEORGIA
Republic of Georgia

Area Sq Km 69 700
Area Sq Miles 26 911
Population 4 395 000
Capital T'bilisi
Languages Georgian, Russian, Armenian, Azeri, Ossetian, Abkhaz
Religions Georgian Orthodox, Russian Orthodox, Sunni Muslim
Currency Lari
Organizations CIS, UN
Map page 81

GERMANY
Federal Republic of Germany

Area Sq Km 357 022
Area Sq Miles 137 847
Population 82 599 000
Capital Berlin
Languages German, Turkish
Religions Protestant, Roman Catholic
Currency Euro
Organizations EU, OECD, UN
Map page 102

GHANA
Republic of Ghana

Area Sq Km 238 537
Area Sq Miles 92 100
Population 23 478 000
Capital Accra
Languages English, Hausa, Akan, local languages
Religions Christian, Sunni Muslim, traditional beliefs
Currency Cedi
Organizations Comm., UN
Map page 114

Gibraltar
United Kingdom Overseas Territory

Area Sq Km	7	**Religions**	Roman Catholic, Protestant, Sunni Muslim
Area Sq Miles	3		
Population	29 000		
Capital	Gibraltar	**Currency**	Gibraltar pound
Languages	English, Spanish	**Map page**	106

GREECE
Hellenic Republic

Area Sq Km	131 957	**Religions**	Greek Orthodox, Sunni Muslim
Area Sq Miles	50 949		
Population	11 147 000	**Currency**	Euro
Capital	Athens (Athina)	**Organizations**	EU, OECD, UN
Languages	Greek	**Map page**	111

Greenland
Self governing Danish Territory

Area Sq Km	2 175 600	**Religions**	Protestant
Area Sq Miles	840 004	**Currency**	Danish krone
Population	58 000	**Map page**	127
Capital	Nuuk (Godthåb)		
Languages	Greenlandic, Danish		

GRENADA

Area Sq Km	378	**Religions**	Roman Catholic, Protestant
Area Sq Miles	146		
Population	106 000	**Currency**	East Caribbean dollar
Capital	St George's	**Organizations**	CARICOM, Comm., UN
Languages	English, creole	**Map page**	147

Guadeloupe
French Overseas Department

Area Sq Km	1 780	**Religions**	Roman Catholic
Area Sq Miles	687	**Currency**	Euro
Population	445 000	**Map page**	147
Capital	Basse-Terre		
Languages	French, creole		

Guam
United States Unincorporated Territory

Area Sq Km	541	**Religions**	Roman Catholic
Area Sq Miles	209	**Currency**	United States dollar
Population	173 000	**Map page**	59
Capital	Hagåtña		
Languages	Chamorro, English, Tagalog		

GUATEMALA
Republic of Guatemala

Area Sq Km	108 890	**Religion**	Roman Catholic, Protestant
Area Sq Miles	42 043		
Population	13 354 000	**Currency**	Quetzal, United States dollar
Capital	Guatemala City		
Languages	Spanish, Mayan languages	**Organizations**	UN
		Map page	146

Guernsey
United Kingdom Crown Dependency

Area Sq Km	78	**Religions**	Protestant, Roman Catholic
Area Sq Miles	30		
Population	63 923	**Currency**	Pound sterling
Capital	St Peter Port	**Map page**	95
Languages	English, French		

GUINEA
Republic of Guinea

Area Sq Km	245 857	**Religions**	Sunni Muslim, traditional beliefs, Christian
Area Sq Miles	94 926		
Population	9 370 000		
Capital	Conakry	**Currency**	Guinea franc
Languages	French, Fulani, Malinke, local languages	**Organizations**	UN
		Map page	114

GUINEA-BISSAU
Republic of Guinea-Bissau

Area Sq Km	36 125	**Religions**	Traditional beliefs, Sunni Muslim, Christian
Area Sq Miles	13 948		
Population	1 695 000		
Capital	Bissau	**Currency**	CFA franc
Languages	Portuguese, crioulo, local languages	**Organizations**	UN
		Map page	114

GUYANA
Co-operative Republic of Guyana

Area Sq Km	214 969	**Religions**	Protestant, Hindu, Roman Catholic, Sunni Muslim
Area Sq Miles	83 000		
Population	738 000		
Capital	Georgetown	**Currency**	Guyana dollar
Languages	English, creole, Amerindian languages	**Organizations**	CARICOM, Comm., UN
		Map page	150

HAITI
Republic of Haiti

Area Sq Km	27 750	**Religions**	Roman Catholic, Protestant, Voodoo
Area Sq Miles	10 714		
Population	9 598 000	**Currency**	Gourde
Capital	Port-au-Prince	**Organizations**	CARICOM, UN
Languages	French, creole	**Map page**	147

HONDURAS
Republic of Honduras

Area Sq Km	112 088	**Religions**	Roman Catholic, Protestant
Area Sq Miles	43 277		
Population	7 106 000	**Currency**	Lempira
Capital	Tegucigalpa	**Organizations**	UN
Languages	Spanish, Amerindian languages	**Map page**	147

HUNGARY
Republic of Hungary

Area Sq Km	93 030	**Religions**	Roman Catholic, Protestant
Area Sq Miles	35 919		
Population	10 030 000	**Currency**	Forint
Capital	Budapest	**Organizations**	EU, OECD, UN
Languages	Hungarian	**Map page**	103

ICELAND
Republic of Iceland

Area Sq Km	102 820	**Religions**	Protestant
Area Sq Miles	39 699	**Currency**	Icelandic króna
Population	301 000	**Organizations**	OECD, UN
Capital	Reykjavík	**Map page**	92
Languages	Icelandic		

INDIA
Republic of India

Area Sq Km	3 064 898	**Religions**	Hindu, Sunni Muslim, Shi'a Muslim, Sikh, Christian
Area Sq Miles	1 183 364	**Currency**	Indian rupee
Population	1 169 016 000	**Organizations**	Comm., UN
Capital	New Delhi	**Map page**	72–73
Languages	Hindi, English, many regional languages		

INDONESIA
Republic of Indonesia

Area Sq Km	1 919 445	**Religions**	Sunni Muslim, Protestant, Roman Catholic, Hindu, Buddhist
Area Sq Miles	741 102	**Currency**	Rupiah
Population	231 627 000	**Organizations**	APEC, ASEAN, OPEC, UN
Capital	Jakarta	**Map page**	58–59
Languages	Indonesian, local languages		

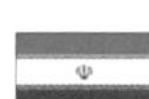

IRAN
Islamic Republic of Iran

Area Sq Km	1 648 000	**Religions**	Shi'a Muslim, Sunni Muslim
Area Sq Miles	636 296	**Currency**	Iranian rial
Population	71 208 000	**Organizations**	OPEC, UN
Capital	Tehrān	**Map page**	81
Languages	Farsi, Azeri, Kurdish, regional languages		

IRAQ
Republic of Iraq

Area Sq Km	438 317	**Religions**	Shi'a Muslim, Sunni Muslim, Christian
Area Sq Miles	169 235	**Currency**	Iraqi dinar
Population	28 993 000	**Organizations**	OPEC, UN
Capital	Baghdād	**Map page**	81
Languages	Arabic, Kurdish, Turkmen		

IRELAND, REPUBLIC OF

Area Sq Km	70 282	**Religions**	Roman Catholic, Protestant
Area Sq Miles	27 136	**Currency**	Euro
Population	4 301 000	**Organizations**	EU, OECD, UN
Capital	Dublin (Baile Átha Cliath)	**Map page**	97
Languages	English, Irish		

Isle of Man
United Kingdom Crown Dependency

Area Sq Km	572	**Religions**	Protestant, Roman Catholic
Area Sq Miles	221	**Currency**	Pound sterling
Population	79 000	**Map page**	98
Capital	Douglas		
Languages	English		

ISRAEL
State of Israel

Area Sq Km	20 770	**Religions**	Jewish, Sunni Muslim, Christian, Druze
Area Sq Miles	8 019	**Currency**	Shekel
Population	6 928 000	**Organizations**	UN
Capital	Jerusalem* (Yerushalayim) (El Quds)	**Map page**	80
Languages	Hebrew, Arabic		

*De facto capital. Disputed.

ITALY
Italian Republic

Area Sq Km	301 245	**Religions**	Roman Catholic
Area Sq Miles	116 311	**Currency**	Euro
Population	58 877 000	**Organizations**	EU, OECD, UN
Capital	Rome (Roma)	**Map page**	108–109
Languages	Italian		

JAMAICA

Area Sq Km	10 991	**Religions**	Protestant, Roman Catholic
Area Sq Miles	4 244	**Currency**	Jamaican dollar
Population	2 714 000	**Organizations**	CARICOM, Comm., UN
Capital	Kingston	**Map page**	146
Languages	English, creole		

Jammu and Kashmir
Disputed territory (India/Pakistan/China)

Area Sq Km	222 236	**Map page**	74–75
Area Sq Miles	85 806		
Population	13 000 000		
Capital	Srinagar		

JAPAN

Area Sq Km	377 727	**Religions**	Shintoist, Buddhist, Christian
Area Sq Miles	145 841	**Currency**	Yen
Population	127 967 000	**Organizations**	APEC, OECD, UN
Capital	Tōkyō	**Map page**	66–67
Languages	Japanese		

Jersey
United Kingdom Crown Dependency

Area Sq Km	116	**Religions**	Protestant, Roman Catholic
Area Sq Miles	45	**Currency**	Pound sterling
Population	88 200	**Map page**	95
Capital	St Helier		
Languages	English, French		

JORDAN
Hashemite Kingdom of Jordan

Area Sq Km	89 206	**Religions**	Sunni Muslim, Christian
Area Sq Miles	34 443	**Currency**	Jordanian dinar
Population	5 924 000	**Organizations**	UN
Capital	'Ammān	**Map page**	80
Languages	Arabic		

Juan Fernández Islands
part of Chile

Area Sq Km	179	**Religions**	Roman Catholic, Protestant
Area Sq Miles	69	**Currency**	Chilean peso
Population	633	**Map page**	157
Capital	San Juan Bautista		
Languages	Spanish, Amerindian languages		

KAZAKHSTAN
Republic of Kazakhstan

Area Sq Km	2 717 300	**Religions**	Sunni Muslim, Russian Orthodox, Protestant
Area Sq Miles	1 049 155	**Currency**	Tenge
Population	15 422 000	**Organizations**	CIS, UN
Capital	Astana (Akmola)	**Map page**	76–77
Languages	Kazakh, Russian, Ukrainian, German, Uzbek, Tatar		

KENYA
Republic of Kenya

Area Sq Km	582 646	**Religions**	Christian, traditional beliefs
Area Sq Miles	224 961	**Currency**	Kenyan shilling
Population	37 538 000	**Organizations**	Comm., UN
Capital	Nairobi	**Map page**	119
Languages	Swahili, English, local languages		

KIRIBATI
Republic of Kiribati

Area Sq Km	717	**Religions**	Roman Catholic, Protestant
Area Sq Miles	277	**Currency**	Australian dollar
Population	95 000	**Organizations**	Comm., UN
Capital	Bairiki	**Map page**	49
Languages	Gilbertese, English		

KOSOVO
Republic of Kosovo

Area Sq Km	10 908	**Religions**	Sunni Muslim, Serbian Orthodox
Area Sq Miles	4 212	**Currency**	Euro
Population	2 070 000	**Map page**	109
Capital	Prishtinë (Priština)		
Languages	Albanian, Serbian		

KUWAIT
State of Kuwait

Area Sq Km	17 818	**Religions**	Sunni Muslim, Shi'a Muslim, Christian, Hindu
Area Sq Miles	6 880	**Currency**	Kuwaiti dinar
Population	2 851 000	**Organizations**	OPEC, UN
Capital	Kuwait (Al Kuwayt)	**Map page**	78
Languages	Arabic		

KYRGYZSTAN
Kyrgyz Republic

Area Sq Km	198 500	**Religions**	Sunni Muslim, Russian Orthodox
Area Sq Miles	76 641	**Currency**	Kyrgyz som
Population	5 317 000	**Organizations**	CIS, UN
Capital	Bishkek (Frunze)	**Map page**	77
Languages	Kyrgyz, Russian, Uzbek		

LAOS
Lao People's Democratic Republic

Area Sq Km	236 800	**Religions**	Buddhist, traditional beliefs
Area Sq Miles	91 429	**Currency**	Kip
Population	5 859 000	**Organizations**	ASEAN, UN
Capital	Vientiane (Viangchan)	**Map page**	62–63
Languages	Lao, local languages		

LATVIA
Republic of Latvia

Area Sq Km	63 700	**Religions**	Protestant, Roman Catholic, Russian Orthodox
Area Sq Miles	24 595	**Currency**	Lats
Population	2 277 000	**Organizations**	EU, UN
Capital	Rīga	**Map page**	88
Languages	Latvian, Russian		

LEBANON
Republic of Lebanon

Area Sq Km	10 452	**Religions**	Shi'a Muslim, Sunni Muslim, Christian
Area Sq Miles	4 036	**Currency**	Lebanese pound
Population	4 099 000	**Organizations**	UN
Capital	Beirut (Beyrouth)	**Map page**	80
Languages	Arabic, Armenian, French		

LESOTHO
Kingdom of Lesotho

Area Sq Km	30 355	**Religions**	Christian, traditional beliefs
Area Sq Miles	11 720	**Currency**	Loti, South African rand
Population	2 008 000	**Organizations**	Comm., SADC, UN
Capital	Maseru	**Map page**	123
Languages	Sesotho, English, Zulu		

LIBERIA
Republic of Liberia

Area Sq Km	111 369	**Religions**	Traditional beliefs, Christian, Sunni Muslim
Area Sq Miles	43 000	**Currency**	Liberian dollar
Population	3 750 000	**Organizations**	UN
Capital	Monrovia	**Map page**	114
Languages	English, creole, local languages		

LIBYA
Socialist People's Libyan Arab Jamahiriya

Area Sq Km	1 759 540	**Religions**	Sunni Muslim
Area Sq Miles	679 362	**Currency**	Libyan dinar
Population	6 160 000	**Organizations**	OPEC, UN
Capital	Tripoli (Ţarābulus)	**Map page**	115
Languages	Arabic, Berber		

LIECHTENSTEIN
Principality of Liechtenstein

Area Sq Km	160	**Religions**	Roman Catholic, Protestant
Area Sq Miles	62	**Currency**	Swiss franc
Population	35 000	**Organizations**	UN
Capital	Vaduz	**Map page**	105
Languages	German		

LITHUANIA
Republic of Lithuania

Area Sq Km	65 200	**Religions**	Roman Catholic, Protestant, Russian Orthodox
Area Sq Miles	25 174	**Currency**	Litas
Population	3 390 000	**Organizations**	EU, UN
Capital	Vilnius	**Map page**	88
Languages	Lithuanian, Russian, Polish		

Lord Howe Island
part of Australia

Area Sq Km	17	**Religions**	Protestant, Roman Catholic
Area Sq Miles	6	**Currency**	Australian dollar
Population	343	**Map page**	51
Languages	English		

LUXEMBOURG
Grand Duchy of Luxembourg

Area Sq Km	2 586	**Religions**	Roman Catholic
Area Sq Miles	998	**Currency**	Euro
Population	467 000	**Organizations**	EU, OECD, UN
Capital	Luxembourg	**Map page**	100
Languages	Letzeburgish, German, French		

MACEDONIA (F.Y.R.O.M.)
Republic of Macedonia

Area Sq Km	25 713	**Religions**	Macedonian Orthodox, Sunni Muslim
Area Sq Miles	9 928	**Currency**	Macedonian denar
Population	2 038 000	**Organizations**	UN
Capital	Skopje	**Map page**	111
Languages	Macedonian, Albanian, Turkish		

MADAGASCAR
Republic of Madagascar

Area Sq Km	587 041	**Religions**	Traditional beliefs, Christian, Sunni Muslim
Area Sq Miles	226 658	**Currency**	Malagasy ariary, Malagasy franc
Population	19 683 000	**Organizations**	SADC, UN
Capital	Antananarivo	**Map page**	121
Languages	Malagasy, French		

Madeira
Autonomous Region of Portugal

Area Sq Km	779	**Religions**	Roman Catholic, Protestant
Area Sq Miles	301	**Currency**	Euro
Population	245 197	**Map page**	114
Capital	Funchal		
Languages	Portuguese		

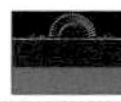

MALAWI
Republic of Malawi

Area Sq Km	118 484	**Religions**	Christian, traditional beliefs, Sunni Muslim
Area Sq Miles	45 747	**Currency**	Malawian kwacha
Population	13 925 000	**Organizations**	Comm., SADC, UN
Capital	Lilongwe	**Map page**	121
Languages	Chichewa, English, local languages		

MALAYSIA
Federation of Malaysia

Area Sq Km	332 965	**Religions**	Sunni Muslim, Buddhist, Hindu, Christian, traditional beliefs
Area Sq Miles	128 559	**Currency**	Ringgit
Population	26 572 000	**Organizations**	APEC, ASEAN, Comm., UN
Capital	Kuala Lumpur/ Putrajaya	**Map page**	60–61
Languages	Malay, English, Chinese, Tamil, local languages		

MALDIVES
Republic of the Maldives

Area Sq Km	298	**Religions**	Sunni Muslim
Area Sq Miles	115	**Currency**	Rufiyaa
Population	306 000	**Organizations**	Comm., UN
Capital	Male	**Map page**	56
Languages	Divehi (Maldivian)		

MALI
Republic of Mali

Area Sq Km	1 240 140	**Religions**	Sunni Muslim, traditional beliefs, Christian
Area Sq Miles	478 821	**Currency**	CFA franc
Population	12 337 000	**Organizations**	UN
Capital	Bamako	**Map page**	114
Languages	French, Bambara, local languages		

MALTA
Republic of Malta

Area Sq Km	316	**Religions**	Roman Catholic
Area Sq Miles	122	**Currency**	Euro
Population	407 000	**Organizations**	Comm., EU, UN
Capital	Valletta	**Map page**	84
Languages	Maltese, English		

MARSHALL ISLANDS
Republic of the Marshall Islands

Area Sq Km	181	**Religions**	Protestant, Roman Catholic
Area Sq Miles	70	**Currency**	United States dollar
Population	59 000	**Organizations**	UN
Capital	Delap-Uliga-Djarrit	**Map page**	48
Languages	English, Marshallese		

Martinique
French Overseas Department

Area Sq Km	1 079	**Religions**	Roman Catholic, traditional beliefs
Area Sq Miles	417	**Currency**	Euro
Population	399 000	**Map page**	147
Capital	Fort-de-France		
Languages	French, creole		

MAURITANIA
Islamic Arab and African Republic of Mauritania

Area Sq Km	1 030 700	**Religions**	Sunni Muslim
Area Sq Miles	397 955	**Currency**	Ouguiya
Population	3 124 000	**Organizations**	UN
Capital	Nouakchott	**Map page**	114
Languages	Arabic, French, local languages		

MAURITIUS
Republic of Mauritius

Area Sq Km	2 040	**Religions**	Hindu, Roman Catholic, Sunni Muslim
Area Sq Miles	788	**Currency**	Mauritius rupee
Population	1 262 000	**Organizations**	Comm., SADC, UN
Capital	Port Louis	**Map page**	113
Languages	English, creole, Hindi, Bhojpuri, French		

Mayotte
French Territorial Collectivity

Area Sq Km	373	**Religions**	Sunni Muslim, Christian
Area Sq Miles	144	**Currency**	Euro
Population	186 026	**Map page**	121
Capital	Dzaoudzi		
Languages	French, Mahorian		

Melilla
Autonomous Community of Spain

Area Sq Km	13	**Religions**	Roman Catholic, Muslim
Area Sq Miles	5	**Currency**	Euro
Population	66 871	**Map page**	114
Capital	Melilla		
Languages	Spanish, Arabic		

MEXICO
United Mexican States

Area Sq Km	1 972 545	**Religions**	Roman Catholic, Protestant
Area Sq Miles	761 604	**Currency**	Mexican peso
Population	106 535 000	**Organizations**	APEC, OECD, UN
Capital	Mexico City	**Map page**	144–145
Languages	Spanish, Amerindian languages		

MICRONESIA, FEDERATED STATES OF

Area Sq Km	701	**Religions**	Roman Catholic, Protestant
Area Sq Miles	271	**Currency**	United States dollar
Population	111 000	**Organizations**	UN
Capital	Palikir	**Map page**	48
Languages	English, Chuukese, Pohnpeian, local languages		

MOLDOVA
Republic of Moldova

Area Sq Km	33 700	**Religions**	Romanian Orthodox, Russian Orthodox
Area Sq Miles	13 012	**Currency**	Moldovan leu
Population	3 794 000	**Organizations**	CIS, UN
Capital	Chişinău (Kishinev)	**Map page**	90
Languages	Romanian, Ukrainian, Gagauz, Russian		

MONACO
Principality of Monaco

Area Sq Km	2	**Religions**	Roman Catholic
Area Sq Miles	1	**Currency**	Euro
Population	33 000	**Organizations**	UN
Capital	Monaco-Ville	**Map page**	105
Languages	French, Monégasque, Italian		

MONGOLIA

Area Sq Km	1 565 000	**Religions**	Buddhist, Sunni Muslim
Area Sq Miles	604 250	**Currency**	Tugrik (tögrög)
Population	2 629 000	**Organizations**	UN
Capital	Ulan Bator (Ulaanbaatar)	**Map page**	68–69
Languages	Khalka (Mongolian), Kazakh, local languages		

MONTENEGRO

Area Sq Km	13 812	**Religions**	Montenegrin, Orthodox, Sunni Muslim
Area Sq Miles	5 333	**Currency**	Euro
Population	598 000	**Organizations**	UN
Capital	Podgorica	**Map page**	109
Languages	Serbian, (Montenegrin), Albanian		

Montserrat
United Kingdom Overseas Territory

Area Sq Km	100	**Religions**	Protestant, Roman Catholic
Area Sq Miles	39	**Currency**	East Caribbean dollar
Population	6 000	**Organizations**	CARICOM
Capital	Brades	**Map page**	147
Languages	English		

MOROCCO
Kingdom of Morocco

Area Sq Km	446 550	**Religions**	Sunni Muslim
Area Sq Miles	172 414	**Currency**	Moroccan dirham
Population	31 224 000	**Organizations**	UN
Capital	Rabat	**Map page**	114
Languages	Arabic, Berber, French		

MOZAMBIQUE
Republic of Mozambique

Area Sq Km	799 380	**Religions**	Traditional beliefs, Roman Catholic, Sunni Muslim
Area Sq Miles	308 642	**Currency**	Metical
Population	21 397 000	**Organizations**	Comm., SADC, UN
Capital	Maputo	**Map page**	121
Languages	Portuguese, Makua, Tsonga, local languages		

MYANMAR (Burma)
Union of Myanmar

Area Sq Km	676 577	**Religions**	Buddhist, Christian, Sunni Muslim
Area Sq Miles	261 228	**Currency**	Kyat
Population	48 798 000	**Organizations**	ASEAN, UN
Capital	Nay Pyi Taw/ Rangoon (Yangôn)	**Map page**	62–63
Languages	Burmese, Shan, Karen, local languages		

NAMIBIA
Republic of Namibia

Area Sq Km	824 292	**Religions**	Protestant, Roman Catholic
Area Sq Miles	318 261	**Currency**	Namibian dollar
Population	2 074 000	**Organizations**	Comm., SADC, UN
Capital	Windhoek	**Map page**	121
Languages	English, Afrikaans, German, Ovambo, local languages		

NAURU
Republic of Nauru

Area Sq Km	21	**Religions**	Protestant, Roman Catholic
Area Sq Miles	8	**Currency**	Australian dollar
Population	10 000	**Organizations**	Comm., UN
Capital	Yaren	**Map page**	48
Languages	Nauruan, English		

NEPAL
Federal Democratic Republic of Nepal

Area Sq Km	147 181	**Religions**	Hindu, Buddhist, Sunni Muslim
Area Sq Miles	56 827	**Currency**	Nepalese rupee
Population	28 196 000	**Organizations**	UN
Capital	Kathmandu	**Map page**	75
Languages	Nepali, Maithili, Bhojpuri, English, local languages		

NETHERLANDS
Kingdom of the Netherlands

Area Sq Km	41 526	**Religions**	Roman Catholic, Protestant, Sunni Muslim
Area Sq Miles	16 033	**Currency**	Euro
Population	16 419 000	**Organizations**	EU, OECD, UN
Capital	Amsterdam/ The Hague ('s-Gravenhage)	**Map page**	100
Languages	Dutch, Frisian		

Netherlands Antilles
Self-governing Netherlands Territory

Area Sq Km	800	**Religions**	Roman Catholic, Protestant
Area Sq Miles	309	**Currency**	Netherlands Antilles guilder
Population	192 000	**Map page**	147
Capital	Willemstad		
Languages	Dutch, Papiamento, English		

New Caledonia
French Overseas Territory

Area Sq Km	19 058	**Religions**	Roman Catholic, Protestant, Sunni Muslim
Area Sq Miles	7 358	**Currency**	CFP franc
Population	242 000	**Map page**	48
Capital	Nouméa		
Languages	French, local languages		

NEW ZEALAND

Area Sq Km	270 534	**Religions**	Protestant, Roman Catholic
Area Sq Miles	104 454	**Currency**	New Zealand dollar
Population	4 179 000	**Organizations**	APEC, Comm., OECD, UN
Capital	Wellington	**Map page**	54
Languages	English, Maori		

NICARAGUA
Republic of Nicaragua

Area Sq Km	130 000	**Religions**	Roman Catholic, Protestant
Area Sq Miles	50 193	**Currency**	Córdoba
Population	5 603 000	**Organizations**	UN
Capital	Managua	**Map page**	146
Languages	Spanish, Amerindian languages		

NIGER
Republic of Niger

Area Sq Km	1 267 000	**Religions**	Sunni Muslim, traditional beliefs
Area Sq Miles	489 191	**Currency**	CFA franc
Population	14 226 000	**Organizations**	UN
Capital	Niamey	**Map page**	115
Languages	French, Hausa, Fulani, local languages		

NIGERIA
Federal Republic of Nigeria

Area Sq Km	923 768	**Religions**	Sunni Muslim, Christian, traditional beliefs
Area Sq Miles	356 669	**Currency**	Naira
Population	148 093 000	**Organizations**	Comm., OPEC, UN
Capital	Abuja	**Map page**	115
Languages	English, Hausa, Yoruba, Ibo, Fulani, local languages		

Niue
Self-governing New Zealand Overseas Territory

Area Sq Km	258	**Religions**	Christian
Area Sq Miles	100	**Currency**	New Zealand dollar
Population	2 000	**Map page**	48
Capital	Alofi		
Languages	English, Nivean		

Norfolk Island
Australian External Territory

Area Sq Km	35	**Religions**	Protestant, Roman Catholic
Area Sq Miles	14	**Currency**	Australian dollar
Population	2 523	**Map page**	48
Capital	Kingston		
Languages	English		

Northern Mariana Islands
United States Commonwealth

Area Sq Km	477	**Religions**	Roman Catholic
Area Sq Miles	184	**Currency**	United States dollar
Population	84 000	**Map page**	59
Capital	Capitol Hill		
Languages	English, Chamorro, local languages		

NORTH KOREA
Democratic People's Republic of Korea

Area Sq Km	120 538	**Religions**	Traditional beliefs, Chondoist, Buddhist
Area Sq Miles	46 540	**Currency**	North Korean won
Population	23 790 000	**Organizations**	UN
Capital	P'yŏngyang	**Map page**	65
Languages	Korean		

NORWAY
Kingdom of Norway

Area Sq Km 323 878
Area Sq Miles 125 050
Population 4 698 000
Capital Oslo
Languages Norwegian
Religions Protestant, Roman Catholic
Currency Norwegian krone
Organizations OECD, UN
Map page 92–93

OMAN
Sultanate of Oman

Area Sq Km 309 500
Area Sq Miles 119 499
Population 2 595 000
Capital Muscat (Masqaṭ)
Languages Arabic, Baluchi, Indian languages
Religions Ibadhi Muslim, Sunni Muslim
Currency Omani riyal
Organizations UN
Map page 79

PAKISTAN
Islamic Republic of Pakistan

Area Sq Km 803 940
Area Sq Miles 310 403
Population 163 902 000
Capital Islamabad
Languages Urdu, Punjabi, Sindhi, Pushtu, English
Religions Sunni Muslim, Shi'a Muslim, Christian, Hindu
Currency Pakistani rupee
Organizations Comm., UN
Map page 74

PALAU
Republic of Palau

Area Sq Km 497
Area Sq Miles 192
Population 20 000
Capital Melekeok
Languages Palauan, English
Religions Roman Catholic, Protestant, traditional beliefs
Currency United States dollar
Organizations UN
Map page 59

PANAMA
Republic of Panama

Area Sq Km 77 082
Area Sq Miles 29 762
Population 3 343 000
Capital Panama City
Languages Spanish, English, Amerindian languages
Religions Roman Catholic, Protestant, Sunni Muslim
Currency Balboa
Organizations UN
Map page 146

PAPUA NEW GUINEA
Independent State of Papua New Guinea

Area Sq Km 462 840
Area Sq Miles 178 704
Population 6 331 000
Capital Port Moresby
Languages English, Tok Pisin (creole), local languages
Religions Protestant, Roman Catholic, traditional beliefs
Currency Kina
Organizations APEC, Comm., UN
Map page 59

PARAGUAY
Republic of Paraguay

Area Sq Km 406 752
Area Sq Miles 157 048
Population 6 127 000
Capital Asunción
Languages Spanish, Guaraní
Religions Roman Catholic, Protestant
Currency Guaraní
Organizations UN
Map page 152

PERU
Republic of Peru

Area Sq Km 1 285 216
Area Sq Miles 496 225
Population 27 903 000
Capital Lima
Languages Spanish, Quechua, Aymara
Religions Roman Catholic, Protestant
Currency Sol
Organizations APEC, UN
Map page 150

PHILIPPINES
Republic of the Philippines

Area Sq Km 300 000
Area Sq Miles 115 831
Population 87 960 000
Capital Manila
Languages English, Filipino, Tagalog, Cebuano, local languages
Religions Roman Catholic, Protestant, Sunni Muslim, Aglipayan
Currency Philippine peso
Organizations APEC, ASEAN, UN
Map page 64

Pitcairn Islands
United Kingdom Overseas Territory

Area Sq Km 45
Area Sq Miles 17
Population 48
Capital Adamstown
Languages English
Religions Protestant
Currency New Zealand dollar
Map page 49

POLAND
Polish Republic

Area Sq Km 312 683
Area Sq Miles 120 728
Population 38 082 000
Capital Warsaw (Warszawa)
Languages Polish, German
Religions Roman Catholic, Polish Orthodox
Currency Złoty
Organizations EU, OECD, UN
Map page 103

PORTUGAL
Portuguese Republic

Area Sq Km 88 940
Area Sq Miles 34 340
Population 10 623 000
Capital Lisbon (Lisboa)
Languages Portuguese
Religions Roman Catholic, Protestant
Currency Euro
Organizations EU, OECD, UN
Map page 106

Puerto Rico
United States Commonwealth

Area Sq Km 9 104
Area Sq Miles 3 515
Population 3 991 000
Capital San Juan
Languages Spanish, English
Religions Roman Catholic, Protestant
Currency United States dollar
Map page 147

QATAR
State of Qatar

Area Sq Km 11 437
Area Sq Miles 4 416
Population 841 000
Capital Doha (Ad Dawḥah)
Languages Arabic
Religions Sunni Muslim
Currency Qatari riyal
Organizations OPEC, UN
Map page 79

Réunion
French Overseas Department

Area Sq Km	2 551	**Religions**	Roman Catholic
Area Sq Miles	985	**Currency**	Euro
Population	807 000	**Map page**	113
Capital	St-Denis		
Languages	French, creole		

Rodrigues Island
part of Mauritius

Area Sq Km	104	**Religions**	Christian
Area Sq Miles	40	**Currency**	Rupee
Population	36 690	**Map page**	159
Capital	Port Mathurin		
Languages	English, creole		

ROMANIA

Area Sq Km	237 500	**Religions**	Romanian Orthodox, Protestant, Roman Catholic
Area Sq Miles	91 699	**Currency**	Romanian leu
Population	21 438 000	**Organizations**	EU, UN
Capital	Bucharest (București)	**Map page**	110
Languages	Romanian, Hungarian		

RUSSIAN FEDERATION

Area Sq Km	17 075 400	**Religions**	Russian Orthodox, Sunni Muslim, Protestant
Area Sq Miles	6 592 849	**Currency**	Russian rouble
Population	142 499 000	**Organizations**	APEC, CIS, UN
Capital	Moscow (Moskva)	**Map page**	82–83
Languages	Russian, Tatar, Ukrainian, local languages		

RWANDA
Republic of Rwanda

Area Sq Km	26 338	**Religions**	Roman Catholic, traditional beliefs, Protestant
Area Sq Miles	10 169	**Currency**	Rwandan franc
Population	9 725 000	**Organizations**	UN
Capital	Kigali	**Map page**	119
Languages	Kinyarwanda, French, English		

Saba
part of Netherlands Antilles

Area Sq Km	13	**Religions**	Roman Catholic, Protestant
Area Sq Miles	5	**Currency**	Netherlands Antilles guilder
Population	1 434	**Map page**	147
Capital	Bottom		
Languages	Dutch, English		

St-Barthélémy
French Overseas Collectivity

Area Sq Km	21	**Religions**	Roman Catholic
Area Sq Miles	8	**Currency**	Euro
Population	6 852	**Map page**	147
Capital	Gustavia		
Languages	French		

St Helena, Ascension and Tristan da Cunha
United Kingdom Overseas Territory

Area Sq Km	121	**Religions**	Protestant, Roman Catholic,
Area Sq Miles	47	**Currency**	St Helena pound
Population	7 000	**Map page**	113
Capital	Jamestown		
Languages	English		

ST KITTS AND NEVIS
Federation of St Kitts and Nevis

Area Sq Km	261	**Religions**	Protestant, Roman Catholic
Area Sq Miles	101	**Currency**	East Caribbean dollar
Population	50 000	**Organizations**	CARICOM, Comm., UN
Capital	Basseterre	**Map page**	147
Languages	English, creole		

ST LUCIA

Area Sq Km	616	**Religions**	Roman Catholic, Protestant
Area Sq Miles	238	**Currency**	East Caribbean dollar
Population	165 000	**Organizations**	CARICOM, Comm., UN
Capital	Castries	**Map page**	147
Languages	English, creole		

St-Martin
French Overseas Collectivity

Area Sq Km	54	**Religions**	Roman Catholic
Area Sq Miles	21	**Currency**	Euro
Population	33 102	**Map page**	147
Capital	Marigot		
Languages	French		

St Pierre and Miquelon
French Territorial Collectivity

Area Sq Km	242	**Religions**	Roman Catholic
Area Sq Miles	93	**Currency**	Euro
Population	6 000	**Map page**	131
Capital	St-Pierre		
Languages	French		

ST VINCENT AND THE GRENADINES

Area Sq Km	389	**Religions**	Protestant, Roman Catholic
Area Sq Miles	150	**Currency**	East Caribbean dollar
Population	120 000	**Organizations**	CARICOM, Comm., UN
Capital	Kingstown	**Map page**	147
Languages	English, creole		

SAMOA
Independent State of Samoa

Area Sq Km	2 831	**Religions**	Protestant, Roman Catholic
Area Sq Miles	1 093	**Currency**	Tala
Population	187 000	**Organizations**	Comm., UN
Capital	Apia	**Map page**	49
Languages	Samoan, English		

SAN MARINO
Republic of San Marino

Area Sq Km	61
Area Sq Miles	24
Population	31 000
Capital	San Marino
Languages	Italian
Religions	Roman Catholic
Currency	Euro
Organizations	UN
Map page	108

SÃO TOMÉ AND PRÍNCIPE
Democratic Republic of São Tomé and Príncipe

Area Sq Km	964
Area Sq Miles	372
Population	158 000
Capital	São Tomé
Languages	Portuguese, creole
Religions	Roman Catholic, Protestant
Currency	Dobra
Organizations	UN
Map page	113

SAUDI ARABIA
Kingdom of Saudi Arabia

Area Sq Km	2 200 000
Area Sq Miles	849 425
Population	24 735 000
Capital	Riyadh (Ar Riyāḍ)
Languages	Arabic
Religions	Sunni Muslim, Shi'a Muslim
Currency	Saudi Arabian riyal
Organizations	OPEC, UN
Map page	78–79

SENEGAL
Republic of Senegal

Area Sq Km	196 720
Area Sq Miles	75 954
Population	12 379 000
Capital	Dakar
Languages	French, Wolof, Fulani, local languages
Religions	Sunni Muslim, Roman Catholic, traditional beliefs
Currency	CFA franc
Organizations	UN
Map page	114

SERBIA
Republic of Serbia

Area Sq Km	88 361
Area Sq Miles	34 116
Population	7 788 448
Capital	Belgrade (Beograd)
Languages	Serbian, Hungarian
Religions	Roman Catholic, Serbian Orthodox, Sunni Muslim
Currency	Serbian dinar
Organizations	UN
Map page	109

SEYCHELLES
Republic of the Seychelles

Area Sq Km	455
Area Sq Miles	176
Population	87 000
Capital	Victoria
Languages	English, French, creole
Religions	Roman Catholic, Protestant
Currency	Seychelles rupee
Organizations	Comm., SADC, UN
Map page	113

SIERRA LEONE
Republic of Sierra Leone

Area Sq Km	71 740
Area Sq Miles	27 699
Population	5 866 000
Capital	Freetown
Languages	English, creole, Mende, Temne, local languages
Religions	Sunni Muslim, traditional beliefs
Currency	Leone
Organizations	Comm., UN
Map page	114

SINGAPORE
Republic of Singapore

Area Sq Km	639
Area Sq Miles	247
Population	4 436 000
Capital	Singapore
Languages	Chinese, English, Malay, Tamil
Religions	Buddhist, Taoist, Sunni Muslim, Christian, Hindu
Currency	Singapore dollar
Organizations	APEC, ASEAN, Comm., UN
Map page	60

Sint Eustatius
part of Netherlands Antilles

Area Sq Km	21
Area Sq Miles	8
Population	2 584
Capital	Oranjestad
Languages	Dutch, English
Religions	Protestant, Roman Catholic
Currency	Netherlands Antilles guilder
Map page	147

Sint Maarten
part of Netherlands Antilles

Area Sq Km	34
Area Sq Miles	13
Population	35 035
Capital	Philipsburg
Languages	Dutch, English
Religions	Protestant, Roman Catholic
Currency	Netherlands Antilles guilder
Map page	147

SLOVAKIA
Slovak Republic

Area Sq Km	49 035
Area Sq Miles	18 933
Population	5 390 000
Capital	Bratislava
Languages	Slovakian, Hungarian, Czech
Religions	Roman Catholic, Protestant, Orthodox
Currency	Euro
Organizations	EU, OECD, UN
Map page	103

SLOVENIA
Republic of Slovenia

Area Sq Km	20 251
Area Sq Miles	7 819
Population	2 002 000
Capital	Ljubljana
Languages	Slovenian, Croatian, Serbian
Religions	Roman Catholic, Protestant
Currency	Euro
Organizations	EU, UN
Map page	108–109

SOLOMON ISLANDS

Area Sq Km	28 370
Area Sq Miles	10 954
Population	496 000
Capital	Honiara
Languages	English, creole, local languages
Religions	Protestant, Roman Catholic
Currency	Solomon Islands dollar
Organizations	Comm., UN
Map page	48

SOMALIA
Somali Democratic Republic

Area Sq Km	637 657	**Religions**	Sunni Muslim
Area Sq Miles	246 201	**Currency**	Somali shilling
Population	8 699 000	**Organizations**	UN
Capital	Mogadishu (Muqdisho)	**Map page**	117
Languages	Somali, Arabic		

SOUTH AFRICA, REPUBLIC OF

Area Sq Km	1 219 080	**Religions**	Protestant, Roman Catholic, Sunni Muslim, Hindu
Area Sq Miles	470 689	**Currency**	Rand
Population	48 577 000	**Organizations**	Comm., SADC, UN
Capital	Pretoria (Tshwane)/ Cape Town	**Map page**	122–123
Languages	Afrikaans, English, nine official local languages		

SOUTH KOREA
Republic of Korea

Area Sq Km	99 274	**Religions**	Buddhist, Protestant, Roman Catholic
Area Sq Miles	38 330	**Currency**	South Korean won
Population	48 224 000	**Organizations**	APEC, OECD, UN
Capital	Seoul (Sŏul)	**Map page**	65
Languages	Korean		

SPAIN
Kingdom of Spain

Area Sq Km	504 782	**Religions**	Roman Catholic
Area Sq Miles	194 897	**Currency**	Euro
Population	44 279 000	**Organizations**	EU, OECD, UN
Capital	Madrid	**Map page**	106–107
Languages	Spanish, Castilian, Catalan, Galician, Basque		

SRI LANKA
Democratic Socialist Republic of Sri Lanka

Area Sq Km	65 610	**Religions**	Buddhist, Hindu, Sunni Muslim, Roman Catholic
Area Sq Miles	25 332	**Currency**	Sri Lankan rupee
Population	19 299 000	**Organizations**	Comm., UN
Capital	Sri Jayewardenepura Kotte	**Map page**	73
Languages	Sinhalese, Tamil, English		

SUDAN
Republic of the Sudan

Area Sq Km	2 505 813	**Religions**	Sunni Muslim, traditional beliefs, Christian
Area Sq Miles	967 500	**Currency**	Sudanese pound (Sudani)
Population	38 560 000	**Organizations**	UN
Capital	Khartoum	**Map page**	116–117
Languages	Arabic, Dinka, Nubian, Beja, Nuer, local languages		

SURINAME
Republic of Suriname

Area Sq Km	163 820	**Religions**	Hindu, Roman Catholic, Protestant, Sunni Muslim
Area Sq Miles	63 251	**Currency**	Suriname guilder
Population	458 000	**Organizations**	CARICOM, UN
Capital	Paramaribo	**Map page**	151
Languages	Dutch, Surinamese, English, Hindi		

Svalbard
part of Norway

Area Sq Km	61 229	**Religions**	Protestant
Area Sq Miles	23 641	**Currency**	Norwegian krone
Population	2 400	**Map page**	82
Capital	Longyearbyen		
Languages	Norwegian		

SWAZILAND
Kingdom of Swaziland

Area Sq Km	17 364	**Currency**	Emalangeni, South African rand
Area Sq Miles	6 704	**Organizations**	Comm., SADC, UN
Population	1 141 000	**Map page**	123
Capital	Mbabane		
Languages	Swazi, English		
Religions	Christian, traditional beliefs		

SWEDEN
Kingdom of Sweden

Area Sq Km	449 964	**Religions**	Protestant, Roman Catholic
Area Sq Miles	173 732	**Currency**	Swedish krona
Population	9 119 000	**Organizations**	EU, OECD, UN
Capital	Stockholm	**Map page**	92–93
Languages	Swedish		

SWITZERLAND
Swiss Confederation

Area Sq Km	41 293	**Religions**	Roman Catholic, Protestant,
Area Sq Miles	15 943	**Currency**	Swiss franc
Population	7 484 000	**Organizations**	OECD, UN
Capital	Bern	**Map page**	105
Languages	German, French, Italian, Romansch		

SYRIA
Syrian Arab Republic

Area Sq Km	185 180	**Religions**	Sunni Muslim, Shi'a Muslim, Christian
Area Sq Miles	71 498	**Currency**	Syrian pound
Population	19 929 000	**Organizations**	UN
Capital	Damascus (Dimashq)	**Map page**	80
Languages	Arabic, Kurdish, Armenian		

TAIWAN
Republic of China

Area Sq Km	36 179	**Religions**	Buddhist, Taoist, Confucian, Christian
Area Sq Miles	13 969	**Currency**	Taiwan dollar
Population	22 880 000	**Organizations**	APEC
Capital	T'aipei	**Map page**	71
Languages	Mandarin, Min, Hakka, local languages		

The People's Republic of China claims Taiwan as its 23rd province

TAJIKISTAN
Republic of Tajikistan

Area Sq Km 143 100
Area Sq Miles 55 251
Population 6 736 000
Capital Dushanbe
Languages Tajik, Uzbek, Russian
Religions Sunni Muslim
Currency Somoni
Organizations CIS, UN
Map page 77

TANZANIA
United Republic of Tanzania

Area Sq Km 945 087
Area Sq Miles 364 900
Population 40 454 000
Capital Dodoma
Languages Swahili, English, Nyamwezi, local languages
Religions Shi'a Muslim, Sunni Muslim, traditional beliefs, Christian
Currency Tanzanian shilling
Organizations Comm., SADC, UN
Map page 119

THAILAND
Kingdom of Thailand

Area Sq Km 513 115
Area Sq Miles 198 115
Population 63 884 000
Capital Bangkok (Krung Thep)
Languages Thai, Lao, Chinese, Malay, Mon-Khmer languages
Religions Buddhist, Sunni Muslim
Currency Baht
Organizations APEC, ASEAN, UN
Map page 62–63

TOGO
Republic of Togo

Area Sq Km 56 785
Area Sq Miles 21 925
Population 6 585 000
Capital Lomé
Languages French, Ewe, Kabre, local languages
Religions Traditional beliefs, Christian, Sunni Muslim
Currency CFA franc
Organizations UN
Map page 114

Tokelau
New Zealand Overseas Territory

Area Sq Km 10
Area Sq Miles 4
Population 1 000
Capital none
Languages English, Tokelauan
Religions Christian
Currency New Zealand dollar
Map page 49

TONGA
Kingdom of Tonga

Area Sq Km 748
Area Sq Miles 289
Population 100 000
Capital Nuku'alofa
Languages Tongan, English
Religions Protestant, Roman Catholic
Currency Pa'anga
Organizations Comm., UN
Map page 49

TRINIDAD AND TOBAGO
Republic of Trinidad and Tobago

Area Sq Km 5 130
Area Sq Miles 1 981
Population 1 333 000
Capital Port of Spain
Languages English, creole, Hindi
Religions Roman Catholic, Hindu, Protestant, Sunni Muslim
Currency Trinidad and Tobago dollar
Organizations CARICOM, Comm., UN
Map page 147

Tristan da Cunha
Dependency of St Helena

Area Sq Km 98
Area Sq Miles 38
Population 284
Capital Settlement of Edinburgh
Languages English
Religions Protestant, Roman Catholic
Currency Pound sterling
Map page 113

TUNISIA
Republic of Tunisia

Area Sq Km 164 150
Area Sq Miles 63 379
Population 10 327 000
Capital Tunis
Languages Arabic, French
Religions Sunni Muslim
Currency Tunisian dinar
Organizations UN
Map page 116

TURKEY
Republic of Turkey

Area Sq Km 779 452
Area Sq Miles 300 948
Population 74 877 000
Capital Ankara
Languages Turkish, Kurdish
Religions Sunni Muslim, Shi'a Muslim
Currency Lira
Organizations OECD, UN
Map page 80

TURKMENISTAN
Republic of Turkmenistan

Area Sq Km 488 100
Area Sq Miles 188 456
Population 4 965 000
Capital Aşgabat (Ashkhabad)
Languages Turkmen, Uzbek, Russian
Religions Sunni Muslim, Russian Orthodox
Currency Turkmen manat
Organizations UN
Map page 76

Turks and Caicos Islands
United Kingdom Overseas Territory

Area Sq Km 430
Area Sq Miles 166
Population 26 000
Capital Grand Turk (Cockburn Town)
Languages English
Religions Protestant
Currency United States dollar
Map page 147

TUVALU

Area Sq Km 25
Area Sq Miles 10
Population 11 000
Capital Vaiaku
Languages Tuvaluan, English
Religions Protestant
Currency Australian dollar
Organizations Comm., UN
Map page 49

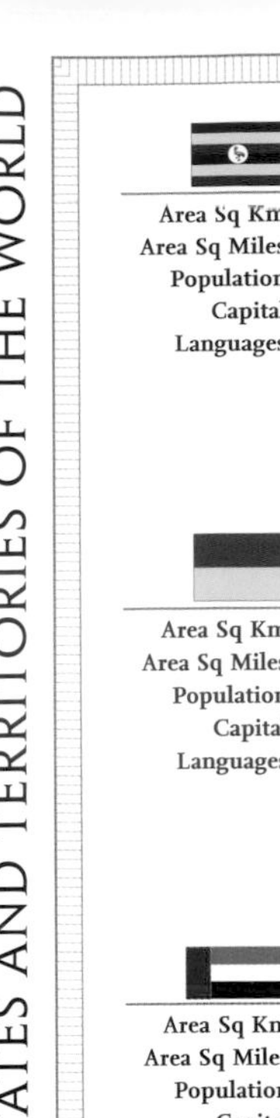

UGANDA
Republic of Uganda

Area Sq Km 241 038
Area Sq Miles 93 065
Population 30 884 000
Capital Kampala
Languages English, Swahili, Luganda, local languages
Religions Roman Catholic, Protestant, Sunni Muslim, traditional beliefs
Currency Ugandan shilling
Organizations Comm., UN
Map page 119

UKRAINE
Republic of Ukraine

Area Sq Km 603 700
Area Sq Miles 233 090
Population 46 205 000
Capital Kiev (Kyiv)
Languages Ukrainian, Russian
Religions Ukrainian Orthodox, Ukrainian Catholic, Roman Catholic
Currency Hryvnia
Organizations CIS, UN
Map page 90–91

UNITED ARAB EMIRATES
Federation of Emirates

Area Sq Km 77 700
Area Sq Miles 30 000
Population 4 380 000
Capital Abu Dhabi (Abū Ẓabī)
Languages Arabic, English
Religions Sunni Muslim, Shi'a Muslim
Currency United Arab Emirates dirham
Organizations OPEC, UN
Map page 79

Abu Dhabi (Abū Ẓabī) (Emirate)

Area Sq Km 67 340
Area Sq Miles 26 000
Population 1 292 119
Capital Abu Dhabi (Abū Ẓabī)

Ajman (Emirate)

Area Sq Km 259
Area Sq Miles 100
Population 189 849
Capital Ajman

Dubai (Emirate)

Area Sq Km 3 885
Area Sq Miles 1 500
Population 1 200 309
Capital Dubai

Fujairah (Emirate)

Area Sq Km 1 165
Area Sq Miles 450
Population 118 617
Capital Fujairah

Ra's al Khaymah (Emirate)

Area Sq Km 1 684
Area Sq Miles 650
Population 197 571
Capital Ra's al Khaymah

Sharjah (Emirate)

Area Sq Km 2 590
Area Sq Miles 1 000
Population 724 859
Capital Sharjah

Umm al Qaywayn (Emirate)

Area Sq Km 777
Area Sq Miles 300
Population 45 756
Capital Umm al Qaywayn

UNITED KINGDOM
of Great Britain and Northern Ireland

Area Sq Km 243 609
Area Sq Miles 94 058
Population 60 769 000
Capital London
Languages English, Welsh, Gaelic
Religions Protestant, Roman Catholic, Muslim
Currency Pound sterling
Organizations Comm., EU, OECD, UN
Map page 94–95

England (Constituent country)

Area Sq Km 130 433
Area Sq Miles 50 360
Population 50 431 700
Capital London

Northern Ireland (Province)

Area Sq Km 13 576
Area Sq Miles 5 242
Population 1 724 400
Capital Belfast

Scotland (Constituent country)

Area Sq Km 78 822
Area Sq Miles 30 433
Population 5 094 800
Capital Edinburgh

Wales (Principality)

Area Sq Km 20 778
Area Sq Miles 8 022
Population 2 958 600
Capital Cardiff

UNITED STATES OF AMERICA
Federal Republic

Area Sq Km 9 826 635
Area Sq Miles 3 794 085
Population 305 826 000
Capital Washington D.C.
Languages English, Spanish
Religions Protestant, Roman Catholic, Sunni Muslim, Jewish
Currency United States dollar
Organizations APEC, OECD, UN
Map page 132–133

Alabama (State)

Area Sq Km 135 765
Area Sq Miles 52 419
Population 4 599 030
Capital Montgomery

Alaska (State)

Area Sq Km 1 717 854
Area Sq Miles 663 267
Population 670 053
Capital Juneau

Arizona (State)

Area Sq Km 295 253
Area Sq Miles 113 998
Population 6 166 318
Capital Phoenix

Arkansas (State)

Area Sq Km 137 733
Area Sq Miles 53 179
Population 2 810 872
Capital Little Rock

California (State)

Area Sq Km 423 971
Area Sq Miles 163 696
Population 36 457 549
Capital Sacramento

Colorado (State)

Area Sq Km	269 602	**Population**	4 753 377
Area Sq Miles	104 094	**Capital**	Denver

Connecticut (State)

Area Sq Km	14 356	**Population**	3 504 809
Area Sq Miles	5 543	**Capital**	Hartford

Delaware (State)

Area Sq Km	6 446	**Population**	853 476
Area Sq Miles	2 489	**Capital**	Dover

District of Columbia (District)

Area Sq Km	176	**Population**	581 530
Area Sq Miles	68	**Capital**	Washington

Florida (State)

Area Sq Km	170 305	**Population**	18 089 888
Area Sq Miles	65 755	**Capital**	Tallahassee

Georgia (State)

Area Sq Km	153 910	**Population**	9 363 941
Area Sq Miles	59 425	**Capital**	Atlanta

Hawaii (State)

Area Sq Km	28 311	**Population**	1 285 498
Area Sq Miles	10 931	**Capital**	Honolulu

Idaho (State)

Area Sq Km	216 445	**Population**	1 466 465
Area Sq Miles	83 570	**Capital**	Boise

Illinois (State)

Area Sq Km	149 997	**Population**	12 831 970
Area Sq Miles	57 914	**Capital**	Springfield

Indiana (State)

Area Sq Km	94 322	**Population**	6 313 520
Area Sq Miles	36 418	**Capital**	Indianapolis

Iowa (State)

Area Sq Km	145 744	**Population**	2 982 085
Area Sq Miles	56 272	**Capital**	Des Moines

Kansas (State)

Area Sq Km	213 096	**Population**	2 764 075
Area Sq Miles	82 277	**Capital**	Topeka

Kentucky (State)

Area Sq Km	104 659	**Population**	4 206 074
Area Sq Miles	40 409	**Capital**	Frankfort

Louisiana (State)

Area Sq Km	134 265	**Population**	4 287 768
Area Sq Miles	51 840	**Capital**	Baton Rouge

Maine (State)

Area Sq Km	91 647	**Population**	1 321 574
Area Sq Miles	35 385	**Capital**	Augusta

Maryland (State)

Area Sq Km	32 134	**Population**	5 615 727
Area Sq Miles	12 407	**Capital**	Annapolis

Massachusetts (State)

Area Sq Km	27 337	**Population**	6 437 193
Area Sq Miles	10 555	**Capital**	Boston

Michigan (State)

Area Sq Km	250 493	**Population**	10 095 643
Area Sq Miles	96 716	**Capital**	Lansing

Minnesota (State)

Area Sq Km	225 171	**Population**	5 167 101
Area Sq Miles	86 939	**Capital**	St Paul

Mississippi (State)

Area Sq Km	125 433	**Population**	2 910 540
Area Sq Miles	48 430	**Capital**	Jackson

Missouri (State)

Area Sq Km	180 533	**Population**	5 842 713
Area Sq Miles	69 704	**Capital**	Jefferson City

Montana (State)

Area Sq Km	380 837	**Population**	944 632
Area Sq Miles	147 042	**Capital**	Helena

Nebraska (State)

Area Sq Km	200 346	**Population**	1 768 331
Area Sq Miles	77 354	**Capital**	Lincoln

Nevada (State)

Area Sq Km	286 352	**Population**	2 495 529
Area Sq Miles	110 561	**Capital**	Carson City

New Hampshire (State)

Area Sq Km	24 216	**Population**	1 314 895
Area Sq Miles	9 350	**Capital**	Concord

New Jersey (State)

Area Sq Km	22 587	**Population**	8 724 560
Area Sq Miles	8 721	**Capital**	Trenton

UNITED STATES OF AMERICA
Federal Republic

New Mexico (State)
Area Sq Km 314 914 | **Population** 1 954 599
Area Sq Miles 121 589 | **Capital** Santa Fe

New York (State)
Area Sq Km 141 299 | **Population** 19 306 183
Area Sq Miles 54 556 | **Capital** Albany

North Carolina (State)
Area Sq Km 139 391 | **Population** 8 856 505
Area Sq Miles 53 819 | **Capital** Raleigh

North Dakota (State)
Area Sq Km 183 112 | **Population** 635 867
Area Sq Miles 70 700 | **Capital** Bismarck

Ohio (State)
Area Sq Km 116 096 | **Population** 11 478 006
Area Sq Miles 44 825 | **Capital** Columbus

Oklahoma (State)
Area Sq Km 181 035 | **Population** 3 579 212
Area Sq Miles 69 898 | **Capital** Oklahoma City

Oregon (State)
Area Sq Km 254 806 | **Population** 3 700 758
Area Sq Miles 98 381 | **Capital** Salem

Pennsylvania (State)
Area Sq Km 119 282 | **Population** 12 440 621
Area Sq Miles 46 055 | **Capital** Harrisburg

Rhode Island (State)
Area Sq Km 4 002 | **Population** 1 067 610
Area Sq Miles 1 545 | **Capital** Providence

South Carolina (State)
Area Sq Km 82 931 | **Population** 4 321 249
Area Sq Miles 32 020 | **Capital** Columbia

South Dakota (State)
Area Sq Km 199 730 | **Population** 781 919
Area Sq Miles 77 116 | **Capital** Pierre

Tennessee (State)
Area Sq Km 109 150 | **Population** 6 038 803
Area Sq Miles 42 143 | **Capital** Nashville

Texas (State)
Area Sq Km 695 622 | **Population** 23 507 783
Area Sq Miles 268 581 | **Capital** Austin

Utah (State)
Area Sq Km 219 887 | **Population** 2 550 063
Area Sq Miles 84 899 | **Capital** Salt Lake City

Vermont (State)
Area Sq Km 24 900 | **Population** 623 908
Area Sq Miles 9 614 | **Capital** Montpelier

Virginia (State)
Area Sq Km 110 784 | **Population** 7 642 884
Area Sq Miles 42 774 | **Capital** Richmond

Washington (State)
Area Sq Km 184 666 | **Population** 6 395 798
Area Sq Miles 71 300 | **Capital** Olympia

West Virginia (State)
Area Sq Km 62 755 | **Population** 1 818 470
Area Sq Miles 24 230 | **Capital** Charleston

Wisconsin (State)
Area Sq Km 169 639 | **Population** 5 556 506
Area Sq Miles 65 498 | **Capital** Madison

Wyoming (State)
Area Sq Km 253 337 | **Population** 515 004
Area Sq Miles 97 814 | **Capital** Cheyenne

URUGUAY
Oriental Republic of Uruguay

Area Sq Km 176 215
Area Sq Miles 68 037
Population 3 340 000
Capital Montevideo
Languages Spanish
Religions Roman Catholic, Protestant, Jewish
Currency Uruguayan peso
Organizations UN
Map page 153

UZBEKISTAN
Republic of Uzbekistan

Area Sq Km 447 400
Area Sq Miles 172 742
Population 27 372 000
Capital Tashkent
Languages Uzbek, Russian, Tajik, Kazakh
Religions Sunni Muslim, Russian Orthodox
Currency Uzbek som
Organizations CIS, UN
Map page 76–77

VANUATU
Republic of Vanuatu

Area Sq Km	12 190	**Religions**	Protestant, Roman Catholic, traditional beliefs
Area Sq Miles	4 707	**Currency**	Vatu
Population	226 000	**Organizations**	Comm., UN
Capital	Port Vila	**Map page**	48
Languages	English, Bislama (creole), French		

VATICAN CITY
Vatican City State

Area Sq Km	0.5	**Religions**	Roman Catholic
Area Sq Miles	0.2	**Currency**	Euro
Population	557	**Map page**	108
Capital	Vatican City		
Languages	Italian		

VENEZUELA
Republic of Venezuela

Area Sq Km	912 050	**Religions**	Roman Catholic, Protestant
Area Sq Miles	352 144	**Currency**	Bolívar fuerte
Population	27 657 000	**Organizations**	OPEC, UN
Capital	Caracas	**Map page**	150
Languages	Spanish, Amerindian languages		

VIETNAM
Socialist Republic of Vietnam

Area Sq Km	329 565	**Religions**	Buddhist, Taoist, Roman Catholic, Cao Dai, Hoa Hoa
Area Sq Miles	127 246	**Currency**	Dong
Population	87 375 000	**Organizations**	APEC, ASEAN, UN
Capital	Ha Nôi (Hanoi)	**Map page**	62–63
Languages	Vietnamese, Thai, Khmer, Chinese, local languages		

Virgin Islands (U.K.)
United Kingdom Overseas Territory

Area Sq Km	153	**Religions**	Protestant, Roman Catholic
Area Sq Miles	59	**Currency**	United States dollar
Population	23 000	**Map page**	147
Capital	Road Town		
Languages	English		

Virgin Islands (U.S.)
United States Unincorporated Territory

Area Sq Km	352	**Religions**	Protestant, Roman Catholic
Area Sq Miles	136	**Currency**	United States dollar
Population	111 000	**Map page**	147
Capital	Charlotte Amalie		
Languages	English, Spanish		

Wallis and Futuna Islands
French Overseas Territory

Area Sq Km	274	**Religions**	Roman Catholic
Area Sq Miles	106	**Currency**	CFP franc
Population	15 000	**Map page**	49
Capital	Matā'utu		
Languages	French, Wallisian, Futunian		

West Bank
Disputed Territory

Area Sq Km	5 860	**Religions**	Sunni Muslim, Jewish, Shi'a Muslim, Christian
Area Sq Miles	2 263	**Currency**	Jordanian dinar, Israeli shekel
Population	2 676 284	**Map page**	80
Capital	none		
Languages	Arabic, Hebrew		

Western Sahara
Disputed Territory (Morocco)

Area Sq Km	266 000	**Religions**	Sunni Muslim
Area Sq Miles	102 703	**Currency**	Moroccan dirham
Population	480 000	**Map page**	114
Capital	Laâyoune		
Languages	Arabic		

YEMEN
Republic of Yemen

Area Sq Km	527 968	**Religions**	Sunni Muslim, Shi'a Muslim
Area Sq Miles	203 850	**Currency**	Yemeni riyal
Population	22 389 000	**Organizations**	UN
Capital	Ṣan'ā'	**Map page**	78–79
Languages	Arabic		

ZAMBIA
Republic of Zambia

Area Sq Km	752 614	**Religions**	Christian, traditional beliefs
Area Sq Miles	290 586	**Currency**	Zambian kwacha
Population	11 922 000	**Organizations**	Comm., SADC, UN
Capital	Lusaka	**Map page**	120–121
Languages	English, Bemba, Nyanja, Tonga, local languages		

ZIMBABWE
Republic of Zimbabwe

Area Sq Km	390 759	**Religions**	Christian, traditional beliefs
Area Sq Miles	150 873	**Currency**	Zimbabwean dollar
Population	13 349 000	**Organizations**	SADC, UN
Capital	Harare	**Map page**	121
Languages	English, Shona, Ndebele		

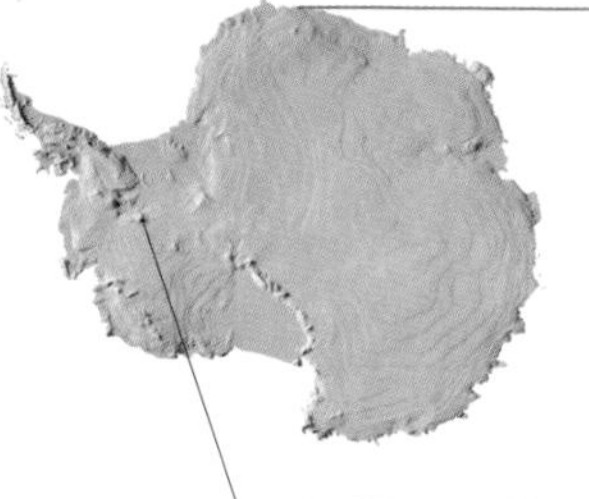

ANTARCTICA

Total Land Area
12 093 000 sq km
4 669 133 sq miles
(excluding ice shelves)

HIGHEST MOUNTAINS	metres	feet
Vinson Massif	4 897	16 066
Mt Tyree	4 852	15 918
Mt Kirkpatrick	4 528	14 855
Mt Markham	4 351	14 275
Mt Jackson	4 190	13 747
Mt Sidley	4 181	13 717

OCEANIA

Total land area
8 844 516 sq km
3 414 887 sq miles
(includes New Guinea and Pacific Island nations)

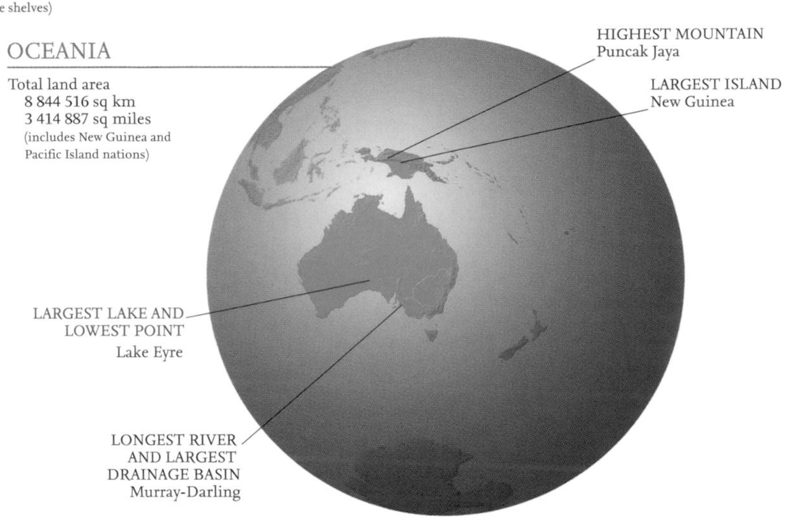

HIGHEST MOUNTAINS	metres	feet	LARGEST ISLANDS	sq km	sq miles	LARGEST LAKES	sq km	sq miles	LONGEST RIVERS	km	miles
Puncak Jaya	5 030	16 502	New Guinea	808 510	312 167	Lake Eyre	0–8 900	0–3 436	Murray-Darling	3 750	2 330
Puncak Trikora	4 730	15 518	South Island	151 215	58 384	Lake Torrens	0–5 780	0–2 232	Darling	2 739	1 702
Puncak Mandala	4 700	15 420	North Island	115 777	44 701				Murray	2 589	1 609
Puncak Yamin	4 595	15 075	Tasmania	67 800	26 178				Murrumbidgee	1 690	1 050
Mt Wilhelm	4 509	14 793							Lachlan	1 480	920
Mt Kubor	4 359	14 301							Macquarie	950	590

ASIA

Total Land Area
45 036 492 sq km
17 388 686 sq miles

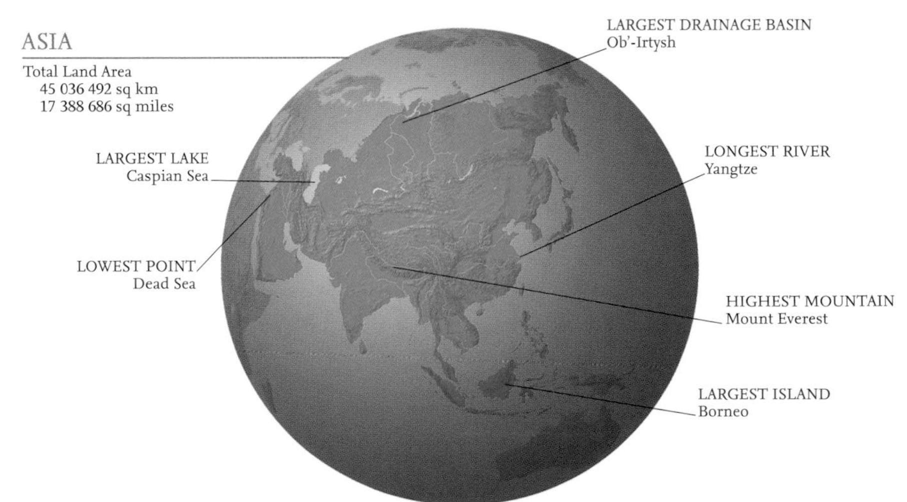

HIGHEST MOUNTAINS	metres	feet	LARGEST ISLANDS	sq km	sq miles	LARGEST LAKES	sq km	sq miles	LONGEST RIVERS	km	miles
Mt Everest	8 848	29 028	Borneo	745 561	287 861	Caspian Sea	371 000	143 243	Yangtze	6 380	3 965
K2	8 611	28 251	Sumatra	473 606	182 859	Lake Baikal	30 500	11 776	Ob'-Irtysh	5 568	3 460
Kangchenjunga	8 586	28 169	Honshū	227 414	87 805	Lake Balkhash	17 400	6 718	Yenisey-Angara-Selenga	5 550	3 449
Lhotse	8 516	27 939	Celebes	189 216	73 056	Aral Sea	17 158	6 625	Yellow	5 464	3 395
Makalu	8 463	27 765	Java	132 188	51 038	Ysyk-Köl	6 200	2 394	Irtysh	4 440	2 759
Cho Oyu	8 201	26 906	Luzon	104 690	40 421						

EUROPE

Total Land Area
9 908 599 sq km
3 825 731 sq miles

HIGHEST MOUNTAINS	metres	feet	LARGEST ISLANDS	sq km	sq miles	LARGEST LAKES	sq km	sq miles	LONGEST RIVERS	km	miles
El'brus	5 642	18 510	Great Britain	218 476	84 354	Caspian Sea	371 000	143 243	Volga	3 688	2 292
Gora Dykh-Tau	5 204	17 073	Iceland	102 820	39 699	Lake Ladoga	18 390	7 100	Danube	2 850	1 771
Shkhara	5 201	17 063	Novaya Zemlya	90 650	35 000	Lake Onega	9 600	3 707	Dnieper	2 285	1 420
Kazbek	5 047	16 558	Ireland	83 045	32 064	Vänern	5 585	2 156	Kama	2 028	1 260
Mont Blanc	4 808	15 774	Spitsbergen	37 814	14 600	Rybinskoye Vodokhranilishche	5 180	2 000	Don	1 931	1 200
Dufourspitze	4 634	15 203	Sicily (Sicilia)	25 426	9 817				Pechora	1 802	1 120

AFRICA

Total Land Area
30 343 578 sq km
11 715 721 sq miles

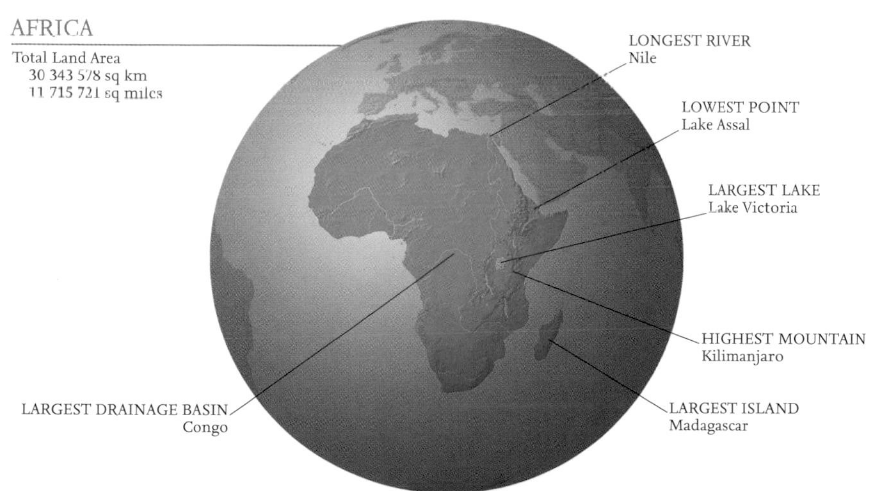

HIGHEST MOUNTAINS	metres	feet	LARGEST ISLANDS	sq km	sq miles	LARGEST LAKES	sq km	sq miles	LONGEST RIVERS	km	miles
Kilimanjaro	5 892	19 330	Madagascar	587 040	226 656	Lake Victoria	68 870	26 591	Nile	6 695	4 160
Mt Kenya	5 199	17 057				Lake Tanganyika	32 600	12 587	Congo	4 667	2 900
Margherita Peak	5 110	16 765				Lake Nyasa	29 500	11 390	Niger	4 184	2 600
Meru	4 565	14 977				Lake Volta	8 482	3 275	Zambezi	2 736	1 700
Ras Dejen	4 533	14 872				Lake Turkana	6 500	2 510	Webi Shabeelle	2 490	1 547
Mt Karisimbi	4 510	14 796				Lake Albert	5 600	2 162	Ubangi	2 250	1 398

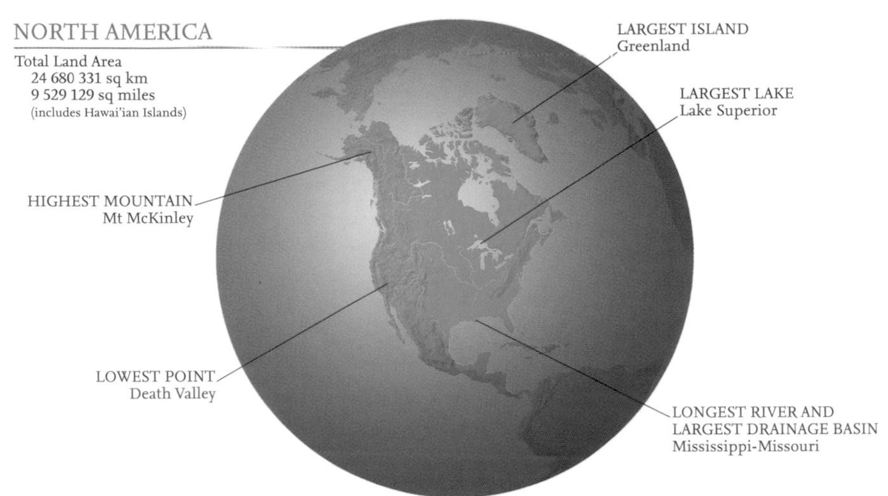

HIGHEST MOUNTAINS	metres	feet
Mt McKinley	6 194	20 321
Mt Logan	5 959	19 550
Pico de Orizaba	5 610	18 405
Mt St Elias	5 489	18 008
Volcán Popocatépetl	5 452	17 887

LARGEST ISLANDS	sq km	sq miles
Greenland	2 175 600	839 999
Baffin Island	507 451	195 927
Victoria Island	217 291	83 896
Ellesmere Island	196 236	75 767
Cuba	110 860	42 803
Newfoundland	108 860	42 031

LARGEST LAKES	sq km	sq miles
Lake Superior	82 100	31 699
Lake Huron	59 600	23 012
Lake Michigan	57 800	22 317
Great Bear Lake	31 328	12 096
Great Slave Lake	28 568	11 030
Lake Erie	25 700	9 923

LONGEST RIVERS	km	miles
Mississippi-Missouri	5 969	3 709
Mackenzie-Peace-Finlay	4 241	2 635
Missouri	4 086	2 539
Mississippi	3 765	2 340
Yukon	3 185	1 979

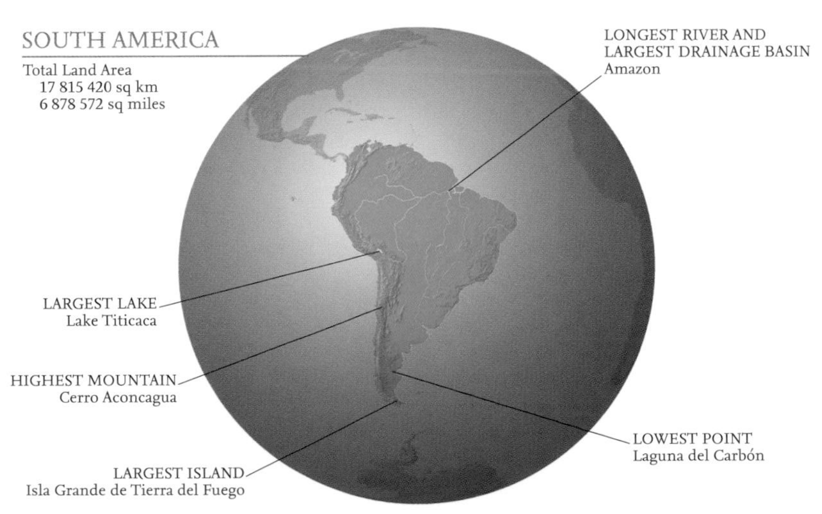

HIGHEST MOUNTAINS	metres	feet
Cerro Aconcagua	6 959	22 831
Nevado Ojos del Salado	6 908	22 664
Cerro Bonete	6 872	22 546
Cerro Pissis	6 858	22 500
Cerro Tupungato	6 800	22 309

LARGEST ISLANDS	sq km	sq miles
Isla Grande de Tierra del Fuego	47 000	18 147
Isla de Chiloé	8 394	3 241
East Falkland	6 760	2 610
West Falkland	5 413	2 090

LARGEST LAKES	sq km	sq miles
Lake Titicaca	8 340	3 220

LONGEST RIVERS	km	miles
Amazon	6 516	4 049
Río de la Plata-Paraná	4 500	2 796
Purus	3 218	2 000
Madeira	3 200	1 988
São Francisco	2 900	1 802

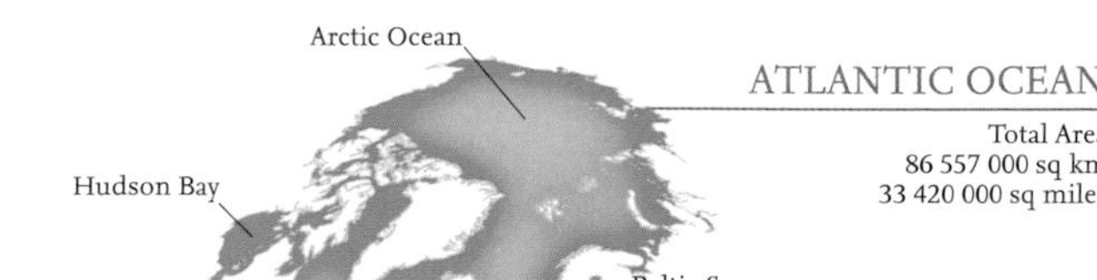

ATLANTIC OCEAN

Total Area
86 557 000 sq km
33 420 000 sq miles

ATLANTIC OCEAN	Area		Deepest Point	
	square km	square miles	metres	feet
Extent	86 557 000	33 420 000	8 605	28 231
Arctic Ocean	9 485 000	3 662 000	5 450	17 880
Caribbean Sea	2 512 000	970 000	7 680	25 196
Mediterranean Sea	2 510 000	969 000	5 121	16 800
Gulf of Mexico	1 544 000	596 000	3 504	11 495
Hudson Bay	1 233 000	476 000	259	849
North Sea	575 000	222 000	661	2 168
Black Sea	508 000	196 000	2 245	7 365
Baltic Sea	382 000	147 000	460	1 509

Bering Sea
Sea of Okhotsk
Sea of Japan (East Sea)
East China Sea and Yellow Sea
Deepest Point Challenger Deep
South China Sea

PACIFIC OCEAN

Total Area
166 241 000 sq km
64 186 000 sq miles

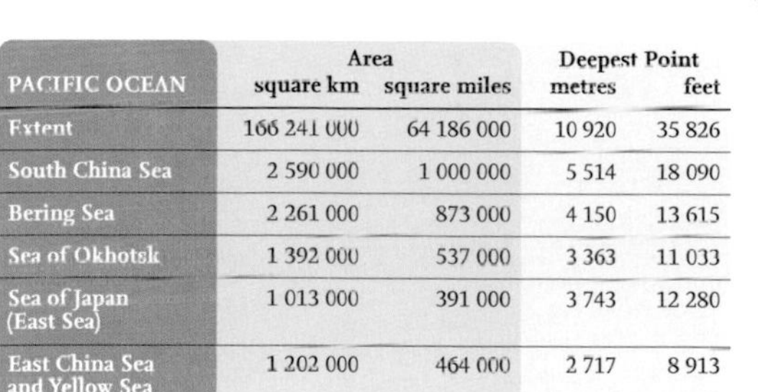

PACIFIC OCEAN	Area		Deepest Point	
	square km	square miles	metres	feet
Extent	166 241 000	64 186 000	10 920	35 826
South China Sea	2 590 000	1 000 000	5 514	18 090
Bering Sea	2 261 000	873 000	4 150	13 615
Sea of Okhotsk	1 392 000	537 000	3 363	11 033
Sea of Japan (East Sea)	1 013 000	391 000	3 743	12 280
East China Sea and Yellow Sea	1 202 000	464 000	2 717	8 913

The Gulf
Red Sea
Bay of Bengal
Deepest Point Java Trench

INDIAN OCEAN	Area		Deepest Point	
	square km	square miles	metres	feet
Extent	73 427 000	28 350 000	7 125	23 376
Bay of Bengal	2 172 000	839 000	4 500	14 763
Red Sea	453 000	175 000	3 040	9 973
The Gulf	238 000	92 000	73	239

INDIAN OCEAN

Total Area
73 427 000 sq km
28 350 000 sq miles

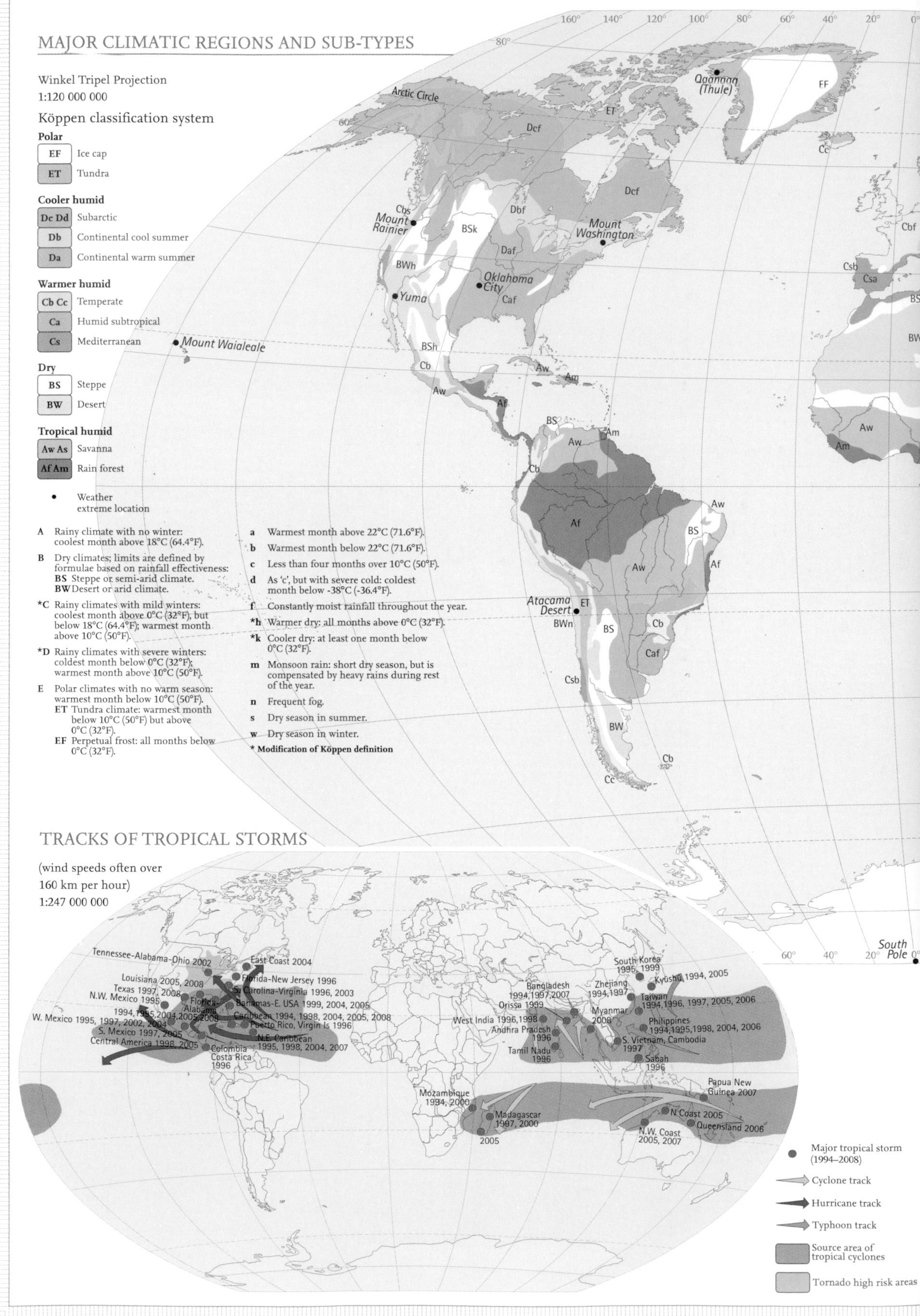

MAJOR CLIMATIC REGIONS AND SUB-TYPES
Winkel Tripel Projection
1:120 000 000
Köppen classification system
Polar
EF Ice cap
ET Tundra
Cooler humid
Dc Dd Subarctic
Db Continental cool summer
Da Continental warm summer
Warmer humid
Cb Cc Temperate
Ca Humid subtropical
Cs Mediterranean
Dry
BS Steppe
BW Desert
Tropical humid
Aw As Savanna
Af Am Rain forest
• Weather extreme location
A Rainy climate with no winter: coolest month above 18°C (64.4°F).
B Dry climates; limits are defined by formulae based on rainfall effectiveness:
BS Steppe or semi-arid climate.
BW Desert or arid climate.
*C Rainy climates with mild winters: coolest month above 0°C (32°F), but below 18°C (64.4°F); warmest month above 10°C (50°F).
*D Rainy climates with severe winters: coldest month below 0°C (32°F); warmest month above 10°C (50°F).
E Polar climates with no warm season: warmest month below 10°C (50°F).
ET Tundra climate: warmest month below 10°C (50°F) but above 0°C (32°F).
EF Perpetual frost: all months below 0°C (32°F).
a Warmest month above 22°C (71.6°F).
b Warmest month below 22°C (71.6°F).
c Less than four months over 10°C (50°F).
d As 'c', but with severe cold: coldest month below -38°C (-36.4°F).
f Constantly moist rainfall throughout the year.
*h Warmer dry: all months above 0°C (32°F).
*k Cooler dry: at least one month below 0°C (32°F).
m Monsoon rain: short dry season, but is compensated by heavy rains during rest of the year.
n Frequent fog.
s Dry season in summer.
w Dry season in winter.
* Modification of Köppen definition
Arctic Circle
Qaanaaq (Thule)
Mount Rainier
Mount Washington
Oklahoma City
Yuma
Mount Waialeale
Atacama Desert
South Pole
TRACKS OF TROPICAL STORMS
(wind speeds often over 160 km per hour)
1:247 000 000
Tennessee-Alabama-Ohio 2002
East Coast 2004
Louisiana 2005, 2008
Florida-New Jersey 1996
Texas 1997, 2008
S. Carolina-Virginia 1996, 2003
N.W. Mexico 1995
Bahamas-E. USA 1999, 2004, 2005
Florida-Alabama 1994, 1995, 2004, 2005, 2008
Caribbean 1994, 1998, 2004, 2005, 2008
W. Mexico 1995, 1997, 2002, 2004
Puerto Rico, Virgin Is 1996
S. Mexico 1997, 2005
N.E. Caribbean 1995, 1998, 2004, 2007
Central America 1998, 2005
Colombia Costa Rica 1996
South Korea 1996, 1999
Kyushu 1994, 2005
Bangladesh 1994, 1997, 2007
Zhejiang 1994, 1997
Taiwan 1994, 1996, 1997, 2005, 2006
Orissa 1999
Myanmar 2008
West India 1996, 1998
Andhra Pradesh 1996
Philippines 1994, 1995, 1998, 2004, 2006
S. Vietnam, Cambodia 1997
Tamil Nadu 1996
Sabah 1996
Papua New Guinea 2007
Mozambique 1994, 2000
Madagascar 1997, 2000
2005
N Coast 2005
Queensland 2006
N.W. Coast 2005, 2007
Major tropical storm (1994–2008)
Cyclone track
Hurricane track
Typhoon track
Source area of tropical cyclones
Tornado high risk areas

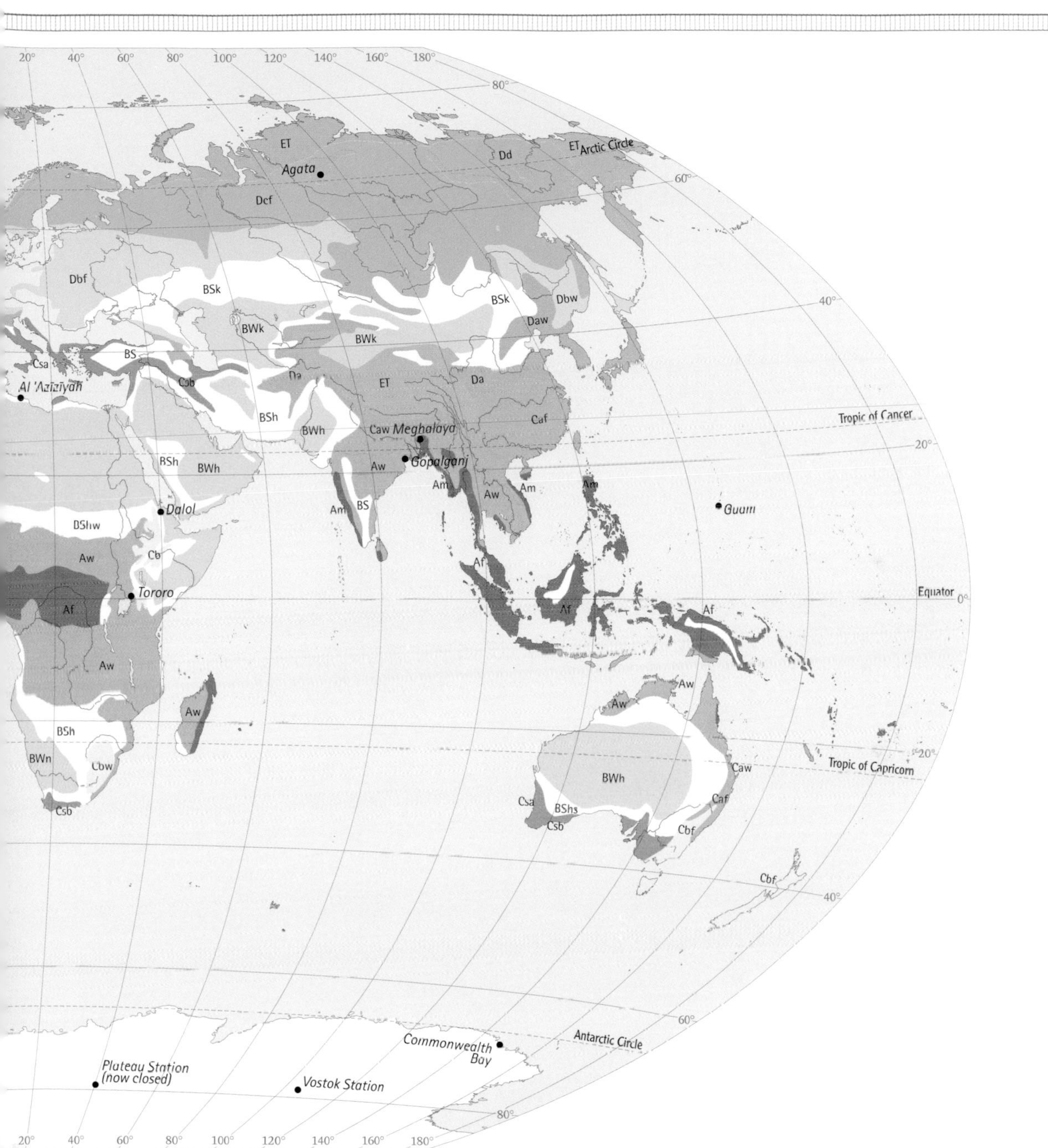

WORLD WEATHER EXTREMES

	Location
Highest shade temperature	57.8°C/136°F Al 'Azīzīyah, Libya (13th September 1922)
Hottest place — Annual mean	34.4°C/93.9°F Dalol, Ethiopia
Driest place — Annual mean	0.1 mm/0.004 inches Atacama Desert, Chile
Most sunshine — Annual mean	90% Yuma, Arizona, USA (over 4 000 hours)
Least sunshine	Nil for 182 days each year, South Pole
Lowest screen temperature	-89.2°C/-128.6°F Vostok Station, Antarctica (21st July 1983)
Coldest place — Annual mean	-56.6°C/-69.9°F Plateau Station, Antarctica
Wettest place — Annual mean	11 873 mm/467.4 inches Meghalaya, India
Most rainy days	Up to 350 per year Mount Waialeale, Hawaii, USA
Windiest place	322 km per hour/200 miles per hour in gales, Commonwealth Bay, Antarctica

	Location
Highest surface wind speed	
High altitude	372 km per hour/231 miles per hour Mount Washington, New Hampshire, USA (12th April 1934)
Low altitude	333 km per hour/207 miles per hour Qaanaaq (Thule), Greenland (8th March 1972)
Tornado	512 km per hour/318 miles per hour Oklahoma City, Oklahoma, USA (3rd May 1999)
Greatest snowfall	31 102 mm/1 224.5 inches Mount Rainier, Washington, USA (19th February 1971 — 18th February 1972)
Heaviest hailstones	1 kg/2.21 lb Gopalganj, Bangladesh (14th April 1986)
Thunder-days average	251 days per year Tororo, Uganda
Highest barometric pressure	1 083.8 mb Agata, Siberia, Rus. Fed. (31st December 1968)
Lowest barometric pressure	870 mb 483 km/300 miles west of Guam, Pacific Ocean (12th October 1979)

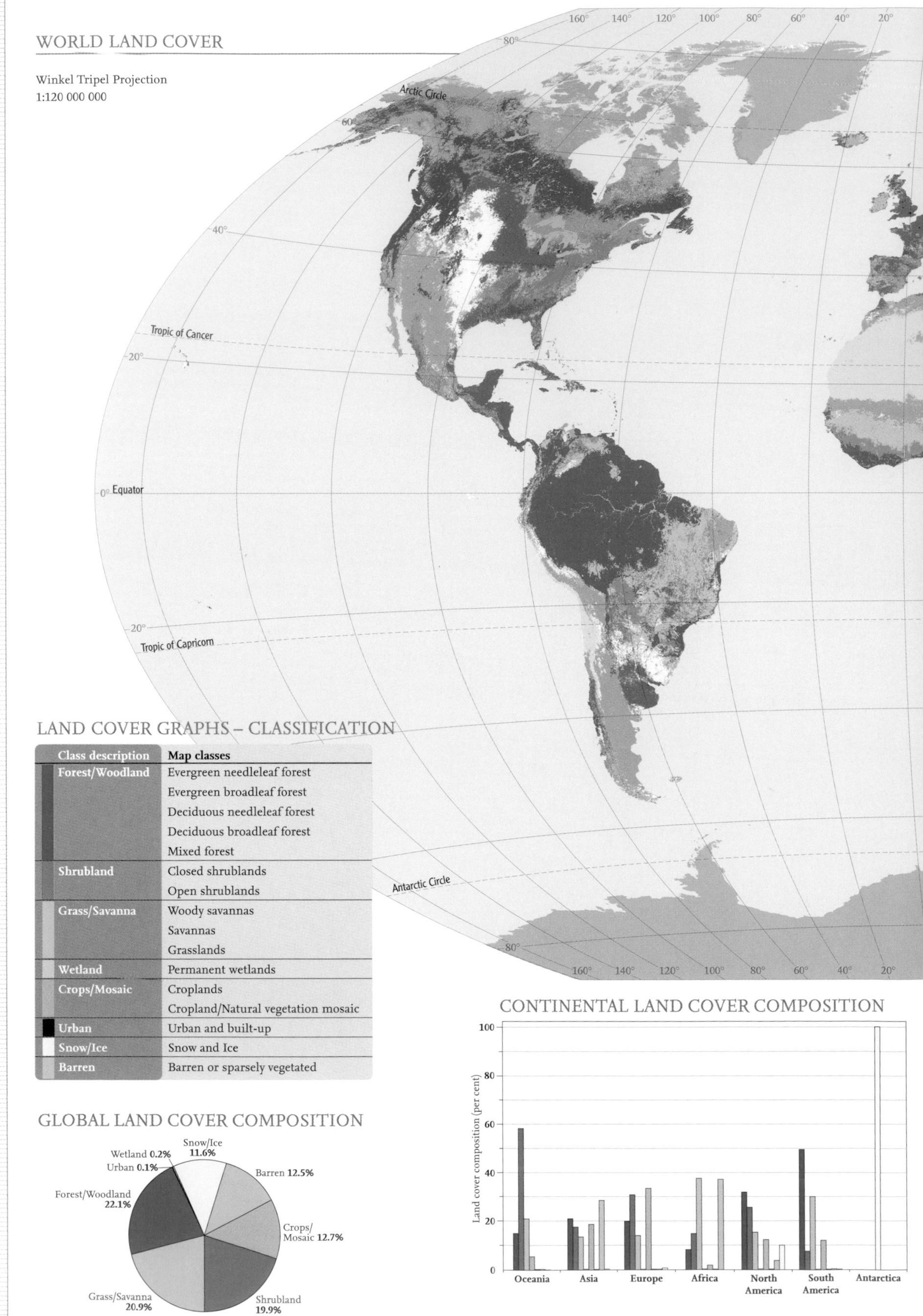

Class description	Map classes
Forest/Woodland	Evergreen needleleaf forest
	Evergreen broadleaf forest
	Deciduous needleleaf forest
	Deciduous broadleaf forest
	Mixed forest
Shrubland	Closed shrublands
	Open shrublands
Grass/Savanna	Woody savannas
	Savannas
	Grasslands
Wetland	Permanent wetlands
Crops/Mosaic	Croplands
	Cropland/Natural vegetation mosaic
Urban	Urban and built-up
Snow/Ice	Snow and Ice
Barren	Barren or sparsely vegetated

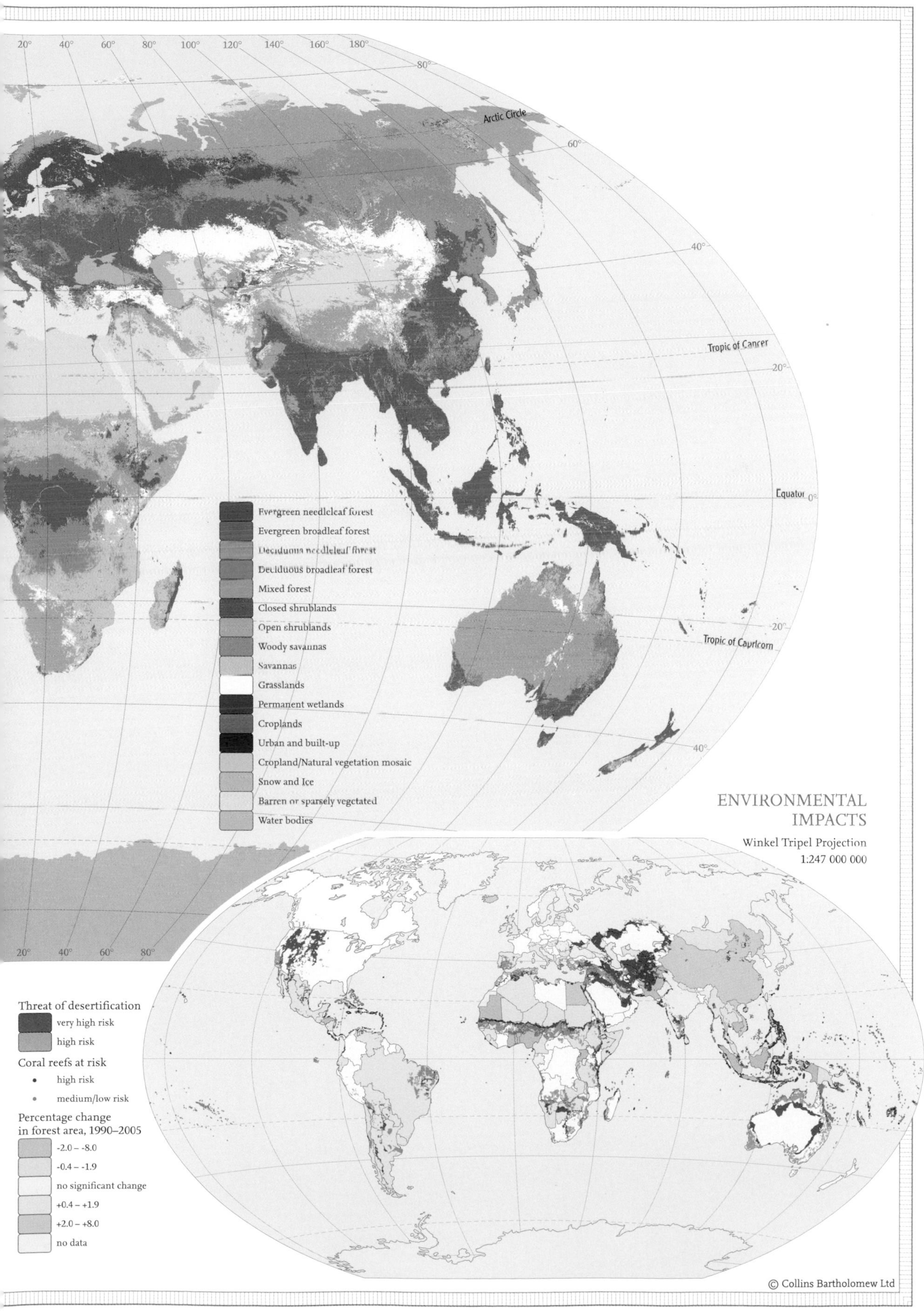

Arctic Circle
Tropic of Cancer
Equator
Tropic of Capricorn
Evergreen needleleaf forest
Evergreen broadleaf forest
Deciduous needleleaf forest
Deciduous broadleaf forest
Mixed forest
Closed shrublands
Open shrublands
Woody savannas
Savannas
Grasslands
Permanent wetlands
Croplands
Urban and built-up
Cropland/Natural vegetation mosaic
Snow and Ice
Barren or sparsely vegetated
Water bodies
Threat of desertification
very high risk
high risk
Coral reefs at risk
high risk
medium/low risk
Percentage change in forest area, 1990–2005
-2.0 – -8.0
-0.4 – -1.9
no significant change
+0.4 – +1.9
+2.0 – +8.0
no data

ENVIRONMENTAL IMPACTS

Winkel Tripel Projection
1:247 000 000

WORLD POPULATION DISTRIBUTION AND THE WORLD'S MAJOR CITIES

Winkel Tripel Projection
1:120 000 000

Major Urban Agglomerations

- over 20 million
- 10 million – 20 million
- 5 million – 10 million

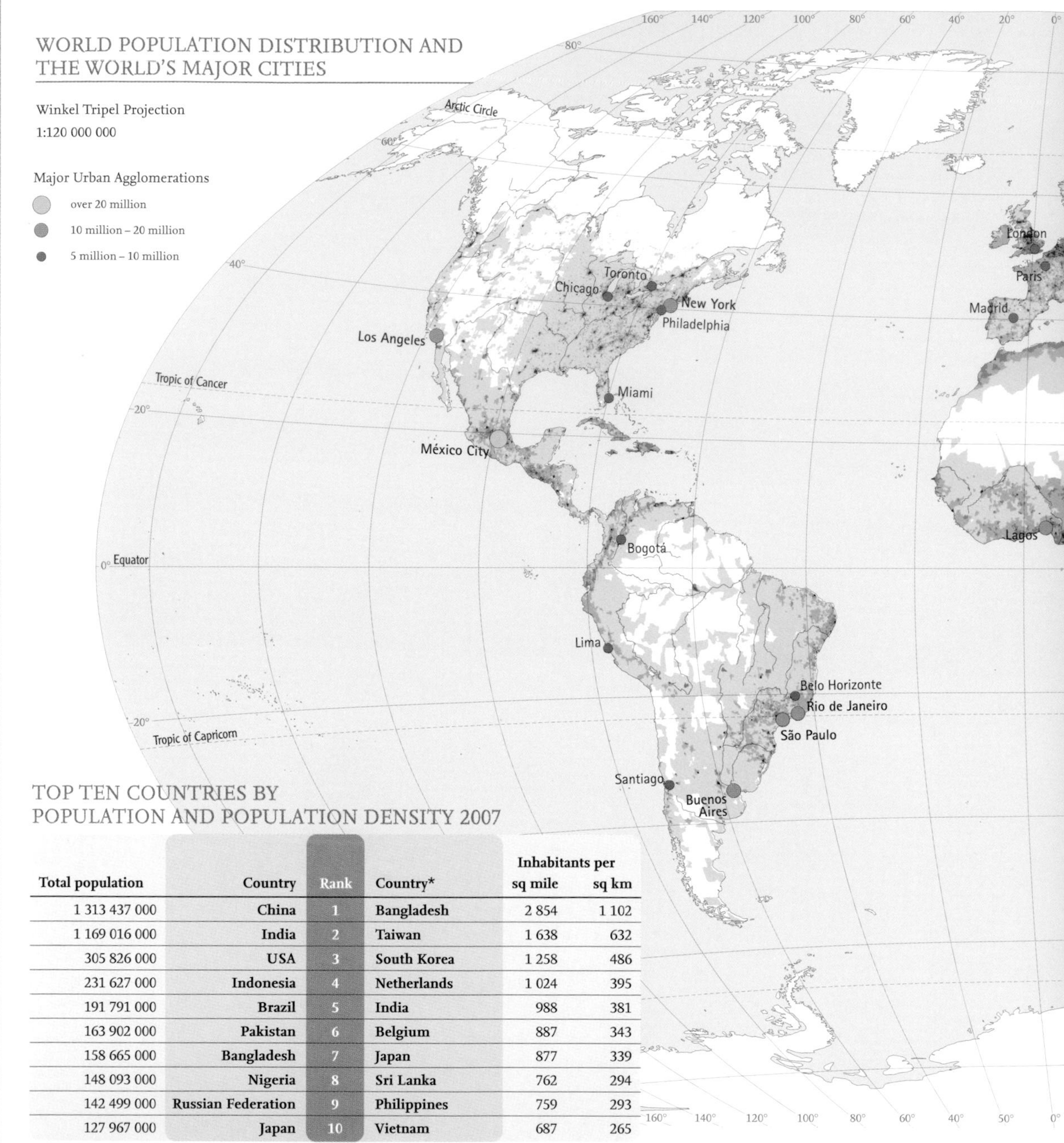

TOP TEN COUNTRIES BY POPULATION AND POPULATION DENSITY 2007

Total population	Country	Rank	Country*	Inhabitants per sq mile	Inhabitants per sq km
1 313 437 000	China	1	Bangladesh	2 854	1 102
1 169 016 000	India	2	Taiwan	1 638	632
305 826 000	USA	3	South Korea	1 258	486
231 627 000	Indonesia	4	Netherlands	1 024	395
191 791 000	Brazil	5	India	988	381
163 902 000	Pakistan	6	Belgium	887	343
158 665 000	Bangladesh	7	Japan	877	339
148 093 000	Nigeria	8	Sri Lanka	762	294
142 499 000	Russian Federation	9	Philippines	759	293
127 967 000	Japan	10	Vietnam	687	265

* Only countries with a population of over 10 million are considered.

KEY POPULATION STATISTICS FOR MAJOR REGIONS

	Population 2007 (millions)	Growth (per cent)	Infant mortality rate	Total fertility rate	Life expectancy (years)	% aged 60 and over 2005	% aged 60 and over 2050
World	6 671	1.2	49	2.6	67	10	22
More developed regions	1 223	0.3	7	1.6	77	20	33
Less developed regions	5 448	1.4	54	2.8	65	8	20
Africa	965	2.3	87	4.7	53	5	10
Asia	4 030	1.1	43	2.3	69	9	24
Europe	731	0.0	8	1.5	75	21	35
Latin America and the Caribbean	572	1.2	22	2.4	73	9	24
North America	339	1.0	6	2	79	17	27
Oceania	34	1.2	26	2.3	75	14	25

Except for population and % aged 60 and over figures, the data are annual averages projected for the period 2005–2010.

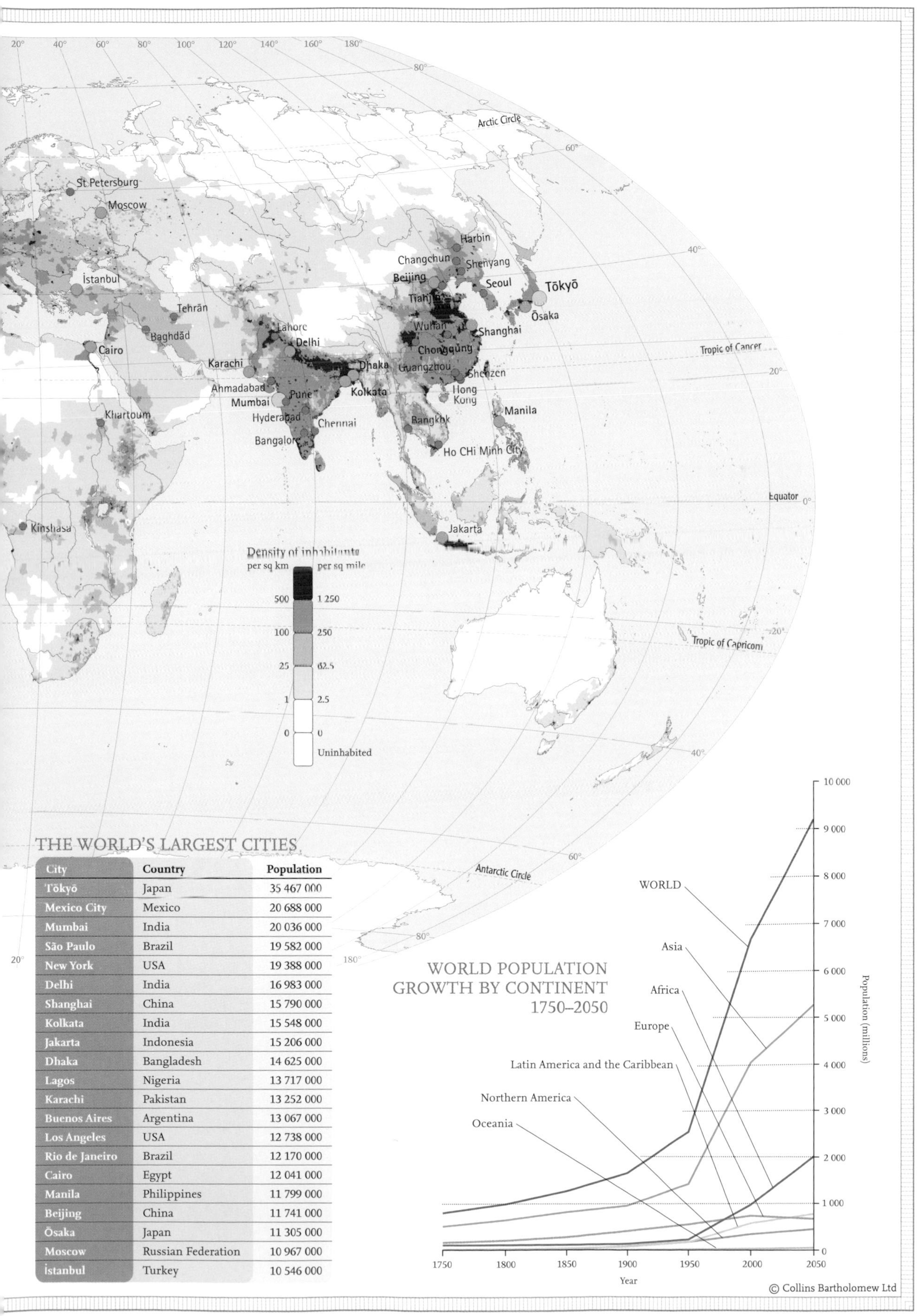

THE WORLD'S LARGEST CITIES

City	Country	Population
Tōkyō	Japan	35 467 000
Mexico City	Mexico	20 688 000
Mumbai	India	20 036 000
São Paulo	Brazil	19 582 000
New York	USA	19 388 000
Delhi	India	16 983 000
Shanghai	China	15 790 000
Kolkata	India	15 548 000
Jakarta	Indonesia	15 206 000
Dhaka	Bangladesh	14 625 000
Lagos	Nigeria	13 717 000
Karachi	Pakistan	13 252 000
Buenos Aires	Argentina	13 067 000
Los Angeles	USA	12 738 000
Rio de Janeiro	Brazil	12 170 000
Cairo	Egypt	12 041 000
Manila	Philippines	11 799 000
Beijing	China	11 741 000
Ōsaka	Japan	11 305 000
Moscow	Russian Federation	10 967 000
İstanbul	Turkey	10 546 000

INTERNATIONAL TELECOMMUNICATIONS TRAFFIC

RUSSIAN FEDERATION

CANADA

UNITED STATES

CHINA

INDIA

AUSTRALIA

Telephone lines per 100 inhabitants 2006

- over 50
- 35.0–50.0
- 15.0–34.9
- 10.0–14.9
- 5.0–9.9
- 1.0–4.9
- 0–0.9
- no data

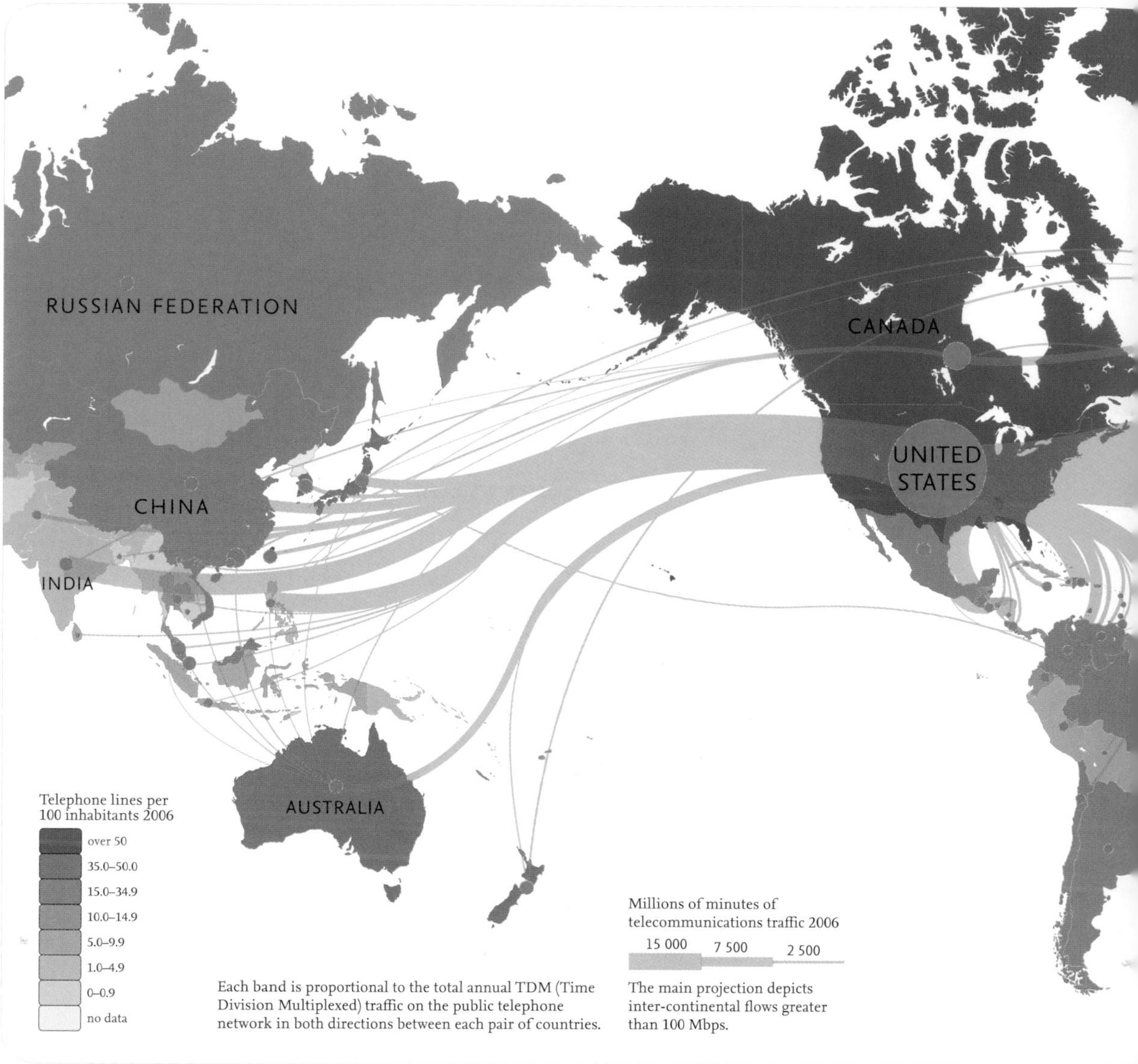

Each band is proportional to the total annual TDM (Time Division Multiplexed) traffic on the public telephone network in both directions between each pair of countries.

Millions of minutes of telecommunications traffic 2006

15 000 7 500 2 500

The main projection depicts inter-continental flows greater than 100 Mbps.

WORLD COMMUNICATION EQUIPMENT 1993–2007

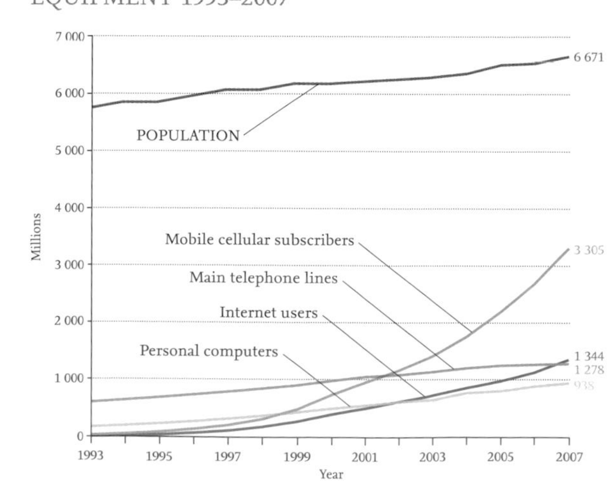

INTERNET USERS 2000 AND 2007

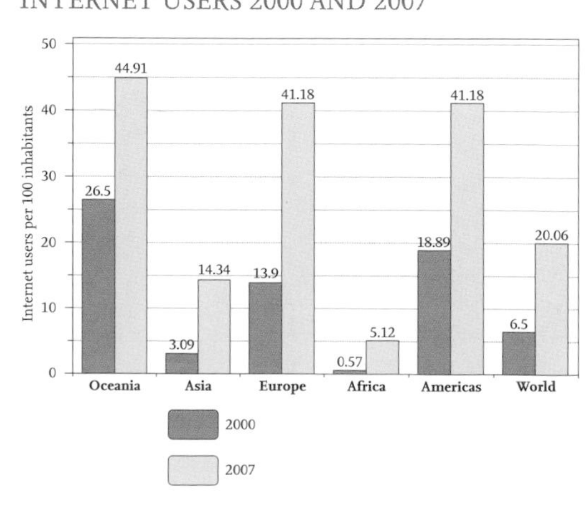

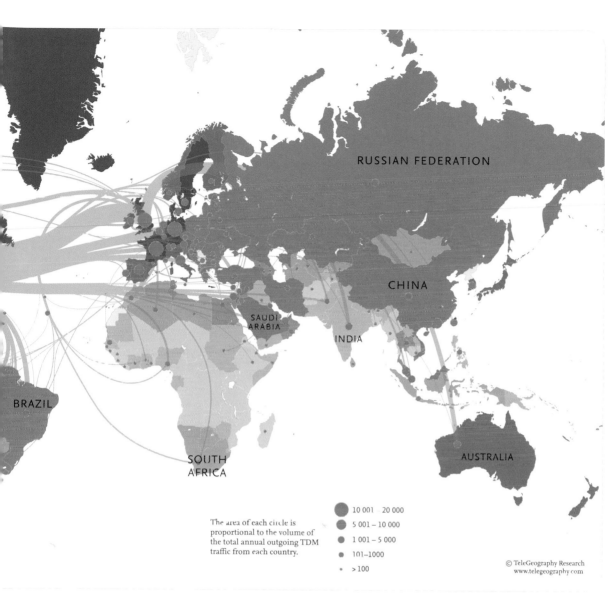

RUSSIAN FEDERATION

CHINA

SAUDI ARABIA

INDIA

BRAZIL

SOUTH AFRICA

AUSTRALIA

The area of each circle is proportional to the volume of the total annual outgoing TDM traffic from each country.

10 001 – 20 000

5 001 – 10 000

1 001 – 5 000

101–1000

> 100

TOP BROADBAND ECONOMIES 2007

Countries with highest broadband penetration rate – subscribers per 100 inhabitants

	Top Economies	Rate
1	Denmark	36.3
2	Iceland	34.8
3	Netherlands	33.5
4	Finland	33.3
5	Switzerland	32.1
6	South Korea	30.6
7	Norway	29.0
8	Sweden	25.9
9	United Kingdom	25.6
10	France	25.2
11	Luxembourg	24.2
12	Germany	24.0
13	Canada	22.9
14	Belgium	22.6
15	Japan	22.1

INTERNET USERS

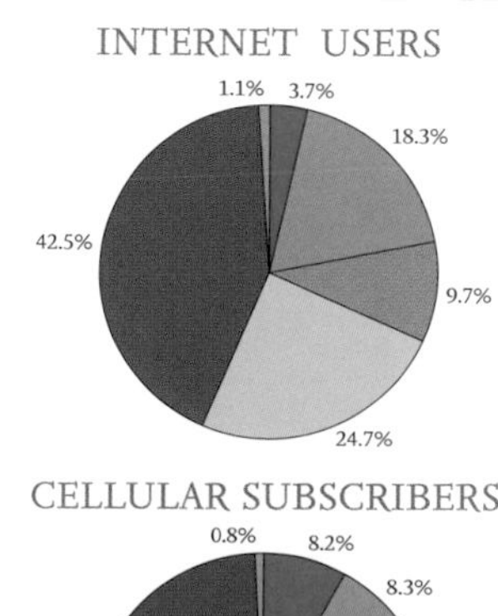

CELLULAR SUBSCRIBERS

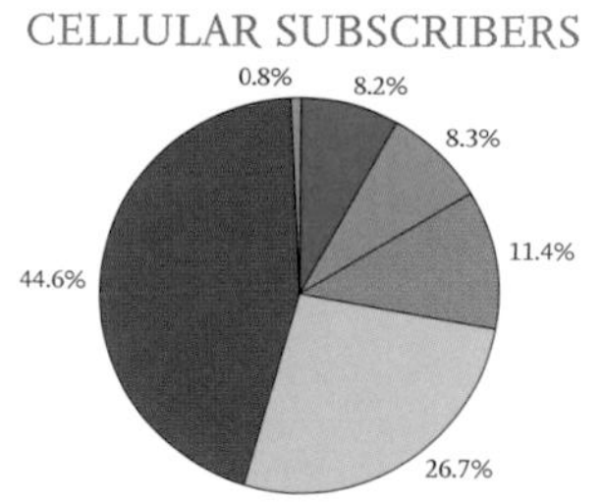

TELEPHONE MAIN LINES

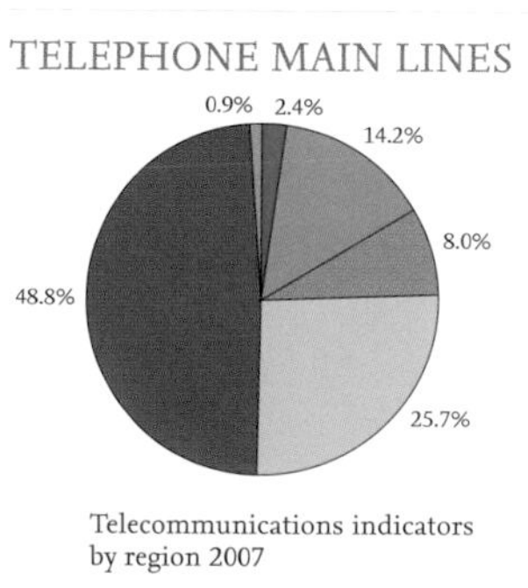

Telecommunications indicators by region 2007

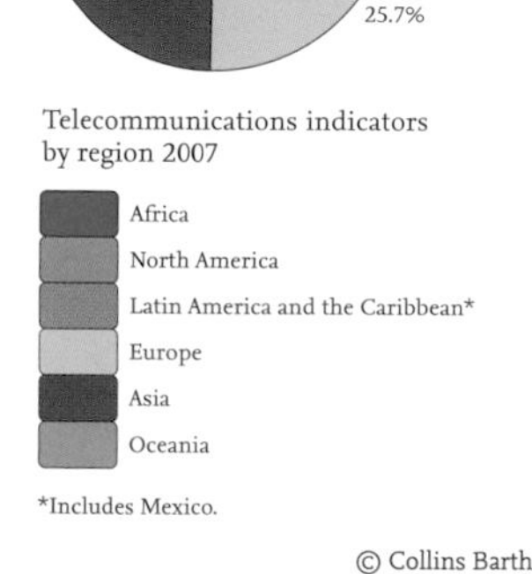

*Includes Mexico.

MAP POLICIES

PLACE NAMES

The spelling of place names on maps has always been a matter of great complexity, because of the variety of the world's languages and the systems used to write them down. There is no standard way of spelling names or of converting them from one alphabet, or symbol set, to another. Instead, conventional ways of spelling have evolved in each of the world's major languages, and the results often differ significantly from the name as it is spelled in the original language. Familiar examples of English conventional names include Munich (München), Florence (Firenze) and Moscow (from the transliterated form, Moskva).

In this atlas, local name forms are used where these are in the Roman alphabet, though for major cities, and main physical features, conventional English names are given first. The local forms are those which are officially recognized by the government of the country concerned, usually as represented by its official mapping agency. This is a basic principle laid down by the United Kingdom government's Permanent Committee on Geographical Names (PCGN) and the equivalent United States Board on Geographic Names, (BGN). Prominent English-language and historic names are not neglected, however. These, and significant superseded names and alternate spellings, are included in brackets on the maps where space permits, and are cross-referenced in the index.

Country names are shown in conventional English form and include any recent changes promulgated by national governments and adopted by the United Nations. The names of continents, oceans, seas and under-water features in international waters also appear in English throughout the atlas, as do those of other international features where such an English form exists and is in common use. International features are defined as features crossing one or more international boundary.

BOUNDARIES

The status of nations, their names and their boundaries, are shown in this atlas as they are at the time of going to press, as far as can be ascertained. Where an international boundary symbol appears in the sea or ocean it does not necessarily infer a legal maritime boundary, but shows which offshore islands belong to which country. The extent of island nations is shown by a short boundary symbol at the extreme limits of the area of sea or ocean within which all land is part of that nation.

Where international boundaries are the subject of dispute it may be that no portrayal of them will meet with the approval of any of the countries involved, but it is not seen as the function of this atlas to try to adjudicate between the rights and wrongs of political issues. Although reference mapping at atlas scales is not the ideal medium for indicating the claims of many separatist and irredentist movements, every reasonable attempt is made to show where an active territorial dispute exists, and where there is an important difference between 'de facto' (existing in fact, on the ground) and 'de jure' (according to law) boundaries. This is done by the use of a different symbol where international boundaries are disputed, or where the alignment is unconfirmed, to that used for settled international boundaries. Ceasefire lines are also shown by a separate symbol. For clarity, disputed boundaries and areas are annotated where this is considered necessary. The atlas aims to take a strictly neutral viewpoint of all such cases, based on advice from expert consultants.

MAP PROJECTIONS

Map projections have been selected specifically for the area and scale of each map, or suite of maps. As the only way to show the Earth with absolute accuracy is on a globe, all map projections are compromises. Some projections seek to maintain correct area relationships (equal area projections), true distances and bearings from a point (equidistant projections) or correct angles and shapes (conformal projections); others attempt to achieve a balance between these properties. The choice of projections used in this atlas has been made on an individual continental and regional basis. Projections used, and their individual parameters, have been defined to minimize distortion and to reduce scale errors as much as possible. The projection used is indicated at the bottom left of each map page.

SCALE

In order to directly compare like with like throughout the world it would be necessary to maintain a single scale throughout the atlas. However, the desirability of mapping the more densely populated areas of the world at larger scales, and other geographical considerations, such as the need to fit a homogeneous physical region within a uniform rectangular page format, mean that a range of scales have been used. Scales for continental maps range between 1:20 000 000 and 1:44 000 000, depending on the size of the continental land mass being covered. Scales for regional maps are typically in the range 1:12 000 000 to 1:20 000 000. Mapping for most countries is at scales between 1:4 800 000 and 1:12 000 000, although for the more densely populated areas of Europe the scale increases to 1:2 400 000.

ABBREVIATIONS

Arch.	Archipelago		
B.	Bay		
	Bahia, Baía	Portuguese	bay
	Bahía	Spanish	bay
	Baie	French	bay
C.	Cape		
	Cabo	Portuguese, Spanish	cape, headland
	Cap	French	cape, headland
Co	Cerro	Spanish	hill, peak, summit
E.	East, Eastern		
Est.	Estrecho	Spanish	strait
G.	Gebel	Arabic	hill, mountain
Gt	Great		
I.	Island, Isle		
	Ilha	Portuguese	island
	Islas	Spanish	island
Is	Islands, Isles		
	Islas	Spanish	islands
Kep.	Kepulauan	Indonesian	islands
Khr.	Khrebet	Russian	mountain range

L.	Lake		
	Loch	(Scotland)	lake
	Lough	(Ireland)	lake
	Lac	French	lake
	Lago	Portuguese, Spanish	lake
M.	Mys	Russian	cape, point
Mt	Mount		
	Mont	French	hill, mountain
Mt.	Mountain		
Mte	Monte	Portuguese, Spanish	hill, mountain
Mts	Mountains		
	Monts	French	hills, mountains
N.	North, Northern		
O.	Ostrov	Russian	island
Pk	Puncak	Indonesian, Malay	hill, mountain
Pt	Point		
Pta	Punta	Italian, Spanish	cape, point
R.	River		
	Rio	Portuguese	river
	Río	Spanish	river
	Rivière	French	river

Ra.	Range		mountain range
S.	South, Southern		
	Salar, Salina, Salinas	Spanish	salt pan, salt pans
Sa	Serra	Portuguese,	mountain range
	Sierra	Spanish	mountain range
Sd	Sound		
S.E.	Southeast, Southeastern		
St	Saint		
	Sankt	German	Saint
	Sint	Dutch	Saint
Sta	Santa	Italian, Portuguese, Spanish	Saint
Ste	Sainte	French	Saint
Str.	Strait		
Tk	Teluk	Indonesian, Malay	bay, gulf
Tg	Tanjong, Tanjung	Indonesian, Malay	cape, point
Vdkhr.	Vodokhranilishche	Russian	reservoir
W.	West, Western		strait
	Wadi, Wâdi, Wādī	Arabic	watercourse

MAP SYMBOLS

LAND AND WATER FEATURES

Lake
Impermanent lake
Salt lake or lagoon
Impermanent salt lake
Dry salt lake or salt pan

River
Impermanent river
Ice cap / Glacier
123 Pass
Height in metres
Site of special interest
Oasis
Wall

TRANSPORT

Motorway
Main road
Track
Main railway
Canal
Main airport

BOUNDARIES

International boundary
Disputed international boundary or alignment unconfirmed
Undefined international boundary in the sea.
All land within this boundary is part of state or territory named.
Administrative boundary
Shown for selected countries only.
Ceasefire line or other boundary described on the map

RELIEF

Contour intervals used in layer-colouring, for land height and sea depth

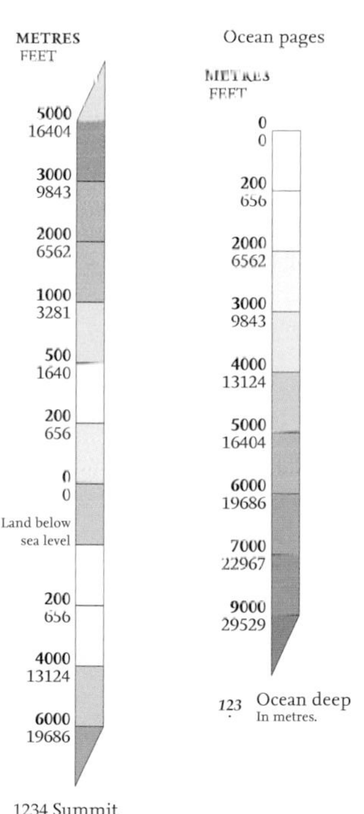

123 Ocean deep
In metres.

1234 Summit
Height in metres

1234 Volcano
Height in metres

STYLES OF LETTERING

Cities and towns are explained separately

Country	FRANCE
Overseas Territory/Dependency	Guadeloupe
Disputed Territory	AKSAI CHIN
Administrative name Shown for selected countries only.	SCOTLAND
Area name	PATAGONIA

Physical features

Island	*Gran Canaria*
Lake	*Lake Erie*
Mountain	*Mt Blanc*
River	*Thames*
Region	*LAPPLAND*

CITIES AND TOWNS

Population	National Capital	Administrative Capital Shown for selected countries only	Other City or Town
over 10 million	DHAKA	Karachi	New York
5 million to 10 million	MADRID	Toronto	Philadelphia
1 million to 5 million	KĀBUL	Sydney	Koahsiung
500 000 to 1 million	BANGUI	Winnipeg	Jeddah
100 000 to 500 000	WELLINGTON	Edinburgh	Apucarana
50 000 to 100 000	PORT OF SPAIN	Bismarck	Invercargill
under 50 000	MALABO	Charlottetown	Ceres

CONTINENTAL MAPS

BOUNDARIES — International boundary — Disputed international boundary — Ceasefire line

CITIES AND TOWNS — National Capital **Beijing** — Other City or Town **New York**

WORLD PHYSICAL FEATURES

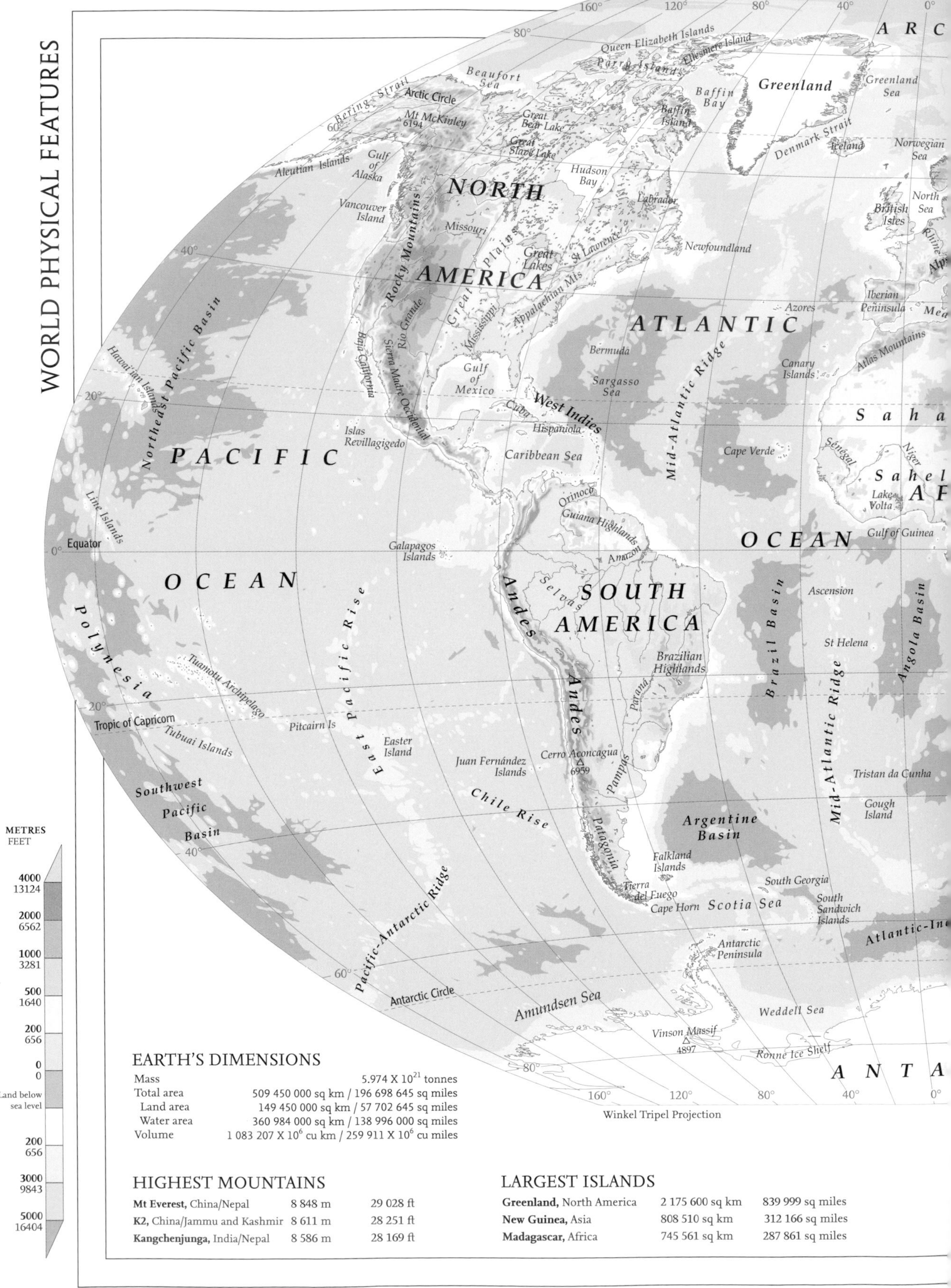

EARTH'S DIMENSIONS

Mass	5.974 X 10^{21} tonnes
Total area	509 450 000 sq km / 196 698 645 sq miles
Land area	149 450 000 sq km / 57 702 645 sq miles
Water area	360 984 000 sq km / 138 996 000 sq miles
Volume	1 083 207 X 10^6 cu km / 259 911 X 10^6 cu miles

Winkel Tripel Projection

HIGHEST MOUNTAINS

Mt Everest, China/Nepal	8 848 m	29 028 ft
K2, China/Jammu and Kashmir	8 611 m	28 251 ft
Kangchenjunga, India/Nepal	8 586 m	28 169 ft

LARGEST ISLANDS

Greenland, North America	2 175 600 sq km	839 999 sq miles
New Guinea, Asia	808 510 sq km	312 166 sq miles
Madagascar, Africa	745 561 sq km	287 861 sq miles

Lambert Azimuthal Equal Area Projection

1: 100 800 000

Equatorial diameter	12 756 km / 7 927 miles
Polar diameter	12 714 km / 7 901 miles
Equatorial circumference	40 075 km / 24 903 miles
Meridional circumference	40 008 km / 24 861 miles

LARGEST LAKES

Caspian Sea, Asia / Europe	371 000 sq km	143 243 sq miles
Lake Superior, North America	82 100 sq km	31 366 sq miles
Lake Victoria, Africa	68 800 sq km	6 591 sq miles

LONGEST RIVERS

Nile, Africa	6 695 km	4 160 miles
Amazon, South America	6 516 km	4 049 miles
Yangtze, Asia	6 380 km	3 965 miles

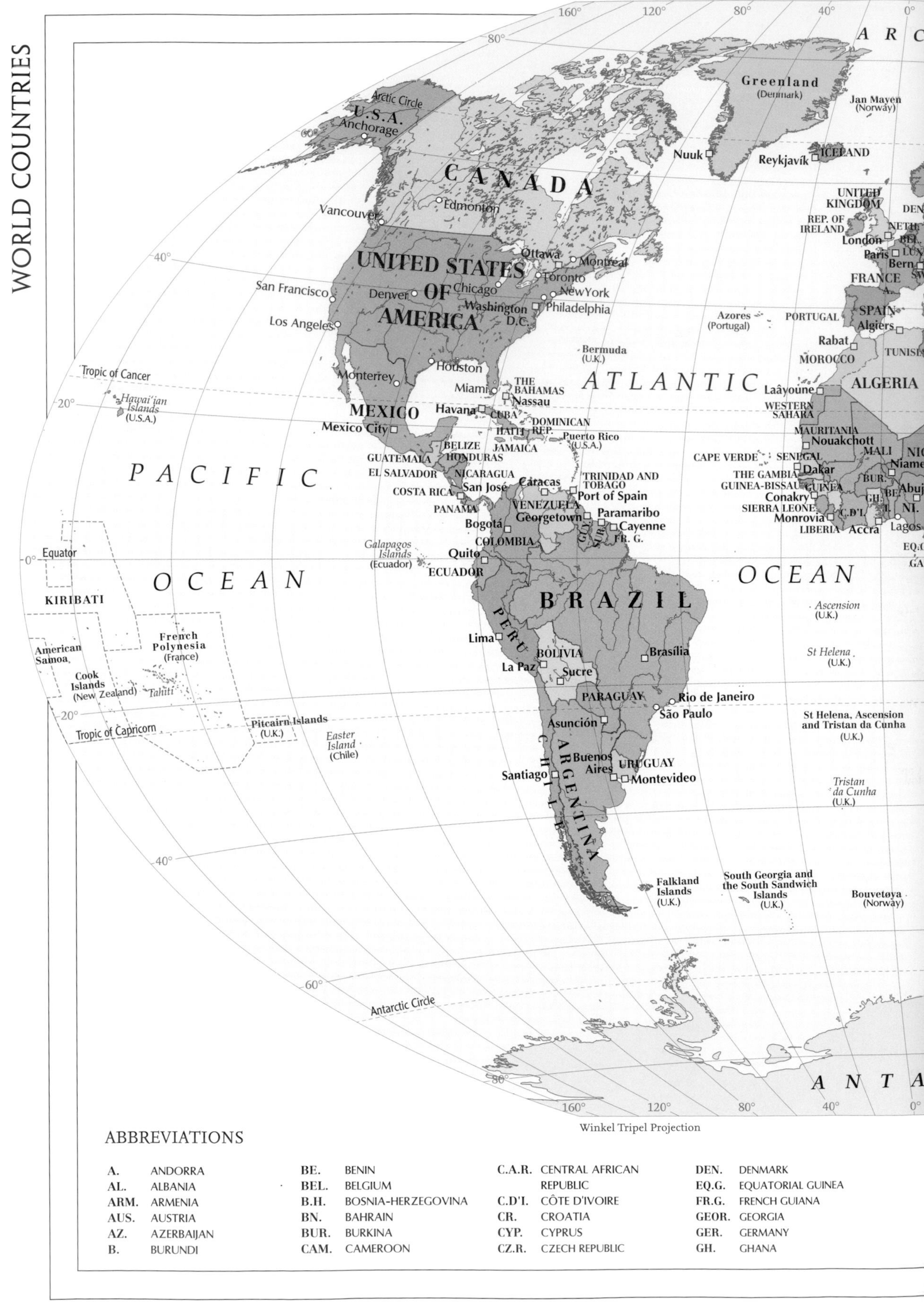

ABBREVIATIONS

A.	ANDORRA	BE.	BENIN	C.A.R.	CENTRAL AFRICAN REPUBLIC	DEN.	DENMARK
AL.	ALBANIA	BEL.	BELGIUM			EQ.G.	EQUATORIAL GUINEA
ARM.	ARMENIA	B.H.	BOSNIA-HERZEGOVINA	C.D'I.	CÔTE D'IVOIRE	FR.G.	FRENCH GUIANA
AUS.	AUSTRIA	BN.	BAHRAIN	CR.	CROATIA	GEOR.	GEORGIA
AZ.	AZERBAIJAN	BUR.	BURKINA	CYP.	CYPRUS	GER.	GERMANY
B.	BURUNDI	CAM.	CAMEROON	CZ.R.	CZECH REPUBLIC	GH.	GHANA

GUY.	GUYANA	LEB.	LEBANON	NI.	NIGERIA	SW.	SWITZERLAND
HUN.	HUNGARY	LITH.	LITHUA	Q.	QATAR	T.	TOGO
ISR.	ISRAEL	LUX.	LUXEMBOURG	R.	RWANDA	TAJIK.	TAJIKISTAN
JOR.	JORDAN	M.	MONTENEGRO	S.	SERBIA	TURKM.	TURKMENISTAN
K.	KOSOVO	MA.	MACEDONIA	SLA.	SLOVAKIA	U.A.E.	UNITED ARAB EMIRATES
KU.	KUWAIT	MO.	MOLDOVA	SL.	SLOVENIA	UZBEK.	UZBEKISTAN
KYR.	KYRGYZSTAN	NETH.	NETHERLANDS	SUR.	SURINAME		

TAIWAN
Tropic of Cancer
Luzon Strait
Luzon
PHILIPPINES
Palawan
Sulu Sea
Mindanao
Celebes Sea
Palau Islands
Kepulauan Talaud
Halmahera
Equator
Moluccas (Maluku)
Seram
Celebes (Sulawesi)
Laut Banda (Banda Sea)
INDONESIA
Laut Flores (Flores Sea)
Flores
Sumba
Timor
EAST TIMOR
Wetar
Kep. Aru
Kep. Tanimbar
Pulau Dolak
Puncak Jaya 5030
New Guinea
Mount Wilhelm 4509
Pagan
Northern Mariana Islands (U.S.A.)
Capitol Hill
Saipan
Hagåtña
Guam (U.S.A.)
Wake Island (U.S.A.)
MARSHALL ISLANDS
Ratak Chain
Ralik Chain
Delap-Uliga-Djarrit
Yap
Hall Islands
Chuuk
Pohnpei
Palikir
Caroline Islands
Mortlock Islands
Kosrae
FEDERATED STATES OF MICRONESIA
Bairiki
Tarawa
Gilbert Islands
Yaren
NAURU
Admiralty Islands
New Ireland
Wewak
Bismarck Sea
Rabaul
Madang
New Britain
Bougainville Island
Solomon Sea
PAPUA NEW GUINEA
Daru
G. of Papua
Port Moresby
Louisiade Arch.
Nukumanu Islands
Choiseul
Santa Isabel
Malaita
SOLOMON ISLANDS
New Georgia Islands
Honiara
Guadalcanal
San Cristobal
Rennell
Duff Islands
Santa Cruz Islands
Banks Islands
Espíritu Santo
VANUATU
Malakula
Port Vila
Erromango
Tanna
New Caledonia (Fr.)
Nouméa
Îles Loyauté
Hunter Island
Île des Pins
Arafura Sea
Torres Strait
Melville Island
Cape Arnhem
Darwin
Gulf of Carpentaria
Timor Sea
Cape Londonderry
Wyndham
Cape Lévêque
Broome
Halls Creek
Coral Sea Islands Territory (Aust.)
Coral Sea
Cairns
Normanton
Townsville
Great Barrier Reef
Great Dividing Range
Mount Isa
Rockhampton
NORTHERN TERRITORY
QUEENSLAND
Port Hedland
Great Sandy Desert
Alice Springs
AUSTRALIA
Charleville
Brisbane
Gold Coast
Toowoomba
Norfolk Island (Aust.)
Newman
Tropic of Capricorn
WESTERN AUSTRALIA
Oodnadatta
Tamworth
Lord Howe Island (Aust.)
SOUTH AUSTRALIA
Broken Hill
Darling
NEW SOUTH WALES
Newcastle
Sydney
Wollongong
Mt Magnet
Port Augusta
Kalgoorlie
Canberra
A.C.T.
Geraldton
Great Australian Bight
Adelaide
Murray
Port Lincoln
VICTORIA
Melbourne
Geelong
Kangaroo Island
TASMAN SEA
Perth
Fremantle
Bass Strait
Flinders Island
King Island
Launceston
TASMANIA
Hobart
South East Cape
Cape Leeuwin
Christchurch
South Island
Dunedin
Invercargill
Stewart Island
Auckland Islands
Campbell Island (N.Z.)
Macquarie Island (Aust.)
Longitude 150° east of Greenwich

Lambert Azimuthal Equal Area Projection

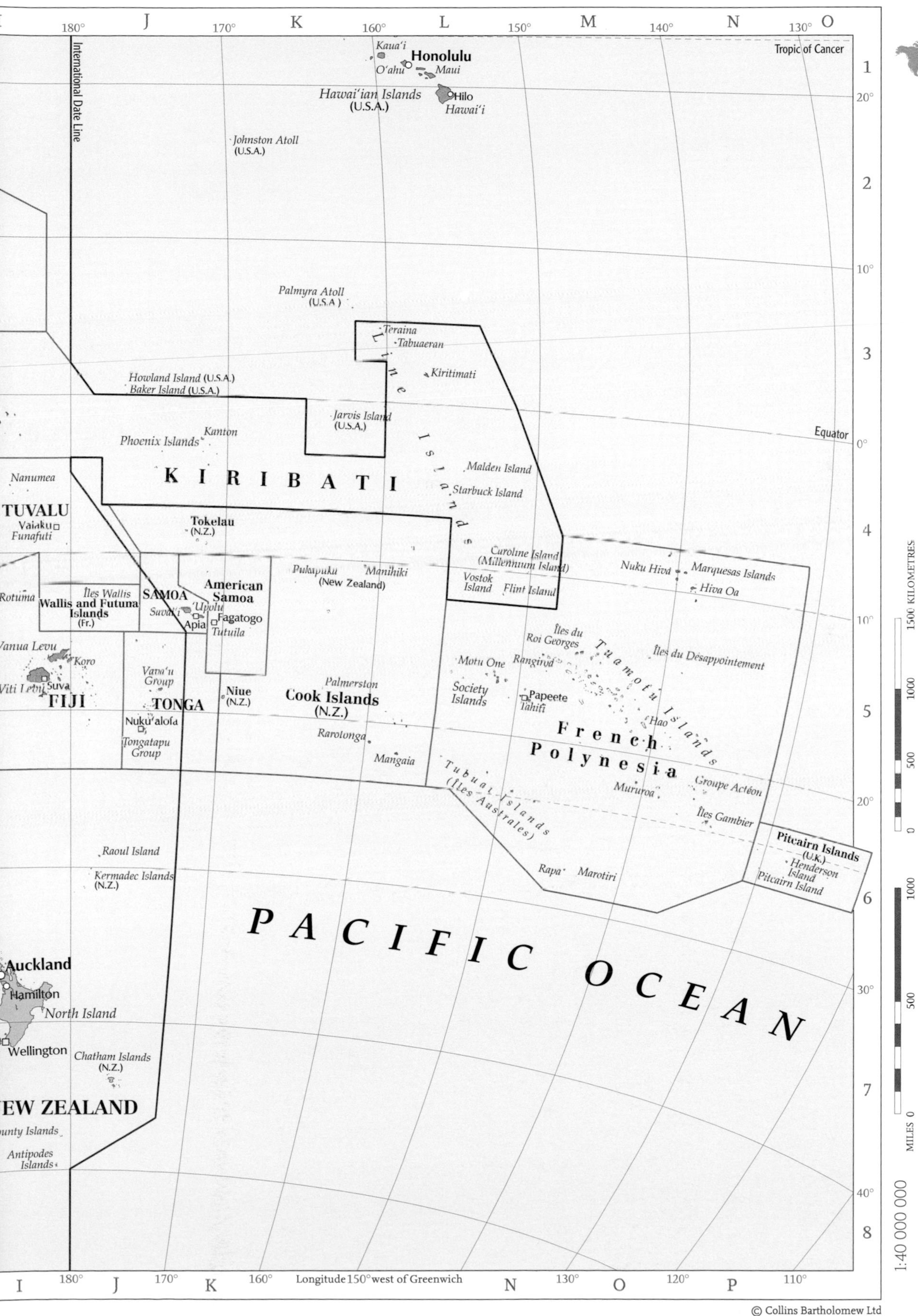

Tropic of Cancer
Kaua'i
Honolulu
O'ahu
Maui
Hawai'ian Islands
(U.S.A.)
Hilo
Hawai'i
International Date Line
Johnston Atoll
(U.S.A.)
Palmyra Atoll
(U.S.A.)
Teraina
Tabuaeran
Line Islands
Kiritimati
Howland Island (U.S.A.)
Baker Island (U.S.A.)
Jarvis Island
(U.S.A.)
Kanton
Phoenix Islands
Equator
Malden Island
Starbuck Island
KIRIBATI
Nanumea
TUVALU
Vaiaku
Funafuti
Tokelau
(N.Z.)
Caroline Island
(Millennium Island)
Nuku Hiva
Marquesas Islands
Hiva Oa
Pukapuka
Manihiki
(New Zealand)
Vostok Island
Flint Island
Rotuma
Îles Wallis
Wallis and Futuna Islands
(Fr.)
SAMOA
Savai'i
'Upolu
Apia
American Samoa
Fagatogo
Tutuila
Îles du Roi Georges
Tuamotu Islands
Îles du Désappointement
Vanua Levu
Koro
Viti Levu
Suva
FIJI
Vava'u Group
TONGA
Nuku'alofa
Tongatapu Group
Niue
(N.Z.)
Palmerston
Cook Islands
(N.Z.)
Rarotonga
Mangaia
Motu One
Rangiroa
Society Islands
Papeete
Tahiti
Hao
French Polynesia
Tubuai Islands
(Îles Australes)
Mururoa
Groupe Actéon
Îles Gambier
Pitcairn Islands
(U.K.)
Henderson Island
Pitcairn Island
Raoul Island
Kermadec Islands
(N.Z.)
Rapa
Marotiri
PACIFIC OCEAN
Auckland
Hamilton
North Island
Wellington
Chatham Islands
(N.Z.)
NEW ZEALAND
Bounty Islands
Antipodes Islands
Longitude 150° west of Greenwich
MILES 0 500 1000
0 500 1000 1500 KILOMETRES
1:40 000 000

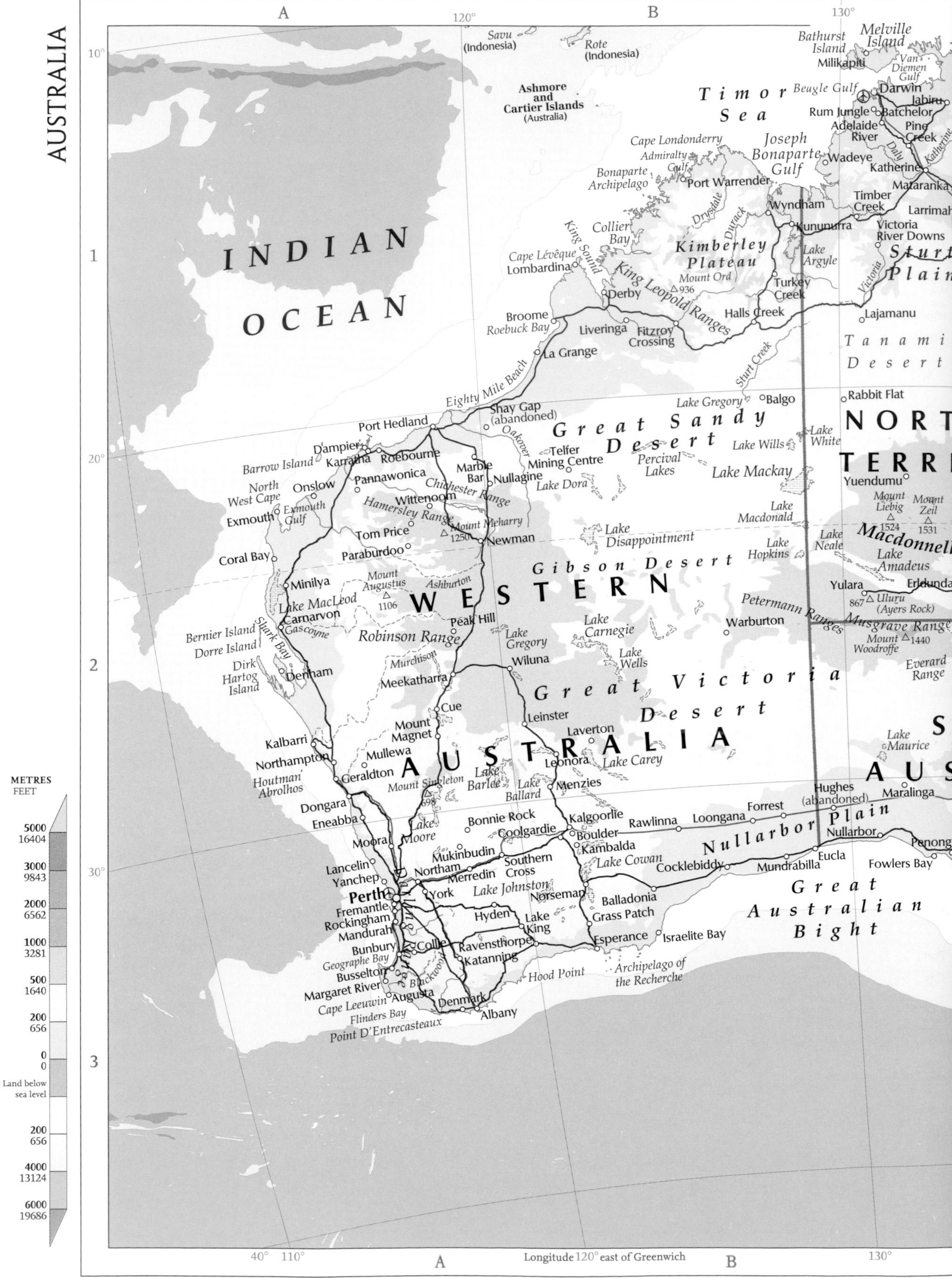
A
B
120°
130°
10°
20°
30°
1
2
3
INDIAN OCEAN
Savu (Indonesia)
Rote (Indonesia)
Ashmore and Cartier Islands (Australia)
Timor Sea
Bathurst Island
Melville Island
Milikapiti
Van Diemen Gulf
Beagle Gulf
Darwin
Jabiru
Rum Jungle
Batchelor
Adelaide River
Pine Creek
Daly
Katherine
Wadeye
Joseph Bonaparte Gulf
Cape Londonderry
Admiralty Gulf
Bonaparte Archipelago
Port Warrender
Mataranka
Timber Creek
Larrimah
Wyndham
Kununurra
Victoria River Downs
Sturt Plain
Lake Argyle
Victoria
Drysdale
Durack
King Sound
Collier Bay
Kimberley Plateau
Mount Ord 936
King Leopold Ranges
Cape Lévêque
Lombardina
Derby
Turkey Creek
Halls Creek
Lajamanu
Broome
Roebuck Bay
Liveringa
Fitzroy Crossing
La Grange
Tanami Desert
Sturt Creek
Eighty Mile Beach
Shay Gap (abandoned)
Lake Gregory
Balgo
Rabbit Flat
Port Hedland
Oakover
Great Sandy Desert
Lake White
NORTHERN TERRITORY
Dampier
Karratha
Roebourne
Barrow Island
Telfer Mining Centre
Lake Wills
Percival Lakes
Lake Mackay
Marble Bar
Nullagine
Lake Dora
Yuendumu
North West Cape
Onslow
Pannawonica
Chichester Range
Exmouth
Exmouth Gulf
Wittenoom
Hamersley Range
Mount Meharry 1250
Lake Macdonald
Mount Liebig 1524
Mount Zeil 1531
Macdonnell
Tom Price
Lake Disappointment
Lake Neale
Newman
Lake Hopkins
Lake Amadeus
Coral Bay
Paraburdoo
Gibson Desert
Minilya
Mount Augustus 1106
Ashburton
Yulara
Erldunda
WESTERN AUSTRALIA
Lake MacLeod
Carnarvon
Uluru (Ayers Rock) 867
Petermann Ranges
Musgrave Ranges
Gascoyne
Peak Hill
Lake Carnegie
Warburton
Mount Woodroffe 1440
Bernier Island
Dorre Island
Shark Bay
Robinson Range
Lake Gregory
Dirk Hartog Island
Denham
Murchison
Wiluna
Lake Wells
Everard Range
Meekatharra
Great Victoria Desert
Cue
Leinster
Mount Magnet
Laverton
Lake Maurice
Kalbarri
Mullewa
Leonora
Lake Carey
Northampton
Geraldton
Houtman Abrolhos
Mount Singleton 698
Lake Barlee
Lake Ballard
Menzies
Hughes (abandoned)
Maralinga
Dongara
Eneabba
Bonnie Rock
Kalgoorlie
Rawlinna
Loongana
Forrest
Nullarbor Plain
Lake Moore
Coolgardie
Boulder
Nullarbor
Moora
Mukinbudin
Kambalda
Penong
Lancelin
Northam
Southern Cross
Lake Cowan
Cocklebiddy
Mundrabilla
Eucla
Fowlers Bay
Yanchep
Merredin
Perth
York
Lake Johnston
Norseman
Great Australian Bight
Fremantle
Rockingham
Balladonia
Hyden
Mandurah
Lake King
Grass Patch
Bunbury
Collie
Ravensthorpe
Esperance
Israelite Bay
Geographe Bay
Busselton
Katanning
Blackwood
Margaret River
Hood Point
Archipelago of the Recherche
Cape Leeuwin
Augusta
Denmark
Albany
Flinders Bay
Point D'Entrecasteaux
METRES
FEET
5000 16404
3000 9843
2000 6562
1000 3281
500 1640
200 656
0 0
Land below sea level
200 656
4000 13124
6000 19686
40° 110°
Longitude 120° east of Greenwich

Lambert Azimuthal Equal Area Projection

PORT MORESBY
Kwikila
Abau
Owen Stanley Range
PAPUA NEW GUINEA
Fergusson Island
D'Entrecasteaux Islands
Conflict Group
Misima Island
Rossel Island
Louisiade Archipelago
Tagula Island
Prince of Wales Island
Cape York
Bamaga
Wessel Islands
Cape Wessel
Buckingham Bay
Nhulunbuy
Milingimbi
Cape Arnhem
Arnhem Land
Arnhem Bay
Isle Woodah
Alyangula
Numbulwar
Groote Eylandt
Gulf of Carpentaria
Sir Edward Pellew Group
Borroloola
Mornington Island
Gununa
Wellesley Islands
Cape Grenville
Albatross Bay
Weipa
Cape York Peninsula
Lockhart River
Cape Direction
Archer
Coen
Princess Charlotte Bay
Cape Melville
Cape Flattery
Cooktown
Kowanyama
Laura
Mitchell
Mossman
Cairns
Mareeba
Atherton
Mount Bartle Frere
1612
Innisfail
Gilbert
Normanton
Tully
Hinchinbrook Island
Ingham
Forsayth
Gregory Range
Townsville
Ayr
Bowen
GREAT BARRIER REEF
CORAL SEA
Daly Waters
Newcastle Waters
Lake Woods
Lake Sylvester
Barkly Tableland
Burketown
Doomadgee
Leichhardt
Flinders
Tennant Creek
Camooweal
Kajabbi
NORTHERN TERRITORY
Barrow Creek
Mount Isa
Cloncurry
Richmond
Charters Towers
McKinlay
Hughenden
Whitsunday Island
Proserpine
Mount Dalrymple
1277
Mackay
Selwyn Range
Dajarra
Corfield
Winton
Thomson
Belyando
Glenden
Sarina
Percy Isles
Arthur Point
Moranbah
Boulia
Georgina
Alice Springs
Ranges
Clermont
Dysart
QUEENSLAND
GREAT DIVIDING RANGE
Lake Philippi
Longreach
Barcaldine
Emerald
Blackwater
Yeppoon
Curtis Island
Rockhampton
Capricorn Channel
Tropic of Capricorn
Simpson Desert
Cluny
Diamantina
Barcoo
Springsure
Gladstone
Moura
Biloela
Bilpa Morea Claypan
Betoota
Yaraka
Windorah
Blackall
Caldervale
Buckland Tableland
Monto
Bundaberg
Hervey Bay
Sandy Cape
Birdsville
Lake Yamma Yamma
Charleville
Warrego
Taroom
Maryborough
Fraser Island
Marla
Alberga
Macumba
Oodnadatta
Lake Eyre (North)
Warburton
Cooper Creek
Mungeranie
Quilpie
Mitchell
Roma
Kingaroy
Gympie
Tewantin
Wyandra
Balonne
Nambour
Maroochydore
Dalby
Caboolture
Sturt Stony Desert
Bulloo Downs
Paroo
St George
Toowoomba
Ipswich
Brisbane
Beenleigh
Gold Coast
SOUTH AUSTRALIA
Coober Pedy
Lake Eyre (South)
Marree
Hungerford
Cunnamulla
Goondiwindi
Warwick
Dirranbandi
Darling Downs
Mungindi
Lismore
Byron Bay
Lake Blanche
Grey Range
Tibooburra
Lightning Ridge
Moree
Glen Innes
Casino
Ballina
Tarcoola
Lake Torrens
Leigh Creek
Brewarrina
Barwon
Walgett
Inverell
Grafton
Lake Frome
Bourke
Narrabri
Armidale
Coffs Harbour
Lake Gairdner
Woomera
Island Lagoon
Flinders Ranges
Barrier Range
Darling
Macquarie
Gunnedah
Wilcannia
Cobar
Tamworth
Macksville
Ceduna
Broken Hill
Barnato
Warren
Dubbo
Streaky Bay
Port Augusta
Port Pirie
Whyalla
NEW SOUTH WALES
Muswellbrook
Port Macquarie
Anxious Bay
Kyancutta
Jamestown
Burra
Ivanhoe
Parkes
Taree
Eyre Peninsula
Spencer Gulf
Wallaroo
Garnpung Lake
Maitland
Lord Howe Island
Murray
Wentworth
Lachlan
Forbes
Orange
Newcastle
Port Lincoln
Gawler
Mildura
Lithgow
Penrith
Cape Carnot
Yorke Pen.
Adelaide
Hay
Griffith
Grenfell
Sydney
Murray Bridge
Ouyen
Goulburn
Botany Bay
Investigator Strait
Lake Alexandrina
Wagga Wagga
Yass
Wollongong
Kingscote
Swan Hill
CANBERRA
A.C.T.
Nowra
Kangaroo Island
Nhill
Albury
Shepparton
Wangaratta
Batemans Bay
Cape Jaffa
Horsham
VICTORIA
Wodonga
Narooma
Mount William
1167
Stawell
Bendigo
Cooma
Bega
Mount Kosciuszko
2229
Mount Gambier
Ballarat
Melbourne
Eden
Discovery Bay
Portland
Geelong
Gippsland
Cape Howe
Warrnambool
Colac
Frankston
Moe
Sale
Bairnsdale
TASMAN SEA
Cape Otway
Bass Strait
Wilson's Promontory
Currie
King Island
Flinders Island
Hunter Islands
Whitemark
Furneaux Group
Cape Barren I.
Banks Strait
Burnie
Devonport
Eddystone Point
Mount Ossa
1617
Launceston
Queenstown
Fingal
TASMANIA
Lake Gordon
Hobart
Sorell
Kingston
Port Arthur
140°
150°
160°
10°
20°
30°
C
D
E
1
2
3
600 KILOMETRES
400
200
0
MILES
300
100
1:16 000 000

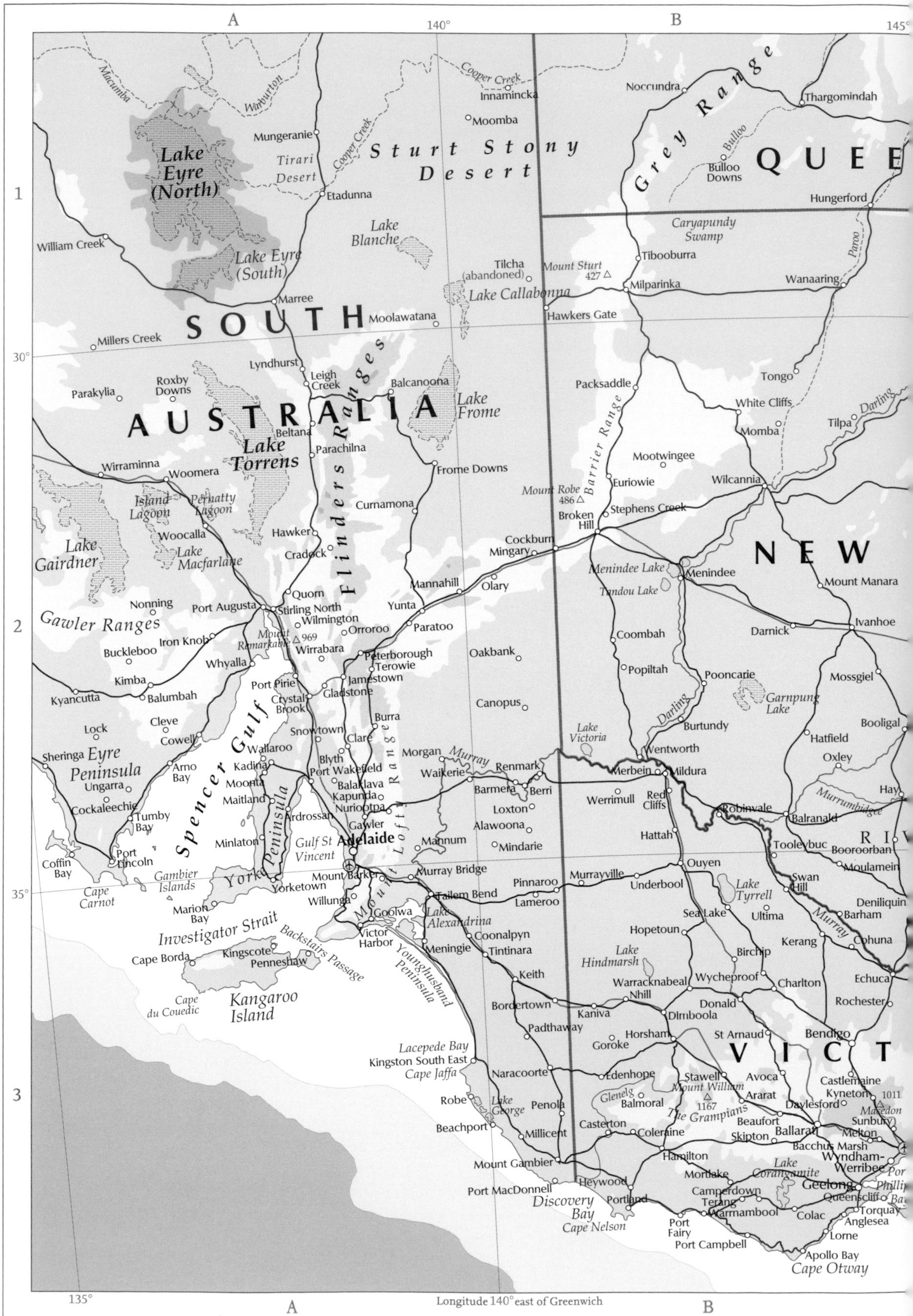

AUSTRALIA SOUTHEAST

A B 140° 145°

1 2 3

30° 35° 135°

SOUTH AUSTRALIA

QUEE

NEW

VICT

RI

Lake Eyre (North)
Lake Eyre (South)
Macumba
Warburton
Cooper Creek
Innamincka
Moomba
Mungeranie
Tirari Desert
Sturt Stony Desert
Etadunna
William Creek
Lake Blanche
Tilcha (abandoned)
Mount Sturt 427
Lake Callabonna
Marree
Moolawatana
Hawkers Gate
Millers Creek
Lyndhurst
Leigh Creek
Balcanoona
Lake Frome
Parakylia
Roxby Downs
Beltana
Lake Torrens
Parachilna
Flinders Ranges
Frome Downs
Wirraminna
Woomera
Island Lagoon
Pernatty Lagoon
Woocalla
Lake Macfarlane
Lake Gairdner
Hawker
Cradock
Curnamona
Quorn
Nonning
Port Augusta
Stirling North
Wilmington
Mount Remarkable 969
Orroroo
Gawler Ranges
Iron Knob
Buckleboo
Whyalla
Wirrabara
Kimba
Kyancutta
Balumbah
Port Pirie
Crystal Brook
Gladstone
Jamestown
Peterborough
Terowie
Mannahill
Olary
Yunta
Paratoo
Oakbank
Canopus
Cleve
Lock
Cowell
Snowtown
Burra
Clare
Sheringa
Eyre Peninsula
Arno Bay
Ungarra
Cockaleechie
Tumby Bay
Port Lincoln
Coffin Bay
Spencer Gulf
Wallaroo
Kadina
Moonta
Maitland
Yorke Peninsula
Ardrossan
Minlaton
Blyth
Port Wakefield
Balaklava
Kapunda
Nuriootpa
Gawler
Adelaide
Gulf St Vincent
Mount Lofty Ranges
Morgan
Murray
Waikerie
Renmark
Barmera
Berri
Loxton
Alawoona
Mannum
Mindarie
Murray Bridge
Mount Barker
Cape Carnot
Gambier Islands
Yorketown
Marion Bay
Willunga
Goolwa
Victor Harbor
Tailem Bend
Lake Alexandrina
Pinnaroo
Lameroo
Coonalpyn
Meningie
Tintinara
Investigator Strait
Backstairs Passage
Kingscote
Penneshaw
Cape Borda
Kangaroo Island
Cape du Couedic
Younghusband Peninsula
Keith
Bordertown
Padthaway
Lacepede Bay
Kingston South East
Cape Jaffa
Naracoorte
Robe
Lake George
Penola
Beachport
Millicent
Mount Gambier
Port MacDonnell
Discovery Bay
Cape Nelson
Nocundra
Grey Range
Thargomindah
Bulloo
Bulloo Downs
Hungerford
Caryapundy Swamp
Paroo
Tibooburra
Milparinka
Wanaaring
Tongo
Packsaddle
Barrier Range
White Cliffs
Darling
Tilpa
Momba
Mootwingee
Mount Robe 486
Euriowie
Wilcannia
Broken Hill
Stephens Creek
Cockburn
Mingary
Menindee Lake
Menindee
Tandou Lake
Mount Manara
Darnick
Ivanhoe
Coombah
Popiltah
Pooncarie
Mossgiel
Garnpung Lake
Burtundy
Lake Victoria
Wentworth
Merbein
Mildura
Hatfield
Booligal
Oxley
Hay
Werrimull
Red Cliffs
Robinvale
Murrumbidgee
Balranald
Hattah
Tooleybuc
Booroorban
Moulamein
Murrayville
Underbool
Ouyen
Lake Tyrrell
Swan Hill
Deniliquin
Ultima
Barham
Sea Lake
Hopetoun
Kerang
Cohuna
Lake Hindmarsh
Birchip
Warracknabeal
Wycheproof
Charlton
Echuca
Nhill
Kaniva
Dimboola
Donald
Rochester
Horsham
Goroke
St Arnaud
Bendigo
Edenhope
Stawell
Avoca
Castlemaine
Glenelg
Balmoral
Mount William 1167
Ararat
Kyneton
Macedon 1011
The Grampians
Daylesford
Sunbury
Casterton
Coleraine
Beaufort
Ballarat
Melton
Skipton
Bacchus Marsh
Hamilton
Wyndham-Werribee
Lake Corangamite
Mortlake
Geelong
Port Phillip Bay
Heywood
Portland
Camperdown
Terang
Queenscliff
Warrnambool
Colac
Torquay
Anglesea
Port Fairy
Lorne
Port Campbell
Apollo Bay
Cape Otway

A B

Longitude 140° east of Greenwich

METRES FEET

METRES	FEET
5000	16404
3000	9843
2000	6562
1000	3281
500	1640
200	656
0	0
Land below sea level	
200	656
4000	13124
6000	19686

Conic Equidistant Projection

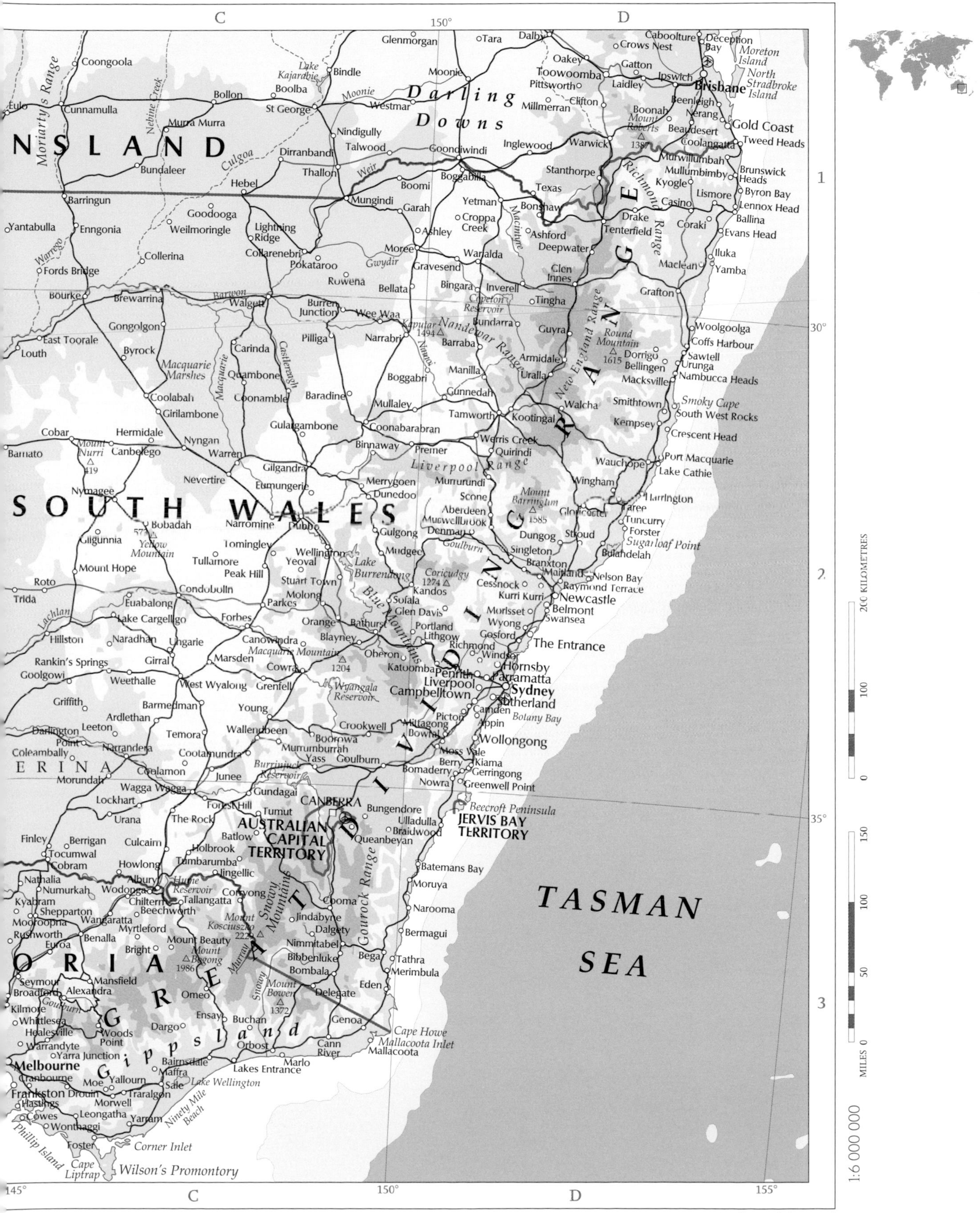

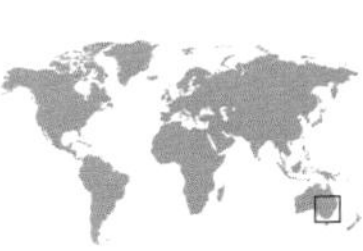

0 100 200 KILOMETRES

MILES 0 50 100 150

1:6 000 000

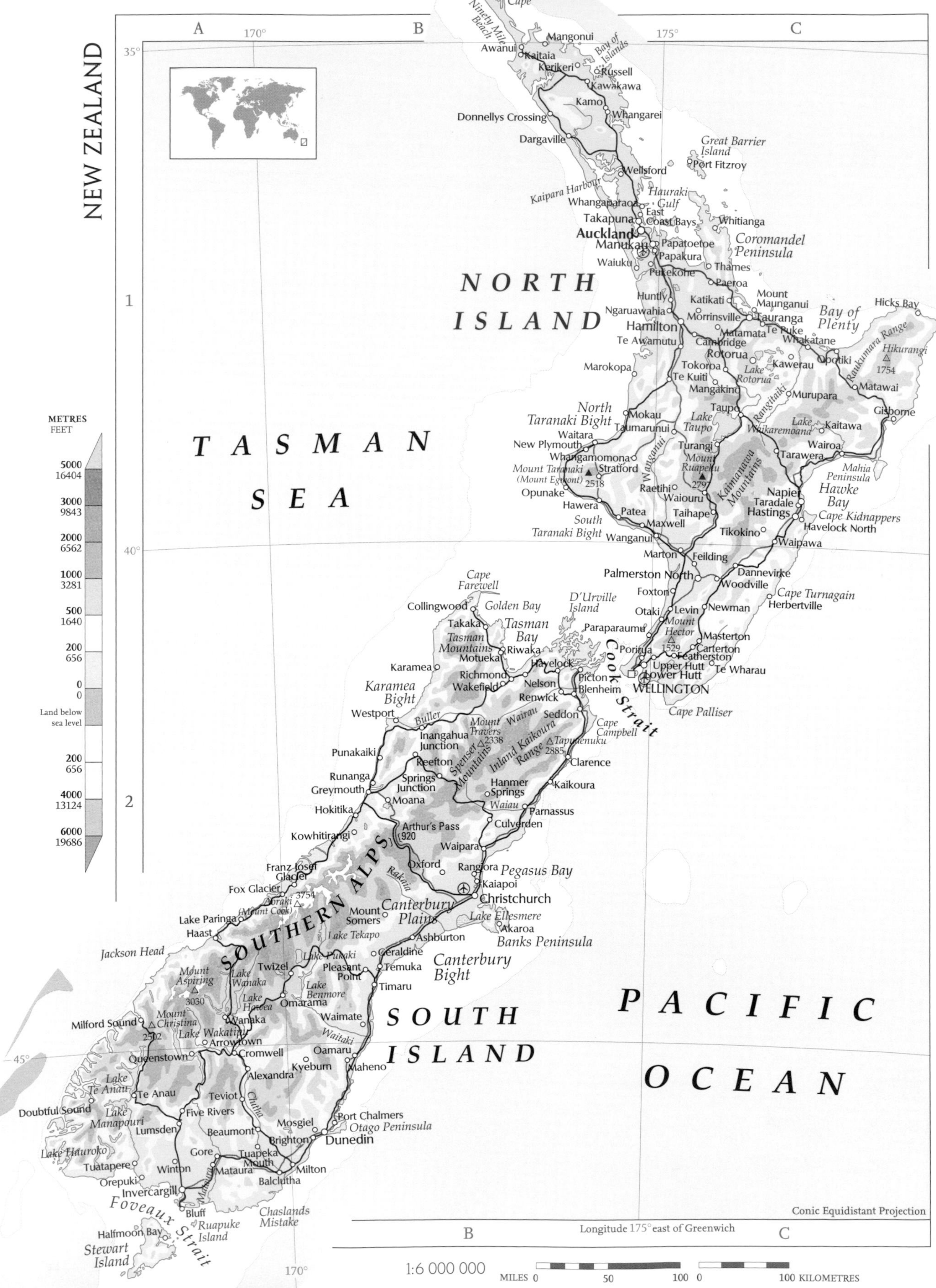

NEW ZEALAND
METRES
FEET
5000
16404
3000
9843
2000
6562
1000
3281
500
1640
200
656
0
0
Land below sea level
200
656
4000
13124
6000
19686
A
B
C
1
2
35°
40°
45°
170°
175°
TASMAN SEA
NORTH ISLAND
SOUTH ISLAND
PACIFIC OCEAN
Te Paki
North Cape
Ninety Mile Beach
Mangonui
Awanui
Kaitaia
Bay of Islands
Kerikeri
Russell
Kawakawa
Kamo
Whangarei
Donnellys Crossing
Dargaville
Great Barrier Island
Port Fitzroy
Wellsford
Kaipara Harbour
Hauraki Gulf
Whangaparaoa
East Coast Bays
Takapuna
Whitianga
Auckland
Manukau
Papatoetoe
Papakura
Coromandel Peninsula
Waiuku
Thames
Pukekohe
Paeroa
Huntly
Katikati
Mount Maunganui
Ngaruawahia
Morrinsville
Tauranga
Bay of Plenty
Hicks Bay
Hamilton
Matamata
Te Puke
Whakatane
Te Awamutu
Cambridge
Rotorua
Raukumara Range
Hikurangi
1754
Opotiki
Marokopa
Tokoroa
Kawerau
Te Kuiti
Lake Rotorua
Mangakino
Matawai
Rangitaiki
Murupara
Taupo
Mokau
Gisborne
North Taranaki Bight
Taumarunui
Lake Taupo
Lake Waikaremoana
Kaitawa
Waitara
New Plymouth
Turangi
Wairoa
Whangamomona
Mount Ruapehu
Tarawera
Mount Taranaki (Mount Egmont)
2518
Stratford
Wanganui
2797
Kaimanawa Mountains
Mahia Peninsula
Opunake
Raetihi
Waiouru
Napier
Hawke Bay
Hawera
Taradale
Hastings
Cape Kidnappers
Patea
Taihape
Havelock North
South Taranaki Bight
Maxwell
Tikokino
Wanganui
Waipawa
Marton
Feilding
Palmerston North
Dannevirke
Foxton
Woodville
Cape Turnagain
Herbertville
Otaki
Levin
Newman
Paraparaumu
Mount Hector
1529
Masterton
Porirua
Carterton
Featherston
Upper Hutt
Lower Hutt
Te Wharau
WELLINGTON
Cape Palliser
Cook Strait
Cape Farewell
Golden Bay
D'Urville Island
Collingwood
Takaka
Tasman Bay
Tasman Mountains
Riwaka
Motueka
Karamea
Havelock
Richmond
Picton
Nelson
Blenheim
Wakefield
Renwick
Karamea Bight
Seddon
Westport
Buller
Mount Travers
Wairau
Cape Campbell
Inangahua Junction
2338
Tapuaenuku
2885
Punakaiki
Inland Kaikoura Range
Spenser Mountains
Reefton
Clarence
Runanga
Springs Junction
Greymouth
Hanmer Springs
Kaikoura
Moana
Hokitika
Waiau
Parnassus
Arthur's Pass
920
Culverden
Kowhitirangi
Waipara
Franz Josef Glacier
Oxford
Rangiora
Pegasus Bay
Rakaia
Kaiapoi
Fox Glacier
3754
Christchurch
Aoraki (Mount Cook)
SOUTHERN ALPS
Mount Somers
Canterbury Plains
Lake Paringa
Lake Ellesmere
Akaroa
Haast
Lake Tekapo
Ashburton
Banks Peninsula
Jackson Head
Geraldine
Lake Pukaki
Canterbury Bight
Twizel
Pleasant Point
Temuka
Mount Aspiring
Lake Wanaka
Lake Benmore
Timaru
3030
Lake Hawea
Omarama
Mount Christina
Waimate
Milford Sound
Wanaka
2502
Lake Wakatipu
Waitaki
Arrowtown
Oamaru
Queenstown
Cromwell
Kyeburn
Maheno
Lake Te Anau
Alexandra
Te Anau
Teviot
Clutha
Doubtful Sound
Lake Manapouri
Five Rivers
Port Chalmers
Lumsden
Otago Peninsula
Mosgiel
Beaumont
Brighton
Dunedin
Lake Hauroko
Gore
Tuapeka Mouth
Tuatapere
Winton
Milton
Mataura
Orepuki
Balclutha
Invercargill
Foveaux Strait
Bluff
Chaslands Mistake
Halfmoon Bay
Ruapuke Island
Stewart Island
Conic Equidistant Projection
Longitude 175° east of Greenwich
1:6 000 000
MILES 0
50
100
0
100 KILOMETRES

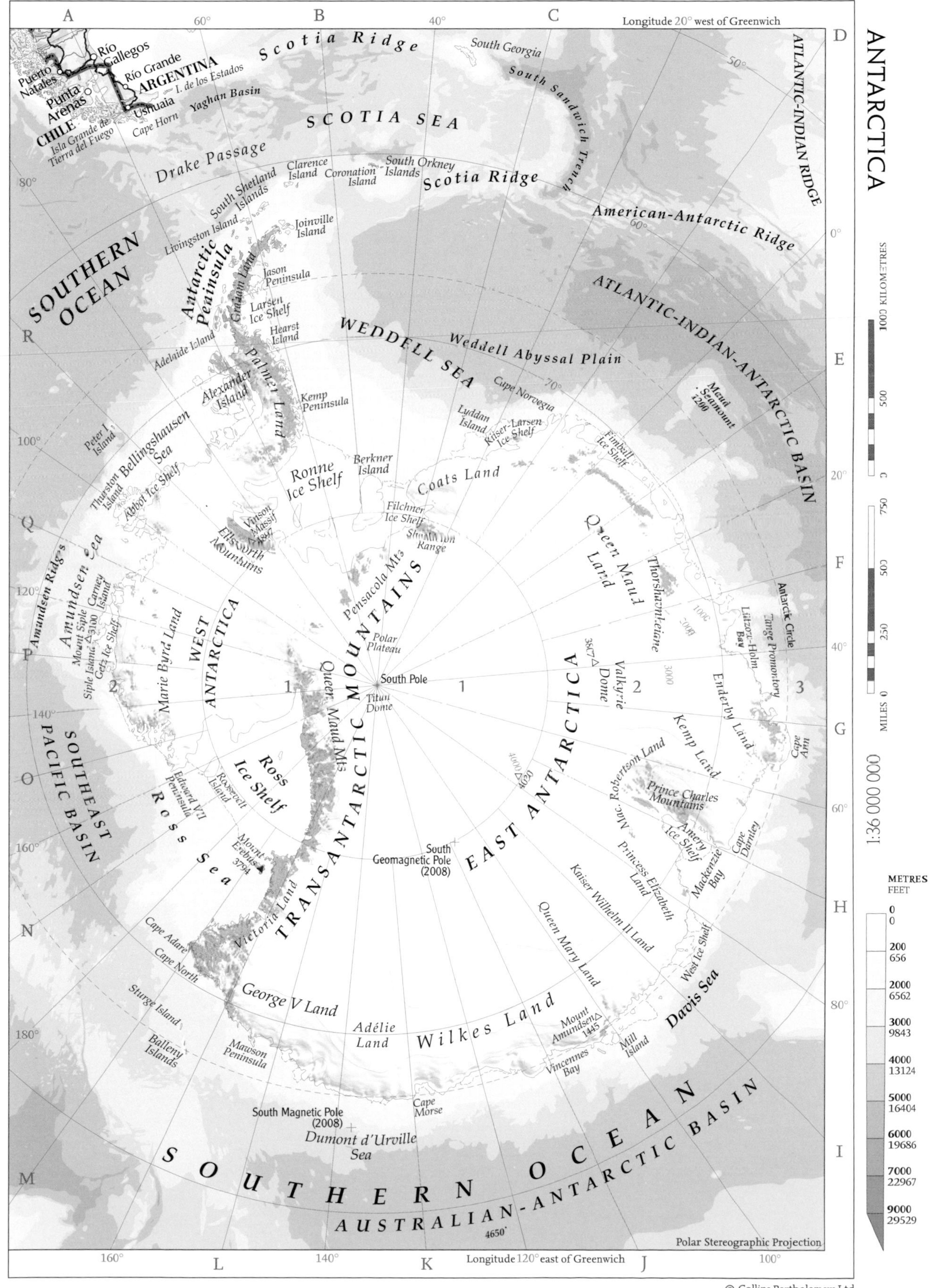
Longitude 20° west of Greenwich
Longitude 120° east of Greenwich
Polar Stereographic Projection
SOUTHERN OCEAN
SCOTIA SEA
Scotia Ridge
South Georgia
South Sandwich Trench
ATLANTIC-INDIAN RIDGE
American-Antarctic Ridge
ATLANTIC-INDIAN-ANTARCTIC BASIN
Weddell Abyssal Plain
WEDDELL SEA
Drake Passage
ARGENTINA
CHILE
Río Gallegos
Río Grande
Puerto Natales
Punta Arenas
Ushuaia
I. de los Estados
Yaghan Basin
Cape Horn
Isla Grande de Tierra del Fuego
South Shetland Islands
Clarence Island
Coronation Island
South Orkney Islands
Livingston Island
Joinville Island
Antarctic Peninsula
Graham Land
Jason Peninsula
Larsen Ice Shelf
Hearst Island
Adelaide Island
Alexander Island
Palmer Land
Kemp Peninsula
Cape Norvegia
Maud Seamount 1290
Lyddan Island
Riiser-Larsen Ice Shelf
Fimbull Ice Shelf
Peter I Island
Bellingshausen Sea
Thurston Island
Abbot Ice Shelf
Ronne Ice Shelf
Berkner Island
Coats Land
Filchner Ice Shelf
Shackleton Range
Vinson Massif 4897
Ellsworth Mountains
Queen Maud Land
Thorshavnheiane
Amundsen Ridges
Amundsen Sea
Carney Island
Mount Siple 3100
Siple Island
Getz Ice Shelf
Marie Byrd Land
WEST ANTARCTICA
Pensacola Mts
TRANSANTARCTIC MOUNTAINS
Polar Plateau
South Pole
Titan Dome
Queen Maud Mts
Valkyrie Dome
3677
Lützow-Holm Bay
Lange Promontory
Antarctic Circle
Enderby Land
Cape Ann
Kemp Land
EAST ANTARCTICA
SOUTHEAST PACIFIC BASIN
Ross Ice Shelf
Roosevelt Island
Edward VII Peninsula
Ross Sea
Mount Erebus 3794
Robertson Land
Prince Charles Mountains
Mac. Robertson Land
Amery Ice Shelf
Cape Darnley
Mackenzie Bay
Princess Elizabeth Land
Kaiser Wilhelm II Land
Queen Mary Land
West Ice Shelf
Davis Sea
South Geomagnetic Pole (2008)
Victoria Land
Cape Adare
Cape North
Sturge Island
Balleny Islands
George V Land
Adélie Land
Wilkes Land
Mount Amundsen 1445
Mill Island
Vincennes Bay
Mawson Peninsula
Cape Morse
South Magnetic Pole (2008)
Dumont d'Urville Sea
AUSTRALIAN-ANTARCTIC BASIN
4650
1:36 000 000
0 500 1000 KILOMETRES
0 250 500 750 MILES
METRES FEET
0 0
200 656
2000 6562
3000 9843
4000 13124
5000 16404
6000 19686
7000 22967
9000 29529

ARCTIC OCEAN
RUSSIAN FED
KAZAKHSTAN
TURKEY
IRAN
IRAQ
SAUDI ARABIA
YEMEN
OMAN
AFGHANISTAN
PAKISTAN
INDIA
CHI
MON
TIBET
SINKIANG
ARABIAN SEA
INDIAN OCEAN
BAY OF BENGAL
Barents Sea
Kara Sea
Black Sea
Caspian Sea
Mediterranean Sea
Red Sea
Gulf of Aden
Gulf of Oman
The Gulf
Rub' al Khālī
Ural Mountains
Himalaya
Istanbul
Ankara
Yekaterinburg
Chelyabinsk
Omsk
Novosibirsk
Barnaul
Astana
Almaty
Tashkent
Bishkek
Dushanbe
Kābul
Islamabad
Lahore
Delhi
New Delhi
Kathmandu
Dhaka
Kolkata (Calcutta)
Mumbai (Bombay)
Hyderabad
Bangalore (Bengaluru)
Chennai (Madras)
Thiruvananthapuram (Trivandrum)
Colombo
Sri Jayewardenepura Kotte
Karachi
Tehrān
Baghdād
Riyadh
Jeddah
Şan'ā
Aden
Muscat
Mashhad
Eşfahān
Shīrāz
Ürümqi
Rangoon (Yangôn)
Nay Pyi Taw
Mandalay
Two Point Equidistant Projection
Longitude 80° east of Greenwich

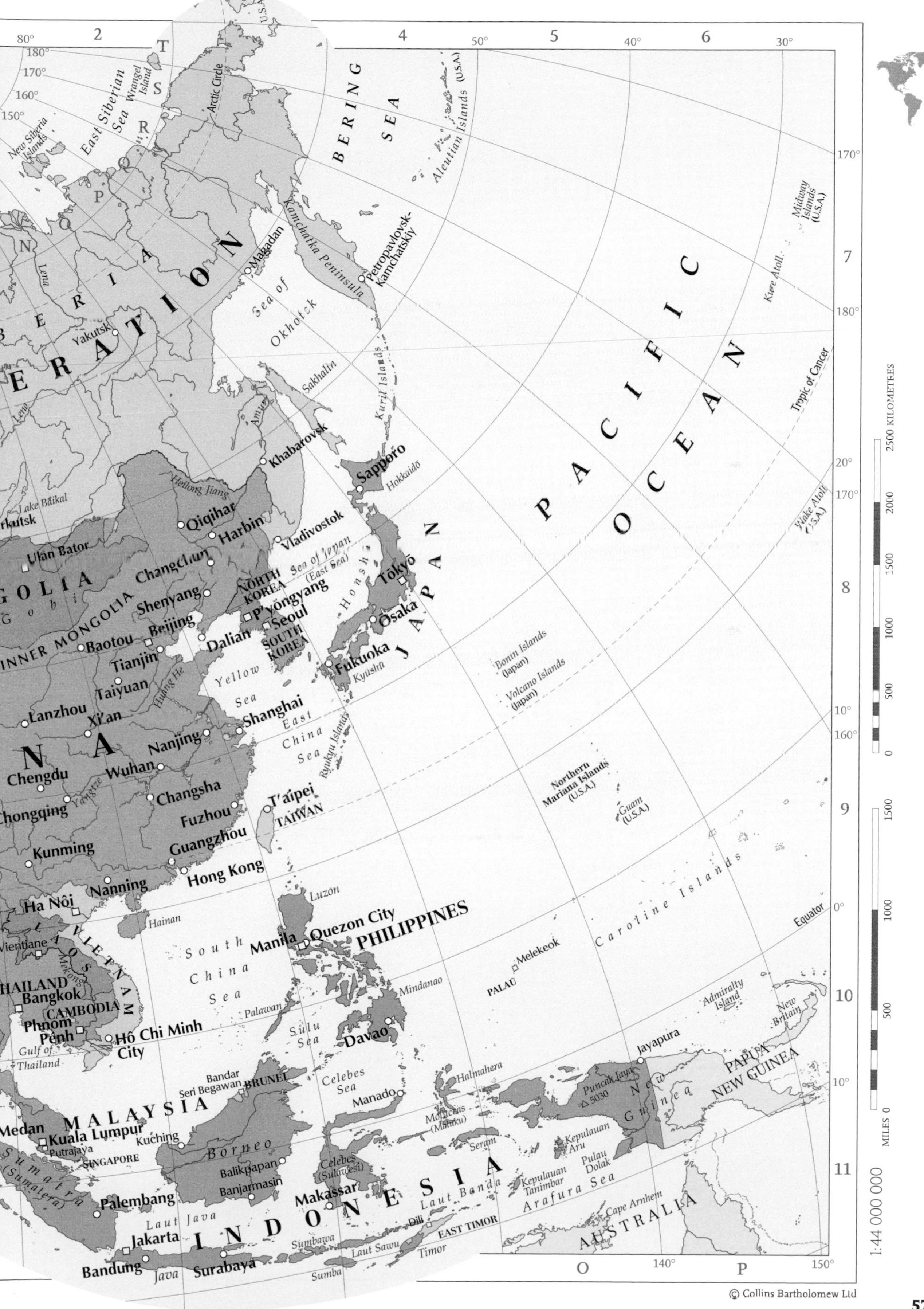
PACIFIC OCEAN
JAPAN
CHINA
MONGOLIA
RUSSIAN FEDERATION
NORTH KOREA
SOUTH KOREA
TAIWAN
PHILIPPINES
VIETNAM
LAOS
THAILAND
CAMBODIA
MALAYSIA
SINGAPORE
BRUNEI
INDONESIA
EAST TIMOR
PAPUA NEW GUINEA
AUSTRALIA
PALAU
INNER MONGOLIA
BERING SEA
East Siberian Sea
Sea of Okhotsk
Sea of Japan (East Sea)
Yellow Sea
East China Sea
South China Sea
Sulu Sea
Celebes Sea
Laut Java
Laut Banda
Laut Sawu
Arafura Sea
Gulf of Thailand
Tōkyō
Ōsaka
Fukuoka
Sapporo
Beijing
Shanghai
Seoul
P'yŏngyang
Hong Kong
Manila
Quezon City
Jakarta
Kuala Lumpur
Putrajaya
Bangkok
Ha Nôi
Hô Chi Minh City
Phnom Penh
Vientiane
Ulan Bator
Irkutsk
Yakutsk
Magadan
Petropavlovsk-Kamchatskiy
Khabarovsk
Vladivostok
Harbin
Qiqihar
Changchun
Shenyang
Dalian
Tianjin
Baotou
Taiyuan
Lanzhou
Xi'an
Nanjing
Wuhan
Chengdu
Chongqing
Changsha
Fuzhou
T'aipei
Guangzhou
Kunming
Nanning
Davao
Manado
Makassar
Dili
Jayapura
Medan
Palembang
Bandung
Surabaya
Kuching
Balikpapan
Banjarmasin
Bandar Seri Begawan
Melekeok
Kamchatka Peninsula
Sakhalin
Kuril Islands
Hokkaidō
Honshū
Kyūshū
Ryukyu Islands
Bonin Islands (Japan)
Volcano Islands (Japan)
Northern Mariana Islands (U.S.A.)
Guam (U.S.A.)
Caroline Islands
Aleutian Islands (U.S.A.)
Midway Islands (U.S.A.)
Kure Atoll
Wake Atoll (U.S.A.)
Wrangel Island
New Siberia Islands
Arctic Circle
Tropic of Cancer
Equator
Lake Baikal
Lena
Amur
Heilong Jiang
Huang He
Yangtze
Mekong
Gobi
Hainan
Luzon
Mindanao
Palawan
Borneo
Sumatra (Sumatera)
Java
Celebes (Sulawesi)
Halmahera
Moluccas (Maluku)
Seram
Sumbawa
Sumba
Timor
Kepulauan Aru
Kepulauan Tanimbar
Pulau Dolak
New Guinea
Puncak Jaya 5030
Admiralty Island
New Britain
Cape Arnhem
2500 KILOMETRES
1500 MILES
1:44 000 000
© Collins Bartholomew Ltd

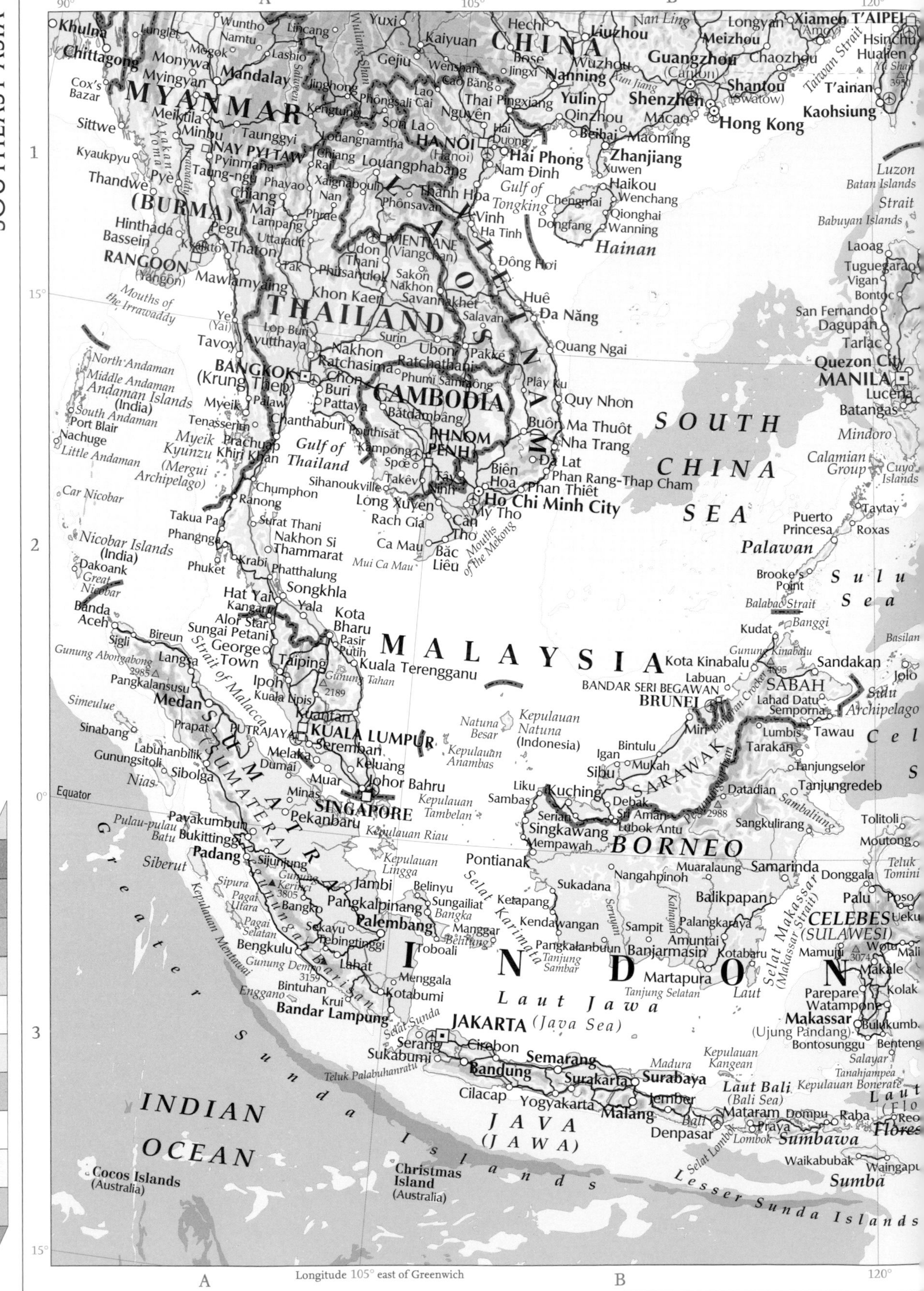

Albers Equal Area Conic Projection

C
D
E
135°
150°
Tropic of Cancer
Ryukyu Islands (Nansei-shotō) (Japan)
TAIWAN
The People's Republic of China claims Taiwan as its 23rd Province.
PACIFIC OCEAN
Philippine Sea
Northern Mariana Islands (U.S.A.)
Pagan
CAPITOL HILL
Saipan
Tinian
Rota
HAGÅTÑA
Guam (U.S.A.)
Mariana Trench
Aparri
Ilagan
Luzon
Polillo Islands
PHILIPPINES
Daet
Catanduanes
Legaspi
Sorsogon
Romblon
Irosin
Catarman
Masbate
Samar
Roxas
Catbalogan
Panay
Tacloban
Bacolod
Iloilo
Cebu
Negros
Bohol
Surigao
Butuan
Cagayan de Oro
Oroquieta
Iligan
Mindanao
Pagadian
Cotabato
Davao
Zamboanga
Mati
Isabela
Moro Gulf
General Santos
FEDERATED STATES OF MICRONESIA
Ulithi
Fais
Yap
Colonia
Faraulep
Ngulu
Sorol
PALAU
MELEKEOK
Babeldaob
Eauripik
Caroline Islands
East Caroline Basin
Equator
Kepulauan Talaud
Sangir
Kepulauan Sangir
Morotai
Daruba
Tobelo
Manado
Halmahera
Ternate
Sao-Siu
Tondano
Kwandang
Gorontalo
Laut Maluku (Molucca Sea)
Kepulauan Togian
Luwuk
Labuna
Bacan
Obi
Peleng
Tataba
Banggai
Todeli
Mangole
Taliabu
Dofa
Moluccas (Maluku)
Kepulauan Banggai
Kepulauan Sula
Waigeo
Selat Dampir
Salawati
Sorong
Kwoka
Jazirah Doberai
Manokwari
Biak
Numfoor
Ransiki
Selat Yapen
Yapen
Serui
Sarmi
Jayapura
Vanimo
Aitape
Misoöl
Fafanlap
Inanwatan
Teluk Cenderawasih
Teluk Berau
Babo
Nabire
Pegunungan Van Rees
PAPUA (IRIAN JAYA)
Taritatu
Puncak Trikora
Pegunungan Maoke
Puncak Jaya
Puncak Mandala
Enarotali
Seram
Piru
Laut Seram (Ceram Sea)
Fakfak
Namlea
Buru
Ambon
Saparua
Bula
Kaimana
Adi
Amamapare
Lorentz
Kendari
Manui
Wowoni
Raha
Buton
Baubau
Kepulauan Tukangbesi
Kepulauan Watubela
Kepulauan Banda
Kepulauan Kai
Kai Kecil
Tual
Kai Besar
Dobo
Wokam
Benjina
Kobroör
Kepulauan Aru
Trangan
Sia
Laut Banda (Banda Sea)
Tanjung Deyong
Digul
Pulau Dolok
Merauke
Tanjung Vals
Tanjung d'Urville
Wuvulu Island
Hermit Islands
Pelleluhu Islands
Admiralty Islands
Manus Island
Lorengau
St Matthias Group
Mussau Island
Ysabel Channel
New Hanover
Kavieng
Umbukul
New Ireland
Bismarck Archipelago
Bismarck Sea
Rabaul
Schouten Islands
Maprik
Wewak
Sepik
Bogia
Manam Island
Ulamona
Long Island
Kimbe
New Britain
Madang
Umboi
Lau
Gasmata
Huon Peninsula
PAPUA NEW GUINEA
NEW GUINEA
Central Ra.
Mt Wilhelm
Mendi
Mount Hagen
Goroka
Kikori
Kiunga
Lae
Morobe
Wau
Trobriand Islands
Losuia
Lake Murray
Balimo
Kerema
Mount Victoria
D'Entrecasteaux Is.
Morehead
Daru
Gulf of Papua
Bereina
Bolubolu
Goschen Strait
Kwikila
Alotau
PORT MORESBY
Abau
Samarai
Flores Sea
Kepulauan Alor
Kepulauan Barat Daya
Damar
Wuliaru
Larat
Kepulauan Tanimbar
Pulau Romang
Tepa
Babar
Kalabahi
Alor
Huaki
Kaiwatu
Saumlakki
Wetar
Larantuka
Ende
Dili
Kepulauan Sermata
Selaru
Maliana
Manatuto
Leti
OCUSSI
EAST TIMOR
Laut Sawu (Savu Sea)
Kefamenanu
Timor
Kupang
Savu
Rote
Arafura Sea
Timor Sea
AUSTRALIA
Melville Island
Milikapiti
Croker Island
Bathurst Island
Van Diemen Gulf
Beagle Gulf
Darwin
Jabiru
Batchelor
Adelaide River
Pine Creek
Arnhem Land
Cape Wessel
Wessel Islands
Nhulunbuy
Milingimbi
Cape Arnhem
Alyangula
Gulf of Carpentaria
Thursday Island
Prince of Wales Island
Cape York
Bamaga
Cape Grenville
Weipa
Lockhart River
Coen
Cape Melville
Cape Flattery
Cape York Peninsula
Cooktown
Laura
1:20 000 000
KILOMETRES 0 250 500
MILES 0 250 500
15°
0°
1
2

Albers Equal Area Conic Projection

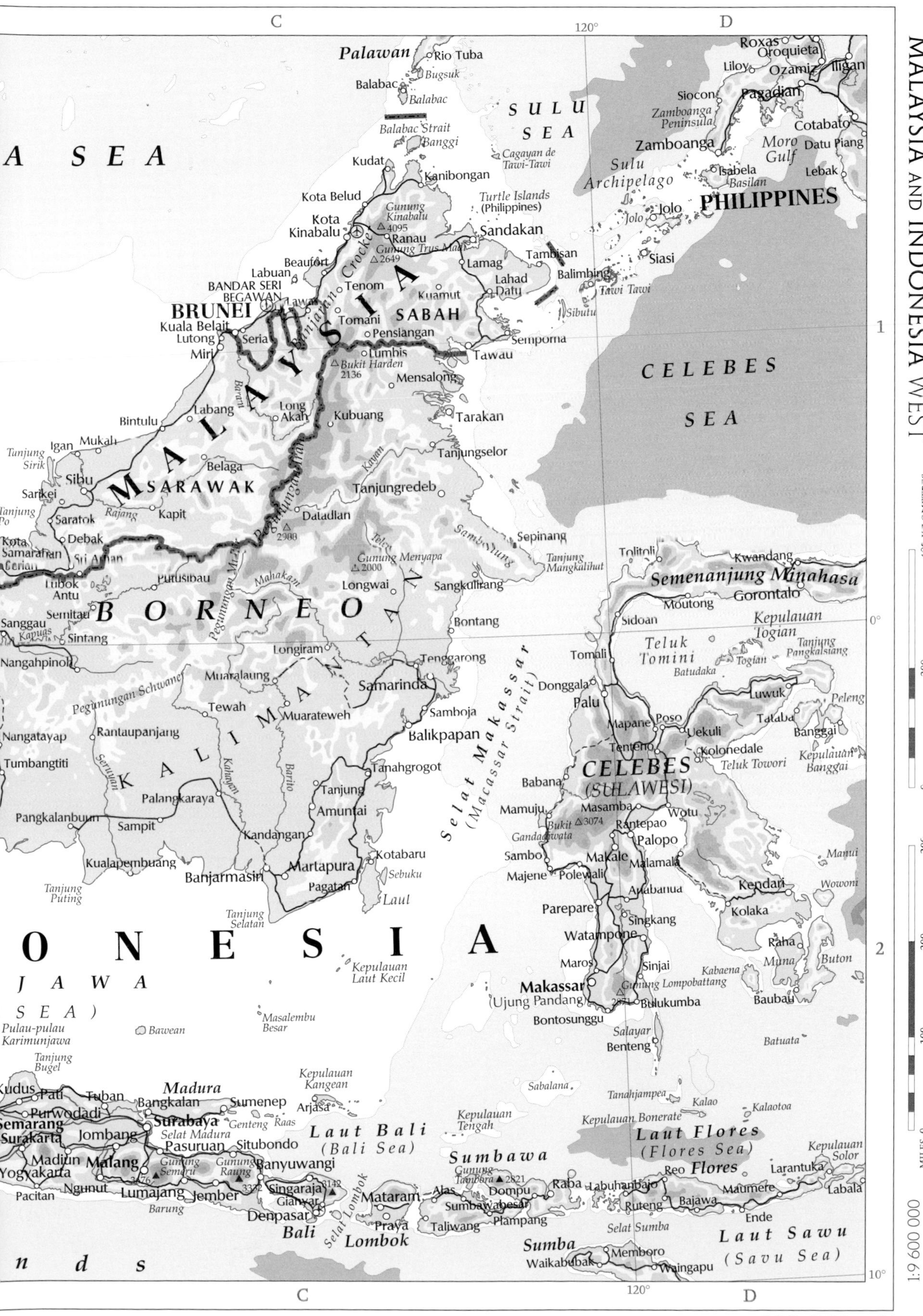
C
120°
D
Palawan
Rio Tuba
Bugsuk
Balabac
Balabac Strait
Banggi
SULU SEA
Cagayan de Tawi-Tawi
Roxas
Oroquieta
Liloy
Ozamiz
Iligan
Siocon
Pagadian
Zamboanga Peninsula
Cotabato
Zamboanga
Moro Gulf
Datu Piang
Sulu Archipelago
Isabela
Basilan
Lebak
PHILIPPINES
Jolo
Siasi
Tawi Tawi
Sibutu
A SEA
Kudat
Kanibongan
Turtle Islands (Philippines)
Kota Belud
Gunung Kinabalu 4095
Kota Kinabalu
Ranau
Gunung Trus Madi 2649
Sandakan
Tambisan
Beaufort
Lamag
Labuan
Lahad Datu
Balimbing
BANDAR SERI BEGAWAN
Tenom
Kuamut
BRUNEI
SABAH
Tomani
Kuala Belait
Seria
Lutong
Miri
Pensiangan
Semporna
Lumbis
Tawau
Bukit Harden 2136
Mensalong
CELEBES SEA
Labang
Long Akah
Baram
Bintulu
Kubuang
Tarakan
Mukah
Igan
Tanjung Sirik
Tanjungselor
Belaga
Sibu
MALAYSIA
SARAWAK
Sarikei
Tanjungredeb
Kayan
Tanjung Po
Kapit
Rajang
Saratok
Datadian
Debak
2988
Kota Samarahan
Sri Aman
Sambaliung
Sepinang
Tanjung Mangkalihat
Gunung Menyapa 2000
Putussibau
Mahakam
Lubok Antu
Longwai
Sangkulirang
Tolitoli
Kwandang
Semenanjung Minahasa
Moutong
Gorontalo
Semitau
BORNEO
Sanggau
Kapuas
Sintang
Bontang
Sidoan
Kepulauan Togian
Teluk Tomini
Tanjung Pangkalsiang
Togian
Batudaka
Longiram
Nangahpinoh
Tenggarong
Tomali
Muaralaung
Samarinda
Donggala
Luwuk
Peleng
Pegunungan Schwaner
Tewah
Palu
Muarateweh
Samboja
Mapane
Poso
Tataba
Banggai
Nangatayap
Rantaupanjang
Balikpapan
Selat Makassar (Macassar Strait)
Uekuli
Tentena
Kolonedale
Teluk Towori
Kepulauan Banggai
Tumbangtiti
KALIMANTAN
Tanahgrogot
CELEBES (SULAWESI)
Babana
Tanjung
Palangkaraya
Kahayan
Barito
Amuntai
Mamuju
Masamba
Wotu
Pangkalanbuun
Sampit
3074
Rantepao
Bukit Gandadiwata
Kandangan
Palopo
Kotabaru
Sambo
Makale
Kualapembuang
Martapura
Sebuku
Majene
Polewali
Malamala
Manui
Banjarmasin
Pagatan
Kendari
Wowoni
Tanjung Puting
Laut
Anabanua
Kolaka
Parepare
Tanjung Selatan
Singkang
INDONESIA
Watampone
Raha
Muna
Buton
Kepulauan Laut Kecil
Maros
Sinjai
Kabaena
JAWA
Makassar (Ujung Pandang)
Gunung Lompobattang
2871
Bulukumba
Baubau
SEA)
Bontosunggu
Pulau-pulau Karimunjawa
Bawean
Masalembu Besar
Salayar
Benteng
Batuata
Tanjung Bugel
Kepulauan Kangean
Sabalana
Kudus
Pati
Tuban
Madura
Bangkalan
Sumenep
Tanahjampea
Kalao
Kalaotoa
Semarang
Purwodadi
Surabaya
Arjasa
Genteng
Raas
Kepulauan Tengah
Kepulauan Bonerate
Surakarta
Jombang
Selat Madura
Laut Bali (Bali Sea)
Laut Flores (Flores Sea)
Kepulauan Solor
Pasuruan
Situbondo
Madiun
Malang
Gunung Semeru
Gunung Raung
Banyuwangi
Sumbawa
Gunung Tambora 2821
Reo
Flores
Larantuka
Yogyakarta
3676
3332
3142
Ngunut
Lumajang
Singaraja
Alas
Dompu
Raba
Labuhanbajo
Maumere
Labala
Pacitan
Jember
Gianyar
Mataram
Sumbawabesar
Ruteng
Bajawa
Barung
Denpasar
Selat Lombok
Praya
Taliwang
Plampang
Ende
Selat Sumba
Bali
Lombok
Sumba
Laut Sawu (Savu Sea)
Memboro
Waikabubak
Waingapu
nds
10°
0°
1
2
KILOMETRES 400 200 0
MILES 300 200 100 0
1:6 000 000

CONTINENTAL SOUTHEAST ASIA

Albers Equal Area Conic Projection

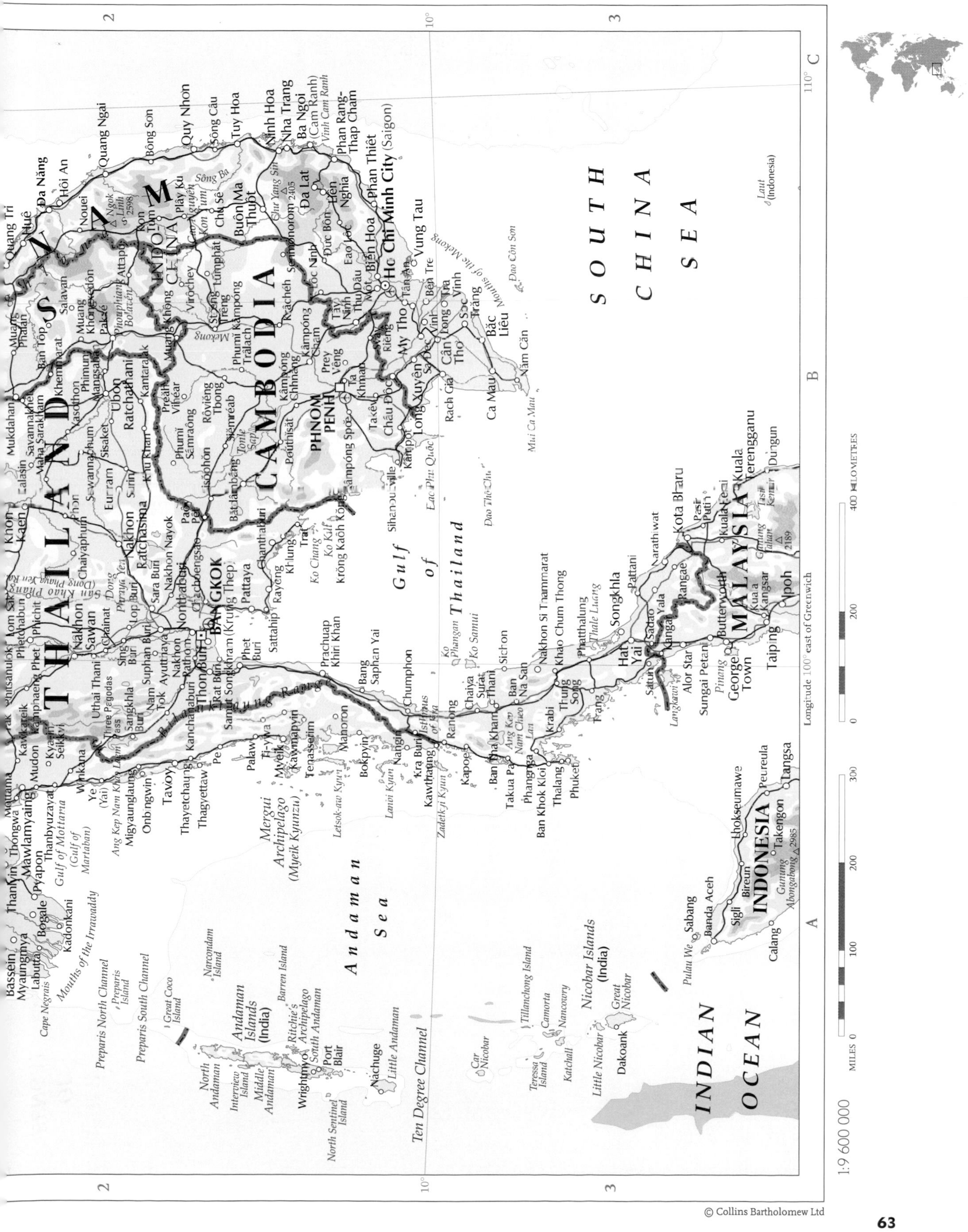

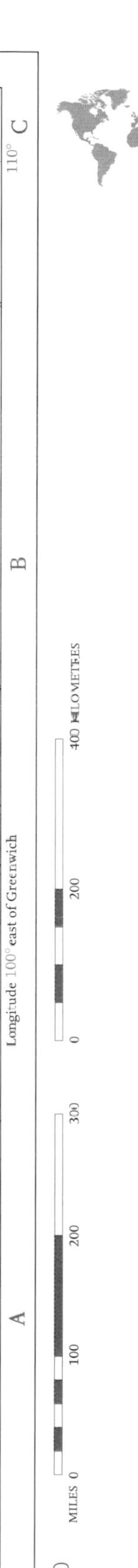

1:9 600 000

Albers Equal Area Conic Projection

1:9 600 000

MILES 0 100 150
0 100 200 KILOMETRES

METRES FEET
5000 16404
3000 9843
2000 6562
1000 3281
500 1640
200 656
0 0
Land below sea level
200 656
4000 13124
6000 19686

NORTH KOREA AND SOUTH KOREA

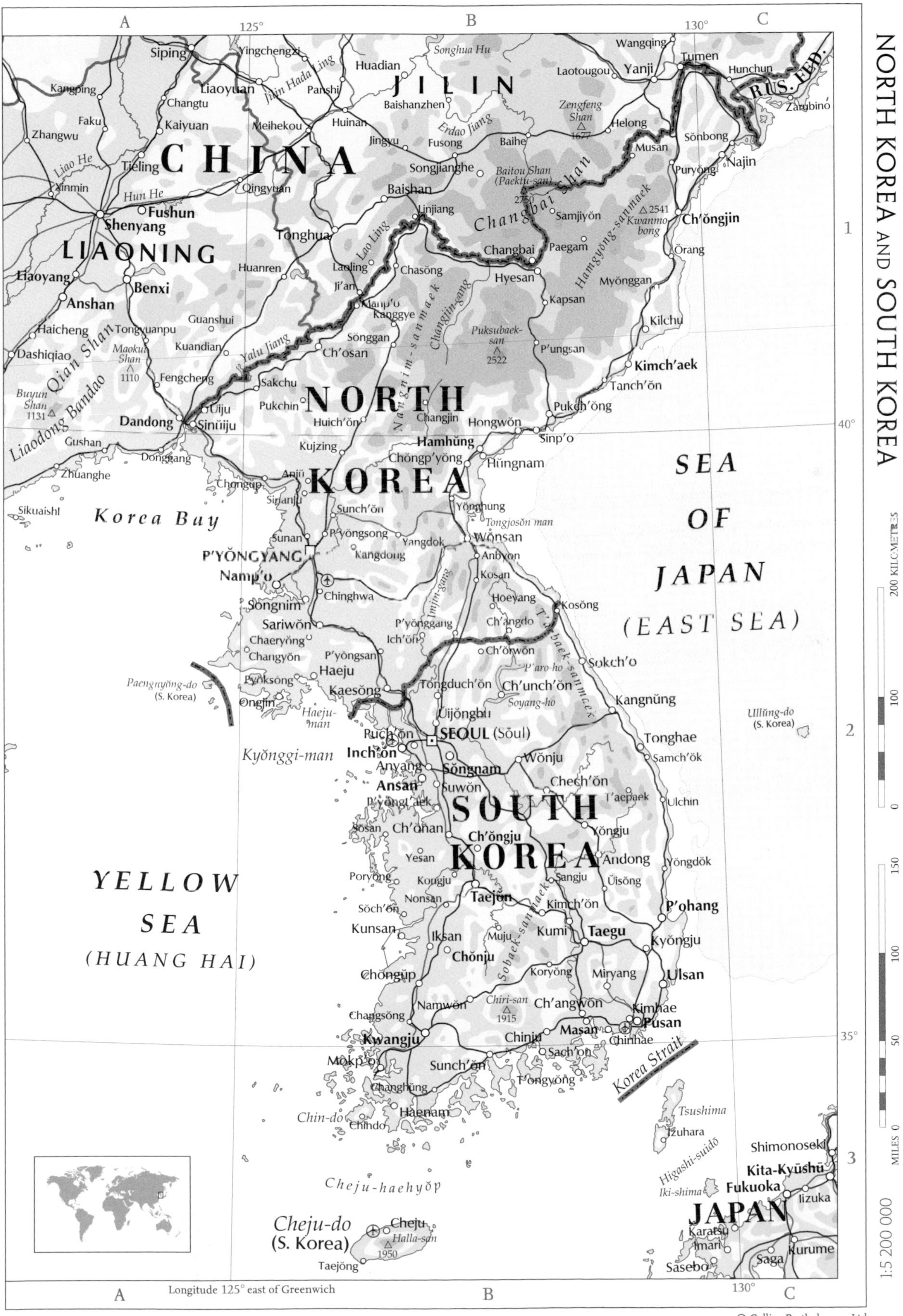

1:5 200 000

Albers Equal Area Conic Projection

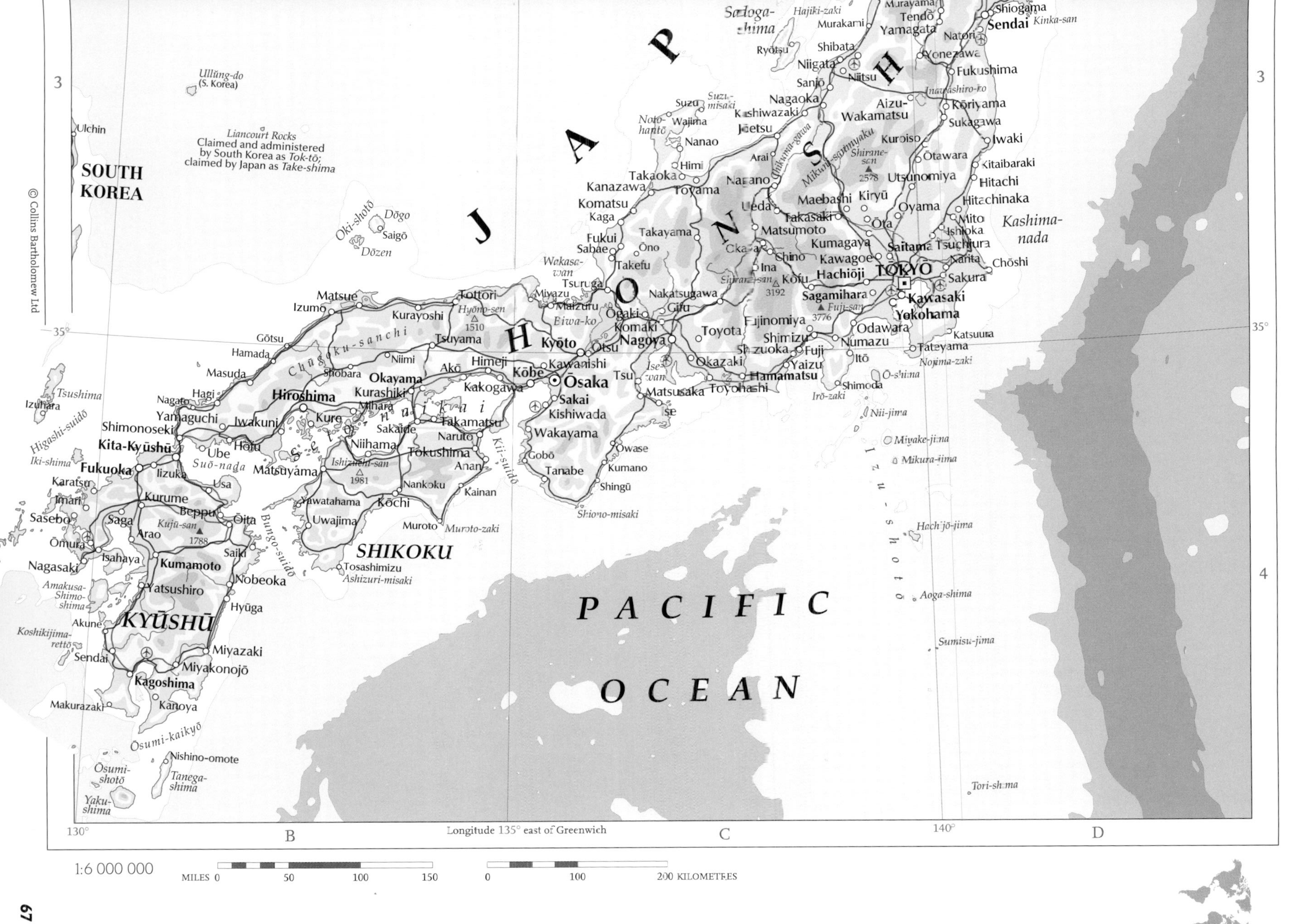

JAPAN
HONSHU
SHIKOKU
KYŪSHŪ
PACIFIC OCEAN
SOUTH KOREA
Ulchin
Ullŭng-do (S. Korea)
Liancourt Rocks
Claimed and administered by South Korea as Tok-tō; claimed by Japan as Take-shima
Oki-shotō
Dōgo
Saigō
Dōzen
Sado-shima
Hajiki-zaki
Murakami
Ryōtsu
Shibata
Niigata
Sanjō
Nagaoka
Kashiwazaki
Jōetsu
Suzu
Suzu-misaki
Noto-hantō
Wajima
Nanao
Himi
Takaoka
Toyama
Kanazawa
Komatsu
Kaga
Fukui
Sabae
Ōno
Takefu
Takayama
Tsuruga
Wakasa-wan
Miyazu
Maizuru
Biwa-ko
Murayama
Tendō
Yamagata
Shiogama
Sendai
Kinka-san
Natori
Yonezawa
Fukushima
Inawashiro-ko
Aizu-Wakamatsu
Kōriyama
Sukagawa
Iwaki
Kuroiso
Ōtawara
Shirane-san
2578
Utsunomiya
Kitaibaraki
Hitachi
Hitachinaka
Mito
Ishioka
Tsuchiura
Kashima-nada
Narita
Chōshi
Sakura
Arai
Nagano
Ueda
Maebashi
Kiryū
Oyama
Ōta
Takasaki
Matsumoto
Kumagaya
Kawagoe
Saitama
Tōkyō
Hachiōji
Chino
Ina
Kōfu
3192
Sagamihara
Kawasaki
Yokohama
Fuji-san
3776
Fujinomiya
Odawara
Shimizu
Numazu
Shizuoka
Fuji
Itō
Yaizu
Tateyama
Katsuura
Nojima-zaki
Shimoda
Irō-zaki
Ō-shima
Nii-jima
Miyake-jima
Mikura-jima
Izu-shotō
Hachijō-jima
Aoga-shima
Sumisu-jima
Tori-shima
Nakatsugawa
Gifu
Ōgaki
Komaki
Nagoya
Toyota
Okazaki
Hamamatsu
Toyohashi
Tsu
Ise-wan
Matsusaka
Ise
Owase
Kumano
Shingū
Shiono-misaki
Kyōto
Ōtsu
Kawanishi
Kōbe
Ōsaka
Sakai
Kishiwada
Wakayama
Gobō
Tanabe
Kii-suidō
Tottori
Hyōno-sen
1510
Matsue
Izumo
Kurayoshi
Tsuyama
Chūgoku-sanchi
Gōtsu
Hamada
Masuda
Niimi
Shōbara
Akō
Himeji
Kakogawa
Okayama
Kurashiki
Hiroshima
Mihara
Kure
Seto-naikai
Sakaide
Takamatsu
Naruto
Tokushima
Anan
Niihama
Ishizuchi-san
1981
Matsuyama
Nankoku
Kōchi
Kainan
Yawatahama
Uwajima
Muroto
Muroto-zaki
Tosashimizu
Ashizuri-misaki
Hagi
Nagato
Yamaguchi
Iwakuni
Hōfu
Ube
Suō-nada
Shimonoseki
Kita-Kyūshū
Tsushima
Izuhara
Higashi-suidō
Iki-shima
Fukuoka
Iizuka
Usa
Karatsu
Imari
Kurume
Beppu
Ōita
Kujū-san
1788
Bungo-suidō
Saga
Sasebo
Arao
Ōmura
Isahaya
Saiki
Nagasaki
Kumamoto
Nobeoka
Amakusa-Shimo-shima
Yatsushiro
Hyūga
Akune
Koshikijima-rettō
Sendai
Miyazaki
Miyakonojō
Kagoshima
Makurazaki
Kanoya
Ōsumi-kaikyō
Nishino-omote
Ōsumi-shotō
Tanega-shima
Yaku-shima
3
4
35°
130°
140°
B
C
D
Longitude 135° east of Greenwich
1:6 000 000
MILES 0 50 100 150
0 100 200 KILOMETRES

METRES
FEET

5000
16404

3000
9843

2000
6562

1000
3281

500
1640

200
656

0
0

Land below sea level

200
656

4000
13124

6000
19686

Albers Equal Area Conic Projection

PACIFIC OCEAN
JAPAN
NORTH KOREA
SOUTH KOREA
TAIWAN
PHILIPPINES
EAST CHINA SEA
SOUTH CHINA SEA
Sea of Japan (East Sea)
Yellow Sea (Huang Hai)
BEIJING
SEOUL
P'YONGYANG
TŌKYŌ
T'AIPEI
ULAN BATOR (Ulaanbaatar)
Shanghai
Hong Kong
Sakhalin
Hokkaidō
Kyūshū
Shikoku
Hainan
Luzon
The People's Republic of China claims Taiwan as its 23rd Province.
Tropic of Cancer
1:20 000 000
1000 KILOMETRES
MILES 0

CHINA CENTRAL

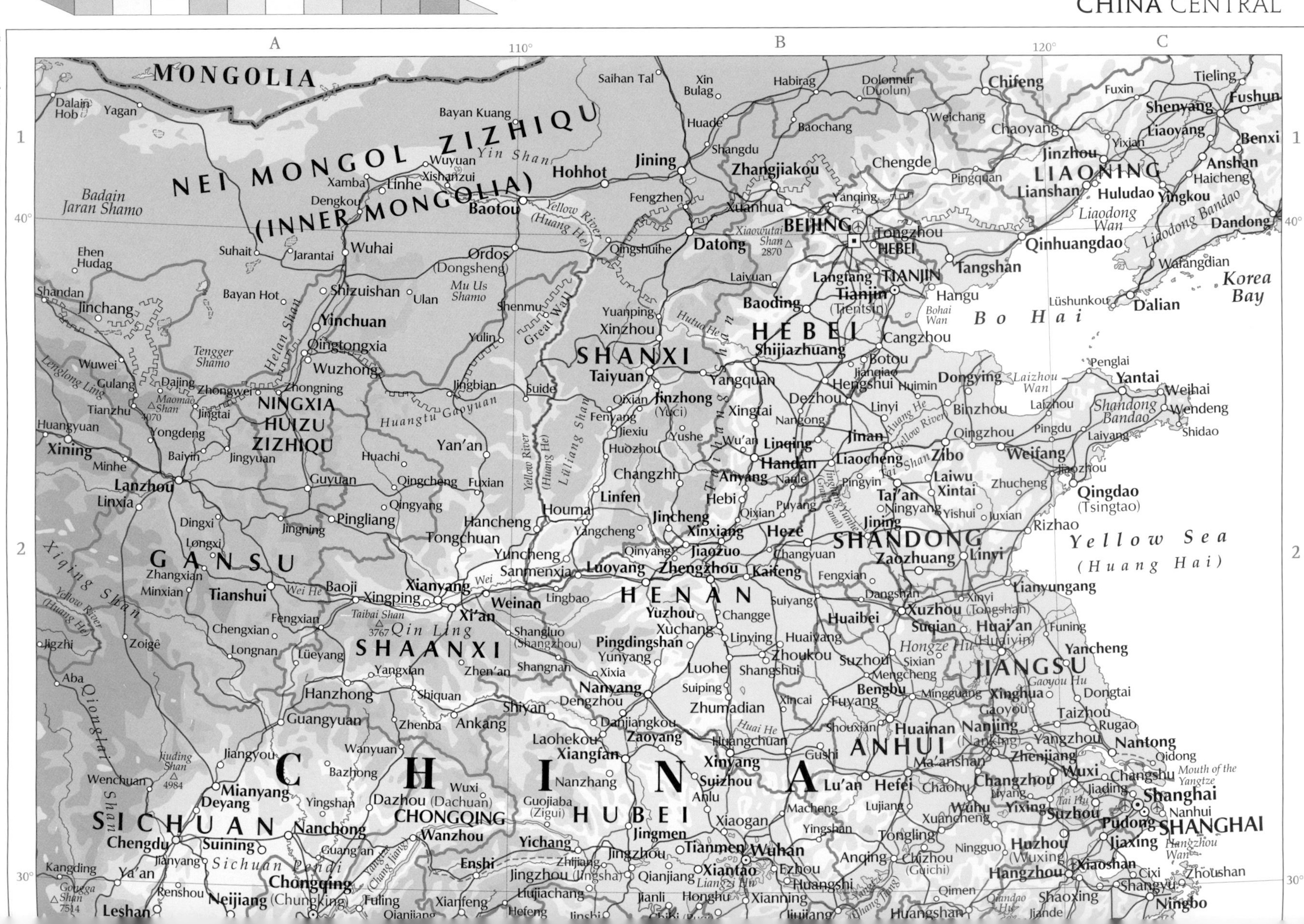

Albers Equal Area Conic Projection

EAST CHINA SEA
SOUTH CHINA SEA
Gulf of Tongking
Luzon Strait
Taiwan Strait
Bashi Channel
Balintang Channel
Babuyan Channel
TAIWAN
T'AIPEI
Kaohsiung
T'aichung
T'ainan
Hualien
The People's Republic of China claims Taiwan as its 23rd Province.
Tropic of Cancer
LUZON
PHILIPPINES
ZHEJIANG
FUJIAN
JIANGXI
HUNAN
GUANGDONG
GUANGXI ZHUANGZU ZIZHIQU
GUIZHOU
YUNNAN
HAINAN
VIETNAM
LAOS
THAILAND
HA NOI
VIENTIANE
Hong Kong
Macao
Guangzhou
Shenzhen
Xiamen
Fuzhou
Wenzhou
Nanchang
Changsha
Guiyang
Kunming
Nanning
Haikou
Zhanjiang
Hai Phong
Longitude 110° east of Greenwich
1:9 600 000
MILES 0 100 200 300
0 200 400 KILOMETRES
A B C
3 4
20° 120°

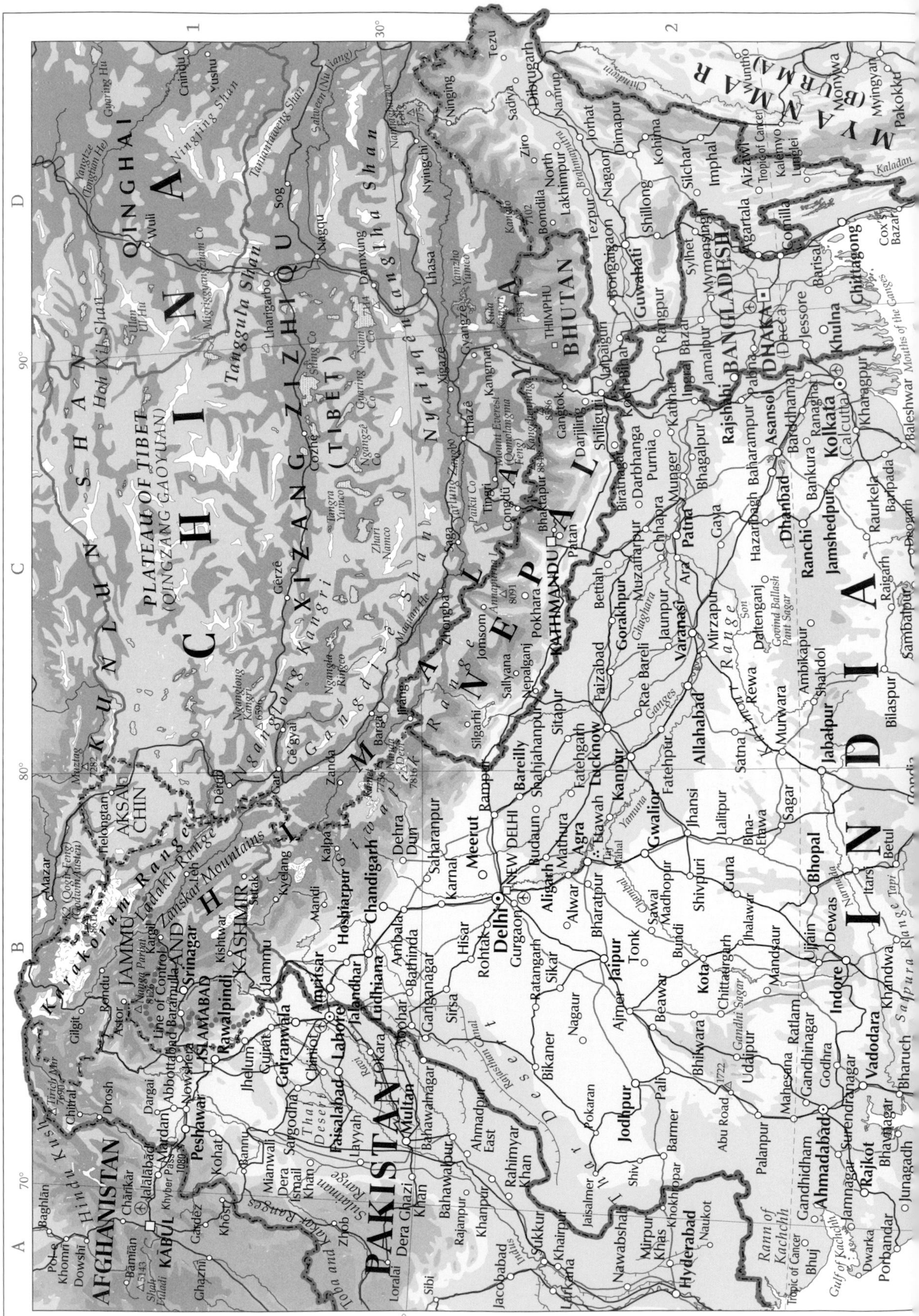

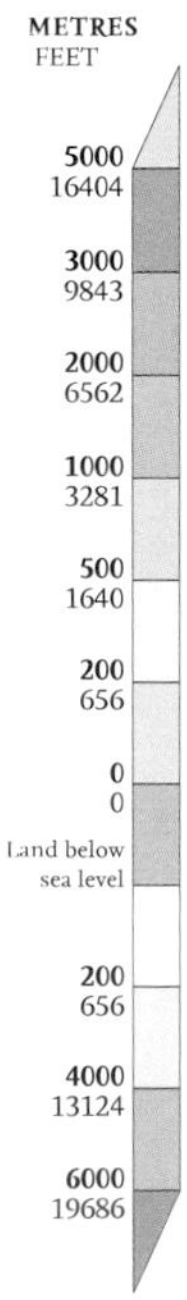

Albers Equal Area Conic Projection

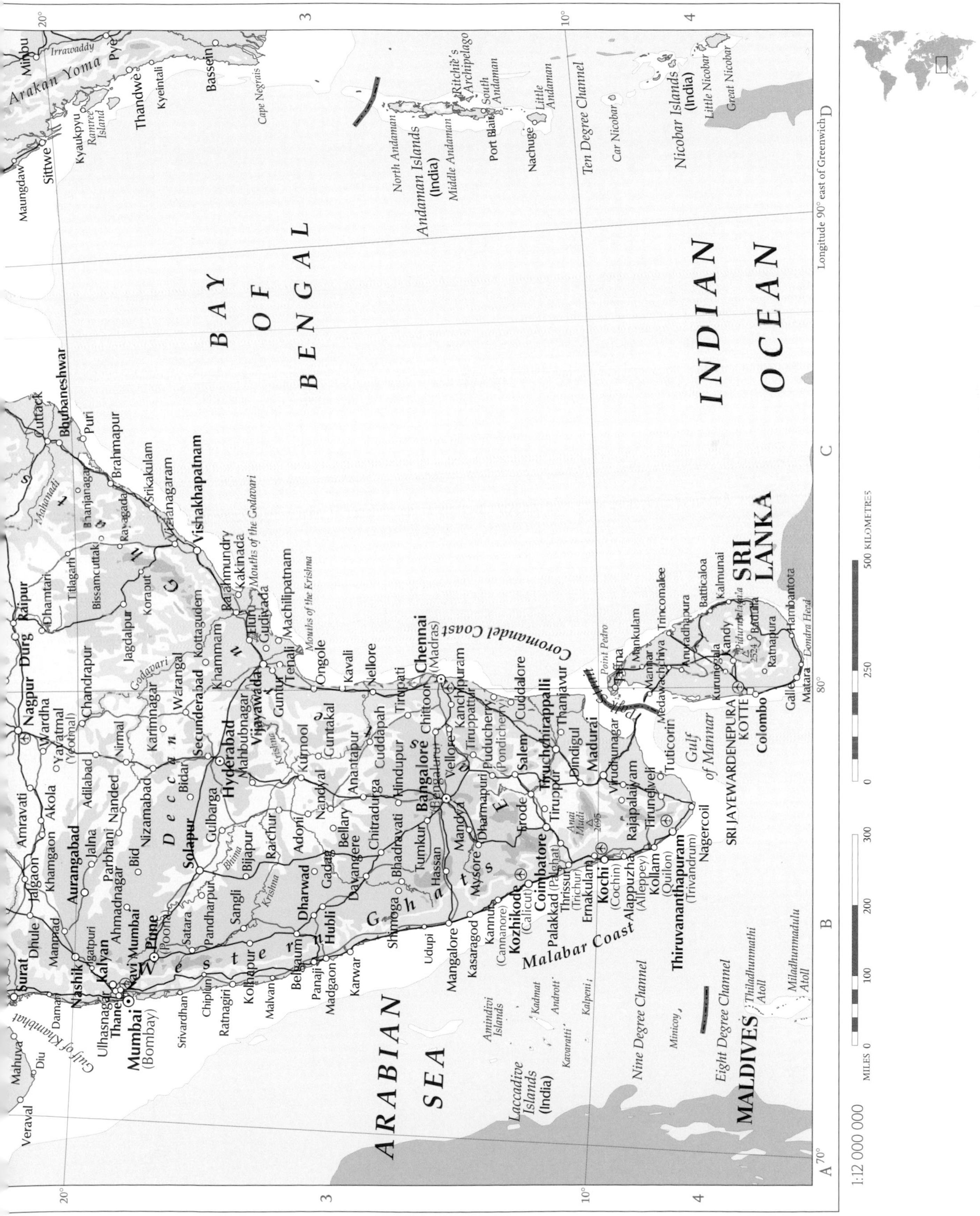

ARABIAN SEA

BAY OF BENGAL

INDIAN OCEAN

SRI LANKA

MALDIVES

Andaman Islands (India)

Nicobar Islands (India)

Laccadive Islands (India)

Longitude 90° east of Greenwich

1:12 000 000

MILES 0 100 200 300

0 250 500 KILOMETRES

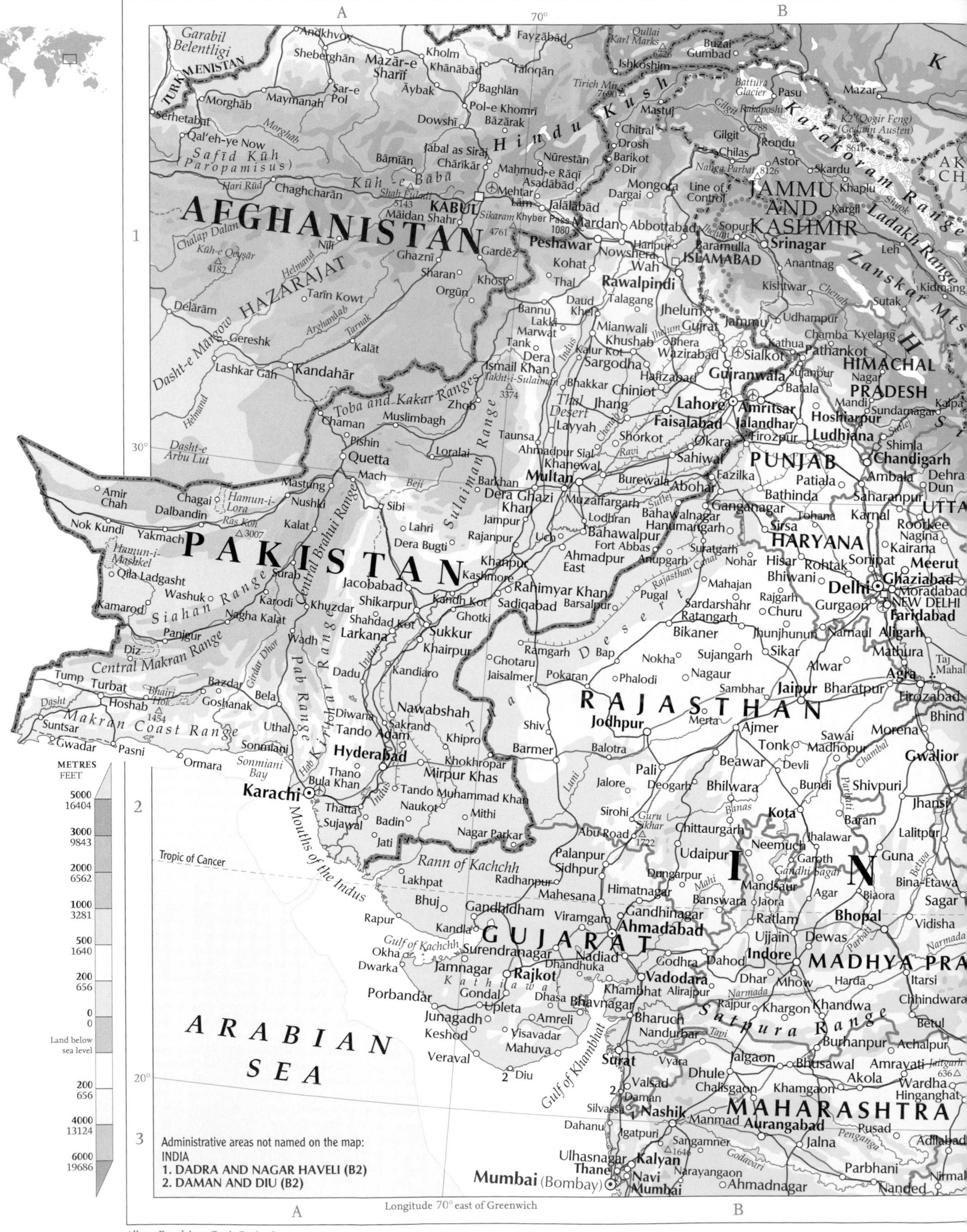

A
70°
B
1
2
3
30°
20°
Longitude 70° east of Greenwich
Albers Equal Area Conic Projection
METRES
FEET
5000
16404
3000
9843
2000
6562
1000
3281
500
1640
200
656
0
0
Land below sea level
200
656
4000
13124
6000
19686
Administrative areas not named on the map:
INDIA
1. DADRA AND NAGAR HAVELI (B2)
2. DAMAN AND DIU (B2)
AFGHANISTAN
PAKISTAN
INDIA
TURKMENISTAN
JAMMU AND KASHMIR
HIMACHAL PRADESH
PUNJAB
HARYANA
RAJASTHAN
GUJARAT
MADHYA PRADESH
MAHARASHTRA
ARABIAN SEA
HAZARAJAT
Hindu Kush
Karakoram Range
Ladakh Range
Zanskar Mts
Safīd Kūh (Paropamisus)
Kūh-e Bābā
Toba and Kakar Ranges
Sulaiman Range
Central Brahui Range
Kirthar Range
Pab Range
Siahan Range
Central Makran Range
Makran Coast Range
Satpura Range
Thar Desert
Thal Desert
Dasht-e Mārgow
Dasht-e Arbu Lut
Rann of Kachchh
Gulf of Kachchh
Gulf of Khambhat
Mouths of the Indus
Tropic of Cancer
Kathiawar
Sonmiani Bay
Garabil Belentligi
KABUL
ISLAMABAD
NEW DELHI
Karachi
Mumbai (Bombay)
Lahore
Delhi
Ahmadabad
Hyderabad
Peshawar
Rawalpindi
Faisalabad
Multan
Quetta
Kandahār
Herat
Mazār-e Sharīf
Srinagar
Amritsar
Jaipur
Jodhpur
Surat
Vadodara
Rajkot
Indore
Bhopal
Nashik
Kalyan
Thane
Navi Mumbai
Aurangabad
Chandigarh
Ludhiana
Jalandhar
Gujranwala
Sialkot
Sukkur
Bikaner
Ajmer
Kota
Udaipur
Gwalior
Agra
Meerut
Ghaziabad
Faridabad
K2 (Qogir Feng) (Godwin Austen) 8611
Nanga Parbat 8126
Tirich Mir 7690
Rakaposhi 7788
Khyber Pass 1080
Sikaram 4761
Shah Fuladi 5143
Takht-i-Sulaiman 3374
Guru Sikhar 1722
Indus
Helmand
Jhelum
Chenab
Ravi
Sutlej
Beas
Luni
Narmada
Tapi
Chambal
Mahi
Godavari
Taj Mahal

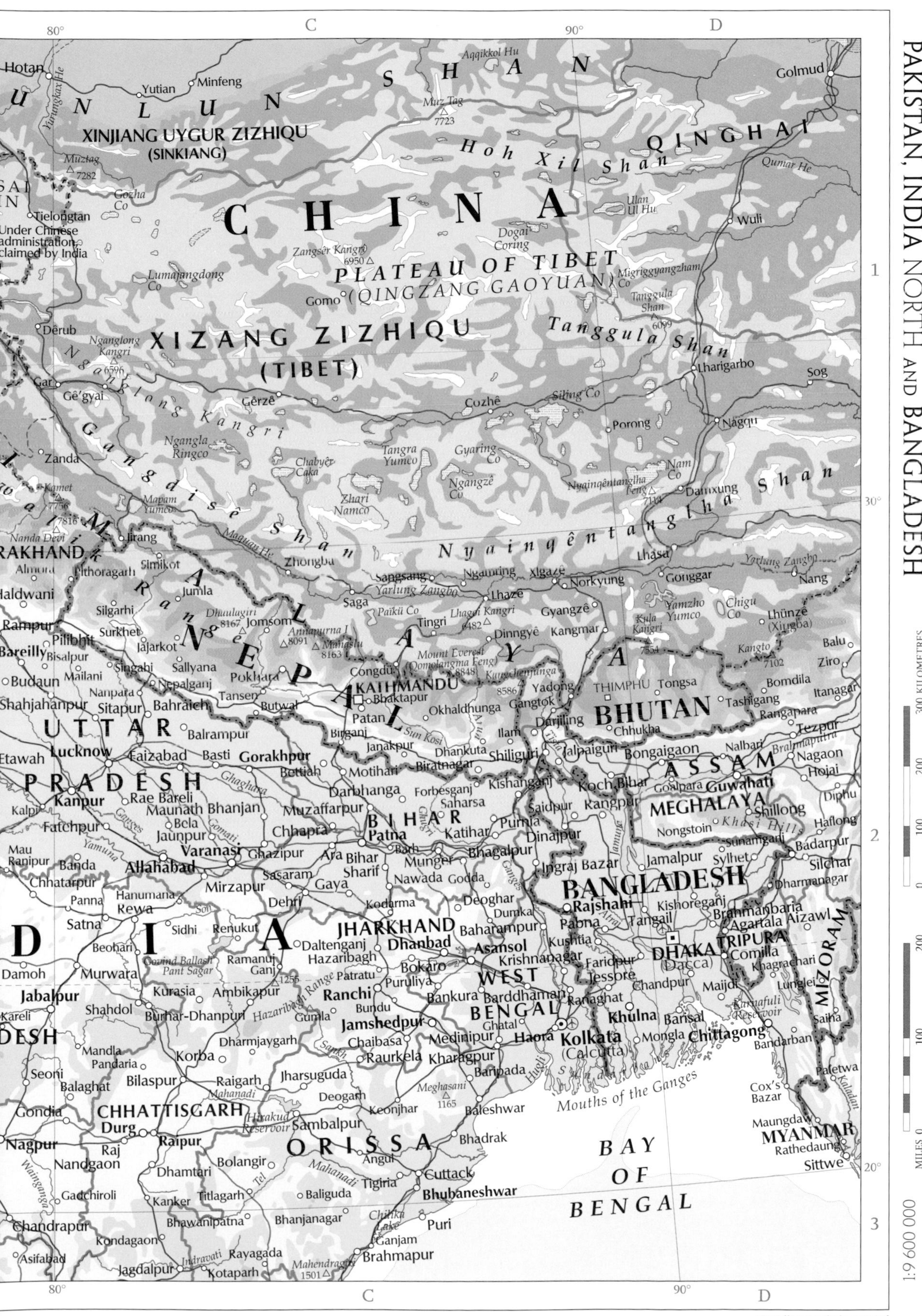

C
D
80°
90°
1
2
3
30°
20°
CHINA
XINJIANG UYGUR ZIZHIQU
(SINKIANG)
KUNLUN SHAN
QINGHAI
Hoh Xil Shan
PLATEAU OF TIBET
(QINGZANG GAOYUAN)
XIZANG ZIZHIQU
(TIBET)
Tanggula Shan
Nganglong Kangri
Gangdisê Shan
Nyainqêntanglha Shan
Under Chinese administration, claimed by India
Hotan
Yutian
Minfeng
Golmud
Muztag
7282
Muz Tag
7723
Aqqikkol Hu
Qumar He
Gozha Co
Tielongtan
Ulan Ul Hu
Wuli
Dogai Coring
Zangsêr Kangri
6950
Lumajangdong Co
Migriggyangzham Co
Tanggula Shan
6099
Gomo
Dêrub
Lharigarbo
Sog
Gar
Gê'gyai
Gêrzê
Cozhê
Siling Co
Porong
Nagqu
Ngangla Ringco
Tangra Yumco
Gyaring Co
Chabyêr Caka
Ngangzê Co
Zhari Namco
Nam Co
Damxung
Zanda
Kamet
7756
Mapam Yumco
Nanda Devi
7816
Jirang
Zhongba
Lhasa
Yarlung Zangbo
Nang
Sangsang
Ngamring
Xigazê
Norkyung
Gonggar
Saga
Lhazê
Yamzho Yumco
Chigu Co
Lhünzê (Xingba)
Paikü Co
Tingri
Gyangzê
Kula Kangri
7554
Kangto
7102
Dinngyê
Kangmar
Balu
Ziro
Bomdila
Itanagar
Dhaulagiri
8167
Jomsom
Annapurna I
8091
Manaslu
8163
Mount Everest (Qomolangma Feng)
8848
Kangchenjunga
8586
NEPAL
KATHMANDU
Bhaktapur
Patan
Okhaldhunga
Yadong
THIMPHU
Tongsa
Gangtok
BHUTAN
Tashigang
Rangapara
Tezpur
Darjiling
Chhukha
Ilam
Dhankuta
Biratnagar
Shiliguri
Jalpaiguri
Bongaigaon
Nalbari
Nagaon
Hojai
ASSAM
Goalpara
Guwahati
Koch Bihar
Rangpur
MEGHALAYA
Shillong
Nongstoin
Khasi Hills
Diphu
Haflong
Badarpur
Silchar
Sunamganj
Sylhet
Jamalpur
Dharmanagar
BANGLADESH
Rajshahi
Pabna
Tangail
Kishoreganj
Brahmanbaria
Agartala
Aizawl
TRIPURA
DHAKA
(Dacca)
Comilla
MIZORAM
Kushtia
Faridpur
Jessore
Chandpur
Maijdi
Khagrachari
Lunglei
Karnafuli Reservoir
Khulna
Barisal
Chittagong
Saiha
Bandarban
Mongla
Paletwa
Cox's Bazar
Maungdaw
MYANMAR
Rathedaung
Sittwe
Mouths of the Ganges
BAY OF BENGAL
RAKHAND
Almora
Pithoragarh
Simikot
Jumla
Haldwani
Silgarhi
Rampur
Pilibhit
Surkhet
Jajarkot
Bareilly
Bisalpur
Singahi
Sallyana
Pokhara
Budaun
Mailani
Nepalganj
Tansen
Nanpara
Shahjahanpur
Sitapur
Bahraich
Butwal
Birganj
Janakpur
UTTAR PRADESH
Balrampur
Lucknow
Etawah
Faizabad
Basti
Gorakhpur
Bettiah
Motihari
Kishanganj
Forbesganj
Saharsa
Darbhanga
Kanpur
Rae Bareli
Maunath Bhanjan
Muzaffarpur
BIHAR
Katihar
Purnia
Saidpur
Dinajpur
Kalpi
Fatehpur
Bela
Jaunpur
Chhapra
Patna
Barh
Mau Ranipur
Banda
Varanasi
Ghazipur
Ara
Bihar Sharif
Munger
Bhagalpur
Ingraj Bazar
Allahabad
Sasaram
Gaya
Nawada
Godda
Chhatarpur
Mirzapur
Dehri
Deoghar
Panna
Hanumana
Rewa
Koderma
Dumka
Satna
Sidhi
Renukut
JHARKHAND
Baharampur
INDIA
Daltenganj
Dhanbad
Asansol
Beohari
Hazaribagh
Krishnanagar
Govind Ballash Pant Sagar
Ramanuj Ganj
Bokaro
Damoh
Murwara
Patratu
WEST BENGAL
Jabalpur
Kurasia
Ambikapur
Ranchi
Purulia
Bankura
Barddhaman
Ranaghat
Shahdol
Burhar-Dhanpuri
Hazaribagh Range
Gumla
Bundu
Kareli
Jamshedpur
Ghatal
DESH
Haora
Kolkata (Calcutta)
Dharmjaygarh
Chaibasa
Medinipur
Mandla
Pandaria
Korba
Raurkela
Kharagpur
Seoni
Balaghat
Bilaspur
Raigarh
Jharsuguda
Baripada
Mahanadi
Deogarh
Meghasani
1165
Gondia
CHHATTISGARH
Keonjhar
Baleshwar
Durg
Hirakud Reservoir
Sambalpur
Nagpur
Raipur
ORISSA
Bhadrak
Rajnandgaon
Angul
Dhamtari
Bolangir
Cuttack
Tigiria
Bhubaneshwar
Gadchiroli
Kanker
Titlagarh
Baliguda
Bhawanipatna
Bhanjanagar
Chilika Lake
Puri
Chandrapur
Kondagaon
Ganjam
Asifabad
Indravati
Rayagada
Brahmapur
Jagdalpur
Kotaparh
Mahendragiri
1501
MILES 0 100 200
0 100 200 300 KILOMETRES

1:6 000 000

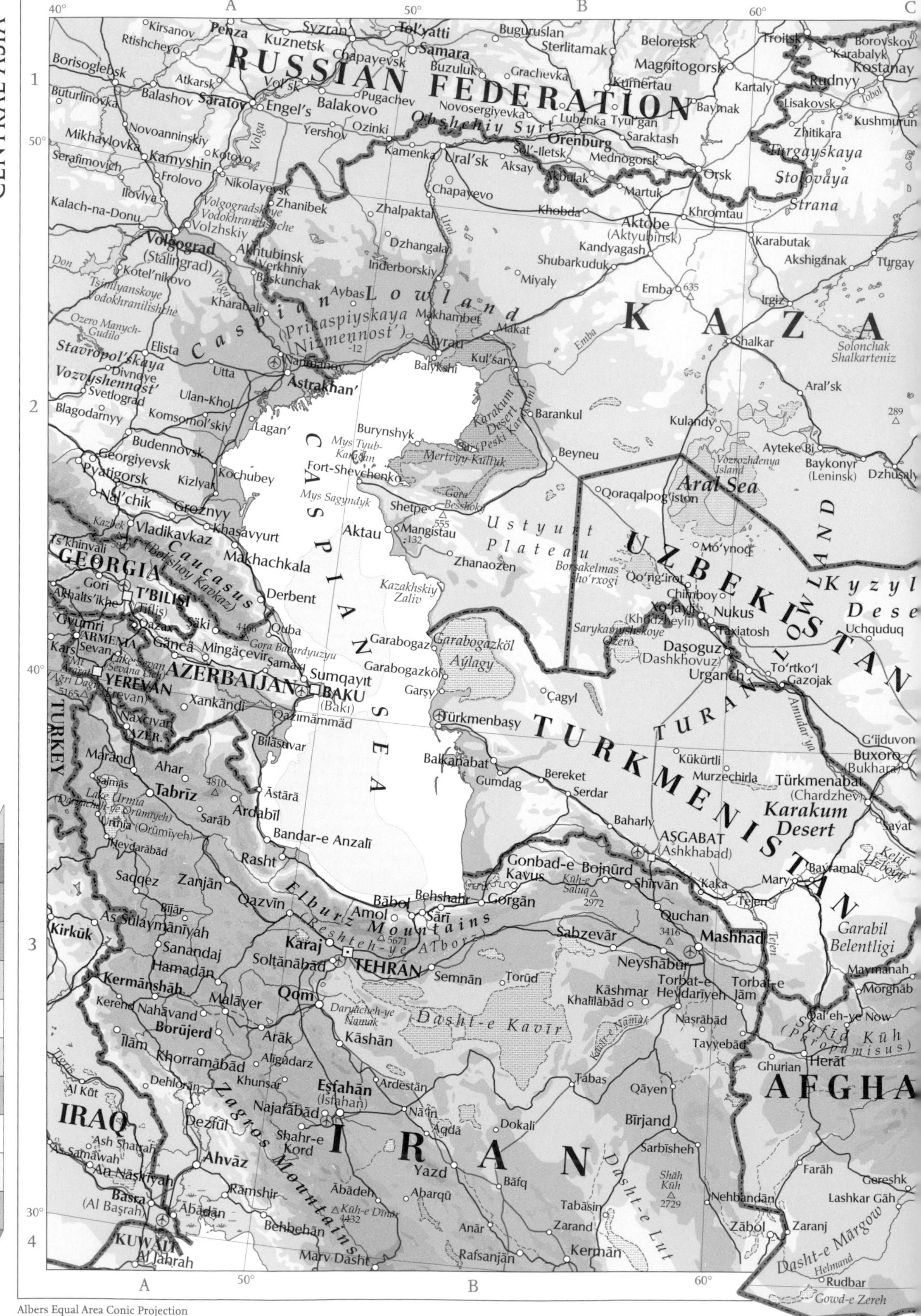

METRES
FEET

5000
16404

3000
9843

2000
6562

1000
3281

500
1640

200
656

0
0

Land below sea level

200
656

4000
13124

6000
19686

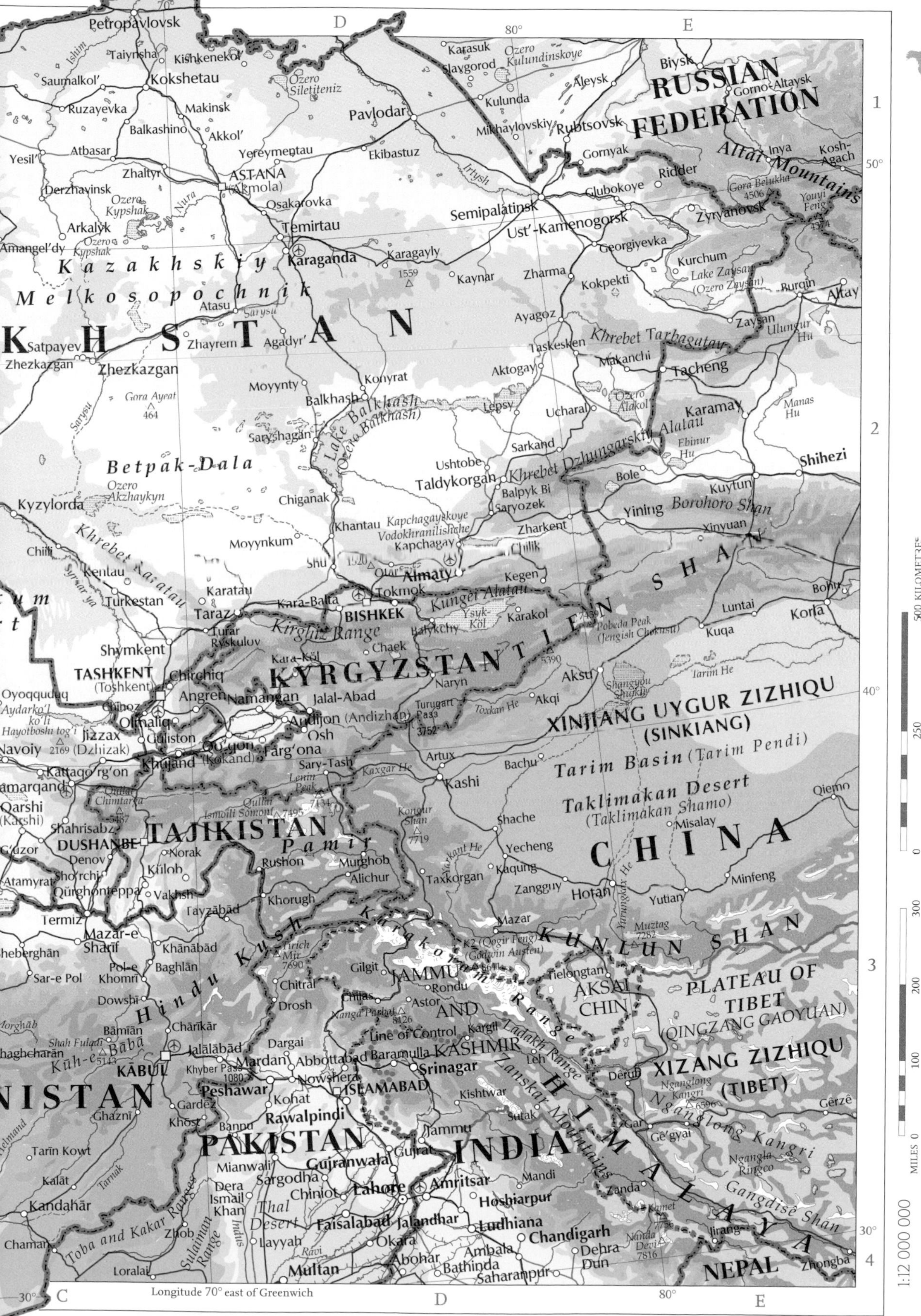

1:12 000 000

0 100 200 300 MILES

0 250 500 KILOMETRES

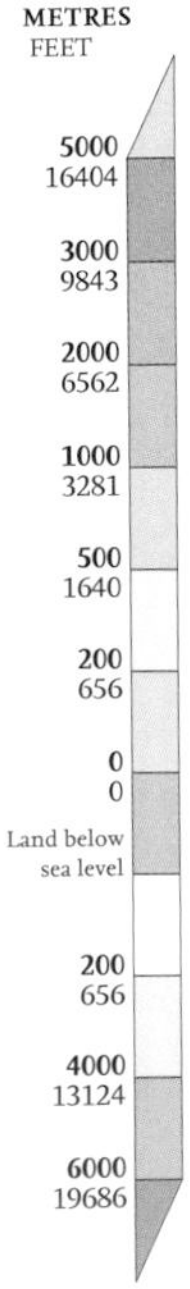

A B

Port Said (Būr Sa'īd) GAZA Al 'Arīsh Beersheba Dead Sea Al Karak At Tafilah Suez Canal Al Ismā'īlīyah ISRAEL JORDAN Petra Ma'ān Ţurayf Wādī as Sirḥān Al 'Īsāwīyah 'Ar'ar Al Widyān An Najaf Ad Dīwānīyah Al Ḥayy 'Amārah Ash Shaţrah Euphrates Tigris As Samāwah An Nāşirīyah Sūq ash Shuyūkh Ash Shabakah IRAQ Hawr al Ḥammār Basra (Al Başrah)

Suez (As Suways) 30° Sinai Eilat Al 'Aqabah Gulf of Suez Gulf of Aqaba Za'farānah Nuwaybi' al Muzayyinah Ḥaql Al Mudawwarah Ḥālat 'Ammār Al Bi'r Dawmat al Jandal Sakākah Raudhatain KUWAIT Hawalli Al Jahrah Rafḥā' Ra's Ghārib Jabal Kātrīnā (Mount Catherine) 2637 Jabal al Lawz 2579 Raf 979 Jabal Ghārib 1751 Aţ Ţūr Tabūk An Nafūd Ash Shu'bah Wādī al Bāţin Aş Şubayḥīyah

Jamsah Sharm ash Shaykh Jabal ad Dubbagh 2350 Ḥarrat al 'Uwayrid Qal'at al Mu'azzam Jubbah Ḥafar al Bāţin Al Ghurdaqah (Hurghada) Al Muwayliḥ Dubā Taymā' Ash Shu'āybah Mawqaq Ḥā'il Jabal al Kū' 325 Qal'at al Azlam Ad Dār al Ḥamrā' Jabal az Zalmā 1258 Qaryat al Ulyā Būr Safājah Al 'Ulā Al Badā'i' Ghazzālah Ţābah Al Kahfah Al Quwārah AD DAHNĀ' Ash Shumlūl Al Quşayr Al Wajh Samīrah As Sulaymī Jabal Ţīn Buraydah Al Arţāwīyah Ḥulayfah 'Uqlat aş Şuqūr Hujr 'Unayzah Az Zilfī Al Majma'ah Khaybar Ar Rass Wādī al Ḥamḍ Wādī ar Rimah Şafrā' as Sark Jabal Ţuwayq

EGYPT HIJAZ NAJD 2 Marsá al 'Alam Ḥanak Umm Lajj Nuqrah Asharat Rumāh ŞAḤŪQ SAUDI Ash Shubaykīyah Nafy Jabal Ḥamāţah 1977 Jabal Raḍwá 1814 Buwāţah Al Ḥanākīyah Sūq Suwayq Medina (Al Madīnah) 'Arjah Ad Dir'īyah Al Jubaylah Jabal Shi'r RIYADH (Ar Riyāḍ) Tropic of Cancer Baranīs Yanbu' al Baḥr Al Musayjīd Al Qā'īyah Ad Dawādimī Wādī al Miyāh RED SEA Rayyis Badr Ḥunayn 'Afīf Al Quwayīyah As Salamiyah Ad Dilam Mahd adh Dhahab Al Ḥillah Bi'r Shalatayn Mastūrah Umm al Birak Ḥalabān Ar Ruwaydah Wādī al 'Allāqī HALAIB TRIANGLE UNDER SUDANESE ADMINISTRATION Jabal Umm Mukhbar Ad Dafīnah ARABIAN Rābigh Khashm Māwān 1025 Ḥādhah Ẓalim Jabal Kursh Tuwwal Halaib Jabal Ḥasan ARABIA Jebel Asoteriba 2215 Khulays Madrakah Laylá Marsa Delwein As Sūq Al Badī' Salâla Jeddah (Jiddah) Al Ḥawīyah Dungunab Mecca (Makkah) Aţ Ţā'if Turabah Wādī Ranyah Amā'ir Wadi Oko Muhammad Qol Nubian Desert Jebel Oda 2259 Mastābah Jabal Abū Şādī Al 'Aqīq Jabal Ţuwayq Al 'Arḍ PENINSULA 20° Al Līth Al Junaynah Al Mindak Qal'at Bīshah Wādī Tathlīth Al Khamāsīn Al Kumdah As Sulayyil SUDAN Port Sudan Baljurshī Wādī 'Amur Kamob Sanha Dawqah Al 'Alāyyah Banī Ma'āriḍ Suakin Sinkat Al Qunfidhah Qam Ḥadīl An Nimāş Tathlīth 'Urūq al 'Awārik ASĪR Ḥamḍah Musmar Erheib Tokar Haiya Dirs RUB' AL KHALI (EMPTY QUARTER) Al Birk Abhā Khamis Mushayţ Derudeb Ḥarajā Ẓahrān Najrān 2780 Karora Ash Shuqayq Ad Darb Ash Sharawrah Algena Hagar Nish Plateau Nakfa Şabyā Ramlat Dahm Atbara Barka Suara 2603 3 Abū 'Arīsh Şa'dah Jīzān Jazā'ir Farasān Afabet Agirrat Hills Mīdī Aroma ERITREA Khamir Al Ḥazm al Jawf Ḥusn Āl 'Ali Akordat Keren Dahlak Archipelago Ḥajjah Raydah Kassala 'Amrān New Halfa Teseney Massawa Aş Şalīf Al Maḥwīt ASMARA Kamarān 3760 Ma'rib Khashm el Girba Dam Khashm el Girba Barentu Mendefera Dekemhare Az Zaydīyah ŞAN'Ā' Showak Adi Keyih Mersa Fatma Hodeidah (Al Ḥudaydah) Bājil YEMEN Tekezē Wenz Koluli Manākhah Ma'bar Bayḥan al Qişab Gedaref Om Hajēr Āksum 3293 Ādīgrat Bayt al Faqīh Dhamār Radā' 'Ataq Inda Silasē Ādwa Āsale Az Zuqur Zabīd Ibb Yarīm Habbān Rahad ETHIOPIA Denakil Ed Al Khawkhah Hays Qa'ţabah Al Bayḍā' Lawdar Ādī Ārk'ay Ras Dejen 4533 3267 Jabal Thamar 2512 Ta'izz Simēn Mek'elē Mocha (Al Mukhā) Shuqrah Gallabat Atbara 2131 Mawza Musaymīr Zinjibār Dhubāb Lahij Bāb al Mandab Assab Am Nābiyah Ash Shaykh 'Uthman Al Turbah Aden ('Adan)

A

Longitude 40° east of Greenwich

METRES	FEET
5000	16404
3000	9843
2000	6562
1000	3281
500	1640
200	656
0	0
Land below sea level	
200	656
4000	13124
6000	19686

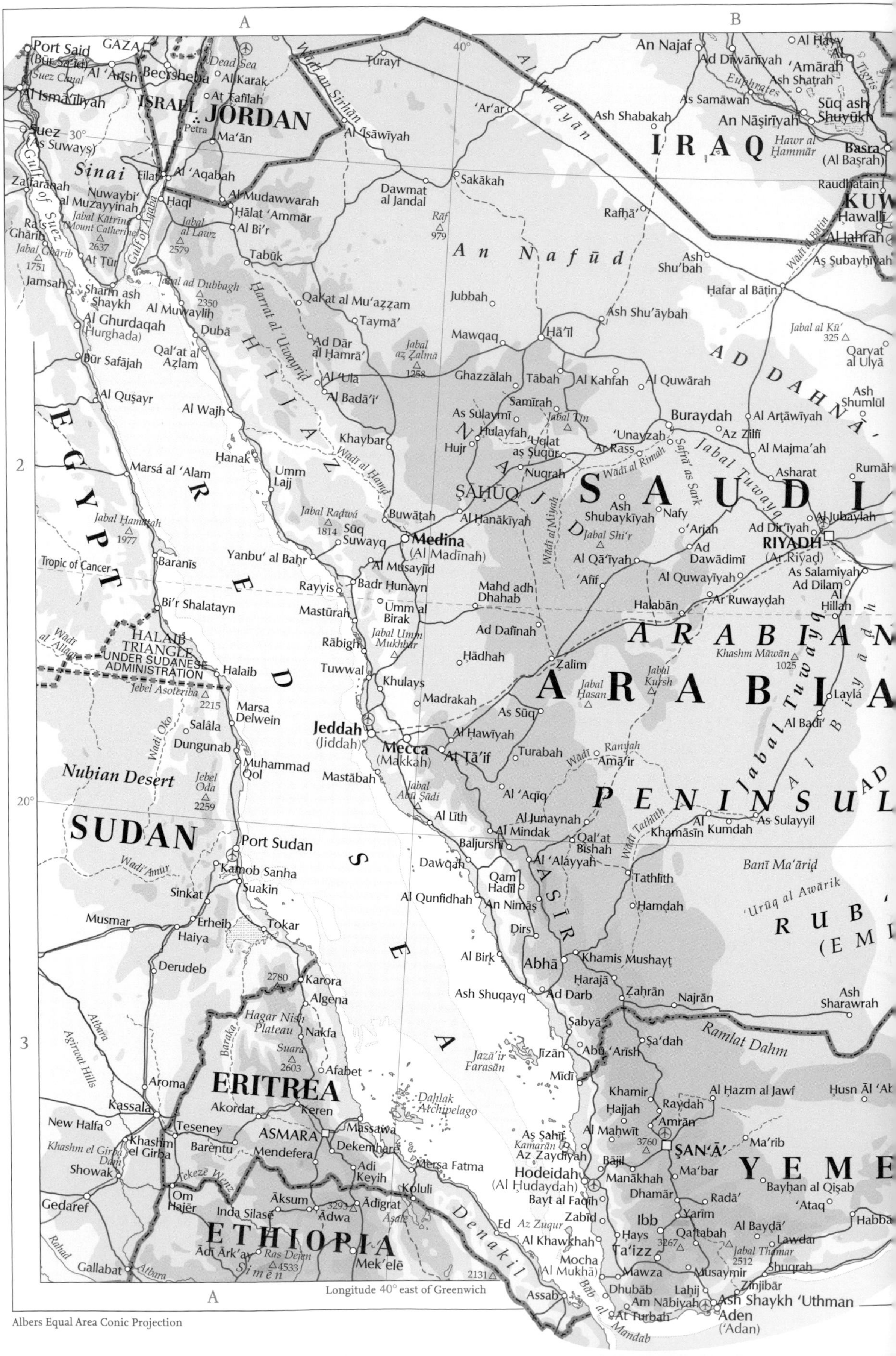

Albers Equal Area Conic Projection

IRAN
Zagros Mountains
(Kūhhā-ye Zagros)
Shāhrezā
Yazd
Bāfq
Ṭabasin
Nehbandān
Zābol
Zaranj
Dasht-e Mārgow
Helmand
Rudbar
Namakzar-e Shadad
Abādeh
Abarqū
Anār
Zarand
Rafsanjān
Kermān
Safāshahr
Lāvar Meydān
Shahr-e Bābak
Bāghīn
Zeynālābād
Nosratābād
Hormak
AFGHANISTAN
Gowd-e Zereh
Kūh-e Dīnār
4432
Yāsūj
Masjed Soleymān
Shushtar
Susangerd
Ahvāz
Rāmhormoz
Rāmshir
Omīdīyeh
Behbehān
Khorrāmshahr
Bandar-e Emām Khomeynī
Ābādān
Al Fāw
KUWAIT
(Al Kuwayt)
Al Aḥmadī
Mīnā' Sa'ūd
Al Mish'āb
Manīfah
An Nu'ayrīyah
Al Jubayl
Ras Tannūrah
Dammām
(Ad Dammām)
Dhahran
Al Mubarrez
Al Hufūf
Harad
Jabal Shāh
239
Ḥaraḍh
Marv Dasht
Arsenajān
Kūh-e Tābask
3218
Kāzerūn
Genāveh
Borāzjān
Būshehr
Shīrāz
Zarqān
Daryācheh-ye Tashk
Kherāmeh
Sarvestān
Estahbān
Neyrīz
Zeydābād
Sīrjān
Bardsīr
Beshneh
Bāft
Kūh-e Ilazārān
4420
Tahrūd
Dārzīn
Bam
Kahūrak
Zāhedān
Mirjāveh
Amir Chah
PAKISTAN
Nok Kundi
Kūh-e Taftān
4042
Vakīlābād
Rīgān
SARHAD
Khāsh
Qila Ladgasht
Saravan
Farrāshband
Fīrūzābād
Ahram
Khvormūj
Fasā
Dārāb
Jahrom
Jūyom
Qīr
Dowlatābād
Zīr Rūd
Dayyer
Kangān
Hājjīābād
Rostāq
Sa'ādatābād
Kūh-e Fūrgun
3267
Alīābād
Kharān
Jīroft
Dowlatābād
Fāryāb
Kahnūj
Hāmūn-e Jaz Mūrīān
Kūh-e Bazmān
3489
Bazmān
Īrānshahr
Bampūr
Zābolī
Khonj
Evaz
Lār
Lamard
Bastak
Mehrān
Bandar-e 'Abbās
Qotbābād
Fāryāb
Jaghīn
Īspakeh
Sarbāz
Kūh-e Bam Posht
Hāleh
Gavbandī
Bandar-e Maqām
Bandar-e Chārak
Bandar-e Lengeh
Khamīr
Lāft
Qeshm
Sūzā
Strait of Hormuz
Tiāb
Mīnāb
Kūh-e Kūhrān
2161
Sīrīk
Angohrān
Remeshk
Marākī
Nīkshahr
MAKRAN
Qasr-e Qand
Pīshīn
Bāhū Kalāt
Turbat
Dasht
Suntsar
Jāsk
Gābrīk
Kalāt
Pozm Tiāb
Chābahār
Jiwani
Gwadar
BAHRAIN
MANAMA
THE GULF
QATAR
DOHA (Ad Dawḥah)
Fuwayriṭ
Al Khawr
Al Jamaliyah
Dukhān
Ar Rayyān
Al Wakrah
Al Kir'ānah
Salwah
'Uyun
Al Ghwaybiyah
Khurays
OMAN
Al Khaṣab
Līmah
Dibā al Ḥiṣn
Ra's al Khaymah
Ajman
Adh Dhayd
Dubai
(Dubayy)
Sharjah
Fujairah
Mina Jebel Ali
Gulf of Oman
Ash Shinas
Ṣuḥār
ABU DHABI
(Abū Ẓabī)
Trucial Coast
Al 'Ayn
Buraymī
Tarīf
Ruweis
Jirwān
Sabkhat Maṭṭī
UNITED ARAB EMIRATES
Al Mariyyah
'Arādah
Al Khunn
Al Qaṣab
Al Bāṭinah
Al Hajar al Gharbī
Al Khābūrah
As Suwayq
Barka
MUSCAT
(Masqaṭ)
Maṭraḥ
Ar Rustāq
Quraiyat
Dibab
Sumāil
Ibrā
Ṣunaynah
Dank
J. Akhḍar
'Ibrī
Bahla
Nazwa
Al Muḍaibī
Ṭīwī
Ṣūr
Ra's al Ḥadd
Jabal Sulukh
1055
Adam
Al Kāmil
Bilād Banī Bū 'Alī
Tropic of Cancer
Al Kidan
Umm as Samīm
AR RIMAL
Qalamat Abū Shafrah
As Ṣanām
OMAN
Dawwah
Jazīrat Maṣīrah
Ra's Ṣīrāb
Khalīj Maṣīrah
AL KHĀLĪ
(EMPTY QUARTER)
Al Ḥibāk
Hajmā'
Jiddat al Ḥarāsīs
Ra's Madrakah
Al Qa'āmīyāt
Dawḥat Ṣawqirah
Wādī al Amilhayt
Dawqah
Fararah
Thamarīt
Ḥabarūt
Jūzur al Ḥalānīyāt
Thamūd
Ṣalālah
Mirbāṭ
Al Ghaydah
Ghubbat al Qamar
Wādī Ḥaḍramawt
Tarīm
Shibām
Al Qaṭn
Wādī al Masīlah
Ra's Fartak
Ḥaḍramawt
Qishn
Sayḥūt
Ash Shiḥr
Mukalla
(Al Mukallā)
Bālḥaf
ARABIAN SEA
50°
60°
30°
20°
C
D
1
2
3
KILOMETRES
MILES
0
100
200
300
400
1:9 600 000

METRES
FEET

METRES	FEET
5000	16404
3000	9843
2000	6562
1000	3281
500	1640
200	656
0	0
Land below sea level	
200	656
4000	13124
6000	19686

Albers Equal Area Conic Projection

C
D
40°
50°
Novocherkassk
Zernograd
Sal'sk
Ozero Manych-Gudilo
Elista
Utta
Volga
Astrakhan
Balykshi
Karakum Desert (Peski Karakum)
Sor Donyztau
Barankul
Sor Mertvyy Kultuk
Beyneu
RUSSIAN FEDERATION
Tikhoretsk
Ipatovo
Divnoye
Ulan-Khol
Kropotkin
Stavropol'skaya Vozvyshennost'
Komsomol'skiy
Lagan'
Burynshyk
KAZAKHSTAN
UZBEKISTAN
Laba
Kuban'
Stavropol'
Armavir
Labinsk
Budennovsk
Nevinnomyssk
Kochubey
Mys Tyub-Karagan
Fort-Shevchenko
Shetpe
Gora Besshoky
555
Ustyurt Plateau
Borsakelmas sho'rxogi
Maykop
Psebay
Cherkessk
Georgiyevsk
Pyatigorsk
Kizlyar
Mys Sagyndyk
Mangistau
132
Aktau
Karachayevsk
Kislovodsk
Prokhladnyy
Mozdok
Nal'chik
Groznyy
Khasavyurt
Kuryk
Zhanaozen
Uzboy Karabaur
Gagra
El'brus 5642
CAUCASUS (BOL'SHOY KAVKAZ)
Alagir
Vladikavkaz
Makhachkala
Sokhumi
Tqvarch'eli
Buynaksk
Izberbash
Kazakhskiy Zaliv
Sarykamyshskoye Ozero
Zugdidi
Kut'aisi
GEORGIA
Derbent
CASPIAN SEA
P'ot'i
Samtredia
Khashuri
Gori
T'elavi
Garabogaz
Garabogazköl Aylagy
Bat'umi
Akhalts'ikhe
T'BILISI (Tiflis)
Zaqatala
Gora Bazardyuzyu 4466
Çagyl
Akhalk'alak'i
Rust'avi
Quba
Garabogazköl
Pazar
Artvin
Ardahan
Lesser Caucasus (Malyy Kavkaz)
Qazax
Garsy
TURKMENISTAN
Kaçkar Dağı 3932
Vanadzor
Gäncä
Mingäçevir
Göyçay
Şamaxı
Sumqayıt
Abşeron Yarımadası
Rize
Yusufeli
Gyumri
Sevan
AZERBAIJAN
BAKU (Bakı)
Janna
Bayburt
Oltu
Kars
ARMENIA
YEREVAN (Erevan)
Qazımämmäd
Kür
Türkmenbaşy
Jebel
Balkanabat
Horasan
Sarıkamış
Araks
Agdam
Äli Bayramlı
Älät
Hazar
Bereket
Erzurum
Ağrı
Iğdır
Ararat
Mt Ararat (Ağrı Dağı) 5165
Xankändi
Salyan
Gumdag
Gyzylarbat
Tutak
Doğubeyazıt
AZER.
Sisian
Biläsuvar
Cälilabad
Magtymguly
Hınıs
Patnos
Erciş
Naxçıvan
Ogurjaly Adasy
Bingöl
Malazgirt
Süphan Dağı 4058
Mākū
Länkäran
Murat
Muş
Ahlat
Khvoy
Marand
Ahar
4810
Ästärä
Tatvan
Van
Silvan
Bitlis
Lake Van (Van Gölü)
Salmās
Tabrīz
Sarāb
Ardabīl
Diyarbakır
Siirt
Başkale
Urmia (Orūmīyeh)
Lake Urmia (Daryācheh-ye Orūmīyeh)
Bandar-e Anzalī
Gonbad-e Kavus
Batman
Tigris (Dicle)
Şırnak
Hakkâri
Samdi Dag 3791
Mīāneh
Rasht
Gomīshān
Gorgan
Mardin
Marāghéh
Lāhījān
Fowman
Behshahr
Mayamey
Al 'Amādīyah
Sendīnī
Heydarābād
Tonkābon
Nowshahr
Bābol
Sārī
Al Qāmishlī
Zākhō
Dahūk
Oshnovīyeh
Mīāndowāb
Amol
Elburz Mountains (Reshteh-ye Alborz)
Emāmrūd
Tall 'Afar
Mahābād
Zanjān
Qazvīn
Damghan
Al Hasakah
Mosul
Arbīl
Saqqez
5671
Bījār
Abhar
Karaj
TEHRĀN
Semnān
Torūd
Dayr az Zawr
As Sulaymānīyah
Sanandaj
Soltānābād
Ash Sharqāt
Tigris
Kirkūk
Halabja
Qorveh
Dasht-e Kavīr
Al Mayādīn
Tuz Khurmātū
Hamadān
Qom
Daryācheh-ye Namak
Abū Kamāl
'Ānah
Bayjī
Tikrīt
Ravānsar
Kangāvar
Malāyer
Buhayrat ath Tharthār
Qasr-e Shīrīn
Kermānshāh
Arāk
Kāshān
Jandaq
Sāmarrā'
Kerend
Nahāvand
IRAN
Al Hadīthah
Al Muqdādīyah
Eslāmābād-e Gharb
Borūjerd
Dow Rūd
Ardestān
Hīt
Ba'qūbah
Īlām
Golpāyegān
Ar Ramādī
Al Kāzimīyah
Khorramābād
Alīgūdarz
Khunsar
Nā'īn
Dokali
Ar Rutbah
Hawr al Habbānīyah
BAGHDĀD
Dārān
Kūh-e Garbosh 4294
Najafābād
Esfahān (Isfahan)
Āqdā
Meybod
Buhayrat ar Razāzah
Dehlorān
Karbalā'
Hillah
Dezfūl
Zagros Mountains (Kūhhā-ye Zagros)
Shahr-e Kord
Shāhrezā
Yazd
IRAQ
Al Kūt
Shushtar
Bāfq
Al Hayy
Al 'Amārah
Masjed Soleymān
An Najaf
Ad Dīwānīyah
Ābādeh
Abarqū
Ash Shatrah
Susangerd
Euphrates
Ahvāz
Rūd-e Kārūn
Kūh-e Dīnār 4432
Anār
As Samāwah
Sūq ash Shuyūkh
Rāmhormoz
Safāshahr
An Nāsirīyah
Rāmshīr
Omīdīyeh
Yāsūj
Lāvar Meydān
Shahr-e Bābak
Al Widyān
'Ar'ar
Ash Shabakah
Hawr al Hammār
Khorramshahr
Behbahān
Basra (Al Basrah)
Ābādān
Bandar-e Emām Khomeynī
Kūh-e Tābask 3218
Marv Dasht
Arsenajān
Ābādeh Tashk
Daryācheh-ye Tashk
Zarqān
Al Fāw
Kherāmeh
Beshneh
Sakākah
Raudhatain
KUWAIT
Genāveh
Kāzerūn
Shīrāz
Sarvestān
Neyrīz
Hawallī
KUWAIT (Al Kuwayt)
Borāzjān
Estahbān
Rūd-e Mand
Rafhā'
ARABIA
Al Jahrah
Al Ahmadī
Būshehr
Farrāshband
Fasā
Dārāb
Fīrūzābād
Rostāq
Wādī al Bātin
Ahram
Qīr
Jahrom
Hājjīābād
An Nafūd
Ash Shu'bah
As Subayhīyah
Mīnā' Sa'ūd
Khvormūj
Dowlatābād
Jūyom
1
2
3
40°
30°
KILOMETRES 0 200 400
MILES 0 100 200 300
1:9 600 000

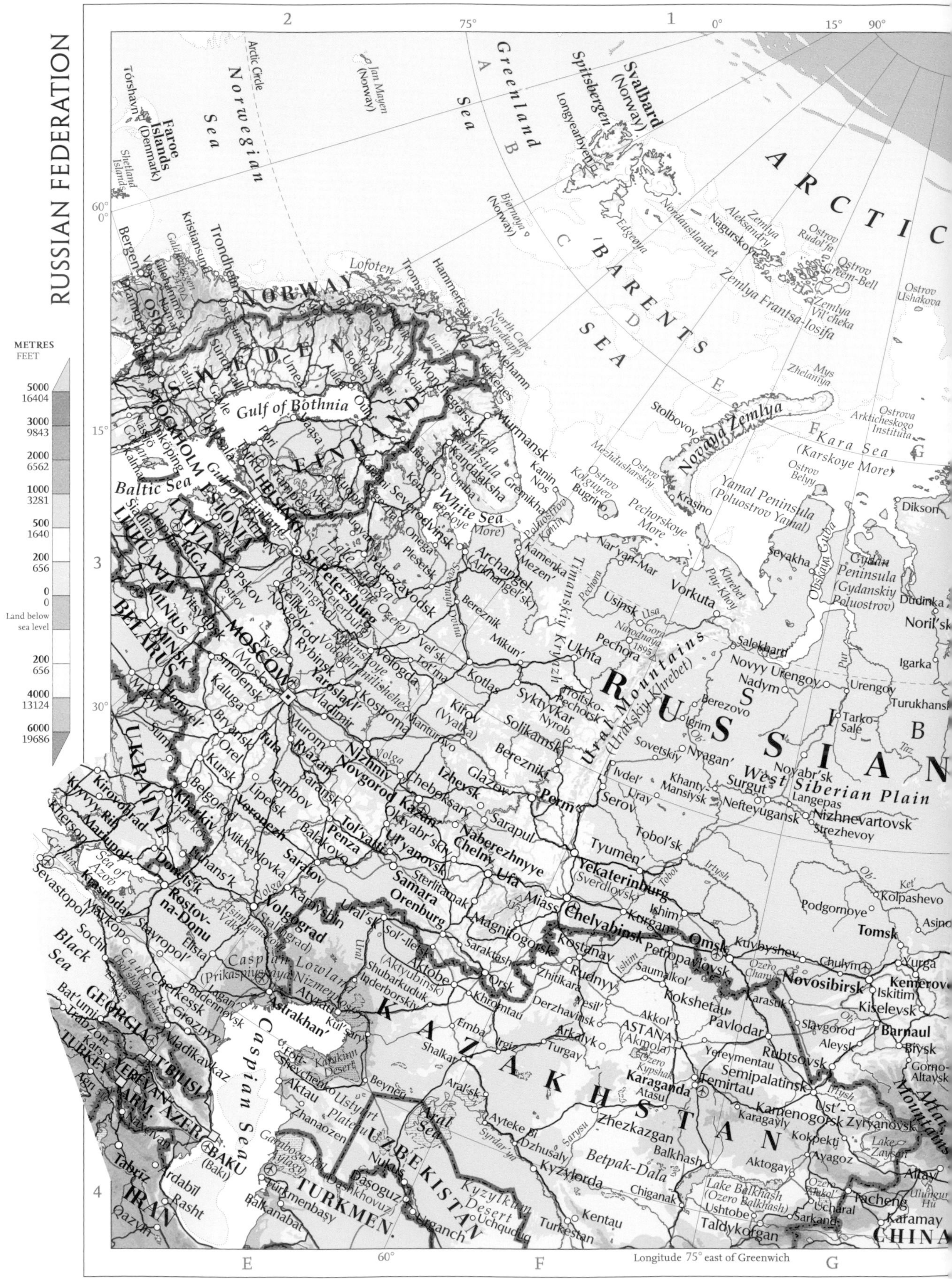

Conic Equidistant Projection

OCEAN
Chukchi Sea
Bering Strait
U.S.A.
St Lawrence Island
Wrangel Island (Ostrov Vrangelya)
Mys Shmidta
Providenıya
East Siberian Sea (Vostochno-Sibirskoye More)
New Siberia Islands (Novosibirskiye Ostrova)
Laptev Sea (More Laptevykh)
Severnaya Zemlya
Ostrov Komsomolets
Ostrov Oktyabr'skoy Revolyutsii
Ostrov Bol'shevik
Ostrov Shmidta
Taymyr Peninsula (Poluostrov Taymyr)
Khatanga
Saskylakh
Olenek
Tiksi
Chokurdakh
Deputatskiy
Srednekolymsk
Zyryanka
Khrebet Cherskogo
Verkhoyanskiy Khrebet
Khrebet Kolymskiy
Koryakskoye Nagor'ye
Kamchatka Peninsula
Sredinnyy Khrebet
Petropavlovsk-Kamchatskiy
Sea of Okhotsk
Magadan
Okhotsk
Ayan
Sakhalin
Okha
Poronaysk
Yuzhno-Sakhalinsk
Tatarskiy Proliv
FEDERATION
Central Siberian Plateau
Yakutsk
Mirnyy
Lensk
Olekminsk
Neryungri
Stanovoye Nagor'ye
Stanovoy Khrebet
Komsomol'sk-na-Amure
Khabarovsk
Blagoveshchensk
Sikhote-Alin
Vladivostok
Nakhodka
Krasnoyarsk
Kansk
Bratsk
Ust'-Ilimsk
Irkutsk
Lake Baikal
Ulan-Ude
Chita
Abakan
Kyzyl
Vostochnyy Sayan
MONGOLIA
ULAN BATOR (Ulaanbaatar)
GOBI
Darhan
Sühbaatar
Choybalsan
Mandalgovi
CHINA
Harbin
Qiqihar
Changchun
Jilin
Shenyang
Anshan
Dandong
Chifeng
N. KOREA
P'YONGYANG
SEOUL
S. KOREA
1:24 000 000
500 KILOMETRES
MILES

40° A 30° B 20° C 10° D 0° E 10° F 20° G

2

60°

Greenland (Denmark)

Arctic Circle

Denmark Strait

Jan Mayen (Nor.)

Bjørnøya (Nor.)

ICELAND

Reykjavík

Tromsø

NORWEGIAN SEA

3

ATLANTIC OCEAN

Faroe Islands (Den.)

Tórshavn

Trondheim

NORWAY

SWEDEN

Gulf of Bothnia

Shetland Islands

Orkney Islands

Bergen

Oslo

Turku

Stockholm

Vänern

SCOTLAND

Glasgow

Edinburgh

NORTH SEA

50°

Gothenburg

Gotland

N. IRELAND

Belfast

UNITED KINGDOM

DENMARK

Copenhagen

Malmö

Baltic Sea

IRELAND

Dublin

Manchester

LITH.

RUS. FED.

WALES

ENGLAND

NETHERLANDS

Amsterdam

Hamburg

Cardiff

Birmingham

The Hague

Hannover

Berlin

POLAND

London

Poznań

Warsaw

English Channel

Brussels

Essen

Channel Is (U.K.)

BELGIUM

Rhine

GERMANY

Łódź

4

K. KOSOVO
LIE. LIECHTENSTEIN
MACE. MACEDONIA
MONT. MONTENEGRO

Seine

Luxembourg

LUXEMBOURG

Frankfurt

Prague

Katowice

Paris

CZECH REPUBLIC

Loire

Danube

Bay of Biscay

FRANCE

Munich

Vienna

Bratislava

SLOVAKIA

Cape Finisterre

Bern

LIE.

SWITZERLAND

AUSTRIA

Budapest

ALPS

Lyon

Mont Blanc 4808

HUNGARY

Bordeaux

SLOVENIA

40°

Ljubljana

Zagreb

Milan

Rhône

Bilbao

CROATIA

Oporto

Turin

Belgrade

Pyrenees

SAN MARINO

BOSNIA-HERZ.

SPAIN

Andorra la Vella

ANDORRA

Marseille

MONACO

Adriatic Sea

Sarajevo

SERBIA

PORTUGAL

Madrid

Corsica

VATICAN CITY

Prishtina

Lisbon

Barcelona

ITALY

MONT.

Podgorica

K.

Skopje

Rome

MACE.

Valencia

Balearic Islands

Sardinia

Tirana

Cabo de São Vicente

ALBANIA

5

Naples

Seville

MEDITERRANEAN SEA

Gibraltar (U.K.)

Palermo

Sicily

Ionian Sea

MOROCCO

ALGERIA

TUNISIA

MALTA

Valletta

10° D Greenwich 0° meridian E 10° F 20°

Chamberlin Trimetric Projection

BARENTS SEA
Novaya Zemlya
Nordkapp
Ostrov Kolguyev
Vorkuta
Murmansk
White Sea
Archangel
Ural Mountains
Ob'
RUSSIAN FEDERATION
Syktyvkar
FINLAND
Lake Onega
Perm'
Lake Ladoga
Helsinki
St Petersburg
Tallinn
Nizhniy Novgorod
Kazan'
Volga
Yaroslavl'
Riga
Orenburg
Samara
Moscow
Ryazan'
Minsk
Saratov
KAZAKHSTAN
BELARUS
Homyel'
Voronezh
Aral Sea
Volgograd
Don
Kiev
Kharkiv
UZBEKISTAN
UKRAINE
Donets'k
Astrakhan'
Dnipropetrovs'k
Rostov na-Donu
Caspian Sea
MOLDOVA
Chişinău
Dnieper
Sea of Azov
Odessa
Krasnodar
Groznyy
TURKMENISTAN
ROMANIA
Caucasus
Bucharest
Black Sea
GEORGIA
AZERBAIJAN
ARMENIA
AZER.
Sofia
BULGARIA
İstanbul
Thessaloniki
TURKEY
IRAN
Aegean Sea
Athens
Euphrates
SYRIA
CYPRUS
IRAQ
Tigris
Crete
LEBANON
1:20 000 000
KILOMETRES
MILES

EUROPEAN RUSSIAN FEDERATION

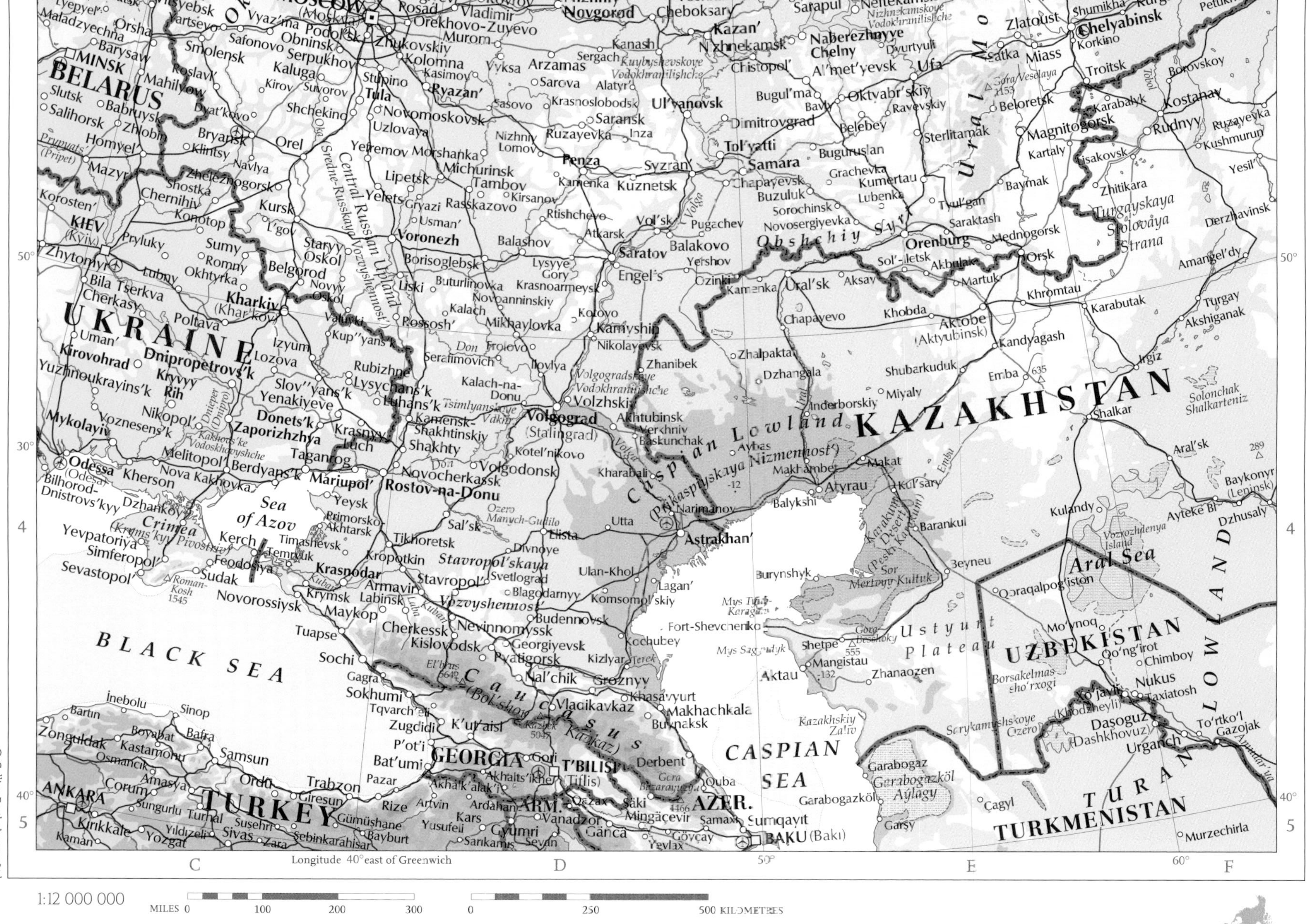

1:12 000 000

MILES 0 100 200 300

0 250 500 KILOMETRES

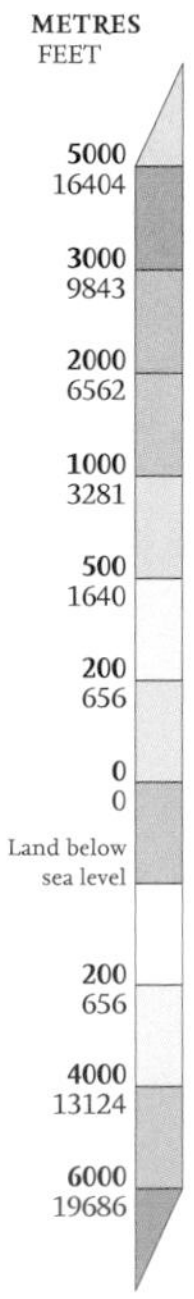

METRES
FEET

METRES	FEET
5000	16404
3000	9843
2000	6562
1000	3281
500	1640
200	656
0	0
Land below sea level	
200	656
4000	13124
6000	19686

Longitude 25° east of Greenwich

Conic Equidistant Projection

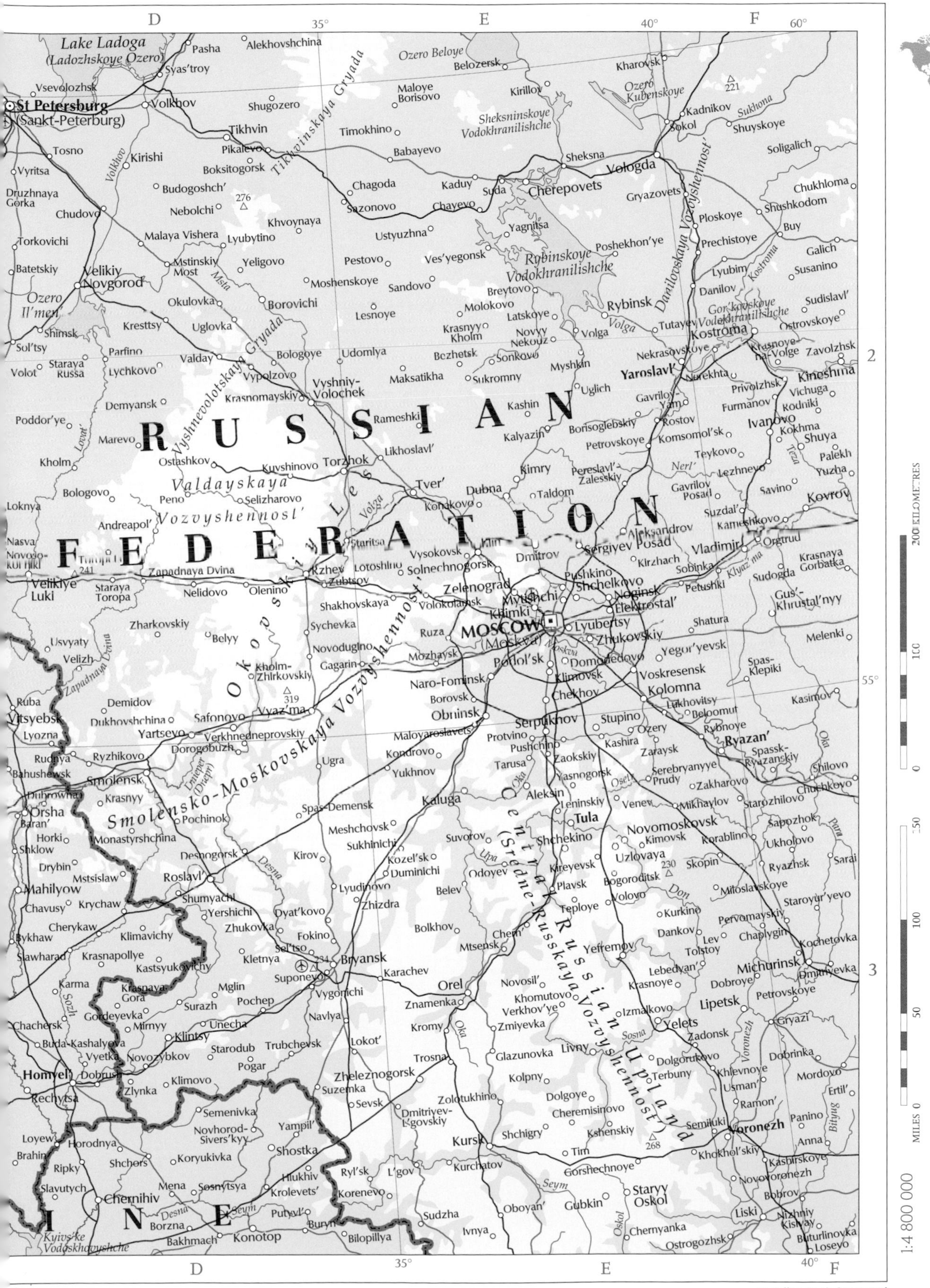

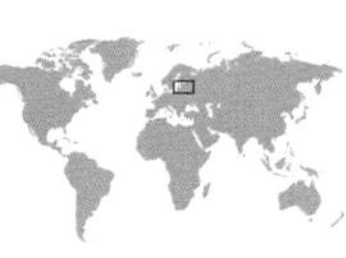

D 35° E 40° F 60°

Lake Ladoga (Ladozhskoye Ozero)
Pasha
Alekhovshchina
Syas'troy
Vsevolozhsk
St Petersburg (Sankt-Peterburg)
Volkhov
Shugozero
Ozero Beloye
Belozersk
Maloye Borisovo
Kirillov
Kharovsk
Ozero Kubenskoye
221
Kadnikov
Sokol
Sukhona
Shuyskoye
Tikhvinskaya Gryada
Sheksninskoye Vodokhranilishche
Tikhvin
Timokhino
Tosno
Kirishi
Pikalevo
Babayevo
Volkhov
Soligalich
Sheksna
Vologda
Vyritsa
Boksitogorsk
Chagoda
Kaduy
Suda
Cherepovets
Gryazovets
Druzhnaya Gorka
Budogoshch'
276
Nebolchi
Sazonovo
Chayevo
Chukhloma
Shushkodom
Chudovo
Ploskoye
Khvoynaya
Yagnitsa
Danilovskaya Vozvyshennost'
Buy
Torkovichi
Malaya Vishera
Lyubytino
Ustyuzhna
Poshekhon'ye
Prechistoye
Galich
Batetskiy
Velikiy Novgorod
Mstinskiy Most
Yeligovo
Pestovo
Ves'yegonsk
Rybinskoye Vodokhranilishche
Lyubim
Kostroma
Susanino
Ozero Il'men'
Msta
Moshenskoye
Sandovo
Breytovo
Danilov
Okulovka
Borovichi
Molokovo
Rybinsk
Gor'kovskoye Vodokhranilishche
Sudislavl'
Lesnoye
Latskoye
Shimsk
Kresttsy
Uglovka
Krasnyy Kholm
Novyy Nekouz
Volga
Tutayev
Kostroma
Ostrovskoye
Sol'tsy
Parfino
Valday
Bologoye
Udomlya
Bezhetsk
Sonkovo
Nekrasovskoye
Krasnoye-na-Volge
Zavolzhsk
2
Volot
Staraya Russa
Lychkovo
Vypolzovo
Maksatikha
Sukromny
Myshkin
Yaroslavl'
Nerekhta
Kineshma
Vyshniy-Volochek
Uglich
Privolzhsk
Vichuga
Demyansk
Krasnomayskiy
Kashin
Gavrilov-Yam
Furmanov
Rodniki
Poddor'ye
Vyshnevolotskaya Gryada
Rameshki
Borisoglebskiy
Rostov
Ivanovo
Kokhma
Lovat'
Marevo
RUSSIAN
Kalyazin
Komsomol'sk
Shuya
Petrovskoye
Teykovo
Palekh
Kholm
Ostashkov
Kuvshinovo
Torzhok
Likhoslavl'
Kimry
Pereslavl'-Zalesskiy
Nerl'
Lezhnevo
Teza
Yuzha
Valdayskaya
Tver'
Dubna
Taldom
Gavrilov Posad
Savino
Kovrov
Bologovo
Peno
Selizharovo
Konakovo
Suzdal'
Loknya
Vozvyshennost'
Volga
FEDERATION
Aleksandrov
Kameshkovo
Andreapol'
Orgtrud
Nasva
Novosokol'niki
Toropets
241
Staritsa
Klin
Sergiyev Posad
Vladimir
Vysokovsk
Dmitrov
Kirzhach
Krasnaya Gorbatka
Lotoshino
Solnechnogorsk
Zapadnaya Dvina
Rzhev
Pushkino
Sobinka
Klyaz'ma
Sudogda
Velikiye Luki
Staraya Toropa
Nelidovo
Olenino
Zubtsov
Zelenograd
Shchelkovo
Petushki
Gus'-Khrustal'nyy
Mytishchi
Noginsk
Shakhovskaya
Volokolamsk
Khimki
Elektrostal'
Zharkovskiy
Sychevka
MOSCOW (Moskva)
Lyubertsy
Shatura
Usvyaty
Belyy
Ruza
Zhukovskiy
Melenki
Novodugino
Moskva
Yegor'yevsk
Velizh
Zapadnaya Dvina
Mozhaysk
Podol'sk
Domodedovo
Spas-Klepiki
Okovskiy Les
Kholm-Zhirkovskiy
Gagarin
Naro-Fominsk
Klimovsk
Voskresensk
55°
Ruba
Demidov
319
Borovsk
Chekhov
Kolomna
Kasimov
Vitsyebsk
Dukhovshchina
Safonovo
Vyaz'ma
Obninsk
Lukhovitsy
Beloomut
Lyozna
Yartsevo
Verkhnedneprovskiy
Maloyaroslavets
Serpukhov
Stupino
Ozery
Rybnoye
Ryazan'
Dorogobuzh
Smolensko-Moskovskaya Vozvyshennost'
Protvino
Kashira
Pushchino
Zaraysk
Spassk-Ryazanskiy
Oka
Rudnya
Ryzhikovo
Kondrovo
Tarusa
Zaokskiy
Ugra
Serebryanyye Prudy
Bahushewsk
Smolensk
Dnieper (Dnepr)
Yukhnov
Shilovo
Oka
Yasnogorsk
Osetr
Zakharovo
Dubrowna
Krasnyy
Aleksin
Mikhaylov
Chuchkovo
Kaluga
Orsha
Starozhilovo
Spas-Demensk
Leninskiy
Venev
Central Russian Upland (Sredne-Russkaya Vozvyshennost')
Baran'
Pochinok
Tula
Novomoskovsk
Sapozhok
Smolensko-Moskovskaya
Horki
Meshchovsk
Suvorov
Shchekino
Kimovsk
Korablino
Para
Shklow
Monastyrshchina
Sukhinichi
Ukholovo
Kozel'sk
Uzlovaya
Drybin
Desnogorsk
Kirov
Duminichi
Skopin
Sarai
Upa
Odoyev
Kireyevsk
230
Ryazhsk
Mstsislaw
Desna
Mahilyow
Roslavl'
Lyudinovo
Belev
Plavsk
Bogoroditsk
Miloslavskoye
Shumyachi
Don
Chavusy
Krychaw
Zhizdra
Volovo
Staroyur'yevo
Yershichi
Dyat'kovo
Teploye
Kurkino
Cherykaw
Zhukovka
Bolkhov
Pervomayskiy
Klimavichy
Fokino
Chern'
Dankov
Chaplygin
Bykhaw
Lev Tolstoy
Sel'tso
Mtsensk
Yefremov
Kochetovka
Slawharad
Krasnapollye
Kletnya
234
Bryansk
Kastsyukovichy
Karachev
Lebedyan'
Michurinsk
3
Suponevo
Dmitriyevka
Karma
Orel
Novosil'
Krasnoye
Dobroye
Krasnaya Gora
Mglin
Vygonichi
Khomutovo
Verkhov'ye
Petrovskoye
Sozh
Pochep
Znamenka
Izmalkovo
Lipetsk
Gordeyevka
Surazh
Navlya
Zmiyevka
Gryazi
Chachersk
Mirnyy
Unecha
Kromy
Yelets
Oka
Sosna
Voronezh
Buda-Kashalyova
Klintsy
Starodub
Trubchevsk
Lokot'
Zadonsk
Vyetka
Novozybkov
Trosna
Glazunovka
Livny
Dolgorukovo
Dobrinka
Pogar
Homyel'
Dobrush
Klimovo
Zheleznogorsk
Terbuny
Khlevnoye
Mordovo
Rechytsa
Zlynka
Suzemka
Kolpny
Usman'
Ertil'
Sevsk
Zolotukhino
Dolgoye
Ramon'
Semenivka
Dmitriyev-L'govskiy
Cheremisinovo
Yampil'
Novhorod-Sivers'kyy
Semiluki
Panino
Bityug
Loyew
Shostka
Voronezh
Horodnya
Kursk
Shchigry
Kshenskiy
Brahin
268
Anna
Koryukivka
Tim
Khokhol'skiy
Ripky
Shchors
Rыl'sk
L'gov
Kurchatov
Kashirskoye
Hlukhiv
Gorshechnoye
Slavutych
Mena
Sosnytsya
Seym
Novovoronezh
Krolevets'
Korenevo
Staryy Oskol
Chernihiv
Bobrov
Desna
Seym
Putyvl'
Gubkin
UKRAINE
Oboyan'
Liski
Borzna
Buryn'
Sudzha
Nizhniy Kislyay
Oskol
Kyivs'ke Vodoskhovyshche
Bakhmach
Konotop
Bilopillya
Ivnya
Chernyanka
Buturlinovka
Ostrogozhsk
Losevo

D 35° E 40° F

KILOMETRES 200 100 0
MILES 0 50 100 150
1:4 800 000

METRES
FEET

METRES	FEET
5000	16404
3000	9843
2000	6562
1000	3281
500	1640
200	656
0	0
Land below sea level	
200	656
4000	13124
6000	19686

Conic Equidistant Projection

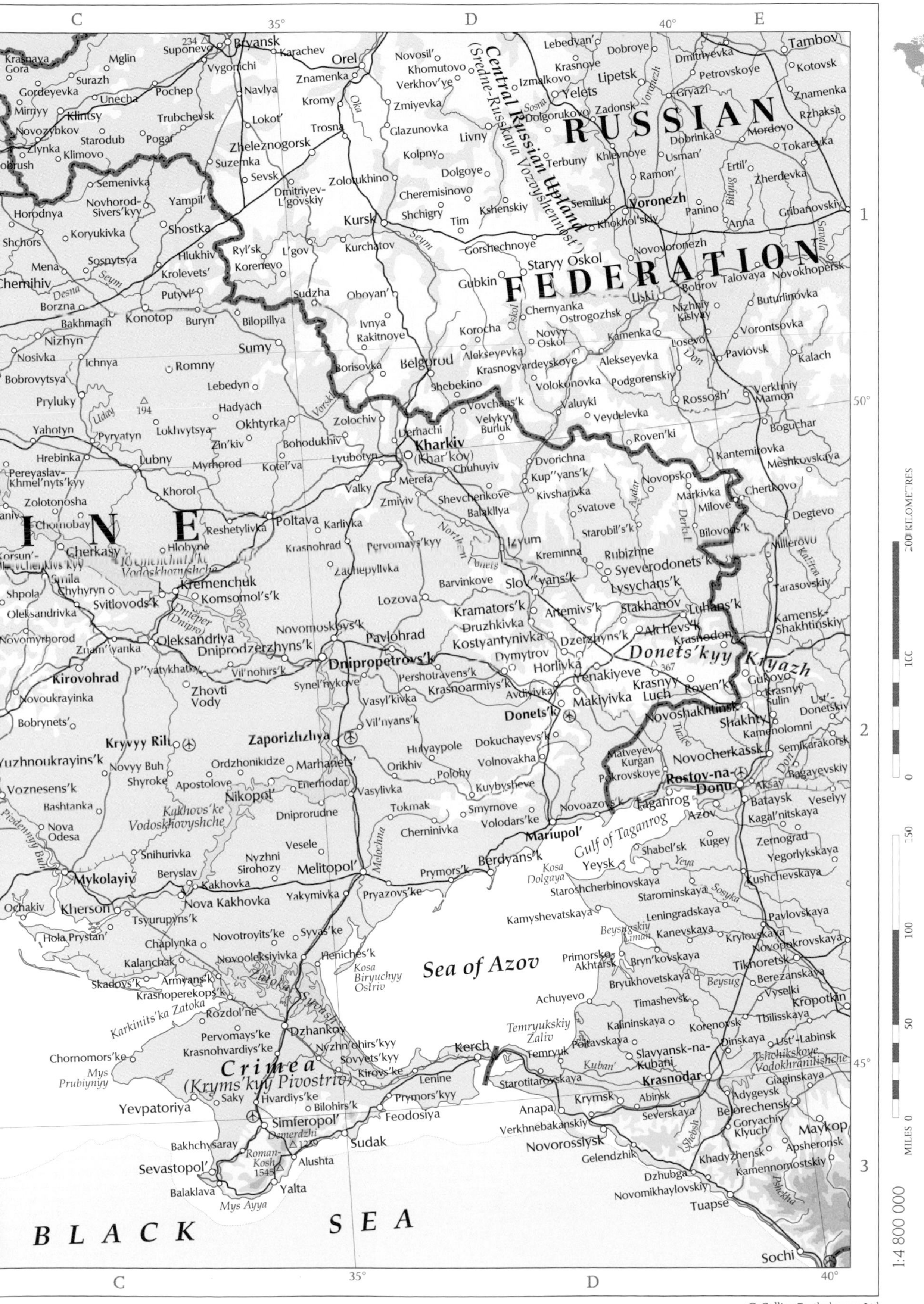

0 50 100 150 200 KILOMETRES
0 50 100 MILES
1:4 800 000

SCANDINAVIA AND ICELAND

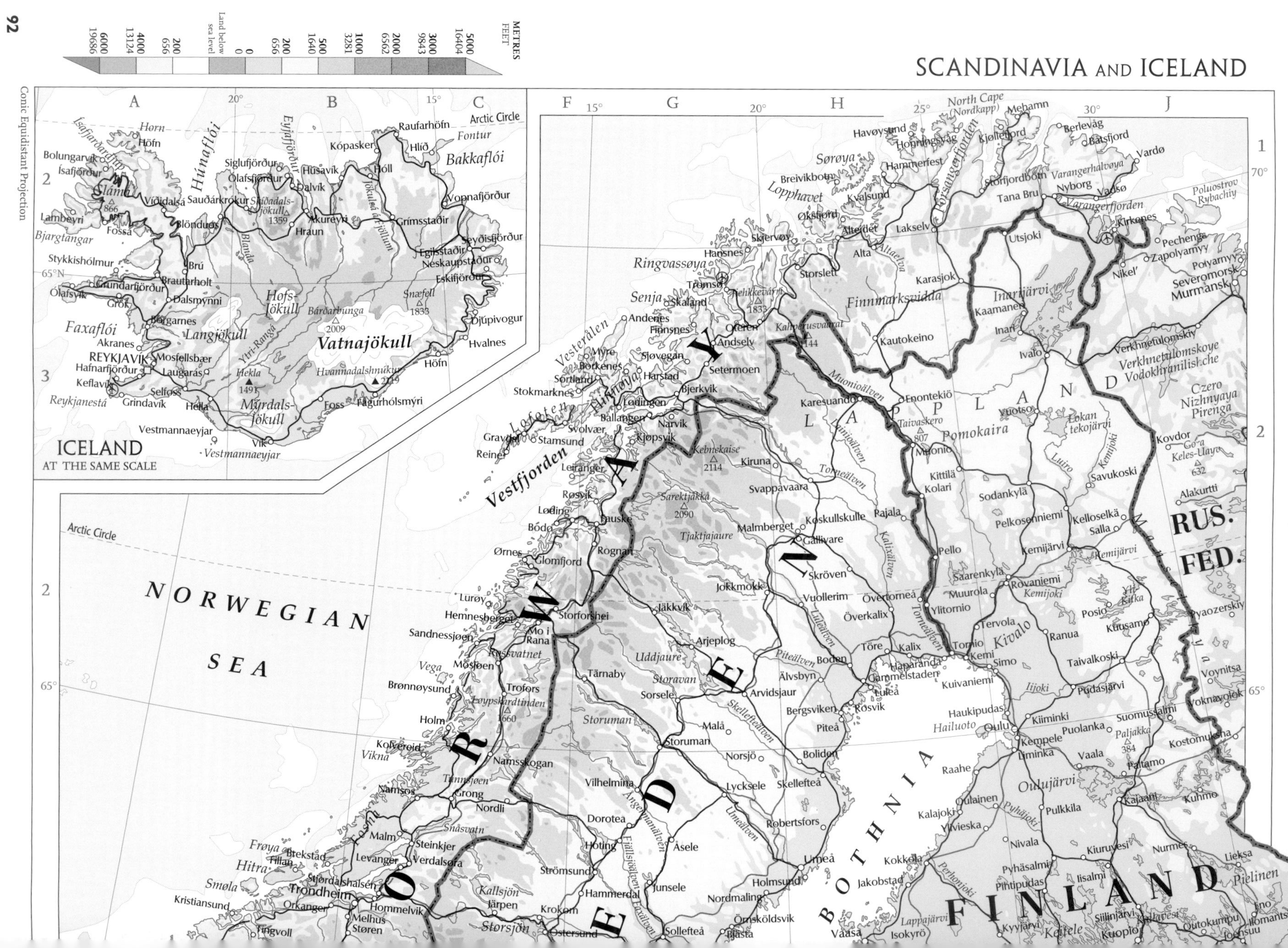

Conic Equidistant Projection

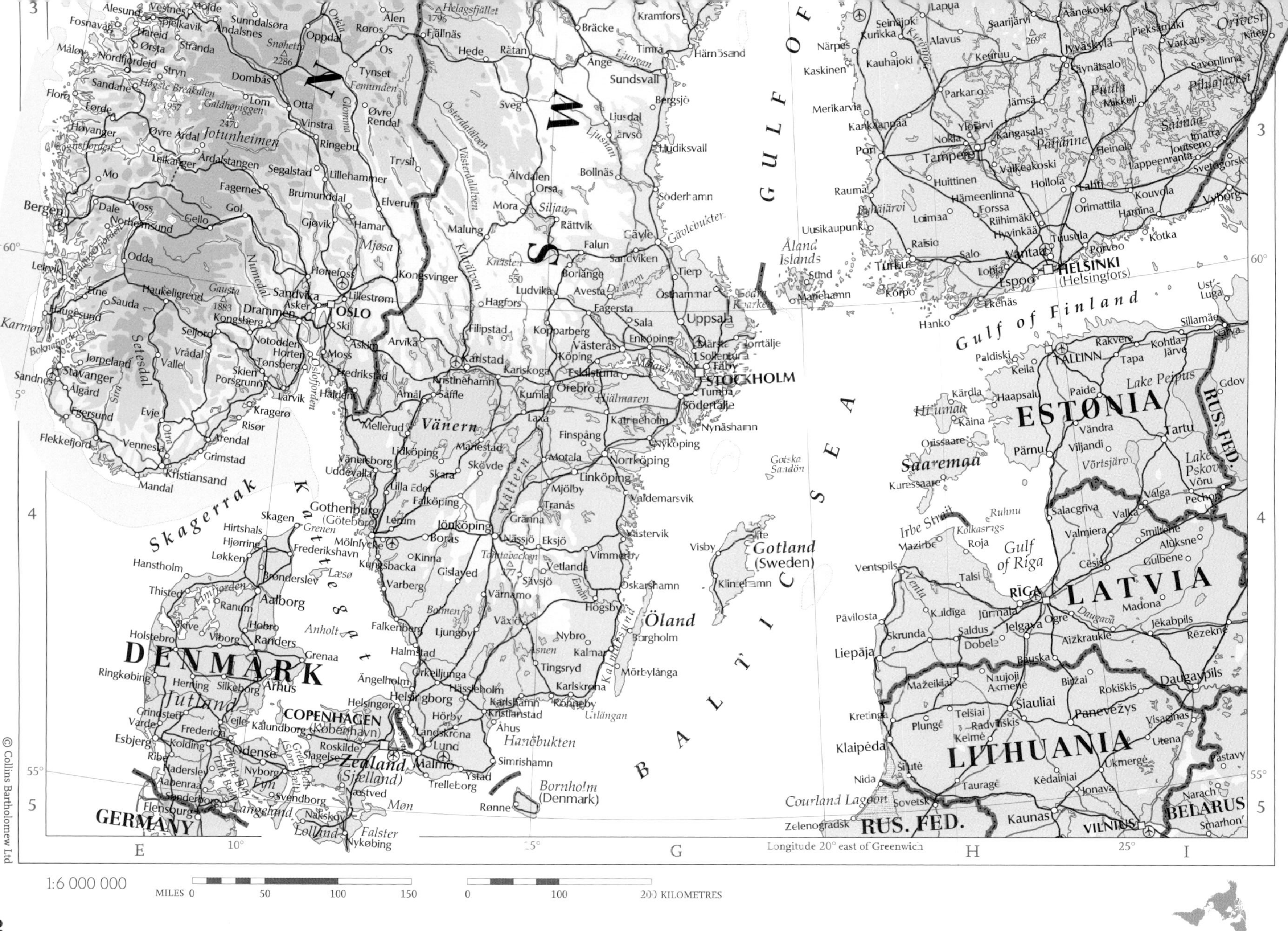
GULF OF
S W E D E N
N O R W A Y
B A L T I C S E A
Gulf of Finland
Gulf of Riga
Skagerrak
Kattegat
ESTONIA
LATVIA
LITHUANIA
RUS. FED.
BELARUS
DENMARK
GERMANY
HELSINKI (Helsingfors)
TALLINN
RIGA
VILNIUS
STOCKHOLM
OSLO
COPENHAGEN (København)
Gotland (Sweden)
Öland
Bornholm (Denmark)
Åland Islands
Saaremaa
Zealand (Sjælland)
Jutland
Vänern
Vättern
Lake Peipus
Courland Lagoon
Setesdal
Jotunheimen
1:6 000 000
MILES
KILOMETRES
Longitude 20° east of Greenwich

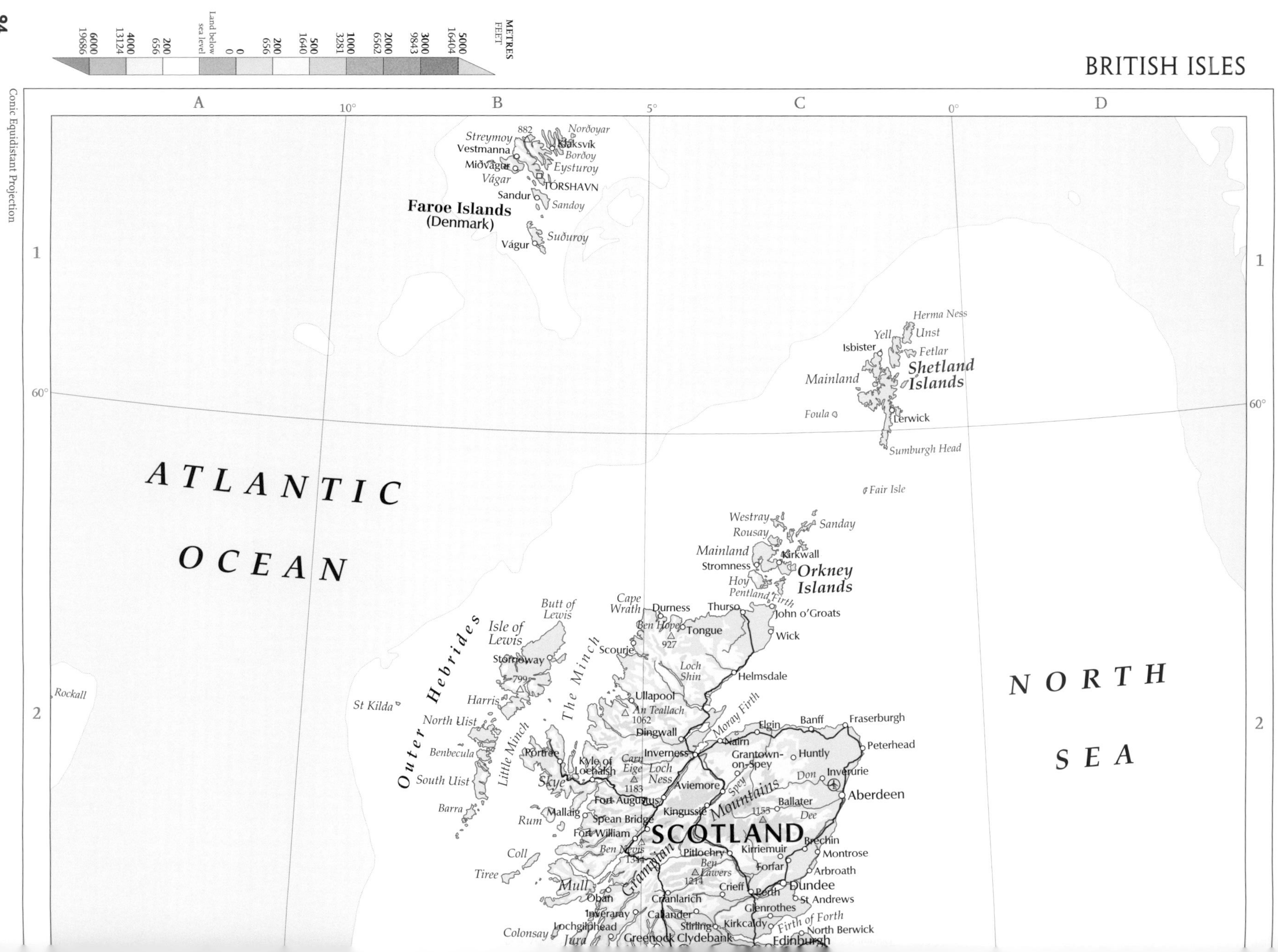

Conic Equidistant Projection

UNITED KINGDOM
IRELAND
NORTHERN IRELAND
ENGLAND
WALES
FRANCE
CELTIC SEA
Irish Sea
English Channel
(La Manche)
North Channel
St George's Channel
Bristol Channel
Strait of Dover
Channel Islands
(Îles Normandes)
Great Britain
British Isles
Pennines
Southern Uplands
North York Moors
LONDON
DUBLIN
DOUGLAS
Belfast
Cardiff
Liverpool
Manchester
Birmingham
Bristol
Leeds
Sheffield
Newcastle upon Tyne
Glasgow
Cork
Limerick
Galway
Isle of Man (U.K.)
Guernsey (U.K.)
Jersey (U.K.)
ST PETER PORT
ST HELIER
Isle of Wight
Isles of Scilly
Land's End
Lizard Point
Longitude 5° west of Greenwich
1:4 800 000
MILES 0 50 100 150
0 100 200 KILOMETRES

SCOTLAND

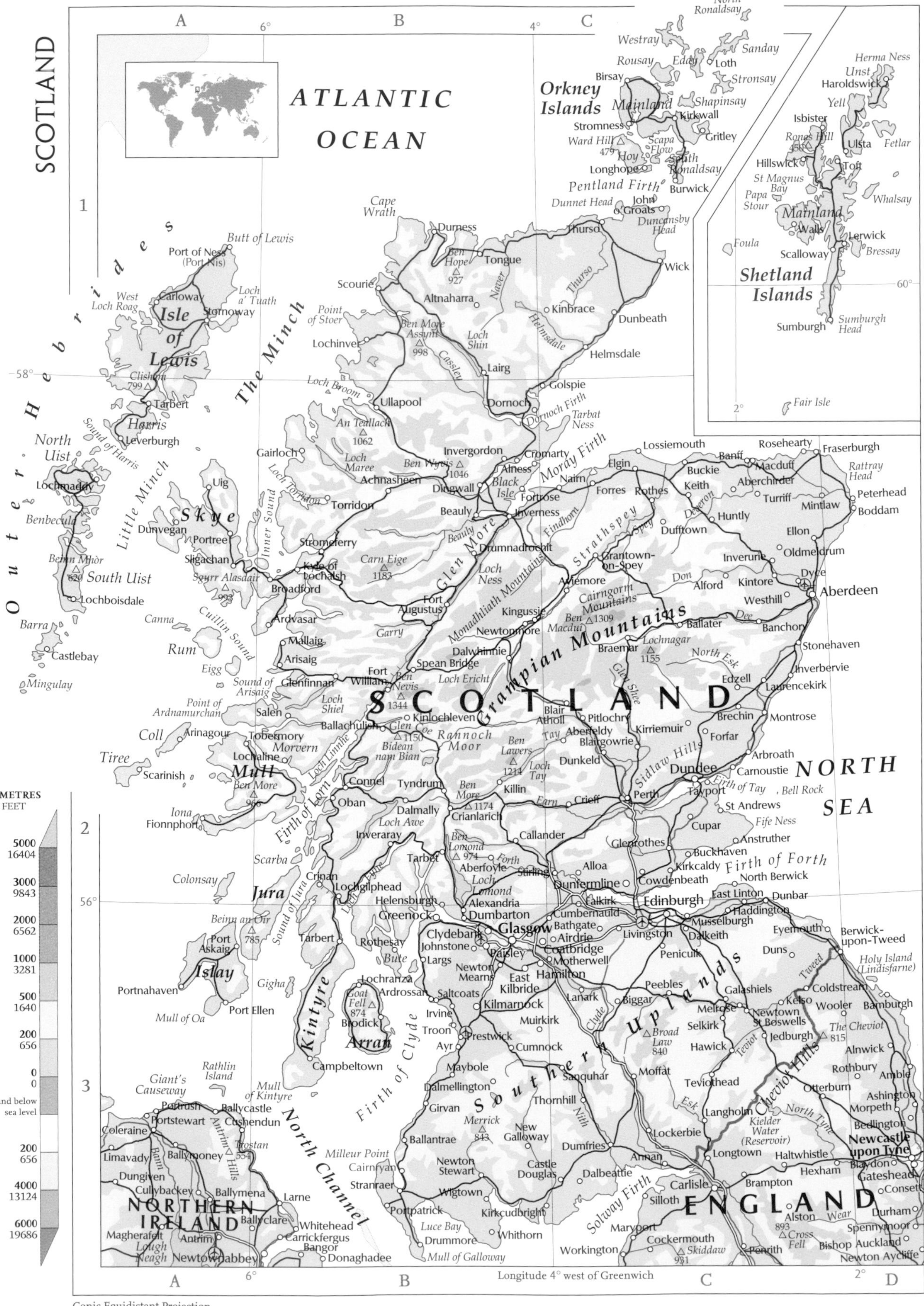

Conic Equidistant Projection

IRELAND

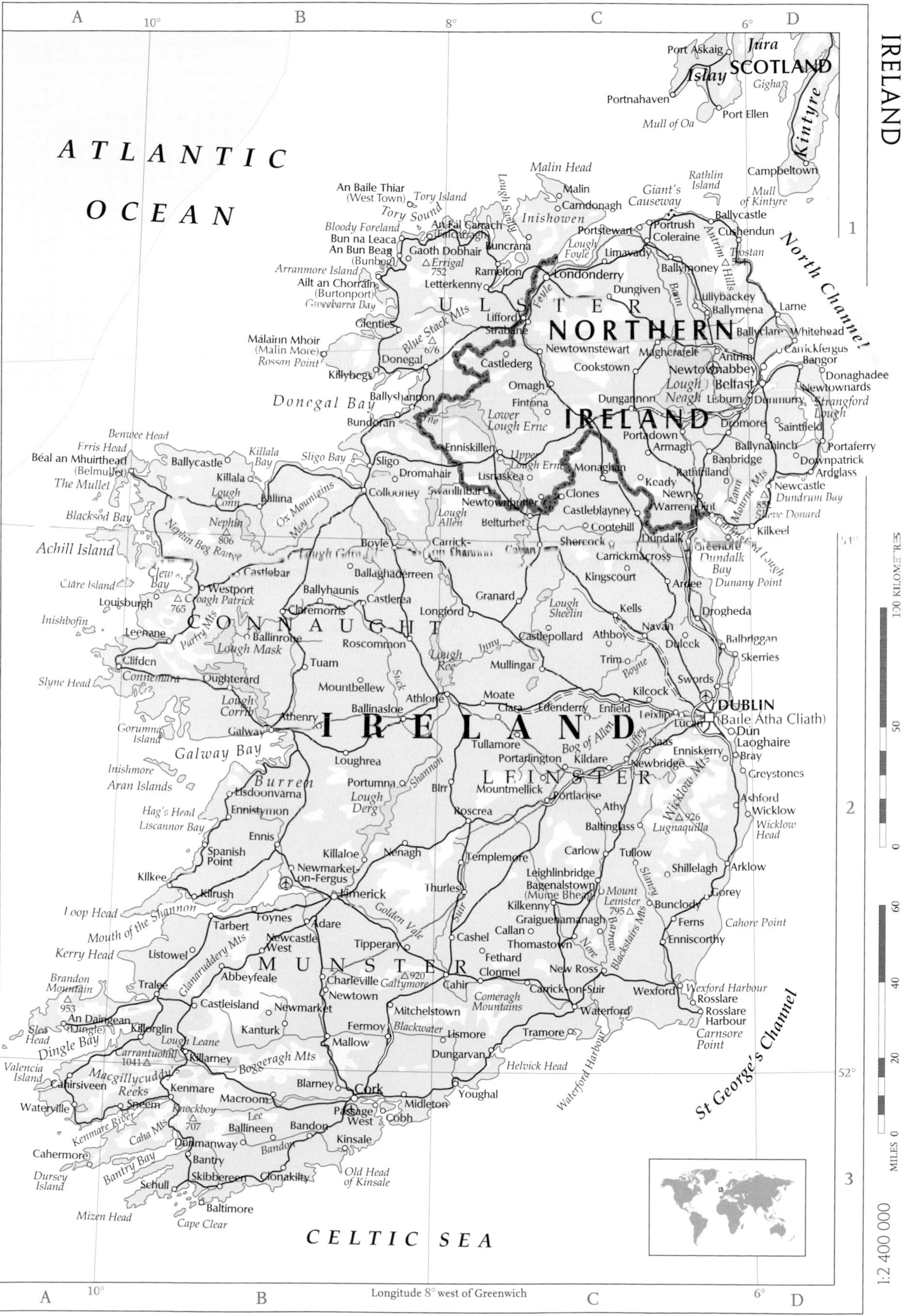

1:2 400 000

Conic Equidistant Projection

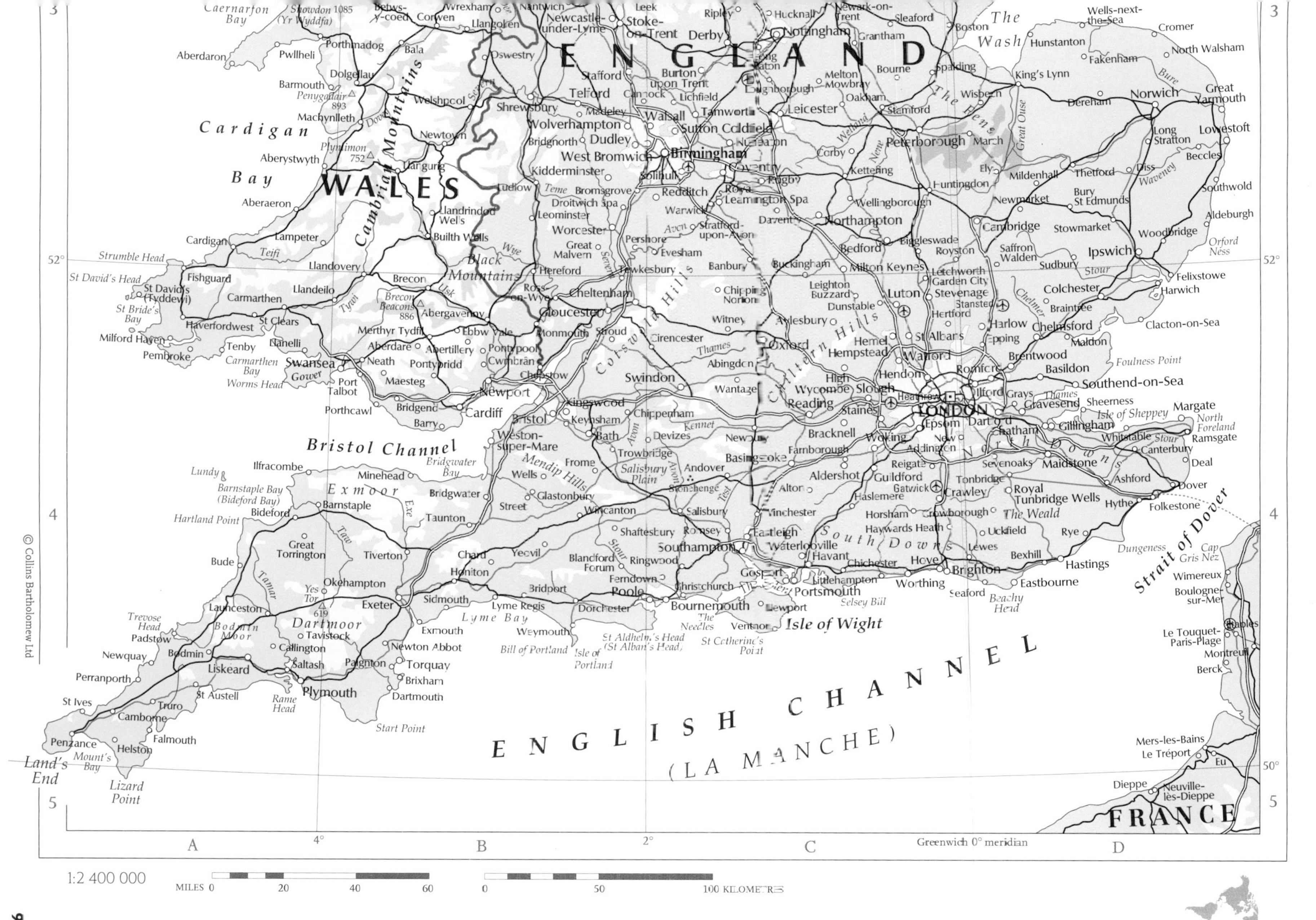
ENGLAND
WALES
FRANCE
ENGLISH CHANNEL
(LA MANCHE)
Strait of Dover
Bristol Channel
Cardigan Bay
The Wash
Isle of Wight
LONDON
Birmingham
Bristol
Cardiff
Swansea
Plymouth
Southampton
Portsmouth
Brighton
Norwich
Ipswich
Nottingham
Leicester
Derby
Oxford
Reading
Cambridge
Peterborough
Gloucester
Exeter
Bournemouth
Dover
Boulogne-sur-Mer
Dieppe
Cambrian Mountains
Black Mountains
Cotswold Hills
Chiltern Hills
North Downs
South Downs
Mendip Hills
Salisbury Plain
Exmoor
Dartmoor
Bodmin Moor
The Fens
The Weald
Land's End
Lizard Point
Snowdon 1085 (Yr Wyddfa)
Greenwich 0° meridian
1:2 400 000
MILES 0 20 40 60
0 50 100 KILOMETRES
52°
50°
4°
2°
A
B
C
D
3
4
5

A B C

4° 6°

1 2 3

52° 50°

NORTH SEA

West Frisian Islands

East Frisian Islands

Waddenzee

IJsselmeer

Markermeer

NETHERLANDS

AMSTERDAM

THE HAGUE ('s-Gravenhage) (Den Haag)

Rotterdam

BELGIUM

BRUSSELS (Bruxelles)

LUXEMBOURG

FRANCE

OSTFRIESLAND

MÜNSTERLAND

Cologne (Köln)

Eifel

Ardennes

Hohes Venn

METRES
FEET

METRES	FEET
5000	16404
3000	9843
2000	6562
1000	3281
500	1640
200	656
0	0
Land below sea level	
200	656
4000	13124
6000	19686

Longitude 6° east of Greenwich

Conic Equidistant Projection

GERMANY
CZECH REP.
LÜNEBURGER HEIDE
MECKLENBURGISCHE SEENPLATTE
Hamburg
Bremen
Hannover
BERLIN
Magdeburg
Leipzig
Kassel
Erfurt
Frankfurt am Main
Nuremberg
Würzburg
Mannheim
Thüringer Wald
Erzgebirge
Böhmer Wald
ODENWALD
1:2 400 000
100 KILOMETRES
MILES

METRES
FEET

METRES	FEET
5000	16404
3000	9843
2000	6562
1000	3281
500	1640
200	656
0	0
Land below sea level	
200	656
4000	13124
6000	19686

Conic Equidistant Projection

15°
D
20°
E
25°
F
Bornholm
BALTIC SEA
RUS. FED.
LITHUANIA
BELARUS
POLAND
UKRAINE
REPUBLIC
SLOVAKIA
HUNGARY
ROMANIA
AUSTRIA
CROATIA
SERBIA
SLOVENIA
CARPATHIAN MTS
Gulf of Gdańsk
Mys Taran
Zelenogradsk
Svetlogorsk
Baltiysk
Svetlyy
Kaliningrad
Gvardeysk
Chernyakhovsk
Gusev
Kybartai
Ozersk
Mamonovo
Bagrationovsk
Noreikiškės
Vilkaviškis
Prienai
Marijampolė
Grigiškės
Trakai
VILNIUS
Astravyets
Ashmyany
Lazdijai
Alytus
Šalčininkai
Merkinė
Varėna
Druskininkai
Voranava
Iwye
Lida
Byarozawka
Hrodna
Shchuchyn
Navahrudak
Masty
Nyoman
Vawkavysk
Slonim
Zel'va
Svislach
Ivatsevichy
Pruzhany
Byaroza
Kamyanyets
Drahichyn
Zhabinka
Kobryn
Ivanava
Brest
Malaryta
Kamin'-Kashyrs'kyy
Ratne
Turiya
Lyuboml'
Kovel'
Turiys'k
Volodymyr-Volyns'kyy
Novovolyns'k
Horokhiv
Sokal'
Chervonohrad
Brody
Kam"yanka-Buz'ka
Zhovkva
L'viv (L'vov)
Zolochiv
Yavoriv
Peremyshlyany
Horodok
Mykolayiv
Berezhany
Sambir
Zhydachiv
Drohobych
Boryslav
Stryy
Kalush
Dniester (Dnister)
Dolyna
Ivano-Frankivs'k
Nadvirna
Uzhhorod
Svalyava
Mizhhir"ya
Mukacheve
Berehove
Khust
Rakhiv
Hora Hoverla 2061
Vynohradiv
Tisza
Władysławowo
Puck
Rumia
Wejherowo
Ustka
Lębork
Gdynia
Gdańsk
Darłowo
Sławno
Słupsk
Kołobrzeg
Koszalin
Bytów
Wieżyca 328
Pruszcz Gdański
Elbląg
Frombork
Braniewo
Bartoszyce
Korsze
Węgorzewo
Gołdap
Suwałki
Sejny
Olecko
Giżycko
Augustów
Trzebiatów
Białogard
Miastko
Tczew
Malbork
Pasłęk
Dobre Miasto
Olsztyn
Pojezierze Mazurskie
Ełk
Grajewo
Jezioro Śniardwy
Gryfice
Świdwin
Starogard Gdański
Kwidzyn
Ostróda
Nowogard
Szczecinek
Czersk
Chojnice
Iława
Dylewska Góra 312
Szczytno
Mońki
Łobez
Goleniów
Grudziądz
Świecie
Nidzica
Działdowo
Łomża
Stargard Szczeciński
Wałcz
Złotów
Chełmno
Wąbrzeźno
Brodnica
Ostrołęka
Narew
Zambrów
Białystok
Piła
Bydgoszcz
Toruń
Mława
Choszczno
Noteć
Vistula (Wisła)
Ciechanów
Nizina
Ostrów Mazowiecka
Hajnówka
Pyrzyce
Myślibórz
Inowrocław
Gorzów Wielkopolski
Wyszków
Bug
Warta
Oborniki
Włocławek
Płock
Węgrów
Legionowo
WARSAW (Warszawa)
Siedlce
Bukowiec 225
Poznań
Gniezno
Konin
Kutno
Pruszków
Mińsk Mazowiecki
Świebodzin
Września
Koło
Łowicz
Skierniewice
Łuków
Biała Podlaska
Grodzisk Wielkopolski
Mazowiecka
Zielona Góra
Kościan
Jarocin
Zgierz
Łódź
Parczew
Leszno
Kalisz
Pabianice
Dęblin
Lubartów
Żary
Odra
Krotoszyn
Tomaszów Mazowiecki
Puławy
Głogów
Rawicz
Ostrów Wielkopolski
Sieradz
Pionki
Polkowice
Piotrków Trybunalski
Radom
Lublin
Chełm
Lubin
Trzebnica
Bełchatów
Końskie
Legnica
Wieluń
Radomsko
Skarżysko-Kamienna
Starachowice
Ostrowiec Świętokrzyski
Krasnystaw
Zamość
Görlitz
Lubań
Jawor
Wrocław
Oława
Kluczbork
Łysica 611
Jelenia Góra
Świdnica
Olesno
Częstochowa
Kielce
Sandomierz
Stalowa Wola
Biłgoraj
Zittau
Śnieżka 1603
Wałbrzych
Brzeg
Staszów
Tomaszów Lubelski
Liberec
Opole
Pińczów
Tarnobrzeg
Nysa
Kędzierzyn-Koźle
Dąbrowa Górnicza
Zawiercie
Mielec
Lubaczów
Trutnov
Paczków
Bytom
Gliwice
Sosnowiec
Przeworsk
Mladá Boleslav
Náchod
Kłodzko
Katowice
Jaworzno
Rzeszów
Hradec Králové
Racibórz
Kraków
Dębica
Jarosław
Pardubice
Šumperk
Praděd 1491
Rybnik
Jastrzębie-Zdrój
Bochnia
Tarnów
Przemyśl
Skawina
Jasło
Krosno
Opava
Ostrava
Bielsko-Biała
Nowy Sącz
Gorlice
Sanok
Děvět skal 836
Svitavy
Olomouc
Nový Jičín
Frýdek-Místek
Rabka
Ustrzyki Dolne
Havlíčkův Brod
Prostějov
Nowy Targ
Pelhřimov
Blansko
Přerov
Čadca
Žilina
Dolný Kubín
Tatra Mountains
Gerlachovský štít 2655
Bardejov
Svidník
Křemešník 765
Jihlava
Vyškov
Považská Bystrica
Martin
Poprad
Prešov
Humenné
Brno
Zlín
Jindřichův Hradec
Třebíč
Břeclav
Uherské Hradiště
Trenčín
Prievidza
Banská Bystrica
Ďumbier 2043
Spišská Nová Ves
Košice
Michalovce
Znojmo
Dyje
Trebišov
Gmünd
Senica
Malé Karpaty
Rožňava
Sátoraljaújhely
Horn
Mistelbach
Zistersdorf
Váh
Žiar nad Hronom
Zvolen
Rimavská Sobota
Sárospatak
Zwettl
Hollabrunn
Stockerau
Trnava
Nitra
Kazincbarcika
Kisvárda
Krems an der Donau
Morava
Levice
Lučenec
Szerencs
Klosterneuburg
Galanta
Salgótarján
Miskolc
Nyíregyháza
VIENNA (Wien)
BRATISLAVA
Nové Zámky
Pásztó
Kékes 1014
Eger
Amstetten
Baden
Eisenstadt
Danube (Duna)
Komárno
Vác
Gyöngyös
Hajdúböszörmény
Wiener Neustadt
Mosonmagyaróvár
Dunakeszi
Debrecen
Sopron
Csorna
Győr
Ács
BUDAPEST
Hajdúszoboszló
Mürzzuschlag
Tatabánya
Jászberény
Karcag
2277
Aspang-Markt
Kapuvár
Bruck an der Mur
Kőszeg
Papa
Kőris-hegy 709
Mór
Érd
Szolnok
Leoben
Hartberg
Zirc
Székesfehérvár
Dabas
Túrkeve
Veszprém
Knittelfeld
Szombathely
Sárvár
Mezőtúr
Graz
Szentgotthárd
Körmend
Kecskemét
Körös
Békés
Großer Speikkogel 2140
Raab
Mur
Zalaegerszeg
Siófok
Dunaújváros
Csongrád
Gyula
Leibnitz
Murska Sobota
Balatonboglár
Kiskunfélegyháza
Szentes
Békéscsaba
Keszthely
Lenti
Lake Balaton
Paks
Orosháza
Hódmezővásárhely
Pesnica
Isten dombja
Marcali
Kiskunhalas
Maribor
Ptuj
Čakovec
Nagykanizsa
Dombóvár
Tolna
Szeged
Makó
Velenje
Kaposvár
Szekszárd
Tompa
Varaždin
Drava
Nagyatád
Baja
Ivanec
Koprivnica
Szigetvár
Komló
Subotica
Križevci
Mohács
Pécs
Bačka Topola
Senta
Kikinda
Trebnje
Sava
Barcs
Siklós
Beli Manastir
Sombor
Novo Mesto
ZAGREB
Bjelovar
Virovitica
Suhopolje
Sânnicolau Mare
Jimbolia
Timișoara
Lugoj
Timiș
Lipova
Arad
Sântana
Salonta
Crișul Alb
Oradea
Aleșd
Săcueni
Carei
Satu Mare
Acâș
Șimleu Silvaniei
Zalău
Someș
Dej
Gherla
Cluj-Napoca
Baia Mare
Sighetu Marmației
Viseu de Sus
Borșa
Bistrița
Târgu Lăpuș
Vârful Bihor 1849
Ștei
Turda
Aiud
Alba Iulia
Ocna Mureș
Târnăveni
Mediaș
Sebeș
Sibiu
Orăștie
Cisnădie
Deva
Mureșul
Hunedoara
Hațeg
Petroșani
Nyomen
1
2
50°
KILOMETRES
200
100
150
100
50
0
MILES 0
1:4 800 000

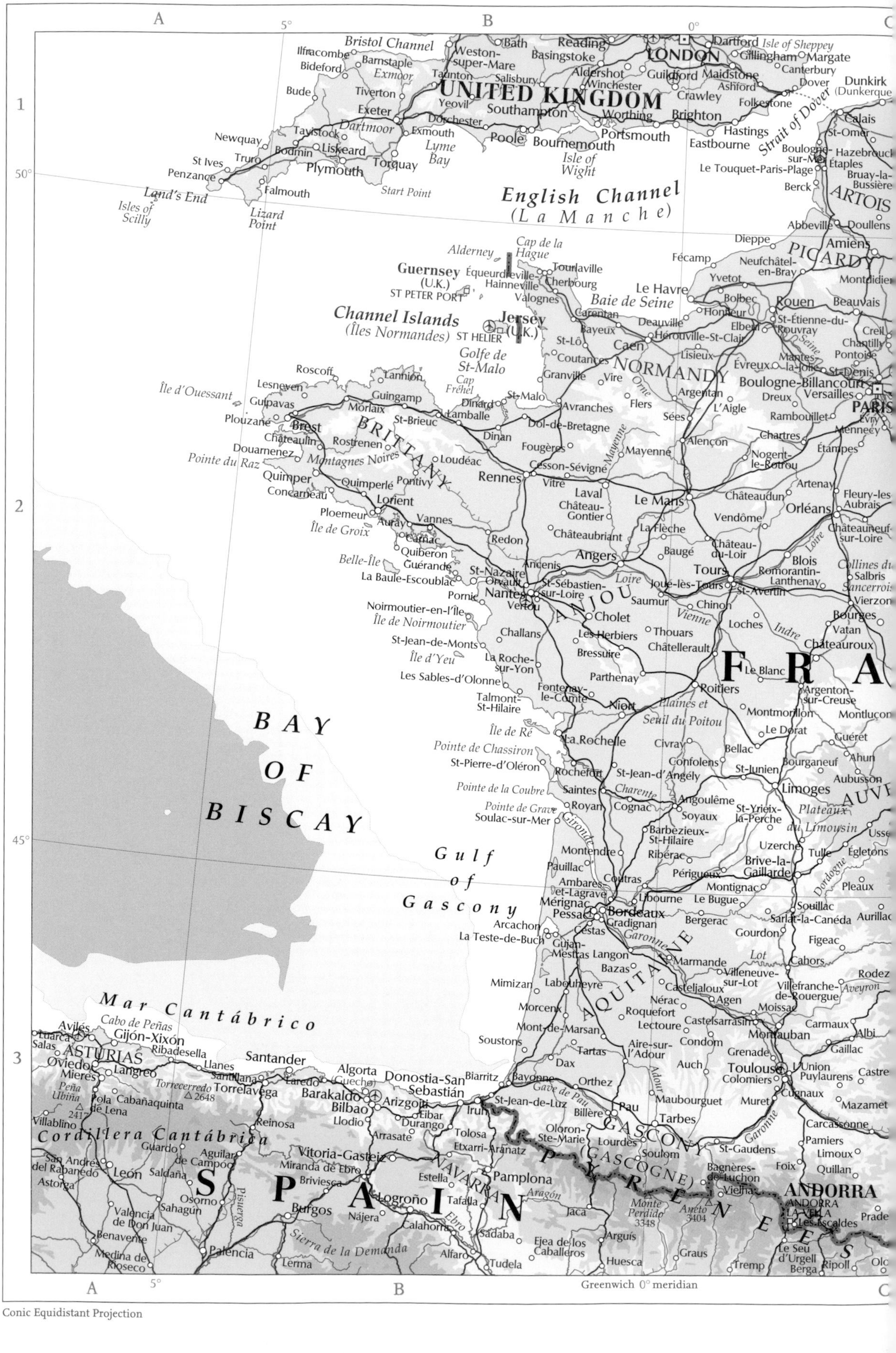

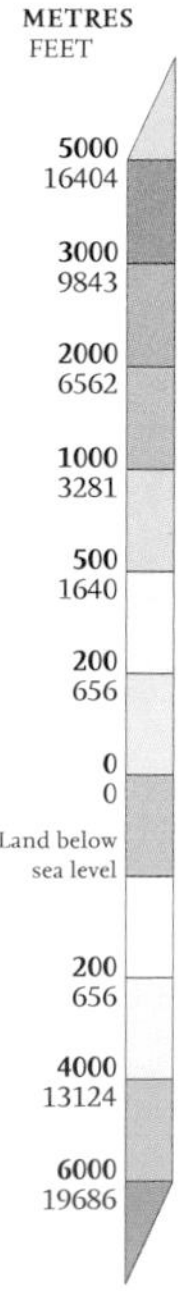

A B C 5° 0° 1 2 3 50° 45°

Bristol Channel
Ilfracombe Barnstaple Bideford Exmoor Bude Tiverton Exeter Taunton Weston-super-Mare Bath Reading Basingstoke LONDON Dartford Isle of Sheppey Gillingham Margate Canterbury Maidstone Aldershot Guildford Salisbury Winchester Ashford Dover Dunkirk (Dunkerque)
UNITED KINGDOM
Yeovil Southampton Crawley Folkestone Dorchester Worthing Brighton Calais St-Omer Strait of Dover
Newquay Tavistock Dartmoor Exmouth Portsmouth Hastings Eastbourne Poole Bournemouth Boulogne-sur-Mer Hazebrouck Étaples
St Ives Truro Bodmin Liskeard Lyme Bay Torquay Plymouth Isle of Wight Le Touquet-Paris-Plage Bruay-la-Bussière
Penzance Land's End Isles of Scilly Falmouth Lizard Point Start Point Berck ARTOIS
English Channel (La Manche)
Abbeville Doullens Amiens Dieppe PICARDY Fécamp Neufchâtel-en-Bray Montdidier
Alderney Cap de la Hague Tourlaville Guernsey (U.K.) ST PETER PORT Équeurdreville-Hainneville Cherbourg Valognes Le Havre Yvetot Bolbec Baie de Seine Rouen Beauvais
Channel Islands (Îles Normandes) Jersey (U.K.) ST HELIER Carentan Deauville Honfleur Elbeuf St-Étienne-du-Rouvray Creil Chantilly
Bayeux Hérouville-St-Clair Caen St-Lô Lisieux Seine Pontoise Mantes-la-Jolie St-Denis
Golfe de St-Malo Coutances NORMANDY Évreux Boulogne-Billancourt Versailles PARIS
Roscoff Lannion Cap Fréhel Granville Vire Orne Argentan Dreux
Île d'Ouessant Lesneven Guingamp St-Malo Dinard Avranches Flers L'Aigle Rambouillet Évry
Guipavas Morlaix Lamballe Sées Mennecy
Plouzané Brest St-Brieuc Dol-de-Bretagne Chartres Étampes
Châteaulin BRITTANY Rostrenen Dinan Alençon Nogent-le-Rotrou
Douarnenez Montagnes Noires Loudéac Fougères Mayenne
Pointe du Raz Quimper Pontivy Rennes Cesson-Sévigné Artenay Fleury-les-Aubrais
Concarneau Quimperlé Vitré Laval Château-Gontier Le Mans Châteaudun Orléans
Lorient Ploemeur Vendôme
Île de Groix Auray Vannes Redon Châteaubriant La Flèche Châteauneuf-sur-Loire
Carnac Quiberon Baugé Château-du-Loir Loire
Belle-Île Guérande Ancenis Angers Blois Collines du
La Baule-Escoublac St-Nazaire Tours Romorantin-Lanthenay Salbris
Orvault Loire St-Sébastien-sur-Loire Joué-lès-Tours St-Avertin Sancerrois
Pornic Nantes ANJOU Saumur Chinon Vierzon
Noirmoutier-en-l'Île Île de Noirmoutier Vertou Cholet Vienne Loches Bourges
Challans Les Herbiers Thouars Indre Vatan
St-Jean-de-Monts Bressuire Châtellerault Châteauroux
Île d'Yeu La Roche-sur-Yon FRA
Les Sables-d'Olonne Parthenay Le Blanc
Talmont-St-Hilaire Fontenay-le-Comte Poitiers Argenton-sur-Creuse
BAY OF BISCAY
Niort Plaines et Seuil du Poitou Montmorillon Montluçon
Île de Ré Le Dorat Guéret
Pointe de Chassiron La Rochelle Civray Bellac Ahun
St-Pierre-d'Oléron Rochefort Confolens Bourganeuf Aubusson
Pointe de la Coubre St-Jean-d'Angély St-Junien
Saintes Charente Angoulême Limoges AUVE
Pointe de Grave Royan Cognac Soyaux St-Yrieix-la-Perche Plateaux du Limousin
Soulac-sur-Mer Gironde Barbezieux-St-Hilaire Ussel
Gulf of Gascony
Montendre Ribérac Uzerche Égletons
Pauillac Périgueux Brive-la-Gaillarde Tulle
Ambarès-et-Lagrave Coutras Montignac Dordogne Pleaux
Mérignac Libourne Le Bugue
Pessac Bordeaux Bergerac Souillac Sarlat-la-Canéda Aurillac
Arcachon Gradignan Cestas Gourdon
La Teste-de-Buch Gujan-Mestras Garonne Figeac
Langon AQUITAINE Marmande Lot Cahors
Bazas Villeneuve-sur-Lot Rodez
Mimizan Labouheyre Casteljaloux Villefranche-de-Rouergue Aveyron
Nérac Agen Moissac
Morcenx Roquefort Castelsarrasin Carmaux
Mont-de-Marsan Lectoure Montauban Albi
Mar Cantábrico
Cabo de Peñas Avilés Gijón-Xixón
Luarca Salas ASTURIAS Ribadesella Llanes Santander
Soustons Tartas Condom Gaillac
Aire-sur-l'Adour Grenade
Dax Auch Toulouse Castres
Oviedo Langreo Santillana Laredo Algorta (Getxo) Donostia-San Sebastián Biarritz Bayonne Orthez Colomiers L'Union Puylaurens
Mieres Torrecerredo 2648 Torrelavega Barakaldo Bilbao Arizgoiti Eibar St-Jean-de-Luz Gave de Pau Adour Muret Cugnaux Mazamet
Peña Ubiña 2417 Pola de Lena Cabañaquinta Irun Pau Maubourguet
Villablino Reinosa Llodio Durango Tolosa Billère Tarbes Carcassonne
Cordillera Cantábrica Arrasate Etxarri-Aranatz Oloron-Ste-Marie Lourdes GASCONY (GASCOGNE) St-Gaudens Garonne Pamiers
Guardo Aguilar de Campoo Vitoria-Gasteiz Soulom Limoux
San Andrés del Rabanedo Miranda de Ebro NAVARRA Bagnères-de-Luchon Foix Quillan
Astorga León Saldaña Briviesca Estella Pamplona Viella ANDORRA
SPAIN Osorno Pisuerga Logroño Tafalla Aragón PYRENEES ANDORRA LA VELLA Les Escaldes Prade
Sahagún Burgos Nájera Ebro Jaca Monte Perdido 3348 Aneto 3404
Valencia de Don Juan Calahorra Sádaba Ejea de los Caballeros Arguís
Benavente Sierra de la Demanda Alfaro Tudela Graus Le Seu d'Urgell Ripoll Olot
Medina de Rioseco Palencia Lerma Huesca Tremp Berga

A 5° B Greenwich 0° meridian C

METRES
FEET

METRES	FEET
5000	16404
3000	9843
2000	6562
1000	3281
500	1640
200	656
0	0
Land below sea level	
200	656
4000	13124
6000	19686

Conic Equidistant Projection

D
E
5°
10°
1
2
3
50°
45°
NETHERLANDS
BELGIUM
GERMANY
LUXEMBOURG
SWITZERLAND
LIECHTENSTEIN
AUSTRIA
ITALY
MONACO
BRUSSELS (Bruxelles)
LUXEMBOURG
BERN
VADUZ
LORRAINE
CHAMPAGNE
BURGUNDY
SAVOY
PROVENCE
LANGUEDOC
BAVARIA
MASSIF CENTRAL
Corsica (Corse) (France)
Ardennes
Vosges
Black Forest (Schwarzwald)
Schwäbische Alb
Fränkische Alb
Côtes de Meuse
Val de Seine
Monts d'Auvergne
Cévennes
VERCORS
Cottian Alps
Maritime Alps
Apennines
Dolomites
Rhine
Mosel
Meuse
Seine
Marne
Yonne
Saône
Doubs
Rhône
Isère
Durance
Verdon
Tarn
Danube (Donau)
Isar
Naab
Lech
Inn
Adige
Ticino
Toce
Tanaro
Reno
Lake Constance (Bodensee)
Zürichsee
Lac de Neuchâtel
Lake Geneva (Lac Léman)
Lake Como
Lake Maggiore
Lake Garda
Jungfrau 4158
Matterhorn 4478
Mont Blanc 4808
Barre des Écrins 4102
Weisskugel 3738
Ortles 3905
St Gotthard Pass 2108
Brenner Pass 1375
Lemberg 1015
Monte Cimone 2165
Col de Tende 1871
Monte Stello 1307
Monte Rotondo 2622
Gulf of Genoa
Ligurian Sea
MEDITERRANEAN SEA
Golfe du Lion
Côte d'Azur
Cap de St-Tropez
Cap Sicié
Îles d'Hyères
Étang de Leucate
Cap de Creus
Capo Mele
Cap Corse
Capo Rosso
Capo di Feno
Isola di Capraia
Isola d'Elba
Arcipelago Toscano
Middelburg
Vlissingen
Ostend (Oostende)
Brugge (Bruges)
Ghent (Gent)
Antwerp (Anvers)
Eindhoven
Duisburg
Essen
Düsseldorf
Neuss
Hagen
Arnsberg
Remscheid
Leverkusen
Cologne (Köln)
Siegen
Kassel
Eschwege
Mühlhausen (Thüringen)
Eisenach
Gotha
Erfurt
Weimar
Jena
Gera
Chemnitz
Zwickau
Saalfeld
Schwarzenberg
Plauen
Karlovy Vary
Ieper
Roeselare
Mouscron
Hasselt
Genk
Maastricht
Leuven
Düren
Bonn
Aachen
Liège
Verviers
Malmédy
Lille
Roubaix
Béthune
Lens
Mons
Charleroi
Andenne
Namur
Ciney
Dinant
Douai
Valenciennes
Maubeuge
Arras
Cambrai
Fumay
La Capelle
Péronne
Vervins
Hirson
St-Quentin
Chauny
Noyon
Laon
Compiègne
Soissons
Senlis
Fismes
Reims
Rethel
Charleville-Mézières
Sedan
Bouillon
Bastogne
Clervaux
Ettelbruck
Arlon
Pétange
Longwy
Vouziers
Stenay
Verdun
Thionville
Rombas
Metz
Épernay
Châlons-en-Champagne
Marne-la-Vallée
Château Thierry
Coulommiers
Sézanne
Provins
Melun
Nemours
Sens
Romilly-sur-Seine
Troyes
Vitry-le-François
St-Dizier
Joinville
Bar-le-Duc
Bar-sur-Aube
Chaumont
Montigny-le-Roi
Langres
Montargis
Auxerre
Châtillon-sur-Seine
Gien
Montbard
Avallon
Semur-en-Auxois
Cosne-Cours-sur-Loire
Saulieu
Prémery
Nevers
Dijon
Nuits-St-Georges
Beaune
Auxonne
Dole
Gray
Selongey
Vesoul
Autun
Le Creusot
Chalon-sur-Saône
Louhans
Tournus
Sancoins
Moulins
Digoin
Paray-le-Monial
St-Pourçain-sur-Sioule
Commentry
Gannat
Vichy
Mâcon
Bourg-en-Bresse
Roanne
Thiers
Riom
Clermont-Ferrand
Issoire
Villefranche-sur-Saône
Rillieux-la-Pape
Villeurbanne
Lyon
Givors
Vienne
Montbrison
St-Étienne
Firminy
Annonay
Yssingeaux
Le Puy-en-Velay
St-Flour
Saugues
Langogne
Marvejols
Mende
Espalion
Aubenas
Privas
Valence
Die
Montélimar
Pierrelatte
Valréas
Nyons
Les Vans
Bollène
Séverac-le-Château
Millau
Alès
Ganges
Bagnols-sur-Cèze
Uzès
Orange
Carpentras
Avignon
Cavaillon
Nîmes
Lodève
Montpellier
Arles
Vauvert
Sète
Agde
Béziers
Narbonne
Durban-Corbières
Rivesaltes
Perpignan
Céret
Port-Vendres
Figueres
Banyoles
Salon-de-Provence
Istres
Martigues
Châteauneuf-les-Martigues
Marignane
Marseille
Aubagne
La Ciotat
Six-Fours-les-Plages
Toulon
Hyères
Aix-en-Provence
Pertuis
Manosque
Brignoles
Draguignan
Fréjus
St-Raphaël
St-Tropez
Cannes
Grasse
Antibes
Nice
MONTE-CARLO
Castellane
Digne-les-Bains
Sisteron
Barcelonnette
Gap
St-Bonnet-en-Champsaur
Briançon
Oulx
Modane
Grenoble
La Mure
St-Égrève
Voiron
Romans-sur-Isère
Bourgoin-Jallieu
Chambéry
Albertville
Aix-les-Bains
Rumilly
Annecy
Cluses
Bonneville
Chamonix-Mont-Blanc
Geneva (Genève)
St-Claude
Oyonnax
Lons-le-Saunier
Poligny
Pontarlier
Besançon
Baume-les-Dames
Montbéliard
Belfort
Lure
Luxeuil-les-Bains
Remiremont
Épinal
Vittel
Neufchâteau
Toul
Nancy
Lunéville
St-Dié
Sélestat
Colmar
Guebwiller
Mulhouse
Saverne
Sarrebourg
Strasbourg
Pont-à-Mousson
Freyming-Merlebach
Bitche
Saarlouis
Saarbrücken
Neunkirchen
Merzig
Trier
Bitburg
Idar-Oberstein
Koblenz
Neuwied
Wetzlar
Gießen
Marburg an der Lahn
Bad Hersfeld
Fulda
Bad Salzungen
Meiningen
Suhl
Coburg
Lichtenfels
Hof
Kulmbach
Bayreuth
Cheb
Bad Kissingen
Schweinfurt
Bamberg
Würzburg
Aschaffenburg
Frankfurt am Main
Offenbach am Main
Wiesbaden
Mainz
Darmstadt
Wertheim
Worms
Mannheim
Ludwigshafen am Rhein
Heidelberg
Mosbach
Speyer
Karlsruhe
Pforzheim
Baden-Baden
Offenburg
Heilbronn
Ludwigsburg
Stuttgart
Göppingen
Tübingen
Reutlingen
Ulm
Balingen
Rottweil
Villingen
Sigmaringen
Biberach an der Riß
Freiburg im Breisgau
Ansbach
Crailsheim
Nördlingen
Aalen
Donauwörth
Fürth
Erlangen
Nuremberg (Nürnberg)
Amberg
Weiden in der Oberpfalz
Roth
Gunzenhausen
Schwandorf
Cham
Regensburg
Straubing
Kelheim
Ingolstadt
Dingolfing
Landshut
Freising
Altötting
Günzburg
Augsburg
Dachau
Munich (München)
Starnberg
Geretsried
Memmingen
Kempten (Allgäu)
Ravensburg
Friedrichshafen
Rosenheim
Garmisch-Partenkirchen
Kufstein
Wörgl
Kitzbühel
Tachov
Domažlice
Konstanz
Schaffhausen
Winterthur
Zürich
St Gallen
Basel (Basle)
Delémont
Aarau
Solothurn
Biel
La Chaux-de-Fonds
Neuchâtel
Lucerne (Luzern)
Zug
Schwyz
Altdorf
Yverdon
Lausanne
Vevey
Montreux
Morges
Interlaken
Frutigen
Andermatt
Bludenz
Chur
Landeck
Pfunds
Innsbruck
Brennero
Vipiteno
Bressanone
Merano
Bolzano
Scuol
Davos
St Moritz
Chiavenna
Sondrio
Tirano
Monthey
Martigny
Sion
Sierre
Brig
Zermatt
Biasca
Bellinzona
Locarno
Luino
Lugano
Varese
Como
Lecco
Bergamo
Arona
Busto Arsizio
Rho
Monza
Milan (Milano)
Crema
Treviglio
Lodi
Brescia
Riva del Garda
Trento
Rovereto
Schio
Valdagno
Vicenza
Verona
Lonigo
Legnago
Padua (Padova)
Mantua (Mantova)
Rovigo
Ferrara
Feltre
Belluno
Laives
Aosta
Borgosesia
Biella
Ivrea
Novara
Vercelli
Cirié
Cuorgnè
Rivoli
Turin (Torino)
Avigliana
Moncalieri
Pinerolo
Saluzzo
Fossano
Cuneo
Mondovì
Alba
Asti
Alessandria
Casale Monferrato
Tortona
Novi Ligure
Acqui Terme
Savona
Genoa (Genova)
Rapallo
Sestri Levante
La Spezia
Carrara
Massa
Tende
Sanremo
Ventimiglia
Imperia
Albenga
Cremona
Piacenza
Parma
Reggio nell'Emilia
Carpi
Modena
Bologna
Imola
Faenza
Argenta
Fivizzano
Barga
Pistoia
Prato
Florence (Firenze)
Lucca
Viareggio
Pisa
Empoli
Scandicci
Livorno
Poggibonsi
Siena
Cecina
Sinalunga
Montepulciano
San Vincenzo
Piombino
Follonica
Grosseto
Castiglione della Pescaia
Orbetello
Portoferraio
Bastia
St-Florent
L'Île-Rousse
Calvi
Vescovato
Cervione
Corte
Ghisonaccia
Prunelli-di-Fiumorbo
Ajaccio
Olmeto
Zonza
Sartène
Porto-Vecchio
Bonifacio
KILOMETRES 0 100 200
MILES 0 50 100 150
1:4 800 000

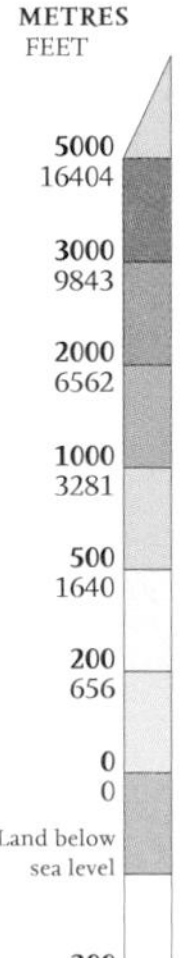

SPAIN AND PORTUGAL

METRES
FEET

METRES	FEET
5000	16404
3000	9843
2000	6562
1000	3281
500	1640
200	656
0	0
Land below sea level	
200	656
4000	13124
6000	19686

Conic Equidistant Projection

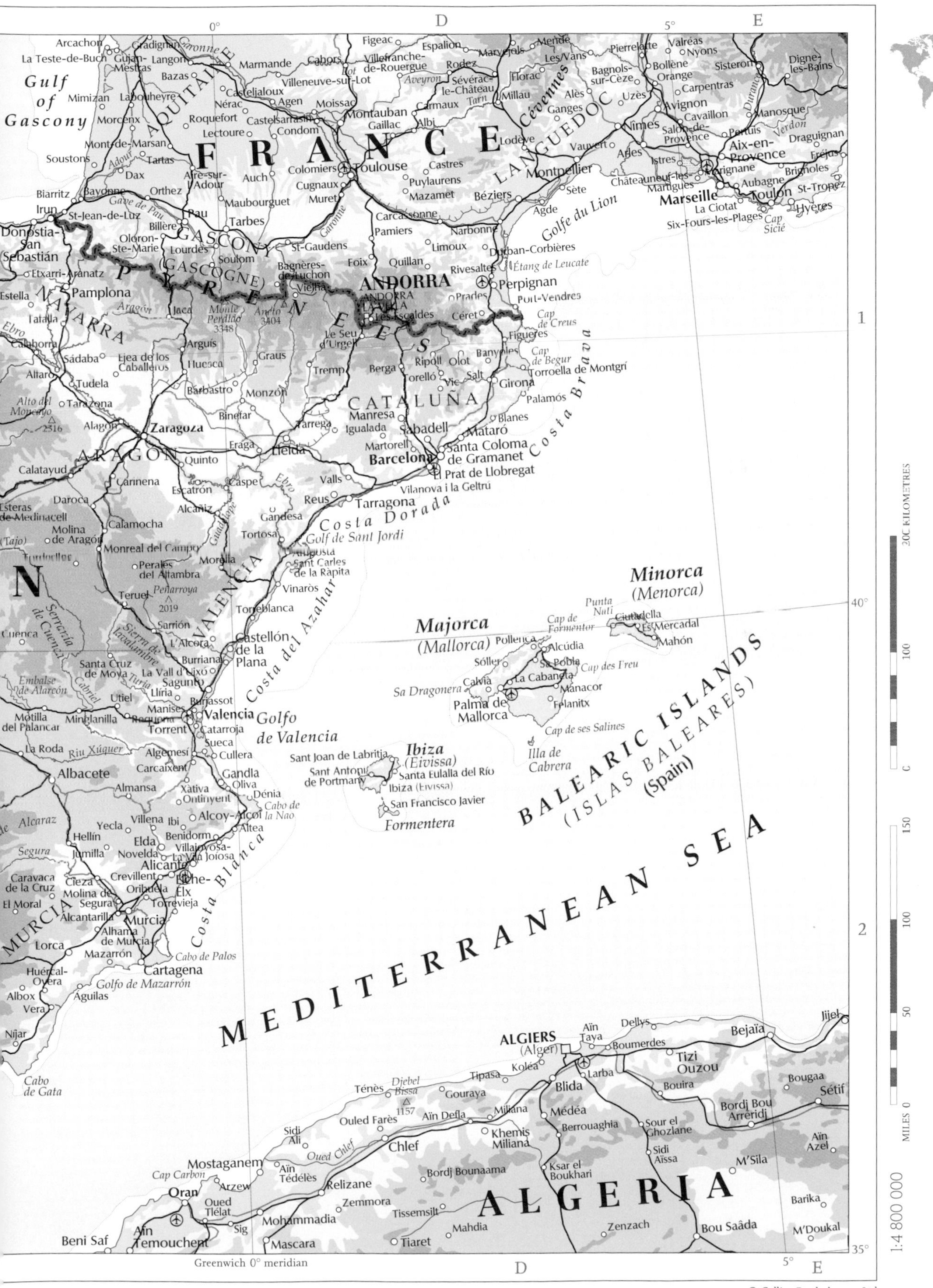

FRANCE
ANDORRA
ALGERIA
MEDITERRANEAN SEA
BALEARIC ISLANDS
(ISLAS BALEARES)
(Spain)
Gulf of Gascony
Golfe du Lion
Golfo de Valencia
Golf de Sant Jordi
Golfo de Mazarrón
Costa Brava
Costa Dorada
Costa del Azahar
Costa Blanca
AQUITAINE
LANGUEDOC
GASCONY
(GASCOGNE)
PYRENEES
NAVARRA
ARAGON
CATALUÑA
VALENCIA
MURCIA
Cévennes
Minorca
(Menorca)
Majorca
(Mallorca)
Ibiza
(Eivissa)
Formentera
Illa de Cabrera
Sa Dragonera
Cap de Formentor
Cap des Freu
Cap de ses Salines
Punta Nati
Ciutadella
Es Mercadal
Mahón
Pollença
Alcúdia
Sóller
Sa Pobla
La Cabaneta
Calvià
Palma de Mallorca
Manacor
Felanitx
Sant Joan de Labritja
Sant Antoni de Portmany
Santa Eulalia del Río
Ibiza (Eivissa)
San Francisco Javier
Arcachon
La Teste-de-Buch
Mimizan
Morcenx
Mont-de-Marsan
Soustons
Dax
Biarritz
Bayonne
Irun
St-Jean-de-Luz
Donostia-San Sebastián
Orthez
Pau
Tarbes
Lourdes
Oloron-Ste-Marie
Toulouse
Colomiers
Montauban
Albi
Carcassonne
Narbonne
Perpignan
Montpellier
Nîmes
Avignon
Arles
Marseille
Toulon
Aix-en-Provence
Béziers
Sète
Agde
Rodez
Cahors
Agen
Auch
Figeac
Mende
Millau
Orange
Digne-les-Bains
Draguignan
Hyères
St-Tropez
La Ciotat
Six-Fours-les-Plages
Cap Sicié
Figueres
Girona
Cap de Creus
Cap de Begur
Pamplona
Estella
Tudela
Zaragoza
Huesca
Lleida
Barcelona
Sabadell
Mataró
Manresa
Tarragona
Reus
Tortosa
Vinaròs
Castellón de la Plana
Sagunto
Valencia
Teruel
Cuenca
Albacete
Alicante
Elche-Elx
Murcia
Cartagena
Lorca
Torrevieja
Benidorm
Dénia
Cabo de la Nao
Cabo de Palos
Cabo de Gata
Monte Perdido 3348
Aneto 3404
Peñarroya 2019
Alto del Moncayo 2316
Serranía de Cuenca
Sierra de Javalambre
Embalse de Alarcón
Ebro
Segura
Turia
Cabriel
Riu Xúquer
Garonne
Adour
ALGIERS
(Alger)
Blida
Médéa
Boumerdes
Tizi Ouzou
Béjaïa
Jijel
Sétif
Bordj Bou Arreridj
Bouira
M'Sila
Bou Saâda
Chlef
Relizane
Mostaganem
Oran
Arzew
Aïn Témouchent
Mascara
Tiaret
Tissemsilt
Djebel Bissa 1157
Cap Carbon
Oued Chlef
Greenwich 0° meridian
0°
5°
40°
35°
D
E
1
2
KILOMETRES 0 100 200
MILES 0 50 100 150
1:4 800 000

ITALY AND THE BALKANS

METRES / FEET

METRES	FEET
5000	16404
3000	9843
2000	6562
1000	3281
500	1640
200	656
0	0
Land below sea level	
200	656
4000	13124
6000	19686

A B 1 2 3 45° 40°

FRANCE ALPS Dolomites SLOV Apennines ITALY SAN MARINO VATICAN CITY MONACO

Ligurian Sea TYRRHENIAN SEA MEDITERRANEAN SEA ADRIATIC Sicilian Channel

Gulf of Genoa Gulf of Venice Golfo di Gaeta Golfo di Salerno Golfo di Orosei Golfo di Cagliari Golfo di Gela Golfe de Tunis Strait of Bonifacio Côte d'Azur Laguna Veneta Arcipelago Toscano

Corsica (Corse) (France) Sardinia (Sardegna) (Italy) Sicily (Sicilia) Isole Lipari Istria

Bonneville Cluses Rumilly Annecy Aix-les-Bains Albertville Chambéry Voiron St-Egrève Grenoble La Mure Gap St-Bonnet-en-Champsaur Barcelonnette Sisteron Digne-les-Bains Manosque Castellane Draguignan Grasse Cannes Nice Antibes Fréjus St-Raphaël St-Tropez Brignoles Toulon Hyères Cap Sicié Îles d'Hyères Cap de St-Tropez MONTE-CARLO Menton Ventimiglia San Remo Imperia Capo Mele Tende Col de Tende 1871 Albenga Savona Mondovì Cuneo Fossano Saluzzo Pinerolo Briançon Oulx Modane Barre des Écrins 4102 Mont Blanc 4808 Chamonix Martigny Matterhorn 4478 Aosta Borgosesia Biella Ivrea Cuorgnè Ciriè Rivoli Giaveno Turin (Torino) Moncalieri Asti Alba Acqui Terme Alessandria Novi Ligure Tortona Casale Monferrato Vercelli Novara Vigevano Milan (Milano) Pavia Lodi Monza Rho Busto Arsizio Como Varese Lugano Bellinzona Verbania Lake Maggiore Lake Como Chiavenna Sondrio Tirano Lecco Bergamo Treviglio Crema Cremona Brescia Manerbio Mantua (Mantova) Piacenza Parma Reggio nell'Emilia Carpi Modena Bologna Ferrara Rovigo Legnago Lonigo Verona Lake Garda Riva del Garda Rovereto Trento Bolzano Merano Ortles 3905 Adige 3738 Cortina d'Ampezzo Belluno Feltre Vittorio Veneto Schio Valdagno Vicenza Padua (Padova) Venice (Venezia) Chioggia Treviso Conegliano Pordenone Udine Maniago Tolmezzo Gemona del Friuli Cividale del Friuli Tarvisio Triglav 2864 Jesenice Tolmin Gorizia Monfalcone Portogruaro Trieste LJUBLJANA Logatec Postojna Snežnik 1796 Koper Rijeka Pazin Crikvenica Krk Poreč Rovinj Labin Pula Cres Rt Kamenjak Veli Lošinj Lošinj Porto Tolle Codigoro Portomaggiore Comacchio Argenta Ravenna Cesenatico Rimini Forlì Faenza Imola Cesena Pesaro Fano Senigallia Ancona Osimo Jesi Cagli Gubbio Macerata Civitanova Marche Fermo San Benedetto del Tronto Ascoli Piceno Giulianova Teramo Pescara Penne Chieti Ortona Vasto Atessa Monte Amaro 2793 L'Aquila Monte Corno 2912 Avezzano Sulmona Trivento Campobasso Venafro Sessa Aurunca Caserta Aversa Naples (Napoli) Vesuvius 1281 Pompei Pozzuoli Sorrento Isola d'Ischia Isola di Capri Isole Ponziane Gaeta Fondi Latina Sezze Cassino Frosinone Sora Velletri Aprilia Anzio Pomezia Sabaudia Rome (Roma) Tivoli Guidonia-Montecelio Civitavecchia Tarquinia Orbetello Viterbo Orvieto Terni Narni Rieti Todi Marsciano Foligno Perugia Fabriano Cortona Arezzo Sansepolcro Montepulciano Siena Grosseto Follonica Piombino Castiglione della Pescaia San Vincenzo Cecina Livorno Pisa Lucca Viareggio Massa Carrara La Spezia Sestri Levante Rapallo Genoa (Genova) Fivizzano Monte Cimone 2165 Barga Pistoia Prato Florence (Firenze) Empoli Scandicci Isola di Capraia Isola d'Elba Portoferraio Isola Pianosa Isola di Montecristo

Cap Corse Monte Stello 1307 St-Florent Bastia L'Île-Rousse Calvi Vescovato Cervione Corte Monte Rotondo 2622 Capo Rosso Capo di Feno Ajaccio Ghisonaccia Prunelli-di-Fiumorbo Olmeto Zonza Sartène Punta d'Ovace 1340 Porto-Vecchio Bonifacio Capo Pertusato

Punta Caprara Isola Asinara Golfo dell' Asinara Arzachena La Maddalena Capo Ferro Punta Balestrieri 1359 Olbia Porto Torres Sassari Capo Caccia Alghero Ploaghe Oschiri Budoni Buddusò Capo Comino Siniscola Bonorva Nuoro Orosei Macomer Abbasanta Punta La Marmora 1834 Capo di Monte Santu Oristano Capo della Frasca Laconi Tortolì Mandas Tertenia Guspini Monte Linas 1236 San Gavino Monreale Serramanna Villaputzu Iglesias Assemini Portoscuso Isola di San Pietro Quartu Sant'Elena Punta Maxia 1017 Cagliari Capo Carbonara Sant'Antioco Isola di Sant'Antioco Pula

Isola di Ustica Isola Filicudi Capo San Vito Monte Sparagio 1110 Isola Marettimo Trapani Partinico Palermo Cefalù Rocca Busambra 1613 Alcamo Termini Imerese Monti Madonie Marsala Partanna Mazara del Vallo Castelvetrano Capo Granitola Leonforte Enna Caltanissetta Sciacca Canicattì Agrigento Caltagirone Niscemi Licata Gela Vittoria Dittaino

La Galite Cap de Fer Collo Skikda Chetaïbi Annaba Cap de Garde ALGERIA Azzaba El Hadjar El Kala El Tarf Nefza Tabarka Mateur Menzel Bourguiba Bizerte Rass Jebel Cap Bon TUNISIA Jedeida

Longitude 10° east of Greenwich

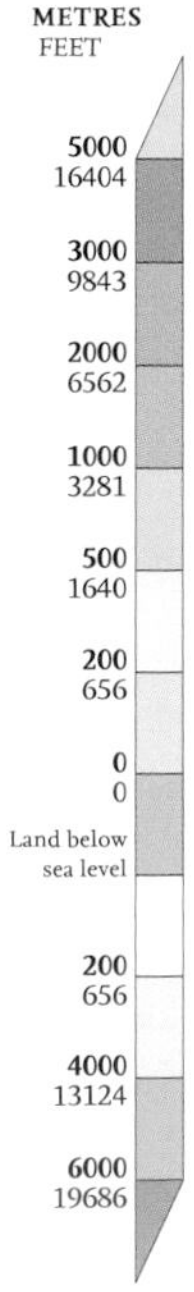

Conic Equidistant Projection

HUNGARY
CROATIA
BOSNIA-HERZEGOVINA
SERBIA
VOJVODINA
ROMANIA
MONTENEGRO
KOSOVO
ALBANIA
MACEDONIA (F.Y.R.O.M.)
BULGARIA
GREECE
DALMATIA
ADRIATIC SEA
IONIAN SEA
Ionian Islands (Ionoi Nisoi)
Strait of Otranto
Golfo di Taranto
Golfo di Manfredonia
Golfo di Squillace
Strait of Messina
Gulf of Corinth
Transylvanian Alps
Pindus Mountains (Pindos)
Le Murge
LA SILA
Danube (Dunav)
ZAGREB
BELGRADE (Beograd)
SARAJEVO
PODGORICA
PRISHTINË (Priština)
SKOPJE
TIRANA (Tiranë)
SOFIA (Sofiya)
Thessaloniki
Maribor
Osijek
Novi Sad
Zrenjanin
Timisoara
Banja Luka
Split
Dubrovnik
Mostar
Zenica
Tuzla
Niš
Kragujevac
Shkodër
Durrës
Elbasan
Vlorë
Bitola
Ohrid
Corfu (Kerkyra)
Cephalonia (Kefallonia)
Zakynthos (Zante)
Lefkada
Patras
Larisa
Volos
Ioannina
Bari
Brindisi
Taranto
Lecce
Foggia
Salerno
Potenza
Cosenza
Catanzaro
Messina
Reggio di Calabria
Catania
Syracuse
Craiova
Sibiu
Mount Olympus 2911
Mount Etna 3323
C
D
1
2
3
45°
40°
20°
15°
KILOMETRES 0 100 200
MILES 0 50 100 150
1:4 800 000

METRES
FEET

Metres	Feet
5000	16404
3000	9843
2000	6562
1000	3281
500	1640
200	656
0	0
Land below sea level	
200	656
4000	13124
6000	19686

Conic Equidistant Projection

ALBANIA
MACEDONIA (F.Y.R.O.M.)
GREECE
TURKEY
AEGEAN SEA
IONIAN SEA
MEDITERRANEAN SEA
Sea of Marmara (Marmara Denizi)
Strait of Otranto
Ionian Islands (Ionoi Nisoi)
Rhodope Mountains
Pindus Mountains (Pindos)
Dodecanese (Dodekanisos)
Cyclades (Kyklades)
Kritiko Pelagos
Mirtoö Pelagos
CRETE (KRITI)
Rhodes (Rodos)
Karpathos (Scarpanto)
Lesbos (Lesvos)
Chios
Samos
Ikaria
Naxos
Andros
Tinos
Milos
Evvoia (Euboea)
Skyros
Thasos
Limnos
Corfu (Kerkyra)
Lefkada
Cephalonia (Kefallonia)
Zakynthos (Zante)
Kythira
ATHENS (Athina)
Thessaloniki
Larisa
Patras
Ioannina
Irakleio
Chania
TIRANA (Tiranë)
SKOPJE
İstanbul
Bursa
İzmir
Edirne
Kütahya
Uşak
Denizli
Manisa
Balıkesir
Çanakkale
Tekirdağ
Gulf of Corinth
Thermaikos Kolpos
Saronikos Kolpos
Argolikos Kolpos
Lakonikos Kolpos
Messiniakos Kolpos
Saros Körfezi
Longitude 20° east of Greenwich
1:4 800 000
MILES 0 50 100 150
KILOMETRES 0 100 200

Oblated Stereographic Projection

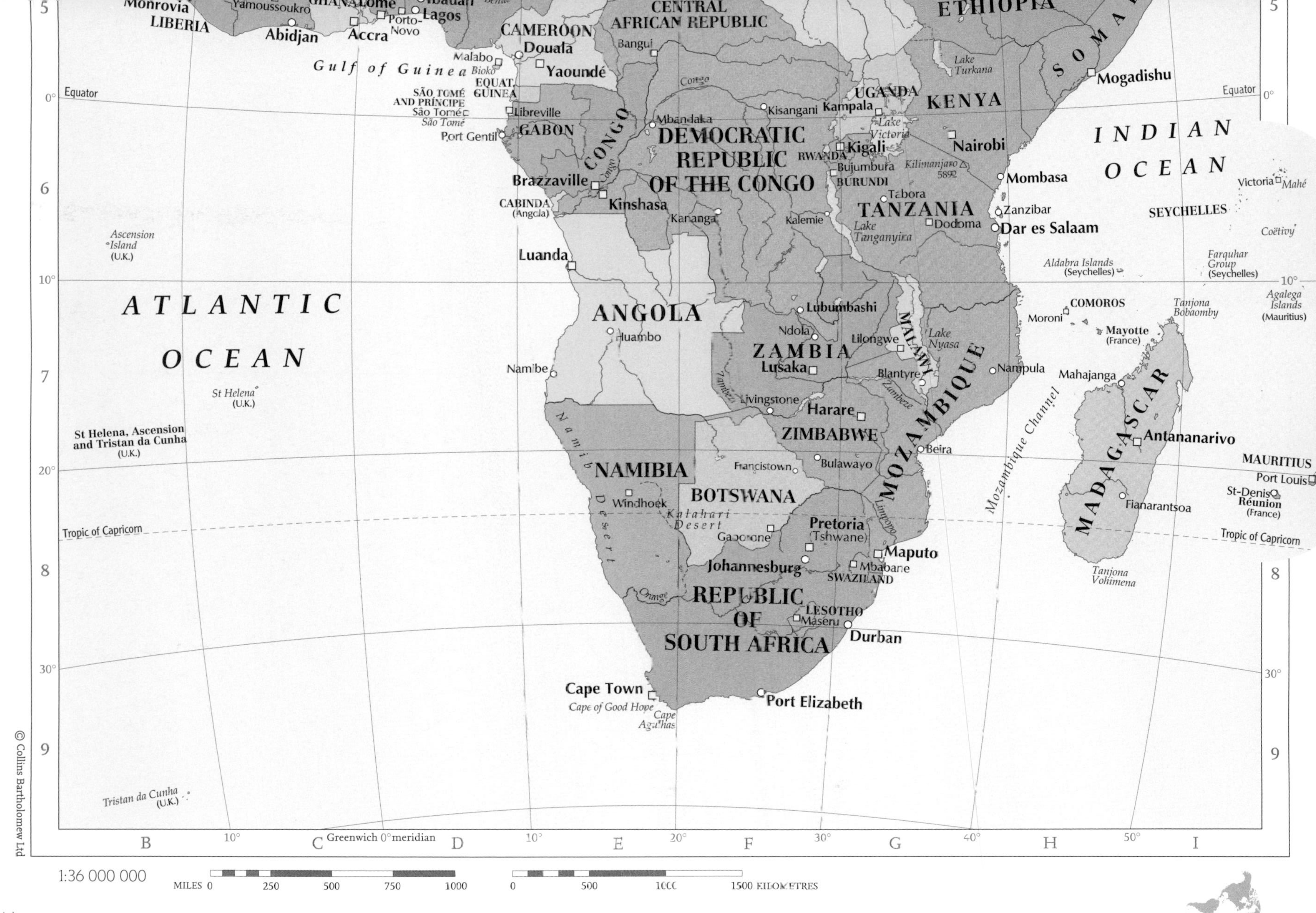

ATLANTIC OCEAN
INDIAN OCEAN
Gulf of Guinea
Mozambique Channel
Equator
Tropic of Capricorn
Greenwich 0° meridian
LIBERIA
Monrovia
Yamoussoukro
Abidjan
Accra
Lomé
Porto-Novo
Lagos
CAMEROON
Douala
Yaoundé
Malabo
Bioko
EQUAT. GUINEA
SÃO TOMÉ AND PRÍNCIPE
São Tomé
Libreville
GABON
Port Gentil
CONGO
Brazzaville
Kinshasa
CABINDA (Angola)
CENTRAL AFRICAN REPUBLIC
Bangui
DEMOCRATIC REPUBLIC OF THE CONGO
Mbandaka
Kisangani
Kananga
Kalemie
Lubumbashi
Congo
ANGOLA
Luanda
Huambo
Namibe
NAMIBIA
Windhoek
Namib Desert
BOTSWANA
Francistown
Gaborone
Kalahari Desert
ZAMBIA
Lusaka
Ndola
Livingstone
Zambeze
ZIMBABWE
Harare
Bulawayo
MALAWI
Lilongwe
Blantyre
Lake Nyasa
MOZAMBIQUE
Beira
Nampula
Maputo
Limpopo
REPUBLIC OF SOUTH AFRICA
Pretoria (Tshwane)
Johannesburg
Durban
Port Elizabeth
Cape Town
Cape of Good Hope
Cape Agulhas
Orange
SWAZILAND
Mbabane
LESOTHO
Maseru
TANZANIA
Dodoma
Dar es Salaam
Zanzibar
Tabora
Lake Tanganyika
Kilimanjaro 5892
BURUNDI
Bujumbura
RWANDA
Kigali
UGANDA
Kampala
Lake Victoria
KENYA
Nairobi
Mombasa
Lake Turkana
ETHIOPIA
Mogadishu
COMOROS
Moroni
Mayotte (France)
Aldabra Islands (Seychelles)
MADAGASCAR
Antananarivo
Mahajanga
Fianarantsoa
Tanjona Bobaomby
Tanjona Vohimena
SEYCHELLES
Victoria
Mahé
Coëtivy
Farquhar Group (Seychelles)
Agalega Islands (Mauritius)
MAURITIUS
Port Louis
St-Denis
Réunion (France)
Ascension Island (U.K.)
St Helena (U.K.)
St Helena, Ascension and Tristan da Cunha (U.K.)
Tristan da Cunha (U.K.)
1:36 000 000
MILES 0 250 500 750 1000
0 500 1000 1500 KILOMETRES

NORTHWEST AFRICA

Lambert Azimuthal Equal Area Projection

METRES	FEET
5000	16404
3000	9843
2000	6562
1000	3281
500	1640
200	656
0	0
Land below sea level	
200	656
4000	13124
6000	19686

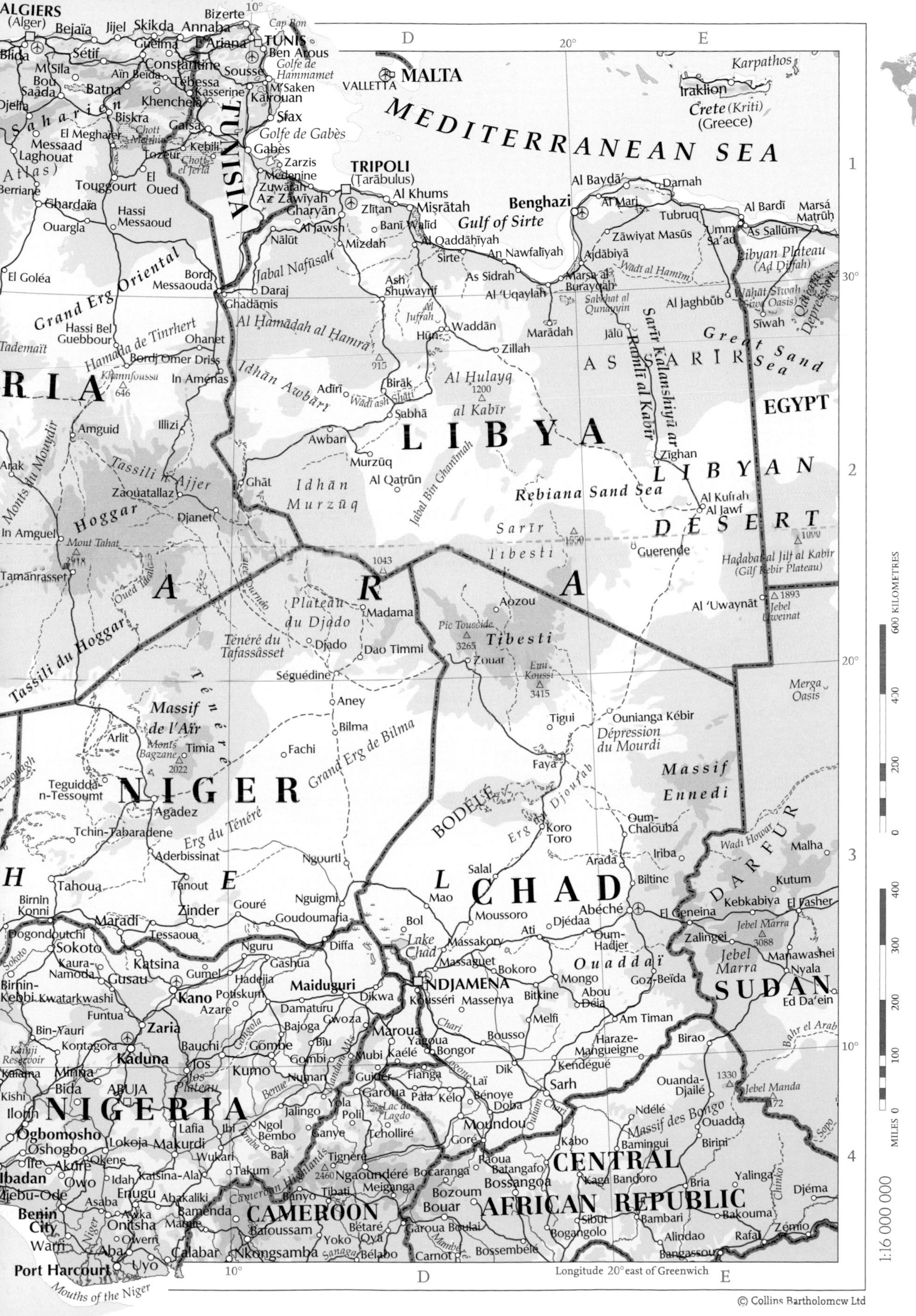
ALGIERS
(Alger)
Bejaïa
Jijel
Skikda
Annaba
Bizerte
Cap Bon
TUNIS
L'Ariana
Ben Arous
Golfe de Hammamet
Sousse
M'Saken
Kairouan
Sfax
Golfe de Gabès
Gabès
Zarzis
Medenine
Blida
Sétif
M'Sila
Bou Saâda
Batna
Constantine
Guelma
Aïn Beïda
Tébessa
Kasserine
Khenchela
Djelfa
Biskra
Gafsa
El Meghaier
Chott Melrhir
Kebili
Tozeur
Chott el Jerid
Messaad
Laghouat
Saharien Atlas
Berriane
Touggourt
El Oued
TUNISIA
Ghardaïa
Ouargla
Hassi Messaoud
El Goléa
Bordj Messaouda
Grand Erg Oriental
Ghadāmis
Daraj
Hassi Bel Guebbour
Tademaït
Hamada de Tinrhert
Ohanet
Bordj Omer Driss
Khanfoussa
646
In Aménas
Amguid
Illizi
Arak
Monts du Mouydir
Tassili n'Ajjer
Zaouatallaz
Djanet
Hoggar
In Amguel
Mont Tahat
2918
Tamanrasset
Oued Tafassasset
Tassili du Hoggar
MALTA
VALLETTA
MEDITERRANEAN SEA
Karpathos
Iraklion
Crete (Kriti)
(Greece)
TRIPOLI
(Ţarābulus)
Zuwārah
Az Zāwīyah
Gharyān
Al Khums
Zlīţan
Mişrātah
Banī Walīd
Nālūt
Al Jawsh
Mizdah
Jabal Nafūsah
Al Qaddāhīyah
Sirte
Benghazi
Gulf of Sirte
Al Baydā'
Al Marj
Darnah
Tubruq
Al Bardī
Marsá Maţrūh
As Sallūm
Umm Sa'ad
Libyan Plateau
(Ad Diffah)
Zāwiyat Masūs
Ajdābiyā
Wādī al Hamīm
An Nawfalīyah
As Sidrah
Marsá al Buraygah
Al 'Uqaylah
Sabkhat al Qunayyin
Al Jaghbūb
Wāhāt Sīwah
(Siwa Oasis)
Sīwah
Qattara Depression
Ash Shuwayrif
Al Juffrah
Hūn
Waddān
Zillah
Marādah
Jālū
Al Hamādah al Hamrā'
915
Idhān Awbārī
Adīrī
Birāk
Wādī ash Shāţi'
Sabhā
Al Hulayq al Kabīr
1200
AS SARIR
Ramlat al Kabir
Sarīr Kalanshiyū ar
Great Sand Sea
EGYPT
LIBYA
Awbari
Murzūq
Al Qaţrūn
Ghāt
Idhān Murzūq
Jabal Bin Ghanīmah
Zīghan
LIBYAN DESERT
Rebiana Sand Sea
Al Kufrah
Al Jawf
Sarīr Tibesti
1550
1000
Guerende
Hadabat al Jilf al Kabir
(Gilf Kebir Plateau)
1893
Jebel Uweinat
Al 'Uwaynāt
1043
Madama
Plateau du Djado
Djado
Dao Timmi
Ténéré du Tafassâsset
Séguédine
Aozou
Pic Toussidé
3265
Tibesti
Zouar
Emi Koussi
3415
Merga Oasis
RIA
ARA
Aney
Bilma
Massif de l'Aïr
Arlit
Monts Bagzane
2022
Timia
Fachi
Grand Erg de Bilma
Ténéré
Tigui
Ounianga Kébir
Dépression du Mourdi
Faya
Massif Ennedi
Teguidda-n-Tessoumt
NIGER
Agadez
Tchin-Tabaradene
Erg du Ténéré
Aderbissinat
Ngourti
BODÉLÉ
Erg du Djourab
Koro Toro
Oum-Chalouba
Arada
Iriba
Wadi Howar
DARFUR
Malha
Tahoua
Tanout
SAHEL
Birnin Konni
Zinder
Gouré
Nguigmi
Goudoumaria
Maradi
Tessaoua
Mao
Salal
CHAD
Biltine
Abéché
El Geneina
Kebkabiya
El Fasher
Kutum
Moussoro
Bol
Ati
Djédaa
Oum-Hadjer
Jebel Marra
3088
Zalingei
Manawashei
Nyala
Dogondoutchi
Sokoto
Katsina
Kaura-Namoda
Gusau
Diffa
Nguru
Gashua
Gumel
Hadejia
Lake Chad
Massakory
Massaguet
Bokoro
Ouaddaï
Mongo
Goz-Beïda
SUDAN
Birnin-Kebbi
Kwatarkwashi
Kano
Potiskum
Azare
Maiduguri
Dikwa
NDJAMENA
Kousséri
Massenya
Bitkine
Abou Déïa
Am Timan
Ed Da'ein
Funtua
Zaria
Damaturu
Gwoza
Bajoga
Maroua
Melfi
Chari
Bousso
Bin-Yauri
Kontagora
Kainji Reservoir
Kaduna
Bauchi
Gombe
Biu
Mubi
Kaélé
Yagoua
Bongor
Haraze-Mangueigne
Birao
Bahr el Arab
Jos
Jos Plateau
Kumo
Gombi
Numan
Guider
Fianga
Laï
Dik
Kendégué
Minna
Kalama
Bida
ABUJA
Kishi
Ilorin
NIGERIA
Benue
Yola
Garoua
Pala
Kélo
Bénoye
Doba
Sarh
Ouanda-Djailé
1330
Jebel Manda
1172
Jalingo
Poli
Lac de Lagdo
Moundou
Ndélé
Massif des Bongo
Ouadda
Ogbomosho
Oshogbo
Lafia
Ibi
Ngol Bembo
Ganye
Tcholliré
Goré
Kabo
Bamingui
Birini
Ilé
Akure
Lokoja
Makurdi
Wukari
Bali
Tignère
Paoua
Batangafo
CENTRAL
Ibadan
Owo
Okene
Takum
2460
Ngaoundéré
Bocaranga
Bossangoa
Kaga Bandoro
Bria
Yalinga
Djéma
Ijebu-Ode
Idah
Enugu
Katsina-Ala
Cameroon Highlands
Banyo
Tibati
Meiganga
Bozoum
Bouar
AFRICAN REPUBLIC
Chinko
Benin City
Asaba
Awka
Onitsha
Abakaliki
Bamenda
CAMEROON
Sibut
Bambari
Bakouma
Warri
Owerri
Niger
Mamfe
Bafoussam
Yoko
Bétaré Oya
Garoua Boulaï
Bogangolo
Alindao
Rafaï
Zémio
Aba
Uyo
Calabar
Nkongsamba
Sanaga
Bélabo
Carnot
Bossembélé
Bangassou
Port Harcourt
Mouths of the Niger
Mambéré
Sopo
Logone
Ouham
D
E
10°
20°
30°
1
2
3
4
Longitude 20° east of Greenwich
600 KILOMETRES
400
200
0
MILES 0
100
200
300
400
1:16 000 000

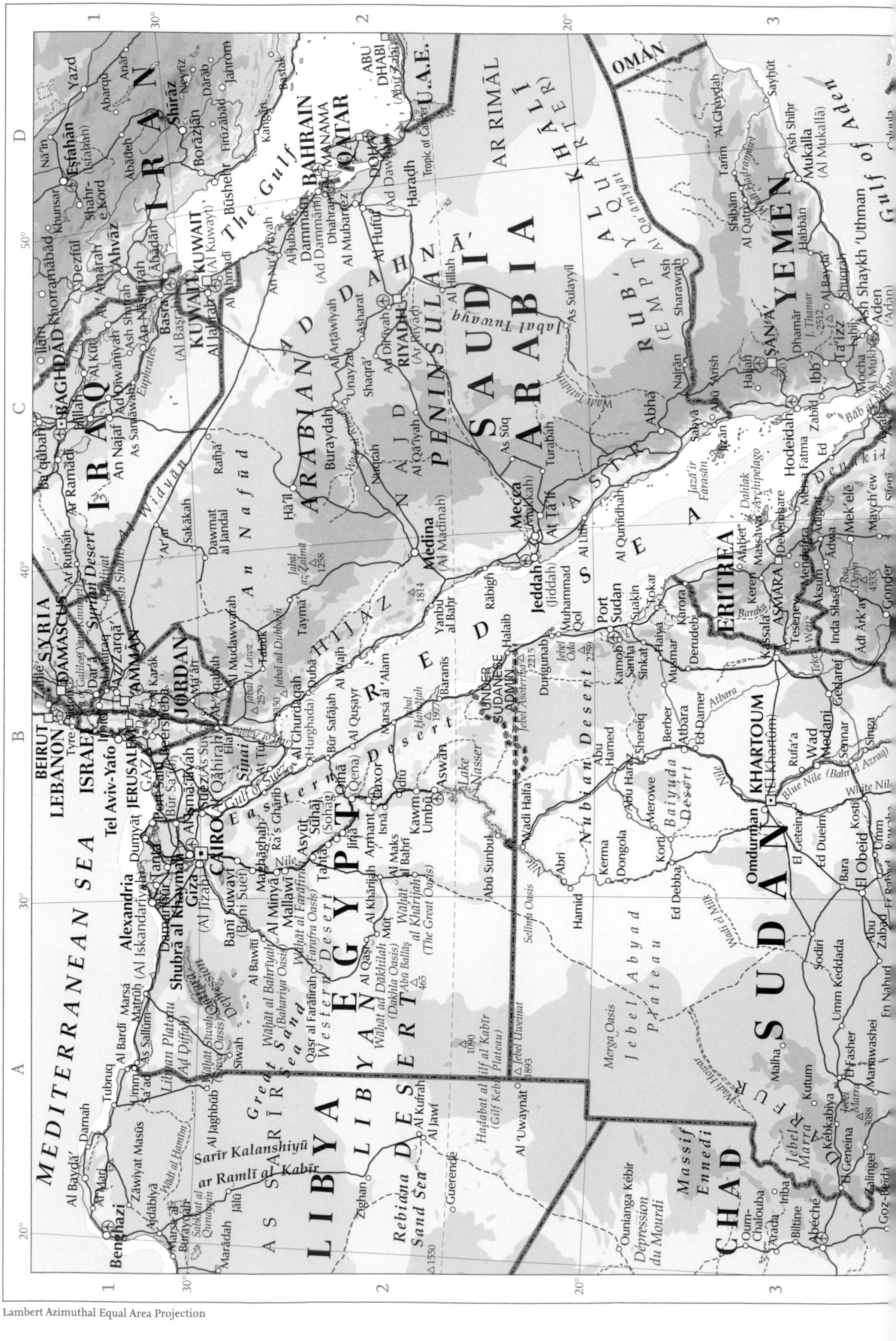

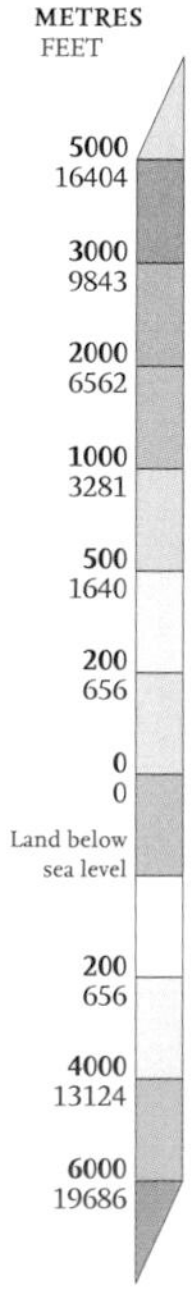

METRES	FEET
5000	16404
3000	9843
2000	6562
1000	3281
500	1640
200	656
0	0
Land below sea level	
200	656
4000	13124
6000	19686

MEDITERRANEAN SEA
LIBYA
EGYPT
SUDAN
CHAD
ERITREA
SAUDI ARABIA
YEMEN
IRAQ
IRAN
JORDAN
SYRIA
LEBANON
ISRAEL
KUWAIT
BAHRAIN
QATAR
U.A.E.
OMAN
RED SEA
Gulf of Aden
The Gulf
ARABIAN PENINSULA
RUB' AL KHĀLĪ (EMPTY QUARTER)
LIBYAN DESERT
Nubian Desert
CAIRO
KHARTOUM
RIYADH
BAGHDĀD
DAMASCUS
BEIRUT
AMMĀN
JERUSALEM
ASMARA
ŞAN'Ā'

Lambert Azimuthal Equal Area Projection

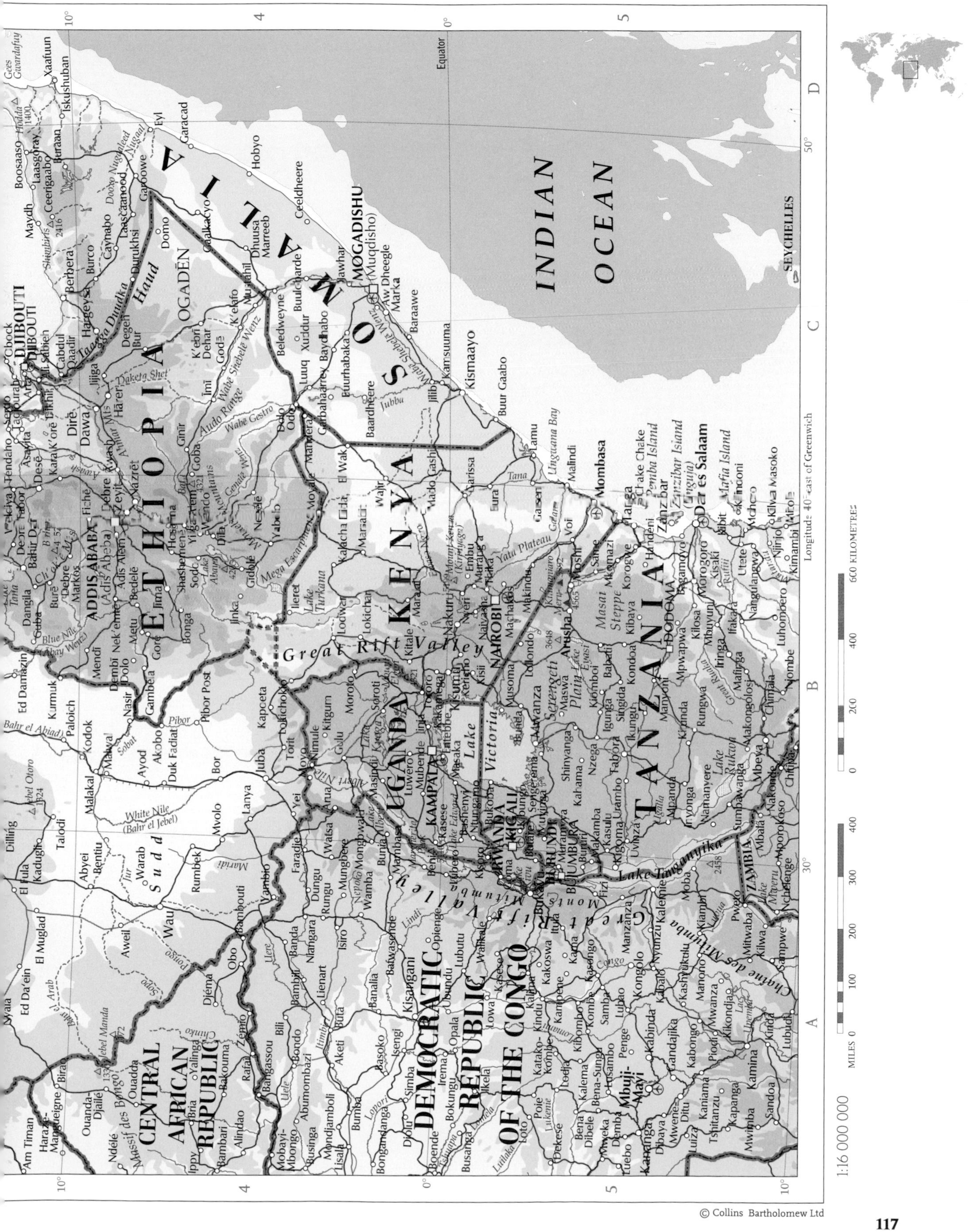

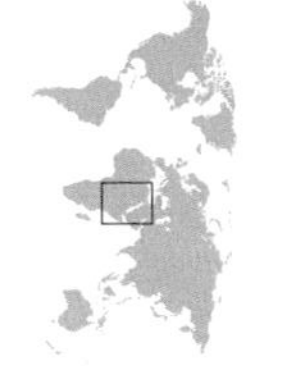

ETHIOPIA
SOMALIA
KENYA
UGANDA
TANZANIA
DEMOCRATIC REPUBLIC OF THE CONGO
CENTRAL AFRICAN REPUBLIC
RWANDA
BURUNDI
DJIBOUTI
ZAMBIA
INDIAN OCEAN
SEYCHELLES

Longitude 40° east of Greenwich

1:16 000 000

MILES 0 100 200 300 400

0 200 400 600 KILOMETRES

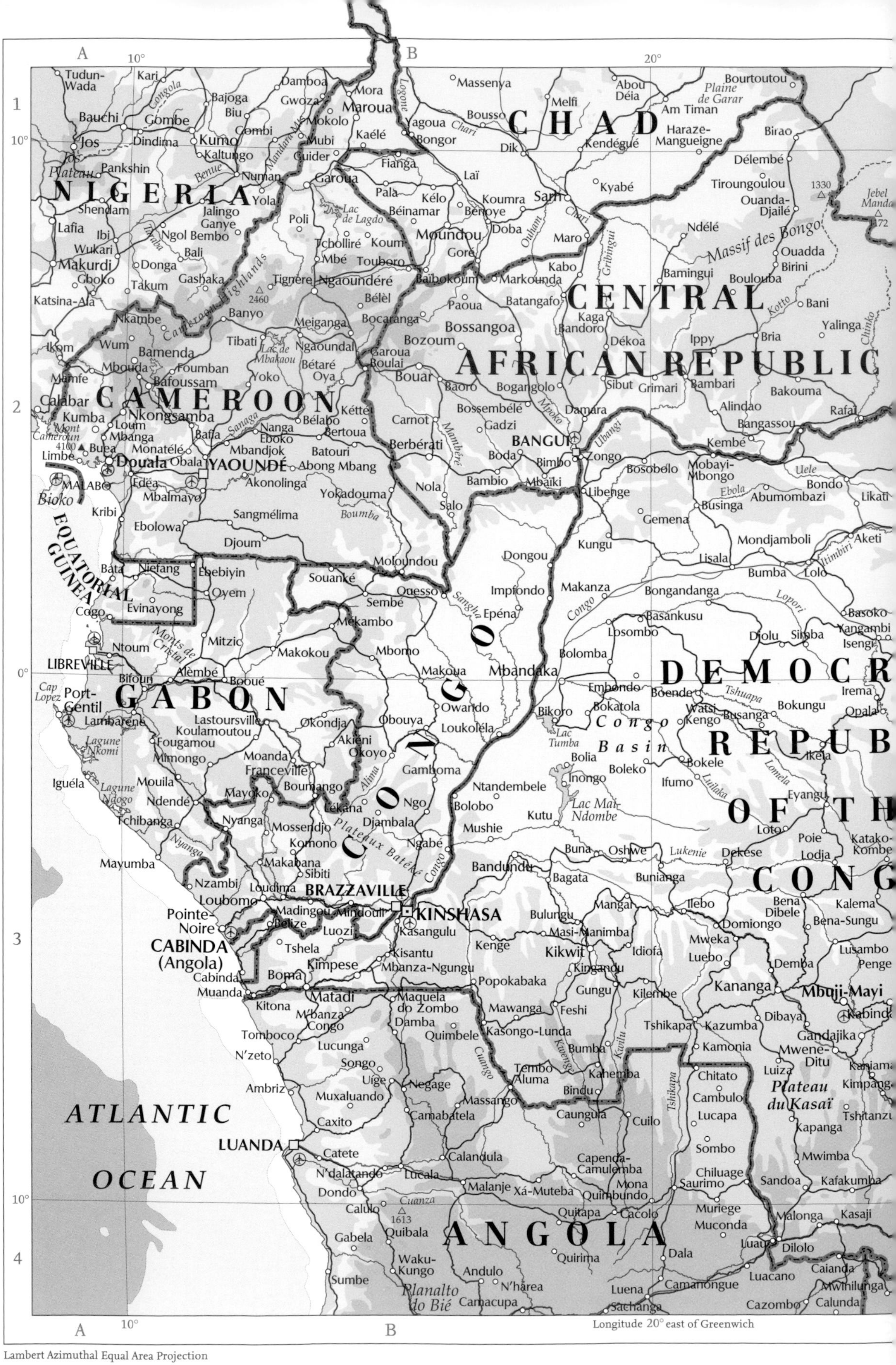

CENTRAL AFRICA

A 10° B 20°

1 2 3 4

10° 0° 10°

NIGERIA
Tudun-Wada
Kari
Bauchi
Gombe
Jos
Dindima
Kumo
Jos Plateau
Pankshin
Kaltungo
Shendam
Lafia
Ibi
Wukari
Makurdi
Gboko
Katsina-Ala
Donga
Takum
Jalingo
Ganye
Ngol Bembo
Bali
Gashaka
Yola
Numan
Bajoga
Biu
Gombi
Damboa
Gwoza
Mokolo
Mubi
Guider
Mandara Mts
Benue
Congola
Taraba
Calabar
Ikom
Mamfe

CAMEROON
Mora
Maroua
Kaélé
Garoua
Lac de Lagdo
Poli
Tchollíré
Mbé
Touboro
Tignère
Ngaoundéré
2460
Cameroon Highlands
Banyo
Tibati
Lac de Mbakaou
Meiganga
Ngaoundal
Bétaré Oya
Yoko
Nkambe
Wum
Bamenda
Mbouda
Foumban
Bafoussam
Kumba
Nkongsamba
Mont Cameroun 4100
Buea
Loum
Mbanga
Limbe
Douala
Monatélé
Bafia
Sanaga
Obala
YAOUNDÉ
Nanga Eboko
Mbandjok
Bélabo
Bertoua
Batouri
Abong Mbang
Akonolinga
Edéa
Mbalmayo
Kribi
Ebolowa
Sangmélima
Djoum
Yokadouma
Boumba
Moloundou
Kétté
Fianga
Pala
Kélo
Béinamar
Koum
Moundou

CHAD
Massenya
Bousso
Chari
Logone
Yagoua
Bongor
Dik
Laï
Koumra
Sarh
Doba
Gore
Baïbokoum
Markounda
Bénoye
Melfi
Abou Déia
Am Timan
Kendégué
Haraze-Mangueigne
Bourtoutou
Plaine de Garar
Kyabé
Ouham
Maro
Kabo
Gribingui

CENTRAL AFRICAN REPUBLIC
Birao
Délembé
Tiroungoulou
Ouanda-Djailé
1330
Jebel Manda
Ndélé
Massif des Bongo
Ouadda
Birini
Bamingui
Bouloba
Kotto
Bani
Yalinga
Chinko
Batangafo
Kaga Bandoro
Paoua
Bocaranga
Bossangoa
Bozoum
Dékoa
Ippy
Bria
Garoua Boulai
Bouar
Baoro
Bogangolo
Sibut
Grimari
Bambari
Bakouma
Bossembélé
Damara
Mpoko
Alindao
Bangassou
Rafai
Carnot
Gadzi
Mambéré
Berbérati
BANGUI
Ubangi
Kembé
Boda
Bimbo
Zongo
Bambio
Mbaïki
Nola
Salo
Mobayi-Mbongo
Bosobolo
Libenge
Uele
Bondo
Ebola
Abumombazi
Likati
Businga
Gemena
Kungu
Mondjamboli
Aketi
Itimbiri
Lisala
Bumba
Lolo

EQUATORIAL GUINEA
MALABO
Bioko
Bata
Niefang
Evinayong
Cogo

GABON
Ebebiyin
Oyem
Souanké
Mitzic
Monts de Cristal
Ntoum
LIBREVILLE
Bifoun
Alèmbé
Booué
Makokou
Cap Lopez
Port-Gentil
Lambaréné
Lastoursville
Koulamoutou
Fougamou
Lagune Nkomi
Mimongo
Moanda
Franceville
Okondja
Iguéla
Lagune Ndogo
Mouila
Ndendé
Tchibanga
Mayoko
Nyanga
Mayumba
Boumango

CONGO
Sembé
Ouesso
Mékambo
Mbomo
Sangha
Epéna
Impfondo
Dongou
Makoua
Owando
Obouya
Loukoléla
Akiéni
Okoyo
Alima
Gamboma
Léкana
Ngo
Djambala
Plateaux Batéké
Mossendjo
Komono
Ngabé
Makabana
Sibiti
Nzambi
Loudima
Loubomo
BRAZZAVILLE
Pointe-Noire
Madingou
Mindouli
Belize
Luozi

CABINDA (Angola)
Cabinda

DEMOCRATIC REPUBLIC OF THE CONGO
Makanza
Congo
Bongandanga
Lopori
Basankusu
Basoko
Yangambi
Isengi
Djolu
Simba
Losombo
Bolomba
Mbandaka
Embondo
Boende
Tshuapa
Bokungu
Irema
Opala
Bikoro
Bokatola
Watsi Kengo
Busanga
Lac Tumba
Congo Basin
Bolia
Inongo
Boleko
Bokele
Ifumo
Lomela
Ikela
Luilaka
Ntandembele
Lac Mai-Ndombe
Kutu
Bolobo
Mushie
Eyangu
Loto
Poie
Lodja
Katako-Kombe
Dekese
Lukenie
Buna
Oshwe
Bandundu
Bagata
Buniangu
Ilebo
Mangai
Bena Dibele
Kalema
Bena-Sungu
Domiongo
KINSHASA
Kasangulu
Bulungu
Masi-Manimba
Mweka
Luebo
Lusambo
Penge
Idiofa
Kenge
Kikwit
Kingandu
Demba
Kananga
Mbuji-Mayi
Kabinda
Gungu
Kilembe
Popokabaka
Feshi
Mawanga
Kasongo-Lunda
Tshikapa
Kazumba
Dibaya
Gandajika
Mwene-Ditu
Kamonia
Kwango
Kwilu
Bumba
Tembo Aluma
Kahemba
Bindu
Tshikapa
Luiza
Kaniama
Kimpanga
Plateau du Kasaï
Tshitanzu
Tshela
Kisantu
Kimpese
Mbanza-Ngungu
Boma
Muanda
Matadi
Kitona

ANGOLA
Maquela do Zombo
Damba
Quimbele
Cuango
M'banza Congo
Tomboco
Lucunga
N'zeto
Songo
Uíge
Negage
Ambriz
Muxaluando
Massango
Camabatela
Caxito
LUANDA
Catete
Calandula
N'dalatando
Lucala
Malanje
Xá-Muteba
Capenda-Camulemba
Mona Quimbundo
Caungula
Cuilo
Chitato
Cambulo
Lucapa
Sombo
Chiluage
Saurimo
Sandoa
Kapanga
Mwimba
Kafakumba
Dondo
Cuanza
1613
Calulo
Quitapa
Cacolo
Muriege
Muconda
Malonga
Kasaji
Gabela
Quibala
Quirima
Dala
Luau
Dilolo
Waku-Kungo
Sumbe
Andulo
N'harea
Planalto do Bié
Camacupa
Luena
Sachanga
Camanongue
Luacano
Caianda
Mwinilunga
Cazombo
Calunda

ATLANTIC OCEAN

METRES
FEET
5000 16404
3000 9843
2000 6562
1000 3281
500 1640
200 656
0 0
Land below sea level
200 656
4000 13124
6000 19686

Longitude 20° east of Greenwich

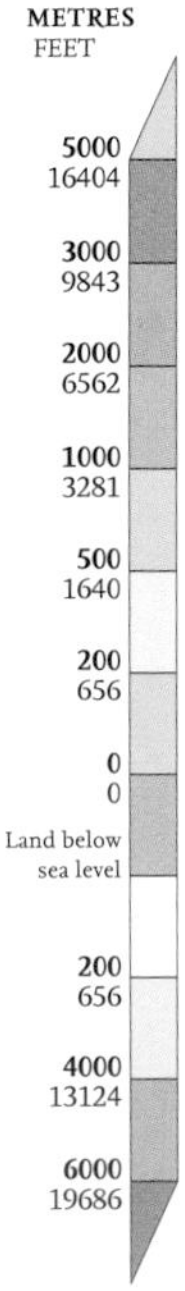

Lambert Azimuthal Equal Area Projection

SUDAN
ETHIOPIA
UGANDA
KENYA
TANZANIA
ZAMBIA
RWANDA
BURUNDI
MALAWI
MOZAMBIQUE
SOMALIA
ADDIS ABABA
NAIROBI
KAMPALA
KIGALI
BUJUMBURA
DODOMA
Lake Victoria
Lake Turkana
Lake Tanganyika
Lake Nyasa
Lake Rukwa
Lake Albert
Lake Edward
Lake Kivu
Lake Mweru
Great Rift Valley
Serengeti Plain
Masai Steppe
Juba
Malakal
Wau
Mombasa
Dar es Salaam
Zanzibar
Lubumbashi
Kisangani
Kinshasa
Arusha
Mwanza
Tabora
Kigoma
Mbeya
Kasama
Ndola
1:12 000 000
MILES 0 100 200 300
0 250 500 KILOMETRE

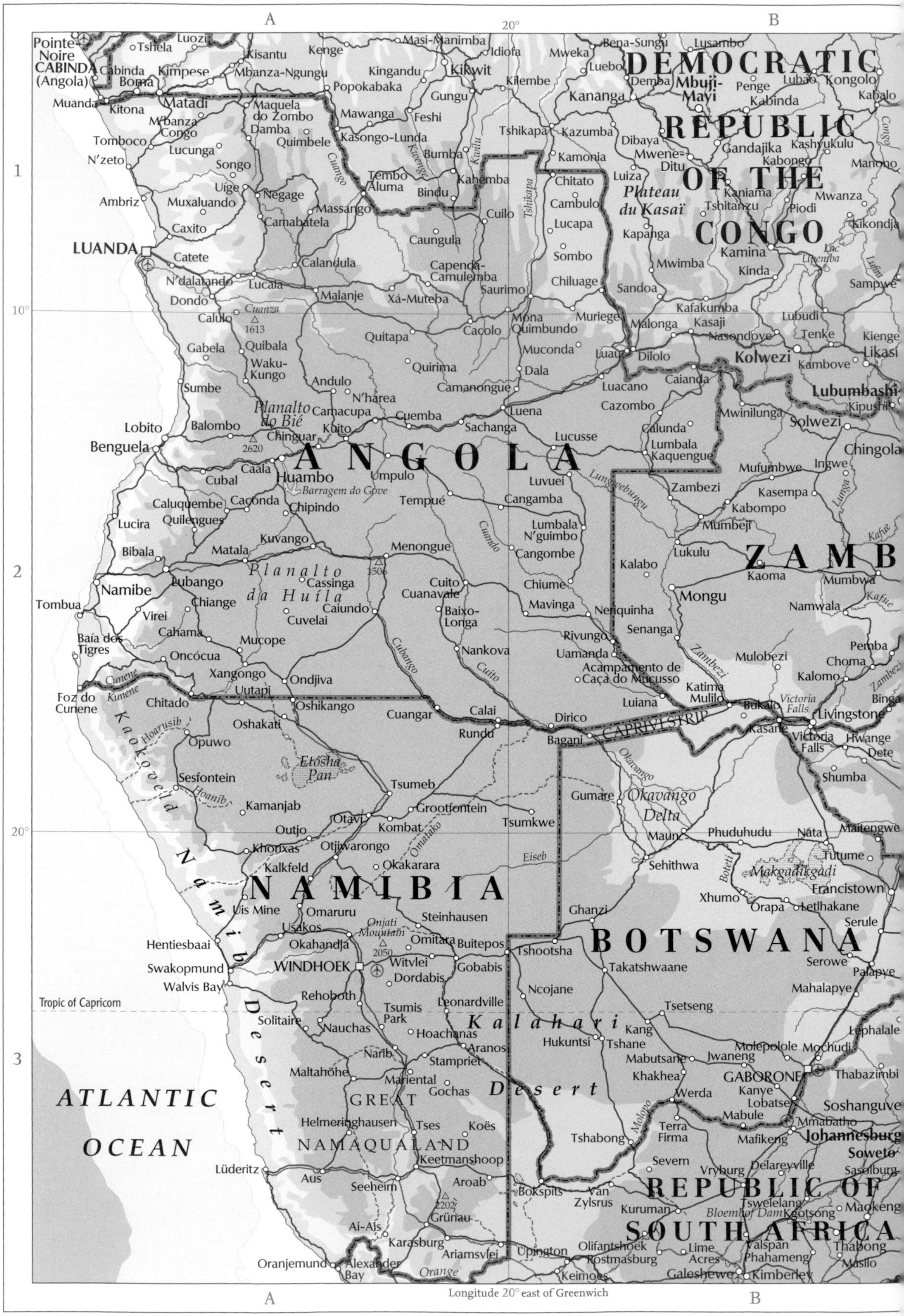

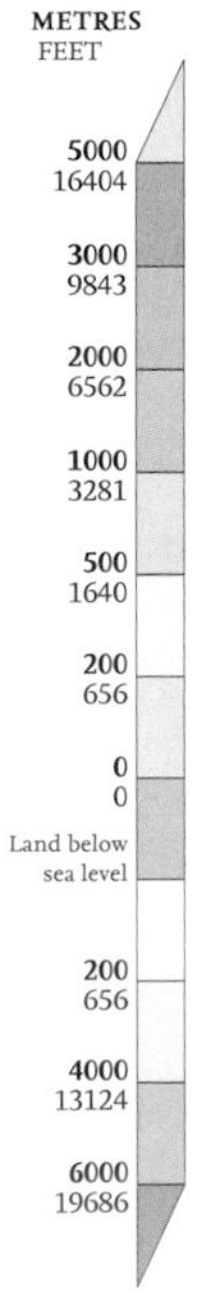

A 20° B

DEMOCRATIC REPUBLIC OF THE CONGO

ANGOLA

ZAMB

NAMIBIA

BOTSWANA

REPUBLIC OF SOUTH AFRICA

ATLANTIC OCEAN

LUANDA

WINDHOEK

GABORONE

Tropic of Capricorn

Namib Desert

Kalahari Desert

GREAT NAMAQUALAND

CAPRIVI STRIP

Okavango Delta

Etosha Pan

Makgadikgadi

Planalto do Bié

Planalto da Huíla

Plateau du Kasaï

METRES	FEET
5000	16404
3000	9843
2000	6562
1000	3281
500	1640
200	656
0	0
Land below sea level	
200	656
4000	13124
6000	19686

A Longitude 20° east of Greenwich B

Lambert Azimuthal Equal Area Projection

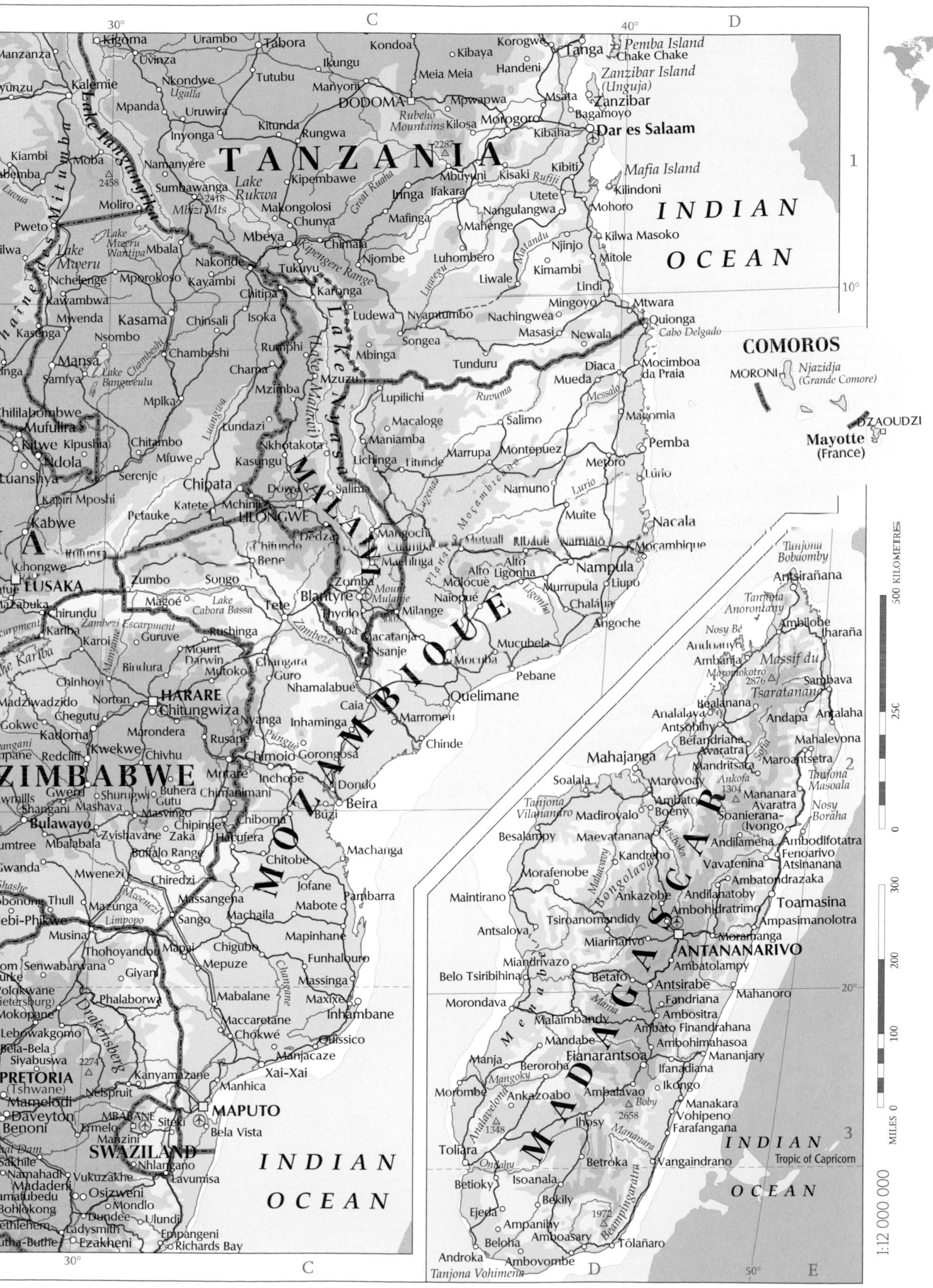

TANZANIA
MALAWI
MOZAMBIQUE
ZIMBABWE
MADAGASCAR
COMOROS
SWAZILAND
INDIAN OCEAN
INDIAN OCEAN
INDIAN OCEAN
DODOMA
Dar es Salaam
Zanzibar
Zanzibar Island (Unguja)
Pemba Island
Mafia Island
Tanga
Chake Chake
Bagamoyo
Morogoro
Kigoma
Tabora
Urambo
Kondoa
Kibaya
Korogwe
Handeni
Mpwapwa
Kilosa
Rubeho Mountains
Iringa
Mbeya
Mbala
Sumbawanga
Lake Rukwa
Lake Tanganyika
Lake Mweru
Lake Bangweulu
Kasama
Mansa
Samfya
Nakonde
Chinsali
Karonga
Chitipa
Rumphi
Mzuzu
Lake Nyasa (Lake Malawi)
Songea
Tunduru
Mbinga
Lindi
Mtwara
Newala
Masasi
Quionga
Cabo Delgado
Mocimboa da Praia
Mueda
Macomia
Pemba
Metoro
Lúrio
Nacala
Moçambique
Nampula
Angoche
Quelimane
Pebane
Chinde
Marromeu
Caia
Beira
Dondo
Búzi
Machanga
Inhambane
Maxixe
Massinga
Quissico
Xai-Xai
Manjacaze
MAPUTO
Manhica
Bela Vista
MBABANE
Manzini
Siteki
Nhlangano
LILONGWE
Dedza
Zomba
Blantyre
Mulanje
Mangochi
Salima
Nkhotakota
Kasungu
Mzimba
Lichinga
Cuamba
Tete
Lake Cabora Bassa
Zambeze
Zumbo
Songo
LUSAKA
Kafue
Chirundu
Kariba
Lake Kariba
Kabwe
Ndola
Kitwe
Mufulira
Chililabombwe
Luanshya
Kapiri Mposhi
Serenje
Chipata
Petauke
Katete
HARARE
Chitungwiza
Marondera
Mutare
Rusape
Chimanimani
Chimoio
Gorongosa
Kwekwe
Kadoma
Gweru
Masvingo
Bulawayo
Gwanda
Beitbridge
Musina
Thohoyandou
Polokwane (Pietersburg)
Mokopane
PRETORIA (Tshwane)
Mamelodi
Daveyton
Benoni
Nelspruit
Ermelo
Vukuzakhe
Ladysmith
Dundee
Ulundi
Empangeni
Richards Bay
Drakensberg
Limpopo
MORONI
Njazidja (Grande Comore)
DZAOUDZI
Mayotte (France)
ANTANANARIVO
Antsirañana
Ambilobe
Sambava
Antalaha
Iharaña
Mahajanga
Toamasina
Moramanga
Antsirabe
Ambositra
Fianarantsoa
Mananjary
Manakara
Farafangana
Vangaindrano
Tôlañaro
Ambovombe
Toliara
Morondava
Maintirano
Morombe
Ihosy
Massif du Tsaratanana
Tropic of Capricorn
1:12 000 000
KILOMETRES
MILES

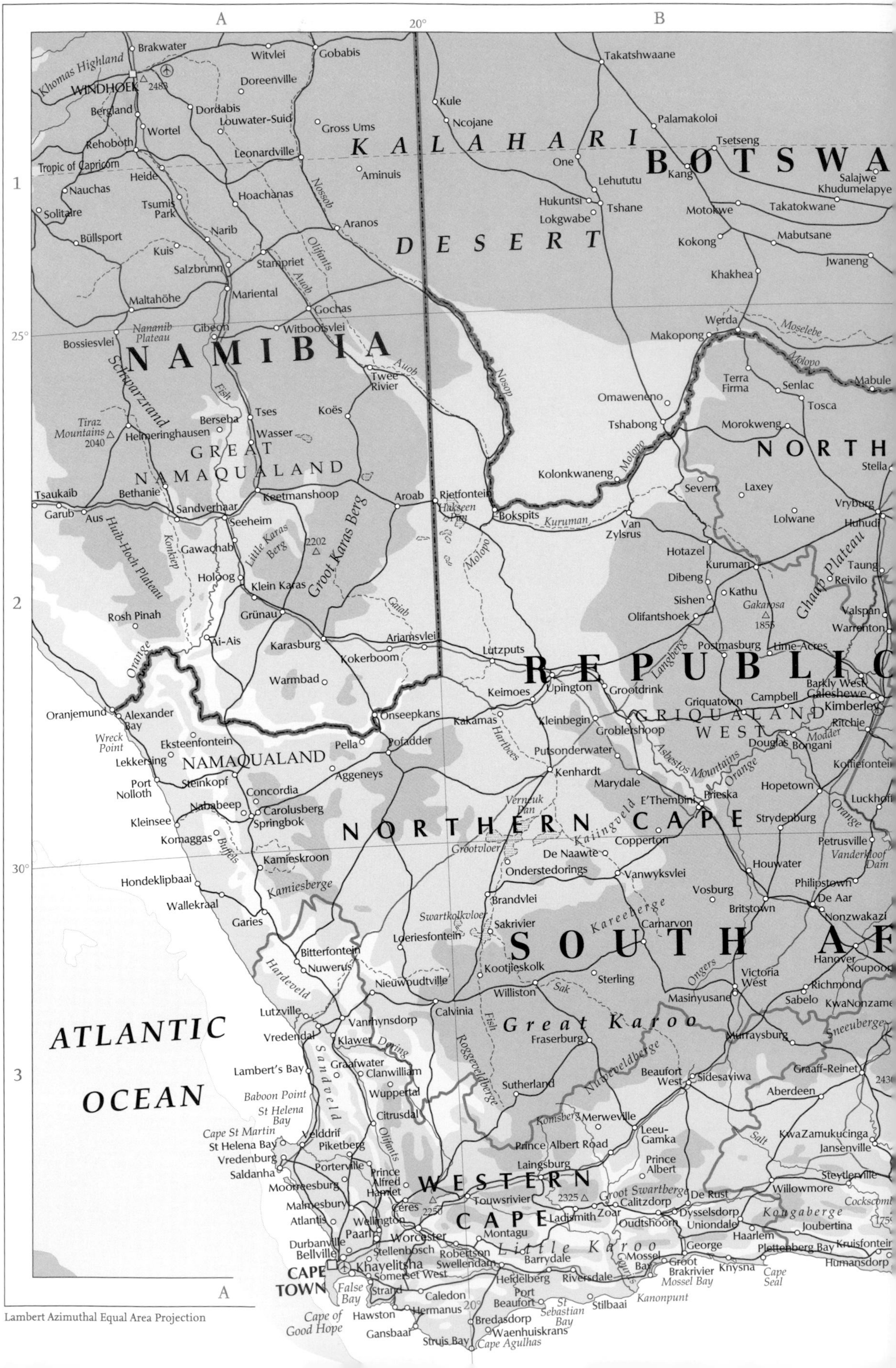

A B 20°

Brakwater Witvlei Gobabis Takatshwaane
Khomas Highland WINDHOEK 2483 Doreenville
Kule Ncojane
Bergland Dordabis Louwater-Suid Gross Ums Palamakoloi
Wortel
Rehoboth KALAHARI Tsetseng
Leonardville One BOTSWA
Tropic of Capricorn Aminuis Kang Salajwe Khudumelapye
Heide Lehututu
1 Nauchas Hoachanas Nossob Hukuntsi Tshane Motokwe Takatokwane
Solitaire Tsumis Park Lokgwabe
Narib Aranos Mabutsane
Büllsport Olifants DESERT Kokong
Kuis Stampriet Jwaneng
Salzbrunn Auob Khakhea
Maltahöhe Mariental
Gochas Werda
Nananib Plateau Gibeon Witbooisvlei Moselebe
25° Bossiesvlei Makopong
NAMIBIA Molopo
Schwarzrand Auob Twee Rivier Nosop Terra Firma Senlac Mabule
Fish Tosca
Tses Koës Omawenenao
Tiraz Mountains 2040 Helmeringhausen Berseba Wasser Tshabong Morokweng
GREAT NORTH
NAMAQUALAND Stella
Kolonkwaneng Molopo
Tsaukaib Bethanie Keetmanshoop Aroab Rietfontein Severn Laxey
Garub Aus Sandverhaar Hakseen Pan Bokspits Vryburg
Seeheim Groot Karas Berg Kuruman Van Zylsrus Lolwane Huhudi
Huib-Hoch Plateau Little Karas Berg 2202
Konkiep Gawachab Hotazel Ghaap Plateau
Molopo Kuruman Taung
Holoog Klein Karas Dibeng Kathu Reivilo
2 Sishen Gakarosa
Grünau Gaiab Olifantshoek 1855 Valspan
Rosh Pinah Warrenton
Ai-Ais Karasburg Ariamsvlei Postmasburg Lime-Acres
Orange Kokerboom Lutzputs REPUBLIC
Langberg Barkly West
Warmbad Keimoes Upington Grootdrink Galeshewe
Oranjemund Alexander Bay Griquatown Campbell Kimberley
Onseepkans Kakamas Kleinbegin GRIQUALAND Ritchie
Wreck Point WEST
Eksteenfontein Pella Pofadder Groblershoop Douglas Modder
Lekkersing Hartbees Bongani
NAMAQUALAND Putsonderwater Asbestos Mountains Koffiefontein
Port Nolloth Steinkopf Aggeneys Kenhardt Orange
Marydale Hopetown
Concordia Verneuk Pan E'Thembini Prieska Luckhoff
Kleinsee Nababeep Carolusberg NORTHERN CAPE
Springbok Kaiingveld Strydenburg Orange
Komaggas Buffels Grootvloer Copperton Petrusville
De Naawte Vanderkloof Dam
30° Kamieskroon Onderstedorings Houwater
Hondeklipbaai Vanwyksvlei Philipstown
Kamiesberge Brandvlei Vosburg De Aar
Wallekraal Britstown
Garies Swartkolkvloer Kareeberge Nonzwakazi
Sakrivier Carnarvon
Loeriesfontein SOUTH AF
Bitterfontein Hanover
Hardeveld Nuwerus Kootjieskolk Noupoort
Sterling Ongers Victoria West
Nieuwoudtville Williston Sak Richmond
Masinyusane Sabelo KwaNonzame
ATLANTIC Lutzville Calvinia Fish Great Karoo
Vredendal Vanrhynsdorp Sneeuberge
OCEAN Klawer Doring Fraserburg Murraysburg
3 Sandveld Graafwater Nuweveldberge
Lambert's Bay Clanwilliam Roggeveldberge Beaufort West Sidesaviwa Graaff-Reinet
Baboon Point Sutherland 2430
Wuppertal Aberdeen
St Helena Bay Citrusdal
Cape St Martin Velddrif Olifants Komsberg Merweville Leeu-Gamka
St Helena Bay Piketberg Salt KwaZamukucinga
Vredenburg Prince Albert Road Jansenville
Saldanha Porterville Laingsburg Prince Albert
Prince Alfred Hamlet Steytlerville
Moorreesburg WESTERN Willowmore
Malmesbury Ceres Touwsrivier 2325 Groot Swartberge De Rust Cockscomb
Atlantis Wellington 2250 CAPE Ladismith Zoar Calitzdorp Kouga Berge
Paarl Worcester Oudtshoorn Dysselsdorp Uniondale Joubertina 1758
Durbanville Montagu Haarlem
Bellville Stellenbosch Robertson Little Karoo Kruisfontein
CAPE TOWN Khayelitsha Swellendam Barrydale George Plettenberg Bay Humansdorp
Somerset West Gouritz Mossel Bay Groot Brakrivier Knysna Cape Seal
False Bay Strand Heidelberg Riversdale Mossel Bay
Cape of Good Hope Hawston Caledon Port Beaufort St Sebastian Bay Stilbaai Kanonpunt
Hermanus 20°
Gansbaai Bredasdorp
Waenhuiskrans
Struis Bay Cape Agulhas

METRES FEET
5000 16404
3000 9843
2000 6562
1000 3281
500 1640
200 656
0 0
Land below sea level
200 656
4000 13124
6000 19686

Lambert Azimuthal Equal Area Projection

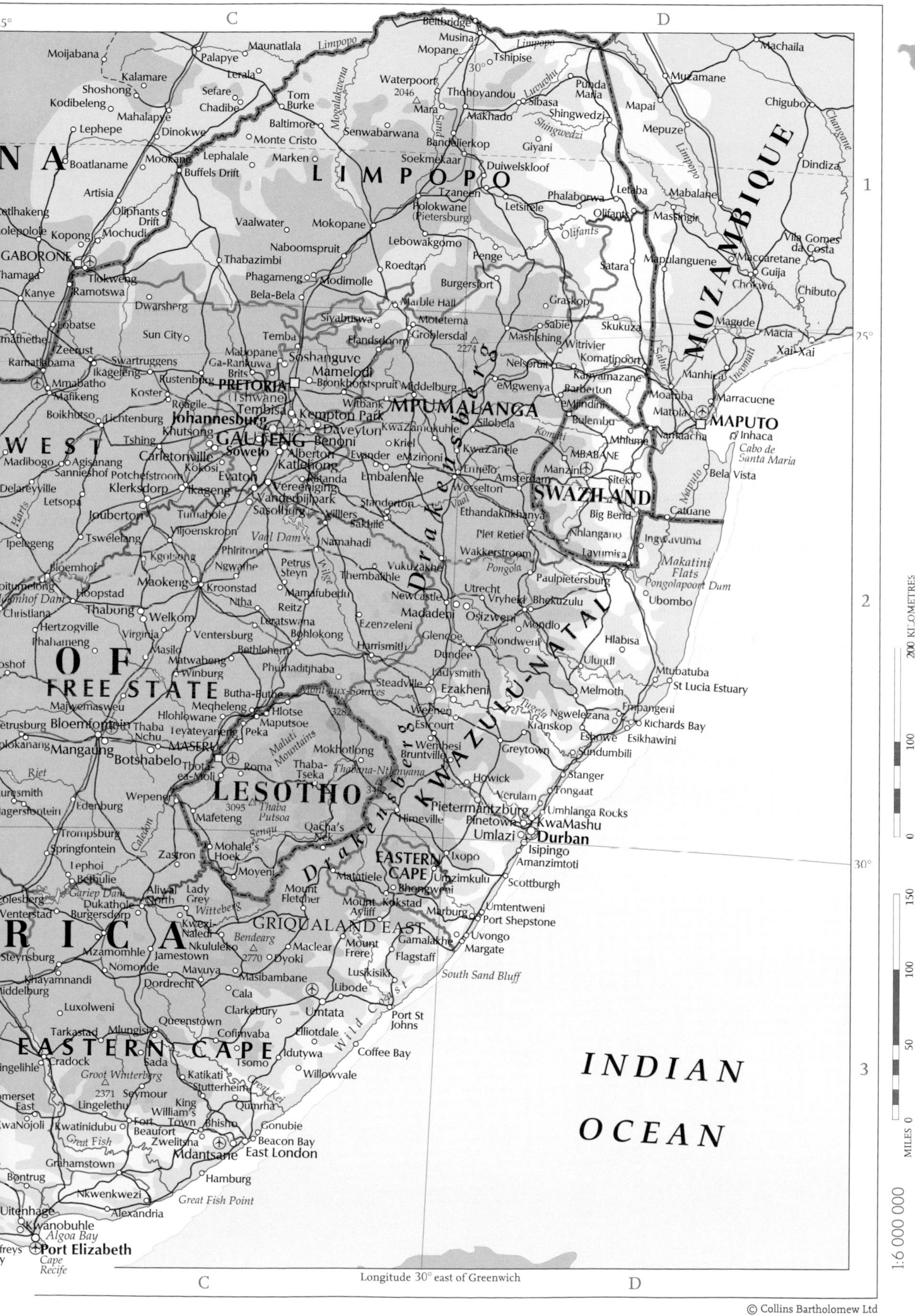
C
D
25°
30°
1
2
3
LIMPOPO
MOZAMBIQUE
MPUMALANGA
GAUTENG
KWAZULU-NATAL
SWAZILAND
LESOTHO
FREE STATE
EASTERN CAPE
GRIQUALAND EAST
INDIAN OCEAN
Drakensberg
Beitbridge
Musina
Mopane
Tshipise
Waterpoort
Thohoyandou
Makhado
Punda Maria
Sibasa
Shingwedzi
Giyani
Polokwane (Pietersburg)
Tzaneen
Phalaborwa
Mokopane
Lebowakgomo
Thabazimbi
Modimolle
Bela-Bela
Burgersfort
Graskop
Sabie
Nelspruit
Mbombela
Komatipoort
Barberton
Witbank
Middelburg
Groblersdal
Marble Hall
Skukuza
Maputo
Matola
Inhaca
Cabo de Santa Maria
Bela Vista
Marracuene
Manhiça
Xai-Xai
Macia
Chokwé
Guija
Chibuto
Chigubo
Mapai
Machaila
Massingir
Mapulanguene
Gaborone
Mochudi
Kanye
Lobatse
Ramotswa
Mahalapye
Palapye
Mmabatho
Mafikeng
Zeerust
Rustenburg
Brits
PRETORIA (Tshwane)
Soshanguve
Mamelodi
Johannesburg
Soweto
Kempton Park
Benoni
Daveyton
Alberton
Katlehong
Vereeniging
Vanderbijlpark
Sasolburg
Klerksdorp
Potchefstroom
Carletonville
Lichtenburg
Welkom
Kroonstad
Virginia
Bethlehem
Harrismith
Bloemfontein
Mangaung
Botshabelo
Thaba Nchu
MASERU
Roma
Mafeteng
Mohale's Hoek
Qacha's Nek
Thaba Putsoa
Thabana-Ntlenyana
Maluti Mountains
Mbabane
Manzini
Siteki
Big Bend
Nhlangano
Piet Retief
Ermelo
Standerton
Volksrust
Newcastle
Madadeni
Osizweni
Vryheid
Ulundi
Dundee
Ladysmith
Estcourt
Pietermaritzburg
Howick
Durban
KwaMashu
Umlazi
Pinetown
Umhlanga Rocks
Amanzimtoti
Scottburgh
Port Shepstone
Margate
Richards Bay
Empangeni
Eshowe
Mtubatuba
St Lucia Estuary
Hlabisa
Ubombo
Pongolapoort Dam
Makatini Flats
Kokstad
Matatiele
Mount Fletcher
Flagstaff
Lusikisiki
Port St Johns
Umtata
Coffee Bay
Wild Coast
South Sand Bluff
Queenstown
Cradock
Dordrecht
Aliwal North
Burgersdorp
Colesberg
Middelburg
Graaff-Reinet
King William's Town
Bhisho
Mdantsane
East London
Beacon Bay
Gonubie
Hamburg
Grahamstown
Great Fish Point
Alexandria
Uitenhage
Kwanobuhle
Port Elizabeth
Algoa Bay
Cape Recife
Longitude 30° east of Greenwich

0 100 200 KILOMETRES
MILES 0 50 100 150
1:6 000 000

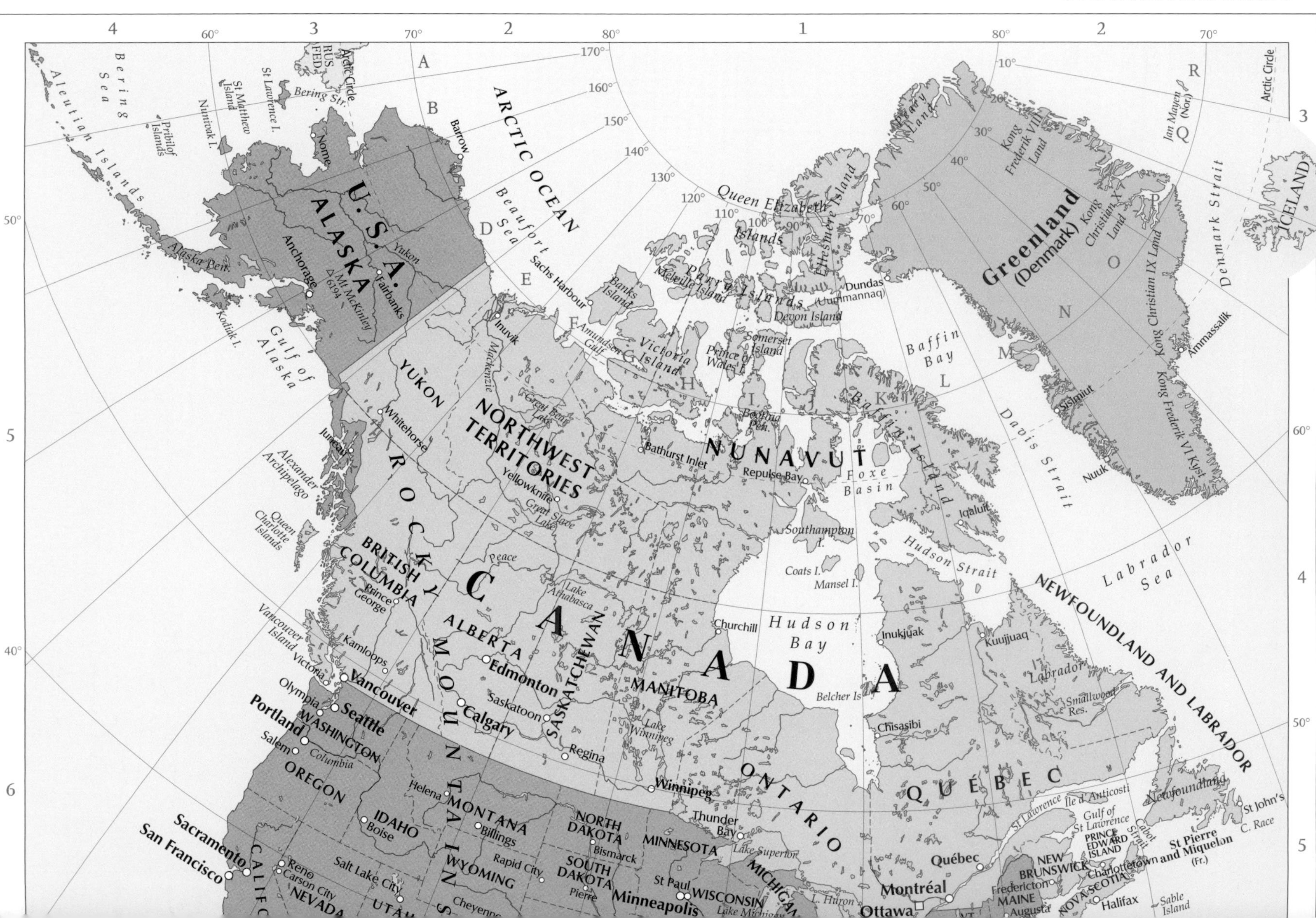

Bi-Polar Oblique Projection

UNITED STATES OF AMERICA
MEXICO
GULF OF MEXICO
ATLANTIC OCEAN
PACIFIC OCEAN
CARIBBEAN SEA
THE BAHAMAS
CUBA
HAITI
DOMINICAN REP.
JAMAICA
BELIZE
GUATEMALA
HONDURAS
EL SALVADOR
NICARAGUA
COSTA RICA
PANAMA
COLOMBIA
VENEZUELA
GUYANA
BRAZIL
ECUADOR
Bermuda (U.K.)
Tropic of Cancer
Equator
C. CONNECTICUT
DEL. DELAWARE
KEN. KENTUCKY
MASS. MASSACHUSETTS
MD. MARYLAND
MISS. MISSISSIPPI
N.H. NEW HAMPSHIRE
N.J. NEW JERSEY
R.I. RHODE ISLAND
VT. VERMONT
W.V. WEST VIRGINIA
Longitude 90° west of Greenwich
1:32 000 000
MILES 0 200 400 600 800
0 400 800 1200 KILOMETRES

ARCTIC OCEAN
BEAUFORT SEA
PACIFIC OCEAN
Gulf of Alaska
ALASKA
U.S.A.
CANADA
YUKON
NORTHWEST TERRITORIES
NUNA
BRITISH COLUMBIA
ALBERTA
SASKATCHEWAN
MANITOBA
WASHINGTON
OREGON
IDAHO
MONTANA
WYOMING
CALIFORNIA
NEVADA
N. DAKOTA
S. DAKOTA
NEBRASKA
MINNESOT
IOW
RUS. FED.
Bering Strait
Brooks Range
Kuskokwim Mountains
Alaska Range
Mackenzie Mountains
Selwyn Mountains
Cassiar Mountains
Coast Mountains
ROCKY MOUNTAINS
Caribou Mountains
Queen Elizabeth Islands
Parry Islands
Victoria Island
Banks Island
Melville Island
Great Bear Lake
Great Slave Lake
Lake Athabasca
Lake Winnipeg
Vancouver Island
Queen Charlotte Is
Alexander Archipelago
Alaska Peninsula
Kodiak Island
Nunivak Island
St Lawrence Island
Anchorage
Fairbanks
Juneau
Whitehorse
Dawson
Yellowknife
Inuvik
Edmonton
Calgary
Vancouver
Victoria
Seattle
Portland
Spokane
Boise
Regina
Saskatoon
Winnipeg
Sacramento
Reno
Salt Lake City
Helena
Billings
Bismarck
Minneapolis
Churchill
Resolute
METRES
FEET
5000 16404
3000 9843
2000 6562
1000 3281
500 1640
200 656
0 0
Land below sea level
200 656
4000 13124
6000 19686
A
B
C
D
E
F
3
4
165°
150°
135°
120°
105°
90°
75°
60°
45°
Longitude 105° west of Greenwich
Lambert Azimuthal Equal Area Projection

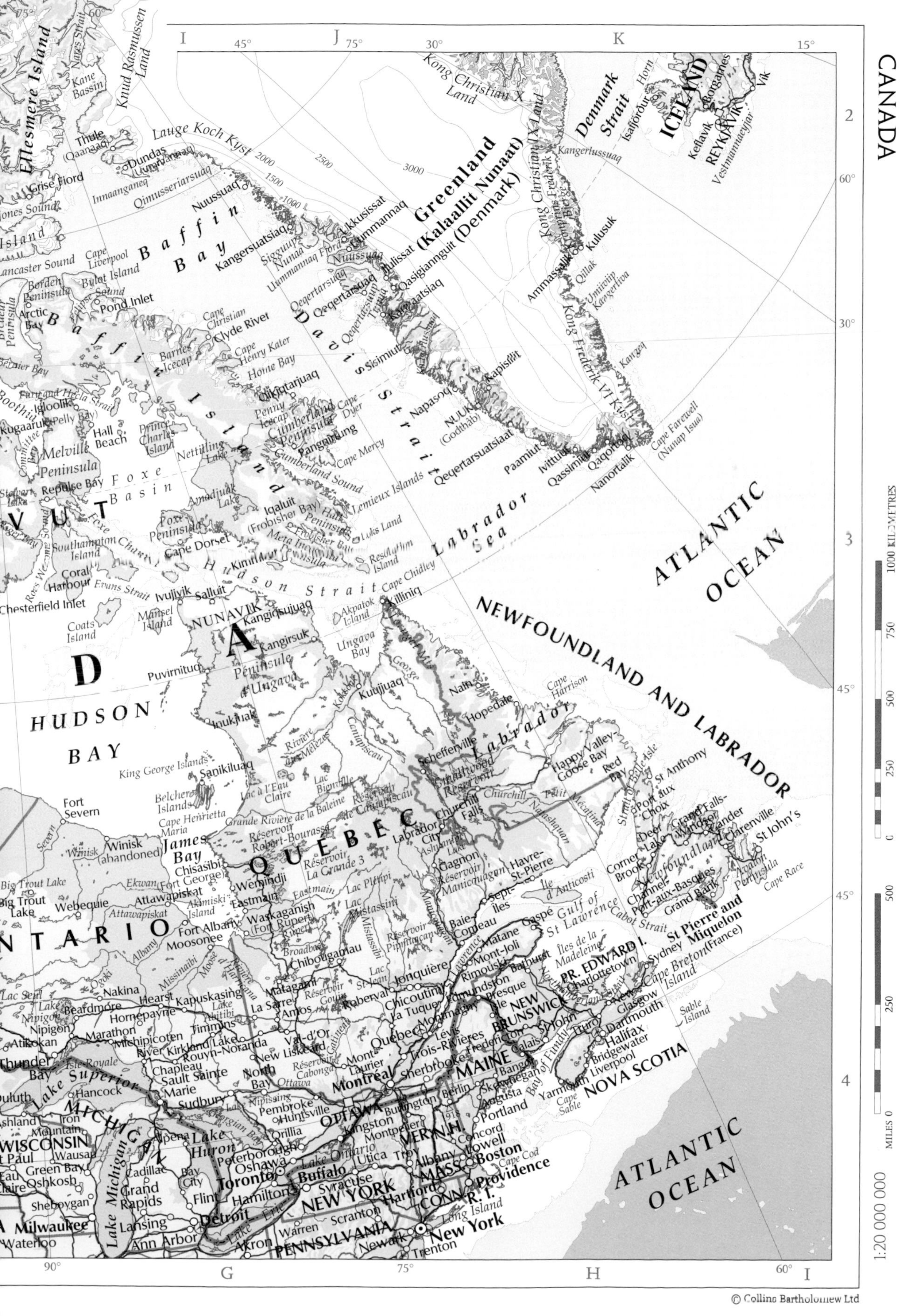
Greenland
(Kalaallit Nunaat)
(Denmark)
ICELAND
REYKJAVIK
Denmark Strait
Baffin Bay
Baffin Island
Davis Strait
Labrador Sea
ATLANTIC OCEAN
NEWFOUNDLAND AND LABRADOR
HUDSON BAY
Hudson Strait
Foxe Basin
Ungava Bay
James Bay
QUÉBEC
NUNAVIK
Péninsule d'Ungava
Labrador
Gulf of St Lawrence
NOVA SCOTIA
NEW BRUNSWICK
PR. EDWARD I.
MAINE
St Pierre and Miquelon (France)
ONTARIO
MICHIGAN
WISCONSIN
NEW YORK
PENNSYLVANIA
Lake Superior
Lake Huron
Lake Michigan
Lake Ontario
OTTAWA
Montreal
Québec
Toronto
Halifax
St John's
Boston
New York
Detroit
Buffalo
Ellesmere Island
Melville Peninsula
Southampton Island
Coats Island
Cumberland Peninsula
Iqaluit (Frobisher Bay)
NUUK (Godthåb)
Cape Farewell (Nunap Isua)
Kangerlussuaq
Sable Island
Cape Breton Island
Île d'Anticosti
Long Island
ATLANTIC OCEAN
1000 KILOMETRES
MILES 0
1:20 000 000

A
B
C
140°
130°
120°
1
2
3
60°
50°
METRES
FEET
5000
16404
3000
9843
2000
6562
1000
3281
500
1640
200
656
0
0
Land below sea level
200
656
4000
13124
6000
19686
YUKON
NORTHWEST TERR
BRITISH COLUMBIA
ALBERTA
ALASKA
U.S.A.
WASHINGTON
PACIFIC OCEAN
ROCKY MOUNTAINS
COAST MOUNTAINS
Mackenzie Mountains
Selwyn Mountains
Franklin Mountains
Pelly Mountains
Cassiar Mountains
Skeena Mountains
Cariboo Mts
Columbia Mts
Selkirk Mountains
Caribou Mountains
Birch Mountains
St Elias Mountains
Great Bear Lake
Great Slave Lake
McTavish Arm
Keith Arm
Norman Wells
(Fort Norman)
Tulita
Déline
Elsa
Mayo
Mount Patterson 2098
Stewart
Grey Hunter Peak 2214
Keele Peak 2972
Beaver Creek
Snag (abandoned)
Koidern
White
Yukon
Pelly
Carmacks
Faro
Fox Mountain 2404
Ross River
Kluane Lake
Aishihik Lake
Mount Logan 5959
Destruction Bay
Haines Junction
Whitehorse
Lake Laberge
Mount Skukum 2382
Jakes Corner
Johnson's Crossing
Carcross
Bennett
Teslin
Teslin Lake
Atlin
Atlin Lake
Tuchitua
Upper Liard
Watson Lake
Lower Post
Tungsten (abandoned)
Mount Sir James MacBrien 2762
North Nahanni
Nahanni Butte
Yakutat Bay
Yakutat
Klukwan
Mount Fairweather 4670
Haines
Skagway
Gustavus
Hoonah
Juneau
Douglas
Chichagof Island
Admiralty Island
Kruzof Island
Sitka
Angoon
Baranof Island
Alexander Archipelago
Frederick Sound
Kupreanof Island
Petersburg
Kate's Needle 3046
Wrangell
Port Alexander
Mount Pattullo 2739
Stewart
Klawock
Prince of Wales Island
Revillagigedo Island
Ketchikan
Dall Island
Dixon Entrance
Cassiar
Stikine Plateau
Taku
Telegraph Creek
Dease Lake
Hyland Post
Coal River
Toad River
Mount Roosevelt 2896
Mount Lloyd George 2972
Fort Nelson
Fort Liard
Prophet River
Ware
Williston Lake
Wonowon
Hudson's Hope
Fort St John
Taylor
Dawson Creek
Chetwynd
Mackenzie
Sentinel Peak 2515
Tumbler Ridge
Beaverlodge
Grande Prairie
Spirit River
Hazelton
New Hazelton
New Aiyansh
Kitwanga
Smithers
Prince Rupert
Port Edward
Masset
Graham Island
Queen Charlotte
Hecate Strait
Queen Charlotte Islands
Mount Moresby
Sewell Inlet
Moresby Island
Cape St James
Terrace
Kitimat
Telkwa
Houston
Granisle
Takla Landing
McLeod Lake
Pendleton Bay
Burns Lake
Fort St James
Vanderhoof
Fraser Lake
Ootsa Lake
Kemano (abandoned)
Hartley Bay
Prince George
Summit Lake
Dome Creek
Grande Cache
Fraser Plateau
Quesnel
Wells
McBride
Mount Robson 3954
Valemount
Jasper
Ocean Falls
Bella Bella
Bella Coola
Hagensborg
Williams Lake
Alexis Creek
Likely
Queen Charlotte Sound
Dawsons Landing
Kleena Kleene
Tatla Lake
Mount Waddington 4042
Dog Creek
100 Mile House
Blue River
Mica Creek
Clearwater
Barrière
Clinton
Cache Creek
Lillooet
Kamloops
Sicamous
Chase
Salmon Arm
Revelstoke
Golden
Vernon
Kelowna
Penticton
Merritt
Princeton
Keremeos
Osoyoos
Nakusp
New Denver
Slocan
Nelson
Castlegar
Trail
Rossland
Grand Forks
Salmo
Creston
Cranbrook
Kimberley
Fernie
Yahk
Invermere
Holberg
Cape Scott
Port Hardy
Port Alice
Port McNeill
Alert Bay
Kyuquot
Thompson Sound
Sayward
Tahsis
Gold River
Campbell River
Courtenay
Comox
Powell River
Pemberton
Whistler
Squamish
Vancouver Island
Tofino
Ucluelet
Alberni
Port Sechelt
Nanaimo
Vancouver
Mission
Hope
Chilliwack
Ladysmith
Lake Cowichan
North Cowichan
Duncan
Juan de Fuca Strait
Port Renfrew
Victoria
Cape Flattery
Port Angeles
Forks
Mount Olympus 2428
Mount Baker 3285
Bellingham
Mount Vernon
Port Townsend
Everett
Lynnwood
Seattle
Bremerton
Bellevue
Shelton
Tacoma
Aberdeen
Olympia
Wenatchee
Ephrata
Moses Lake
Okanogan
Grand Coulee
Colville
Spokane
Coeur d'Alene
Kellogg
Bonners Ferry
Sandpoint
Thompson Falls
Eureka
Libby
Kalispell
Whitefish
Polson
Browning
Fort Simpson
Jean Marie River
Fort Providence
Wrigley
Keller Lake
Blackwater Lake
Lac Grandin
Lac la Martre
Whatì
Behchokö
Yellowknife
Detah
Wekweètì (Snare Lakes)
Gamètì
Hardisty Lake
Hottah Lake
Point Lake
MacKay Lake
Hay River
Fort Resolution
Pine Point (abandoned)
Enterprise
Kakisa
Trout Lake
Fort Smith
Fitzgerald
Tathlina Lake
Bistcho Lake
Steen River
Zama City
Meander River
Chateh
John D'Or Prairie
Fox Lake
Lake Claire
High Level
Rainbow Lake
La Crete
Fort Vermilion
Keg River
Manning
Peerless Lake
Trout Lake
Fort Mackay
Fort McMurray
Cadotte Lake
Grimshaw
Peace River
Gift Lake
Fairview
Falher
McLennan
Wabasca-Desmarais
Sexsmith
High Prairie
Slave Lake
Lesser Slave Lake
Valleyview
Swan Hills
Fox Creek
Fort Assiniboine
Athabasca
Whitecourt
Barrhead
Westlock
Mayerthorpe
Edson
Hinton
Edmonton
Drayton Valley
Devon
Leduc
Camrose
Wetaskiwin
Rimbey
Lacombe
Ponoka
Nordegg
Rocky Mountain House
Red Deer
Olds
Stettler
Three Hills
Sundre
Drumheller
Airdrie
Cochrane
Calgary
Banff
Canmore
Lake Louise
Rogers Pass
Mount Assiniboine 3618
Mount Farnham 3457
Okotoks
High River
Strathmore
Bassano
Claresholm
Elkford
Lethbridge
Coaldale
Crowsnest Pass
Mount Cleveland 3184
Cardston
Pincher Creek
McDonald Peak 2993
Longitude 120° west of Greenwich

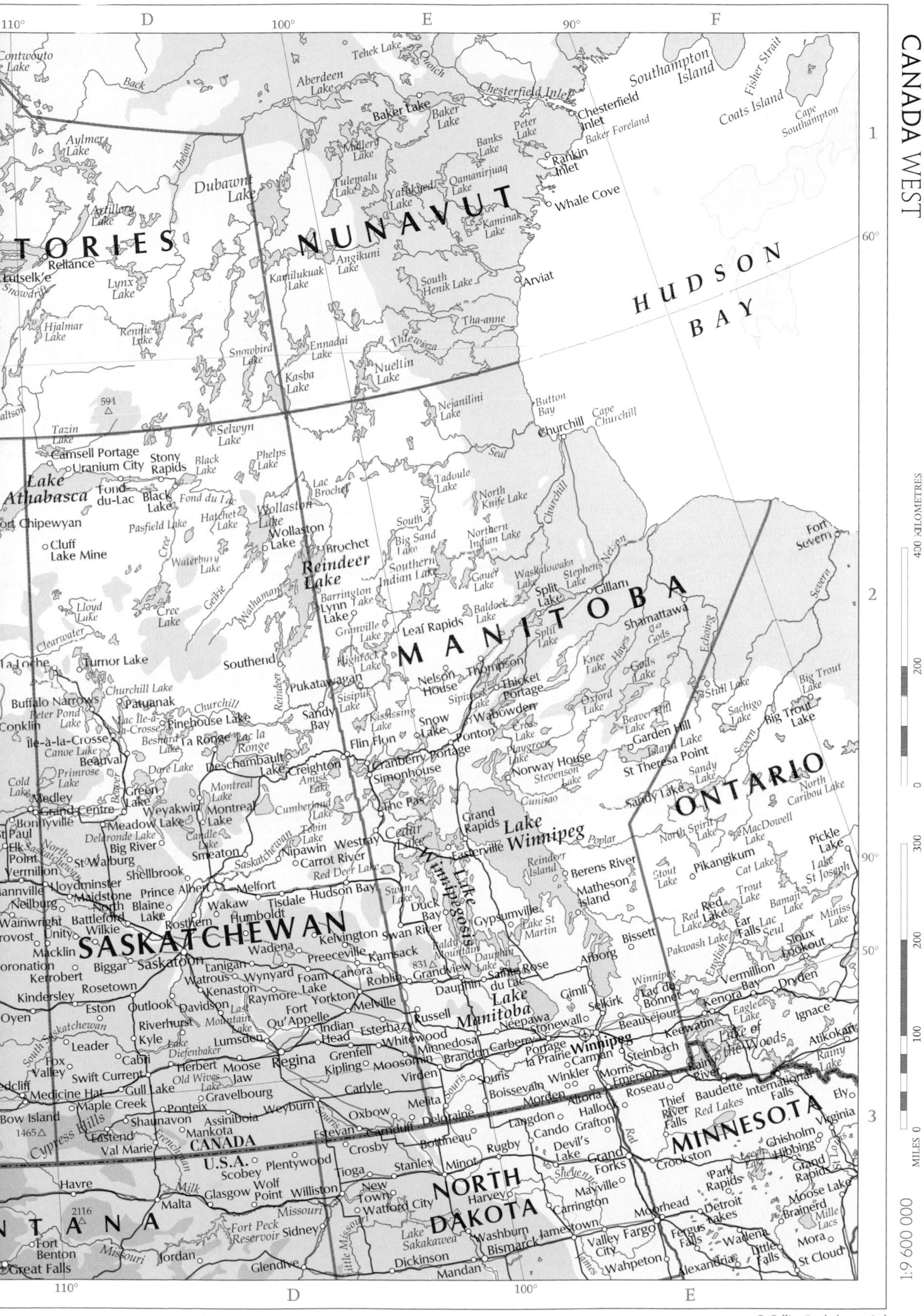
110°
D
100°
E
90°
F
Contwoyto Lake
Tehek Lake
Aberdeen Lake
Back
Chesterfield Inlet
Southampton Island
Fisher Strait
Coats Island
Cape Southampton
Baker Lake
Chesterfield Inlet
Baker Foreland
Aylmer Lake
Thelon
Peter Lake
Banks Lake
Rankin Inlet
Dubawnt Lake
Tulemalu Lake
Qamanirjuaq Lake
Whale Cove
Artillery Lake
NUNAVUT
Kaminak Lake
TORIES
Reliance
Lutselk'e
Snowdrift
Lynx Lake
Kamilukuak Lake
Angikuni Lake
South Henik Lake
Arviat
HUDSON
BAY
Hjalmar Lake
Rennie Lake
Tha-anne
Snowbird Lake
Ennadai Lake
Thlewiaza
Kasba Lake
Nueltin Lake
591
Tazin Lake
Selwyn Lake
Nejanilini Lake
Button Bay
Churchill
Cape Churchill
Seal
Camsell Portage
Uranium City
Stony Rapids
Black Lake
Phelps Lake
Lake Athabasca
Fond-du-Lac
Black Lake
Fond du Lac
Lac Brochet
Tadoule Lake
North Knife Lake
Hatchet Lake
Wollaston Lake
Fort Chipewyan
Pasfield Lake
Wollaston Lake
South Seal
Big Sand Lake
Northern Indian Lake
Churchill
Fort Severn
Cluff Lake Mine
Brochet
Reindeer Lake
Southern Indian Lake
Waterbury Lake
Cree
Geikie
Wathaman
Gauer Lake
Waskaiowaka Lake
Stephens Lake
Nelson
Barrington Lake
Lynn Lake
Split Lake
Gillam
MANITOBA
Lloyd Lake
Cree Lake
Baldock Lake
Shamattawa
Severn
Granville Lake
Leaf Rapids
Split Lake
Gods
Echoing
Clearwater
La Loche
Turnor Lake
Southend
Highrock Lake
Thompson
Hayes
Knee Lake
Gods Lake
Nelson House
Reindeer
Pukatawagan
Sipiwesk Lake
Thicket Portage
Oxford Lake
Stull Lake
Big Trout Lake
Churchill Lake
Buffalo Narrows
Patuanak
Churchill
Sisipuk Lake
Sandy Bay
Kississing Lake
Snow Lake
Wabowden
Beaver Hill Lake
Sachigo Lake
Big Trout Lake
Peter Pond Lake
Lac Île-à-la-Crosse
Pinehouse Lake
Conklin
Île-à-la-Crosse
La Ronge
Lac la Ronge
Flin Flon
Ponton
Cross Lake
Garden Hill
Island Lake
Canoe Lake
Beauval
Besnard Lake
Deschambault Lake
Creighton
Cranberry Portage
Playgreen Lake
Norway House
St Theresa Point
Sandy Lake
Primrose Lake
Dore Lake
Amisk Lake
Simonhouse
Stevenson Lake
ONTARIO
Cold Lake
Medley
Grand Centre
Green Lake
Beaver
Montreal Lake
Weyakwin
Montreal Lake
Cumberland Lake
The Pas
Cunisao
Sandy Lake
North Caribou Lake
Bonnyville
Meadow Lake
Candle Lake
Tobin Lake
Grand Rapids
Lake Winnipeg
North Spirit Lake
MacDowell Lake
St Paul
Elk Point
Delaronde Lake
Big River
Smeaton
Saskatchewan
Nipawin
Cedar Lake
Westray
Easterville
Poplar
Pikangikum
Pickle Lake
North Saskatchewan
St Walburg
Carrot River
Red Deer Lake
Reindeer Island
Berens River
Cat Lake
Lake St Joseph
Vermilion
Shellbrook
Stout Lake
Mannville
Lloydminster
Maidstone
Prince Albert
Melfort
Hudson Bay
Swan Lake
Lake Winnipegosis
Matheson Island
Trout Lake
Neilburg
North Battleford
Blaine Lake
Wakaw
Tisdale
Duck Bay
Red Lake
Red Lake
Bamaji Lake
Miniss Lake
Wainwright
Battleford
Rosthern
Humboldt
Gypsumville
Ear Falls
Lac Seul
Provost
Unity
Wilkie
SASKATCHEWAN
Kelvington
Swan River
Baldy Mountain
Lake St Martin
Bissett
Pakwash Lake
English
Sioux Lookout
Macklin
Wadena
Preeceville
Kamsack
Dauphin Lake
Arborg
Coronation
Biggar
Saskatoon
Lanigan
Canora
831
Grandview
Sainte Rose du Lac
Winnipeg
Vermillion Bay
Dryden
Kerrobert
Watrous
Wynyard
Foam Lake
Roblin
Dauphin
Lac du Bonnet
Rosetown
Kenaston
Raymore
Yorkton
Gimli
Kindersley
Lake Manitoba
Selkirk
Kenora
Eagle Lake
Ignace
Eston
Outlook
Davidson
Last Mountain Lake
Fort Qu'Appelle
Melville
Russell
Oyen
Riverhurst
Indian Head
Esterhazy
Neepawa
Stonewall
Beausejour
Keewatin
Lake of the Woods
South Saskatchewan
Kyle
Lake Diefenbaker
Lumsden
Whitewood
Minnedosa
Winnipeg
Atikokan
Leader
Regina
Grenfell
Carberry
Portage la Prairie
Steinbach
Fox Valley
Cabri
Herbert
Moose Jaw
Kipling
Moosomin
Brandon
Carman
Rainy Lake
Swift Current
Gull Lake
Old Wives Lake
Virden
Souris
Winkler
Morris
Emerson
Rainy River
International Falls
Medicine Hat
Maple Creek
Gravelbourg
Carlyle
Boissevain
Morden
Altona
Roseau
Baudette
Ely
Ponteix
Melita
Thief River Falls
Red Lakes
Bow Island
Shaunavon
Assiniboia
Weyburn
Oxbow
Deloraine
Hallock
Virginia
1465
Cypress Hills
Eastend
Mankota
Estevan
Carnduff
Langdon
Grafton
MINNESOTA
Val Marie
Frenchman
CANADA
Crosby
Bottineau
Cando
Rugby
Devil's Lake
Grand Forks
Chisholm
Hibbing
U.S.A.
Scobey
Plentywood
Tioga
Stanley
Minot
Crookston
Grand Rapids
Havre
Milk
Glasgow
Wolf Point
Williston
New Town
NORTH
Sheyenne
Mayville
Park Rapids
2116
Malta
Missouri
Watford City
Harvey
DAKOTA
Carrington
Moorhead
Detroit Lakes
Brainerd
Moose Lake
NTANA
Fort Peck Reservoir
Sidney
Lake Sakakawea
Washburn
Jamestown
Fergus Falls
Wadena
Mille Lacs
Fort Benton
Missouri
Jordan
Bismarck
Valley City
Fargo
Little Falls
Mora
Great Falls
Glendive
Dickinson
Mandan
James
Wahpeton
Alexandria
St Cloud
Little Missouri
110°
D
100°
E
1
2
3
60°
90°
50°
KILOMETRES
MILES
1:6 000 000

Lambert Azimuthal Equal Area Projection

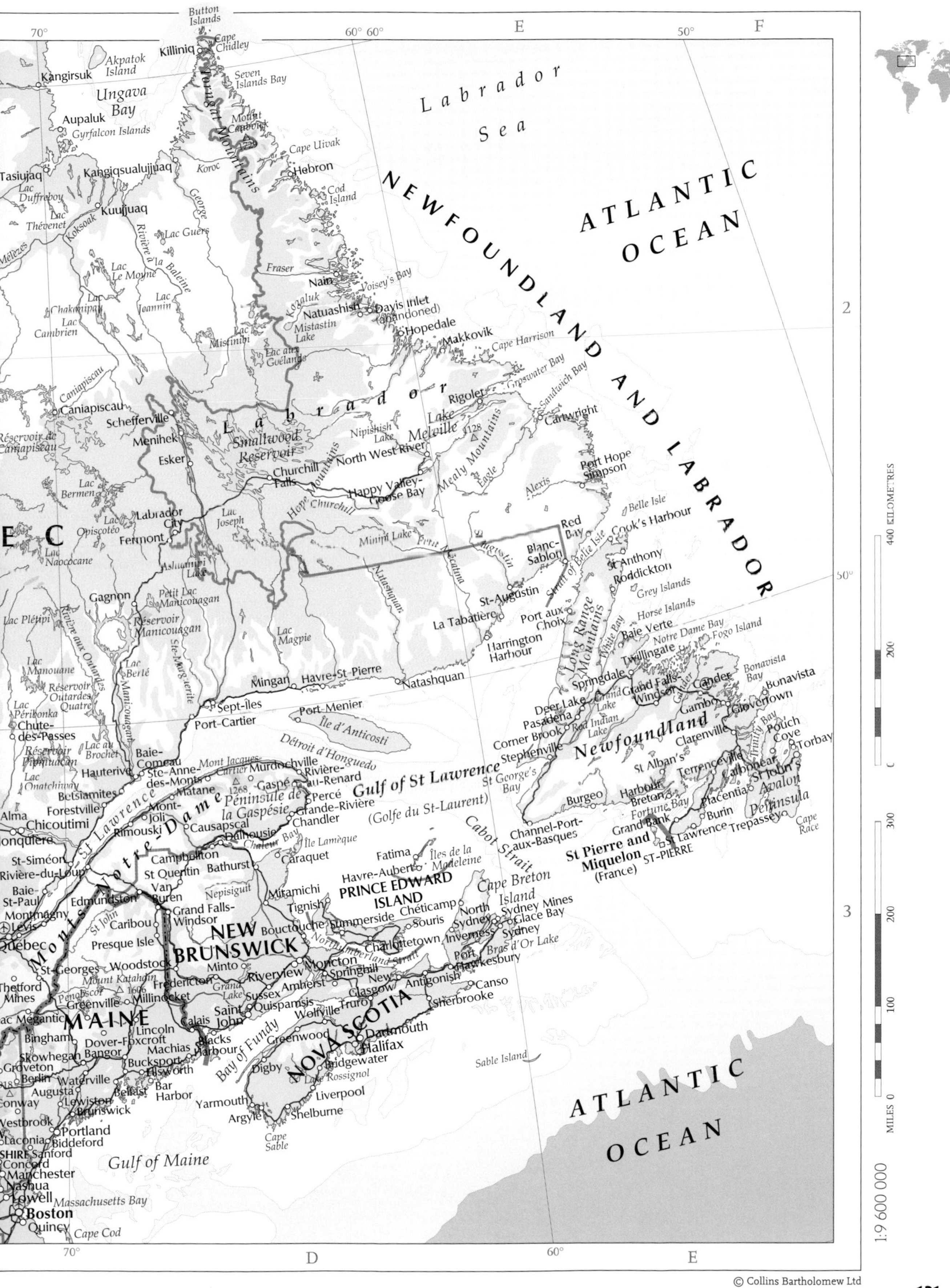
Labrador Sea
ATLANTIC OCEAN
NEWFOUNDLAND AND LABRADOR
Labrador
Newfoundland
Gulf of St Lawrence
(Golfe du St-Laurent)
Cabot Strait
NEW BRUNSWICK
NOVA SCOTIA
PRINCE EDWARD ISLAND
MAINE
St Pierre and Miquelon (France)
Cape Breton Island
Bay of Fundy
Gulf of Maine
Ungava Bay
Smallwood Reservoir
Lake Melville
Île d'Anticosti
Péninsule de la Gaspésie
Avalon Peninsula
Sable Island
Halifax
Boston
Québec
Sydney
Charlottetown
Fredericton
Moncton
Saint John
Portland
Corner Brook
Happy Valley-Goose Bay
Labrador City
Sept-Îles
Gander
St John's
Gulf of Maine
Massachusetts Bay
Cape Cod
1:9 600 000
KILOMETRES
MILES
© Collins Bartholomew Ltd

UNITED STATES OF AMERICA

METRES
FEET

METRES	FEET
5000	16404
3000	9843
2000	6562
1000	3281
500	1640
200	656
0	0
Land below sea level	
200	656
4000	13124
6000	19686

Longitude 110° west of Greenwich

Lambert Azimuthal Equal Area Projection

ONTARIO
QUÉBEC
CANADA
MINNESOTA
WISCONSIN
MICHIGAN
IOWA
ILLINOIS
INDIANA
OHIO
PENNSYLVANIA
NEW YORK
NEW JERSEY
MAINE
N.H.
VER.
MASS.
CONN.
R.I.
MD.
DEL.
W.VIRG.
VIRGINIA
KENTUCKY
TENNESSEE
N. CAROLINA
SOUTH CAROLINA
GEORGIA
ALABAMA
MISSISSIPPI
LOUISIANA
ARKANSAS
MISSOURI
FLORIDA
NEW BRUNSWICK
UNITED STATES OF AMERICA
ATLANTIC OCEAN
GULF OF MEXICO
THE BAHAMAS
CUBA
Lake Winnipeg
Lake Superior
Lake Michigan
Lake Huron
Lake Erie
Lake Ontario
Lake Nipigon
Lake Nipissing
Georgian Bay
Winnipeg
Thunder Bay
Sault Ste Marie
Sudbury
Ottawa
Montréal
Québec
Toronto
Hamilton
London
Detroit
Chicago
Milwaukee
Minneapolis
St Paul
Duluth
Des Moines
Omaha
Kansas City
St Louis
Indianapolis
Columbus
Cincinnati
Cleveland
Pittsburgh
Buffalo
Rochester
Albany
Boston
Providence
Hartford
New York
Philadelphia
Baltimore
WASHINGTON D.C.
Richmond
Norfolk
Raleigh
Charlotte
Nashville
Knoxville
Memphis
Atlanta
Birmingham
Jackson
New Orleans
Baton Rouge
Houston
Galveston
Dallas
Fort Worth
Austin
Corpus Christi
Brownsville
Matamoros
Oklahoma City
Tulsa
Little Rock
Jacksonville
Orlando
Tampa
St Petersburg
West Palm Beach
Fort Lauderdale
Hollywood
Miami
Key West
Straits of Florida
NASSAU
HAVANA (La Habana)
Cape Hatteras
Cape Cod
Long Island
Mississippi Delta
Apalachee Bay
1:16 000 000
MILES 0 100 200 300 400
0 200 400 600 KILOMETRES
90°
80°
70°
50°
40°
30°
20°
D
E
F
G
2
3
4

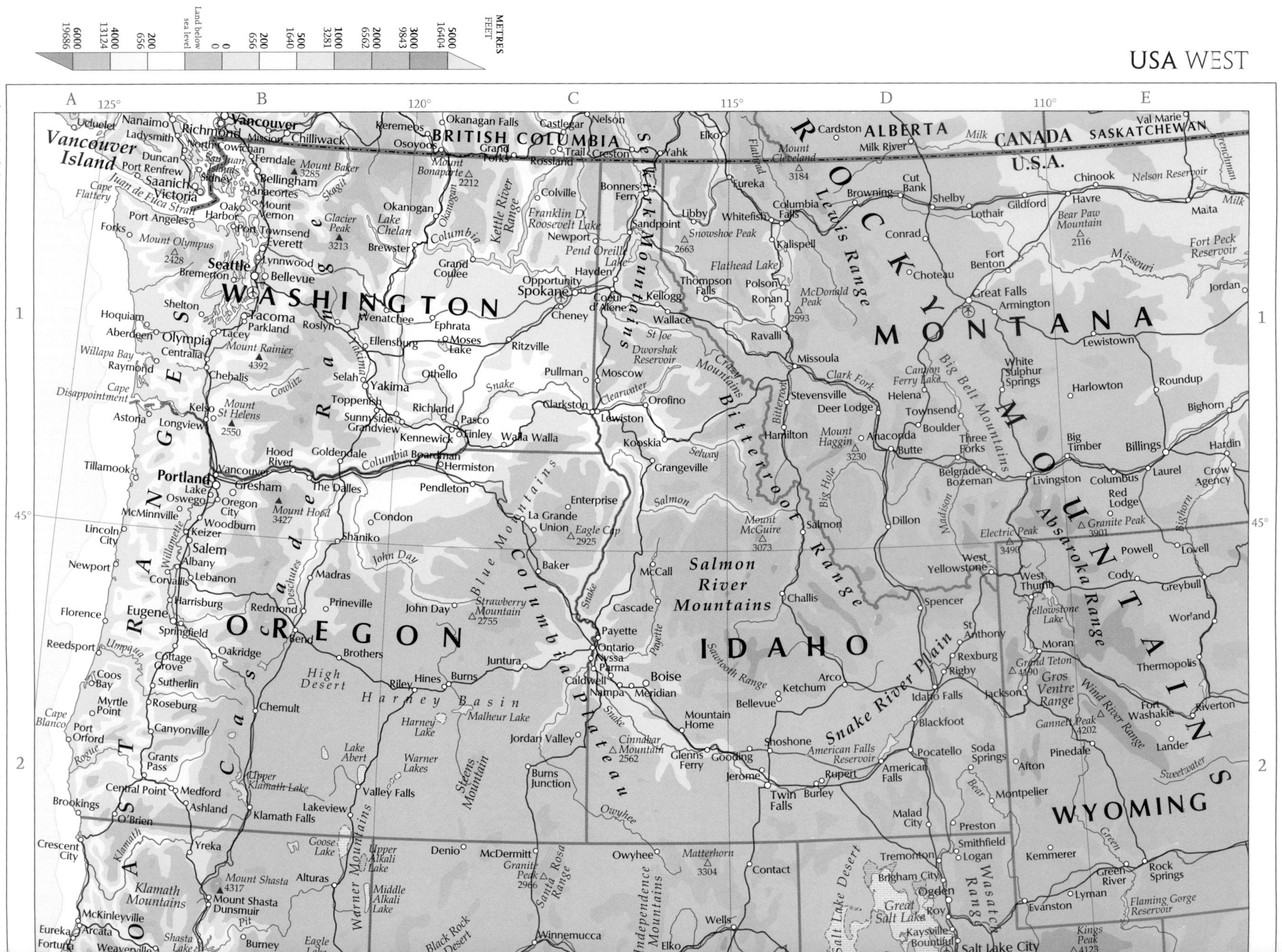

Lambert Azimuthal Equal Area Projection

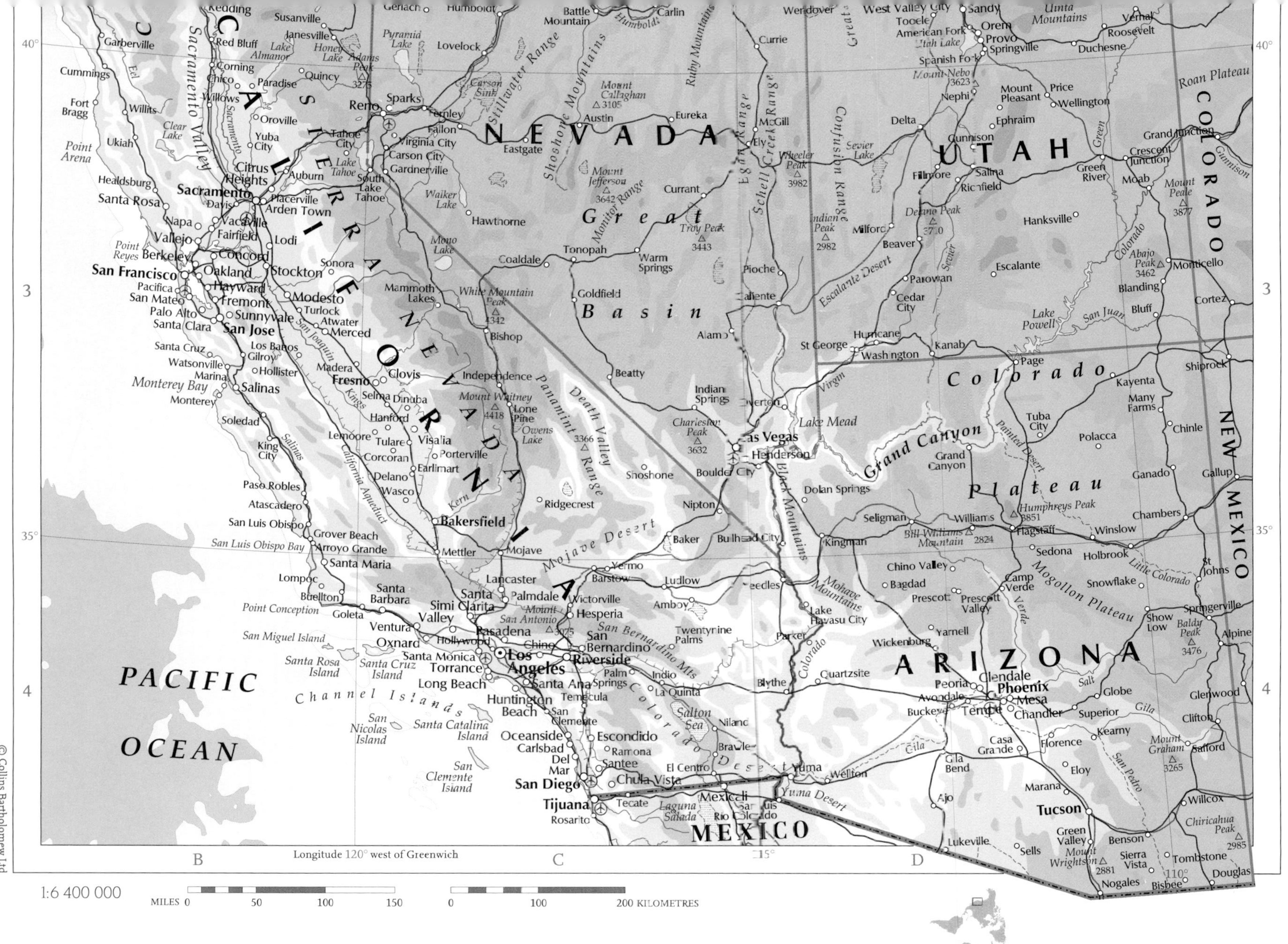
COLORADO
NEW MEXICO
UTAH
NEVADA
CALIFORNIA
SIERRA NEVADA
ARIZONA
MEXICO
PACIFIC OCEAN
Great Basin
Colorado Plateau
Grand Canyon
Mojave Desert
Death Valley
Sacramento Valley
Mogollon Plateau
Painted Desert
Yuma Desert
Channel Islands
Confusion Range
Black Mountains
Lake Mead
Lake Powell
Salton Sea
Las Vegas
Phoenix
Tucson
Los Angeles
San Diego
San Francisco
Sacramento
San Jose
Fresno
Bakersfield
Reno
Flagstaff
Tijuana
Longitude 120° west of Greenwich
1:6 400 000
MILES 0 50 100 150
0 100 200 KILOMETRES

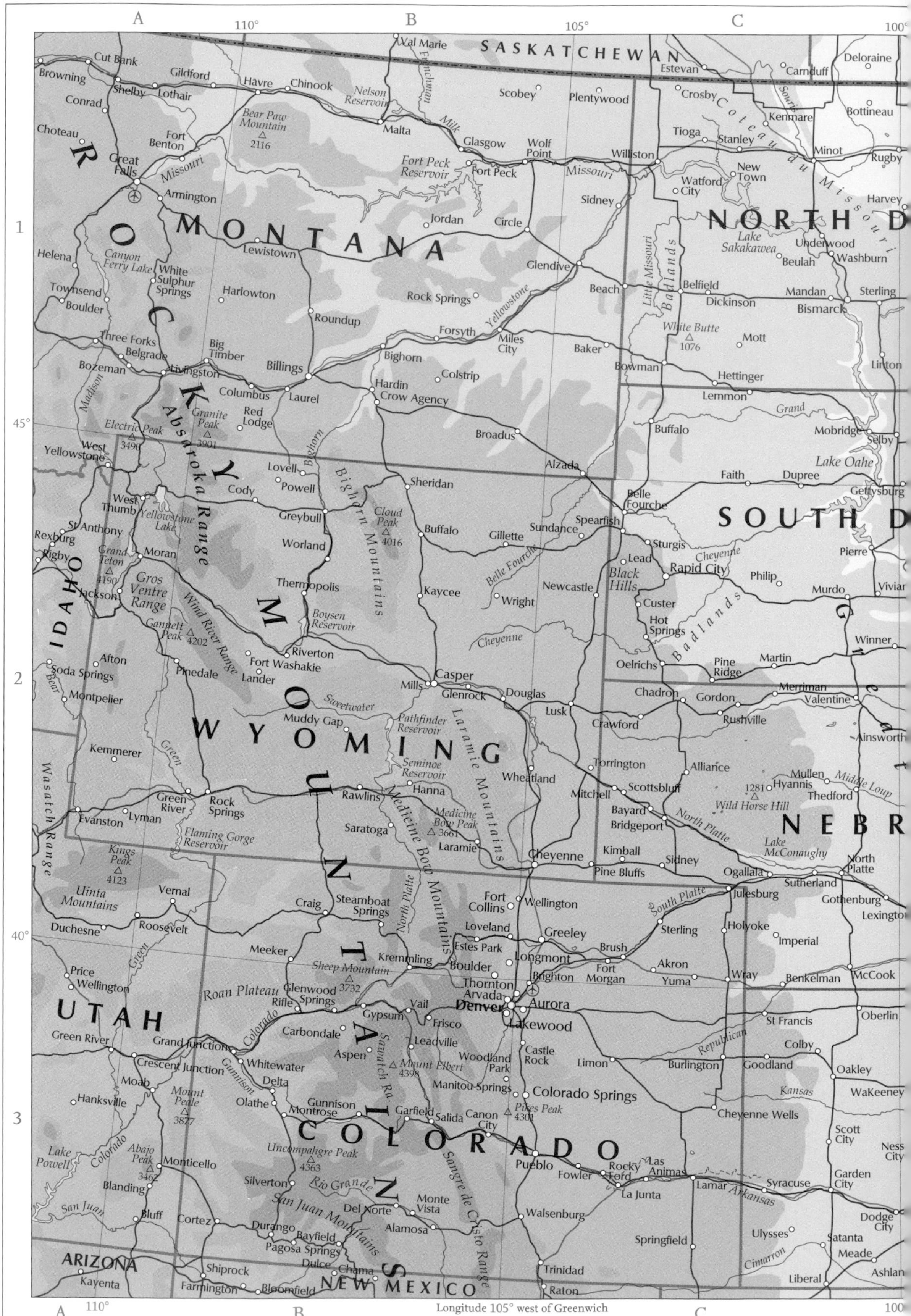

A B C
110° 105° 100°

SASKATCHEWAN
MONTANA
NORTH D
SOUTH D
NEBR
WYOMING
IDAHO
UTAH
COLORADO
ARIZONA
NEW MEXICO
ROCKY MOUNTAINS

Cut Bank, Browning, Shelby, Conrad, Lothair, Gildford, Havre, Chinook, Choteau, Fort Benton, Great Falls, Armington, Malta, Glasgow, Wolf Point, Scobey, Plentywood, Val Marie, Estevan, Carnduff, Deloraine, Crosby, Kenmare, Bottineau, Tioga, Stanley, Minot, Rugby, Williston, New Town, Watford City, Harvey, Fort Peck, Sidney, Jordan, Circle, Helena, Lewistown, White Sulphur Springs, Townsend, Boulder, Harlowton, Roundup, Glendive, Beach, Belfield, Dickinson, Mandan, Bismarck, Sterling, Underwood, Washburn, Beulah, Rock Springs, Forsyth, Miles City, Baker, Bowman, Mott, Hettinger, Lemmon, Linton, Three Forks, Belgrade, Bozeman, Livingston, Big Timber, Billings, Columbus, Laurel, Red Lodge, Bighorn, Hardin, Crow Agency, Colstrip, Broadus, West Yellowstone, Lovell, Powell, Cody, Sheridan, Alzada, Buffalo, Mobridge, Selby, Faith, Dupree, Gettysburg, Belle Fourche, Spearfish, Sundance, Gillette, Sturgis, Lead, Rapid City, Pierre, Philip, Murdo, Vivian, Custer, Hot Springs, Newcastle, Wright, Kaycee, Greybull, Worland, Thermopolis, Riverton, Fort Washakie, Lander, Moran, Jackson, Rexburg, Rigby, St Anthony, West Thumb, Afton, Soda Springs, Montpelier, Pinedale, Casper, Mills, Glenrock, Douglas, Lusk, Oelrichs, Chadron, Gordon, Rushville, Pine Ridge, Martin, Merriman, Valentine, Winner, Ainsworth, Crawford, Muddy Gap, Kemmerer, Torrington, Alliance, Wheatland, Mitchell, Scottsbluff, Hyannis, Mullen, Thedford, Bayard, Bridgeport, Hanna, Rawlins, Green River, Rock Springs, Evanston, Lyman, Saratoga, Laramie, Cheyenne, Kimball, Sidney, Pine Bluffs, Ogallala, North Platte, Sutherland, Gothenburg, Lexington, Julesburg, Vernal, Craig, Steamboat Springs, Fort Collins, Wellington, Duchesne, Roosevelt, Loveland, Greeley, Sterling, Holyoke, Imperial, Meeker, Kremmling, Estes Park, Longmont, Boulder, Brush, Fort Morgan, Akron, Yuma, Wray, Benkelman, McCook, Price, Wellington, Rifle, Glenwood Springs, Thornton, Arvada, Brighton, Denver, Aurora, Lakewood, Vail, Gypsum, Frisco, Oberlin, St Francis, Green River, Grand Junction, Carbondale, Leadville, Aspen, Woodland Park, Castle Rock, Limon, Burlington, Goodland, Colby, Oakley, WaKeeney, Crescent Junction, Whitewater, Delta, Moab, Hanksville, Olathe, Montrose, Gunnison, Garfield, Salida, Manitou Springs, Colorado Springs, Canon City, Cheyenne Wells, Scott City, Ness City, Monticello, Blanding, Silverton, Pueblo, Fowler, Rocky Ford, Las Animas, La Junta, Lamar, Syracuse, Garden City, Bluff, Cortez, Del Norte, Monte Vista, Alamosa, Walsenburg, Durango, Bayfield, Pagosa Springs, Dulce, Chama, Springfield, Ulysses, Satanta, Dodge City, Meade, Liberal, Ashland, Shiprock, Kayenta, Farmington, Bloomfield, Trinidad, Raton

Bear Paw Mountain 2116, Electric Peak 3490, Granite Peak 3901, Cloud Peak 4016, White Butte 1076, Grand Teton 4190, Gannett Peak 4202, Medicine Bow Peak 3661, Kings Peak 4123, 1281 Wild Horse Hill, Sheep Mountain 3732, Mount Elbert 4398, Pikes Peak 4301, Mount Peale 3877, Abajo Peak 3462, Uncompahgre Peak 4363

Absaroka Range, Bighorn Mountains, Gros Ventre Range, Wind River Range, Laramie Mountains, Medicine Bow Mountains, Wasatch Range, Uinta Mountains, Roan Plateau, Sawatch Ra., Sangre de Cristo Range, San Juan Mountains, Black Hills, Badlands, Coteau du Missouri

Missouri, Milk, Frenchman, Yellowstone, Little Missouri, Bighorn, Madison, Belle Fourche, Cheyenne, Sweetwater, Green, Bear, North Platte, South Platte, Middle Loup, Colorado, Gunnison, Republican, Kansas, Arkansas, Rio Grande, San Juan, Cimarron, Souris, Grand

Nelson Reservoir, Fort Peck Reservoir, Canyon Ferry Lake, Lake Sakakawea, Lake Oahe, Yellowstone Lake, Boysen Reservoir, Pathfinder Reservoir, Seminoe Reservoir, Flaming Gorge Reservoir, Lake McConaughy, Lake Powell

1 2 3
45° 40°

Longitude 105° west of Greenwich

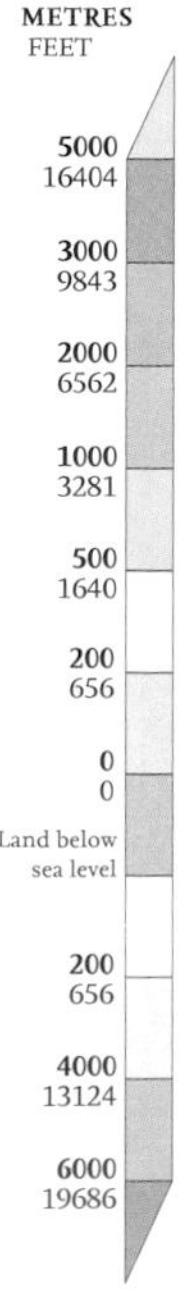

METRES / FEET
5000 / 16404
3000 / 9843
2000 / 6562
1000 / 3281
500 / 1640
200 / 656
0 / 0
Land below sea level
200 / 656
4000 / 13124
6000 / 19686

Lambert Azimuthal Equal Area Projection

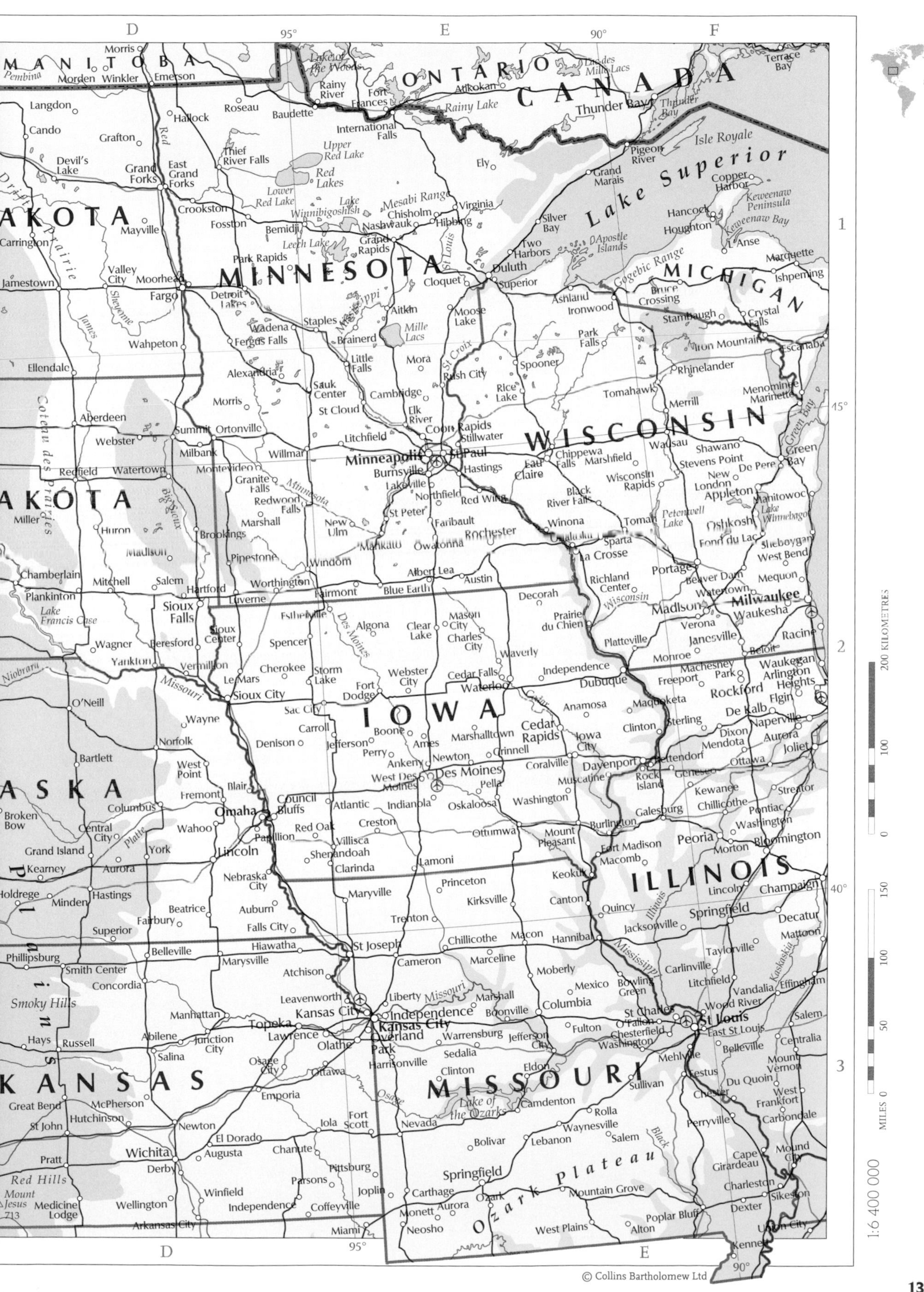
D
95°
E
90°
F
MANITOBA
Morris
Pembina
Morden
Winkler
Emerson
Lake of the Woods
Rainy River
Fort Frances
ONTARIO
Atikokan
Lac des Mille Lacs
CANADA
Thunder Bay
Terrace Bay
Rainy Lake
International Falls
Langdon
Cando
Hallock
Roseau
Baudette
Grafton
Red
Upper Red Lake
Red Lakes
Lower Red Lake
Isle Royale
Pigeon River
Devil's Lake
Grand Forks
East Grand Forks
Thief River Falls
Ely
Grand Marais
Lake Superior
Copper Harbor
Keweenaw Peninsula
Keweenaw Bay
Drift Prairie
AKOTA
Crookston
Mayville
Fosston
Bemidji
Lake Winnibigoshish
Mesabi Range
Chisholm
Nashwauk
Hibbing
Virginia
Silver Bay
Hancock
Houghton
L'Anse
Carrington
Leech Lake
Grand Rapids
Two Harbors
Apostle Islands
Park Rapids
St Louis
Duluth
Superior
Gogebic Range
Marquette
Ishpeming
Valley City
Moorhead
Fargo
Jamestown
MINNESOTA
Cloquet
MICHIGAN
Detroit Lakes
Ashland
Ironwood
Bruce Crossing
Sheyenne
James
Mississippi
Aitkin
Moose Lake
Stambaugh
Crystal Falls
Wadena
Staples
Mille Lacs
Fergus Falls
Brainerd
Park Falls
Iron Mountain
Escanaba
Wahpeton
St Croix
Ellendale
Alexandria
Little Falls
Mora
Spooner
Rhinelander
Rush City
Rice Lake
Sauk Center
Cambridge
Tomahawk
Menominee
Marinette
Coteau des Prairies
Morris
St Cloud
Merrill
Green Bay
15°
Aberdeen
Elk River
Coon Rapids
Stillwater
WISCONSIN
Summit
Ortonville
Litchfield
Webster
Milbank
Willmar
Minneapolis
St Paul
Chippewa Falls
Marshfield
Wausau
Shawano
Green Bay
Redfield
Watertown
Montevideo
Burnsville
Hastings
Eau Claire
Stevens Point
De Pere
Granite Falls
Minnesota
Lakeville
Wisconsin Rapids
New London
Big Sioux
AKOTA
Redwood Falls
Northfield
Red Wing
Black River Falls
Appleton
Manitowoc
Miller
Marshall
St Peter
Faribault
Petenwell Lake
Lake Winnebago
Huron
Brookings
New Ulm
Rochester
Winona
Tomah
Oshkosh
Madison
Mankato
Owatonna
Sparta
Fond du Lac
Sheboygan
Pipestone
Windom
La Crosse
West Bend
Chamberlain
Albert Lea
Portage
Plankinton
Mitchell
Salem
Hartford
Worthington
Austin
Beaver Dam
Mequon
Fairmont
Blue Earth
Richland Center
Watertown
Lake Francis Case
Sioux Falls
Luverne
Decorah
Wisconsin
Milwaukee
Madison
Waukesha
Estherville
Algona
Mason City
Prairie du Chien
Verona
Sioux Center
Des Moines
Clear Lake
Charles City
Wagner
Beresford
Spencer
Janesville
Racine
Platteville
2
Yankton
Waverly
Monroe
Beloit
Niobrara
Vermillion
Cherokee
Storm Lake
Webster City
Cedar Falls
Independence
Machesney Park
Waukegan
Arlington Heights
Missouri
Le Mars
Dubuque
Freeport
Rockford
Sioux City
Fort Dodge
Waterloo
Elgin
O'Neill
Sac City
IOWA
Anamosa
Maquoketa
De Kalb
Wayne
Carroll
Cedar
Cedar Rapids
Sterling
Naperville
Boone
Clinton
Norfolk
Denison
Jefferson
Ames
Marshalltown
Iowa City
Dixon
Aurora
Perry
Grinnell
Mendota
Joliet
Bartlett
Ankeny
Newton
Bettendorf
West Point
Coralville
Davenport
Ottawa
West Des Moines
Des Moines
Muscatine
Rock Island
Geneseo
ASKA
Blair
Pella
Fremont
Council Bluffs
Kewanee
Streator
Columbus
Atlantic
Indianola
Oskaloosa
Washington
Chillicothe
Broken Bow
Omaha
Galesburg
Pontiac
Central City
Wahoo
Red Oak
Creston
Burlington
Washington
Platte
Papillion
Mount Pleasant
Peoria
Bloomington
Ottumwa
Grand Island
York
Villisca
Morton
Lincoln
Shenandoah
Fort Madison
Kearney
Aurora
Clarinda
Lamoni
Macomb
Nebraska City
Keokuk
ILLINOIS
Holdrege
Hastings
Princeton
Lincoln
Champaign
Minden
Maryville
Kirksville
Canton
40°
Beatrice
Auburn
Illinois
Springfield
Quincy
Decatur
Fairbury
Trenton
Jacksonville
Superior
Falls City
Mattoon
Macon
Hannibal
Chillicothe
Hiawatha
St Joseph
Taylorville
Belleville
Phillipsburg
Marysville
Cameron
Marceline
Mississippi
Carlinville
Smith Center
Atchison
Moberly
Kaskaskia
Litchfield
Mexico
Bowling Green
Concordia
Vandalia
Effingham
Leavenworth
Liberty
Missouri
Marshall
Smoky Hills
Kansas City
Columbia
Wood River
Manhattan
Independence
Boonville
St Charles
St Louis
Salem
Topeka
Kansas City
Fulton
O'Fallon
Chesterfield
East St Louis
Hays
Russell
Abilene
Junction City
Lawrence
Olathe
Overland Park
Warrensburg
Jefferson City
Washington
Belleville
Centralia
Salina
Sedalia
Mehlville
Osage City
Harrisonville
Eldon
Mount Vernon
Ottawa
Clinton
3
KANSAS
MISSOURI
Sullivan
Festus
Du Quoin
Emporia
Chester
West Frankfort
Great Bend
McPherson
Osage
Lake of the Ozarks
Camdenton
Hutchinson
Carbondale
Rolla
St John
Newton
Iola
Fort Scott
Nevada
Waynesville
Perryville
El Dorado
Salem
Black
Bolivar
Lebanon
Wichita
Augusta
Chanute
Mound City
Pratt
Derby
Cape Girardeau
Pittsburg
Springfield
Ozark Plateau
Red Hills
Parsons
Charleston
Winfield
Joplin
Carthage
Ozark
Mountain Grove
Sikeston
Mount Jesus
713
Medicine Lodge
Wellington
Independence
Coffeyville
Aurora
Dexter
Monett
Poplar Bluff
Union City
Arkansas City
Miami
Neosho
West Plains
Alton
Kennett
D
95°
E
90°
200 KILOMETRES
100
0
150
100
50
MILES 0
1:6 400 000

METRES
FEET

METRES	FEET
5000	16404
3000	9843
2000	6562
1000	3281
500	1640
200	656
0	0
Land below sea level	
200	656
4000	13124
6000	19686

Lambert Azimuthal Equal Area Projection

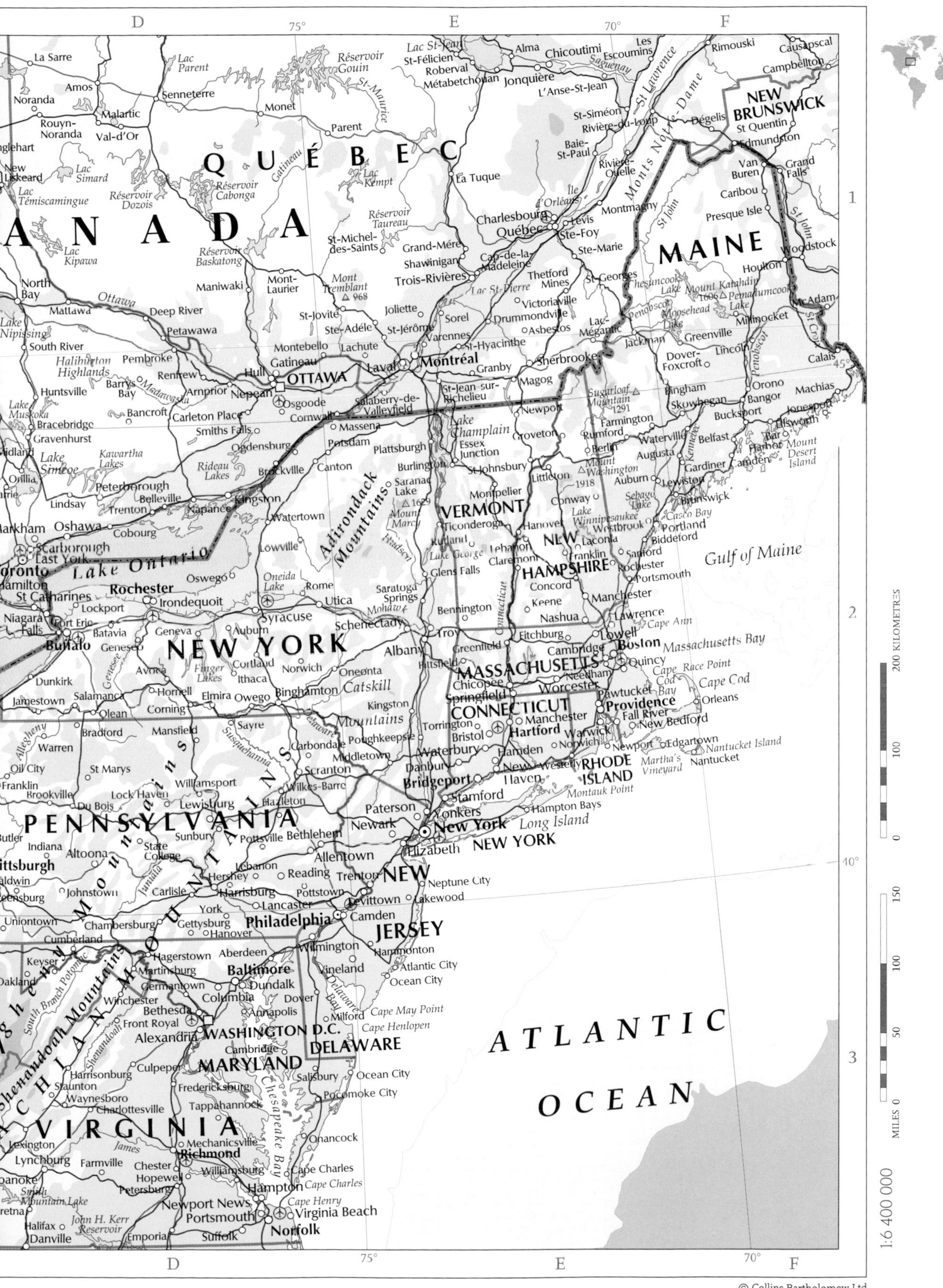
D
75°
E
70°
F
1
2
3
10°
45°
QUÉBEC
CANADA
NEW BRUNSWICK
MAINE
VERMONT
NEW HAMPSHIRE
MASSACHUSETTS
CONNECTICUT
RHODE ISLAND
NEW YORK
PENNSYLVANIA
NEW JERSEY
MARYLAND
DELAWARE
VIRGINIA
WASHINGTON D.C.
ATLANTIC OCEAN
Gulf of Maine
Massachusetts Bay
Lake Ontario
Adirondack Mountains
Catskill Mountains
Long Island
Chesapeake Bay
Lake Champlain
Monts Notre-Dame
St Lawrence
La Sarre
Amos
Noranda
Rouyn-Noranda
Malartic
Val-d'Or
Senneterre
Lac Parent
Réservoir Gouin
Monet
Parent
St-Maurice
Lac St-Jean
St-Félicien
Roberval
Métabetchouan
Alma
Chicoutimi
Jonquière
Saguenay
Les Escoumins
L'Anse-St-Jean
Rimouski
Causapscal
Campbellton
Dégelis
St Quentin
Edmundston
St-Siméon
Rivière-du-Loup
Baie-St-Paul
Rivière-Ouelle
Île d'Orléans
Montmagny
La Tuque
Lac Kempt
Réservoir Taureau
St-Michel-des-Saints
Grand-Mère
Shawinigan
Trois-Rivières
Cap-de-la-Madeleine
Charlesbourg
Québec
Lévis
Ste-Foy
Ste-Marie
Thetford Mines
Lac St-Pierre
Victoriaville
Drummondville
Asbestos
Lac-Mégantic
St-Georges
Mont Tremblant
968
Joliette
Sorel
St-Jovite
Ste-Adèle
St-Jérôme
Varennes
St-Hyacinthe
Montebello
Lachute
Laval
Montréal
Granby
Sherbrooke
Magog
St-Jean-sur-Richelieu
Salaberry-de-Valleyfield
Gatineau
Hull
OTTAWA
Nepean
Osgoode
Cornwall
Englehart
New Liskeard
Lac Simard
Lac Témiscamingue
Réservoir Dozois
Réservoir Cabonga
Gatineau
Lac Kipawa
Réservoir Baskatong
Maniwaki
Mont-Laurier
North Bay
Mattawa
Ottawa
Deep River
Petawawa
Lake Nipissing
South River
Haliburton Highlands
Pembroke
Renfrew
Arnprior
Barrys Bay
Madawaska
Huntsville
Lake Muskoka
Bracebridge
Gravenhurst
Bancroft
Carleton Place
Smiths Falls
Midland
Lake Simcoe
Orillia
Barrie
Kawartha Lakes
Rideau Lakes
Peterborough
Lindsay
Belleville
Trenton
Napanee
Kingston
Brockville
Ogdensburg
Massena
Potsdam
Canton
Plattsburgh
Burlington
Essex Junction
St Johnsbury
Montpelier
Saranac Lake
Mount Marcy
1629
Watertown
Markham
Oshawa
Cobourg
Scarborough
East York
Toronto
Hamilton
St Catharines
Niagara Falls
Fort Erie
Buffalo
Lockport
Rochester
Irondequoit
Oswego
Oneida Lake
Rome
Utica
Syracuse
Lowville
Hudson
Geneva
Auburn
Batavia
Geneseo
Finger Lakes
Cortland
Ithaca
Norwich
Oneonta
Avoca
Hornell
Elmira
Owego
Binghamton
Dunkirk
Jamestown
Salamanca
Olean
Corning
Bradford
Warren
Oil City
Franklin
Brookville
Du Bois
St Marys
Mansfield
Sayre
Susquehanna
Williamsport
Lock Haven
Lewisburg
Hazleton
Wilkes-Barre
Scranton
Carbondale
Kingston
Poughkeepsie
Middletown
Delaware
Saratoga Springs
Mohawk
Schenectady
Albany
Troy
Glens Falls
Lake George
Ticonderoga
Rutland
Bennington
Pittsfield
Greenfield
Connecticut
Lebanon
Claremont
Hanover
Keene
Concord
Nashua
Manchester
Fitchburg
Lowell
Lawrence
Cape Ann
Boston
Cambridge
Quincy
Needham
Worcester
Chicopee
Springfield
Hartford
Manchester
Torrington
Bristol
Waterbury
Danbury
Hamden
New Haven
Norwich
Westerly
Warwick
Providence
Pawtucket
Fall River
New Bedford
Newport
Cape Cod
Cape Cod Bay
Race Point
Orleans
Edgartown
Martha's Vineyard
Nantucket Island
Nantucket
Montauk Point
Hampton Bays
Bridgeport
Stamford
Yonkers
Paterson
Newark
New York
Elizabeth
Trenton
Neptune City
Lakewood
Levittown
Camden
Philadelphia
Wilmington
Hammonton
Vineland
Atlantic City
Ocean City
Cape May Point
Cape Henlopen
Milford
Dover
Delaware Bay
Salisbury
Ocean City
Pocomoke City
Onancock
Cape Charles
Cape Henry
Virginia Beach
Norfolk
Portsmouth
Suffolk
Newport News
Hampton
Williamsburg
Mechanicsville
Richmond
Chester
Hopewell
Petersburg
Emporia
Tappahannock
Cambridge
Annapolis
Baltimore
Dundalk
Columbia
Aberdeen
Hagerstown
Martinsburg
Germantown
Bethesda
Alexandria
Front Royal
Winchester
Culpeper
Fredericksburg
Harrisonburg
Staunton
Waynesboro
Charlottesville
Lexington
Lynchburg
Farmville
Roanoke
Smith Mountain Lake
Gretna
Halifax
John H. Kerr Reservoir
Danville
James
Shenandoah
South Branch Potomac
Allegheny Mountains
Appalachian Mountains
Cumberland
Keyser
Oakland
Uniontown
Greensburg
Baldwin
Pittsburgh
Butler
Indiana
Altoona
State College
Johnstown
Juniata
Chambersburg
Gettysburg
Hanover
York
Carlisle
Harrisburg
Hershey
Lebanon
Reading
Pottstown
Lancaster
Allentown
Bethlehem
Pottsville
Sunbury
Jackman
Moosehead Lake
Greenville
Chesuncook Lake
Mount Katahdin
1606
Pemadumcook Lake
Millinocket
Dover-Foxcroft
Lincoln
Penobscot
St John
Van Buren
Grand Falls
Caribou
Presque Isle
Houlton
Woodstock
McAdam
St Croix
Calais
Sugarloaf Mountain
1291
Bingham
Skowhegan
Farmington
Orono
Bangor
Machias
Bucksport
Jonesport
Ellsworth
Bar Harbor
Mount Desert Island
Belfast
Camden
Rumford
Berlin
Waterville
Augusta
Kennebec
Gardiner
Newport
Groveton
Littleton
Mount Washington
1918
Auburn
Lewiston
Brunswick
Sebago Lake
Casco Bay
Portland
Biddeford
Sanford
Conway
Lake Winnipesaukee
Westbrook
Laconia
Franklin
Rochester
Portsmouth
Dover
200 KILOMETRES
100
0
150
100
50
0
MILES
1:6 400 000

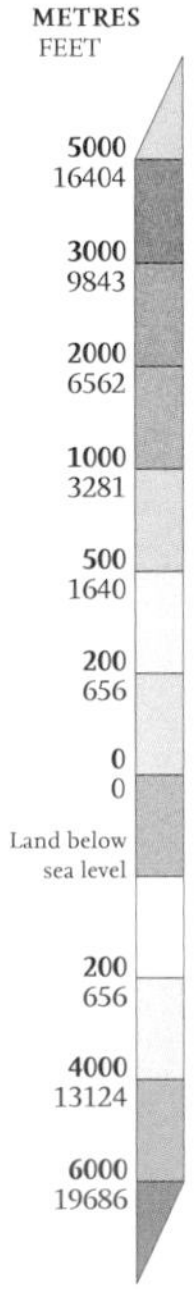

METRES
FEET

METRES	FEET
5000	16404
3000	9843
2000	6562
1000	3281
500	1640
200	656
0	0
Land below sea level	
200	656
4000	13124
6000	19686

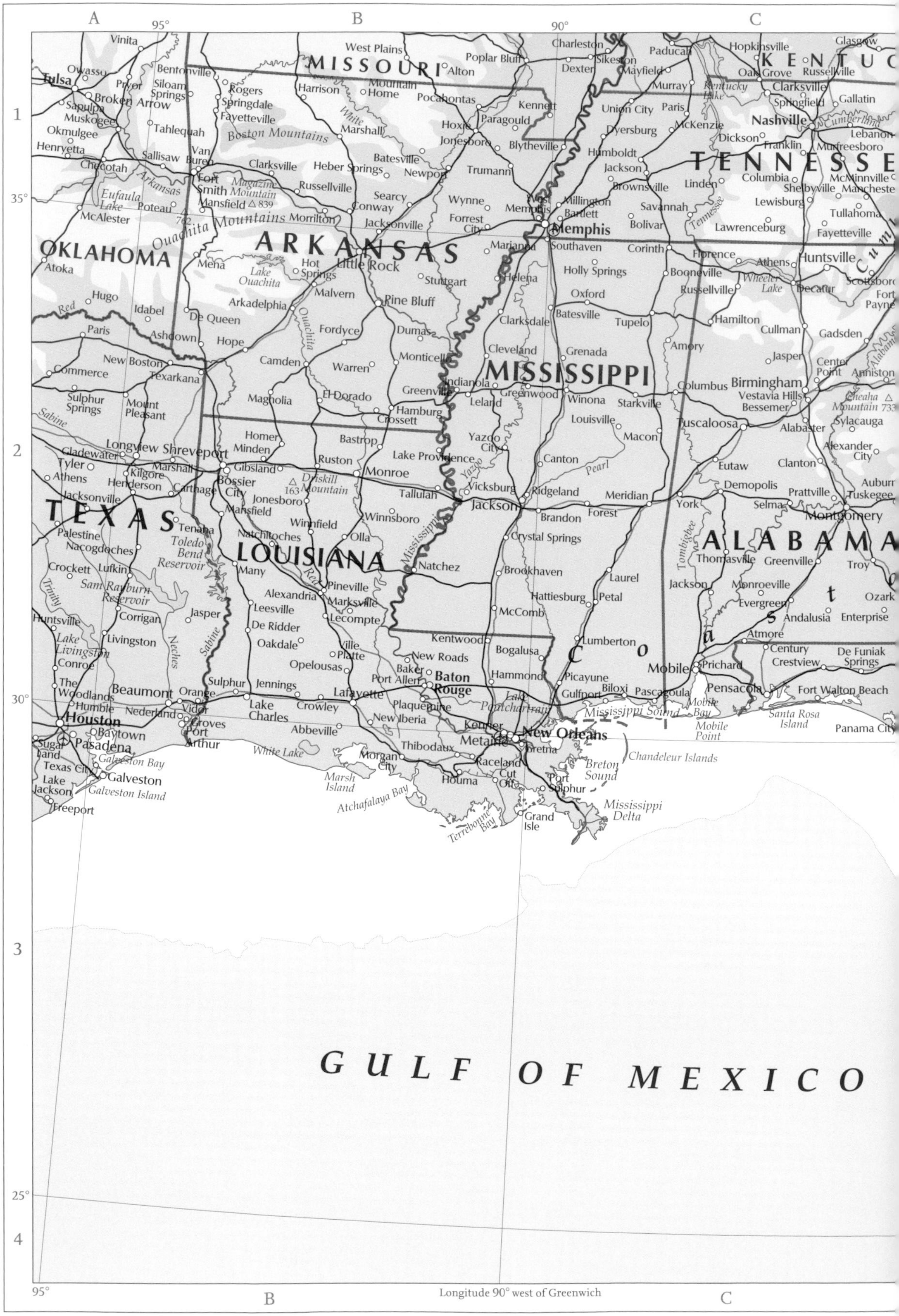

OKLAHOMA

ARKANSAS

MISSOURI

TENNESSEE

MISSISSIPPI

ALABAMA

TEXAS

LOUISIANA

GULF OF MEXICO

Longitude 90° west of Greenwich

Lambert Azimuthal Equal Area Projection

85° D 80° E 75°

1 2 3 4

35° 30° 25°

VIRGINIA
Columbia
Somerset
Norton
Marion
Halifax
Emporia
Suffolk
Williamsburg
Dale Hollow Lake
Middlesboro
Holston
Abingdon
Martinsville
Danville
John H. Kerr Reservoir
Lake Gaston
Roanoke Rapids
Dismal Swamp
Elizabeth City
Kitty Hawk
Kingsport
Bristol
Mount Airy
Reidsville
Roanoke
Edenton
Nags Head
La Follette
Gray
Johnson City
Burlington
Henderson
Albemarle Sound
Oregon Inlet
Cookeville
Morristown
Greeneville
Yadkin
High Point
Durham
Rocky Mount
Tarboro
Manteo
Crossville
Oak Ridge
Newport
Lenoir
Winston-Salem
Chapel Hill
Wilson
Williamston
Knoxville
Maryville
Morganton
Statesville
Raleigh
Smithfield
Greenville
Rockwood
Great Smoky Mountains
Appalachian Mountains
Blue Ridge
Cumberland Plateau
2037
Hickory
Salisbury
Sanford
Cape Hatteras
Tennessee
Athens
Asheville
NORTH CAROLINA
Goldsboro
Washington
Pamlico Sound
Kinston
Ocracoke Island
Waynesville
Hendersonville
Gastonia
Albemarle
Southern Pines
New Bern
Red Bank
Shelby
Charlotte
Fayetteville
Raleigh Bay
Cleveland
Matthews
Murphy
Spartanburg
Gaffney
Chattanooga
Rock Hill
Laurinburg
Jacksonville
Morehead City
Cape Lookout
Greenville
Broad
Cape Fear
Dalton
Mount Oglethorpe
Seneca
Mauldin
Chester
Cheraw
Wallace
Lancaster
Lumberton
Onslow Bay
La Fayette
1003
Toccoa
Anderson
Dillon
Whiteville
Rome
Lake Sidney Lanier
Hartwell Reservoir
Newberry
Florence
Green Swamp
Wilmington
Gainesville
Elberton
Greenwood
Saluda
SOUTH
Marion
Southport
Lake Murray
Dentsville
Pee Dee
Cape Fear
Marietta
Lawrenceville
Athens
Columbia
Sumter
Long Bay
Sandy Springs
Lake City
Atlanta
Clark Hill Reservoir
Aiken
Lake Marion
Myrtle Beach
Carrollton
Covington
Orangeburg
Martinez
Thomson
Augusta
CAROLINA
Georgetown
Chattahoochee
Newnan
Griffin
Barnwell
Lake Moultrie
Cape Romain
Milledgeville
Oconee
Waynesboro
Summerville
La Grange
Walterboro
Ladson
North Charleston
Lanett
Macon
Mount Pleasant
Charleston
Opelika
Swainsboro
Columbus
Warner Robins
Savannah
Statesboro
Beaufort
Phenix City
Perry
Dublin
Eastman
Vidalia
Hilton Head Island
Wilmington Island
GEORGIA
Savannah
Eufaula
Americus
Cordele
Hinesville
Richmond Hill
Altamaha
Dawson
Fitzgerald
St Catherines Island
Abbeville
Albany
Douglas
Jesup
Blakely
Tifton
Waycross
Nahunta
Dothan
Moultrie
Adel
Brunswick
Bainbridge
Okefenokee Swamp
Cumberland Island
Folkston
Marianna
Lake Seminole
Thomasville
Valdosta
Fernandina Beach
Monticello
Atlantic Beach
Quincy
Tallahassee
Jacksonville
Live Oak
Orange Park
Lake City
Perry
Port St Joe
Carrabelle
Apalachee Bay
Starke
St Augustine
Gainesville
St Johns
Cape San Blas
St George Island
Deadman Bay
Cross City
Palatka
Suwannee
FLORIDA
Lake George
Ormond Beach
Daytona Beach
Suwannee Sound
Ocala
De Land
Edgewater
Waccasassa Bay
Sanford
Oviedo
Homosassa Springs
Leesburg
Apopka
Titusville
Brooksville
Lake Apopka
Orlando
Cape Canaveral
Spring Hill
Dade City
Kissimmee
Cape Canaveral
Melbourne
Tarpon Springs
Lakeland
Lake Tohopekaliga
Palm Bay
Clearwater
Winter Haven
Largo
Tampa
Lake Kissimmee
St Petersburg
Orchid Island
Vero Beach
Tampa Bay
Sebring
Fort Pierce
Bradenton
Lake Istokpoga
Hutchinson Island
Arcadia
Sarasota
Okeechobee
Port St Lucie City
Venice
Lake Okeechobee
Jupiter
Port Charlotte
Englewood
West Palm Beach
Charlotte Harbor
Clewiston
Belle Glade
Lake Worth
Cape Coral
Fort Myers
Delray Beach
Pine Islands
Boca Raton
Immokalee
Fort Lauderdale
Sunrise
Naples
Hollywood
Pembroke Pines
Hialeah
Miami Beach
Everglades
Miami
Kendall
Biscayne Bay
Ten Thousand Islands
Homestead
Cape Sable
Florida Bay
Key Largo
Islamorada
Pine Islands
Marathon
Florida Keys
Marquesas Keys
Key West
Straits of Florida
Bimini Islands
ATLANTIC
OCEAN
Appalachian
THE BAHAMAS
Little Abaco
Cooper's Town
Little Bahama Bank
Marsh Harbour
Freeport City
Grand Bahama
Great Abaco
Northwest Providence Channel
Northeast Providence Channel
Berry Islands
Eleuthera
New Providence
Governor's Harbour
NASSAU
Bannerman Town
Andros Town
Exuma Cays
Andros

0 100 200 KILOMETRES
MILES 0 50 100 150

1:6 400 000

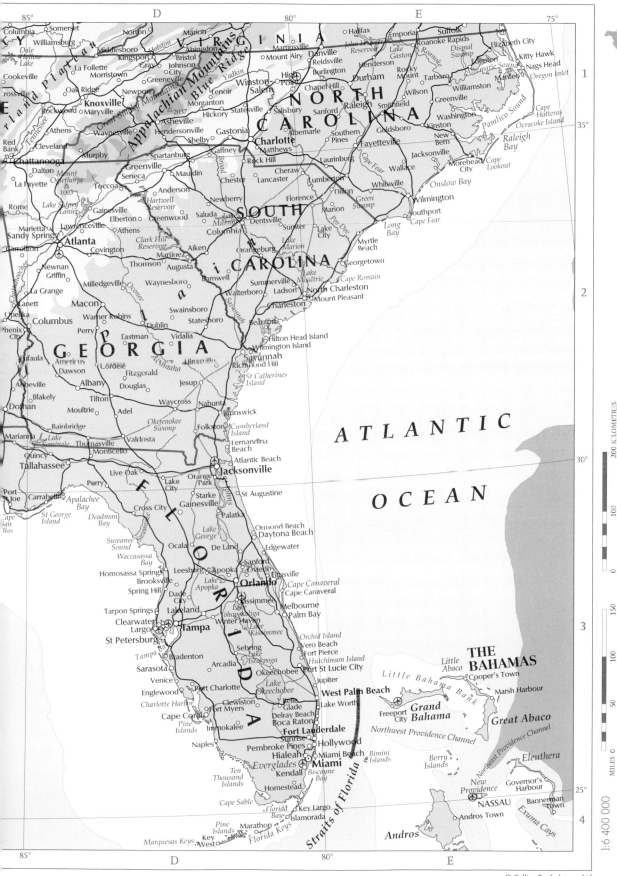

115° A 110° B 105°

1 2 3

35° 30°

UTAH
COLORADO
NEVADA
ARIZONA
NEW MEXICO
SONORA
CHIHUAHUA
BAJA CALIFORNIA
BAJA CALIFORNIA SUR
SINALOA
DURANGO
MEXICO

Colorado Plateau
Grand Canyon
ROCKY MOUNTAINS
Sangre de Cristo Range
San Juan Mountains
Chuska Mountains
Zuni Mountains
Mogollon Plateau
Black Range
San Andres Mountains
Sacramento Mountains
Sierra Madre Occidental
Gulf of California
Desierto de Altar
Desierto de Vizcaíno
Chaco Mesa
Diablo Plateau
Bolsón de Mapimí
Black Mountains
Mohave Mountains
Painted Desert
Escalante Desert

Lake Powell
Lake Mead
Lake Havasu City
Colorado
San Juan
Virgin
Gila
Salt
Verde
Little Colorado
San Pedro
Rio Grande
Río Bravo del Norte
Pecos
Conchos
Yaqui
Sonora
Bavispe
Santa María
Aros
Sextín

Uncompahgre Peak 4363
Abajo Peak 3462
Humphreys Peak 3851
Bill Williams Mountain 2824
Wheeler Peak 4011
Laughlin Peak 2688
Hosta Butte 2693
Baldy Peak 3476
South Baldy 3287
Whitewater Baldy 3320
Mount Graham 3265
Chiricahua Peak 2985
Mount Wrightson 2881
Sierra Cibuta 2034
Guadalupe Peak 2667
Sierra Libre 1180
Pico Echeverría 1908
Volcán Las Tres Vírgenes 1996

Phoenix
Tucson
Albuquerque
Santa Fe
El Paso
Ciudad Juárez
Chihuahua
Hermosillo
Flagstaff
Las Cruces
Nogales
Yuma
Guaymas
Ciudad Obregón
Los Mochis

Longitude 110° west of Greenwich

Lambert Azimuthal Equal Area Projection

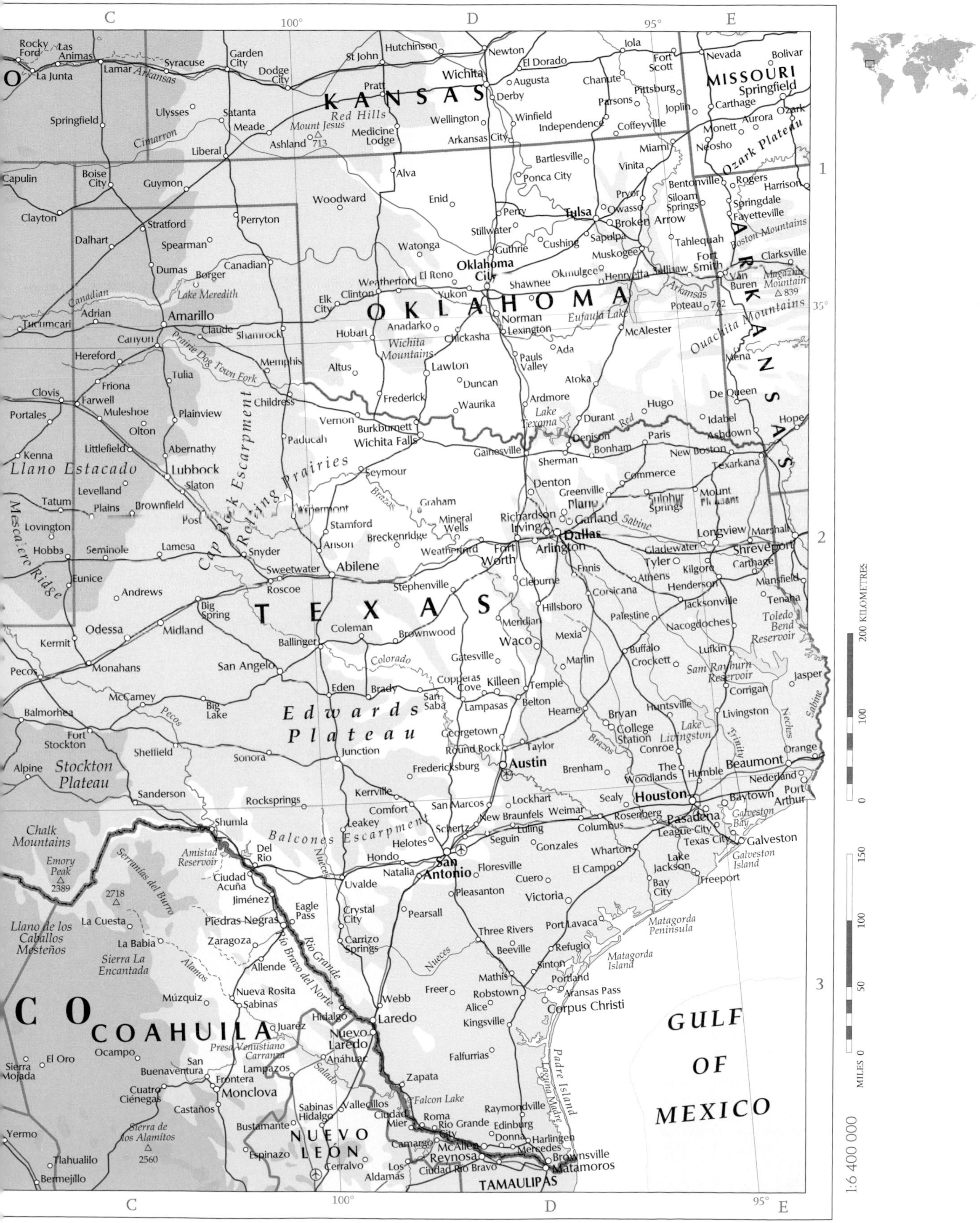

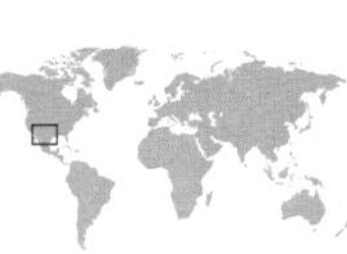

C D E

100° 95°

KANSAS

Rocky Ford, Las Animas, La Junta, Lamar, Arkansas, Syracuse, Garden City, Dodge City, St John, Hutchinson, Newton, Iola, Fort Scott, Nevada, Bolivar, Wichita, El Dorado, Augusta, Derby, Chanute, Pittsburg, Parsons, Joplin, Carthage, Springfield, Pratt, Red Hills, Mount Jesus, 713, Medicine Lodge, Ulysses, Satanta, Meade, Ashland, Springfield, Cimarron, Liberal, Wellington, Winfield, Independence, Coffeyville, Arkansas City

MISSOURI

Monett, Aurora, Ozark, Neosho, Ozark Plateau, Miami, Vinita, Bentonville, Rogers, Harrison, Siloam Springs, Springdale, Fayetteville

1

Capulin, Boise City, Guymon, Clayton, Alva, Woodward, Enid, Bartlesville, Ponca City, Perry, Pryor, Owasso, Tulsa, Broken Arrow, Stillwater, Cushing, Sapulpa, Tahlequah, Boston Mountains, Dalhart, Stratford, Perryton, Spearman, Watonga, Guthrie, Muskogee, Fort Smith, Clarksville, Dumas, Borger, Canadian, Oklahoma City, El Reno, Weatherford, Yukon, Shawnee, Okmulgee, Henryetta, Van Buren, Magazine Mountain, 839, Lake Meredith, Canadian, Elk City, Clinton

OKLAHOMA

ARKANSAS

Adrian, Tucumcari, Amarillo, Anadarko, Norman, Lexington, Eufaula Lake, Arkansas, Poteau, 762, McAlester, Ouachita Mountains, 35°, Claude, Shamrock, Hobart, Canyon, Chickasha, Wichita Mountains, Ada, Hereford, Prairie Dog Town Fork, Memphis, Altus, Lawton, Pauls Valley, Mena, Tulia, Duncan, Atoka, Friona, Clovis, Farwell, Childress, Frederick, Ardmore, De Queen, Muleshoe, Waurika, Lake Texoma, Hugo, Portales, Plainview, Olton, Vernon, Burkburnett, Durant, Red, Idabel, Hope, Wichita Falls, Denison, Paris, Ashdown, Littlefield, Abernathy, Paducah, Bonham, Gainesville, Sherman, New Boston, Kenna, Texarkana, Llano Estacado, Lubbock, Seymour, Commerce, Caprock Escarpment, Rolling Prairies, Slaton, Denton, Mount Pleasant, Levelland, Greenville, Tatum, Plains, Brownfield, Brazos, Graham, Sulphur Springs, Post, Aspermont, Plano, Mescalero Ridge, Stamford, Mineral Wells, Richardson, Garland, Sabine, Lovington, Irving, Marshall, Longview, Breckenridge, Dallas, Hobbs, Seminole, Lamesa, Anson, Gladewater

2

Snyder, Weatherford, Fort Worth, Arlington, Shreveport, Tyler, Kilgore, Carthage, Sweetwater, Abilene, Eunice, Ennis, Athens, Mansfield, Roscoe, Cleburne, Henderson, Andrews, Stephenville, Corsicana, Tenaha, Big Spring, Jacksonville, Hillsboro

TEXAS

Toledo Bend Reservoir, Odessa, Midland, Palestine, Nacogdoches, Meridian, Coleman, Brownwood, Mexia, Kermit, Ballinger, Waco, Buffalo, Lufkin, Colorado, Gatesville, Marlin, Crockett, Pecos, Monahans, San Angelo, Sam Rayburn Reservoir, Jasper, Copperas Cove, Killeen, Eden, Brady, Temple, Corrigan, McCamey, San Saba, Belton, Lampasas, Huntsville, Bryan, Hearne, Balmorhea, Big Lake, Livingston, Neches, Sabine, Pecos, College Station, Lake Livingston, Trinity, Edwards Plateau, Georgetown, Fort Stockton, Taylor, Brazos, Orange, Round Rock, Conroe, Sheffield, Junction, Austin, Beaumont, Sonora, Alpine, Stockton Plateau, Fredericksburg, Brenham, The Woodlands, Humble, Nederland, Port Arthur, Sanderson, Kerrville, Lockhart, Sealy, Houston, Baytown, Rockprings, Comfort, San Marcos, Weimar, Rosenberg, Pasadena, Galveston Bay, Chalk Mountains, Shumla, New Braunfels, Columbus, Leakey, Schertz, Luling, League City, Balcones Escarpment, Seguin, Gonzales, Texas City, Galveston, Amistad Reservoir, Del Rio, Helotes, Emory Peak, 2389, Nueces, San Antonio, Wharton, Galveston Island, Hondo, Lake Jackson, Floresville, Ciudad Acuña, Natalia, El Campo, Serranías del Burro, Cuero, Freeport, Uvalde, Bay City, 2718, Jiménez, Pleasanton, Victoria, Eagle Pass, Crystal City, Pearsall, Piedras Negras, Port Lavaca, Matagorda Peninsula, La Cuesta, Llano de los Caballos Mesteños, Zaragoza, Three Rivers, La Babia, Carrizo Springs, Beeville, Refugio, Sierra La Encantada, Alamos, Allende, Rio Bravo del Norte, Rio Grande, Nueces, Matagorda Island, Sinton, Mathis, Portland, Múzquiz, Nueva Rosita, Freer, Robstown, Aransas Pass

3

Sabinas, Webb, Alice, Corpus Christi, Kingsville, Hidalgo, Laredo

COAHUILA

Juarez, Nuevo Laredo, Ocampo, Presa Venustiano Carranza, Anáhuac, Falfurrias

GULF OF MEXICO

Sierra Mojada, El Oro, San Buenaventura, Lampazos, Salado, Padre Island, Laguna Madre, Frontera, Zapata, Monclova, Cuatro Ciénegas, Castaños, Falcon Lake, Sabinas Hidalgo, Vallecillos, Raymondville, Ciudad Mier, Roma, Rio Grande City, Edinburg, Yermo, Bustamante, Sierra de los Alamitos, 2560, Donna, Harlingen, Mercedes

NUEVO LEÓN

Camargo, McAllen, Brownsville, Tlahualilo, Espinazo, Reynosa, Matamoros, Cerralvo, Los Aldamas, Ciudad Río Bravo, Bermejillo

TAMAULIPAS

C 100° D 95° E

200 KILOMETRES, 100, 0

150 MILES, 100, 50, 0

1:6 400 000

METRES
FEET

METRES	FEET
5000	16404
3000	9843
2000	6562
1000	3281
500	1640
200	656
0	0
Land below sea level	
200	656
4000	13124
6000	19686

Lambert Azimuthal Equal Area Projection

100°
C
90°
D
1
2
3
30°
20°
UNITED STATES OF AMERICA
TEXAS
LOUISIANA
MISSISSIPPI
ALABAMA
FLORIDA
MEXICO
YUCATÁN
BELIZE
GUATEMALA
HONDURAS
GULF OF MEXICO
Bahía de Campeche
Gulf of Tehuantepec
Yucatan Channel
Tropic of Cancer
Edwards Plateau
Sierra Madre Oriental
Sierra Madre del Sur
Istmo de Tehuantepec
Dallas
Fort Worth
Houston
San Antonio
Austin
New Orleans
Baton Rouge
Shreveport
Jackson
Mobile
Montgomery
Pensacola
Corpus Christi
Laredo
Brownsville
Matamoros
Monterrey
Reynosa
McAllen
Nuevo Laredo
Ciudad Victoria
Tampico
Ciudad Madero
San Luis Potosí
Querétaro
Pachuca
MEXICO CITY
Nezahualcóyotl
Toluca
Puebla
Cuernavaca
Veracruz
Jalapa
Córdoba
Orizaba
Coatzacoalcos
Minatitlán
Villahermosa
Oaxaca
Acapulco
Chilpancingo
Tuxtla Gutiérrez
Mérida
Campeche
Progreso
Cancún
Cozumel
Chetumal
Belize
BELMOPAN
GUATEMALA CITY
Quetzaltenango
Tapachula
San Pedro Sula
Galveston
Beaumont
Port Arthur
Lake Charles
Lafayette
Waco
Abilene
Mississippi Delta
Arrecife Alacrán
Laguna Madre
Padre Island
Matagorda Island
Laguna de Términos
Cabo Catoche
Banco Chinchorro
Ambergris Cay
Turneffe Islands
1:9 600 000
200 KILOMETRES
MILES

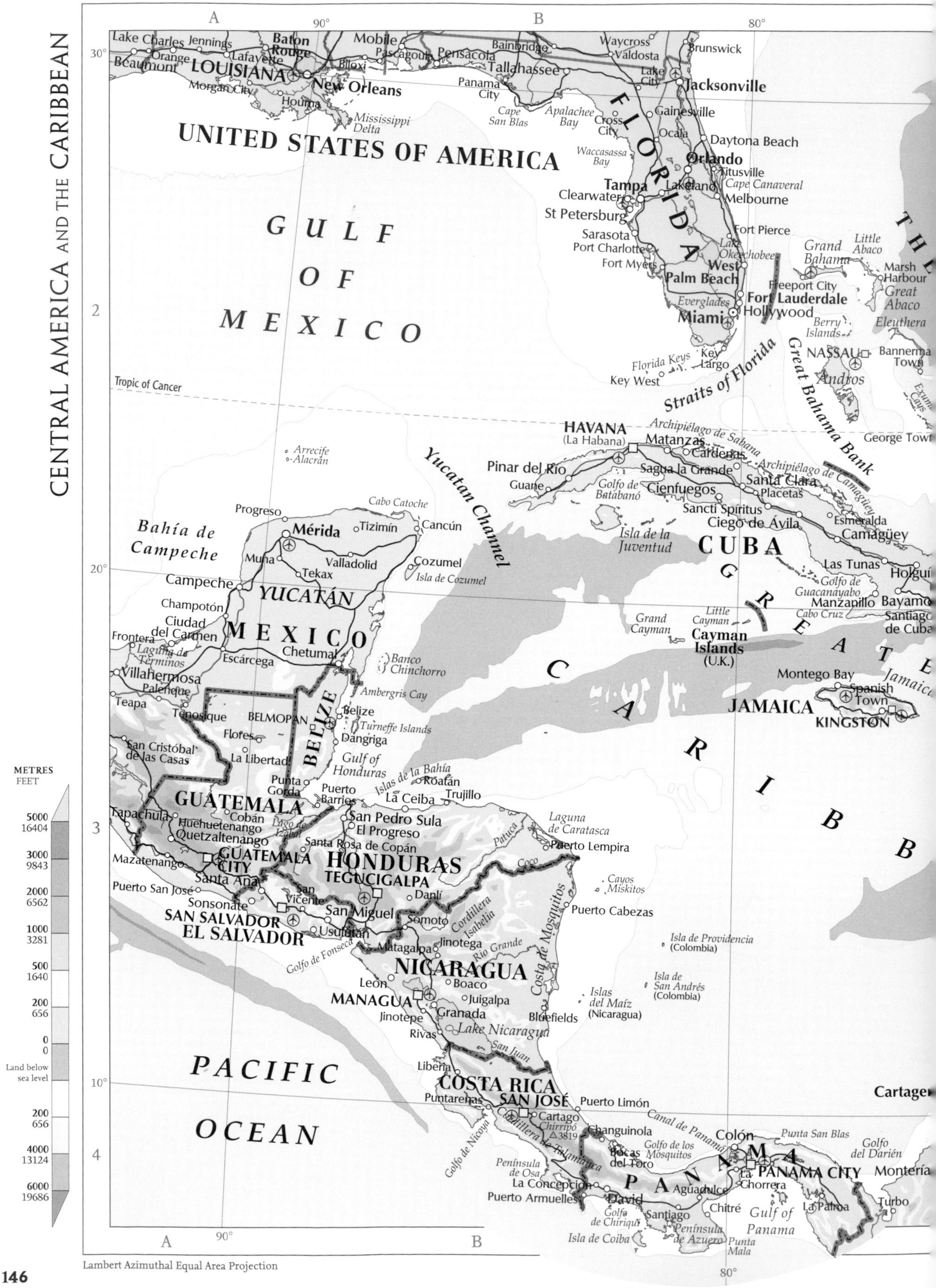

A B
90° 80°
30° 20° 10°
2 3 4

Lake Charles
Jennings
Baton Rouge
Mobile
Orange
Lafayette
Pascagoula
Pensacola
Bainbridge
Waycross
Valdosta
Brunswick
Beaumont
LOUISIANA
Biloxi
Tallahassee
Lake City
Jacksonville
Morgan City
New Orleans
Panama City
Houma
Mississippi Delta
Cape San Blas
Apalachee Bay
Cross City
Gainesville
Ocala
FLORIDA
UNITED STATES OF AMERICA
Daytona Beach
Waccasassa Bay
Orlando
Titusville
Tampa
Lakeland
Cape Canaveral
Clearwater
Melbourne
St Petersburg
GULF OF MEXICO
Sarasota
Port Charlotte
Fort Myers
Fort Pierce
Lake Okeechobee
West Palm Beach
Grand Bahama
Little Abaco
Marsh Harbour
Great Abaco
Freeport City
Fort Lauderdale
Everglades
Miami
Hollywood
Berry Islands
Eleuthera
NASSAU
Bannerman Town
Florida Keys
Key Largo
Key West
Straits of Florida
Great Bahama Bank
Andros
Exuma Cays
Tropic of Cancer
HAVANA (La Habana)
Matanzas
Archipiélago de Sabana
Cárdenas
George Town
Arrecife Alacrán
Yucatan Channel
Pinar del Río
Sagua la Grande
Archipiélago de Camagüey
Santa Clara
Guane
Golfo de Batabanó
Cienfuegos
Placetas
Sancti Spíritus
Cabo Catoche
Progreso
Ciego de Ávila
Esmeralda
Bahía de Campeche
Mérida
Tizimín
Cancún
Isla de la Juventud
CUBA
Camagüey
Muna
Valladolid
Cozumel
Tekax
Isla de Cozumel
Las Tunas
Holguín
Campeche
YUCATÁN
Golfo de Guacanayabo
Manzanillo
Bayamo
Champotón
Cabo Cruz
Santiago de Cuba
Ciudad del Carmen
Little Cayman
Grand Cayman
Cayman Islands (U.K.)
MEXICO
Frontera
Laguna de Términos
Chetumal
Escárcega
Banco Chinchorro
GREATER
Villahermosa
CARIBBEAN
Palenque
Ambergris Cay
Montego Bay
Jamaica
Teapa
Spanish Town
Tenosique
BELMOPAN
Belize
JAMAICA
KINGSTON
Turneffe Islands
BELIZE
Flores
Dangriga
San Cristóbal de las Casas
La Libertad
Gulf of Honduras
Islas de la Bahía
Punta Gorda
Roatán
Puerto Barrios
La Ceiba
Trujillo
GUATEMALA
Tapachula
Cobán
Lago de Izabal
San Pedro Sula
Huehuetenango
El Progreso
Laguna de Caratasca
Quetzaltenango
Santa Rosa de Copán
Patuca
Puerto Lempira
Mazatenango
GUATEMALA CITY
HONDURAS
Santa Ana
Coco
TEGUCIGALPA
Cayos Miskitos
Puerto San José
San Vicente
Danlí
Sonsonate
San Miguel
Puerto Cabezas
SAN SALVADOR
Somoto
Cordillera Isabelia
EL SALVADOR
Usulután
Costa de Mosquitos
Jinotega
Matagalpa
Golfo de Fonseca
Rio Grande
Isla de Providencia (Colombia)
NICARAGUA
León
Boaco
Isla de San Andrés (Colombia)
MANAGUA
Juigalpa
Islas del Maíz (Nicaragua)
Jinotepe
Granada
Bluefields
Rivas
Lake Nicaragua
San Juan
PACIFIC OCEAN
Liberia
COSTA RICA
Cartagena
Puntarenas
SAN JOSÉ
Puerto Limón
Cartago
Canal de Panamá
Chirripó 3819
Changuinola
Colón
Punta San Blas
Golfo del Darién
Golfo de Nicoya
Cordillera de Talamanca
Golfo de los Mosquitos
Bocas del Toro
PANAMA
PANAMA CITY
Montería
Península de Osa
La Chorrera
La Concepción
Aguadulce
Puerto Armuelles
David
Chitré
Gulf of Panama
La Palma
Turbo
Golfo de Chiriquí
Santiago
Península de Azuero
Isla de Coiba
Punta Mala

METRES FEET
5000 16404
3000 9843
2000 6562
1000 3281
500 1640
200 656
0 0
Land below sea level
200 656
4000 13124
6000 19686

Lambert Azimuthal Equal Area Projection

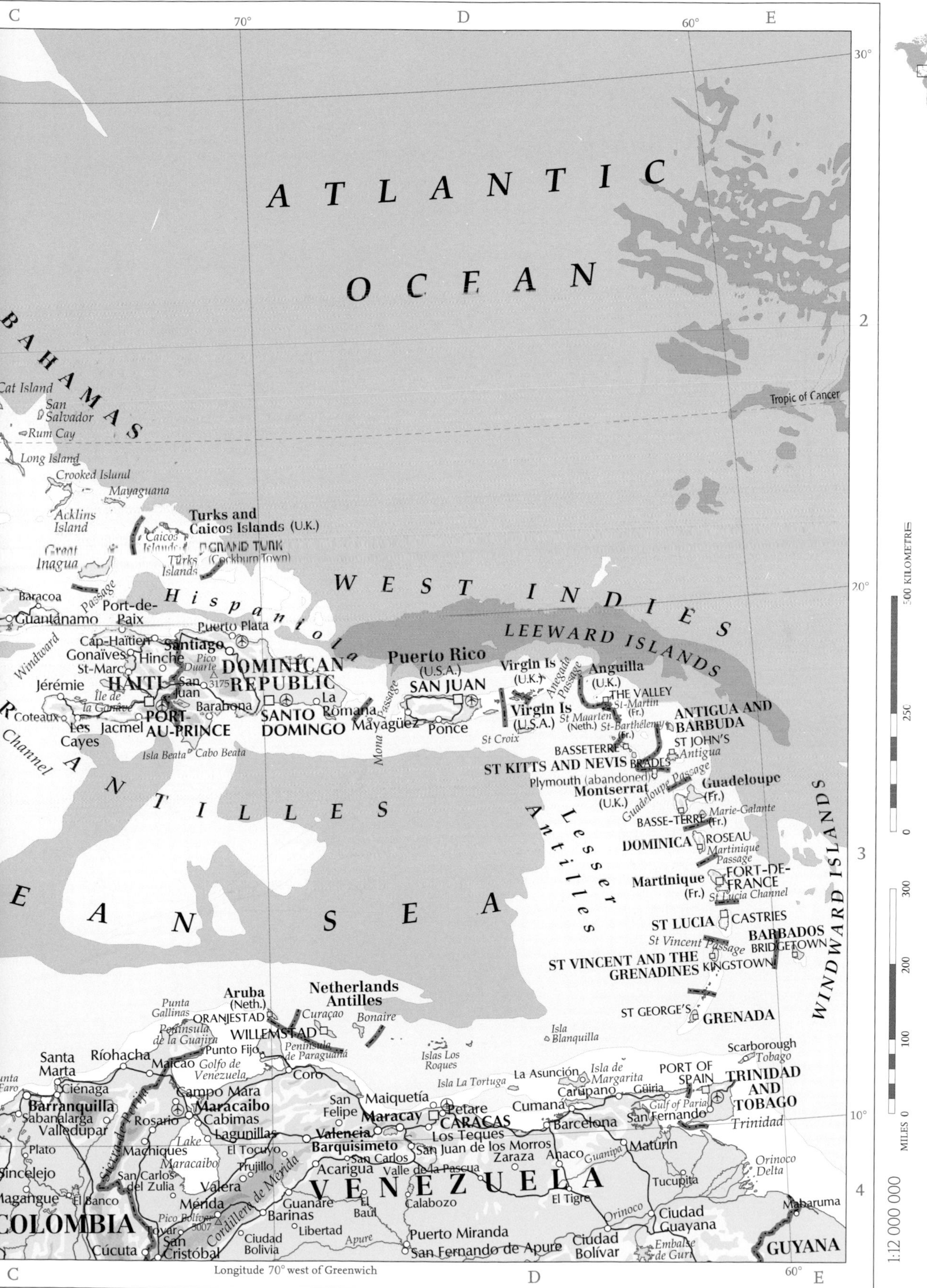
ATLANTIC
OCEAN
BAHAMAS
Cat Island
San Salvador
Rum Cay
Long Island
Crooked Island
Mayaguana
Acklins Island
Great Inagua
Turks and Caicos Islands (U.K.)
Caicos Islands
GRAND TURK (Cockburn Town)
Turks Islands
Tropic of Cancer
WEST INDIES
Hispaniola
Baracoa
Guantánamo
Windward Passage
Port-de-Paix
Cap-Haïtien
Gonaïves
St-Marc
Jérémie
Île de la Gonâve
HAITI
Hinche
PORT-AU-PRINCE
Coteaux
Les Cayes
Jacmel
Puerto Plata
Santiago
Pico Duarte 3175
DOMINICAN REPUBLIC
San Juan
Barahona
SANTO DOMINGO
La Romana
Isla Beata
Cabo Beata
Mona Passage
Mayagüez
Puerto Rico (U.S.A.)
SAN JUAN
Ponce
Virgin Is (U.K.)
Virgin Is (U.S.A.)
St Croix
Anegada Passage
LEEWARD ISLANDS
Anguilla (U.K.)
THE VALLEY
St-Martin (Fr.)
St Maarten (Neth.)
St-Barthélemy (Fr.)
ANTIGUA AND BARBUDA
ST JOHN'S
Antigua
BASSETERRE
ST KITTS AND NEVIS
BRADES
Plymouth (abandoned)
Montserrat (U.K.)
Guadeloupe Passage
Guadeloupe (Fr.)
BASSE-TERRE
Marie-Galante (Fr.)
DOMINICA
ROSEAU
Martinique Passage
Martinique (Fr.)
FORT-DE-FRANCE
St Lucia Channel
ST LUCIA
CASTRIES
St Vincent Passage
BARBADOS
BRIDGETOWN
ST VINCENT AND THE GRENADINES
KINGSTOWN
ST GEORGE'S
GRENADA
WINDWARD ISLANDS
Lesser Antilles
ANTILLES
CARIBBEAN SEA
Aruba (Neth.)
ORANJESTAD
Netherlands Antilles
Curaçao
WILLEMSTAD
Bonaire
Punta Gallinas
Península de la Guajira
Punto Fijo
Península de Paraguaná
Islas Los Roques
Isla La Tortuga
Isla Blanquilla
La Asunción
Isla de Margarita
Scarborough
Tobago
Santa Marta
Ríohacha
Maicao
Golfo de Venezuela
Coro
Ciénaga
Barranquilla
Sabanalarga
Valledupar
Campo Mara
Maracaibo
Cabimas
Rosario
Lagunillas
Lake Maracaibo
Machiques
Plato
Sincelejo
San Carlos del Zulia
Magangue
El Banco
Sierra de Perijá
COLOMBIA
Pico Bolívar 5007
Tovar
San Cristóbal
Cúcuta
San Felipe
Maiquetía
Maracay
Petare
CARACAS
Los Teques
Valencia
Barquisimeto
El Tocuyo
Trujillo
Valera
Mérida
Cordillera de Mérida
San Carlos
Acarigua
Guanare
Barinas
Libertad
Ciudad Bolivia
El Baúl
VENEZUELA
Calabozo
Valle de la Pascua
San Juan de los Morros
Zaraza
Cumaná
Barcelona
Carúpano
Güiria
PORT OF SPAIN
Gulf of Paria
San Fernando
TRINIDAD AND TOBAGO
Trinidad
Anaco
Guanipa
Maturín
El Tigre
Tucupita
Orinoco Delta
Orinoco
Ciudad Guayana
Ciudad Bolívar
Embalse de Guri
Puerto Miranda
San Fernando de Apure
Apure
Mabaruma
GUYANA
Longitude 70° west of Greenwich
500 KILOMETRES
250
0
300
200
100
0 MILES
1:12 000 000

Bi-Polar Oblique Projection

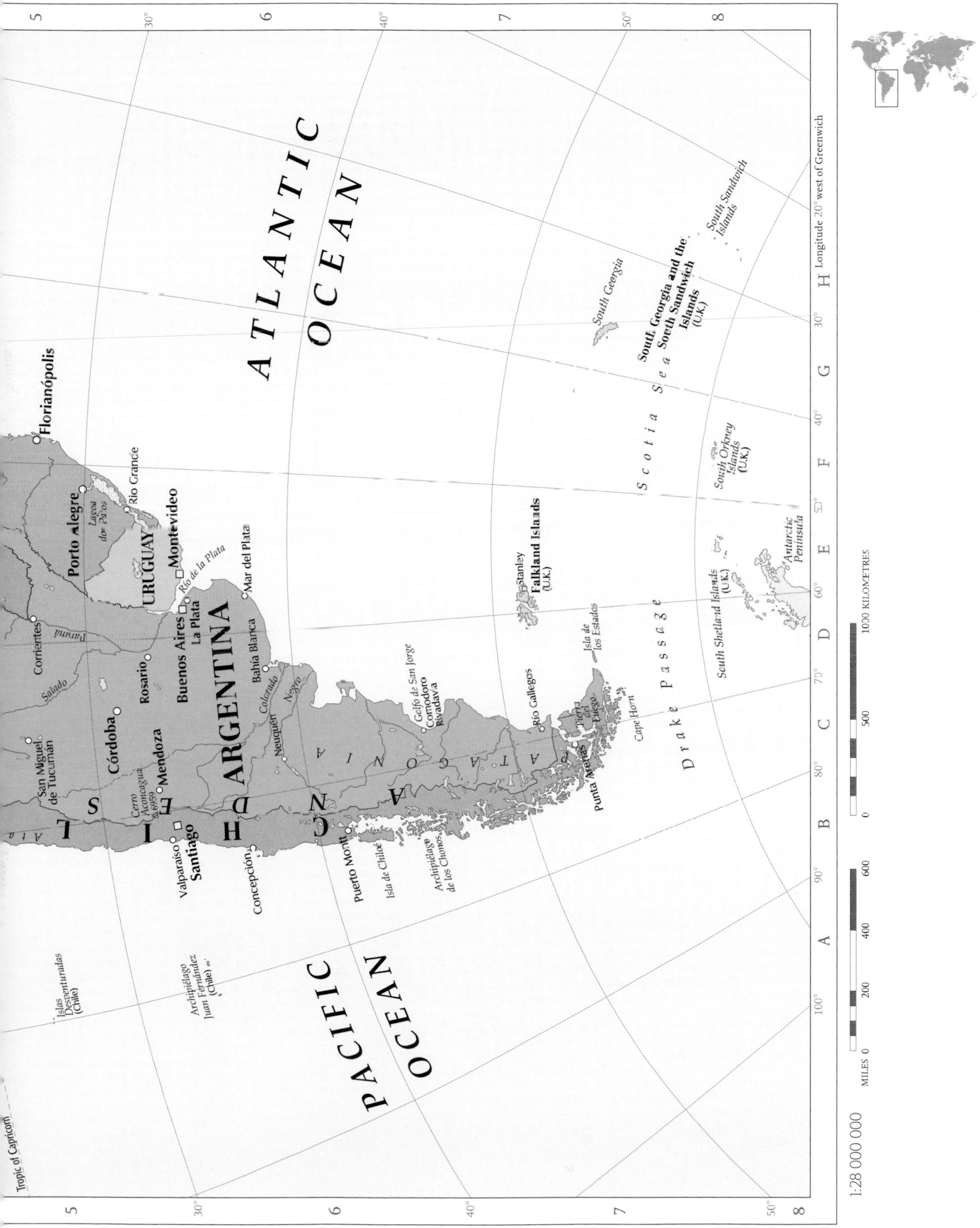

Tropic of Capricorn

Islas Desventuradas (Chile)

Archipiélago Juan Fernández (Chile)

San Miguel de Tucumán

Corrientes

Florianópolis

Porto Alegre

Lagoa dos Patos

Salado

Paraná

Córdoba

Cerro Aconcagua 6959

Mendoza

Rosario

URUGUAY

Rio Grande

Montevideo

Valparaíso

Santiago

Buenos Aires

La Plata

Río de la Plata

CHILE

ARGENTINA

Mar del Plata

Concepción

Bahía Blanca

Colorado

Neuquén

Negro

ANDES

PATAGONIA

ATLANTIC OCEAN

PACIFIC OCEAN

Puerto Montt

Isla de Chiloé

Archipiélago de los Chonos

Golfo de San Jorge

Comodoro Rivadavia

Stanley

Falkland Islands (U.K.)

Río Gallegos

Punta Arenas

Tierra del Fuego

Isla de los Estados

Cape Horn

South Georgia

Scotia Sea

South Georgia and the South Sandwich Islands (U.K.)

Drake Passage

South Sandwich Islands

South Shetland Islands (U.K.)

South Orkney Islands (U.K.)

Antarctic Peninsula

5 6 7 8

A B C D E F G H

30° 40° 50°

100° 90° 80° 70° 60° 50° 40° 30° Longitude 20° west of Greenwich

1:28 000 000

MILES 0 200 400 600

0 500 1000 KILOMETRES

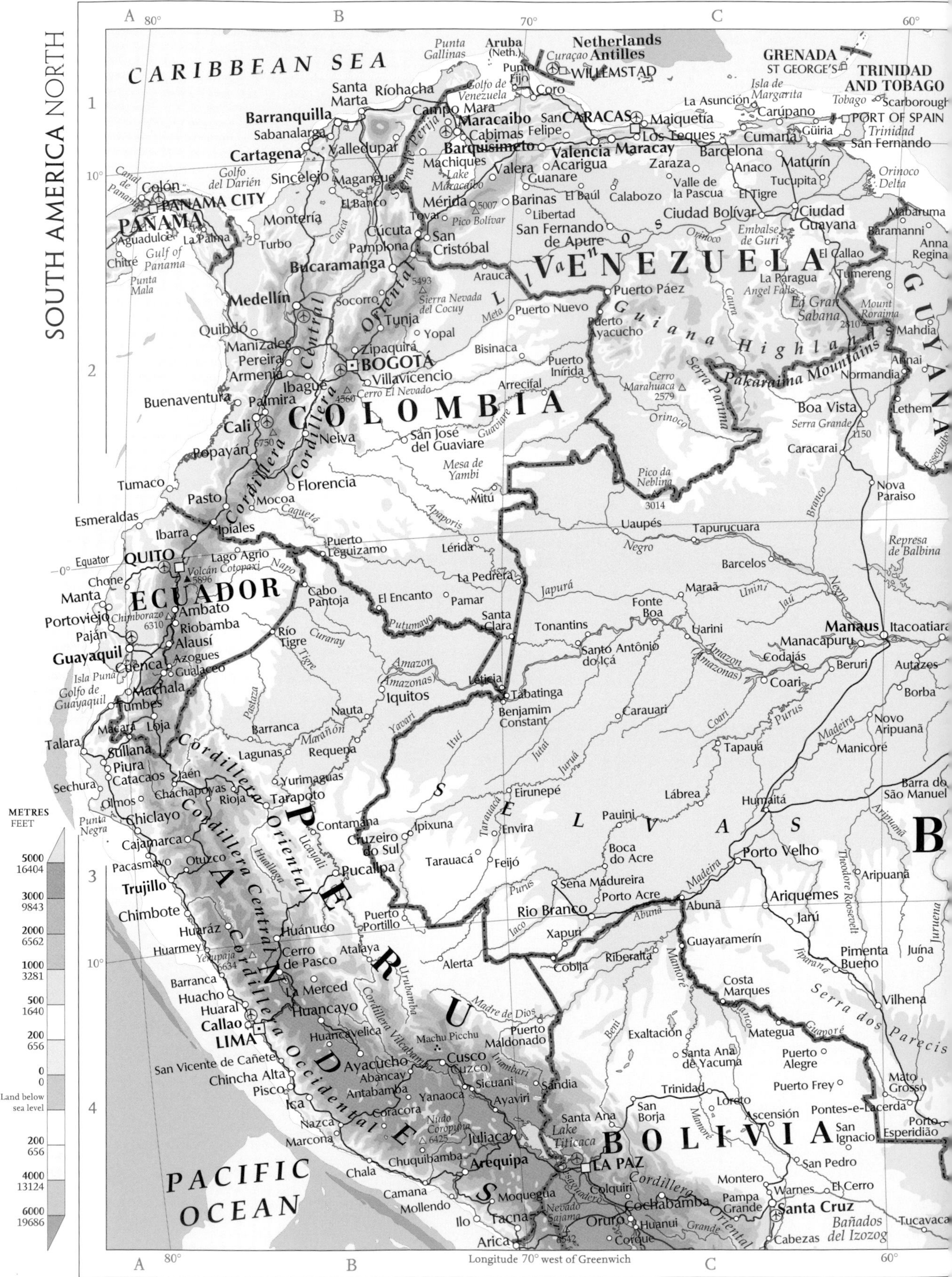

Lambert Azimuthal Equal Area Projection

D
50°
E
40°
F
1
2
3
4
10°
0°
10°
Equator
ATLANTIC
OCEAN
400 KILOMETRES
200
0
MILES 0
100
200
300
1:16 000 000
GEORGETOWN
Paradise
New Amsterdam
Linden
Totness
PARAMARIBO
Albina
St-Laurent-du-Maroni
Nieuw Nickerie
Brokopondo
Sinnamary
Kourou
CAYENNE
Professor van Blommestein Meer
SURINAME
French Guiana
Guisanbourg
Oiapoque
Juliana Top
1230
Inini
Pontoetoe
Lourenço
Calçoene
Amapá
Ilha de Maracá
Serra Tumucumaque
Mouths of the Amazon
Macapá
Ilha Caviana
Porto Santana
Mazagão
Chaves
Cabo Maguarinho
Baía de Marajó
Arere
Ilha de Marajó
Salinópolis
Bragança
Serra Parauaquara
359
Almeirim
Belém
Oriximiná
Óbidos
Breves
Viseu
Juruti
Monte Alegre
Portel
Castanhal
Cururupu
Urucara
Parintins
Cametá
Acará
Pinheiro
Baía de São Marcos
Urucurituba
Santarém
Capim
São Luís
Parnaíba
Camocim
Altamira
Tucuruí
Viana
Itapicuru Mirim
Luzilândia
Tapajós
Represa Tucuruí
Pindaré
Caucaia
Fortaleza
Itaituba
Iriri
Santa Luzia
Bacabal
Codó
Tianguá
Sobral
Jacunda
Pedreiras
Piripiri
Cascavel
Serra dos Carajás
Marabá
Pres. Dutra
Caxias
Campo Maior
Canindé
Aracati
Imperatriz
Grajaú
Timon
Teresina
Quixadá
Macau
Ponta do Calcanhar
Jacareacanga
Araras
São Félix
Tocantinópolis
Barra do Corda
Buriti Bravo
Crateús
Boa Viagem
Mossoró
Touros
Xinguara
Porto Franco
Açude Boa Esperança
Palmeirais
Taua
Natal
Manuelzinho
Araguaína
Jerumenha
Floriano
Iguatu
Icó
Balsas
Picos
Sousa
Campina Grande
Mamanguape
Carolina
Uruçuí
Oeiras
Crato
Juazeiro do Norte
João Pessoa
RAZIL
Conceição do Araguaia
Canto do Buriti
Paulistana
Jaboatão dos Guararapes
Olinda
Salgueiro
Recife
Santa Maria das Barreiras
Pedro Afonso
São Raimundo Nonato
Floresta
Caruaru
Cabo de Santo Agostinho
Caracol
Petrolina
Garanhuns
Serra do Cachimbo
Gilbués
Nova Remanso
Paulo Afonso
Rio Largo
Peixoto de Azevedo
Palmas
Juazeiro
Maceió
Barragem de Sobradinho
Senhor do Bonfim
Arapiraca
Ilha do Bananal
Porto Nacional
Corrente
Monte Santo
São Félix
Dianópolis
Xique Xique
Lagarto
Aracaju
Porto dos Gauchos
Óbidos
Gurupi
Natividade
Barreiras
Irecê
Jacobina
Estância
Serra do Roncador
Serra Geral de Goiás
Ibotirama
Feira de Santana
Serrinha
Alagoinhas
Porto Artur
Santana
Bom Jesus da Lapa
Itaberaba
Camaçari
Chapada Diamantina
Salvador
Porangatu
Cavalcante
Correntina
Jequié
Santo Antônio de Jesus
Diamantino
Planalto do Mato Grosso
Represa Serra da Mesa
Posse
Brumado
Ipiaú
Rosário Oeste
Uruaçu
Niquelândia
Guanambi
Ubaitaba
Barra do Bugres
Itabuna
Ilhéus
Cuiabá
Barra do Garças
BRASÍLIA
Formosa
Januária
Espinosa
Vitória da Conquista
Una
Cáceres
Rondonópolis
Goiás
Anápolis
Luziânia
Arinos
Itapetinga
Alto Garças
Iporá
Trindade
Vianópolis
Unaí
Montes Claros
Janaúba
Salinas
Serra do Caiapó
Goiânia
Paraúna
Almenara
Porto Seguro
Itiquira
Paracatu
Jequitaí
Puerto Isabel
Taquarí
Jataí
Rio Verde
Serra do Espinhaço
Teófilo Otôni
Alcobaça
Coxim
Itumbiara
Araguari
Patos de Minas
Corumbá
Rio Verde de Mato Grosso
Uberlândia

SOUTH AMERICA SOUTH

METRES	FEET
5000	16404
3000	9843
2000	6562
1000	3281
500	1640
200	656
0	0
Land below sea level	
200	656
4000	13124
6000	19686

Lambert Azimuthal Equal Area Projection

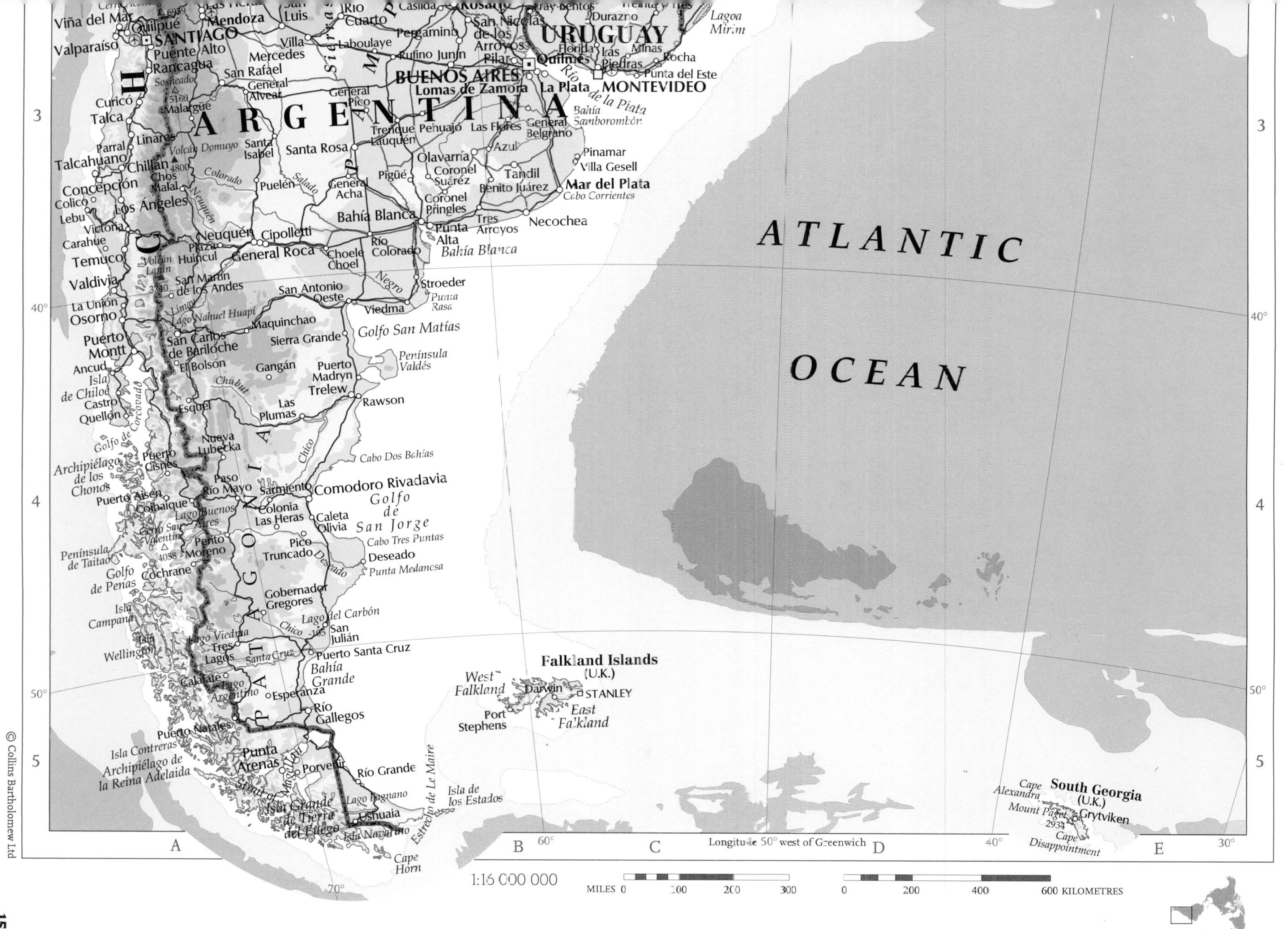
ATLANTIC
OCEAN
ARGENTINA
PATAGONIA
URUGUAY
BUENOS AIRES
MONTEVIDEO
SANTIAGO
Mendoza
Mar del Plata
Bahía Blanca
Golfo San Matías
Comodoro Rivadavia
Golfo de San Jorge
Río Gallegos
Punta Arenas
Ushuaia
Cape Horn
Falkland Islands
(U.K.)
STANLEY
West Falkland
East Falkland
South Georgia
(U.K.)
Grytviken
Longitude 50° west of Greenwich
1:16 000 000
MILES 0 100 200 300
0 200 400 600 KILOMETRES

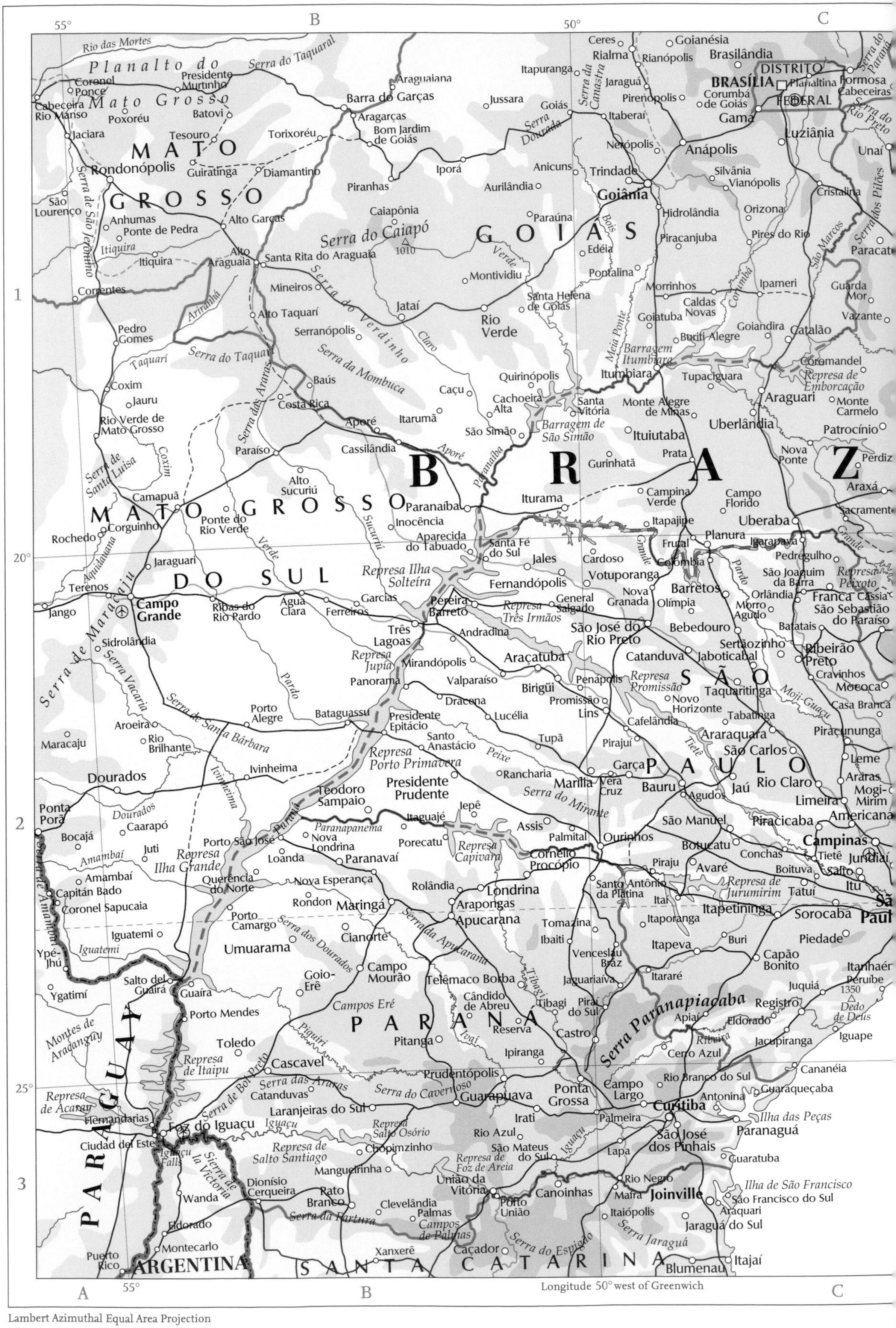

55° B 50° C

Rio das Mortes
Planalto do Mato Grosso
Serra do Taquaral
Coronel Ponce
Presidente Murtinho
Cabeceira Rio Manso
Poxoréu
Batovi
Barra do Garças
Araguaiana
Aragarças
Bom Jardim de Goiás
Jaciara
Tesouro
Torixoréu
MATO GROSSO
Rondonópolis
Guiratinga
Diamantino
Piranhas
Iporá
Jussara
Itapuranga
Goiás
Serra Dourada
Serra da Canastra
Ceres
Rialma
Rianópolis
Goianésia
Brasilândia
Jaraguá
Pirenópolis
Itaberaí
Nerópolis
Anicuns
Trindade
Goiânia
Aurilândia
Anápolis
DISTRITO FEDERAL
BRASÍLIA
Planaltina
Formosa
Cabeceiras
Corumbá de Goiás
Gama
Luziânia
Unaí
Serra do Paranã
Serra do Rio Preto
Silvânia
Vianópolis
Cristalina
Serra dos Pilões
São Lourenço
Serra de São Jerônimo
Anhumas
Ponte de Pedra
Alto Garças
Caiapônia
Paraúna
Serra do Caiapó
1010
GOIÁS
Hidrolândia
Orizona
Pires do Rio
Paracatu
Itiquira
Alto Araguaia
Santa Rita do Araguaia
Serra do Verdinho
Bois
Verde
Edéia
Montividiu
Pontalina
Piracanjuba
São Marcos
Correntes
Mineiros
Alto Taquarí
Araguaia
Ariranha
Jataí
Rio Verde
Santa Helena de Goiás
Morrinhos
Caldas Novas
Ipameri
Guarda Mor
Vazante
Corumbá
Meia Ponte
Goiatuba
Buriti Alegre
Goiandira
Catalão
Pedro Gomes
Serranópolis
Claro
Taquarí
Serra do Taquari
Serra da Mombuca
Barragem Itumbiara
Itumbiara
Tupaciguara
Coromandel
Represa de Emborcação
Coxim
Jauru
Baús
Serra das Araras
Costa Rica
Caçu
Quirinópolis
Cachoeira Alta
Santa Vitória
Monte Alegre de Minas
Araguari
Monte Carmelo
Rio Verde de Mato Grosso
Aporé
Itarumã
São Simão
Barragem de São Simão
Ituiutaba
Uberlândia
Patrocínio
Serra de Santa Luísa
Coxim
Paraíso
Cassilândia
BRAZ
Paranaíba
Gurinhatã
Prata
Nova Ponte
Perdiz
Araxá
Camapuã
Alto Sucuriú
MATO GROSSO DO SUL
Ponte do Rio Verde
Sucuriú
Paranaíba
Inocência
Iturama
Campina Verde
Campo Florido
Sacramento
Rochedo
Corguinho
Aparecida do Tabuado
Santa Fé do Sul
Itapajipe
Uberaba
Planura
Frutal
Igarapava
Verde
Jaraguari
Jales
Cardoso
Grande
Colômbia
Pedregulho
20°
Aquidauana
Terenos
Represa Ilha Solteira
Fernandópolis
Votuporanga
Nova Granada
Barretos
São Joaquim da Barra
Represa Peixoto
Orlândia
Franca
Cássia
São Sebastião do Paraíso
Jango
Campo Grande
Ribas do Rio Pardo
Água Clara
Garcias
Ferreiros
Pereira Barreto
Represa Três Irmãos
General Salgado
Olímpia
Morro Agudo
Pardo
Batatais
Serra de Maracaju
Sidrolândia
Três Lagoas
Andradina
São José do Rio Preto
Bebedouro
Sertãozinho
Ribeirão Preto
Represa Jupiá
Mirandópolis
Araçatuba
Catanduva
Jaboticabal
Cravinhos
Serra Vacaria
Pardo
Panorama
Valparaíso
Birigüi
Penápolis
Represa Promissão
SÃO PAULO
Taquaritinga
Mococa
Moji-Guaçu
Dracena
Promissão
Novo Horizonte
Casa Branca
Porto Alegre
Bataguassu
Lucélia
Lins
Tabatinga
Aroeira
Serra de Santa Bárbara
Presidente Epitácio
Cafelândia
Araraquara
Pirassununga
Maracaju
Rio Brilhante
Santo Anastácio
Peixe
Tupã
Pirajuí
Tietê
São Carlos
Leme
Represa Porto Primavera
Garça
Rio Claro
Araras
Dourados
Ivinheima
Ivinheima
Presidente Prudente
Rancharia
Marília
Vera Cruz
Bauru
Jaú
Mogi-Mirim
Limeira
Teodoro Sampaio
Serra do Mirante
Agudos
Americana
Ponta Porã
Dourados
Iepê
São Manuel
Piracicaba
Bocajá
Caarapó
Paraná
Paranapanema
Itaguajé
Assis
Palmital
Ourinhos
Campinas
Porto São José
Nova Londrina
Porecatu
Represa Capivara
Cornélio Procópio
Botucatu
Conchas
Tietê
Jundiaí
Juti
Amambaí
Represa Ilha Grande
Loanda
Paranavaí
Piraju
Avaré
Boituva
Salto
Itu
Amambaí
Querência do Norte
Nova Esperança
Rolândia
Londrina
Santo Antônio da Platina
Represa de Jurumirim
Tatuí
Serra de Amambaí
Capitán Bado
Rondon
Maringá
Arapongas
Itaí
Itapetininga
Sorocaba
São Paulo
Coronel Sapucaia
Porto Camargo
Serra dos Dourados
Serra da Apucarana
Apucarana
Tomazina
Itaporanga
Iguatemi
Cianorte
Ibaiti
Piedade
Iguatemi
Umuarama
Itapeva
Buri
Ypé-Jhú
Venceslau Braz
Capão Bonito
Campo Mourão
Telêmaco Borba
Tibagi
Jaguariaíva
Itararé
Itanhaém
Peruíbe
Salto del Guairá
Guaíra
Goio-Erê
Cândido de Abreu
Juquiá
1350
Ygatimí
Campos Eré
Tibagi
Piraí do Sul
Serra Paranapiacaba
Registro
Dedo de Deus
Porto Mendes
PARANÁ
Reserva
Apiaí
Eldorado
Montes de Aracanguy
Toledo
Piquiri
Pitanga
Ivaí
Castro
Ribeira
Jacupiranga
Iguape
Represa de Itaipu
Cascavel
Ipiranga
Cerro Azul
Serra das Araras
Prudentópolis
Rio Branco do Sul
Cananéia
25°
Represa de Acaray
Catanduvas
Serra do Boi Preto
Serra do Cavernoso
Guarapuava
Ponta Grossa
Campo Largo
Curitiba
Antonina
Guaraqueçaba
Hernandarias
Laranjeiras do Sul
Represa Salto Osório
Irati
Palmeira
Ilha das Peças
Foz do Iguaçu
Iguaçu
Paranaguá
Ciudad del Este
Iguaçu Falls
Sierra de la Victoria
Represa de Salto Santiago
Chopinzinho
Rio Azul
São Mateus do Sul
Iguaçu
São José dos Pinhais
Lapa
Mangueirinha
Represa de Foz de Areia
Guaratuba
Dionísio Cerqueira
Rato Branco
União da Vitória
Rio Negro
Ilha de São Francisco
Wanda
Canoinhas
Mafra
Joinville
São Francisco do Sul
PARAGUAY
Clevelândia
Palmas
Porto União
Itaiópolis
Araquari
Serra da Partura
Campos de Palmas
Jaraguá do Sul
Eldorado
Serra do Espigão
Serra Jaraguá
Montecarlo
Xanxerê
Caçador
Puerto Rico
ARGENTINA
SANTA CATARINA
Blumenau
Itajaí

1 2 3

A 55° B Longitude 50° west of Greenwich C

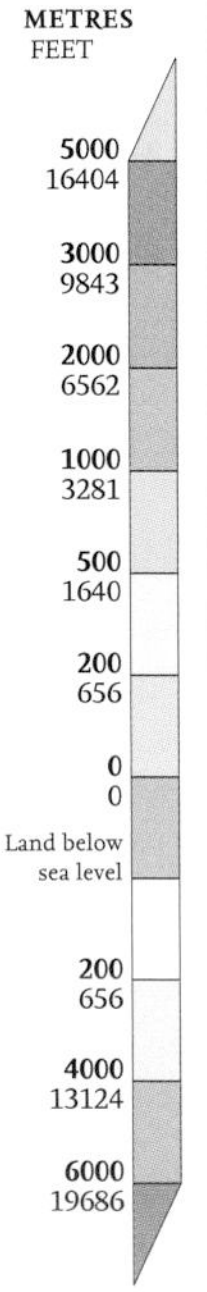

METRES / FEET

METRES	FEET
5000	16404
3000	9843
2000	6562
1000	3281
500	1640
200	656
0	0
Land below sea level	
200	656
2000	6562
4000	13124
6000	19686

Lambert Azimuthal Equal Area Projection

D
E
45°
40°
20°
25°
1
2
3
MINAS GERAIS
BAHIA
ESPÍRITO SANTO
RIO DE JANEIRO
ATLANTIC
OCEAN
Tropic of Capricorn
Januária
Buritis
Serra das Araras
Chapadão de Santa Maria
Serra de São Felipe
Verde Grande
Arinos
São Francisco
Janaúba
São João da Ponte
Ubaí
Brasília de Minas
Mirabela
São Romão
Bonfinópolis de Minas
Preto
Coração de Jesus
Miralta
Montes Claros
Ibiaí
Caatinga
Paracatu
Pirapora
Jequitaí
Bocaiúva
Várzea da Palma
Lassance
João Pinheiro
Serra do Cabral
Buenópolis
Augusto de Lima
Diamantina
São Gonçalo do Abaeté
Presidente Olegário
Represa Três Marias
Corinto
Curvelo
Patos de Minas
Serra da Canastra
Biquinhas
Felixlândia
Tiros
Carmo do Paranaíba
Abaeté
Pompéu
Cordisburgo
Velhas
Ibiá
São Gotardo
Martinho Campos
Bom Despacho
Pitangui
Sete Lagoas
Lagoa Santa
Belo Horizonte
Campos Altos
Pará de Minas
Sabará
Nova Lima
Bambuí
Santo Antônio do Monte
Itaúna
Divinópolis
Itabirito
1800
Piumhí
Formiga
Candeias
Oliveira
Passa Tempo
Conselheiro Lafaiete
Ouro Preto
Passos
Represa Furnas
Campo Belo
Carandaí
Barbacena
Guaxupe
Muzambinho
Alfenas
Três Pontas
Lavras
São João del Rei
Varginha
Grande
Machado
Andrelândia
Poços de Caldas
Três Corações
Campanha
São João da Boa Vista
Pinhal
São Lourenço
Agulhas Negras
2797
Pouso Alegre
Itapira
Itajubá
Amparo
Campos do Jordão
Serra da Mantiqueira
Cruzeiro
Lorena
Guaratinguetá
Bragança Paulista
Taubaté
São José dos Campos
Jacareí
Moji das Cruzes
Santo André
São Bernardo do Campo
Santos
São Vicente
Guarujá
Caraguatatuba
Ilhabela
Ilha do São Sebastião
Ponta do Boi
Parati
Angra dos Reis
Ilha Grande
Baía da Ilha Grande
Baía de Sepetiba
Itaguaí
Rio de Janeiro
Niterói
São Gonçalo
Nova Iguaçu
Volta Redonda
Marquês de Valença
Três Rios
Juiz de Fora
Lima Duarte
Santos Dumont
Bicas
Além Paraíba
Paraíba do Sul
Teresópolis
Nova Friburgo
Cantagalo
Rio Bonito
São Pedro da Aldeia
Cabo Frio
Ilha do Cabo Frio
Lago de Araruama
Macaé
Campos
Lagoa Feia
Santo Amaro de Campos
Cabo de São Tomé
São João da Barra
São Fidélis
Itaperuna
Bom Jesus do Itabapoana
Itabapoana
São João Nepomuceno
Leopoldina
Cataguases
Muriaé
Ubá
Viçosa
Tombos
Carangola
Ponte Nova
Rio Casca
Manhuaçu
Pico da Bandeira
2890
Serra do Caparaó
Muqui
Alegre
Iconha
Cachoeiro de Itapemirim
Itapemirim
Mimoso do Sul
Guarapari
Muniz Freire
Castelo
Vila Velha
Vitória
Serra
Cariacica
Fundão
Ibiraçu
Aracruz
Santa Teresa
Regência
Ponta de Monsarás
Doce
Colatina
Linhares
Mutum
Caratinga
Coronel Fabriciano
Ipatinga
Itabira
Piracicaba
Tarumirim
Aimorés
Resplendor
Conselheiro Pena
Mantena
Governador Valadares
Serra dos Aimorés
Serra das Safiras
Nova Venécia
São Mateus
Conceição da Barra
Itaúnas
Morro d'Anta
Mucuri
Campanário
Coroaci
Peçanha
Guanhães
Sêrro
Conceição do Mato Dentro
São João Evangelista
Santa Maria do Suaçuí
Suaçuí Grande
Pico de Itambé
2033
Serra Negra
Serra do Espinhaço
Itamarandiba
Capelinha
Carbonita
Turmalina
Minas Novas
Itambacuri
Malacacheta
Ladainha
Teófilo Otôni
Ataléia
Carlos Chagas
Planalto do Brasil
Nanuque
Pavão
Itanhém
Águas Formosas
Serra do Chifre
Caraí
Araçuaí
Virgem da Lapa
Jequitinhonha
Itinga
Itaobím
Joaíma
Grão Mogol
Francisco Sá
Salinas
Riacho dos Machados
Porteirinha
Taiobeiras
Rio Pardo de Minas
São João do Paraíso
Encruzilhada
Medina
Pedra Azul
Almenara
Jacinto
Salto da Divisa
Jordânia
Macarani
Itapetinga
Pardo
Potiraguá
Itapebi
Arataca
Una
Mascote
Canavieiras
Belmonte
Santa Cruz Cabrália
Porto Seguro
Monte Pascoal
536
Jucuruçu
Itamaraju
Prado
Alcobaça
Juerana
Ponta da Baleia
Caravelas
1:6 000 000
KILOMETRES
MILES
0
50
100
150
200

PACIFIC OCEAN

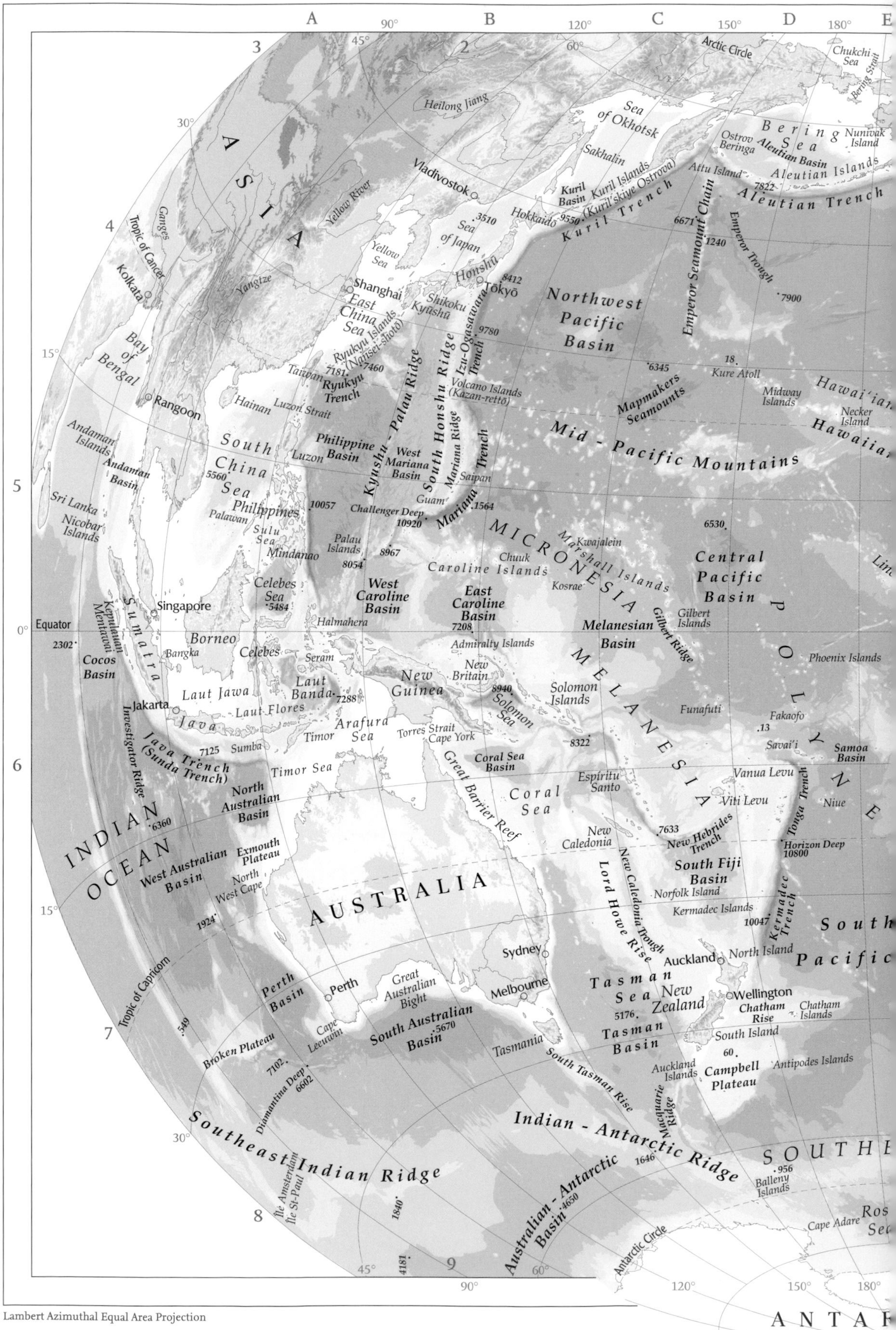

A 90° B 120° C 150° D 180° E

ASIA
Heilong Jiang
Sea of Okhotsk
Bering Sea
Chukchi Sea
Bering Strait
Nunivak Island
Ostrov Beringa
Aleutian Basin
Aleutian Islands
Attu Island
7822
Aleutian Trench
Sakhalin
Kuril Basin
Kuril Islands (Kuril'skiye Ostrova)
9550
Kuril Trench
Vladivostok
Hokkaido
Sea of Japan
3510
Yellow River
Yellow Sea
Ganges
Tropic of Cancer
Kolkata
Yangtze
Shanghai
East China Sea
Honshū
Tōkyō
8412
Shikoku
Kyūshū
Ryukyu Islands (Nansei-shotō)
Izu-Ogasawara Trench
9780
Emperor Seamount Chain
6671
1240
Emperor Trough
7900
Northwest Pacific Basin
Bay of Bengal
Taiwan
7181
7460
Ryukyu Trench
Kyushu - Palau Ridge
South Honshu Ridge
Volcano Islands (Kazan-retto)
6345
18
Kure Atoll
Midway Islands
Hawai'ian
Necker Island
Hawaiian
Mapmakers Seamounts
Mid - Pacific Mountains
Rangoon
Hainan
Luzon Strait
Andaman Islands
Andaman Basin
South China Sea
5560
Luzon
Philippine Basin
West Mariana Basin
Mariana Ridge
Mariana Trench
Saipan
Sri Lanka
Nicobar Islands
Philippines
Palawan
10057
Challenger Deep
10920
Guam
1564
Sulu Sea
Mindanao
Palau Islands
8054
8967
MICRONESIA
Marshall Islands
Kwajalein
Chuuk
Caroline Islands
Kosrae
6530
Central Pacific Basin
Celebes Sea
5484
West Caroline Basin
East Caroline Basin
7208
Singapore
Equator
0°
2302
Kepulauan Mentawai
Sumatra
Cocos Basin
Borneo
Bangka
Celebes
Halmahera
Seram
Gilbert Islands
Gilbert Ridge
Melanesian Basin
Admiralty Islands
New Britain
New Guinea
Laut Banda
7288
Laut Jawa
Jakarta
Java
Laut Flores
Timor
Arafura Sea
Torres Strait
Cape York
8940
Solomon Sea
Solomon Islands
MELANESIA
8322
Funafuti
Phoenix Islands
Fakaofo
13
Savai'i
Samoa Basin
POLYNESIA
Investigator Ridge
Java Trench (Sunda Trench)
7125
Sumba
Timor Sea
Great Barrier Reef
Coral Sea Basin
Coral Sea
Espiritu Santo
Vanua Levu
Viti Levu
Tonga Trench
Niue
North Australian Basin
6360
INDIAN OCEAN
West Australian Basin
Exmouth Plateau
North West Cape
New Caledonia
7633
New Hebrides Trench
Horizon Deep 10800
South Fiji Basin
Norfolk Island
Kermadec Islands
Kermadec Trench
10047
AUSTRALIA
Lord Howe Rise
New Caledonia Trough
1924
Tropic of Capricorn
Perth Basin
Perth
Great Australian Bight
Sydney
Melbourne
Auckland
North Island
South Pacific
Tasman Sea
New Zealand
Wellington
Chatham Rise
Chatham Islands
5176
Tasman Basin
South Island
549
Broken Plateau
Cape Leeuwin
South Australian Basin
5670
Tasmania
South Tasman Rise
60
Auckland Islands
Campbell Plateau
Antipodes Islands
7102
Diamantina Deep
6602
Macquarie Ridge
Southeast Indian Ridge
Indian - Antarctic Ridge
1646
SOUTHE
956
Balleny Islands
Île Amsterdam
Île St-Paul
1840
Australian - Antarctic Basin
4650
Cape Adare
Ross Sea
Antarctic Circle
4181
ANTA

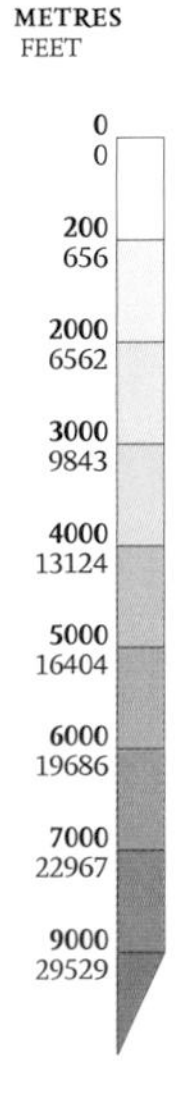

METRES FEET

METRES	FEET
0	0
200	656
2000	6562
3000	9843
4000	13124
5000	16404
6000	19686
7000	22967
9000	29529

Lambert Azimuthal Equal Area Projection

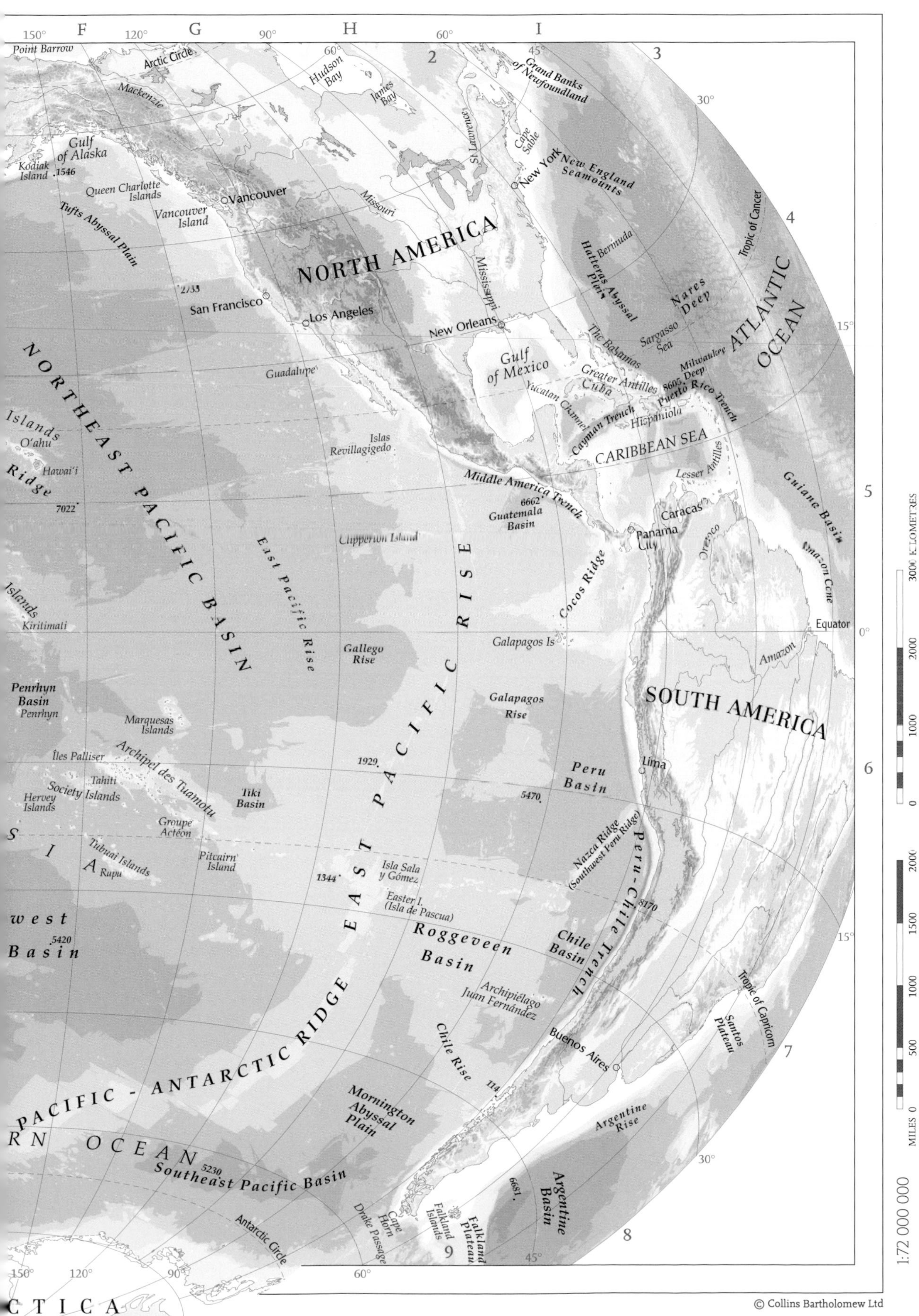

NORTH AMERICA
SOUTH AMERICA
ATLANTIC OCEAN
NORTHEAST PACIFIC BASIN
EAST PACIFIC RISE
PACIFIC - ANTARCTIC RIDGE
Gulf of Alaska
Gulf of Mexico
CARIBBEAN SEA
Hudson Bay
James Bay
Vancouver
San Francisco
Los Angeles
New Orleans
New York
Panama City
Caracas
Lima
Buenos Aires
Equator
Tropic of Cancer
Tropic of Capricorn
Arctic Circle
Antarctic Circle
Southeast Pacific Basin
Peru-Chile Trench
Middle America Trench
Galapagos Is
Easter I. (Isla de Pascua)
Drake Passage
Falkland Islands
Argentine Basin
1:72 000 000

ATLANTIC OCEAN

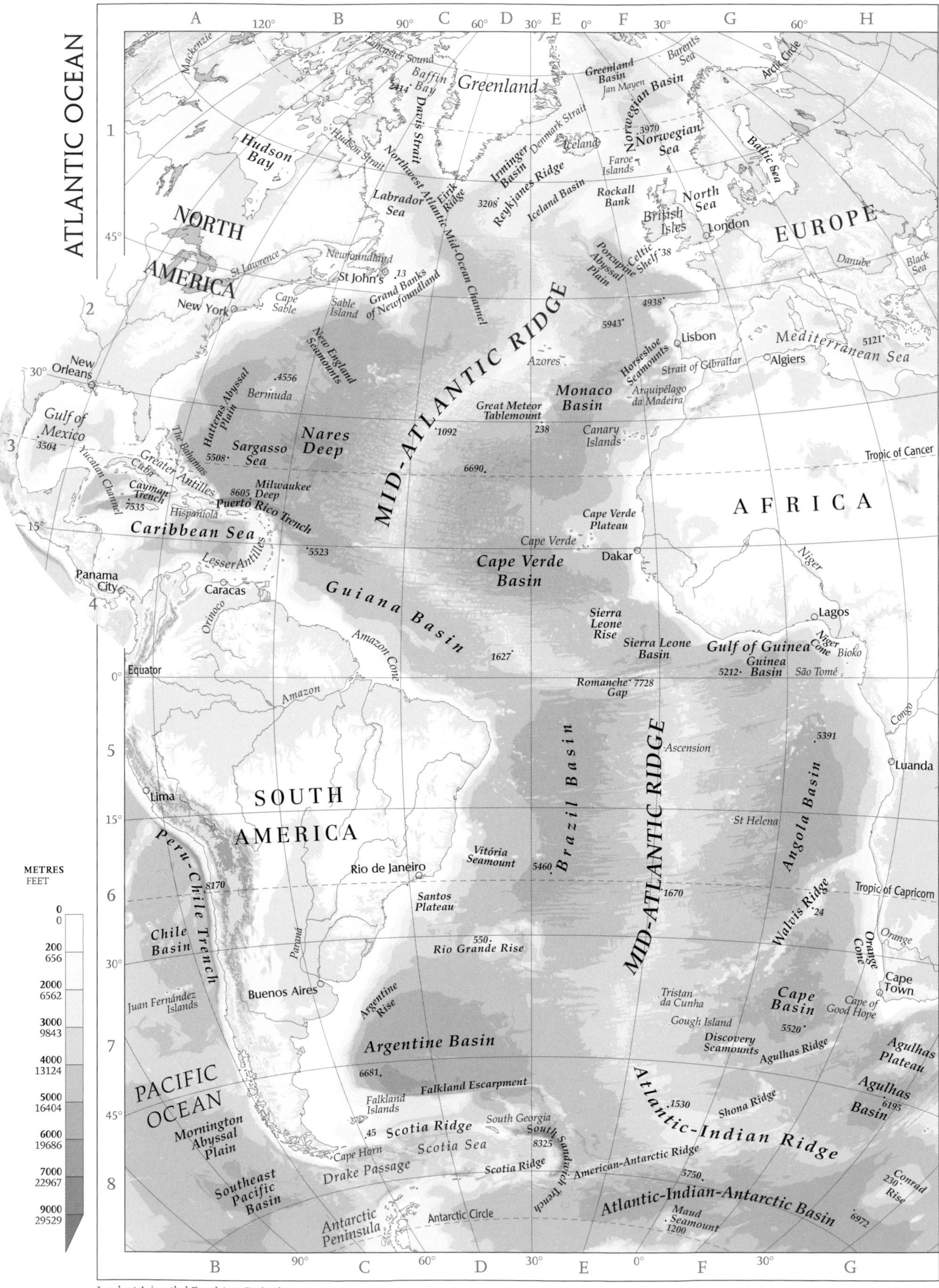

Lambert Azimuthal Equal Area Projection

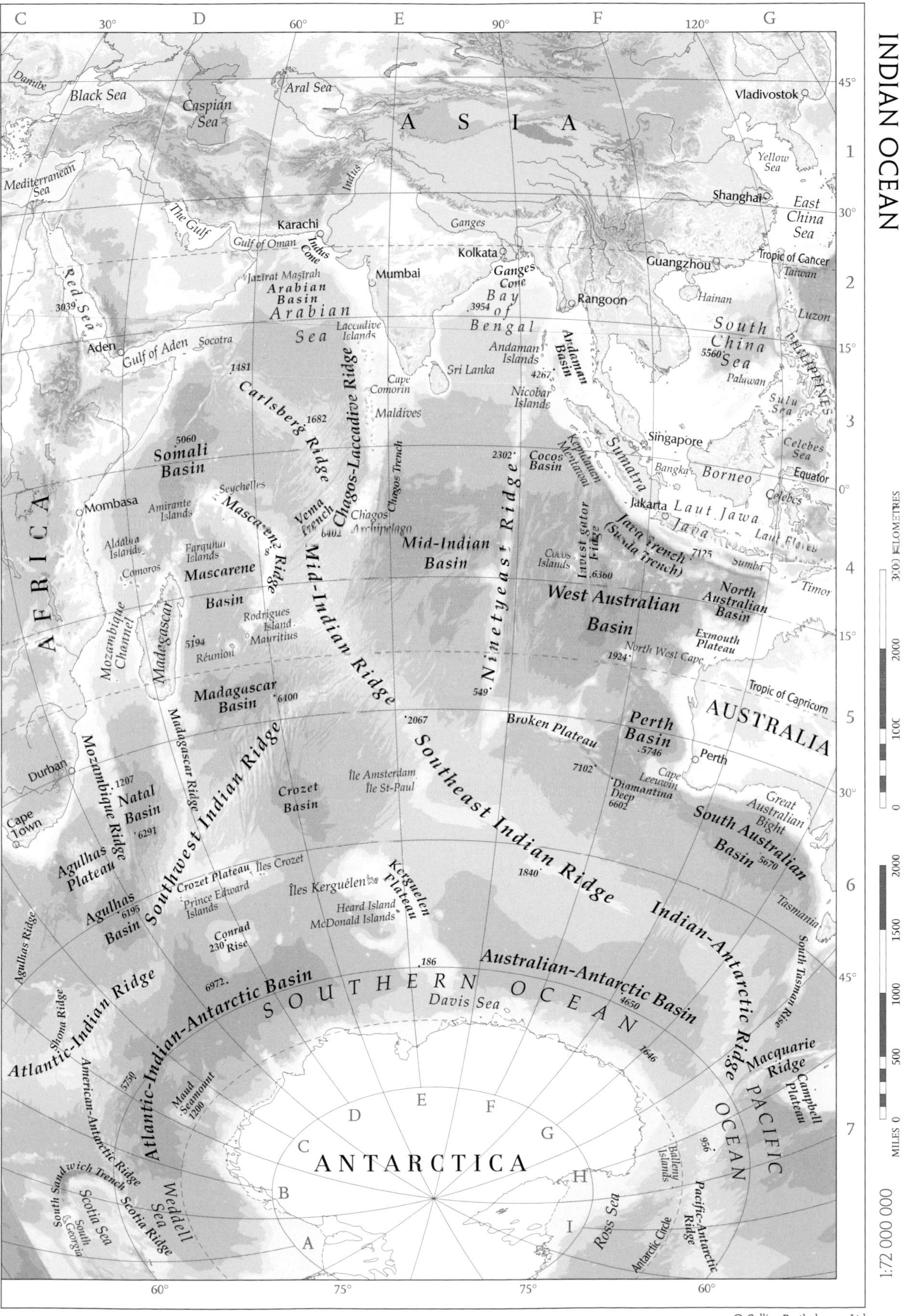
ASIA
AFRICA
AUSTRALIA
ANTARCTICA
SOUTHERN OCEAN
PACIFIC OCEAN
Black Sea
Caspian Sea
Aral Sea
Mediterranean Sea
The Gulf
Gulf of Oman
Karachi
Indus Cone
Red Sea
Aden
Gulf of Aden
Socotra
Arabian Basin
Arabian Sea
Mumbai
Kolkata
Ganges Cone
Bay of Bengal
Rangoon
Andaman Islands
Andaman Basin
Nicobar Islands
Sri Lanka
Laccadive Islands
Cape Comorin
Maldives
Carlsberg Ridge
Chagos-Laccadive Ridge
Chagos Trench
Chagos Archipelago
Vema Trench
Somali Basin
Seychelles
Amirante Islands
Mombasa
Aldabra Islands
Farquhar Islands
Comoros
Mascarene Ridge
Mascarene Basin
Mozambique Channel
Madagascar
Rodrigues Island
Mauritius
Réunion
Madagascar Basin
Madagascar Ridge
Mid-Indian Ridge
Mid-Indian Basin
Ninetyeast Ridge
Cocos Basin
Cocos Islands
Investigator Ridge
Kepulauan Mentawai
Sumatra
Singapore
Bangka
Borneo
Jakarta
Laut Jawa
Jawa
Java Trench (Sunda Trench)
Sumba
Timor
West Australian Basin
North Australian Basin
Exmouth Plateau
North West Cape
Tropic of Capricorn
Broken Plateau
Perth Basin
Perth
Cape Leeuwin
Diamantina Deep 6602
Great Australian Bight
South Australian Basin
Southeast Indian Ridge
Île Amsterdam
Île St-Paul
Crozet Basin
Southwest Indian Ridge
Natal Basin
Mozambique Ridge
Durban
Cape Town
Agulhas Plateau
Agulhas Basin
Agulhas Ridge
Crozet Plateau
Îles Crozet
Prince Edward Islands
Îles Kerguelen
Kerguelen Plateau
Heard Island
McDonald Islands
Conrad Rise
Indian-Antarctic Ridge
Tasmania
South Tasman Rise
Australian-Antarctic Basin
Atlantic-Indian-Antarctic Basin
Atlantic-Indian Ridge
Shona Ridge
American-Antarctic Ridge
Davis Sea
Maud Seamount 1200
Macquarie Ridge
Campbell Plateau
Balleny Islands
Ross Sea
Antarctic Circle
Pacific-Antarctic Ridge
South Sandwich Trench
Scotia Sea
South Georgia
Scotia Ridge
Weddell Sea
Vladivostok
Yellow Sea
Shanghai
East China Sea
Tropic of Cancer
Taiwan
Guangzhou
Hainan
Luzon
South China Sea
PHILIPPINES
Palawan
Sulu Sea
Celebes Sea
Equator
Celebes
Laut Flores
Danube
Indus
Ganges
Jazīrat Maşīrah
3039
3954
1481
1682
5060
6402
4267
5560
2302
7125
6360
5194
6400
1924
549
2067
5746
7102
1207
6291
1840
5670
6195
230
186
6972
4650
1646
5750
956
C
D
E
F
G
H
I
A
B
30°
60°
90°
120°
45°
15°
0°
75°
1
2
3
4
5
6
7
KILOMETRES
MILES
0
500
1000
1500
2000
3000
1:72 000 000

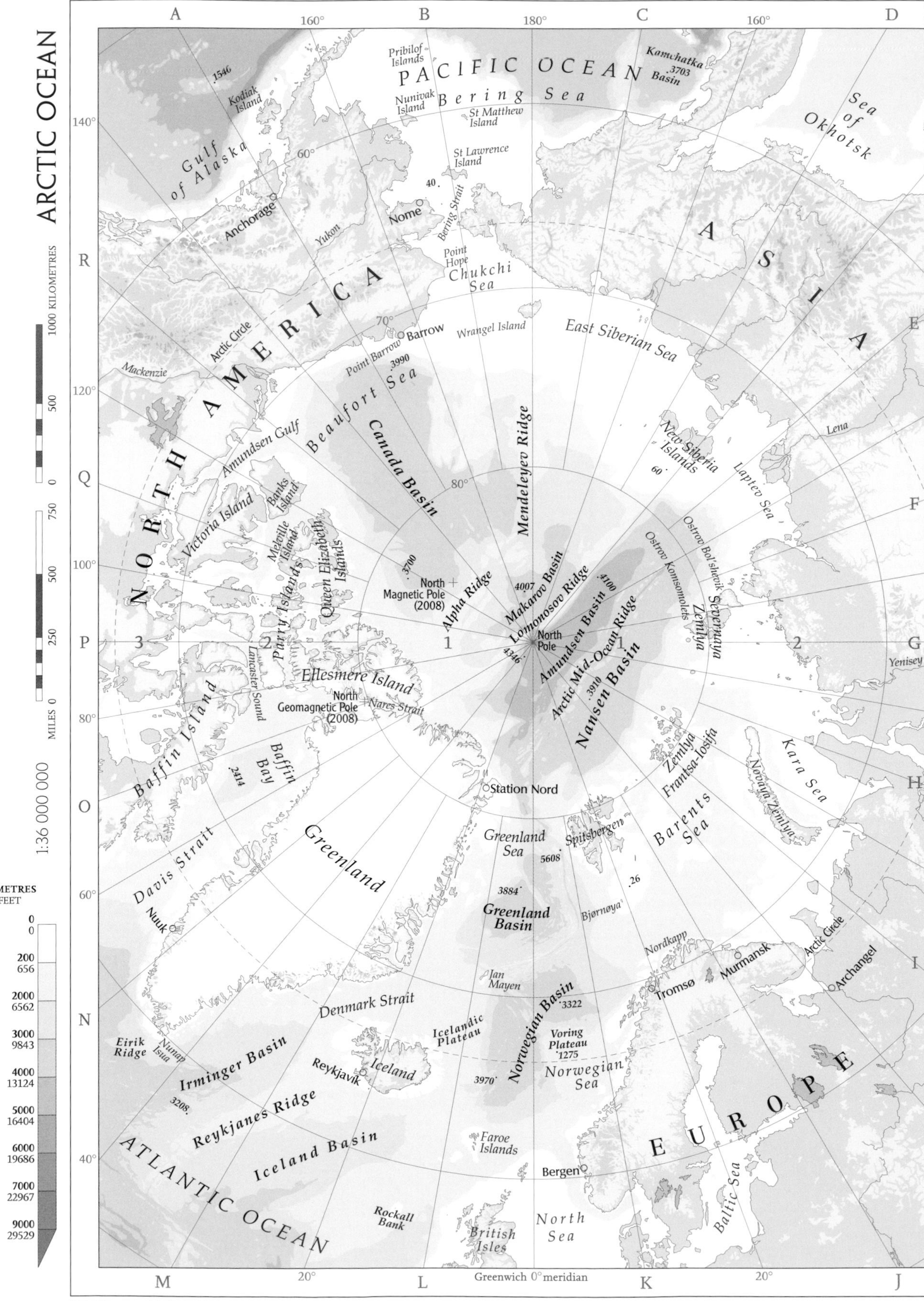
A
B
C
D
160°
180°
160°
PACIFIC OCEAN
Bering Sea
Pribilof Islands
Nunivak Island
St Matthew Island
St Lawrence Island
Kamchatka Basin
3703
Sea of Okhotsk
1546
Kodiak Island
Gulf of Alaska
140°
60°
40
Anchorage
Nome
Bering Strait
Yukon
Point Hope
Chukchi Sea
ASIA
R
E
NORTH AMERICA
Arctic Circle
70°
Barrow
Point Barrow
Wrangel Island
East Siberian Sea
3990
Beaufort Sea
Mackenzie
120°
Amundsen Gulf
Canada Basin
Mendeleyev Ridge
New Siberia Islands
60
Lena
Laptev Sea
Q
Banks Island
Victoria Island
80°
F
Melville Island
Queen Elizabeth Islands
Ostrov Bol'shevik
Ostrov Komsomolets
Severnaya Zemlya
100°
3700
North Magnetic Pole (2008)
Alpha Ridge
4007
Makarov Basin
Lomonosov Ridge
4010
Parry Islands
Amundsen Basin
P
3
2
1
North Pole
1
2
G
4346
Arctic Mid-Ocean Ridge
Yenisey
Lancaster Sound
Ellesmere Island
3910
Nansen Basin
80°
North Geomagnetic Pole (2008)
Nares Strait
Baffin Island
Baffin Bay
2414
Zemlya Frantsa-Iosifa
Kara Sea
H
Novaya Zemlya
Station Nord
O
Greenland
Greenland Sea
5608
Spitsbergen
Barents Sea
Davis Strait
60°
26
3884
Greenland Basin
Bjørnøya
Nuuk
Nordkapp
Murmansk
Arctic Circle
I
Archangel
Jan Mayen
Tromsø
Denmark Strait
Norwegian Basin
3322
N
Eirik Ridge
Nunap Isua
Irminger Basin
Icelandic Plateau
Voring Plateau
1275
Reykjavik
Iceland
3970
Norwegian Sea
EUROPE
3208
Reykjanes Ridge
Faroe Islands
40°
ATLANTIC OCEAN
Iceland Basin
Bergen
Baltic Sea
Rockall Bank
British Isles
North Sea
M
20°
L
Greenwich 0° meridian
K
20°
J
1000 KILOMETRES
500
0
750
500
250
0
MILES
1:36 000 000
METRES
FEET
0
0
200
656
2000
6562
3000
9843
4000
13124
5000
16404
6000
19686
7000
22967
9000
29529

Polar Stereographic Projection

WORLD FACTS AND FIGURES

162–167 WORLD STATISTICS
- Population
- 2050 projected population
- Gross National Income per capita
- Literacy Rate
- International dialling codes
- Time zones
- Official websites
- Tourism websites

168–169 WORLD TIME ZONES

170–171 GEOGRAPHICAL TABLES
- Highest mountains
- Longest rivers
- Largest lakes
- Largest drainage basins
- Ocean areas and deepest points
- Largest islands
- Deepest lakes
- Lowest points on land
- Highest waterfalls
- Earth's dimensions
- Largest countries by population
- Largest countries by area
- Largest cities
- Busiest airports

172–173 CLIMATE AROUND THE WORLD

174–175 USEFUL FACTS AND WEB LINKS
- Environment
- Oceans
- Climate
- Population
- Countries
- Travel
- Organizations

176 DISTANCE AND CONVERSION CHARTS

	Total Population	2050 Projected Population	Gross National Income (GNI) Per Capita (US$)	Literacy Rate (%)	International Dialling Code	Time Zone	Official Website *Tourism Website*
WORLD	6 651 873 557	9 075 903 000	1 700	80.1	...	...	
AFGHANISTAN	27 145 000	97 324 000	...	28.0	93	+4.5	... ...
ALBANIA	3 190 000	3 458 000	2 930	99.0	355	+1	www.km.gov.al *www.albaniantourism.com*
ALGERIA	33 858 000	49 500 000	3 030	75.4	213	+1	www.el-mouradia.dz *www.matet.dz*
ANDORRA	75 000	58 000	...	...	376	+1	www.andorra.ad *www.andorra.ad*
ANGOLA	17 024 000	43 501 000	1 970	67.4	244	+1	www.angola.org *www.angola.org.uk/prov_tourism.htm*
ANTIGUA AND BARBUDA	85 000	112 000	11 050	...	1 268	-4	www.ab.gov.ag *www.antigua-barbuda.org*
ARGENTINA	39 531 000	51 382 000	5 150	97.6	54	-3	www.info.gov.ar *www.turismo.gov.ar*
ARMENIA	3 002 000	2 506 000	1 920	99.5	374	+4	www.gov.am *www.turismo.gov.ar*
AUSTRALIA	20 743 000	27 940 000	35 860	...	61	+8 to +10.5	www.gov.au *www.australia.com*
AUSTRIA	8 361 000	8 073 000	39 750	...	43	+1	www.oesterreich.at *www.austria.info*
AZERBAIJAN	8 467 000	9 631 000	1 840	99.4	994	+4	www.president.az ...
THE BAHAMAS	331 000	466 000	...	...	1 242	-5	www.bahamas.gov.bs *www.bahamas.com*
BAHRAIN	753 000	1 155 000	19 350	88.8	973	+3	www.bahrain.gov.bh *www.bahraintourism.com*
BANGLADESH	158 665 000	242 937 000	450	53.5	880	+6	www.bangladesh.gov.bd *www.parjatan.org*
BARBADOS	294 000	255 000	...	...	1 246	-4	www.barbados.gov.bb *www.barbados.org/bta.htm*
BELARUS	9 689 000	7 017 000	3 470	99.7	375	+2	www.government.by *www.mst.by*
BELGIUM	10 457 000	10 302 000	38 460	...	32	+1	www.belgium.be *www.visitflanders.com Wallonia: www.opt.be*
BELIZE	288 000	442 000	3 740	...	501	-6	www.belize.gov.bz *www.travelbelize.org*
BENIN	9 033 000	22 123 000	530	40.5	229	+1	www.gouv.bj *www.benintourisme.com*
BHUTAN	658 000	4 393 000	1 430	55.6	975	+6	www.bhutan.gov.bt *www.tourism.gov.bt*
BOLIVIA	9 525 000	14 908 000	1 100	90.3	591	-4	www.bolivia.gov.bo ...
BOSNIA-HERZEGOVINA	3 935 000	3 170 000	3 230	96.7	387	+1	www.fbihvlada.gov.ba *www.bhtourism.ba*
BOTSWANA	1 882 000	1 658 000	5 570	82.9	267	+2	www.gov.bw ...
BRAZIL	191 791 000	253 105 000	4 710	90.5	55	-2 to -5	www.brazil.gov.br *www.braziltour.com*
BRUNEI	390 000	681 000	26 930	94.9	673	+8	www.brunei.gov.bn *www.tourismbrunei.com*
BULGARIA	7 639 000	5 065 000	3 990	98.3	359	+2	www.government.bg *www.bulgariatravel.org*
BURKINA	14 784 000	39 093 000	440	28.7	226	GMT	www.primature.gov.bf *www.culture.gov.bf*
BURUNDI	8 508 000	25 812 000	100	59.3	257	+2	www.burundi.gov.bi ...
CAMBODIA	14 444 000	25 972 000	490	76.3	855	+7	www.cambodia.gov.kh *www.visit-mekong.com/cambodia/mot/*
CAMEROON	18 549 000	26 891 000	990	67.9	237	+1	... ...
CANADA	32 876 000	42 844 000	36 650	...	1	-3.5 to -8	canada.gc.ca *www.canada.travel*
CAPE VERDE	530 000	1 002 000	2 130	83.8	238	-1	www.governo.cv ...
CENTRAL AFRICAN REPUBLIC	4 343 000	6 747 000	350	48.6	236	+1	www.spm.gov.cm ...
CHAD	10 781 000	31 497 000	450	25.7	235	+1	www.primature-tchad.org ...
CHILE	16 635 000	20 657 000	6 810	96.5	56	-4	www.gobiernodechile.cl *www.visit-chile.org*

	Total Population	2050 Projected Population	Gross National Income (GNI) Per Capita (US$)	Literacy Rate (%)	International Dialling Code	Time Zone	Official Website *Tourism Website*
CHINA	1 313 437 000	1 402 062 000	2 000	93.3	86	+8	www.china.org.cn ...
COLOMBIA	46 156 000	65 679 000	3 120	93.6	57	-5	www.gobiernoenlinea.gov.co *www.idct.gov.co*
COMOROS	839 000	1 781 000	660	75.1	269	+3	www.beit-salam.km ...
CONGO	3 768 000	13 721 000	1 050	86.8	242	+1	www.congo-site.com ...
CONGO, DEMOCRATIC REPUBLIC OF THE	62 636 000	177 271 000	130	67.2	243	+1 to +2	www.un.int/drcongo ...
COSTA RICA	4 468 000	6 426 000	4 980	95.9	506	-6	www.casapres.go.cr *www.visitcostarica.com*
CÔTE D'IVOIRE	19 262 000	33 959 000	880	48.7	225	GMT	www.cotedivoire-pr.ci *www.tourismeci.org*
CROATIA	4 555 000	3 686 000	9 310	98.7	385	+1	www.vlada.hr *www.croatia.hr*
CUBA	11 268 000	9 749 000	...	99.8	53	-5	www.cubagob.gov.cu *www.cubatravel.cu*
CYPRUS	855 000	1 174 000	23 270	97.7	357	+2	www.cyprus.gov.cy *www.visitcyprus.com*
CZECH REPUBLIC	10 186 000	8 452 000	12 790	...	420	+1	www.czech.cz *www.czechtourism.com*
DENMARK	5 442 000	5 851 000	52 110	...	45	+1	www.denmark.dk *www.visitdenmark.com*
DJIBOUTI	833 000	1 547 000	1 060	...	253	+3	www.presidence.dj *www.office-tourisme.dj*
DOMINICA	67 000	98 000	4 100	...	1 767	-4	www.ndcdominica.dm *www.ndcdominica.dm*
DOMINICAN REPUBLIC	9 760 000	12 668 000	2 910	89.1	1 809	-4	www.cig.gov.do ...
EAST TIMOR	1 155 000	3 265 000	840	...	670	+9	www.timor-leste.gov.tl ...
ECUADOR	13 341 000	19 214 000	2 910	92.6	593	-5	... *www.vivecuador.com*
EGYPT	75 498 000	125 916 000	1 360	72.0	20	+2	www.sis.gov.eg ...
EL SALVADOR	6 857 000	10 823 000	2 680	85.5	503	-6	www.casapres.gob.sv *www.elsalvador.travel*
EQUATORIAL GUINEA	507 000	1 146 000	8 510	...	240	+1	www.ceiba-equatorial-guinea.org ...
ERITREA	4 851 000	11 229 000	190	...	291	+3	shabait.com ...
ESTONIA	1 335 000	1 119 000	11 400	99.8	372	+2	www.valitsus.ee *visitestonia.com*
ETHIOPIA	83 099 000	170 190 000	170	35.9	251	+3	www.ethiopar.net *www.tourismethiopia.org*
FIJI	839 000	934 000	3 720	...	679	+12	www.fiji.gov.fj *www.bulafiji.com*
FINLAND	5 277 000	5 329 000	41 360	...	358	+2	www.valtioneuvosto.fi *www.visitfinland.com*
FRANCE	61 647 000	63 116 000	36 560	...	33	+1	www.premier-ministre.gouv.fr *www.franceguide.com*
GABON	1 331 000	2 279 000	5 360	86.2	241	+1	www.legabon.org *www.tourisme-gabon.com*
THE GAMBIA	1 709 000	3 106 000	290	...	220	GMT	www.statehouse.gm ...
GEORGIA	4 395 000	2 985 000	1 580	...	995	+4	www.parliament.ge ...
GERMANY	82 599 000	78 765 000	36 810	...	49	+1	www.bundesregierung.de *www.germany-tourism.de*
GHANA	23 478 000	40 573 000	510	65.0	233	GMT	www.ghana.gov.gh *www.touringghana.com*
GREECE	11 147 000	10 742 000	27 390	97.1	30	+2	www.greece.gov.gr *www.gnto.gr*
GRENADA	106 000	157 000	4 650	...	1 473	-4	www.gov.gd *grenadagrenadines.com*
GUATEMALA	13 354 000	25 612 000	2 590	73.2	502	-6	www.congreso.gob.gt ...
GUINEA	9 370 000	22 987 000	400	29.5	224	GMT	... *www.mirinet.net.gn/ont/*
GUINEA-BISSAU	1 695 000	5 312 000	190	64.6	245	GMT	www.republica-da-guine-bissau.org ...

	Total Population	2050 Projected Population	Gross National Income (GNI) Per Capita (US$)	Literacy Rate (%)	International Dialling Code	Time Zone	Official Website *Tourism Website*
GUYANA	738 000	488 000	1 150	...	592	-4	www.gina.gov.gy *www.guyana-tourism.com*
HAITI	9 598 000	12 996 000	430	62.1	509	-5	www.haiti.org *www.haititourisme.org*
HONDURAS	7 106 000	12 776 000	1 270	83.1	504	-6	www.congreso.gob.hn *www.letsgohonduras.com*
HUNGARY	10 030 000	8 262 000	10 870	98.9	36	+1	www.magyarorszag.hu *www.hungarytourism.hu*
ICELAND	301 000	370 000	49 960	...	354	GMT	www.iceland.is *www.visiticeland.com*
INDIA	1 169 016 000	1 592 704 000	820	66.0	91	+5.5	www.india.gov.in *www.tourismofindia.com*
INDONESIA	231 627 000	284 640 000	1 420	91.4	62	+7 to +9	... *www.budpar.go.id*
IRAN	71 208 000	101 944 000	2 930	84.7	98	+3.5	www.president.ir *www.itto.org*
IRAQ	28 993 000	63 693 000	...	74.1	964	+3	www.cabinet.iq ...
IRELAND	4 301 000	5 762 000	44 830	...	353	GMT	www.irlgov.ie *www.discoverireland.ie*
ISRAEL	6 928 000	10 403 000	20 170	...	972	+2	www.gov.il *www.tourism.gov.il*
ITALY	58 877 000	50 912 000	31 990	98.9	39	+1	www.governo.it *www.enit.it*
JAMAICA	2 714 000	2 586 000	3 560	86.0	1 876	-5	www.jis.gov.jm *www.visitjamaica.com*
JAPAN	127 967 000	112 198 000	38 630	...	81	+9	web-japan.org *www.jnto.go.jp*
JORDAN	5 924 000	10 225 000	2 650	93.1	962	+2	www.jordan.gov.jo *www.see-jordan.com*
KAZAKHSTAN	15 422 000	13 086 000	3 870	99.6	7	+5 to +6	www.government.kz ...
KENYA	37 538 000	83 073 000	580	73.6	254	+3	www.kenya.go.ke *www.magicalkenya.com*
KIRIBATI	95 000	177 000	1 240	...	686	+12 to +14	... ...
KOSOVO	2 070 000	...	...	...			... ...
KUWAIT	2 851 000	5 279 000	30 630	93.9	965	+3	www.kuwaitmission.com ...
KYRGYZSTAN	5 317 000	6 664 000	500	99.3	996	+6	www.gov.kg ...
LAOS	5 859 000	11 586 000	500	73.2	856	+7	www.un.int/lao ...
LATVIA	2 277 000	1 678 000	8 100	99.8	371	+2	www.saeima.lv *www.latviatourism.lv*
LEBANON	4 099 000	4 702 000	5 580	...	961	+2	www.presidency.gov.lb *www.destinationlebanon.com*
LESOTHO	2 008 000	1 601 000	980	82.2	266	+2	www.lesotho.gov.ls ...
LIBERIA	3 750 000	10 653 000	130	55.5	231	GMT	www.embassyofliberia.org ...
LIBYA	6 160 000	9 553 000	7 290	86.8	218	+2	www.micat.gov.lr ...
LIECHTENSTEIN	35 000	44 000	...	...	423	+1	www.liechtenstein.li *www.tourismus.li*
LITHUANIA	3 390 000	2 565 000	7 930	99.7	370	+2	www.lrv.lt *www.tourism.lt*
LUXEMBOURG	467 000	721 000	71 240	...	352	+1	www.gouvernement.lu *www.ont.lu*
MACEDONIA (F.Y.R.O.M.)	2 038 000	1 884 000	3 070	97.0	389	+1	www.vlada.mk *www.exploringmacedonia.com*
MADAGASCAR	19 683 000	43 508 000	280	70.7	261	+3	www.madagascar.gov.mg ...
MALAWI	13 925 000	29 452 000	230	71.8	265	+2	www.malawi.gov.mw ...
MALAYSIA	26 572 000	38 924 000	5 620	91.9	60	+8	www.gov.my *www.tourism.gov.my*
MALDIVES	306 000	682 000	3 010	97.0	960	+5	www.maldivesinfo.gov.mv *www.visitmaldives.com*
MALI	12 337 000	41 976 000	460	23.3	223	GMT	www.maliensdelexterieur.gov.ml *www.malitourisme.com*

	Total Population	2050 Projected Population	Gross National Income (GNI) Per Capita (US$)	Literacy Rate (%)	International Dialling Code	Time Zone	Official Website *Tourism Website*
MALTA	407 000	428 000	15 310	91.6	356	+1	www.gov.mt *www.visitmalta.com*
MARSHALL ISLANDS	59 000	150 000	2 980	...	692	+12	www.rmiembassyus.org *www.visitmarshallislands.com*
MAURITANIA	3 124 000	7 497 000	760	55.8	222	GMT	www.mauritania.mr ...
MAURITIUS	1 262 000	1 465 000	5 430	87.4	230	+4	www.gov.mu *www.mauritius.net*
MEXICO	106 535 000	139 015 000	7 830	92.4	52	-6 to -8	www.gob.mx *www.visitmexico.com*
MICRONESIA, FEDERATED STATES OF	111 000	99 000	2 390	...	691	+10 to +11	www.fsmgov.org *visit-fsm.org*
MOLDOVA	3 794 000	3 312 000	1 080	99.2	373	+2	www.moldova.md *www.turism.md*
MONACO	33 000	55 000	...	...	377	+1	www.visitmonaco.com *www.monaco-congres.com*
MONGOLIA	2 629 000	3 625 000	1 000	97.3	976	+8	www.pmis.gov.mn *www.mongoliatourism.gov.mn*
MONTENEGRO	598 000	650 000	4 130	...	382	+1	www.montenegro.yu *www.visit-montenegro.com*
MOROCCO	31 224 000	46 397 000	2 160	55.6	212	GMT	www.maroc.ma *www.tourism-in-morocco.com*
MOZAMBIQUE	21 397 000	37 604 000	310	44.4	258	+2	www.mozambique.mz ...
MYANMAR	48 798 000	63 657 000	...	89.9	95	+6.5	www.myanmar.com *www.myanmar-tourism.com*
NAMIBIA	2 074 000	3 060 000	3 210	88.0	264	+1	www.grnnet.gov.na *www.namibiatourism.com.na*
NAURU	10 000	18 000	...	...	674	+12	www.un.int/nauru ...
NEPAL	28 196 000	51 172 000	320	56.5	977	+5.75	www.nepalhmg.gov.np *www.welcomenepal.com*
NETHERLANDS	16 419 000	17 139 000	43 050	...	31	+1	www.overheid.nl *www.us.holland.com*
NEW ZEALAND	4 179 000	4 790 000	26 750	...	64	+12 to +12.75	www.newzealand.govt.nz *www.newzealand.com*
NICARAGUA	5 603 000	9 371 000	930	80.5	505	-6	www.asamblea.gob.ni *www.visit-nicaragua.com*
NIGER	14 226 000	50 156 000	270	30.4	227	+1	... ...
NIGERIA	148 093 000	258 108 000	620	72.0	234	+1	www.nigeria.gov.ng *www.nigeriatourism.net*
NORTH KOREA	23 790 000	24 192 000	...	...	850	+9	www.korea-dpr.com ...
NORWAY	4 698 000	5 435 000	68 440	...	47	+1	www.norway.no *www.visitnorway.com*
OMAN	2 595 000	4 958 000	11 120	84.4	968	+4	www.omanet.om *www.omantourism.gov.om*
PAKISTAN	163 902 000	304 700 000	800	54.9	92	+5	www.infopak.gov.pk *www.tourism.gov.pk*
PALAU	20 000	21 000	7 990	...	680	+9	www.palauembassy.com *visit-palau.com*
PANAMA	3 343 000	5 093 000	5 000	93.4	507	-5	www.pa *www.visitpanama.com*
PAPUA NEW GUINEA	6 331 000	10 619 000	740	57.8	675	+10	www.pngonline.gov.pg *www.pngtourism.org.pg/*
PARAGUAY	6 127 000	12 095 000	1 410	93.7	595	-4	www.presidencia.gov.py *www.senatur.gov.py*
PERU	27 903 000	42 552 000	2 980	90.5	51	-5	www.peru.gob.pe *www.peru.info*
PHILIPPINES	87 960 000	127 068 000	1 390	93.4	63	+8	www.gov.ph *www.tourism.gov.ph*
POLAND	38 082 000	31 916 000	8 210	99.3	48	+1	www.poland.gov.pl *www.poland.travel/en/*
PORTUGAL	10 623 000	10 723 000	17 850	94.9	351	GMT	www.portugal.gov.pt *www.visitportugal.com*
QATAR	841 000	1 330 000	...	90.2	974	+3	www.mofa.gov.qa *www.experienceqatar.com*
ROMANIA	21 438 000	16 757 000	4 830	97.6	40	+2	www.guv.ro *www.romaniatravel.com*
RUSSIAN FEDERATION	142 499 000	111 752 000	5 770	99.5	7	+2 to +12	www.gov.ru *www.russiatourism.ru*

	Total Population	2050 Projected Population	Gross National Income (GNI) Per Capita (US$)	Literacy Rate (%)	International Dialling Code	Time Zone	Official Website *Tourism Website*
RWANDA	9 725 000	18 153 000	250	64.9	250	+2	www.gov.rw *www.rwandatourism.com*
ST KITTS AND NEVIS	50 000	59 000	8 460	...	1 869	-4	www.gov.kn *www.stkittstourism.kn*
ST LUCIA	165 000	188 000	5 060	...	1 758	-4	www.stlucia.gov.lc *www.stlucia.org*
ST VINCENT AND THE GRENADINES	120 000	105 000	3 320	...	1 784	-4	... *www.svgtourism.com*
SAMOA	187 000	157 000	2 270	98.7	685	-11	www.govt.ws *www.visitsamoa.ws*
SAN MARINO	31 000	30 000	45 130	...	378	+1	www.consigliograndeegenerale.sm *www.visitsanmarino.com*
SÃO TOMÉ AND PRÍNCIPE	158 000	295 000	800	87.9	239	GMT	www.parlamento.st *www.saotome.st*
SAUDI ARABIA	24 735 000	49 464 000	13 980	85.0	966	+3	www.saudinf.com ...
SENEGAL	12 379 000	23 108 000	760	42.6	221	GMT	www.gouv.sn *www.senegal-tourism.com*
SERBIA	7 788 000	...	4 030	...	381	+1	www.srbija.gov.rs *www.serbia-tourism.org*
SEYCHELLES	87 000	99 000	8 870	91.8	248	+4	www.virtualseychelles.sc *www.virtualseychelles.sc*
SIERRA LEONE	5 866 000	13 786 000	240	38.1	232	GMT	www.statehouse-sl.org ...
SINGAPORE	4 436 000	5 213 000	28 730	94.4	65	+8	www.gov.sg *www.visitsingapore.com*
SLOVAKIA	5 390 000	4 612 000	9 610	...	421	+1	www.government.gov.sk *www.slovakia.travel*
SLOVENIA	2 002 000	1 630 000	18 660	99.7	386	+1	www.gov.si *www.slovenia.info*
SOLOMON ISLANDS	496 000	921 000	690	...	677	+11	www.commerce.gov.sb *www.commerce.gov.sb*
SOMALIA	8 699 000	21 329 000	...	...	252	+3	www.somali-gov.info ...
SOUTH AFRICA, REPUBLIC OF	48 577 000	48 660 000	5 390	88.0	27	+2	www.gov.za *www.southafrica.net*
SOUTH KOREA	48 224 000	44 629 000	17 690	...	82	+9	www.korea.net *english.visitkorea.or.kr*
SPAIN	44 279 000	42 541 000	27 340	97.4	34	+1	www.la-moncloa.es *www.spain.info*
SRI LANKA	19 299 000	23 554 000	1 310	91.5	94	+5.5	www.priu.gov.lk *www.srilankatourism.org*
SUDAN	38 560 000	66 705 000	800	60.9	249	+3	www.sudan.gov.sd ...
SURINAME	458 000	429 000	4 210	90.4	597	-3	www.kabinet.sr.org *www.mintct.sr*
SWAZILAND	1 141 000	1 026 000	2 400	79.6	268	+2	www.gov.sz ...
SWEDEN	9 119 000	10 054 000	43 530	...	46	+1	www.sweden.se *www.visitsweden.com*
SWITZERLAND	7 484 000	7 252 000	58 050	...	41	+1	www.admin.ch *www.myswitzerland.com*
SYRIA	19 929 000	35 935 000	1 560	83.1	963	+2	www.moi-syria.com *www.syriatourism.org*
TAIWAN	22 880 000	...	...	...	886	+8	www.gov.tw *www.tbroc.gov.tw*
TAJIKISTAN	6 736 000	10 423 000	390	99.6	992	+5	www.tjus.org ...
TANZANIA	40 454 000	66 845 000	350	72.3	255	+3	www.tanzania.go.tz *www.tanzaniatouristboard.com*
THAILAND	63 884 000	74 594 000	3 050	94.1	66	+7	www.thaigov.go.th *www.tourismthailand.org*
TOGO	6 585 000	13 544 000	350	53.2	228	GMT	www.republicoftogo.com ...
TONGO	100 000	75 000	2 250	99.2	676	+13	www.pmo.gov.to *www.tongaholiday.com*
TRINIDAD AND TOBAGO	1 333 000	1 230 000	12 500	98.7	1 868	-4	www.gov.tt *www.gotrinidadandtobago.com*
TUNISIA	10 327 000	12 927 000	2 970	77.7	216	+1	www.tunisiaonline.com *www.tourismtunisia.coom*
TURKEY	74 877 000	101 208 000	5 400	88.7	90	+2	www.mfa.gov.tr *www.kultur.gov.tr*

	Total Population	2050 Projected Population	Gross National Income (GNI) Per Capita (US$)	Literacy Rate (%)	International Dialling Code	Time Zone	Official Website *Tourism Website*
TURKMENISTAN	4 965 000	6 780 000	...	99.5	993	+5	www.turkmenistanembassy.org *www.turkmenistanembassy.org*
TUVALU	11 000	12 000	...	...	688	+12	... *www.timelesstuvalu.com*
UGANDA	30 884 000	126 950 000	300	73.6	256	+3	www.mofa.go.ug *www.visituganda.com*
UKRAINE	46 205 000	26 393 000	1 940	99.7	380	+2	www.kmu.gov.ua *www.tourism.gov.ua*
UNITED ARAB EMIRATES	4 380 000	9 056 000	...	90.4	971	+4	www.government.ae ...
UNITED KINGDOM	60 769 000	67 143 000	40 560	...	44	GMT	www.direct.gov.uk *www.visitbritain.com*
UNITED STATES OF AMERICA	305 826 000	394 976 000	44 710	...	1	-5 to -10	www.usa.gov *www.seeamerica.org*
URUGUAY	3 340 000	4 043 000	5 310	98.0	598	-3	www.presidencia.gub.uy *www.turismo.gub.uy*
UZBEKISTAN	27 372 000	38 665 000	610	96.9	998	+5	www.gov.uz *www.uzbektourism.uz*
VANUATU	226 000	375 000	1 690	78.1	678	+11	www.vanuatugovernment.gov.vu *www.vanuatutourism.com*
VATICAN CITY	557	1 000	...	...	39	+1	www.vatican.va *www.vaticanstate.va*
VENEZUELA	27 657 000	41 991 000	6 070	93.0	58	-4.5	www.gobiernoenlinea.ve ...
VIETNAM	87 375 000	116 654 000	700	...	84	+7	www.na.gov.vn *www.vietnamtourism.com*
YEMEN	22 389 000	59 454 000	700	[illegible]	967	+3	www.nic.gov.ye *www.yementourism.com*
ZAMBIA	11 922 000	22 781 000	630	...	260	+2	www.statehouse.gov.zm *www.zambiatourism.com*
ZIMBABWE	13 349 000	15 805 000	340	91.2	263	+2	www.zim.gov.zw www.zimbabwetourism.co.zw

INDICATOR	DEFINITION
Total population	Interpolated mid-year population, 2007.
2050 projected population	Projected total population for the year 2050.
GNI per capita	Gross National Income per person in U.S. dollars using the World Bank Atlas method, from latest available data.
Literacy rate	Percentage of population aged 15–24 with at least a basic ability to read and write, 2007.
International dialling code	The country code prefix to be used when dialling from another country.
Time zone	Time difference in hours between local standard time and Greenwich Mean Time (GMT).
Official website	The official country website where available.
Tourism website	The country website for tourists where available.

MAIN STATISTICAL SOURCES	WEB LINKS
United Nations Department of Economic and Social Affairs (UDESA) World Population Prospects: The 2006 Revision World Urbanization Prospects: The 2005 Revision	www.un.org/esa/population/unpop
World Bank World Development Indicators online	www.worldbank.org/data
UNESCO Education Data Centre	stats.uis.unesco.org
International Telecommunications Union (ITU)	www.itu.int

The system of timekeeping throughout the world is based on twenty-four time zones, each stretching over fifteen degrees of longitude – the distance equivalent to a time difference of one hour. The Prime, or Greenwich Meridian (0 degrees west), is the basis for Greenwich Mean Time (GMT) or Universal Coordinated Time (UTC), by which other times are measured. This universal reference point was agreed at an international conference in 1884.

Times are the local Standard Times observed compared with 12:00 (noon) Greenwich Mean Time (GMT). Daylight Saving Time, normally one hour ahead of local Standard Time, which is observed by certain countries for part of the year, is not shown on the map.

Organization	Web Address	Theme
Greenwich Royal Observatory	www.rog.nmm.ac.uk	The home of time
Greenwich Mean Time	wwp.greenwichmeantime.com	World time since 1884
World time zones	www.worldtimezones.com	Detailed time zones information
The Official US time	www.time.gov/	The home of US time
International Date Line	aa.usno.navy.mil/faq/docs/international_date.php	Understanding the international date line

Time zone boundaries can be altered to suit international or internal boundaries. China uses only one time zone although it should theoretically have five, while the Russian Federation stretches over eleven zones. The four mainland USA time zones do not always follow state boundaries.

The International Date Line is an imaginary line at approximately 180° west (or east) of Greenwich, across which the date changes by one day. The line has no international legal status and countries near to the line can choose which date they will observe. The line was amended recently so that Caroline Island, in Kiribati in the Pacific Ocean, would be the first land area to greet the year 2000. The island was renamed Millennium Island in recognition of this.

Daylight Saving Time allows nations to adjust their clocks to extend daylight during the working day. It was first introduced to the UK during the First World War to reduce the demand for artificial heating and lighting.

TIME DIFFERENCES FOR MAJOR CITIES FROM GMT

	hours
Los Angeles	-8
New York	-5
Buenos Aires	-3
Berlin	+1
Cape Town	+2
Mumbai	+5.5
Singapore	+8
Beijing	+8
Tōkyō	+9
Sydney	+10

HIGHEST MOUNTAINS	Height metres	feet	Location
Mt Everest	8 848	29 028	China/Nepal
K2	8 611	28 251	Pakistan
Kangchenjunga	8 586	28 169	India/Nepal
Lhotse	8 516	27 939	China/Nepal
Makalu	8 463	27 765	China/Nepal
Cho Oyu	8 201	26 906	China/Nepal
Dhaulagiri	8 167	26 794	Nepal
Manaslu	8 163	26 781	Nepal
Nanga Parbat	8 126	26 660	Pakistan
Annapurna I	8 091	26 545	Nepal
Gasherbrum I	8 068	26 469	China/Pakistan
Broad Peak	8 047	26 401	China/Pakistan
Gasherbrum II	8 035	26 361	China/Pakistan
Xixabangma Feng	8 012	26 286	China
Annapurna II	7 937	26 040	Nepal

LONGEST RIVERS	Length km	miles	Continent
Nile	6 695	4 160	Africa
Amazon	6 516	4 049	South America
Yangtze	6 380	3 965	Asia
Mississippi-Missouri	5 969	3 709	North America
Ob'-Irtysh	5 568	3 460	Asia
Yenisey-Angara-Selenga	5 550	3 449	Asia
Yellow River	5 464	3 395	Asia
Congo	4 667	2 900	Africa
Río de la Plata-Paraná	4 500	2 796	South America
Irtysh	4 440	2 759	Asia
Mekong	4 425	2 750	Asia
Heilong Jiang-Argun'	4 416	2 744	Asia
Lena-Kirenga	4 400	2 734	Asia
MacKenzie-Peace-Finlay	4 241	2 635	North America
Niger	4 184	2 600	Africa

LARGEST LAKES	Area sq km	sq miles	Continent
Caspian Sea	371 000	143 243	Asia/Europe
Lake Superior	82 100	31 699	North America
Lake Victoria	68 870	26 591	Africa
Lake Huron	59 600	23 012	North America
Lake Michigan	57 800	22 317	North America
Lake Tanganyika	32 600	12 587	Africa
Great Bear Lake	31 328	12 096	North America
Lake Baikal	30 500	11 776	Asia
Lake Nyasa	29 500	11 390	Africa
Great Slave Lake	28 568	11 030	North America
Lake Erie	25 700	9 923	North America
Lake Winnipeg	24 387	9 416	North America
Lake Ontario	18 960	7 320	North America
Lake Ladoga	18 390	7 100	Europe
Lake Balkhash	17 400	6 718	Asia

LARGEST DRAINAGE BASINS	Area sq km	sq miles	Continent
Amazon	7 050 000	2 722 000	South America
Congo	3 700 000	1 429 000	Africa
Nile	3 349 000	1 293 000	Africa
Mississippi-Missouri	3 250 000	1 255 000	North America
Río de la Plata-Paraná	3 100 000	1 197 000	South America
Ob'-Irtysh	2 990 000	1 154 000	Asia
Yenisey-Angara-Selenga	2 580 000	996 000	Asia
Lena-Kirenga	2 490 000	961 000	Asia
Yangtze	1 959 000	756 000	Asia
Niger	1 890 000	730 000	Africa
Heilong Jiang-Argun'	1 855 000	716 000	Asia
Mackenzie-Peace-Finlay	1 805 000	697 000	North America
Ganges-Brahmaputra	1 621 000	626 000	Asia
St Lawrence-St Louis	1 463 000	565 000	North America
Volga	1 380 000	533 000	Europe

ATLANTIC OCEAN	Area sq km	sq miles	Deepest Point metres		feet
Total extent	86 557 000	33 420 000	8 605	Milwaukee Deep	28 231
Arctic Ocean	9 485 000	3 662 000	5 450		17 880
Caribbean Sea	2 512 000	970 000	7 680		25 196
Mediterranean Sea	2 510 000	969 000	5 121		16 800
Gulf of Mexico	1 544 000	596 000	3 504		11 495
Hudson Bay	1 233 000	476 000	259		849
North Sea	575 000	222 000	661		2 168
Black Sea	508 000	196 000	2 245		7 365
Baltic Sea	382 000	147 000	460		1 509
INDIAN OCEAN	**Area sq km**	**sq miles**	**Deepest Point metres**		**feet**
Total extent	73 427 000	28 350 000	7 125	Java Trench	23 376
Bay of Bengal	2 172 000	839 000	4 500		14 763
Red Sea	453 000	175 000	3 040		9 973
The Gulf	238 000	92 000	73		239
PACIFIC OCEAN	**Area sq km**	**sq miles**	**Deepest Point metres**		**feet**
Total extent	166 241 000	64 186 000	10 920	Challenger Deep	35 826
South China Sea	2 590 000	1 000 000	5 514		18 090
Bering Sea	2 261 000	873 000	4 150		13 615
Sea of Okhotsk	1 392 000	537 000	3 363		11 033
Sea of Japan (East Sea)	1 013 000	391 000	3 743		12 280
East China Sea and Yellow Sea	1 202 000	464 000	2 717		8 913

LARGEST ISLANDS	Area sq km	Area sq miles	Continent
Greenland	2 175 600	839 999	North America
New Guinea	808 510	312 166	Oceania
Borneo	745 561	287 861	Asia
Madagascar	587 040	266 656	Africa
Baffin Island	507 451	195 927	North America
Sumatra	473 606	182 859	Asia
Honshū	227 414	87 805	Asia
Great Britain	218 476	84 354	Europe
Victoria Island	217 291	83 896	North America
Ellesmere Island	196 236	75 767	North America
Celebes	189 216	73 056	Asia
South Island, New Zealand	151 215	58 384	Oceania
Java	132 188	51 038	Asia
North Island, New Zealand	115 777	44 701	Oceania
Cuba	110 860	42 803	North America

DEEPEST LAKES	Depth metres	Depth feet	Continent
Lake Baikal	1 741	5 712	Asia
Lake Tanganyika	1 471	4 826	Africa
Caspian Sea	1 025	3 363	Asia/Europe
Lake Nyasa	706	2 316	Africa
Ysyk-Köl	702	2 303	Asia

LOWEST POINTS ON LAND	Depth below sea level metres	Depth below sea level feet	Location
Dead Sea	-421	-1 381	Asia
Lake Assal	-156	-512	Djibouti
Turpan Pendi	-154	-505	China
Qattara Depression	-133	-436	Egypt
Poluostrov Mangyshlak	-132	-433	Kazakhstan

HIGHEST WATERFALLS	Height metres	Height feet	Location
Angel Falls	979	3 212	Venezuela
Tugela	948	3 110	South Africa
Utigård	800	2 625	Norway
Mongfossen	774	2 539	Norway
Mtarazi	762	2 500	Zimbabwe

EARTH'S DIMENSIONS	
Mass	5.974×10^{21} tonnes
Total area	509 450 000 sq km /196 698 645 sq miles
Land area	149 450 000 sq km / 57 702 645 sq miles
Water area	360 000 000 sq km /138 996 000 sq miles
Volume	$1\ 083\ 207 \times 10^{6}$ cubic km /
	$259\ 911 \times 10^{6}$ cubic miles
Equatorial diameter	12 756 km / 7 927 miles
Polar diameter	12 714 km / 7 901 miles
Equatorial circumference	40 075 km / 24 903 miles
Meridional circumference	40 008 km / 24 861 miles

LARGEST COUNTRIES BY POPULATION	Population
China	1 313 437 000
India	1 169 016 000
United States of America	305 826 000
Indonesia	231 627 000
Brazil	191 791 000
Pakistan	163 902 000
Bangladesh	158 665 000
Nigeria	148 093 000
Russian Federation	142 499 000
Japan	127 967 000

LARGEST COUNTRIES BY AREA	Area sq km	Area sq miles
Russian Federation	17 075 400	6 592 849
Canada	9 984 670	3 855 103
United States of America	9 826 635	3 794 085
China	9 584 492	3 700 593
Brazil	8 514 879	3 287 613
Australia	7 692 024	2 969 907
India	3 064 898	1 183 364
Argentina	2 766 889	1 068 302
Kazakhstan	2 717 300	1 049 155
Sudan	2 505 813	967 500

LARGEST CITIES	Population	Location
Tōkyō	35 467 000	Japan
Mexico City	20 688 000	Mexico
Mumbai	20 036 000	India
São Paulo	19 582 000	Brazil
New York	19 388 000	United States of America
Delhi	16 983 000	India
Shanghai	15 790 000	China
Kolkata	15 548 000	India
Jakarta	15 206 000	Indonesia
Dhaka	14 625 000	Bangladesh
Lagos	13 717 000	Nigeria
Karachi	13 252 000	Pakistan
Buenos Aires	13 067 000	Argentina
Los Angeles	12 738 000	United States of America
Rio de Janeiro	12 170 000	Brazil

BUSIEST AIRPORTS (2007)	Location	Passengers
Atlanta (ATL)	USA	89 379 287
Chicago (ORD)	USA	76 177 855
London (LHR)	UK	68 068 304
Tōkyō (HND)	Japan	66 823 414
Los Angeles (LAX)	USA	61 896 075
Paris (CDG)	France	59 922 177
Dallas/Fort Worth Airport (DFW)	USA	59 786 476
Frankfurt am Main (FRA)	Germany	54 161 856
Beijing (PEK)	China	53 583 664
Madrid (MAD)	Spain	52 122 702
Denver (DEN)	USA	49 863 352
Amsterdam (AMS)	Netherlands	47 794 994
New York (JFK)	USA	47 716 941
Hong Kong (HKG)	China	47 042 419
Las Vegas (LAS)	USA	46 961 011

Climate is defined by the long-term weather conditions prevalent in any part of the world. The classification of climate types is based on the relationship between temperature and humidity and also on how these are affected by latitude, altitude, ocean currents and wind. Weather is how climatic conditions affect local areas. Weather stations collect data on temperature and rainfall, which can be plotted on graphs as shown here. These are based on average monthly figures over a minimum period of thirty years and can help to monitor climate change.

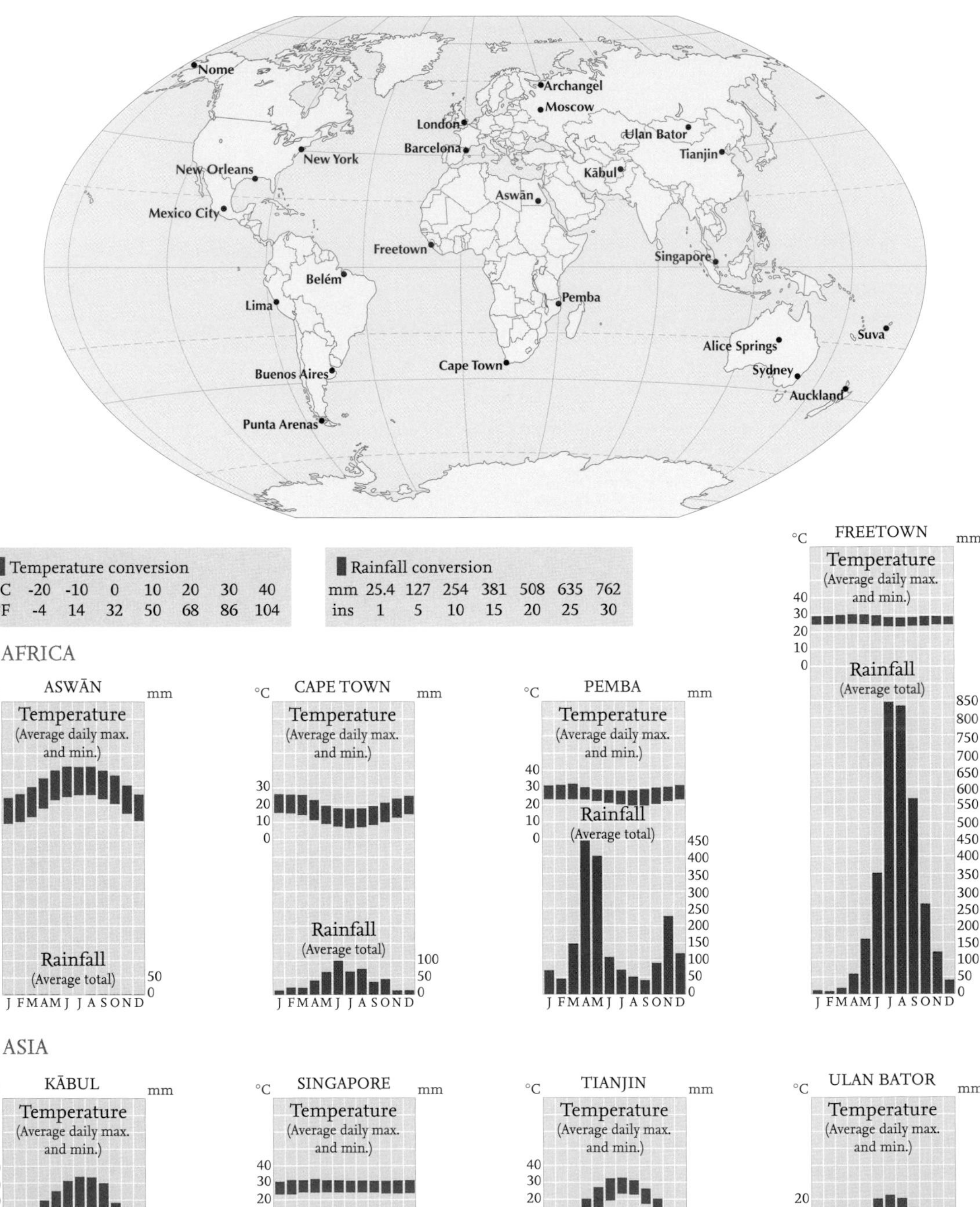

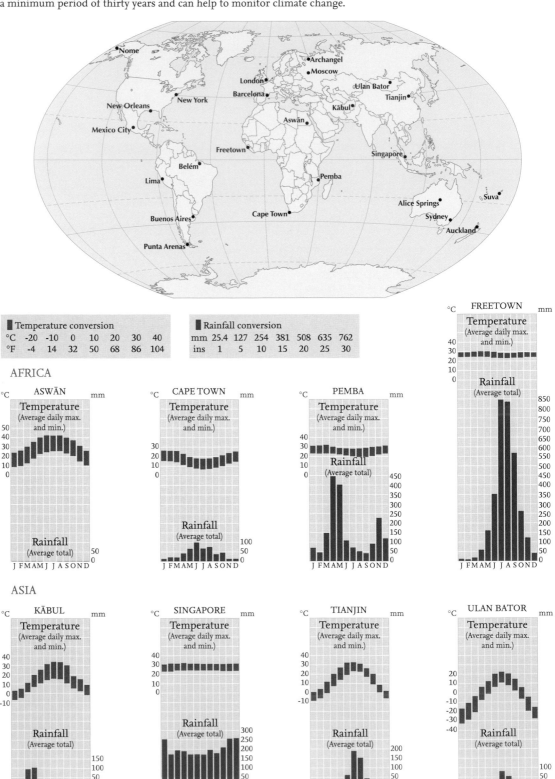

▮ Temperature conversion							
°C	-20	-10	0	10	20	30	40
°F	-4	14	32	50	68	86	104

▮ Rainfall conversion							
mm	25.4	127	254	381	508	635	762
ins	1	5	10	15	20	25	30

AFRICA

ASIA

EUROPE

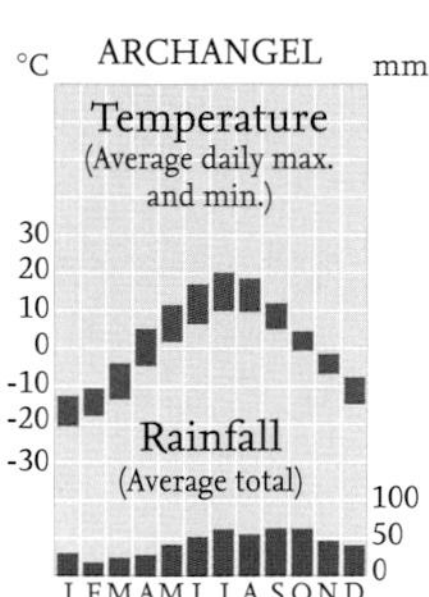

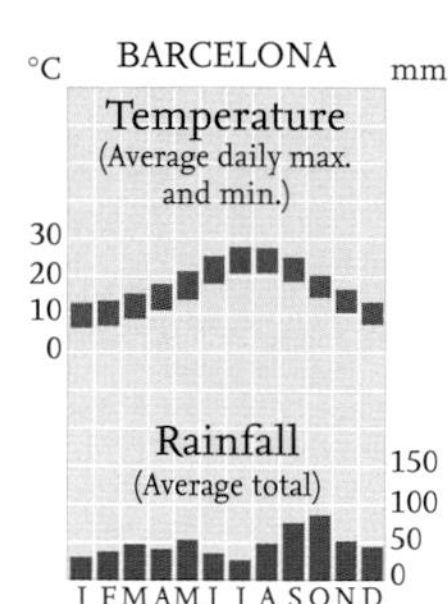

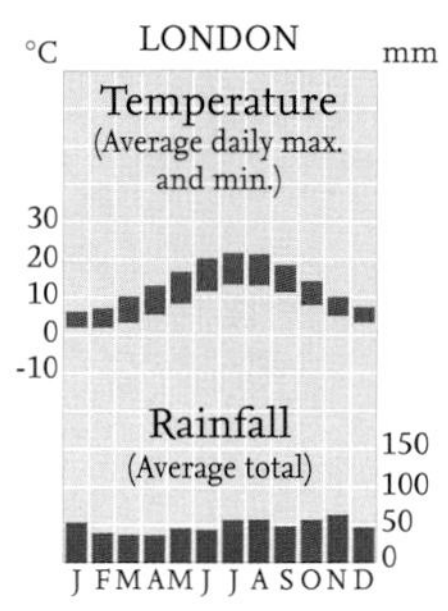

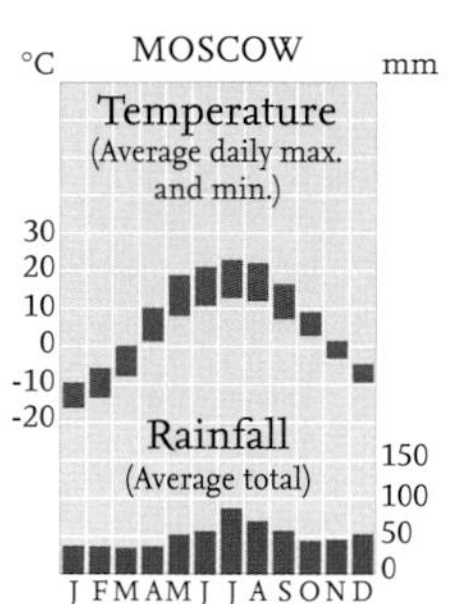

NORTH AMERICA

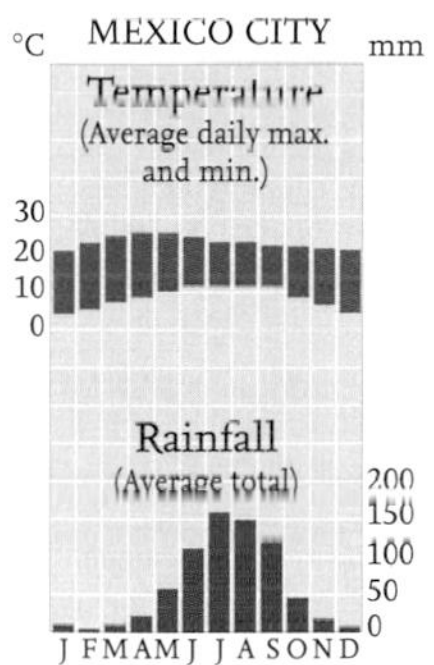

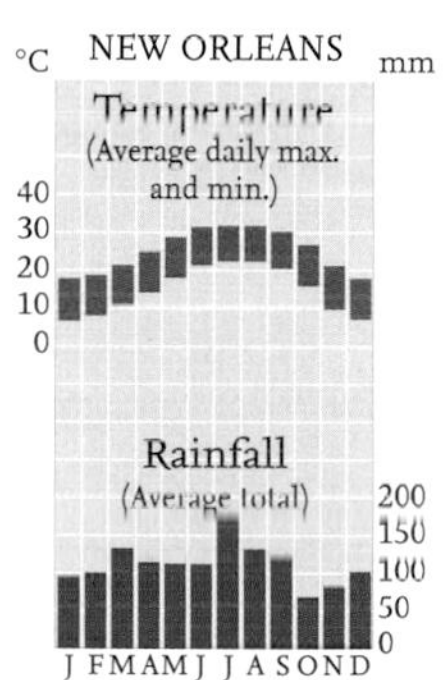

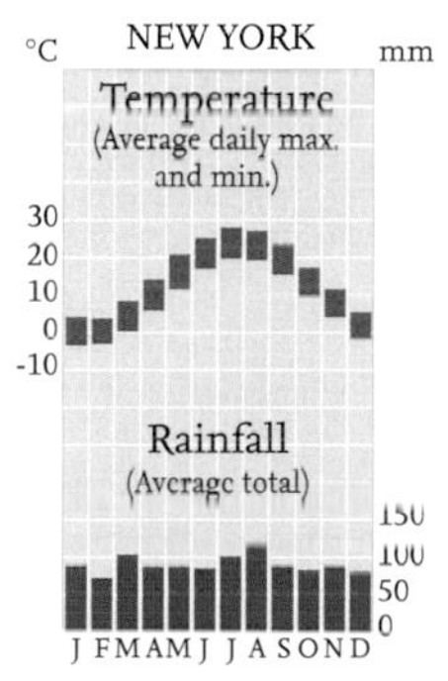

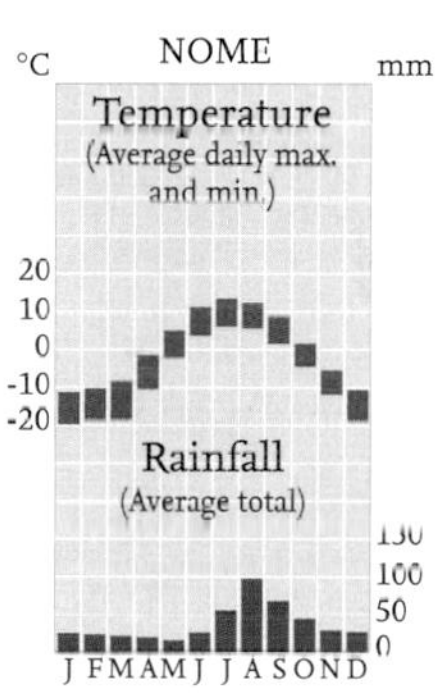

SOUTH AMERICA

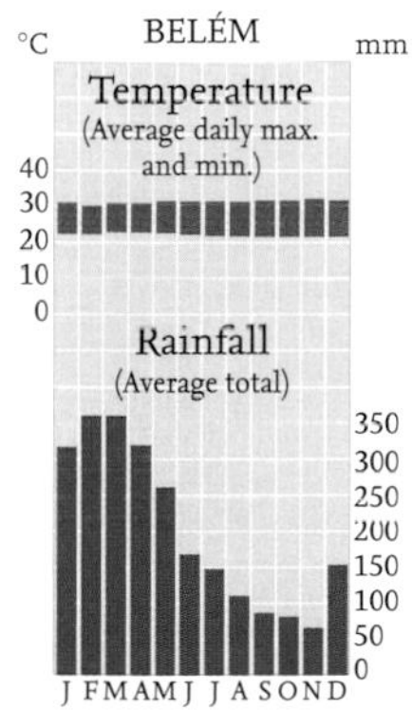

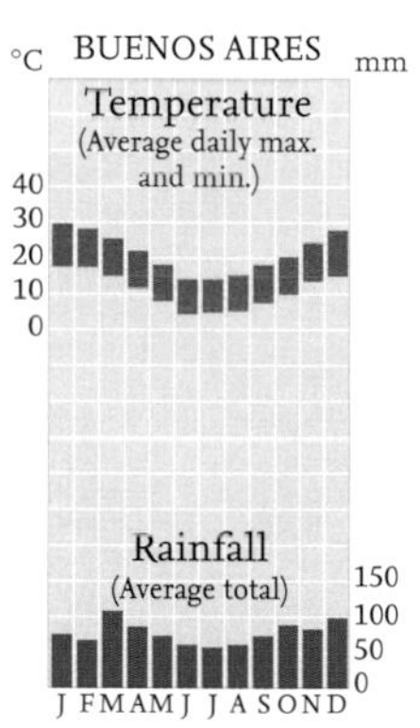

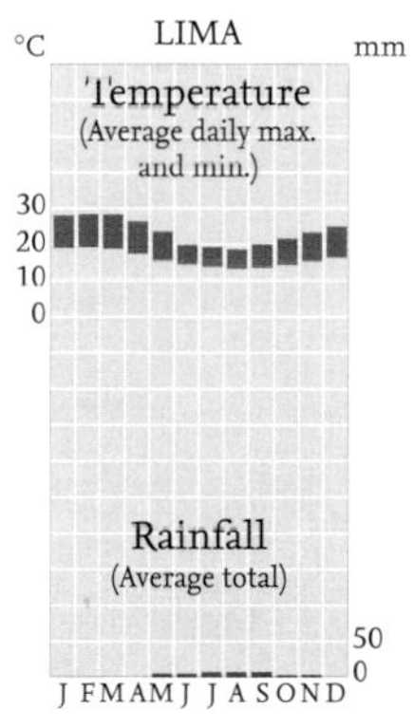

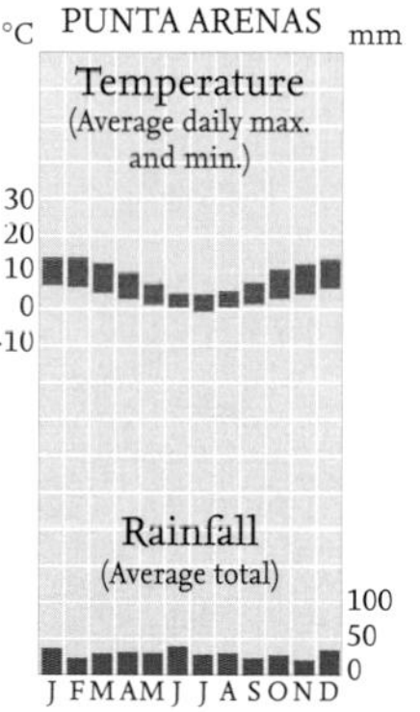

OCEANIA

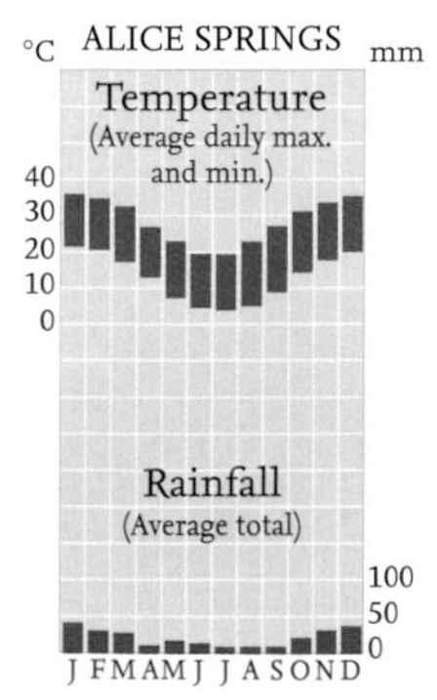

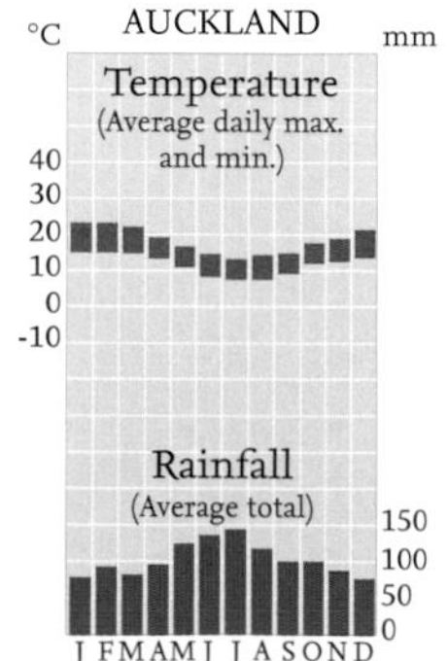

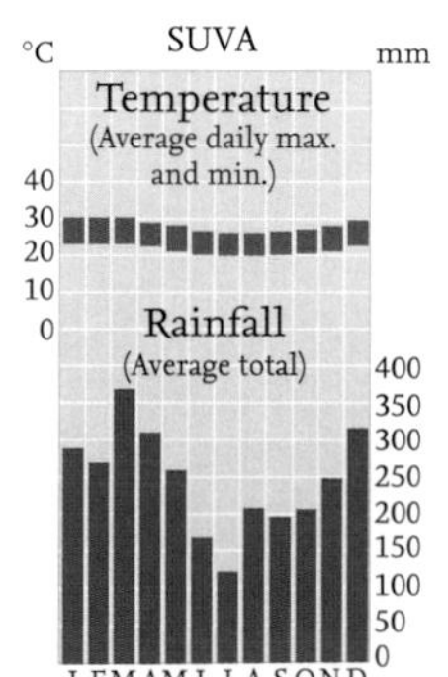

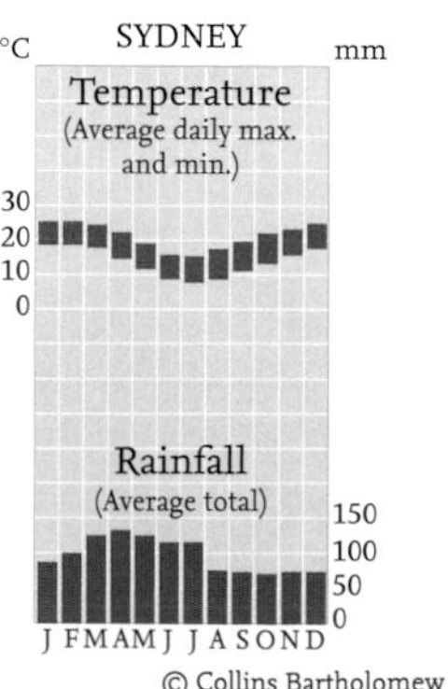

ENVIRONMENT

The earth has a rich environment with a wide range of habitats. Forest and woodland form the predominant natural land cover and tropical rain forests are believed to be home to the majority of the world's bird, animal and plant species. These forests are part of a delicate land-atmosphere relationship disturbed by changes in land use. Grassland, shrubland and deserts cover most of the unwooded areas of the earth with low-growing tundra in the far northern latitudes. Grassland and shrubland regions in particular have been altered greatly by man through agriculture, livestock grazing and settlements.

Organization	Web address	Theme
Earth Observatory	earthobservatory.nasa.gov	Observing the earth
USGS National Earthquake Information Center	neic.usgs.gov	Monitoring earthquakes
Scripps Institution of Oceanography	sio.ucsd.edu	Exploration of the oceans
Visible Earth	visibleearth.nasa.gov	Satellite images of the earth
USGS Volcano Hazards Program	volcanoes.usgs.gov	Volcanic activity
UNESCO World Heritage Centre	whc.unesco.org	World Heritage Sites
British Geological Survey	www.bgs.ac.uk	Geology
International Union for the Conservation of Nature	www.iucn.org	World and ocean conservation
World Rainforest Information Portal	www.rainforestweb.org	Rainforest information and resources
United Nations Environment Programme	www.unep.org	Environmental protection by the UN
World Conservation Monitoring Centre	www.unep-wcmc.org	Conservation and the environment
World Resources Institute	www.wri.org	Monitoring the environment and resources
IUCN Red List	www.iucnredlist.org	Threatened species

OCEANS

Between them, the world's oceans cover approximately 70 per cent of the earth's surface. They contain 96 per cent of the earth's water and a vast range of flora and fauna. They are a major influence on the world's climate, particularly through ocean currents – the circulation of water within and between the oceans. Our understanding of the oceans has increased enormously over the last twenty years through the development of new technologies, including that of satellite images, which can generate vast amounts of data relating to the sea floor, ocean currents and sea surface temperatures.

Organization	Web address	Theme
International Maritime Organization	www.imo.org	Shipping and the environment
General Bathymetric Chart of the Oceans	www.gebco.net	Mapping the oceans
National Oceanography Centre	www.soc.soton.ac.uk	Researching the oceans
Scott Polar Research Institute	www.spri.cam.ac.uk	Polar research

CLIMATE

The Earth's climate system is highly complex. It is recognized and accepted that man's activities are affecting this system, and monitoring climate change, including human influences upon it, is now a major issue. Future climate change depends critically on how quickly and to what extent the concentration of greenhouse gases in the atmosphere increase. Change will not be uniform across the globe and the information from sophisticated mathematical climate models is invaluable in helping governments and industry to assess the impacts climate change will have.

Organization	Web address	Theme
BBC Weather	www.bbc.co.uk/weather	Worldwide weather forecasts
Climatic Research Unit	www.cru.uea.ac.uk	Climatic research
Meteorological Office	www.met-office.gov.uk	Weather information and climatic research
National Climatic Data Center	www.ncdc.noaa.gov	Global climate data
US National Hurricane Center	www.nhc.noaa.gov	Tracking hurricanes
National Oceanic and Atmospheric Administration	www.noaa.gov	Monitoring climate and the oceans
World Meteorological Organization	www.wmo.ch	The world's climate
El Niño	www.elnino.noaa.gov	El Niño research and observations

POPULATION

The world's population reached 6 billion in 1999. Rates of population growth vary between continents, but overall, the rate of growth has been increasing and it is predicted that by 2050 another 3 billion people will inhabit the planet. The process of urbanization, in particular migration from countryside to city, has led to the rapid growth of many cities. It is estimated that by the end of 2008, more people will be living in urban areas than in rural areas, and that by 2010 there will be 473 cities with over 1 million inhabitants and twenty-one with over 10 million.

Organization	Web address	Theme
Office for National Statistics	www.statistics.gov.uk/census	UK census information
City Population	www.citypopulation.de	Statistics and maps about population
US Census Bureau	www.census.gov	US and world population
UN World Urbanization Prospects	www.un.org/esa/population/publications/2007_PopDevt	Population estimates and projections
UN Population Information Network	www.un.org/popin	World population statistics
UN Population Division	www.un.org/esa/population/unpop	Monitoring world population

COUNTRIES

The present picture of the political world is the result of a long history of exploration, colonialism, conflict and negotiation. In 1950 there were eighty-two independent countries. Since then there has been a significant trend away from colonial influences and although many dependent territories still exist, there are now 195 independent countries. The newest country is Kosovo which declared independence from Serbia in February 2008. The shapes of countries reflect a combination of natural features, such as mountain ranges, and political agreements. There are still areas of the world where boundaries are disputed or only temporarily settled as ceasefire lines.

Organization	Web address	Theme
European Union	europa.eu	Gateway to the European Union
Permanent Committee on Geographical Names	www.pcgn.org.uk	Place names research in the UK
The World Factbook	www.odci.gov/cia/publications/factbook	Country profiles
US Board on Geographic Names	geonames.usgs.gov	Place names research in the USA
United Nations	www.un.org	The United Nations
International Boundaries Research Unit	www.dur.ac.uk/ibru	International boundaries resources and research
Organisation for Economic Cooperation and Development	www.oecd.org	Economic statistics
The World Bank	www.worldbank.org/data	World development data and statistics

TRAVEL

Travelling as a tourist or on business to some countries, or travelling within certain areas can be dangerous because of wars and political unrest. The UK Foreign Office provides the latest travel advice and security warnings. Some areas of the world, particularly tropical regions in the developing world, also carry many risks of disease. Advice should be sought on precautions to take and medications required.

Organization	Web address	Theme
UK Foreign and Commonwealth Office	www.fco.gov.uk	Travel, trade and country information
US Department of State	www.state.gov	Travel, trade and country information
World Health Organization	www.who.int	Health advice and world health issues
Centers for Disease Control and Prevention	www.cdc.gov/travel	Advice for travellers
Airports Council International	www.airports.org	The voice of the world's airports
Travel Daily News	www.traveldailynews.com	Travel and tourism newsletter

ORGANIZATIONS

Throughout the world there are many international, national and local organizations representing the interests of individual countries, groups of countries, regions and specialist groups. These can provide enormous amounts of information on economic, social, cultural, environmental and general geographical issues facing the world. The following is a selection of such sites.

Organization	Web address	Theme
United Nations	www.un.org	The United Nations
United Nations Educational, Scientific and Cultural Organization	www.unesco.org	International collaboration
United Nations Children's Fund	www.unicef.org	Children's health, education, equality and protection
United Nations High Commissioner for Refugees	www.unhcr.org	The UN refugee agency
Food and Agriculture Organization of the United Nations	www.fao.org	Agriculture and defeating hunger
United Nations Development Programme	www.undp.org	The UN global development network
North Atlantic Treaty Organization	www.nato.int	North Atlantic freedom and security
European Environment Agency	www.eea.europa.eu/	Europe's environment
European Centre for Nature Conservation	www.ecnc.nl/	Nature conservation in Europe
Europa - The European Union On-line	europa.eu/index.en.htm	European Union facts and statistics
World Health Organisation	www.who.int	Health issues and advice
Association of Southeast Asian Nations	www.aseansec.org	Economic, social and cultural development
Africawater	www.africawater.org	Water resources in Africa
Joint United Nations Programme on HIV/AIDS	www.unaids.org	The AIDS crisis
African Union	www.africa-union.org	African international relations
World Lakes Network	www.worldlakes.org/	Lakes around the world
Secretariat of the Pacific Commmunity	www.spc.int	The Pacific community
The Maori world	www.maori.org.nz	Maori culture
US National Park Service	www.nps.gov	National Parks of the USA
Parks Canada	www.pc.gc.ca	Natural heritage of Canada
Panama Canal Authority	www.pancanal.com	Explore the Panama Canal
Caribbean Community Secretariat	www.caricom.org	Caribbean Community
Organization of American States	www.oas.org	Inter-American cooperation
The Latin American Network Information Center	lanic.utexas.edu	Latin America
World Wildlife Fund	www.worldwildlife.org	Global environmental conservation
Amazon Conservation Team	www.amazonteam.org	Conservation in tropical America

DISTANCES

This table shows air distances in both kilometres and *miles* for 27 cities around the world. These are the shortest distances between cities and are known as Great Circle routes.

	Tōkyō	Sydney	Singapore	Seoul	Rome	Rio de Janiero	Paris	New York	Nairobi	Moscow	Montréal	Mexico City	Melbourne	Madrid	Los Angeles	London	Jerusalem	İstanbul	Delhi	Cape Town	Cairo	Buenos Aires	Berlin	Beijing	Bangkok	Auckland
Abu Dhabi	8075 / *5018*	9793 / *6085*	5905 / *3669*	6918 / *4299*	4303 / *2674*	11764 / *7310*	5247 / *3260*	11040 / *6860*	3422 / *2126*	3735 / *2321*	10647 / *6616*	14374 / *8932*	11689 / *7263*	5632 / *3500*	13481 / *8377*	5478 / *3404*	2043 / *1270*	2987 / *1856*	2317 / *1440*	7498 / *4659*	2367 / *1471*	13534 / *8410*	4637 / *2881*	5972 / *3711*	4795 / *3091*	14244 / *8851*
Auckland	8811 / *5475*	2161 / *1343*	8411 / *5227*	9596 / *5963*	18400 / *11433*	12288 / *7636*	18540 / *11521*	14187 / *8816*	13966 / *8678*	16194 / *10063*	14379 / *8935*	10947 / *6802*	2629 / *1634*	19592 / *12174*	10479 / *6512*	18330 / *11390*	16287 / *10121*	17042 / *10590*	12482 / *7756*	11796 / *7330*	16573 / *10298*	10372 / *6445*	17743 / *11025*	10388 / *6455*	9566 / *5944*	
Bangkok	4610 / *2865*	7523 / *4675*	1427 / *887*	3720 / *2312*	8842 / *5494*	16081 / *9993*	9457 / *5877*	13949 / *8668*	7218 / *4485*	7070 / *4393*	13417 / *8337*	15760 / *9739*	7359 / *4573*	10196 / *6336*	13319 / *8276*	9544 / *5931*	6895 / *4285*	7477 / *4646*	2917 / *1813*	10144 / *6303*	7279 / *4523*	16885 / *10492*	8613 / *5352*	3291 / *2045*		
Beijing	2104 / *1307*	8923 / *5545*	4465 / *2775*	958 / *595*	8144 / *5061*	17325 / *10766*	8236 / *5118*	11012 / *6843*	9216 / *5727*	5809 / *3610*	10490 / *6518*	12478 / *7754*	9093 / *5650*	9243 / *5744*	10082 / *6265*	8160 / *5071*	7135 / *4434*	7072 / *4394*	3788 / *2354*	12947 / *8045*	7557 / *4696*	19265 / *11971*	7375 / *4583*			
Berlin	8942 / *5556*	16090 / *9998*	9927 / *6169*	8150 / *5064*	1182 / *735*	9989 / *6207*	880 / *547*	6403 / *3979*	6353 / *3948*	1612 / *1002*	6018 / *3740*	9746 / *6056*	15970 / *9924*	1871 / *1163*	9332 / *5799*	934 / *580*	2903 / *1804*	1739 / *1081*	5791 / *3599*	9588 / *5958*	2891 / *1796*	11890 / *7388*				
Buenos Aires	18365 / *11412*	11821 / *7345*	15889 / *9873*	19429 / *12073*	11135 / *6919*	1968 / *1223*	11029 / *6853*	8490 / *5276*	10416 / *6472*	13461 / *8365*	9001 / *5593*	7366 / *4577*	11629 / *7226*	10024 / *6229*	9828 / *6107*	11105 / *6901*	12236 / *7603*	12235 / *7603*	15800 / *9818*	6891 / *4282*	11811 / *7339*					
Cairo	9587 / *5957*	14415 / *8957*	8270 / *5139*	8504 / *5284*	2135 / *1327*	9882 / *6141*	3215 / *1998*	9042 / *5618*	3518 / *2186*	2899 / *1801*	8733 / *5427*	12392 / *7700*	13966 / *8678*	3355 / *2085*	12223 / *7595*	3513 / *2183*	426 / *265*	1234 / *767*	4436 / *2757*	7208 / *4479*						
Cape Town	14737 / *9157*	11034 / *6856*	9671 / *6009*	13710 / *8519*	8417 / *5230*	6075 / *3775*	9307 / *5783*	12551 / *7799*	4090 / *2542*	10101 / *6277*	12744 / *7919*	13703 / *8515*	10338 / *6424*	8536 / *5304*	16054 / *9976*	9635 / *5987*	7481 / *4649*	8367 / *5199*	9284 / *5769*							
Delhi	5857 / *3640*	10415 / *6472*	4142 / *2574*	4699 / *2920*	5929 / *3684*	14080 / *8749*	6601 / *4102*	11779 / *7319*	5428 / *3373*	4349 / *2702*	11286 / *7013*	14679 / *9121*	10192 / *6333*	7288 / *4529*	12882 / *8005*	6724 / *4178*	4032 / *2505*	4560 / *2834*								
İstanbul	8970 / *5574*	14944 / *9286*	8652 / *5376*	7975 / *4956*	1379 / *857*	10268 / *6380*	2261 / *1405*	8089 / *5026*	4751 / *2952*	1755 / *1091*	7730 / *4803*	11448 / *7114*	14628 / *9090*	2744 / *1705*	11043 / *6862*	2504 / *1556*	1170 / *727*									
Jerusalem	9171 / *5699*	14126 / *8778*	7924 / *4924*	8083 / *5023*	2310 / *1435*	10308 / *6405*	3339 / *2075*	9190 / *5711*	3662 / *2276*	2671 / *1660*	8854 / *5502*	12552 / *7800*	13713 / *8521*	3602 / *2238*	12210 / *7587*	3615 / *2246*										
London	9585 / *5956*	16990 / *10557*	10860 / *6748*	8882 / *5519*	1434 / *891*	9254 / *5750*	341 / *212*	5586 / *3471*	6805 / *4229*	5206 / *1557*	5240 / *3256*	8947 / *5560*	16902 / *10503*	1264 / *785*	8778 / *5455*											
Los Angeles	8828 / *5486*	12065 / *7497*	14136 / *8784*	9605 / *5968*	10212 / *6346*	10129 / *6294*	9106 / *5658*	3945 / *2451*	15553 / *9664*	9793 / *6085*	3973 / *2469*	2492 / *1549*	12762 / *7930*	9387 / *5833*												
Madrid	10789 / *6704*	17687 / *10990*	10021 / *7081*	11396 / *6227*	1365 / *848*	8118 / *5044*	1054 / *655*	5785 / *3595*	6177 / *3838*	3446 / *2141*	5551 / *3449*	9083 / *5644*	17315 / *10759*													
Melbourne	8159 / *5070*	711 / *442*	6050 / *3759*	8551 / *5314*	15987 / *9934*	13227 / *8219*	16793 / *10435*	16671 / *10359*	11513 / *7154*	14418 / *8959*	16730 / *10396*	13557 / *8424*														
Mexico City	11319 / *7034*	12972 / *8061*	16623 / *10329*	12071 / *7501*	10260 / *6375*	7669 / *4765*	9213 / *5725*	3362 / *2089*	14834 / *9218*	10740 / *6674*	3728 / *2317*															
Montréal	10409 / *6468*	16026 / *9958*	14816 / *9207*	10577 / *6572*	6601 / *4102*	8175 / *5080*	5522 / *3431*	533 / *331*	11692 / *7265*	7077 / *4398*																
Moscow	7502 / *4662*	14487 / *9002*	8426 / *5236*	6626 / *4117*	2378 / *1478*	11529 / *7164*	2492 / *1549*	7530 / *4679*	6323 / *3929*																	
Nairobi	11266 / *7001*	12162 / *7557*	7467 / *4640*	10115 / *6285*	5374 / *3339*	8941 / *5556*	6471 / *4021*	11849 / *7363*																		
New York	10870 / *6755*	15990 / *9936*	15349 / *9538*	11078 / *6884*	6907 / *4292*	7729 / *4803*	5851 / *3636*																			
Paris	9738 / *6051*	16959 / *10538*	10743 / *6676*	8990 / *5586*	1108 / *689*	9146 / *5683*																				
Rio de Janiero	18557 / *10288*	13539 / *8413*	15740 / *9781*	18135 / *11269*	9181 / *5705*																					
Rome	9881 / *6140*	16322 / *10142*	10030 / *6232*	8991 / *5587*																						
Seoul	1160 / *721*	8298 / *5156*	4666 / *2899*																							
Singapore	5317 / *3304*	6293 / *3910*																								
Sydney	7794 / *4843*																									

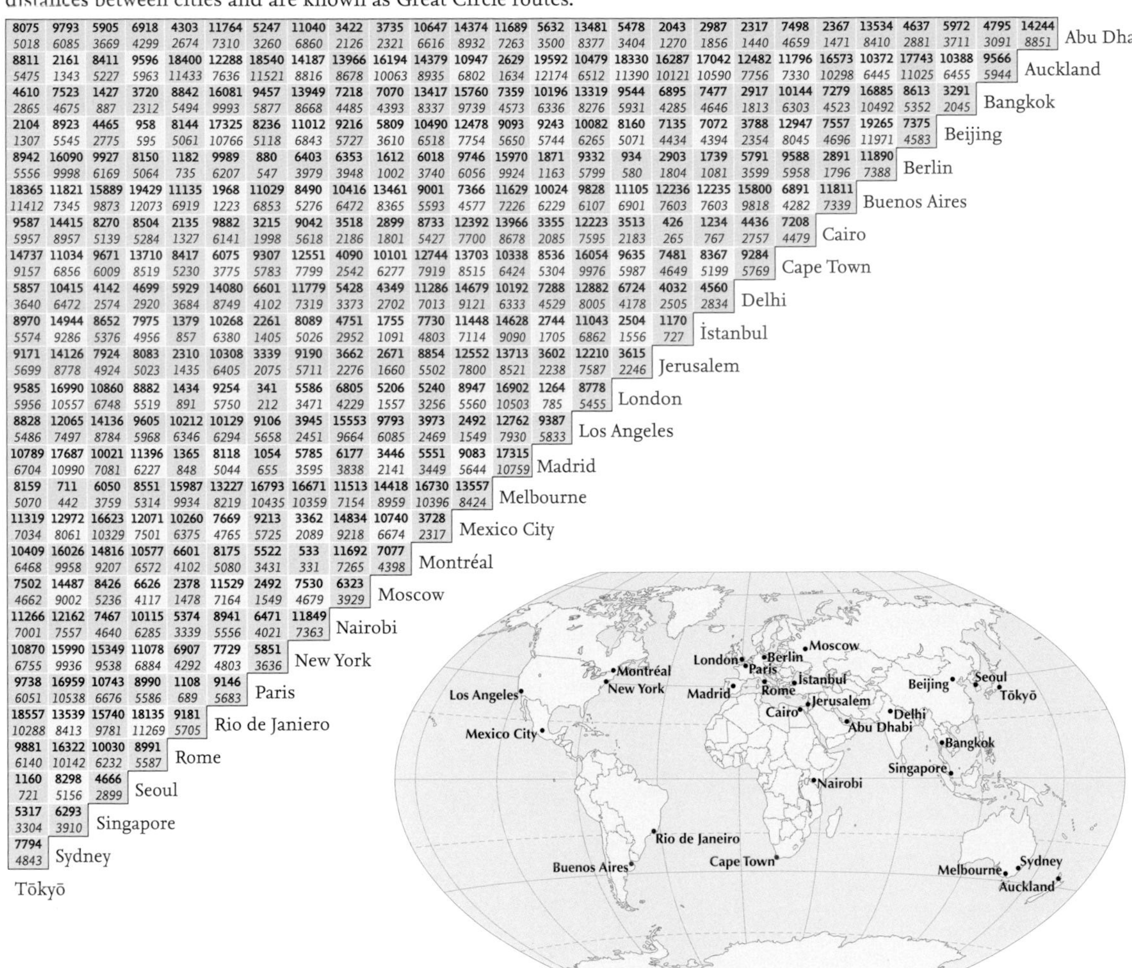

CONVERSION CHARTS

To convert	into	multiply by
LENGTH AND AREA		
millimetres	inches	0.0394
centimetres	inches	0.3937
metres	feet	3.2808
metres	yards	1.0936
kilometres	miles	0.6214
inches	millimetres	25.4
inches	centimetres	2.54
feet	metres	0.3048
yards	metres	0.9144
miles	kilometres	1.6093
acres	hectares	0.4047
hectares	acres	2.4711
square miles	square kilometres	2.5900
square kilometres	square miles	0.3861
TEMPERATURE		
°C	°F	multiply by 1.8 and add 32
°F	°C	subtract 32 and divide by 1.8

To convert	into	multiply by
WEIGHT		
grams	ounces	0.0353
kilograms	pounds	2.2046
metric tonnes (1000 kg)	tons (2 240lbs)	0.9842
ounces	grams	28.3495
pounds	kilograms	0.4536
tons (2 240lbs)	metric tonnes (1000 kg)	1.0161
VOLUME		
pints (20fl oz)	litres	0.5683
imperial gallons	litres	4.5461
litres	pints (20fl oz)	1.7598
litres	imperial gallons	0.2200
SPEED		
km/h	mph	0.6214
mph	km/h	1.6093

INTRODUCTION TO THE INDEX

The index includes all names shown on the maps in the Atlas of the World. Names are referenced by page number and by a grid reference. The grid reference correlates to the alphanumeric values which appear within each map frame. Each entry also includes the country or geographical area in which the feature is located. Entries relating to names appearing on insets are indicated by a small box symbol: □, followed by a grid reference if the inset has its own alphanumeric values.

Name forms are as they appear on the maps, with additional alternative names or name forms included as cross-references which refer the user to the entry for the map form of the name. Names beginning with Mc or Mac are alphabetized exactly as they appear. The terms Saint, Sainte, Sankt, etc, are abbreviated to St, Ste, St, etc, but alphabetized as if in the full form.

Names of physical features beginning with generic geographical terms are permuted – the descriptive term is placed after the main part of the name. For example, Lake Superior is indexed as Superior, Lake; Mount Everest as Everest, Mount. This policy is applied to all languages.

Entries, other than those for towns and cities, include a descriptor indicating the type of geographical feature. Descriptors are not included where the type of feature is implicit in the name itself.

Administrative divisions are included to differentiate entries of the same name and feature type within the one country. In such cases, duplicate names are alphabetized in order of administrative division. Additional qualifiers are also included for names within selected geographical areas.

INDEX ABBREVIATIONS

admin. div.	administrative division
Afgh.	Afghanistan
Alg.	Algeria
Arg.	Argentina
Austr.	Australia
aut. comm.	autonomous community
aut. reg.	autonomous region
aut. rep.	autonomous republic
Azer.	Azerbaijan
b.	bay
B.I.O.T.	British Indian Ocean Territory
Bangl.	Bangladesh
Bol.	Bolivia
Bos.-Herz.	Bosnia Herzegovina
Bulg.	Bulgaria
c.	cape
Can.	Canada
C.A.R.	Central African Republic
Col.	Colombia
Czech Rep.	Czech Republic
Dem. Rep. Congo	Democratic Republic of the Congo
depr.	depression
des.	desert
Dom. Rep.	Dominican Republic
Equat. Guinea	Equatorial Guinea
esc.	escarpment
est.	estuary
Eth.	Ethiopia
Fin.	Finland
for.	forest
Fr. Guiana	French Guiana
Fr. Polynesia	French Polynesia
g.	gulf
Ger.	Germany
Guat.	Guatemala
hd	headland
Hond.	Honduras
i.	island
imp. l.	impermanent lake
Indon.	Indonesia
is.	islands
isth.	isthmus
Kazakh.	Kazakhstan
Kyrg.	Kyrgyzstan
l.	lake
lag.	lagoon
Lith.	Lithuania
Lux.	Luxembourg
Madag.	Madagascar
Maur.	Mauritania
Mex.	Mexico
Moz.	Mozambique
mt.	mountain
mts	mountains
mun.	municipality
N.	North
Neth.	Netherlands
Neth. Antilles	Netherlands Antilles
Nic.	Nicaragua
N.Z.	New Zealand
Pak.	Pakistan
Para.	Paraguay
pen.	peninsula
Phil.	Philippines
plat.	plateau
P.N.G.	Papua New Guinea
Pol.	Poland
Port.	Portugal
prov.	province
pt	point
r.	river
r. mouth	river mouth
reg.	region
resr	reservoir
rf	reef
Rus. Fed.	Russian Federation
S.	South
salt l.	salt lake
sea chan.	sea channel
special admin. reg.	special administrative region
str.	strait
Switz.	Switzerland
Tajik.	Tajikistan
Tanz.	Tanzania
terr.	territory
Thai.	Thailand
Trin. and Tob.	Trinidad and Tobago
Turkm.	Turkmenistan
U.A.E.	United Arab Emirates
U.K.	United Kingdom
Ukr.	Ukraine
union terr.	union territory
Uru.	Uruguay
U.S.A.	United States of America
Uzbek.	Uzbekistan
val.	valley
Venez.	Venezuela
vol.	volcano
vol. crater	volcanic crater

1

128 B2 100 Mile House Can.

A

93 E4 Aabenraa Denmark
100 C2 Aachen Ger.
93 E4 Aalborg Denmark
102 C2 Aalen Ger.
100 B2 Aalst Belgium
93 I3 Äänekoski Fin.
105 D2 Aarau Switz.
100 B2 Aarschot Belgium
70 A2 Aba China
119 D2 Aba Dem. Rep. Congo
115 C4 Aba Nigeria
81 C2 Ābādān Iran
81 D2 Ābādeh Iran
81 D3 Ābādeh Ţashk Iran
114 B1 Abadla Alg.
155 C1 Abaeté Brazil
Abagnar Qi China see Xilinhot
135 E3 Abajo Peak U.S.A.
115 C4 Abakaliki Nigeria
83 H3 Abakan Rus. Fed.
150 B4 Abancay Peru
81 D2 Abarqū Iran
66 D2 Abashiri Japan
66 D2 Abashiri-wan b. Japan
59 D3 Abau P.N.G.
Abaya, Lake l. Eth. see Lake Abaya
Ābay Wenz r. Eth. see Blue Nile
83 H3 Abaza Rus. Fed.
108 A2 Abbasanta Italy
104 C1 Abbeville France
141 C2 Abbeville AL U.S.A.
140 B3 Abbeville LA U.S.A.
97 B2 Abbeyfeale Ireland
55 R2 Abbot Ice Shelf Antarctica
74 B1 Abbottabad Pak.
115 E3 Abéché Chad
114 B4 Abengourou Côte d'Ivoire
114 C4 Abeokuta Nigeria
99 A3 Aberaeron U.K.
96 C2 Aberchirder U.K.
Abercorn Zambia see Mbala
99 B4 Aberdare U.K.
99 A3 Aberdaron U.K.
53 D2 Aberdeen Austr.
122 B3 Aberdeen S. Africa
96 C2 Aberdeen U.K.
139 D3 Aberdeen MD U.S.A.
137 D1 Aberdeen SD U.S.A.
134 B1 Aberdeen WA U.S.A.
129 E1 Aberdeen Lake Can.
96 C2 Aberfeldy U.K.
96 B2 Aberfoyle U.K.
99 B4 Abergavenny U.K.
Abergwaun U.K. see Fishguard
Aberhonddu U.K. see Brecon
143 C2 Abernathy U.S.A.
134 B2 Abert, Lake U.S.A.
Abertawe U.K. see Swansea
Aberteifi U.K. see Cardigan
99 B4 Abertillery U.K.
99 A3 Aberystwyth U.K.
86 F2 Abez' Rus. Fed.
78 B3 Abhā Saudi Arabia
81 C2 Abhar Iran
Abiad, Bahr el r. Sudan/Uganda see White Nile
114 B4 Abidjan Côte d'Ivoire
137 D3 Abilene KS U.S.A.
143 D2 Abilene TX U.S.A.
99 C4 Abingdon U.K.
138 C3 Abingdon U.S.A.
91 D3 Abinsk Rus. Fed.
130 B3 Abitibi, Lake Can.
Åbo Fin. see Turku
74 B1 Abohar India
114 B4 Aboisso Côte d'Ivoire
114 C4 Abomey Benin
60 A1 Abongabong, Gunung mt. Indon.
118 B2 Abong Mbang Cameroon
64 A3 Aborlan Phil.
115 D3 Abou Déia Chad
106 B2 Abrantes Port.
152 B2 Abra Pampa Arg.
142 A3 Abreojos, Punta pt Mex.
116 B2 'Abri Sudan
136 A2 Absaroka Range mts U.S.A.
81 C1 Abşeron Yarımadası pen. Azer.
78 B3 Abū 'Arīsh Saudi Arabia
116 A2 Abū Ballāş h. Egypt
79 C2 Abu Dhabi U.A.E.
116 B3 Abu Hamed Sudan
116 B3 Abu Haraz Sudan
115 C4 Abuja Nigeria
81 C2 Abū Kamāl Syria
118 C2 Abumombazi Dem. Rep. Congo
152 B1 Abunã r. Bol./Brazil
150 C3 Abunã Brazil
74 B2 Abu Road India
78 B2 Abū Şādi, Jabal h. Saudi Arabia
116 B2 Abū Sunbul Egypt
116 A3 Abu Zabad Sudan
Abū Ẓabī U.A.E. see Abu Dhabi
117 A4 Abyei Sudan
145 B2 Acambaro Mex.
120 B2 Acampamento de Caça do Mucusso Angola
106 B1 A Cañiza Spain
144 B2 Acaponeta Mex.
145 C3 Acapulco Mex.
151 E3 Acará Brazil
154 A3 Acaray, Represa de resr Para.
150 C2 Acarigua Venez.
110 B1 Acâş Romania
145 C3 Acatlán Mex.
145 C3 Acayucán Mex.
114 B4 Accra Ghana
98 B3 Accrington U.K.
74 B2 Achalpur India
97 A2 Achill Island Ireland
101 D1 Achim Ger.
96 B2 Achnasheen U.K.
91 D2 Achuyevo Rus. Fed.
111 C3 Acıpayam Turkey
109 C3 Acireale Italy
147 C2 Acklins Island Bahamas
153 A3 Aconcagua, Cerro mt. Arg.
106 B1 A Coruña Spain
108 A2 Acqui Terme Italy
103 D2 Ács Hungary
49 N6 Actéon, Groupe is Fr. Polynesia
145 C2 Actopán Mex.
143 D2 Ada U.S.A.
Adabazar Turkey see Adapazarı
79 C2 Adam Oman
111 B3 Adamas Greece
135 B3 Adams Peak U.S.A.
'Adan Yemen see Aden
80 B2 Adana Turkey
111 D2 Adapazarı Turkey
97 B2 Adare Ireland
55 M2 Adare, Cape Antarctica
108 A1 Adda r. Italy
78 B2 Ad Dafīnah Saudi Arabia
78 B2 Ad Dahnā' des. Saudi Arabia
79 B2 Ad Dahnā' des. Saudi Arabia
114 A2 Ad Dakhla Western Sahara
Ad Dammām Saudi Arabia see Dammam
78 A2 Ad Dār al Ḩamrā' Saudi Arabia
78 B3 Ad Darb Saudi Arabia
78 B2 Ad Dawādimī Saudi Arabia
Ad Dawḩah Qatar see Doha
Aḑ Ḑiffah plat. Egypt/Libya see Libyan Plateau
78 B2 Ad Dilam Saudi Arabia
78 B2 Ad Dir'īyah Saudi Arabia
117 B4 Addis Ababa Eth.
81 C2 Ad Dīwānīyah Iraq
141 D2 Adel U.S.A.
52 A2 Adelaide Austr.
55 A3 Adelaide Island Antarctica
50 C1 Adelaide River Austr.
101 D2 Adelebsen Ger.
55 K2 Adélie Land reg. Antarctica
78 B3 Aden Yemen
116 C3 Aden, Gulf of Somalia/Yemen
100 C2 Adenau Ger.
115 C3 Aderbissinat Niger
79 C2 Adh Dhayd U.A.E.
59 C3 Adi i. Indon.
116 B3 Ādī Ārk'ay Eth.
108 B1 Adige r. Italy
116 B3 Ādīgrat Eth.
78 A3 Adi Keyih Eritrea
74 B3 Adilabad India
115 D2 Adīrī Libya
139 E2 Adirondack Mountains U.S.A.
Ādīs Ābeba Eth. see Addis Ababa
117 B4 Ādīs Alem Eth.
80 B2 Adıyaman Turkey
110 C1 Adjud Romania
50 B1 Admiralty Gulf Austr.
128 A2 Admiralty Island U.S.A.
59 D3 Admiralty Islands P.N.G.
73 B3 Adoni India
104 B3 Adour r. France
106 C2 Adra Spain
114 B2 Adrar Alg.
138 C2 Adrian MI U.S.A.
143 C1 Adrian TX U.S.A.
108 B2 Adriatic Sea Europe
Adua Eth. see Ādwa
116 B3 Ādwa Eth.
83 K2 Adycha r. Rus. Fed.
91 D3 Adygeysk Rus. Fed.
114 B4 Adzopé Côte d'Ivoire
111 B3 Aegean Sea Greece/Turkey
101 D1 Aerzen Ger.
106 B1 A Estrada Spain
116 B3 Afabet Eritrea
Affreville Alg. see Khemis Miliana
76 C3 Afghanistan country Asia
78 B2 'Afīf Saudi Arabia
136 A2 Afton U.S.A.
80 B2 Afyon Turkey
115 C3 Agadez Niger
114 B1 Agadir Morocco
77 D2 Agadyr' Kazakh.
113 I7 Agalega Islands Mauritius
Agana Guam see Hagåtña
106 B1 A Gándara de Altea Spain
74 B2 Agar India
119 D2 Āgaro Eth.
75 D2 Agartala India
81 C2 Ağdam Azer.
105 C3 Agde France
Agedabia Libya see Ajdābiyā
104 C3 Agen France
122 A2 Aggeneys S. Africa
111 C3 Agia Varvara Greece
111 B3 Agios Dimitrios Greece
111 C3 Agios Efstratios i. Greece
111 C3 Agios Kirykos Greece
111 C3 Agios Nikolaos Greece
78 A3 Agirwat Hills Sudan
123 C2 Agisanang S. Africa
110 B1 Agnita Romania
74 B2 Agra India
81 C2 Ağrı Turkey
Ağrı Dağı mt. Turkey see Ararat, Mount
108 B3 Agrigento Italy
111 B3 Agrinio Greece
109 B2 Agropoli Italy
87 E3 Agryz Rus. Fed.
144 B2 Agua Brava, Laguna lag. Mex.
154 B2 Água Clara Brazil
145 C3 Aguada Mex.
146 B4 Aguadulce Panama
144 B2 Aguanaval r. Mex.
144 B1 Agua Prieta Mex.
144 B2 Aguascalientes Mex.
155 D1 Águas Formosas Brazil
154 C2 Agudos Brazil
106 B1 Águeda Port.
114 C3 Aguelhok Mali
106 C1 Aguilar de Campóo Spain
107 C2 Águilas Spain
144 B3 Aguililla Mex.
122 B3 Agulhas, Cape S. Africa
158 F7 Agulhas Basin Southern Ocean
155 D2 Agulhas Negras mt. Brazil
158 F7 Agulhas Plateau Southern Ocean
158 F7 Agulhas Ridge S. Atlantic Ocean
111 C2 Ağva Turkey
81 C2 Ahar Iran
100 C1 Ahaus Ger.
81 C2 Ahlat Turkey
100 C2 Ahlen Ger.
74 B2 Ahmadabad India
74 B3 Ahmadnagar India
74 B2 Ahmadpur East Pak.
74 B1 Ahmadpur Sial Pak.
117 C4 Ahmar Eth.
Ahmedabad India see Ahmadabad
Ahmednagar India see Ahmadnagar
144 B2 Ahome Mex.
81 D3 Ahram Iran
101 E1 Ahrensburg Ger.
104 C2 Ahun France
93 F4 Åhus Sweden
81 C2 Ahvāz Iran
Ahvenanmaa is Fin. see Åland Islands
122 A2 Ai-Ais Namibia
80 B2 Aigialousa Cyprus
111 B3 Aigio Greece
Aihui China see Heihe
Aijal India see Aizawl
141 D2 Aiken U.S.A.
97 B1 Ailt an Chorráin Ireland
155 D1 Aimorés Brazil
155 D1 Aimorés, Serra dos hills Brazil
105 D2 Ain r. France
107 E2 Aïn Azel Alg.
115 C1 Aïn Beïda Alg.
114 B2 'Aïn Ben Tili Maur.
107 D2 Aïn Defla Alg.
114 B1 Aïn Sefra Alg.
136 D2 Ainsworth U.S.A.
Aintab Turkey see Gaziantep
107 D2 Aïn Taya Alg.
107 D2 Aïn Tédélès Alg.
107 C2 Aïn Temouchent Alg.
115 C3 Aïr, Massif de l' mts Niger
60 A1 Airbangis Indon.
128 C2 Airdrie Can.
96 C3 Airdrie U.K.
104 B3 Aire-sur-l'Adour France
101 E3 Aisch r. Ger.
128 A1 Aishihik Lake Can.
100 A3 Aisne r. France
59 D3 Aitape P.N.G.
137 E1 Aitkin U.S.A.
110 B1 Aiud Romania
105 D3 Aix-en-Provence France
Aix-la-Chapelle Ger. see Aachen
105 D2 Aix-les-Bains France
75 D2 Aizawl India
88 C2 Aizkraukle Latvia
88 B2 Aizpute Latvia
67 C3 Aizu-Wakamatsu Japan
105 D3 Ajaccio France
Ajayameru India see Ajmer
115 E1 Ajdābiyā Libya
79 C2 'Ajman U.A.E.
74 B2 Ajmer India
Ajmer-Merwara India see Ajmer
142 A2 Ajo U.S.A.
119 D2 Āk'ak'ī Beseka Eth.
Akamagaseki Japan see Shimonoseki
54 B2 Akaroa N.Z.
87 E3 Akbulak Rus. Fed.
80 B2 Akçakale Turkey
114 A3 Akchâr reg. Maur.
111 C3 Akdağ mt. Turkey
80 B2 Akdağmadeni Turkey
88 A2 Åkersberga Sweden
118 C2 Aketi Dem. Rep. Congo
81 C1 Akhalk'alak'i Georgia
81 C1 Akhalts'ikhe Georgia
79 C2 Akhḑar, Jabal mts Oman
111 C3 Akhisar Turkey
87 D4 Akhtubinsk Rus. Fed.
118 B3 Akiéni Gabon
130 B2 Akimiski Island Can.
66 D3 Akita Japan
114 A3 Akjoujt Maur.
Akkerman Ukr. see Bilhorod-Dnistrovs'kyy
77 D1 Akkol' Kazakh.
Ak-Mechet Kazakh. see Kyzylorda
88 B2 Akmenrags pt Latvia
Akmola Kazakh. see Astana
Akmolinsk Kazakh. see Astana
67 B4 Akō Japan
117 B4 Akobo Sudan
74 B2 Akola India
118 B2 Akonolinga Cameroon
78 A3 Akordat Eritrea
131 D1 Akpatok Island Can.
77 D2 Akqi China
92 □A3 Akranes Iceland
136 C2 Akron CO U.S.A.
138 C2 Akron OH U.S.A.
75 B1 Aksai Chin terr. Asia
80 B2 Aksaray Turkey
86 F2 Aksarka Rus. Fed.
76 B1 Aksay Kazakh.
91 D2 Aksay Rus. Fed.
80 B2 Akşehir Turkey
76 C2 Akshiganak Kazakh.
77 E2 Aksu China
116 B3 Āksum Eth.
76 B2 Aktau Kazakh.
76 B1 Aktobe Kazakh.
77 D2 Aktogay Kazakh.
88 C3 Aktsyabrski Belarus
Aktyubinsk Kazakh. see Aktobe
67 B4 Akune Japan
115 C4 Akure Nigeria
92 □B2 Akureyri Iceland
Akyab Myanmar see Sittwe
111 D2 Akyazı Turkey
77 C2 Akzhaykyn, Ozero salt l. Kazakh.
140 C2 Alabama r. U.S.A.
140 C2 Alabama state U.S.A.
140 C2 Alabaster U.S.A.
111 C3 Alaçatı Turkey
145 D2 Alacrán, Arrecife rf Mex.
81 C1 Alagir Rus. Fed.
151 F4 Alagoinhas Brazil
107 C1 Alagón Spain
78 B2 Al Aḩmadī Kuwait
77 E2 Alakol', Ozero salt l. Kazakh.
92 J2 Alakurtti Rus. Fed.
78 B3 Al 'Alayyah Saudi Arabia
81 C2 Al 'Amādīyah Iraq
81 C2 Al 'Amārah Iraq
80 A2 Al 'Āmirīyah Egypt
143 C3 Alamítos, Sierra de los mt. Mex.
135 C3 Alamo U.S.A.
142 B2 Alamogordo U.S.A.
144 A2 Alamos Mex.
144 B2 Alamos Mex.
144 B2 Alamos r. Mex.
136 B3 Alamosa U.S.A.
Åland is Fin. see Åland Islands
93 G3 Åland Islands is Fin.
80 B2 Alanya Turkey
73 B4 Alappuzha India
80 B3 Al 'Aqabah Jordan
78 B3 Al 'Aqīq Saudi Arabia
107 C2 Alarcón, Embalse de resr Spain
80 B2 Al 'Arīsh Egypt
78 B2 Al Arţāwīyah Saudi Arabia
61 C2 Alas Indon.
111 C3 Alaşehir Turkey
128 A2 Alaska state U.S.A.
124 D4 Alaska, Gulf of U.S.A.
126 B3 Alaska Peninsula U.S.A.
126 C2 Alaska Range mts U.S.A.
81 C2 Ālāt Azer.
87 D3 Alatyr' Rus. Fed.
150 B3 Alausí Ecuador
93 H3 Alavus Fin.
52 B2 Alawoona Austr.
79 C2 Al 'Ayn U.A.E.
108 A2 Alba Italy
107 C2 Albacete Spain
78 A2 Al Badā'i' Saudi Arabia
78 B2 Al Badī' Saudi Arabia
110 B1 Alba Iulia Romania
109 C2 Albania country Europe
50 A3 Albany Austr.
130 B2 Albany r. Can.
141 D2 Albany GA U.S.A.
139 E2 Albany NY U.S.A.
134 B2 Albany OR U.S.A.
115 E1 Al Bardī Libya
Al Başrah Iraq see Basra
51 D1 Albatross Bay Austr.
116 A2 Al Bawītī Egypt
115 E1 Al Bayḑā' Libya
78 B3 Al Bayḑā' Yemen
141 D1 Albemarle U.S.A.
141 E1 Albemarle Sound sea chan. U.S.A.
108 A2 Albenga Italy
51 C2 Alberga watercourse Austr.
119 D2 Albert, Lake Dem. Rep. Congo/Uganda
128 C2 Alberta prov. Can.
100 B2 Albert Kanaal canal Belgium
137 E2 Albert Lea U.S.A.
117 B4 Albert Nile r. Sudan/Uganda
123 C2 Alberton S. Africa

Albertville Dem. Rep. Congo *see* **Kalemie**
105 D2 **Albertville** France
104 C3 **Albi** France
151 D2 **Albina** Suriname
78 A2 **Al Bi'r** Saudi Arabia
78 B3 **Al Birk** Saudi Arabia
78 B2 **Al Biyāḍh** *reg.* Saudi Arabia
106 C2 **Alborán, Isla de** *i.* Spain
106 C2 **Alborán Sea** Europe
Alborz, Reshteh-ye *mts* Iran *see* **Elburz Mountains**
107 C2 **Albox** Spain
106 B2 **Albufeira** Port.
142 B1 **Albuquerque** U.S.A.
79 C2 **Al Buraymī** Oman
53 C3 **Albury** Austr.
106 B2 **Alcácer do Sal** Port.
106 C1 **Alcalá de Henares** Spain
106 C2 **Alcalá la Real** Spain
108 B3 **Alcamo** Italy
107 C1 **Alcañiz** Spain
106 B2 **Alcántara** Spain
107 C2 **Alcantarilla** Spain
106 C2 **Alcaraz** Spain
106 C2 **Alcaraz, Sierra de** *mts* Spain
106 C2 **Alcaudete** Spain
106 C2 **Alcázar de San Juan** Spain
Alcazarquivir Morocco *see* **Ksar el Kebir**
91 D2 **Alchevs'k** Ukr.
155 E1 **Alcobaça** Brazil
107 C2 **Alcoy-Alcoi** Spain
107 D2 **Alcúdia** Spain
113 H6 **Aldabra Islands** Seychelles
142 B3 **Aldama** Mex.
145 C2 **Aldama** Mex.
83 J3 **Aldan** Rus. Fed.
83 J2 **Aldan** *r.* Rus. Fed.
99 D3 **Aldeburgh** U.K.
95 C4 **Alderney** *i.* Channel Is
99 C4 **Aldershot** U.K.
114 A3 **Aleg** Maur.
155 D2 **Alegre** Brazil
152 C2 **Alegrete** Brazil
89 D1 **Alekhovshchina** Rus. Fed.
89 E2 **Aleksandrov** Rus. Fed.
Aleksandrovsk Ukr. *see* **Zaporizhzhya**
83 K3 **Aleksandrovsk-Sakhalinskiy** Rus. Fed.
82 E1 **Aleksandry, Zemlya** *i.* Rus. Fed.
Alekseyevka Kazakh. *see* **Akkol'**
91 D1 **Alekseyevka** Rus. Fed.
91 D1 **Alekseyevka** Rus. Fed.
89 E3 **Aleksin** Rus. Fed.
109 D2 **Aleksinac** Serbia
118 B3 **Alèmbé** Gabon
155 D2 **Além Paraíba** Brazil
93 F3 **Ålen** Norway
104 C2 **Alençon** France
80 B2 **Aleppo** Syria
150 B4 **Alerta** Peru
128 B2 **Alert Bay** Can.
105 C3 **Alès** France
110 B1 **Aleşd** Romania
Aleshki Ukr. *see* **Tsyurupyns'k**
108 A2 **Alessandria** Italy
Alessio Albania *see* **Lezhë**
93 E3 **Ålesund** Norway
156 D2 **Aleutian Basin** Bering Sea
124 A4 **Aleutian Islands** U.S.A.
83 L3 **Alevina, Mys** *c.* Rus. Fed.
128 A2 **Alexander Archipelago** *is* U.S.A.
122 A2 **Alexander Bay** S. Africa
140 C2 **Alexander City** U.S.A.
55 A2 **Alexander Island** Antarctica
53 C3 **Alexandra** Austr.
54 A3 **Alexandra** N.Z.
153 E5 **Alexandra, Cape** S. Georgia
Alexandra Land *i.* Rus. Fed. *see* **Aleksandry, Zemlya**
111 B2 **Alexandreia** Greece
116 A1 **Alexandria** Egypt
110 C2 **Alexandria** Romania
123 C3 **Alexandria** S. Africa
96 B3 **Alexandria** U.K.
140 B2 **Alexandria** *LA* U.S.A.
137 D1 **Alexandria** *MN* U.S.A.
139 D3 **Alexandria** *VA* U.S.A.
52 A3 **Alexandrina, Lake** Austr.
111 C2 **Alexandroupoli** Greece
131 E2 **Alexis** *r.* Can.
128 B2 **Alexis Creek** Can.
77 E1 **Aleysk** Rus. Fed.
107 C1 **Alfaro** Spain
81 C3 **Al Fāw** Iraq
80 B3 **Al Fayyūm** Egypt
101 D2 **Alfeld (Leine)** Ger.
155 C2 **Alfenas** Brazil
96 C2 **Alford** U.K.
Al Fujayrah U.A.E. *see* **Fujairah**
Al Furāt *r.* Iraq/Syria *see* **Euphrates**
93 E4 **Ålgård** Norway
106 B2 **Algarve** *reg.* Port.
106 B2 **Algeciras** Spain
107 C2 **Algemesí** Spain
78 A3 **Algena** Eritrea
Alger Alg. *see* **Algiers**
114 C2 **Algeria** *country* Africa
79 C3 **Al Ghayḍah** Yemen
108 A2 **Alghero** Italy
116 B2 **Al Ghurdaqah** Egypt
79 B2 **Al Ghwaybiyah** Saudi Arabia
115 C1 **Algiers** Alg.
123 C3 **Algoa Bay** S. Africa
137 E2 **Algona** U.S.A.
106 C1 **Algorta** Spain
Algueirao Moz. *see* **Hacufera**
81 C2 **Al Ḥadīthah** Iraq
79 C2 **Al Ḥajar al Gharbī** *mts* Oman
107 C2 **Alhama de Murcia** Spain
80 A2 **Al Ḥammām** Egypt
78 B2 **Al Ḥanākīyah** Saudi Arabia
81 C2 **Al Ḥasakah** Syria
78 B2 **Al Ḥawīyah** Saudi Arabia
81 C2 **Al Ḥayy** Iraq
78 B3 **Al Ḥazm al Jawf** Yemen
79 C3 **Al Ḥibāk** *des.* Saudi Arabia
Al Ḥillah Iraq *see* **Hillah**
78 B2 **Al Ḥillah** Saudi Arabia
79 B2 **Al Ḥinnāh** Saudi Arabia
Al Ḥudaydah Yemen *see* **Hodeidah**
79 B2 **Al Hufūf** Saudi Arabia
115 D2 **Al Ḥulayq al Kabīr** *hills* Libya
79 C2 **'Alīābād** Iran
111 C3 **Aliağa** Turkey
111 B2 **Aliakmonas** *r.* Greece
81 C2 **Äli Bayramlı** Azer.
107 C2 **Alicante** Spain
143 D3 **Alice** U.S.A.
109 C3 **Alice, Punta** *pt* Italy
51 C2 **Alice Springs** Austr.
77 D3 **Alichur** Tajik.
74 B2 **Aligarh** India
81 C2 **Alīgūdarz** Iran
69 E1 **Alihe** China
118 B3 **Alima** *r.* Congo
118 C2 **Alindao** C.A.R.
111 C3 **Aliova** *r.* Turkey
74 B2 **Alirajpur** India
117 C3 **Ali Sabieh** Djibouti
78 A1 **Al 'Īsāwīyah** Saudi Arabia
Al Iskandarīyah Egypt *see* **Alexandria**
116 B1 **Al Ismā'īlīyah** Egypt
123 C3 **Aliwal North** S. Africa
115 E2 **Al Jaghbūb** Libya
78 B2 **Al Jahrah** Kuwait
79 C2 **Al Jamalīyah** Qatar
115 E2 **Al Jawf** Libya
115 D1 **Al Jawsh** Libya
106 B2 **Aljezur** Port.
Al Jīzah Egypt *see* **Giza**
79 B2 **Al Jubayl** Saudi Arabia
78 B2 **Al Jubaylah** Saudi Arabia
115 D2 **Al Jufrah** Libya
78 B2 **Al Junaynah** Saudi Arabia
106 B2 **Aljustrel** Port.
78 B2 **Al Kahfah** Saudi Arabia
79 C2 **Al Kāmil** Oman
80 B2 **Al Karak** Jordan
81 C2 **Al Kāẓimīyah** Iraq
79 C2 **Al Khābūrah** Oman
78 B2 **Al Khamāsīn** Saudi Arabia
116 B2 **Al Khārijah** Egypt
79 C2 **Al Khaṣab** Oman
78 B3 **Al Khawkhah** Yemen
79 C2 **Al Khawr** Qatar
115 D1 **Al Khums** Libya
79 B2 **Al Khunn** Saudi Arabia
79 C2 **Al Kidan** *well* Saudi Arabia
79 C2 **Al Kir'ānah** Qatar
100 B1 **Alkmaar** Neth.
115 E2 **Al Kufrah** Libya
81 C2 **Al Kūt** Iraq
Al Kuwayt Kuwait *see* **Kuwait**
Al Lādhiqīyah Syria *see* **Latakia**
75 C2 **Allahabad** India
83 K2 **Allakh-Yun'** Rus. Fed.
78 A2 **'Allāqī, Wādī al** *watercourse* Egypt
139 D2 **Allegheny** *r.* U.S.A.
139 C3 **Allegheny Mountains** U.S.A.
97 B1 **Allen, Lough** *l.* Ireland
145 B2 **Allende** Mex.
145 B2 **Allende** Mex.
139 D2 **Allentown** U.S.A.
Alleppey India *see* **Alappuzha**
101 D1 **Aller** *r.* Ger.
136 C2 **Alliance** *NE* U.S.A.
138 C2 **Alliance** *OH* U.S.A.
78 B2 **Al Līth** Saudi Arabia
96 C2 **Alloa** U.K.
131 C3 **Alma** Can.
Alma-Ata Kazakh. *see* **Almaty**
106 B2 **Almada** Port.
106 C2 **Almadén** Spain
Al Madīnah Saudi Arabia *see* **Medina**
80 B2 **Al Mafraq** Jordan
114 B2 **Al Mahbas** Western Sahara
78 B3 **Al Maḥwīt** Yemen
78 B2 **Al Majma'ah** Saudi Arabia
116 B2 **Al Maks al Baḥrī** Egypt
Al Manāmah Bahrain *see* **Manama**
135 B2 **Almanor, Lake** U.S.A.
107 C2 **Almansa** Spain
80 B2 **Al Manṣūrah** Egypt
79 C2 **Al Mariyyah** U.A.E.
115 E1 **Al Marj** Libya
77 D2 **Almaty** Kazakh.
Al Mawṣil Iraq *see* **Mosul**
81 C2 **Al Mayādīn** Syria
106 C1 **Almazán** Spain
151 D3 **Almeirim** Brazil
100 C1 **Almelo** Neth.
155 D1 **Almenara** Brazil
106 B1 **Almendra, Embalse de** *resr* Spain
106 B2 **Almendralejo** Spain
106 C2 **Almería** Spain
106 C2 **Almería, Golfo de** *b.* Spain
87 E3 **Al'met'yevsk** Rus. Fed.
78 B2 **Al Mindak** Saudi Arabia
116 B2 **Al Minyā** Egypt
79 B2 **Al Mish'āb** Saudi Arabia
106 B2 **Almodôvar** Port.
106 B2 **Almonte** Spain
75 B2 **Almora** India
78 B2 **Al Mubarrez** Saudi Arabia
79 C2 **Al Muḍaibī** Oman
80 B3 **Al Mudawwarah** Jordan
Al Mukallā Yemen *see* **Mukalla**
Al Mukhā Yemen *see* **Mocha**
106 C2 **Almuñécar** Spain
81 C2 **Al Muqdādīyah** Iraq
78 A2 **Al Musayjīd** Saudi Arabia
78 A2 **Al Muwayliḥ** Saudi Arabia
111 B3 **Almyros** Greece
96 B2 **Alness** U.K.
98 C2 **Alnwick** U.K.
62 A1 **Along** India
111 B3 **Alonnisos** *i.* Greece
59 C3 **Alor** *i.* Indon.
59 C3 **Alor, Kepulauan** *is* Indon.
Alor Setar Malaysia *see* **Alor Star**
60 B1 **Alor Star** Malaysia
Alost Belgium *see* **Aalst**
59 E3 **Alotau** P.N.G.
86 C2 **Alozero** Rus. Fed.
138 C1 **Alpena** U.S.A.
160 Q1 **Alpha Ridge** Arctic Ocean
100 B1 **Alphen aan den Rijn** Neth.
142 B2 **Alpine** *AZ* U.S.A.
143 C2 **Alpine** *TX* U.S.A.
84 E4 **Alps** *mts* Europe
79 B3 **Al Qa'āmīyāt** *reg.* Saudi Arabia
115 D1 **Al Qaddaḥīyah** Libya
Al Qāhirah Egypt *see* **Cairo**
78 B2 **Al Qā'īyah** Saudi Arabia
81 C2 **Al Qāmishlī** Syria
80 B2 **Al Qaryatayn** Syria
79 B2 **Al Qaṣab** Saudi Arabia
116 A2 **Al Qaṣr** Egypt
79 B3 **Al Qaṭn** Yemen
115 D2 **Al Qaṭrūn** Libya
106 B2 **Alqueva, Barragem de** *resr* Port.
80 B2 **Al Quṭayfah** Syria
78 B3 **Al Qunfidhah** Saudi Arabia
116 B2 **Al Quṣayr** Egypt
78 B2 **Al Quwārah** Saudi Arabia
78 B2 **Al Quwayīyah** Saudi Arabia
101 D2 **Alsfeld** Ger.
98 B2 **Alston** U.K.
92 H2 **Alta** Norway
92 H2 **Altaelva** *r.* Norway
68 B1 **Altai Mountains** Asia
141 D2 **Altamaha** *r.* U.S.A.
151 D3 **Altamira** Brazil
109 C2 **Altamura** Italy
144 A1 **Altar, Desierto de** *des.* Mex.
77 F2 **Altay** China
68 C1 **Altay** Mongolia
105 D2 **Altdorf** Switz.
107 C2 **Altea** Spain
92 H1 **Alteidet** Norway
101 F2 **Altenburg** Ger.
100 C2 **Altenkirchen (Westerwald)** Ger.
101 F1 **Altentreptow** Ger.
111 C3 **Altınoluk** Turkey
111 D3 **Altıntaş** Turkey
152 B1 **Altiplano** *plain* Bol.
96 B1 **Altnaharra** U.K.
154 B1 **Alto Araguaia** Brazil
107 C1 **Alto del Moncayo** *mt.* Spain
154 B1 **Alto Garças** Brazil
121 C2 **Alto Ligonha** Moz.
121 C2 **Alto Molócuè** Moz.
99 C4 **Alton** U.K.
137 E3 **Alton** U.S.A.
129 E3 **Altona** Can.
139 D2 **Altoona** U.S.A.
154 B1 **Alto Sucuriú** Brazil
154 B1 **Alto Taquarí** Brazil
102 C2 **Altötting** Ger.
68 C2 **Altun Shan** *mt.* China
68 B2 **Altun Shan** *mts* China
134 B2 **Alturas** U.S.A.
143 D2 **Altus** U.S.A.
88 C2 **Alūksne** Latvia
78 A2 **Al 'Ulā** Saudi Arabia
115 D1 **Al 'Uqaylah** Libya
Al Uqṣur Egypt *see* **Luxor**
91 C3 **Alushta** Ukr.
115 E2 **Al 'Uwaynāt** Libya
143 D1 **Alva** U.S.A.
145 C3 **Alvarado** Mex.
93 F3 **Älvdalen** Sweden
93 F3 **Älvdalen** *val.* Sweden
92 H2 **Älvsbyn** Sweden
78 A2 **Al Wajh** Saudi Arabia
79 C2 **Al Wakrah** Qatar
74 B2 **Alwar** India
81 C2 **Al Widyān** *plat.* Iraq/Saudi Arabia
Alxa Youqi China *see* **Ehen Hudag**
Alxa Zuoqi China *see* **Bayan Hot**
51 C1 **Alyangula** Austr.
88 B3 **Alytus** Lith.
136 C1 **Alzada** U.S.A.
101 D3 **Alzey** Ger.
50 C2 **Amadeus, Lake** *imp. l.* Austr.
127 H2 **Amadjuak Lake** Can.
106 B2 **Amadora** Port.
78 B2 **Amā'ir** Saudi Arabia
67 B4 **Amakusa-Shimo-shima** *i.* Japan
93 F4 **Åmål** Sweden
111 B3 **Amaliada** Greece
59 D3 **Amamapare** Indon.
154 A2 **Amambaí** Brazil
154 B2 **Amambaí** *r.* Brazil
154 A2 **Amambaí, Serra de** *hills* Brazil/Para.
69 E3 **Amami-Ō-shima** *i.* Japan
69 E3 **Amami-shotō** *is* Japan
77 C1 **Amangel'dy** Kazakh.
109 C3 **Amantea** Italy
123 D3 **Amanzimtoti** S. Africa
151 D2 **Amapá** Brazil
106 B2 **Amareleja** Port.
88 B2 **Āmari** Estonia
143 C1 **Amarillo** U.S.A.
108 B2 **Amaro, Monte** *mt.* Italy
80 B1 **Amasya** Turkey
150 D2 **Amazon** *r.* S. America
151 E2 **Amazon, Mouths of the** Brazil
Amazonas *r.* S. America *see* **Amazon**
157 I5 **Amazon Cone** S. Atlantic Ocean
74 B1 **Ambala** India
121 □D3 **Ambalavao** Madag.
121 □D2 **Ambanja** Madag.
104 B3 **Ambarès-et-Lagrave** France
150 B3 **Ambato** Ecuador
121 □D2 **Ambato Boeny** Madag.
121 □D3 **Ambato Finandrahana** Madag.
121 □D2 **Ambatolampy** Madag.
121 □D2 **Ambatondrazaka** Madag.
101 E3 **Amberg** Ger.
146 B3 **Ambergris Cay** *i.* Belize
75 C2 **Ambikapur** India
121 □D2 **Ambilobe** Madag.
98 C2 **Amble** U.K.
98 B2 **Ambleside** U.K.
121 □D3 **Amboasary** Madag.
121 □D2 **Ambodifotatra** Madag.
121 □D2 **Ambohidratrimo** Madag.
121 □D3 **Ambohimahasoa** Madag.
Amboina Indon. *see* **Ambon**
59 C3 **Ambon** Indon.
59 C3 **Ambon** *i.* Indon.
121 □D3 **Ambositra** Madag.
121 □D3 **Ambovombe** Madag.
135 C4 **Amboy** U.S.A.
Ambre, Cap d' *c.* Madag. *see* **Bobaomby, Tanjona**
120 A1 **Ambriz** Angola
Ambrizete Angola *see* **N'zeto**
86 F2 **Amderma** Rus. Fed.
Amdo China *see* **Lharigarbo**
145 B2 **Amealco** Mex.
144 B2 **Ameca** Mex.
100 B1 **Ameland** *i.* Neth.
154 C2 **Americana** Brazil
55 D4 **American-Antarctic Ridge** S. Atlantic Ocean
134 D2 **American Falls** U.S.A.
134 D2 **American Falls Reservoir** U.S.A.
135 D2 **American Fork** U.S.A.
49 J5 **American Samoa** *terr.* S. Pacific Ocean
141 D2 **Americus** U.S.A.
100 B1 **Amersfoort** Neth.
55 H2 **Amery Ice Shelf** Antarctica
137 E2 **Ames** U.S.A.
111 B3 **Amfissa** Greece
83 J2 **Amga** Rus. Fed.
66 C1 **Amgu** Rus. Fed.
115 C2 **Amguid** Alg.
83 K3 **Amgun'** *r.* Rus. Fed.
131 D3 **Amherst** Can.
104 C2 **Amiens** France
79 C3 **Amilḥayt, Wādī al** *r.* Oman
73 B3 **Amindivi Islands** India
122 A1 **Aminuis** Namibia
74 A2 **Amir Chah** Pak.
129 D2 **Amisk Lake** Can.
143 C3 **Amistad Reservoir** Mex./U.S.A.
98 A3 **Amlwch** U.K.
80 B2 **'Ammān** Jordan
127 J2 **Ammassalik** Greenland
78 B3 **Am Nābiyah** Yemen
81 D2 **Amol** Iran
111 C3 **Amorgos** *i.* Greece
140 C2 **Amory** U.S.A.
130 C3 **Amos** Can.
Amoy China *see* **Xiamen**
121 □D3 **Ampanihy** Madag.
155 C2 **Amparo** Brazil
121 □D2 **Ampasimanolotra** Madag.
107 D1 **Amposta** Spain
78 B3 **'Amrān** Yemen
Amraoti India *see* **Amravati**
74 B2 **Amravati** India
74 B2 **Amreli** India
74 B1 **Amritsar** India
100 B1 **Amstelveen** Neth.
100 B1 **Amsterdam** Neth.
123 D2 **Amsterdam** S. Africa
156 A8 **Amsterdam, Île** *i.* Indian Ocean
103 C2 **Amstetten** Austria
115 E3 **Am Timan** Chad
76 B2 **Amudar'ya** *r.* Asia
126 F1 **Amund Ringnes Island** Can.
55 J3 **Amundsen, Mount** Antarctica
160 H1 **Amundsen Basin** Arctic Ocean
126 D2 **Amundsen Gulf** Can.
55 P2 **Amundsen Ridges** Southern Ocean
55 P2 **Amundsen Sea** Antarctica
61 C2 **Amuntai** Indon.
Amur *r.* China *see* **Heilong Jiang**
78 A3 **'Amur, Wadi** *watercourse* Sudan

61 D2 **Anabanua** Indon.
83 I2 **Anabar** *r.* Rus. Fed.
83 I2 **Anabarskiy Zaliv** *b.* Rus. Fed.
150 C2 **Anaco** Venez.
134 D1 **Anaconda** U.S.A.
134 B1 **Anacortes** U.S.A.
143 D1 **Anadarko** U.S.A.
80 B1 **Anadolu Dağları** *mts* Turkey
83 M2 **Anadyr'** Rus. Fed.
83 M2 **Anadyr'** *r.* Rus. Fed.
81 C2 **'Ānah** Iraq
145 B2 **Anáhuac** Mex.
73 B3 **Anai Mudi** India
121 □D2 **Analalava** Madag.
121 □D3 **Analavelona** *mts* Madag.
60 B1 **Anambas, Kepulauan** *is* Indon.
137 E2 **Anamosa** U.S.A.
80 B2 **Anamur** Turkey
67 B4 **Anan** Japan
73 B3 **Anantapur** India
74 B1 **Anantnag** India
90 B2 **Anan'yiv** Ukr.
91 D3 **Anapa** Rus. Fed.
154 C1 **Anápolis** Brazil
81 D2 **Anār** Iran
152 B2 **Añatuya** Arg.
97 B1 **An Baile Thiar** Ireland
97 B1 **An Bun Beag** Ireland
65 B2 **Anbyon** N. Korea
104 B2 **Ancenis** France
126 C2 **Anchorage** U.S.A.
108 B2 **Ancona** Italy
153 A4 **Ancud** Chile
Anda China *see* **Daqing**
97 A2 **An Daingean** Ireland
93 E3 **Åndalsnes** Norway
106 C2 **Andalucía** *aut. comm.* Spain
Andalusia *aut. comm.* Spain *see* **Andalucía**
140 C2 **Andalusia** U.S.A.
159 F3 **Andaman Basin** Indian Ocean
73 D3 **Andaman Islands** India
63 A2 **Andaman Sea** Indian Ocean
121 □D2 **Andapa** Madag.
100 B2 **Andelst** Neth.
92 G2 **Andenes** Norway
100 B2 **Andenne** Belgium
100 B2 **Anderlecht** Belgium
105 D2 **Andermatt** Switz.
126 D2 **Anderson** *r.* Can.
126 C2 **Anderson** *AK* U.S.A.
138 B2 **Anderson** *IN* U.S.A.
141 D2 **Anderson** *SC* U.S.A.
148 C3 **Andes** *mts* S. America
77 D2 **Andijon** Uzbek.
121 □D2 **Andilamena** Madag.
121 □D2 **Andilanatoby** Madag.
Andizhan Uzbek. *see* **Andijon**
74 A1 **Andkhvoy** Afgh.
121 □D2 **Andoany** Madag.
Andong China *see* **Dandong**
65 B2 **Andong** S. Korea
104 C3 **Andorra** *country* Europe
104 C3 **Andorra la Vella** Andorra
99 C4 **Andover** U.K.
154 B2 **Andradina** Brazil
89 D2 **Andreapol'** Rus. Fed.
155 D2 **Andrelândia** Brazil
143 C2 **Andrews** U.S.A.
109 C2 **Andria** Italy
121 □D3 **Androka** Madag.
Andropov Rus. Fed. *see* **Rybinsk**
146 C2 **Andros** *i.* Bahamas
111 B3 **Andros** Greece
111 B3 **Andros** *i.* Greece
141 E4 **Andros Town** Bahamas
73 B3 **Andrott** *i.* India
90 B1 **Andrushivka** Ukr.
92 G2 **Andselv** Norway
106 C2 **Andújar** Spain
120 A2 **Andulo** Angola
114 C3 **Anéfis** Mali
147 D3 **Anegada Passage** Virgin Is (U.K.)
114 C4 **Aného** Togo
107 D1 **Aneto** *mt.* Spain
115 D3 **Aney** Niger
97 B1 **An Fál Carrach** Ireland
83 H3 **Angara** *r.* Rus. Fed.
68 C1 **Angarsk** Rus. Fed.
93 G3 **Ånge** Sweden
Angel, Salto del *waterfall* Venez. *see* **Angel Falls**
144 A2 **Ángel de la Guarda, Isla** *i.* Mex.
64 B2 **Angeles** Phil.
150 C2 **Angel Falls** Venez.
93 F4 **Ängelholm** Sweden
92 G3 **Ångermanälven** *r.* Sweden
104 B2 **Angers** France
129 E1 **Angikuni Lake** Can.
52 B3 **Anglesea** Austr.
98 A3 **Anglesey** *i.* U.K.
121 C2 **Angoche** Moz.
79 C2 **Angohrān** Iran
120 A2 **Angola** *country* Africa
138 C2 **Angola** U.S.A.
158 F6 **Angola Basin** S. Atlantic Ocean
128 A2 **Angoon** U.S.A.
104 C2 **Angoulême** France
155 D2 **Angra dos Reis** Brazil
77 D2 **Angren** Uzbek.
147 D3 **Anguilla** *terr.* West Indies
75 C2 **Angul** India
93 F4 **Anholt** *i.* Denmark
71 B3 **Anhua** China
70 B2 **Anhui** *prov.* China
154 B1 **Anhumas** Brazil
Anhwei *prov.* China *see* **Anhui**
154 C1 **Anicuns** Brazil
66 D1 **Aniva, Mys** *c.* Rus. Fed.
66 D1 **Aniva, Zaliv** *b.* Rus. Fed.
88 C1 **Anjalankoski** Fin.
104 B2 **Anjou** *reg.* France
65 B2 **Anjŭ** N. Korea
70 A2 **Ankang** China
80 B2 **Ankara** Turkey
121 □D3 **Ankazoabo** Madag.
121 □D2 **Ankazobe** Madag.
137 E2 **Ankeny** U.S.A.
102 C1 **Anklam** Ger.
121 □D2 **Ankofa** *mt.* Madag.
70 B2 **Anlu** China
55 G3 **Ann, Cape** Antarctica
139 E2 **Ann, Cape** U.S.A.
89 F3 **Anna** Rus. Fed.
115 C1 **Annaba** Alg.
101 F2 **Annaberg-Buchholtz** Ger.
80 B2 **An Nabk** Syria
78 B2 **An Nafūd** *des.* Saudi Arabia
150 D2 **Annai** Guyana
81 C2 **An Najaf** Iraq
63 B2 **Annam Highlands** *mts* Laos/Vietnam
96 C3 **Annan** U.K.
139 D3 **Annapolis** U.S.A.
75 C2 **Annapurna I** *mt.* Nepal
138 C2 **Ann Arbor** U.S.A.
150 D2 **Anna Regina** Guyana
An Nás Ireland *see* **Naas**
81 C2 **An Nāṣirīyah** Iraq
115 D1 **An Nawfalīyah** Libya
105 D2 **Annecy** France
78 B3 **An Nimāş** Saudi Arabia
71 A3 **Anning** China
140 C2 **Anniston** U.S.A.
105 C2 **Annonay** France
79 B2 **An Nu'ayrīyah** Saudi Arabia
121 □D2 **Anorontany, Tanjona** *hd* Madag.
71 B3 **Anpu** China
70 B2 **Anqing** China
65 B2 **Ansan** S. Korea
101 E3 **Ansbach** Ger.
70 C1 **Anshan** China
71 A3 **Anshun** China
143 D2 **Anson** U.S.A.
114 C3 **Ansongo** Mali
96 C2 **Anstruther** U.K.
150 B4 **Antabamba** Peru
80 B2 **Antakya** Turkey
121 □E2 **Antalaha** Madag.
80 B2 **Antalya** Turkey
80 B2 **Antalya Körfezi** *g.* Turkey
121 □D2 **Antananarivo** Madag.
55 A2 **Antarctic Peninsula** Antarctica
96 B2 **An Teallach** *mt.* U.K.
106 C2 **Antequera** Spain
142 B2 **Anthony** U.S.A.
114 B2 **Anti-Atlas** *mts* Morocco
105 D3 **Antibes** France
131 D3 **Anticosti, Île d'** *i.* Can.
131 D3 **Antigonish** Can.
147 D3 **Antigua** *i.* Antigua
147 D3 **Antigua and Barbuda** *country* West Indies
145 C2 **Antiguo-Morelos** Mex.
111 B3 **Antikythira** *i.* Greece
Antioch Turkey *see* **Antakya**
49 I8 **Antipodes Islands** N.Z.
An t-Ob U.K. *see* **Leverburgh**
152 A2 **Antofagasta** Chile
154 C3 **Antonina** Brazil
António Enes Moz. *see* **Angoche**
97 C1 **Antrim** U.K.
97 C1 **Antrim Hills** U.K.
121 □D2 **Antsalova** Madag.
Antseranana Madag. *see* **Antsirañana**
121 □D2 **Antsirabe** Madag.
121 □D2 **Antsirañana** Madag.
121 □D2 **Antsohihy** Madag.
100 B2 **Antwerp** Belgium
Antwerpen Belgium *see* **Antwerp**
An Uaimh Ireland *see* **Navan**
74 B2 **Anupgarh** India
73 C4 **Anuradhapura** Sri Lanka
Anvers Belgium *see* **Antwerp**
51 C3 **Anxious Bay** Austr.
70 B2 **Anyang** China
65 B2 **Anyang** S. Korea
108 B2 **Anzio** Italy
67 C4 **Aoga-shima** *i.* Japan
66 D2 **Aomori** Japan
54 B2 **Aoraki** N.Z.
108 A1 **Aosta** Italy
114 B2 **Aoukâr** *reg.* Mali/Maur.
114 C2 **Aoulef** Alg.
115 D2 **Aozou** Chad
141 D3 **Apalachee Bay** U.S.A.
150 C3 **Apaporis** *r.* Col.
154 B2 **Aparecida do Tabuado** Brazil
64 B2 **Aparri** Phil.
86 C2 **Apatity** Rus. Fed.
144 B3 **Apatzingán** Mex.
100 B1 **Apeldoorn** Neth.
100 C1 **Apen** Ger.
108 A2 **Apennines** *mts* Italy
49 J5 **Apia** Samoa
154 C2 **Apiaí** Brazil
64 B3 **Apo, Mount** *vol.* Phil.
101 E2 **Apolda** Ger.
52 B3 **Apollo Bay** Austr.
141 D3 **Apopka** U.S.A.
141 D3 **Apopka, Lake** U.S.A.
154 B1 **Aporé** Brazil
154 B1 **Aporé** *r.* Brazil
138 A1 **Apostle Islands** U.S.A.
80 B2 **Apostolos Andreas, Cape** Cyprus
91 C2 **Apostolove** Ukr.
133 F3 **Appalachian Mountains** U.S.A.
Appennino *mts* Italy *see* **Apennines**
53 D2 **Appin** Austr.
100 C1 **Appingedam** Neth.
98 B2 **Appleby-in-Westmorland** U.K.
138 B2 **Appleton** U.S.A.
108 B2 **Aprilia** Italy
62 A1 **Aprunyi** India
91 D3 **Apsheronsk** Rus. Fed.
Apsheronskaya Rus. Fed. *see* **Apsheronsk**
154 B2 **Apucarana** Brazil
154 B2 **Apucarana, Serra da** *hills* Brazil
64 A3 **Apurahuan** Phil.
147 D4 **Apure** *r.* Venez.
78 A2 **Aqaba, Gulf of** Asia
81 D2 **'Aqdā** Iran
75 C1 **Aqqikkol Hu** *salt l.* China
154 A1 **Aquidauana** *r.* Brazil
104 B3 **Aquitaine** *reg.* France
75 C2 **Ara** India
117 A4 **Arab, Bahr el** *watercourse* Sudan
Arabian Gulf *g.* Asia *see* **The Gulf**
78 B2 **Arabian Peninsula** Asia
56 B4 **Arabian Sea** Indian Ocean
151 F4 **Aracaju** Brazil
154 A2 **Aracanguy, Montes de** *hills* Para.
151 F3 **Aracati** Brazil
154 B2 **Araçatuba** Brazil
155 D1 **Aracruz** Brazil
155 D1 **Araçuaí** Brazil
110 B1 **Arad** Romania
115 E3 **Arada** Chad
79 C2 **'Arādah** U.A.E.
156 C6 **Arafura Sea** Austr./Indon.
154 B1 **Aragarças** Brazil
107 C1 **Aragón** *aut. comm.* Spain
107 C1 **Aragón** *r.* Spain
151 E3 **Araguaia** *r.* Brazil
154 B1 **Araguaiana** Brazil
151 E3 **Araguaína** Brazil
154 C1 **Araguari** Brazil
67 C3 **Arai** Japan
115 C2 **Arak** Alg.
81 C2 **Arāk** Iran
62 A1 **Arakan Yoma** *mts* Myanmar
81 C1 **Arak's** *r.* Armenia
76 C2 **Aral Sea** *salt l.* Kazakh./Uzbek.
76 C2 **Aral'sk** Kazakh.
Aral'skoye More *salt l.* Kazakh./Uzbek. *see* **Aral Sea**
106 C1 **Aranda de Duero** Spain
109 D2 **Aranđelovac** Serbia
97 B2 **Aran Islands** Ireland
106 C1 **Aranjuez** Spain
122 A1 **Aranos** Namibia
143 D3 **Aransas Pass** U.S.A.
67 B4 **Arao** Japan
114 B3 **Araouane** Mali
151 F3 **Arapiraca** Brazil
154 B2 **Arapongas** Brazil
154 C3 **Araquari** Brazil
78 B1 **'Ar'ar** Saudi Arabia
154 C2 **Araraquara** Brazil
151 D3 **Araras** Brazil
154 C2 **Araras** Brazil
154 B1 **Araras, Serra das** *hills* Brazil
154 B3 **Araras, Serra das** *mts* Brazil
81 C2 **Ararat** Armenia
52 B3 **Ararat** Austr.
81 C2 **Ararat, Mount** Turkey
155 D2 **Araruama, Lago de** *lag.* Brazil
155 E1 **Arataca** Brazil
Aratürük China *see* **Yiwu**
150 B2 **Arauca** Col.
154 C1 **Araxá** Brazil
81 C2 **Arbīl** Iraq
129 E2 **Arborg** Can.
96 C2 **Arbroath** U.K.
74 A2 **Arbu Lut, Dasht-e** *des.* Afgh.
104 B3 **Arcachon** France
141 D3 **Arcadia** U.S.A.
134 B2 **Arcata** U.S.A.
145 B3 **Arcelia** Mex.
86 D2 **Archangel** Rus. Fed.
51 D1 **Archer** *r.* Austr.
49 M5 **Archipel des Tuamotu** *is* Fr. Polynesia
149 B6 **Archipiélago Juan Fernández** S. Pacific Ocean
134 D2 **Arco** U.S.A.
106 B2 **Arcos de la Frontera** Spain
127 G2 **Arctic Bay** Can.
Arctic Institute Islands *is* Rus. Fed. *see* **Arkticheskogo Instituta, Ostrova**
160 J1 **Arctic Mid-Ocean Ridge** Arctic Ocean
160 **Arctic Ocean**
126 D2 **Arctic Red** *r.* Can.
81 C2 **Ardabīl** Iran
81 C1 **Ardahan** Turkey
93 E3 **Årdalstangen** Norway
97 C2 **Ardee** Ireland
100 B3 **Ardennes** *plat.* Belgium
135 B3 **Arden Town** U.S.A.
81 D2 **Ardestān** Iran
97 D1 **Ardglass** U.K.
53 C2 **Ardlethan** Austr.
143 D2 **Ardmore** U.S.A.
96 A2 **Ardnamurchan, Point of** U.K.
52 A2 **Ardrossan** Austr.
96 B3 **Ardrossan** U.K.
96 B2 **Ardvasar** U.K.
135 B3 **Arena, Point** U.S.A.
93 E4 **Arendal** Norway
100 B2 **Arendonk** Belgium
101 E1 **Arendsee (Altmark)** Ger.
150 B4 **Arequipa** Peru
151 D3 **Arere** Brazil
106 C1 **Arévalo** Spain
108 B2 **Arezzo** Italy
108 B2 **Argenta** Italy
104 B2 **Argentan** France
153 C2 **Argentina** *country* S. America
158 D7 **Argentine Basin** S. Atlantic Ocean
157 I8 **Argentine Rise** S. Atlantic Ocean
153 A5 **Argentino, Lago** *l.* Arg.
104 C2 **Argenton-sur-Creuse** France
110 C2 **Argeş** *r.* Romania
74 A1 **Arghandab** *r.* Afgh.
111 B3 **Argolikos Kolpos** *b.* Greece
111 B3 **Argos** Greece
111 B3 **Argostoli** Greece
107 C1 **Arguís** Spain
69 E1 **Argun'** *r.* China/Rus. Fed.
131 D3 **Argyle** Can.
50 B1 **Argyle, Lake** Austr.
Argyrokastron Albania *see* **Gjirokastër**
Ar Horqin Qi China *see* **Tianshan**
93 F4 **Århus** Denmark
122 A2 **Ariamsvlei** Namibia
152 A1 **Arica** Chile
96 A2 **Arinagour** U.K.
155 C1 **Arinos** Brazil
150 D4 **Aripuanã** Brazil
150 C3 **Aripuanã** *r.* Brazil
150 C3 **Ariquemes** Brazil
154 B1 **Ariranhá** *r.* Brazil
96 B2 **Arisaig** U.K.
96 B2 **Arisaig, Sound of** *sea chan.* U.K.
104 B3 **Arizgoiti** Spain
142 A2 **Arizona** *state* U.S.A.
144 A1 **Arizpe** Mex.
78 B2 **'Arjah** Saudi Arabia
61 C2 **Arjasa** Indon.
92 G2 **Arjeplog** Sweden
140 B2 **Arkadelphia** U.S.A.
77 C1 **Arkalyk** Kazakh.
140 B2 **Arkansas** *r.* U.S.A.
140 B1 **Arkansas** *state* U.S.A.
137 D3 **Arkansas City** U.S.A.
Arkhangel'sk Rus. Fed. *see* **Archangel**
97 C2 **Arklow** Ireland
102 C1 **Arkona, Kap** *c.* Ger.
82 G1 **Arkticheskogo Instituta, Ostrova** *is* Rus. Fed.
105 C3 **Arles** France
143 D2 **Arlington** U.S.A.
138 B2 **Arlington Heights** U.S.A.
115 C3 **Arlit** Niger
100 B3 **Arlon** Belgium
97 C1 **Armagh** U.K.
116 B2 **Armant** Egypt
87 D4 **Armavir** Rus. Fed.
81 C1 **Armenia** *country* Asia
150 B2 **Armenia** Col.
Armenopolis Romania *see* **Gherla**
144 B3 **Armeria** Mex.
53 D2 **Armidale** Austr.
134 D1 **Armington** U.S.A.
130 B2 **Armstrong** Can.
91 C2 **Armyans'k** Ukr.
Armyanskaya S.S.R. *country* Asia *see* **Armenia**
Arnaoutis, Cape *c.* Cyprus *see* **Arnauti, Cape**
130 D2 **Arnaud** *r.* Can.
80 B2 **Arnauti, Cape** Cyprus
100 B2 **Arnhem** Neth.
51 C1 **Arnhem, Cape** Austr.
51 C1 **Arnhem Bay** Austr.
51 C1 **Arnhem Land** *reg.* Austr.
108 B2 **Arno** *r.* Italy
52 A2 **Arno Bay** Austr.
130 C3 **Arnprior** Can.
101 D2 **Arnsberg** Ger.
101 E2 **Arnstadt** Ger.
122 A2 **Aroab** Namibia
154 B2 **Aroeira** Brazil
101 D2 **Arolsen** Ger.
78 A3 **Aroma** Sudan
108 A1 **Arona** Italy
144 B2 **Aros** *r.* Mex.
Arquipélago dos Açores *aut. reg.* Port. *see* **Azores**
Arrah India *see* **Ara**
81 C2 **Ar Ramādī** Iraq
96 B3 **Arran** *i.* U.K.
97 B1 **Arranmore Island** Ireland
80 B2 **Ar Raqqah** Syria
105 C1 **Arras** France
106 C1 **Arrasate** Spain
78 B2 **Ar Rass** Saudi Arabia
79 C2 **Ar Rayyān** Qatar
150 C2 **Arrecifal** Col.
145 C3 **Arriagá** Mex.
79 C2 **Ar Rimāl** *reg.* Saudi Arabia
Ar Riyāḍ Saudi Arabia *see* **Riyadh**
54 A2 **Arrowtown** N.Z.

135 B3 **Arroyo Grande** U.S.A.
145 C2 **Arroyo Seco** Mex.
79 C2 **Ar Rustāq** Oman
81 C2 **Ar Ruţbah** Iraq
78 B2 **Ar Ruwayḑah** Saudi Arabia
81 D3 **Arsenajān** Iran
66 B2 **Arsen'yev** Rus. Fed.
117 C3 **Arta** Djibouti
111 B3 **Arta** Greece
144 B3 **Arteaga** Mex.
66 B2 **Artem** Rus. Fed.
91 D2 **Artemivs'k** Ukr.
104 C2 **Artenay** France
142 C2 **Artesia** U.S.A.
51 E2 **Arthur Point** Austr.
54 B2 **Arthur's Pass** N.Z.
152 C3 **Artigas** Uru.
129 D1 **Artillery Lake** Can.
123 C1 **Artisia** Botswana
104 C1 **Artois** *reg.* France
90 B2 **Artsyz** Ukr.
Artur de Paiva Angola *see* **Kuvango**
77 D3 **Artux** China
81 C1 **Artvin** Turkey
59 C3 **Aru, Kepulauan** *is* Indon.
119 D2 **Arua** Uganda
147 D3 **Aruba** *terr.* West Indies
75 C2 **Arun** *r.* Nepal
119 D3 **Arusha** Tanz.
136 B3 **Arvada** U.S.A.
68 C1 **Arvayheer** Mongolia
129 E1 **Arviat** Can.
92 G2 **Arvidsjaur** Sweden
93 F4 **Arvika** Sweden
108 A2 **Arzachena** Italy
87 D3 **Arzamas** Rus. Fed.
107 C2 **Arzew** Alg.
100 C2 **Arzfeld** Ger.
Arzila Morocco *see* **Asilah**
101 F2 **Aš** Czech Rep.
115 C4 **Asaba** Nigeria
74 B1 **Asadābād** Afgh.
66 D2 **Asahi-dake** *vol.* Japan
66 D2 **Asahikawa** Japan
78 B3 **Āsalē** *l.* Eth.
75 C2 **Asansol** India
117 C3 **Āsayita** Eth.
130 C3 **Asbestos** Can.
122 B2 **Asbestos Mountains** S. Africa
119 E2 **Āsbe Teferi** Eth.
109 C2 **Ascea** Italy
152 B1 **Ascensión** Bol.
113 B6 **Ascension** *i.* S. Atlantic Ocean
145 D3 **Ascensión, Bahía de la** *b.* Mex.
101 D3 **Aschaffenburg** Ger.
100 C2 **Ascheberg** Ger.
101 E2 **Aschersleben** Ger.
108 B2 **Ascoli Piceno** Italy
119 D2 **Āsela** Eth.
92 G3 **Åsele** Sweden
111 B2 **Asenovgrad** Bulg.
76 B3 **Aşgabat** Turkm.
78 B2 **Asharat** Saudi Arabia
50 A2 **Ashburton** *watercourse* Austr.
54 B2 **Ashburton** N.Z.
140 B2 **Ashdown** U.S.A.
141 D1 **Asheville** U.S.A.
53 D1 **Ashford** Austr.
97 C2 **Ashford** Ireland
99 D4 **Ashford** U.K.
66 D2 **Ashibetsu** Japan
98 C2 **Ashington** U.K.
67 B4 **Ashizuri-misaki** *pt* Japan
Ashkhabad Turkm. *see* **Aşgabat**
136 D3 **Ashland** *KS* U.S.A.
138 C3 **Ashland** *KY* U.S.A.
138 C2 **Ashland** *OH* U.S.A.
134 B2 **Ashland** *OR* U.S.A.
138 A1 **Ashland** *WI* U.S.A.
53 C1 **Ashley** Austr.
88 C3 **Ashmyany** Belarus
66 D2 **Ashoro** Japan
81 C2 **Ash Shabakah** Iraq
78 B3 **Ash Sharawrah** Saudi Arabia
Ash Shāriqah U.A.E. *see* **Sharjah**
81 C2 **Ash Sharqāţ** Iraq
81 C2 **Ash Shaţrah** Iraq
78 B3 **Ash Shaykh 'Uthman** Yemen
79 B3 **Ash Shiḩr** Yemen
79 C2 **Ash Shināş** Oman
78 B2 **Ash Shu'aybah** Saudi Arabia
78 B2 **Ash Shu'bah** Saudi Arabia
78 B2 **Ash Shubaykīyah** Saudi Arabia
78 B2 **Ash Shumlūl** Saudi Arabia
78 B3 **Ash Shuqayq** Saudi Arabia
115 D2 **Ash Shuwayrif** Libya
138 C2 **Ashtabula** U.S.A.
131 D2 **Ashuanipi Lake** Can.
75 B3 **Asifabad** India
106 B2 **Asilah** Morocco
108 A2 **Asinara, Golfo dell'** *b.* Italy
108 A2 **Asinara, Isola** *i.* Italy
82 G3 **Asino** Rus. Fed.
88 C3 **Asipovichy** Belarus
78 B2 **'Asīr** *reg.* Saudi Arabia
93 F4 **Asker** Norway
93 F4 **Askim** Norway
68 C1 **Askiz** Rus. Fed.
116 B3 **Asmara** Eritrea
93 F4 **Åsnen** *l.* Sweden
116 B2 **Asoteriba, Jebel** *mt.* Sudan
103 D2 **Aspang-Markt** Austria
136 B3 **Aspen** U.S.A.
143 C2 **Aspermont** U.S.A.
54 A2 **Aspiring, Mount** N.Z.
116 C3 **Assab** Eritrea
78 B3 **Aş Şahīf** Yemen
Aş Şaḩrā' al Gharbīyah *des.* Egypt *see* **Western Desert**
Aş Şaḩrā' ash Sharqīyah *des.* Egypt *see* **Eastern Desert**
78 B2 **As Salamiyah** Saudi Arabia
75 D2 **Assam** *state* India
81 C2 **As Samāwah** Iraq
79 C2 **Aş Şanām** *reg.* Saudi Arabia
115 E2 **As Sarīr** *reg.* Libya
108 A3 **Assemini** Italy
100 C1 **Assen** Neth.
100 B2 **Assesse** Belgium
115 D1 **As Sidrah** Libya
129 D3 **Assiniboia** Can.
128 C2 **Assiniboine, Mount** Can.
154 B2 **Assis** Brazil
78 B2 **Aş Şubayḩīyah** Kuwait
81 C2 **As Sulaymānīyah** Iraq
78 B2 **As Sulaymī** Saudi Arabia
78 B2 **As Sulayyil** Saudi Arabia
78 B2 **As Sūq** Saudi Arabia
80 B2 **As Suwaydā'** Syria
79 C2 **As Suwayq** Oman
As Suways Egypt *see* **Suez**
111 B3 **Astakos** Greece
77 D1 **Astana** Kazakh.
81 C2 **Āstārā** Iran
100 B2 **Asten** Neth.
Asterabad Iran *see* **Gorgān**
108 A2 **Asti** Italy
74 B1 **Astor** Pak.
106 B1 **Astorga** Spain
134 B1 **Astoria** U.S.A.
Astrabad Iran *see* **Gorgān**
87 D4 **Astrakhan'** Rus. Fed.
Astrakhan' Bazar Azer. *see* **Cälilabad**
88 C3 **Astravyets** Belarus
Astrida Rwanda *see* **Butare**
106 B1 **Asturias** *aut. comm.* Spain
111 C3 **Astypalaia** *i.* Greece
152 C2 **Asunción** Para.
116 B2 **Aswān** Egypt
116 B2 **Asyūţ** Egypt
Atacama, Desierto de *des.* Chile *see* **Atacama Desert**
152 B2 **Atacama, Puna de** *plat.* Arg.
152 B2 **Atacama, Salar de** *salt flat* Chile
152 B3 **Atacama Desert** *des.* Chile
114 C4 **Atakpamé** Togo
111 B3 **Atalanti** Greece
150 B4 **Atalaya** Peru
155 D1 **Ataléia** Brazil
77 C3 **Atamyrat** Turkm.
78 B3 **'Ataq** Yemen
114 A2 **Atâr** Maur.
135 B3 **Atascadero** U.S.A.
77 D2 **Atasu** Kazakh.
111 C3 **Atavyros** *mt.* Greece
116 B3 **Atbara** Sudan
116 B3 **Atbara** *r.* Sudan
77 C1 **Atbasar** Kazakh.
140 B3 **Atchafalaya Bay** U.S.A.
137 D3 **Atchison** U.S.A.
Ateransk Kazakh. *see* **Atyrau**
108 B2 **Aterno** *r.* Italy
108 B2 **Atessa** Italy
100 A2 **Ath** Belgium
128 C2 **Athabasca** Can.
129 C2 **Athabasca** *r.* Can.
129 D2 **Athabasca, Lake** Can.
97 C2 **Athboy** Ireland
97 B2 **Athenry** Ireland
111 B3 **Athens** Greece
140 C2 **Athens** *AL* U.S.A.
141 D2 **Athens** *GA* U.S.A.
138 C3 **Athens** *OH* U.S.A.
141 D1 **Athens** *TN* U.S.A.
143 D2 **Athens** *TX* U.S.A.
51 D1 **Atherton** Austr.
Athina Greece *see* **Athens**
97 C2 **Athlone** Ireland
111 B2 **Athos** *mt.* Greece
97 C2 **Athy** Ireland
115 D3 **Ati** Chad
130 A3 **Atikokan** Can.
87 D3 **Atkarsk** Rus. Fed.
141 D2 **Atlanta** U.S.A.
137 D2 **Atlantic** U.S.A.
141 D2 **Atlantic Beach** U.S.A.
139 E3 **Atlantic City** U.S.A.
55 D3 **Atlantic-Indian-Antarctic Basin** S. Atlantic Ocean
158 E8 **Atlantic-Indian Ridge** Southern Ocean
158 **Atlantic Ocean**
122 A3 **Atlantis** S. Africa
114 B1 **Atlas Mountains** Africa
114 C1 **Atlas Saharien** *mts* Alg.
128 A2 **Atlin** Can.
128 A2 **Atlin Lake** Can.
140 C2 **Atmore** U.S.A.
152 B2 **Atocha** Bol.
143 D2 **Atoka** U.S.A.
75 C2 **Atrai** *r.* India
80 B2 **Aţ Ţafīlah** Jordan
78 B2 **Aţ Ţā'if** Saudi Arabia
63 B2 **Attapu** Laos
130 B2 **Attawapiskat** Can.
130 B2 **Attawapiskat** *r.* Can.
130 B2 **Attawapiskat Lake** Can.
100 C2 **Attendorn** Ger.
100 A3 **Attichy** France
116 B2 **Aţ Ţūr** Egypt
78 B3 **At Turbah** Yemen
135 B3 **Atwater** U.S.A.
76 B2 **Atyrau** Kazakh.
105 D3 **Aubagne** France
105 C3 **Aubenas** France
126 D2 **Aubry Lake** Can.
140 C2 **Auburn** *AL* U.S.A.
135 B3 **Auburn** *CA* U.S.A.
138 B2 **Auburn** *IN* U.S.A.
139 E2 **Auburn** *ME* U.S.A.
137 D2 **Auburn** *NE* U.S.A.
139 D2 **Auburn** *NY* U.S.A.
104 C2 **Aubusson** France
104 C3 **Auch** France
54 B1 **Auckland** N.Z.
48 H9 **Auckland Islands** N.Z.
117 C4 **Audo** *mts* Eth.
101 F2 **Aue** Ger.
101 F2 **Auerbach** Ger.
102 C2 **Augsburg** Ger.
50 A3 **Augusta** Austr.
109 C3 **Augusta** Italy
141 D2 **Augusta** *GA* U.S.A.
137 D3 **Augusta** *KS* U.S.A.
139 F2 **Augusta** *ME* U.S.A.
155 D1 **Augusto de Lima** Brazil
103 E1 **Augustów** Pol.
50 A2 **Augustus, Mount** Austr.
100 A2 **Aulnoye-Aymeries** France
Aumale Alg. *see* **Sour el Ghozlane**
62 A2 **Aunglan** Myanmar
122 B2 **Auob** *watercourse* Namibia/S. Africa
131 D2 **Aupaluk** Can.
74 B3 **Aurangabad** India
104 B2 **Auray** France
100 C1 **Aurich** Ger.
154 B1 **Aurilândia** Brazil
104 C3 **Aurillac** France
136 C3 **Aurora** *CO* U.S.A.
138 B2 **Aurora** *IL* U.S.A.
137 E3 **Aurora** *MO* U.S.A.
137 D2 **Aurora** *NE* U.S.A.
122 A2 **Aus** Namibia
138 C2 **Au Sable** *r.* U.S.A.
137 E2 **Austin** *MN* U.S.A.
135 C3 **Austin** *NV* U.S.A.
143 D2 **Austin** *TX* U.S.A.
Australes, Îles *is* Fr. Polynesia *see* **Tubuai Islands**
50 B2 **Australia** *country* Oceania
55 K4 **Australian-Antarctic Basin** *sea feature* Southern Ocean
53 C3 **Australian Capital Territory** *admin. div.* Austr.
102 C2 **Austria** *country* Europe
150 D3 **Autazes** Brazil
144 B3 **Autlán** Mex.
105 C2 **Autun** France
104 C3 **Auvergne** *reg.* France
105 C2 **Auvergne, Monts d'** *mts* France
105 C2 **Auxerre** France
105 D2 **Auxonne** France
105 C2 **Avallon** France
131 E3 **Avalon Peninsula** Can.
154 C2 **Avaré** Brazil
91 D2 **Avdiyivka** Ukr.
106 B1 **Aveiro** Port.
109 B2 **Avellino** Italy
108 B2 **Aversa** Italy
100 A2 **Avesnes-sur-Helpe** France
93 G3 **Avesta** Sweden
104 C3 **Aveyron** *r.* France
108 B2 **Avezzano** Italy
96 C2 **Aviemore** U.K.
109 C2 **Avigliano** Italy
105 C3 **Avignon** France
106 C1 **Ávila** Spain
106 B1 **Avilés** Spain
52 B3 **Avoca** Austr.
139 D2 **Avoca** U.S.A.
109 C3 **Avola** Italy
99 B3 **Avon** *r. England* U.K.
99 B4 **Avon** *r. England* U.K.
99 C4 **Avon** *r. England* U.K.
142 A2 **Avondale** U.S.A.
104 B2 **Avranches** France
54 B1 **Awanui** N.Z.
78 B3 **Awārik, 'Urūq al** *des.* Saudi Arabia
119 D2 **Āwasa** Eth.
117 C4 **Āwash** Eth.
117 C3 **Āwash** *r.* Eth.
115 D2 **Awbārī** Libya
115 D2 **Awbārī, Idhān** *des.* Libya
117 C4 **Aw Dheegle** Somalia
96 B2 **Awe, Loch** *l.* U.K.
117 A4 **Aweil** Sudan
115 C4 **Awka** Nigeria
114 A2 **Awserd** Western Sahara
126 F1 **Axel Heiberg Island** Can.
114 B4 **Axim** Ghana
150 B4 **Ayacucho** Peru
77 E2 **Ayagoz** Kazakh.
Ayaguz Kazakh. *see* **Ayagoz**
68 B2 **Ayakkum Hu** *salt l.* China
106 B2 **Ayamonte** Spain
83 K3 **Ayan** Rus. Fed.
150 B4 **Ayaviri** Peru
74 A1 **Aybak** Afgh.
76 A2 **Aybas** Kazakh.
91 D2 **Aydar** *r.* Ukr.
77 C2 **Aydarko'l ko'li** *l.* Uzbek.
111 C3 **Aydın** Turkey
77 C2 **Ayeat, Gora** *h.* Kazakh.
Ayers Rock *h.* Austr. *see* **Uluru**
83 I2 **Aykhal** Rus. Fed.
99 C4 **Aylesbury** U.K.
106 C1 **Ayllón** Spain
129 D1 **Aylmer Lake** Can.
117 B4 **Ayod** Sudan
83 M2 **Ayon, Ostrov** *i.* Rus. Fed.
114 B3 **'Ayoûn el 'Atroûs** Maur.
51 D1 **Ayr** Austr.
96 B3 **Ayr** U.K.
98 A2 **Ayre, Point of** Isle of Man
76 C2 **Ayteke Bi** Kazakh.
110 C2 **Aytos** Bulg.
145 C3 **Ayutla** Mex.
63 B2 **Ayutthaya** Thai.
111 C3 **Ayvacık** Turkey
111 C3 **Ayvalık** Turkey
91 C3 **Ayya, Mys** *pt* Ukr.
114 B3 **Azaouâd** *reg.* Mali
114 C3 **Azaouagh, Vallée de** *watercourse* Mali/Niger
115 D3 **Azare** Nigeria
Azbine *mts* Niger *see* **Aïr, Massif de l'**
81 C1 **Azerbaijan** *country* Asia
Azerbaydzhanskaya S.S.R. *country* Asia *see* **Azerbaijan**
150 B3 **Azogues** Ecuador
86 D2 **Azopol'ye** Rus. Fed.
112 A2 **Azores** *aut. reg.* Port.
91 D2 **Azov** Rus. Fed.
91 D2 **Azov, Sea of** Rus. Fed./Ukr.
Azraq, Bahr el *r.* Sudan *see* **Blue Nile**
106 B2 **Azuaga** Spain
146 B4 **Azuero, Península de** *pen.* Panama
153 C3 **Azul** Arg.
108 A3 **Azzaba** Alg.
Az Zahran Saudi Arabia *see* **Dhahran**
80 B2 **Az Zaqāzīq** Egypt
80 B2 **Az Zarqā'** Jordan
115 D1 **Az Zāwiyah** Libya
78 B3 **Az Zaydīyah** Yemen
114 C2 **Azzel Matti, Sebkha** *salt pan* Alg.
78 B2 **Az Zilfī** Saudi Arabia
78 B3 **Az Zuqur** *i.* Yemen

B

63 B2 **Ba, Sông** *r.* Vietnam
117 C4 **Baardheere** Somalia
77 C3 **Bābā, Kūh-e** *mts* Afgh.
111 C3 **Baba Burnu** *pt* Turkey
110 C2 **Babadag** Romania
111 C2 **Babaeski** Turkey
116 C3 **Bāb al Mandab** *str.* Africa/Asia
61 C2 **Babana** Indon.
119 C1 **Babanusa** Sudan
59 C3 **Babar** *i.* Indon.
119 D3 **Babati** Tanz.
89 E2 **Babayevo** Rus. Fed.
59 C2 **Babeldaob** *i.* Palau
128 B2 **Babine** *r.* Can.
128 B2 **Babine Lake** Can.
59 C3 **Babo** Indon.
81 D2 **Bābol** Iran
122 A3 **Baboon Point** S. Africa
88 C3 **Babruysk** Belarus
Babu China *see* **Hezhou**
64 B2 **Babuyan** *i.* Phil.
64 B2 **Babuyan Channel** Phil.
64 B2 **Babuyan Islands** Phil.
151 E3 **Bacabal** Brazil
145 D3 **Bacalar** Mex.
59 C3 **Bacan** *i.* Indon.
110 C1 **Bacău** Romania
52 B3 **Bacchus Marsh** Austr.
62 B1 **Bắc Giang** Vietnam
77 D3 **Bachu** China
129 E1 **Back** *r.* Can.
109 C1 **Bačka Palanka** Serbia
109 C1 **Bačka Topola** Serbia
52 A3 **Backstairs Passage** Austr.
63 B3 **Bạc Liêu** Vietnam
142 B3 **Bacobampo** Mex.
64 B2 **Bacolod** Phil.
130 C2 **Bacqueville, Lac** *l.* Can.
Bada China *see* **Xilin**
70 A1 **Badain Jaran Shamo** *des.* China
106 B2 **Badajoz** Spain
Badaojiang China *see* **Baishan**
75 D2 **Badarpur** India
101 E2 **Bad Berka** Ger.
101 D2 **Bad Berleburg** Ger.
101 E1 **Bad Bevensen** Ger.
101 D3 **Bad Dürkheim** Ger.
100 C2 **Bad Ems** Ger.
103 D2 **Baden** Austria
102 B2 **Baden-Baden** Ger.
101 E2 **Bad Harzburg** Ger.
101 D2 **Bad Hersfeld** Ger.
102 C2 **Bad Hofgastein** Austria
101 D2 **Bad Homburg vor der Höhe** Ger.
101 D1 **Bad Iburg** Ger.
74 A2 **Badin** Pak.
Bādiyat ash Shām *des.* Asia *see* **Syrian Desert**
101 E2 **Bad Kissingen** Ger.
100 C3 **Bad Kreuznach** Ger.
136 C1 **Badlands** *reg.* *ND* U.S.A.
136 C2 **Badlands** *reg.* *SD* U.S.A.
101 E2 **Bad Lauterberg im Harz** Ger.

101 D2 **Bad Lippspringe** Ger.
101 D3 **Bad Mergentheim** Ger.
101 D2 **Bad Nauheim** Ger.
100 C2 **Bad Neuenahr-Ahrweiler** Ger.
101 E2 **Bad Neustadt an der Saale** Ger.
101 E1 **Bad Oldesloe** Ger.
101 D2 **Bad Pyrmont** Ger.
78 A2 **Badr Ḥunayn** Saudi Arabia
101 D1 **Bad Salzuflen** Ger.
101 E2 **Bad Salzungen** Ger.
102 C1 **Bad Schwartau** Ger.
101 E1 **Bad Segeberg** Ger.
100 C3 **Bad Sobernheim** Ger.
73 C4 **Badulla** Sri Lanka
101 D1 **Bad Zwischenahn** Ger.
106 C2 **Baeza** Spain
114 A3 **Bafatá** Guinea-Bissau
127 H2 **Baffin Bay** *sea* Can./Greenland
127 H2 **Baffin Island** Can.
118 B2 **Bafia** Cameroon
114 A3 **Bafing** *r.* Africa
114 A3 **Bafoulabé** Mali
118 B2 **Bafoussam** Cameroon
81 D2 **Bāfq** Iran
80 B1 **Bafra** Turkey
79 C2 **Bāft** Iran
119 C2 **Bafwasende** Dem. Rep. Congo
119 D3 **Bagamoyo** Tanz.
Bagan Datoh Malaysia *see* **Bagan Datuk**
60 B1 **Bagan Datuk** Malaysia
64 B3 **Baganga** Phil.
120 B2 **Bagani** Namibia
60 B1 **Bagansiapiapi** Indon.
118 B3 **Bagata** Dem. Rep. Congo
91 E2 **Bagayevskiy** Rus. Fed.
142 A2 **Bagdad** U.S.A.
152 C3 **Bagé** Brazil
97 C2 **Bagenalstown** Ireland
81 C2 **Baghdād** Iraq
79 C1 **Bāghīn** Iran
77 C3 **Baghlān** Afgh.
104 C3 **Bagnères-de-Luchon** France
105 C3 **Bagnols-sur-Cèze** France
Bago Myanmar *see* **Pegu**
88 B3 **Bagrationovsk** Rus. Fed.
Bagrax China *see* **Bohu**
64 B2 **Baguio** Phil.
115 C3 **Bagzane, Monts** *mts* Niger
146 C2 **Bahamas, The** *country* West Indies
75 C2 **Baharampur** India
Bahariya Oasis *oasis* Egypt *see* **Wāḥāt al Baḥrīyah**
76 B3 **Baharly** Turkm.
60 B1 **Bahau** Malaysia
74 B2 **Bahawalnagar** Pak.
74 B2 **Bahawalpur** Pak.
Bahia Brazil *see* **Salvador**
155 E1 **Bahia** *state* Brazil
146 B3 **Bahía, Islas de la** *is* Hond.
153 B3 **Bahía Blanca** Arg.
144 A2 **Bahía Kino** Mex.
152 C2 **Bahía Negra** Para.
144 A2 **Bahía Tortugas** Mex.
117 B3 **Bahir Dar** Eth.
79 C2 **Bahlā** Oman
75 C2 **Bahraich** India
79 C2 **Bahrain** *country* Asia
79 D2 **Bāhū Kālāt** Iran
89 D3 **Bahushewsk** Belarus
110 C2 **Baia** Romania
120 A2 **Baía dos Tigres** Angola
110 B1 **Baia Mare** Romania
118 B2 **Baïbokoum** Chad
69 E1 **Baicheng** China
Baidoa Somalia *see* **Baydhabo**
Baie-aux-Feuilles Can. *see* **Tasiujaq**
131 D3 **Baie-Comeau** Can.
Baie-du-Poste Can. *see* **Mistissini**
131 C3 **Baie-St-Paul** Can.
131 E3 **Baie Verte** Can.
62 A1 **Baihanchang** China
65 B1 **Baihe** China
69 D1 **Baikal, Lake** Rus. Fed.
Baile Átha Cliath Ireland *see* **Dublin**
110 B2 **Băileşti** Romania
68 C2 **Baima** China
141 D2 **Bainbridge** U.S.A.
Baingoin China *see* **Porong**
48 I3 **Bairiki** Kiribati
Bairin Youqi China *see* **Daban**
53 C3 **Bairnsdale** Austr.
65 B1 **Baishan** *Jilin* China
65 B1 **Baishan** *Jilin* China
65 B1 **Baitou Shan** *mt.* China/N. Korea
120 A2 **Baixo-Longa** Angola
70 A2 **Baiyin** China
116 B3 **Baiyuda Desert** Sudan
103 D2 **Baja** Hungary
144 A1 **Baja California** *pen.* Mex.
61 D2 **Bajawa** Indon.
78 B3 **Bājil** Yemen
115 D3 **Bajoga** Nigeria
109 D2 **Bajram Curri** Albania
114 A3 **Bakel** Senegal
135 C3 **Baker** *CA* U.S.A.
140 B2 **Baker** *LA* U.S.A.
136 C1 **Baker** *MT* U.S.A.
134 C2 **Baker** *OR* U.S.A.
134 B1 **Baker, Mount** *vol.* U.S.A.
129 E1 **Baker Foreland** *hd* Can.
49 J3 **Baker Island** *terr.* N. Pacific Ocean
129 E1 **Baker Lake** Can.
129 E1 **Baker Lake** *l.* Can.
135 C3 **Bakersfield** U.S.A.
Bakharden Turkm. *see* **Baharly**
91 C3 **Bakhchysaray** Ukr.
91 C1 **Bakhmach** Ukr.
Bakhmut Ukr. *see* **Artemivs'k**
Bākhtarān Iran *see* **Kermānshāh**
Bakı Azer. *see* **Baku**
111 C2 **Bakırköy** Turkey
92 □C2 **Bakkaflói** *b.* Iceland
118 C2 **Bakouma** C.A.R.
81 C1 **Baku** Azer.
99 B3 **Bala** U.K.
64 A3 **Balabac** Phil.
64 A3 **Balabac** *i.* Phil.
61 C1 **Balabac Strait** Malaysia/Phil.
75 C2 **Balaghat** India
60 C2 **Balaiberkuak** Indon.
52 A2 **Balaklava** Austr.
91 C3 **Balaklava** Ukr.
91 D2 **Balakliya** Ukr.
87 D3 **Balakovo** Rus. Fed.
145 C3 **Balancán** Mex.
111 C3 **Balan Dağı** *h.* Turkey
64 B2 **Balanga** Phil.
87 D3 **Balashov** Rus. Fed.
Balaton, Lake *l.* Hungary *see* **Lake Balaton**
103 D2 **Balatonboglár** Hungary
150 D3 **Balbina, Represa de** *resr* Brazil
97 C2 **Balbriggan** Ireland
52 A2 **Balcanoona** Austr.
110 C2 **Balchik** Bulg.
54 A3 **Balclutha** N.Z.
143 C3 **Balcones Escarpment** U.S.A.
129 E2 **Baldock Lake** Can.
138 D2 **Baldwin** U.S.A.
129 D2 **Baldy Mountain** *h.* Can.
142 B2 **Baldy Peak** U.S.A.
Baleares, Islas *is* Spain *see* **Balearic Islands**
107 D2 **Balearic Islands** *is* Spain
155 E1 **Baleia, Ponta da** *pt* Brazil
130 C2 **Baleine, Grande Rivière de la** *r.* Can.
131 D2 **Baleine, Rivière à la** *r.* Can.
75 C2 **Baleshwar** India
108 A2 **Balestrieri, Punta** *mt.* Italy
50 B2 **Balgo** Austr.
78 B3 **Balḥaf** Yemen
61 C2 **Bali** *i.* Indon.
115 D4 **Bali** Nigeria
60 A1 **Balige** Indon.
75 C2 **Baliguda** India
111 C3 **Balıkesir** Turkey
61 C2 **Balikpapan** Indon.
64 A3 **Balimbing** Phil.
59 D3 **Balimo** P.N.G.
102 B2 **Balingen** Ger.
64 B2 **Balintang Channel** Phil.
Bali Sea *sea* Indon. *see* **Laut Bali**
78 B3 **Baljurshī** Saudi Arabia
76 B3 **Balkanabat** Turkm.
110 B2 **Balkan Mountains** Bulg./Serbia
77 C1 **Balkashino** Kazakh.
77 D2 **Balkhash** Kazakh.
77 D2 **Balkhash, Lake** Kazakh.
Balkhash, Ozero *l.* Kazakh. *see* **Balkhash, Lake**
Balla Balla Zimbabwe *see* **Mbalabala**
96 B2 **Ballachulish** U.K.
50 B3 **Balladonia** Austr.
97 B2 **Ballaghaderreen** Ireland
92 G2 **Ballangen** Norway
96 B3 **Ballantrae** U.K.
52 B3 **Ballarat** Austr.
50 B2 **Ballard, Lake** *imp. l.* Austr.
96 C2 **Ballater** U.K.
114 B3 **Ballé** Mali
55 M3 **Balleny Islands** Antarctica
53 D1 **Ballina** Austr.
97 B1 **Ballina** Ireland
97 B2 **Ballinasloe** Ireland
97 B3 **Ballineen** Ireland
143 D2 **Ballinger** U.S.A.
97 B2 **Ballinrobe** Ireland
97 B1 **Ballycastle** Ireland
97 C1 **Ballycastle** U.K.
97 D1 **Ballyclare** U.K.
97 B2 **Ballyhaunis** Ireland
97 C1 **Ballymena** U.K.
97 C1 **Ballymoney** U.K.
97 D1 **Ballynahinch** U.K.
97 B1 **Ballyshannon** Ireland
95 B2 **Ballyvoy** U.K.
52 B3 **Balmoral** Austr.
143 C2 **Balmorhea** U.S.A.
120 A2 **Balombo** Angola
53 C1 **Balonne** *r.* Austr.
74 B2 **Balotra** India
77 D2 **Balpyk Bi** Kazakh.
75 C2 **Balrampur** India
52 B2 **Balranald** Austr.
110 B2 **Balş** Romania
151 E3 **Balsas** Brazil
145 C3 **Balsas** Mex.
145 B3 **Balsas** *r.* Mex.
90 B2 **Balta** Ukr.
90 B2 **Bălţi** Moldova
93 G4 **Baltic Sea** *g.* Europe
80 B2 **Balṭīm** Egypt
97 B3 **Baltimore** Ireland
123 C1 **Baltimore** S. Africa
139 D3 **Baltimore** U.S.A.
97 C2 **Baltinglass** Ireland
88 A3 **Baltiysk** Rus. Fed.
75 D2 **Balu** India
52 A2 **Balumbah** Austr.
88 C2 **Balvi** Latvia
77 D2 **Balykchy** Kyrg.
87 E4 **Balykshi** Kazakh.
79 C2 **Bam** Iran
71 A3 **Bama** China
51 D1 **Bamaga** Austr.
130 A2 **Bamaji Lake** Can.
114 B3 **Bamako** Mali
118 C2 **Bambari** C.A.R.
101 E3 **Bamberg** Ger.
119 C2 **Bambili** Dem. Rep. Congo
118 B2 **Bambio** C.A.R.
119 C2 **Bambouti** C.A.R.
155 C2 **Bambuí** Brazil
98 C2 **Bamburgh** U.K.
118 B2 **Bamenda** Cameroon
77 C3 **Bāmīān** Afgh.
118 C2 **Bamingui** C.A.R.
79 D2 **Bampūr** Iran
79 C2 **Bampūr** *watercourse* Iran
119 C2 **Banalia** Dem. Rep. Congo
71 A3 **Banan** China
151 D4 **Bananal, Ilha do** *i.* Brazil
74 B2 **Banas** *r.* India
111 C3 **Banaz** Turkey
62 B2 **Ban Ban** Laos
97 C1 **Banbridge** U.K.
99 C3 **Banbury** U.K.
96 C2 **Banchory** U.K.
130 C3 **Bancroft** Can.
Bancroft Zambia *see* **Chililabombwe**
119 C2 **Banda** Dem. Rep. Congo
75 C2 **Banda** India
59 C3 **Banda, Kepulauan** *is* Indon.
59 C3 **Banda, Laut** Indon.
60 A1 **Banda Aceh** Indon.
Bandar India *see* **Machilipatnam**
Bandar Abbas Iran *see* **Bandar-e 'Abbās**
75 D2 **Bandarban** Bangl.
79 C2 **Bandar-e 'Abbās** Iran
81 C2 **Bandar-e Anzalī** Iran
79 C2 **Bandar-e Chārak** Iran
81 C2 **Bandar-e Emām Khomeynī** Iran
79 C2 **Bandar-e Lengeh** Iran
79 C2 **Bandar-e Maqām** Iran
Bandar-e Pahlavī Iran *see* **Bandar-e Anzalī**
Bandar-e Shāhpūr Iran *see* **Bandar-e Emām Khomeynī**
60 B2 **Bandar Lampung** Indon.
61 C1 **Bandar Seri Begawan** Brunei
Banda Sea *sea* Indon. *see* **Banda, Laut**
155 D2 **Bandeiras, Pico de** *mt.* Brazil
123 C1 **Bandelierkop** S. Africa
144 B2 **Banderas, Bahía de** *b.* Mex.
114 B3 **Bandiagara** Mali
111 C2 **Bandırma** Turkey
Bandjarmasin Indon. *see* **Banjarmasin**
97 B3 **Bandon** Ireland
97 B3 **Bandon** *r.* Ireland
118 B3 **Bandundu** Dem. Rep. Congo
60 B2 **Bandung** Indon.
128 C2 **Banff** Can.
96 C2 **Banff** U.K.
114 B3 **Banfora** Burkina
64 B3 **Banga** Phil.
73 B3 **Bangalore** India
118 C2 **Bangassou** C.A.R.
61 D2 **Banggai** Indon.
61 D2 **Banggai, Kepulauan** *is* Indon.
61 C1 **Banggi** *i.* Malaysia
Banghāzī Libya *see* **Benghazi**
60 B2 **Bangka** *i.* Indon.
60 B2 **Bangka, Selat** *sea chan.* Indon.
61 C2 **Bangkalan** Indon.
60 B1 **Bangkinang** Indon.
60 B2 **Bangko** Indon.
63 B2 **Bangkok** Thai.
75 C2 **Bangladesh** *country* Asia
63 B2 **Ba Ngoi** Vietnam
97 D1 **Bangor** *Northern Ireland* U.K.
98 A3 **Bangor** *Wales* U.K.
139 F2 **Bangor** U.S.A.
63 A2 **Bang Saphan Yai** Thai.
64 B2 **Bangued** Phil.
118 B2 **Bangui** C.A.R.
64 B2 **Bangui** Phil.
121 B2 **Bangweulu, Lake** Zambia
80 B2 **Banhā** Egypt
62 B2 **Ban Huai Khon** Thai.
118 C2 **Bani** C.A.R.
80 B3 **Banī Mazār** Egypt
116 B2 **Banī Suwayf** Egypt
115 D1 **Banī Walīd** Libya
80 B2 **Bāniyās** Syria
109 C2 **Banja Luka** Bos.-Herz.
61 C2 **Banjarmasin** Indon.
114 A3 **Banjul** Gambia
63 A3 **Ban Khok Kloi** Thai.
128 A2 **Banks Island** *B.C.* Can.
126 D2 **Banks Island** *N.W.T.* Can.
48 H5 **Banks Islands** Vanuatu
129 E1 **Banks Lake** Can.
54 B2 **Banks Peninsula** N.Z.
51 D4 **Banks Strait** Austr.
75 C2 **Bankura** India
62 A1 **Banmauk** Myanmar
62 B2 **Ban Mouang** Laos
97 C1 **Bann** *r.* U.K.
62 B2 **Ban Napè** Laos
63 A3 **Ban Na San** Thai.
146 C2 **Bannerman Town** Bahamas
Banningville Dem. Rep. Congo *see* **Bandundu**
71 A4 **Ban Nong Kung** Thai.
74 B1 **Bannu** Pak.
62 B2 **Ban Phôn-Hông** Laos
103 D2 **Banská Bystrica** Slovakia
111 B2 **Bansko** Bulg.
74 B2 **Banswara** India
62 B2 **Ban Taviang** Laos
63 A3 **Ban Tha Kham** Thai.
62 A2 **Ban Tha Song Yang** Thai.
63 B2 **Ban Tôp** Laos
97 B3 **Bantry** Ireland
97 B3 **Bantry Bay** Ireland
60 A1 **Banyak, Pulau-pulau** *is* Indon.
118 B2 **Banyo** Cameroon
107 D1 **Banyoles** Spain
61 C2 **Banyuwangi** Indon.
Banzyville Dem. Rep. Congo *see* **Mobayi-Mbongo**
Bao'an China *see* **Shenzhen**
70 B1 **Baochang** China
70 B2 **Baoding** China
70 A2 **Baoji** China
62 B1 **Bao Lac** Vietnam
63 B2 **Bao Lôc** Vietnam
66 B1 **Baoqing** China
118 B2 **Baoro** C.A.R.
62 A1 **Baoshan** China
70 B1 **Baotou** China
74 B2 **Bap** India
81 C2 **Ba'qūbah** Iraq
109 C2 **Bar** Montenegro
90 B2 **Bar** Ukr.
116 B3 **Bara** Sudan
117 C4 **Baraawe** Somalia
147 C2 **Baracoa** Cuba
53 C2 **Baradine** Austr.
147 C3 **Barahona** Dom. Rep.
116 B3 **Baraka** *watercourse* Eritrea/Sudan
106 C1 **Barakaldo** Spain
61 C1 **Baram** *r.* Malaysia
150 D2 **Baramanni** Guyana
74 B1 **Baramulla** India
89 D3 **Baran'** Belarus
74 B2 **Baran** India
88 C3 **Baranavichy** Belarus
116 B2 **Baranīs** Egypt
90 B1 **Baranivka** Ukr.
76 B2 **Barankul** Kazakh.
128 A2 **Baranof Island** U.S.A.
Baranowicze Belarus *see* **Baranavichy**
59 C3 **Barat Daya, Kepulauan** *is* Indon.
155 D2 **Barbacena** Brazil
147 E3 **Barbados** *country* West Indies
107 D1 **Barbastro** Spain
106 B2 **Barbate de Franco** Spain
123 D2 **Barberton** S. Africa
104 B2 **Barbezieux-St-Hilaire** France
51 D2 **Barcaldine** Austr.
107 D1 **Barcelona** Spain
150 C1 **Barcelona** Venez.
105 D3 **Barcelonnette** France
150 C3 **Barcelos** Brazil
114 B4 **Barclayville** Liberia
51 D2 **Barcoo** *watercourse* Austr.
Barcoo Creek *watercourse* Austr. *see* **Cooper Creek**
103 D2 **Barcs** Hungary
92 □B3 **Bárðarbunga** *mt.* Iceland
75 C2 **Barddhaman** India
103 E2 **Bardejov** Slovakia
Bardera Somalia *see* **Baardheere**
79 C2 **Bardsīr** Iran
75 B2 **Bareilly** India
82 D1 **Barents Sea** Arctic Ocean
78 A3 **Barentu** Eritrea
72 C1 **Barga** China
108 B2 **Barga** Italy
75 C2 **Barh** India
52 B3 **Barham** Austr.
139 F2 **Bar Harbor** U.S.A.
109 C2 **Bari** Italy
107 E2 **Barika** Alg.
74 B1 **Barikot** Afgh.
150 B2 **Barinas** Venez.
75 C2 **Baripada** India
75 D2 **Barisal** Bangl.
60 B2 **Barisan, Pegunungan** *mts* Indon.
61 C2 **Barito** *r.* Indon.
79 C2 **Barkā** Oman
88 C2 **Barkava** Latvia
74 A2 **Barkhan** Pak.
51 C1 **Barkly Tableland** *reg.* Austr.
122 B2 **Barkly West** S. Africa
68 C2 **Barkol** China
110 C1 **Bârlad** Romania
105 D2 **Bar-le-Duc** France
50 A2 **Barlee, Lake** *imp. l.* Austr.
109 C2 **Barletta** Italy
53 C2 **Barmedman** Austr.
Barmen-Elberfeld Ger. *see* **Wuppertal**
74 B2 **Barmer** India
52 B2 **Barmera** Austr.
99 A3 **Barmouth** U.K.
101 D1 **Barmstedt** Ger.
98 C2 **Barnard Castle** U.K.
53 B2 **Barnato** Austr.
82 G3 **Barnaul** Rus. Fed.

127 H2 **Barnes Icecap** Can.
100 B1 **Barneveld** Neth.
98 C3 **Barnsley** U.K.
99 A4 **Barnstaple** U.K.
99 A4 **Barnstaple Bay** U.K.
Bideford Bay *b.* U.K. *see* **Barnstaple Bay**
141 D2 **Barnwell** U.S.A.
Baroda India *see* **Vadodara**
150 C1 **Barquisimeto** Venez.
96 A2 **Barra** *i.* U.K.
53 D2 **Barraba** Austr.
151 D4 **Barra do Bugres** Brazil
151 E3 **Barra do Corda** Brazil
154 B1 **Barra do Garças** Brazil
150 D3 **Barra do São Manuel** Brazil
Barraigh *i.* U.K. *see* **Barra**
150 B4 **Barranca** *Lima* Peru
150 B3 **Barranca** *Loreto* Peru
152 C2 **Barranqueras** Arg.
150 B1 **Barranquilla** Col.
105 D3 **Barre des Écrins** *mt.* France
151 E4 **Barreiras** Brazil
63 A2 **Barren Island** India
154 C2 **Barretos** Brazil
128 C2 **Barrhead** Can.
130 C3 **Barrie** Can.
128 B2 **Barrière** Can.
52 B2 **Barrier Range** *hills* Austr.
53 D2 **Barrington, Mount** Austr.
129 D2 **Barrington Lake** Can.
53 C1 **Barringun** Austr.
97 C2 **Barrow** *r.* Ireland
126 B2 **Barrow** U.S.A.
126 B2 **Barrow, Point** U.S.A.
51 C2 **Barrow Creek** Austr.
98 B2 **Barrow-in-Furness** U.K.
50 A2 **Barrow Island** Austr.
126 F2 **Barrow Strait** Can.
99 B4 **Barry** U.K.
122 B3 **Barrydale** S. Africa
130 C3 **Barrys Bay** Can.
74 B2 **Barsalpur** India
101 D1 **Barsinghausen** Ger.
135 C4 **Barstow** U.S.A.
105 C2 **Bar-sur-Aube** France
102 C1 **Barth** Ger.
80 B1 **Bartın** Turkey
51 D1 **Bartle Frere, Mount** Austr.
143 D1 **Bartlesville** U.S.A.
137 D2 **Bartlett** *NE* U.S.A.
140 C1 **Bartlett** *TN* U.S.A.
98 C3 **Barton-upon-Humber** U.K.
103 E1 **Bartoszyce** Pol.
61 C2 **Barung** *i.* Indon.
69 D1 **Baruun-Urt** Mongolia
91 D2 **Barvinkove** Ukr.
53 C2 **Barwon** *r.* Austr.
88 C3 **Barysaw** Belarus
118 B2 **Basankusu** Dem. Rep. Congo
110 C2 **Basarabi** Romania
64 B1 **Basco** Phil.
105 D2 **Basel** Switz.
71 C3 **Bashi Channel** Phil./Taiwan
91 C2 **Bashtanka** Ukr.
64 B3 **Basilan** *i.* Phil.
99 D4 **Basildon** U.K.
99 C4 **Basingstoke** U.K.
81 C2 **Başkale** Turkey
130 C3 **Baskatong, Réservoir** *resr* Can.
Basle Switz. *see* **Basel**
118 C2 **Basoko** Dem. Rep. Congo
81 C2 **Basra** Iraq
128 C2 **Bassano** Can.
114 C4 **Bassar** Togo
63 A2 **Bassein** Myanmar
147 D3 **Basse-Terre** Guadeloupe
147 D3 **Basseterre** St Kitts and Nevis
114 B3 **Bassikounou** Maur.
114 C4 **Bassila** Benin
51 D3 **Bass Strait** Austr.
79 C2 **Bastak** Iran
101 E2 **Bastheim** Ger.
75 C2 **Basti** India
105 D3 **Bastia** France
100 B2 **Bastogne** Belgium
140 B2 **Bastrop** U.S.A.
Basuo China *see* **Dongfang**
Basutoland *country* Africa *see* **Lesotho**
118 A2 **Bata** Equat. Guinea
146 B2 **Batabanó, Golfo de** *b.* Cuba
83 J2 **Batagay** Rus. Fed.
154 B2 **Bataguassu** Brazil
74 B1 **Batala** India
106 B2 **Batalha** Port.
64 B1 **Batan** *i.* Phil.
118 B2 **Batangafo** C.A.R.
64 B2 **Batangas** Phil.
60 B2 **Batanghari** *r.* Indon.
64 B1 **Batan Islands** Phil.
154 C2 **Batatais** Brazil
139 D2 **Batavia** U.S.A.
91 D2 **Bataysk** Rus. Fed.
130 B3 **Batchawana Mountain** *h.* Can.
50 C1 **Batchelor** Austr.
63 B2 **Bătdâmbâng** Cambodia
118 B3 **Batéké, Plateaux** Congo
53 D3 **Batemans Bay** Austr.
140 B1 **Batesville** *AR* U.S.A.
140 C2 **Batesville** *MS* U.S.A.
89 D2 **Batetskiy** Rus. Fed.
99 B4 **Bath** U.K.
96 C3 **Bathgate** U.K.
74 B1 **Bathinda** India
53 C2 **Bathurst** Austr.
131 D3 **Bathurst** Can.
Bathurst Gambia *see* **Banjul**
126 E2 **Bathurst Inlet** *inlet* Can.
126 E2 **Bathurst Inlet (abandoned)** Can.
50 C1 **Bathurst Island** Austr.
126 F1 **Bathurst Island** Can.
78 B1 **Bāţin, Wādī al** *watercourse* Asia
53 C3 **Batlow** Austr.
81 C2 **Batman** Turkey
115 C1 **Batna** Alg.
140 B2 **Baton Rouge** U.S.A.
144 B2 **Batopilas** Mex.
118 B2 **Batouri** Cameroon
154 B1 **Batovi** Brazil
Batrā' *tourist site* Jordan *see* **Petra**
92 I1 **Båtsfjord** Norway
73 C4 **Batticaloa** Sri Lanka
109 B2 **Battipaglia** Italy
128 D2 **Battle** *r.* Can.
138 B2 **Battle Creek** U.S.A.
135 C2 **Battle Mountain** U.S.A.
74 B1 **Battura Glacier** Pak.
117 B4 **Batu** *mt.* Eth.
60 A2 **Batu, Pulau-pulau** *is* Indon.
61 D2 **Batuata** *i.* Indon.
61 D2 **Batudaka** *i.* Indon.
64 B3 **Batulaki** Phil.
Batum Georgia *see* **Bat'umi**
81 C1 **Bat'umi** Georgia
60 B1 **Batu Pahat** Malaysia
61 D2 **Baubau** Indon.
115 C3 **Bauchi** Nigeria
137 E1 **Baudette** U.S.A.
Baudouinville Dem. Rep. Congo *see* **Moba**
104 B2 **Baugé** France
105 D2 **Baume-les-Dames** France
154 C2 **Bauru** Brazil
154 B1 **Baús** Brazil
88 B2 **Bauska** Latvia
102 C1 **Bautzen** Ger.
144 B2 **Bavispe** *r.* Mex.
87 E3 **Bavly** Rus. Fed.
62 A1 **Bawdwin** Myanmar
61 C2 **Bawean** *i.* Indon.
114 B3 **Bawku** Ghana
Baxian China *see* **Banan**
146 C2 **Bayamo** Cuba
Bayan Gol China *see* **Dengkou**
68 C1 **Bayanhongor** Mongolia
70 A2 **Bayan Hot** China
70 A1 **Bayan Kuang** China
69 D1 **Bayan-Uul** Mongolia
136 C2 **Bayard** *NE* U.S.A.
142 B2 **Bayard** *NM* U.S.A.
64 B3 **Bayawan** Phil.
81 C1 **Bayburt** Turkey
138 C2 **Bay City** *MI* U.S.A.
143 D3 **Bay City** *TX* U.S.A.
86 F2 **Baydaratskaya Guba** Rus. Fed.
117 C4 **Baydhabo** Somalia
102 C2 **Bayern** *reg.* Ger.
104 B2 **Bayeux** France
136 B3 **Bayfield** U.S.A.
78 B3 **Bayḩan al Qişab** Yemen
Bay Islands *is* Hond. *see* **Bahía, Islas de la**
81 C2 **Bayjī** Iraq
Baykal, Ozero *l.* Rus. Fed. *see* **Baikal, Lake**
Baykal Range *mts* Rus. Fed. *see* **Baykal'skiy Khrebet**
83 I3 **Baykal'skiy Khrebet** *mts* Rus. Fed.
76 C2 **Baykonyr** Kazakh.
87 E3 **Baymak** Rus. Fed.
64 B2 **Bayombong** Phil.
104 B3 **Bayonne** France
76 C3 **Baýramaly** Turkm.
111 C3 **Bayramiç** Turkey
101 E3 **Bayreuth** Ger.
78 B3 **Bayt al Faqīh** Yemen
143 D3 **Baytown** U.S.A.
106 C2 **Baza** Spain
106 C2 **Baza, Sierra de** *mts* Spain
74 A1 **Bāzārak** Afgh.
76 A2 **Bazardyuzyu, Gora** *mt.* Azer./Rus. Fed.
104 B3 **Bazas** France
74 A2 **Bazdar** Pak.
70 A2 **Bazhong** China
79 D2 **Bazmān** Iran
79 D2 **Bazmān, Kūh-e** *mt.* Iran
Bé, Nossi *i.* Madag. *see* **Bé, Nosy**
121 □D2 **Bé, Nosy** *i.* Madag.
136 C1 **Beach** U.S.A.
52 B3 **Beachport** Austr.
99 D4 **Beachy Head** *hd* U.K.
123 C3 **Beacon Bay** S. Africa
50 B1 **Beagle Gulf** Austr.
121 □D2 **Bealanana** Madag.
97 B1 **Béal an Mhuirthead** Ireland
121 □D3 **Beampingaratra** *mts* Madag.
134 D2 **Bear** *r.* U.S.A.
130 B3 **Beardmore** Can.
Bear Island *i.* Arctic Ocean *see* **Bjørnøya**
134 E1 **Bear Paw Mountain** U.S.A.
147 C3 **Beata, Cabo** *c.* Dom. Rep.
147 C3 **Beata, Isla** *i.* Dom. Rep.
137 D2 **Beatrice** U.S.A.
135 C3 **Beatty** U.S.A.
53 D1 **Beaudesert** Austr.
52 B3 **Beaufort** Austr.
61 C1 **Beaufort** Malaysia
141 D2 **Beaufort** U.S.A.
126 D2 **Beaufort Sea** Can./U.S.A.
122 B3 **Beaufort West** S. Africa
96 B2 **Beauly** U.K.
96 B2 **Beauly** *r.* U.K.
100 B2 **Beaumont** Belgium
54 A3 **Beaumont** N.Z.
143 E2 **Beaumont** U.S.A.
105 C2 **Beaune** France
100 B2 **Beauraing** Belgium
129 E2 **Beauséjour** Can.
104 C2 **Beauvais** France
129 D2 **Beauval** Can.
129 D2 **Beaver** *r.* Can.
135 D3 **Beaver** U.S.A.
128 A1 **Beaver Creek** Can.
138 B2 **Beaver Dam** U.S.A.
129 E2 **Beaver Hill Lake** Can.
138 B1 **Beaver Island** U.S.A.
128 C2 **Beaverlodge** Can.
74 B2 **Beawar** India
154 C2 **Bebedouro** Brazil
101 D2 **Bebra** Ger.
99 D3 **Beccles** U.K.
109 D1 **Bečej** Serbia
106 B1 **Becerreá** Spain
114 B1 **Béchar** Alg.
Bechuanaland *country* Africa *see* **Botswana**
138 C3 **Beckley** U.S.A.
117 B4 **Bedelē** Eth.
99 C3 **Bedford** U.K.
138 B3 **Bedford** U.S.A.
98 C2 **Bedlington** U.K.
100 C1 **Bedum** Neth.
53 C3 **Beechworth** Austr.
53 D2 **Beecroft Peninsula** Austr.
101 F1 **Beelitz** Ger.
53 D1 **Beenleigh** Austr.
80 B2 **Beersheba** Israel
Be'ér Sheva' Israel *see* **Beersheba**
143 D3 **Beeville** U.S.A.
121 □D2 **Befandriana Avaratra** Madag.
53 C3 **Bega** Austr.
107 D1 **Begur, Cap de** *c.* Spain
81 D2 **Behbehān** Iran
128 C1 **Behchokô** Can.
81 D2 **Behshahr** Iran
69 E1 **Bei'an** China
71 A3 **Beihai** China
70 B2 **Beijing** China
100 C1 **Beilen** Neth.
118 B2 **Béinamar** Chad
96 B3 **Beinn an Oir** *h.* U.K.
96 A2 **Beinn Mhòr** *h.* U.K.
Beinn na Faoghlia *i.* U.K. *see* **Benbecula**
121 C2 **Beira** Moz.
80 B2 **Beirut** Lebanon
123 C1 **Beitbridge** Zimbabwe
106 B2 **Beja** Port.
115 C1 **Bejaïa** Alg.
106 B1 **Béjar** Spain
74 A2 **Beji** *r.* Pak.
103 E2 **Békés** Hungary
103 E2 **Békéscsaba** Hungary
121 □D3 **Bekily** Madag.
66 D2 **Bekkai** Japan
114 B4 **Bekwai** Ghana
75 C2 **Bela** India
74 A2 **Bela** Pak.
123 C1 **Bela-Bela** S. Africa
118 B2 **Bélabo** Cameroon
109 D2 **Bela Crkva** Serbia
61 C1 **Belaga** Malaysia
88 C3 **Belarus** *country* Europe
121 C3 **Bela Vista** Moz.
60 A1 **Belawan** Indon.
83 M2 **Belaya** *r.* Rus. Fed.
103 D1 **Bełchatów** Pol.
Belchatow Pol. *see* **Bełchatów**
130 C2 **Belcher Islands** Can.
87 E3 **Belebey** Rus. Fed.
117 C4 **Beledweyne** Somalia
118 B2 **Bélèl** Cameroon
151 E3 **Belém** Brazil
142 B2 **Belen** U.S.A.
110 C2 **Belene** Bulg.
89 E3 **Belev** Rus. Fed.
97 D1 **Belfast** U.K.
139 F2 **Belfast** U.S.A.
136 C1 **Belfield** U.S.A.
105 D2 **Belfort** France
73 B3 **Belgaum** India
Belgian Congo *country* Africa *see* **Congo, Democratic Republic of the**
100 B2 **Belgium** *country* Europe
91 D1 **Belgorod** Rus. Fed.
109 D2 **Belgrade** Serbia
134 D1 **Belgrade** U.S.A.
109 C1 **Beli Manastir** Croatia
60 B2 **Belinyu** Indon.
60 B2 **Belitung** *i.* Indon.
118 B3 **Belize** Angola
146 B3 **Belize** Belize
146 B3 **Belize** *country* Central America
83 K1 **Bel'kovskiy, Ostrov** *i.* Rus. Fed.
128 B2 **Bella Bella** Can.
104 C2 **Bellac** France
128 B2 **Bella Coola** Can.
73 B3 **Bellary** India
53 C1 **Bellata** Austr.
138 C2 **Bellefontaine** U.S.A.
136 C2 **Belle Fourche** U.S.A.
136 C2 **Belle Fourche** *r.* U.S.A.
141 D3 **Belle Glade** U.S.A.
104 B2 **Belle-Île** *i.* France
131 E2 **Belle Isle** *i.* Can.
131 E2 **Belle Isle, Strait of** Can.
130 C3 **Belleville** Can.
138 B3 **Belleville** *IL* U.S.A.
137 D3 **Belleville** *KS* U.S.A.
134 D2 **Bellevue** *ID* U.S.A.
134 B1 **Bellevue** *WA* U.S.A.
Bellin Can. *see* **Kangirsuk**
53 D2 **Bellingen** Austr.
134 B1 **Bellingham** U.S.A.
55 R2 **Bellingshausen Sea** Antarctica
105 D2 **Bellinzona** Switz.
96 C2 **Bell Rock** *i.* U.K.
108 B1 **Belluno** Italy
122 A3 **Bellville** S. Africa
53 D2 **Belmont** Austr.
155 E1 **Belmonte** Brazil
146 B3 **Belmopan** Belize
Belmullet Ireland *see* **Béal an Mhuirthead**
69 E1 **Belogorsk** Rus. Fed.
121 □D3 **Beloha** Madag.
155 D1 **Belo Horizonte** Brazil
138 B2 **Beloit** U.S.A.
86 C2 **Belomorsk** Rus. Fed.
89 E3 **Beloomut** Rus. Fed.
91 D3 **Belorechensk** Rus. Fed.
Belorechenskaya Rus. Fed. *see* **Belorechensk**
87 E3 **Beloretsk** Rus. Fed.
Belorussia *country* Europe *see* **Belarus**
Belorusskaya S.S.R. *country* Europe *see* **Belarus**
Belostok Pol. *see* **Białystok**
121 □D2 **Belo Tsiribihina** Madag.
86 F2 **Beloyarskiy** Rus. Fed.
89 E1 **Beloye, Ozero** *l.* Rus. Fed.
Beloye More *sea* Rus. Fed. *see* **White Sea**
89 E1 **Belozersk** Rus. Fed.
52 A2 **Beltana** Austr.
143 D2 **Belton** U.S.A.
Bel'tsi Moldova *see* **Bălţi**
Bel'tsy Moldova *see* **Bălţi**
97 C1 **Belturbet** Ireland
77 E2 **Belukha, Gora** *mt.* Kazakh./Rus. Fed.
86 D2 **Belush'ye** Rus. Fed.
138 B2 **Belvidere** U.S.A.
51 D2 **Belyando** *r.* Austr.
89 D2 **Belyy** Rus. Fed.
82 F2 **Belyy, Ostrov** *i.* Rus. Fed.
101 F1 **Belzig** Ger.
137 E1 **Bemidji** U.S.A.
118 C3 **Bena Dibele** Dem. Rep. Congo
53 C3 **Benalla** Austr.
Benares India *see* **Varanasi**
115 D1 **Ben Arous** Tunisia
118 C3 **Bena-Sungu** Dem. Rep. Congo
106 B1 **Benavente** Spain
96 A2 **Benbecula** *i.* U.K.
134 B2 **Bend** U.S.A.
123 C3 **Bendearg** *mt.* S. Africa
Bender Moldova *see* **Tighina**
Bendery Moldova *see* **Tighina**
52 B3 **Bendigo** Austr.
121 C2 **Bene** Moz.
102 C2 **Benešov** Czech Rep.
109 B2 **Benevento** Italy
73 C3 **Bengal, Bay of** *sea* Indian Ocean
Bengaluru India *see* **Bangalore**
70 B2 **Bengbu** China
115 E1 **Benghazi** Libya
60 B1 **Bengkalis** Indon.
60 B1 **Bengkayang** Indon.
60 B2 **Bengkulu** Indon.
120 A2 **Benguela** Angola
Benha Egypt *see* **Banhā**
96 B1 **Ben Hope** *h.* U.K.
152 B1 **Beni** *r.* Bol.
119 C2 **Beni** Dem. Rep. Congo
114 B1 **Beni Abbès** Alg.
107 C2 **Benidorm** Spain
114 B1 **Beni Mellal** Morocco
114 C3 **Benin** *country* Africa
114 C4 **Benin, Bight of** *g.* Africa
115 C4 **Benin City** Nigeria
107 C2 **Beni Saf** Alg.
Beni Suef Egypt *see* **Banī Suwayf**
153 C3 **Benito Juárez** Arg.
150 C3 **Benjamim Constant** Brazil
144 A1 **Benjamín Hill** Mex.
59 C3 **Benjina** Indon.
136 C2 **Benkelman** U.S.A.
96 B2 **Ben Lawers** *mt.* U.K.
96 B2 **Ben Lomond** *h.* U.K.
96 C2 **Ben Macdui** *mt.* U.K.
96 A2 **Ben More** *h.* U.K.
96 B2 **Ben More** *mt.* U.K.
54 B2 **Benmore, Lake** N.Z.
96 B1 **Ben More Assynt** *h.* U.K.
128 A2 **Bennett** Can.
83 K1 **Bennetta, Ostrov** *i.* Rus. Fed.
Bennett Island *i.* Rus. Fed. *see* **Bennetta, Ostrov**
96 B2 **Ben Nevis** *mt.* U.K.
139 E2 **Bennington** U.S.A.
123 C2 **Benoni** S. Africa
115 D4 **Bénoye** Chad

101 D3 Bensheim Ger.
114 B1 Ben Slimane Morocco
142 A2 Benson U.S.A.
61 D2 Benteng Indon.
117 A4 Bentiu Sudan
138 B2 Benton Harbor U.S.A.
140 B1 Bentonville U.S.A.
63 B2 Bên Tre Vietnam
115 C4 Benue r. Nigeria
97 B1 Benwee Head hd Ireland
96 B2 Ben Wyvis mt. U.K.
70 C1 Benxi China
Beograd Serbia see Belgrade
75 C2 Beohari India
114 B4 Béoumi Côte d'Ivoire
67 B4 Beppu Japan
109 C2 Berane Montenegro
109 C2 Berat Albania
59 C3 Berau, Teluk b. Indon.
116 B3 Berber Sudan
117 C3 Berbera Somalia
118 B2 Berbérati C.A.R.
104 C1 Berck France
91 D2 Berdyans'k Ukr.
90 B2 Berdychiv Ukr.
90 A2 Berehove Ukr.
59 D3 Bereina P.N.G.
76 B3 Bereket Turkm.
129 E2 Berens River Can.
137 D2 Beresford U.S.A.
91 D2 Berezanskaya Rus. Fed.
90 A2 Berezhany Ukr.
90 C2 Berezivka Ukr.
90 B1 Berezne Ukr.
86 D2 Bereznik Rus. Fed.
86 E3 Berezniki Rus. Fed.
Berezov Rus. Fed. see Berezovo
86 F2 Berezovo Rus. Fed.
107 D1 Berga Spain
111 C3 Bergama Turkey
108 A1 Bergamo Italy
102 C1 Bergen Ger.
101 D1 Bergen Ger.
100 B1 Bergen Neth.
93 E3 Bergen Norway
100 B2 Bergen op Zoom Neth.
104 C3 Bergerac France
100 C2 Bergheim (Erft) Ger.
100 C2 Bergisch Gladbach Ger.
122 A1 Bergland Namibia
93 G3 Bergsjö Sweden
92 H2 Bergsviken Sweden
Berhampur India see Baharampur
83 M3 Beringa, Ostrov i. Rus. Fed.
100 B2 Beringen Belgium
124 A4 Bering Sea N. Pacific Ocean
124 B3 Bering Strait Rus. Fed./U.S.A.
100 C1 Berkel r. Neth.
135 B3 Berkeley U.S.A.
100 B1 Berkhout Neth.
55 B2 Berkner Island Antarctica
110 B2 Berkovitsa Bulg.
92 I1 Berlevåg Norway
101 F1 Berlin Ger.
139 E2 Berlin U.S.A.
101 E2 Berlingerode Ger.
53 D3 Bermagui Austr.
144 B2 Bermejíllo Mex.
152 B2 Bermejo Bol.
131 D2 Bermen, Lac l. Can.
125 L6 Bermuda terr. N. Atlantic Ocean
105 D2 Bern Switz.
101 E2 Bernburg (Saale) Ger.
127 G2 Bernier Bay Can.
50 A2 Bernier Island Austr.
100 C3 Bernkastel-Kues Ger.
121 □D3 Beroroha Madag.
52 B2 Berri Austr.
115 C1 Berriane Alg.
53 C3 Berrigan Austr.
107 D2 Berrouaghia Alg.
53 D2 Berry Austr.
146 C2 Berry Islands Bahamas
122 A2 Berseba Namibia
101 C1 Bersenbrück Ger.
90 B2 Bershad' Ukr.
131 D2 Berté, Lac l. Can.
118 B2 Bertoua Cameroon
150 C3 Beruri Brazil
98 B2 Berwick-upon-Tweed U.K.
91 C2 Beryslav Ukr.
121 □D2 Besalampy Madag.
105 D2 Besançon France
81 D3 Beshneh Iran
129 D2 Besnard Lake Can.
140 C2 Bessemer U.S.A.
76 B2 Besshoky, Gora h. Kazakh.
100 B2 Best Neth.
121 □D2 Betafo Madag.
106 B1 Betanzos Spain
118 B2 Bétaré Oya Cameroon
122 A2 Bethanie Namibia
100 B3 Bétheny France
139 D3 Bethesda U.S.A.
123 C2 Bethlehem S. Africa
139 D2 Bethlehem U.S.A.
123 C3 Bethulie S. Africa
105 C1 Béthune France
121 □D3 Betioky Madag.
51 D2 Betoota Austr.
77 D2 Betpak-Dala plain Kazakh.
121 □D3 Betroka Madag.
131 D3 Betsiamites Can.
121 □D2 Betsiboka r. Madag.
137 E2 Bettendorf U.S.A.
75 C2 Bettiah India
74 B2 Betul India
74 B2 Betwa r. India
99 B3 Betws-y-coed U.K.
100 C2 Betzdorf Ger.
136 C1 Beulah U.S.A.
98 C3 Beverley U.K.
101 D2 Beverungen Ger.
100 B1 Beverwijk Neth.
99 D4 Bexhill U.K.
111 C2 Beykoz Turkey
114 B4 Beyla Guinea
76 B2 Beyneu Kazakh.
80 B1 Beypazarı Turkey
Beyrouth Lebanon see Beirut
80 B2 Beyşehir Turkey
80 B2 Beyşehir Gölü l. Turkey
91 D2 Beysug r. Rus. Fed.
91 D2 Beysugskiy Liman lag. Rus. Fed.
88 C2 Bezhanitsy Rus. Fed.
89 E2 Bezhetsk Rus. Fed.
105 C3 Béziers France
Bhadgaon Nepal see Bhaktapur
75 C2 Bhadrak India
73 B3 Bhadravati India
75 C2 Bhagalpur India
74 A2 Bhairi Hol mt. Pak.
74 B1 Bhakkar Pak.
75 C2 Bhaktapur Nepal
62 A1 Bhamo Myanmar
75 C3 Bhanjanagar India
74 B2 Bharatpur India
74 B2 Bharuch India
74 B2 Bhavnagar India
75 C3 Bhawanipatna India
123 D2 Bhekuzulu S. Africa
74 B1 Bhera Pak.
74 B2 Bhilwara India
73 B3 Bhima r. India
74 B2 Bhind India
123 C3 Bhisho S. Africa
74 B2 Bhiwani India
123 C3 Bhongweni S. Africa
74 B2 Bhopal India
75 C2 Bhubaneshwar India
Bhubaneswar India see Bhubaneshwar
74 A2 Bhuj India
74 B2 Bhusawal India
75 D2 Bhutan country Asia
62 B2 Bia, Phou mt. Laos
Biafra, Bight of g. Africa see Benin, Bight of
59 D3 Biak Indon.
59 D3 Biak i. Indon.
103 E1 Biała Podlaska Pol.
103 D1 Białogard Pol.
103 E1 Białystok Pol.
109 C3 Bianco Italy
74 B2 Biaora India
104 B3 Biarritz France
105 D2 Biasca Switz.
66 D2 Bibai Japan
120 A2 Bibala Angola
53 C3 Bibbenluke Austr.
102 B2 Biberach an der Riß Ger.
155 D2 Bicas Brazil
73 B3 Bid India
115 C4 Bida Nigeria
73 B3 Bidar India
139 E2 Biddeford U.S.A.
96 B2 Bidean nam Bian mt. U.K.
99 A4 Bideford U.K.
Bié Angola see Kuito
120 A2 Bié, Planalto do Angola
101 D2 Biedenkopf Ger.
105 D2 Biel Switz.
101 D1 Bielefeld Ger.
108 A1 Biella Italy
103 D2 Bielsko-Biała Pol.
63 B2 Biên Hoa Vietnam
130 C2 Bienville, Lac l. Can.
100 B3 Bièvre Belgium
118 B3 Bifoun Gabon
111 C2 Biga Turkey
134 D1 Big Belt Mountains U.S.A.
123 D2 Big Bend Swaziland
129 D2 Biggar Can.
96 C3 Biggar U.K.
99 C3 Biggleswade U.K.
134 D1 Big Hole r. U.S.A.
134 E1 Bighorn U.S.A.
136 B1 Bighorn r. U.S.A.
136 B2 Bighorn Mountains U.S.A.
143 C2 Big Lake U.S.A.
138 B2 Big Rapids U.S.A.
129 D2 Big River Can.
129 E2 Big Sand Lake Can.
137 D2 Big Sioux r. U.S.A.
143 C2 Big Spring U.S.A.
134 E1 Big Timber U.S.A.
130 B2 Big Trout Lake Can.
130 A2 Big Trout Lake l. Can.
109 C2 Bihać Bos.-Herz.
75 C2 Bihar state India
75 C2 Bihar Sharif India
110 B1 Bihor, Vârful mt. Romania
114 A3 Bijagós, Arquipélago dos is Guinea-Bissau
73 B3 Bijapur India
81 C2 Bījār Iran
109 C2 Bijeljina Bos.-Herz.
109 C2 Bijelo Polje Montenegro
71 A3 Bijie China
74 B2 Bikaner India
66 B1 Bikin Rus. Fed.
66 B1 Bikin r. Rus. Fed.
118 B3 Bikoro Dem. Rep. Congo
79 C2 Bilād Banī Bū 'Alī Oman
75 C2 Bilaspur India
81 C2 Biläsuvar Azer.
90 C2 Bila Tserkva Ukr.
63 A2 Bilauktaung Range mts Myanmar/Thai.
106 C1 Bilbao Spain
109 C2 Bileća Bos.-Herz.
111 C2 Bilecik Turkey
103 E1 Biłgoraj Pol.
119 D3 Bilharamulo Tanz.
90 C2 Bilhorod-Dnistrovs'kyy Ukr.
119 C2 Bili Dem. Rep. Congo
83 M2 Bilibino Rus. Fed.
109 D2 Bilisht Albania
104 B3 Billère France
134 E1 Billings U.S.A.
99 B4 Bill of Portland hd U.K.
142 A1 Bill Williams Mountain U.S.A.
115 D3 Bilma Niger
115 D3 Bilma, Grand Erg de des. Niger
51 E2 Biloela Austr.
91 C2 Bilohirs'k Ukr.
90 B1 Bilohir"ya Ukr.
91 C1 Bilopillya Ukr.
91 D2 Bilovods'k Ukr.
140 C2 Biloxi U.S.A.
51 C2 Bilpa Morea Claypan salt flat Austr.
101 E2 Bilshausen Ger.
115 E3 Biltine Chad
90 C2 Bilyayivka Ukr.
114 C4 Bimbila Ghana
118 B2 Bimbo C.A.R.
141 E3 Bimini Islands Bahamas
74 B2 Bina-Etawa India
59 C3 Binaija, Gunung mt. Indon.
53 C1 Bindle Austr.
118 B3 Bindu Dem. Rep. Congo
121 C2 Bindura Zimbabwe
107 D1 Binefar Spain
120 B2 Binga Zimbabwe
53 D1 Bingara Austr.
100 C3 Bingen am Rhein Ger.
114 B4 Bingerville Côte d'Ivoire
139 F1 Bingham U.S.A.
139 D2 Binghamton U.S.A.
115 D2 Bin Ghanīmah, Jabal hills Libya
81 C2 Bingöl Turkey
62 A1 Bingzhongluo China
60 A1 Binjai Indon.
53 C2 Binnaway Austr.
60 B1 Bintan i. Indon.
60 B2 Bintuhan Indon.
61 C1 Bintulu Malaysia
115 C3 Bin-Yauri Nigeria
70 B2 Binzhou China
109 C2 Biograd na Moru Croatia
118 A2 Bioko i. Equat. Guinea
155 C1 Biquinhas Brazil
115 D2 Birāk Libya
118 C1 Birao C.A.R.
75 C2 Biratnagar Nepal
52 B3 Birchip Austr.
128 C2 Birch Mountains Can.
51 C2 Birdsville Austr.
80 B2 Birecik Turkey
Birendranagar Nepal see Surkhet
60 A1 Bireun Indon.
75 C2 Birganj Nepal
117 B3 Birhan mt. Eth.
154 B2 Birigüi Brazil
118 C2 Birini C.A.R.
76 B3 Bīrjand Iran
98 B3 Birkenhead U.K.
99 C3 Birmingham U.K.
140 C2 Birmingham U.S.A.
114 A2 Bîr Mogreïn Maur.
115 C3 Birnin-Kebbi Nigeria
115 C3 Birnin Konni Niger
69 E1 Birobidzhan Rus. Fed.
97 C2 Birr Ireland
96 C1 Birsay U.K.
78 A2 Bi'r Shalatayn Egypt
88 B2 Biržai Lith.
75 B2 Bisalpur India
142 B2 Bisbee U.S.A.
104 A2 Biscay, Bay of sea France/Spain
141 D3 Biscayne Bay U.S.A.
102 C2 Bischofshofen Austria
77 D2 Bishkek Kyrg.
135 C3 Bishop U.S.A.
98 C2 Bishop Auckland U.K.
69 E1 Bishui China
150 C2 Bisinaca Col.
115 C1 Biskra Alg.
64 B3 Bislig Phil.
136 C1 Bismarck U.S.A.
59 D3 Bismarck Archipelago is P.N.G.
59 D3 Bismarck Sea P.N.G.
107 D2 Bissa, Djebel mt. Alg.
114 A3 Bissau Guinea-Bissau
129 E2 Bissett Can.
128 C2 Bistcho Lake Can.
110 B1 Bistrița Romania
110 C1 Bistrița r. Romania
100 C3 Bitburg Ger.
105 D2 Bitche France
115 D3 Bitkine Chad
81 C2 Bitlis Turkey
111 B2 Bitola Macedonia
Bitolj Macedonia see Bitola
109 C2 Bitonto Italy
101 F2 Bitterfeld Ger.
122 A3 Bitterfontein S. Africa
134 D1 Bitterroot r. U.S.A.
134 C1 Bitterroot Range mts U.S.A.
89 E3 Bityug r. Rus. Fed.
115 D3 Biu Nigeria
67 C3 Biwa-ko l. Japan
77 E1 Biysk Rus. Fed.
Bizerta Tunisia see Bizerte
115 C1 Bizerte Tunisia
92 □A2 Bjargtangar hd Iceland
92 G3 Bjästa Sweden
109 C1 Bjelovar Croatia
92 G2 Bjerkvik Norway
Björneborg Fin. see Pori
82 C2 Bjørnøya Arctic Ocean
114 B3 Bla Mali
137 E3 Black r. U.S.A.
51 D2 Blackall Austr.
98 B3 Blackburn U.K.
134 D2 Blackfoot U.S.A.
102 B2 Black Forest mts Ger.
136 C2 Black Hills U.S.A.
96 B2 Black Isle pen. U.K.
129 D2 Black Lake Can.
129 D2 Black Lake l. Can.
99 B4 Black Mountains hills U.K.
142 A1 Black Mountains U.S.A.
98 B3 Blackpool U.K.
142 B2 Black Range mts U.S.A.
62 B1 Black River r. Vietnam
138 A2 Black River Falls U.S.A.
134 C2 Black Rock Desert U.S.A.
138 C3 Blacksburg U.S.A.
80 B1 Black Sea Asia/Europe
131 D3 Blacks Harbour Can.
97 A1 Blacksod Bay Ireland
97 C2 Blackstairs Mountains hills Ireland
114 B4 Black Volta r. Africa
51 D2 Blackwater Austr.
97 C2 Blackwater r. Ireland
128 B1 Blackwater Lake Can.
50 A3 Blackwood r. Austr.
87 D4 Blagodarnyy Rus. Fed.
111 B2 Blagoevgrad Bulg.
69 E1 Blagoveshchensk Rus. Fed.
129 D2 Blaine Lake Can.
137 D2 Blair U.S.A.
96 C2 Blair Atholl U.K.
96 C2 Blairgowrie U.K.
141 D2 Blakely U.S.A.
105 D2 Blanc, Mont mt. France/Italy
153 B3 Blanca, Bahía b. Arg.
52 A1 Blanche, Lake imp. l. Austr.
152 B1 Blanco r. Bol.
134 B2 Blanco, Cape U.S.A.
131 E2 Blanc-Sablon Can.
92 □A2 Blanda r. Iceland
99 B4 Blandford Forum U.K.
135 E3 Blanding U.S.A.
107 D1 Blanes Spain
60 A1 Blangkejeren Indon.
100 A2 Blankenberge Belgium
100 C2 Blankenheim Ger.
100 C2 Blankenrath Ger.
147 D3 Blanquilla, Isla i. Venez.
103 D2 Blansko Czech Rep.
121 C2 Blantyre Malawi
97 B3 Blarney Ireland
98 C2 Blaydon U.K.
53 C2 Blayney Austr.
54 B2 Blenheim N.Z.
115 C1 Blida Alg.
130 B3 Blind River Can.
123 C2 Bloemfontein S. Africa
123 C2 Bloemhof S. Africa
123 C2 Bloemhof Dam S. Africa
104 C2 Blois France
92 □A2 Blönduós Iceland
97 B1 Bloody Foreland pt Ireland
142 B1 Bloomfield U.S.A.
138 B2 Bloomington IL U.S.A.
138 B3 Bloomington IN U.S.A.
102 B2 Bludenz Austria
137 E2 Blue Earth U.S.A.
138 C3 Bluefield U.S.A.
146 B3 Bluefields Nic.
53 C2 Blue Mountains Austr.
134 C1 Blue Mountains U.S.A.
116 B3 Blue Nile r. Eth./Sudan
126 E2 Bluenose Lake Can.
138 C3 Blue Ridge mts U.S.A.
128 C2 Blue River Can.
97 B1 Blue Stack Mountains hills Ireland
54 A3 Bluff N.Z.
135 E3 Bluff U.S.A.
154 C3 Blumenau Brazil
52 A2 Blyth Austr.
98 C2 Blyth U.K.
135 D4 Blythe U.S.A.
140 C1 Blytheville U.S.A.
114 A4 Bo Sierra Leone
64 B2 Boac Phil.
146 B3 Boaco Nic.
151 E3 Boa Esperança, Açude resr Brazil
134 C1 Boardman U.S.A.
123 C1 Boatlaname Botswana
151 F3 Boa Viagem Brazil
150 C2 Boa Vista Brazil
53 C2 Bobadah Austr.
71 B3 Bobai China

121 □D2 Bobaomby, Tanjona c. Madag.
114 B3 Bobo-Dioulasso Burkina
121 B3 Bobonong Botswana
Bobriki Rus. Fed. see Novomoskovsk
89 F3 Bobrov Rus. Fed.
91 C1 Bobrovytsya Ukr.
91 C2 Bobrynets' Ukr.
121 □D3 Boby mt. Madag.
150 C3 Boca do Acre Brazil
155 D1 Bocaiúva Brazil
154 A2 Bocajá Brazil
118 B2 Bocaranga C.A.R.
141 D3 Boca Raton U.S.A.
146 B4 Bocas del Toro Panama
103 E2 Bochnia Pol.
100 B2 Bocholt Belgium
100 C2 Bocholt Ger.
100 C2 Bochum Ger.
101 E1 Bockenem Ger.
110 B1 Bocşa Romania
118 B2 Boda C.A.R.
83 I3 Bodaybo Rus. Fed.
96 D2 Boddam U.K.
115 D3 Bodélé reg. Chad
92 H2 Boden Sweden
Bodensee l. Ger./Switz. see Constance, Lake
99 A4 Bodmin U.K.
99 A4 Bodmin Moor moorland U.K.
92 F2 Bodø Norway
111 C3 Bodrum Turkey
118 C3 Boende Dem. Rep. Congo
63 A2 Bogale Myanmar
140 C2 Bogalusa U.S.A.
114 B3 Bogandé Burkina
118 B2 Bogangolo C.A.R.
80 B2 Boğazlıyan Turkey
68 B2 Bogda Shan mts China
53 D1 Boggabilla Austr.
53 D2 Boggabri Austr.
97 B2 Boggeragh Mountains hills Ireland
Boghari Alg. see Ksar el Boukhari
59 D3 Bogia P.N.G.
100 B3 Bogny-sur-Meuse France
97 C2 Bog of Allen reg. Ireland
53 C3 Bogong, Mount Austr.
60 B2 Bogor Indon.
89 E3 Bogoroditsk Rus. Fed.
150 B2 Bogotá Col.
83 G3 Bogotol Rus. Fed.
Bogoyavlenskoye Rus. Fed. see Pervomayskiy
83 H3 Boguchany Rus. Fed.
91 E2 Boguchar Rus. Fed.
114 A3 Bogué Maur.
70 B2 Bo Hai g. China
100 A3 Bohain-en-Vermandois France
70 B2 Bohai Wan b. China
Bohemian Forest mts Ger. see Böhmer Wald
123 C2 Bohlokong S. Africa
101 F3 Böhmer Wald mts Ger.
91 D1 Bohodukhiv Ukr.
64 B3 Bohol i. Phil.
64 B3 Bohol Sea Phil.
77 E2 Bohu China
155 C2 Boi, Ponta do pt Brazil
123 C2 Boikhutso S. Africa
154 B3 Boi Preto, Serra de hills Brazil
154 B1 Bois r. Brazil
126 D2 Bois, Lac des l. Can.
134 C2 Boise U.S.A.
143 C1 Boise City U.S.A.
129 D3 Boissevain Can.
123 C2 Boitumelong S. Africa
154 C2 Boituva Brazil
101 E1 Boizenburg Ger.
76 B3 Bojnūrd Iran
75 C2 Bokaro India
118 B3 Bokatola Dem. Rep. Congo
114 A3 Boké Guinea
118 C3 Bokele Dem. Rep. Congo
93 E4 Boknafjorden sea chan. Norway
115 D3 Bokoro Chad
63 A2 Bokpyin Myanmar
89 D2 Boksitogorsk Rus. Fed.
122 B2 Bokspits Botswana
118 C3 Bokungu Dem. Rep. Congo
115 D3 Bol Chad
114 A3 Bolama Guinea-Bissau
75 C2 Bolangir India
63 B2 Bolavén, Phouphiang plat. Laos
104 C2 Bolbec France
77 E2 Bole China
118 B3 Boleko Dem. Rep. Congo
114 B3 Bolgatanga Ghana
90 B2 Bolhrad Ukr.
66 B1 Boli China
118 B3 Bolia Dem. Rep. Congo
92 H3 Boliden Sweden
110 C2 Bolintin-Vale Romania
137 E3 Bolivar MO U.S.A.
140 C1 Bolivar TN U.S.A.
150 B2 Bolívar, Pico mt. Venez.
152 B1 Bolivia country S. America
89 E3 Bolkhov Rus. Fed.
105 C3 Bollène France
93 G3 Bollnäs Sweden
53 C1 Bollon Austr.
101 E2 Bollstedt Ger.
93 F4 Bolmen l. Sweden
118 B3 Bolobo Dem. Rep. Congo
108 B2 Bologna Italy
89 D2 Bologovo Rus. Fed.
89 D2 Bologoye Rus. Fed.
123 C2 Bolokanang S. Africa
118 B2 Bolomba Dem. Rep. Congo
108 B2 Bolsena, Lago di l. Italy
83 H1 Bol'shevik, Ostrov i. Rus. Fed.
86 E2 Bol'shezemel'skaya Tundra lowland Rus. Fed.
66 B2 Bol'shoy Kamen' Rus. Fed.
Bol'shoy Kavkaz mts Asia/Europe see Caucasus
83 K2 Bol'shoy Lyakhovskiy, Ostrov i. Rus. Fed.
Bol'shoy Tokmak Kyrg. see Tokmok
Bol'shoy Tokmak Ukr. see Tokmak
144 B2 Bolsón de Mapimí des. Mex.
100 B1 Bolsward Neth.
98 B3 Bolton U.K.
80 B1 Bolu Turkey
59 E3 Bolubolu P.N.G.
92 □A2 Bolungarvík Iceland
108 B1 Bolzano Italy
118 B3 Boma Dem. Rep. Congo
53 D2 Bomaderry Austr.
53 C3 Bombala Austr.
Bombay India see Mumbai
155 C1 Bom Despacho Brazil
75 D2 Bomdila India
154 B1 Bom Jardim de Goiás Brazil
151 E4 Bom Jesus da Lapa Brazil
155 D2 Bom Jesus do Itabapoana Brazil
115 D1 Bon, Cap c. Tunisia
147 D3 Bonaire i. Neth. Antilles
134 C1 Bonaparte, Mount U.S.A.
50 B1 Bonaparte Archipelago is Austr.
131 E3 Bonavista Can.
131 E3 Bonavista Bay Can.
118 C2 Bondo Dem. Rep. Congo
114 B4 Bondoukou Côte d'Ivoire
Bône Alg. see Annaba
61 D2 Bonerate, Kepulauan is Indon.
155 C1 Bonfinópolis de Minas Brazil
117 B4 Bonga Eth.
75 D2 Bongaigaon India
118 C2 Bongandanga Dem. Rep. Congo
122 B2 Bongani S. Africa
118 C2 Bongo, Massif des mts C.A.R.
121 □D2 Bongolava mts Madag.
115 D3 Bongor Chad
114 B4 Bongouanou Côte d'Ivoire
63 B2 Bông Sơn Vietnam
143 D2 Bonham U.S.A.
105 D3 Bonifacio France
108 A2 Bonifacio, Strait of France/Italy
69 F3 Bonin Islands is Japan
100 C2 Bonn Ger.
134 C1 Bonners Ferry U.S.A.
105 D2 Bonneville France
50 A3 Bonnie Rock Austr.
129 C2 Bonnyville Can.
108 A2 Bonorva Italy
53 D1 Bonshaw Austr.
61 C1 Bontang Indon.
114 A4 Bonthe Sierra Leone
64 B2 Bontoc Phil.
61 C2 Bontosunggu Indon.
123 C3 Bontrug S. Africa
53 C1 Boolba Austr.
52 B2 Booligal Austr.
53 C1 Boomi Austr.
53 D1 Boonah Austr.
137 E2 Boone U.S.A.
140 C2 Booneville U.S.A.
137 E3 Boonville U.S.A.
52 B2 Booroorban Austr.
53 C2 Boorowa Austr.
117 C3 Boosaaso Somalia
126 G2 Boothia, Gulf of Can.
126 F2 Boothia Peninsula Can.
118 B3 Booué Gabon
100 C2 Boppard Ger.
144 B2 Boquilla, Presa de la resr Mex.
109 D2 Bor Serbia
117 B4 Bor Sudan
80 B2 Bor Turkey
119 E2 Bor, Lagh watercourse Kenya/Somalia
121 □E2 Boraha, Nosy i. Madag.
93 F4 Borås Sweden
81 D3 Borāzjān Iran
150 D3 Borba Brazil
104 B3 Bordeaux France
126 E1 Borden Island Can.
127 G2 Borden Peninsula Can.
52 B3 Bordertown Austr.
107 D2 Bordj Bou Arréridj Alg.
107 D2 Bordj Bounaama Alg.
114 B2 Bordj Flye Ste-Marie Alg.
115 C1 Bordj Messaouda Alg.
114 C2 Bordj Mokhtar Alg.
Bordj Omar Driss Alg. see Bordj Omer Driss
115 C2 Bordj Omer Driss Alg.
94 B1 Borðoy i. Faroe Is
Borgå Fin. see Porvoo
92 □A3 Borgarnes Iceland
143 C1 Borger U.S.A.
93 G4 Borgholm Sweden
100 B2 Borgloon Belgium
108 A1 Borgosesia Italy
87 D3 Borisoglebsk Rus. Fed.
89 E2 Borisoglebskiy Rus. Fed.
91 D1 Borisovka Rus. Fed.
119 C2 Bo River Post Sudan
100 C2 Borken Ger.
92 G2 Borkenes Norway
100 C1 Borkum Ger.
100 C1 Borkum i. Ger.
93 G3 Borlänge Sweden
101 F2 Borna Ger.
100 C1 Borne Neth.
61 C1 Borneo i. Asia
93 F4 Bornholm i. Denmark
111 C3 Bornova Turkey
90 B1 Borodyanka Ukr.
77 E2 Borohoro Shan mts China
114 B3 Boron Mali
89 D2 Borovichi Rus. Fed.
89 E2 Borovsk Rus. Fed.
76 C1 Borovskoy Kazakh.
51 C1 Borroloola Austr.
110 B1 Borşa Romania
76 B2 Borsakelmas sho'rxogi salt marsh Uzbek.
90 B2 Borshchiv Ukr.
69 D1 Borshchovochnyy Khrebet mts Rus. Fed.
101 E1 Börßum Ger.
Bortala China see Bole
81 C2 Borujerd Iran
90 A2 Boryslav Ukr.
90 C1 Boryspil' Ukr.
91 C1 Borzna Ukr.
69 D1 Borzya Rus. Fed.
109 C1 Bosanska Dubica Bos.-Herz.
109 C1 Bosanska Gradiška Bos.-Herz.
109 C2 Bosanska Krupa Bos.-Herz.
109 C1 Bosanski Novi Bos.-Herz.
109 C2 Bosansko Grahovo Bos.-Herz.
71 A3 Bose China
123 C2 Boshof S. Africa
109 C2 Bosnia-Herzegovina country Europe
118 B2 Bosobolo Dem. Rep. Congo
111 C2 Bosporus str. Turkey
142 B2 Bosque U.S.A.
118 B2 Bossangoa C.A.R.
118 B2 Bossembélé C.A.R.
140 B2 Bossier City U.S.A.
122 A2 Bossiesvlei Namibia
68 B2 Bosten Hu l. China
99 C3 Boston U.K.
139 E2 Boston U.S.A.
140 B1 Boston Mountains U.S.A.
53 D2 Botany Bay Austr.
120 B3 Boteti r. Botswana
110 B2 Botev mt. Bulg.
80 A1 Botevgrad Bulg.
92 G3 Bothnia, Gulf of Fin./Sweden
110 C1 Botoşani Romania
70 B2 Botou China
123 C2 Botshabelo S. Africa
120 B3 Botswana country Africa
109 C3 Botte Donato, Monte mt. Italy
136 C1 Bottineau U.S.A.
100 C2 Bottrop Ger.
154 C2 Botucatu Brazil
114 B4 Bouaké Côte d'Ivoire
118 B2 Bouar C.A.R.
114 B1 Bouârfa Morocco
131 D3 Bouctouche Can.
107 E2 Bougaa Alg.
48 G4 Bougainville Island P.N.G.
Bougie Alg. see Bejaïa
114 B3 Bougouni Mali
100 B3 Bouillon Belgium
107 D2 Bouira Alg.
114 A2 Boujdour Western Sahara
50 B3 Boulder Austr.
136 B2 Boulder CO U.S.A.
134 D1 Boulder MT U.S.A.
135 D3 Boulder City U.S.A.
Boulhaut Morocco see Ben Slimane
51 C2 Boulia Austr.
104 C2 Boulogne-Billancourt France
104 C1 Boulogne-sur-Mer France
118 C2 Boulouba C.A.R.
118 B3 Boumango Gabon
118 B2 Boumba r. Cameroon
107 D2 Boumerdes Alg.
114 B4 Bouna Côte d'Ivoire
114 B4 Boundiali Côte d'Ivoire
134 D2 Bountiful U.S.A.
49 I8 Bounty Islands N.Z.
114 B3 Bourem Mali
104 C2 Bourganeuf France
105 D2 Bourg-en-Bresse France
104 C2 Bourges France
Bourgogne reg. France see Burgundy
105 D2 Bourgoin-Jallieu France
53 C2 Bourke Austr.
99 C3 Bourne U.K.
99 C4 Bournemouth U.K.
118 C1 Bourtoutou Chad
115 C1 Bou Saâda Alg.
115 D3 Bousso Chad
100 A2 Boussu Belgium
114 A3 Boutilimit Maur.
128 C3 Bow r. Can.
Bowa China see Muli
51 D2 Bowen Austr.
53 C3 Bowen, Mount Austr.
129 C3 Bow Island Can.
138 B3 Bowling Green KY U.S.A.
137 E3 Bowling Green MO U.S.A.
138 C2 Bowling Green OH U.S.A.
136 C1 Bowman U.S.A.
53 D2 Bowral Austr.
101 D3 Boxberg Ger.
100 B2 Boxtel Neth.
80 B1 Boyabat Turkey
Boyang China see Poyang
97 B2 Boyle Ireland
97 C2 Boyne r. Ireland
136 B2 Boysen Reservoir U.S.A.
152 B2 Boyuibe Bol.
111 C3 Bozburun Turkey
111 C3 Bozcaada i. Turkey
111 C3 Bozdağ mt. Turkey
111 C3 Boz Dağları mts Turkey
111 C3 Bozdoğan Turkey
134 D1 Bozeman U.S.A.
118 B2 Bozoum C.A.R.
111 D3 Bozüyük Turkey
109 C2 Brač i. Croatia
130 C3 Bracebridge Can.
93 G3 Bräcke Sweden
99 C4 Bracknell U.K.
109 C2 Bradano r. Italy
141 D3 Bradenton U.S.A.
147 B3 Brades Montserrat
98 C3 Bradford U.K.
139 D2 Bradford U.S.A.
143 D2 Brady U.S.A.
96 C2 Braemar U.K.
106 B1 Braga Port.
151 E3 Bragança Brazil
106 B1 Bragança Port.
155 C2 Bragança Paulista Brazil
89 D3 Brahin Belarus
75 D2 Brahmanbaria Bangl.
75 C3 Brahmapur India
62 A1 Brahmaputra r. China/India
53 C3 Braidwood Austr.
110 C1 Brăila Romania
137 E1 Brainerd U.S.A.
99 D4 Braintree U.K.
100 B2 Braives Belgium
101 D1 Brake (Unterweser) Ger.
122 A1 Brakwater Namibia
98 B2 Brampton U.K.
101 D1 Bramsche Ger.
150 C3 Branco r. Brazil
101 F1 Brandenburg Ger.
129 E3 Brandon Can.
140 C2 Brandon U.S.A.
97 A2 Brandon Mountain h. Ireland
122 B3 Brandvlei S. Africa
103 D1 Braniewo Pol.
130 B3 Brantford Can.
53 D2 Branxton Austr.
131 D3 Bras d'Or Lake Can.
155 D1 Brasil, Planalto do plat. Brazil
154 C1 Brasilândia Brazil
154 C1 Brasília Brazil
155 D1 Brasília de Minas Brazil
88 C2 Braslaw Belarus
110 C1 Braşov Romania
103 D2 Bratislava Slovakia
83 H3 Bratsk Rus. Fed.
102 C2 Braunau am Inn Austria
101 E1 Braunschweig Ger.
92 □A2 Brautarholt Iceland
Bravo del Norte, Río r. Mex./U.S.A. see Rio Grande
135 C4 Brawley U.S.A.
97 C2 Bray Ireland
150 D2 Brazil country S. America
158 E6 Brazil Basin S. Atlantic Ocean
143 D3 Brazos r. U.S.A.
118 B3 Brazzaville Congo
109 C2 Brčko Bos.-Herz.
96 C2 Brechin U.K.
100 B2 Brecht Belgium
143 D2 Breckenridge U.S.A.
103 D2 Břeclav Czech Rep.
99 B4 Brecon U.K.
99 B4 Brecon Beacons reg. U.K.
100 B2 Breda Neth.
122 B3 Bredasdorp S. Africa
102 B2 Bregenz Austria
92 H1 Breivikbotn Norway
92 E3 Brekstad Norway
101 D1 Bremen Ger.
101 D1 Bremerhaven Ger.
Bremersdorp Swaziland see Manzini
134 B1 Bremerton U.S.A.
101 D1 Bremervörde Ger.
143 D2 Brenham U.S.A.
105 E2 Brennero Italy
102 C2 Brenner Pass Austria/Italy
99 D4 Brentwood U.K.
108 B1 Brescia Italy
100 A2 Breskens Neth.
105 E2 Bressanone Italy
96 □ Bressay i. U.K.
104 B2 Bressuire France
88 B3 Brest Belarus
104 B2 Brest France
Brest-Litovsk Belarus see Brest
Bretagne reg. France see Brittany
140 C3 Breton Sound b. U.S.A.
151 D3 Breves Brazil
53 C1 Brewarrina Austr.
134 C1 Brewster U.S.A.
89 E2 Breytovo Rus. Fed.
Brezhnev Rus. Fed. see Naberezhnyye Chelny
109 C1 Brezovo Polje plain Croatia
118 C2 Bria C.A.R.
105 D3 Briançon France
90 B2 Briceni Moldova
Brichany Moldova see Briceni
99 B4 Bridgend U.K.

139 E2 **Bridgeport** *CT* U.S.A.
136 C2 **Bridgeport** *NE* U.S.A.
147 E3 **Bridgetown** Barbados
131 D3 **Bridgewater** Can.
99 B3 **Bridgnorth** U.K.
99 B4 **Bridgwater** U.K.
99 B4 **Bridgwater Bay** U.K.
98 C2 **Bridlington** U.K.
98 C2 **Bridlington Bay** U.K.
99 B4 **Bridport** U.K.
105 D2 **Brig** Switz.
134 D2 **Brigham City** U.S.A.
53 C3 **Bright** Austr.
54 B3 **Brighton** N.Z.
99 C4 **Brighton** U.K.
136 C3 **Brighton** *CO* U.S.A.
138 C2 **Brighton** *MI* U.S.A.
105 D3 **Brignoles** France
114 A3 **Brikama** Gambia
101 D2 **Brilon** Ger.
109 C2 **Brindisi** Italy
Brinlack Ireland *see* **Bun na Leaca**
53 D1 **Brisbane** Austr.
99 B4 **Bristol** U.K.
139 E2 **Bristol** *CT* U.S.A.
141 D1 **Bristol** *TN* U.S.A.
99 A4 **Bristol Channel** *est.* U.K.
128 B2 **British Columbia** *prov.* Can.
British Guiana *country* S. America *see* **Guyana**
British Honduras *country* Central America *see* **Belize**
56 C6 **British Indian Ocean Territory** *terr.* Indian Ocean
95 B2 **British Isles** *is* Europe
British Solomon Islands *country* S. Pacific Ocean *see* **Solomon Islands**
123 C2 **Brits** S. Africa
122 B3 **Britstown** S. Africa
104 B2 **Brittany** *reg.* France
104 C2 **Brive-la-Gaillarde** France
106 C1 **Briviesca** Spain
99 B4 **Brixham** U.K.
103 D2 **Brno** Czech Rep.
Broach India *see* **Bharuch**
141 D2 **Broad** *r.* U.S.A.
130 C2 **Broadback** *r.* Can.
53 C3 **Broadford** Austr.
96 B2 **Broadford** U.K.
96 C3 **Broad Law** *h.* U.K.
136 B1 **Broadus** U.S.A.
129 D2 **Brochet** Can.
129 D2 **Brochet, Lac** *l.* Can.
131 D3 **Brochet, Lac au** *l.* Can.
101 E1 **Bröckel** Ger.
101 E2 **Brocken** *mt.* Ger.
126 E1 **Brock Island** Can.
130 C3 **Brockville** Can.
127 G2 **Brodeur Peninsula** Can.
96 B3 **Brodick** U.K.
103 D1 **Brodnica** Pol.
90 B1 **Brody** Ukr.
143 D1 **Broken Arrow** U.S.A.
137 D2 **Broken Bow** U.S.A.
52 B2 **Broken Hill** Austr.
Broken Hill Zambia *see* **Kabwe**
159 F6 **Broken Plateau** Indian Ocean
151 D2 **Brokopondo** Suriname
99 B3 **Bromsgrove** U.K.
93 E4 **Brønderslev** Denmark
123 C2 **Bronkhorstspruit** S. Africa
92 F2 **Brønnøysund** Norway
64 A3 **Brooke's Point** Phil.
140 B2 **Brookhaven** U.S.A.
134 B2 **Brookings** *OR* U.S.A.
137 D2 **Brookings** *SD* U.S.A.
128 C2 **Brooks** Can.
126 C2 **Brooks Range** *mts* U.S.A.
141 D3 **Brooksville** U.S.A.
139 D2 **Brookville** U.S.A.
96 B2 **Broom, Loch** *inlet* U.K.
50 B1 **Broome** Austr.
134 B2 **Brothers** U.S.A.
Broughton Island Can. *see* **Qikiqtarjuaq**
90 C1 **Brovary** Ukr.
143 C2 **Brownfield** U.S.A.
128 C3 **Browning** U.S.A.
140 C1 **Brownsville** *TN* U.S.A.
143 D3 **Brownsville** *TX* U.S.A.
143 D2 **Brownwood** U.S.A.
92 □A2 **Brú** Iceland
104 C1 **Bruay-la-Bussière** France
138 B1 **Bruce Crossing** U.S.A.
130 B3 **Bruce Peninsula** Can.
103 D2 **Bruck an der Mur** Austria
Bruges Belgium *see* **Brugge**
100 A2 **Brugge** Belgium
62 A1 **Bruint** India
128 C2 **Brûlé** Can.
151 E4 **Brumado** Brazil
93 F3 **Brumunddal** Norway
61 C1 **Brunei** *country* Asia
Brunei Brunei *see* **Bandar Seri Begawan**
102 C2 **Brunico** Italy
Brünn Czech Rep. *see* **Brno**
101 D1 **Brunsbüttel** Ger.
141 D2 **Brunswick** *GA* U.S.A.
139 F2 **Brunswick** *ME* U.S.A.
53 D1 **Brunswick Heads** Austr.
123 D2 **Bruntville** S. Africa
136 C2 **Brush** U.S.A.
100 B2 **Brussels** Belgium
Bruxelles Belgium *see* **Brussels**
143 D2 **Bryan** U.S.A.
89 D3 **Bryansk** Rus. Fed.
91 D2 **Bryn'kovskaya** Rus. Fed.
91 D2 **Bryukhovetskaya** Rus. Fed.
103 D1 **Brzeg** Pol.
Brześć nad Bugiem Belarus *see* **Brest**
114 A3 **Buba** Guinea-Bissau
111 C3 **Buca** Turkey
80 B2 **Bucak** Turkey
150 B2 **Bucaramanga** Col.
90 B2 **Buchach** Ukr.
53 C3 **Buchan** Austr.
114 A4 **Buchanan** Liberia
110 C2 **Bucharest** Romania
101 D1 **Bucholz in der Nordheide** Ger.
110 C1 **Bucin, Pasul** *pass* Romania
101 D1 **Bückeburg** Ger.
142 A2 **Buckeye** U.S.A.
96 C2 **Buckhaven** U.K.
96 C2 **Buckie** U.K.
99 C3 **Buckingham** U.K.
51 C1 **Buckingham Bay** Austr.
51 D2 **Buckland Tableland** *reg.* Austr.
52 A2 **Buckleboo** Austr.
139 F2 **Bucksport** U.S.A.
103 D2 **Bučovice** Czech Rep.
București Romania *see* **Bucharest**
89 D3 **Buda-Kashalyova** Belarus
103 D2 **Budapest** Hungary
75 B2 **Budaun** India
108 A2 **Buddusò** Italy
99 A4 **Bude** U.K.
87 D4 **Budennovsk** Rus. Fed.
Budennoye Rus. Fed. *see* **Krasnogvardeyskoye**
89 D2 **Budogoshch'** Rus. Fed.
108 A2 **Budoni** Italy
Budweis Czech Rep. *see* **České Budějovice**
118 A2 **Buea** Cameroon
135 B4 **Buellton** U.S.A.
150 B2 **Buenaventura** Col.
144 B2 **Buenaventura** Mex.
Buena Vista *i.* N. Mariana Is *see* **Tinian**
106 C1 **Buendia, Embalse de** *resr* Spain
155 D1 **Buenópolis** Brazil
153 C3 **Buenos Aires** Arg.
153 A4 **Buenos Aires, Lago** *l.* Arg./Chile
139 D2 **Buffalo** *NY* U.S.A.
136 C1 **Buffalo** *SD* U.S.A.
143 D2 **Buffalo** *TX* U.S.A.
136 B2 **Buffalo** *WY* U.S.A.
129 D2 **Buffalo Narrows** Can.
121 C3 **Buffalo Range** Zimbabwe
122 A2 **Buffels** *watercourse* S. Africa
123 C1 **Buffels Drift** S. Africa
110 C2 **Buftea** Romania
103 E1 **Bug** *r.* Pol.
61 C2 **Bugel, Tanjung** *pt* Indon.
109 C2 **Bugojno** Bos.-Herz.
86 D2 **Bugrino** Rus. Fed.
64 A3 **Bugsuk** *i.* Phil.
87 E3 **Bugul'ma** Rus. Fed.
87 E3 **Buguruslan** Rus. Fed.
121 C2 **Buhera** Zimbabwe
110 C1 **Buhuşi** Romania
99 B3 **Builth Wells** U.K.
69 D1 **Buir Nur** *l.* Mongolia
120 A3 **Buitepos** Namibia
109 D2 **Bujanovac** Serbia
119 C3 **Bujumbura** Burundi
69 D1 **Bukachacha** Rus. Fed.
120 B2 **Bukalo** Namibia
119 C3 **Bukavu** Dem. Rep. Congo
Bukhara Uzbek. *see* **Buxoro**
60 B2 **Bukittinggi** Indon.
119 D3 **Bukoba** Tanz.
103 D1 **Bukowiec** *h.* Pol.
59 C3 **Bula** Indon.
53 D2 **Bulahdelah** Austr.
121 B3 **Bulawayo** Zimbabwe
111 C3 **Buldan** Turkey
123 D2 **Bulembu** Swaziland
68 C1 **Bulgan** Mongolia
110 C2 **Bulgaria** *country* Europe
54 B2 **Buller** *r.* N.Z.
142 A1 **Bullhead City** U.S.A.
52 B1 **Bulloo** *watercourse* Austr.
52 B1 **Bulloo Downs** Austr.
122 A1 **Büllsport** Namibia
61 D2 **Bulukumba** Indon.
118 B3 **Bulungu** Dem. Rep. Congo
118 B3 **Bumba** Dem. Rep. Congo
118 C2 **Bumba** Dem. Rep. Congo
62 A1 **Bumhkang** Myanmar
118 B3 **Buna** Dem. Rep. Congo
Bun Beg Ireland *see* **An Bun Beag**
50 A3 **Bunbury** Austr.
97 C2 **Bunclody** Ireland
97 C1 **Buncrana** Ireland
119 D3 **Bunda** Tanz.
51 E2 **Bundaberg** Austr.
53 C1 **Bundaleer** Austr.
53 D2 **Bundarra** Austr.
74 B2 **Bundi** India
97 B1 **Bundoran** Ireland
75 C2 **Bundu** India
53 C3 **Bungendore** Austr.
119 D2 **Bungoma** Kenya
67 B4 **Bungo-suidō** *sea chan.* Japan
119 D2 **Bunia** Dem. Rep. Congo
118 C3 **Bunianga** Dem. Rep. Congo
97 B1 **Bun na Leaca** Ireland
63 B2 **Buôn Ma Thuột** Vietnam
119 D3 **Bura** Kenya
117 C3 **Buraan** Somalia
Burang China *see* **Jirang**
78 B2 **Buraydah** Saudi Arabia
101 D2 **Burbach** Ger.
117 C4 **Burco** Somalia
100 B1 **Burdaard** Neth.
111 D3 **Burdur** Turkey
Burdwan India *see* **Barddhaman**
117 B3 **Burē** Eth.
99 D3 **Bure** *r.* U.K.
69 E1 **Bureinskiy Khrebet** *mts* Rus. Fed.
101 D2 **Büren** Ger.
74 B1 **Burewala** Pak.
Bureya Range *mts* Rus. Fed. *see* **Bureinskiy Khrebet**
110 C2 **Burgas** Bulg.
101 E1 **Burg bei Magdeburg** Ger.
101 E1 **Burgdorf** *Niedersachsen* Ger.
101 E1 **Burgdorf** *Niedersachsen* Ger.
131 E3 **Burgeo** Can.
123 C3 **Burgersdorp** S. Africa
123 D1 **Burgersfort** S. Africa
100 A2 **Burgh-Haamstede** Neth.
101 F3 **Burglengenfeld** Ger.
145 C2 **Burgos** Mex.
106 C1 **Burgos** Spain
105 C2 **Burgundy** *reg.* France
111 C3 **Burhaniye** Turkey
74 B2 **Burhanpur** India
75 C2 **Burhar-Dhanpuri** India
101 D1 **Burhave (Butjadingen)** Ger.
154 C2 **Buri** Brazil
60 B2 **Buriai** Indon.
64 B2 **Burias** *i.* Phil.
131 E3 **Burin** Can.
63 B2 **Buriram** Thai.
154 C1 **Buriti Alegre** Brazil
151 E3 **Buriti Bravo** Brazil
155 C1 **Buritis** Brazil
107 C2 **Burjassot** Spain
143 D2 **Burkburnett** U.S.A.
51 C1 **Burketown** Austr.
114 B3 **Burkina** *country* Africa
134 D2 **Burley** U.S.A.
136 C3 **Burlington** *CO* U.S.A.
137 E2 **Burlington** *IA* U.S.A.
141 E1 **Burlington** *NC* U.S.A.
139 E2 **Burlington** *VT* U.S.A.
134 B2 **Burney** U.S.A.
51 D4 **Burnie** Austr.
98 B3 **Burnley** U.K.
134 C2 **Burns** U.S.A.
134 C2 **Burns Junction** U.S.A.
128 B2 **Burns Lake** Can.
137 E2 **Burnsville** U.S.A.
101 F1 **Burow** Ger.
77 E2 **Burqin** China
52 A2 **Burra** Austr.
109 D2 **Burrel** Albania
97 B2 **Burren** *reg.* Ireland
53 C2 **Burrendong, Lake** Austr.
53 C2 **Burren Junction** Austr.
107 C2 **Burriana** Spain
53 C2 **Burrinjuck Reservoir** Austr.
144 B2 **Burro, Serranías del** *mts* Mex.
111 C2 **Bursa** Turkey
116 B2 **Būr Safājah** Egypt
Būr Sa'īd Egypt *see* **Port Said**
Būr Sa'īd Egypt *see* **Port Said**
Būr Sudan Sudan *see* **Port Sudan**
130 C2 **Burton, Lac** *l.* Can.
Burtonport Ireland *see* **Ailt an Chorráin**
99 C3 **Burton upon Trent** U.K.
52 B2 **Burtundy** Austr.
59 C3 **Buru** *i.* Indon.
119 C3 **Burundi** *country* Africa
119 C3 **Bururi** Burundi
96 C1 **Burwick** U.K.
98 B3 **Bury** U.K.
91 C1 **Buryn'** Ukr.
76 B2 **Burynshyk** Kazakh.
99 D3 **Bury St Edmunds** U.K.
118 C3 **Busanga** Dem. Rep. Congo
81 D3 **Būshehr** Iran
119 D3 **Bushenyi** Uganda
Bushire Iran *see* **Būshehr**
118 C2 **Businga** Dem. Rep. Congo
50 A3 **Busselton** Austr.
143 C3 **Bustamante** Mex.
108 A1 **Busto Arsizio** Italy
64 A2 **Busuanga** Phil.
118 C2 **Buta** Dem. Rep. Congo
119 C3 **Butare** Rwanda
96 B3 **Bute** *i.* U.K.
119 C2 **Butembo** Dem. Rep. Congo
123 C2 **Butha-Buthe** Lesotho
139 D2 **Butler** U.S.A.
61 D2 **Buton** *i.* Indon.
134 D1 **Butte** U.S.A.
60 B1 **Butterworth** Malaysia
96 A1 **Butt of Lewis** *hd* U.K.
129 E2 **Button Bay** Can.
131 D1 **Button Islands** Can.
64 B3 **Butuan** Phil.
89 F3 **Buturlinovka** Rus. Fed.
75 C2 **Butwal** Nepal
101 D2 **Butzbach** Ger.
117 C4 **Buulobarde** Somalia
117 C5 **Buur Gaabo** Somalia
117 C4 **Buurhabaka** Somalia
78 A2 **Buwāṭah** Saudi Arabia
76 C3 **Buxoro** Uzbek.
101 D1 **Buxtehude** Ger.
98 C3 **Buxton** U.K.
89 F2 **Buy** Rus. Fed.
87 D4 **Buynaksk** Rus. Fed.
111 C3 **Büyükmenderes** *r.* Turkey
65 A1 **Buyun Shan** *mt.* China
74 B1 **Buzai Gumbad** Afgh.
110 C1 **Buzău** Romania
110 C1 **Buzău** *r.* Romania
121 C2 **Búzi** Moz.
87 E3 **Buzuluk** Rus. Fed.
88 C3 **Byahoml'** Belarus
110 C2 **Byala** *Sliven* Bulg.
110 C2 **Byala** *Varna* Bulg.
88 C3 **Byalynichy** Belarus
88 D3 **Byarezina** *r.* Belarus
88 B3 **Byaroza** Belarus
88 C3 **Byarozawka** Belarus
103 D1 **Bydgoszcz** Pol.
Byelorussia *country* Europe *see* **Belarus**
88 C3 **Byerazino** Belarus
88 C2 **Byeshankovichy** Belarus
89 D3 **Bykhaw** Belarus
127 G2 **Bylot Island** Can.
53 C2 **Byrock** Austr.
53 D1 **Byron Bay** Austr.
83 J2 **Bytantay** *r.* Rus. Fed.
103 D1 **Bytom** Pol.
103 D1 **Bytów** Pol.

C

120 A2 **Caála** Angola
154 B2 **Caarapó** Brazil
155 C1 **Caatinga** Brazil
144 B2 **Caballos Mesteños, Llano de los** *plain* Mex.
106 B1 **Cabañaquinta** Spain
64 B2 **Cabanatuan** Phil.
117 C3 **Cabdul Qaadir** Somalia
154 A1 **Cabeceira Rio Manso** Brazil
154 C1 **Cabeceiras** Brazil
106 B2 **Cabeza del Buey** Spain
152 B1 **Cabezas** Bol.
150 B1 **Cabimas** Venez.
120 A1 **Cabinda** Angola
118 B3 **Cabinda** *prov.* Angola
151 F3 **Cabo de Santo Agostinho** Brazil
155 D2 **Cabo Frio** Brazil
155 D2 **Cabo Frio, Ilha do** *i.* Brazil
130 C3 **Cabonga, Réservoir** *resr* Can.
53 D1 **Caboolture** Austr.
150 B3 **Cabo Pantoja** Peru
121 C2 **Cabora Bassa, Lake** *resr* Moz.
144 A1 **Caborca** Mex.
131 D3 **Cabot Strait** Can.
106 C2 **Cabra** Spain
155 D1 **Cabral, Serra do** *mts* Brazil
107 D2 **Cabrera, Illa de** *i.* Spain
106 B1 **Cabrera, Sierra de la** *mts* Spain
129 D2 **Cabri** Can.
107 C2 **Cabriel** *r.* Spain
154 B3 **Caçador** Brazil
109 D2 **Čačak** Serbia
108 A2 **Caccia, Capo** *c.* Italy
106 B2 **Cacém** Port.
151 D4 **Cáceres** Brazil
106 B2 **Cáceres** Spain
128 B2 **Cache Creek** Can.
114 A3 **Cacheu** Guinea-Bissau
151 D3 **Cachimbo, Serra do** *hills* Brazil
154 B1 **Cachoeira Alta** Brazil
155 D2 **Cachoeiro de Itapemirim** Brazil
114 A3 **Cacine** Guinea-Bissau
120 A2 **Cacolo** Angola
120 A2 **Caconda** Angola
154 B1 **Caçu** Brazil
103 D2 **Čadca** Slovakia
101 D1 **Cadenberge** Ger.
145 B2 **Cadereyta** Mex.
138 B2 **Cadillac** U.S.A.
64 B2 **Cadiz** Phil.
106 B2 **Cádiz** Spain
106 B2 **Cádiz, Golfo de** *g.* Spain
128 C2 **Cadotte Lake** Can.
104 B2 **Caen** France
Caerdydd U.K. *see* **Cardiff**
Caerfyrddin U.K. *see* **Carmarthen**
Caergybi U.K. *see* **Holyhead**
98 A3 **Caernarfon** U.K.
99 A3 **Caernarfon Bay** U.K.
Caernarvon U.K. *see* **Caernarfon**
152 B2 **Cafayate** Arg.
154 C2 **Cafelândia** Brazil
64 B3 **Cagayan de Oro** Phil.
64 A3 **Cagayan de Tawi-Tawi** *i.* Phil.
108 B2 **Cagli** Italy
108 A3 **Cagliari** Italy
108 A3 **Cagliari, Golfo di** *b.* Italy
76 B2 **Çagyl** Turkm.
120 A2 **Cahama** Angola
97 B3 **Caha Mountains** *hills* Ireland
97 A3 **Cahermore** Ireland
97 C2 **Cahir** Ireland
97 A3 **Cahirsiveen** Ireland
Cahora Bassa, Lago de *resr* Moz. *see* **Cabora Bassa, Lake**

97 C2 **Cahore Point** Ireland
104 C3 **Cahors** France
90 B2 **Cahul** Moldova
121 C2 **Caia** Moz.
151 D4 **Caiabis, Serra dos** *hills* Brazil
120 B2 **Caianda** Angola
154 B1 **Caiapó, Serra do** *mts* Brazil
154 B1 **Caiapônia** Brazil
147 C2 **Caicos Islands** Turks and Caicos Is
96 C2 **Cairngorm Mountains** U.K.
96 B3 **Cairnryan** U.K.
51 D1 **Cairns** Austr.
116 B1 **Cairo** Egypt
Caisleán an Bharraigh Ireland *see* **Castlebar**
98 C3 **Caistor** U.K.
120 A2 **Caiundo** Angola
150 B3 **Cajamarca** Peru
109 C1 **Čakovec** Croatia
123 C3 **Cala** S. Africa
115 C4 **Calabar** Nigeria
150 C2 **Calabozo** Venez.
110 B2 **Calafat** Romania
153 A5 **Calafate** Arg.
107 C1 **Calahorra** Spain
120 A2 **Calai** Angola
104 C1 **Calais** France
139 F1 **Calais** U.S.A.
152 B2 **Calama** Chile
64 A2 **Calamian Group** *is* Phil.
107 C1 **Calamocha** Spain
120 A1 **Calandula** Angola
60 A1 **Calang** Indon.
64 B2 **Calapan** Phil.
110 C2 **Călărași** Romania
107 C1 **Calatayud** Spain
64 B2 **Calayan** *i.* Phil.
64 B2 **Calbayog** Phil.
151 F3 **Calcanhar, Ponta do** *pt* Brazil
151 D2 **Calçoene** Brazil
Calcutta India *see* **Kolkata**
106 B2 **Caldas da Rainha** Port.
154 C1 **Caldas Novas** Brazil
152 A2 **Caldera** Chile
51 D2 **Caldervale** Austr.
134 C2 **Caldwell** U.S.A.
123 C3 **Caledon** *r.* Lesotho/S. Africa
122 A3 **Caledon** S. Africa
153 B4 **Caleta Olivia** Arg.
98 A2 **Calf of Man** *i.* Isle of Man
128 C2 **Calgary** Can.
150 B2 **Cali** Col.
Calicut India *see* **Kozhikode**
135 D3 **Caliente** U.S.A.
135 B2 **California** *state* U.S.A.
144 A1 **California, Gulf of** *g.* Mex.
135 B3 **California Aqueduct** *canal* U.S.A.
81 C2 **Cälilabad** Azer.
122 B3 **Calitzdorp** S. Africa
145 C2 **Calkiní** Mex.
52 B1 **Callabonna, Lake** *imp. l.* Austr.
135 C3 **Callaghan, Mount** U.S.A.
97 C2 **Callan** Ireland
96 B2 **Callander** U.K.
150 B4 **Callao** Peru
99 A4 **Callington** U.K.
108 B3 **Caltagirone** Italy
108 B3 **Caltanissetta** Italy
120 A1 **Calulo** Angola
120 B2 **Calunda** Angola
120 A2 **Caluquembe** Angola
117 D3 **Caluula** Somalia
105 D3 **Calvi** France
107 D2 **Calvià** Spain
144 B2 **Calvillo** Mex.
122 A3 **Calvinia** S. Africa
109 C2 **Calvo, Monte** *mt.* Italy
120 A1 **Camabatela** Angola
151 F4 **Camaçari** Brazil
144 B2 **Camacho** Mex.
120 A2 **Camacupa** Angola
146 C2 **Camagüey** Cuba
146 C2 **Camagüey, Archipiélago de** *is* Cuba
150 B4 **Camana** Peru
120 B2 **Camanongue** Angola
154 B1 **Camapuã** Brazil
145 C2 **Camargo** Mex.
63 B3 **Ca Mau** Vietnam
63 B3 **Ca Mau, Mui** *c.* Vietnam
Cambay India *see* **Khambhat**
63 B2 **Cambodia** *country* Asia
99 A4 **Camborne** U.K.
105 C1 **Cambrai** France
99 B3 **Cambrian Mountains** *hills* U.K.
138 C2 **Cambridge** Can.
54 C1 **Cambridge** N.Z.
99 D3 **Cambridge** U.K.
139 E2 **Cambridge** *MA* U.S.A.
139 D3 **Cambridge** *MD* U.S.A.
137 E1 **Cambridge** *MN* U.S.A.
138 C2 **Cambridge** *OH* U.S.A.
126 E2 **Cambridge Bay** Can.
131 D2 **Cambrien, Lac** *l.* Can.
120 B1 **Cambulo** Angola
53 D2 **Camden** Austr.
140 B2 **Camden** *AR* U.S.A.
139 F2 **Camden** *ME* U.S.A.
139 D3 **Camden** *NJ* U.S.A.
137 E3 **Camdenton** U.S.A.
137 E3 **Cameron** U.S.A.
118 B2 **Cameroon** *country* Africa
118 B2 **Cameroon Highlands** *slope* Cameroon/Nigeria
118 A2 **Cameroun, Mont** *vol.* Cameroon
151 E3 **Cametá** Brazil
64 B2 **Camiguin** *i.* Phil.
64 B3 **Camiguin** *i.* Phil.
152 B2 **Camiri** Bol.
151 E3 **Camocim** Brazil
51 C1 **Camooweal** Austr.
63 A3 **Camorta** *i.* India
153 A4 **Campana, Isla** *i.* Chile
155 D1 **Campanário** Brazil
155 C2 **Campanha** Brazil
122 B2 **Campbell** S. Africa
54 B2 **Campbell, Cape** N.Z.
48 H9 **Campbell Island** N.Z.
156 D9 **Campbell Plateau** S. Pacific Ocean
128 B2 **Campbell River** Can.
138 B3 **Campbellsville** U.S.A.
131 D3 **Campbellton** Can.
53 D2 **Campbelltown** Austr.
96 B3 **Campbeltown** U.K.
145 C3 **Campeche** Mex.
145 C3 **Campeche, Bahía de** *g.* Mex.
52 B3 **Camperdown** Austr.
110 C1 **Câmpina** Romania
151 F3 **Campina Grande** Brazil
154 C2 **Campinas** Brazil
154 C1 **Campina Verde** Brazil
108 B2 **Campobasso** Italy
155 C2 **Campo Belo** Brazil
154 C1 **Campo Florido** Brazil
152 B2 **Campo Gallo** Arg.
154 B2 **Campo Grande** Brazil
154 C3 **Campo Largo** Brazil
151 E3 **Campo Maior** Brazil
106 B2 **Campo Maior** Port.
150 B1 **Campo Mara** Venez.
109 C2 **Campomarino** Italy
154 B2 **Campo Mourão** Brazil
155 D2 **Campos** Brazil
155 C1 **Campos Altos** Brazil
155 C2 **Campos do Jordão** Brazil
110 C1 **Câmpulung** Romania
142 A2 **Camp Verde** U.S.A.
Cam Ranh Vietnam *see* **Ba Ngoi**
63 B2 **Cam Ranh, Vinh** *b.* Vietnam
Cam Ranh Bay *b.* Vietnam *see* **Cam Ranh, Vinh**
128 C2 **Camrose** Can.
129 D2 **Camsell Portage** Can.
111 C2 **Çan** Turkey
126 F2 **Canada** *country* N. America
160 A2 **Canada Basin** Arctic Ocean
143 C1 **Canadian** U.S.A.
143 D1 **Canadian** *r.* U.S.A.
111 C2 **Çanakkale** Turkey
144 A1 **Cananea** Mex.
154 C2 **Cananéia** Brazil
114 A2 **Canary Islands** *is* N. Atlantic Ocean
154 C1 **Canastra, Serra da** *mts Goiás* Brazil
155 C1 **Canastra, Serra da** *mts Minas Gerais* Brazil
144 B2 **Canatlán** Mex.
141 D3 **Canaveral, Cape** U.S.A.
155 E1 **Canavieiras** Brazil
53 C2 **Canbelego** Austr.
53 C3 **Canberra** Austr.
145 D2 **Cancún** Mex.
111 C3 **Çandarlı** Turkey
155 C2 **Candeias** Brazil
145 C3 **Candelaria** Mex.
154 B2 **Cândido de Abreu** Brazil
129 D2 **Candle Lake** Can.
137 D1 **Cando** U.S.A.
120 A2 **Cangamba** Angola
106 B1 **Cangas** Spain
106 B1 **Cangas del Narcea** Spain
120 B2 **Cangombe** Angola
152 C3 **Canguçu** Brazil
70 B2 **Cangzhou** China
131 D2 **Caniapiscau** Can.
131 D2 **Caniapiscau** *r.* Can.
131 C2 **Caniapiscau, Réservoir de** *resr* Can.
Caniçado Moz. *see* **Guija**
108 B3 **Canicattì** Italy
151 F3 **Canindé** Brazil
144 B2 **Cañitas de Felipe Pescador** Mex.
80 B1 **Çankırı** Turkey
128 C2 **Canmore** Can.
96 A2 **Canna** *i.* U.K.
Cannanore India *see* **Kannur**
105 D3 **Cannes** France
99 B3 **Cannock** U.K.
53 C3 **Cann River** Austr.
152 C2 **Canoas** Brazil
129 D2 **Canoe Lake** Can.
154 B3 **Canoinhas** Brazil
136 B3 **Canon City** U.S.A.
52 B2 **Canopus** Austr.
129 D2 **Canora** Can.
53 C2 **Canowindra** Austr.
131 D3 **Canso** Can.
Cantabrian Mountains *mts* Spain *see* **Cantábrica, Cordillera**
Cantabrian Sea *sea* Spain *see* **Cantábrico, Mar**
106 C1 **Cantábrica, Cordillera** *mts* Spain
106 B1 **Cantábrico, Mar** *sea* Spain
99 D4 **Canterbury** U.K.
54 B2 **Canterbury Bight** *b.* N.Z.
54 B2 **Canterbury Plains** N.Z.
63 B2 **Cần Thơ** Vietnam
151 E3 **Canto do Buriti** Brazil
Canton China *see* **Guangzhou**
137 E2 **Canton** *MO* U.S.A.
140 C2 **Canton** *MS* U.S.A.
139 D2 **Canton** *NY* U.S.A.
138 C2 **Canton** *OH* U.S.A.
143 C1 **Canyon** U.S.A.
134 D1 **Canyon Ferry Lake** U.S.A.
134 B2 **Canyonville** U.S.A.
62 B1 **Cao Băng** Vietnam
109 C2 **Capaccio** Italy
154 C2 **Capão Bonito** Brazil
155 D2 **Caparaó, Serra do** *mts* Brazil
139 E1 **Cap-de-la-Madeleine** Can.
51 D4 **Cape Barren Island** Austr.
158 F7 **Cape Basin** S. Atlantic Ocean
52 A3 **Cape Borda** Austr.
131 D3 **Cape Breton Island** Can.
141 D3 **Cape Canaveral** U.S.A.
139 D3 **Cape Charles** U.S.A.
114 B4 **Cape Coast** Ghana
139 E2 **Cape Cod Bay** U.S.A.
141 D3 **Cape Coral** U.S.A.
127 G2 **Cape Dorset** Can.
141 E2 **Cape Fear** *r.* U.S.A.
137 F3 **Cape Girardeau** U.S.A.
155 D1 **Capelinha** Brazil
100 B2 **Capelle aan de IJssel** Neth.
Capelongo Angola *see* **Kuvango**
139 E3 **Cape May Point** U.S.A.
120 A1 **Capenda-Camulemba** Angola
122 A3 **Cape Town** S. Africa
158 E3 **Cape Verde** *country* N. Atlantic Ocean
158 D4 **Cape Verde Basin** N. Atlantic Ocean
51 D1 **Cape York Peninsula** Austr.
147 C3 **Cap-Haïtien** Haiti
151 E3 **Capim** *r.* Brazil
154 A2 **Capitán Bado** Para.
58 D1 **Capitol Hill** N. Mariana Is
154 B2 **Capivara, Represa** *resr* Brazil
109 C2 **Čapljina** Bos.-Herz.
109 B3 **Capo d'Orlando** Italy
108 A2 **Capraia, Isola di** *i.* Italy
108 A2 **Caprara, Punta** *pt* Italy
108 B2 **Capri, Isola di** *i.* Italy
51 E2 **Capricorn Channel** Austr.
120 B2 **Caprivi Strip** *reg.* Namibia
143 C2 **Cap Rock Escarpment** U.S.A.
143 C1 **Capulin** U.S.A.
150 C3 **Caquetá** *r.* Col.
110 B2 **Caracal** Romania
150 C2 **Caracaraí** Brazil
150 C1 **Caracas** Venez.
151 E3 **Caracol** Brazil
155 C2 **Caraguatatuba** Brazil
153 A3 **Carahue** Chile
155 D1 **Caraí** Brazil
151 D3 **Carajás, Serra dos** *hills* Brazil
155 D2 **Carandaí** Brazil
155 D2 **Carangola** Brazil
110 B1 **Caransebeș** Romania
131 D3 **Caraquet** Can.
146 B3 **Caratasca, Laguna de** *lag.* Hond.
155 D1 **Caratinga** Brazil
150 C3 **Carauari** Brazil
107 C2 **Caravaca de la Cruz** Spain
155 F1 **Caravelas** Brazil
129 E3 **Carberry** Can.
144 A2 **Carbó** Mex.
107 C2 **Carbon, Cap** *c.* Alg.
153 B5 **Carbón, Laguna del** *l.* Arg.
108 A3 **Carbonara, Capo** *c.* Italy
136 B3 **Carbondale** *CO* U.S.A.
138 B3 **Carbondale** *IL* U.S.A.
139 D2 **Carbondale** *PA* U.S.A.
131 E3 **Carbonear** Can.
155 D1 **Carbonita** Brazil
107 C2 **Carcaixent** Spain
104 C3 **Carcassonne** France
128 A1 **Carcross** Can.
146 B2 **Cárdenas** Cuba
145 C3 **Cárdenas** Mex.
99 B4 **Cardiff** U.K.
99 A3 **Cardigan** U.K.
99 A3 **Cardigan Bay** U.K.
154 C2 **Cardoso** Brazil
128 C3 **Cardston** Can.
110 B1 **Carei** Romania
104 B2 **Carentan** France
50 B2 **Carey, Lake** *imp. l.* Austr.
155 D2 **Cariacica** Brazil
146 B3 **Caribbean Sea** N. Atlantic Ocean
128 B2 **Cariboo Mountains** Can.
139 F1 **Caribou** U.S.A.
130 B2 **Caribou Lake** Can.
128 C2 **Caribou Mountains** Can.
144 B2 **Carichic** Mex.
100 B3 **Carignan** France
53 C2 **Carinda** Austr.
107 C1 **Cariñena** Spain
130 C3 **Carleton Place** Can.
123 C2 **Carletonville** S. Africa
135 C2 **Carlin** U.S.A.
97 C1 **Carlingford Lough** *inlet* Ireland/U.K.
138 B3 **Carlinville** U.S.A.
98 B2 **Carlisle** U.K.
139 D2 **Carlisle** U.S.A.
155 D1 **Carlos Chagas** Brazil
97 C2 **Carlow** Ireland
96 A1 **Carloway** U.K.
135 C4 **Carlsbad** *CA* U.S.A.
142 C2 **Carlsbad** *NM* U.S.A.
129 D3 **Carlyle** Can.
128 A1 **Carmacks** Can.
129 E3 **Carman** Can.
99 A4 **Carmarthen** U.K.
99 A4 **Carmarthen Bay** U.K.
104 C3 **Carmaux** France
145 C3 **Carmelita** Guat.
144 A2 **Carmen, Isla** *i.* Mex.
155 C1 **Carmo do Paranaíba** Brazil
Carmona Angola *see* **Uíge**
106 B2 **Carmona** Spain
104 B2 **Carnac** France
50 A2 **Carnarvon** Austr.
122 B3 **Carnarvon** S. Africa
97 C1 **Carndonagh** Ireland
129 D3 **Carnduff** Can.
50 B2 **Carnegie, Lake** *imp. l.* Austr.
96 B2 **Carn Eige** *mt.* U.K.
55 P2 **Carney Island** Antarctica
73 D4 **Car Nicobar** *i.* India
118 B2 **Carnot** C.A.R.
52 A2 **Carnot, Cape** Austr.
96 C2 **Carnoustie** U.K.
97 C2 **Carnsore Point** Ireland
151 E3 **Carolina** Brazil
49 L4 **Caroline Island** Kiribati
59 D2 **Caroline Islands** N. Pacific Ocean
122 A2 **Carolusberg** S. Africa
103 D2 **Carpathian Mountains** Europe
Carpații Meridionali *mts* Romania *see* **Transylvanian Alps**
51 C1 **Carpentaria, Gulf of** Austr.
105 D3 **Carpentras** France
108 B2 **Carpi** Italy
141 D3 **Carrabelle** U.S.A.
97 B3 **Carrantuohill** *mt.* Ireland
108 B2 **Carrara** Italy
97 D1 **Carrickfergus** U.K.
97 C2 **Carrickmacross** Ireland
97 B2 **Carrick-on-Shannon** Ireland
97 C2 **Carrick-on-Suir** Ireland
137 D1 **Carrington** U.S.A.
143 D3 **Carrizo Springs** U.S.A.
142 B2 **Carrizozo** U.S.A.
137 E2 **Carroll** U.S.A.
141 C2 **Carrollton** U.S.A.
129 D2 **Carrot River** Can.
135 C3 **Carson City** U.S.A.
135 C3 **Carson Sink** *l.* U.S.A.
Carstensz-top *mt.* Indon. *see* **Jaya, Puncak**
150 B1 **Cartagena** Col.
107 C2 **Cartagena** Spain
146 B4 **Cartago** Costa Rica
54 C2 **Carterton** N.Z.
137 E3 **Carthage** *MO* U.S.A.
143 E2 **Carthage** *TX* U.S.A.
131 E2 **Cartwright** Can.
151 F3 **Caruarú** Brazil
150 C1 **Carúpano** Venez.
52 B1 **Caryapundy Swamp** Austr.
114 B1 **Casablanca** Morocco
154 C2 **Casa Branca** Brazil
144 B1 **Casa de Janos** Mex.
142 A2 **Casa Grande** U.S.A.
108 A1 **Casale Monferrato** Italy
109 C2 **Casarano** Italy
144 B1 **Casas Grandes** Mex.
134 C2 **Cascade** U.S.A.
134 B2 **Cascade Range** *mts* Can./U.S.A.
106 B2 **Cascais** Port.
151 F3 **Cascavel** Brazil
154 B2 **Cascavel** Brazil
139 F2 **Casco Bay** U.S.A.
108 B2 **Caserta** Italy
97 C2 **Cashel** Ireland
153 B3 **Casilda** Arg.
53 D1 **Casino** Austr.
Casnewydd U.K. *see* **Newport**
107 C1 **Caspe** Spain
136 B2 **Casper** U.S.A.
76 A2 **Caspian Lowland** Kazakh./Rus. Fed.
81 C1 **Caspian Sea** Asia/Europe
Cassaigne Alg. *see* **Sidi Ali**
154 C2 **Cássia** Brazil
128 B2 **Cassiar** Can.
128 A2 **Cassiar Mountains** Can.
154 B1 **Cassilândia** Brazil
120 A2 **Cassinga** Angola
108 B2 **Cassino** Italy
96 B2 **Cassley** *r.* U.K.
151 E3 **Castanhal** Brazil
152 B3 **Castaño** *r.* Arg.
144 B2 **Castaños** Mex.
104 C3 **Casteljaloux** France
105 D3 **Castellane** France
107 C2 **Castellón de la Plana** Spain
155 D2 **Castelo** Brazil
106 B2 **Castelo Branco** Port.
104 C3 **Castelsarrasin** France
108 B3 **Castelvetrano** Italy
52 B3 **Casterton** Austr.
108 B2 **Castiglione della Pescaia** Italy
106 C2 **Castilla-La Mancha** *aut. comm.* Spain
106 C1 **Castilla y León** *aut. comm.* Spain
97 B2 **Castlebar** Ireland
96 A2 **Castlebay** U.K.
97 C1 **Castleblayney** Ireland
97 C1 **Castlederg** U.K.
96 C3 **Castle Douglas** U.K.
128 C3 **Castlegar** Can.
97 B2 **Castleisland** Ireland
52 B3 **Castlemaine** Austr.
97 C2 **Castlepollard** Ireland
97 B2 **Castlerea** Ireland
53 C2 **Castlereagh** *r.* Austr.
136 C3 **Castle Rock** U.S.A.
128 C2 **Castor** Can.

104 C3 **Castres** France
100 B1 **Castricum** Neth.
147 D3 **Castries** St Lucia
154 C2 **Castro** Brazil
153 A4 **Castro** Chile
106 B2 **Castro Verde** Port.
109 C3 **Castrovillari** Italy
150 A3 **Catacaos** Peru
155 D2 **Cataguases** Brazil
154 C1 **Catalão** Brazil
Catalonia *aut. comm.* Spain *see* **Cataluña**
107 D1 **Cataluña** *aut. comm.* Spain
152 B2 **Catamarca** Arg.
64 B2 **Catanduanes** *i.* Phil.
154 C2 **Catanduva** Brazil
154 B3 **Catanduvas** Brazil
109 C3 **Catania** Italy
109 C3 **Catanzaro** Italy
64 B2 **Catarman** Phil.
107 C2 **Catarroja** Spain
64 B2 **Catbalogan** Phil.
145 C3 **Catemaco** Mex.
120 A1 **Catete** Angola
Catherine, Mount *mt.* Egypt *see* **Kātrīnā, Jabal**
147 C2 **Cat Island** Bahamas
130 A2 **Cat Lake** Can.
145 D2 **Catoche, Cabo** *c.* Mex.
139 E2 **Catskill Mountains** U.S.A.
123 D2 **Catuane** Moz.
64 B3 **Cauayan** Phil.
131 D2 **Caubvick, Mount** Can.
150 B2 **Cauca** *r.* Col.
151 F3 **Caucaia** Brazil
81 C1 **Caucasus** *mts* Asia/Europe
100 A2 **Caudry** France
109 C3 **Caulonia** Italy
120 A1 **Caungula** Angola
150 C2 **Caura** *r.* Venez.
131 D3 **Causapscal** Can.
90 B2 **Căușeni** Moldova
105 D3 **Cavaillon** France
151 E4 **Cavalcante** Brazil
114 B4 **Cavally** *r.* Côte d'Ivoire/Liberia
97 C2 **Cavan** Ireland
154 B3 **Cavernoso, Serra do** *mts* Brazil
151 D2 **Caviana, Ilha** *i.* Brazil
Cawnpore India *see* **Kanpur**
151 E3 **Caxias** Brazil
152 C2 **Caxias do Sul** Brazil
120 A1 **Caxito** Angola
151 D2 **Cayenne** Fr. Guiana
146 B3 **Cayman Islands** *terr.* West Indies
158 C3 **Cayman Trench** Caribbean Sea
117 C4 **Caynabo** Somalia
120 B2 **Cazombo** Angola
Ceará Brazil *see* **Fortaleza**
Ceatharlach Ireland *see* **Carlow**
144 B2 **Ceballos** Mex.
64 B2 **Cebu** Phil.
64 B2 **Cebu** *i.* Phil.
108 B2 **Cecina** Italy
137 F2 **Cedar** *r.* U.S.A.
135 D3 **Cedar City** U.S.A.
137 E2 **Cedar Falls** U.S.A.
129 D2 **Cedar Lake** Can.
137 E2 **Cedar Rapids** U.S.A.
144 A2 **Cedros, Isla** *i.* Mex.
51 C3 **Ceduna** Austr.
117 C4 **Ceeldheere** Somalia
117 C3 **Ceerigaabo** Somalia
108 B3 **Cefalù** Italy
145 B2 **Celaya** Mex.
61 D2 **Celebes** *i.* Indon.
156 C5 **Celebes Sea** Indon./Phil.
145 C2 **Celestún** Mex.
101 E1 **Celle** Ger.
95 B3 **Celtic Sea** Ireland/U.K.
59 D3 **Cenderawasih, Teluk** *b.* Indon.
140 C2 **Center Point** U.S.A.
150 B2 **Central, Cordillera** *mts* Col.
150 B4 **Central, Cordillera** *mts* Peru
64 B2 **Central, Cordillera** *mts* Phil.
Central African Empire *country* Africa *see* **Central African Republic**
118 C2 **Central African Republic** *country* Africa
74 A2 **Central Brahui Range** *mts* Pak.
137 D2 **Central City** U.S.A.
138 B3 **Centralia** *IL* U.S.A.
134 B1 **Centralia** *WA* U.S.A.
74 A2 **Central Makran Range** *mts* Pak.
156 D5 **Central Pacific Basin** Pacific Ocean
134 B2 **Central Point** U.S.A.
Central Provinces *state* India *see* **Madhya Pradesh**
59 D3 **Central Range** *mts* P.N.G.
89 E3 **Central Russian Upland** *hills* Rus. Fed.
83 I2 **Central Siberian Plateau** *plat.* Rus. Fed.
140 C2 **Century** U.S.A.
Ceos *i.* Greece *see* **Kea**
111 B3 **Cephalonia** *i.* Greece
Ceram *i.* Indon. *see* **Seram**
Ceram Sea *sea* Indon. *see* **Laut Seram**
101 F3 **Čerchov** *mt.* Czech Rep.
152 B2 **Ceres** Arg.
154 C1 **Ceres** Brazil
122 A3 **Ceres** S. Africa
105 C3 **Céret** France
106 C1 **Cerezo de Abajo** Spain
109 C2 **Cerignola** Italy
Cerigo *i.* Greece *see* **Kythira**
110 C2 **Cernavodă** Romania
145 C2 **Cerralvo** Mex.
144 B2 **Cerralvo, Isla** *i.* Mex.
145 B2 **Cerritos** Mex.
154 C2 **Cerro Azul** Brazil
145 C2 **Cerro Azul** Mex.
150 B4 **Cerro de Pasco** Peru
105 D3 **Cervione** France
106 B1 **Cervo** Spain
108 B2 **Cesena** Italy
108 B2 **Cesenatico** Italy
88 C2 **Cēsis** Latvia
102 C2 **České Budějovice** Czech Rep.
101 F3 **Český les** *mts* Czech Rep.
111 C3 **Çeşme** Turkey
53 D2 **Cessnock** Austr.
104 B2 **Cesson-Sévigné** France
104 B3 **Cestas** France
109 C2 **Cetinje** Montenegro
109 C3 **Cetraro** Italy
106 B2 **Ceuta** N. Africa
105 C3 **Cévennes** *mts* France
Ceylon *country* Asia *see* **Sri Lanka**
79 D2 **Chābahār** Iran
75 C1 **Chabyêr Caka** *salt l.* China
150 B3 **Chachapoyas** Peru
89 D3 **Chachersk** Belarus
63 B2 **Chachoengsao** Thai.
152 C2 **Chaco Boreal** *reg.* Para.
142 B1 **Chaco Mesa** *plat.* U.S.A.
115 D3 **Chad** *country* Africa
115 D3 **Chad, Lake** Africa
68 C1 **Chadaasan** Mongolia
68 C1 **Chadan** Rus. Fed.
123 C1 **Chadibe** Botswana
136 C2 **Chadron** U.S.A.
Chadyr-Lunga Moldova *see* **Ciadîr-Lunga**
77 D2 **Chaek** Kyrg.
65 B2 **Chaeryŏng** N. Korea
74 A2 **Chagai** Pak.
77 C3 **Chaghcharān** Afgh.
89 E2 **Chagoda** Rus. Fed.
56 I10 **Chagos Archipelago** *is* B.I.O.T.
159 E4 **Chagos-Laccadive Ridge** Indian Ocean
159 E4 **Chagos Trench** Indian Ocean
75 C2 **Chaibasa** India
63 B2 **Chainat** Thai.
63 A3 **Chaiya** Thai.
63 B2 **Chaiyaphum** Thai.
152 C3 **Chajarí** Arg.
119 D3 **Chake Chake** Tanz.
131 D2 **Chakonipau, Lac** Can.
150 B4 **Chala** Peru
74 A1 **Chalap Dalan** *mts* Afgh.
121 C2 **Chaláua** Moz.
131 D3 **Chaleur Bay** *inlet* Can.
74 B2 **Chalisgaon** India
111 C3 **Chalki** *i.* Greece
111 B3 **Chalkida** Greece
143 C3 **Chalk Mountains** U.S.A.
104 B2 **Challans** France
134 D2 **Challis** U.S.A.
105 C2 **Châlons-en-Champagne** France
Châlons-sur-Marne France *see* **Châlons-en-Champagne**
105 C2 **Chalon-sur-Saône** France
101 F3 **Cham** Ger.
142 B1 **Chama** U.S.A.
121 C2 **Chama** Zambia
74 A1 **Chaman** Pak.
74 B1 **Chamba** India
74 B2 **Chambal** *r.* India
137 D2 **Chamberlain** U.S.A.
142 B1 **Chambers** U.S.A.
139 D3 **Chambersburg** U.S.A.
105 D2 **Chambéry** France
121 C2 **Chambeshi** Zambia
121 B2 **Chambeshi** *r.* Zambia
Chamdo China *see* **Qamdo**
119 D2 **Ch'amo Hāyk'** *l.* Eth.
105 D2 **Chamonix-Mont-Blanc** France
105 C2 **Champagne** *reg.* France
138 B2 **Champaign** U.S.A.
139 E2 **Champlain, Lake** Can./U.S.A.
145 C3 **Champotón** Mex.
Chanak Turkey *see* **Çanakkale**
152 A2 **Chañaral** Chile
Chanda India *see* **Chandrapur**
126 C2 **Chandalar** *r.* U.S.A.
140 C3 **Chandeleur Islands** U.S.A.
74 B1 **Chandigarh** India
131 D3 **Chandler** Can.
142 A2 **Chandler** U.S.A.
75 D2 **Chandpur** Bangl.
75 B3 **Chandrapur** India
63 B2 **Chang, Ko** *i.* Thai.
Chang'an China *see* **Rong'an**
121 C3 **Changane** *r.* Moz.
121 C2 **Changara** Moz.
65 B1 **Changbai** China
65 B1 **Changbai Shan** *mts* China/N. Korea
Changchow *Fujian* China *see* **Zhangzhou**
Changchow *Jiangsu* China *see* **Changzhou**
69 E2 **Changchun** China
71 B3 **Changde** China
65 B2 **Ch'angdo** N. Korea
70 B2 **Changge** China
71 C3 **Changhua** Taiwan
65 B3 **Changhŭng** S. Korea
Chang Jiang *r.* China *see* **Yangtze**
Changjiang Kou *r. mouth* China *see* **Yangtze, Mouth of the**
65 B1 **Changjin** N. Korea
65 B1 **Changjin-gang** *r.* N. Korea
Changkiang China *see* **Zhanjiang**
Changning China *see* **Xunwu**
Ch'ang-pai Shan *mts* China/N. Korea *see* **Changbai Shan**
71 B3 **Changsha** China
70 C2 **Changshu** China
65 B2 **Changsŏng** S. Korea
Changteh China *see* **Changde**
71 B3 **Changting** *Fujian* China
66 A2 **Changting** *Heilong.* China
65 A1 **Changtu** China
146 B4 **Changuinola** Panama
65 B2 **Ch'angwŏn** S. Korea
65 B2 **Changyŏn** N. Korea
70 B2 **Changyuan** China
70 B2 **Changzhi** China
70 B2 **Changzhou** China
111 B3 **Chania** Greece
95 C4 **Channel Islands** English Chan.
135 C4 **Channel Islands** U.S.A.
131 E3 **Channel-Port-aux-Basques** Can.
106 B1 **Chantada** Spain
63 B2 **Chanthaburi** Thai.
104 C2 **Chantilly** France
137 D3 **Chanute** U.S.A.
82 G3 **Chany, Ozero** *salt l.* Rus. Fed.
70 B2 **Chaohu** China
Chaoyang China *see* **Huinan**
71 B3 **Chaoyang** *Guangdong* China
70 C1 **Chaoyang** *Liaoning* China
71 B3 **Chaozhou** China
144 B2 **Chapala, Laguna de** *l.* Mex.
76 B1 **Chapayevo** Kazakh.
87 D3 **Chapayevsk** Rus. Fed.
152 C2 **Chapecó** Brazil
141 E1 **Chapel Hill** U.S.A.
130 B3 **Chapleau** Can.
89 E3 **Chaplygin** Rus. Fed.
91 C2 **Chaplynka** Ukr.
Chapra India *see* **Chhapra**
145 B2 **Charcas** Mex.
99 B4 **Chard** U.K.
Chardzhev Turkm. *see* **Türkmenabat**
Chardzhou Turkm. *see* **Türkmenabat**
104 B2 **Charente** *r.* France
118 B1 **Chari** *r.* Cameroon/Chad
77 C3 **Chārīkār** Afgh.
86 E2 **Charkayuvom** Rus. Fed.
Charkhlik China *see* **Ruoqiang**
100 B2 **Charleroi** Belgium
139 D3 **Charles, Cape** U.S.A.
139 E1 **Charlesbourg** Can.
137 E2 **Charles City** U.S.A.
138 B3 **Charleston** *IL* U.S.A.
137 F3 **Charleston** *MO* U.S.A.
141 E2 **Charleston** *SC* U.S.A.
138 C3 **Charleston** *WV* U.S.A.
135 C3 **Charleston Peak** U.S.A.
51 D2 **Charleville** Austr.
97 B2 **Charleville** Ireland
105 C2 **Charleville-Mézières** France
138 B1 **Charlevoix** U.S.A.
141 D1 **Charlotte** U.S.A.
141 D3 **Charlotte Harbor** *b.* U.S.A.
139 D3 **Charlottesville** U.S.A.
131 D3 **Charlottetown** Can.
52 B3 **Charlton** Austr.
130 C2 **Charlton Island** Can.
51 D2 **Charters Towers** Austr.
104 C2 **Chartres** France
128 C2 **Chase** Can.
88 C3 **Chashniki** Belarus
54 A3 **Chaslands Mistake** *c.* N.Z.
65 B1 **Chasŏng** N. Korea
104 B2 **Chassiron, Pointe de** *pt* France
104 B2 **Châteaubriant** France
104 C2 **Château-du-Loir** France
104 C2 **Châteaudun** France
104 B2 **Château-Gontier** France
104 B2 **Châteaulin** France
105 D3 **Châteauneuf-les-Martigues** France
104 C2 **Châteauneuf-sur-Loire** France
104 C2 **Châteauroux** France
105 C2 **Château-Thierry** France
128 C2 **Chateh** Can.
100 B2 **Châtelet** Belgium
104 C2 **Châtellerault** France
138 C2 **Chatham** Can.
99 D4 **Chatham** U.K.
49 J8 **Chatham Islands** N.Z.
105 C2 **Châtillon-sur-Seine** France
141 D2 **Chattahoochee** *r.* U.S.A.
141 C1 **Chattanooga** U.S.A.
63 B2 **Châu Đốc** Vietnam
62 A1 **Chauk** Myanmar
105 D2 **Chaumont** France
105 C2 **Chauny** France
Chau Phu Vietnam *see* **Châu Đốc**
151 E3 **Chaves** Brazil
106 B1 **Chaves** Port.
130 C2 **Chavigny, Lac** *l.* Can.
89 D3 **Chavusy** Belarus
89 E2 **Chayevo** Rus. Fed.
86 E3 **Chaykovskiy** Rus. Fed.
140 C2 **Cheaha Mountain** *h.* U.S.A.
102 C1 **Cheb** Czech Rep.
87 D3 **Cheboksary** Rus. Fed.
138 C1 **Cheboygan** U.S.A.
65 B2 **Chech'ŏn** S. Korea
140 A1 **Checotah** U.S.A.
Chefoo China *see* **Yantai**
126 B2 **Chefornak** U.S.A.
114 B2 **Chegga** Maur.
121 C2 **Chegutu** Zimbabwe
134 B1 **Chehalis** U.S.A.
65 B3 **Cheju** S. Korea
65 B3 **Cheju-do** *i.* S. Korea
65 B3 **Cheju-haehyŏp** *sea chan.* S. Korea
89 E2 **Chekhov** Rus. Fed.
Chekiang *prov.* China *see* **Zhejiang**
134 B1 **Chelan, Lake** U.S.A.
103 E1 **Chełm** Pol.
99 D4 **Chelmer** *r.* U.K.
103 D1 **Chełmno** Pol.
99 D4 **Chelmsford** U.K.
99 B4 **Cheltenham** U.K.
87 F3 **Chelyabinsk** Rus. Fed.
83 H1 **Chelyuskin** Rus. Fed.
101 F2 **Chemnitz** Ger.
Chemulpo S. Korea *see* **Inch'ŏn**
134 B2 **Chemult** U.S.A.
74 B2 **Chenab** *r.* India/Pak.
114 B2 **Chenachane** Alg.
134 C1 **Cheney** U.S.A.
Chengchow China *see* **Zhengzhou**
70 B1 **Chengde** China
70 A2 **Chengdu** China
Chengjiang China *see* **Taihe**
71 B4 **Chengmai** China
Chengshou China *see* **Yingshan**
Chengtu China *see* **Chengdu**
70 A2 **Chengxian** China
Chengxiang China *see* **Wuxi**
Chengxiang China *see* **Mianning**
Chengyang China *see* **Juxian**
73 C3 **Chennai** India
Chenstokhov Pol. *see* **Częstochowa**
71 B3 **Chenzhou** China
99 B4 **Chepstow** U.K.
141 E2 **Cheraw** U.S.A.
104 B2 **Cherbourg** France
Cherchen China *see* **Qiemo**
89 E3 **Cheremisinovo** Rus. Fed.
68 C1 **Cheremkhovo** Rus. Fed.
89 E2 **Cherepovets** Rus. Fed.
91 C2 **Cherkasy** Ukr.
87 D4 **Cherkessk** Rus. Fed.
89 E3 **Chern'** Rus. Fed.
91 C1 **Chernihiv** Ukr.
91 D2 **Cherninivka** Ukr.
90 B2 **Chernivtsi** Ukr.
68 C1 **Chernogorsk** Rus. Fed.
90 B1 **Chernyakhiv** Ukr.
88 B3 **Chernyakhovsk** Rus. Fed.
89 E3 **Chernyanka** Rus. Fed.
69 D1 **Chernyshevsk** Rus. Fed.
83 I2 **Chernyshevskiy** Rus. Fed.
Chernyy Rynok Rus. Fed. *see* **Kochubey**
137 D2 **Cherokee** U.S.A.
83 L2 **Cherskiy** Rus. Fed.
83 K2 **Cherskogo, Khrebet** *mts* Rus. Fed.
91 E2 **Chertkovo** Rus. Fed.
Chervonoarmeyskoye Ukr. *see* **Vil'nyans'k**
Chervonoarmiys'k Ukr. *see* **Krasnoarmiys'k**
Chervonoarmiys'k Ukr. *see* **Radyvyliv**
90 A1 **Chervonohrad** Ukr.
88 C3 **Chervyen'** Belarus
89 D3 **Cherykaw** Belarus
139 D3 **Chesapeake Bay** U.S.A.
86 D2 **Cheshskaya Guba** *b.* Rus. Fed.
98 B3 **Chester** U.K.
138 B3 **Chester** *IL* U.S.A.
141 D2 **Chester** *SC* U.S.A.
139 D3 **Chester** *VA* U.S.A.
98 C3 **Chesterfield** U.K.
137 E3 **Chesterfield** U.S.A.
129 E1 **Chesterfield Inlet** Can.
129 E1 **Chesterfield Inlet** *inlet* Can.
139 F1 **Chesuncook Lake** U.S.A.
108 A3 **Chetaïbi** Alg.
131 D3 **Chéticamp** Can.
145 D3 **Chetumal** Mex.
128 B2 **Chetwynd** Can.
98 B2 **Cheviot Hills** U.K.
119 D2 **Che'w Bahir** *salt l.* Eth.
136 C2 **Cheyenne** U.S.A.
136 C2 **Cheyenne** *r.* U.S.A.
136 C3 **Cheyenne Wells** U.S.A.
75 C2 **Chhapra** India
75 B2 **Chhatarpur** India
75 C2 **Chhattisgarh** *state* India
74 B2 **Chhindwara** India
75 C2 **Chhukha** Bhutan
71 C3 **Chiai** Taiwan
62 A2 **Chiang Dao** Thai.
120 A2 **Chiange** Angola
62 A2 **Chiang Mai** Thai.
62 A2 **Chiang Rai** Thai.
145 C3 **Chiapa** Mex.
108 A1 **Chiavenna** Italy
69 F2 **Chiba** Japan
70 B3 **Chibi** China
Chibizovka Rus. Fed. *see* **Zherdevka**
121 C3 **Chiboma** Moz.
130 C3 **Chibougamau** Can.
123 D1 **Chibuto** Moz.
138 B2 **Chicago** U.S.A.
128 A2 **Chichagof Island** U.S.A.
99 C4 **Chichester** U.K.

50 A2 **Chichester Range** *mts* Austr.
143 D1 **Chickasha** U.S.A.
106 B2 **Chiclana de la Frontera** Spain
150 B3 **Chiclayo** Peru
153 B4 **Chico** *Chubut r.* Arg.
153 B4 **Chico** *Santa Cruz r.* Arg.
135 B3 **Chico** U.S.A.
139 E2 **Chicopee** U.S.A.
64 B2 **Chico Sapocoy, Mount** Phil.
131 C3 **Chicoutimi** Can.
131 D1 **Chidley, Cape** Can.
63 A3 **Chieo Lan, Ang Kep Nam** Thai.
108 B2 **Chieti** Italy
145 C3 **Chietla** Mex.
70 B1 **Chifeng** China
155 D1 **Chifre, Serra do** *mts* Brazil
121 C2 **Chifunde** Moz.
77 D2 **Chiganak** Kazakh.
145 C3 **Chignahuapán** Mex.
121 C3 **Chigubo** Moz.
62 A1 **Chigu Co** *l.* China
144 B2 **Chihuahua** Mex.
77 C2 **Chiili** Kazakh.
88 C2 **Chikhachevo** Rus. Fed.
67 C3 **Chikuma-gawa** *r.* Japan
128 B2 **Chilanko** *r.* Can.
74 B1 **Chilas** Pak.
143 C2 **Childress** U.S.A.
153 A3 **Chile** *country* S. America
158 C6 **Chile Basin** S. Pacific Ocean
152 B2 **Chilecito** Arg.
157 G8 **Chile Rise** S. Pacific Ocean
77 D2 **Chilik** Kazakh.
75 C3 **Chilika Lake** India
121 B2 **Chililabombwe** Zambia
128 B2 **Chilko** *r.* Can.
128 B2 **Chilko Lake** Can.
153 A3 **Chillán** Chile
138 B2 **Chillicothe** *IL* U.S.A.
137 E3 **Chillicothe** *MO* U.S.A.
138 C3 **Chillicothe** *OH* U.S.A.
128 B3 **Chilliwack** Can.
153 A4 **Chiloé, Isla de** *i.* Chile
145 C3 **Chilpancingo** Mex.
53 C3 **Chiltern** Austr.
99 C4 **Chiltern Hills** U.K.
120 B1 **Chiluage** Angola
71 C3 **Chilung** Taiwan
119 D3 **Chimala** Tanz.
121 C2 **Chimanimani** Zimbabwe
152 B3 **Chimbas** Arg.
150 B3 **Chimborazo** *mt.* Ecuador
150 B3 **Chimbote** Peru
76 B2 **Chimboy** Uzbek.
Chimishliya Moldova *see* **Cimişlia**
Chimkent Kazakh. *see* **Shymkent**
121 C2 **Chimoio** Moz.
77 C3 **Chimtargha, Qullai** *mt.* Tajik.
68 C2 **China** *country* Asia
145 C2 **China** Mex.
150 B4 **Chincha Alta** Peru
128 C2 **Chinchaga** *r.* Can.
145 D3 **Chinchorro, Banco** Mex.
121 C2 **Chinde** Moz.
65 B3 **Chindo** S. Korea
65 B3 **Chin-do** *i.* S. Korea
68 C2 **Chindu** China
62 A1 **Chindwin** *r.* Myanmar
65 B2 **Chinghwa** N. Korea
121 B2 **Chingola** Zambia
120 A2 **Chinguar** Angola
65 B2 **Chinhae** S. Korea
121 C2 **Chinhoyi** Zimbabwe
Chini India *see* **Kalpa**
Chining China *see* **Jining**
74 B1 **Chiniot** Pak.
144 B2 **Chinipas** Mex.
65 B2 **Chinju** S. Korea
118 C2 **Chinko** *r.* C.A.R.
142 B1 **Chinle** U.S.A.
71 B3 **Chinmen** Taiwan
Chinnamp'o N. Korea *see* **Namp'o**
67 C3 **Chino** Japan
135 C4 **Chino** U.S.A.
104 C2 **Chinon** France
134 E1 **Chinook** U.S.A.
142 A2 **Chino Valley** U.S.A.
77 C2 **Chinoz** Uzbek.
121 C2 **Chinsali** Zambia
108 B1 **Chioggia** Italy
111 C3 **Chios** Greece
111 C3 **Chios** *i.* Greece
121 C2 **Chipata** Zambia
120 A2 **Chipindo** Angola
Chipinga Zimbabwe *see* **Chipinge**
121 C3 **Chipinge** Zimbabwe
73 B3 **Chiplun** India
99 B4 **Chippenham** U.K.
138 A2 **Chippewa Falls** U.S.A.
99 C4 **Chipping Norton** U.K.
Chipuriro Zimbabwe *see* **Guruve**
145 D3 **Chiquimula** Guat.
77 C2 **Chirchiq** Uzbek.
121 C3 **Chiredzi** Zimbabwe
142 B2 **Chiricahua Peak** U.S.A.
146 B4 **Chiriquí, Golfo de** *b.* Panama
65 B2 **Chiri-san** *mt.* S. Korea
146 B4 **Chirripó** *mt.* Costa Rica
121 B2 **Chirundu** Zimbabwe
130 C2 **Chisasibi** Can.
137 E1 **Chisholm** U.S.A.
Chisimaio Somalia *see* **Kismaayo**
90 B2 **Chişinău** Moldova
87 E3 **Chistopol'** Rus. Fed.
69 D1 **Chita** Rus. Fed.
120 A2 **Chitado** Angola
Chitaldrug India *see* **Chitradurga**
121 C2 **Chitambo** Zambia
120 B1 **Chitato** Angola
121 C1 **Chitipa** Malawi
121 C3 **Chitobe** Moz.
Chitor India *see* **Chittaurgarh**
66 D2 **Chitose** Japan
73 B3 **Chitradurga** India
74 B1 **Chitral** Pak.
146 B4 **Chitré** Panama
75 D2 **Chittagong** Bangl.
74 B2 **Chittaurgarh** India
73 B3 **Chittoor** India
Chittorgarh India *see* **Chittaurgarh**
121 C2 **Chitungwiza** Zimbabwe
120 B2 **Chiume** Angola
121 C2 **Chivhu** Zimbabwe
70 B2 **Chizhou** China
Chkalov Rus. Fed. *see* **Orenburg**
114 C1 **Chlef** Alg.
107 D2 **Chlef, Oued** *r.* Alg.
101 F2 **Chodov** Czech Rep.
153 B3 **Choele Choel** Arg.
Chogori Feng *mt.* China/Pakistan *see* **K2**
48 G4 **Choiseul** *i.* Solomon Is
144 B2 **Choix** Mex.
102 C1 **Chojna** Pol.
103 D1 **Chojnice** Pol.
117 B3 **Ch'ok'ē** Eth.
Chokue Moz. *see* **Chókwè**
83 K2 **Chokurdakh** Rus. Fed.
121 C3 **Chókwè** Moz.
104 B2 **Cholet** France
145 C3 **Cholula** Mex.
120 B2 **Choma** Zambia
Chomo China *see* **Yadong**
102 C1 **Chomutov** Czech Rep.
83 I2 **Chona** *r.* Rus. Fed.
65 B2 **Ch'ŏnan** S. Korea
58 A2 **Chon Buri** Thai.
150 A3 **Chone** Ecuador
Chong'an China *see* **Wuyishan**
65 B1 **Ch'ŏngjin** N. Korea
65 B2 **Chŏngju** N. Korea
65 B2 **Ch'ŏngju** S. Korea
65 B2 **Chŏngp'yŏng** N. Korea
70 A3 **Chongqing** China
70 A2 **Chongqing** *mun.* China
65 B2 **Chŏngŭp** S. Korea
121 B2 **Chongwe** Zambia
71 A3 **Chongzuo** China
65 B2 **Chŏnju** S. Korea
153 A4 **Chonos, Archipiélago de los** *is* Chile
154 B3 **Chopimzinho** Brazil
111 B3 **Chora Sfakion** Greece
98 B3 **Chorley** U.K.
91 C2 **Chornobay** Ukr.
90 C1 **Chornobyl'** Ukr.
91 C2 **Chornomors'ke** Ukr.
90 B2 **Chortkiv** Ukr.
65 B2 **Ch'ŏrwŏn** S. Korea
65 B1 **Ch'osan** N. Korea
67 D3 **Chōshi** Japan
153 A3 **Chos Malal** Arg.
103 D1 **Choszczno** Pol.
134 D1 **Choteau** U.S.A.
114 A2 **Choûm** Maur.
69 D1 **Choybalsan** Mongolia
69 D1 **Choyr** Mongolia
54 B2 **Christchurch** N.Z.
99 C4 **Christchurch** U.K.
127 H2 **Christian, Cape** Can.
123 C2 **Christiana** S. Africa
Christianshåb Greenland *see* **Qasigiannguit**
54 A2 **Christina, Mount** N.Z.
58 B3 **Christmas Island** *terr.* Indian Ocean
111 B2 **Chrysoupoli** Greece
Chu Kazakh. *see* **Shu**
Chubarovka Ukr. *see* **Polohy**
153 B4 **Chubut** *r.* Arg.
89 F3 **Chuchkovo** Rus. Fed.
90 B1 **Chudniv** Ukr.
89 D2 **Chudovo** Rus. Fed.
126 C2 **Chugach Mountains** U.S.A.
67 B4 **Chūgoku-sanchi** *mts* Japan
Chuguchak China *see* **Tacheng**
66 B2 **Chuguyevka** Rus. Fed.
91 D2 **Chuhuyiv** Ukr.
Chukchi Peninsula *pen.* Rus. Fed. *see* **Chukotskiy Poluostrov**
160 J3 **Chukchi Sea** *sea* Rus. Fed./U.S.A.
89 F2 **Chukhloma** Rus. Fed.
83 N2 **Chukotskiy Poluostrov** *pen.* Rus. Fed.
Chulaktau Kazakh. *see* **Karatau**
135 C4 **Chula Vista** U.S.A.
82 G3 **Chulym** Rus. Fed.
152 B2 **Chumbicha** Arg.
83 K3 **Chumikan** Rus. Fed.
63 A2 **Chumphon** Thai.
65 B2 **Ch'unch'ŏn** S. Korea
Chungking China *see* **Chongqing**
Ch'ungmu S. Korea *see* **T'ongyŏng**
71 C3 **Chungyang Shanmo** *mts* Taiwan
83 H2 **Chunya** *r.* Rus. Fed.
119 D3 **Chunya** Tanz.
150 B4 **Chuquibamba** Peru
152 B2 **Chuquicamata** Chile
105 D2 **Chur** Switz.
62 A1 **Churachandpur** India
83 J2 **Churapcha** Rus. Fed.
129 E2 **Churchill** Can.
129 E2 **Churchill** *r. Man.* Can.
131 D2 **Churchill** *r. Nfld. and Lab.* Can.
129 E2 **Churchill, Cape** Can.
131 D2 **Churchill Falls** Can.
129 D2 **Churchill Lake** Can.
74 B2 **Churu** India
63 B2 **Chu Sê** Vietnam
142 B1 **Chuska Mountains** U.S.A.
86 E3 **Chusovoy** Rus. Fed.
131 C3 **Chute-des-Passes** Can.
48 G3 **Chuuk** *is* Micronesia
62 B1 **Chuxiong** China
91 C2 **Chyhyryn** Ukr.
Chymyshliya Moldova *see* **Cimişlia**
Ciadâr-Lunga Moldova *see* **Ciadîr-Lunga**
90 B2 **Ciadîr-Lunga** Moldova
60 B2 **Ciamis** Indon.
60 B2 **Cianjur** Indon.
154 B2 **Cianorte** Brazil
142 A2 **Cibuta, Sierra** *mt.* Mex.
80 B1 **Cide** Turkey
103 E1 **Ciechanów** Pol.
146 C2 **Ciego de Ávila** Cuba
147 C3 **Ciénaga** Col.
146 B2 **Cienfuegos** Cuba
107 C2 **Cieza** Spain
106 C2 **Cigüela** *r.* Spain
80 B2 **Cihanbeyli** Turkey
144 B3 **Cihuatlán** Mex.
106 C2 **Cijara, Embalse de** *resr* Spain
109 C2 **Çikës, Maja e** *mt.* Albania
60 B2 **Cilacap** Indon.
Cill Airne Ireland *see* **Killarney**
Cill Chainnigh Ireland *see* **Kilkenny**
143 C1 **Cimarron** *r.* U.S.A.
90 B2 **Cimişlia** Moldova
108 B2 **Cimone, Monte** *mt.* Italy
Cîmpina Romania *see* **Câmpina**
Cîmpulung Romania *see* **Câmpulung**
60 B2 **Cina, Tanjung** *c.* Indon.
138 C3 **Cincinnati** U.S.A.
Cinco de Outubro Angola *see* **Xá-Muteba**
111 C3 **Çine** Turkey
100 B2 **Ciney** Belgium
134 C2 **Cinnabar Mountain** U.S.A.
145 C3 **Cintalapa** Mex.
71 B3 **Ciping** China
Ciping China *see* **Ciping**
153 B3 **Cipolletti** Arg.
126 C2 **Circle** *AK* U.S.A.
136 B1 **Circle** *MT* U.S.A.
60 B2 **Cirebon** Indon.
99 C4 **Cirencester** U.K.
108 A1 **Ciriè** Italy
109 C3 **Cirò Marina** Italy
110 B1 **Cisnădie** Romania
109 C2 **Čitluk** Bos.-Herz.
122 A3 **Citrusdal** S. Africa
135 B3 **Citrus Heights** U.S.A.
110 C1 **Ciucaş, Vârful** *mt.* Romania
145 B2 **Ciudad Acuña** Mex.
145 B3 **Ciudad Altamirano** Mex.
150 C2 **Ciudad Bolívar** Venez.
147 C4 **Ciudad Bolivia** Venez.
144 B2 **Ciudad Camargo** Mex.
144 A2 **Ciudad Constitución** Mex.
145 C3 **Ciudad Cuauhtémoc** Mex.
145 C3 **Ciudad del Carmen** Mex.
154 B3 **Ciudad del Este** Para.
144 B2 **Ciudad Delicias** Mex.
145 C2 **Ciudad de Valles** Mex.
150 C2 **Ciudad Guayana** Venez.
142 B3 **Ciudad Guerrero** Mex.
144 B3 **Ciudad Guzmán** Mex.
145 C3 **Ciudad Hidalgo** Mex.
145 C3 **Ciudad Ixtepec** Mex.
144 B1 **Ciudad Juárez** Mex.
145 C2 **Ciudad Madero** Mex.
145 C2 **Ciudad Mante** Mex.
145 C2 **Ciudad Mier** Mex.
144 B2 **Ciudad Obregón** Mex.
106 C2 **Ciudad Real** Spain
145 C2 **Ciudad Río Bravo** Mex.
106 B1 **Ciudad Rodrigo** Spain
Ciudad Trujillo Dom. Rep. *see* **Santo Domingo**
145 C2 **Ciudad Victoria** Mex.
107 D1 **Ciutadella** Spain
108 B1 **Cividale del Friuli** Italy
108 B2 **Civitanova Marche** Italy
108 B2 **Civitavecchia** Italy
104 C2 **Civray** France
111 C3 **Çivril** Turkey
70 C2 **Cixi** China
99 D4 **Clacton-on-Sea** U.K.
128 C2 **Claire, Lake** Can.
105 C2 **Clamecy** France
140 C2 **Clanton** U.S.A.
122 A3 **Clanwilliam** S. Africa
97 C2 **Clara** Ireland
52 A2 **Clare** Austr.
138 C2 **Clare** U.S.A.
97 A2 **Clare Island** Ireland
139 E2 **Claremont** U.S.A.
97 B2 **Claremorris** Ireland
54 B2 **Clarence** N.Z.
55 B3 **Clarence Island** Antarctica
131 E3 **Clarenville** Can.
128 C2 **Claresholm** Can.
137 D2 **Clarinda** U.S.A.
144 A3 **Clarión, Isla** *i.* Mex.
123 C3 **Clarkebury** S. Africa
134 C1 **Clark Fork** *r.* U.S.A.
141 D2 **Clark Hill Reservoir** U.S.A.
138 C3 **Clarksburg** U.S.A.
140 B2 **Clarksdale** U.S.A.
134 C1 **Clarkston** U.S.A.
140 B1 **Clarksville** *AR* U.S.A.
140 C1 **Clarksville** *TN* U.S.A.
154 B1 **Claro** *r.* Brazil
143 C1 **Claude** U.S.A.
143 C1 **Clayton** U.S.A.
97 B3 **Clear, Cape** Ireland
126 C3 **Cleare, Cape** U.S.A.
137 E2 **Clear Lake** U.S.A.
135 B3 **Clear Lake** *l.* U.S.A.
128 C2 **Clearwater** Can.
129 C2 **Clearwater** *r.* Can.
141 D3 **Clearwater** U.S.A.
134 C1 **Clearwater** *r.* U.S.A.
143 D2 **Cleburne** U.S.A.
101 E1 **Clenze** Ger.
51 D2 **Clermont** Austr.
105 C2 **Clermont-Ferrand** France
100 C2 **Clervaux** Lux.
52 A2 **Cleve** Austr.
140 B2 **Cleveland** *MS* U.S.A.
138 C2 **Cleveland** *OH* U.S.A.
141 D1 **Cleveland** *TN* U.S.A.
134 D1 **Cleveland, Mount** U.S.A.
154 B3 **Clevelândia** Brazil
97 B2 **Clew Bay** Ireland
141 D3 **Clewiston** U.S.A.
97 A2 **Clifden** Ireland
53 D1 **Clifton** Austr.
142 B2 **Clifton** U.S.A.
142 B1 **Clines Corners** U.S.A.
128 B2 **Clinton** Can.
137 E2 **Clinton** *IA* U.S.A.
137 E3 **Clinton** *MO* U.S.A.
143 D1 **Clinton** *OK* U.S.A.
125 H8 **Clipperton, Île** *terr.* N. Pacific Ocean
96 A2 **Clisham** *h.* U.K.
98 B3 **Clitheroe** U.K.
97 B3 **Clonakilty** Ireland
51 D2 **Cloncurry** Austr.
97 C1 **Clones** Ireland
97 C2 **Clonmel** Ireland
101 D1 **Cloppenburg** Ger.
137 E1 **Cloquet** U.S.A.
136 B2 **Cloud Peak** U.S.A.
135 C3 **Clovis** *CA* U.S.A.
143 C2 **Clovis** *NM* U.S.A.
Cluain Meala Ireland *see* **Clonmel**
129 D2 **Cluff Lake Mine** Can.
110 B1 **Cluj-Napoca** Romania
51 C2 **Cluny** Austr.
105 D2 **Cluses** France
54 A3 **Clutha** *r.* N.Z.
96 B3 **Clyde** *r.* U.K.
96 B3 **Clyde, Firth of** *est.* U.K.
96 B3 **Clydebank** U.K.
127 H2 **Clyde River** Can.
144 B3 **Coalcomán** Mex.
128 C3 **Coaldale** Can.
135 C3 **Coaldale** U.S.A.
128 B2 **Coal River** Can.
150 C3 **Coari** Brazil
150 C3 **Coari** *r.* Brazil
141 C2 **Coastal Plain** U.S.A.
128 B2 **Coast Mountains** Can.
134 B2 **Coast Ranges** *mts* U.S.A.
96 B3 **Coatbridge** U.K.
129 F1 **Coats Island** Can.
55 C2 **Coats Land** *reg.* Antarctica
145 C3 **Coatzacoalcos** Mex.
146 A3 **Cobán** Guat.
53 C2 **Cobar** Austr.
97 B3 **Cobh** Ireland
152 B1 **Cobija** Bol.
Coblenz Ger. *see* **Koblenz**
130 C3 **Cobourg** Can.
50 C1 **Cobourg Peninsula** Austr.
53 C3 **Cobram** Austr.
101 E2 **Coburg** Ger.
152 B1 **Cochabamba** Bol.
100 C2 **Cochem** Ger.
Cochin India *see* **Kochi**
128 C2 **Cochrane** *Alta* Can.
130 B3 **Cochrane** *Ont.* Can.
153 A4 **Cochrane** Chile
52 A2 **Cockaleechie** Austr.
52 B2 **Cockburn** Austr.
Cockburn Town Turks and Caicos Is *see* **Grand Turk**
98 B2 **Cockermouth** U.K.
50 B3 **Cocklebiddy** Austr.
122 B3 **Cockscomb** *mt.* S. Africa
146 B3 **Coco** *r.* Hond./Nic.
125 J9 **Coco, Isla de** *i.* N. Pacific Ocean
159 F4 **Cocos Basin** Indian Ocean
58 A3 **Cocos Islands** *terr.* Indian Ocean
144 B2 **Cocula** Mex.
150 B2 **Cocuy, Sierra Nevada del** *mt.* Col.
139 E2 **Cod, Cape** U.S.A.
150 C3 **Codajás** Brazil
108 B2 **Codigoro** Italy
131 D2 **Cod Island** Can.
151 E3 **Codó** Brazil
136 B2 **Cody** U.S.A.
51 D1 **Coen** Austr.
100 C2 **Coesfeld** Ger.
113 I6 **Coëtivy** *i.* Seychelles

134 C1 **Coeur d'Alene** U.S.A.
100 C1 **Coevorden** Neth.
123 C3 **Coffee Bay** S. Africa
137 D3 **Coffeyville** U.S.A.
52 A2 **Coffin Bay** Austr.
53 D2 **Coffs Harbour** Austr.
123 C3 **Cofimvaba** S. Africa
104 B2 **Cognac** France
118 A2 **Cogo** Equat. Guinea
52 B3 **Cohuna** Austr.
146 B4 **Coiba, Isla de** *i.* Panama
153 A4 **Coihaique** Chile
73 B3 **Coimbatore** India
106 B1 **Coimbra** Port.
152 B1 **Coipasa, Salar de** *salt flat* Bol.
52 B3 **Colac** Austr.
155 D1 **Colatina** Brazil
136 C3 **Colby** U.S.A.
99 D4 **Colchester** U.K.
129 C2 **Cold Lake** Can.
96 C3 **Coldstream** U.K.
53 C2 **Coleambally** Austr.
143 D2 **Coleman** U.S.A.
52 B3 **Coleraine** Austr.
97 C1 **Coleraine** U.K.
123 C3 **Colesberg** S. Africa
153 A3 **Colico** Chile
144 B3 **Colima** Mex.
144 B3 **Colima, Nevado de** *vol.* Mex.
96 A2 **Coll** *i.* U.K.
53 C1 **Collarenebri** Austr.
143 D2 **College Station** U.S.A.
53 C1 **Collerina** Austr.
50 A3 **Collie** Austr.
50 B1 **Collier Bay** Austr.
138 C2 **Collingwood** Can.
54 B2 **Collingwood** N.Z.
126 F2 **Collinson Peninsula** Can.
101 F2 **Collmberg** *h.* Ger.
108 A3 **Collo** Alg.
97 B1 **Collooney** Ireland
105 D2 **Colmar** France
98 B3 **Colne** U.K.
100 C2 **Cologne** Ger.
Colomb-Béchar Alg. *see* **Béchar**
154 C2 **Colômbia** Brazil
150 B2 **Colombia** *country* S. America
73 B4 **Colombo** Sri Lanka
104 C3 **Colomiers** France
152 C3 **Colón** Arg.
146 C4 **Colón** Panama
59 D2 **Colonia** Micronesia
153 B4 **Colonia Las Heras** Arg.
109 C3 **Colonna, Capo** *c.* Italy
96 A2 **Colonsay** *i.* U.K.
153 B3 **Colorado** *r.* Arg.
142 A2 **Colorado** *r.* Mex./U.S.A.
143 D2 **Colorado** *r. Texas* U.S.A.
136 B3 **Colorado** *state* U.S.A.
135 C4 **Colorado Desert** U.S.A.
135 E3 **Colorado Plateau** U.S.A.
136 C3 **Colorado Springs** U.S.A.
144 B2 **Colotlán** Mex.
152 B1 **Colquiri** Bol.
136 B1 **Colstrip** U.S.A.
138 B3 **Columbia** *KY* U.S.A.
139 D3 **Columbia** *MD* U.S.A.
137 E3 **Columbia** *MO* U.S.A.
141 D2 **Columbia** *SC* U.S.A.
140 C1 **Columbia** *TN* U.S.A.
134 B1 **Columbia** *r.* U.S.A.
128 C2 **Columbia, Mount** Can.
134 D1 **Columbia Falls** U.S.A.
128 B2 **Columbia Mountains** Can.
134 C1 **Columbia Plateau** U.S.A.
141 D2 **Columbus** *GA* U.S.A.
138 B3 **Columbus** *IN* U.S.A.
140 C2 **Columbus** *MS* U.S.A.
134 E1 **Columbus** *MT* U.S.A.
137 D2 **Columbus** *NE* U.S.A.
142 B2 **Columbus** *NM* U.S.A.
138 C3 **Columbus** *OH* U.S.A.
143 D3 **Columbus** *TX* U.S.A.
134 C1 **Colville** U.S.A.
126 B2 **Colville** *r.* U.S.A.
126 D2 **Colville Lake** Can.
98 B3 **Colwyn Bay** U.K.
108 B2 **Comacchio** Italy
145 C3 **Comalcalco** Mex.
110 C1 **Comănești** Romania
130 C2 **Comencho, Lac** *l.* Can.
97 C2 **Comeragh Mountains** *hills* Ireland
143 D2 **Comfort** U.S.A.
75 D2 **Comilla** Bangl.
108 A2 **Comino, Capo** *c.* Italy
145 C3 **Comitán de Domínguez** Mex.
105 C2 **Commentry** France
143 D2 **Commerce** U.S.A.
127 G2 **Committee Bay** Can.
108 A1 **Como** Italy
Como, Lago di *l.* Italy *see* **Como, Lake**
108 A1 **Como, Lake** *l.* Italy
153 B4 **Comodoro Rivadavia** Arg.
145 B2 **Comonfort** Mex.
121 D2 **Comoros** *country* Africa
128 B3 **Comox** Can.
105 C2 **Compiègne** France
144 B2 **Compostela** Mex.
90 B2 **Comrat** Moldova
114 A4 **Conakry** Guinea
104 B2 **Concarneau** France
155 E1 **Conceição da Barra** Brazil
151 E3 **Conceição do Araguaia** Brazil
155 D1 **Conceição do Mato Dentro** Brazil
152 B2 **Concepción** Arg.
153 A3 **Concepción** Chile
144 B2 **Concepción** Mex.
135 B4 **Conception, Point** U.S.A.
154 C2 **Conchas** Brazil
142 C1 **Conchas Lake** U.S.A.
144 B2 **Conchos** *r.* Mex.
145 C2 **Conchos** *r.* Mex.
135 B3 **Concord** *CA* U.S.A.
139 E2 **Concord** *NH* U.S.A.
152 C3 **Concordia** Arg.
122 A2 **Concordia** S. Africa
137 D3 **Concordia** U.S.A.
53 C2 **Condobolin** Austr.
104 C3 **Condom** France
134 B1 **Condon** U.S.A.
108 B1 **Conegliano** Italy
51 E1 **Conflict Group** *is* P.N.G.
104 C2 **Confolens** France
135 D3 **Confusion Range** *mts* U.S.A.
75 C2 **Congdü** China
98 B3 **Congleton** U.K.
118 B3 **Congo** *country* Africa
118 B3 **Congo** *r.* Congo/Dem. Rep. Congo
Congo (Brazzaville) *country* Africa *see* **Congo**
Congo (Kinshasa) *country* Africa *see* **Congo, Democratic Republic of the**
118 C3 **Congo, Democratic Republic of the** *country* Africa
118 C3 **Congo Basin** Dem. Rep. Congo
Congo Free State *country* Africa *see* **Congo, Democratic Republic of the**
129 C2 **Conklin** Can.
97 B1 **Conn, Lough** *l.* Ireland
97 B2 **Connaught** *reg.* Ireland
139 E2 **Connecticut** *r.* U.S.A.
139 E2 **Connecticut** *state* U.S.A.
96 B2 **Connel** U.K.
97 B2 **Connemara** *reg.* Ireland
134 D1 **Conrad** U.S.A.
159 D7 **Conrad Rise** Southern Ocean
143 D2 **Conroe** U.S.A.
155 D2 **Conselheiro Lafaiete** Brazil
155 D1 **Conselheiro Pena** Brazil
100 B3 **Consenvoye** France
98 C2 **Consett** U.K.
63 B3 **Côn Sơn, Đao** *i.* Vietnam
Constance Ger. *see* **Konstanz**
105 D2 **Constance, Lake** Ger./Switz.
110 C2 **Constanța** Romania
106 B2 **Constantina** Spain
115 C1 **Constantine** Alg.
134 D2 **Contact** U.S.A.
155 D2 **Contagalo** Brazil
150 B3 **Contamana** Peru
153 A5 **Contreras, Isla** *i.* Chile
126 E2 **Contwoyto Lake** Can.
140 B1 **Conway** *AR* U.S.A.
139 E2 **Conway** *NH* U.S.A.
51 C2 **Coober Pedy** Austr.
Cooch Behar India *see* **Koch Bihar**
Cook, Mount *mt.* N.Z. *see* **Aoraki**
141 C1 **Cookeville** U.S.A.
126 B2 **Cook Inlet** *sea chan.* U.S.A.
49 K5 **Cook Islands** *terr.* S. Pacific Ocean
131 E2 **Cook's Harbour** Can.
97 C1 **Cookstown** U.K.
54 B2 **Cook Strait** N.Z.
51 D1 **Cooktown** Austr.
53 C2 **Coolabah** Austr.
53 C2 **Coolamon** Austr.
53 D1 **Coolangatta** Austr.
50 B3 **Coolgardie** Austr.
53 C3 **Cooma** Austr.
52 B2 **Coombah** Austr.
53 C2 **Coonabarabran** Austr.
52 A3 **Coonalpyn** Austr.
53 C2 **Coonamble** Austr.
53 C1 **Coongoola** Austr.
137 E1 **Coon Rapids** U.S.A.
52 A1 **Cooper Creek** *watercourse* Austr.
141 E3 **Cooper's Town** Bahamas
134 B2 **Coos Bay** U.S.A.
53 C2 **Cootamundra** Austr.
97 C1 **Cootehill** Ireland
145 C3 **Copainalá** Mex.
145 C3 **Copala** Mex.
93 F4 **Copenhagen** Denmark
109 C2 **Copertino** Italy
53 D1 **Copeton Reservoir** Austr.
152 A2 **Copiapó** Chile
143 D2 **Copperas Cove** U.S.A.
138 B1 **Copper Harbor** U.S.A.
Coppermine Can. *see* **Kugluktuk**
126 E2 **Coppermine** *r.* Can.
122 B2 **Copperton** S. Africa
Coquilhatville Dem. Rep. Congo *see* **Mbandaka**
152 A2 **Coquimbo** Chile
152 A2 **Coquimbo, Bahía de** *b.* Chile
110 B2 **Corabia** Romania
155 D1 **Coração de Jesus** Brazil
150 B4 **Coracora** Peru
53 D1 **Coraki** Austr.
50 A2 **Coral Bay** Austr.
127 G2 **Coral Harbour** Can.
156 D7 **Coral Sea** S. Pacific Ocean
48 G5 **Coral Sea Islands Territory** *terr.* Austr.
137 E2 **Coralville** U.S.A.
52 B3 **Corangamite, Lake** Austr.
99 C3 **Corby** U.K.
Corcaigh Ireland *see* **Cork**
135 C3 **Corcoran** U.S.A.
153 A4 **Corcovado, Golfo de** *sea chan.* Chile
141 D2 **Cordele** U.S.A.
64 B2 **Cordilleras Range** *mts* Phil.
155 D1 **Cordisburgo** Brazil
152 B3 **Córdoba** Arg.
145 C3 **Córdoba** Mex.
106 C2 **Córdoba** Spain
153 B3 **Córdoba, Sierras de** *mts* Arg.
126 C2 **Cordova** U.S.A.
51 D2 **Corfield** Austr.
111 A3 **Corfu** *i.* Greece
154 B1 **Corguinho** Brazil
106 B2 **Coria** Spain
106 B2 **Coria del Río** Spain
53 D2 **Coricudgy** *mt.* Austr.
111 B3 **Corinth** Greece
140 C2 **Corinth** U.S.A.
Corinth, Gulf of *sea chan.* Greece *see* **Gulf of Corinth**
155 D1 **Corinto** Brazil
97 B3 **Cork** Ireland
111 C2 **Çorlu** Turkey
154 B2 **Cornélio Procópio** Brazil
131 E3 **Corner Brook** Can.
53 C3 **Corner Inlet** *b.* Austr.
135 B3 **Corning** *CA* U.S.A.
139 D2 **Corning** *NY* U.S.A.
Corn Islands *is* Nic. *see* **Maíz, Islas del**
108 B2 **Corno, Monte** *mt.* Italy
130 C3 **Cornwall** Can.
126 F1 **Cornwallis Island** Can.
150 C1 **Coro** Venez.
155 D1 **Coroaci** Brazil
154 C1 **Coromandel** Brazil
73 C3 **Coromandel Coast** India
54 C1 **Coromandel Peninsula** N.Z.
64 B2 **Coron** Phil.
129 C2 **Coronation** Can.
126 E2 **Coronation Gulf** Can.
55 B3 **Coronation Island** S. Atlantic Ocean
155 D1 **Coronel Fabriciano** Brazil
152 C2 **Coronel Oviedo** Para.
154 B1 **Coronel Ponce** Brazil
153 B3 **Coronel Pringles** Arg.
154 A2 **Coronel Sapucaia** Brazil
153 B3 **Coronel Suárez** Arg.
109 D2 **Çorovodë** Albania
145 D3 **Corozal** Belize
143 D3 **Corpus Christi** U.S.A.
152 B1 **Corque** Bol.
151 E4 **Corrente** Brazil
154 B1 **Correntes** Brazil
151 E4 **Correntina** Brazil
97 B2 **Corrib, Lough** *l.* Ireland
152 C2 **Corrientes** Arg.
153 C3 **Corrientes, Cabo** *c.* Arg.
144 B2 **Corrientes, Cabo** *c.* Mex.
143 E2 **Corrigan** U.S.A.
53 C3 **Corryong** Austr.
Corse *i.* France *see* **Corsica**
105 D3 **Corse, Cap** *c.* France
105 D3 **Corsica** *i.* France
143 D2 **Corsicana** U.S.A.
105 D3 **Corte** France
106 B2 **Cortegana** Spain
136 B3 **Cortez** U.S.A.
108 B1 **Cortina d'Ampezzo** Italy
139 D2 **Cortland** U.S.A.
108 B2 **Cortona** Italy
106 B2 **Coruche** Port.
Çoruh Turkey *see* **Artvin**
80 B1 **Çorum** Turkey
151 D4 **Corumbá** Brazil
154 C1 **Corumbá** *r.* Brazil
154 C1 **Corumbá de Goiás** Brazil
Corunna Spain *see* **A Coruña**
134 B2 **Corvallis** U.S.A.
99 B3 **Corwen** U.K.
Cos *i.* Greece *see* **Kos**
144 B2 **Cosalá** Mex.
145 C3 **Cosamaloapan** Mex.
109 C3 **Cosenza** Italy
105 C2 **Cosne-Cours-sur-Loire** France
152 B3 **Cosquín** Arg.
107 C2 **Costa Blanca** *coastal area* Spain
107 D1 **Costa Brava** *coastal area* Spain
106 B2 **Costa de la Luz** *coastal area* Spain
107 C2 **Costa del Azahar** *coastal area* Spain
106 B2 **Costa del Sol** *coastal area* Spain
146 B3 **Costa de Mosquitos** *coastal area* Nic.
107 D1 **Costa Dorada** *coastal area* Spain
150 C4 **Costa Marques** Brazil
154 B1 **Costa Rica** Brazil
146 B3 **Costa Rica** *country* Central America
144 B2 **Costa Rica** Mex.
Costermansville Dem. Rep. Congo *see* **Bukavu**
110 B2 **Costești** Romania
64 B3 **Cotabato** Phil.
137 D1 **Coteau des Prairies** *reg.* U.S.A.
136 C1 **Coteau du Missouri** *reg.* U.S.A.
147 C3 **Coteaux** Haiti
105 D3 **Côte d'Azur** *coastal area* France
114 B4 **Côte d'Ivoire** *country* Africa
Côte Française de Somalis *country* Africa *see* **Djibouti**
105 C2 **Côtes de Meuse** *ridge* France
150 B3 **Cotopaxi, Volcán** *vol.* Ecuador
99 B4 **Cotswold Hills** U.K.
134 B2 **Cottage Grove** U.S.A.
102 C1 **Cottbus** Ger.
105 D3 **Cottian Alps** *mts* France/Italy
104 B2 **Coubre, Pointe de la** *pt* France
52 A3 **Couedic, Cape du** Austr.
105 C2 **Coulommiers** France
137 D2 **Council Bluffs** U.S.A.
88 B2 **Courland Lagoon** *b.* Lith./Rus. Fed.
100 A3 **Courmelles** France
128 B3 **Courtenay** Can.
104 B2 **Coutances** France
104 B2 **Coutras** France
100 B2 **Couvin** Belgium
99 C3 **Coventry** U.K.
106 B1 **Covilhã** Port.
141 D2 **Covington** *GA* U.S.A.
138 C3 **Covington** *KY* U.S.A.
138 C3 **Covington** *VA* U.S.A.
50 B3 **Cowan, Lake** *imp. l.* Austr.
96 C2 **Cowdenbeath** U.K.
52 A2 **Cowell** Austr.
53 C3 **Cowes** Austr.
134 B1 **Cowlitz** *r.* U.S.A.
53 C2 **Cowra** Austr.
154 B1 **Coxim** Brazil
154 B1 **Coxim** *r.* Brazil
75 D2 **Cox's Bazar** Bangl.
145 B3 **Coyuca de Benitez** Mex.
75 C1 **Cozhê** China
145 D2 **Cozumel** Mex.
145 D2 **Cozumel, Isla de** *i.* Mex.
52 A2 **Cradock** Austr.
123 C3 **Cradock** S. Africa
136 B2 **Craig** U.S.A.
102 C2 **Crailsheim** Ger.
110 B2 **Craiova** Romania
129 D2 **Cranberry Portage** Can.
53 C3 **Cranbourne** Austr.
128 C3 **Cranbrook** Can.
151 E3 **Crateús** Brazil
151 F3 **Crato** Brazil
154 C2 **Cravinhos** Brazil
136 C2 **Crawford** U.S.A.
138 B2 **Crawfordsville** U.S.A.
99 C4 **Crawley** U.K.
134 D1 **Crazy Mountains** U.S.A.
129 D2 **Cree** *r.* Can.
144 B2 **Creel** Mex.
129 D2 **Cree Lake** Can.
129 D2 **Creighton** Can.
104 C2 **Creil** France
100 B1 **Creil** Neth.
108 A1 **Crema** Italy
108 B1 **Cremona** Italy
108 B2 **Cres** *i.* Croatia
134 B2 **Crescent City** U.S.A.
53 D2 **Crescent Head** Austr.
135 E3 **Crescent Junction** U.S.A.
128 C3 **Creston** Can.
137 E2 **Creston** U.S.A.
140 C2 **Crestview** U.S.A.
111 B3 **Crete** *i.* Greece
107 D1 **Creus, Cap de** *c.* Spain
107 C2 **Crevillent** Spain
98 B3 **Crewe** U.K.
96 B2 **Crianlarich** U.K.
152 D2 **Criciúma** Brazil
96 C2 **Crieff** U.K.
108 B1 **Crikvenica** Croatia
91 C2 **Crimea** *pen.* Ukr.
101 F2 **Crimmitschau** Ger.
96 B2 **Crinan** U.K.
118 B2 **Cristal, Monts de** *mts* Equat. Guinea/Gabon
154 C1 **Cristalina** Brazil
110 B1 **Crișul Alb** *r.* Romania
101 E1 **Crivitz** Ger.
Crna Gora *country* Europe *see* **Montenegro**
109 C1 **Črnomelj** Slovenia
97 B2 **Croagh Patrick** *h.* Ireland
109 C1 **Croatia** *country* Europe
61 C1 **Crocker, Banjaran** *mts* Malaysia
143 D2 **Crockett** U.S.A.
59 C3 **Croker Island** Austr.
96 B2 **Cromarty** U.K.
99 D3 **Cromer** U.K.
54 A3 **Cromwell** N.Z.
147 C2 **Crooked Island** Bahamas
137 D1 **Crookston** U.S.A.
53 C2 **Crookwell** Austr.
53 D1 **Croppa Creek** Austr.
136 C1 **Crosby** U.S.A.
141 D3 **Cross City** U.S.A.
140 B2 **Crossett** U.S.A.
98 B2 **Cross Fell** *h.* U.K.
129 E2 **Cross Lake** Can.
141 C1 **Crossville** U.S.A.
109 C3 **Crotone** Italy
134 E1 **Crow Agency** U.S.A.
99 D4 **Crowborough** U.K.
140 B2 **Crowley** U.S.A.
53 D1 **Crows Nest** Austr.
128 C3 **Crowsnest Pass** Can.
159 D7 **Crozet, Îles** *is* Indian Ocean
146 C3 **Cruz, Cabo** *c.* Cuba
152 C2 **Cruz Alta** Brazil
152 B3 **Cruz del Eje** Arg.
155 D2 **Cruzeiro** Brazil
150 B3 **Cruzeiro do Sul** Brazil
52 A2 **Crystal Brook** Austr.
143 D3 **Crystal City** U.S.A.
138 B1 **Crystal Falls** U.S.A.
140 B2 **Crystal Springs** U.S.A.
103 E2 **Csongrád** Hungary
103 D2 **Csorna** Hungary

121 C2 **Cuamba** Moz.
120 B2 **Cuando** *r.* Angola/Zambia
120 A2 **Cuangar** Angola
118 B3 **Cuango** *r.* Angola/Dem. Rep. Congo
120 A1 **Cuanza** *r.* Angola
144 B2 **Cuatro Ciénegas** Mex.
144 B2 **Cuauhtémoc** Mex.
145 C3 **Cuautla** Mex.
146 B2 **Cuba** *country* West Indies
120 A2 **Cubal** Angola
120 B2 **Cubango** *r.* Angola/Namibia
150 B2 **Cúcuta** Col.
73 B3 **Cuddalore** India
73 B3 **Cuddapah** India
50 A2 **Cue** Austr.
106 C1 **Cuéllar** Spain
120 A2 **Cuemba** Angola
150 B3 **Cuenca** Ecuador
107 C1 **Cuenca** Spain
107 C1 **Cuenca, Serranía de** *mts* Spain
145 C3 **Cuernavaca** Mex.
143 D3 **Cuero** U.S.A.
104 C3 **Cugnaux** France
151 D4 **Cuiabá** Brazil
151 D4 **Cuiabá** *r.* Brazil
96 A2 **Cuillin Sound** *sea chan.* U.K.
120 A1 **Cuilo** Angola
120 B2 **Cuito** *r.* Angola
120 A2 **Cuito Cuanavale** Angola
60 B1 **Cukai** Malaysia
64 B2 **Culasi** Phil.
53 C3 **Culcairn** Austr.
100 B2 **Culemborg** Neth.
53 C1 **Culgoa** *r.* Austr.
144 B2 **Culiacán** Mex.
64 A2 **Culion** *i.* Phil.
107 C2 **Cullera** Spain
140 C2 **Cullman** U.S.A.
97 C1 **Cullybackey** U.K.
139 D3 **Culpeper** U.S.A.
151 D4 **Culuene** *r.* Brazil
54 B2 **Culverden** N.Z.
150 C1 **Cumaná** Venez.
139 D3 **Cumberland** U.S.A.
138 B3 **Cumberland** *r.* U.S.A.
141 D2 **Cumberland Island** U.S.A.
129 D2 **Cumberland Lake** Can.
127 H2 **Cumberland Peninsula** Can.
[illegible] **Cumberland Plateau** U.S.A.
127 H2 **Cumberland Sound** *sea chan.* Can.
96 C3 **Cumbernauld** U.K.
135 B3 **Cummings** U.S.A.
96 B3 **Cumnock** U.K.
144 B1 **Cumpas** Mex.
145 C3 **Cunduacán** Mex.
108 A2 **Cuneo** Italy
53 C1 **Cunnamulla** Austr.
108 A1 **Cuorgnè** Italy
96 C2 **Cupar** U.K.
110 B2 **Ćuprija** Serbia
147 D3 **Curaçao** *i.* Neth. Antilles
150 B3 **Curaray** *r.* Ecuador
153 A3 **Curicó** Chile
154 C3 **Curitiba** Brazil
52 A2 **Curnamona** Austr.
135 C3 **Currant** U.S.A.
51 D3 **Currie** Austr.
135 D2 **Currie** U.S.A.
51 E2 **Curtis Island** Austr.
151 D3 **Curuá** *r.* Brazil
60 B2 **Curup** Indon.
151 E3 **Cururupu** Brazil
155 D1 **Curvelo** Brazil
150 B4 **Cusco** Peru
97 C1 **Cushendun** U.K.
143 D1 **Cushing** U.S.A.
136 C2 **Custer** U.S.A.
134 D1 **Cut Bank** U.S.A.
140 B3 **Cut Off** U.S.A.
75 C2 **Cuttack** India
120 A2 **Cuvelai** Angola
101 D1 **Cuxhaven** Ger.
64 B2 **Cuyo Islands** Phil.
Cuzco Peru *see* **Cusco**
99 B4 **Cwmbrân** U.K.
119 C3 **Cyangugu** Rwanda
111 B3 **Cyclades** *is* Greece
129 C3 **Cypress Hills** Can.
80 B2 **Cyprus** *country* Asia
80 B2 **Cyprus** *i.* Asia
102 C2 **Czech Republic** *country* Europe
103 D1 **Czersk** Pol.
103 D1 **Częstochowa** Pol.

D

Đa, Sông *r.* Vietnam *see* **Black River**
69 D2 **Daban** China
103 D2 **Dabas** Hungary
114 A3 **Dabola** Guinea
103 D1 **Dąbrowa Górnicza** Pol.
110 B2 **Dăbuleni** Romania
Dacca Bangl. *see* **Dhaka**
102 C2 **Dachau** Ger.
Dachuan China *see* **Dazhou**
141 D3 **Dade City** U.S.A.
Dadong China *see* **Donggang**
Dadra India *see* **Achalpur**
74 B2 **Dadra and Nagar Haveli** *union terr.* India
74 A2 **Dadu** Pak.
Daegu S. Korea *see* **Taegu**
64 B2 **Daet** Phil.
114 A3 **Dagana** Senegal
119 D2 **Daga Post** Sudan
88 C2 **Dagda** Latvia
64 B2 **Dagupan** Phil.
Dahalach, Isole *is* Eritrea *see* **Dahlak Archipelago**
74 B3 **Dahanu** India
69 D2 **Da Hinggan Ling** *mts* China
116 C3 **Dahlak Archipelago** *is* Eritrea
100 C2 **Dahlem** Ger.
78 B3 **Dahm, Ramlat** *des.* Saudi Arabia/Yemen
74 B2 **Dahod** India
Dahomey *country* Africa *see* **Benin**
Dahra Senegal *see* **Dara**
81 C2 **Dahūk** Iraq
60 B2 **Daik** Indon.
106 C2 **Daimiel** Spain
Dairen China *see* **Dalian**
51 C2 **Dajarra** Austr.
70 A2 **Dajing** China
114 A3 **Dakar** Senegal
117 C4 **Daketa Shet'** *watercourse* Eth.
Dakhla Oasis *oasis* Egypt *see* **Wāḩāt ad Dākhilah**
63 A3 **Dakoank** India
88 C3 **Dakol'ka** *r.* Belarus
Đakovica Kosovo *see* **Gjakovë**
109 C1 **Đakovo** Croatia
120 B2 **Dala** Angola
70 A1 **Dalain Hob** China
93 G3 **Dalälven** *r.* Sweden
111 C3 **Dalaman** Turkey
111 C3 **Dalaman** *r.* Turkey
68 C2 **Dalandzadgad** Mongolia
64 B2 **Dalanganem Islands** Phil.
63 B2 **Đa Lat** Vietnam
Dalatando Angola *see* **N'dalatando**
74 A2 **Dalbandin** Pak.
96 C3 **Dalbeattie** U.K.
53 D1 **Dalby** Austr.
93 E3 **Dale** Norway
141 C1 **Dale Hollow Lake** U.S.A.
53 C3 **Dalgety** Austr.
143 C1 **Dalhart** U.S.A.
131 D3 **Dalhousie** Can.
62 B1 **Dali** China
70 C2 **Dalian** China
96 C3 **Dalkeith** U.K.
143 D2 **Dallas** U.S.A.
128 A2 **Dall Island** U.S.A.
Dalmacija *reg.* Bos.-Herz./Croatia *see* **Dalmatia**
96 B2 **Dalmally** U.K.
109 C2 **Dalmatia** *reg.* Bos.-Herz./Croatia
96 B3 **Dalmellington** U.K.
66 C2 **Dal'negorsk** Rus. Fed.
66 B1 **Dal'nerechensk** Rus. Fed.
Dalny China *see* **Dalian**
114 B4 **Daloa** Côte d'Ivoire
71 A3 **Dalou Shan** *mts* China
51 D2 **Dalrymple, Mount** Austr.
92 □A3 **Dalsmynni** Iceland
75 C2 **Daltenganj** India
141 D2 **Dalton** U.S.A.
Daltonganj India *see* **Daltenganj**
60 B1 **Daludalu** Indon.
71 B3 **Daluo Shan** *mt.* China
92 □B2 **Dalvík** Iceland
96 B2 **Dalwhinnie** U.K.
50 C1 **Daly** *r.* Austr.
51 C1 **Daly Waters** Austr.
74 B2 **Daman** India
74 B2 **Daman and Diu** *union terr.* India
116 B1 **Damanhūr** Egypt
59 C3 **Damar** *i.* Indon.
118 B2 **Damara** C.A.R.
80 B2 **Damascus** Syria
115 D3 **Damaturu** Nigeria
76 B3 **Damāvand, Qolleh-ye** *mt.* Iran
120 A1 **Damba** Angola
118 B1 **Damboa** Nigeria
81 D2 **Damghan** Iran
Damietta Egypt *see* **Dumyāţ**
79 C2 **Dammam** Saudi Arabia
101 D1 **Damme** Ger.
75 B2 **Damoh** India
114 B4 **Damongo** Ghana
50 A2 **Dampier** Austr.
59 C3 **Dampir, Selat** *sea chan.* Indon.
75 D1 **Damxung** China
114 B4 **Danané** Côte d'Ivoire
63 B2 **Đa Năng** Vietnam
139 E2 **Danbury** U.S.A.
70 C1 **Dandong** China
117 B3 **Dangila** Eth.
146 B3 **Dangriga** Belize
70 B2 **Dangshan** China
89 F2 **Danilov** Rus. Fed.
89 E2 **Danilovskaya Vozvyshennost'** *hills* Rus. Fed.
70 B2 **Danjiangkou** China
79 C2 **Ḑank** Oman
89 E3 **Dankov** Rus. Fed.
146 B3 **Danlí** Hond.
101 E1 **Dannenberg (Elbe)** Ger.
54 C2 **Dannevirke** N.Z.
62 B2 **Dan Sai** Thai.
110 A1 **Danube** *r.* Europe
110 C1 **Danube Delta** Romania/Ukr.
138 B2 **Danville** *IL* U.S.A.
138 C3 **Danville** *KY* U.S.A.
139 D3 **Danville** *VA* U.S.A.
Danxian China *see* **Danzhou**
71 A4 **Danzhou** China
Danzig, Gulf of *g.* Pol./Rus. Fed. *see* **Gdańsk, Gulf of**
Daojiang China *see* **Daoxian**
115 D2 **Dao Timmi** Niger
Daoud Alg. *see* **Aïn Beïda**
114 B4 **Daoukro** Côte d'Ivoire
71 B3 **Daoxian** China
64 B3 **Dapa** Phil.
114 C3 **Dapaong** Togo
68 C2 **Da Qaidam Zhen** China
69 E1 **Daqing** China
114 A3 **Dara** Senegal
80 B2 **Dar'ā** Syria
81 D3 **Dārāb** Iran
115 D1 **Daraj** Libya
81 D2 **Dārān** Iran
Đaravica Kosovo *see* **Gjeravicë**
75 C2 **Darbhanga** India
Dardo China *see* **Kangding**
119 D3 **Dar es Salaam** Tanz.
117 A3 **Darfur** *reg.* Sudan
74 B1 **Dargai** Pak.
54 B1 **Dargaville** N.Z.
53 C3 **Dargo** Austr.
68 D1 **Darhan** Mongolia
150 B2 **Darién, Golfo del** *g.* Col.
Darjeeling India *see* **Darjiling**
75 C2 **Darjiling** India
68 C2 **Darlag** China
52 B2 **Darling** *r.* Austr.
53 C1 **Darling Downs** *hills* Austr.
50 A3 **Darling Range** *hills* Austr.
98 C2 **Darlington** U.K.
53 C2 **Darlington Point** Austr.
103 D1 **Darłowo** Pol.
101 D3 **Darmstadt** Ger.
115 E1 **Darnah** Libya
52 B2 **Darnick** Austr.
55 H3 **Darnley, Cape** Antarctica
107 C1 **Daroca** Spain
99 D4 **Dartford** U.K.
99 A4 **Dartmoor** *hills* U.K.
131 D3 **Dartmouth** Can.
99 B4 **Dartmouth** U.K.
59 D3 **Daru** P.N.G.
59 C2 **Daruba** Indon.
50 C1 **Darwin** Austr.
153 C5 **Darwin** Falkland Is
79 C2 **Dārzīn** Iran
65 A1 **Dashiqiao** China
Dashkhovuz Turkm. *see* **Daşoguz**
74 A2 **Dasht** *r.* Pak.
76 B2 **Daşoguz** Turkm.
61 C1 **Datadian** Indon.
111 C3 **Datça** Turkey
66 D2 **Date** Japan
71 B3 **Datian** China
70 B1 **Datong** China
64 B3 **Datu Piang** Phil.
74 B1 **Daud Khel** Pak.
88 B2 **Daugava** *r.* Latvia
88 C2 **Daugavpils** Latvia
100 C2 **Daun** Ger.
129 D2 **Dauphin** Can.
129 E2 **Dauphin Lake** Can.
73 B3 **Davangere** India
64 B3 **Davao** Phil.
64 B3 **Davao Gulf** Phil.
137 E2 **Davenport** U.S.A.
99 C3 **Daventry** U.K.
123 C2 **Daveyton** S. Africa
146 B4 **David** Panama
129 D2 **Davidson** Can.
126 F3 **Davidson Lake** Can.
135 B3 **Davis** U.S.A.
131 D2 **Davis Inlet (abandoned)** Can.
55 I3 **Davis Sea** *sea* Antarctica
160 P3 **Davis Strait** *str.* Can./Greenland
105 D2 **Davos** Switz.
88 C3 **Davyd-Haradok** Belarus
78 A2 **Dawmat al Jandal** Saudi Arabia
79 C3 **Dawqah** Oman
78 B3 **Dawqah** Saudi Arabia
126 C2 **Dawson** Can.
141 D2 **Dawson** U.S.A.
128 B2 **Dawson Creek** Can.
128 B2 **Dawsons Landing** Can.
68 C2 **Dawu** China
Dawukou China *see* **Shizuishan**
79 C2 **Dawwah** Oman
104 B3 **Dax** France
Daxian China *see* **Dazhou**
68 C2 **Da Xueshan** *mts* China
52 B3 **Daylesford** Austr.
Dayong China *see* **Zhangjiajie**
81 C2 **Dayr az Zawr** Syria
138 C3 **Dayton** U.S.A.
141 D3 **Daytona Beach** U.S.A.
71 B3 **Dayu** China
Da Yunhe *canal* China *see* **Jinghang Yunhe**
79 C2 **Dayyer** Iran
70 A2 **Dazhou** China
122 B3 **De Aar** S. Africa
141 D3 **Deadman Bay** U.S.A.
80 B2 **Dead Sea** *salt l.* Asia
99 D4 **Deal** U.K.
71 B3 **De'an** China
152 B3 **Deán Funes** Arg.
128 B2 **Dease Lake** Can.
126 E2 **Dease Strait** Can.
135 C3 **Death Valley** *depr.* U.S.A.
104 C2 **Deauville** France
61 C1 **Debak** Malaysia
111 B2 **Debar** Macedonia
103 E1 **Dębica** Pol.
103 E1 **Dęblin** Pol.
114 B3 **Débo, Lac** *l.* Mali
103 E2 **Debrecen** Hungary
117 B3 **Debre Markos** Eth.
119 D2 **Debre Sīna** Eth.
117 B3 **Debre Tabor** Eth.
117 B4 **Debre Zeyit** Eth.
140 C2 **Decatur** *AL* U.S.A.
138 B3 **Decatur** *IL* U.S.A.
73 B3 **Deccan** *plat.* India
53 D1 **Deception Bay** Austr.
71 A3 **Dechang** China
102 C1 **Děčín** Czech Rep.
137 E2 **Decorah** U.S.A.
154 C2 **Dedo de Deus** *mt.* Brazil
88 C2 **Dedovichi** Rus. Fed.
121 C2 **Dedza** Malawi
99 B3 **Dee** *r. England/Wales* U.K.
96 C2 **Dee** *r. Scotland* U.K.
130 C3 **Deep River** Can.
53 D1 **Deepwater** Austr.
131 E3 **Deer Lake** Can.
134 D1 **Deer Lodge** U.S.A.
138 C2 **Defiance** U.S.A.
140 C2 **De Funiak Springs** U.S.A.
68 C2 **Dêgê** China
117 C4 **Degeh Bur** Eth.
139 F1 **Dégelis** Can.
102 C2 **Deggendorf** Ger.
91 E2 **Degtevo** Rus. Fed.
81 C2 **Dehlorān** Iran
74 B1 **Dehra Dun** India
75 C2 **Dehri** India
69 E2 **Dehui** China
100 A2 **Deinze** Belgium
110 B1 **Dej** Romania
138 B2 **De Kalb** U.S.A.
116 B3 **Dekemhare** Eritrea
118 C3 **Dekese** Dem. Rep. Congo
118 B2 **Dékoa** C.A.R.
141 D3 **De Land** U.S.A.
135 C3 **Delano** U.S.A.
135 D3 **Delano Peak** U.S.A.
[illegible] I3 **Delap-Uliga-Djarrit** Marshall Is
74 A1 **Delārām** Afgh.
123 C2 **Delareyville** S. Africa
129 D2 **Delaronde Lake** Can.
138 C2 **Delaware** U.S.A.
139 D3 **Delaware** *r.* U.S.A.
139 D3 **Delaware** *state* U.S.A.
139 D3 **Delaware Bay** U.S.A.
53 C3 **Delegate** Austr.
118 C2 **Délembé** C.A.R.
105 D2 **Delémont** Switz.
100 B1 **Delft** Neth.
100 C1 **Delfzijl** Neth.
121 D2 **Delgado, Cabo** *c.* Moz.
68 C1 **Delgerhaan** Mongolia
68 C2 **Delhi** China
74 B2 **Delhi** India
60 B2 **Deli** *i.* Indon.
128 B1 **Déline** Can.
Delingha China *see* **Delhi**
101 F2 **Delitzsch** Ger.
107 D2 **Dellys** Alg.
135 C4 **Del Mar** U.S.A.
101 D1 **Delmenhorst** Ger.
109 B1 **Delnice** Croatia
136 B3 **Del Norte** U.S.A.
83 L1 **De-Longa, Ostrova** *is* Rus. Fed.
De Long Islands *is* Rus. Fed. *see* **De-Longa, Ostrova**
De Long Strait *sea chan.* Rus. Fed. *see* **Longa, Proliv**
129 D3 **Deloraine** Can.
111 B3 **Delphi** *tourist site* Greece
141 D3 **Delray Beach** U.S.A.
143 C3 **Del Rio** U.S.A.
136 B3 **Delta** *CO* U.S.A.
135 D3 **Delta** *UT* U.S.A.
126 C2 **Delta Junction** U.S.A.
109 D3 **Delvinë** Albania
106 C1 **Demanda, Sierra de la** *mts* Spain
Demavend *mt.* Iran *see* **Damāvand, Qolleh-ye**
118 C3 **Demba** Dem. Rep. Congo
119 D1 **Dembech'a** Eth.
117 B4 **Dembī Dolo** Eth.
Demerara Guyana *see* **Georgetown**
91 C3 **Demerdzhi** *mt.* Ukr.
89 D2 **Demidov** Rus. Fed.
142 B2 **Deming** U.S.A.
111 C3 **Demirci** Turkey
111 C2 **Demirköy** Turkey
102 C1 **Demmin** Ger.
140 C2 **Demopolis** U.S.A.
60 B2 **Dempo, Gunung** *vol.* Indon.
89 D2 **Demyansk** Rus. Fed.
122 B3 **De Naawte** S. Africa
117 C3 **Denakil** *reg.* Africa
98 B3 **Denbigh** U.K.
100 B1 **Den Burg** Neth.
62 B2 **Den Chai** Thai.
60 B2 **Dendang** Indon.
100 B2 **Dendermonde** Belgium
100 B2 **Dendre** *r.* Belgium
Dengjiabu China *see* **Yujiang**
70 A1 **Dengkou** China
Dengxian China *see* **Dengzhou**
70 B2 **Dengzhou** China

Dengzhou China see Penglai
Den Haag Neth. see The Hague
50 A2 Denham Austr.
100 B1 Den Helder Neth.
107 D2 Dénia Spain
52 B3 Deniliquin Austr.
134 C2 Denio U.S.A.
137 D2 Denison IA U.S.A.
143 D2 Denison TX U.S.A.
111 C3 Denizli Turkey
53 D2 Denman Austr.
50 A3 Denmark Austr.
93 E4 Denmark country Europe
84 B2 Denmark Strait Greenland/Iceland
77 C3 Denov Uzbek.
61 C2 Denpasar Indon.
143 D2 Denton U.S.A.
50 A3 D'Entrecasteaux, Point Austr.
59 E3 D'Entrecasteaux Islands P.N.G.
141 D2 Dentsville U.S.A.
136 B3 Denver U.S.A.
75 C2 Deogarh Orissa India
74 B2 Deogarh Rajasthan India
75 C2 Deoghar India
138 B2 De Pere U.S.A.
83 K2 Deputatskiy Rus. Fed.
62 A1 Dêqên China
140 B2 De Queen U.S.A.
74 A2 Dera Bugti Pak.
74 B1 Dera Ghazi Khan Pak.
74 B1 Dera Ismail Khan Pak.
87 D4 Derbent Rus. Fed.
50 B1 Derby Austr.
99 C3 Derby U.K.
137 D3 Derby U.S.A.
99 D3 Dereham U.K.
97 B2 Derg, Lough l. Ireland
91 D1 Derhachi Ukr.
140 B2 De Ridder U.S.A.
91 D2 Derkul r. Rus. Fed./Ukr.
75 B1 Dêrub China
116 B3 Derudeb Sudan
122 B3 De Rust S. Africa
109 C2 Derventa Bos.-Herz.
98 C3 Derwent r. England U.K.
98 C3 Derwent r. England U.K.
98 B2 Derwent Water l. U.K.
77 C1 Derzhavinsk Kazakh.
Derzhavinskiy Kazakh. see Derzhavinsk
152 B1 Desaguadero r. Bol.
49 M5 Désappointement, Îles du is Fr. Polynesia
129 D2 Deschambault Lake Can.
134 B1 Deschutes r. U.S.A.
117 B3 Desē Eth.
153 B4 Deseado Arg.
153 B4 Deseado r. Arg.
142 A2 Desemboque Mex.
137 E2 Des Moines U.S.A.
137 E2 Des Moines r. U.S.A.
91 C1 Desna r. Rus. Fed./Ukr.
89 D3 Desnogorsk Rus. Fed.
101 F2 Dessau Ger.
Dessye Eth. see Desē
128 A1 Destruction Bay Can.
149 C4 Desventuradas, Islas is S. Pacific Ocean
128 C1 Detah Can.
120 B2 Dete Zimbabwe
101 D2 Detmold Ger.
138 C2 Detroit U.S.A.
137 D1 Detroit Lakes U.S.A.
Dett Zimbabwe see Dete
100 B2 Deurne Neth.
110 B1 Deva Romania
100 C1 Deventer Neth.
96 C2 Deveron r. U.K.
103 D2 Devét skal h. Czech Rep.
137 D1 Devil's Lake U.S.A.
128 A2 Devil's Paw mt. U.S.A.
99 C4 Devizes U.K.
74 B2 Devli India
110 C2 Devnya Bulg.
128 C2 Devon Can.
126 F1 Devon Island Can.
51 D4 Devonport Austr.
74 B2 Dewas India
137 F3 Dexter U.S.A.
70 A2 Deyang China
59 D3 Deyong, Tanjung pt Indon.
81 C2 Dezfūl Iran
70 B2 Dezhou China
79 C2 Dhahran Saudi Arabia
75 D2 Dhaka Bangl.
78 B3 Dhamār Yemen
75 C2 Dhamtari India
75 C2 Dhanbad India
74 B2 Dhandhuka India
75 C2 Dhankuta Nepal
74 B2 Dhar India
75 D2 Dharmanagar India
73 B3 Dharmapuri India
75 C2 Dharmjaygarh India
114 B3 Ḑhar Oualâta hills Maur.
114 B3 Ḑhar Tîchît hills Maur.
73 B3 Dharwad India
Dharwar India see Dharwad
74 B2 Dhasa India
75 C2 Dhaulagiri mt. Nepal
78 B3 Dhubāb Yemen
74 B2 Dhule India
Dhulia India see Dhule
117 C4 Dhuusa Marreeb Somalia
144 A1 Diablo, Picacho del mt. Mex.
142 B2 Diablo Plateau U.S.A.
121 C2 Diaca Moz.
51 C2 Diamantina watercourse Austr.
155 D1 Diamantina Brazil
151 E4 Diamantina, Chapada plat. Brazil
159 F6 Diamantina Deep sea feature Indian Ocean
151 D4 Diamantino Mato Grosso Brazil
154 B1 Diamantino Mato Grosso Brazil
71 B3 Dianbai China
151 E4 Dianópolis Brazil
114 B4 Dianra Côte d'Ivoire
114 C3 Diapaga Burkina
79 C2 Dibā al Ḩiṣn U.A.E.
79 C2 Ḑibab Oman
118 C3 Dibaya Dem. Rep. Congo
122 B2 Dibeng S. Africa
72 D2 Dibrugarh India
136 C1 Dickinson U.S.A.
140 C1 Dickson U.S.A.
Dicle r. Turkey see Tigris
105 D3 Die France
Diedenhofen France see Thionville
129 D2 Diefenbaker, Lake Can.
Diégo Suarez Madag. see Antsirañana
114 B3 Diéma Mali
101 D2 Diemel r. Ger.
62 B1 Điên Biên Phu Vietnam
62 B2 Diên Châu Vietnam
101 D1 Diepholz Ger.
104 C2 Dieppe France
100 B2 Diest Belgium
115 D3 Diffa Niger
131 D3 Digby Can.
105 D3 Digne-les-Bains France
105 C2 Digoin France
64 B3 Digos Phil.
59 D3 Digul r. Indon.
105 D2 Dijon France
115 D4 Dik Chad
117 C3 Dikhil Djibouti
111 C3 Dikili Turkey
100 A2 Diksmuide Belgium
82 G2 Dikson Rus. Fed.
115 D3 Dikwa Nigeria
117 B4 Dīla Eth.
59 C3 Dili East Timor
101 D2 Dillenburg Ger.
117 A3 Dilling Sudan
126 B3 Dillingham U.S.A.
134 D1 Dillon MT U.S.A.
141 E2 Dillon SC U.S.A.
118 C4 Dilolo Dem. Rep. Congo
72 D2 Dimapur India
Dimashq Syria see Damascus
52 B3 Dimboola Austr.
110 C2 Dimitrovgrad Bulg.
87 D3 Dimitrovgrad Rus. Fed.
Dimitrovo Bulg. see Pernik
64 B2 Dinagat i. Phil.
75 C2 Dinajpur Bangl.
104 B2 Dinan France
100 B2 Dinant Belgium
111 D3 Dinar Turkey
81 D2 Dīnār, Kūh-e mt. Iran
104 B2 Dinard France
Dinbych U.K. see Denbigh
73 B3 Dindigul India
118 B1 Dindima Nigeria
123 D1 Dindiza Moz.
101 E2 Dingelstädt Ger.
75 C2 Dinggyê China
Dingle Ireland see An Daingean
97 A2 Dingle Bay Ireland
71 B3 Dingnan China
102 C2 Dingolfing Ger.
114 A3 Dinguiraye Guinea
96 B2 Dingwall U.K.
70 A2 Dingxi China
123 C1 Dinokwe Botswana
91 D2 Dinskaya Rus. Fed.
100 C2 Dinslaken Ger.
135 C3 Dinuba U.S.A.
114 B3 Dioïla Mali
154 B3 Dionísio Cerqueira Brazil
114 A3 Diourbel Senegal
75 D2 Diphu India
64 B3 Dipolog Phil.
74 B1 Dir Pak.
51 D1 Direction, Cape Austr.
117 C4 Dirē Dawa Eth.
120 B2 Dirico Angola
50 A2 Dirk Hartog Island Austr.
53 C1 Dirranbandi Austr.
78 B3 Ḑirs Saudi Arabia
153 E5 Disappointment, Cape S. Georgia
134 B1 Disappointment, Cape U.S.A.
50 B2 Disappointment, Lake imp. l. Austr.
52 B3 Discovery Bay Austr.
Disko i. Greenland see Qeqertarsuaq
141 E1 Dismal Swamp U.S.A.
99 D3 Diss U.K.
154 C1 Distrito Federal admin. dist. Brazil
108 B3 Dittaino r. Italy
74 B2 Diu India
155 D2 Divinópolis Brazil
87 D4 Divnoye Rus. Fed.
114 B4 Divo Côte d'Ivoire
80 B2 Divriği Turkey
74 A2 Diwana Pak.
138 B2 Dixon U.S.A.
128 A2 Dixon Entrance sea chan. Can./U.S.A.
81 C2 Diyarbakır Turkey
74 A2 Diz Pak.
115 D2 Djado Niger
115 D2 Djado, Plateau du Niger
Djakarta Indon. see Jakarta
118 B3 Djambala Congo
115 C2 Djanet Alg.
115 D3 Djédaa Chad
115 C1 Djelfa Alg.
119 C2 Djéma C.A.R.
114 B3 Djenné Mali
114 B3 Djibo Burkina
117 C3 Djibouti country Africa
117 C3 Djibouti Djibouti
Djidjelli Alg. see Jijel
118 C2 Djolu Dem. Rep. Congo
114 C4 Djougou Benin
118 B2 Djoum Cameroon
115 D3 Djourab, Erg du des. Chad
92 □C3 Djúpivogur Iceland
89 F3 Dmitriyevka Rus. Fed.
89 E3 Dmitriyev-L'govskiy Rus. Fed.
Dmitriyevsk Ukr. see Makiyivka
89 E2 Dmitrov Rus. Fed.
Dmytriyevs'k Ukr. see Makiyivka
89 D3 Dnieper r. Rus. Fed.
91 C2 Dnieper r. Ukr.
90 B2 Dniester r. Ukr.
Dnipro r. Ukr. see Dnieper
Dnepr r. Rus. Fed. see Dnieper
91 C2 Dniprodzerzhyns'k Ukr.
91 D2 Dnipropetrovs'k Ukr.
91 C2 Dniprorudne Ukr.
Dnister r. Ukr. see Dniester
90 C2 Dnistrovs'kyy Lyman lag. Ukr.
88 C2 Dno Rus. Fed.
121 C2 Doa Moz.
115 D4 Doba Chad
88 B2 Dobele Latvia
101 F2 Döbeln Ger.
59 C3 Doberai, Jazirah pen. Indon.
Doberai Peninsula pen. Indon. see Doberai, Jazirah
59 C3 Dobo Indon.
109 C2 Doboj Bos.-Herz.
103 E1 Dobre Miasto Pol.
110 C2 Dobrich Bulg.
89 F3 Dobrinka Rus. Fed.
89 E3 Dobroye Rus. Fed.
89 D3 Dobrush Belarus
86 E3 Dobryanka Rus. Fed.
155 E1 Doce r. Brazil
145 B2 Doctor Arroyo Mex.
144 B2 Doctor Belisario Domínguez Mex.
Doctor Petru Groza Romania see Ştei
111 C3 Dodecanese is Greece
Dodekanisos is Greece see Dodecanese
136 C3 Dodge City U.S.A.
119 D3 Dodoma Tanz.
100 C1 Doesburg Neth.
100 C2 Doetinchem Neth.
59 C3 Dofa Indon.
75 C1 Dogai Coring salt l. China
128 B2 Dog Creek Can.
67 B3 Dōgo i. Japan
115 C3 Dogondoutchi Niger
81 C2 Doğubeyazıt Turkey
79 C2 Doha Qatar
62 A2 Doi Saket Thai.
81 D2 Dokali Iran
100 B1 Dokkum Neth.
88 C3 Dokshytsy Belarus
91 D2 Dokuchayevs'k Ukr.
142 A1 Dolan Springs U.S.A.
130 C3 Dolbeau-Mistassini Can.
104 B2 Dol-de-Bretagne France
105 D2 Dole France
91 D2 Dolgaya, Kosa spit Rus. Fed.
99 B3 Dolgellau U.K.
89 E3 Dolgorukovo Rus. Fed.
89 E3 Dolgoye Rus. Fed.
69 F1 Dolinsk Rus. Fed.
103 D2 Dolný Kubín Slovakia
59 D3 Dolok, Pulau i. Indon.
108 B1 Dolomites mts Italy
Dolomiti mts Italy see Dolomites
70 B1 Dolonnur China
117 C4 Dolo Odo Eth.
144 A2 Dolores Mex.
126 E2 Dolphin and Union Strait Can.
90 A2 Dolyna Ukr.
102 C2 Domažlice Czech Rep.
93 E3 Dombås Norway
103 D2 Dombóvár Hungary
Dombrovitsa Ukr. see Dubrovytsya
Dombrowa Pol. see Dąbrowa Górnicza
128 B2 Dome Creek Can.
147 D3 Dominica country West Indies
147 C3 Dominican Republic country West Indies
118 C3 Domiongo Dem. Rep. Congo
117 C4 Domo Eth.
89 E2 Domodedovo Rus. Fed.
111 B3 Domokos Greece
61 C2 Dompu Indon.
153 A3 Domuyo, Volcán vol. Arg.
142 B3 Don Mex.
89 E3 Don r. Rus. Fed.
96 C2 Don r. U.K.
97 D1 Donaghadee U.K.
52 B3 Donald Austr.
Donau r. Austria/Ger. see Danube
102 C2 Donauwörth Ger.
106 B2 Don Benito Spain
98 C3 Doncaster U.K.
120 A1 Dondo Angola
121 C2 Dondo Moz.
73 C4 Dondra Head hd Sri Lanka
97 B1 Donegal Ireland
97 B1 Donegal Bay Ireland
91 D2 Donets'k Ukr.
91 D2 Donets'kyy Kryazh hills Rus. Fed./Ukr.
118 B2 Donga Nigeria
50 A2 Dongara Austr.
71 A3 Dongchuan China
71 A4 Dongfang China
66 B1 Dongfanghong China
61 C2 Donggala Indon.
65 A2 Donggang China
Donggou China see Donggang
71 B3 Dongguan China
62 B2 Đông Ha Vietnam
Dong Hai sea N. Pacific Ocean see East China Sea
62 B2 Đông Hơi Vietnam
116 B3 Dongola Sudan
118 B2 Dongou Congo
Dong Phaya Yen Range mts Thai. see San Khao Phang Hoei
63 B2 Dong Phraya Yen esc. Thai.
Dongping China see Anhua
71 B3 Dongshan China
Dongsheng China see Ordos
70 C2 Dongtai China
71 B3 Dongting Hu l. China
Dong Ujimqin Qi China see Uliastai
71 C3 Dongyang China
70 B2 Dongying China
143 D3 Donna U.S.A.
54 B1 Donnellys Crossing N.Z.
100 C3 Donnersberg h. Ger.
107 C1 Donostia-San Sebastián Spain
81 D1 Donyztau, Sor dry lake Kazakh.
51 C1 Doomadgee Austr.
138 B2 Door Peninsula U.S.A.
117 C4 Dooxo Nugaaleed val. Somalia
50 B2 Dora, Lake imp. l. Austr.
99 B4 Dorchester U.K.
122 A1 Dordabis Namibia
104 B2 Dordogne r. France
100 B2 Dordrecht Neth.
123 C3 Dordrecht S. Africa
122 A1 Doreenville Namibia
129 D2 Doré Lake Can.
101 D1 Dorfmark Ger.
114 B3 Dori Burkina
122 A3 Doring r. S. Africa
100 C2 Dormagen Ger.
96 B2 Dornoch U.K.
96 B2 Dornoch Firth est. U.K.
114 B3 Doro Mali
89 D3 Dorogobuzh Rus. Fed.
110 C1 Dorohoi Romania
68 C1 Döröö Nuur salt l. Mongolia
92 G3 Dorotea Sweden
50 A2 Dorre Island Austr.
53 D2 Dorrigo Austr.
100 C2 Dorsten Ger.
100 C2 Dortmund Ger.
100 C2 Dortmund-Ems-Kanal canal Ger.
153 B4 Dos Bahías, Cabo c. Arg.
101 F1 Dosse r. Ger.
114 C3 Dosso Niger
141 C2 Dothan U.S.A.
101 D1 Dötlingen Ger.
105 C1 Douai France
118 A2 Douala Cameroon
104 B2 Douarnenez France
105 D2 Doubs r. France/Switz.
54 A3 Doubtful Sound N.Z.
114 B3 Douentza Mali
98 A2 Douglas Isle of Man
122 B2 Douglas S. Africa
128 A2 Douglas AK U.S.A.
142 B2 Douglas AZ U.S.A.
141 D2 Douglas GA U.S.A.
136 B2 Douglas WY U.S.A.
104 C1 Doullens France
154 B1 Dourada, Serra hills Brazil
154 B2 Dourados Brazil
154 B2 Dourados r. Brazil
154 B2 Dourados, Serra dos hills Brazil
106 B1 Douro r. Port.
99 D4 Dover U.K.
139 D3 Dover U.S.A.
95 D3 Dover, Strait of France/U.K.
139 F1 Dover-Foxcroft U.S.A.
99 B3 Dovey r. U.K.
121 C2 Dowa Malawi
79 C2 Dowlatābād Būshehr Iran
79 C2 Dowlatābād Kermān Iran
97 D1 Downpatrick U.K.
81 C2 Dow Rūd Iran
77 C3 Dowshī Afgh.
67 B3 Dōzen is Japan
130 C3 Dozois, Réservoir resr Can.
114 B2 Drâa, Hamada du plat. Alg.
154 B2 Dracena Brazil
100 C1 Drachten Neth.
110 B2 Drăgănești-Olt Romania
110 B2 Drăgășani Romania
105 D3 Draguignan France
88 C3 Drahichyn Belarus

53 D1 **Drake** Austr.
123 C2 **Drakensberg** *mts* Lesotho/S. Africa
123 C2 **Drakensberg** *mts* S. Africa
149 C8 **Drake Passage** S. Atlantic Ocean
111 B2 **Drama** Greece
93 F4 **Drammen** Norway
109 C1 **Drava** *r.* Europe
128 C2 **Drayton Valley** Can.
101 D2 **Dreieich** Ger.
102 C1 **Dresden** Ger.
104 C2 **Dreux** France
100 B1 **Driemond** Neth.
98 C2 **Driffield** U.K.
137 D1 **Drift Prairie** *reg.* U.S.A.
109 C2 **Drina** *r.* Bosnia-Herzegovina/Serbia
140 B2 **Driskill Mountain** *h.* U.S.A.
Drissa Belarus *see* **Vyerkhnyadzvinsk**
109 C2 **Drniš** Croatia
110 B2 **Drobeta-Turnu Severin** Romania
90 B2 **Drochia** Moldova
101 D1 **Drochtersen** Ger.
97 C2 **Drogheda** Ireland
90 A2 **Drohobych** Ukr.
99 B3 **Droitwich Spa** U.K.
Drokiya Moldova *see* **Drochia**
97 B1 **Dromahair** Ireland
97 C1 **Dromore** U.K.
100 B1 **Dronten** Neth.
74 B1 **Drosh** Pak.
53 C3 **Drouin** Austr.
128 C2 **Drumheller** Can.
138 C1 **Drummond Island** U.S.A.
131 C3 **Drummondville** Can.
96 B3 **Drummore** U.K.
96 B2 **Drumnadrochit** U.K.
Druskieniki Lith. *see* **Druskininkai**
88 B3 **Druskininkai** Lith.
88 C2 **Druya** Belarus
91 D2 **Druzhkivka** Ukr.
88 D2 **Druzhnaya Gorka** Rus. Fed.
89 D3 **Drybin** Belarus
130 A3 **Dryden** Can.
50 B1 **Drysdale** *r.* Austr.
147 C3 **Duarte, Pico** *mt.* Dom. Rep.
78 A2 **Ḍubā** Saudi Arabia
79 C2 **Dubai** U.A.E.
90 B2 **Dubăsari** Moldova
129 D1 **Dubawnt Lake** Can.
Dubayy U.A.E. *see* **Dubai**
78 A2 **Dubbagh, Jabal ad** *mt.* Saudi Arabia
53 C2 **Dubbo** Austr.
Dubesar' Moldova *see* **Dubăsari**
97 C2 **Dublin** Ireland
141 D2 **Dublin** U.S.A.
89 E2 **Dubna** Rus. Fed.
90 B1 **Dubno** Ukr.
139 D2 **Du Bois** U.S.A.
Dubossary Moldova *see* **Dubăsari**
114 A4 **Dubréka** Guinea
109 C2 **Dubrovnik** Croatia
90 B1 **Dubrovytsya** Ukr.
89 D3 **Dubrowna** Belarus
137 E2 **Dubuque** U.S.A.
63 B2 **Đức Bôn** Vietnam
135 D2 **Duchesne** U.S.A.
129 D2 **Duck Bay** Can.
101 E2 **Duderstadt** Ger.
82 G2 **Dudinka** Rus. Fed.
99 B3 **Dudley** U.K.
106 B1 **Duero** *r.* Spain
48 H4 **Duff Islands** Solomon Is
131 C2 **Duffreboy, Lac** *l.* Can.
96 C2 **Dufftown** U.K.
109 C2 **Dugi Otok** *i.* Croatia
109 C2 **Dugi Rat** Croatia
100 C2 **Duisburg** Ger.
123 D1 **Duiwelskloof** S. Africa
123 C3 **Dukathole** S. Africa
117 B4 **Duk Fadiat** Sudan
79 C2 **Dukhān** Qatar
89 D2 **Dukhovshchina** Rus. Fed.
Dukou China *see* **Panzhihua**
88 C2 **Dūkštas** Lith.
68 C2 **Dulan** China
152 B3 **Dulce** *r.* Arg.
142 B1 **Dulce** U.S.A.
97 C2 **Duleek** Ireland
100 C2 **Dülmen** Ger.
110 C2 **Dulovo** Bulg.
137 E1 **Duluth** U.S.A.
64 B3 **Dumaguete** Phil.
60 B1 **Dumai** Indon.
64 B2 **Dumaran** *i.* Phil.
140 B2 **Dumas** *AR* U.S.A.
143 C1 **Dumas** *TX* U.S.A.
96 B3 **Dumbarton** U.K.
103 D2 **Ďumbier** *mt.* Slovakia
96 C3 **Dumfries** U.K.
89 E3 **Duminichi** Rus. Fed.
75 C2 **Dumka** India
55 L3 **Dumont d'Urville Sea** Antarctica
116 B1 **Dumyāṭ** Egypt
Duna *r.* Hungary *see* **Danube**
Dünaburg Latvia *see* **Daugavpils**
Dunaj *r.* Slovakia *see* **Danube**
103 D2 **Dunakeszi** Hungary
97 C2 **Dunany Point** Ireland
Dunărea *r.* Romania *see* **Danube**
Dunării, Delta *delta* Romania/Ukr. *see* **Danube Delta**
103 D2 **Dunaújváros** Hungary
Dunav *r.* Bulg./Croatia/Serbia *see* **Danube**
90 B2 **Dunayivtsi** Ukr.
96 C2 **Dunbar** U.K.
96 C1 **Dunbeath** U.K.
128 B3 **Duncan** Can.
143 D2 **Duncan** U.S.A.
96 C1 **Duncansby Head** *hd* U.K.
88 B2 **Dundaga** Latvia
97 C1 **Dundalk** Ireland
139 D3 **Dundalk** U.S.A.
97 C2 **Dundalk Bay** Ireland
127 H1 **Dundas** Greenland
Dún Dealgan Ireland *see* **Dundalk**
123 D2 **Dundee** S. Africa
96 C2 **Dundee** U.K.
97 D1 **Dundrum Bay** U.K.
54 B3 **Dunedin** N.Z.
53 C2 **Dunedoo** Austr.
96 C2 **Dunfermline** U.K.
97 C1 **Dungannon** U.K.
74 B2 **Dungarpur** India
97 C2 **Dungarvan** Ireland
99 D4 **Dungeness** *hd* U.K.
97 C1 **Dungiven** U.K.
53 D2 **Dungog** Austr.
119 C2 **Dungu** Dem. Rep. Congo
60 B1 **Dungun** Malaysia
116 B2 **Dungunab** Sudan
69 E2 **Dunhua** China
68 C2 **Dunhuang** China
96 C2 **Dunkeld** U.K.
Dunkerque France *see* **Dunkirk**
104 C1 **Dunkirk** France
139 D2 **Dunkirk** U.S.A.
97 C2 **Dún Laoghaire** Ireland
97 B3 **Dunmanway** Ireland
97 D1 **Dunmurry** U.K.
96 C1 **Dunnet Head** *hd* U.K.
96 C3 **Duns** U.K.
134 B2 **Dunsmuir** U.S.A.
99 C4 **Dunstable** U.K.
100 B3 **Dun-sur-Meuse** France
96 A2 **Dunvegan** U.K.
Duolun China *see* **Dolonnur**
Duperré Alg. *see* **Aïn Defla**
110 B2 **Dupnitsa** Bulg.
136 C1 **Dupree** U.S.A.
Duque de Bragança Angola *see* **Calandula**
138 B3 **Du Quoin** U.S.A.
50 B1 **Durack** *r.* Austr.
105 C3 **Durance** *r.* France
144 B2 **Durango** Mex.
106 C1 **Durango** Spain
136 B3 **Durango** U.S.A.
143 D2 **Durant** U.S.A.
153 C3 **Durazno** Uru.
Durazzo Albania *see* **Durrës**
123 D2 **Durban** S. Africa
105 C3 **Durban-Corbières** France
122 A3 **Durbanville** S. Africa
100 B2 **Durbuy** Belgium
100 C2 **Düren** Ger.
75 C2 **Durg** India
98 C2 **Durham** U.K.
141 E1 **Durham** U.S.A.
60 B1 **Duri** Indon.
109 C2 **Durmitor** *mt.* Montenegro
96 B1 **Durness** U.K.
109 C2 **Durrës** Albania
97 A3 **Dursey Island** Ireland
111 C3 **Dursunbey** Turkey
117 C4 **Durukhsi** Somalia
59 D3 **D'Urville, Tanjung** *pt* Indon.
54 B2 **D'Urville Island** N.Z.
71 A3 **Dushan** China
77 C3 **Dushanbe** Tajik.
100 C2 **Düsseldorf** Ger.
Dutch East Indies *country* Asia *see* **Indonesia**
Dutch Guiana *country* S. America *see* **Suriname**
Dutch West Indies *terr.* West Indies *see* **Netherlands Antilles**
Duvno Bos.-Herz. *see* **Tomislavgrad**
71 A3 **Duyun** China
80 B1 **Düzce** Turkey
91 D2 **Dvorichna** Ukr.
74 A2 **Dwarka** India
123 C1 **Dwarsberg** S. Africa
134 C1 **Dworshak Reservoir** U.S.A.
89 D3 **Dyat'kovo** Rus. Fed.
96 C2 **Dyce** U.K.
127 H2 **Dyer, Cape** Can.
140 C1 **Dyersburg** U.S.A.
Dyfrdwy *r.* U.K. *see* **Dee**
103 D2 **Dyje** *r.* Austria/Czech Rep.
103 D1 **Dylewska Góra** *h.* Pol.
91 D2 **Dymytrov** Ukr.
123 C3 **Dyoki** S. Africa
51 D2 **Dysart** Austr.
122 B3 **Dysselsdorp** S. Africa
87 E3 **Dyurtyuli** Rus. Fed.
69 D2 **Dzamīn Üüd** Mongolia
121 D2 **Dzaoudzi** Mayotte
91 D2 **Dzerzhyns'k** Ukr.
Dzhaltyr Kazakh. *see* **Zhaltyr**
Dzhambul Kazakh. *see* **Taraz**
76 B2 **Dzhangala** Kazakh.
91 C2 **Dzhankoy** Ukr.
Dzharkent Kazakh. *see* **Zharkent**
Dzhetygara Kazakh. *see* **Zhitikara**
Dzhezkazgan Kazakh. *see* **Zhezkazgan**
Dzhizak Uzbek. *see* **Jizzax**
91 D3 **Dzhubga** Rus. Fed.
83 K3 **Dzhugdzhur, Khrebet** *mts* Rus. Fed.
77 D2 **Dzhungarskiy Alatau, Khrebet** *mts* China/Kazakh.
76 C2 **Dzhusaly** Kazakh.
103 E1 **Działdowo** Pol.
145 D2 **Dzilam de Bravo** Mex.
69 D1 **Dzuunmod** Mongolia
88 C3 **Dzyarzhynsk** Belarus
88 C3 **Dzyatlavichy** Belarus

E

131 E2 **Eagle** *r.* Can.
134 C1 **Eagle Cap** *mt.* U.S.A.
130 A3 **Eagle Lake** Can.
134 B2 **Eagle Lake** U.S.A.
143 C3 **Eagle Pass** U.S.A.
126 C2 **Eagle Plain** Can.
Eap *i.* Micronesia *see* **Yap**
130 A2 **Ear Falls** Can.
135 C3 **Earlimart** U.S.A.
96 C2 **Earn** *r.* U.K.
55 J2 **East Antarctica** *reg.* Antarctica
East Bengal *country* Asia *see* **Bangladesh**
99 D4 **Eastbourne** U.K.
59 D2 **East Caroline Basin** N. Pacific Ocean
69 E2 **East China Sea** N. Pacific Ocean
54 B1 **East Coast Bays** N.Z.
East Dereham U.K. *see* **Dereham**
129 D3 **Eastend** Can.
157 G7 **Easter Island** S. Pacific Ocean
123 C3 **Eastern Cape** *prov.* S. Africa
116 B2 **Eastern Desert** Egypt
73 B3 **Eastern Ghats** *mts* India
Eastern Samoa *terr.* S. Pacific Ocean *see* **American Samoa**
Eastern Sayan Mountains *mts* Rus. Fed. *see* **Vostochnyy Sayan**
Eastern Transvaal *prov.* S. Africa *see* **Mpumalanga**
129 E2 **Easterville** Can.
153 C5 **East Falkland** *i.* Falkland Is
100 C1 **East Frisian Islands** Ger.
135 C3 **Eastgate** U.S.A.
137 D1 **East Grand Forks** U.S.A.
96 B3 **East Kilbride** U.K.
138 C2 **East Lansing** U.S.A.
99 C4 **Eastleigh** U.K.
96 C3 **East Linton** U.K.
138 C2 **East Liverpool** U.S.A.
123 C3 **East London** S. Africa
130 C2 **Eastmain** Can.
130 C2 **Eastmain** *r.* Can.
141 D2 **Eastman** U.S.A.
157 G8 **East Pacific Rise** N. Pacific Ocean
East Pakistan *country* Asia *see* **Bangladesh**
138 A3 **East St Louis** U.S.A.
East Sea *sea* N. Pacific Ocean *see* **Japan, Sea of**
83 K2 **East Siberian Sea** Rus. Fed.
59 C3 **East Timor** *country* Asia
53 C2 **East Toorale** Austr.
139 D2 **East York** Can.
138 A2 **Eau Claire** U.S.A.
130 C2 **Eau Claire, Lac à l'** *l.* Can.
59 D2 **Eauripik** *atoll* Micronesia
145 C2 **Ebano** Mex.
99 B4 **Ebbw Vale** U.K.
118 B2 **Ebebiyin** Equat. Guinea
102 C1 **Eberswalde-Finow** Ger.
66 D2 **Ebetsu** Japan
77 E2 **Ebinur Hu** *salt l.* China
118 C2 **Ebola** *r.* Dem. Rep. Congo
109 C2 **Eboli** Italy
118 B2 **Ebolowa** Cameroon
107 D1 **Ebro** *r.* Spain
Echeng China *see* **Ezhou**
144 A2 **Echeverria, Pico** *mt.* Mex.
129 E2 **Echoing** *r.* Can.
100 C3 **Echternach** Lux.
52 B3 **Echuca** Austr.
106 B2 **Écija** Spain
102 B1 **Eckernförde** Ger.
127 G2 **Eclipse Sound** *sea chan.* Can.
150 B3 **Ecuador** *country* S. America
116 C3 **Ed** Eritrea
96 C1 **Eday** *i.* U.K.
117 A3 **Ed Da'ein** Sudan
117 B3 **Ed Damazin** Sudan
116 B3 **Ed Damer** Sudan
116 B3 **Ed Debba** Sudan
116 B3 **Ed Dueim** Sudan
51 D4 **Eddystone Point** Austr.
100 B1 **Ede** Neth.
118 B2 **Edéa** Cameroon
154 C1 **Edéia** Brazil
53 C3 **Eden** Austr.
98 B2 **Eden** *r.* U.K.
143 D2 **Eden** U.S.A.
123 C2 **Edenburg** S. Africa
97 C2 **Edenderry** Ireland
52 B3 **Edenhope** Austr.
141 E1 **Edenton** U.S.A.
111 B2 **Edessa** Greece
139 E2 **Edgartown** U.S.A.
Edge Island *i.* Svalbard *see* **Edgeøya**
82 C1 **Edgeøya** *i.* Svalbard
141 D3 **Edgewater** U.S.A.
138 C2 **Edinboro** U.S.A.
143 D3 **Edinburg** U.S.A.
96 C3 **Edinburgh** U.K.
90 B2 **Edineț** Moldova
111 C2 **Edirne** Turkey
Edith Ronne Land Antarctica *see* **Ronne Ice Shelf**
128 C2 **Edmonton** Can.
131 D3 **Edmundston** Can.
111 C3 **Edremit** Turkey
111 C3 **Edremit Körfezi** *b.* Turkey
128 C2 **Edson** Can.
119 C3 **Edward, Lake** Dem. Rep. Congo/Uganda
Edwardesabad Pak. *see* **Bannu**
143 D2 **Edwards Plateau** U.S.A.
55 O2 **Edward VII Peninsula** Antarctica
96 C2 **Edzell** U.K.
100 A2 **Eeklo** Belgium
135 B2 **Eel** *r.* U.S.A.
100 C1 **Eemskanaal** *canal* Neth.
100 C1 **Eenrum** Neth.
138 B3 **Effingham** U.S.A.
135 C3 **Egan Range** *mts* U.S.A.
103 E2 **Eger** Hungary
93 E4 **Egersund** Norway
100 B2 **Eghezée** Belgium
92 □C2 **Egilsstaðir** Iceland
80 B2 **Eğirdir** Turkey
80 B2 **Eğirdir Gölü** *l.* Turkey
104 C2 **Égletons** France
Egmont, Mount *vol.* N.Z. *see* **Taranaki, Mount**
83 M2 **Egvekinot** Rus. Fed.
116 A2 **Egypt** *country* Africa
70 A2 **Ehen Hudag** China
106 C1 **Eibar** Spain
100 C1 **Eibergen** Neth.
100 C2 **Eifel** *hills* Ger.
96 A2 **Eigg** *i.* U.K.
73 B4 **Eight Degree Channel** India/Maldives
50 B1 **Eighty Mile Beach** Austr.
80 B3 **Eilat** Israel
101 F2 **Eilenburg** Ger.
101 D2 **Einbeck** Ger.
100 B2 **Eindhoven** Neth.
160 N4 **Eirik Ridge** N. Atlantic Ocean
150 C3 **Eirunepé** Brazil
120 B2 **Eiseb** *watercourse* Namibia
101 E2 **Eisenach** Ger.
101 E2 **Eisenberg** Ger.
102 C1 **Eisenhüttenstadt** Ger.
103 D2 **Eisenstadt** Austria
101 E2 **Eisleben Lutherstadt** Ger.
Eivissa Spain *see* **Ibiza**
Eivissa *i.* Spain *see* **Ibiza**
107 C1 **Ejea de los Caballeros** Spain
121 □D3 **Ejeda** Madag.
Ejin Qi China *see* **Dalain Hob**
93 H4 **Ekenäs** Fin.
77 D1 **Ekibastuz** Kazakh.
93 F4 **Eksjö** Sweden
122 A2 **Eksteenfontein** S. Africa
130 B2 **Ekwan** *r.* Can.
62 A2 **Ela** Myanmar
El Aaiún Western Sahara *see* **Laâyoune**
123 C2 **Elandsdoorn** S. Africa
El Araïche Morocco *see* **Larache**
El Asnam Alg. *see* **Chlef**
111 B3 **Elassona** Greece
Elat Israel *see* **Eilat**
80 B2 **Elazığ** Turkey
108 B2 **Elba, Isola d'** *i.* Italy
150 B2 **El Banco** Col.
142 B2 **El Barreal** *l.* Mex.
109 D2 **Elbasan** Albania
150 C2 **El Baúl** Venez.
114 C1 **El Bayadh** Alg.
101 D1 **Elbe** *r.* Ger.
136 B3 **Elbert, Mount** U.S.A.
141 D2 **Elberton** U.S.A.
104 C2 **Elbeuf** France
80 B2 **Elbistan** Turkey
103 D1 **Elbląg** Pol.
153 A4 **El Bolsón** Arg.
87 D4 **El'brus** *mt.* Rus. Fed.
81 C2 **Elburz Mountains** *mts* Iran
150 C2 **El Callao** Venez.
143 D3 **El Campo** U.S.A.
135 C4 **El Centro** U.S.A.
152 B1 **El Cerro** Bol.
107 C2 **Elche-Elx** Spain
145 C3 **El Chichónal** *vol.* Mex.
107 C2 **Elda** Spain
119 D2 **Eldama Ravine** Kenya
137 E3 **Eldon** U.S.A.
154 B3 **Eldorado** Arg.
154 C2 **Eldorado** Brazil
144 B2 **El Dorado** Mex.
140 B2 **El Dorado** *AR* U.S.A.
137 D3 **El Dorado** *KS* U.S.A.
134 D1 **Electric Peak** U.S.A.
114 B2 **El Eglab** *plat.* Alg.
106 C2 **El Ejido** Spain
89 E2 **Elektrostal'** Rus. Fed.
150 B3 **El Encanto** Col.
146 C2 **Eleuthera** *i.* Bahamas
116 A3 **El Fasher** Sudan
144 B2 **El Fuerte** Mex.
117 A3 **El Fula** Sudan
116 A3 **El Geneina** Sudan
116 B3 **El Geteina** Sudan
96 C2 **Elgin** U.K.

138 B2 **Elgin** U.S.A.
83 K2 **El'ginskiy** Rus. Fed.
El Gîza Egypt *see* **Giza**
115 C1 **El Goléa** Alg.
144 A1 **El Golfo de Santa Clara** Mex.
119 D2 **Elgon, Mount** Kenya/Uganda
108 A3 **El Hadjar** Alg.
114 A2 **El Ḥammâmi** *reg.* Maur.
114 B2 **El Ḥank** *esc.* Mali/Maur.
114 A2 **El Hierro** *i.* Islas Canarias
145 C2 **El Higo** Mex.
114 C2 **El Homr** Alg.
Elichpur India *see* **Achalpur**
126 B2 **Elim** U.S.A.
Élisabethville Dem. Rep. Congo *see* **Lubumbashi**
El Iskandarîya Egypt *see* **Alexandria**
87 D4 **Elista** Rus. Fed.
139 E2 **Elizabeth** U.S.A.
141 E1 **Elizabeth City** U.S.A.
138 B3 **Elizabethtown** U.S.A.
114 B1 **El Jadida** Morocco
103 E1 **Ełk** Pol.
108 A3 **El Kala** Alg.
88 C2 **Elkas kalns** *h.* Latvia
143 D1 **Elk City** U.S.A.
114 B1 **El Kelaâ des Srarhna** Morocco
128 C2 **Elkford** Can.
138 B2 **Elkhart** U.S.A.
El Khartûm Sudan *see* **Khartoum**
110 C2 **Elkhovo** Bulg.
139 D3 **Elkins** U.S.A.
128 C3 **Elko** Can.
134 C2 **Elko** U.S.A.
129 C2 **Elk Point** Can.
137 E1 **Elk River** U.S.A.
126 F1 **Ellef Ringnes Island** Can.
137 D1 **Ellendale** U.S.A.
134 B1 **Ellensburg** U.S.A.
54 B2 **Ellesmere, Lake** N.Z.
127 G1 **Ellesmere Island** Can.
98 B3 **Ellesmere Port** U.K.
126 F2 **Ellice** *r.* Can.
Ellice Islands *country* S. Pacific Ocean *see* **Tuvalu**
123 C3 **Elliotdale** S. Africa
138 C1 **Elliot Lake** Can.
96 C2 **Ellon** U.K.
139 F2 **Ellsworth** U.S.A.
55 R2 **Ellsworth Mountains** Antarctica
111 C3 **Elmalı** Turkey
115 C1 **El Meghaïer** Alg.
139 D2 **Elmira** U.S.A.
107 C2 **El Moral** Spain
101 D1 **Elmshorn** Ger.
117 A3 **El Muglad** Sudan
150 B2 **El Nevado, Cerro** *mt.* Col.
64 A2 **El Nido** Phil.
116 B3 **El Obeid** Sudan
144 B2 **El Oro** Mex.
115 C1 **El Oued** Alg.
142 A2 **Eloy** U.S.A.
El Paso U.S.A. *see* **Derby**
142 B2 **El Paso** U.S.A.
145 D3 **El Pinalón, Cerro** *mt.* Guat.
144 B1 **El Porvenir** Mex.
107 D1 **El Prat de Llobregat** Spain
146 B3 **El Progreso** Hond.
106 B2 **El Puerto de Santa María** Spain
El Qâhira Egypt *see* **Cairo**
El Quds Israel/West Bank *see* **Jerusalem**
143 D1 **El Reno** U.S.A.
128 A1 **Elsa** Can.
145 B2 **El Salado** Mex.
144 B2 **El Salto** Mex.
146 B3 **El Salvador** *country* Central America
152 B2 **El Salvador** Chile
145 B2 **El Salvador** Mex.
142 B3 **El Sauz** Mex.
144 A1 **El Socorro** Mex.
142 B3 **El Sueco** Mex.
El Suweis Egypt *see* **Suez**
108 A3 **El Tarf** Alg.
106 B1 **El Teleno** *mt.* Spain
145 C2 **El Temascal** Mex.
150 C2 **El Tigre** Venez.
147 D4 **El Tocuyo** Venez.
El Uqşur Egypt *see* **Luxor**
73 C3 **Eluru** India
88 C2 **Elva** Estonia
106 B2 **Elvas** Port.
93 F3 **Elverum** Norway
119 E2 **El Wak** Kenya
99 D3 **Ely** U.K.
137 E1 **Ely** *MN* U.S.A.
135 D3 **Ely** *NV* U.S.A.
81 D2 **Emāmrūd** Iran
93 G4 **Emån** *r.* Sweden
76 B2 **Emba** Kazakh.
76 B2 **Emba** *r.* Kazakh.
123 C2 **Embalenhle** S. Africa
118 B2 **Embondo** Dem. Rep. Congo
154 C1 **Emborcação, Represa de** *resr* Brazil
119 D3 **Embu** Kenya
100 C1 **Emden** Ger.
51 D2 **Emerald** Austr.
129 E3 **Emerson** Can.
111 C3 **Emet** Turkey
123 D2 **eMgwenya** S. Africa
115 D3 **Emi Koussi** *mt.* Chad
145 C3 **Emiliano Zapata** Mex.
110 C2 **Emine, Nos** *pt* Bulg.
80 B2 **Emirdağ** Turkey
123 D2 **eMjindini** S. Africa
88 B2 **Emmaste** Estonia
100 B1 **Emmeloord** Neth.
100 C2 **Emmelshausen** Ger.
100 C1 **Emmen** Neth.
143 C3 **Emory Peak** U.S.A.
144 A2 **Empalme** Mex.
123 D2 **Empangeni** S. Africa
156 D2 **Emperor Trough** N. Pacific Ocean
108 B2 **Empoli** Italy
111 C3 **Emponas** Greece
137 D3 **Emporia** *KS* U.S.A.
139 D3 **Emporia** *VA* U.S.A.
Empty Quarter *des.* Saudi Arabia *see* **Rub' al Khālī**
100 C1 **Ems** *r.* Ger.
100 C1 **Emsdetten** Ger.
88 C2 **Emumägi** *h.* Estonia
123 C2 **eMzinoni** S. Africa
59 D3 **Enarotali** Indon.
144 B2 **Encarnación** Mex.
152 C2 **Encarnación** Para.
155 D1 **Encruzilhada** Brazil
61 D2 **Ende** Indon.
55 G2 **Enderby Land** *reg.* Antarctica
126 B2 **Endicott Mountains** U.S.A.
50 A2 **Eneabba** Austr.
91 C2 **Enerhodar** Ukr.
111 C2 **Enez** Turkey
97 C2 **Enfield** Ireland
87 D3 **Engel's** Rus. Fed.
60 B2 **Enggano** *i.* Indon.
99 C3 **England** *admin. div.* U.K.
130 C3 **Englehart** Can.
141 D3 **Englewood** U.S.A.
130 A2 **English** *r.* Can.
English Bazar India *see* **Ingraj Bazar**
95 C4 **English Channel** France/U.K.
143 D1 **Enid** U.S.A.
Enkeldoorn Zimbabwe *see* **Chivhu**
100 B1 **Enkhuizen** Neth.
93 G4 **Enköping** Sweden
108 B3 **Enna** Italy
129 D1 **Ennadai Lake** Can.
116 A3 **En Nahud** Sudan
115 E3 **Ennedi, Massif** *mts* Chad
53 C1 **Enngonia** Austr.
97 B2 **Ennis** Ireland
143 D2 **Ennis** U.S.A.
97 C2 **Enniscorthy** Ireland
97 C2 **Enniskerry** Ireland
97 C1 **Enniskillen** U.K.
97 B2 **Ennistymon** Ireland
102 C2 **Enns** Austria
102 C2 **Enns** *r.* Austria
92 J3 **Eno** Fin.
92 H2 **Enontekiö** Fin.
53 C3 **Ensay** Austr.
100 C1 **Enschede** Neth.
144 A1 **Ensenada** Mex.
70 A2 **Enshi** China
119 D2 **Entebbe** Uganda
128 C1 **Enterprise** Can.
140 C2 **Enterprise** *AL* U.S.A.
134 C1 **Enterprise** *OR* U.S.A.
152 B2 **Entre Ríos** Bol.
106 B2 **Entroncamento** Port.
115 C4 **Enugu** Nigeria
150 B3 **Envira** Brazil
118 B2 **Epéna** Congo
105 C2 **Épernay** France
135 D3 **Ephraim** U.S.A.
134 C1 **Ephrata** U.S.A.
105 D2 **Épinal** France
99 D4 **Epping** U.K.
99 C4 **Epsom** U.K.
118 A2 **Equatorial Guinea** *country* Africa
104 B2 **Équeurdreville-Hainneville** France
101 D3 **Erbach** Ger.
101 F3 **Erbendorf** Ger.
100 C3 **Erbeskopf** *h.* Ger.
81 C2 **Erciş** Turkey
80 B2 **Erciyes Dağı** *mt.* Turkey
103 D2 **Érd** Hungary
Erdaobaihe China *see* **Baihe**
65 B1 **Erdao Jiang** *r.* China
111 C2 **Erdek** Turkey
80 B2 **Erdemli** Turkey
154 B2 **Eré, Campos** *hills* Brazil
55 M2 **Erebus, Mount** *vol.* Antarctica
152 C2 **Erechim** Brazil
69 D1 **Ereentsav** Mongolia
80 B2 **Ereğli** *Konya* Turkey
80 B1 **Ereğli** *Zonguldak* Turkey
69 D2 **Erenhot** China
Erevan Armenia *see* **Yerevan**
101 E2 **Erfurt** Ger.
80 B2 **Ergani** Turkey
114 B2 **'Erg Chech** *des.* Alg./Mali
111 C2 **Ergene** *r.* Turkey
78 A3 **Erheib** Sudan
96 B2 **Ericht, Loch** *l.* U.K.
138 C2 **Erie** U.S.A.
138 C2 **Erie, Lake** Can./U.S.A.
66 D2 **Erimo-misaki** *c.* Japan
116 B3 **Eritrea** *country* Africa
101 E3 **Erlangen** Ger.
50 C2 **Erldunda** Austr.
123 C2 **Ermelo** S. Africa
80 B2 **Ermenek** Turkey
111 B3 **Ermoupoli** Greece
73 B4 **Ernakulam** India
97 B1 **Erne** *r.* Ireland/U.K.
73 B3 **Erode** India
100 B2 **Erp** Neth.
114 B1 **Er Rachidia** Morocco
116 B3 **Er Rahad** Sudan
97 B1 **Errigal** *h.* Ireland
97 A1 **Erris Head** *hd* Ireland
48 H5 **Erromango** *i.* Vanuatu
109 D2 **Ersekë** Albania
62 B1 **Ertan Reservoir** China
89 F3 **Ertil'** Rus. Fed.
101 D2 **Erwitte** Ger.
101 F2 **Erzgebirge** *mts* Czech Rep./Ger.
80 B2 **Erzincan** Turkey
81 C2 **Erzurum** Turkey
66 D2 **Esashi** Japan
93 E4 **Esbjerg** Denmark
135 D3 **Escalante** U.S.A.
135 D3 **Escalante Desert** U.S.A.
144 B2 **Escalón** Mex.
138 B1 **Escanaba** U.S.A.
145 C3 **Escárcega** Mex.
107 C1 **Escatrón** Spain
100 A2 **Escaut** *r.* Belgium/France
101 E1 **Eschede** Ger.
100 B3 **Esch-sur-Alzette** Lux.
101 E2 **Eschwege** Ger.
100 C2 **Eschweiler** Ger.
135 C4 **Escondido** U.S.A.
144 B2 **Escuinapa** Mex.
111 C3 **Eşen** Turkey
81 D2 **Eşfahān** Iran
123 D2 **Eshowe** S. Africa
123 D2 **Esikhawini** S. Africa
98 B2 **Esk** *r.* U.K.
131 D2 **Esker** Can.
92 □C2 **Eskifjörður** Iceland
93 G4 **Eskilstuna** Sweden
Eskimo Point Can. *see* **Arviat**
111 D3 **Eskişehir** Turkey
81 C2 **Eslāmābād-e Gharb** Iran
111 C3 **Esler Dağı** *mt.* Turkey
111 C3 **Eşme** Turkey
146 C2 **Esmeralda** Cuba
150 B2 **Esmeraldas** Ecuador
107 D2 **Es Mercadal** Spain
79 D2 **Espakeh** Iran
105 C3 **Espalion** France
130 B3 **Espanola** Can.
142 B1 **Espanola** U.S.A.
50 B3 **Esperance** Austr.
153 A5 **Esperanza** Arg.
144 B2 **Esperanza** Mex.
106 B2 **Espichel, Cabo** *c.* Port.
154 B3 **Espigão, Serra do** *mts* Brazil
143 C3 **Espinazo** Mex.
155 D1 **Espinhaço, Serra do** *mts* Brazil
151 E4 **Espinosa** Brazil
Espirito Santo Brazil *see* **Vila Velha**
155 D1 **Espírito Santo** *state* Brazil
48 H5 **Espíritu Santo** *i.* Vanuatu
144 A2 **Espíritu Santo, Isla** *i.* Mex.
93 H3 **Espoo** Fin.
153 A4 **Esquel** Arg.
114 B1 **Essaouira** Morocco
114 A2 **Es Semara** Western Sahara
100 C2 **Essen** Ger.
150 D2 **Essequibo** *r.* Guyana
139 E2 **Essex Junction** U.S.A.
83 L3 **Esso** Rus. Fed.
106 B1 **Estaca de Bares, Punta de** *pt* Spain
153 B5 **Estados, Isla de los** *i.* Arg.
81 D3 **Eşţahbān** Iran
151 F4 **Estância** Brazil
123 C2 **Estcourt** S. Africa
107 C1 **Estella** Spain
106 B2 **Estepona** Spain
106 C1 **Esteras de Medinaceli** Spain
129 D2 **Esterhazy** Can.
152 B2 **Esteros** Para.
136 B2 **Estes Park** U.S.A.
129 D3 **Estevan** Can.
137 E2 **Estherville** U.S.A.
129 D2 **Eston** Can.
88 C2 **Estonia** *country* Europe
Estonskaya S.S.R. *country* Europe *see* **Estonia**
106 B1 **Estrela, Serra da** *mts* Port.
106 B2 **Estremoz** Port.
52 A1 **Etadunna** Austr.
104 C2 **Étampes** France
104 C1 **Étaples** France
75 B2 **Etawah** India
123 D2 **Ethandakukhanya** S. Africa
122 B2 **E'Thembini** S. Africa
117 B4 **Ethiopia** *country* Africa
Etna, Monte *vol.* Italy *see* **Etna, Mount**
109 C3 **Etna, Mount** *vol.* Italy
93 E4 **Etne** Norway
128 A2 **Etolin Island** U.S.A.
120 A2 **Etosha Pan** *salt pan* Namibia
110 B2 **Etropole** Bulg.
100 C3 **Ettelbruck** Lux.
100 B2 **Etten-Leur** Neth.
107 C1 **Etxarri-Aranatz** Spain
99 D4 **Eu** France
53 C2 **Euabalong** Austr.
Euboea *i.* Greece *see* **Evvoia**
50 B3 **Eucla** Austr.
138 C2 **Euclid** U.S.A.
141 C2 **Eufaula** U.S.A.
143 D1 **Eufaula Lake** *resr* U.S.A.
134 B2 **Eugene** U.S.A.
144 A2 **Eugenia, Punta** *pt* Mex.
53 C1 **Eulo** Austr.
53 C2 **Eumungerie** Austr.
143 C2 **Eunice** U.S.A.
81 C2 **Euphrates** *r.* Asia
134 B2 **Eureka** *CA* U.S.A.
134 C1 **Eureka** *MT* U.S.A.
135 C3 **Eureka** *NV* U.S.A.
52 B2 **Euriowie** Austr.
53 C3 **Euroa** Austr.
106 B2 **Europa Point** Gibraltar
140 C2 **Eutaw** U.S.A.
128 B2 **Eutsuk Lake** Can.
123 C2 **Evander** S. Africa
130 C2 **Evans, Lac** *l.* Can.
53 D1 **Evans Head** Austr.
127 G2 **Evans Strait** Can.
138 B2 **Evanston** *IL* U.S.A.
136 A2 **Evanston** *WY* U.S.A.
138 B3 **Evansville** U.S.A.
Eva Perón Arg. *see* **La Plata**
123 C2 **Evaton** S. Africa
79 C2 **Evaz** Iran
83 L2 **Evensk** Rus. Fed.
50 C2 **Everard Range** *hills* Austr.
75 C2 **Everest, Mount** China/Nepal
134 B1 **Everett** U.S.A.
100 A2 **Evergem** Belgium
141 D3 **Everglades** *swamp* U.S.A.
140 C2 **Evergreen** U.S.A.
99 C3 **Evesham** U.K.
118 B2 **Evinayong** Equat. Guinea
93 E4 **Evje** Norway
106 B2 **Évora** Port.
69 F1 **Evoron, Ozero** *l.* Rus. Fed.
111 B2 **Evosmos** Greece
104 C2 **Évreux** France
111 C2 **Evros** *r.* Greece/Turkey
111 B3 **Evrotas** *r.* Greece
104 C2 **Évry** France
80 B2 **Evrychou** Cyprus
111 B3 **Evvoia** *i.* Greece
119 E2 **Ewaso Ngiro** *r.* Kenya
152 B1 **Exaltación** Bol.
99 B4 **Exe** *r.* U.K.
99 B4 **Exeter** U.K.
99 B4 **Exmoor** *hills* U.K.
50 A2 **Exmouth** Austr.
99 B4 **Exmouth** U.K.
50 A2 **Exmouth Gulf** Austr.
106 B2 **Extremadura** *aut. comm.* Spain
146 C2 **Exuma Cays** *is* Bahamas
118 C3 **Eyangu** Dem. Rep. Congo
119 D3 **Eyasi, Lake** *salt l.* Tanz.
96 C3 **Eyemouth** U.K.
92 □B2 **Eyjafjörður** *inlet* Iceland
117 C4 **Eyl** Somalia
52 A1 **Eyre (North), Lake** *imp. l.* Austr.
52 A2 **Eyre Peninsula** Austr.
94 B1 **Eysturoy** *i.* Faroe Is
123 D2 **Ezakheni** S. Africa
123 C2 **Ezenzeleni** S. Africa
70 B2 **Ezhou** China
86 E2 **Ezhva** Rus. Fed.
111 C3 **Ezine** Turkey

F

102 C1 **Faaborg** Denmark
142 B2 **Fabens** U.S.A.
108 B2 **Fabriano** Italy
115 D3 **Fachi** Niger
114 C3 **Fada-N'Gourma** Burkina
108 B2 **Faenza** Italy
Faeroes *terr.* N. Atlantic Ocean *see* **Faroe Islands**
59 C3 **Fafanlap** Indon.
110 B1 **Făgăraş** Romania
49 J5 **Fagatogo** American Samoa
93 E3 **Fagernes** Norway
93 G4 **Fagersta** Sweden
153 B5 **Fagnano, Lago** *l.* Arg./Chile
114 B3 **Faguibine, Lac** *l.* Mali
92 □B3 **Fagurhólsmýri** Iceland
126 C2 **Fairbanks** U.S.A.
137 D2 **Fairbury** U.S.A.
135 B3 **Fairfield** *CA* U.S.A.
138 C3 **Fairfield** *OH* U.S.A.
96 □ **Fair Isle** *i.* U.K.
137 E2 **Fairmont** *MN* U.S.A.
138 C3 **Fairmont** *WV* U.S.A.
128 C2 **Fairview** Can.
128 A2 **Fairweather, Mount** Can./U.S.A.
59 D2 **Fais** *i.* Micronesia
74 B1 **Faisalabad** Pak.
136 C1 **Faith** U.S.A.
75 C2 **Faizabad** India
156 E6 **Fakaofo** *atoll* Tokelau
99 D3 **Fakenham** U.K.
59 C3 **Fakfak** Indon.
65 A1 **Faku** China
114 A4 **Falaba** Sierra Leone
Falcarragh Ireland *see* **An Fál Carrach**
143 D3 **Falcon Lake** Mex./U.S.A.
Faleshty Moldova *see* **Făleşti**
90 B2 **Făleşti** Moldova
143 D3 **Falfurrias** U.S.A.
128 C2 **Falher** Can.
101 F2 **Falkenberg** Ger.
93 F4 **Falkenberg** Sweden
101 F1 **Falkensee** Ger.
96 C3 **Falkirk** U.K.

158 D8 **Falkland Escarpment** S. Atlantic Ocean
153 C5 **Falkland Islands** *terr.* S. Atlantic Ocean
157 I9 **Falkland Plateau** S. Atlantic Ocean
93 F4 **Falköping** Sweden
101 D1 **Fallingbostel** Ger.
135 C3 **Fallon** U.S.A.
139 E2 **Fall River** U.S.A.
137 D2 **Falls City** U.S.A.
99 A4 **Falmouth** U.K.
122 A3 **False Bay** S. Africa
144 B2 **Falso, Cabo** *c.* Mex.
93 F5 **Falster** *i.* Denmark
110 C1 **Fălticeni** Romania
93 G3 **Falun** Sweden
152 B2 **Famailla** Arg.
121 □D3 **Fandriana** Madag.
Fangcheng China *see* **Fangchenggang**
71 A3 **Fangchenggang** China
71 C3 **Fangshan** Taiwan
66 A1 **Fangzheng** China
108 B2 **Fano** Italy
119 C2 **Faradje** Dem. Rep. Congo
121 □D3 **Farafangana** Madag.
Farafra Oasis *oasis* Egypt *see* **Wāḥāt al Farāfirah**
76 C3 **Farāh** Afgh.
114 A3 **Faranah** Guinea
79 C3 **Fararah** Oman
78 B3 **Farasān, Jazā'ir** *is* Saudi Arabia
59 D2 **Faraulep** *atoll* Micronesia
127 J2 **Farewell, Cape** *c.* Greenland
54 B2 **Farewell, Cape** N.Z.
137 D1 **Fargo** U.S.A.
77 D2 **Farg'ona** Uzbek.
137 E2 **Faribault** U.S.A.
130 C2 **Faribault, Lac** *l.* Can.
74 B2 **Faridabad** India
75 C2 **Faridpur** Bangl.
139 E2 **Farmington** *ME* U.S.A.
142 B1 **Farmington** *NM* U.S.A.
139 D3 **Farmville** U.S.A.
99 C4 **Farnborough** U.K.
128 C2 **Farnham, Mount** Can.
128 A1 **Faro** Can.
106 B2 **Faro** Port.
88 A2 **Fårö** *i.* Sweden
147 C3 **Faro, Punta** *pt* Col.
106 B1 **Faro, Serra do** *mts* Spain
94 B1 **Faroe Islands** *terr.* N. Atlantic Ocean
113 I6 **Farquhar Group** *is* Seychelles
81 D3 **Farrāshband** Iran
Farrukhabad India *see* **Fatehgarh**
79 C3 **Fartak, Ra's** *c.* Yemen
154 B3 **Fartura, Serra da** *mts* Brazil
143 C2 **Farwell** U.S.A.
79 C2 **Fāryāb** *Hormozgān* Iran
79 C2 **Fāryāb** *Kermān* Iran
81 D3 **Fasā** Iran
109 C2 **Fasano** Italy
90 B1 **Fastiv** Ukr.
119 D2 **Fataki** Dem. Rep. Congo
75 B2 **Fatehgarh** India
75 C2 **Fatehpur** India
114 A3 **Fatick** Senegal
131 D3 **Fatima** Can.
123 C2 **Fauresmith** S. Africa
92 G2 **Fauske** Norway
92 □A3 **Faxaflói** *b.* Iceland
92 G3 **Faxälven** *r.* Sweden
115 D3 **Faya** Chad
140 B1 **Fayetteville** *AR* U.S.A.
141 F1 **Fayetteville** *NC* U.S.A.
140 C1 **Fayetteville** *TN* U.S.A.
77 D3 **Fayzābād** Afgh.
74 B1 **Fazilka** India
114 A2 **Fdérik** Maur.
141 E2 **Fear, Cape** U.S.A.
54 C2 **Featherston** N.Z.
104 C2 **Fécamp** France
Federated Malay States *country* Asia *see* **Malaysia**
102 C1 **Fehmarn** *i.* Ger.
101 F1 **Fehrbellin** Ger.
155 D2 **Feia, Lagoa** *lag.* Brazil
150 B3 **Feijó** Brazil
54 C2 **Feilding** N.Z.
151 F4 **Feira de Santana** Brazil
107 D2 **Felanitx** Spain
101 F1 **Feldberg** Ger.
145 D3 **Felipe C. Puerto** Mex.
155 D1 **Felixlândia** Brazil
99 D4 **Felixstowe** U.K.
101 D2 **Felsberg** Ger.
108 B1 **Feltre** Italy
93 F3 **Femunden** *l.* Norway
Fénérive Madag. *see* **Fenoarivo Atsinanana**
Fengcheng China *see* **Fengshan**
71 B3 **Fengcheng** *Jiangxi* China
65 A1 **Fengcheng** *Liaoning* China
62 A1 **Fengqing** China
71 A3 **Fengshan** China
Fengshan China *see* **Fengqing**
70 B2 **Fengxian** *Jiangsu* China
70 A2 **Fengxian** *Shaanxi* China
Fengxiang China *see* **Lincang**
Fengyi China *see* **Zheng'an**
71 C3 **Fengyüan** Taiwan
70 B1 **Fengzhen** China
105 D3 **Feno, Capo di** *c.* France
121 □D2 **Fenoarivo Atsinanana** Madag.
70 B2 **Fenyang** China
91 D2 **Feodosiya** Ukr.
108 A3 **Fer, Cap de** *c.* Alg.
137 D1 **Fergus Falls** U.S.A.
51 E1 **Fergusson Island** P.N.G.
110 D2 **Ferizaj** Kosovo
114 B4 **Ferkessédougou** Côte d'Ivoire
108 B2 **Fermo** Italy
131 D2 **Fermont** Can.
106 B1 **Fermoselle** Spain
97 B2 **Fermoy** Ireland
141 D2 **Fernandina Beach** U.S.A.
154 B2 **Fernandópolis** Brazil
Fernando Poó *i.* Equat. Guinea *see* **Bioko**
134 B1 **Ferndale** U.S.A.
99 C4 **Ferndown** U.K.
128 C3 **Fernie** Can.
135 C3 **Fernley** U.S.A.
97 C2 **Ferns** Ireland
Ferozepore India *see* **Firozpur**
108 B2 **Ferrara** Italy
154 B2 **Ferreiros** Brazil
108 A2 **Ferro, Capo** *c.* Italy
106 B1 **Ferrol** Spain
Ferryville Tunisia *see* **Menzel Bourguiba**
100 B1 **Ferwert** Neth.
114 B1 **Fès** Morocco
118 B3 **Feshi** Dem. Rep. Congo
137 F3 **Festus** U.S.A.
110 C2 **Fetești** Romania
97 C2 **Fethard** Ireland
111 C3 **Fethiye** Turkey
96 □ **Fetlar** *i.* U.K.
130 C2 **Feuilles, Rivière aux** *r.* Can.
Fez Morocco *see* **Fès**
121 □D3 **Fianarantsoa** Madag.
115 D4 **Fianga** Chad
117 B4 **Fichē** Eth.
109 C2 **Fier** Albania
96 C2 **Fife Ness** *pt* U.K.
104 C3 **Figeac** France
106 B1 **Figueira da Foz** Port.
107 D1 **Figueres** Spain
114 B1 **Figuig** Morocco
49 I5 **Fiji** *country* S. Pacific Ocean
152 B2 **Filadelfia** Para.
55 B2 **Filchner Ice Shelf** Antarctica
98 C2 **Filey** U.K.
108 B3 **Filicudi, Isola** *i.* Italy
114 C3 **Filingué** Niger
111 B3 **Filippiada** Greece
93 F4 **Filipstad** Sweden
92 E3 **Fillan** Norway
135 D3 **Fillmore** U.S.A.
119 E2 **Filtu** Eth.
55 D2 **Fimbull Ice Shelf** Antarctica
96 C2 **Findhorn** *r.* U.K.
138 C2 **Findlay** U.S.A.
51 D4 **Fingal** Austr.
139 D2 **Finger Lakes** U.S.A.
111 D3 **Finike** Turkey
106 B1 **Finisterre, Cape** *c.* Spain
93 I3 **Finland** *country* Europe
93 H4 **Finland, Gulf of** Europe
128 B2 **Finlay** *r.* Can.
53 C3 **Finley** Austr.
134 C1 **Finley** U.S.A.
101 E2 **Finne** *ridge* Ger.
92 H2 **Finnmarksvidda** *reg.* Norway
92 G2 **Finnsnes** Norway
93 G4 **Finspång** Sweden
97 C1 **Fintona** U.K.
96 A2 **Fionnphort** U.K.
111 C3 **Fira** Greece
Fırat *r.* Turkey *see* **Euphrates**
Firenze Italy *see* **Florence**
105 C2 **Firminy** France
74 B2 **Firozabad** India
74 B1 **Firozpur** India
81 D3 **Fīrūzābād** Iran
122 A2 **Fish** *watercourse* Namibia
122 B3 **Fish** *r.* S. Africa
129 F1 **Fisher Strait** Can.
99 A4 **Fishguard** U.K.
105 C2 **Fismes** France
Fisterra, Cabo *c.* Spain *see* **Finisterre, Cape**
139 E2 **Fitchburg** U.S.A.
128 C2 **Fitzgerald** Can.
141 D2 **Fitzgerald** U.S.A.
50 B1 **Fitzroy Crossing** Austr.
Fiume Croatia *see* **Rijeka**
54 A3 **Five Rivers** N.Z.
108 B2 **Fivizzano** Italy
119 C3 **Fizi** Dem. Rep. Congo
93 F3 **Fjällnäs** Sweden
92 G3 **Fjällsjöälven** *r.* Sweden
123 C3 **Flagstaff** S. Africa
142 A1 **Flagstaff** U.S.A.
130 C2 **Flaherty Island** Can.
98 C2 **Flamborough Head** *hd* U.K.
101 F1 **Fläming** *hills* Ger.
136 B2 **Flaming Gorge Reservoir** U.S.A.
134 D1 **Flathead** *r.* U.S.A.
134 D1 **Flathead Lake** U.S.A.
51 D1 **Flattery, Cape** Austr.
134 B1 **Flattery, Cape** U.S.A.
98 B3 **Fleetwood** U.K.
93 E4 **Flekkefjord** Norway
102 B1 **Flensburg** Ger.
104 B2 **Flers** France
100 B2 **Fleurus** Belgium
104 C2 **Fleury-les-Aubrais** France
51 D1 **Flinders** *r.* Austr.
50 A3 **Flinders Bay** Austr.
51 D3 **Flinders Island** Austr.
52 A2 **Flinders Ranges** *mts* Austr.
129 D2 **Flin Flon** Can.
98 B3 **Flint** U.K.
138 C2 **Flint** U.S.A.
49 L5 **Flint Island** Kiribati
101 F2 **Flöha** Ger.
107 D1 **Florac** France
100 C3 **Florange** France
108 B2 **Florence** Italy
140 C2 **Florence** *AL* U.S.A.
142 A2 **Florence** *AZ* U.S.A.
134 B2 **Florence** *OR* U.S.A.
141 E2 **Florence** *SC* U.S.A.
150 B2 **Florencia** Col.
146 B3 **Flores** Guat.
61 D2 **Flores** *i.* Indon.
61 C2 **Flores, Laut** Indon.
Floreshty Moldova *see* **Florești**
Flores Sea *sea* Indon. *see* **Flores, Laut**
151 F3 **Floresta** Brazil
90 B2 **Florești** Moldova
143 D3 **Floresville** U.S.A.
151 E3 **Floriano** Brazil
152 D2 **Florianópolis** Brazil
153 C3 **Florida** Uru.
141 D2 **Florida** *state* U.S.A.
141 D4 **Florida, Straits of** N. Atlantic Ocean
141 D4 **Florida Bay** U.S.A.
141 D4 **Florida Keys** *is* U.S.A.
111 B2 **Florina** Greece
93 E3 **Florø** Norway
129 D2 **Foam Lake** Can.
109 C2 **Foča** Bos.-Herz.
110 C1 **Focșani** Romania
71 B3 **Fogang** China
109 C2 **Foggia** Italy
131 E3 **Fogo Island** Can.
104 C3 **Foix** France
89 D3 **Fokino** Rus. Fed.
130 B3 **Foleyet** Can.
108 B2 **Foligno** Italy
99 D4 **Folkestone** U.K.
141 D2 **Folkston** U.S.A.
108 B2 **Follonica** Italy
129 D2 **Fond-du-Lac** Can.
129 D2 **Fond du Lac** *r.* Can.
138 B2 **Fond du Lac** U.S.A.
106 B1 **Fondevila** Spain
108 B2 **Fondi** Italy
146 B3 **Fonseca, Golfo do** *b.* Central America
150 C3 **Fonte Boa** Brazil
104 B2 **Fontenay-le-Comte** France
92 □C2 **Fontur** *pt* Iceland
Foochow China *see* **Fuzhou**
53 C2 **Forbes** Austr.
75 C2 **Forbesganj** India
101 E3 **Forchheim** Ger.
93 E3 **Førde** Norway
53 C1 **Fords Bridge** Austr.
140 B2 **Fordyce** U.S.A.
140 C2 **Forest** U.S.A.
53 C3 **Forest Hill** Austr.
131 D3 **Forestville** Can.
96 C2 **Forfar** U.K.
134 B1 **Forks** U.S.A.
108 B2 **Forlì** Italy
107 D2 **Formentera** *i.* Spain
107 D2 **Formentor, Cap de** *c.* Spain
155 C2 **Formiga** Brazil
152 C2 **Formosa** Arg.
Formosa *country* Asia *see* **Taiwan**
154 C1 **Formosa** Brazil
Formosa Strait *str.* China/Taiwan *see* **Taiwan Strait**
Føroyar *terr.* N. Atlantic Ocean *see* **Faroe Islands**
96 C2 **Forres** U.K.
50 B3 **Forrest** Austr.
140 B1 **Forrest City** U.S.A.
51 D1 **Forsayth** Austr.
93 H3 **Forssa** Fin.
53 D2 **Forster** Austr.
136 B1 **Forsyth** U.S.A.
74 B2 **Fort Abbas** Pak.
130 B2 **Fort Albany** Can.
151 F3 **Fortaleza** Brazil
Fort Archambault Chad *see* **Sarh**
128 C2 **Fort Assiniboine** Can.
96 B2 **Fort Augustus** U.K.
123 C3 **Fort Beaufort** S. Africa
134 D1 **Fort Benton** U.S.A.
Fort Brabant Can. *see* **Tuktoyaktuk**
135 B3 **Fort Bragg** U.S.A.
Fort Carnot Madag. *see* **Ikongo**
Fort Charlet Alg. *see* **Djanet**
Fort Chimo Can. *see* **Kuujjuaq**
129 C2 **Fort Chipewyan** Can.
136 B2 **Fort Collins** U.S.A.
Fort Crampel C.A.R. *see* **Kaga Bandoro**
Fort-Dauphin Madag. *see* **Tôlañaro**
147 D3 **Fort-de-France** Martinique
Fort de Polignac Alg. *see* **Illizi**
137 E2 **Fort Dodge** U.S.A.
139 D2 **Fort Erie** Can.
Fort Flatters Alg. *see* **Bordj Omer Driss**
Fort Foureau Cameroon *see* **Kousséri**
130 A3 **Fort Frances** Can.
Fort Franklin Can. *see* **Déljne**
Fort Gardel Alg. *see* **Zaouatallaz**
Fort George Can. *see* **Chisasibi**
126 D2 **Fort Good Hope** Can.
Fort Gouraud Maur. *see* **Fdérik**
96 C2 **Forth** *r.* U.K.
96 C2 **Forth, Firth of** *est.* U.K.
Fort Hall Kenya *see* **Murang'a**
Fort Hertz Myanmar *see* **Putao**
152 C2 **Fortín Madrejón** Para.
Fort Jameson Zambia *see* **Chipata**
Fort Johnston Malawi *see* **Mangochi**
Fort Lamy Chad *see* **Ndjamena**
Fort Laperrine Alg. *see* **Tamanrasset**
141 D3 **Fort Lauderdale** U.S.A.
128 B1 **Fort Liard** Can.
128 C2 **Fort Mackay** Can.
137 E2 **Fort Madison** U.S.A.
Fort Manning Malawi *see* **Mchinji**
128 C2 **Fort McMurray** Can.
126 D2 **Fort McPherson** Can.
136 C2 **Fort Morgan** U.S.A.
141 D3 **Fort Myers** U.S.A.
128 B2 **Fort Nelson** Can.
128 B2 **Fort Nelson** *r.* Can.
Fort Norman Can. *see* **Tulita**
140 C2 **Fort Payne** U.S.A.
136 B1 **Fort Peck** U.S.A.
136 B1 **Fort Peck Reservoir** U.S.A.
141 D3 **Fort Pierce** U.S.A.
119 D2 **Fort Portal** Uganda
128 C1 **Fort Providence** Can.
129 D2 **Fort Qu'Appelle** Can.
128 C1 **Fort Resolution** Can.
96 B2 **Fortrose** U.K.
Fort Rosebery Zambia *see* **Mansa**
Fort Rousset Congo *see* **Owando**
Fort Rupert Can. *see* **Waskaganish**
128 B2 **Fort St James** Can.
128 B2 **Fort St John** Can.
Fort Sandeman Pak. *see* **Zhob**
128 C2 **Fort Saskatchewan** Can.
137 E3 **Fort Scott** U.S.A.
130 B2 **Fort Severn** Can.
76 B2 **Fort-Shevchenko** Kazakh.
128 B1 **Fort Simpson** Can.
128 C1 **Fort Smith** Can.
140 B1 **Fort Smith** U.S.A.
143 C2 **Fort Stockton** U.S.A.
142 C2 **Fort Sumner** U.S.A.
Fort Trinquet Maur. *see* **Bîr Mogreïn**
134 B2 **Fortuna** U.S.A.
131 E3 **Fortune Bay** Can.
128 C2 **Fort Vermilion** Can.
Fort Victoria Zimbabwe *see* **Masvingo**
Fort Walton U.S.A. *see* **Fort Walton Beach**
140 C2 **Fort Walton Beach** U.S.A.
136 B2 **Fort Washakie** U.S.A.
138 B2 **Fort Wayne** U.S.A.
96 B2 **Fort William** U.K.
143 D2 **Fort Worth** U.S.A.
126 C2 **Fort Yukon** U.S.A.
71 B3 **Foshan** China
92 F3 **Fosna** *pen.* Norway
93 E3 **Fosnavåg** Norway
92 □B3 **Foss** Iceland
92 □A2 **Fossá** Iceland
108 A2 **Fossano** Italy
137 D1 **Fosston** U.S.A.
53 C3 **Foster** Austr.
118 B3 **Fougamou** Gabon
104 B2 **Fougères** France
96 □ **Foula** *i.* U.K.
99 D4 **Foulness Point** U.K.
118 B2 **Foumban** Cameroon
111 C3 **Fournoi** *i.* Greece
114 A3 **Fouta Djallon** *reg.* Guinea
54 A3 **Foveaux Strait** N.Z.
136 C3 **Fowler** U.S.A.
50 C3 **Fowlers Bay** Austr.
81 C2 **Fowman** Iran
128 C2 **Fox Creek** Can.
127 G2 **Foxe Basin** *g.* Can.
127 G2 **Foxe Channel** Can.
127 G2 **Foxe Peninsula** Can.
54 B2 **Fox Glacier** N.Z.
128 C2 **Fox Lake** Can.
128 A1 **Fox Mountain** Can.
54 C2 **Foxton** N.Z.
129 D2 **Fox Valley** Can.
97 C1 **Foyle** *r.* Ireland/U.K.
97 C1 **Foyle, Lough** *b.* Ireland/U.K.
97 B2 **Foynes** Ireland
154 B3 **Foz de Areia, Represa de** *resr* Brazil
120 A2 **Foz do Cunene** Angola
154 B3 **Foz do Iguaçu** Brazil
107 D1 **Fraga** Spain
100 A2 **Frameries** Belgium
154 C2 **Franca** Brazil
109 C2 **Francavilla Fontana** Italy
104 C2 **France** *country* Europe
118 B3 **Franceville** Gabon
137 D2 **Francis Case, Lake** U.S.A.
155 D1 **Francisco Sá** Brazil
120 B3 **Francistown** Botswana
128 B2 **François Lake** Can.
100 B1 **Franeker** Neth.
101 D2 **Frankenberg (Eder)** Ger.
101 D3 **Frankenthal (Pfalz)** Ger.

101 E2 **Frankenwald** *mts* Ger.
138 C3 **Frankfort** *KY* U.S.A.
138 B2 **Frankfort** *MI* U.S.A.
Frankfurt Ger. *see* **Frankfurt am Main**
101 D2 **Frankfurt am Main** Ger.
102 C1 **Frankfurt an der Oder** Ger.
102 C2 **Fränkische Alb** *hills* Ger.
101 E3 **Fränkische Schweiz** *reg.* Ger.
139 E2 **Franklin** *NH* U.S.A.
139 D2 **Franklin** *PA* U.S.A.
140 C1 **Franklin** *TN* U.S.A.
126 D2 **Franklin Bay** Can.
134 C1 **Franklin D. Roosevelt Lake** U.S.A.
128 B1 **Franklin Mountains** Can.
126 F2 **Franklin Strait** Can.
53 C3 **Frankston** Austr.
82 E1 **Frantsa-Iosifa, Zemlya** *is* Rus. Fed.
54 B2 **Franz Josef Glacier** N.Z.
Franz Josef Land *is* Rus. Fed. *see* **Frantsa-Iosifa, Zemlya**
108 A3 **Frasca, Capo della** *c.* Italy
128 B3 **Fraser** *r. B.C.* Can.
131 D2 **Fraser** *r. Nfld. and Lab.* Can.
122 B3 **Fraserburg** S. Africa
96 C2 **Fraserburgh** U.K.
130 B3 **Fraserdale** Can.
51 E2 **Fraser Island** Austr.
128 B2 **Fraser Lake** Can.
128 B2 **Fraser Plateau** Can.
153 C3 **Fray Bentos** Uru.
93 E4 **Fredericia** Denmark
143 D2 **Frederick** U.S.A.
143 D2 **Fredericksburg** *TX* U.S.A.
139 D3 **Fredericksburg** *VA* U.S.A.
128 A2 **Frederick Sound** *sea chan.* U.S.A.
131 D3 **Fredericton** Can.
Frederikshåb Greenland *see* **Paamiut**
93 F4 **Frederikshavn** Denmark
Fredrikshamn Fin. *see* **Hamina**
93 F4 **Fredrikstad** Norway
138 B2 **Freeport** *IL* U.S.A.
143 D3 **Freeport** *TX* U.S.A.
146 C2 **Freeport City** Bahamas
143 D3 **Freer** U.S.A.
123 C2 **Free State** *prov.* S. Africa
114 A4 **Freetown** Sierra Leone
106 B2 **Fregenal de la Sierra** Spain
104 B2 **Fréhel, Cap** *c.* France
102 B2 **Freiburg im Breisgau** Ger.
102 C2 **Freising** Ger.
102 C2 **Freistadt** Austria
105 D3 **Fréjus** France
50 A3 **Fremantle** Austr.
135 B3 **Fremont** *CA* U.S.A.
137 D2 **Fremont** *NE* U.S.A.
138 C2 **Fremont** *OH* U.S.A.
French Congo *country* Africa *see* **Congo**
151 D2 **French Guiana** *terr.* S. America
French Guinea *country* Africa *see* **Guinea**
134 E1 **Frenchman** *r.* U.S.A.
49 M5 **French Polynesia** *terr.* S. Pacific Ocean
French Somaliland *country* Africa *see* **Djibouti**
French Sudan *country* Africa *see* **Mali**
French Territory of the Afars and Issas *country* Africa *see* **Djibouti**
151 D3 **Fresco** *r.* Brazil
144 B2 **Fresnillo** Mex.
135 C3 **Fresno** U.S.A.
107 D2 **Freu, Cap des** *c.* Spain
105 D2 **Freyming-Merlebach** France
114 A3 **Fria** Guinea
152 B2 **Frias** Arg.
101 D2 **Friedberg (Hessen)** Ger.
102 B2 **Friedrichshafen** Ger.
101 F1 **Friesack** Ger.
100 C1 **Friesoythe** Ger.
143 C2 **Friona** U.S.A.
136 B3 **Frisco** U.S.A.
Frobisher Bay Can. *see* **Iqaluit**
127 H2 **Frobisher Bay** *b.* Can.
101 F2 **Frohburg** Ger.
87 D4 **Frolovo** Rus. Fed.
103 D1 **Frombork** Pol.
99 B4 **Frome** U.K.
52 A2 **Frome, Lake** *imp. l.* Austr.
52 A2 **Frome Downs** Austr.
100 C2 **Fröndenberg** Ger.
143 C3 **Frontera** Mex.
145 C3 **Frontera** Mex.
144 B1 **Fronteras** Mex.
139 D3 **Front Royal** U.S.A.
108 B2 **Frosinone** Italy
92 E3 **Frøya** *i.* Norway
Frunze Kyrg. *see* **Bishkek**
154 C2 **Frutal** Brazil
105 D2 **Frutigen** Switz.
103 D2 **Frýdek-Místek** Czech Rep.
71 B3 **Fu'an** China
71 C3 **Fuding** China
106 C1 **Fuenlabrada** Spain
152 C2 **Fuerte Olimpo** Para.
114 A2 **Fuerteventura** *i.* Islas Canarias
64 B2 **Fuga** *i.* Phil.
79 C2 **Fujairah** U.A.E.
67 C3 **Fuji** Japan
71 B3 **Fujian** *prov.* China
67 C3 **Fujinomiya** Japan
67 C3 **Fuji-san** *vol.* Japan
Fukien *prov.* China *see* **Fujian**
67 C3 **Fukui** Japan
67 B4 **Fukuoka** Japan
67 D3 **Fukushima** Japan
101 D2 **Fulda** Ger.
101 D2 **Fulda** *r.* Ger.
70 A3 **Fuling** China
137 E3 **Fulton** U.S.A.
105 C2 **Fumay** France
49 I4 **Funafuti** *atoll* Tuvalu
114 A1 **Funchal** Arquipélago da Madeira
155 D1 **Fundão** Brazil
106 B1 **Fundão** Port.
131 D3 **Fundy, Bay of** *g.* Can.
121 C3 **Funhalouro** Moz.
70 B2 **Funing** *Jiangsu* China
71 A3 **Funing** *Yunnan* China
115 C3 **Funtua** Nigeria
79 C2 **Fürgun, Kūh-e** *mt.* Iran
89 F2 **Furmanov** Rus. Fed.
Furmanovka Kazakh. *see* **Moyynkum**
Furmanovo Kazakh. *see* **Zhalpaktal**
155 C2 **Furnas, Represa** *resr* Brazil
51 D4 **Furneaux Group** *is* Austr.
Furong China *see* **Wan'an**
100 C1 **Fürstenau** Ger.
101 E3 **Fürth** Ger.
66 D3 **Furukawa** Japan
127 G2 **Fury and Hecla Strait** Can.
70 C1 **Fushun** China
65 B1 **Fusong** China
79 C2 **Fuwayriṭ** Qatar
Fuxian China *see* **Wafangdian**
70 A2 **Fuxian** China
70 C1 **Fuxin** China
70 B2 **Fuyang** China
69 E1 **Fuyu** China
Fuyu China *see* **Songyuan**
68 B1 **Fuyun** China
71 B3 **Fuzhou** *Fujian* China
71 B3 **Fuzhou** *Jiangxi* China
93 F4 **Fyn** *i.* Denmark
96 B3 **Fyne, Loch** *inlet* U.K.
F.Y.R.O.M. *country* Europe *see* **Macedonia**

G

117 C4 **Gaalkacyo** Somalia
120 A2 **Gabela** Angola
Gaberones Botswana *see* **Gaborone**
115 D1 **Gabès** Tunisia
115 D1 **Gabès, Golfe de** *g.* Tunisia
118 B3 **Gabon** *country* Africa
123 C1 **Gaborone** Botswana
79 C2 **Gābrīk** Iran
110 C2 **Gabrovo** Bulg.
114 A3 **Gabú** Guinea-Bissau
73 B3 **Gadag** India
75 C2 **Gadchiroli** India
101 E1 **Gadebusch** Ger.
140 C2 **Gadsden** U.S.A.
118 B2 **Gadzi** C.A.R.
110 C2 **Găeşti** Romania
108 B2 **Gaeta** Italy
108 B2 **Gaeta, Golfo di** *g.* Italy
141 D1 **Gaffney** U.S.A.
115 C1 **Gafsa** Tunisia
89 E2 **Gagarin** Rus. Fed.
109 C3 **Gagliano del Capo** Italy
114 B4 **Gagnoa** Côte d'Ivoire
131 D2 **Gagnon** Can.
Gago Coutinho Angola *see* **Lumbala N'guimbo**
81 C1 **Gagra** Georgia
122 A2 **Gaiab** *watercourse* Namibia
111 C3 **Gaïdouronisi** *i.* Greece
104 C3 **Gaillac** France
Gaillimh Ireland *see* **Galway**
141 D3 **Gainesville** *FL* U.S.A.
141 D2 **Gainesville** *GA* U.S.A.
143 D2 **Gainesville** *TX* U.S.A.
98 C3 **Gainsborough** U.K.
52 A2 **Gairdner, Lake** *imp. l.* Austr.
96 B2 **Gairloch** U.K.
122 B2 **Gakarosa** *mt.* S. Africa
119 E3 **Galana** *r.* Kenya
103 D2 **Galanta** Slovakia
Galápagos, Islas *is* Ecuador *see* **Galapagos Islands**
125 I10 **Galapagos Islands** *is* Ecuador
157 G6 **Galapagos Rise** Pacific Ocean
96 C3 **Galashiels** U.K.
110 C1 **Galați** Romania
93 E3 **Galdhøpiggen** *mt.* Norway
145 B2 **Galeana** Mex.
128 C2 **Galena Bay** Can.
138 A2 **Galesburg** U.S.A.
122 B2 **Galeshewe** S. Africa
89 F2 **Galich** Rus. Fed.
106 B1 **Galicia** *aut. comm.* Spain
80 B2 **Galilee, Sea of** *l.* Israel
78 A3 **Gallabat** Sudan
140 C1 **Gallatin** U.S.A.
73 C4 **Galle** Sri Lanka
157 G6 **Gallego Rise** Pacific Ocean
150 B1 **Gallinas, Punta** *pt* Col.
109 C2 **Gallipoli** Italy
111 C2 **Gallipoli** Turkey
92 H2 **Gällivare** Sweden
142 B1 **Gallup** U.S.A.
114 A2 **Galtat Zemmour** Western Sahara
97 B2 **Galtymore** *h.* Ireland
143 E3 **Galveston** U.S.A.
143 E3 **Galveston Bay** U.S.A.
143 E3 **Galveston Island** U.S.A.
97 B2 **Galway** Ireland
97 B2 **Galway Bay** Ireland
154 C1 **Gamá** Brazil
123 D3 **Gamalakhe** S. Africa
117 B4 **Gambēla** Eth.
114 A3 **Gambia** *r.* Gambia
114 A3 **Gambia, The** *country* Africa
49 N6 **Gambier, Îles** *is* Fr. Polynesia
52 A3 **Gambier Islands** Austr.
131 E3 **Gambo** Can.
118 B3 **Gamboma** Congo
128 C1 **Gamêtì** Can.
92 H2 **Gammelstaden** Sweden
142 B1 **Ganado** U.S.A.
81 C1 **Gäncä** Azer.
61 C2 **Gandadiwata, Bukit** *mt.* Indon.
118 C3 **Gandajika** Dem. Rep. Congo
131 E3 **Gander** Can.
131 E3 **Gander** *r.* Can.
101 D1 **Ganderkesee** Ger.
107 D1 **Gandesa** Spain
74 B2 **Gandhidham** India
74 B2 **Gandhinagar** India
74 B2 **Gandhi Sagar** *resr* India
107 C2 **Gandia** Spain
Ganga *r.* Bangl./India *see* **Ganges**
153 B4 **Gangán** Arg.
74 B2 **Ganganagar** India
62 A1 **Gangaw** Myanmar
68 C2 **Gangca** China
75 C1 **Gangdisê Shan** *mts* China
75 D2 **Ganges** *r.* Bangl./India
105 C3 **Ganges** France
75 C2 **Ganges, Mouths of the** Bangl./India
159 E2 **Ganges Cone** Indian Ocean
75 C2 **Gangtok** India
75 C3 **Ganjam** India
71 A3 **Ganluo** China
105 C2 **Gannat** France
136 B2 **Gannett Peak** U.S.A.
122 A3 **Gansbaai** S. Africa
70 A1 **Gansu** *prov.* China
115 D4 **Ganye** Nigeria
71 B3 **Ganzhou** China
114 B3 **Gao** Mali
Gaoleshan China *see* **Xianfeng**
97 B1 **Gaoth Dobhair** Ireland
114 B3 **Gaoua** Burkina
114 A3 **Gaoual** Guinea
70 B2 **Gaoyou** China
70 B2 **Gaoyou Hu** *l.* China
105 D3 **Gap** France
64 B2 **Gapan** Phil.
75 C1 **Gar** China
97 B2 **Gara, Lough** *l.* Ireland
76 C3 **Garabil Belentligi** *hills* Turkm.
76 B2 **Garabogaz** Turkm.
76 B2 **Garabogazköl** Turkm.
76 B2 **Garabogazköl Aýlagy** *b.* Turkm.
117 C4 **Garacad** Somalia
53 C1 **Garah** Austr.
151 F3 **Garanhuns** Brazil
123 C2 **Ga-Rankuwa** S. Africa
118 C1 **Garar, Plaine de** *plain* Chad
117 C4 **Garbahaarrey** Somalia
135 B2 **Garberville** U.S.A.
81 D2 **Garbosh, Kūh-e** *mt.* Iran
101 D1 **Garbsen** Ger.
154 C2 **Garça** Brazil
154 B2 **Garcias** Brazil
108 B1 **Garda, Lake** *l.* Italy
108 A3 **Garde, Cap de** *c.* Alg.
101 E1 **Gardelegen** Ger.
136 C3 **Garden City** U.S.A.
129 E2 **Garden Hill** Can.
77 C3 **Gardēz** Afgh.
139 F2 **Gardiner** U.S.A.
Gardner *atoll* Micronesia *see* **Faraulep**
135 C3 **Gardnerville** U.S.A.
136 B3 **Garfield** U.S.A.
88 B2 **Gargždai** Lith.
123 C3 **Gariep Dam** *dam* S. Africa
122 A3 **Garies** S. Africa
119 D3 **Garissa** Kenya
88 B2 **Garkalne** Latvia
143 D2 **Garland** U.S.A.
102 C2 **Garmisch-Partenkirchen** Ger.
52 B2 **Garnpung Lake** *imp. l.* Austr.
104 B3 **Garonne** *r.* France
117 C4 **Garoowe** Somalia
74 B2 **Garoth** India
118 B2 **Garoua** Cameroon
118 B2 **Garoua Boulai** Cameroon
Garqêntang China *see* **Sog**
96 B2 **Garry** *r.* U.K.
126 F2 **Garry Lake** Can.
119 E3 **Garsen** Kenya
76 B2 **Garşy** Turkm.
122 A2 **Garub** Namibia
60 B2 **Garut** Indon.
138 B2 **Gary** U.S.A.
145 B2 **Garza García** Mex.
68 C2 **Garzê** China
Gascogne *reg.* France *see* **Gascony**
Gascogne, Golfe de *g.* France *see* **Gascony, Gulf of**
104 B3 **Gascony** *reg.* France
104 B3 **Gascony, Gulf of** France
50 A2 **Gascoyne** *r.* Austr.
118 B2 **Gashaka** Nigeria
115 D3 **Gashua** Nigeria
59 E3 **Gasmata** P.N.G.
131 D3 **Gaspé** Can.
131 D3 **Gaspésie, Péninsule de la** *pen.* Can.
141 E1 **Gaston, Lake** U.S.A.
141 D1 **Gastonia** U.S.A.
107 C2 **Gata, Cabo de** *c.* Spain
88 D2 **Gatchina** Rus. Fed.
98 C2 **Gateshead** U.K.
143 D2 **Gatesville** U.S.A.
139 D1 **Gatineau** Can.
130 C3 **Gatineau** *r.* Can.
Gatooma Zimbabwe *see* **Kadoma**
53 D1 **Gatton** Austr.
129 E2 **Gauer Lake** Can.
93 E4 **Gausta** *mt.* Norway
123 C2 **Gauteng** *prov.* S. Africa
79 C2 **Gāvbandī** Iran
111 B3 **Gavdos** *i.* Greece
93 G3 **Gävle** Sweden
93 G3 **Gävlebukten** *b.* Sweden
89 F2 **Gavrilov Posad** Rus. Fed.
89 E2 **Gavrilov-Yam** Rus. Fed.
122 A2 **Gawachab** Namibia
62 A1 **Gawai** Myanmar
52 A2 **Gawler** Austr.
52 A2 **Gawler Ranges** *hills* Austr.
75 C2 **Gaya** India
114 C3 **Gaya** Niger
114 C3 **Gayéri** Burkina
138 C1 **Gaylord** U.S.A.
86 E2 **Gayny** Rus. Fed.
116 B1 **Gaza** *terr.* Asia
80 B2 **Gaza** Gaza
80 B2 **Gaziantep** Turkey
76 C2 **Gazojak** Turkm.
114 B4 **Gbarnga** Liberia
118 A2 **Gboko** Nigeria
103 D1 **Gdańsk** Pol.
88 A3 **Gdańsk, Gulf of** Pol./Rus. Fed.
88 C2 **Gdov** Rus. Fed.
103 D1 **Gdynia** Pol.
116 B3 **Gedaref** Sudan
101 D2 **Gedern** Ger.
111 C3 **Gediz** Turkey
111 C3 **Gediz** *r.* Turkey
102 C1 **Gedser** Denmark
100 B2 **Geel** Belgium
52 B3 **Geelong** Austr.
101 E1 **Geesthacht** Ger.
75 C1 **Gê'gyai** China
129 D2 **Geikie** *r.* Can.
93 E3 **Geilo** Norway
119 D3 **Geita** Tanz.
71 A3 **Gejiu** China
108 B3 **Gela** Italy
108 B3 **Gela, Golfo di** *g.* Italy
91 D3 **Gelendzhik** Rus. Fed.
Gelibolu Turkey *see* **Gallipoli**
100 C2 **Gelsenkirchen** Ger.
118 B2 **Gemena** Dem. Rep. Congo
111 C2 **Gemlik** Turkey
108 B1 **Gemona del Friuli** Italy
117 C4 **Genalē Wenz** *r.* Eth.
81 D3 **Genāveh** Iran
153 B3 **General Acha** Arg.
153 B3 **General Alvear** Arg.
153 C3 **General Belgrano** Arg.
144 B2 **General Cepeda** Mex.
General Freire Angola *see* **Muxaluando**
General Machado Angola *see* **Camacupa**
153 B3 **General Pico** Arg.
153 B3 **General Roca** Arg.
154 B2 **General Salgado** Brazil
64 B3 **General Santos** Phil.
139 D2 **Genesee** *r.* U.S.A.
138 A2 **Geneseo** *IL* U.S.A.
139 D2 **Geneseo** *NY* U.S.A.
105 D2 **Geneva** Switz.
139 D2 **Geneva** U.S.A.
105 D2 **Geneva, Lake** *l.* France/Switz.
Genève Switz. *see* **Geneva**
106 B2 **Genil** *r.* Spain
100 B2 **Genk** Belgium
53 C3 **Genoa** Austr.
108 A2 **Genoa** Italy
108 A2 **Genoa, Gulf of** *g.* Italy
Genova Italy *see* **Genoa**
Gent Belgium *see* **Ghent**
61 C2 **Genteng** *i.* Indon.
101 F1 **Genthin** Ger.
50 A3 **Geographe Bay** Austr.
131 D2 **George** *r.* Can.
122 B3 **George** S. Africa
52 A3 **George, Lake** Austr.
141 D3 **George, Lake** *FL* U.S.A.
139 E2 **George, Lake** *NY* U.S.A.
146 C2 **George Town** Bahamas
114 A3 **Georgetown** Gambia
151 D2 **Georgetown** Guyana
60 B1 **George Town** Malaysia
138 C3 **Georgetown** *KY* U.S.A.
141 E2 **Georgetown** *SC* U.S.A.
143 D2 **Georgetown** *TX* U.S.A.
55 L2 **George V Land** *reg.* Antarctica
81 C1 **Georgia** *country* Asia
141 D2 **Georgia** *state* U.S.A.
130 B3 **Georgian Bay** Can.
51 C2 **Georgina** *watercourse* Austr.
Georgiu-Dezh Rus. Fed. *see* **Liski**
77 E2 **Georgiyevka** Kazakh.
87 D4 **Georgiyevsk** Rus. Fed.

101 F2 **Gera** Ger.
151 E4 **Geral de Goiás, Serra** *hills* Brazil
54 B2 **Geraldine** N.Z.
50 A2 **Geraldton** Austr.
80 B1 **Gerede** Turkey
76 C3 **Gereshk** Afgh.
102 C2 **Geretsried** Ger.
135 C2 **Gerlach** U.S.A.
103 E2 **Gerlachovský štít** *mt.* Slovakia
139 D3 **Germantown** U.S.A.
102 C1 **Germany** *country* Europe
100 C2 **Gerolstein** Ger.
101 E3 **Gerolzhofen** Ger.
53 D2 **Gerringong** Austr.
101 D2 **Gersfeld (Rhön)** Ger.
Géryville Alg. *see* **El Bayadh**
75 C1 **Gêrzê** China
117 C4 **Gestro, Wabē** *r.* Eth.
106 C1 **Getafe** Spain
139 D3 **Gettysburg** *PA* U.S.A.
136 D1 **Gettysburg** *SD* U.S.A.
55 P2 **Getz Ice Shelf** Antarctica
111 B2 **Gevgelija** Macedonia
111 C3 **Geyikli** Turkey
122 B2 **Ghaap Plateau** S. Africa
Ghadamés Libya *see* **Ghadāmis**
115 C1 **Ghadāmis** Libya
75 C2 **Ghaghara** *r.* India
114 B4 **Ghana** *country* Africa
120 B3 **Ghanzi** Botswana
115 C1 **Ghardaïa** Alg.
78 A2 **Ghārib, Jabal** *mt.* Egypt
115 D1 **Gharyān** Libya
115 D2 **Ghāt** Libya
75 C2 **Ghatal** India
75 B2 **Ghaziabad** India
75 C2 **Ghazipur** India
77 C3 **Ghaznī** Afgh.
78 B2 **Ghazzālah** Saudi Arabia
100 A2 **Ghent** Belgium
Gheorghe Gheorghiu-Dej Romania *see* **Onești**
110 C1 **Gheorgheni** Romania
110 B1 **Gherla** Romania
105 D3 **Ghisonaccia** France
74 B2 **Ghotaru** India
74 A2 **Ghotki** Pak.
75 C2 **Ghugri** *r.* India
76 C3 **Ghurian** Afgh.
91 E3 **Giaginskaya** Rus. Fed.
97 C1 **Giant's Causeway** *lava field* U.K.
61 C2 **Gianyar** Indon.
109 C3 **Giarre** Italy
108 A1 **Giaveno** Italy
122 A2 **Gibeon** Namibia
106 B2 **Gibraltar** Gibraltar
106 B2 **Gibraltar, Strait of** Morocco/Spain
140 B2 **Gibsland** U.S.A.
50 B2 **Gibson Desert** Austr.
68 C1 **Gichgeniyn Nuruu** *mts* Mongolia
117 B4 **Gīdolē** Eth.
105 C2 **Gien** France
101 D2 **Gießen** Ger.
101 E1 **Gifhorn** Ger.
128 C2 **Gift Lake** Can.
67 C3 **Gifu** Japan
96 B3 **Gigha** *i.* U.K.
76 C2 **G'ijduvon** Uzbek.
106 B1 **Gijón-Xixón** Spain
142 A2 **Gila** *r.* U.S.A.
142 A2 **Gila Bend** U.S.A.
51 D1 **Gilbert** *r.* Austr.
48 I4 **Gilbert Islands** *is* Kiribati
156 D5 **Gilbert Ridge** Pacific Ocean
151 E3 **Gilbués** Brazil
134 D1 **Gildford** U.S.A.
Gilf Kebir Plateau *plat.* Egypt *see* **Haḍabat al Jilf al Kabīr**
53 C2 **Gilgandra** Austr.
74 B1 **Gilgit** Pak.
74 B1 **Gilgit** *r.* Pak.
53 C2 **Gilgunnia** Austr.
129 E2 **Gillam** Can.
136 B2 **Gillette** U.S.A.
99 D4 **Gillingham** U.K.
130 C2 **Gilmour Island** Can.
135 B3 **Gilroy** U.S.A.
129 E2 **Gimli** Can.
64 B3 **Gingoog** Phil.
117 C4 **Gīnīr** Eth.
109 C2 **Ginosa** Italy
109 C2 **Gioia del Colle** Italy
53 C3 **Gippsland** *reg.* Austr.
74 A2 **Girdar Dhor** *r.* Pak.
79 D1 **Girdi** Iran
80 B1 **Giresun** Turkey
Girgenti Italy *see* **Agrigento**
53 C2 **Girilambone** Austr.
Giron Sweden *see* **Kiruna**
107 D1 **Girona** Spain
104 B2 **Gironde** *est.* France
53 C2 **Girral** Austr.
96 B3 **Girvan** U.K.
54 C1 **Gisborne** N.Z.
93 F4 **Gislaved** Sweden
119 C3 **Gitarama** Rwanda
119 C3 **Gitega** Burundi
Giuba *r.* Somalia *see* **Jubba**
108 B2 **Giulianova** Italy
110 C2 **Giurgiu** Romania
110 C1 **Giuvala, Pasul** *pass* Romania
105 C2 **Givors** France
123 D1 **Giyani** S. Africa
119 D2 **Giyon** Eth.
116 B2 **Giza** Egypt
103 E1 **Giżycko** Pol.
109 D2 **Gjakovë** Kosovo
109 D2 **Gjeravicë** *mt.* Kosovo
110 D2 **Gjilan** Kosovo
109 D2 **Gjirokastër** Albania
126 F2 **Gjoa Haven** Can.
93 F3 **Gjøvik** Norway
131 E3 **Glace Bay** Can.
134 B1 **Glacier Peak** *vol.* U.S.A.
143 E2 **Gladewater** U.S.A.
51 E2 **Gladstone** *Qld* Austr.
52 A2 **Gladstone** *S.A.* Austr.
92 □A2 **Gláma** *mts* Iceland
109 C2 **Glamoč** Bos.-Herz.
100 C3 **Glan** *r.* Ger.
97 B2 **Glanaruddery Mountains** *hills* Ireland
96 B3 **Glasgow** U.K.
138 B3 **Glasgow** *KY* U.S.A.
136 B1 **Glasgow** *MT* U.S.A.
99 B4 **Glastonbury** U.K.
101 F2 **Glauchau** Ger.
86 E3 **Glazov** Rus. Fed.
89 E3 **Glazunovka** Rus. Fed.
123 D2 **Glencoe** S. Africa
96 B2 **Glen Coe** *val.* U.K.
142 A2 **Glendale** *AZ* U.S.A.
138 B2 **Glendale** *WI* U.S.A.
53 D2 **Glen Davis** Austr.
51 D2 **Glenden** Austr.
136 C1 **Glendive** U.S.A.
52 B3 **Glenelg** *r.* Austr.
96 B2 **Glenfinnan** U.K.
53 D1 **Glen Innes** Austr.
96 B2 **Glen More** *val.* U.K.
53 C1 **Glenmorgan** Austr.
126 C2 **Glennallen** U.S.A.
134 C2 **Glenns Ferry** U.S.A.
136 B2 **Glenrock** U.S.A.
96 C2 **Glenrothes** U.K.
139 E2 **Glens Falls** U.S.A.
96 C2 **Glen Shee** *val.* U.K.
97 B1 **Glenties** Ireland
142 B2 **Glenwood** U.S.A.
130 D3 **Glenwood Springs** U.S.A.
101 F1 **Glinde** Ger.
103 D1 **Gliwice** Pol.
142 A2 **Globe** U.S.A.
103 D1 **Głogów** Pol.
92 F2 **Glomfjord** Norway
93 F4 **Glomma** *r.* Norway
53 D2 **Gloucester** Austr.
99 B4 **Gloucester** U.K.
131 E3 **Glovertown** Can.
101 E1 **Glöwen** Ger.
77 E1 **Glubokoye** Kazakh.
101 D1 **Glückstadt** Ger.
103 C2 **Gmünd** Austria
102 C2 **Gmunden** Austria
101 D1 **Gnarrenburg** Ger.
103 D1 **Gniezno** Pol.
Gnjilane Kosovo *see* **Gjilan**
75 D2 **Goalpara** India
96 B3 **Goat Fell** *h.* U.K.
117 C4 **Goba** Eth.
122 A1 **Gobabis** Namibia
153 A4 **Gobernador Gregores** Arg.
152 C2 **Gobernador Virasoro** Arg.
68 D2 **Gobi** *des.* China/Mongolia
67 C4 **Gobō** Japan
100 C2 **Goch** Ger.
122 A1 **Gochas** Namibia
74 B3 **Godavari** *r.* India
73 C3 **Godavari, Mouths of the** India
75 C2 **Godda** India
117 C4 **Godē** Eth.
130 B3 **Goderich** Can.
Godhavn Greenland *see* **Qeqertarsuaq**
74 B2 **Godhra** India
129 E2 **Gods** *r.* Can.
129 E2 **Gods Lake** Can.
Godthåb Greenland *see* **Nuuk**
Godwin-Austen, Mount *mt.* China/Pakistan *see* **K2**
Goedgegun Swaziland *see* **Nhlangano**
130 C3 **Goéland, Lac au** *l.* Can.
131 D2 **Goélands, Lac aux** *l.* Can.
100 A2 **Goes** Neth.
138 B1 **Gogebic Range** *hills* U.S.A.
88 C1 **Gogland, Ostrov** *i.* Rus. Fed.
Gogra *r.* India *see* **Ghaghara**
119 C2 **Gogrial** Sudan
154 C1 **Goiandira** Brazil
154 C1 **Goianésia** Brazil
154 C1 **Goiânia** Brazil
154 B1 **Goiás** Brazil
154 B1 **Goiás** *state* Brazil
154 C1 **Goiatuba** Brazil
154 B2 **Goio-Erê** Brazil
111 C2 **Gökçeada** *i.* Turkey
111 C3 **Gökçedağ** Turkey
121 B2 **Gokwe** Zimbabwe
93 E3 **Gol** Norway
62 A1 **Golaghat** India
111 C2 **Gölcük** Turkey
103 E1 **Gołdap** Pol.
101 F1 **Goldberg** Ger.
Gold Coast *country* Africa *see* **Ghana**
53 D1 **Gold Coast** Austr.
114 B4 **Gold Coast** *coastal area* Ghana
128 C2 **Golden** Can.
54 B2 **Golden Bay** N.Z.
134 B1 **Goldendale** U.S.A.
128 B3 **Golden Hinde** *mt.* Can.
97 B2 **Golden Vale** *lowland* Ireland
135 C3 **Goldfield** U.S.A.
128 B3 **Gold River** Can.
141 E1 **Goldsboro** U.S.A.
103 C1 **Goleniów** Pol.
135 C4 **Goleta** U.S.A.
Golfe du St-Laurent *g.* Can. *see* **St Lawrence, Gulf of**
111 C3 **Gölhisar** Turkey
Gollel Swaziland *see* **Lavumisa**
75 D1 **Golmud** China
81 D2 **Golpāyegān** Iran
96 C2 **Golspie** U.K.
Golyshi Rus. Fed. *see* **Vetluzhskiy**
119 C3 **Goma** Dem. Rep. Congo
75 C2 **Gomati** *r.* India
115 D3 **Gombe** Nigeria
115 D3 **Gombi** Nigeria
Gomel' Belarus *see* **Homyel'**
144 B2 **Gómez Palacio** Mex.
81 D2 **Gomīshān** Iran
75 C1 **Gomo** China
147 C3 **Gonaïves** Haiti
147 C3 **Gonâve, Île de la** *i.* Haiti
81 D2 **Gonbad-e Kavus** Iran
74 B2 **Gondal** India
Gondar Eth. *see* **Gonder**
116 B3 **Gonder** Eth.
75 C2 **Gondia** India
111 C2 **Gönen** Turkey
62 A1 **Gonggar** China
70 A3 **Gongga Shan** *mt.* China
68 C2 **Gonghe** China
115 D4 **Gongola** *r.* Nigeria
53 C2 **Gongolgon** Austr.
Gongtang China *see* **Damxung**
123 C3 **Gonubie** S. Africa
145 C2 **Gonzáles** Mex.
143 D3 **Gonzales** U.S.A.
122 A3 **Good Hope, Cape of** S. Africa
134 D2 **Gooding** U.S.A.
136 C3 **Goodland** U.S.A.
53 C1 **Goodooga** Austr.
98 C3 **Goole** U.K.
53 C2 **Goolgowi** Austr.
52 A3 **Goolwa** Austr.
53 D1 **Goondiwindi** Austr.
134 B2 **Goose Lake** U.S.A.
102 B2 **Göppingen** Ger.
75 C2 **Gorakhpur** India
109 C2 **Goražde** Bos.-Herz.
111 C3 **Gördes** Turkey
89 D3 **Gordeyevka** Rus. Fed.
136 C2 **Gordon** U.S.A.
51 D4 **Gordon, Lake** Austr.
115 D4 **Goré** Chad
117 B4 **Gorē** Eth.
54 A3 **Gore** N.Z.
97 C2 **Gorey** Ireland
81 D2 **Gorgān** Iran
81 C1 **Gori** Georgia
100 B2 **Gorinchem** Neth.
108 B1 **Gorizia** Italy
Gor'kiy Rus. Fed. *see* **Nizhniy Novgorod**
89 F2 **Gor'kovskoye Vodokhranilishche** *resr* Rus. Fed.
103 E2 **Gorlice** Pol.
103 C1 **Görlitz** Ger.
Gorna Dzhumaya Bulg. *see* **Blagoevgrad**
109 D2 **Gornji Milanovac** Serbia
109 C2 **Gornji Vakuf** Bos.-Herz.
77 E1 **Gorno-Altaysk** Rus. Fed.
86 F2 **Gornopravdinsk** Rus. Fed.
110 C2 **Gornotrakiyska Nizina** *lowland* Bulg.
66 D1 **Gornozavodsk** Rus. Fed.
77 E1 **Gornyak** Rus. Fed.
59 D3 **Goroka** P.N.G.
52 B3 **Goroke** Austr.
114 B3 **Gorom Gorom** Burkina
121 C2 **Gorongosa** Moz.
61 D1 **Gorontalo** Indon.
89 E3 **Gorshechnoye** Rus. Fed.
97 B2 **Gorumna Island** Ireland
91 D3 **Goryachiy Klyuch** Rus. Fed.
103 D1 **Gorzów Wielkopolski** Pol.
59 E3 **Goschen Strait** P.N.G.
53 D2 **Gosford** Austr.
74 A2 **Goshanak** Pak.
66 D2 **Goshogawara** Japan
101 E2 **Goslar** Ger.
109 C2 **Gospić** Croatia
99 C4 **Gosport** U.K.
111 B2 **Gostivar** Macedonia
Göteborg Sweden *see* **Gothenburg**
101 E2 **Gotha** Ger.
93 F4 **Gothenburg** Sweden
136 C2 **Gothenburg** U.S.A.
93 G4 **Gotland** *i.* Sweden
111 B2 **Gotse Delchev** Bulg.
93 G4 **Gotska Sandön** *i.* Sweden
67 B4 **Gōtsu** Japan
101 D2 **Göttingen** Ger.
128 B2 **Gott Peak** Can.
Gottwaldow Czech Rep. *see* **Zlín**
Gotval'd Ukr. *see* **Zmiyiv**
100 B1 **Gouda** Neth.
114 A3 **Goudiri** Senegal
115 D3 **Goudoumaria** Niger
158 E7 **Gough Island** S. Atlantic Ocean
130 C3 **Gouin, Réservoir** *resr* Can.
53 C2 **Goulburn** Austr.
53 D2 **Goulburn** *r.* *N.S.W.* Austr.
53 C3 **Goulburn** *r.* *Vic.* Austr.
114 B3 **Goundam** Mali
107 D2 **Gouraya** Alg.
114 B3 **Gourcy** Burkina
104 C3 **Gourdon** France
115 D3 **Gouré** Niger
122 B3 **Gourits** *r.* S. Africa
114 B3 **Gourma-Rharous** Mali
53 C3 **Gourock Range** *mts* Austr.
155 D1 **Governador Valadares** Brazil
141 E3 **Governor's Harbour** Bahamas
68 C2 **Govĭ Altayn Nuruu** *mts* Mongolia
75 C2 **Govind Ballash Pant Sagar** *resr* India
99 A3 **Gower** *pen.* U.K.
152 C2 **Goya** Arg.
81 C1 **Göyçay** Azer.
80 B1 **Göynük** Turkey
115 E3 **Goz-Beïda** Chad
75 C1 **Gozha Co** *salt l.* China
122 B3 **Graaff-Reinet** S. Africa
122 A3 **Graafwater** S. Africa
101 E1 **Grabow** Ger.
109 C2 **Gračac** Croatia
87 E3 **Grachevka** Rus. Fed.
109 C2 **Gradačac** Bos.-Herz.
104 B3 **Gradignan** France
101 F2 **Gräfenhainichen** Ger.
53 D1 **Grafton** Austr.
137 D1 **Grafton** U.S.A.
143 D2 **Graham** U.S.A.
142 B2 **Graham, Mount** U.S.A.
Graham Bell Island *i.* Rus. Fed. *see* **Greem-Bell, Ostrov**
128 A2 **Graham Island** Can.
55 A3 **Graham Land** *pen.* Antarctica
123 C3 **Grahamstown** S. Africa
97 C2 **Graiguenamanagh** Ireland
151 F3 **Grajaú** Brazil
103 E1 **Grajewo** Pol.
111 B2 **Grammos** *mt.* Greece
96 B2 **Grampian Mountains** U.K.
146 B3 **Granada** Nic.
106 C4 **Granada** Spain
97 C2 **Granard** Ireland
139 E1 **Granby** Can.
114 A2 **Gran Canaria** *i.* Islas Canarias
152 B3 **Gran Chaco** *reg.* Arg./Para.
136 F2 **Grand** *r.* *MO* U.S.A.
136 C1 **Grand** *r.* *SD* U.S.A.
146 C2 **Grand Bahama** *i.* Bahamas
131 E3 **Grand Bank** Can.
158 D2 **Grand Banks of Newfoundland** N. Atlantic Ocean
Grand Canal *canal* China *see* **Jinghang Yunhe**
Grand Canary *i.* Islas Canarias *see* **Gran Canaria**
142 A1 **Grand Canyon** U.S.A.
142 A1 **Grand Canyon** *gorge* U.S.A.
146 B3 **Grand Cayman** *i.* Cayman Is
129 C2 **Grand Centre** Can.
134 C1 **Grand Coulee** U.S.A.
152 B1 **Grande** *r.* Bol.
154 B2 **Grande** *r.* Brazil
153 B5 **Grande, Bahía** *b.* Arg.
155 D2 **Grande, Ilha** *i.* Brazil
150 C2 **Grande, Serra** *mt.* Brazil
128 C2 **Grande Cache** Can.
Grande Comore *i.* Comoros *see* **Njazidja**
128 C2 **Grande Prairie** Can.
114 B1 **Grand Erg Occidental** *des.* Alg.
115 C2 **Grand Erg Oriental** *des.* Alg.
131 D3 **Grande-Rivière** Can.
152 B3 **Grandes, Salinas** *salt flat* Arg.
131 D3 **Grand Falls** *N.B.* Can.
131 E3 **Grand Falls-Windsor** *Nfld. and Lab.* Can.
128 C3 **Grand Forks** Can.
137 D1 **Grand Forks** U.S.A.
138 B2 **Grand Haven** U.S.A.
128 C1 **Grandin, Lac** *l.* Can.
137 D2 **Grand Island** U.S.A.
140 B3 **Grand Isle** U.S.A.
136 B3 **Grand Junction** U.S.A.
114 B4 **Grand-Lahou** Côte d'Ivoire
131 D3 **Grand Lake** *N.B.* Can.
131 E3 **Grand Lake** *Nfld. and Lab.* Can.
137 E1 **Grand Marais** U.S.A.
130 C3 **Grand-Mère** Can.
106 B2 **Grândola** Port.
129 E2 **Grand Rapids** Can.
138 B2 **Grand Rapids** *MI* U.S.A.
137 E1 **Grand Rapids** *MN* U.S.A.
136 A2 **Grand Teton** *mt.* U.S.A.
147 C2 **Grand Turk** Turks and Caicos Is
129 D2 **Grandview** Can.
134 C1 **Grandview** U.S.A.
134 C1 **Grangeville** U.S.A.
128 B2 **Granisle** Can.
137 D2 **Granite Falls** U.S.A.
134 E1 **Granite Peak** *MT* U.S.A.
134 C2 **Granite Peak** *NV* U.S.A.
108 B3 **Granitola, Capo** *c.* Italy
93 F4 **Gränna** Sweden
101 F1 **Gransee** Ger.
99 C3 **Grantham** U.K.
96 C2 **Grantown-on-Spey** U.K.
142 B1 **Grants** U.S.A.
134 B2 **Grants Pass** U.S.A.

104 B2 Granville France
129 D2 Granville Lake Can.
155 D1 Grão Mogol Brazil
123 D1 Graskop S. Africa
105 D3 Grasse France
50 B3 Grass Patch Austr.
107 D1 Graus Spain
92 F2 Gravdal Norway
104 B2 Grave, Pointe de pt France
129 D3 Gravelbourg Can.
130 C3 Gravenhurst Can.
53 D1 Gravesend Austr.
99 D4 Gravesend U.K.
105 D2 Gray France
141 D1 Gray U.S.A.
138 C2 Grayling U.S.A.
99 D4 Grays U.K.
103 D2 Graz Austria
146 C2 Great Abaco i. Bahamas
50 B3 Great Australian Bight g. Austr.
146 C2 Great Bahama Bank Bahamas
54 C1 Great Barrier Island N.Z.
51 D1 Great Barrier Reef Austr.
135 C3 Great Basin U.S.A.
128 C1 Great Bear Lake Can.
93 F4 Great Belt sea chan. Denmark
137 D3 Great Bend U.S.A.
95 C3 Great Britain i. Europe
63 A2 Great Coco Island Cocos Is
53 B3 Great Dividing Range mts Austr.
Great Eastern Erg des. Alg. see Grand Erg Oriental
146 B2 Greater Antilles is Caribbean Sea
Greater Khingan Mountains mts China see Da Hinggan Ling
58 A3 Greater Sunda Islands Indon.
134 D1 Great Falls U.S.A.
123 C3 Great Fish r. S. Africa
123 C3 Great Fish Point S. Africa
147 C2 Great Inagua i. Bahamas
122 B3 Great Karoo plat. S. Africa
123 C3 Great Kei r. S. Africa
99 B3 Great Malvern U.K.
122 A2 Great Namaqualand reg. Namibia
73 D4 Great Nicobar i. India
98 B3 Great Ormes Head hd U.K.
99 D3 Great Ouse r. U.K.
136 C2 Great Plains U.S.A.
119 D3 Great Rift Valley Africa
119 D3 Great Ruaha r. Tanz.
134 D2 Great Salt Lake U.S.A.
134 D2 Great Salt Lake Desert U.S.A.
116 A2 Great Sand Sea des. Egypt/Libya
50 B2 Great Sandy Desert Austr.
128 C1 Great Slave Lake Can.
141 D1 Great Smoky Mountains U.S.A.
99 A4 Great Torrington U.K.
50 B2 Great Victoria Desert Austr.
70 B1 Great Wall tourist site China
Great Western Erg des. Alg. see Grand Erg Occidental
99 D3 Great Yarmouth U.K.
Grebenkovskiy Ukr. see Hrebinka
106 B1 Gredos, Sierra de mts Spain
111 B3 Greece country Europe
136 C2 Greeley U.S.A.
82 F1 Greem-Bell, Ostrov i. Rus. Fed.
138 F1 Green r. Can.
138 B3 Green r. KY U.S.A.
136 B3 Green r. WY U.S.A.
138 B2 Green Bay U.S.A.
138 B1 Green Bay b. U.S.A.
138 C3 Greenbrier r. U.S.A.
138 B3 Greencastle U.S.A.
141 D1 Greeneville U.S.A.
139 E2 Greenfield U.S.A.
129 D2 Green Lake Can.
127 J2 Greenland terr. N. America
160 L2 Greenland Basin Arctic Ocean
160 R2 Greenland Sea sea Greenland/Svalbard
96 B3 Greenock U.K.
97 C1 Greenore Ireland
135 D3 Green River UT U.S.A.
136 B2 Green River WY U.S.A.
138 B3 Greensburg IN U.S.A.
139 D2 Greensburg PA U.S.A.
141 E2 Green Swamp U.S.A.
142 A2 Green Valley U.S.A.
114 B4 Greenville Liberia
140 C2 Greenville AL U.S.A.
139 F1 Greenville ME U.S.A.
140 B2 Greenville MS U.S.A.
141 E1 Greenville NC U.S.A.
141 D2 Greenville SC U.S.A.
143 D2 Greenville TX U.S.A.
53 D2 Greenwell Point Austr.
131 D3 Greenwood Can.
140 B2 Greenwood MS U.S.A.
141 D2 Greenwood SC U.S.A.
50 B2 Gregory, Lake imp. l. Austr.
51 D1 Gregory Range hills Austr.
102 C1 Greifswald Ger.
101 F2 Greiz Ger.
86 C2 Gremikha Rus. Fed.
93 F4 Grenaa Denmark
140 C2 Grenada U.S.A.
147 D3 Grenada country West Indies
104 C3 Grenade France
93 F4 Grenen spit Denmark
53 C2 Grenfell Austr.
129 D2 Grenfell Can.
105 D2 Grenoble France
51 D1 Grenville, Cape Austr.
134 B1 Gresham U.S.A.
140 B3 Gretna LA U.S.A.
139 D3 Gretna VA U.S.A.
100 C1 Greven Ger.
111 B2 Grevena Greece
100 C2 Grevenbroich Ger.
101 E1 Grevesmühlen Ger.
136 B2 Greybull U.S.A.
128 A1 Grey Hunter Peak Can.
131 E2 Grey Islands Can.
54 B2 Greymouth N.Z.
52 B1 Grey Range hills Austr.
97 C2 Greystones Ireland
123 D2 Greytown S. Africa
91 E1 Gribanovskiy Rus. Fed.
118 B2 Gribingui r. C.A.R.
101 D3 Griesheim Ger.
141 D2 Griffin U.S.A.
53 C2 Griffith Austr.
88 C3 Grigiškės Lith.
118 C2 Grimari C.A.R.
101 F2 Grimma Ger.
102 C1 Grimmen Ger.
98 C3 Grimsby U.K.
128 C2 Grimshaw Can.
92 □B2 Grímsstaðir Iceland
93 E4 Grimstad Norway
92 □A3 Grindavík Iceland
93 E4 Grindsted Denmark
137 E2 Grinnell U.S.A.
123 C3 Griqualand East reg. S. Africa
122 B2 Griqualand West reg. S. Africa
122 B2 Griquatown S. Africa
127 G1 Grise Fiord Can.
Grishino Ukr. see Krasnoarmiys'k
99 D4 Gris Nez, Cap c. France
96 C1 Gritley U.K.
123 C2 Groblersdal S. Africa
122 B2 Groblershoop S. Africa
Grodno Belarus see Hrodna
103 D1 Grodzisk Wielkopolski Pol.
92 □A3 Gröf Iceland
104 B2 Groix, Île de i. France
100 C1 Gronau (Westfalen) Ger.
92 F3 Grong Norway
100 C1 Groningen Neth.
122 B3 Groot Brakrivier S. Africa
122 B3 Grootdrink S. Africa
51 C1 Groote Eylandt i. Austr.
120 A2 Grootfontein Namibia
122 A2 Groot Karas Berg plat. Namibia
122 B3 Groot Swartberge mts S. Africa
122 B2 Grootvloer salt pan S. Africa
123 C3 Groot Winterberg mt. S. Africa
101 D2 Großenlüder Ger.
101 E2 Großer Beerberg h. Ger.
102 C2 Großer Rachel mt. Ger.
103 C2 Grosser Speikkogel mt. Austria
108 B2 Grosseto Italy
101 D3 Groß-Gerau Ger.
103 C2 Großglockner mt. Austria
100 C1 Groß-Hesepe Ger.
101 E2 Großlohra Ger.
122 A1 Gross Ums Namibia
136 A2 Gros Ventre Range mts U.S.A.
131 E2 Groswater Bay Can.
130 B3 Groundhog r. Can.
135 B3 Grover Beach U.S.A.
140 B3 Groves U.S.A.
139 E2 Groveton U.S.A.
87 D4 Groznyy Rus. Fed.
109 C1 Grubišno Polje Croatia
Grudovo Bulg. see Sredets
103 D1 Grudziądz Pol.
122 A2 Grünau Namibia
92 □A3 Grundarfjörður Iceland
Gruzinskaya S.S.R. country Asia see Georgia
89 E3 Gryazi Rus. Fed.
89 F2 Gryazovets Rus. Fed.
103 D1 Gryfice Pol.
102 C1 Gryfino Pol.
153 E5 Grytviken S. Georgia
146 C2 Guacanayabo, Golfo de b. Cuba
144 B2 Guadalajara Mex.
106 C1 Guadalajara Spain
106 C1 Guadalajara reg. Spain
48 H4 Guadalcanal i. Solomon Is
107 C1 Guadalope r. Spain
106 B2 Guadalquivir r. Spain
132 B4 Guadalupe i. Mex.
106 B2 Guadalupe, Sierra de mts Spain
142 C2 Guadalupe Peak U.S.A.
144 B2 Guadalupe Victoria Mex.
144 B2 Guadalupe y Calvo Mex.
106 C1 Guadarrama, Sierra de mts Spain
147 D3 Guadeloupe terr. West Indies
147 D3 Guadeloupe Passage Caribbean Sea
106 B2 Guadiana r. Port./Spain
106 C2 Guadix Spain
154 B2 Guaíra Brazil
147 C3 Guajira, Península de la pen. Col.
150 B3 Gualaceo Ecuador
59 D2 Guam terr. N. Pacific Ocean
144 B2 Guamúchil Mex.
144 B2 Guanacevi Mex.
151 E4 Guanambi Brazil
150 C2 Guanare Venez.
146 B2 Guane Cuba
70 A2 Guang'an China
71 B3 Guangchang China
71 B3 Guangdong prov. China
Guanghua China see Laohekou
71 A3 Guangxi Zhuangzu Zizhiqu aut. reg. China
70 A2 Guangyuan China
71 B3 Guangzhou China
155 D1 Guanhães Brazil
147 D4 Guanipa r. Venez.
71 A3 Guanling China
65 A1 Guanshui China
Guansuo China see Guanling
147 C2 Guantánamo Cuba
155 C2 Guapé Brazil
150 C4 Guaporé r. Bol./Brazil
155 D2 Guarapari Brazil
154 B3 Guarapuava Brazil
154 C3 Guaraqueçaba Brazil
155 C2 Guaratinguetá Brazil
154 C3 Guaratuba Brazil
106 B1 Guarda Port.
Guardafui, Cape c. Somalia see Gwardafuy, Gees
154 C1 Guarda Mor Brazil
106 C1 Guardo Spain
155 C2 Guarujá Brazil
144 B2 Guasave Mex.
146 A3 Guatemala country Central America
Guatemala Guat. see Guatemala City
157 G5 Guatemala Basin N. Pacific Ocean
146 A3 Guatemala City Guat.
150 C2 Guaviare r. Col.
155 C2 Guaxupé Brazil
150 B3 Guayaquil Ecuador
150 A3 Guayaquil, Golfo de g. Ecuador
152 B1 Guayaramerín Bol.
144 A2 Guaymas Mex.
68 C2 Guazhou China
117 B3 Guba Eth.
86 E1 Guba Dolgaya Rus. Fed.
108 B2 Gubbio Italy
89 E3 Gubkin Rus. Fed.
73 C3 Gudivada India
105 D2 Guebwiller France
Guecho Spain see Algorta
114 A2 Guelb er Rîchât h. Maur.
115 C1 Guelma Alg.
114 A2 Guelmine Morocco
130 B3 Guelph Can.
145 C2 Guémez Mex.
104 B2 Guérande France
115 E2 Guerende Libya
104 C2 Guéret France
95 C4 Guernsey i. Channel Is
95 C4 Guernsey terr. Channel Is
144 A2 Guerrero Negro Mex.
131 D2 Guers, Lac l. Can.
158 D4 Guiana Basin N. Atlantic Ocean
150 C2 Guiana Highlands mts Guyana/Venez.
Guichi China see Chizhou
118 B2 Guider Cameroon
108 B2 Guidonia-Montecelio Italy
71 A3 Guigang China
100 A3 Guignicourt France
123 D1 Guija Moz.
99 C4 Guildford U.K.
71 B3 Guilin China
130 C2 Guillaume-Delisle, Lac l. Can.
106 B1 Guimarães Port.
114 A3 Guinea country Africa
113 D5 Guinea, Gulf of Africa
114 A3 Guinea-Bissau country Africa
104 B2 Guingamp France
104 B2 Guipavas France
154 B1 Guiratinga Brazil
150 C1 Güiria Venez.
151 D2 Guisanbourg Fr. Guiana
98 C2 Guisborough U.K.
100 A3 Guise France
64 B2 Guiuan Phil.
71 A3 Guiyang China
71 A3 Guizhou prov. China
104 B3 Gujan-Mestras France
74 B2 Gujarat state India
Gujerat state India see Gujarat
74 B1 Gujranwala Pak.
74 B1 Gujrat Pak.
91 D2 Gukovo Rus. Fed.
70 A2 Gulang China
53 C2 Gulargambone Austr.
73 B3 Gulbarga India
88 C2 Gulbene Latvia
Gulf of California g. Mex. see California, Gulf of
Gulf of Chihli g. China see Bo Hai
111 B3 Gulf of Corinth sea chan. Greece
140 C2 Gulfport U.S.A.
79 C2 Gulf, The Asia
53 C2 Gulgong Austr.
69 E1 Gulian China
77 C2 Guliston Uzbek.
Gulja China see Yining
129 D2 Gull Lake Can.
111 C3 Güllük Turkey
Gulü China see Xincai
119 D2 Gulu Uganda
120 B2 Gumare Botswana
76 B3 Gumdag Turkm.
115 C3 Gumel Nigeria
75 C2 Gumla India
100 C2 Gummersbach Ger.
87 C4 Gümüşhane Turkey
74 B2 Guna India
Gunan China see Qijiang
53 C3 Gundagai Austr.
111 C3 Güney Turkey
118 B3 Gungu Dem. Rep. Congo
129 E2 Gunisao r. Can.
53 D2 Gunnedah Austr.
136 B3 Gunnison CO U.S.A.
135 D3 Gunnison UT U.S.A.
136 B3 Gunnison r. U.S.A.
73 B3 Guntakal India
73 C3 Guntur India
51 C1 Gununa Austr.
60 A1 Gunungsitoli Indon.
60 A1 Gunungtua Indon.
102 C2 Günzburg Ger.
102 C2 Gunzenhausen Ger.
70 B2 Guojiaba China
Guoluezhen China see Lingbao
74 B2 Gurgaon India
151 E3 Gurgueia r. Brazil
150 C2 Guri, Embalse de resr Venez.
154 C1 Gurinhatã Brazil
121 C2 Guro Moz.
151 E4 Gurupi Brazil
151 E3 Gurupi r. Brazil
74 B2 Guru Sikhar mt. India
121 C2 Guruve Zimbabwe
Gur'yev Kazakh. see Atyrau
115 C3 Gusau Nigeria
88 B3 Gusev Rus. Fed.
65 A2 Gushan China
70 B2 Gushi China
83 I3 Gusinoozersk Rus. Fed.
89 F2 Gus'-Khrustal'nyy Rus. Fed.
108 A3 Guspini Italy
128 A2 Gustavus U.S.A.
101 F1 Güstrow Ger.
101 D2 Gütersloh Ger.
143 D1 Guthrie U.S.A.
152 B1 Gutiérrez Bol.
121 C2 Gutu Zimbabwe
75 D2 Guwahati India
150 D2 Guyana country S. America
Guyi China see Sanjiang
143 C1 Guymon U.S.A.
53 D2 Guyra Austr.
70 A2 Guyuan China
Guzhou China see Rongjiang
144 B1 Guzmán Mex.
77 C3 G'uzor Uzbek.
88 B3 Gvardeysk Rus. Fed.
74 A2 Gwadar Pak.
Gwador Pak. see Gwadar
74 B2 Gwalior India
121 B3 Gwanda Zimbabwe
117 D3 Gwardafuy, Gees c. Somalia
97 B1 Gweebarra Bay Ireland
Gweedore Ireland see Gaoth Dobhair
Gwelo Zimbabwe see Gweru
121 B2 Gweru Zimbabwe
115 D3 Gwoza Nigeria
53 D2 Gwydir r. Austr.
Gya'gya China see Saga
Gyandzha Azer. see Gäncä
Gyangkar China see Dinggyê
Gyangtse China see Gyangzê
75 C2 Gyangzê China
75 C1 Gyaring Co l. China
68 C2 Gyaring Hu l. China
86 G1 Gydan Peninsula pen. Rus. Fed.
Gydanskiy Poluostrov pen. Rus. Fed. see Gydan Peninsula
Gyêgu China see Yushu
62 A1 Gyigang China
Gyixong China see Gonggar
51 E2 Gympie Austr.
62 A2 Gyobingauk Myanmar
103 D2 Gyöngyös Hungary
103 D2 Győr Hungary
136 B3 Gypsum U.S.A.
129 E2 Gypsumville Can.
131 D2 Gyrfalcon Islands Can.
111 B3 Gytheio Greece
103 E2 Gyula Hungary
81 C1 Gyumri Armenia
Gzhatsk Rus. Fed. see Gagarin

H

88 B2 Haapsalu Estonia
100 B1 Haarlem Neth.
122 B3 Haarlem S. Africa
101 C2 Haarstrang ridge Ger.
54 A2 Haast N.Z.
74 A2 Hab r. Pak.
79 C3 Ḥabarūt Oman
78 B3 Habbān Yemen
81 C2 Ḥabbānīyah, Hawr al l. Iraq
70 B1 Habirag China
67 C4 Hachijō-jima i. Japan
66 D2 Hachinohe Japan
67 C3 Hachiōji Japan
121 C3 Hacufera Moz.
116 A2 Ḥaḍabat al Jilf al Kabīr Egypt
79 C2 Ḥadd, Ra's al pt Oman
96 C3 Haddington U.K.
115 D3 Hadejia Nigeria
93 E4 Haderslev Denmark
78 B2 Ḥādhah Saudi Arabia
79 B3 Ḥaḍramawt reg. Yemen
79 B3 Ḥaḍramawt, Wādī watercourse Yemen
91 C1 Hadyach Ukr.
65 B2 Haeju N. Korea

65 B2 **Haeju-man** *b.* N. Korea
65 B3 **Haenam** S. Korea
78 B2 **Ḥafar al Bāṭin** Saudi Arabia
74 B1 **Hafizabad** Pak.
75 D2 **Haflong** India
92 □A3 **Hafnarfjörður** Iceland
78 A3 **Hagar Nish Plateau** Eritrea/Sudan
59 D2 **Hagåtña** Guam
101 F1 **Hagelberg** *h.* Ger.
100 C2 **Hagen** Ger.
101 E1 **Hagenow** Ger.
128 B2 **Hagensborg** Can.
139 D3 **Hagerstown** U.S.A.
93 F3 **Hagfors** Sweden
134 D1 **Haggin, Mount** U.S.A.
67 B4 **Hagi** Japan
62 B1 **Ha Giang** Vietnam
97 B2 **Hag's Head** *hd* Ireland
104 B2 **Hague, Cap de la** *c.* France
69 F3 **Hahajima-rettō** *is* Japan
119 D3 **Hai** Tanz.
Haicheng China *see* **Haifeng**
70 C1 **Haicheng** China
62 B1 **Hai Dương** Vietnam
80 B2 **Haifa** Israel
71 B3 **Haifeng** China
Haikang China *see* **Leizhou**
71 B3 **Haikou** China
78 B2 **Ḥā'īl** Saudi Arabia
Hailar China *see* **Hulun Buir**
Hailong China *see* **Meihekou**
92 H2 **Hailuoto** *i.* Fin.
69 D3 **Hainan** *i.* China
71 A4 **Hainan** *prov.* China
128 A2 **Haines** U.S.A.
128 A1 **Haines Junction** Can.
101 E2 **Hainich** *ridge* Ger.
101 E2 **Hainleite** *ridge* Ger.
62 B1 **Hai Phong** Vietnam
Haiphong Vietnam *see* **Hai Phong**
147 C3 **Haiti** *country* West Indies
116 B3 **Haiya** Sudan
103 E2 **Hajdúböszörmény** Hungary
103 E2 **Hajdúszoboszló** Hungary
67 C3 **Hajiki-zaki** *pt* Japan
78 B3 **Ḥajjah** Yemen
81 D3 **Ḥājjīābād** Iran
103 E1 **Hajnówka** Pol.
62 A1 **Haka** Myanmar
81 C2 **Hakkârı** Turkey
66 D2 **Hakodate** Japan
122 B2 **Hakseen Pan** *salt pan* S. Africa
Ḥalab Syria *see* **Aleppo**
78 B2 **Halabān** Saudi Arabia
81 C2 **Ḥalabja** Iraq
116 B2 **Halaib** Sudan
78 A2 **Halaib Triangle** *terr.* Egypt/Sudan
79 C3 **Ḥalāniyāt, Juzur al** *is* Oman
78 A2 **Ḥālat 'Ammār** Saudi Arabia
Halban Mongolia *see* **Tsetserleg**
101 E2 **Halberstadt** Ger.
64 B2 **Halcon, Mount** Phil.
93 F4 **Halden** Norway
101 E1 **Haldensleben** Ger.
75 B2 **Haldwani** India
79 C2 **Hāleh** Iran
54 A3 **Halfmoon Bay** N.Z.
139 D1 **Haliburton Highlands** *hills* Can.
131 D3 **Halifax** Can.
98 C3 **Halifax** U.K.
139 D3 **Halifax** U.S.A.
65 B3 **Halla-san** *mt.* S. Korea
127 G2 **Hall Beach** Can.
100 B2 **Halle** Belgium
101 E2 **Halle (Saale)** Ger.
102 C2 **Hallein** Austria
101 E2 **Halle-Neustadt** Ger.
48 G3 **Hall Islands** Micronesia
137 D1 **Hallock** U.S.A.
127 H2 **Hall Peninsula** Can.
50 B1 **Halls Creek** Austr.
59 C2 **Halmahera** *i.* Indon.
93 F4 **Halmstad** Sweden
62 B1 **Ha Long** Vietnam
Hälsingborg Sweden *see* **Helsingborg**
100 B2 **Halsteren** Neth.
98 B2 **Haltwhistle** U.K.
67 B4 **Hamada** Japan
81 C2 **Hamadān** Iran
80 B2 **Ḥamāh** Syria
67 C4 **Hamamatsu** Japan
93 F3 **Hamar** Norway
116 B2 **Ḥamāṭah, Jabal** *mt.* Egypt
73 C4 **Hambantota** Sri Lanka
101 D1 **Hamburg** Ger.
123 C3 **Hamburg** S. Africa
140 B2 **Hamburg** U.S.A.
78 A2 **Ḥamḍ, Wādī al** *watercourse* Saudi Arabia
78 B3 **Ḥamḍah** Saudi Arabia
139 E2 **Hamden** U.S.A.
93 H3 **Hämeenlinna** Fin.
101 D1 **Hameln** Ger.
50 A2 **Hamersley Range** *mts* Austr.
65 B1 **Hamgyŏng-sanmaek** *mts* N. Korea
65 B2 **Hamhŭng** N. Korea
68 C2 **Hami** China
116 B2 **Hamid** Sudan
52 B3 **Hamilton** Austr.
130 C3 **Hamilton** Can.
Hamilton *r.* Can. *see* **Churchill**
54 C1 **Hamilton** N.Z.
96 B3 **Hamilton** U.K.
140 C2 **Hamilton** *AL* U.S.A.
134 D1 **Hamilton** *MT* U.S.A.
138 C3 **Hamilton** *OH* U.S.A.
115 E1 **Hamīm, Wādī al** *watercourse* Libya
93 I3 **Hamina** Fin.
100 C2 **Hamm** Ger.
115 D1 **Hammamet, Golfe de** *g.* Tunisia
81 C2 **Ḥammār, Hawr al** *imp. l.* Iraq
101 D2 **Hammelburg** Ger.
92 G3 **Hammerdal** Sweden
92 H1 **Hammerfest** Norway
140 B2 **Hammond** U.S.A.
139 E3 **Hammonton** U.S.A.
139 D3 **Hampton** U.S.A.
139 E2 **Hampton Bays** U.S.A.
115 D2 **Ḥamrā', Al Ḥamādah al** *plat.* Libya
78 A2 **Ḥanak** Saudi Arabia
66 D3 **Hanamaki** Japan
101 D2 **Hanau** Ger.
69 D2 **Hanbogd** Mongolia
70 B2 **Hancheng** China
138 B1 **Hancock** U.S.A.
70 B2 **Handan** China
119 D3 **Handeni** Tanz.
135 C3 **Hanford** U.S.A.
68 C1 **Hangayn Nuruu** *mts* Mongolia
Hangchow China *see* **Hangzhou**
Hanggin Houqi China *see* **Xamba**
Hangö Fin. *see* **Hanko**
70 B2 **Hangu** China
70 C2 **Hangzhou** China
70 C2 **Hangzhou Wan** *b.* China
79 B2 **Ḥanīdh** Saudi Arabia
Hanjia China *see* **Pengshui**
Hanjiang China *see* **Yangzhou**
93 H4 **Hanko** Fin.
135 D3 **Hanksville** U.S.A.
54 B2 **Hanmer Springs** N.Z.
128 C2 **Hanna** Can.
136 B2 **Hanna** U.S.A.
137 E3 **Hannibal** U.S.A.
101 D1 **Hannover** Ger.
101 D2 **Hannoversch Münden** Ger.
93 F4 **Hanöbukten** *b.* Sweden
62 B1 **Ha Nôi** Vietnam
Hanoi Vietnam *see* **Ha Nôi**
130 B3 **Hanover** Can.
Hanover Ger. *see* **Hannover**
122 B3 **Hanover** S. Africa
139 E2 **Hanover** *NH* U.S.A.
139 D3 **Hanover** *PA* U.S.A.
92 G2 **Hansnes** Norway
93 E4 **Hanstholm** Denmark
88 C3 **Hantsavichy** Belarus
75 C2 **Hanumana** India
74 D2 **Hanumangarh** India
70 A2 **Hanzhong** China
49 M5 **Hao** *atoll* Fr. Polynesia
75 C2 **Haora** India
92 H2 **Haparanda** Sweden
100 B2 **Hapert** Neth.
131 D2 **Happy Valley-Goose Bay** Can.
78 A2 **Ḥaql** Saudi Arabia
79 B2 **Ḥaraḍh** Saudi Arabia
88 C2 **Haradok** Belarus
78 B3 **Ḥarajā** Saudi Arabia
121 C2 **Harare** Zimbabwe
79 C3 **Ḥarāsīs, Jiddat al** *des.* Oman
69 D1 **Har-Ayrag** Mongolia
115 E3 **Haraze-Mangueigne** Chad
114 A4 **Harbel** Liberia
69 E1 **Harbin** China
138 C2 **Harbor Beach** U.S.A.
131 E3 **Harbour Breton** Can.
74 B2 **Harda** India
92 E4 **Hardangerfjorden** *sea chan.* Norway
61 C1 **Harden, Bukit** *mt.* Indon.
100 C1 **Hardenberg** Neth.
100 B1 **Harderwijk** Neth.
122 A3 **Hardeveld** *mts* S. Africa
134 E1 **Hardin** U.S.A.
128 C1 **Hardisty Lake** Can.
93 E3 **Hareid** Norway
100 C1 **Haren (Ems)** Ger.
117 C4 **Hārer** Eth.
117 C4 **Hargeysa** Somalia
110 C1 **Harghita-Mădăraș, Vârful** *mt.* Romania
68 C2 **Har Hu** *l.* China
88 B2 **Hari kurk** *sea chan.* Estonia
74 B1 **Haripur** Pak.
74 A1 **Hari Rūd** *r.* Afgh./Iran
110 C1 **Hârlău** Romania
100 B1 **Harlingen** Neth.
143 D3 **Harlingen** U.S.A.
99 D4 **Harlow** U.K.
134 E1 **Harlowton** U.S.A.
134 C2 **Harney Basin** U.S.A.
134 C2 **Harney Lake** U.S.A.
93 G3 **Härnösand** Sweden
69 E1 **Har Nur** China
68 C1 **Har Nuur** *l.* Mongolia
96 □ **Haroldswick** U.K.
114 B4 **Harper** Liberia
101 D1 **Harpstedt** Ger.
130 C2 **Harricana, Rivière d'** *r.* Can.
53 D2 **Harrington** Austr.
131 E2 **Harrington Harbour** Can.
96 A2 **Harris** *reg.* U.K.
96 A2 **Harris, Sound of** *sea chan.* U.K.
138 B3 **Harrisburg** *IL* U.S.A.
134 B2 **Harrisburg** *OR* U.S.A.
139 D2 **Harrisburg** *PA* U.S.A.
123 C2 **Harrismith** S. Africa
140 B1 **Harrison** U.S.A.
131 E2 **Harrison, Cape** Can.
126 B2 **Harrison Bay** U.S.A.
139 D3 **Harrisonburg** U.S.A.
128 B3 **Harrison Lake** Can.
137 E3 **Harrisonville** U.S.A.
98 C3 **Harrogate** U.K.
110 C2 **Hârșova** Romania
92 G2 **Harstad** Norway
122 B2 **Hartbees** *watercourse* S. Africa
103 D2 **Hartberg** Austria
139 E2 **Hartford** *CT* U.S.A.
137 D2 **Hartford** *SD* U.S.A.
99 A4 **Hartland Point** U.K.
98 C2 **Hartlepool** U.K.
Hartley Zimbabwe *see* **Chegutu**
128 B2 **Hartley Bay** Can.
123 B2 **Harts** *r.* S. Africa
141 D2 **Hartwell Reservoir** U.S.A.
68 C1 **Har Us Nuur** *l.* Mongolia
136 C1 **Harvey** U.S.A.
99 D4 **Harwich** U.K.
74 B2 **Haryana** *state* India
101 E2 **Harz** *hills* Ger.
101 E2 **Harzgerode** Ger.
78 B2 **Ḥasan, Jabal** *h.* Saudi Arabia
80 B2 **Hasan Dağı** *mts* Turkey
99 C4 **Haslemere** U.K.
73 B3 **Hassan** India
100 B2 **Hasselt** Belgium
101 E2 **Haßfurt** Ger.
115 C2 **Hassi Bel Guebbour** Alg.
115 C1 **Hassi Messaoud** Alg.
93 F4 **Hässleholm** Sweden
100 B2 **Hastière-Lavaux** Belgium
53 C3 **Hastings** Austr.
54 C1 **Hastings** N.Z.
99 D4 **Hastings** U.K.
137 E2 **Hastings** *MN* U.S.A.
137 D2 **Hastings** *NE* U.S.A.
Hatay Turkey *see* **Antakya**
142 B2 **Hatch** U.S.A.
129 D2 **Hatchet Lake** Can.
110 B1 **Hațeg** Romania
52 B2 **Hatfield** Austr.
68 C1 **Hatgal** Mongolia
62 B2 **Hà Tinh** Vietnam
52 D2 **Hattah** Austr.
141 E1 **Hatteras, Cape** U.S.A.
157 H3 **Hatteras Abyssal Plain** S. Atlantic Ocean
140 C2 **Hattiesburg** U.S.A.
100 C2 **Hattingen** Ger.
63 B3 **Hat Yai** Thai.
117 C4 **Haud** *reg.* Eth.
93 E4 **Haugesund** Norway
93 E4 **Haukeligrend** Norway
92 I2 **Haukipudas** Fin.
54 C1 **Hauraki Gulf** N.Z.
54 A3 **Hauroko, Lake** N.Z.
114 B1 **Haut Atlas** *mts* Morocco
131 D3 **Hauterive** Can.
Haute-Volta *country* Africa *see* **Burkina**
114 B1 **Hauts Plateaux** Alg.
146 B2 **Havana** Cuba
99 C4 **Havant** U.K.
101 F1 **Havel** *r.* Ger.
101 F1 **Havelberg** Ger.
54 B2 **Havelock** N.Z.
Havelock Swaziland *see* **Bulembu**
54 C1 **Havelock North** N.Z.
99 A4 **Haverfordwest** U.K.
100 C2 **Havixbeck** Ger.
103 D2 **Havlíčkův Brod** Czech Rep.
92 H1 **Havøysund** Norway
111 C3 **Havran** Turkey
134 E1 **Havre** U.S.A.
131 D3 **Havre-Aubert** Can.
131 D2 **Havre-St-Pierre** Can.
49 L2 **Hawai'i** *i.* U.S.A.
156 E4 **Hawai'ian Islands** *is* N. Pacific Ocean
78 B2 **Ḥawallī** Kuwait
98 B3 **Hawarden** U.K.
54 A2 **Hawea, Lake** N.Z.
54 B1 **Hawera** N.Z.
98 B2 **Hawes** U.K.
96 C3 **Hawick** U.K.
54 C1 **Hawke Bay** N.Z.
52 A2 **Hawker** Austr.
52 B1 **Hawkers Gate** Austr.
122 A3 **Hawston** S. Africa
135 C3 **Hawthorne** U.S.A.
52 B2 **Hay** Austr.
128 C1 **Hay** *r.* Can.
100 C3 **Hayange** France
134 C1 **Hayden** U.S.A.
129 E2 **Hayes** *r. Man.* Can.
126 F2 **Hayes** *r. Nunavut* Can.
79 C3 **Haymā'** Oman
77 C2 **Hayotboshi tog'i** *mt.* Uzbek.
111 C2 **Hayrabolu** Turkey
128 C1 **Hay River** Can.
137 D3 **Hays** U.S.A.
78 B3 **Ḥays** Yemen
90 B2 **Haysyn** Ukr.
135 B3 **Hayward** U.S.A.
99 C4 **Haywards Heath** U.K.
81 D2 **Hazar** Turkm.
74 A1 **Hazarajat** *reg.* Afgh.
138 C3 **Hazard** U.S.A.
75 C2 **Hazaribagh** India
75 C2 **Hazaribagh Range** *mts* India
104 C1 **Hazebrouck** France
128 B2 **Hazelton** Can.
139 D2 **Hazleton** U.S.A.
135 B3 **Healdsburg** U.S.A.
53 C3 **Healesville** Austr.
159 E7 **Heard Island** Indian Ocean
143 D2 **Hearne** U.S.A.
130 B3 **Hearst** Can.
55 A3 **Hearst Island** Antarctica
70 B2 **Hebei** *prov.* China
53 C1 **Hebel** Austr.
140 B1 **Heber Springs** U.S.A.
70 B2 **Hebi** China
131 D2 **Hebron** Can.
128 A2 **Hecate Strait** Can.
71 A3 **Hechi** China
100 B2 **Hechtel** Belgium
54 C2 **Hector, Mount** N.Z.
93 F3 **Hede** Sweden
100 C1 **Heerde** Neth.
100 B1 **Heerenveen** Neth.
100 B1 **Heerhugowaard** Neth.
100 B2 **Heerlen** Neth.
Ḥefa Israel *see* **Haifa**
70 B2 **Hefei** China
70 B3 **Hefeng** China
69 E1 **Hegang** China
119 D1 **Heiban** Sudan
102 B1 **Heide** Ger.
122 A1 **Heide** Namibia
101 D3 **Heidelberg** Ger.
122 B3 **Heidelberg** S. Africa
69 E1 **Heihe** China
102 B2 **Heilbronn** Ger.
69 E1 **Heilong Jiang** *r.* China
93 I3 **Heinola** Fin.
Hejaz *reg.* Saudi Arabia *see* **Hijaz**
92 A3 **Hekla** *vol.* Iceland
92 F3 **Helagsfjället** *mt.* Sweden
70 A2 **Helan Shan** *mts* China
140 B2 **Helena** *AR* U.S.A.
134 D1 **Helena** *MT* U.S.A.
96 B2 **Helensburgh** U.K.
102 B1 **Helgoland** *i.* Ger.
102 B1 **Helgoländer Bucht** *g.* Ger.
Heligoland *i.* Ger. *see* **Helgoland**
Heligoland Bight *g.* Ger. *see* **Helgoländer Bucht**
Helixi China *see* **Ningguo**
92 □A3 **Hella** Iceland
100 B2 **Hellevoetsluis** Neth.
107 C2 **Hellín** Spain
Hell-Ville Madag. *see* **Andoany**
76 C3 **Helmand** *r.* Afgh.
101 E2 **Helmbrechts** Ger.
122 A2 **Helmeringhausen** Namibia
100 B2 **Helmond** Neth.
96 C1 **Helmsdale** U.K.
96 C1 **Helmsdale** *r.* U.K.
98 C2 **Helmsley** U.K.
101 E1 **Helmstedt** Ger.
65 B1 **Helong** China
143 D3 **Helotes** U.S.A.
93 F4 **Helsingborg** Sweden
Helsingfors Fin. *see* **Helsinki**
93 F4 **Helsingør** Denmark
93 H3 **Helsinki** Fin.
99 A4 **Helston** U.K.
97 C2 **Helvick Head** *hd* Ireland
99 C4 **Hemel Hempstead** U.K.
101 D1 **Hemmoor** Ger.
92 F2 **Hemnesberget** Norway
70 B2 **Henan** *prov.* China
111 D2 **Hendek** Turkey
138 B3 **Henderson** *KY* U.S.A.
141 E1 **Henderson** *NC* U.S.A.
135 D3 **Henderson** *NV* U.S.A.
143 E2 **Henderson** *TX* U.S.A.
49 O6 **Henderson Island** Pitcairn Is
141 D1 **Hendersonville** U.S.A.
99 C4 **Hendon** U.K.
62 A1 **Hengduan Shan** *mts* China
100 C1 **Hengelo** Neth.
Hengnan China *see* **Hengyang**
71 B3 **Hengshan** China
70 B2 **Hengshui** China
71 A3 **Hengxian** China
71 B3 **Hengyang** China
Hengzhou China *see* **Hengxian**
91 C2 **Heniches'k** Ukr.
139 D3 **Henlopen, Cape** U.S.A.
100 C2 **Hennef (Sieg)** Ger.
130 B2 **Henrietta Maria, Cape** Can.
Henrique de Carvalho Angola *see* **Saurimo**
139 D3 **Henry, Cape** U.S.A.
143 D1 **Henryetta** U.S.A.
127 H2 **Henry Kater, Cape** Can.
101 D1 **Henstedt-Ulzburg** Ger.
120 A3 **Hentiesbaai** Namibia
101 D3 **Heppenheim (Bergstraße)** Ger.
71 A3 **Hepu** China
76 C3 **Herāt** Afgh.
129 D2 **Herbert** Can.
54 C2 **Herbertville** N.Z.
101 D2 **Herbstein** Ger.
109 C2 **Herceg-Novi** Montenegro
99 B3 **Hereford** U.K.
143 C2 **Hereford** U.S.A.
101 D1 **Herford** Ger.
100 C2 **Herkenbosch** Neth.
96 □ **Herma Ness** *hd* U.K.
122 A3 **Hermanus** S. Africa
53 C2 **Hermidale** Austr.

134 C1 **Hermiston** U.S.A.
59 D3 **Hermit Islands** P.N.G.
144 A2 **Hermosillo** Mex.
154 B3 **Hernandarias** Para.
100 C2 **Herne** Ger.
93 E4 **Herning** Denmark
104 B2 **Hérouville-St-Clair** France
106 B2 **Herrera del Duque** Spain
139 D2 **Hershey** U.S.A.
99 C4 **Hertford** U.K.
123 C2 **Hertzogville** S. Africa
51 E2 **Hervey Bay** Austr.
101 F2 **Herzberg** Ger.
101 E3 **Herzogenaurach** Ger.
71 A3 **Heshan** China
135 C4 **Hesperia** U.S.A.
128 A1 **Hess** *r.* Can.
101 E1 **Hessen** Ger.
101 D2 **Hessisch Lichtenau** Ger.
136 C1 **Hettinger** U.S.A.
101 E2 **Hettstedt** Ger.
98 B2 **Hexham** U.K.
81 C2 **Ḥeydarābād** Iran
98 B2 **Heysham** U.K.
71 B3 **Heyuan** China
52 B3 **Heywood** Austr.
70 B2 **Heze** China
71 B3 **Hezhou** China
141 D3 **Hialeah** U.S.A.
137 D3 **Hiawatha** U.S.A.
137 E1 **Hibbing** U.S.A.
141 D1 **Hickory** U.S.A.
54 C1 **Hicks Bay** N.Z.
66 D2 **Hidaka-sanmyaku** *mts* Japan
143 D3 **Hidalgo** Mex.
145 C2 **Hidalgo** Mex.
144 B2 **Hidalgo del Parral** Mex.
154 C1 **Hidrolândia** Brazil
67 A4 **Higashi-suidō** *str.* Japan
High Atlas *mts* Morocco *see* **Haut Atlas**
134 B2 **High Desert** U.S.A.
128 C2 **High Level** Can.
141 E1 **High Point** U.S.A.
128 C2 **High Prairie** Can.
128 C2 **High River** Can.
129 D2 **Highrock Lake** Can.
High Tatras *mts* Pol./Slovakia *see* **Tatry**
99 C4 **High Wycombe** U.K.
88 B2 **Hiiumaa** *i.* Estonia
78 A2 **Hijaz** *reg.* Saudi Arabia
54 C1 **Hikurangi** *mt.* N.Z.
101 E2 **Hildburghausen** Ger.
100 C2 **Hilden** Ger.
101 E2 **Hilders** Ger.
101 D1 **Hildesheim** Ger.
81 C2 **Hillah** Iraq
100 B1 **Hillegom** Neth.
100 C2 **Hillesheim** Ger.
138 C3 **Hillsboro** *OH* U.S.A.
143 D2 **Hillsboro** *TX* U.S.A.
53 C2 **Hillston** Austr.
96 □ **Hillswick** U.K.
49 L2 **Hilo** U.S.A.
141 D2 **Hilton Head Island** U.S.A.
100 B1 **Hilversum** Neth.
74 B1 **Himachal Pradesh** *state* India
68 B2 **Himalaya** *mts* Asia
74 B2 **Himatnagar** India
67 B4 **Himeji** Japan
123 C2 **Himeville** S. Africa
67 C3 **Himi** Japan
Ḥimş Syria *see* **Homs**
147 C3 **Hinche** Haiti
51 D1 **Hinchinbrook Island** Austr.
52 B3 **Hindmarsh, Lake** *dry lake* Austr.
74 A1 **Hindu Kush** *mts* Afgh./Pak.
73 B3 **Hindupur** India
134 C2 **Hines** U.S.A.
141 D2 **Hinesville** U.S.A.
74 B2 **Hinganghat** India
81 C2 **Hınıs** Turkey
92 G2 **Hinnøya** *i.* Norway
106 B2 **Hinojosa del Duque** Spain
100 C1 **Hinte** Ger.
62 A2 **Hinthada** Myanmar
128 C2 **Hinton** Can.
75 C2 **Hirakud Reservoir** India
Hîrlău Romania *see* **Hârlău**
66 D2 **Hiroo** Japan
66 D2 **Hirosaki** Japan
67 B4 **Hiroshima** Japan
101 E3 **Hirschaid** Ger.
101 E2 **Hirschberg** Ger.
105 C2 **Hirson** France
Hîrşova Romania *see* **Hârşova**
93 E4 **Hirtshals** Denmark
74 B2 **Hisar** India
147 C2 **Hispaniola** *i.* Caribbean Sea
81 C2 **Hīt** Iraq
67 D3 **Hitachi** Japan
67 D3 **Hitachinaka** Japan
92 E3 **Hitra** *i.* Norway
49 N4 **Hiva Oa** *i.* Fr. Polynesia
93 G4 **Hjälmaren** *l.* Sweden
129 D1 **Hjalmar Lake** Can.
93 F4 **Hjørring** Denmark
123 D2 **Hlabisa** S. Africa
92 □B2 **Hlíð** Iceland
91 C2 **Hlobyne** Ukr.
123 C2 **Hlohlowane** S. Africa
123 C2 **Hlotse** Lesotho
91 C1 **Hlukhiv** Ukr.
88 C3 **Hlusk** Belarus
88 C2 **Hlybokaye** Belarus
114 C4 **Ho** Ghana
62 B2 **Hoa Binh** Vietnam
122 A1 **Hoachanas** Namibia
120 A2 **Hoanib** *watercourse* Namibia
120 A2 **Hoarusib** *watercourse* Namibia
51 D4 **Hobart** Austr.
143 D1 **Hobart** U.S.A.
143 C2 **Hobbs** U.S.A.
93 E4 **Hobro** Denmark
117 C4 **Hobyo** Somalia
Hồ Chi Minh Vietnam *see* **Ho Chi Minh City**
63 B2 **Ho Chi Minh City** Vietnam
114 B3 **Ḥôḍ** *reg.* Maur.
117 D3 **Hodda** *mt.* Somalia
78 B3 **Hodeidah** Yemen
103 E2 **Hódmezővásárhely** Hungary
Hoek van Holland Neth. *see* **Hook of Holland**
65 B2 **Hoeyang** N. Korea
101 E2 **Hof** Ger.
101 E2 **Hofheim in Unterfranken** Ger.
92 □B3 **Höfn** Iceland
92 □A2 **Höfn** Iceland
92 □B3 **Hofsjökull** Iceland
67 B4 **Hōfu** Japan
115 C2 **Hoggar** *plat.* Alg.
93 G4 **Högsby** Sweden
93 E3 **Høgste Breakulen** *mt.* Norway
101 D2 **Hohe Rhön** *mts* Ger.
100 C2 **Hohe Venn** *moorland* Belgium
70 B1 **Hohhot** China
75 C1 **Hoh Xil Shan** *mts* China
63 B2 **Hôi An** Vietnam
119 D2 **Hoima** Uganda
75 D2 **Hojai** India
54 B2 **Hokitika** N.Z.
66 D2 **Hokkaidō** *i.* Japan
91 C2 **Hola Prystan'** Ukr.
128 B2 **Holberg** Can.
53 C3 **Holbrook** Austr.
142 A2 **Holbrook** U.S.A.
137 D2 **Holdrege** U.S.A.
146 C2 **Holguín** Cuba
92 □B2 **Höll** Iceland
103 D2 **Hollabrunn** Austria
138 B2 **Holland** U.S.A.
Hollandia Indon. *see* **Jayapura**
135 B3 **Hollister** U.S.A.
103 E2 **Hollóháza** Hungary
93 I3 **Hollola** Fin.
100 B1 **Hollum** Neth.
140 C2 **Holly Springs** U.S.A.
134 C4 **Hollywood** U.S.A.
141 D3 **Hollywood** U.S.A.
92 F2 **Holm** Norway
Holman Can. *see* **Ulukhaktok**
92 H3 **Holmsund** Sweden
122 A2 **Holoog** Namibia
93 E4 **Holstebro** Denmark
141 D1 **Holston** *r.* U.S.A.
98 A3 **Holyhead** U.K.
98 C2 **Holy Island** *England* U.K.
98 A3 **Holy Island** *Wales* U.K.
136 C2 **Holyoke** U.S.A.
Holy See Europe *see* **Vatican City**
101 D2 **Holzminden** Ger.
62 A1 **Homalin** Myanmar
101 D2 **Homberg (Efze)** Ger.
114 B3 **Hombori** Mali
100 C3 **Homburg** Ger.
127 H2 **Home Bay** Can.
140 B2 **Homer** U.S.A.
141 D3 **Homestead** U.S.A.
92 F3 **Hommelvik** Norway
141 D3 **Homosassa Springs** U.S.A.
80 B2 **Homs** Syria
89 D3 **Homyel'** Belarus
Honan *prov.* China *see* **Henan**
122 A3 **Hondeklipbaai** S. Africa
145 D3 **Hondo** *r.* Belize/Mex.
142 B2 **Hondo** *NM* U.S.A.
143 D3 **Hondo** *TX* U.S.A.
146 B3 **Honduras** *country* Central America
146 B3 **Honduras, Gulf of** Belize/Hond.
93 F3 **Hønefoss** Norway
135 B2 **Honey Lake** U.S.A.
104 C2 **Honfleur** France
70 B3 **Honghu** China
71 A3 **Hongjiang** China
71 B3 **Hong Kong** China
71 B3 **Hong Kong** *aut. reg.* China
Hongqizhen China *see* **Wuzhishan**
131 D3 **Honguedo, Détroit d'** *sea chan.* Can.
65 B1 **Hongwŏn** N. Korea
70 B2 **Hongze Hu** *l.* China
48 H4 **Honiara** Solomon Is
99 B4 **Honiton** U.K.
66 D3 **Honjō** Japan
92 I1 **Honningsvåg** Norway
49 L1 **Honolulu** U.S.A.
67 B3 **Honshū** *i.* Japan
134 B1 **Hood, Mount** *vol.* U.S.A.
50 A3 **Hood Point** Austr.
134 B1 **Hood River** U.S.A.
100 B2 **Hoogerheide** Neth.
100 C1 **Hoogeveen** Neth.
100 C1 **Hoogezand-Sappemeer** Neth.
100 C2 **Hoog-Keppel** Neth.
100 B2 **Hook of Holland** Neth.
128 A2 **Hoonah** U.S.A.
123 C2 **Hoopstad** S. Africa
100 B1 **Hoorn** Neth.
49 J5 **Hoorn, Îles de** *is* Wallis and Futuna Is
128 B3 **Hope** Can.
140 B2 **Hope** U.S.A.
83 N2 **Hope, Point** U.S.A.
131 D2 **Hopedale** Can.
Hopei *prov.* China *see* **Hebei**
145 D3 **Hopelchén** Mex.
131 D2 **Hope Mountains** Can.
Hopes Advance Bay Can. *see* **Aupaluk**
52 B3 **Hopetoun** Austr.
122 B2 **Hopetown** S. Africa
139 D3 **Hopewell** U.S.A.
130 C2 **Hopewell Islands** Can.
50 B2 **Hopkins, Lake** *imp. l.* Austr.
138 B3 **Hopkinsville** U.S.A.
134 B1 **Hoquiam** U.S.A.
81 C1 **Horasan** Turkey
93 F4 **Hörby** Sweden
89 D3 **Horki** Belarus
91 D2 **Horlivka** Ukr.
79 D2 **Hormak** Iran
79 C2 **Hormuz, Strait of** Iran/Oman
103 D2 **Horn** Austria
92 □A2 **Horn** *c.* Iceland
153 B5 **Horn, Cape** Chile
139 D2 **Hornell** U.S.A.
130 B3 **Hornepayne** Can.
Hornos, Cabo de *c.* Chile *see* **Horn, Cape**
53 D2 **Hornsby** Austr.
98 C3 **Hornsea** U.K.
90 B2 **Horodenka** Ukr.
91 C1 **Horodnya** Ukr.
90 B2 **Horodok** Ukr.
90 A2 **Horodok** Ukr.
90 A1 **Horokhiv** Ukr.
Horqin Youyi Qianqi China *see* **Ulanhot**
131 E2 **Horse Islands** Can.
52 B3 **Horsham** Austr.
99 C4 **Horsham** U.K.
93 F4 **Horten** Norway
126 D2 **Horton** *r.* Can.
117 B4 **Hosa'ina** Eth.
74 A2 **Hoshab** Pak.
74 B1 **Hoshiarpur** India
142 B1 **Hosta Butte** *mt.* U.S.A.
75 C1 **Hotan** China
122 B2 **Hotazel** S. Africa
92 G3 **Hoting** Sweden
Hot Springs U.S.A. *see* **Truth or Consequences**
140 B2 **Hot Springs** *AR* U.S.A.
136 C2 **Hot Springs** *SD* U.S.A.
128 C1 **Hottah Lake** Can.
62 B1 **Houayxay** Laos
100 B2 **Houffalize** Belgium
138 B1 **Houghton** U.S.A.
139 F1 **Houlton** U.S.A.
70 B2 **Houma** China
140 B3 **Houma** U.S.A.
128 B2 **Houston** Can.
143 D3 **Houston** U.S.A.
50 A2 **Houtman Abrolhos** *is* Austr.
122 B3 **Houwater** S. Africa
68 C1 **Hovd** Mongolia
99 C4 **Hove** U.K.
90 A2 **Hoverla, Hora** *mt.* Ukr.
68 C1 **Hövsgöl Nuur** *l.* Mongolia
116 A3 **Howar, Wadi** *watercourse* Sudan
98 C3 **Howden** U.K.
53 C3 **Howe, Cape** Austr.
123 D2 **Howick** S. Africa
49 J3 **Howland Island** *terr.* N. Pacific Ocean
53 C3 **Howlong** Austr.
Howrah India *see* **Haora**
140 B1 **Hoxie** U.S.A.
101 D2 **Höxter** Ger.
96 C1 **Hoy** *i.* U.K.
93 E3 **Høyanger** Norway
102 C1 **Hoyerswerda** Ger.
62 A2 **Hpapun** Myanmar
103 D1 **Hradec Králové** Czech Rep.
109 C2 **Hrasnica** Bos.-Herz.
92 □B2 **Hraun** Iceland
91 C1 **Hrebinka** Ukr.
88 B3 **Hrodna** Belarus
62 A1 **Hsi-hseng** Myanmar
71 C3 **Hsinchu** Taiwan
71 C3 **Hsinying** Taiwan
62 A1 **Hsipaw** Myanmar
70 A2 **Huachi** China
150 B4 **Huacho** Peru
70 B1 **Huade** China
65 B1 **Huadian** China
70 B2 **Huai'an** China
70 B2 **Huaibei** China
70 B2 **Huai He** *r.* China
71 A3 **Huaihua** China
70 B2 **Huainan** China
70 B2 **Huaiyang** China
145 C3 **Huajuápan de León** Mex.
59 C3 **Huaki** Indon.
71 C3 **Hualien** Taiwan
150 B3 **Huallaga** *r.* Peru
120 A2 **Huambo** Angola
150 B4 **Huancavelica** Peru
150 B4 **Huancayo** Peru
Huangcaoba China *see* **Xingyi**
70 B2 **Huangchuan** China
Huang Hai *sea* N. Pacific Ocean *see* **Yellow Sea**
Huang He *r.* China *see* **Yellow River**
71 A4 **Huangliu** China
70 B3 **Huangshan** China
70 B2 **Huangshi** China
70 A2 **Huangtu Gaoyuan** *plat.* China
71 C3 **Huangyan** China
70 A2 **Huangyuan** China
65 B1 **Huanren** China
150 B3 **Huánuco** Peru
152 B1 **Huanuni** Bol.
150 B4 **Huaral** Peru
150 B3 **Huaráz** Peru
150 B4 **Huarmey** Peru
152 A2 **Huasco** Chile
152 A2 **Huasco** *r.* Chile
144 B2 **Huatabampo** Mex.
145 C3 **Huatusco** Mex.
71 A3 **Huayuan** China
70 B2 **Hubei** *prov.* China
73 B3 **Hubli** India
100 C2 **Hückelhoven** Ger.
99 C3 **Hucknall** U.K.
98 C3 **Huddersfield** U.K.
93 G3 **Hudiksvall** Sweden
139 E2 **Hudson** *r.* U.S.A.
129 D2 **Hudson Bay** Can.
127 G3 **Hudson Bay** *sea* Can.
128 B2 **Hudson's Hope** Can.
127 H2 **Hudson Strait** Can.
63 B2 **Huê** Vietnam
146 A3 **Huehuetenango** Guat.
144 B2 **Huehueto, Cerro** *mt.* Mex.
145 C2 **Huejutla** Mex.
106 B2 **Huelva** Spain
107 C2 **Huércal-Overa** Spain
107 C1 **Huesca** Spain
106 C2 **Huéscar** Spain
51 D2 **Hughenden** Austr.
50 B3 **Hughes (abandoned)** Austr.
75 C2 **Hugli** *r. mouth* India
143 D2 **Hugo** U.S.A.
Huhehot China *see* **Hohhot**
122 B2 **Huhudi** S. Africa
122 A2 **Huib-Hoch Plateau** Namibia
71 B3 **Huichang** China
Huicheng China *see* **Huilai**
65 B1 **Huich'ŏn** N. Korea
120 A2 **Huíla, Planalto da** Angola
71 B3 **Huilai** China
71 A3 **Huili** China
70 B2 **Huimin** China
69 E2 **Huinan** China
Huinan China *see* **Nanhui**
93 H3 **Huittinen** Fin.
145 C3 **Huixtla** Mex.
71 A3 **Huize** China
78 B2 **Hujr** Saudi Arabia
122 B1 **Hukuntsi** Botswana
78 B2 **Ḥulayfah** Saudi Arabia
66 B1 **Hulin** China
130 C3 **Hull** Can.
70 C1 **Huludao** China
69 D1 **Hulun Buir** China
69 D1 **Hulun Nur** *l.* China
91 D2 **Hulyaypole** Ukr.
69 E1 **Huma** China
150 C3 **Humaitá** Brazil
122 B3 **Humansdorp** S. Africa
98 C2 **Humber** *est.* U.K.
143 D3 **Humble** U.S.A.
129 D2 **Humboldt** Can.
135 C2 **Humboldt** *NV* U.S.A.
140 C1 **Humboldt** *TN* U.S.A.
135 C2 **Humboldt** *r.* U.S.A.
103 E2 **Humenné** Slovakia
53 C3 **Hume Reservoir** Austr.
142 A1 **Humphreys Peak** U.S.A.
115 D2 **Hūn** Libya
92 □A2 **Húnaflói** *b.* Iceland
71 B3 **Hunan** *prov.* China
65 C1 **Hunchun** China
110 B1 **Hunedoara** Romania
101 D2 **Hünfeld** Ger.
103 D2 **Hungary** *country* Europe
52 B1 **Hungerford** Austr.
65 B2 **Hŭngnam** N. Korea
65 A1 **Hun He** *r.* China
Hunjiang China *see* **Baishan**
99 D3 **Hunstanton** U.K.
101 D1 **Hunte** *r.* Ger.
48 I6 **Hunter Island** S. Pacific Ocean
51 D4 **Hunter Islands** Austr.
99 C3 **Huntingdon** U.K.
138 B2 **Huntington** *IN* U.S.A.
138 C3 **Huntington** *WV* U.S.A.
135 C4 **Huntington Beach** U.S.A.
54 C1 **Huntly** N.Z.
96 C2 **Huntly** U.K.
130 C3 **Huntsville** Can.
140 C2 **Huntsville** *AL* U.S.A.
143 D2 **Huntsville** *TX* U.S.A.
Hunyani *r.* Moz./Zimbabwe *see* **Manyame**
59 D3 **Huon Peninsula** P.N.G.
Huoxian China *see* **Huozhou**
70 B2 **Huozhou** China
Hupeh *prov.* China *see* **Hubei**
Hurghada Egypt *see* **Al Ghurdaqah**
137 D2 **Huron** U.S.A.
138 C2 **Huron, Lake** Can./U.S.A.
135 D3 **Hurricane** U.S.A.
100 C2 **Hürth** Ger.

92 □B2 **Húsavík** Iceland
110 C1 **Huși** Romania
126 B2 **Huslia** U.S.A.
78 B3 **Ḥusn Āl 'Abr** Yemen
102 B1 **Husum** Ger.
68 C1 **Hutag-Öndör** Mongolia
60 A1 **Hutanopan** Indon.
137 D3 **Hutchinson** U.S.A.
141 D3 **Hutchinson Island** U.S.A.
70 B2 **Hutuo He** *r.* China
100 B2 **Huy** Belgium
70 C2 **Huzhou** China
92 □C3 **Hvalnes** Iceland
92 □B3 **Hvannadalshnúkur** *vol.* Iceland
109 C2 **Hvar** Croatia
109 C2 **Hvar** *i.* Croatia
91 C2 **Hvardiys'ke** Ukr.
120 B2 **Hwange** Zimbabwe
Hwang Ho *r.* China *see* **Yellow River**
136 C2 **Hyannis** U.S.A.
68 C1 **Hyargas Nuur** *salt l.* Mongolia
50 A3 **Hyden** Austr.
73 B3 **Hyderabad** India
74 A2 **Hyderabad** Pak.
Hydra *i.* Greece *see* **Ydra**
105 D3 **Hyères** France
105 D3 **Hyères, Îles d'** *is* France
65 B1 **Hyesan** N. Korea
128 B2 **Hyland Post** Can.
67 B3 **Hyōno-sen** *mt.* Japan
99 D4 **Hythe** U.K.
67 B4 **Hyūga** Japan
93 H3 **Hyvinkaa** Fin.

I

114 B2 **Iabès, Erg** *des.* Alg.
150 C3 **Iaco** *r.* Brazil
110 C2 **Ialomița** *r.* Romania
110 C1 **Ianca** Romania
110 C1 **Iași** Romania
64 A2 **Iba** Phil.
115 C4 **Ibadan** Nigeria
150 B2 **Ibagué** Col.
[illegible] **Ibaiti** Brazil
150 B2 **Ibarra** Ecuador
78 B3 **Ibb** Yemen
100 C1 **Ibbenbüren** Ger.
115 C4 **Ibi** Nigeria
107 C2 **Ibi** Spain
155 C1 **Ibiá** Brazil
155 D1 **Ibiaí** Brazil
155 D1 **Ibiraçu** Brazil
107 D2 **Ibiza** Spain
107 D2 **Ibiza** *i.* Spain
151 E4 **Ibotirama** Brazil
79 C2 **Ibrā'** Oman
79 C2 **Ibrī** Oman
150 B4 **Ica** Peru
Icaria *i.* Greece *see* **Ikaria**
İçel Turkey *see* **Mersin**
92 □B2 **Iceland** *country* Europe
160 M4 **Iceland Basin** N. Atlantic Ocean
160 L3 **Icelandic Plateau** N. Atlantic Ocean
66 D3 **Ichinoseki** Japan
91 C1 **Ichnya** Ukr.
65 B2 **Ich'ŏn** N. Korea
151 F3 **Icó** Brazil
155 D2 **Iconha** Brazil
143 E2 **Idabel** U.S.A.
115 C4 **Idah** Nigeria
134 D2 **Idaho** *state* U.S.A.
134 D2 **Idaho Falls** U.S.A.
100 C3 **Idar-Oberstein** Ger.
68 C1 **Ideriyn Gol** *r.* Mongolia
116 B2 **Idfū** Egypt
Idi Amin Dada, Lake Dem. Rep. Congo/Uganda *see* **Edward, Lake**
118 B3 **Idiofa** Dem. Rep. Congo
80 B2 **Idlib** Syria
123 C3 **Idutywa** S. Africa
88 B2 **Iecava** Latvia
154 B2 **Iepê** Brazil
100 A2 **Ieper** Belgium
111 C3 **Ierapetra** Greece
119 D3 **Ifakara** Tanz.
121 □D3 **Ifanadiana** Madag.
115 C4 **Ife** Nigeria
114 C3 **Ifôghas, Adrar des** *hills* Mali
118 C3 **Ifumo** Dem. Rep. Congo
61 C1 **Igan** Malaysia
119 D2 **Iganga** Uganda
154 C2 **Igarapava** Brazil
82 G2 **Igarka** Rus. Fed.
74 B3 **Igatpuri** India
81 C2 **Iğdır** Turkey
108 A3 **Iglesias** Italy
127 G2 **Igloolik** Can.
Igluligaarjuk Can. *see* **Chesterfield Inlet**
130 A3 **Ignace** Can.
88 C2 **Ignalina** Lith.
111 C2 **İğneada** Turkey
110 C2 **İğneada Burnu** *pt* Turkey
111 B3 **Igoumenitsa** Greece
86 E3 **Igra** Rus. Fed.
86 F2 **Igrim** Rus. Fed.
154 B3 **Iguaçu** *r.* Brazil
154 B3 **Iguaçu Falls** Arg./Brazil
145 C3 **Iguala** Mex.
107 D1 **Igualada** Spain
154 C2 **Iguape** Brazil
154 B2 **Iguatemi** Brazil
154 B2 **Iguatemi** *r.* Brazil
151 F3 **Iguatu** Brazil
118 A3 **Iguéla** Gabon
114 B2 **Iguidi, Erg** *des.* Alg./Maur.
119 D3 **Igunga** Tanz.
121 □D2 **Iharaña** Madag.
121 □D3 **Ihosy** Madag.
92 I2 **Iijoki** *r.* Fin.
92 I3 **Iisalmi** Fin.
67 B4 **Iizuka** Japan
115 C4 **Ijebu-Ode** Nigeria
100 B1 **IJmuiden** Neth.
100 B1 **IJssel** *r.* Neth.
100 B1 **IJsselmeer** *l.* Neth.
152 C2 **Ijuí** Brazil
Ikaahuk Can. *see* **Sachs Harbour**
123 C2 **Ikageleng** S. Africa
123 C2 **Ikageng** S. Africa
111 C3 **Ikaria** *i.* Greece
118 C3 **Ikela** Dem. Rep. Congo
110 B2 **Ikhtiman** Bulg.
67 A4 **Iki-shima** *i.* Japan
118 A2 **Ikom** Nigeria
121 □D3 **Ikongo** Madag.
65 B2 **Iksan** S. Korea
119 D3 **Ikungu** Tanz.
114 C2 **Ilaferh, Oued** *watercourse* Alg.
64 B2 **Ilagan** Phil.
81 C2 **Īlām** Iran
75 C2 **Ilam** Nepal
103 D1 **Iława** Pol.
79 C2 **Ilazārān, Kūh-e** *mt.* Iran
129 D2 **Île-à-la-Crosse** Can.
129 D2 **Île-à-la-Crosse, Lac** *l.* Can.
118 C3 **Ilebo** Dem. Rep. Congo
119 D2 **Ileret** Kenya
99 D4 **Ilford** U.K.
99 A4 **Ilfracombe** U.K.
155 C2 **Ilhabela** Brazil
155 D2 **Ilha Grande, Baía da** *b.* Brazil
154 B2 **Ilha Grande, Represa** *resr* Brazil
154 B2 **Ilha Solteíra, Represa** *resr* Brazil
106 B1 **Ílhavo** Port.
151 F4 **Ilhéus** Brazil
Ili Kazakh. *see* **Kapchagay**
[illegible] **Iliamna Lake** U.S.A.
64 B3 **Iligan** Phil.
Iliysk Kazakh. *see* **Kapchagay**
98 C3 **Ilkley** U.K.
152 A3 **Illapel** Chile
90 C2 **Illichivs'k** Ukr.
138 A3 **Illinois** *r.* U.S.A.
138 B3 **Illinois** *state* U.S.A.
90 B2 **Illintsi** Ukr.
115 C2 **Illizi** Alg.
89 D2 **Il'men', Ozero** *l.* Rus. Fed.
101 E2 **Ilmenau** Ger.
150 B4 **Ilo** Peru
64 B2 **Iloilo** Phil.
92 J3 **Ilomantsi** Fin.
115 C4 **Ilorin** Nigeria
87 D4 **Ilovlya** Rus. Fed.
53 D1 **Iluka** Austr.
127 I2 **Ilulissat** Greenland
Iman Rus. Fed. *see* **Dal'nerechensk**
66 B1 **Iman** *r.* Rus. Fed.
67 A4 **Imari** Japan
93 I3 **Imatra** Fin.
imeni Petra Stuchki Latvia *see* **Aizkraukle**
117 C4 **Īmī** Eth.
65 B2 **Imjin-gang** *r.* N. Korea/S. Korea
141 D3 **Immokalee** U.S.A.
108 B2 **Imola** Italy
151 E3 **Imperatriz** Brazil
108 A2 **Imperia** Italy
136 C2 **Imperial** U.S.A.
118 B2 **Impfondo** Congo
72 D2 **Imphal** India
111 C2 **İmroz** Turkey
67 C3 **Ina** Japan
150 C4 **Inambari** *r.* Peru
115 C2 **In Aménas** Alg.
115 C2 **In Amguel** Alg.
54 B2 **Inangahua Junction** N.Z.
59 C3 **Inanwatan** Indon.
92 I2 **Inari** Fin.
92 I2 **Inarijärvi** *l.* Fin.
67 D3 **Inawashiro-ko** *l.* Japan
80 B1 **İnce Burun** *pt* Turkey
65 B2 **Inch'ŏn** S. Korea
121 C3 **Inchope** Moz.
123 D2 **Incomati** *r.* Moz.
116 B3 **Inda Silasē** Eth.
144 B2 **Indé** Mex.
143 C3 **Independence** *CA* U.S.A.
137 E2 **Independence** *IA* U.S.A.
137 D3 **Independence** *KS* U.S.A.
137 E3 **Independence** *MO* U.S.A.
134 C2 **Independence Mountains** U.S.A.
76 B2 **Inderborskiy** Kazakh.
72 B2 **India** *country* Asia
139 D2 **Indiana** U.S.A.
138 B2 **Indiana** *state* U.S.A.
138 B3 **Indianapolis** U.S.A.
129 D2 **Indian Head** Can.
Indian Ocean
137 E2 **Indianola** *IA* U.S.A.
140 B2 **Indianola** *MS* U.S.A.
135 D3 **Indian Peak** U.S.A.
135 C3 **Indian Springs** U.S.A.
86 D2 **Indiga** Rus. Fed.
83 K2 **Indigirka** *r.* Rus. Fed.
109 D1 **Inđija** Serbia
135 C4 **Indio** U.S.A.
58 B3 **Indonesia** *country* Asia
74 B2 **Indore** India
60 B2 **Indramayu, Tanjung** *pt* Indon.
Indrapura, Gunung *vol.* Indon. *see* **Kerinci, Gunung**
75 C3 **Indravati** *r.* India
104 C2 **Indre** *r.* France
74 A2 **Indus** *r.* China/Pak.
74 A2 **Indus, Mouths of the** Pak.
159 E2 **Indus Cone** Indian Ocean
80 B1 **İnebolu** Turkey
111 C2 **İnegöl** Turkey
Infantes Spain *see* **Villanueva de los Infantes**
144 B3 **Infiernillo, Presa** *resr* Mex.
51 D1 **Ingham** Austr.
53 D1 **Inglewood** Austr.
102 C2 **Ingolstadt** Ger.
75 C2 **Ingraj Bazar** India
123 D2 **Ingwavuma** S. Africa
120 B2 **Ingwe** Zambia
123 D2 **Inhaca** Moz.
121 C3 **Inhambane** Moz.
121 C2 **Inhaminga** Moz.
151 D2 **Inini** Fr. Guiana
Inis Ireland *see* **Ennis**
97 A2 **Inishbofin** *i.* Ireland
97 B2 **Inishmore** *i.* Ireland
97 C1 **Inishowen** *pen.* Ireland
54 B2 **Inland Kaikoura Range** *mts* N.Z.
Inland Sea *sea* Japan *see* **Seto-naikai**
102 C2 **Inn** *r.* Europe
127 H1 **Innaanganeq** *c.* Greenland
52 B1 **Innamincka** Austr.
70 A1 **Inner Mongolia** *aut. reg.* China
96 B2 **Inner Sound** *sea chan.* U.K.
51 D1 **Innisfail** Austr.
102 C2 **Innsbruck** Austria
97 C2 **Inny** *r.* Ireland
154 B1 **Inocência** Brazil
118 B3 **Inongo** Dem. Rep. Congo
111 D3 **İnönü** Turkey
Inoucdjouac Can. *see* **Inukjuak**
103 D1 **Inowrocław** Pol.
114 C2 **In Salah** Alg.
62 A2 **Insein** Myanmar
110 C2 **Însurăței** Romania
86 F2 **Inta** Rus. Fed.
105 D2 **Interlaken** Switz.
137 E1 **International Falls** U.S.A.
63 A2 **Interview Island** India
130 C2 **Inukjuak** Can.
126 D2 **Inuvik** Can.
96 B2 **Inveraray** U.K.
96 C2 **Inverbervie** U.K.
54 A3 **Invercargill** N.Z.
53 D1 **Inverell** Austr.
96 B2 **Invergordon** U.K.
128 C2 **Invermere** Can.
131 D3 **Inverness** Can.
96 B2 **Inverness** U.K.
96 C2 **Inverurie** U.K.
159 F4 **Investigator Ridge** Indian Ocean
52 A3 **Investigator Strait** Austr.
77 E1 **Inya** Rus. Fed.
Inyanga Zimbabwe *see* **Nyanga**
119 D3 **Inyonga** Tanz.
87 D3 **Inza** Rus. Fed.
111 B3 **Ioannina** Greece
137 D3 **Iola** U.S.A.
96 A2 **Iona** *i.* U.K.
111 B3 **Ionian Islands** Greece
109 C3 **Ionian Sea** Greece/Italy
Ionioi Nisoi *is* Greece *see* **Ionian Islands**
111 C3 **Ios** *i.* Greece
137 E2 **Iowa** *state* U.S.A.
137 E2 **Iowa City** U.S.A.
154 C1 **Ipameri** Brazil
155 D1 **Ipatinga** Brazil
81 C1 **Ipatovo** Rus. Fed.
123 C2 **Ipelegeng** S. Africa
150 B2 **Ipiales** Col.
151 F4 **Ipiaú** Brazil
154 B3 **Ipiranga** Brazil
150 B3 **Ipixuna** Brazil
60 B1 **Ipoh** Malaysia
154 B1 **Iporá** Brazil
118 C2 **Ippy** C.A.R.
111 C2 **İpsala** Turkey
53 D1 **Ipswich** Austr.
99 D3 **Ipswich** U.K.
127 H2 **Iqaluit** Can.
152 A2 **Iquique** Chile
150 B3 **Iquitos** Peru
Irakleio Greece *see* **Iraklion**
111 C3 **Iraklion** Greece
81 D2 **Iran** *country* Asia
61 C1 **Iran, Pegunungan** *mts* Indon.
79 D2 **Īrānshahr** Iran
144 B2 **Irapuato** Mex.
81 C2 **Iraq** *country* Asia
154 B3 **Irati** Brazil
88 B2 **Irbe Strait** Estonia/Latvia
80 B2 **Irbid** Jordan
86 F3 **Irbit** Rus. Fed.
151 E4 **Irecê** Brazil
97 C2 **Ireland** *country* Europe
118 C3 **Irema** Dem. Rep. Congo
76 C2 **Irgiz** Kazakh.
Iri S. Korea *see* **Iksan**
Irian Jaya *reg.* Indon. *see* **Papua**
115 E3 **Iriba** Chad
114 B3 **Irîgui** *reg.* Mali/Maur.
119 D3 **Iringa** Tanz.
151 D3 **Iriri** *r.* Brazil
Irish Free State *country* Europe *see* **Ireland**
95 B3 **Irish Sea** Ireland/U.K.
68 C1 **Irkutsk** Rus. Fed.
160 M4 **Irminger Basin** N. Atlantic Ocean
139 D2 **Irondequoit** U.S.A.
52 A2 **Iron Knob** Austr.
138 B1 **Iron Mountain** U.S.A.
138 C3 **Ironton** U.S.A.
138 A1 **Ironwood** U.S.A.
130 B3 **Iroquois Falls** Can.
64 B2 **Irosin** Phil.
67 C4 **Irō-zaki** *pt* Japan
90 C1 **Irpin'** Ukr.
62 A2 **Irrawaddy** *r.* Myanmar
63 A2 **Irrawaddy, Mouths of the** Myanmar
86 F2 **Irtysh** *r.* Kazakh./Rus. Fed.
107 C1 **Irun** Spain
96 B3 **Irvine** U.K.
143 D2 **Irving** U.S.A.
64 B3 **Isabela** Phil.
146 B3 **Isabelia, Cordillera** *mts* Nic.
92 □A2 **Ísafjarðardjúp** *est.* Iceland
92 □A2 **Ísafjörður** Iceland
67 B4 **Isahaya** Japan
102 C2 **Isar** *r.* Ger.
96 □ **Isbister** U.K.
108 B2 **Ischia, Isola d'** *i.* Italy
67 C4 **Ise** Japan
118 C2 **Isengi** Dem. Rep. Congo
105 C3 **Isère** *r.* France
100 C2 **Iserlohn** Ger.
101 D1 **Isernhagen** Ger.
67 C4 **Ise-wan** *b.* Japan
114 C4 **Iseyin** Nigeria
Isfahan Iran *see* **Eşfahān**
66 D2 **Ishikari-wan** *b.* Japan
77 D1 **Ishim** *r.* Kazakh./Rus. Fed.
82 F3 **Ishim** Rus. Fed.
67 D3 **Ishinomaki** Japan
67 D3 **Ishioka** Japan
67 B4 **Ishizuchi-san** *mt.* Japan
74 B1 **Ishkoshim** Tajik.
138 B1 **Ishpeming** U.S.A.
111 C2 **Işıklar Dağı** *mts* Turkey
111 C3 **Işıklı** Turkey
123 D2 **Isipingo** S. Africa
119 C2 **Isiro** Dem. Rep. Congo
80 B2 **İskenderun** Turkey
82 G3 **Iskitim** Rus. Fed.
110 B2 **Iskŭr** *r.* Bulg.
117 D3 **Iskushuban** Somalia
128 A2 **Iskut** *r.* Can.
74 B1 **Islamabad** Pak.
141 D4 **Islamorada** U.S.A.
52 A2 **Island Lagoon** *imp. l.* Austr.
129 E2 **Island Lake** Can.
54 B1 **Islands, Bay of** N.Z.
Islas Canarias *is* N. Atlantic Ocean *see* **Canary Islands**
96 A3 **Islay** *i.* U.K.
98 A2 **Isle of Man** *i.* Irish Sea
Ismail Ukr. *see* **Izmayil**
77 D3 **Ismoili Somoní, Qullai** *mt.* Tajik.
116 B2 **Isnā** Egypt
121 □D3 **Isoanala** Madag.
121 C2 **Isoka** Zambia
93 H3 **Isokyrö** Fin.
109 C3 **Isola di Capo Rizzuto** Italy
Ispahan Iran *see* **Eşfahān**
80 B2 **Isparta** Turkey
110 C2 **Isperikh** Bulg.
Ispisar Tajik. *see* **Khŭjand**
80 B2 **Israel** *country* Asia
50 B3 **Israelite Bay** Austr.
105 C2 **Issoire** France
Issyk-Kul' Kyrg. *see* **Balykchy**
111 C2 **İstanbul** Turkey
İstanbul Boğazı *str.* Turkey *see* **Bosporus**
103 D2 **Isten dombja** *h.* Hungary
111 B3 **Istiaia** Greece
141 D3 **Istokpoga, Lake** U.S.A.
Istra *pen.* Croatia *see* **Istria**
105 C3 **Istres** France
108 B1 **Istria** *pen.* Croatia
155 D2 **Itabapoana** Brazil
151 E4 **Itaberaba** Brazil
154 C1 **Itaberaí** Brazil
155 D1 **Itabira** Brazil
155 D2 **Itabirito** Brazil
151 F4 **Itabuna** Brazil
150 D3 **Itacoatiara** Brazil
155 D2 **Itaguaí** Brazil
154 B2 **Itaguajé** Brazil
154 C2 **Itaí** Brazil
154 C3 **Itaiópolis** Brazil
154 B3 **Itaipu, Represa de** *resr* Brazil
151 D3 **Itaituba** Brazil
154 C3 **Itajaí** Brazil
155 C2 **Itajubá** Brazil
108 B2 **Italy** *country* Europe
155 E1 **Itamaraju** Brazil
155 D1 **Itamarandiba** Brazil
155 D1 **Itambacuri** Brazil
155 D1 **Itambé, Pico de** *mt.* Brazil
75 D2 **Itanagar** India
154 C2 **Itanhaém** Brazil
155 D1 **Itanhém** Brazil
155 D1 **Itaobím** Brazil

154 C1 **Itapajipe** Brazil
155 E1 **Itapebi** Brazil
155 D2 **Itapemirim** Brazil
155 D2 **Itaperuna** Brazil
155 D1 **Itapetinga** Brazil
154 C2 **Itapetininga** Brazil
154 C2 **Itapeva** Brazil
151 F4 **Itapicuru** *r.* Brazil
151 E3 **Itapicuru Mirim** Brazil
155 C2 **Itapira** Brazil
154 C2 **Itaporanga** Brazil
154 C1 **Itapuranga** Brazil
154 C2 **Itararé** Brazil
74 B2 **Itarsi** India
154 B1 **Itarumã** Brazil
155 D2 **Itaúna** Brazil
155 E1 **Itaúnas** Brazil
64 B1 **Itbayat** *i.* Phil.
139 D2 **Ithaca** U.S.A.
101 D1 **Ith Hils** *ridge* Ger.
118 C2 **Itimbiri** *r.* Dem. Rep. Congo
155 D1 **Itinga** Brazil
154 B1 **Itiquira** Brazil
154 A1 **Itiquira** *r.* Brazil
67 C4 **Itō** Japan
154 C2 **Itu** Brazil
150 B3 **Ituí** *r.* Brazil
154 C1 **Ituiutaba** Brazil
119 C3 **Itula** Dem. Rep. Congo
154 C1 **Itumbiara** Brazil
154 C1 **Itumbiara, Barragem** *resr* Brazil
154 B1 **Iturama** Brazil
101 D1 **Itzehoe** Ger.
83 N2 **Iul'tin** Rus. Fed.
155 D2 **Iúna** Brazil
154 B2 **Ivaí** *r.* Brazil
92 I2 **Ivalo** Fin.
88 C3 **Ivanava** Belarus
109 C1 **Ivanec** Croatia
Ivangrad Montenegro *see* **Berane**
52 B2 **Ivanhoe** Austr.
90 B1 **Ivankiv** Ukr.
90 A2 **Ivano-Frankivs'k** Ukr.
89 F2 **Ivanovo** Rus. Fed.
88 C3 **Ivatsevichy** Belarus
111 C2 **Ivaylovgrad** Bulg.
86 F2 **Ivdel'** Rus. Fed.
110 C1 **Iveşti** Romania
154 B2 **Ivinheima** Brazil
154 B2 **Ivinheima** *r.* Brazil
127 I2 **Ivittuut** Greenland
Iviza *i.* Spain *see* **Ibiza**
89 E3 **Ivnya** Rus. Fed.
Ivory Coast *country* Africa *see* **Côte d'Ivoire**
108 A1 **Ivrea** Italy
111 C3 **İvrindi** Turkey
Ivugivik Can. *see* **Ivujivik**
127 G2 **Ivujivik** Can.
67 D3 **Iwaki** Japan
67 B4 **Iwakuni** Japan
66 D2 **Iwamizawa** Japan
66 D2 **Iwanai** Japan
66 D3 **Iwate-san** *vol.* Japan
88 C3 **Iwye** Belarus
123 D3 **Ixopo** S. Africa
144 B2 **Ixtlán** Mex.
146 B3 **Izabal, Lago de** *l.* Guat.
145 D2 **Izamal** Mex.
81 C1 **Izberbash** Rus. Fed.
86 E3 **Izhevsk** Rus. Fed.
86 E2 **Izhma** Rus. Fed.
Izhma Rus. Fed. *see* **Sosnogorsk**
89 E3 **Izmalkovo** Rus. Fed.
90 B2 **Izmayil** Ukr.
111 C3 **İzmir** Turkey
111 C2 **İzmit** Turkey
111 C2 **İznik Gölü** *l.* Turkey
152 B1 **Izozog, Bañados del** *swamp* Bol.
67 A4 **Izuhara** Japan
67 B3 **Izumo** Japan
156 C4 **Izu-Ogasawara Trench** N. Pacific Ocean
67 C4 **Izu-shotō** *is* Japan
90 B1 **Izyaslav** Ukr.
91 D2 **Izyum** Ukr.

J

74 A1 **Jabal as Sirāj** Afgh.
106 C2 **Jabalón** *r.* Spain
75 B2 **Jabalpur** India
50 C1 **Jabiru** Austr.
109 C2 **Jablanica** Bos.-Herz.
151 F3 **Jaboatão dos Guararapes** Brazil
154 C2 **Jaboticabal** Brazil
107 C1 **Jaca** Spain
145 C2 **Jacala** Mex.
151 D3 **Jacareacanga** Brazil
155 C2 **Jacareí** Brazil
154 B1 **Jaciara** Brazil
155 D1 **Jacinto** Brazil
139 E1 **Jackman** U.S.A.
140 C2 **Jackson** *AL* U.S.A.
138 C2 **Jackson** *MI* U.S.A.
140 B2 **Jackson** *MS* U.S.A.
140 C1 **Jackson** *TN* U.S.A.
136 A2 **Jackson** *WY* U.S.A.
54 A2 **Jackson Head** *hd* N.Z.
140 B2 **Jacksonville** *AR* U.S.A.
141 D2 **Jacksonville** *FL* U.S.A.
138 A3 **Jacksonville** *IL* U.S.A.
141 E2 **Jacksonville** *NC* U.S.A.
143 D2 **Jacksonville** *TX* U.S.A.
147 C3 **Jacmel** Haiti
74 A2 **Jacobabad** Pak.
151 E4 **Jacobina** Brazil
131 D3 **Jacques-Cartier, Mont** *mt.* Can.
151 E3 **Jacunda** Brazil
154 C2 **Jacupiranga** Brazil
101 D1 **Jadebusen** *b.* Ger.
Jadotville Dem. Rep. Congo *see* **Likasi**
109 C2 **Jadovnik** *mt.* Bos.-Herz.
150 B3 **Jaén** Peru
106 C2 **Jaén** Spain
Jaffa Israel *see* **Tel Aviv-Yafo**
52 A3 **Jaffa, Cape** Austr.
73 B4 **Jaffna** Sri Lanka
75 C3 **Jagdalpur** India
123 C2 **Jagersfontein** S. Africa
79 C2 **Jaghīn** Iran
152 C3 **Jaguarão** Brazil
154 C2 **Jaguariaíva** Brazil
81 D3 **Jahrom** Iran
74 B2 **Jaipur** India
74 B2 **Jaisalmer** India
74 B2 **Jaitgarh** *h.* India
75 C2 **Jajarkot** Nepal
109 C2 **Jajce** Bos.-Herz.
Jajnagar *state* India *see* **Orissa**
60 B2 **Jakarta** Indon.
128 A1 **Jakes Corner** Can.
92 G2 **Jäkkvik** Sweden
Jakobshavn Greenland *see* **Ilulissat**
92 H3 **Jakobstad** Fin.
77 D3 **Jalālābād** Afgh.
77 D2 **Jalal-Abad** Kyrg.
74 B1 **Jalandhar** India
145 C3 **Jalapa** Mex.
154 B2 **Jales** Brazil
74 B2 **Jalgaon** India
115 D4 **Jalingo** Nigeria
74 B3 **Jalna** India
74 B2 **Jalore** India
144 B2 **Jalostotitlán** Mex.
144 B2 **Jalpa** Mex.
75 C2 **Jalpaiguri** India
145 C2 **Jalpan** Mex.
115 E2 **Jālū** Libya
146 C3 **Jamaica** *country* West Indies
146 C3 **Jamaica Channel** Haiti/Jamaica
75 C2 **Jamalpur** Bangl.
60 B2 **Jambi** Indon.
137 D2 **James** *r. N. Dakota/S. Dakota* U.S.A.
139 D3 **James** *r. VA* U.S.A.
130 B2 **James Bay** Can.
52 A2 **Jamestown** Austr.
Jamestown Can. *see* **Wawa**
123 C3 **Jamestown** S. Africa
137 D1 **Jamestown** *ND* U.S.A.
139 D2 **Jamestown** *NY* U.S.A.
74 B1 **Jammu** India
74 B1 **Jammu and Kashmir** *terr.* Asia
74 B2 **Jamnagar** India
74 B2 **Jampur** Pak.
93 I3 **Jämsä** Fin.
78 A2 **Jamsah** Egypt
75 C2 **Jamshedpur** India
75 C2 **Jamuna** *r.* Bangl.
75 C2 **Janakpur** Nepal
155 D1 **Janaúba** Brazil
81 D2 **Jandaq** Iran
114 A2 **Jandía** *h.* Islas Canarias
135 B2 **Janesville** *CA* U.S.A.
138 B2 **Janesville** *WI* U.S.A.
154 A2 **Jango** Brazil
82 A2 **Jan Mayen** *terr.* Arctic Ocean
81 D1 **Jaňňa** Turkm.
122 B3 **Jansenville** S. Africa
155 D1 **Januária** Brazil
74 B2 **Jaora** India
67 C3 **Japan** *country* Asia
66 B3 **Japan, Sea of** N. Pacific Ocean
150 C3 **Japurá** *r.* Brazil
154 C1 **Jaraguá** Brazil
154 C3 **Jaraguá, Serra** *mts* Brazil
154 C3 **Jaraguá do Sul** Brazil
154 B2 **Jaraguari** Brazil
70 A2 **Jarantai** China
152 C2 **Jardim** Brazil
103 D1 **Jarocin** Pol.
103 E1 **Jarosław** Pol.
92 F3 **Järpen** Sweden
150 C4 **Jarú** Brazil
Jarud China *see* **Lubei**
88 C1 **Järvenpää** Fin.
49 K4 **Jarvis Island** *terr.* S. Pacific Ocean
93 G3 **Järvsö** Sweden
79 C2 **Jāsk** Iran
103 E2 **Jasło** Pol.
55 A3 **Jason Peninsula** Antarctica
128 C2 **Jasper** Can.
140 C2 **Jasper** *AL* U.S.A.
138 B3 **Jasper** *IN* U.S.A.
143 E2 **Jasper** *TX* U.S.A.
Jassy Romania *see* **Iaşi**
103 D2 **Jastrzębie-Zdrój** Pol.
103 D2 **Jászberény** Hungary
154 B1 **Jataí** Brazil
74 A2 **Jati** Pak.
154 C2 **Jaú** Brazil
150 C3 **Jaú** *r.* Brazil
145 C2 **Jaumave** Mex.
75 C2 **Jaunpur** India
154 B1 **Jauru** Brazil
61 B2 **Java** *i.* Indon.
107 C1 **Javalambre, Sierra de** *mts* Spain
Java Sea *sea* Indon. *see* **Laut Jawa**
156 B6 **Java Trench** Indian Ocean
Jawa *i.* Indon. *see* **Java**
117 C4 **Jawhar** Somalia
103 D1 **Jawor** Pol.
103 D1 **Jaworzno** Pol.
59 D3 **Jaya, Puncak** *mt.* Indon.
59 D3 **Jayapura** Indon.
79 C2 **Jazīrat Maşīrah** *i.* Oman
79 C2 **Jaz Mūrīān, Hāmūn-e** *imp. l.* Iran
128 B1 **Jean Marie River** Can.
131 D2 **Jeannin, Lac** *l.* Can.
81 D2 **Jebel** Turkm.
Jebel, Bahr el *r.* Sudan/Uganda *see* **White Nile**
116 A3 **Jebel Abyad Plateau** Sudan
96 C3 **Jedburgh** U.K.
78 A2 **Jeddah** Saudi Arabia
108 A3 **Jedeida** Tunisia
101 E1 **Jeetze** *r.* Ger.
137 E2 **Jefferson** U.S.A.
135 C3 **Jefferson, Mount** U.S.A.
137 E3 **Jefferson City** U.S.A.
122 B3 **Jeffreys Bay** S. Africa
88 C2 **Jēkabpils** Latvia
103 D1 **Jelenia Góra** Pol.
88 B2 **Jelgava** Latvia
60 B1 **Jemaja** *i.* Indon.
61 C2 **Jember** Indon.
101 E2 **Jena** Ger.
Jengish Chokusu *mt.* China/Kyrg. *see* **Pobeda Peak**
80 B2 **Jenīn** West Bank
140 B2 **Jennings** U.S.A.
151 E4 **Jequié** Brazil
155 D1 **Jequitaí** Brazil
155 D1 **Jequitinhonha** Brazil
155 E1 **Jequitinhonha** *r.* Brazil
147 C3 **Jérémie** Haiti
144 B2 **Jerez** Mex.
106 B2 **Jerez de la Frontera** Spain
109 D3 **Jergucat** Albania
115 C1 **Jerid, Chott el** *salt l.* Tunisia
134 D2 **Jerome** U.S.A.
95 C4 **Jersey** *i.* Channel Is
95 C4 **Jersey** *terr.* Channel Is
151 E3 **Jerumenha** Brazil
80 B2 **Jerusalem** Israel/West Bank
53 D3 **Jervis Bay Territory** *admin. div.* Austr.
108 B1 **Jesenice** Slovenia
108 B2 **Jesi** Italy
Jesselton Malaysia *see* **Kota Kinabalu**
101 F2 **Jessen** Ger.
75 C2 **Jessore** Bangl.
141 D2 **Jesup** U.S.A.
137 D3 **Jesus, Mount** *h.* U.S.A.
145 C3 **Jesús Carranza** Mex.
100 C1 **Jever** Ger.
74 B2 **Jhalawar** India
74 B1 **Jhang** Pak.
74 B2 **Jhansi** India
75 C2 **Jharkhand** *state* India
75 C2 **Jharsuguda** India
74 B1 **Jhelum** *r.* India/Pak.
74 B1 **Jhelum** Pak.
74 B2 **Jhunjhunun** India
70 C2 **Jiading** China
69 E1 **Jiamusi** China
71 B3 **Ji'an** *Jiangxi* China
65 B1 **Ji'an** *Jilin* China
Jianchang China *see* **Nancheng**
62 A1 **Jianchuan** China
70 B3 **Jiande** China
Jiangling China *see* **Jingzhou**
71 B3 **Jiangmen** China
70 B2 **Jiangsu** *prov.* China
71 B3 **Jiangxi** *prov.* China
70 A2 **Jiangyou** China
70 B3 **Jianli** China
70 B2 **Jianqiao** China
71 B3 **Jianyang** *Fujian* China
70 A2 **Jianyang** *Sichuan* China
69 E2 **Jiaohe** China
Jiaojiang China *see* **Taizhou**
70 C2 **Jiaozhou** China
70 B2 **Jiaozuo** China
Jiashan China *see* **Mingguang**
70 C2 **Jiaxing** China
68 C2 **Jiayuguan** China
Jiddah Saudi Arabia *see* **Jeddah**
92 G2 **Jiehkkevárri** *mt.* Norway
70 B2 **Jiexiu** China
70 A2 **Jigzhi** China
103 D2 **Jihlava** Czech Rep.
115 C1 **Jijel** Alg.
117 C4 **Jijiga** Eth.
117 C4 **Jilib** Somalia
69 E2 **Jilin** China
65 B1 **Jilin** *prov.* China
65 A1 **Jilin Hada Ling** *mts* China
117 B4 **Jīma** Eth.
110 B1 **Jimbolia** Romania
144 B2 **Jiménez** *Chihuahua* Mex.
143 C3 **Jiménez** *Coahuila* Mex.
70 B2 **Jinan** China
70 A2 **Jinchang** China
70 B2 **Jincheng** China
Jinchuan China *see* **Jinchang**
53 C3 **Jindabyne** Austr.
103 D2 **Jindřichův Hradec** Czech Rep.
Jin'e China *see* **Longchang**
70 A2 **Jingbian** China
71 B3 **Jingdezhen** China
62 B1 **Jingdong** China
53 C3 **Jingellic** Austr.
70 B2 **Jinghang Yunhe** *canal* China
62 B1 **Jinghong** China
70 B2 **Jingmen** China
70 A2 **Jingning** China
Jingsha China *see* **Jingzhou**
70 A2 **Jingtai** China
71 A3 **Jingxi** China
Jingxian China *see* **Jingzhou**
65 B1 **Jingyu** China
70 A2 **Jingyuan** China
70 B2 **Jingzhou** *Hubei* China
70 B2 **Jingzhou** *Hubei* China
71 A3 **Jingzhou** *Hunan* China
71 B3 **Jinhua** China
70 B1 **Jining** *Nei Mongol* China
70 B2 **Jining** *Shandong* China
119 D2 **Jinja** Uganda
117 B4 **Jinka** Eth.
146 B3 **Jinotega** Nic.
146 B3 **Jinotepe** Nic.
71 A3 **Jinping** China
Jinsha Jiang *r.* China *see* **Yangtze**
70 B3 **Jinshi** China
Jinshi China *see* **Xinning**
Jinxi China *see* **Lianshan**
70 B2 **Jinzhong** China
70 C1 **Jinzhou** China
150 C3 **Jiparaná** *r.* Brazil
75 C1 **Jirang** China
116 B2 **Jirjā** Egypt
79 C2 **Jīroft** Iran
79 C2 **Jirwān** Saudi Arabia
71 A3 **Jishou** China
110 B2 **Jiu** *r.* Romania
70 A2 **Jiuding Shan** *mt.* China
70 B3 **Jiujiang** China
Jiulian China *see* **Mojiang**
79 D2 **Jiwani** Pak.
66 B1 **Jixi** China
78 B3 **Jīzān** Saudi Arabia
77 C2 **Jizzax** Uzbek.
155 D1 **Joaíma** Brazil
João Belo Moz. *see* **Xai-Xai**
151 F3 **João Pessoa** Brazil
155 C1 **João Pinheiro** Brazil
74 B2 **Jodhpur** India
92 I3 **Joensuu** Fin.
67 C3 **Jōetsu** Japan
121 C3 **Jofane** Moz.
88 C2 **Jõgeva** Estonia
Jogjakarta Indon. *see* **Yogyakarta**
123 C2 **Johannesburg** S. Africa
134 C2 **John Day** U.S.A.
134 B1 **John Day** *r.* U.S.A.
128 C2 **John D'Or Prairie** Can.
141 E1 **John H. Kerr Reservoir** U.S.A.
96 C1 **John o'Groats** U.K.
141 D1 **Johnson City** U.S.A.
128 A1 **Johnson's Crossing** Can.
50 B3 **Johnston, Lake** *imp. l.* Austr.
49 J2 **Johnston Atoll** N. Pacific Ocean
96 B3 **Johnstone** U.K.
Johnstone Lake *l.* Can. *see* **Old Wives Lake**
139 D2 **Johnstown** U.S.A.
60 B1 **Johor Bahru** Malaysia
88 C2 **Jõhvi** Estonia
154 C3 **Joinville** Brazil
105 D2 **Joinville** France
55 B3 **Joinville Island** Antarctica
92 G2 **Jokkmokk** Sweden
92 □B2 **Jökulsá á Fjöllum** *r.* Iceland
138 B2 **Joliet** U.S.A.
130 C3 **Joliette** Can.
64 B3 **Jolo** Phil.
64 B3 **Jolo** *i.* Phil.
61 C2 **Jombang** Indon.
75 C2 **Jomsom** Nepal
88 B2 **Jonava** Lith.
140 B1 **Jonesboro** *AR* U.S.A.
140 B2 **Jonesboro** *LA* U.S.A.
139 F2 **Jonesport** U.S.A.
127 G1 **Jones Sound** *sea chan.* Can.
93 F4 **Jönköping** Sweden
131 C3 **Jonquière** Can.
145 C3 **Jonuta** Mex.
137 E3 **Joplin** U.S.A.
80 B2 **Jordan** *country* Asia
80 B2 **Jordan** *r.* Asia
134 E1 **Jordan** U.S.A.
155 D1 **Jordânia** Brazil
134 C2 **Jordan Valley** U.S.A.
72 D2 **Jorhat** India
101 D1 **Jork** Ger.
93 E4 **Jørpeland** Norway
115 C4 **Jos** Nigeria
145 C3 **José Cardel** Mex.
131 D2 **Joseph, Lac** *l.* Can.
50 B1 **Joseph Bonaparte Gulf** Austr.
115 C4 **Jos Plateau** Nigeria
93 E3 **Jotunheimen** *mts* Norway
122 B3 **Joubertina** S. Africa
123 C2 **Jouberton** S. Africa
104 C2 **Joué-lès-Tours** France
93 I3 **Joutseno** Fin.
134 B1 **Juan de Fuca Strait** Can./U.S.A.
Juanshui China *see* **Tongcheng**
145 B2 **Juaréz** Mex.
144 A1 **Juárez, Sierra de** *mts* Mex.
151 E3 **Juazeiro** Brazil
151 F3 **Juazeiro do Norte** Brazil

117 B4 Juba Sudan
117 C5 Jubba r. Somalia
78 B2 Jubbah Saudi Arabia
Jubbulpore India see Jabalpur
145 C3 Juchitán Mex.
155 E1 Jucuruçu Brazil
102 C2 Judenburg Austria
155 E1 Juerana Brazil
101 D2 Jühnde Ger.
146 B3 Juigalpa Nic.
150 D4 Juína Brazil
100 C1 Juist i. Ger.
155 D2 Juiz de Fora Brazil
136 C2 Julesburg U.S.A.
150 B4 Juliaca Peru
Julianatop mt. Indon. see Mandala, Puncak
151 D2 Juliana Top mt. Suriname
Jullundur India see Jalandhar
107 C2 Jumilla Spain
75 C2 Jumla Nepal
Jumna r. India see Yamuna
74 B2 Junagadh India
143 D2 Junction U.S.A.
137 D3 Junction City U.S.A.
154 C2 Jundiaí Brazil
128 A2 Juneau U.S.A.
53 C2 Junee Austr.
105 D2 Jungfrau mt. Switz.
139 D2 Juniata r. U.S.A.
153 B3 Junín Arg.
92 G3 Junsele Sweden
134 C2 Juntura U.S.A.
Junxi China see Datian
Junxian China see Danjiangkou
154 B2 Jupía, Represa resr Brazil
141 D3 Jupiter U.S.A.
154 C2 Juquiá Brazil
117 A4 Jur r. Sudan
105 D2 Jura mts France/Switz.
96 B2 Jura i. U.K.
96 B3 Jura, Sound of sea chan. U.K.
88 B2 Jurbarkas Lith.
88 B2 Jūrmala Latvia
150 C3 Juruá r. Brazil
150 D3 Juruena r. Brazil
154 C2 Jurumirim, Represa de resr Brazil
151 D3 Juruti Brazil
154 B1 Jussara Brazil
150 C3 Jutaí r. Brazil
101 F2 Jüterbog Ger.
154 B2 Juti Brazil
145 D3 Jutiapa Guat.
93 E4 Jutland pen. Denmark
146 B2 Juventud, Isla de la i. Cuba
70 B2 Juxian China
81 D3 Jüyom Iran
122 B1 Jwaneng Botswana
Jylland pen. Denmark see Jutland
93 I3 Jyväskylä Fin.

K

74 B1 K2 mt. China/Pakistan
Kaakhka Turkm. see Kaka
92 I2 Kaamanen Fin.
61 D2 Kabaena i. Indon.
119 C3 Kabalo Dem. Rep. Congo
119 C3 Kabambare Dem. Rep. Congo
119 C3 Kabare Dem. Rep. Congo
119 C3 Kabemba Dem. Rep. Congo
130 B3 Kabinakagami Lake Can.
118 C3 Kabinda Dem. Rep. Congo
118 B2 Kabo C.A.R.
120 B2 Kabompo Zambia
119 C3 Kabongo Dem. Rep. Congo
77 C3 Kābul Afgh.
64 B3 Kaburuang i. Indon.
121 B2 Kabwe Zambia
109 D2 Kačanik Kosovo
74 A2 Kachchh, Gulf of India
74 B2 Kachchh, Rann of marsh India
83 I3 Kachug Rus. Fed.
81 C1 Kaçkar Dağı mt. Turkey
111 C2 Kadıköy Turkey
52 A2 Kadina Austr.
114 B3 Kadiolo Mali
Kadiyevka Ukr. see Stakhanov
73 B3 Kadmat atoll India
89 F2 Kadnikov Rus. Fed.
121 B2 Kadoma Zimbabwe
63 A2 Kadonkani Myanmar
117 A3 Kadugli Sudan
115 C3 Kaduna Nigeria
89 E2 Kaduy Rus. Fed.
86 E2 Kadzherom Rus. Fed.
114 A3 Kaédi Maur.
118 B1 Kaélé Cameroon
65 B2 Kaesŏng N. Korea
118 C3 Kafakumba Dem. Rep. Congo
114 A3 Kaffrine Senegal
80 B2 Kafr ash Shaykh Egypt
121 B2 Kafue Zambia
120 B2 Kafue r. Zambia
67 C3 Kaga Japan
118 B2 Kaga Bandoro C.A.R.
91 E2 Kagal'nitskaya Rus. Fed.
Kaganovichi Pervyye Ukr. see Polis'ke
60 A2 Kagologolo Indon.
67 B4 Kagoshima Japan
Kagul Moldova see Cahul
119 D3 Kahama Tanz.
90 C2 Kaharlyk Ukr.
61 C2 Kahayan r. Indon.
118 B3 Kahemba Dem. Rep. Congo
101 E2 Kahla Ger.
79 C2 Kahnūj Iran
92 H2 Kahperusvaarat mts Fin.
80 B2 Kahramanmaraş Turkey
79 C2 Kahūrak Iran
59 C3 Kai, Kepulauan is Indon.
115 C4 Kaiama Nigeria
54 B2 Kaiapoi N.Z.
59 C3 Kai Besar i. Indon.
70 B2 Kaifeng China
Kaihua China see Wenshan
122 B2 Kaiingveld reg. S. Africa
59 C3 Kai Kecil i. Indon.
54 B2 Kaikoura N.Z.
114 A4 Kailahun Sierra Leone
Kailas Range mts China see Gangdisê Shan
71 A3 Kaili China
59 C3 Kaimana Indon.
54 C1 Kaimanawa Mountains N.Z.
72 C2 Kaimur Range hills India
88 B2 Käina Estonia
67 C4 Kainan Japan
115 C3 Kainji Reservoir Nigeria
54 B1 Kaipara Harbour N.Z.
74 B2 Kairana India
115 D1 Kairouan Tunisia
100 C3 Kaiserslautern Ger.
55 I2 Kaiser Wilhelm II Land reg. Antarctica
54 B1 Kaitaia N.Z.
54 C1 Kaitawa N.Z.
Kaitong China see Tongyu
59 C3 Kaiwatu Indon.
65 A1 Kaiyuan Liaoning China
71 A3 Kaiyuan Yunnan China
92 I3 Kajaani Fin.
51 D2 Kajabbi Austr.
53 C1 Kajarabie, Lake Austr.
76 B3 Kaka Turkm.
122 B2 Kakamas S. Africa
119 D2 Kakamega Kenya
114 A4 Kakata Liberia
91 C2 Kakhovka Ukr.
91 C2 Kakhovs'ke Vodoskhovyshche resr Ukr.
Kakhul Moldova see Cahul
73 C3 Kakinada India
128 C1 Kakisa Can.
67 B4 Kakogawa Japan
119 C3 Kakoswa Dem. Rep. Congo
126 C2 Kaktovik U.S.A.
Kalaallit Nunaat terr. N. America see Greenland
59 C3 Kalabahi Indon.
120 B2 Kalabo Zambia
91 E1 Kalach Rus. Fed.
119 D2 Kalacha Dida Kenya
87 D4 Kalach-na-Donu Rus. Fed.
62 A1 Kaladan r. India/Myanmar
120 B3 Kalahari Desert Africa
92 H3 Kalajoki Fin.
123 C1 Kalamare Botswana
111 B2 Kalamaria Greece
111 B3 Kalamata Greece
138 B2 Kalamazoo U.S.A.
111 B3 Kalampaka Greece
88 B2 Kalana Estonia
91 C2 Kalanchak Ukr.
115 E2 Kalanshiyū ar Ramlī al Kabīr, Sarīr des. Libya
61 D2 Kalao i. Indon.
61 D2 Kalaotoa i. Indon.
63 B2 Kalasin Thai.
77 C3 Kalāt Afgh.
79 C2 Kalāt Iran
74 A2 Kalat Pak.
50 A2 Kalbarri Austr.
111 C3 Kale Turkey
80 B1 Kalecik Turkey
118 C3 Kalema Dem. Rep. Congo
119 C3 Kalemie Dem. Rep. Congo
62 A1 Kalemyo Myanmar
86 C2 Kalevala Rus. Fed.
Kalgan China see Zhangjiakou
50 B3 Kalgoorlie Austr.
109 C2 Kali Croatia
110 C2 Kaliakra, Nos pt Bulg.
60 A2 Kaliet Indon.
119 C3 Kalima Dem. Rep. Congo
61 C2 Kalimantan reg. Indon.
Kalinin Rus. Fed. see Tver'
88 B3 Kaliningrad Rus. Fed.
91 D2 Kalininskaya Rus. Fed.
88 C3 Kalinkavichy Belarus
134 D1 Kalispell U.S.A.
103 D1 Kalisz Pol.
91 E2 Kalitva r. Rus. Fed.
92 H2 Kalix Sweden
92 H2 Kalixälven r. Sweden
111 C3 Kalkan Turkey
120 A3 Kalkfeld Namibia
100 C2 Kall Ger.
92 I3 Kallavesi l. Fin.
92 F3 Kallsjön l. Sweden
93 G4 Kalmar Sweden
93 G4 Kalmarsund sea chan. Sweden
73 C4 Kalmunai Sri Lanka
119 C3 Kalole Dem. Rep. Congo
120 B2 Kalomo Zambia
128 B2 Kalone Peak Can.
74 B1 Kalpa India
73 B3 Kalpeni atoll India
75 B2 Kalpi India
126 B2 Kaltag U.S.A.
101 D1 Kaltenkirchen Ger.
118 B2 Kaltungo Nigeria
89 E3 Kaluga Rus. Fed.
93 F4 Kalundborg Denmark
74 B1 Kalur Kot Pak.
90 A2 Kalush Ukr.
74 B3 Kalyan India
89 E2 Kalyazin Rus. Fed.
111 C3 Kalymnos Greece
111 C3 Kalymnos i. Greece
119 C3 Kama Dem. Rep. Congo
62 A2 Kama Myanmar
86 E3 Kama r. Rus. Fed.
66 D3 Kamaishi Japan
80 B2 Kaman Turkey
120 A2 Kamanjab Namibia
78 B3 Kamarān i. Yemen
Kamaran Island i. Yemen see Kamarān
74 A2 Kamarod Pak.
50 B3 Kambalda Austr.
119 C4 Kambove Dem. Rep. Congo
160 C4 Kamchatka Basin Bering Sea
83 L3 Kamchatka Peninsula Rus. Fed.
110 C2 Kamchiya r. Bulg.
108 B2 Kamenjak, Rt pt Croatia
76 B1 Kamenka Kazakh.
86 D2 Kamenka Arkhangel'skaya Oblast' Rus. Fed.
87 D3 Kamenka Penzenskaya Oblast' Rus. Fed.
66 C2 Kamenka Primorskiy Kray Rus. Fed.
91 D1 Kamenka Voronezhskaya Oblast' Rus. Fed.
Kamenka-Strumilovskaya Ukr. see Kam"yanka-Buz'ka
91 E3 Kamennomostskiy Rus. Fed.
91 E2 Kamenolomni Rus. Fed.
Kamenongue Angola see Camanongue
83 M2 Kamenskoye Rus. Fed.
Kamenskoye Ukr. see Dniprodzerzhyns'k
91 E2 Kamensk-Shakhtinskiy Rus. Fed.
86 F3 Kamensk-Ural'skiy Rus. Fed.
89 F2 Kameshkovo Rus. Fed.
72 C1 Kamet mt. China/India
75 B1 Kamet mt. China/India
122 A3 Kamiesberge mts S. Africa
122 A3 Kamieskroon S. Africa
129 D1 Kamilukuak Lake Can.
119 C3 Kamina Dem. Rep. Congo
129 E1 Kaminak Lake Can.
90 A1 Kamin'-Kashyrs'kyy Ukr.
119 C3 Kamituga Dem. Rep. Congo
128 B2 Kamloops Can.
54 B1 Kamo N.Z.
116 B3 Kamob Sanha Sudan
118 C3 Kamonia Dem. Rep. Congo
119 D2 Kampala Uganda
60 B1 Kampar r. Indon.
60 B1 Kampar Malaysia
100 B1 Kampen Neth.
119 C3 Kampene Dem. Rep. Congo
63 A2 Kamphaeng Phet Thai.
63 B2 Kâmpóng Cham Cambodia
63 B2 Kâmpóng Chhnăng Cambodia
Kâmpóng Saôm Cambodia see Sihanoukville
63 B2 Kâmpóng Spœ Cambodia
63 B2 Kâmpôt Cambodia
Kampuchea country Asia see Cambodia
129 D2 Kamsack Can.
86 E3 Kamskoye Vodokhranilishche resr Rus. Fed.
117 C4 Kamsuuma Somalia
90 B2 Kam"yanets'-Podil's'kyy Ukr.
90 A1 Kam"yanka-Buz'ka Ukr.
88 B3 Kamyanyets Belarus
91 D2 Kamyshevatskaya Rus. Fed.
87 D3 Kamyshin Rus. Fed.
135 D3 Kanab U.S.A.
118 C3 Kananga Dem. Rep. Congo
87 D3 Kanash Rus. Fed.
138 C3 Kanawha r. U.S.A.
67 C3 Kanazawa Japan
62 A1 Kanbalu Myanmar
63 A2 Kanchanaburi Thai.
73 B3 Kanchipuram India
77 C3 Kandahār Afgh.
86 C2 Kandalaksha Rus. Fed.
61 C2 Kandangan Indon.
74 A2 Kandh Kot Pak.
114 C3 Kandi Benin
74 A2 Kandiaro Pak.
74 B2 Kandla India
53 C2 Kandos Austr.
121 □D2 Kandreho Madag.
73 C4 Kandy Sri Lanka
76 B2 Kandyagash Kazakh.
127 H1 Kane Bassin b. Greenland
91 D2 Kanevskaya Rus. Fed.
122 B1 Kang Botswana
127 I2 Kangaatsiaq Greenland
114 B3 Kangaba Mali
80 B2 Kangal Turkey
79 C2 Kangān Iran
60 B1 Kangar Malaysia
52 A3 Kangaroo Island Austr.
93 H3 Kangasala Fin.
81 C2 Kangāvar Iran
75 C2 Kangchenjunga mt. India/Nepal
70 A2 Kangding China
65 B2 Kangdong N. Korea
61 C2 Kangean, Kepulauan is Indon.
119 D2 Kangen r. Sudan
127 J2 Kangeq c. Greenland
127 I2 Kangerlussuaq inlet Greenland
127 J2 Kangerlussuaq inlet Greenland
127 I2 Kangersuatsiaq Greenland
65 B1 Kanggye N. Korea
131 D2 Kangiqsualujjuaq Can.
127 H2 Kangiqsujuaq Can.
131 C1 Kangirsuk Can.
75 C2 Kangmar China
65 B2 Kangnŭng S. Korea
65 A1 Kangping China
72 D2 Kangto mt. China/India
62 A1 Kani Myanmar
118 C3 Kaniama Dem. Rep. Congo
61 C1 Kanibongan Malaysia
86 D2 Kanin, Poluostrov pen. Rus. Fed.
86 D2 Kanin Nos Rus. Fed.
86 D2 Kanin Nos, Mys c. Rus. Fed.
91 C2 Kaniv Ukr.
52 B3 Kaniva Austr.
93 H3 Kankaanpää Fin.
138 B2 Kankakee U.S.A.
114 B3 Kankan Guinea
75 C2 Kanker India
73 B3 Kannur India
115 C3 Kano Nigeria
122 B3 Kanonpunt pt S. Africa
67 B4 Kanoya Japan
75 C2 Kanpur India
136 C3 Kansas r. U.S.A.
137 D3 Kansas state U.S.A.
137 E3 Kansas City KS U.S.A.
137 E3 Kansas City MO U.S.A.
83 H3 Kansk Rus. Fed.
Kansu prov. China see Gansu
63 B2 Kantaralak Thai.
114 C3 Kantchari Burkina
91 D2 Kantemirovka Rus. Fed.
49 J4 Kanton atoll Kiribati
97 B2 Kanturk Ireland
123 D2 Kanyamazane S. Africa
123 C1 Kanye Botswana
71 C3 Kaohsiung Taiwan
120 A2 Kaokoveld plat. Namibia
114 A3 Kaolack Senegal
120 B2 Kaoma Zambia
118 C3 Kapanga Dem. Rep. Congo
88 C3 Kapatkyevichy Belarus
77 D2 Kapchagay Kazakh.
77 D2 Kapchagayskoye Vodokhranilishche resr Kazakh.
100 B2 Kapellen Belgium
121 B2 Kapiri Mposhi Zambia
127 I2 Kapisillit Greenland
130 B2 Kapiskau r. Can.
61 C1 Kapit Malaysia
63 A3 Kapoe Thai.
117 B4 Kapoeta Sudan
103 D2 Kaposvár Hungary
102 B1 Kappeln Ger.
65 B1 Kapsan N. Korea
Kapsukas Lith. see Marijampolė
61 B2 Kapuas r. Indon.
52 A2 Kapunda Austr.
130 B3 Kapuskasing Can.
53 D2 Kaputar mt. Austr.
103 D2 Kapuvár Hungary
88 C3 Kapyl' Belarus
77 D3 Kaqung China
114 C4 Kara Togo
111 C3 Kara Ada i. Turkey
77 D2 Kara-Balta Kyrg.
76 C1 Karabalyk Kazakh.
81 D1 Karabaur, Uval hills Kazakh./Uzbek.
Kara-Bogaz-Gol Turkm. see Garabogazköl
80 B1 Karabük Turkey
76 C2 Karabutak Kazakh.
111 C2 Karacabey Turkey
111 C2 Karacaköy Turkey
81 C1 Karachayevsk Rus. Fed.
89 D3 Karachev Rus. Fed.
74 A2 Karachi Pak.
77 D2 Karaganda Kazakh.
77 D2 Karagayly Kazakh.
83 L3 Karaginskiy Zaliv b. Rus. Fed.
81 D2 Karaj Iran
Kara-Kala Turkm. see Magtymguly
64 B3 Karakelong i. Indon.
Karaklis Armenia see Vanadzor
77 D2 Kara-Köl Kyrg.
77 D2 Karakol Kyrg.
74 B1 Karakoram Range mts Asia
117 B3 Kara K'orē Eth.
Karakum, Peski des. Kazakh. see Karakum Desert
76 B2 Karakum Desert des. Kazakh.
76 C3 Karakum Desert Turkm.
Karakumy, Peski des. Turkm. see Karakum Desert
80 B2 Karaman Turkey
77 E2 Karamay China
54 B2 Karamea N.Z.
54 B2 Karamea Bight b. N.Z.
80 B2 Karapınar Turkey
122 A2 Karasburg Namibia

86 F1 **Kara Sea** Rus. Fed.
92 I2 **Karasjok** Norway
Kara Strait *str.* Rus. Fed. *see* **Karskiye Vorota, Proliv**
111 D2 **Karasu** Turkey
Karasubazar Ukr. *see* **Bilohirs'k**
77 D1 **Karasuk** Rus. Fed.
77 D2 **Karatau** Kazakh.
77 C2 **Karatau, Khrebet** *mts* Kazakh.
86 F2 **Karatayka** Rus. Fed.
67 A4 **Karatsu** Japan
111 B3 **Karavas** Greece
60 B2 **Karawang** Indon.
81 C2 **Karbalā'** Iraq
103 E2 **Karcag** Hungary
Kardeljevo Croatia *see* **Ploče**
111 B3 **Karditsa** Greece
88 B2 **Kärdla** Estonia
122 B3 **Kareeberge** *mts* S. Africa
75 B2 **Kareli** India
88 C3 **Karelichy** Belarus
92 H2 **Karesuando** Sweden
Karghalik China *see* **Yecheng**
74 B1 **Kargil** India
Kargilik China *see* **Yecheng**
86 C2 **Kargopol'** Rus. Fed.
118 B1 **Kari** Nigeria
121 B2 **Kariba** Zimbabwe
121 B2 **Kariba, Lake** *resr* Zambia/Zimbabwe
60 B2 **Karimata, Pulau-pulau** *is* Indon.
60 B2 **Karimata, Selat** *str.* Indon.
73 B3 **Karimnagar** India
61 C2 **Karimunjawa, Pulau-pulau** *is* Indon.
91 C2 **Karkinits'ka Zatoka** *g.* Ukr.
91 D2 **Karlivka** Ukr.
Karl-Marx-Stadt Ger. *see* **Chemnitz**
109 C1 **Karlovac** Croatia
102 C1 **Karlovy Vary** Czech Rep.
Karlsburg Romania *see* **Alba Iulia**
93 F4 **Karlshamn** Sweden
93 F4 **Karlskoga** Sweden
93 G4 **Karlskrona** Sweden
102 B2 **Karlsruhe** Ger.
93 F4 **Karlstad** Sweden
101 D3 **Karlstadt** Ger.
89 D3 **Karma** Belarus
93 E4 **Karmøy** *i.* Norway
75 D2 **Karnafuli Reservoir** Bangl.
74 B2 **Karnal** India
110 C2 **Karnobat** Bulg.
74 A2 **Karodi** Pak.
121 B2 **Karoi** Zimbabwe
121 C1 **Karonga** Malawi
116 B3 **Karora** Eritrea
111 C3 **Karpathos** Greece
111 C3 **Karpathos** *i.* Greece
111 B3 **Karpenisi** Greece
Karpilovka Belarus *see* **Aktsyabrski**
86 D2 **Karpogory** Rus. Fed.
50 A2 **Karratha** Austr.
81 C1 **Kars** Turkey
88 C2 **Kārsava** Latvia
Karshi Uzbek. *see* **Qarshi**
111 C3 **Karşıyaka** Turkey
86 E2 **Karskiye Vorota, Proliv** *str.* Rus. Fed.
Karskoye More *sea* Rus. Fed. *see* **Kara Sea**
101 E1 **Karstädt** Ger.
111 C2 **Kartal** Turkey
87 F3 **Kartaly** Rus. Fed.
81 C2 **Kārūn, Rūd-e** *r.* Iran
73 B3 **Karwar** India
83 I3 **Karymskoye** Rus. Fed.
111 B3 **Karystos** Greece
111 C3 **Kaş** Turkey
130 B2 **Kasabonika Lake** Can.
118 C3 **Kasaï, Plateau du** Dem. Rep. Congo
118 C4 **Kasaji** Dem. Rep. Congo
121 C2 **Kasama** Zambia
120 B2 **Kasane** Botswana
118 B3 **Kasangulu** Dem. Rep. Congo
73 B3 **Kasaragod** India
129 D1 **Kasba Lake** Can.
120 B2 **Kasempa** Zambia
119 C4 **Kasenga** Dem. Rep. Congo
119 C3 **Kasese** Dem. Rep. Congo
119 D2 **Kasese** Uganda
Kasevo Rus. Fed. *see* **Neftekamsk**
81 D2 **Kāshān** Iran
Kashgar China *see* **Kashi**
77 D3 **Kashi** China
67 D3 **Kashima-nada** *b.* Japan
89 E2 **Kashin** Rus. Fed.
89 E3 **Kashira** Rus. Fed.
89 E3 **Kashirskoye** Rus. Fed.
67 C3 **Kashiwazaki** Japan
76 B3 **Kāshmar** Iran
Kashmir *terr.* Asia *see* **Jammu and Kashmir**
74 A2 **Kashmore** Pak.
119 C3 **Kashyukulu** Dem. Rep. Congo
89 F3 **Kasimov** Rus. Fed.
138 B3 **Kaskaskia** *r.* U.S.A.
93 H3 **Kaskinen** Fin.
119 C3 **Kasongo** Dem. Rep. Congo
118 B3 **Kasongo-Lunda** Dem. Rep. Congo
111 C3 **Kasos** *i.* Greece
Kaspiyskiy Rus. Fed. *see* **Lagan'**
116 B3 **Kassala** Sudan
101 D2 **Kassel** Ger.
115 C1 **Kasserine** Tunisia
80 B1 **Kastamonu** Turkey
Kastellorizon *i.* Greece *see* **Megisti**
111 B2 **Kastoria** Greece
89 D3 **Kastsyukovichy** Belarus
119 D3 **Kasulu** Tanz.
121 C2 **Kasungu** Malawi
139 F1 **Katahdin, Mount** U.S.A.
118 C3 **Katako-Kombe** Dem. Rep. Congo
119 D2 **Katakwi** Uganda
50 A3 **Katanning** Austr.
63 A3 **Katchall** *i.* India
111 B2 **Katerini** Greece
119 D3 **Katesh** Tanz.
128 A2 **Kate's Needle** *mt.* Can./U.S.A.
121 C2 **Katete** Zambia
62 A1 **Katha** Myanmar
50 C1 **Katherine** Austr.
50 C1 **Katherine** *r.* Austr.
74 B2 **Kathiawar** *pen.* India
75 C2 **Kathmandu** Nepal
122 B2 **Kathu** S. Africa
74 B1 **Kathua** India
114 B3 **Kati** Mali
75 C2 **Katihar** India
54 C1 **Katikati** N.Z.
123 C3 **Katikati** S. Africa
120 B2 **Katima Mulilo** Namibia
114 B4 **Katiola** Côte d'Ivoire
123 C2 **Katlehong** S. Africa
Katmandu Nepal *see* **Kathmandu**
111 B3 **Kato Achaïa** Greece
119 C3 **Katompi** Dem. Rep. Congo
53 D2 **Katoomba** Austr.
103 D1 **Katowice** Pol.
80 B3 **Kātrīnā, Jabal** *mt.* Egypt
93 G4 **Katrineholm** Sweden
115 C3 **Katsina** Nigeria
115 C4 **Katsina-Ala** Nigeria
67 D3 **Katsuura** Japan
77 C3 **Kattaqo'rg'on** Uzbek.
93 F4 **Kattegat** *str.* Denmark/Sweden
100 B1 **Katwijk aan Zee** Neth.
101 D3 **Katzenbuckel** *h.* Ger.
49 L1 **Kaua'i** *i.* U.S.A.
93 H3 **Kauhajoki** Fin.
88 B3 **Kaunas** Lith.
115 C3 **Kaura-Namoda** Nigeria
Kaushany Moldova *see* **Căușeni**
92 H2 **Kautokeino** Norway
109 D2 **Kavadarci** Macedonia
109 C2 **Kavajë** Albania
111 B2 **Kavala** Greece
66 C2 **Kavalerovo** Rus. Fed.
73 C3 **Kavali** India
73 B3 **Kavaratti** *atoll* India
110 C2 **Kavarna** Bulg.
59 E3 **Kavieng** P.N.G.
81 D2 **Kavīr, Dasht-e** *des.* Iran
67 C3 **Kawagoe** Japan
54 B1 **Kawakawa** N.Z.
121 B1 **Kawambwa** Zambia
67 C3 **Kawanishi** Japan
130 C3 **Kawartha Lakes** Can.
67 C3 **Kawasaki** Japan
54 C1 **Kawerau** N.Z.
63 A2 **Kawkareik** Myanmar
62 A1 **Kawlin** Myanmar
63 A2 **Kawmapyin** Myanmar
116 B2 **Kawm Umbū** Egypt
63 A2 **Kawthaung** Myanmar
Kaxgar China *see* **Kashi**
77 D3 **Kaxgar He** *r.* China
114 B3 **Kaya** Burkina
111 C3 **Kayacı Dağı** *h.* Turkey
121 C1 **Kayambi** Zambia
61 C1 **Kayan** *r.* Indon.
136 B2 **Kaycee** U.S.A.
Kaydanovo Belarus *see* **Dzyarzhynsk**
142 A1 **Kayenta** U.S.A.
114 A3 **Kayes** Mali
77 D2 **Kaynar** Kazakh.
80 B2 **Kayseri** Turkey
134 D2 **Kaysville** U.S.A.
60 B2 **Kayuagung** Indon.
Kazakhskaya S.S.R. *country* Asia *see* **Kazakhstan**
77 D1 **Kazakhskiy Melkosopochnik** *plain* Kazakh.
76 B2 **Kazakhskiy Zaliv** *b.* Kazakh.
76 C2 **Kazakhstan** *country* Asia
Kazakhstan Kazakh. *see* **Aksay**
87 D3 **Kazan'** Rus. Fed.
Kazandzhik Turkm. *see* **Bereket**
110 C2 **Kazanlŭk** Bulg.
Kazan-rettō *is* Japan *see* **Volcano Islands**
76 A2 **Kazbek** *mt.* Georgia/Rus. Fed.
81 D3 **Kāzerūn** Iran
103 E2 **Kazincbarcika** Hungary
118 C3 **Kazumba** Dem. Rep. Congo
66 D2 **Kazuno** Japan
86 F2 **Kazymskiy Mys** Rus. Fed.
111 B3 **Kea** *i.* Greece
97 C1 **Keady** U.K.
137 D2 **Kearney** U.S.A.
142 A2 **Kearny** U.S.A.
115 C1 **Kebili** Tunisia
116 A3 **Kebkabiya** Sudan
92 G2 **Kebnekaise** *mt.* Sweden
117 C4 **K'ebrī Dehar** Eth.
60 B2 **Kebumen** Indon.
128 B2 **Kechika** *r.* Can.
111 D3 **Keçiborlu** Turkey
103 D2 **Kecskemét** Hungary
88 B2 **Kėdainiai** Lith.
114 A3 **Kédougou** Senegal
103 D1 **Kędzierzyn-Koźle** Pol.
128 B1 **Keele** *r.* Can.
128 A1 **Keele Peak** Can.
Keelung Taiwan *see* **Chilung**
139 E2 **Keene** U.S.A.
122 A2 **Keetmanshoop** Namibia
129 E3 **Keewatin** Can.
Kefallonia *i.* Greece *see* **Cephalonia**
59 C3 **Kefamenanu** Indon.
92 □A3 **Keflavík** Iceland
77 D2 **Kegen** Kazakh.
128 C2 **Keg River** Can.
88 C2 **Kehra** Estonia
62 A1 **Kehsi Mansam** Myanmar
98 C3 **Keighley** U.K.
88 B2 **Keila** Estonia
122 B2 **Keimoes** S. Africa
92 I3 **Keitele** *l.* Fin.
52 B3 **Keith** Austr.
96 C2 **Keith** U.K.
128 B1 **Keith Arm** *b.* Can.
134 B2 **Keizer** U.S.A.
103 E2 **Kékes** *mt.* Hungary
117 C4 **K'elafo** Eth.
Kelang Malaysia *see* **Klang**
92 J2 **Keles-Uayv, Gora** *h.* Rus. Fed.
102 C2 **Kelheim** Ger.
76 C3 **Kelif Uzboýy** *marsh* Turkm.
80 B1 **Kelkit** *r.* Turkey
128 B1 **Keller Lake** Can.
134 C1 **Kellogg** U.S.A.
92 I2 **Kelloselkä** Fin.
97 C2 **Kells** Ireland
88 B2 **Kelmė** Lith.
115 D4 **Kélo** Chad
128 C3 **Kelowna** Can.
96 C3 **Kelso** U.K.
134 B1 **Kelso** U.S.A.
60 B1 **Keluang** Malaysia
129 D2 **Kelvington** Can.
86 C2 **Kem'** Rus. Fed.
Ke Macina Mali *see* **Macina**
128 B2 **Kemano (abandoned)** Can.
118 C2 **Kembé** C.A.R.
111 C3 **Kemer** Turkey
82 G3 **Kemerovo** Rus. Fed.
92 H2 **Kemi** Fin.
92 I2 **Kemijärvi** Fin.
92 I2 **Kemijärvi** *l.* Fin.
92 I2 **Kemijoki** *r.* Fin.
136 A2 **Kemmerer** U.S.A.
92 I3 **Kempele** Fin.
55 G2 **Kemp Land** *reg.* Antarctica
55 A2 **Kemp Peninsula** Antarctica
53 D2 **Kempsey** Austr.
130 C3 **Kempt, Lac** *l.* Can.
102 C2 **Kempten (Allgäu)** Ger.
123 C2 **Kempton Park** S. Africa
61 C2 **Kemujan** *i.* Indon.
126 B2 **Kenai** U.S.A.
129 D2 **Kenaston** Can.
98 B2 **Kendal** U.K.
141 D3 **Kendall** U.S.A.
61 D2 **Kendari** Indon.
60 C2 **Kendawangan** Indon.
115 D3 **Kendégué** Chad
114 A4 **Kenema** Sierra Leone
118 B3 **Kenge** Dem. Rep. Congo
62 A1 **Kengtung** Myanmar
122 B2 **Kenhardt** S. Africa
114 B1 **Kenitra** Morocco
97 B3 **Kenmare** Ireland
136 C1 **Kenmare** U.S.A.
97 A3 **Kenmare River** *inlet* Ireland
100 C3 **Kenn** Ger.
143 C2 **Kenna** U.S.A.
139 F2 **Kennebec** *r.* U.S.A.
Kennedy, Cape *c.* U.S.A. *see* **Canaveral, Cape**
140 B3 **Kenner** U.S.A.
99 C4 **Kennet** *r.* U.K.
137 E3 **Kennett** U.S.A.
134 C1 **Kennewick** U.S.A.
130 A3 **Kenora** Can.
138 B2 **Kenosha** U.S.A.
142 C2 **Kent** U.S.A.
77 C2 **Kentau** Kazakh.
138 B3 **Kentucky** *r.* U.S.A.
138 C3 **Kentucky** *state* U.S.A.
138 B3 **Kentucky Lake** U.S.A.
140 B2 **Kentwood** U.S.A.
119 D2 **Kenya** *country* Africa
119 D3 **Kenya, Mount** *mt.* Kenya
60 B1 **Kenyir, Tasik** *resr* Malaysia
137 E2 **Keokuk** U.S.A.
75 C2 **Keonjhar** India
111 C3 **Kepsut** Turkey
52 B3 **Kerang** Austr.
91 D2 **Kerch** Ukr.
59 D3 **Kerema** P.N.G.
128 C3 **Keremeos** Can.
116 B3 **Keren** Eritrea
81 C2 **Kerend** Iran
159 E7 **Kerguélen, Îles** *is* Indian Ocean
159 E7 **Kerguelen Plateau** Indian Ocean
119 D3 **Kericho** Kenya
54 B1 **Kerikeri** N.Z.
60 B2 **Kerinci, Gunung** *vol.* Indon.
Kerintji *vol.* Indon. *see* **Kerinci, Gunung**
100 C2 **Kerkrade** Neth.
111 A3 **Kerkyra** Greece
Kerkyra *i.* Greece *see* **Corfu**
116 B3 **Kerma** Sudan
49 J7 **Kermadec Islands** S. Pacific Ocean
79 C1 **Kermān** Iran
81 C2 **Kermānshāh** Iran
Kermine Uzbek. *see* **Navoiy**
143 C2 **Kermit** U.S.A.
135 C3 **Kern** *r.* U.S.A.
114 B4 **Kérouané** Guinea
100 C2 **Kerpen** Ger.
129 D2 **Kerrobert** Can.
143 D2 **Kerrville** U.S.A.
97 B2 **Kerry Head** *hd* Ireland
Keryneia Cyprus *see* **Kyrenia**
130 B2 **Kesagami Lake** Can.
111 C2 **Keşan** Turkey
66 D3 **Kesennuma** Japan
74 B2 **Keshod** India
100 C2 **Kessel** Neth.
98 B2 **Keswick** U.K.
103 D2 **Keszthely** Hungary
82 G3 **Ket'** *r.* Rus. Fed.
60 C2 **Ketapang** Indon.
128 A2 **Ketchikan** U.S.A.
134 D2 **Ketchum** U.S.A.
114 B4 **Kete Krachi** Ghana
118 B2 **Kétté** Cameroon
99 C3 **Kettering** U.K.
138 C3 **Kettering** U.S.A.
134 C1 **Kettle River Range** *mts* U.S.A.
93 H3 **Keuruu** Fin.
100 C2 **Kevelaer** Ger.
138 B2 **Kewanee** U.S.A.
138 B1 **Keweenaw Bay** U.S.A.
138 B1 **Keweenaw Peninsula** U.S.A.
141 D3 **Key Largo** U.S.A.
99 B4 **Keynsham** U.K.
139 D3 **Keyser** U.S.A.
141 D4 **Key West** U.S.A.
123 C2 **Kgotsong** S. Africa
69 F1 **Khabarovsk** Rus. Fed.
91 D3 **Khadyzhensk** Rus. Fed.
75 D2 **Khagrachari** Bangl.
74 A2 **Khairpur** Pak.
122 B1 **Khakhea** Botswana
76 B3 **Khalīlābād** Iran
86 F2 **Khal'mer"yu** Rus. Fed.
68 C1 **Khamar-Daban, Khrebet** *mts* Rus. Fed.
74 B2 **Khambhat** India
74 B3 **Khambhat, Gulf of** India
74 B2 **Khamgaon** India
79 C2 **Khamīr** Iran
78 B3 **Khamir** Yemen
78 B3 **Khamis Mushayţ** Saudi Arabia
77 C3 **Khānābād** Afgh.
74 B2 **Khandwa** India
83 K2 **Khandyga** Rus. Fed.
74 B1 **Khanewal** Pak.
Khan Hung Vietnam *see* **Soc Trăng**
83 J3 **Khani** Rus. Fed.
66 B2 **Khanka, Lake** China/Rus. Fed.
115 C2 **Khannfoussa** *h.* Alg.
74 B2 **Khanpur** Pak.
77 D2 **Khantau** Kazakh.
83 H2 **Khantayskoye, Ozero** *l.* Rus. Fed.
86 F2 **Khanty-Mansiysk** Rus. Fed.
63 A3 **Khao Chum Thong** Thai.
63 A2 **Khao Laem, Ang Kep Nam** Thai.
74 B1 **Khaplu** Pak.
87 D4 **Kharabali** Rus. Fed.
75 C2 **Kharagpur** India
79 C2 **Khārān** *r.* Iran
Kharga Oasis *oasis* Egypt *see* **Wāḥāt al Khārijah**
74 B2 **Khargon** India
91 D2 **Kharkiv** Ukr.
Khar'kov Ukr. *see* **Kharkiv**
111 C2 **Kharmanli** Bulg.
89 F2 **Kharovsk** Rus. Fed.
116 B3 **Khartoum** Sudan
87 D4 **Khasavyurt** Rus. Fed.
79 D2 **Khāsh** Iran
86 F2 **Khashgort** Rus. Fed.
78 A3 **Khashm el Girba** Sudan
78 A3 **Khashm el Girba Dam** Sudan
81 C1 **Khashuri** Georgia
75 D2 **Khasi Hills** India
111 C2 **Khaskovo** Bulg.
83 H2 **Khatanga** Rus. Fed.
123 C3 **Khayamnandi** S. Africa
78 A2 **Khaybar** Saudi Arabia
122 A3 **Khayelitsha** S. Africa
107 D2 **Khemis Miliana** Alg.
63 B2 **Khemmarat** Thai.
115 C1 **Khenchela** Alg.
81 D3 **Kherāmeh** Iran
91 C2 **Kherson** Ukr.
83 H2 **Kheta** *r.* Rus. Fed.
69 D1 **Khilok** Rus. Fed.
89 E2 **Khimki** Rus. Fed.
74 A2 **Khipro** Pak.
89 E3 **Khlevnoye** Rus. Fed.
63 B2 **Khlung** Thai.
90 B2 **Khmel'nyts'kyy** Ukr.
Khmer Republic *country* Asia *see* **Cambodia**
76 B1 **Khobda** Kazakh.
Khodzheyli Uzbek. *see* **Xo'jayli**
89 E3 **Khokhol'skiy** Rus. Fed.
74 B2 **Khokhropar** Pak.
74 A1 **Kholm** Afgh.
89 D2 **Kholm** Rus. Fed.
89 D2 **Kholm-Zhirkovskiy** Rus. Fed.
122 A1 **Khomas Highland** *hills* Namibia
89 E3 **Khomutovo** Rus. Fed.
79 C2 **Khonj** Iran

63 B2 Khon Kaen Thai.
62 A1 Khonsa India
83 K2 Khonuu Rus. Fed.
86 E2 Khoreyver Rus. Fed.
69 D1 Khorinsk Rus. Fed.
120 A3 Khorixas Namibia
66 B2 Khorol Rus. Fed.
91 C2 Khorol Ukr.
81 C2 Khorramābād Iran
81 C2 Khorramshahr Iran
77 D3 Khorugh Tajik.
77 C3 Khōst Afgh.
Khotan China see Hotan
90 B2 Khotyn Ukr.
114 B1 Khouribga Morocco
88 C3 Khoyniki Belarus
62 A1 Khreum Myanmar
76 B1 Khromtau Kazakh.
Khrushchev Ukr. see Svitlovods'k
90 B2 Khrystynivka Ukr.
123 B1 Khudumelapye Botswana
77 C2 Khŭjand Tajik.
63 B2 Khu Khan Thai.
78 A2 Khulays Saudi Arabia
75 C2 Khulna Bangl.
Khūnīnshahr Iran see Khorramshahr
81 D2 Khunsar Iran
79 B2 Khurays Saudi Arabia
74 B1 Khushab Pak.
90 A2 Khust Ukr.
123 C2 Khutsong S. Africa
74 A2 Khuzdar Pak.
81 D3 Khvormūj Iran
81 C2 Khvoy Iran
89 D2 Khvoynaya Rus. Fed.
77 D3 Khyber Pass Afgh./Pak.
53 D2 Kiama Austr.
64 B3 Kiamba Phil.
119 C3 Kiambi Dem. Rep. Congo
Kiangsi prov. China see Jiangxi
Kiangsu prov. China see Jiangsu
119 D3 Kibaha Tanz.
119 D3 Kibaya Tanz.
119 D3 Kibiti Tanz.
119 C3 Kibombo Dem. Rep. Congo
119 D3 Kibondo Tanz.
119 D2 Kibre Mengist Eth.
119 D3 Kibungo Rwanda
111 B2 Kičevo Macedonia
114 C3 Kidal Mali
99 B3 Kidderminster U.K.
114 A3 Kidira Senegal
74 B1 Kidmang India
54 C1 Kidnappers, Cape N.Z.
102 C1 Kiel Ger.
103 E1 Kielce Pol.
98 B2 Kielder Water resr U.K.
119 C4 Kienge Dem. Rep. Congo
90 C1 Kiev Ukr.
114 A3 Kiffa Maur.
119 D3 Kigali Rwanda
119 C3 Kigoma Tanz.
88 B2 Kihnu i. Estonia
92 I2 Kiiminki Fin.
67 B4 Kii-suidō sea chan. Japan
109 D1 Kikinda Serbia
119 C3 Kikondja Dem. Rep. Congo
59 D3 Kikori P.N.G.
59 D3 Kikori r. P.N.G.
118 B3 Kikwit Dem. Rep. Congo
65 B1 Kilchu N. Korea
97 C2 Kilcock Ireland
97 C2 Kildare Ireland
118 B3 Kilembe Dem. Rep. Congo
143 E2 Kilgore U.S.A.
119 D3 Kilifi Kenya
119 D3 Kilimanjaro vol. Tanz.
119 D3 Kilindoni Tanz.
80 B2 Kilis Turkey
90 B2 Kiliya Ukr.
97 B2 Kilkee Ireland
97 D1 Kilkeel U.K.
97 C2 Kilkenny Ireland
111 B2 Kilkis Greece
97 B1 Killala Ireland
97 B1 Killala Bay Ireland
97 B2 Killaloe Ireland
128 C2 Killam Can.
97 B2 Killarney Ireland
143 D2 Killeen U.S.A.
96 B2 Killin U.K.
131 D1 Killiniq Can.
97 B2 Killorglin Ireland
97 B1 Killybegs Ireland
96 B3 Kilmarnock U.K.
53 B3 Kilmore Austr.
119 D3 Kilosa Tanz.
97 B2 Kilrush Ireland
119 C3 Kilwa Dem. Rep. Congo
119 D3 Kilwa Masoko Tanz.
119 D3 Kimambi Tanz.
52 A2 Kimba Austr.
136 C2 Kimball U.S.A.
59 E3 Kimbe P.N.G.
128 C3 Kimberley Can.
122 B2 Kimberley S. Africa
50 B1 Kimberley Plateau Austr.
65 B1 Kimch'aek N. Korea
65 B2 Kimch'ŏn S. Korea
65 B2 Kimhae S. Korea
127 H2 Kimmirut Can.
89 E3 Kimovsk Rus. Fed.
118 C3 Kimpanga Dem. Rep. Congo
118 B3 Kimpese Dem. Rep. Congo
89 E2 Kimry Rus. Fed.
61 C1 Kinabalu, Gunung mt. Malaysia
128 C2 Kinbasket Lake Can.
96 C1 Kinbrace U.K.
130 B3 Kincardine Can.
62 A1 Kinchang Myanmar
119 C3 Kinda Dem. Rep. Congo
98 C3 Kinder Scout h. U.K.
129 D2 Kindersley Can.
114 A3 Kindia Guinea
119 C3 Kindu Dem. Rep. Congo
89 F2 Kineshma Rus. Fed.
118 B3 Kingandu Dem. Rep. Congo
51 E2 Kingaroy Austr.
135 B3 King City U.S.A.
130 C2 King George Islands Can.
88 C2 Kingisepp Rus. Fed.
51 D3 King Island Austr.
Kingisseppa Estonia see Kuressaare
50 B1 King Leopold Ranges hills Austr.
142 A1 Kingman U.S.A.
135 B3 Kings r. U.S.A.
52 A3 Kingscote Austr.
97 C2 Kingscourt Ireland
99 D3 King's Lynn U.K.
50 B1 King Sound b. Austr.
134 D2 Kings Peak U.S.A.
141 D1 Kingsport U.S.A.
51 D4 Kingston Austr.
130 C3 Kingston Can.
146 C3 Kingston Jamaica
139 E2 Kingston U.S.A.
52 A3 Kingston South East Austr.
98 C3 Kingston upon Hull U.K.
147 D3 Kingstown St Vincent
143 D3 Kingsville U.S.A.
99 B4 Kingswood U.K.
96 B2 Kingussie U.K.
126 F2 King William Island Can.
123 C3 King William's Town S. Africa
67 D3 Kinka-san i. Japan
96 B2 Kinlochleven U.K.
93 F4 Kinna Sweden
97 B3 Kinsale Ireland
118 B3 Kinshasa Dem. Rep. Congo
141 E1 Kinston U.S.A.
88 B2 Kintai Lith.
114 B4 Kintampo Ghana
96 C2 Kintore U.K.
96 B3 Kintyre pen. U.K.
62 A1 Kin-U Myanmar
119 D3 Kiomboi Tanz.
130 C3 Kipawa, Lac l. Can.
119 D3 Kipembawe Tanz.
119 D3 Kipengere Range mts Tanz.
129 D2 Kipling Can.
Kipling Station Can. see Kipling
119 C4 Kipushi Dem. Rep. Congo
119 C4 Kipushia Dem. Rep. Congo
101 D2 Kirchhain Ger.
101 D3 Kirchheim-Bolanden Ger.
83 I3 Kirenga r. Rus. Fed.
83 I3 Kirensk Rus. Fed.
89 E3 Kireyevsk Rus. Fed.
Kirghizia country Asia see Kyrgyzstan
77 D2 Kirghiz Range mts Kazakh./Kyrg.
Kirgizskaya S.S.R. country Asia see Kyrgyzstan
49 J4 Kiribati country Pacific Ocean
80 B2 Kırıkkale Turkey
89 E2 Kirillov Rus. Fed.
Kirin China see Jilin
Kirin prov. China see Jilin
Kirinyaga mt. Kenya see Kenya, Mount
89 D2 Kirishi Rus. Fed.
48 L3 Kiritimati atoll Kiribati
111 C3 Kırkağaç Turkey
98 B3 Kirkby U.K.
98 B2 Kirkby Stephen U.K.
96 C2 Kirkcaldy U.K.
96 B3 Kirkcudbright U.K.
92 J2 Kirkenes Norway
88 B1 Kirkkonummi Fin.
130 B3 Kirkland Lake Can.
111 C2 Kırklareli Turkey
137 E2 Kirksville U.S.A.
81 C2 Kirkūk Iraq
96 C1 Kirkwall U.K.
Kīrov Kazakh. see Balpyk Bi
89 D3 Kirov Kaluzhskaya Oblast' Rus. Fed.
86 D3 Kirov Kirovskaya Oblast' Rus. Fed.
Kirovabad Azer. see Gäncä
Kirovakan Armenia see Vanadzor
Kirovo Ukr. see Kirovohrad
86 E3 Kirovo-Chepetsk Rus. Fed.
Kirovo-Chepetskiy Rus. Fed. see Kirovo-Chepetsk
91 C2 Kirovohrad Ukr.
86 C2 Kirovsk Rus. Fed.
91 D2 Kirovs'ke Ukr.
Kirovskiy Kazakh. see Balpyk Bi
66 B1 Kirovskiy Rus. Fed.
96 C2 Kirriemuir U.K.
86 E3 Kirs Rus. Fed.
87 D3 Kirsanov Rus. Fed.
80 B2 Kırşehir Turkey
74 A2 Kirthar Range mts Pak.
92 H2 Kiruna Sweden
67 C3 Kiryū Japan
89 E2 Kirzhach Rus. Fed.
119 D3 Kisaki Tanz.
119 C2 Kisangani Dem. Rep. Congo
118 B3 Kisantu Dem. Rep. Congo
60 A1 Kisaran Indon.
82 G3 Kiselevsk Rus. Fed.
75 C2 Kishanganj India
115 C4 Kishi Nigeria
Kishinev Moldova see Chișinău
67 C4 Kishiwada Japan
77 D1 Kishkenekol' Kazakh.
75 D2 Kishoreganj Bangl.
74 B1 Kishtwar India
119 D3 Kisii Kenya
103 D2 Kiskunfélegyháza Hungary
103 D2 Kiskunhalas Hungary
87 D4 Kislovodsk Rus. Fed.
117 C5 Kismaayo Somalia
Kismayu Somalia see Kismaayo
119 C3 Kisoro Uganda
111 B3 Kissamos Greece
114 A4 Kissidougou Guinea
141 D3 Kissimmee U.S.A.
141 D3 Kissimmee, Lake U.S.A.
129 D2 Kississing Lake Can.
Kistna r. India see Krishna
119 D3 Kisumu Kenya
103 E2 Kisvárda Hungary
Kisykkamys Kazakh. see Dzhangala
114 B3 Kita Mali
67 D3 Kitaibaraki Japan
66 D3 Kitakami Japan
66 D3 Kitakami-gawa r. Japan
67 B4 Kita-Kyūshu Japan
119 D2 Kitale Kenya
66 D2 Kitami Japan
130 B3 Kitchener Can.
93 J3 Kitee Fin.
119 D2 Kitgum Uganda
128 B2 Kitimat Can.
118 B3 Kitona Dem. Rep. Congo
92 H2 Kittilä Fin.
141 E1 Kitty Hawk U.S.A.
119 D3 Kitunda Tanz.
128 B2 Kitwanga Can.
121 B2 Kitwe Zambia
102 C2 Kitzbühel Austria
101 E3 Kitzingen Ger.
59 D3 Kiunga P.N.G.
92 I3 Kiuruvesi Fin.
92 I2 Kivalo ridge Fin.
90 B1 Kivertsi Ukr.
88 C2 Kiviõli Estonia
91 D2 Kivsharivka Ukr.
119 C3 Kivu, Lake Dem. Rep. Congo/Rwanda
111 C2 Kıyıköy Turkey
86 E3 Kizel Rus. Fed.
111 C3 Kızılca Dağ mt. Turkey
80 B1 Kızılırmak r. Turkey
87 D4 Kizlyar Rus. Fed.
Kizyl-Arbat Turkm. see Serdar
92 I1 Kjøllefjord Norway
92 G2 Kjøpsvik Norway
102 C1 Kladno Czech Rep.
102 C2 Klagenfurt Austria
88 B2 Klaipėda Lith.
94 B1 Klaksvík Faroe Is
134 B2 Klamath r. U.S.A.
134 B2 Klamath Falls U.S.A.
134 B2 Klamath Mountains U.S.A.
60 B1 Klang Malaysia
102 C2 Klatovy Czech Rep.
122 A3 Klawer S. Africa
128 A2 Klawock U.S.A.
128 B2 Kleena Kleene Can.
122 B2 Kleinbegin S. Africa
122 A2 Klein Karas Namibia
122 A2 Kleinsee S. Africa
123 C2 Klerksdorp S. Africa
90 B1 Klesiv Ukr.
89 D3 Kletnya Rus. Fed.
100 C2 Kleve Ger.
88 C3 Klichaw Belarus
89 D3 Klimavichy Belarus
89 D3 Klimovo Rus. Fed.
89 E2 Klimovsk Rus. Fed.
89 E2 Klin Rus. Fed.
101 F2 Klingenthal Ger.
101 F2 Klínovec mt. Czech Rep.
93 G4 Klintehamn Sweden
89 D3 Klintsy Rus. Fed.
109 C2 Ključ Bos.-Herz.
103 D1 Kłodzko Pol.
100 C1 Kloosterhaar Neth.
103 D2 Klosterneuburg Austria
101 E1 Klötze (Altmark) Ger.
128 A1 Kluane Lake Can.
Kluang Malaysia see Keluang
103 D1 Kluczbork Pol.
Klukhori Rus. Fed. see Karachayevsk
128 A2 Klukwan U.S.A.
89 F2 Klyaz'ma r. Rus. Fed.
88 C3 Klyetsk Belarus
83 L3 Klyuchi Rus. Fed.
98 C2 Knaresborough U.K.
93 F3 Knästen h. Sweden
129 E2 Knee Lake Can.
101 E1 Knesebeck Ger.
101 E3 Knetzgau Ger.
109 C2 Knin Croatia
103 C2 Knittelfeld Austria
109 D2 Knjaževac Serbia
Knob Lake Can. see Schefferville
97 B3 Knockboy h. Ireland
100 A2 Knokke-Heist Belgium
141 D1 Knoxville U.S.A.
127 H1 Knud Rasmussen Land reg. Greenland
122 B3 Knysna S. Africa
60 B2 Koba Indon.
67 C4 Kōbe Japan
København Denmark see Copenhagen
100 C2 Koblenz Ger.
59 C3 Kobroör i. Indon.
88 B3 Kobryn Belarus
Kocaeli Turkey see İzmit
111 B2 Kočani Macedonia
111 C2 Kocasu r. Turkey
109 B1 Kočevje Slovenia
75 C2 Koch Bihar India
89 F3 Kochetovka Rus. Fed.
73 B4 Kochi India
67 B4 Kōchi Japan
87 D4 Kochubey Rus. Fed.
75 C2 Kodarma India
126 B3 Kodiak U.S.A.
126 B3 Kodiak Island U.S.A.
123 C1 Kodibeleng Botswana
117 B4 Kodok Sudan
90 B2 Kodyma Ukr.
111 C2 Kodzhaele mt. Bulg./Greece
122 A2 Koës Namibia
122 C2 Koffiefontein S. Africa
114 B4 Koforidua Ghana
67 C3 Kōfu Japan
131 D2 Kogaluk r. Can.
114 B3 Kogoni Mali
74 B1 Kohat Pak.
72 D2 Kohima India
88 C2 Kohtla-Järve Estonia
128 A1 Koidern Can.
Kokand Uzbek. see Qo'qon
88 B2 Kökar Fin.
Kokchetav Kazakh. see Kokshetau
122 A2 Kokerboom Namibia
88 C3 Kokhanava Belarus
89 F2 Kokhma Rus. Fed.
92 H3 Kokkola Fin.
88 C2 Koknese Latvia
138 B2 Kokomo U.S.A.
122 B1 Kokong Botswana
123 C2 Kokosi S. Africa
77 E2 Kokpekty Kazakh.
77 C1 Kokshetau Kazakh.
131 D2 Koksoak r. Can.
123 C3 Kokstad S. Africa
Koktokay China see Fuyun
61 D2 Kolaka Indon.
86 C2 Kola Peninsula Rus. Fed.
92 H2 Kolari Fin.
Kolarovgrad Bulg. see Shumen
114 A3 Kolda Senegal
93 E4 Kolding Denmark
119 C2 Kole Dem. Rep. Congo
107 D2 Koléa Alg.
86 D2 Kolguyev, Ostrov i. Rus. Fed.
73 B3 Kolhapur India
88 B2 Kolkasrags pt Latvia
75 C2 Kolkata India
73 B4 Kollam India
100 C1 Kollum Neth.
Köln Ger. see Cologne
103 D1 Koło Pol.
103 D1 Kołobrzeg Pol.
114 B3 Kolokani Mali
89 E2 Kolomna Rus. Fed.
90 B2 Kolomyya Ukr.
114 B3 Kolondiéba Mali
61 D2 Kolonedale Indon.
122 B2 Kolonkwaneng Botswana
82 G3 Kolpashevo Rus. Fed.
89 E3 Kolpny Rus. Fed.
Kol'skiy Poluostrov pen. Rus. Fed. see Kola Peninsula
78 B3 Koluli Eritrea
92 F3 Kolvereid Norway
119 C4 Kolwezi Dem. Rep. Congo
83 L2 Kolyma r. Rus. Fed.
Kolyma Lowland lowland Rus. Fed. see Kolymskaya Nizmennost'
Kolyma Range mts Rus. Fed. see Kolymskiy, Khrebet
83 L2 Kolymskaya Nizmennost' lowland Rus. Fed.
83 M2 Kolymskiy, Khrebet mts Rus. Fed.
122 A2 Komaggas S. Africa
67 C3 Komaki Japan
83 M3 Komandorskiye Ostrova is Rus. Fed.
103 D2 Komárno Slovakia
123 D2 Komati r. S. Africa/Swaziland
123 D2 Komatipoort S. Africa
67 C3 Komatsu Japan
120 A2 Kombat Namibia
119 C3 Kombe Dem. Rep. Congo
Komintern Ukr. see Marhanets'
90 C2 Kominternivs'ke Ukr.
109 C2 Komiža Croatia
103 D2 Komló Hungary
Kommunarsk Ukr. see Alchevs'k
118 B3 Komono Congo
111 C2 Komotini Greece
Kompong Som Cambodia see Sihanoukville
Komrat Moldova see Comrat
122 B3 Komsberg mts S. Africa
83 H1 Komsomolets, Ostrov i. Rus. Fed.
89 F2 Komsomol'sk Rus. Fed.
91 C2 Komsomol's'k Ukr.
Komsomol'skiy Rus. Fed. see Yugorsk

83 M2 **Komsomol'skiy** *Chukotskiy Avtonomnyy Okrug* Rus. Fed.
87 D4 **Komsomol'skiy** *Respublika Kalmykiya-Khalm'g-Tangch* Rus. Fed.
83 K3 **Komsomol'sk-na-Amure** Rus. Fed.
89 E2 **Konakovo** Rus. Fed.
75 C3 **Kondagaon** India
86 F2 **Kondinskoye** Rus. Fed.
Kondinskoye Rus. Fed. *see* **Oktyabr'skoye**
119 D3 **Kondoa** Tanz.
86 C2 **Kondopoga** Rus. Fed.
89 E3 **Kondrovo** Rus. Fed.
127 J2 **Kong Christian IX Land** *reg.* Greenland
127 K2 **Kong Christian X Land** *reg.* Greenland
127 J2 **Kong Frederik VI Kyst** *coastal area* Greenland
65 B2 **Kongju** S. Korea
119 C3 **Kongolo** Dem. Rep. Congo
93 E4 **Kongsberg** Norway
93 F3 **Kongsvinger** Norway
77 D3 **Kongur Shan** *mt.* China
100 C2 **Königswinter** Ger.
103 D1 **Konin** Pol.
109 C2 **Konjic** Bos.-Herz.
122 A2 **Konkiep** *watercourse* Namibia
86 D2 **Konosha** Rus. Fed.
91 C1 **Konotop** Ukr.
103 E1 **Końskie** Pol.
Konstantinograd Ukr. *see* **Krasnohrad**
102 B2 **Konstanz** Ger.
115 C3 **Kontagora** Nigeria
63 B2 **Kon Tum** Vietnam
63 B2 **Kon Tum, Cao Nguyên** Vietnam
80 B2 **Konya** Turkey
77 D2 **Konyrat** Kazakh.
100 C3 **Konz** Ger.
86 E3 **Konzhakovskiy Kamen', Gora** *mt.* Rus. Fed.
134 C1 **Kooskia** U.S.A.
128 C3 **Kootenay Lake** Can.
53 D2 **Kootingal** Austr.
122 B3 **Kootjieskolk** S. Africa
92 □B2 **Kópasker** Iceland
108 B1 **Koper** Slovenia
93 G4 **Köping** Sweden
123 C1 **Kopong** Botswana
93 G4 **Kopparberg** Sweden
109 C1 **Koprivnica** Croatia
89 F3 **Korablino** Rus. Fed.
73 C3 **Koraput** India
75 C2 **Korba** India
101 D2 **Korbach** Ger.
109 D2 **Korçë** Albania
109 C2 **Korčula** Croatia
109 C2 **Korčula** *i.* Croatia
70 C2 **Korea Bay** *g.* China/N. Korea
65 B1 **Korea, North** *country* Asia
65 B2 **Korea, South** *country* Asia
65 B3 **Korea Strait** Japan/S. Korea
89 D3 **Korenevo** Rus. Fed.
91 D2 **Korenovsk** Rus. Fed.
Korenovskaya Rus. Fed. *see* **Korenovsk**
90 B1 **Korets'** Ukr.
111 C2 **Körfez** Turkey
114 B4 **Korhogo** Côte d'Ivoire
Korinthos Greece *see* **Corinth**
103 D2 **Kőris-hegy** *h.* Hungary
109 D2 **Koritnik** *mt.* Albania/Kosovo
Koritsa Albania *see* **Korçë**
67 D3 **Kōriyama** Japan
87 F3 **Korkino** Rus. Fed.
111 D3 **Korkuteli** Turkey
77 E2 **Korla** China
103 D2 **Körmend** Hungary
49 I5 **Koro** *i.* Fiji
114 B3 **Koro** Mali
131 D2 **Koroc** *r.* Can.
91 D1 **Korocha** Rus. Fed.
119 D3 **Korogwe** Tanz.
59 C2 **Koror** Palau
103 E2 **Körös** *r.* Hungary
90 B1 **Korosten'** Ukr.
90 B1 **Korostyshiv** Ukr.
115 D3 **Koro Toro** Chad
93 H3 **Korpo** Fin.
66 D1 **Korsakov** Rus. Fed.
91 C2 **Korsun'-Shevchenkivs'kyy** Ukr.
103 E1 **Korsze** Pol.
116 B3 **Korti** Sudan
100 A2 **Kortrijk** Belgium
83 L3 **Koryakskaya, Sopka** *vol.* Rus. Fed.
83 M2 **Koryakskoye Nagor'ye** *mts* Rus. Fed.
86 D2 **Koryazhma** Rus. Fed.
65 B2 **Koryŏng** S. Korea
91 C1 **Koryukivka** Ukr.
111 C3 **Kos** Greece
111 C3 **Kos** *i.* Greece
91 D2 **Kosa Biryuchyy Ostriv** *i.* Ukr.
65 B2 **Kosan** N. Korea
103 D1 **Kościan** Pol.
Kosciusko, Mount *mt.* Austr. *see* **Kosciuszko, Mount**
53 C3 **Kosciuszko, Mount** Austr.
77 E2 **Kosh-Agach** Rus. Fed.
67 A4 **Koshikijima-rettō** *is* Japan
103 E2 **Košice** Slovakia
92 H2 **Koskullskulle** Sweden
65 B2 **Kosŏng** N. Korea
109 D2 **Kosovo** *country* Europe
Kosovska Mitrovica Kosovo *see* **Mitrovicë**
48 H3 **Kosrae** *atoll* Micronesia
114 B4 **Kossou, Lac de** *l.* Côte d'Ivoire
76 C1 **Kostanay** Kazakh.
110 B2 **Kostenets** Bulg.
123 C2 **Koster** S. Africa
116 B3 **Kosti** Sudan
92 J3 **Kostomuksha** Rus. Fed.
90 B1 **Kostopil'** Ukr.
89 F2 **Kostroma** Rus. Fed.
89 F2 **Kostroma** *r.* Rus. Fed.
102 C1 **Kostrzyn** Pol.
91 D2 **Kostyantynivka** Ukr.
103 D1 **Koszalin** Pol.
103 D2 **Kőszeg** Hungary
74 B2 **Kota** India
60 B2 **Kotaagung** Indon.
61 C2 **Kotabaru** Indon.
61 C1 **Kota Belud** Malaysia
60 B1 **Kota Bharu** Malaysia
60 B2 **Kotabumi** Indon.
61 C1 **Kota Kinabalu** Malaysia
75 C3 **Kotaparh** India
61 C1 **Kota Samarahan** Malaysia
86 D3 **Kotel'nich** Rus. Fed.
87 D4 **Kotel'nikovo** Rus. Fed.
83 K1 **Kotel'nyy, Ostrov** *i.* Rus. Fed.
91 C1 **Kotel'va** Ukr.
101 E2 **Köthen (Anhalt)** Ger.
119 D2 **Kotido** Uganda
93 I3 **Kotka** Fin.
86 D2 **Kotlas** Rus. Fed.
126 B2 **Kotlik** U.S.A.
109 C2 **Kotor Varoš** Bos.-Herz.
87 D3 **Kotovo** Rus. Fed.
91 E1 **Kotovsk** Rus. Fed.
90 B2 **Kotovs'k** Ukr.
73 C3 **Kottagudem** India
118 C2 **Kotto** *r.* C.A.R.
83 H2 **Kotuy** *r.* Rus. Fed.
126 B2 **Kotzebue** U.S.A.
126 B2 **Kotzebue Sound** *sea chan.* U.S.A.
114 A3 **Koubia** Guinea
100 A2 **Koudekerke** Neth.
114 B3 **Koudougou** Burkina
122 B3 **Kougaberge** *mts* S. Africa
118 B3 **Koulamoutou** Gabon
114 B3 **Koulikoro** Mali
118 B2 **Koum** Cameroon
118 B2 **Koumra** Chad
114 A3 **Koundâra** Guinea
Kounradskiy Kazakh. *see* **Konyrat**
151 D2 **Kourou** Fr. Guiana
114 B3 **Kouroussa** Guinea
115 D3 **Kousséri** Cameroon
114 B3 **Koutiala** Mali
93 I3 **Kouvola** Fin.
109 D1 **Kovačica** Serbia
92 J2 **Kovdor** Rus. Fed.
90 A1 **Kovel'** Ukr.
Kovno Lith. *see* **Kaunas**
89 F2 **Kovrov** Rus. Fed.
51 D1 **Kowanyama** Austr.
54 B2 **Kowhitirangi** N.Z.
111 C3 **Köyceğiz** Turkey
86 D2 **Koyda** Rus. Fed.
126 B2 **Koyukuk** *r.* U.S.A.
111 B2 **Kozani** Greece
90 C1 **Kozelets'** Ukr.
89 E3 **Kozel'sk** Rus. Fed.
73 B3 **Kozhikode** India
90 B2 **Kozyatyn** Ukr.
114 C4 **Kpalimé** Togo
63 A2 **Kra, Isthmus of** Myanmar/Thai.
63 A3 **Krabi** Thai.
63 A2 **Kra Buri** Thai.
63 B2 **Krâchéh** Cambodia
93 E4 **Kragerø** Norway
100 B1 **Kraggenburg** Neth.
109 D2 **Kragujevac** Serbia
60 B2 **Krakatau** *i.* Indon.
103 D1 **Kraków** Pol.
109 D2 **Kraljevo** Serbia
91 D2 **Kramators'k** Ukr.
93 G3 **Kramfors** Sweden
111 B3 **Kranidi** Greece
102 C2 **Kranj** Slovenia
123 D2 **Kranskop** S. Africa
86 E1 **Krasino** Rus. Fed.
88 C2 **Krāslava** Latvia
101 F2 **Kraslice** Czech Rep.
89 D3 **Krasnapollye** Belarus
89 D3 **Krasnaya Gora** Rus. Fed.
89 F2 **Krasnaya Gorbatka** Rus. Fed.
Krasnoarmeysk Kazakh. *see* **Taiynsha**
87 D3 **Krasnoarmeysk** Rus. Fed.
Krasnoarmeyskaya Rus. Fed. *see* **Poltavskaya**
91 D2 **Krasnoarmiys'k** Ukr.
86 D2 **Krasnoborsk** Rus. Fed.
91 D2 **Krasnodar** Rus. Fed.
91 D2 **Krasnodon** Ukr.
88 C2 **Krasnogorodskoye** Rus. Fed.
91 D1 **Krasnogvardeyskoye** Rus. Fed.
91 C2 **Krasnohrad** Ukr.
91 C2 **Krasnohvardiys'ke** Ukr.
86 E3 **Krasnokamsk** Rus. Fed.
89 D2 **Krasnomayskiy** Rus. Fed.
91 C2 **Krasnoperekops'k** Ukr.
87 D3 **Krasnoslobodsk** Rus. Fed.
86 F3 **Krasnotur'insk** Rus. Fed.
86 E3 **Krasnoufimsk** Rus. Fed.
86 E2 **Krasnovishersk** Rus. Fed.
Krasnovodsk Turkm. *see* **Türkmenbaşy**
83 H3 **Krasnoyarsk** Rus. Fed.
89 E3 **Krasnoye** Rus. Fed.
83 M2 **Krasnoye, Ozero** *l.* Rus. Fed.
89 F2 **Krasnoye-na-Volge** Rus. Fed.
103 E1 **Krasnystaw** Pol.
89 D3 **Krasnyy** Rus. Fed.
Krasnyy Kamyshanik Rus. Fed. *see* **Komsomol'skiy**
89 E2 **Krasnyy Kholm** Rus. Fed.
91 D2 **Krasnyy Luch** Ukr.
91 E2 **Krasnyy Sulin** Rus. Fed.
90 B2 **Krasyliv** Ukr.
Kraulshavn Greenland *see* **Nuussuaq**
100 C2 **Krefeld** Ger.
91 C2 **Kremenchuk** Ukr.
91 C2 **Kremenchuts'ke Vodoskhovyshche** *resr* Ukr.
90 B1 **Kremenets'** Ukr.
103 D2 **Křemešník** *h.* Czech Rep.
Kremges Ukr. *see* **Svitlovods'k**
91 D2 **Kreminna** Ukr.
136 B2 **Kremmling** U.S.A.
103 D2 **Krems an der Donau** Austria
89 D2 **Kresttsy** Rus. Fed.
88 B2 **Kretinga** Lith.
100 C2 **Kreuzau** Ger.
101 C2 **Kreuztal** Ger.
118 A2 **Kribi** Cameroon
123 C2 **Kriel** S. Africa
111 B3 **Krikellos** Greece
66 D1 **Kril'on, Mys** *c.* Rus. Fed.
111 B3 **Krios, Akrotirio** *pt* Greece
73 C3 **Krishna** *r.* India
73 C3 **Krishna, Mouths of the** India
75 C2 **Krishnanagar** India
93 E4 **Kristiansand** Norway
93 F4 **Kristianstad** Sweden
92 E3 **Kristiansund** Norway
93 F4 **Kristinehamn** Sweden
Kristinopol' Ukr. *see* **Chervonohrad**
Kriti *i.* Greece *see* **Crete**
111 C3 **Kritiko Pelagos** *sea* Greece
110 B2 **Kriva Palanka** Macedonia
Krivoy Rog Ukr. *see* **Kryvyy Rih**
109 C1 **Križevci** Croatia
108 B1 **Krk** *i.* Croatia
92 F3 **Krokom** Sweden
91 C1 **Krolevets'** Ukr.
89 E3 **Kromy** Rus. Fed.
101 E2 **Kronach** Ger.
63 B2 **Krŏng Kaôh Kŏng** Cambodia
127 J2 **Kronprins Frederik Bjerge** *nunataks* Greenland
123 C2 **Kroonstad** S. Africa
91 E2 **Kropotkin** Rus. Fed.
103 E2 **Krosno** Pol.
103 D1 **Krotoszyn** Pol.
60 B2 **Krui** Indon.
122 B3 **Kruisfontein** S. Africa
109 C2 **Krujë** Albania
111 C2 **Krumovgrad** Bulg.
Krung Thep Thai. *see* **Bangkok**
88 C3 **Krupki** Belarus
109 D2 **Kruševac** Serbia
101 E2 **Krušné hory** *mts* Czech Rep.
128 A2 **Kruzof Island** U.S.A.
89 D3 **Krychaw** Belarus
91 D2 **Krylovskaya** Rus. Fed.
91 D3 **Krymsk** Rus. Fed.
Krymskaya Rus. Fed. *see* **Krymsk**
Kryms'kyy Pivostriv *pen.* Ukr. *see* **Crimea**
Krystynopol Ukr. *see* **Chervonohrad**
91 C2 **Kryvyy Rih** Ukr.
90 B2 **Kryzhopil'** Ukr.
114 B2 **Ksabi** Alg.
107 D2 **Ksar el Boukhari** Alg.
114 B1 **Ksar el Kebir** Morocco
Ksar-es-Souk Morocco *see* **Er Rachidia**
89 E3 **Kshenskiy** Rus. Fed.
78 B2 **Kū', Jabal al** *h.* Saudi Arabia
61 C1 **Kuala Belait** Brunei
Kuala Dungun Malaysia *see* **Dungun**
60 B1 **Kuala Kangsar** Malaysia
60 B1 **Kuala Kerai** Malaysia
60 B1 **Kuala Lipis** Malaysia
60 B1 **Kuala Lumpur** Malaysia
61 C2 **Kualapembuang** Indon.
60 B1 **Kuala Terengganu** Malaysia
60 B2 **Kualatungal** Indon.
61 C1 **Kuamut** Malaysia
65 A1 **Kuandian** China
60 B1 **Kuantan** Malaysia
91 D2 **Kuban'** *r.* Rus. Fed.
89 E2 **Kubenskoye, Ozero** *l.* Rus. Fed.
110 C2 **Kubrat** Bulg.
60 B2 **Kubu** Indon.
61 C1 **Kubuang** Indon.
60 C1 **Kuching** Malaysia
109 C2 **Kuçovë** Albania
61 C1 **Kudat** Malaysia
61 C2 **Kudus** Indon.
102 C2 **Kufstein** Austria
127 G2 **Kugaaruk** Can.
91 D2 **Kugey** Rus. Fed.
126 E2 **Kugluktuk** Can.
126 D2 **Kugmallit Bay** Can.
92 I3 **Kuhmo** Fin.
79 C2 **Kūhrān, Kūh-e** *mt.* Iran
122 A1 **Kuis** Namibia
Kuitin China *see* **Kuytun**
120 A2 **Kuito** Angola
92 I2 **Kuivaniemi** Fin.
65 B2 **Kujang** N. Korea
66 D2 **Kuji** Japan
67 B4 **Kujū-san** *vol.* Japan
109 D2 **Kukës** Albania
76 B3 **Kükürtli** Turkm.
111 C3 **Kula** Turkey
75 D2 **Kula Kangri** *mt.* Bhutan/China
76 B2 **Kulandy** Kazakh.
88 B2 **Kuldīga** Latvia
Kuldja China *see* **Yining**
122 B1 **Kule** Botswana
101 E2 **Kulmbach** Ger.
77 C3 **Kŭlob** Tajik.
76 B2 **Kul'sary** Kazakh.
111 D3 **Kulübe Tepe** *mt.* Turkey
77 D1 **Kulunda** Rus. Fed.
77 D1 **Kulundinskoye, Ozero** *salt l.* Rus. Fed.
127 J2 **Kulusuk** Greenland
67 C3 **Kumagaya** Japan
67 B4 **Kumamoto** Japan
67 C4 **Kumano** Japan
110 B2 **Kumanovo** Macedonia
114 B4 **Kumasi** Ghana
118 A2 **Kumba** Cameroon
Kum-Dag Turkm. *see* **Gumdag**
78 B2 **Kumdah** Saudi Arabia
87 E3 **Kumertau** Rus. Fed.
65 B2 **Kumi** S. Korea
119 D2 **Kumi** Uganda
111 C3 **Kumkale** Turkey
93 G4 **Kumla** Sweden
115 D3 **Kumo** Nigeria
62 A1 **Kumon Range** *mts* Myanmar
62 B2 **Kumphawapi** Thai.
Kumul China *see* **Hami**
120 A2 **Kunene** *r.* Angola/Namibia
77 D2 **Kungei Alatau** *mts* Kazakh./Kyrg.
93 F4 **Kungsbacka** Sweden
118 B2 **Kungu** Dem. Rep. Congo
86 E3 **Kungur** Rus. Fed.
62 A1 **Kunhing** Myanmar
62 A1 **Kunlong** Myanmar
75 B1 **Kunlun Shan** *mts* China
71 A3 **Kunming** China
65 B2 **Kunsan** S. Korea
50 B1 **Kununurra** Austr.
101 D3 **Künzelsau** Ger.
92 I3 **Kuopio** Fin.
109 C1 **Kupa** *r.* Croatia/Slovenia
59 C3 **Kupang** Indon.
88 B2 **Kupiškis** Lith.
111 C2 **Küplü** Turkey
128 A2 **Kupreanof Island** U.S.A.
91 D2 **Kup''yans'k** Ukr.
77 E2 **Kuqa** China
81 C2 **Kür** *r.* Azer.
67 B4 **Kurashiki** Japan
75 C2 **Kurasia** India
67 B3 **Kurayoshi** Japan
89 E3 **Kurchatov** Rus. Fed.
77 E2 **Kurchum** Kazakh.
111 C2 **Kŭrdzhali** Bulg.
67 B4 **Kure** Japan
57 T7 **Kure Atoll** U.S.A.
88 B2 **Kuressaare** Estonia
87 F3 **Kurgan** Rus. Fed.
Kuria Muria Islands *is* Oman *see* **Ḥalāniyāt, Juzur al**
93 H3 **Kurikka** Fin.
156 C2 **Kuril Basin** Sea of Okhotsk
69 F1 **Kuril Islands** *is* Rus. Fed.
69 F1 **Kuril'sk** Rus. Fed.
Kuril'skiye Ostrova *is* Rus. Fed. *see* **Kuril Islands**
156 C3 **Kuril Trench** N. Pacific Ocean
89 E3 **Kurkino** Rus. Fed.
Kurmashkino Kazakh. *see* **Kurchum**
117 B3 **Kurmuk** Sudan
73 B3 **Kurnool** India
67 D3 **Kuroiso** Japan
53 D2 **Kurri Kurri** Austr.
88 B2 **Kuršėnai** Lith.
78 B2 **Kursh, Jabal** *mt.* Saudi Arabia
89 E3 **Kursk** Rus. Fed.
109 D2 **Kuršumlija** Serbia
122 B2 **Kuruman** S. Africa
122 B2 **Kuruman** *watercourse* S. Africa
67 B4 **Kurume** Japan
83 I3 **Kurumkan** Rus. Fed.
73 C4 **Kurunegala** Sri Lanka
81 D1 **Kuryk** Kazakh.
111 C3 **Kuşadası** Turkey
111 C3 **Kuşadası Körfezi** *b.* Turkey
111 C2 **Kuş Gölü** *l.* Turkey
91 D2 **Kushchevskaya** Rus. Fed.
66 D2 **Kushiro** Japan
Kushka Turkm. *see* **Serhetabat**
76 C1 **Kushmurun** Kazakh.
75 C2 **Kushtia** Bangl.
126 B2 **Kuskokwim** *r.* U.S.A.
126 B2 **Kuskokwim Mountains** U.S.A.
66 D2 **Kussharo-ko** *l.* Japan
Kustanay Kazakh. *see* **Kostanay**
63 B2 **Kut, Ko** *i.* Thai.
111 C3 **Kütahya** Turkey
81 C1 **K'ut'aisi** Georgia
Kutaraja Indon. *see* **Banda Aceh**
Kutch, Gulf of *g.* India *see* **Kachchh, Gulf of**

109 C1 **Kutjevo** Croatia
103 D1 **Kutno** Pol.
118 B3 **Kutu** Dem. Rep. Congo
116 A3 **Kutum** Sudan
126 E2 **Kuujjua** *r.* Can.
131 D2 **Kuujjuaq** Can.
130 C2 **Kuujjuarapik** Can.
92 I2 **Kuusamo** Fin.
120 A2 **Kuvango** Angola
89 D2 **Kuvshinovo** Rus. Fed.
78 B2 **Kuwait** *country* Asia
78 B2 **Kuwait** Kuwait
82 G3 **Kuybyshev** Rus. Fed.
Kuybyshev Rus. Fed. *see* **Samara**
91 D2 **Kuybysheve** Ukr.
Kuybyshevka-Vostochnaya Rus. Fed. *see* **Belogorsk**
87 D3 **Kuybyshevskoye Vodokhranilishche** *resr* Rus. Fed.
77 E2 **Kuytun** China
111 C3 **Kuyucak** Turkey
87 D3 **Kuznetsk** Rus. Fed.
90 B1 **Kuznetsovs'k** Ukr.
86 C2 **Kuzomen'** Rus. Fed.
92 H1 **Kvalsund** Norway
123 D2 **KwaMashu** S. Africa
61 D1 **Kwandang** Indon.
Kwangchow China *see* **Guangzhou**
65 B2 **Kwangju** S. Korea
Kwangtung *prov.* China *see* **Guangdong**
65 B1 **Kwanmo bong** *mt.* N. Korea
123 C3 **Kwanobuhle** S. Africa
123 C3 **KwaNojoli** S. Africa
122 B3 **KwaNonzame** S. Africa
115 C3 **Kwatarkwashi** Nigeria
123 C3 **Kwatinidubu** S. Africa
123 C2 **KwaZamokuhle** S. Africa
122 B3 **KwaZamukucinga** S. Africa
123 C2 **KwaZanele** S. Africa
123 D2 **KwaZulu-Natal** *prov.* S. Africa
Kweichow *prov.* China *see* **Guizhou**
Kweiyang China *see* **Guiyang**
121 B2 **Kwekwe** Zimbabwe
118 B3 **Kwenge** *r.* Dem. Rep. Congo
123 C3 **Kwezi-Naledi** S. Africa
103 D1 **Kwidzyn** Pol.
59 D3 **Kwikila** P.N.G.
118 B3 **Kwilu** *r.* Angola/Dem. Rep. Congo
59 C3 **Kwoka** *mt.* Indon.
118 B2 **Kyabé** Chad
53 C3 **Kyabram** Austr.
62 A2 **Kyaikto** Myanmar
63 A2 **Kya-in Seikkyi** Myanmar
68 D1 **Kyakhta** Rus. Fed.
52 A2 **Kyancutta** Austr.
62 A1 **Kyaukpadaung** Myanmar
62 A2 **Kyaukpyu** Myanmar
88 B3 **Kybartai** Lith.
62 A2 **Kyebogyi** Myanmar
54 B3 **Kyeburn** N.Z.
62 A2 **Kyeintali** Myanmar
74 B1 **Kyelang** India
Kyiv Ukr. *see* **Kiev**
90 C1 **Kyivs'ke Vodoskhovyshche** *resr* Ukr.
Kyklades *is* Greece *see* **Cyclades**
129 D2 **Kyle** Can.
96 B2 **Kyle of Lochalsh** U.K.
100 C3 **Kyll** *r.* Ger.
111 B3 **Kyllini** *mt.* Greece
111 B3 **Kymi** Greece
52 B3 **Kyneton** Austr.
119 D2 **Kyoga, Lake** Uganda
53 D1 **Kyogle** Austr.
65 B2 **Kyŏnggi-man** *b.* S. Korea
65 D2 **Kyŏngju** S. Korea
67 C4 **Kyōto** Japan
111 B3 **Kyparissia** Greece
111 B3 **Kyparissiakos Kolpos** *b.* Greece
77 C1 **Kypshak, Ozero** *salt l.* Kazakh.
111 B3 **Kyra Panagia** *i.* Greece
80 B2 **Kyrenia** Cyprus
77 D2 **Kyrgyzstan** *country* Asia
101 F1 **Kyritz** Ger.
93 H3 **Kyrönjoki** *r.* Fin.
86 E2 **Kyrta** Rus. Fed.
86 D2 **Kyssa** Rus. Fed.
83 J2 **Kytalyktakh** Rus. Fed.
111 B3 **Kythira** *i.* Greece
111 B3 **Kythnos** *i.* Greece
128 B2 **Kyuquot** Can.
67 B4 **Kyūshū** *i.* Japan
110 B2 **Kyustendil** Bulg.
62 A2 **Kywebwe** Myanmar
92 H3 **Kyyjärvi** Fin.
68 C1 **Kyzyl** Rus. Fed.
76 C2 **Kyzylkum Desert** Kazakh./Uzbek.
77 C2 **Kyzylorda** Kazakh.
Kzyl-Orda Kazakh. *see* **Kyzylorda**
Kzyltu Kazakh. *see* **Kishkenekol'**

L

145 C3 **La Angostura, Presa de** *resr* Mex.
117 C4 **Laascaanood** Somalia
117 C3 **Laasgoray** Somalia
150 C1 **La Asunción** Venez.
114 A2 **Laâyoune** Western Sahara
87 D4 **Laba** *r.* Rus. Fed.
144 B2 **La Babia** Mex.
61 D2 **Labala** Indon.
152 B2 **La Banda** Arg.
61 C1 **Labang** Malaysia
104 B2 **La Baule-Escoublac** France
102 C1 **Labe** *r.* Czech Rep.
114 A3 **Labé** Guinea
128 A1 **Laberge, Lake** Can.
128 C2 **La Biche, Lac** *l.* Can.
108 B1 **Labin** Croatia
87 D4 **Labinsk** Rus. Fed.
64 B2 **Labo** Phil.
104 B3 **Labouheyre** France
153 B3 **Laboulaye** Arg.
131 D2 **Labrador** *reg.* Can.
131 D2 **Labrador City** Can.
127 I2 **Labrador Sea** Can./Greenland
150 C3 **Lábrea** Brazil
61 C1 **Labuan** Malaysia
60 C2 **Labuhanbajo** Indon.
60 B1 **Labuhanbilik** Indon.
59 C3 **Labuna** Indon.
63 A2 **Labutta** Myanmar
86 F2 **Labytnangi** Rus. Fed.
109 C2 **Laç** Albania
107 D2 **La Cabaneta** Spain
La Calle Alg. *see* **El Kala**
105 C2 **La Capelle** France
73 B3 **Laccadive Islands** India
129 E2 **Lac du Bonnet** Can.
146 B3 **La Ceiba** Hond.
52 A3 **Lacepede Bay** Austr.
134 B1 **Lacey** U.S.A.
105 D2 **La Chaux-de-Fonds** Switz.
53 B2 **Lachlan** *r.* Austr.
146 C4 **La Chorrera** Panama
139 F1 **Lachute** Can.
105 D3 **La Ciotat** France
128 C2 **Lac La Biche** Can.
Lac la Martre Can. *see* **Whatî**
139 E1 **Lac-Mégantic** Can.
128 C2 **Lacombe** Can.
146 B4 **La Concepción** Panama
145 C3 **La Concordia** Mex.
108 A3 **Laconi** Italy
139 E2 **Laconia** U.S.A.
128 C2 **La Crete** Can.
138 A2 **La Crosse** U.S.A.
144 B2 **La Cruz** Mex.
144 B2 **La Cuesta** Mex.
155 D1 **Ladainha** Brazil
74 B1 **Ladakh Range** *mts* India/Pak.
122 B3 **Ladismith** S. Africa
79 D2 **Lādīz** Iran
89 D1 **Ladoga, Lake** Rus. Fed.
Ladozhskoye Ozero *l.* Rus. Fed. *see* **Ladoga, Lake**
141 D2 **Ladson** U.S.A.
123 C3 **Lady Grey** S. Africa
128 B3 **Ladysmith** Can.
123 C2 **Ladysmith** S. Africa
59 D3 **Lae** P.N.G.
143 C3 **La Encantada, Sierra** *mts* Mex.
152 B2 **La Esmeralda** Bol.
93 F4 **Læsø** *i.* Denmark
Lafayette Alg. *see* **Bougaa**
141 C2 **La Fayette** U.S.A.
138 B2 **Lafayette** *IN* U.S.A.
140 B2 **Lafayette** *LA* U.S.A.
115 C4 **Lafia** Nigeria
104 B2 **La Flèche** France
141 D1 **La Follette** U.S.A.
130 C2 **Laforge** Can.
79 C2 **Lāft** Iran
108 A3 **La Galite** *i.* Tunisia
87 D4 **Lagan'** Rus. Fed.
151 F4 **Lagarto** Brazil
118 B2 **Lagdo, Lac de** *l.* Cameroon
115 C1 **Laghouat** Alg.
155 D1 **Lagoa Santa** Brazil
114 A2 **La Gomera** *i.* Islas Canarias
114 C4 **Lagos** Nigeria
106 B2 **Lagos** Port.
134 C1 **La Grande** U.S.A.
130 C2 **La Grande 3, Réservoir** *resr* Can.
130 C2 **La Grande 4, Réservoir** *resr* Can.
50 B1 **La Grange** Austr.
141 C2 **La Grange** U.S.A.
150 C2 **La Gran Sabana** *plat.* Venez.
152 D2 **Laguna** Brazil
144 A2 **Laguna, Picacho de la** *mt.* Mex.
150 B3 **Lagunas** Peru
147 C3 **Lagunillas** Venez.
La Habana Cuba *see* **Havana**
61 C1 **Lahad Datu** Malaysia
60 B2 **Lahat** Indon.
78 B3 **Laḩij** Yemen
81 C2 **Lāhījān** Iran
100 C2 **Lahnstein** Ger.
74 B1 **Lahore** Pak.
74 A2 **Lahri** Pak.
93 I3 **Lahti** Fin.
115 D4 **Laï** Chad
53 D1 **Laidley** Austr.
104 C2 **L'Aigle** France
111 B3 **Laimos, Akrotirio** *pt* Greece
122 B3 **Laingsburg** S. Africa
92 H2 **Lainioälven** *r.* Sweden
96 B1 **Lairg** U.K.
108 B1 **Laives** Italy
70 B2 **Laiwu** China
70 C2 **Laiyang** China
70 B2 **Laiyuan** China
70 B2 **Laizhou** China
70 B2 **Laizhou Wan** *b.* China
50 C1 **Lajamanu** Austr.
152 C2 **Lajes** Brazil
144 B2 **La Junta** Mex.
136 C3 **La Junta** U.S.A.
117 B4 **Lake Abaya** *l.* Eth.
103 D2 **Lake Balaton** *l.* Hungary
53 C2 **Lake Cargelligo** Austr.
53 D2 **Lake Cathie** Austr.
140 B2 **Lake Charles** U.S.A.
141 D2 **Lake City** *FL* U.S.A.
141 E2 **Lake City** *SC* U.S.A.
128 B3 **Lake Cowichan** Can.
Lake Harbour Can. *see* **Kimmirut**
142 A2 **Lake Havasu City** U.S.A.
143 D3 **Lake Jackson** U.S.A.
50 A3 **Lake King** Austr.
141 D3 **Lakeland** U.S.A.
128 C2 **Lake Louise** Can.
134 B1 **Lake Oswego** U.S.A.
54 A2 **Lake Paringa** N.Z.
140 B2 **Lake Providence** U.S.A.
53 C3 **Lakes Entrance** Austr.
117 B3 **Lake Tana** *l.* Eth.
134 B2 **Lakeview** U.S.A.
137 E2 **Lakeville** U.S.A.
136 B3 **Lakewood** *CO* U.S.A.
139 E2 **Lakewood** *NJ* U.S.A.
141 D3 **Lake Worth** U.S.A.
74 A2 **Lakhpat** India
74 B1 **Lakki Marwat** Pak.
111 B3 **Lakonikos Kolpos** *b.* Greece
114 B4 **Lakota** Côte d'Ivoire
92 H1 **Lakselv** Norway
107 C1 **L'Alcora** Spain
146 A3 **La Libertad** Guat.
106 B1 **Lalín** Spain
106 B2 **La Línea de la Concepción** Spain
74 B2 **Lalitpur** India
Lalitpur Nepal *see* **Patan**
129 D2 **La Loche** Can.
100 B2 **La Louvière** Belgium
108 A2 **La Maddalena** Italy
61 C1 **Lamag** Malaysia
La Manche *str.* France/U.K. *see* **English Channel**
136 C3 **Lamar** U.S.A.
79 C2 **Lamard** Iran
108 A3 **La Marmora, Punta** *mt.* Italy
128 C1 **La Martre, Lac** *l.* Can.
104 B2 **Lamballe** France
118 B3 **Lambaréné** Gabon
122 A3 **Lambert's Bay** S. Africa
92 □A2 **Lambeyri** Iceland
106 B1 **Lamego** Port.
131 D3 **Lamèque, Île** *i.* Can.
150 B4 **La Merced** Peru
52 B3 **Lameroo** Austr.
143 C2 **Lamesa** U.S.A.
111 B3 **Lamia** Greece
137 E2 **Lamoni** U.S.A.
62 A2 **Lampang** Thai.
143 D2 **Lampasas** U.S.A.
145 B2 **Lampazos** Mex.
99 A3 **Lampeter** U.K.
62 A2 **Lamphun** Thai.
119 E3 **Lamu** Kenya
105 D3 **La Mure** France
96 C3 **Lanark** U.K.
63 A2 **Lanbi Kyun** *i.* Myanmar
62 A1 **Lancang** China
Lancang Jiang *r.* China *see* **Mekong**
98 B2 **Lancaster** U.K.
135 C4 **Lancaster** *CA* U.S.A.
138 C3 **Lancaster** *OH* U.S.A.
139 D2 **Lancaster** *PA* U.S.A.
141 D2 **Lancaster** *SC* U.S.A.
127 G2 **Lancaster Sound** *str.* Can.
50 A3 **Lancelin** Austr.
Lanchow China *see* **Lanzhou**
102 C2 **Landeck** Austria
136 B2 **Lander** U.S.A.
99 A4 **Land's End** *pt* U.K.
102 C2 **Landshut** Ger.
93 F4 **Landskrona** Sweden
141 C2 **Lanett** U.S.A.
122 B2 **Langberg** *mts* S. Africa
137 D1 **Langdon** U.S.A.
93 F4 **Langeland** *i.* Denmark
101 D1 **Langen** Ger.
100 C1 **Langeoog** Ger.
100 C1 **Langeoog** *i.* Ger.
82 G2 **Langepas** Rus. Fed.
70 B2 **Langfang** China
101 D2 **Langgöns** Ger.
96 C3 **Langholm** U.K.
92 □A3 **Langjökull** Iceland
60 A1 **Langkawi** *i.* Malaysia
105 C3 **Langogne** France
104 B3 **Langon** France
106 B1 **Langreo** Spain
105 D2 **Langres** France
60 A1 **Langsa** Indon.
62 B1 **Lang Sơn** Vietnam
105 C3 **Languedoc** *reg.* France
101 D1 **Langwedel** Ger.
129 D2 **Lanigan** Can.
153 A3 **Lanín, Volcán** *vol.* Arg./Chile
81 C2 **Länkäran** Azer.
104 B2 **Lannion** France
138 B1 **L'Anse** U.S.A.
139 E1 **L'Anse-St-Jean** Can.
138 C2 **Lansing** U.S.A.
71 B3 **Lanxi** China
117 B4 **Lanya** Sudan
114 A2 **Lanzarote** *i.* Islas Canarias
70 A2 **Lanzhou** China
64 B2 **Laoag** Phil.
62 B1 **Lao Cai** Vietnam
70 B2 **Laohekou** China
68 C2 **Laojunmiao** China
65 B1 **Laoling** China
65 B1 **Lao Ling** *mts* China
105 C2 **Laon** France
62 B2 **Laos** *country* Asia
65 B1 **Laotougou** China
66 A2 **Laoye Ling** *mts* China
154 C3 **Lapa** Brazil
114 A2 **La Palma** *i.* Islas Canarias
146 C4 **La Palma** Panama
150 C2 **La Paragua** Venez.
152 B1 **La Paz** Bol.
145 D3 **La Paz** Hond.
144 A2 **La Paz** Mex.
150 C3 **La Pedrera** Col.
138 C2 **Lapeer** U.S.A.
66 D1 **La Pérouse Strait** Japan/Rus. Fed.
145 C2 **La Pesca** Mex.
144 B2 **La Piedad** Mex.
153 C3 **La Plata** Arg.
153 C3 **La Plata, Río de** *sea chan.* Arg./Uru.
92 H3 **Lappajärvi** *l.* Fin.
93 I3 **Lappeenranta** Fin.
92 G2 **Lappland** *reg.* Europe
111 C2 **Lâpseki** Turkey
Laptevo Rus. Fed. *see* **Yasnogorsk**
83 J1 **Laptev Sea** Rus. Fed.
Laptevykh, More *sea* Rus. Fed. *see* **Laptev Sea**
93 H3 **Lapua** Fin.
152 B2 **La Quiaca** Arg.
108 B2 **L'Aquila** Italy
135 C4 **La Quinta** U.S.A.
79 C2 **Lār** Iran
114 B1 **Larache** Morocco
136 B2 **Laramie** U.S.A.
136 B2 **Laramie Mountains** U.S.A.
154 B3 **Laranjeiras do Sul** Brazil
61 D2 **Larantuka** Indon.
59 C3 **Larat** *i.* Indon.
107 D2 **Larba** Alg.
L'Ardenne, Plateau de *plat.* Belgium *see* **Ardennes**
106 C1 **Laredo** Spain
143 D3 **Laredo** U.S.A.
141 D3 **Largo** U.S.A.
96 B3 **Largs** U.K.
115 D1 **L'Ariana** Tunisia
152 B2 **La Rioja** Arg.
111 B3 **Larisa** Greece
74 A2 **Larkana** Pak.
80 B2 **Larnaca** Cyprus
Larnaka Cyprus *see* **Larnaca**
97 D1 **Larne** U.K.
100 B2 **La Roche-en-Ardenne** Belgium
104 B2 **La Rochelle** France
104 B2 **La Roche-sur-Yon** France
107 C2 **La Roda** Spain
147 D3 **La Romana** Dom. Rep.
129 D2 **La Ronge** Can.
129 D2 **La Ronge, Lac** *l.* Can.
50 C1 **Larrimah** Austr.
55 A3 **Larsen Ice Shelf** Antarctica
93 F4 **Larvik** Norway
136 C3 **Las Animas** U.S.A.
Las Anod Somalia *see* **Laascaanood**
130 C3 **La Sarre** Can.
142 B2 **Las Cruces** U.S.A.
152 A2 **La Serena** Chile
153 C3 **Las Flores** Arg.
153 B3 **Las Heras** Arg.
62 A1 **Lashio** Myanmar
76 C3 **Lashkar Gāh** Afgh.
109 C3 **La Sila** *reg.* Italy
152 B2 **Las Lomitas** Arg.
106 B2 **Las Marismas** *marsh* Spain
144 B2 **Las Nieves** Mex.
114 A2 **Las Palmas de Gran Canaria** Islas Canarias
108 A2 **La Spezia** Italy
153 C3 **Las Piedras** Uru.
153 B4 **Las Plumas** Arg.
155 D1 **Lassance** Brazil
129 D2 **Last Mountain Lake** Can.
152 B2 **Las Tórtolas, Cerro** *mt.* Arg./Chile
118 B3 **Lastoursville** Gabon
109 C2 **Lastovo** *i.* Croatia
144 A2 **Las Tres Vírgenes, Volcán** *vol.* Mex.
146 C2 **Las Tunas** Cuba
144 B2 **Las Varas** *Chihuahua* Mex.
144 B2 **Las Varas** *Nayarit* Mex.
142 B1 **Las Vegas** *NM* U.S.A.
135 C3 **Las Vegas** *NV* U.S.A.
131 E2 **La Tabatière** Can.
80 B2 **Latakia** Syria
104 B3 **La Teste-de-Buch** France
108 B2 **Latina** Italy
147 D3 **La Tortuga, Isla** *i.* Venez.
64 B2 **La Trinidad** Phil.
89 E2 **Latskoye** Rus. Fed.
130 C3 **La Tuque** Can.
88 B2 **Latvia** *country* Europe
Latviyskaya S.S.R. *country* Europe *see* **Latvia**
59 E3 **Lau** P.N.G.
102 C1 **Lauchhammer** Ger.
101 E3 **Lauf an der Pegnitz** Ger.
105 D2 **Laufen** Switz.
92 □A3 **Laugarás** Iceland
127 H1 **Lauge Koch Kyst** *reg.* Greenland
142 C1 **Laughlin Peak** U.S.A.

51 D4 Launceston Austr.
99 A4 Launceston U.K.
62 A1 Launggyaung Myanmar
153 A4 La Unión Chile
51 D1 Laura Austr.
140 C2 Laurel *MS* U.S.A.
134 E1 Laurel *MT* U.S.A.
96 C2 Laurencekirk U.K.
109 C2 Lauria Italy
141 E2 Laurinburg U.S.A.
105 D2 Lausanne Switz.
60 B1 Laut *i.* Indon.
61 C2 Laut *i.* Indon.
61 C2 Laut Bali Indon.
101 D2 Lautersbach (Hessen) Ger.
60 C2 Laut Jawa Indon.
61 C2 Laut Kecil, Kepulauan *is* Indon.
59 C3 Laut Maluku Indon.
61 D2 Laut Sawu Indon.
59 C3 Laut Seram Indon.
100 C1 Lauwersmeer *l.* Neth.
139 E1 Laval Can.
104 B2 Laval France
107 C2 La Vall d'Uixó Spain
81 D2 Lāvar Meydān *salt marsh* Iran
50 B2 Laverton Austr.
155 D2 Lavras Brazil
123 D2 Lavumisa Swaziland
61 C1 Lawas Malaysia
78 B3 Lawdar Yemen
62 A1 Lawksawk Myanmar
114 B3 Lawra Ghana
138 B3 Lawrence *IN* U.S.A.
137 D3 Lawrence *KS* U.S.A.
139 E2 Lawrence *MA* U.S.A.
140 C1 Lawrenceburg U.S.A.
141 D2 Lawrenceville U.S.A.
143 D2 Lawton U.S.A.
78 A2 Lawz, Jabal al *mt.* Saudi Arabia
93 F4 Laxå Sweden
122 B2 Laxey S. Africa
78 B2 Laylá Saudi Arabia
74 B1 Layyah Pak.
109 D2 Lazarevac Serbia
144 A1 Lázaro Cárdenas Mex.
144 B3 Lázaro Cárdenas Mex.
88 B3 Lazdijai Lith.
66 B2 Lazo *Primorskiy Kray* Rus. Fed.
83 K2 Lazo *Respublika Sakha* Rus. Fed.
136 C2 Lead U.S.A.
129 D2 Leader Can.
136 B3 Leadville U.S.A.
Leaf Bay Can. *see* Tasiujaq
129 D2 Leaf Rapids Can.
143 D3 League City U.S.A.
143 D3 Leakey U.S.A.
99 C3 Leamington Spa, Royal U.K.
97 B2 Leane, Lough *l.* Ireland
137 E3 Leavenworth U.S.A.
64 B3 Lebak Phil.
80 B2 Lebanon *country* Asia
137 E3 Lebanon *MO* U.S.A.
139 E2 Lebanon *NH* U.S.A.
134 B2 Lebanon *OR* U.S.A.
139 D2 Lebanon *PA* U.S.A.
140 C1 Lebanon *TN* U.S.A.
89 E3 Lebedyan' Rus. Fed.
91 C1 Lebedyn Ukr.
130 C3 Lebel-sur-Quévillon Can.
104 C2 Le Blanc France
103 D1 Lębork Pol.
123 C1 Lebowakgomo S. Africa
106 B2 Lebrija Spain
153 A3 Lebu Chile
104 C3 Le Bugue France
109 C2 Lecce Italy
108 A1 Lecco Italy
102 C2 Lech *r.* Austria/Ger.
111 B3 Lechaina Greece
71 B3 Lechang China
102 B1 Leck Ger.
140 B2 Lecompte U.S.A.
105 C2 Le Creusot France
104 C3 Lectoure France
106 B1 Ledesma Spain
104 C2 Le Dorat France
128 C2 Leduc Can.
97 B3 Lee *r.* Ireland
137 E1 Leech Lake U.S.A.
98 C3 Leeds U.K.
99 B3 Leek U.K.
97 B2 Leenane Ireland
100 C1 Leer (Ostfriesland) Ger.
141 D3 Leesburg U.S.A.
140 B2 Leesville U.S.A.
53 C2 Leeton Austr.
122 B3 Leeu-Gamka S. Africa
100 B1 Leeuwarden Neth.
50 A3 Leeuwin, Cape Austr.
147 D3 Leeward Islands Caribbean Sea
111 B3 Lefkada Greece
111 B3 Lefkada *i.* Greece
Lefkosia Cyprus *see* Nicosia
64 B2 Legaspi Phil.
103 E1 Legionowo Pol.
108 B1 Legnago Italy
103 D1 Legnica Pol.
74 B1 Leh India
104 C2 Le Havre France
101 E1 Lehre Ger.
122 B1 Lehututu Botswana
103 D2 Leibnitz Austria
99 C3 Leicester U.K.
51 C1 Leichhardt *r.* Austr.
51 D2 Leichhardt Range *mts* Austr.
100 B1 Leiden Neth.
100 A2 Leie *r.* Belgium
52 A2 Leigh Creek Austr.
97 C2 Leighlinbridge Ireland
99 C4 Leighton Buzzard U.K.
93 E3 Leikanger Norway
101 D1 Leine *r.* Ger.
50 B2 Leinster Austr.
97 C2 Leinster *reg.* Ireland
97 C2 Leinster, Mount *h.* Ireland
101 F2 Leipzig Ger.
92 F2 Leiranger Norway
106 B2 Leiria Port.
93 E4 Leirvik Norway
97 C2 Leixlip Ireland
71 B3 Leiyang China
71 B3 Leizhou China
71 A3 Leizhou Bandao *pen.* China
118 B3 Lékana Congo
122 A2 Lekkersing S. Africa
140 B2 Leland U.S.A.
Leli China *see* Tianlin
100 B1 Lelystad Neth.
153 B5 Le Maire, Estrecho de *sea chan.* Arg.
Léman, Lac *l.* France/Switz. *see* Geneva, Lake
104 C2 Le Mans France
137 D2 Le Mars U.S.A.
102 B2 Lemberg *mt.* Ger.
154 C2 Leme Brazil
Lemesos Cyprus *see* Limassol
101 D1 Lemförde Ger.
127 H2 Lemieux Islands Can.
136 C1 Lemmon U.S.A.
135 C3 Lemoore U.S.A.
131 D2 Le Moyne, Lac *l.* Can.
62 A1 Lemro *r.* Myanmar
109 C2 Le Murge *hills* Italy
83 J2 Lena *r.* Rus. Fed.
100 C1 Lengerich Ger.
70 A2 Lenglong Ling *mts* China
71 B3 Lengshuijiang China
71 B3 Lengshuitan China
Leninabad Tajik. *see* Khŭjand
Leninakan Armenia *see* Gyumri
91 D2 Lenine Ukr.
Leningrad Rus. Fed. *see* St Petersburg
91 D2 Leningradskaya Rus. Fed.
Leninobod Tajik. *see* Khŭjand
77 D3 Lenin Peak Kyrg./Tajik.
Leninsk Kazakh. *see* Baykonyr
89 E3 Leninskiy Rus. Fed.
53 D1 Lennox Head Austr.
141 D1 Lenoir U.S.A.
100 A2 Lens Belgium
105 C1 Lens France
83 I2 Lensk Rus. Fed.
103 D2 Lenti Hungary
109 C3 Lentini Italy
114 B3 Léo Burkina
103 D2 Leoben Austria
Leodhais, Eilean *i.* U.K. *see* Lewis, Isle of
99 B3 Leominster U.K.
144 B2 León Mex.
146 B3 León Nic.
106 B1 León Spain
122 A1 Leonardville Namibia
108 B3 Leonforte Italy
53 C3 Leongatha Austr.
50 B2 Leonora Austr.
Léopold II, Lac *l.* Dem. Rep. Congo *see* Mai-Ndombe, Lac
155 D2 Leopoldina Brazil
Léopoldville Dem. Rep. Congo *see* Kinshasa
90 B2 Leova Moldova
Leovo Moldova *see* Leova
123 C1 Lephalale S. Africa
123 C1 Lephepe Botswana
123 C3 Lephoi S. Africa
71 B3 Leping China
77 D2 Lepsy Kazakh.
105 C2 Le Puy-en-Velay France
123 C1 Lerala Botswana
123 C2 Leratswana S. Africa
150 B3 Lérida Col.
Lérida Spain *see* Lleida
106 C1 Lerma Spain
111 C3 Leros *i.* Greece
130 C2 Le Roy, Lac *l.* Can.
93 F4 Lerum Sweden
96 □ Lerwick U.K.
111 C3 Lesbos *i.* Greece
147 C3 Les Cayes Haiti
104 C3 Les Escaldes Andorra
139 F1 Les Escoumins Can.
107 D1 Le Seu d'Urgell Spain
70 A3 Leshan China
104 B2 Les Herbiers France
86 D2 Leshukonskoye Rus. Fed.
Leskhimstroy Ukr. *see* Syeverodonets'k
109 D2 Leskovac Serbia
104 B2 Lesneven France
Lesnoy Rus. Fed. *see* Umba
89 E2 Lesnoye Rus. Fed.
83 H3 Lesosibirsk Rus. Fed.
123 C2 Lesotho *country* Africa
66 B1 Lesozavodsk Rus. Fed.
104 B2 Les Sables-d'Olonne France
147 D3 Lesser Antilles *is* Caribbean Sea
81 C1 Lesser Caucasus *mts* Asia
Lesser Khingan Mountains *mts* China *see* Xiao Hinggan Ling
128 C2 Lesser Slave Lake Can.
58 B3 Lesser Sunda Islands Indon.
105 C3 Les Vans France
Lesvos *i.* Greece *see* Lesbos
103 D1 Leszno Pol.
123 D1 Letaba S. Africa
99 C4 Letchworth Garden City U.K.
128 C3 Lethbridge Can.
150 D2 Lethem Guyana
59 C3 Leti, Kepulauan *is* Indon.
150 C3 Leticia Col.
120 B3 Letlhakane Botswana
123 C1 Letlhakeng Botswana
104 C1 Le Touquet-Paris-Plage France
99 D4 Le Tréport France
123 D1 Letsitele S. Africa
63 A2 Letsok-aw Kyun *i.* Myanmar
123 C2 Letsopa S. Africa
97 C1 Letterkenny Ireland
105 C3 Leucate, Étang de *l.* France
Leukas Greece *see* Lefkada
60 A1 Leuser, Gunung *mt.* Indon.
100 B2 Leuven Belgium
92 F3 Levanger Norway
143 C2 Levelland U.S.A.
50 B1 Lévêque, Cape Austr.
96 A2 Leverburgh U.K.
100 C2 Leverkusen Ger.
103 D2 Levice Slovakia
54 C2 Levin N.Z.
131 C3 Lévis Can.
139 E2 Levittown U.S.A.
89 E3 Lev Tolstoy Rus. Fed.
99 D4 Lewes U.K.
96 A1 Lewis, Isle of *i.* U.K.
139 D2 Lewisburg *PA* U.S.A.
140 C1 Lewisburg *TN* U.S.A.
138 C3 Lewisburg *WV* U.S.A.
134 D1 Lewis Range *mts* U.S.A.
134 C1 Lewiston *ID* U.S.A.
139 E2 Lewiston *ME* U.S.A.
134 E1 Lewistown U.S.A.
138 C3 Lexington *KY* U.S.A.
136 D2 Lexington *NE* U.S.A.
143 D1 Lexington *OK* U.S.A.
139 D3 Lexington *VA* U.S.A.
64 B2 Leyte *i.* Phil.
109 C2 Lezhë Albania
89 F2 Lezhnevo Rus. Fed.
89 E3 L'gov Rus. Fed.
75 C2 Lhagoi Kangri *mt.* China
75 D1 Lharigarbo China
75 D2 Lhasa China
75 C2 Lhazê China
60 A1 Lhokseumawe Indon.
62 A1 Lhünzê China
111 B3 Liakoura *mt.* Greece
67 B3 Liancourt Rocks *is* N. Pacific Ocean
Liangzhou China *see* Wuwei
70 B2 Liangzi Hu *l.* China
Lianhe China *see* Qianjiang
71 B3 Lianhua China
71 B3 Lianjiang China
Lianran China *see* Anning
70 C1 Lianshan China
Liantang China *see* Nanchang
Lianxian China *see* Lianzhou
70 B2 Lianyungang China
71 B3 Lianzhou China
Lianzhou China *see* Hepu
70 B2 Liaocheng China
70 C1 Liaodong Bandao *pen.* China
70 C1 Liaodong Wan *b.* China
65 A1 Liao He *r.* China
70 C1 Liaoning *prov.* China
70 C1 Liaoyang China
65 B1 Liaoyuan China
128 B1 Liard *r.* Can.
134 C1 Libby U.S.A.
118 B2 Libenge Dem. Rep. Congo
136 C3 Liberal U.S.A.
103 D1 Liberec Czech Rep.
114 B4 Liberia *country* Africa
146 B3 Liberia Costa Rica
150 C2 Libertad Venez.
137 E3 Liberty U.S.A.
100 B3 Libin Belgium
64 B2 Libmanan Phil.
71 A3 Libo China
123 C3 Libode S. Africa
119 E2 Liboi Kenya
104 B3 Libourne France
100 B3 Libramont Belgium
142 A3 Libre, Sierra *mts* Mex.
118 A2 Libreville Gabon
115 D2 Libya *country* Africa
115 E2 Libyan Desert Egypt/Libya
116 A1 Libyan Plateau Egypt/Libya
108 B3 Licata Italy
Licheng China *see* Lipu
99 C3 Lichfield U.K.
121 C2 Lichinga Moz.
101 E2 Lichte Ger.
123 C2 Lichtenburg S. Africa
101 E2 Lichtenfels Ger.
88 C3 Lida Belarus
93 F4 Lidköping Sweden
50 C2 Liebig, Mount Austr.
105 D2 Liechtenstein *country* Europe
100 B2 Liège Belgium
92 J3 Lieksa Fin.
119 C2 Lienart Dem. Rep. Congo
63 B2 Liên Nghia Vietnam
102 C2 Lienz Austria
88 B2 Liepāja Latvia
100 B2 Lier Belgium
102 C2 Liezen Austria
97 C2 Liffey *r.* Ireland
97 C1 Lifford Ireland
53 C1 Lightning Ridge Austr.
121 C2 Ligonha *r.* Moz.
105 D3 Ligurian Sea France/Italy
119 C4 Likasi Dem. Rep. Congo
118 C2 Likati Dem. Rep. Congo
128 B2 Likely Can.
Likhachevo Ukr. *see* Pervomays'kyy
Likhachyovo Ukr. *see* Pervomays'kyy
89 E2 Likhoslavl' Rus. Fed.
60 B1 Liku Indon.
105 D3 L'Île-Rousse France
71 B3 Liling China
93 F4 Lilla Edet Sweden
100 B2 Lille Belgium
105 C1 Lille France
Lille Bælt *sea chan.* Denmark *see* Little Belt
93 F3 Lillehammer Norway
93 F4 Lillestrøm Norway
128 B2 Lillooet Can.
121 C2 Lilongwe Malawi
64 B3 Liloy Phil.
150 B4 Lima Peru
138 C2 Lima U.S.A.
155 D2 Lima Duarte Brazil
79 C2 Līmah Oman
80 B2 Limassol Cyprus
97 C1 Limavady U.K.
153 B3 Limay *r.* Arg.
101 F2 Limbach-Oberfrohna Ger.
88 B2 Limbaži Latvia
118 A2 Limbe Cameroon
101 D2 Limburg an der Lahn Ger.
122 B2 Lime Acres S. Africa
154 C2 Limeira Brazil
97 B2 Limerick Ireland
93 E4 Limfjorden *sea chan.* Denmark
92 I3 Liminka Fin.
111 C3 Limnos *i.* Greece
104 C2 Limoges France
136 C3 Limon U.S.A.
104 C2 Limousin, Plateaux du France
104 C3 Limoux France
123 C1 Limpopo *prov.* S. Africa
121 C3 Limpopo *r.* S. Africa/Zimbabwe
64 A2 Linapacan *i.* Phil.
153 A3 Linares Chile
145 C2 Linares Mex.
106 C2 Linares Spain
108 A3 Linas, Monte *mt.* Italy
62 B1 Lincang China
Linchuan China *see* Fuzhou
98 C3 Lincoln U.K.
138 B2 Lincoln *IL* U.S.A.
139 F1 Lincoln *ME* U.S.A.
137 D2 Lincoln *NE* U.S.A.
134 B2 Lincoln City U.S.A.
151 D2 Linden Guyana
140 C1 Linden U.S.A.
119 C2 Lindi *r.* Dem. Rep. Congo
119 D3 Lindi Tanz.
Lindisfarne *i.* U.K. *see* Holy Island
111 C3 Lindos Greece
130 C3 Lindsay Can.
48 K3 Line Islands Kiribati
70 B2 Linfen China
64 B2 Lingayen Phil.
70 B2 Lingbao China
Lingcheng China *see* Lingshan
Lingcheng China *see* Lingshui
123 C3 Lingelethu S. Africa
123 C3 Lingelihle S. Africa
100 C1 Lingen (Ems) Ger.
60 B2 Lingga *i.* Indon.
60 B2 Lingga, Kepulauan *is* Indon.
71 A3 Lingshan China
71 A4 Lingshui China
114 A3 Linguère Senegal
155 D1 Linhares Brazil
70 A1 Linhe China
Linjiang China *see* Shanghang
65 B1 Linjiang China
93 G4 Linköping Sweden
66 B1 Linkou China
71 B3 Linli China
96 B2 Linnhe, Loch *inlet* U.K.
70 B2 Linqing China
154 C2 Lins Brazil
136 C1 Linton U.S.A.
69 D2 Linxi China
70 A2 Linxia China
70 B2 Linyi *Shandong* China
70 B2 Linyi *Shandong* China
70 B2 Linying China
102 C2 Linz Austria
105 C3 Lion, Golfe du *g.* France
Lions, Gulf of *g.* France *see* Lion, Golfe du
109 B3 Lipari Italy
108 B3 Lipari, Isole *is* Italy
89 E3 Lipetsk Rus. Fed.
110 B1 Lipova Romania
101 D2 Lippstadt Ger.
53 C3 Liptrap, Cape Austr.
71 B3 Lipu China

119 D2 **Lira** Uganda
108 B2 **Liri** *r.* Italy
76 C1 **Lisakovsk** Kazakh.
118 C2 **Lisala** Dem. Rep. Congo
Lisboa Port. *see* **Lisbon**
106 B2 **Lisbon** Port.
97 C1 **Lisburn** U.K.
97 B2 **Liscannor Bay** Ireland
97 B2 **Lisdoonvarna** Ireland
Lishi China *see* **Dingnan**
71 B3 **Lishui** China
104 C2 **Lisieux** France
99 A4 **Liskeard** U.K.
89 E3 **Liski** Rus. Fed.
53 D1 **Lismore** Austr.
97 C2 **Lismore** Ireland
97 C1 **Lisnaskea** U.K.
97 B2 **Listowel** Ireland
71 A3 **Litang** *Guangxi* China
68 C2 **Litang** *Sichuan* China
138 B3 **Litchfield** *IL* U.S.A.
137 E1 **Litchfield** *MN* U.S.A.
53 D2 **Lithgow** Austr.
111 B3 **Lithino, Akrotirio** *pt* Greece
88 B2 **Lithuania** *country* Europe
111 B2 **Litochoro** Greece
102 C1 **Litoměřice** Czech Rep.
Litovskaya S.S.R. *country* Europe *see* **Lithuania**
146 C2 **Little Abaco** *i.* Bahamas
73 D3 **Little Andaman** *i.* India
141 E3 **Little Bahama Bank** *sea feature* Bahamas
93 F4 **Little Belt** *sea chan.* Denmark
146 B3 **Little Cayman** *i.* Cayman Is
142 A1 **Little Colorado** *r.* U.S.A.
138 C1 **Little Current** Can.
137 E1 **Little Falls** U.S.A.
143 C2 **Littlefield** U.S.A.
99 C4 **Littlehampton** U.K.
122 A2 **Little Karas Berg** *plat.* Namibia
122 B3 **Little Karoo** *plat.* S. Africa
96 A2 **Little Minch** *sea chan.* U.K.
136 C1 **Little Missouri** *r.* U.S.A.
73 D4 **Little Nicobar** *i.* India
140 B2 **Little Rock** U.S.A.
139 F2 **Littleton** U.S.A.
121 C2 **Litunde** Moz.
90 B2 **Lityn** Ukr.
Liuchow China *see* **Liuzhou**
70 B2 **Liujiachang** China
Liupanshui China *see* **Lupanshui**
121 C2 **Liupo** Moz.
71 A3 **Liuzhou** China
111 B3 **Livadeia** Greece
88 C2 **Līvāni** Latvia
141 D2 **Live Oak** U.S.A.
50 B1 **Liveringa** Austr.
142 C2 **Livermore, Mount** U.S.A.
53 D2 **Liverpool** Austr.
131 D3 **Liverpool** Can.
98 B3 **Liverpool** U.K.
127 G2 **Liverpool, Cape** Can.
53 C2 **Liverpool Range** *mts* Austr.
96 C3 **Livingston** U.K.
134 D1 **Livingston** *MT* U.S.A.
143 E2 **Livingston** *TX* U.S.A.
143 D2 **Livingston, Lake** U.S.A.
120 B2 **Livingstone** Zambia
55 A3 **Livingston Island** Antarctica
109 C2 **Livno** Bos.-Herz.
89 E3 **Livny** Rus. Fed.
138 C2 **Livonia** U.S.A.
108 B2 **Livorno** Italy
119 D3 **Liwale** Tanz.
99 A5 **Lizard Point** U.K.
108 B1 **Ljubljana** Slovenia
93 G3 **Ljungan** *r.* Sweden
93 F4 **Ljungby** Sweden
93 G3 **Ljusdal** Sweden
93 G3 **Ljusnan** *r.* Sweden
99 B4 **Llandeilo** U.K.
99 B4 **Llandovery** U.K.
99 B3 **Llandrindod Wells** U.K.
98 B3 **Llandudno** U.K.
99 A4 **Llanelli** U.K.
106 C1 **Llanes** Spain
98 A3 **Llangefni** U.K.
99 B3 **Llangollen** U.K.
99 B3 **Llangurig** U.K.
143 C2 **Llano Estacado** *plain* U.S.A.
150 C2 **Llanos** *plain* Col./Venez.
107 D1 **Lleida** Spain
99 A3 **Lleyn Peninsula** U.K.
107 C2 **Llíria** Spain
106 C1 **Llodio** Spain
128 B2 **Lloyd George, Mount** Can.
129 D2 **Lloyd Lake** Can.
129 C2 **Lloydminster** Can.
152 B2 **Llullaillaco, Volcán** *vol.* Chile
154 B2 **Loanda** Brazil
123 C2 **Lobatse** Botswana
103 D1 **Łobez** Pol.
120 A2 **Lobito** Angola
101 F1 **Loburg** Ger.
96 B2 **Lochaber** *reg.* U.K.
96 B2 **Lochaline** U.K.
Loch Baghasdail U.K. *see* **Lochboisdale**
96 A2 **Lochboisdale** U.K.
104 C2 **Loches** France
96 B2 **Lochgilphead** U.K.
96 B1 **Lochinver** U.K.
96 A2 **Lochmaddy** U.K.
96 C2 **Lochnagar** *mt.* U.K.
Loch nam Madadh U.K. *see* **Lochmaddy**
96 B3 **Lochranza** U.K.
52 A2 **Lock** Austr.
96 C3 **Lockerbie** U.K.
53 C3 **Lockhart** Austr.
143 D3 **Lockhart** U.S.A.
51 D1 **Lockhart River** Austr.
139 D2 **Lock Haven** U.S.A.
139 D2 **Lockport** U.S.A.
63 B2 **Lôc Ninh** Vietnam
105 C3 **Lodève** France
86 C2 **Lodeynoye Pole** Rus. Fed.
74 B2 **Lodhran** Pak.
108 A1 **Lodi** Italy
135 B3 **Lodi** U.S.A.
92 F2 **Løding** Norway
92 G2 **Lødingen** Norway
118 C3 **Lodja** Dem. Rep. Congo
119 D2 **Lodwar** Kenya
103 D1 **Łódź** Pol.
62 B2 **Loei** Thai.
122 A3 **Loeriesfontein** S. Africa
92 F2 **Lofoten** *is* Norway
134 D2 **Logan** U.S.A.
128 A1 **Logan, Mount** Can.
138 B2 **Logansport** U.S.A.
108 B1 **Logatec** Slovenia
115 D3 **Logone** *r.* Africa
106 C1 **Logroño** Spain
93 H3 **Lohja** Fin.
101 D1 **Löhne** Ger.
101 D1 **Lohne (Oldenburg)** Ger.
62 A2 **Loikaw** Myanmar
62 A2 **Loi Lan** *mt.* Myanmar/Thai.
93 H3 **Loimaa** Fin.
104 B2 **Loire** *r.* France
150 B3 **Loja** Ecuador
106 C2 **Loja** Spain
92 I2 **Lokan tekojärvi** *resr* Fin.
100 B2 **Lokeren** Belgium
122 B1 **Lokgwabe** Botswana
91 C1 **Lokhvytsya** Ukr.
119 D2 **Lokichar** Kenya
119 D2 **Lokichokio** Kenya
93 E4 **Løkken** Denmark
[illegible]
115 C4 **Lokoja** Nigeria
89 D3 **Lokot'** Rus. Fed.
88 C2 **Loksa** Estonia
127 H2 **Loks Land** *i.* Can.
114 B4 **Lola** Guinea
93 F5 **Lolland** *i.* Denmark
119 D3 **Lollondo** Tanz.
118 C2 **Lolo** Dem. Rep. Congo
122 B2 **Lolwane** S. Africa
110 B2 **Lom** Bulg.
93 E3 **Lom** Norway
119 C2 **Lomami** *r.* Dem. Rep. Congo
153 C3 **Lomas de Zamora** Arg.
50 B1 **Lombardina** Austr.
61 C2 **Lombok** *i.* Indon.
61 C2 **Lombok, Selat** *sea chan.* Indon.
114 C4 **Lomé** Togo
118 C3 **Lomela** *r.* Dem. Rep. Congo
100 B2 **Lommel** Belgium
96 B2 **Lomond, Loch** *l.* U.K.
88 C2 **Lomonosov** Rus. Fed.
160 A1 **Lomonosov Ridge** Arctic Ocean
61 C2 **Lompobattang, Gunung** *mt.* Indon.
135 B4 **Lompoc** U.S.A.
63 B2 **Lom Sak** Thai.
103 E1 **Łomża** Pol.
130 B3 **London** Can.
99 C4 **London** U.K.
138 C3 **London** U.S.A.
97 C1 **Londonderry** U.K.
50 B1 **Londonderry, Cape** Austr.
154 B2 **Londrina** Brazil
135 C3 **Lone Pine** U.S.A.
83 M2 **Longa, Proliv** *sea chan.* Rus. Fed.
61 C1 **Long Akah** Malaysia
141 E2 **Long Bay** U.S.A.
135 C4 **Long Beach** U.S.A.
71 A3 **Longchang** China
99 C3 **Long Eaton** U.K.
97 C2 **Longford** Ireland
96 C1 **Longhope** U.K.
119 D3 **Longido** Tanz.
61 C2 **Longiram** Indon.
147 C2 **Long Island** Bahamas
130 C2 **Long Island** Can.
59 D3 **Long Island** P.N.G.
139 E2 **Long Island** U.S.A.
130 B3 **Longlac** Can.
130 B3 **Long Lake** Can.
71 A3 **Longli** China
71 A3 **Longming** China
136 B2 **Longmont** U.S.A.
70 A2 **Longnan** China
Longping China *see* **Luodian**
138 C2 **Long Point** Can.
71 B3 **Longquan** China
131 E3 **Long Range Mountains** Can.
51 D2 **Longreach** Austr.
Longshan China *see* **Longli**
99 D3 **Long Stratton** U.K.
98 B2 **Longtown** U.K.
105 D2 **Longuyon** France
143 E2 **Longview** *TX* U.S.A.
134 B1 **Longview** *WA* U.S.A.
61 C1 **Longwai** Indon.
70 A2 **Longxi** China
Longxian China *see* **Wengyuan**
71 B3 **Longxi Shan** *mt.* China
63 B2 **Long Xuyên** Vietnam
71 B3 **Longyan** China
82 C1 **Longyearbyen** Svalbard
108 B1 **Lonigo** Italy
100 C1 **Löningen** Ger.
105 D2 **Lons-le-Saunier** France
141 E2 **Lookout, Cape** U.S.A.
119 D3 **Loolmalasin** *vol. crater* Tanz.
50 B3 **Loongana** Austr.
97 B2 **Loop Head** *hd* Ireland
Lopasnya Rus. Fed. *see* **Chekhov**
63 B2 **Lop Buri** Thai.
64 B2 **Lopez** Phil.
118 A3 **Lopez, Cap** *c.* Gabon
68 C2 **Lop Nur** *salt flat* China
118 B2 **Lopori** *r.* Dem. Rep. Congo
92 H1 **Lopphavet** *b.* Norway
74 A2 **Lora, Hamun-i-** *dry lake* Afgh./Pak.
106 B2 **Lora del Río** Spain
138 C2 **Lorain** U.S.A.
74 A1 **Loralai** Pak.
107 C2 **Lorca** Spain
51 E3 **Lord Howe Island** Austr.
142 B2 **Lordsburg** U.S.A.
155 C2 **Lorena** Brazil
59 D3 **Lorengau** P.N.G.
59 D3 **Lorentz** *r.* Indon.
152 B1 **Loreto** Bol.
144 A2 **Loreto** Mex.
104 B2 **Lorient** France
96 B2 **Lorn, Firth of** *est.* U.K.
52 B3 **Lorne** Austr.
105 D2 **Lorraine** *reg.* France
140 B2 **Los Alamos** U.S.A.
143 D3 **Los Aldamas** Mex.
153 A3 **Los Ángeles** Chile
135 C4 **Los Angeles** U.S.A.
135 B3 **Los Banos** U.S.A.
152 B2 **Los Blancos** Arg.
89 F3 **Losevo** Rus. Fed.
108 B2 **Lošinj** *i.* Croatia
144 B2 **Los Mochis** Mex.
118 B2 **Losombo** Dem. Rep. Congo
106 B2 **Los Pedroches** *plat.* Spain
147 D3 **Los Roques, Islas** *is* Venez.
96 C2 **Lossiemouth** U.K.
150 C1 **Los Teques** Venez.
59 E3 **Losuia** P.N.G.
152 A3 **Los Vilos** Chile
104 C3 **Lot** *r.* France
96 C1 **Loth** U.K.
134 D1 **Lothair** U.S.A.
Lothringen *reg.* France *see* **Lorraine**
119 D2 **Lotikipi Plain** Kenya/Sudan
118 C3 **Loto** Dem. Rep. Congo
89 E2 **Lotoshino** Rus. Fed.
62 B1 **Louangnamtha** Laos
62 B2 **Louangphabang** Laos
118 B3 **Loubomo** Congo
104 B2 **Loudéac** France
71 B3 **Loudi** China
118 B3 **Loudima** Congo
114 A3 **Louga** Senegal
99 C3 **Loughborough** U.K.
97 B2 **Loughrea** Ireland
105 D2 **Louhans** France
97 B2 **Louisburgh** Ireland
51 E1 **Louisiade Archipelago** *is* P.N.G.
140 B2 **Louisiana** *state* U.S.A.
123 C1 **Louis Trichardt** S. Africa
138 B3 **Louisville** *KY* U.S.A.
140 C2 **Louisville** *MS* U.S.A.
86 C2 **Loukhi** Rus. Fed.
118 B3 **Loukoléla** Congo
106 B2 **Loulé** Port.
118 A2 **Loum** Cameroon
130 C2 **Loups Marins, Lacs des** *lakes* Can.
104 B3 **Lourdes** France
151 D2 **Lourenço** Brazil
Lourenço Marques Moz. *see* **Maputo**
106 B1 **Lousã** Port.
53 C2 **Louth** Austr.
98 C3 **Louth** U.K.
Louvain Belgium *see* **Leuven**
122 A1 **Louwater-Suid** Namibia
89 D2 **Lovat'** *r.* Rus. Fed.
110 B2 **Lovech** Bulg.
136 B2 **Loveland** U.S.A.
136 B2 **Lovell** U.S.A.
135 C2 **Lovelock** U.S.A.
88 C1 **Loviisa** Fin.
143 C2 **Lovington** U.S.A.
86 C2 **Lovozero** Rus. Fed.
119 C3 **Lowa** Dem. Rep. Congo
139 E2 **Lowell** U.S.A.
119 D2 **Lowelli** Sudan
128 C3 **Lower Arrow Lake** Can.
Lower California *pen.* Mex. *see* **Baja California**
54 B2 **Lower Hutt** N.Z.
97 C1 **Lower Lough Erne** *l.* U.K.
128 B2 **Lower Post** Can.
137 E1 **Lower Red Lake** U.S.A.
Lower Tunguska *r.* Rus. Fed. *see* **Nizhnyaya Tunguska**
99 D3 **Lowestoft** U.K.
103 D1 **Łowicz** Pol.
139 D2 **Lowville** U.S.A.
52 B2 **Loxton** Austr.
Loyang China *see* **Luoyang**
48 H6 **Loyauté, Îles** New Caledonia
89 D3 **Loyew** Belarus
92 F2 **Løypskardtinden** *mt.* Norway
109 C2 **Loznica** Serbia
91 D2 **Lozova** Ukr.
120 B2 **Luacano** Angola
70 B2 **Lu'an** China
120 A1 **Luanda** Angola
63 B3 **Luang, Thale** *lag.* Thai.
121 C2 **Luangwa** *r.* Zambia
121 B2 **Luanshya** Zambia
Luao Angola *see* **Luau**
106 B1 **Luarca** Spain
120 B2 **Luau** Angola
103 E1 **Lubaczów** Pol.
103 D1 **Lubań** Pol.
64 A2 **Lubang Islands** Phil.
120 A2 **Lubango** Angola
119 C3 **Lubao** Dem. Rep. Congo
103 E1 **Lubartów** Pol.
101 D1 **Lübbecke** Ger.
102 C1 **Lübben** Ger.
143 C2 **Lubbock** U.S.A.
101 E1 **Lübeck** Ger.
69 E2 **Lubei** China
76 B1 **Lubenka** Kazakh.
119 C3 **Lubero** Dem. Rep. Congo
103 D1 **Lubin** Pol.
103 E1 **Lublin** Pol.
91 C1 **Lubny** Ukr.
61 C1 **Lubok Antu** Malaysia
101 E1 **Lübow** Ger.
101 E1 **Lübtheen** Ger.
119 C3 **Lubudi** Dem. Rep. Congo
60 B2 **Lubuklinggau** Indon.
119 C4 **Lubumbashi** Dem. Rep. Congo
120 B2 **Lubungu** Zambia
119 C3 **Lubutu** Dem. Rep. Congo
120 A1 **Lucala** Angola
97 C2 **Lucan** Ireland
120 B1 **Lucapa** Angola
108 B2 **Lucca** Italy
96 B3 **Luce Bay** U.K.
154 B2 **Lucélia** Brazil
64 B2 **Lucena** Phil.
106 C2 **Lucena** Spain
103 D2 **Lučenec** Slovakia
109 C2 **Lucera** Italy
105 D2 **Lucerne** Switz.
66 B1 **Luchegorsk** Rus. Fed.
101 E1 **Lüchow** Ger.
120 A2 **Lucira** Angola
Łuck Ukr. *see* **Luts'k**
101 F1 **Luckenwalde** Ger.
122 B2 **Luckhoff** S. Africa
75 C2 **Lucknow** India
120 A1 **Lucunga** Angola
120 B2 **Lucusse** Angola
Lüda China *see* **Dalian**
100 C2 **Lüdenscheid** Ger.
101 E1 **Lüder** Ger.
120 A3 **Lüderitz** Namibia
119 D4 **Ludewa** Tanz.
74 B1 **Ludhiana** India
138 B2 **Ludington** U.S.A.
99 B3 **Ludlow** U.K.
135 C4 **Ludlow** U.S.A.
110 C2 **Ludogorie** *reg.* Bulg.
93 G3 **Ludvika** Sweden
102 B2 **Ludwigsburg** Ger.
101 F1 **Ludwigsfelde** Ger.
101 D3 **Ludwigshafen am Rhein** Ger.
101 E1 **Ludwigslust** Ger.
88 C2 **Ludza** Latvia
118 C3 **Luebo** Dem. Rep. Congo
120 A2 **Luena** Angola
70 A2 **Lüeyang** China
71 B3 **Lufeng** China
119 C3 **Lufira** *r.* Dem. Rep. Congo
143 E2 **Lufkin** U.S.A.
88 C2 **Luga** Rus. Fed.
88 C2 **Luga** *r.* Rus. Fed.
105 D2 **Lugano** Switz.
121 C2 **Lugenda** *r.* Moz.
97 C2 **Lugnaquilla** *h.* Ireland
106 B1 **Lugo** Spain
110 B1 **Lugoj** Romania
91 D2 **Luhans'k** Ukr.
119 D3 **Luhombero** Tanz.
90 B1 **Luhyny** Ukr.
120 B2 **Luiana** Angola
Luichow Peninsula *pen.* China *see* **Leizhou Bandao**
118 C3 **Luilaka** *r.* Dem. Rep. Congo
Luimneach Ireland *see* **Limerick**
105 D2 **Luino** Italy
92 I2 **Luiro** *r.* Fin.
118 C3 **Luiza** Dem. Rep. Congo
70 B2 **Lujiang** China
Lukapa Angola *see* **Lucapa**
109 C2 **Lukavac** Bos.-Herz.
118 B3 **Lukenie** *r.* Dem. Rep. Congo
142 A2 **Lukeville** U.S.A.
89 E3 **Lukhovitsy** Rus. Fed.
Lukou China *see* **Zhuzhou**
103 E1 **Łuków** Pol.
120 B2 **Lukulu** Zambia
92 H2 **Luleå** Sweden
92 H2 **Luleälven** *r.* Sweden
111 C2 **Lüleburgaz** Turkey
70 B2 **Lüliang Shan** *mts* China
143 D3 **Luling** U.S.A.
Luluabourg Dem. Rep. Congo *see* **Kananga**
61 C2 **Lumajang** Indon.

75 C1 Lumajangdong Co salt l. China
Lumbala Angola see Lumbala Kaquengue
Lumbala Angola see Lumbala N'guimbo
120 B2 Lumbala Kaquengue Angola
120 B2 Lumbala N'guimbo Angola
140 C2 Lumberton MS U.S.A.
141 E2 Lumberton NC U.S.A.
61 C1 Lumbis Indon.
106 B1 Lumbrales Spain
63 B2 Lumphăt Cambodia
129 D2 Lumsden Can.
54 A3 Lumsden N.Z.
93 F4 Lund Sweden
121 C2 Lundazi Zambia
99 A4 Lundy U.K.
101 E1 Lüneburg Ger.
101 E1 Lüneburger Heide reg. Ger.
100 C2 Lünen Ger.
105 D2 Lunéville France
120 B2 Lunga r. Zambia
114 A4 Lungi Sierra Leone
Lungleh India see Lunglei
75 D2 Lunglei India
120 B2 Lungwebungu r. Zambia
74 B2 Luni r. India
88 C3 Luninyets Belarus
104 C3 L'Union France
114 A4 Lunsar Sierra Leone
77 E2 Luntai China
71 A3 Luodian China
71 B3 Luoding China
70 B2 Luohe China
70 B2 Luoyang China
118 B3 Luozi Dem. Rep. Congo
121 B2 Lupane Zimbabwe
71 A3 Lupanshui China
110 B1 Lupeni Romania
121 C2 Lupilichi Moz.
101 F2 Luppa Ger.
95 B3 Lurgan U.K.
Luring China see Gêrzê
121 D2 Lúrio Moz.
121 D2 Lurio r. Moz.
92 F2 Lurøy Norway
121 B2 Lusaka Zambia
118 C3 Lusambo Dem. Rep. Congo
109 C2 Lushnjë Albania
70 C2 Lüshunkou China
123 C3 Lusikisiki S. Africa
136 C2 Lusk U.S.A.
Luso Angola see Luena
76 B3 Lut, Dasht-e des. Iran
99 C4 Luton U.K.
61 C1 Lutong Malaysia
129 C1 Łutselk'e Can.
90 B1 Luts'k Ukr.
55 F3 Lützow-Holm Bay Antarctica
122 B2 Lutzputs S. Africa
122 A3 Lutzville S. Africa
117 C4 Luuq Somalia
137 D2 Luverne U.S.A.
119 C3 Luvua r. Dem. Rep. Congo
120 B2 Luvuei Angola
123 D1 Luvuvhu r. S. Africa
119 D3 Luwegu r. Tanz.
119 D2 Luwero Uganda
61 D2 Luwuk Indon.
100 C3 Luxembourg country Europe
100 C3 Luxembourg Lux.
105 D2 Luxeuil-les-Bains France
62 A1 Luxi China
123 C3 Luxolweni S. Africa
116 B2 Luxor Egypt
100 B2 Luyksgestel Neth.
86 D2 Luza Rus. Fed.
Luzern Switz. see Lucerne
62 B1 Luzhai China
71 A3 Luzhi China
71 A3 Luzhou China
154 C1 Luziânia Brazil
151 E3 Luzilândia Brazil
64 B2 Luzon i. Phil.
64 B1 Luzon Strait Phil./Taiwan
109 C3 Luzzi Italy
90 A2 L'viv Ukr.
L'vov Ukr. see L'viv
Lwów Ukr. see L'viv
88 C3 Lyakhavichy Belarus
Lyallpur Pak. see Faisalabad
89 D2 Lychkovo Rus. Fed.
92 G3 Lycksele Sweden
55 C2 Lyddan Island Antarctica
88 C3 Lyel'chytsy Belarus
88 C3 Lyepyel' Belarus
136 A2 Lyman U.S.A.
99 B4 Lyme Bay U.K.
99 B4 Lyme Regis U.K.
139 D3 Lynchburg U.S.A.
52 A2 Lyndhurst Austr.
129 D2 Lynn Lake Can.
134 B1 Lynnwood U.S.A.
129 D1 Lynx Lake Can.
105 C2 Lyon France
Lyons France see Lyon
89 D2 Lyozna Belarus
103 E1 Łysica h. Pol.
86 E3 Lys'va Rus. Fed.
91 D2 Lysychans'k Ukr.
87 D3 Lysyye Gory Rus. Fed.
98 B3 Lytham St Anne's U.K.
88 C3 Lyuban' Belarus
90 C2 Lyubashivka Ukr.
89 E2 Lyubertsy Rus. Fed.
90 B1 Lyubeshiv Ukr.
89 F2 Lyubim Rus. Fed.
90 A1 Lyuboml' Ukr.
91 D2 Lyubotyn Ukr.
89 D2 Lyubytino Rus. Fed.
89 D3 Lyudinovo Rus. Fed.

M

80 B2 Ma'ān Jordan
70 B2 Ma'anshan China
88 C2 Maardu Estonia
78 B3 Ma'āriḍ, Banī des. Saudi Arabia
80 B2 Ma'arrat an Nu'mān Syria
100 B1 Maarssen Neth.
100 B2 Maas r. Neth.
100 B2 Maaseik Belgium
64 B2 Maasin Phil.
100 B2 Maastricht Neth.
121 C3 Mabalane Moz.
78 B3 Ma'bar Yemen
150 D2 Mabaruma Guyana
98 D3 Mablethorpe U.K.
123 C2 Mabopane S. Africa
121 C3 Mabote Moz.
122 B2 Mabule Botswana
122 B1 Mabutsane Botswana
155 D2 Macaé Brazil
121 C2 Macaloge Moz.
126 F2 MacAlpine Lake Can.
71 B3 Macao aut. reg. China
151 D2 Macapá Brazil
150 B3 Macará Ecuador
155 D1 Macarani Brazil
Macassar Indon. see Makassar
Macassar Strait str. Indon. see Makassar, Selat
121 C2 Macatanja Moz.
151 F3 Macau Brazil
121 C3 Maccaretane Moz.
98 B3 Macclesfield U.K.
50 B2 Macdonald, Lake imp. l. Austr.
50 C2 Macdonnell Ranges mts Austr.
130 A2 MacDowell Lake Can.
96 C2 Macduff U.K.
106 B1 Macedo de Cavaleiros Port.
52 B3 Macedon mt. Austr.
111 B2 Macedonia country Europe
151 F3 Maceió Brazil
108 B2 Macerata Italy
52 A2 Macfarlane, Lake imp. l. Austr.
97 B3 Macgillycuddy's Reeks mts Ireland
74 A2 Mach Pak.
155 C2 Machado Brazil
121 C3 Machaila Moz.
119 D3 Machakos Kenya
150 B3 Machala Ecuador
121 C3 Machanga Moz.
Machaze Moz. see Chitobe
70 B2 Macheng China
138 B2 Machesney Park U.S.A.
139 F2 Machias U.S.A.
73 C3 Machilipatnam India
121 C2 Machinga Malawi
150 B1 Machiques Venez.
150 B4 Machu Picchu tourist site Peru
99 B3 Machynlleth U.K.
123 D2 Macia Moz.
Macias Nguema i. Equat. Guinea see Bioko
110 C1 Măcin Romania
114 B3 Macina Mali
53 D1 Macintyre r. Austr.
51 D2 Mackay Austr.
50 B2 Mackay, Lake imp. l. Austr.
128 C1 MacKay Lake Can.
128 B2 Mackenzie Can.
128 A1 Mackenzie r. Can.
Mackenzie Guyana see Linden
Mackenzie atoll Micronesia see Ulithi
55 H3 Mackenzie Bay Antarctica
126 C2 Mackenzie Bay Can.
126 E1 Mackenzie King Island Can.
128 A1 Mackenzie Mountains Can.
Mackillop, Lake imp. l. Austr. see Yamma Yamma, Lake
129 D2 Macklin Can.
53 D2 Macksville Austr.
53 D1 Maclean Austr.
123 C3 Maclear S. Africa
50 A2 MacLeod, Lake dry lake Austr.
138 A2 Macomb U.S.A.
108 A2 Macomer Italy
121 D2 Macomia Moz.
105 C2 Mâcon France
141 D2 Macon GA U.S.A.
137 E3 Macon MO U.S.A.
140 C2 Macon MS U.S.A.
53 C2 Macquarie r. Austr.
48 G9 Macquarie Island S. Pacific Ocean
53 C2 Macquarie Marshes Austr.
53 C2 Macquarie Mountain Austr.
156 D9 Macquarie Ridge S. Pacific Ocean
55 H2 Mac. Robertson Land reg. Antarctica
97 B3 Macroom Ireland
52 A1 Macumba watercourse Austr.
145 C3 Macuspana Mex.
144 B2 Macuzari, Presa resr Mex.
123 D2 Madadeni S. Africa
121 □D3 Madagascar country Africa
159 D5 Madagascar Ridge Indian Ocean
115 D2 Madama Niger
111 B2 Madan Bulg.
59 D3 Madang P.N.G.
139 D1 Madawaska r. Can.
62 A1 Madaya Myanmar
150 D3 Madeira r. Brazil
114 A1 Madeira terr. N. Atlantic Ocean
131 D3 Madeleine, Îles de la is Can.
99 B3 Madeley U.K.
144 B2 Madera Mex.
135 B3 Madera U.S.A.
73 B3 Madgaon India
74 B2 Madhya Pradesh state India
123 C2 Madibogo S. Africa
118 B3 Madingou Congo
121 □D2 Madirovalo Madag.
138 B3 Madison IN U.S.A.
137 D2 Madison SD U.S.A.
138 B2 Madison WI U.S.A.
138 C3 Madison WV U.S.A.
134 D1 Madison r. U.S.A.
138 B3 Madisonville U.S.A.
61 C2 Madiun Indon.
119 D2 Mado Gashi Kenya
68 C2 Madoi China
88 C2 Madona Latvia
78 A2 Madrakah Saudi Arabia
79 C3 Madrakah, Ra's c. Oman
Madras India see Chennai
134 B2 Madras U.S.A.
145 C2 Madre, Laguna lag. Mex.
143 D3 Madre, Laguna lag. U.S.A.
150 C4 Madre de Dios r. Peru
145 B3 Madre del Sur, Sierra mts Mex.
144 B2 Madre Occidental, Sierra mts Mex.
145 B2 Madre Oriental, Sierra mts Mex.
106 C1 Madrid Spain
106 C2 Madridejos Spain
61 C2 Madura i. Indon.
61 C2 Madura, Selat sea chan. Indon.
73 B4 Madurai India
121 B2 Madziwadzido Zimbabwe
67 C3 Maebashi Japan
62 A2 Mae Hong Son Thai.
62 A1 Mae Sai Thai.
62 A2 Mae Sariang Thai.
99 B4 Maesteg U.K.
62 A2 Mae Suai Thai.
121 □D2 Maevatanana Madag.
Mafeking S. Africa see Mafikeng
123 C2 Mafeteng Lesotho
53 C3 Maffra Austr.
119 D3 Mafia Island Tanz.
123 C2 Mafikeng S. Africa
119 D3 Mafinga Tanz.
154 C3 Mafra Brazil
83 L3 Magadan Rus. Fed.
Magallanes Chile see Punta Arenas
Magallanes, Estrecho de sea chan. Chile see Magellan, Strait of
150 B2 Magangue Col.
140 B1 Magazine Mountain h. U.S.A.
114 A4 Magburaka Sierra Leone
69 E1 Magdagachi Rus. Fed.
144 A1 Magdalena Mex.
142 B2 Magdalena U.S.A.
144 A2 Magdalena, Bahía b. Mex.
101 E1 Magdeburg Ger.
153 A5 Magellan, Strait of sea chan. Chile
Maggiore, Lago l. Italy see Maggiore, Lake
108 A1 Maggiore, Lake l. Italy
116 B2 Maghāghah Egypt
97 C1 Magherafelt U.K.
87 E3 Magnitogorsk Rus. Fed.
140 B2 Magnolia U.S.A.
121 C2 Màgoé Moz.
130 C3 Magog Can.
131 D2 Magpie, Lac l. Can.
114 A3 Magṭa' Laḥjar Maur.
81 D2 Magtymguly Turkm.
119 D3 Magu Tanz.
151 E3 Maguarinho, Cabo c. Brazil
123 D2 Magude Moz.
90 B2 Măgura, Dealul h. Moldova
62 A1 Magwe Myanmar
81 C2 Mahābād Iran
74 B2 Mahajan India
121 □D2 Mahajanga Madag.
61 C2 Mahakam r. Indon.
123 C1 Mahalapye Botswana
121 □D2 Mahalevona Madag.
75 C2 Mahanadi r. India
121 □D2 Mahanoro Madag.
74 B3 Maharashtra state India
63 B2 Maha Sarakham Thai.
121 □D2 Mahavavy r. Madag.
68 B3 Mahbubnagar India
78 B2 Mahd adh Dhahab Saudi Arabia
107 D2 Mahdia Alg.
150 D2 Mahdia Guyana
113 I6 Mahé i. Seychelles
75 C3 Mahendragiri mt. India
119 D3 Mahenge Tanz.
54 B3 Maheno N.Z.
74 B2 Mahesana India
74 B2 Mahi r. India
54 C1 Mahia Peninsula N.Z.
89 D3 Mahilyow Belarus
107 D2 Mahón Spain
114 B3 Mahou Mali
Mahsana India see Mahesana
74 B2 Mahuva India
111 C2 Mahya Dağı mt. Turkey
106 B1 Maia Port.
Maiaia Moz. see Nacala
147 C3 Maicao Col.
74 A1 Maīdān Shahr Afgh.
129 D2 Maidstone Can.
99 D4 Maidstone U.K.
115 D3 Maiduguri Nigeria
75 D2 Maijdi Bangl.
75 C2 Mailani India
101 D2 Main r. Ger.
118 B3 Mai-Ndombe, Lac l. Dem. Rep. Congo
101 E3 Main-Donau-Kanal canal Ger.
139 F1 Maine state U.S.A.
131 D3 Maine, Gulf of Can./U.S.A.
62 A1 Maingkwan Myanmar
96 C1 Mainland i. Scotland U.K.
96 □ Mainland i. Scotland U.K.
121 □D2 Maintirano Madag.
101 D2 Mainz Ger.
150 C1 Maiquetía Venez.
120 B3 Maitengwe Botswana
53 D2 Maitland N.S.W. Austr.
52 A2 Maitland S.A. Austr.
146 B3 Maíz, Islas del is Nic.
67 C3 Maizuru Japan
109 C2 Maja Jezercë mt. Albania
61 C2 Majene Indon.
119 D2 Majī Eth.
107 D2 Majorca i. Spain
Majunga Madag. see Mahajanga
123 C2 Majwemasweu S. Africa
118 B3 Makabana Congo
61 C2 Makale Indon.
119 C3 Makamba Burundi
77 E2 Makanchi Kazakh.
118 B2 Makanza Dem. Rep. Congo
90 B1 Makariv Ukr.
69 F1 Makarov Rus. Fed.
160 B1 Makarov Basin Arctic Ocean
109 C2 Makarska Croatia
61 C2 Makassar Indon.
61 C2 Makassar, Selat Indon.
76 B2 Makat Kazakh.
119 D3 Makatapora Tanz.
123 D2 Makatini Flats lowland S. Africa
114 A4 Makeni Sierra Leone
120 B3 Makgadikgadi depr. Botswana
87 D4 Makhachkala Rus. Fed.
76 B2 Makhambet Kazakh.
119 D3 Makindu Kenya
77 D1 Makinsk Kazakh.
91 D2 Makiyivka Ukr.
Makkah Saudi Arabia see Mecca
131 E2 Makkovik Can.
103 E2 Makó Hungary
118 B2 Makokou Gabon
119 D3 Makongolosi Tanz.
122 B2 Makopong Botswana
119 C2 Makoro Dem. Rep. Congo
118 B3 Makoua Congo
111 B3 Makrakomi Greece
79 D2 Makran reg. Iran/Pak.
74 A2 Makran Coast Range mts Pak.
89 E2 Maksatikha Rus. Fed.
81 C2 Mākū Iran
62 A1 Makum India
67 B4 Makurazaki Japan
115 C4 Makurdi Nigeria
92 G2 Malå Sweden
146 B4 Mala, Punta pt Panama
73 B3 Malabar Coast India
118 A2 Malabo Equat. Guinea
155 D1 Malacacheta Brazil
Malacca Malaysia see Melaka
60 A1 Malacca, Strait of Indon./Malaysia
134 D2 Malad City U.S.A.
88 C3 Maladzyechna Belarus
106 C2 Málaga Spain
Malagasy Republic country Africa see Madagascar
121 □D3 Malaimbandy Madag.
97 B1 Málainn Mhóir Ireland
48 H4 Malaita i. Solomon Is
117 B4 Malakal Sudan
48 H5 Malakula i. Vanuatu
61 D2 Malamala Indon.
61 C2 Malang Indon.
Malange Angola see Malanje
120 A1 Malanje Angola
93 G4 Mälaren l. Sweden
153 B3 Malargüe Arg.
130 C3 Malartic Can.
88 B3 Malaryta Belarus
80 B2 Malatya Turkey
121 C2 Malawi country Africa
Malawi, Lake l. Africa see Nyasa, Lake
89 D2 Malaya Vishera Rus. Fed.
64 B3 Malaybalay Phil.
81 C2 Malāyer Iran
60 B1 Malaysia country Asia
81 C2 Malazgirt Turkey
103 D1 Malbork Pol.
101 F1 Malchin Ger.
100 A2 Maldegem Belgium
48 L4 Malden Island Kiribati
56 C5 Maldives country Indian Ocean
99 D4 Maldon U.K.
56 I9 Male Maldives
111 B3 Maleas, Akrotirio pt Greece
103 D2 Malé Karpaty hills Slovakia
119 C3 Malela Dem. Rep. Congo

116 A3 **Malha** Sudan
134 C2 **Malheur Lake** U.S.A.
114 B3 **Mali** *country* Africa
114 A3 **Mali** Guinea
59 C3 **Maliana** East Timor
58 C3 **Malili** Indon.
97 C1 **Malin** Ireland
119 E3 **Malindi** Kenya
97 C1 **Malin Head** *hd* Ireland
Malin More Ireland *see* **Málainn Mhór**
111 C2 **Malkara** Turkey
88 C3 **Mal'kavichy** Belarus
110 C2 **Malko Tŭrnovo** Bulg.
53 C3 **Mallacoota** Austr.
53 C3 **Mallacoota Inlet** *b.* Austr.
96 B2 **Mallaig** U.K.
116 B2 **Mallawī** Egypt
129 E1 **Mallery Lake** Can.
Mallorca *i.* Spain *see* **Majorca**
97 B2 **Mallow** Ireland
92 F3 **Malm** Norway
92 H2 **Malmberget** Sweden
100 C2 **Malmédy** Belgium
122 A3 **Malmesbury** S. Africa
93 F4 **Malmö** Sweden
71 A3 **Malong** China
118 C4 **Malonga** Dem. Rep. Congo
86 C2 **Maloshuyka** Rus. Fed.
93 E3 **Måløy** Norway
89 E2 **Maloyaroslavets** Rus. Fed.
89 E2 **Maloye Borisovo** Rus. Fed.
86 D2 **Malozemel'skaya Tundra** *lowland* Rus. Fed.
125 J9 **Malpelo, Isla de** *i.* N. Pacific Ocean
84 F5 **Malta** *country* Europe
88 C2 **Malta** Latvia
134 F1 **Malta** U.S.A.
122 A1 **Maltahöhe** Namibia
98 C2 **Malton** U.K.
Maluku *is* Indon. *see* **Moluccas**
93 F3 **Malung** Sweden
123 C2 **Maluti Mountains** Lesotho
73 B3 **Malvan** India
140 B2 **Malvern** U.S.A.
117 B4 **Malwal** Sudan
90 B1 **Malyn** Ukr.
83 L2 **Malyy Anyuy** *r.* Rus. Fed.
Malyy Kavkaz *mts* Asia *see* **Lesser Caucasus**
83 K2 **Malyy Lyakhovskiy, Ostrov** *i.* Rus. Fed.
123 C2 **Mamafubedu** S. Africa
151 F3 **Mamanguape** Brazil
64 B3 **Mambajao** Phil.
119 C2 **Mambasa** Dem. Rep. Congo
118 B2 **Mambéré** *r.* C.A.R.
64 B2 **Mamburao** Phil.
123 C2 **Mamelodi** S. Africa
118 A2 **Mamfe** Cameroon
135 C3 **Mammoth Lakes** U.S.A.
88 A3 **Mamonovo** Rus. Fed.
150 C4 **Mamoré** *r.* Bol./Brazil
114 A3 **Mamou** Guinea
114 B4 **Mampong** Ghana
61 C2 **Mamuju** Indon.
114 B4 **Man** Côte d'Ivoire
150 C3 **Manacapuru** Brazil
107 D2 **Manacor** Spain
59 C2 **Manado** Indon.
146 B3 **Managua** Nic.
121 □D3 **Manakara** Madag.
78 B3 **Manākhah** Yemen
79 C2 **Manama** Bahrain
59 D3 **Manam Island** P.N.G.
121 □D3 **Mananara** *r.* Madag.
121 □D2 **Mananara Avaratra** Madag.
121 □D3 **Mananjary** Madag.
114 A3 **Manantali, Lac de** *l.* Mali
54 A3 **Manapouri, Lake** N.Z.
77 E2 **Manas Hu** *l.* China
75 C2 **Manaslu** *mt.* Nepal
Manastir Macedonia *see* **Bitola**
59 C3 **Manatuto** East Timor
62 A2 **Man-aung Kyun** Myanmar
150 C3 **Manaus** Brazil
80 B2 **Manavgat** Turkey
116 A3 **Manawashei** Sudan
98 B3 **Manchester** U.K.
139 E2 **Manchester** *CT* U.S.A.
139 E2 **Manchester** *NH* U.S.A.
140 C1 **Manchester** *TN* U.S.A.
81 D3 **Mand, Rūd-e** *r.* Iran
117 A4 **Manda, Jebel** *mt.* Sudan
121 □D3 **Mandabe** Madag.
93 E4 **Mandal** Norway
59 D3 **Mandala, Puncak** *mt.* Indon.
62 A1 **Mandalay** Myanmar
68 D1 **Mandalgovĭ** Mongolia
136 C1 **Mandan** U.S.A.
118 B1 **Mandara Mountains** Cameroon/Nigeria
108 A3 **Mandas** Italy
119 E2 **Mandera** Kenya
100 C2 **Manderscheid** Ger.
74 B1 **Mandi** India
114 B3 **Mandiana** Guinea
Mandidzuzure Zimbabwe *see* **Chimanimani**
75 C2 **Mandla** India
121 □D2 **Mandritsara** Madag.
74 B2 **Mandsaur** India
50 A3 **Mandurah** Austr.
73 B3 **Mandya** India
108 B1 **Manerbio** Italy
90 B1 **Manevychi** Ukr.
109 C2 **Manfredonia** Italy
109 C2 **Manfredonia, Golfo di** *g.* Italy
114 B3 **Manga** Burkina
118 B3 **Mangai** Dem. Rep. Congo
49 L6 **Mangaia** *i.* Cook Is
54 C1 **Mangakino** N.Z.
110 C2 **Mangalia** Romania
73 B3 **Mangalore** India
123 C2 **Mangaung** S. Africa
60 B2 **Manggar** Indon.
Mangghyshlaq Kazakh. *see* **Mangistau**
76 B2 **Mangistau** Kazakh.
61 C1 **Mangkalihat, Tanjung** *pt* Indon.
68 C2 **Mangnai** China
121 C2 **Mangochi** Malawi
121 □D3 **Mangoky** *r.* Madag.
59 C3 **Mangole** *i.* Indon.
54 B1 **Mangonui** N.Z.
Mangshi China *see* **Luxi**
106 B1 **Mangualde** Port.
154 D3 **Mangueirinha** Brazil
69 E1 **Mangui** China
Mangyshlak Kazakh. *see* **Mangistau**
137 D3 **Manhattan** U.S.A.
121 C3 **Manhica** Moz.
155 D2 **Manhuaçu** Brazil
121 □D2 **Mania** *r.* Madag.
108 B1 **Maniago** Italy
121 C2 **Maniamba** Moz.
150 C3 **Manicoré** Brazil
131 D3 **Manicouagan** *r.* Can.
131 D2 **Manicouagan, Petit Lac** *l.* Can.
131 D2 **Manicouagan, Réservoir** *resr* Can.
79 B2 **Manīfah** Saudi Arabia
49 K5 **Manihiki** *atoll* Cook Is
64 B2 **Manila** Phil.
53 D2 **Manilla** Austr.
Manipur India *see* **Imphal**
111 C3 **Manisa** Turkey
107 C2 **Manises** Spain
98 A2 **Man, Isle of** *i.* Irish Sea
138 B2 **Manistee** U.S.A.
138 B1 **Manistique** U.S.A.
129 E2 **Manitoba** *prov.* Can.
129 E2 **Manitoba, Lake** Can.
138 B1 **Manitou Islands** U.S.A.
130 B3 **Manitoulin Island** Can.
136 C3 **Manitou Springs** U.S.A.
130 B3 **Manitouwadge** Can.
138 B2 **Manitowoc** U.S.A.
130 C3 **Maniwaki** Can.
150 B2 **Manizales** Col.
121 □D3 **Manja** Madag.
121 C3 **Manjacaze** Moz.
137 E2 **Mankato** U.S.A.
114 B4 **Mankono** Côte d'Ivoire
129 D3 **Mankota** Can.
73 C4 **Mankulam** Sri Lanka
74 B2 **Manmad** India
52 A2 **Mannahill** Austr.
73 B4 **Mannar** Sri Lanka
73 B4 **Mannar, Gulf of** India/Sri Lanka
101 D3 **Mannheim** Ger.
128 C2 **Manning** Can.
52 A3 **Mannum** Austr.
129 C2 **Mannville** Can.
59 C3 **Manokwari** Indon.
119 C3 **Manono** Dem. Rep. Congo
63 A2 **Manoron** Myanmar
105 D3 **Manosque** France
131 C2 **Manouane, Lac** *l.* Can.
65 B1 **Manp'o** N. Korea
107 D1 **Manresa** Spain
121 B2 **Mansa** Zambia
127 G2 **Mansel Island** Can.
92 I2 **Mansel'kya** *ridge* Fin./Rus. Fed.
53 C3 **Mansfield** Austr.
98 C3 **Mansfield** U.K.
140 B1 **Mansfield** *AR* U.S.A.
140 B2 **Mansfield** *LA* U.S.A.
138 C2 **Mansfield** *OH* U.S.A.
139 D2 **Mansfield** *PA* U.S.A.
150 A3 **Manta** Ecuador
64 A3 **Mantalingajan, Mount** Phil.
155 D1 **Mantena** Brazil
141 E1 **Manteo** U.S.A.
104 C2 **Mantes-la-Jolie** France
155 C2 **Mantiqueira, Serra da** *mts* Brazil
Mantova Italy *see* **Mantua**
88 C1 **Mäntsälä** Fin.
108 B1 **Mantua** Italy
86 D3 **Manturovo** Rus. Fed.
151 D3 **Manuelzinho** Brazil
61 D2 **Manui** *i.* Indon.
54 B1 **Manukau** N.Z.
59 D3 **Manus Island** P.N.G.
140 B2 **Many** U.S.A.
121 C2 **Manyame** *r.* Moz./Zimbabwe
119 D3 **Manyara, Lake** *salt l.* Tanz.
Manyas Gölü *l.* Turkey *see* **Kuş Gölü**
87 D4 **Manych-Gudilo, Ozero** *l.* Rus. Fed.
142 B1 **Many Farms** U.S.A.
119 D3 **Manyoni** Tanz.
106 C2 **Manzanares** Spain
146 C2 **Manzanillo** Cuba
144 B3 **Manzanillo** Mex.
119 C3 **Manzanza** Dem. Rep. Congo
69 D1 **Manzhouli** China
123 D2 **Manzini** Swaziland
115 D3 **Mao** Chad
Maó Spain *see* **Mahón**
59 D3 **Maoke, Pegunungan** *mts* Indon.
123 C2 **Maokeng** S. Africa
65 A1 **Maokui Shan** *mt.* China
70 A2 **Maomao Shan** *mt.* China
71 B3 **Maoming** China
121 C3 **Mapai** Moz.
75 C1 **Mapam Yumco** *l.* China
61 D2 **Mapane** Indon.
145 C3 **Mapastepec** Mex.
144 B2 **Mapimí** Mex.
121 C3 **Mapinhane** Moz.
129 D3 **Maple Creek** Can.
156 D4 **Mapmakers Seamounts** N. Pacific Ocean
59 D3 **Maprik** P.N.G.
123 D1 **Mapulanguene** Moz.
121 C3 **Maputo** Moz.
123 D2 **Maputo** *r.* Moz./S. Africa
123 C2 **Maputsoe** Lesotho
114 A2 **Maqţeïr** *reg.* Maur.
75 C2 **Maquan He** *r.* China
120 A1 **Maquela do Zombo** Angola
153 B4 **Maquinchao** Arg.
137 E2 **Maquoketa** U.S.A.
123 C1 **Mara** S. Africa
150 C3 **Maraã** Brazil
151 E3 **Marabá** Brazil
151 D2 **Maracá, Ilha de** *i.* Brazil
150 B1 **Maracaibo** Venez.
Maracaibo, Lago de *inlet* Venez. *see* **Maracaibo, Lake**
150 B2 **Maracaibo, Lake** *inlet* Venez.
154 A2 **Maracaju** Brazil
154 A2 **Maracaju, Serra de** *hills* Brazil
150 C1 **Maracay** Venez.
115 D2 **Marādah** Libya
115 C3 **Maradi** Niger
81 C2 **Marāgheh** Iran
150 C2 **Marahuaca, Cerro** *mt.* Venez.
151 E3 **Marajó, Baía de** *est.* Brazil
151 D3 **Marajó, Ilha de** *i.* Brazil
79 C2 **Marākī** Iran
119 D2 **Maralal** Kenya
Maralbashi China *see* **Bachu**
50 C3 **Maralinga** Austr.
Maralwexi China *see* **Bachu**
142 A2 **Marana** U.S.A.
81 C2 **Marand** Iran
Marandellas Zimbabwe *see* **Marondera**
150 B3 **Marañón** *r.* Peru
Maraş Turkey *see* **Kahramanmaraş**
110 C1 **Mărăşeşti** Romania
130 B3 **Marathon** Can.
141 D4 **Marathon** U.S.A.
106 C2 **Marbella** Spain
50 A2 **Marble Bar** Austr.
123 C1 **Marble Hall** S. Africa
123 D3 **Marburg** S. Africa
101 D2 **Marburg an der Lahn** Ger.
103 D2 **Marcali** Hungary
137 E3 **Marceline** U.S.A.
99 D3 **March** U.K.
100 B2 **Marche-en-Famenne** Belgium
106 B2 **Marchena** Spain
152 B3 **Mar Chiquita, Laguna** *l.* Arg.
150 B4 **Marcona** Peru
139 E2 **Marcy, Mount** U.S.A.
74 B1 **Mardan** Pak.
153 C3 **Mar del Plata** Arg.
81 C2 **Mardin** Turkey
96 B2 **Maree, Loch** *l.* U.K.
51 D1 **Mareeba** Austr.
108 B3 **Marettimo, Isola** *i.* Italy
89 D2 **Marevo** Rus. Fed.
142 C2 **Marfa** U.S.A.
Margao India *see* **Madgaon**
50 A3 **Margaret River** Austr.
150 C1 **Margarita, Isla de** *i.* Venez.
123 D3 **Margate** S. Africa
99 D4 **Margate** U.K.
62 A1 **Margherita** India
Margherita, Lake *l.* Eth. *see* **Lake Abaya**
119 C2 **Margherita Peak** Dem. Rep. Congo/Uganda
76 C3 **Mārgow, Dasht-e** *des.* Afgh.
91 C2 **Marhanets'** Ukr.
62 A1 **Mari** Myanmar
152 B2 **María Elena** Chile
156 C5 **Mariana Trench** N. Pacific Ocean
Mariánica, Cordillera *mts* Spain *see* **Morena, Sierra**
140 B2 **Marianna** *AR* U.S.A.
141 C2 **Marianna** *FL* U.S.A.
102 C2 **Mariánské Lázně** Czech Rep.
144 B2 **Marías, Islas** *is* Mex.
78 B3 **Ma'rib** Yemen
109 C1 **Maribor** Slovenia
Maricourt Can. *see* **Kangiqsujuaq**
119 C2 **Maridi** Sudan
117 A4 **Maridi** *watercourse* Sudan
55 P2 **Marie Byrd Land** *reg.* Antarctica
147 D3 **Marie-Galante** *i.* Guadeloupe
93 G3 **Mariehamn** Fin.
122 A1 **Mariental** Namibia
93 F4 **Mariestad** Sweden
141 D2 **Marietta** *GA* U.S.A.
138 C3 **Marietta** *OH* U.S.A.
105 D3 **Marignane** France
83 K3 **Marii, Mys** *pt* Rus. Fed.
88 B3 **Marijampolė** Lith.
154 C2 **Marília** Brazil
106 B1 **Marín** Spain
135 B3 **Marina** U.S.A.
109 C3 **Marina di Gioiosa Ionica** Italy
88 C3 **Mar"ina Horka** Belarus
138 B1 **Marinette** U.S.A.
154 B2 **Maringá** Brazil
106 B2 **Marinha Grande** Port.
138 B2 **Marion** *IN* U.S.A.
138 C2 **Marion** *OH* U.S.A.
141 E2 **Marion** *SC* U.S.A.
138 C3 **Marion** *VA* U.S.A.
141 D2 **Marion, Lake** U.S.A.
52 A3 **Marion Bay** Austr.
152 B2 **Mariscal José Félix Estigarribia** Para.
105 D3 **Maritime Alps** *mts* France/Italy
110 C2 **Maritsa** *r.* Bulg.
91 D2 **Mariupol'** Ukr.
117 C4 **Marka** Somalia
68 C3 **Markam** China
123 C1 **Marken** S. Africa
100 B1 **Markermeer** *l.* Neth.
98 C3 **Market Rasen** U.K.
98 C3 **Market Weighton** U.K.
83 I2 **Markha** *r.* Rus. Fed.
139 D2 **Markham** Can.
91 D2 **Markivka** Ukr.
118 B2 **Markounda** C.A.R.
140 B2 **Marksville** U.S.A.
101 D3 **Marktheidenfeld** Ger.
101 F2 **Marktredwitz** Ger.
100 C2 **Marl** Ger.
51 C2 **Marla** Austr.
100 A3 **Marle** France
143 D2 **Marlin** U.S.A.
53 C3 **Marlo** Austr.
104 C3 **Marmande** France
111 C2 **Marmara, Sea of** *g.* Turkey
Marmara Denizi *g.* Turkey *see* **Marmara, Sea of**
111 C3 **Marmaris** Turkey
105 C2 **Marne** *r.* France
105 C2 **Marne-la-Vallée** France
118 B2 **Maro** Chad
121 □D2 **Maroantsetra** Madag.
54 B1 **Marokopa** N.Z.
101 E2 **Maroldsweisach** Ger.
121 □D2 **Maromokotro** *mt.* Madag.
121 C2 **Marondera** Zimbabwe
151 D2 **Maroni** *r.* Fr. Guiana
51 E2 **Maroochydore** Austr.
61 C2 **Maros** Indon.
49 M6 **Marotiri** *is* Fr. Polynesia
118 B1 **Maroua** Cameroon
121 □D2 **Marovoay** Madag.
49 N4 **Marquesas Islands** Fr. Polynesia
141 D4 **Marquesas Keys** *is* U.S.A.
155 D2 **Marquês de Valença** Brazil
138 B1 **Marquette** U.S.A.
116 A3 **Marra, Jebel** *mt.* Sudan
116 A3 **Marra, Jebel** Sudan
123 D2 **Marracuene** Moz.
114 B1 **Marrakech** Morocco
Marrakesh Morocco *see* **Marrakech**
52 A1 **Marree** Austr.
86 F2 **Marresale** Rus. Fed.
121 C2 **Marromeu** Moz.
121 C2 **Marrupa** Moz.
116 B2 **Marsá al 'Alam** Egypt
115 D1 **Marsa al Burayqah** Libya
119 D2 **Marsabit** Kenya
78 A2 **Marsa Delwein** Sudan
108 B3 **Marsala** Italy
116 A1 **Marsá Maţrūḩ** Egypt
101 D2 **Marsberg** Ger.
108 B2 **Marsciano** Italy
53 C2 **Marsden** Austr.
100 B1 **Marsdiep** *sea chan.* Neth.
105 D3 **Marseille** France
Marseilles France *see* **Marseille**
140 B1 **Marshall** *AR* U.S.A.
137 D2 **Marshall** *MN* U.S.A.
137 E3 **Marshall** *MO* U.S.A.
143 E2 **Marshall** *TX* U.S.A.
48 H2 **Marshall Islands** *country* N. Pacific Ocean
137 E2 **Marshalltown** U.S.A.
138 A2 **Marshfield** U.S.A.
146 C2 **Marsh Harbour** Bahamas
140 B3 **Marsh Island** U.S.A.
93 G4 **Märsta** Sweden
Martaban, Gulf of *g.* Myanmar *see* **Mottama, Gulf of**
61 C2 **Martapura** Indon.
60 B2 **Martapura** Indon.
139 E2 **Martha's Vineyard** *i.* U.S.A.
105 D2 **Martigny** Switz.
103 D2 **Martin** Slovakia
136 C2 **Martin** U.S.A.
145 C2 **Martínez** Mex.
141 D2 **Martinez** U.S.A.
155 C1 **Martinho Campos** Brazil
147 D3 **Martinique** *terr.* West Indies
147 D3 **Martinique Passage** Dominica/Martinique
139 D3 **Martinsburg** U.S.A.
138 D3 **Martinsville** U.S.A.
54 C2 **Marton** N.Z.
107 D1 **Martorell** Spain
106 C2 **Martos** Spain
76 B1 **Martuk** Kazakh.
81 D3 **Marv Dasht** Iran
105 C3 **Marvejols** France
76 C3 **Mary** Turkm.
51 E2 **Maryborough** Austr.

122 B2 Marydale S. Africa
139 D3 Maryland *state* U.S.A.
98 B2 Maryport U.K.
137 D3 Marysville U.S.A.
137 E2 Maryville *MO* U.S.A.
141 D1 Maryville *TN* U.S.A.
119 D3 Masai Steppe *plain* Tanz.
119 D3 Masaka Uganda
61 C2 Masalembu Besar *i.* Indon.
61 D2 Masamba Indon.
65 B2 Masan S. Korea
119 D4 Masasi Tanz.
64 B2 Masbate Phil.
64 B2 Masbate *i.* Phil.
107 D2 Mascara Alg.
155 E1 Mascote Brazil
123 C2 Maseru Lesotho
Mashaba Zimbabwe *see* Mashava
121 C3 Mashava Zimbabwe
76 B3 Mashhad Iran
123 D2 Mashishing S. Africa
74 A2 Mashkel, Hamun-i- *salt flat* Pak.
123 C3 Masibambane S. Africa
79 C3 Masīlah, Wādī al *watercourse* Yemen
123 C2 Masilo S. Africa
118 B3 Masi-Manimba Dem. Rep. Congo
119 D2 Masindi Uganda
122 B3 Masinyusane S. Africa
Masira, Gulf of *b.* Oman *see* Maşīrah, Khalīj
79 C3 Maşīrah, Khalīj Oman
81 C2 Masjed Soleymān Iran
97 B2 Mask, Lough *l.* Ireland
121 □E2 Masoala, Tanjona *c.* Madag.
137 E2 Mason City U.S.A.
Masqaţ Oman *see* Muscat
108 B2 Massa Italy
139 E2 Massachusetts *state* U.S.A.
139 E2 Massachusetts Bay U.S.A.
115 D3 Massaguet Chad
115 D3 Massakory Chad
121 C3 Massangena Moz.
120 A1 Massango Angola
116 B3 Massawa Eritrea
139 E2 Massena U.S.A.
115 D3 Massenya Chad
128 A2 Masset Can.
105 C2 Massif Central *mts* France
138 C2 Massillon U.S.A.
121 C3 Massinga Moz.
123 D1 Massingir Moz.
78 A2 Mastābah Saudi Arabia
54 C2 Masterton N.Z.
74 B1 Mastuj Pak.
74 A2 Mastung Pak.
78 A2 Mastūrah Saudi Arabia
88 B3 Masty Belarus
67 B4 Masuda Japan
Masuku Gabon *see* Franceville
121 C3 Masvingo Zimbabwe
119 D3 Maswa Tanz.
69 D1 Matad Mongolia
118 B3 Matadi Dem. Rep. Congo
146 B3 Matagalpa Nic.
130 C3 Matagami Can.
130 C3 Matagami, Lac *l.* Can.
143 D3 Matagorda Island U.S.A.
143 D3 Matagorda Peninsula U.S.A.
120 A2 Matala Angola
114 A3 Matam Senegal
54 C1 Matamata N.Z.
144 B2 Matamoros *Chihuahua* Mex.
145 C2 Matamoros *Tamaulipas* Mex.
119 D3 Matandu *r.* Tanz.
131 D3 Matane Can.
146 B2 Matanzas Cuba
Matapan, Cape *c.* Greece *see* Tainaro, Akra
73 C4 Matara Sri Lanka
61 C2 Mataram Indon.
50 C1 Mataranka Austr.
107 D1 Mataró Spain
123 C3 Matatiele S. Africa
54 A3 Mataura N.Z.
54 A3 Mataura *r.* N.Z.
54 C1 Matawai N.Z.
152 B1 Mategua Bol.
145 B2 Matehuala Mex.
109 C2 Matera Italy
108 A3 Mateur Tunisia
129 E2 Matheson Island Can.
143 D3 Mathis U.S.A.
74 B2 Mathura India
64 B3 Mati Phil.
145 C3 Matías Romero Mex.
98 C3 Matlock U.K.
150 D4 Mato Grosso Brazil
154 B1 Mato Grosso *state* Brazil
154 B1 Mato Grosso, Planalto do *plat.* Brazil
154 B1 Mato Grosso do Sul *state* Brazil
123 D2 Matola Moz.
106 B1 Matosinhos Port.
Matou China *see* Pingguo
79 C2 Maţraḩ Oman
67 B3 Matsue Japan
66 D2 Matsumae Japan
67 C3 Matsumoto Japan
67 C4 Matsusaka Japan
71 C3 Matsu Tao *i.* Taiwan
67 B4 Matsuyama Japan
130 B2 Mattagami *r.* Can.
130 C3 Mattawa Can.
105 D2 Matterhorn *mt.* Italy/Switz.
134 C2 Matterhorn *mt.* U.S.A.
141 D1 Matthews U.S.A.
79 C2 Maţţī, Sabkhat *salt pan* Saudi Arabia
138 B3 Mattoon U.S.A.
150 C2 Maturín Venez.
91 D2 Matveyev Kurgan Rus. Fed.
123 C2 Matwabeng S. Africa
105 C1 Maubeuge France
104 C3 Maubourguet France
55 E3 Maud Seamount *sea feature* S. Atlantic Ocean
49 L1 Maui *i.* U.S.A.
141 D2 Mauldin U.S.A.
138 C2 Maumee *r.* U.S.A.
61 D2 Maumere Indon.
120 B2 Maun Botswana
75 C2 Maunath Bhanjan India
123 C1 Maunatlala Botswana
62 A1 Maungdaw Myanmar
75 B2 Mau Ranipur India
50 C2 Maurice, Lake *imp. l.* Austr.
114 A3 Mauritania *country* Africa
113 I8 Mauritius *country* Indian Ocean
120 B2 Mavinga Angola
123 C3 Mavuya S. Africa
78 B2 Māwān, Khashm *mt.* Saudi Arabia
118 B3 Mawanga Dem. Rep. Congo
71 B3 Mawei China
62 A1 Mawkmai Myanmar
62 A1 Mawlaik Myanmar
63 A2 Mawlamyaing Myanmar
78 B2 Mawqaq Saudi Arabia
55 L3 Mawson Peninsula Antarctica
78 B3 Mawza Yemen
108 A3 Maxia, Punta *mt.* Italy
121 C3 Maxixe Moz.
54 B1 Maxwell N.Z.
83 J2 Maya *r.* Rus. Fed.
147 C2 Mayaguana *i.* Bahamas
147 D3 Mayagüez Puerto Rico
81 D2 Mayamey Iran
96 B3 Maybole U.K.
116 B3 Maych'ew Eth.
117 C3 Maydh Somalia
100 C2 Mayen Ger.
104 B2 Mayenne France
104 B2 Mayenne *r.* France
128 C2 Mayerthorpe Can.
138 B3 Mayfield U.S.A.
91 E3 Maykop Rus. Fed.
76 C3 Maymanah Afgh.
128 A1 Mayo Can.
118 B3 Mayoko Congo
Mayo Landing Can. *see* Mayo
64 B2 Mayon *vol.* Phil.
121 D2 Mayotte *terr.* Africa
83 J3 Mayskiy Rus. Fed.
138 C3 Maysville U.S.A.
118 B3 Mayumba Gabon
137 D1 Mayville U.S.A.
120 B2 Mazabuka Zambia
Mazagan Morocco *see* El Jadida
151 D3 Mazagão Brazil
104 C3 Mazamet France
74 B1 Mazar China
108 B3 Mazara del Vallo Italy
77 C3 Mazār-e Sharīf Afgh.
107 C2 Mazarrón Spain
107 C2 Mazarrón, Golfo de *b.* Spain
144 A2 Mazatán Mex.
146 A3 Mazatenango Guat.
144 B2 Mazatlán Mex.
88 B2 Mažeikiai Lith.
88 B2 Mazirbe Latvia
103 E1 Mazowiecka, Nizina *lowland* Pol.
121 B3 Mazunga Zimbabwe
103 E1 Mazurskie, Pojezierze *reg.* Pol.
88 C3 Mazyr Belarus
123 D2 Mbabane Swaziland
118 B2 Mbaïki C.A.R.
118 B2 Mbakaou, Lac de *l.* Cameroon
121 C1 Mbala Zambia
121 B3 Mbalabala Zimbabwe
119 D2 Mbale Uganda
118 B2 Mbalmayo Cameroon
118 B3 Mbandaka Dem. Rep. Congo
118 B2 Mbandjok Cameroon
118 A2 Mbanga Cameroon
120 A1 M'banza Congo Angola
118 B3 Mbanza-Ngungu Dem. Rep. Congo
119 D3 Mbarara Uganda
118 B2 Mbé Cameroon
119 D3 Mbeya Tanz.
119 D4 Mbinga Tanz.
119 D3 Mbizi Mountains Tanz.
119 C2 Mboki C.A.R.
118 B3 Mbomo Congo
118 B2 Mbouda Cameroon
114 A3 Mbour Senegal
114 A3 Mbout Maur.
118 C3 Mbuji-Mayi Dem. Rep. Congo
119 D3 Mbuyuni Tanz.
139 F1 McAdam Can.
143 D2 McAlester U.S.A.
143 D3 McAllen U.S.A.
128 B2 McBride Can.
134 C2 McCall U.S.A.
143 C2 McCamey U.S.A.
126 F2 McClintock Channel Can.
126 E2 McClure Strait Can.
140 B2 McComb U.S.A.
136 C2 McConaughy, Lake U.S.A.
136 C2 McCook U.S.A.
134 C2 McDermitt U.S.A.
159 E7 McDonald Islands Indian Ocean
134 D1 McDonald Peak U.S.A.
135 D3 McGill U.S.A.
126 B2 McGrath U.S.A.
134 D1 McGuire, Mount U.S.A.
121 C2 Mchinji Malawi
140 C1 McKenzie U.S.A.
51 D2 McKinlay Austr.
134 B2 McKinleyville U.S.A.
128 C2 McLennan Can.
128 B2 McLeod Lake Can.
134 B1 McMinnville *OR* U.S.A.
140 C1 McMinnville *TN* U.S.A.
137 D3 McPherson U.S.A.
128 C1 McTavish Arm *b.* Can.
123 C3 Mdantsane S. Africa
107 E2 M'Doukal Alg.
135 D3 Mead, Lake *resr* U.S.A.
136 C3 Meade U.S.A.
129 D2 Meadow Lake Can.
138 C2 Meadville U.S.A.
66 D2 Meaken-dake *vol.* Japan
106 B1 Mealhada Port.
131 E2 Mealy Mountains Can.
128 C2 Meander River Can.
78 A2 Mecca Saudi Arabia
139 D3 Mechanicsville U.S.A.
100 B2 Mechelen Belgium
100 B2 Mechelen Neth.
100 C2 Mechernich Ger.
100 C2 Meckenheim Ger.
101 E1 Mecklenburgische Seenplatte *reg.* Ger.
106 B1 Meda Port.
60 A1 Medan Indon.
153 B4 Medanosa, Punta *pt* Arg.
73 C4 Medawachchiya Sri Lanka
107 D2 Médéa Alg.
150 B2 Medellín Col.
115 D1 Medenine Tunisia
134 B2 Medford U.S.A.
110 C2 Medgidia Romania
110 B1 Mediaş Romania
136 B2 Medicine Bow Mountains U.S.A.
136 B2 Medicine Bow Peak U.S.A.
129 C2 Medicine Hat Can.
137 D3 Medicine Lodge U.S.A.
155 D1 Medina Brazil
78 A2 Medina Saudi Arabia
106 C1 Medinaceli Spain
106 C1 Medina del Campo Spain
106 B1 Medina de Rioseco Spain
75 C2 Medinipur India
84 E5 Mediterranean Sea
129 C2 Medley Can.
87 E3 Mednogorsk Rus. Fed.
62 A1 Mêdog China
88 B2 Medvėgalio kalnas *h.* Lith.
83 L2 Medvezh'i, Ostrova *is* Rus. Fed.
86 C2 Medvezh'yegorsk Rus. Fed.
50 A2 Meekatharra Austr.
136 B2 Meeker U.S.A.
74 B2 Meerut India
100 A2 Meetkerke Belgium
119 D2 Mēga Eth.
60 B2 Mega *i.* Indon.
119 D2 Mega Escarpment Eth./Kenya
111 B3 Megalopoli Greece
75 D2 Meghalaya *state* India
75 C2 Meghasani *mt.* India
111 C3 Megisti *i.* Greece
92 I1 Mehamn Norway
50 A2 Meharry, Mount Austr.
137 E3 Mehlville U.S.A.
79 C2 Mehrān *watercourse* Iran
74 B1 Mehtar Lām Afgh.
119 D3 Meia Meia Tanz.
154 C1 Meia Ponte *r.* Brazil
118 B2 Meiganga Cameroon
65 B1 Meihekou China
Meijiang China *see* Ningdu
62 A1 Meiktila Myanmar
101 E2 Meiningen Ger.
102 C1 Meißen Ger.
Meixian China *see* Meizhou
71 B3 Meizhou China
152 B2 Mejicana *mt.* Arg.
152 A2 Mejillones Chile
118 B2 Mékambo Gabon
116 B3 Mek'elē Eth.
114 C2 Mekerrhane, Sebkha *salt pan* Alg.
114 B1 Meknès Morocco
63 B2 Mekong *r.* Asia
63 B3 Mekong, Mouths of the Vietnam
60 B1 Melaka Malaysia
156 D6 Melanesia *is* Pacific Ocean
156 D5 Melanesian Basin Pacific Ocean
53 B3 Melbourne Austr.
141 D3 Melbourne U.S.A.
108 A2 Mele, Capo *c.* Italy
Melekess Rus. Fed. *see* Dimitrovgrad
89 F2 Melenki Rus. Fed.
131 C2 Mélèzes, Rivière aux *r.* Can.
115 D3 Melfi Chad
109 C2 Melfi Italy
129 D2 Melfort Can.
92 F3 Melhus Norway
106 B1 Melide Spain
114 B1 Melilla N. Africa
129 D3 Melita Can.
91 D2 Melitopol' Ukr.
119 D2 Melka Guba Eth.
101 D1 Melle Ger.
93 F4 Mellerud Sweden
101 E2 Mellrichstadt Ger.
101 D1 Mellum *i.* Ger.
123 D2 Melmoth S. Africa
152 C3 Melo Uru.
115 C1 Melrhir, Chott *salt l.* Alg.
96 C3 Melrose U.K.
Melsetter Zimbabwe *see* Chimanimani
52 B3 Melton Austr.
99 C3 Melton Mowbray U.K.
105 C2 Melun France
129 D2 Melville Can.
51 D1 Melville, Cape Austr.
131 E2 Melville, Lake Can.
50 C1 Melville Island Austr.
126 E1 Melville Island Can.
127 G2 Melville Peninsula Can.
61 C2 Memboro Indon.
102 C2 Memmingen Ger.
60 B1 Mempawah Indon.
80 B3 Memphis *tourist site* Egypt
140 B1 Memphis *TN* U.S.A.
143 C2 Memphis *TX* U.S.A.
91 C1 Mena Ukr.
140 B2 Mena U.S.A.
121 □D3 Menabe *mts* Madag.
114 C3 Ménaka Mali
Mènam Khong *r.* Laos/Thai. *see* Mekong
105 C3 Mende France
117 B4 Mendebo Eth.
116 B3 Mendefera Eritrea
160 B1 Mendeleyev Ridge Arctic Ocean
145 C2 Méndez Mex.
117 B4 Mendī Eth.
59 D3 Mendi P.N.G.
99 B4 Mendip Hills U.K.
138 B2 Mendota U.S.A.
153 B3 Mendoza Arg.
111 C3 Menemen Turkey
100 A2 Menen Belgium
70 B2 Mengcheng China
60 B2 Menggala Indon.
71 A3 Mengzi China
131 D2 Menihek Can.
52 B2 Menindee Austr.
52 B2 Menindee Lake Austr.
52 A3 Meningie Austr.
104 C2 Mennecy France
138 B1 Menominee U.S.A.
120 A2 Menongue Angola
Menorca *i.* Spain *see* Minorca
61 C1 Mensalong Indon.
60 A2 Mentawai, Kepulauan *is* Indon.
60 B2 Mentok Indon.
61 C1 Menyapa, Gunung *mt.* Indon.
108 A3 Menzel Bourguiba Tunisia
50 B2 Menzies Austr.
144 B2 Meoqui Mex.
100 C1 Meppel Neth.
100 C1 Meppen Ger.
121 C3 Mepuze Moz.
123 C2 Meqheleng S. Africa
138 B2 Mequon U.S.A.
108 B1 Merano Italy
59 D3 Merauke Indon.
52 B2 Merbein Austr.
Merca Somalia *see* Marka
135 B3 Merced U.S.A.
152 C2 Mercedes Arg.
143 D3 Mercedes U.S.A.
127 H2 Mercy, Cape Can.
143 C1 Meredith, Lake U.S.A.
91 D2 Merefa Ukr.
116 A3 Merga Oasis Sudan
63 A2 Mergui Archipelago *is* Myanmar
110 C2 Meriç *r.* Greece/Turkey
111 C2 Meriç Turkey
145 D2 Mérida Mex.
106 B2 Mérida Spain
150 B2 Mérida Venez.
147 C4 Mérida, Cordillera de *mts* Venez.
134 C2 Meridian *ID* U.S.A.
140 C2 Meridian *MS* U.S.A.
143 D2 Meridian *TX* U.S.A.
104 B3 Mérignac France
93 H3 Merikarvia Fin.
53 C3 Merimbula Austr.
88 B3 Merkinė Lith.
116 B3 Merowe Sudan
50 A3 Merredin Austr.
96 B3 Merrick *h.* U.K.
138 B1 Merrill U.S.A.
138 B2 Merrillville U.S.A.
136 C2 Merriman U.S.A.
128 B2 Merritt Can.
53 C2 Merrygoen Austr.
116 C3 Mersa Fatma Eritrea
100 C3 Mersch Lux.
101 E2 Merseburg (Saale) Ger.
98 B2 Mersey *r.* U.K.
80 B2 Mersin Turkey
60 B1 Mersing Malaysia
99 D4 Mers-les-Bains France
74 B2 Merta India
99 B4 Merthyr Tydfil U.K.
119 D2 Merti Plateau Kenya
106 B2 Mértola Port.
76 B2 Mertvyy Kultuk, Sor *dry lake* Kazakh.
119 D3 Meru *vol.* Tanz.
122 B3 Merweville S. Africa
80 B1 Merzifon Turkey
100 C3 Merzig Ger.
142 A2 Mesa *AZ* U.S.A.
142 C2 Mesa *NM* U.S.A.

137 E1 **Mesabi Range** *hills* U.S.A.
109 C2 **Mesagne** Italy
142 B2 **Mescalero** U.S.A.
143 C2 **Mescalero Ridge** U.S.A.
101 D2 **Meschede** Ger.
89 E3 **Meshchovsk** Rus. Fed.
Meshed Iran *see* **Mashhad**
91 E2 **Meshkovskaya** Rus. Fed.
142 B2 **Mesilla** U.S.A.
111 B2 **Mesimeri** Greece
111 B3 **Mesolongi** Greece
115 C1 **Messaad** Alg.
121 D2 **Messalo** *r.* Moz.
109 C3 **Messina** Italy
109 C3 **Messina, Strait of** *str.* Italy
Messina, Stretta di *str.* Italy *see* **Messina, Strait of**
111 B3 **Messini** Greece
111 B3 **Messiniakos Kolpos** *g.* Greece
111 B2 **Mesta** *r.* Bulg.
Mesta *r.* Greece *see* **Nestos**
150 C2 **Meta** *r.* Col./Venez.
130 C3 **Métabetchouan** Can.
127 H2 **Meta Incognita Peninsula** Can.
140 B3 **Metairie** U.S.A.
152 B2 **Metán** Arg.
111 B3 **Methoni** Greece
109 C2 **Metković** Croatia
121 C2 **Metoro** Moz.
60 B2 **Metro** Indon.
100 C3 **Mettlach** Ger.
135 C3 **Mettler** U.S.A.
117 B4 **Metu** Eth.
105 D2 **Metz** France
100 B2 **Meuse** *r.* Belgium/France
143 D2 **Mexia** U.S.A.
144 A1 **Mexicali** Mex.
144 B2 **Mexico** *country* Central America
México Mex. *see* **Mexico City**
137 E3 **Mexico** U.S.A.
125 I7 **Mexico, Gulf of** Mex./U.S.A.
145 C3 **Mexico City** Mex.
81 D2 **Meybod** Iran
101 F1 **Meyenburg** Ger.
83 M2 **Meynypil'gyno** Rus. Fed.
86 D2 **Mezen'** Rus. Fed.
86 D2 **Mezen'** *r.* Rus. Fed.
86 F1 **Mezhdusharskiy, Ostrov** *i.* Rus. Fed.
103 E2 **Mezőtúr** Hungary
132 C4 **Mezquital** *r.* Mex.
144 B2 **Mezquitic** Mex.
88 C2 **Mežvidi** Latvia
121 C2 **Mfuwe** Zambia
89 D3 **Mglin** Rus. Fed.
123 D2 **Mhlume** Swaziland
74 B2 **Mhow** India
145 C3 **Miahuatlán** Mex.
106 B2 **Miajadas** Spain
141 D3 **Miami** *FL* U.S.A.
143 E1 **Miami** *OK* U.S.A.
141 D3 **Miami Beach** U.S.A.
81 C2 **Mīāndowāb** Iran
121 □D2 **Miandrivazo** Madag.
81 C2 **Mīāneh** Iran
71 A3 **Mianning** China
74 B1 **Mianwali** Pak.
Mianyang China *see* **Xiantao**
70 A2 **Mianyang** China
121 □D2 **Miarinarivo** Madag.
87 F3 **Miass** Rus. Fed.
103 D1 **Miastko** Pol.
128 C2 **Mica Creek** Can.
103 E2 **Michalovce** Slovakia
138 B1 **Michigan** *state* U.S.A.
138 B2 **Michigan, Lake** U.S.A.
138 B2 **Michigan City** U.S.A.
138 B1 **Michipicoten Bay** Can.
130 B3 **Michipicoten Island** Can.
130 B3 **Michipicoten River** Can.
Michurin Bulg. *see* **Tsarevo**
89 F3 **Michurinsk** Rus. Fed.
156 D5 **Micronesia** *is* Pacific Ocean
48 G3 **Micronesia, Federated States of** *country* N. Pacific Ocean
158 E6 **Mid-Atlantic Ridge** Atlantic Ocean
100 A2 **Middelburg** Neth.
123 C3 **Middelburg** *E. Cape* S. Africa
123 C2 **Middelburg** *Mpumalanga* S. Africa
100 B2 **Middelharnis** Neth.
134 B2 **Middle Alkali Lake** U.S.A.
73 D3 **Middle Andaman** *i.* India
Middle Congo *country* Africa *see* **Congo**
136 D2 **Middle Loup** *r.* U.S.A.
138 C3 **Middlesboro** U.S.A.
98 C2 **Middlesbrough** U.K.
139 E2 **Middletown** *NY* U.S.A.
138 C3 **Middletown** *OH* U.S.A.
78 B3 **Mīdī** Yemen
130 C3 **Midland** Can.
138 C2 **Midland** *MI* U.S.A.
143 C2 **Midland** *TX* U.S.A.
97 B3 **Midleton** Ireland
Midnapore India *see* **Medinipur**
94 B1 **Miðvágur** Faroe Is
Midway Oman *see* **Thamarīt**
57 T7 **Midway Islands** *terr.* N. Pacific Ocean
109 D2 **Midzhur** *mt.* Bulg./Serbia
103 E1 **Mielec** Pol.
110 C1 **Miercurea-Ciuc** Romania
106 B1 **Mieres** Spain
101 E1 **Mieste** Ger.
75 D1 **Migriggyangzham Co** *l.* China
145 C3 **Miguel Alemán, Presa** *resr* Mex.
144 B2 **Miguel Auza** Mex.
144 B2 **Miguel Hidalgo, Presa** *resr* Mex.
63 A2 **Migyaunglaung** Myanmar
67 B4 **Mihara** Japan
89 E3 **Mikhaylov** Rus. Fed.
Mikhaylovgrad Bulg. *see* **Montana**
Mikhaylovka Rus. Fed. *see* **Kimovsk**
66 B2 **Mikhaylovka** *Primorskiy Kray* Rus. Fed.
87 D3 **Mikhaylovka** *Volvogradskaya Oblast'* Rus. Fed.
77 D1 **Mikhaylovskiy** Rus. Fed.
93 I3 **Mikkeli** Fin.
86 E2 **Mikun'** Rus. Fed.
67 C3 **Mikuni-sanmyaku** *mts* Japan
67 C4 **Mikura-jima** *i.* Japan
73 B4 **Miladhunmadulu Atoll** Maldives
108 A1 **Milan** Italy
121 C2 **Milange** Moz.
Milano Italy *see* **Milan**
111 C3 **Milas** Turkey
137 D1 **Milbank** U.S.A.
99 D3 **Mildenhall** U.K.
52 B2 **Mildura** Austr.
71 A3 **Mile** China
136 B1 **Miles City** U.S.A.
139 D3 **Milford** *DE* U.S.A.
135 D3 **Milford** *UT* U.S.A.
99 A4 **Milford Haven** U.K.
54 A2 **Milford Sound** N.Z.
Milḩ, Baḩr al *l.* Iraq *see* **Razāzah, Buḩayrat ar**
107 D2 **Miliana** Alg.
50 C1 **Milikapiti** Austr.
51 C1 **Milingimbi** Austr.
134 E1 **Milk** *r.* U.S.A.
116 B3 **Milk, Wadi el** *watercourse* Sudan
83 L3 **Mil'kovo** Rus. Fed.
128 C3 **Milk River** Can.
105 C3 **Millau** France
141 D2 **Milledgeville** U.S.A.
137 E1 **Mille Lacs** *lakes* U.S.A.
130 A3 **Mille Lacs, Lac des** *l.* Can.
Millennium Island *atoll* Kiribati *see* **Caroline Island**
137 D2 **Miller** U.S.A.
91 F2 **Millerovo** Rus. Fed.
52 A2 **Millers Creek** Austr.
96 B3 **Milleur Point** U.K.
52 B3 **Millicent** Austr.
140 C1 **Millington** U.S.A.
139 F1 **Millinocket** U.S.A.
55 J3 **Mill Island** Antarctica
53 D1 **Millmerran** Austr.
98 B2 **Millom** U.K.
136 B2 **Mills** U.S.A.
128 C1 **Mills Lake** Can.
111 B3 **Milos** *i.* Greece
89 E3 **Miloslavskoye** Rus. Fed.
91 E2 **Milove** Ukr.
52 B1 **Milparinka** Austr.
54 A3 **Milton** N.Z.
99 C3 **Milton Keynes** U.K.
138 B2 **Milwaukee** U.S.A.
158 C3 **Milwaukee Deep** *sea feature* Caribbean Sea
104 B3 **Mimizan** France
118 B3 **Mimongo** Gabon
155 D2 **Mimoso do Sul** Brazil
79 C2 **Mīnāb** Iran
61 D1 **Minahasa, Semenanjung** *pen.* Indon.
Minahassa Peninsula *pen.* Indon. *see* **Minahasa, Semenanjung**
79 C2 **Mina Jebel Ali** U.A.E.
Minaker Can. *see* **Prophet River**
60 B1 **Minas** Indon.
153 C3 **Minas** Uru.
79 B2 **Mīnā' Sa'ūd** Kuwait
155 D1 **Minas Gerais** *state* Brazil
155 D1 **Minas Novas** Brazil
145 C3 **Minatitlán** Mex.
62 A1 **Minbu** Myanmar
64 B3 **Mindanao** *i.* Phil.
52 B3 **Mindarie** Austr.
101 D1 **Minden** Ger.
140 B2 **Minden** *LA* U.S.A.
137 D2 **Minden** *NE* U.S.A.
64 B2 **Mindoro** *i.* Phil.
64 A2 **Mindoro Strait** Phil.
118 B3 **Mindouli** Congo
99 B4 **Minehead** U.K.
154 B1 **Mineiros** Brazil
143 D2 **Mineral Wells** U.S.A.
71 B3 **Minfeng** China
119 C4 **Minga** Dem. Rep. Congo
81 C1 **Mingäçevir** Azer.
131 D2 **Mingan** Can.
52 B2 **Mingary** Austr.
70 B2 **Mingguang** China
62 A1 **Mingin** Myanmar
107 C2 **Minglanilla** Spain
119 D4 **Mingoyo** Tanz.
69 E1 **Mingshui** China
96 A2 **Mingulay** *i.* U.K.
71 B3 **Mingxi** China
Mingzhou China *see* **Suide**
70 A2 **Minhe** China
73 B4 **Minicoy** *atoll* India
50 A2 **Minilya** Austr.
114 B3 **Mininian** Côte d'Ivoire
131 D2 **Minipi Lake** Can.
130 A2 **Miniss Lake** Can.
52 A2 **Minlaton** Austr.
115 C4 **Minna** Nigeria
137 E2 **Minneapolis** U.S.A.
129 E2 **Minnedosa** Can.
137 E2 **Minnesota** *r.* U.S.A.
137 E1 **Minnesota** *state* U.S.A.
106 B1 **Miño** *r.* Port./Spain
107 D1 **Minorca** *i.* Spain
136 C1 **Minot** U.S.A.
88 C3 **Minsk** Belarus
103 E1 **Mińsk Mazowiecki** Pol.
96 D2 **Mintlaw** U.K.
131 D3 **Minto** Can.
130 C2 **Minto, Lac** *l.* Can.
68 C1 **Minusinsk** Rus. Fed.
62 A1 **Minutang** India
70 A2 **Minxian** China
155 D1 **Mirabela** Brazil
155 D1 **Miralta** Brazil
131 D2 **Miramichi** Can.
111 C3 **Mirampellou, Kolpos** *b.* Greece
152 C2 **Miranda** Brazil
152 C1 **Miranda** *r.* Brazil
Miranda Moz. *see* **Macaloge**
106 C1 **Miranda de Ebro** Spain
106 B1 **Mirandela** Port.
154 B2 **Mirandópolis** Brazil
154 B2 **Mirante, Serra do** *hills* Brazil
79 C3 **Mirbāţ** Oman
61 C1 **Miri** Malaysia
153 C3 **Mirim, Lagoa** *l.* Brazil/Uru.
79 D2 **Mīrjāveh** Iran
89 D3 **Mirnyy** *Bryanskya Oblast'* Rus. Fed.
83 I2 **Mirnyy** *Respublika Sakha* Rus. Fed.
101 F1 **Mirow** Ger.
74 A2 **Mirpur Khas** Pak.
Mirtoan Sea *sea* Greece *see* **Mirtoö Pelagos**
111 B3 **Mirtoö Pelagos** *sea* Greece
65 B2 **Miryang** S. Korea
Mirzachirla Turkm. *see* **Murzechirla**
Mirzachul Uzbek. *see* **Guliston**
75 C2 **Mirzapur** India
77 E3 **Misalay** China
66 B1 **Mishan** China
51 E1 **Misima Island** P.N.G.
146 B3 **Miskitos, Cayos** *is* Nic.
103 E2 **Miskolc** Hungary
59 C3 **Misoöl** *i.* Indon.
115 D1 **Mişratah** Libya
130 B2 **Missinaibi** *r.* Can.
130 B3 **Missinaibi Lake** Can.
128 B3 **Mission** Can.
130 B2 **Missisa Lake** Can.
140 C3 **Mississippi** *r.* U.S.A.
140 C2 **Mississippi** *state* U.S.A.
140 C3 **Mississippi Delta** U.S.A.
140 C2 **Mississippi Sound** *sea chan.* U.S.A.
Missolonghi Greece *see* **Mesolongi**
134 D1 **Missoula** U.S.A.
137 E3 **Missouri** *r.* U.S.A.
137 E3 **Missouri** *state* U.S.A.
130 C3 **Mistassibi** *r.* Can.
130 C2 **Mistassini, Lac** *l.* Can.
131 D2 **Mistastin Lake** Can.
103 D2 **Mistelbach** Austria
131 D2 **Mistinibi, Lac** *l.* Can.
130 C2 **Mistissini** Can.
51 D2 **Mitchell** Austr.
51 D1 **Mitchell** *r.* Austr.
136 C2 **Mitchell** *NE* U.S.A.
137 D2 **Mitchell** *SD* U.S.A.
97 B2 **Mitchelstown** Ireland
74 A2 **Mithi** Pak.
67 D3 **Mito** Japan
119 D3 **Mitole** Tanz.
109 D2 **Mitrovicë** Kosovo
53 D2 **Mittagong** Austr.
101 E2 **Mittelhausen** Ger.
101 D1 **Mittellandkanal** *canal* Ger.
101 F3 **Mitterteich** Ger.
Mittimatalik Can. *see* **Pond Inlet**
150 B2 **Mitú** Col.
119 C4 **Mitumba, Chaîne des** *mts* Dem. Rep. Congo
119 C3 **Mitumba, Monts** *mts* Dem. Rep. Congo
119 C3 **Mitwaba** Dem. Rep. Congo
118 B2 **Mitzic** Gabon
78 B2 **Miyah, Wādī al** *watercourse* Saudi Arabia
67 C4 **Miyake-jima** *i.* Japan
66 D3 **Miyako** Japan
67 B4 **Miyakonojō** Japan
76 B2 **Miyaly** Kazakh.
Miyang China *see* **Mile**
67 B4 **Miyazaki** Japan
67 C3 **Miyazu** Japan
115 D1 **Mizdah** Libya
97 B3 **Mizen Head** *hd* Ireland
90 A2 **Mizhhirr"ya** Ukr.
Mizo Hills *state* India *see* **Mizoram**
75 D2 **Mizoram** *state* India
93 G4 **Mjölby** Sweden
93 F3 **Mjøsa** *l.* Norway
119 D3 **Mkomazi** Tanz.
103 C1 **Mladá Boleslav** Czech Rep.
109 D2 **Mladenovac** Serbia
103 E1 **Mława** Pol.
109 C2 **Mljet** *i.* Croatia
123 C3 **Mlungisi** S. Africa
90 B1 **Mlyniv** Ukr.
123 C2 **Mmabatho** S. Africa
123 C2 **Mmathethe** Botswana
93 E3 **Mo** Norway
135 E3 **Moab** U.S.A.
123 D2 **Moamba** Moz.
54 B2 **Moana** N.Z.
118 B3 **Moanda** Gabon
97 C2 **Moate** Ireland
119 C3 **Moba** Dem. Rep. Congo
118 C2 **Mobayi-Mbongo** Dem. Rep. Congo
137 E3 **Moberly** U.S.A.
140 C2 **Mobile** U.S.A.
140 C2 **Mobile Bay** U.S.A.
140 C2 **Mobile Point** U.S.A.
136 C1 **Mobridge** U.S.A.
Mobutu, Lake *l.* Dem. Rep. Congo/ Uganda *see* **Albert, Lake**
Mobutu Sese Seko, Lake *l.* Dem. Rep. Congo/ Uganda *see* **Albert, Lake**
121 C2 **Moçambicano, Planalto** *plat.* Moz.
121 D2 **Moçambique** Moz.
Moçâmedes Angola *see* **Namibe**
62 B1 **Môc Châu** Vietnam
78 B3 **Mocha** Yemen
123 C1 **Mochudi** Botswana
121 D2 **Mocimboa da Praia** Moz.
101 D3 **Möckmühl** Ger.
150 B2 **Mocoa** Col.
154 C2 **Mococa** Brazil
144 B2 **Mocorito** Mex.
144 B1 **Moctezuma** Mex.
145 B2 **Moctezuma** Mex.
144 B2 **Moctezuma** Mex.
121 C2 **Mocuba** Moz.
105 D2 **Modane** France
122 B2 **Modder** *r.* S. Africa
108 B2 **Modena** Italy
135 B3 **Modesto** U.S.A.
109 B3 **Modica** Italy
123 C1 **Modimolle** S. Africa
53 C3 **Moe** Austr.
Moero, Lake *l.* Dem. Rep. Congo/ Zambia *see* **Mweru, Lake**
100 C2 **Moers** Ger.
96 C3 **Moffat** U.K.
117 C4 **Mogadishu** Somalia
Mogador Morocco *see* **Essaouira**
106 B1 **Mogadouro, Serra de** *mts* Port.
123 C1 **Mogalakwena** *r.* S. Africa
62 A1 **Mogaung** Myanmar
Mogilev Belarus *see* **Mahilyow**
154 C2 **Mogi-Mirim** Brazil
83 I3 **Mogocha** Rus. Fed.
123 C1 **Mogoditshane** Botswana
62 A1 **Mogok** Myanmar
142 A2 **Mogollon Plateau** U.S.A.
103 D2 **Mohács** Hungary
123 C3 **Mohale's Hoek** Lesotho
107 D2 **Mohammadia** Alg.
142 A2 **Mohave Mountains** U.S.A.
139 E2 **Mohawk** *r.* U.S.A.
62 A1 **Mohnyin** Myanmar
119 D3 **Mohoro** Tanz.
90 B2 **Mohyliv-Podil's'kyy** Ukr.
123 C1 **Moijabana** Botswana
110 C1 **Moinești** Romania
Mointy Kazakh. *see* **Moyynty**
92 F2 **Mo i Rana** Norway
88 C2 **Mõisaküla** Estonia
104 C3 **Moissac** France
135 C3 **Mojave** U.S.A.
135 C3 **Mojave Desert** U.S.A.
62 B1 **Mojiang** China
155 C2 **Moji das Cruzes** Brazil
154 C2 **Moji-Guaçu** *r.* Brazil
109 C2 **Mojkovac** Montenegro
54 B1 **Mokau** N.Z.
123 C2 **Mokhotlong** Lesotho
83 J2 **Mokhsogollokh** Rus. Fed.
118 B1 **Mokolo** Cameroon
123 C1 **Mokopane** S. Africa
65 B3 **Mokp'o** S. Korea
109 C2 **Mola di Bari** Italy
145 C2 **Molango** Mex.
Moldavia *country* Europe *see* **Moldova**
Moldavskaya S.S.R. *country* Europe *see* **Moldova**
93 E3 **Molde** Norway
90 B2 **Moldova** *country* Europe
110 B1 **Moldova Nouă** Romania
110 B1 **Moldoveanu, Vârful** *mt.* Romania
110 B1 **Moldovei, Podișul** *plat.* Romania
90 B2 **Moldovei Centrale, Podișul** *plat.* Moldova
123 C1 **Molepolole** Botswana
88 C2 **Molėtai** Lith.
109 C2 **Molfetta** Italy
Molière Alg. *see* **Bordj Bounaama**
107 C1 **Molina de Aragón** Spain
107 C2 **Molina de Segura** Spain
119 D3 **Moliro** Dem. Rep. Congo
150 B4 **Mollendo** Peru
93 F4 **Mölnlycke** Sweden
91 D2 **Molochna** *r.* Ukr.
89 E2 **Molokovo** Rus. Fed.
53 C2 **Molong** Austr.
122 B2 **Molopo** *watercourse* Botswana/ S. Africa
Molotov Rus. Fed. *see* **Perm'**
Molotovsk Rus. Fed. *see* **Severodvinsk**
Molotovsk Rus. Fed. *see* **Nolinsk**
118 B2 **Moloundou** Cameroon
59 C3 **Moluccas** *is* Indon.

Molucca Sea *sea* Indon. *see* **Laut Maluku**
52 B2 **Momba** Austr.
119 D3 **Mombasa** Kenya
154 B1 **Mombuca, Serra da** *hills* Brazil
111 C2 **Momchilgrad** Bulg.
93 F4 **Møn** *i.* Denmark
105 D3 **Monaco** *country* Europe
96 B2 **Monadhliath Mountains** U.K.
97 C1 **Monaghan** Ireland
143 C2 **Monahans** U.S.A.
147 D3 **Mona Passage** Dom. Rep./Puerto Rico
120 A1 **Mona Quimbundo** Angola
Monastir Macedonia *see* **Bitola**
89 D3 **Monastyrshchina** Rus. Fed.
90 B2 **Monastyryshche** Ukr.
118 B2 **Monatélé** Cameroon
66 D2 **Monbetsu** Japan
108 A1 **Moncalieri** Italy
86 C2 **Monchegorsk** Rus. Fed.
100 C2 **Mönchengladbach** Ger.
144 B2 **Monclova** Mex.
131 D3 **Moncton** Can.
106 B1 **Mondego** *r.* Port.
118 C2 **Mondjamboli** Dem. Rep. Congo
123 D2 **Mondlo** S. Africa
108 A2 **Mondovì** Italy
111 B3 **Monemvasia** Greece
66 D1 **Moneron, Ostrov** *i.* Rus. Fed.
139 D1 **Monet** Can.
137 E3 **Monett** U.S.A.
108 B1 **Monfalcone** Italy
106 B1 **Monforte de Lemos** Spain
119 D2 **Mongbwalu** Dem. Rep. Congo
62 B1 **Mông Cai** Vietnam
62 A1 **Mong Hang** Myanmar
Monghyr India *see* **Munger**
75 C2 **Mongla** Bangl.
62 B1 **Mong Lin** Myanmar
62 A1 **Mong Nawng** Myanmar
115 D3 **Mongo** Chad
68 C1 **Mongolia** *country* Asia
74 B1 **Mongora** Pak.
62 A1 **Mong Pawk** Myanmar
62 A1 **Mong Ping** Myanmar
120 B2 **Mongu** Zambia
135 C3 **Monitor Range** *mts* U.S.A.
103 E1 **Mońki** Pol.
99 B4 **Monmouth** U.K.
114 C4 **Mono** *r.* Benin/Togo
135 C3 **Mono Lake** U.S.A.
109 C2 **Monopoli** Italy
107 C1 **Monreal del Campo** Spain
140 B2 **Monroe** *LA* U.S.A.
138 C2 **Monroe** *MI* U.S.A.
138 B2 **Monroe** *WI* U.S.A.
140 C2 **Monroeville** U.S.A.
114 A4 **Monrovia** Liberia
100 A2 **Mons** Belgium
155 E1 **Monsarás, Ponta de** *pt* Brazil
100 C2 **Montabaur** Ger.
122 B3 **Montagu** S. Africa
109 C3 **Montalto** *mt.* Italy
110 B2 **Montana** Bulg.
134 E1 **Montana** *state* U.S.A.
105 C2 **Montargis** France
104 C3 **Montauban** France
139 E2 **Montauk Point** U.S.A.
123 C2 **Mont-aux-Sources** *mt.* Lesotho
105 C2 **Montbard** France
105 D2 **Montbéliard** France
105 C2 **Montbrison** France
100 B3 **Montcornet** France
104 B3 **Mont-de-Marsan** France
104 C2 **Montdidier** France
151 D3 **Monte Alegre** Brazil
154 C1 **Monte Alegre de Minas** Brazil
139 E1 **Montebello** Can.
154 B3 **Montecarlo** Arg.
105 D3 **Monte-Carlo** Monaco
154 C1 **Monte Carmelo** Brazil
152 C3 **Monte Caseros** Arg.
123 C1 **Monte Cristo** S. Africa
108 B2 **Montecristo, Isola di** *i.* Italy
146 C3 **Montego Bay** Jamaica
105 C3 **Montélimar** France
109 C2 **Montella** Italy
145 C2 **Montemorelos** Mex.
104 B2 **Montendre** France
109 C2 **Montenegro** *country* Europe
121 C2 **Montepuez** Moz.
108 B2 **Montepulciano** Italy
135 B3 **Monterey** U.S.A.
135 B3 **Monterey Bay** U.S.A.
150 B2 **Montería** Col.
152 B1 **Montero** Bol.
145 B2 **Monterrey** Mex.
109 C2 **Montesano sulla Marcellana** Italy
109 C2 **Monte Sant'Angelo** Italy
151 F4 **Monte Santo** Brazil
108 A2 **Monte Santu, Capo di** *c.* Italy
155 D1 **Montes Claros** Brazil
153 C3 **Montevideo** Uru.
137 D2 **Montevideo** U.S.A.
136 B3 **Monte Vista** U.S.A.
140 C2 **Montgomery** U.S.A.
100 B3 **Monthermé** France
105 D2 **Monthey** Switz.
140 B2 **Monticello** *AR* U.S.A.
141 D2 **Monticello** *FL* U.S.A.
135 E3 **Monticello** *UT* U.S.A.
104 C2 **Montignac** France
100 B2 **Montignies-le-Tilleul** Belgium
105 D2 **Montigny-le-Roi** France
106 B2 **Montijo** Port.
106 B2 **Montijo** Spain
106 C2 **Montilla** Spain
154 B1 **Montividiu** Brazil
131 D3 **Mont-Joli** Can.
130 C3 **Mont-Laurier** Can.
104 C2 **Montluçon** France
131 C3 **Montmagny** Can.
104 C2 **Montmorillon** France
51 E2 **Monto** Austr.
134 D2 **Montpelier** *ID* U.S.A.
139 E2 **Montpelier** *VT* U.S.A.
105 C3 **Montpellier** France
130 C3 **Montréal** Can.
129 D2 **Montreal Lake** Can.
129 D2 **Montreal Lake** *l.* Can.
99 D4 **Montreuil** France
105 D2 **Montreux** Switz.
96 C2 **Montrose** U.K.
136 B3 **Montrose** U.S.A.
147 D3 **Montserrat** *terr.* West Indies
62 A1 **Monywa** Myanmar
108 A1 **Monza** Italy
107 D1 **Monzón** Spain
123 C1 **Mookane** Botswana
52 A1 **Moolawatana** Austr.
52 B1 **Moomba** Austr.
53 D1 **Moonie** Austr.
53 C1 **Moonie** *r.* Austr.
52 A2 **Moonta** Austr.
50 A3 **Moora** Austr.
50 A2 **Moore, Lake** *imp. l.* Austr.
137 D1 **Moorhead** U.S.A.
53 C3 **Mooroopna** Austr.
122 A3 **Moorreesburg** S. Africa
130 B2 **Moose** *r.* Can.
130 B2 **Moose Factory** Can.
139 F1 **Moosehead Lake** U.S.A.
129 D2 **Moose Jaw** Can.
137 E1 **Moose Lake** U.S.A.
129 D2 **Moosomin** Can.
130 B2 **Moosonee** Can.
52 B2 **Mootwingee** Austr.
123 C1 **Mopane** S. Africa
114 B3 **Mopti** Mali
150 B4 **Moquegua** Peru
103 D2 **Mór** Hungary
118 B1 **Mora** Cameroon
93 F3 **Mora** Sweden
137 E1 **Mora** U.S.A.
74 B2 **Moradabad** India
121 □D2 **Morafenobe** Madag.
121 □D2 **Moramanga** Madag.
136 A2 **Moran** U.S.A.
51 D2 **Moranbah** Austr.
103 D2 **Morava** *r.* Europe
96 B2 **Moray Firth** *b.* U.K.
100 C3 **Morbach** Ger.
74 B2 **Morbi** India
93 G4 **Mörbylånga** Sweden
104 B3 **Morcenx** France
69 E1 **Mordaga** China
129 E3 **Morden** Can.
89 F3 **Mordovo** Rus. Fed.
98 B2 **Morecambe** U.K.
98 B2 **Morecambe Bay** U.K.
53 C1 **Moree** Austr.
59 D3 **Morehead** P.N.G.
138 C3 **Morehead** U.S.A.
141 E2 **Morehead City** U.S.A.
145 B3 **Morelia** Mex.
107 C1 **Morella** Spain
74 B2 **Morena** India
106 B2 **Morena, Sierra** *mts* Spain
110 C2 **Moreni** Romania
142 A3 **Moreno** Mex.
128 A2 **Moresby, Mount** Can.
128 A2 **Moresby Island** Can.
53 D1 **Moreton Island** Austr.
52 A2 **Morgan** Austr.
140 B3 **Morgan City** U.S.A.
141 D1 **Morganton** U.S.A.
139 D3 **Morgantown** U.S.A.
105 D2 **Morges** Switz.
76 C3 **Morghāb** Afgh.
77 C3 **Morghāb** *r.* Afgh.
68 C2 **Mori** China
66 D2 **Mori** Japan
53 C1 **Moriarty's Range** *hills* Austr.
128 B2 **Morice Lake** Can.
66 D3 **Morioka** Japan
53 D2 **Morisset** Austr.
104 B2 **Morlaix** France
98 C3 **Morley** U.K.
157 G9 **Mornington Abyssal Plain** S. Atlantic Ocean
51 C1 **Mornington Island** Austr.
59 D3 **Morobe** P.N.G.
114 B1 **Morocco** *country* Africa
119 D3 **Morogoro** Tanz.
64 B3 **Moro Gulf** Phil.
122 B2 **Morokweng** S. Africa
121 □D3 **Morombe** Madag.
68 C1 **Mörön** Mongolia
121 □D3 **Morondava** Madag.
106 B2 **Morón de la Frontera** Spain
121 D2 **Moroni** Comoros
59 C2 **Morotai** *i.* Indon.
119 D2 **Moroto** Uganda
98 C2 **Morpeth** U.K.
140 B1 **Morrilton** U.S.A.
154 C1 **Morrinhos** Brazil
54 C1 **Morrinsville** N.Z.
129 E3 **Morris** Can.
137 D1 **Morris** U.S.A.
141 D1 **Morristown** U.S.A.
154 C2 **Morro Agudo** Brazil
155 E1 **Morro d'Anta** Brazil
55 K3 **Morse, Cape** Antarctica
87 D3 **Morshanka** Rus. Fed.
Morshansk Rus. Fed. *see* **Morshanka**
151 C3 **Mortes, Rio das** *r.* Brazil
52 B3 **Mortlake** Austr.
48 G3 **Mortlock Islands** Micronesia
138 B2 **Morton** U.S.A.
53 C2 **Morundah** Austr.
53 D3 **Moruya** Austr.
96 B2 **Morvern** *reg.* U.K.
Morvi India *see* **Morbi**
53 C3 **Morwell** Austr.
101 D3 **Mosbach** Ger.
89 E2 **Moscow** Rus. Fed.
134 C1 **Moscow** U.S.A.
100 C2 **Mosel** *r.* Ger.
122 B2 **Moselebe** *watercourse* Botswana
105 D2 **Moselle** *r.* France
134 C1 **Moses Lake** U.S.A.
92 □A3 **Mosfellsbær** Iceland
54 B3 **Mosgiel** N.Z.
88 C2 **Moshchnyy, Ostrov** *i.* Rus. Fed.
89 D2 **Moshenskoye** Rus. Fed.
119 D3 **Moshi** Tanz.
92 F2 **Mosjøen** Norway
Moskva Rus. Fed. *see* **Moscow**
89 E2 **Moskva** *r.* Rus. Fed.
103 D2 **Mosonmagyaróvár** Hungary
146 B4 **Mosquitos, Golfo de los** *b.* Panama
93 F4 **Moss** Norway
Mossâmedes Angola *see* **Namibe**
122 B3 **Mossel Bay** S. Africa
122 B3 **Mossel Bay** *b.* S. Africa
118 B3 **Mossendjo** Congo
52 B2 **Mossgiel** Austr.
51 D1 **Mossman** Austr.
151 F3 **Mossoró** Brazil
53 D2 **Moss Vale** Austr.
102 C1 **Most** Czech Rep.
114 C1 **Mostaganem** Alg.
109 C2 **Mostar** Bos.-Herz.
152 C3 **Mostardas** Brazil
106 C1 **Móstoles** Spain
81 C2 **Mosul** Iraq
145 D3 **Motagua** *r.* Guat.
93 G4 **Motala** Sweden
123 C2 **Motetema** S. Africa
96 C3 **Motherwell** U.K.
75 C2 **Motihari** India
107 C2 **Motilla del Palancar** Spain
122 B1 **Motokwe** Botswana
106 C2 **Motril** Spain
110 B2 **Motru** Romania
136 C1 **Mott** U.S.A.
63 A2 **Mottama** Myanmar
63 A2 **Mottama, Gulf of** Myanmar
54 B2 **Motueka** N.Z.
145 D2 **Motul** Mex.
49 L5 **Motu One** *atoll* Fr. Polynesia
114 A3 **Moudjéria** Maur.
111 C3 **Moudros** Greece
118 B3 **Mouila** Gabon
52 B3 **Moulamein** Austr.
105 C2 **Moulins** France
141 D2 **Moultrie** U.S.A.
141 E2 **Moultrie, Lake** U.S.A.
138 B3 **Mound City** U.S.A.
115 D4 **Moundou** Chad
138 C3 **Moundsville** U.S.A.
137 E3 **Mountain Grove** U.S.A.
140 B1 **Mountain Home** *AR* U.S.A.
134 C2 **Mountain Home** *ID* U.S.A.
141 D1 **Mount Airy** U.S.A.
123 C3 **Mount Ayliff** S. Africa
52 A3 **Mount Barker** Austr.
53 C3 **Mount Beauty** Austr.
97 B2 **Mountbellew** Ireland
121 C2 **Mount Darwin** Zimbabwe
139 F2 **Mount Desert Island** U.S.A.
123 C3 **Mount Fletcher** S. Africa
123 C3 **Mount Frere** S. Africa
52 B3 **Mount Gambier** Austr.
59 D3 **Mount Hagen** P.N.G.
53 C2 **Mount Hope** Austr.
51 C2 **Mount Isa** Austr.
52 A3 **Mount Lofty Range** *mts* Austr.
50 A2 **Mount Magnet** Austr.
52 B2 **Mount Manara** Austr.
54 C1 **Mount Maunganui** N.Z.
97 C2 **Mountmellick** Ireland
111 B2 **Mount Olympus** *mt.* Greece
137 E2 **Mount Pleasant** *IA* U.S.A.
138 C2 **Mount Pleasant** *MI* U.S.A.
141 E2 **Mount Pleasant** *SC* U.S.A.
143 E2 **Mount Pleasant** *TX* U.S.A.
135 D3 **Mount Pleasant** *UT* U.S.A.
99 A4 **Mount's Bay** U.K.
134 B2 **Mount Shasta** U.S.A.
54 B2 **Mount Somers** N.Z.
138 B3 **Mount Vernon** *IL* U.S.A.
138 C2 **Mount Vernon** *OH* U.S.A.
134 B1 **Mount Vernon** *WA* U.S.A.
51 D2 **Moura** Austr.
106 B2 **Moura** Port.
115 E3 **Mourdi, Dépression du** *depr.* Chad
97 C1 **Mourne Mountains** *hills* U.K.
100 A2 **Mouscron** Belgium
115 D3 **Moussoro** Chad
61 D1 **Moutong** Indon.
115 C2 **Mouydir, Monts du** *plat.* Alg.
100 B3 **Mouzon** France
97 B1 **Moy** *r.* Ireland
117 B4 **Moyale** Eth.
Moyen Congo *country* Africa *see* **Congo**
123 C3 **Moyeni** Lesotho
76 B2 **Mo'ynoq** Uzbek.
119 D2 **Moyo** Uganda
77 D2 **Moyynkum** Kazakh.
77 D2 **Moyynty** Kazakh.
121 C3 **Mozambique** *country* Africa
113 G8 **Mozambique Channel** Africa
81 C1 **Mozdok** Rus. Fed.
89 E2 **Mozhaysk** Rus. Fed.
119 D3 **Mpanda** Tanz.
121 C2 **Mpika** Zambia
118 B2 **Mpoko** *r.* C.A.R.
121 C1 **Mporokoso** Zambia
123 C2 **Mpumalanga** *prov.* S. Africa
119 D3 **Mpwapwa** Tanz.
62 A1 **Mrauk-U** Myanmar
115 D1 **M'Saken** Tunisia
119 D3 **Msambweni** Kenya
119 D3 **Msata** Tanz.
88 C2 **Mshinskaya** Rus. Fed.
115 C1 **M'Sila** Alg.
89 D2 **Msta** *r.* Rus. Fed.
89 D2 **Mstinskiy Most** Rus. Fed.
89 D3 **Mstsislaw** Belarus
Mtoko Zimbabwe *see* **Mutoko**
89 E3 **Mtsensk** Rus. Fed.
123 D2 **Mtubatuba** S. Africa
119 E4 **Mtwara** Tanz.
151 E3 **Muana** Brazil
118 B3 **Muanda** Dem. Rep. Congo
62 B1 **Muang Hiam** Laos
62 B2 **Muang Hinboun** Laos
63 B2 **Muang Không** Laos
63 B2 **Muang Khôngxédôn** Laos
62 B1 **Muang Ngoy** Laos
62 B2 **Muang Pakbeng** Laos
63 B2 **Muang Phalan** Laos
62 B1 **Muang Sing** Laos
62 B2 **Muang Vangviang** Laos
60 B1 **Muar** Malaysia
60 B2 **Muarabungo** Indon.
60 B2 **Muaradua** Indon.
61 C2 **Muaralaung** Indon.
60 A2 **Muarasiberut** Indon.
60 B2 **Muaratembesi** Indon.
61 C2 **Muarateweh** Indon.
Muara Tuang Malaysia *see* **Kota Samarahan**
119 D2 **Mubende** Uganda
115 D3 **Mubi** Nigeria
120 B2 **Muconda** Angola
120 A2 **Mucope** Angola
121 C2 **Mucubela** Moz.
155 E1 **Mucuri** Brazil
155 E1 **Mucuri** *r.* Brazil
66 A2 **Mudanjiang** China
66 A1 **Mudan Jiang** *r.* China
111 C2 **Mudanya** Turkey
136 B2 **Muddy Gap** U.S.A.
101 E1 **Müden (Örtze)** Ger.
53 C2 **Mudgee** Austr.
63 A2 **Mudon** Myanmar
80 B1 **Mudurnu** Turkey
121 C2 **Mueda** Moz.
121 B2 **Mufulira** Zambia
120 B2 **Mufumbwe** Zambia
111 C3 **Muğla** Turkey
116 B2 **Muhammad Qol** Sudan
Muhammarah Iran *see* **Khorramshahr**
101 F2 **Mühlberg** Ger.
101 E2 **Mühlhausen (Thüringen)** Ger.
88 B2 **Muhu** *i.* Estonia
96 B3 **Muirkirk** U.K.
121 C2 **Muite** Moz.
65 B2 **Muju** S. Korea
Mukačevo Ukr. *see* **Mukacheve**
90 A2 **Mukacheve** Ukr.
61 C1 **Mukah** Malaysia
79 B3 **Mukalla** Yemen
63 B2 **Mukdahan** Thai.
Mukden China *see* **Shenyang**
Mukhtuya Rus. Fed. *see* **Lensk**
50 A3 **Mukinbudin** Austr.
60 B2 **Mukomuko** Indon.
121 C2 **Mulanje, Mount** Malawi
101 F2 **Mulde** *r.* Ger.
119 D3 **Muleba** Tanz.
144 A2 **Mulegé** Mex.
143 C2 **Muleshoe** U.S.A.
106 C2 **Mulhacén** *mt.* Spain
100 C2 **Mülheim an der Ruhr** Ger.
105 D2 **Mulhouse** France
62 B1 **Muli** China
66 B2 **Muling** China
66 B1 **Muling He** *r.* China
96 B2 **Mull** *i.* U.K.
53 C2 **Mullaley** Austr.
136 C2 **Mullen** U.S.A.
61 C1 **Muller, Pegunungan** *mts* Indon.
50 A2 **Mullewa** Austr.
97 C2 **Mullingar** Ireland
96 B3 **Mull of Galloway** *c.* U.K.
96 B3 **Mull of Kintyre** *hd* U.K.
96 A3 **Mull of Oa** *hd* U.K.
53 D1 **Mullumbimby** Austr.
120 B2 **Mulobezi** Zambia
74 B1 **Multan** Pak.

86 F2 **Mulym'ya** Rus. Fed.
74 B3 **Mumbai** India
120 B2 **Mumbeji** Zambia
120 B2 **Mumbwa** Zambia
61 D2 **Muna** *i.* Indon.
145 D2 **Muna** Mex.
101 E2 **Münchberg** Ger.
München Ger. *see* **Munich**
München-Gladbach Ger. *see* **Mönchengladbach**
138 B2 **Muncie** U.S.A.
50 B3 **Mundrabilla** Austr.
138 B3 **Munfordville** U.S.A.
119 C2 **Mungbere** Dem. Rep. Congo
75 C2 **Munger** India
52 A1 **Mungeranie** Austr.
53 C1 **Mungindi** Austr.
102 C2 **Munich** Ger.
155 D2 **Muniz Freire** Brazil
101 E1 **Münster** Ger.
100 C2 **Münster** Ger.
97 B2 **Munster** *reg.* Ireland
100 C2 **Münsterland** *reg.* Ger.
62 B1 **Mường Nhe** Vietnam
92 H2 **Muonio** Fin.
92 H2 **Muonioälven** *r.* Fin./Sweden
Muqdisho Somalia *see* **Mogadishu**
155 D2 **Muqui** Brazil
103 D2 **Mur** *r.* Austria
67 C3 **Murakami** Japan
119 C3 **Muramvya** Burundi
119 D3 **Murang'a** Kenya
86 D3 **Murashi** Rus. Fed.
81 B2 **Murat** *r.* Turkey
111 C2 **Muratlı** Turkey
67 D3 **Murayama** Japan
50 A2 **Murchison** *watercourse* Austr.
107 C2 **Murcia** Spain
107 C2 **Murcia** *aut. comm.* Spain
136 C2 **Murdo** U.S.A.
131 D3 **Murdochville** Can.
111 C2 **Mürefte** Turkey
110 B1 **Mureşul** *r.* Romania
104 C3 **Muret** France
140 C1 **Murfreesboro** U.S.A.
77 D3 **Murghob** Tajik.
155 D2 **Muriaé** Brazil
120 B1 **Muriege** Angola
101 F1 **Müritz** *l.* Ger.
92 J2 **Murmansk** Rus. Fed.
86 C2 **Murmanskiy Bereg** *coastal area* Rus. Fed.
87 D3 **Murom** Rus. Fed.
66 D2 **Muroran** Japan
106 B1 **Muros** Spain
67 B4 **Muroto** Japan
67 B4 **Muroto-zaki** *pt* Japan
141 D1 **Murphy** U.S.A.
53 C1 **Murra Murra** Austr.
52 A3 **Murray** *r.* Austr.
128 B2 **Murray** *r.* Can.
138 B3 **Murray** U.S.A.
59 D3 **Murray, Lake** P.N.G.
141 D2 **Murray, Lake** U.S.A.
52 A3 **Murray Bridge** Austr.
122 B3 **Murraysburg** S. Africa
52 B3 **Murrayville** Austr.
52 B2 **Murrumbidgee** *r.* Austr.
53 C2 **Murrumburrah** Austr.
121 C2 **Murrupula** Moz.
53 D2 **Murrurundi** Austr.
109 C1 **Murska Sobota** Slovenia
54 C1 **Murupara** N.Z.
49 N6 **Mururoa** *atoll* Fr. Polynesia
75 C2 **Murwara** India
53 D1 **Murwillumbah** Austr.
76 C3 **Murzechirla** Turkm.
115 D2 **Murzūq** Libya
115 D2 **Murzūq, Idhān** *des.* Libya
103 D2 **Mürzzuschlag** Austria
81 C2 **Muş** Turkey
110 B2 **Musala** *mt.* Bulg.
65 B1 **Musan** N. Korea
78 B3 **Musaymir** Yemen
79 C2 **Muscat** Oman
Muscat and Oman *country* Asia *see* **Oman**
137 E2 **Muscatine** U.S.A.
50 C2 **Musgrave Ranges** *mts* Austr.
118 B3 **Mushie** Dem. Rep. Congo
60 B2 **Musi** *r.* Indon.
123 D1 **Musina** S. Africa
138 B2 **Muskegon** U.S.A.
138 B2 **Muskegon** *r.* U.S.A.
138 C3 **Muskingum** *r.* U.S.A.
143 D1 **Muskogee** U.S.A.
139 D1 **Muskoka, Lake** Can.
128 B2 **Muskwa** *r.* Can.
74 A1 **Muslimbagh** Pak.
116 B3 **Musmar** Sudan
119 D3 **Musoma** Tanz.
59 D3 **Mussau Island** P.N.G.
96 C3 **Musselburgh** U.K.
117 C4 **Mustahīl** Eth.
88 B2 **Mustjala** Estonia
53 D2 **Muswellbrook** Austr.
116 A2 **Mūţ** Egypt
121 C2 **Mutare** Zimbabwe
121 C2 **Mutoko** Zimbabwe
66 D2 **Mutsu** Japan
66 D2 **Mutsu-wan** *b.* Japan
121 C2 **Mutuali** Moz.
155 D1 **Mutum** Brazil
92 I2 **Muurola** Fin.
70 A2 **Mu Us Shamo** *des.* China
120 A1 **Muxaluando** Angola
86 C2 **Muyezerskiy** Rus. Fed.
119 D3 **Muyinga** Burundi
74 B1 **Muzaffargarh** Pak.
75 C2 **Muzaffarpur** India
123 D1 **Muzamane** Moz.
155 C2 **Muzambinho** Brazil
144 B2 **Múzquiz** Mex.
75 C1 **Muz Tag** *mt.* China
117 A4 **Mvolo** Sudan
119 C3 **Mwanza** Dem. Rep. Congo
119 D3 **Mwanza** Tanz.
118 C3 **Mweka** Dem. Rep. Congo
121 B2 **Mwenda** Zambia
118 C3 **Mwene-Ditu** Dem. Rep. Congo
121 C3 **Mwenezi** Zimbabwe
121 C3 **Mwenezi** *r.* Zimbabwe
119 C3 **Mweru, Lake** Dem. Rep. Congo/Zambia
121 B1 **Mweru Wantipa, Lake** Zambia
118 C3 **Mwimba** Dem. Rep. Congo
120 B2 **Mwinilunga** Zambia
88 C3 **Myadzyel** Belarus
62 A2 **Myanaung** Myanmar
62 A1 **Myanmar** *country* Asia
Myanmar *country* Asia *see* **Myanmar**
63 A2 **Myaungmya** Myanmar
63 A2 **Myeik** Myanmar
Myeik Kyunzu *is* Myanmar *see* **Mergui Archipelago**
62 A1 **Myingyan** Myanmar
62 A1 **Myitkyina**Myanmar
90 A2 **Mykolayiv** *L'vivs'ka Oblast'* Ukr.
91 C2 **Mykolayiv** *Mykolayivs'ka Oblast'* Ukr.
111 C3 **Mykonos** Greece
111 C3 **Mykonos** *i.* Greece
86 E2 **Myla** Rus. Fed.
75 D2 **Mymensingh** Bangl.
65 B1 **Myŏnggan** N. Korea
88 C2 **Myory** Belarus
92 □B3 **Mýrdalsjökull** Iceland
92 G2 **Myre** Norway
91 C2 **Myrhorod** Ukr.
111 C3 **Myrina** Greece
90 C2 **Myronivka** Ukr.
141 E2 **Myrtle Beach** U.S.A.
53 C3 **Myrtleford** Austr.
134 B2 **Myrtle Point** U.S.A.
89 E2 **Myshkin** Rus. Fed.
Myshkino Rus. Fed. *see* **Myshkin**
103 C1 **Myślibórz** Pol.
73 B3 **Mysore** India
83 N2 **Mys Shmidta** Rus. Fed.
63 B2 **My Tho** Vietnam
111 C3 **Mytilini** Greece
89 E3 **Mytishchi** Rus. Fed.
123 C3 **Mzamomhle** S. Africa
121 C2 **Mzimba** Malawi
121 C2 **Mzuzu** Malawi

N

101 F3 **Naab** *r.* Ger.
100 B1 **Naarden** Neth.
97 C2 **Naas** Ireland
122 A2 **Nababeep** S. Africa
87 E3 **Naberezhnyye Chelny** Rus. Fed.
59 D3 **Nabire** Indon.
80 B2 **Nāblus** West Bank
123 C1 **Naboomspruit** S. Africa
121 D2 **Nacala** Moz.
119 D4 **Nachingwea** Tanz.
103 D1 **Náchod** Czech Rep.
73 D3 **Nachuge** India
143 E2 **Nacogdoches** U.S.A.
144 B1 **Nacozari de García** Mex.
Nada China *see* **Danzhou**
74 B2 **Nadiad** India
90 A2 **Nadvirna** Ukr.
86 C2 **Nadvoitsy** Rus. Fed.
86 G2 **Nadym** Rus. Fed.
93 F4 **Næstved** Denmark
111 B3 **Nafpaktos** Greece
111 B3 **Nafplio** Greece
115 D1 **Nafūsah, Jabal** *hills* Libya
78 B2 **Nafy** Saudi Arabia
64 B2 **Naga** Phil.
130 B2 **Nagagami** *r.* Can.
67 C3 **Nagano** Japan
67 C3 **Nagaoka** Japan
75 D2 **Nagaon** India
74 B1 **Nagar** India
74 B2 **Nagar Parkar** Pak.
67 A4 **Nagasaki** Japan
67 B4 **Nagato** Japan
74 B2 **Nagaur** India
73 B4 **Nagercoil** India
74 A2 **Nagha Kalat** Pak.
74 B2 **Nagina** India
67 C3 **Nagoya** Japan
75 B2 **Nagpur** India
75 D1 **Nagqu** China
141 E1 **Nags Head** U.S.A.
82 E1 **Nagurskoye** Rus. Fed.
103 D2 **Nagyatád** Hungary
103 D2 **Nagykanizsa** Hungary
128 B1 **Nahanni Butte** Can.
81 C2 **Nahāvand** Iran
101 E1 **Nahrendorf** Ger.
153 A4 **Nahuel Huapí, Lago** *l.* Arg.
141 D2 **Nahunta** U.S.A.
131 D2 **Nain** Can.
81 D2 **Nā'īn** Iran
121 C2 **Naiopué** Moz.
96 C2 **Nairn** U.K.
119 D3 **Nairobi** Kenya
Naissus Serbia *see* **Niš**
119 D3 **Naivasha** Kenya
81 D2 **Najafābād** Iran
78 B2 **Najd** *reg.* Saudi Arabia
106 C1 **Nájera** Spain
65 C1 **Najin** N. Korea
78 B3 **Najrān** Saudi Arabia
119 D2 **Nakasongola** Uganda
67 C3 **Nakatsugawa** Japan
78 A3 **Nakfa** Eritrea
66 B2 **Nakhodka** Rus. Fed.
63 B2 **Nakhon Nayok** Thai.
63 B2 **Nakhon Pathom** Thai.
62 B2 **Nakhon Phanom** Thai.
63 B2 **Nakhon Ratchasima** Thai.
63 B2 **Nakhon Sawan** Thai.
63 A3 **Nakhon Si Thammarat** Thai.
Nakhrachi Rus. Fed. *see* **Kondinskoye**
130 B2 **Nakina** Can.
126 B3 **Naknek** U.S.A.
121 C1 **Nakonde** Zambia
93 F5 **Nakskov** Denmark
119 D3 **Nakuru** Kenya
128 C2 **Nakusp** Can.
75 D2 **Nalbari** India
87 D4 **Nal'chik** Rus. Fed.
115 D1 **Nalut** Libya
123 D2 **Namaacha** Moz.
123 C2 **Namahadi** S. Africa
81 D2 **Namak, Daryācheh-ye** *imp. l.* Iran
76 B3 **Namak, Kavīr-e** *salt flat* Iran
79 C1 **Namakzar-e Shadad** *salt flat* Iran
77 D2 **Namangan** Uzbek.
119 D3 **Namanyere** Tanz.
122 A2 **Namaqualand** *reg.* S. Africa
51 E2 **Nambour** Austr.
53 D2 **Nambucca Heads** Austr.
63 B3 **Năm Căn** Vietnam
75 D1 **Nam Co** *salt l.* China
62 B1 **Nam Định** Vietnam
121 C2 **Namialo** Moz.
120 A3 **Namib Desert** Namibia
120 A2 **Namibe** Angola
120 A3 **Namibia** *country* Africa
72 D2 **Namjagbarwa Feng** *mt.* China
59 C3 **Namlea** Indon.
62 B2 **Nam Ngum Reservoir** Laos
53 C2 **Namoi** *r.* Austr.
134 C2 **Nampa** U.S.A.
114 B3 **Nampala** Mali
65 B2 **Namp'o** N. Korea
121 C2 **Nampula** Moz.
72 D2 **Namrup** India
62 A1 **Namsang** Myanmar
92 F3 **Namsos** Norway
92 F3 **Namsskogan** Norway
63 A2 **Nam Tok** Thai.
83 J2 **Namtsy** Rus. Fed.
62 A1 **Namtu** Myanmar
121 C2 **Namuno** Moz.
100 B2 **Namur** Belgium
120 B2 **Namwala** Zambia
65 B2 **Namwŏn** S. Korea
62 A1 **Namya Ra** Myanmar
62 B2 **Nan** Thai.
128 B3 **Nanaimo** Can.
71 B3 **Nan'an** China
122 A1 **Nananib Plateau** Namibia
Nan'ao China *see* **Dayu**
67 C3 **Nanao** Japan
71 B3 **Nanchang** *Jiangxi* China
71 B3 **Nanchang** *Jiangxi* China
71 B3 **Nancheng** China
70 A2 **Nanchong** China
63 A3 **Nancowry** *i.* India
105 D2 **Nancy** France
75 C1 **Nanda Devi** *mt.* India
71 A3 **Nandan** China
74 B3 **Nanded** India
Nander India *see* **Nanded**
53 D2 **Nandewar Range** *mts* Austr.
74 B2 **Nandurbar** India
73 B3 **Nandyal** India
71 B3 **Nanfeng** China
62 A1 **Nang** China
118 B2 **Nanga Eboko** Cameroon
61 C2 **Nangahpinoh** Indon.
77 D3 **Nanga Parbat** *mt.* Pak.
61 C2 **Nangatayap** Indon.
63 A2 **Nangin** Myanmar
65 B1 **Nangnim-sanmaek** *mts* N. Korea
70 B2 **Nangong** China
119 D3 **Nangulangwa** Tanz.
70 C2 **Nanhui** China
70 B2 **Nanjing** China
Nanking China *see* **Nanjing**
67 B4 **Nankoku** Japan
120 A2 **Nankova** Angola
70 B2 **Nanle** China
71 B3 **Nan Ling** *mts* China
71 A3 **Nanning** China
127 I2 **Nanortalik** Greenland
71 A3 **Nanpan Jiang** *r.* China
75 C2 **Nanpara** India
71 B3 **Nanping** China
Nanpu China *see* **Pucheng**
Nansei-shotō *is* Japan *see* **Ryukyu Islands**
160 I1 **Nansen Basin** Arctic Ocean
126 F1 **Nansen Sound** *sea chan.* Can.
104 B2 **Nantes** France
70 C2 **Nantong** China
139 E2 **Nantucket** U.S.A.
139 F2 **Nantucket Island** U.S.A.
99 B3 **Nantwich** U.K.
49 I4 **Nanumea** *atoll* Tuvalu
155 D1 **Nanuque** Brazil
64 B3 **Nanusa, Kepulauan** *is* Indon.
71 B3 **Nanxiong** China
70 B2 **Nanyang** China
119 D3 **Nanyuki** Kenya
70 B2 **Nanzhang** China
Nanzhao China *see* **Zhao'an**
107 D2 **Nao, Cabo de la** *c.* Spain
131 C2 **Naococane, Lac** *l.* Can.
71 B3 **Naozhou Dao** *i.* China
135 B3 **Napa** U.S.A.
126 E2 **Napaktulik Lake** Can.
139 D2 **Napanee** Can.
127 I2 **Napasoq** Greenland
137 F2 **Naperville** U.S.A.
54 C1 **Napier** N.Z.
108 B2 **Naples** Italy
141 D3 **Naples** U.S.A.
150 B3 **Napo** *r.* Ecuador/Peru
Napoli Italy *see* **Naples**
Napug China *see* **Gê'gyai**
114 B3 **Nara** Mali
88 C3 **Narach** Belarus
52 B3 **Naracoorte** Austr.
53 C2 **Naradhan** Austr.
145 C2 **Naranjos** Mex.
63 B3 **Narathiwat** Thai.
74 B3 **Narayangaon** India
105 C3 **Narbonne** France
63 A2 **Narcondam Island** India
127 H1 **Nares Strait** Can./Greenland
103 E1 **Narew** *r.* Pol.
122 A1 **Narib** Namibia
87 D4 **Narimanov** Rus. Fed.
67 D3 **Narita** Japan
74 B2 **Narmada** *r.* India
74 D2 **Narnaul** India
108 B2 **Narni** Italy
86 F2 **Narodnaya, Gora** *mt.* Rus. Fed.
90 D1 **Narodychi** Ukr.
89 E2 **Naro-Fominsk** Rus. Fed.
53 D3 **Narooma** Austr.
88 C3 **Narowlya** Belarus
93 H3 **Närpes** Fin.
53 C2 **Narrabri** Austr.
53 C2 **Narrandera** Austr.
53 C2 **Narromine** Austr.
67 B4 **Naruto** Japan
88 C2 **Narva** Estonia
88 C2 **Narva Bay** Estonia/Rus. Fed.
92 G2 **Narvik** Norway
88 C2 **Narvskoye Vodokhranilishche** *resr* Estonia/Rus. Fed.
86 E2 **Nar'yan-Mar** Rus. Fed.
77 D2 **Naryn** Kyrg.
74 B2 **Nashik** India
139 E2 **Nashua** U.S.A.
140 C1 **Nashville** U.S.A.
137 E1 **Nashwauk** U.S.A.
109 C1 **Našice** Croatia
117 B4 **Nasir** Sudan
Nasirabad Bangl. *see* **Mymensingh**
119 C4 **Nasondoye** Dem. Rep. Congo
76 B3 **Naşrābād** Iran
128 B2 **Nass** *r.* Can.
146 C2 **Nassau** Bahamas
116 B2 **Nasser, Lake** *resr* Egypt
93 F4 **Nässjö** Sweden
130 C2 **Nastapoca** *r.* Can.
130 C2 **Nastapoka Islands** Can.
89 D2 **Nasva** Rus. Fed.
120 B3 **Nata** Botswana
151 F3 **Natal** Brazil
60 A1 **Natal** Indon.
Natal *prov.* S. Africa *see* **KwaZulu-Natal**
159 D6 **Natal Basin** Indian Ocean
143 D3 **Natalia** U.S.A.
131 D2 **Natashquan** Can.
131 D2 **Natashquan** *r.* Can.
140 B2 **Natchez** U.S.A.
140 B2 **Natchitoches** U.S.A.
53 C3 **Nathalia** Austr.
107 D1 **Nati, Punta** *pt* Spain
114 C3 **Natitingou** Benin
151 E4 **Natividade** Brazil
67 D3 **Natori** Japan
119 D3 **Natron, Lake** *salt l.* Tanz.
60 B1 **Natuna, Kepulauan** *is* Indon.
60 B1 **Natuna Besar** *i.* Indon.
122 A1 **Nauchas** Namibia
101 F1 **Nauen** Ger.
64 B2 **Naujan** Phil.
88 B2 **Naujoji Akmenė** Lith.
74 A2 **Naukot** Pak.
101 E2 **Naumburg (Saale)** Ger.
48 H34 **Nauru** *country* S. Pacific Ocean
150 B3 **Nauta** Peru
145 C2 **Nautla** Mex.
88 C3 **Navahrudak** Belarus
106 B2 **Navalmoral de la Mata** Spain
106 B2 **Navalvillar de Pela** Spain
97 C2 **Navan** Ireland
Navangar India *see* **Jamnagar**
88 C2 **Navapolatsk** Belarus
83 M2 **Navarin, Mys** *c.* Rus. Fed.

153 B5 **Navarino, Isla** *i.* Chile
107 C1 **Navarra** *aut. comm.* Spain
Navarre *aut. comm.* Spain *see* **Navarra**
96 B1 **Naver** *r.* U.K.
73 B3 **Navi Mumbai** India
89 D3 **Navlya** Rus. Fed.
110 C2 **Năvodari** Romania
77 C2 **Navoiy** Uzbek.
144 B2 **Navojoa** Mex.
144 B2 **Navolato** Mex.
74 A2 **Nawabshah** Pak.
75 C2 **Nawada** India
62 A1 **Nawnghkio** Myanmar
62 A1 **Nawngleng** Myanmar
81 C2 **Naxçıvan** Azer.
111 C3 **Naxos** Greece
111 C3 **Naxos** *i.* Greece
144 B2 **Nayar** Mex.
66 D2 **Nayoro** Japan
62 A2 **Nay Pyi Taw** Myanmar
Nazareth Israel *see* **Naẕerat**
144 B2 **Nazas** Mex.
144 B2 **Nazas** *r.* Mex.
150 B4 **Nazca** Peru
157 H7 **Nazca Ridge** S. Pacific Ocean
80 B2 **Naẕerat** Israel
111 C3 **Nazilli** Turkey
117 B4 **Nazrēt** Eth.
79 C2 **Nazwá** Oman
121 B1 **Nchelenge** Zambia
122 B1 **Ncojane** Botswana
120 A1 **N'dalatando** Angola
118 C2 **Ndélé** C.A.R.
118 B3 **Ndendé** Gabon
115 D3 **Ndjamena** Chad
118 A3 **Ndogo, Lagune** *lag.* Gabon
121 B2 **Ndola** Zambia
97 C1 **Neagh, Lough** *l.* U.K.
50 C2 **Neale, Lake** *imp. l.* Austr.
111 B3 **Neapoli** Greece
111 B2 **Nea Roda** Greece
99 B4 **Neath** U.K.
119 D2 **Nebbi** Uganda
53 C1 **Nebine Creek** *r.* Austr.
150 C2 **Neblina, Pico da** *mt.* Brazil
135 D3 **Nebo, Mount** U.S.A.
89 D2 **Nebolchi** Rus. Fed.
136 C2 **Nebraska** *state* U.S.A.
137 D2 **Nebraska City** U.S.A.
108 B3 **Nebrodi, Monti** *mts* Italy
143 E3 **Neches** *r.* U.S.A.
156 E4 **Necker Island** U.S.A.
153 C3 **Necochea** Arg.
143 E3 **Nederland** U.S.A.
100 B2 **Neder Rijn** *r.* Neth.
130 C2 **Nedlouc, Lac** *l.* Can.
139 E2 **Needham** U.S.A.
135 D4 **Needles** U.S.A.
74 B2 **Neemuch** India
129 E2 **Neepawa** Can.
87 E3 **Neftekamsk** Rus. Fed.
82 F2 **Nefteyugansk** Rus. Fed.
108 A3 **Nefza** Tunisia
120 A1 **Negage** Angola
117 B4 **Negēlē** Eth.
109 D2 **Negotin** Serbia
111 B2 **Negotino** Macedonia
150 A3 **Negra, Punta** *pt* Peru
155 D1 **Negra, Serra** *mts* Brazil
63 A2 **Negrais, Cape** Myanmar
153 B4 **Negro** *r.* Arg.
150 D3 **Negro** *r.* S. America
152 C3 **Negro** *r.* Uru.
106 B2 **Negro, Cabo** *c.* Morocco
64 B3 **Negros** *i.* Phil.
79 D1 **Nehbandān** Iran
69 E1 **Nehe** China
70 A3 **Neijiang** China
129 D2 **Neilburg** Can.
150 B2 **Neiva** Col.
129 E2 **Nejanilini Lake** Can.
Nejd *reg.* Saudi Arabia *see* **Najd**
117 B4 **Nek'emtē** Eth.
89 F2 **Nekrasovskoye** Rus. Fed.
89 D2 **Nelidovo** Rus. Fed.
73 B3 **Nellore** India
128 C3 **Nelson** Can.
129 E2 **Nelson** *r.* Can.
54 B2 **Nelson** N.Z.
52 B3 **Nelson, Cape** Austr.
53 D2 **Nelson Bay** Austr.
129 E2 **Nelson House** Can.
134 E1 **Nelson Reservoir** U.S.A.
123 D2 **Nelspruit** S. Africa
114 B3 **Néma** Maur.
88 B2 **Neman** Rus. Fed.
105 C2 **Nemours** France
66 D2 **Nemuro** Japan
90 B2 **Nemyriv** Ukr.
97 B2 **Nenagh** Ireland
99 D3 **Nene** *r.* U.K.
69 E1 **Nenjiang** China
137 E3 **Neosho** U.S.A.
75 C2 **Nepal** *country* Asia
75 C2 **Nepalganj** Nepal
139 D1 **Nepean** Can.
135 D3 **Nephi** U.S.A.
97 B1 **Nephin** *h.* Ireland
97 B1 **Nephin Beg Range** *hills* Ireland
131 D3 **Nepisiguit** *r.* Can.
119 C2 **Nepoko** *r.* Dem. Rep. Congo
139 E2 **Neptune City** U.S.A.
108 B2 **Nera** *r.* Italy
104 C3 **Nérac** France
53 D1 **Nerang** Austr.
69 D1 **Nerchinsk** Rus. Fed.
89 F2 **Nerekhta** Rus. Fed.
109 C2 **Neretva** *r.* Bos.-Herz./Croatia
120 B2 **Neriquinha** Angola
88 B3 **Neris** *r.* Lith.
89 E2 **Nerl'** *r.* Rus. Fed.
86 F2 **Nerokhi** Rus. Fed.
154 C1 **Nerópolis** Brazil
83 J3 **Neryungri** Rus. Fed.
92 □C2 **Neskaupstaður** Iceland
96 B2 **Ness, Loch** *l.* U.K.
136 D3 **Ness City** U.S.A.
Nesterov Ukr. *see* **Zhovkva**
111 B2 **Nestos** *r.* Greece
100 B1 **Netherlands** *country* Europe
147 D3 **Netherlands Antilles** *terr.* West Indies
127 H2 **Nettilling Lake** Can.
101 F1 **Neubrandenburg** Ger.
105 D2 **Neuchâtel** Switz.
105 D2 **Neuchâtel, Lac de** *l.* Switz.
100 C2 **Neuerburg** Ger.
100 B3 **Neufchâteau** Belgium
105 D2 **Neufchâteau** France
104 C2 **Neufchâtel-en-Bray** France
101 D2 **Neuhof** Ger.
101 E3 **Neumarkt in der Oberpfalz** Ger.
102 B1 **Neumünster** Ger.
100 C3 **Neunkirchen** Ger.
153 B3 **Neuquén** Arg.
153 B3 **Neuquén** *r.* Arg.
101 F1 **Neuruppin** Ger.
100 C2 **Neuss** Ger.
101 D1 **Neustadt am Rübenberge** Ger.
101 E3 **Neustadt an der Aisch** Ger.
Neustadt an der Hardt Ger. *see* **Neustadt an der Weinstraße**
101 D3 **Neustadt an der Weinstraße** Ger.
101 E1 **Neustadt-Glewe** Ger.
101 F1 **Neustrelitz** Ger.
99 D5 **Neuville-lès-Dieppe** France
100 C2 **Neuwied** Ger.
137 E3 **Nevada** U.S.A.
135 C3 **Nevada** *state* U.S.A.
106 C2 **Nevada, Sierra** *mts* Spain
135 B2 **Nevada, Sierra** *mts* U.S.A.
88 C2 **Nevaišių kalnas** *h.* Lith.
88 C2 **Nevel'** Rus. Fed.
105 C2 **Nevers** France
53 C2 **Nevertire** Austr.
109 C2 **Nevesinje** Bos.-Herz.
87 D4 **Nevinnomyssk** Rus. Fed.
80 B2 **Nevşehir** Turkey
99 C4 **New Addington** U.K.
128 B2 **New Aiyansh** Can.
119 D4 **Newala** Tanz.
138 B3 **New Albany** U.S.A.
151 D2 **New Amsterdam** Guyana
139 E2 **Newark** *NJ* U.S.A.
138 C2 **Newark** *OH* U.S.A.
99 C3 **Newark-on-Trent** U.K.
139 E2 **New Bedford** U.S.A.
141 E1 **New Bern** U.S.A.
138 B1 **Newberry** *MI* U.S.A.
141 D2 **Newberry** *SC* U.S.A.
143 E2 **New Boston** U.S.A.
143 D3 **New Braunfels** U.S.A.
97 C2 **Newbridge** Ireland
59 D3 **New Britain** *i.* P.N.G.
131 D3 **New Brunswick** *prov.* Can.
99 C4 **Newbury** U.K.
48 H6 **New Caledonia** *terr.* S. Pacific Ocean
156 D7 **New Caledonia Trough** Tasman Sea
53 D2 **Newcastle** Austr.
123 C2 **Newcastle** S. Africa
97 D1 **Newcastle** U.K.
138 C2 **New Castle** U.S.A.
136 C2 **Newcastle** U.S.A.
99 B3 **Newcastle-under-Lyme** U.K.
98 C2 **Newcastle upon Tyne** U.K.
51 C1 **Newcastle Waters** Austr.
97 B2 **Newcastle West** Ireland
74 B2 **New Delhi** India
128 C3 **New Denver** Can.
53 D2 **New England Range** *mts* Austr.
157 H3 **New England Seamounts** N. Atlantic Ocean
131 E3 **Newfoundland** *i.* Can.
131 E2 **Newfoundland and Labrador** *prov.* Can.
96 B3 **New Galloway** U.K.
48 G4 **New Georgia Islands** Solomon Is
131 D3 **New Glasgow** Can.
59 D3 **New Guinea** *i.* Indon./P.N.G.
78 A3 **New Halfa** Sudan
139 E2 **New Hampshire** *state* U.S.A.
59 E3 **New Hanover** *i.* P.N.G.
139 E2 **New Haven** U.S.A.
128 B2 **New Hazelton** Can.
New Hebrides *country* S. Pacific Ocean *see* **Vanuatu**
156 D7 **New Hebrides Trench** S. Pacific Ocean
140 B2 **New Iberia** U.S.A.
59 E3 **New Ireland** *i.* P.N.G.
139 E3 **New Jersey** *state* U.S.A.
130 C3 **New Liskeard** Can.
138 B2 **New London** U.S.A.
50 A2 **Newman** Austr.
54 C2 **Newman** N.Z.
97 B2 **Newmarket** Ireland
99 D3 **Newmarket** U.K.
97 B2 **Newmarket-on-Fergus** Ireland
142 B2 **New Mexico** *state* U.S.A.
141 D2 **Newnan** U.S.A.
140 B3 **New Orleans** U.S.A.
138 C2 **New Philadelphia** U.S.A.
54 B1 **New Plymouth** N.Z.
99 C4 **Newport** *England* U.K.
99 B4 **Newport** *Wales* U.K.
140 B1 **Newport** *AR* U.S.A.
134 B2 **Newport** *OR* U.S.A.
139 E2 **Newport** *RI* U.S.A.
141 D1 **Newport** *TN* U.S.A.
139 E2 **Newport** *VT* U.S.A.
134 C1 **Newport** *WA* U.S.A.
139 D3 **Newport News** U.S.A.
141 E3 **New Providence** *i.* Bahamas
99 A4 **Newquay** U.K.
140 B2 **New Roads** U.S.A.
97 C2 **New Ross** Ireland
97 C1 **Newry** U.K.
83 K1 **New Siberia Islands** Rus. Fed.
52 B2 **New South Wales** *state* Austr.
137 E2 **Newton** *IA* U.S.A.
137 D3 **Newton** *KS* U.S.A.
99 B4 **Newton Abbot** U.K.
98 C2 **Newton Aycliffe** U.K.
96 B3 **Newton Mearns** U.K.
96 B2 **Newtonmore** U.K.
96 B3 **Newton Stewart** U.K.
97 B2 **Newtown** Ireland
99 B3 **Newtown** U.K.
136 C1 **New Town** U.S.A.
97 D1 **Newtownabbey** U.K.
97 D1 **Newtownards** U.K.
Newtownbarry Ireland *see* **Bunclody**
97 C1 **Newtownbutler** U.K.
96 C3 **Newtown St Boswells** U.K.
97 C1 **Newtownstewart** U.K.
137 E2 **New Ulm** U.S.A.
139 E2 **New York** U.S.A.
139 D2 **New York** *state* U.S.A.
54 B2 **New Zealand** *country* Oceania
86 D3 **Neya** Rus. Fed.
81 D3 **Neyrīz** Iran
76 B3 **Neyshābūr** Iran
145 C3 **Nezahualcóyotl, Presa** *resr* Mex.
60 B1 **Ngabang** Indon.
118 B3 **Ngabé** Congo
75 C2 **Ngamring** China
119 D2 **Ngangala** Sudan
75 C1 **Ngangla Ringco** *salt l.* China
75 C1 **Nganglong Kangri** *mt.* China
75 C1 **Nganglong Kangri** *mts* China
75 C1 **Ngangzê Co** *salt l.* China
62 B1 **Ngân Sơn** Vietnam
62 A2 **Ngao** Thai.
118 B2 **Ngaoundal** Cameroon
118 B2 **Ngaoundéré** Cameroon
54 C1 **Ngaruawahia** N.Z.
62 A2 **Ngathainggyaung** Myanmar
Ngiva Angola *see* **Ondjiva**
118 B3 **Ngo** Congo
63 B2 **Ngok Linh** *mt.* Vietnam
115 D4 **Ngol Bembo** Nigeria
68 C2 **Ngoring Hu** *l.* China
115 D3 **Ngourti** Niger
115 D3 **Nguigmi** Niger
59 D2 **Ngulu** *atoll* Micronesia
61 C2 **Ngunut** Indon.
Ngunza Angola *see* **Sumbe**
Ngunza-Kabolu Angola *see* **Sumbe**
115 D3 **Nguru** Nigeria
123 C2 **Ngwathe** S. Africa
123 D2 **Ngwelezana** S. Africa
121 C2 **Nhamalabué** Moz.
120 A2 **N'harea** Angola
63 B2 **Nha Trang** Vietnam
52 B3 **Nhill** Austr.
123 D2 **Nhlangano** Swaziland
51 C1 **Nhulunbuy** Austr.
139 D2 **Niagara Falls** Can.
114 C3 **Niamey** Niger
119 C2 **Niangara** Dem. Rep. Congo
114 B3 **Niangay, Lac** *l.* Mali
119 C2 **Nia-Nia** Dem. Rep. Congo
60 A1 **Nias** *i.* Indon.
88 B2 **Nīca** Latvia
146 B3 **Nicaragua** *country* Central America
Nicaragua, Lago de *l.* Nic. *see* **Nicaragua, Lake**
146 B3 **Nicaragua, Lake** *l.* Nic.
109 C3 **Nicastro** Italy
105 D3 **Nice** France
73 D4 **Nicobar Islands** India
80 B2 **Nicosia** Cyprus
146 B4 **Nicoya, Golfo de** *b.* Costa Rica
88 B2 **Nida** Lith.
103 E1 **Nidzica** Pol.
102 B1 **Niebüll** Ger.
101 D2 **Niederaula** Ger.
118 B2 **Niefang** Equat. Guinea
101 F1 **Niemegk** Ger.
101 D1 **Nienburg (Weser)** Ger.
103 C1 **Niesky** Ger.
100 B1 **Nieuwegein** Neth.
100 B1 **Nieuwe-Niedorp** Neth.
151 D2 **Nieuw Nickerie** Suriname
122 A3 **Nieuwoudtville** S. Africa
100 A2 **Nieuwpoort** Belgium
80 B2 **Niğde** Turkey
115 C3 **Niger** *country* Africa
115 C4 **Niger** *r.* Africa
115 C4 **Niger, Mouths of the** Nigeria
115 C4 **Nigeria** *country* Africa
130 B3 **Nighthawk Lake** Can.
111 B2 **Nigrita** Greece
67 C3 **Niigata** Japan
67 B4 **Niihama** Japan
67 C4 **Nii-jima** *i.* Japan
67 B4 **Niimi** Japan
67 C3 **Niitsu** Japan
107 C2 **Níjar** Spain
100 B1 **Nijkerk** Neth.
100 B2 **Nijmegen** Neth.
100 C1 **Nijverdal** Neth.
92 J2 **Nikel'** Rus. Fed.
Nikolayev Ukr. *see* **Mykolayiv**
87 D3 **Nikolayevsk** Rus. Fed.
Nikolayevskiy Rus. Fed. *see* **Nikolayevsk**
86 D3 **Nikol'sk** Rus. Fed.
Nikol'skiy Kazakh. *see* **Satpayev**
83 M3 **Nikol'skoye** Rus. Fed.
Nikol'skoye Rus. Fed. *see* **Sheksna**
91 C2 **Nikopol'** Ukr.
80 B1 **Niksar** Turkey
79 D2 **Nīkshahr** Iran
109 C2 **Nikšić** Montenegro
Nīl, Bahr el *r.* Africa *see* **Nile**
135 C4 **Niland** U.S.A.
116 B1 **Nile** *r.* Africa
138 B2 **Niles** U.S.A.
74 A1 **Nīlī** Afgh.
Nimach India *see* **Neemuch**
105 C3 **Nîmes** France
53 C3 **Nimmitabel** Austr.
117 B4 **Nimule** Sudan
Nimwegen Neth. *see* **Nijmegen**
53 C1 **Nindigully** Austr.
73 B4 **Nine Degree Channel** India
53 C3 **Ninety Mile Beach** Austr.
54 B1 **Ninety Mile Beach** N.Z.
70 C3 **Ningbo** China
71 B3 **Ningde** China
71 B3 **Ningdu** China
70 B2 **Ningguo** China
71 C3 **Ninghai** China
72 D2 **Ninging** India
Ningjiang China *see* **Songyuan**
68 C2 **Ningjing Shan** *mts* China
70 A2 **Ningxia Huizu Zizhiqu** *aut. reg.* China
70 B2 **Ningyang** China
62 B1 **Ninh Binh** Vietnam
63 B2 **Ninh Hoa** Vietnam
66 D2 **Ninohe** Japan
137 D2 **Niobrara** *r.* U.S.A.
62 A1 **Nioko** India
114 B3 **Niono** Mali
114 B3 **Nioro** Mali
104 B2 **Niort** France
129 D2 **Nipawin** Can.
130 B3 **Nipigon** Can.
130 B3 **Nipigon, Lake** Can.
131 D2 **Nipishish Lake** Can.
130 C3 **Nipissing, Lake** Can.
135 C3 **Nipton** U.S.A.
151 E4 **Niquelândia** Brazil
74 B3 **Nirmal** India
109 D2 **Niš** Serbia
109 D2 **Nišava** *r.* Serbia
108 B3 **Niscemi** Italy
67 B4 **Nishino-omote** Japan
90 B2 **Nisporeni** Moldova
155 D2 **Niterói** Brazil
96 C3 **Nith** *r.* U.K.
103 D2 **Nitra** Slovakia
49 K5 **Niue** *terr.* S. Pacific Ocean
92 H3 **Nivala** Fin.
100 B2 **Nivelles** Belgium
73 B3 **Nizamabad** India
87 E3 **Nizhnekamsk** Rus. Fed.
87 E3 **Nizhnekamskoye Vodokhranilishche** *resr* Rus. Fed.
83 H3 **Nizhneudinsk** Rus. Fed.
82 G2 **Nizhnevartovsk** Rus. Fed.
Nizhnevolzhsk Rus. Fed. *see* **Narimanov**
83 K2 **Nizhneyansk** Rus. Fed.
Nizhniye Kresty Rus. Fed. *see* **Cherskiy**
Nizhniye Ustriki Pol. *see* **Ustrzyki Dolne**
89 F3 **Nizhniy Kislyay** Rus. Fed.
87 D3 **Nizhniy Lomov** Rus. Fed.
87 D3 **Nizhniy Novgorod** Rus. Fed.
86 E2 **Nizhniy Odes** Rus. Fed.
86 E3 **Nizhniy Tagil** Rus. Fed.
83 G2 **Nizhnyaya Tunguska** *r.* Rus. Fed.
86 E3 **Nizhnyaya Tura** Rus. Fed.
91 C1 **Nizhyn** Ukr.
121 D2 **Njazidja** *i.* Comoros
119 D3 **Njinjo** Tanz.
119 D3 **Njombe** Tanz.
118 B2 **Nkambe** Cameroon
119 D4 **Nkhata Bay** Malawi
121 C2 **Nkhotakota** Malawi
118 A3 **Nkomi, Lagune** *lag.* Gabon
119 D3 **Nkondwe** Tanz.
118 A2 **Nkongsamba** Cameroon
123 C3 **Nkululeko** S. Africa
123 C3 **Nkwenkwezi** S. Africa
67 B4 **Nobeoka** Japan
138 B2 **Noblesville** U.S.A.
52 B1 **Noccundra** Austr.
144 A1 **Nogales** Mex.
142 A2 **Nogales** U.S.A.
104 C2 **Nogent-le-Rotrou** France

89 E2 **Noginsk** *Moscovskiya Oblast'* Rus. Fed.
83 H2 **Noginsk** *Krasnoyarskiy Kray* Rus. Fed.
83 K3 **Nogliki** Rus. Fed.
74 B2 **Nohar** India
100 C3 **Nohfelden** Ger.
104 B2 **Noires, Montagnes** *hills* France
104 B2 **Noirmoutier, Île de** *i.* France
104 B2 **Noirmoutier-en-l'Île** France
67 C4 **Nojima-zaki** *c.* Japan
74 B2 **Nokha** India
93 H3 **Nokia** Fin.
74 A2 **Nok Kundi** Pak.
118 B2 **Nola** C.A.R.
86 D3 **Nolinsk** Rus. Fed.
126 A2 **Nome** U.S.A.
123 C3 **Nomonde** S. Africa
123 D2 **Nondweni** S. Africa
Nonghui China *see* **Guang'an**
62 B2 **Nong Khai** Thai.
75 D2 **Nongstoin** India
52 A2 **Nonning** Austr.
144 B2 **Nonoava** Mex.
65 B2 **Nonsan** S. Korea
63 B2 **Nonthaburi** Thai.
122 B3 **Nonzwakazi** S. Africa
100 B1 **Noordwijk-Binnen** Neth.
77 C3 **Norak** Tajik.
82 C1 **Nordaustlandet** *i.* Svalbard
128 C2 **Nordegg** Can.
100 C1 **Norden** Ger.
83 H1 **Nordenshel'da, Arkhipelag** *is* Rus. Fed.
Nordenskjold Archipelago *is* Rus. Fed. *see* **Nordenshel'da, Arkhipelag**
100 C1 **Norderney** Ger.
100 C1 **Norderney** *i.* Ger.
101 E1 **Norderstedt** Ger.
93 E3 **Nordfjordeid** Norway
Nordfriesische Inseln *is* Ger. *see* **North Frisian Islands**
101 E2 **Nordhausen** Ger.
101 D1 **Nordholz** Ger.
100 C1 **Nordhorn** Ger.
Nordkapp *c.* Norway *see* **North Cape**
92 F3 **Nordli** Norway
102 C2 **Nördlingen** Ger.
92 G3 **Nordmaling** Sweden
94 B1 **Norðoyar** *is* Faroe Is
97 C2 **Nore** *r.* Ireland
88 B3 **Noreikiškės** Lith.
137 D2 **Norfolk** *NE* U.S.A.
139 D3 **Norfolk** *VA* U.S.A.
48 H6 **Norfolk Island** *terr.* S. Pacific Ocean
93 E3 **Norheimsund** Norway
82 G2 **Noril'sk** Rus. Fed.
75 C2 **Norkyung** China
143 D1 **Norman** U.S.A.
Normandes, Îles *is* English Chan. *see* **Channel Islands**
150 D2 **Normandia** Brazil
Normandie *reg.* France *see* **Normandy**
104 B2 **Normandy** *reg.* France
51 D1 **Normanton** Austr.
128 B1 **Norman Wells** Can.
93 G4 **Norrköping** Sweden
93 G4 **Norrtälje** Sweden
50 B3 **Norseman** Austr.
92 G3 **Norsjö** Sweden
55 M2 **North, Cape** Antarctica
98 C2 **Northallerton** U.K.
50 A3 **Northam** Austr.
50 A2 **Northampton** Austr.
99 C3 **Northampton** U.K.
73 D3 **North Andaman** *i.* India
159 F4 **North Australian Basin** Indian Ocean
129 D2 **North Battleford** Can.
130 C3 **North Bay** Can.
130 C2 **North Belcher Islands** Can.
96 C2 **North Berwick** U.K.
North Borneo *state* Malaysia *see* **Sabah**
92 I1 **North Cape** *c.* Norway
54 B1 **North Cape** N.Z.
130 A2 **North Caribou Lake** Can.
141 E1 **North Carolina** *state* U.S.A.
130 B3 **North Channel** *lake channel* Can.
96 A3 **North Channel** U.K.
141 E2 **North Charleston** U.S.A.
128 B3 **North Cowichan** Can.
136 C1 **North Dakota** *state* U.S.A.
99 C4 **North Downs** *hills* U.K.
157 E3 **Northeast Pacific Basin** N. Pacific Ocean
141 E3 **Northeast Providence Channel** Bahamas
101 D2 **Northeim** Ger.
122 A2 **Northern Cape** *prov.* S. Africa
91 D2 **Northern Donets** *r.* Rus. Fed./Ukr.
Northern Dvina *r.* Rus. Fed. *see* **Severnaya Dvina**
129 E2 **Northern Indian Lake** Can.
97 C1 **Northern Ireland** *prov.* U.K.
59 D1 **Northern Mariana Islands** *terr.* N. Pacific Ocean
Northern Rhodesia *country* Africa *see* **Zambia**
50 C1 **Northern Territory** *admin. div.* Austr.
Northern Transvaal *prov.* S. Africa *see* **Limpopo**
96 C2 **North Esk** *r.* U.K.
137 E2 **Northfield** U.S.A.
99 D4 **North Foreland** *c.* U.K.
102 B1 **North Frisian Islands** *is* Ger.
160 P2 **North Geomagnetic Pole (2008)**
54 B1 **North Island** N.Z.
129 E2 **North Knife Lake** Can.
65 B1 **North Korea** *country* Asia
72 D2 **North Lakhimpur** India
North Land *is* Rus. Fed. *see* **Severnaya Zemlya**
160 R1 **North Magnetic Pole (2008)**
128 B1 **North Nahanni** *r.* Can.
136 C2 **North Platte** U.S.A.
136 C2 **North Platte** *r.* U.S.A.
96 C1 **North Ronaldsay** *i.* U.K.
129 D2 **North Saskatchewan** *r.* Can.
94 D2 **North Sea** Europe
63 A2 **North Sentinel Island** India
130 A2 **North Spirit Lake** Can.
53 D1 **North Stradbroke Island** Austr.
131 D3 **North Sydney** Can.
54 B1 **North Taranaki Bight** *b.* N.Z.
130 C2 **North Twin Island** Can.
98 B2 **North Tyne** *r.* U.K.
96 A2 **North Uist** *i.* U.K.
131 D3 **Northumberland Strait** Can.
99 D3 **North Walsham** U.K.
123 C2 **North West** *prov.* S. Africa
158 D1 **Northwest Atlantic Mid-Ocean Channel** *sea chan.* N. Atlantic Ocean
50 A2 **North West Cape** Austr.
156 D3 **Northwest Pacific Basin** N. Pacific Ocean
141 E3 **Northwest Providence Channel** Bahamas
131 E2 **North West River** Can.
128 B1 **Northwest Territories** *admin. div.* Can.
98 C2 **North York Moors** *moorland* U.K.
138 C3 **Norton** U.S.A.
121 C2 **Norton** Zimbabwe
Norton de Matos Angola *see* **Balombo**
126 B2 **Norton Sound** *sea chan.* U.S.A.
55 D2 **Norvegia, Cape** Antarctica
138 C2 **Norwalk** U.S.A.
93 F3 **Norway** *country* Europe
129 E2 **Norway House** Can.
160 L3 **Norwegian Basin** N. Atlantic Ocean
92 E2 **Norwegian Sea** N. Atlantic Ocean
99 D3 **Norwich** U.K.
139 E2 **Norwich** *CT* U.S.A.
139 D2 **Norwich** *NY* U.S.A.
66 D2 **Noshiro** Japan
91 C1 **Nosivka** Ukr.
122 B2 **Nosop** *watercourse* Africa
86 E2 **Nosovaya** Rus. Fed.
79 C2 **Noșratābād** Iran
122 A1 **Nossob** *watercourse* Africa
103 D1 **Noteć** *r.* Pol.
93 E4 **Notodden** Norway
67 C3 **Noto-hantō** *pen.* Japan
131 D3 **Notre-Dame, Monts** *mts* Can.
131 E3 **Notre Dame Bay** Can.
130 C2 **Nottaway** *r.* Can.
99 C3 **Nottingham** U.K.
114 A2 **Nouâdhibou** Maur.
114 A3 **Nouakchott** Maur.
114 A3 **Nouâmghâr** Maur.
63 B2 **Nouei** Vietnam
48 H6 **Nouméa** New Caledonia
114 B3 **Nouna** Burkina
122 B3 **Noupoort** S. Africa
Nouveau-Comptoir Can. *see* **Wemindji**
Nouvelle Anvers Dem. Rep. Congo *see* **Makanza**
Nouvelles Hébrides *country* S. Pacific Ocean *see* **Vanuatu**
Nova Chaves Angola *see* **Muconda**
154 B2 **Nova Esperança** Brazil
Nova Freixa Moz. *see* **Cuamba**
155 D2 **Nova Friburgo** Brazil
109 C1 **Nova Gradiška** Croatia
154 C2 **Nova Granada** Brazil
155 D2 **Nova Iguaçu** Brazil
91 C2 **Nova Kakhovka** Ukr.
155 D1 **Nova Lima** Brazil
Nova Lisboa Angola *see* **Huambo**
154 B2 **Nova Londrina** Brazil
91 C2 **Nova Odesa** Ukr.
150 C2 **Nova Paraiso** Brazil
154 C1 **Nova Ponte** Brazil
108 A1 **Novara** Italy
151 E3 **Nova Remanso** Brazil
131 D3 **Nova Scotia** *prov.* Can.
155 D1 **Nova Venécia** Brazil
83 K1 **Novaya Sibir', Ostrov** *i.* Rus. Fed.
86 E1 **Novaya Zemlya** *is* Rus. Fed.
107 C2 **Novelda** Spain
103 D2 **Nové Zámky** Slovakia
Novgorod Rus. Fed. *see* **Velikiy Novgorod**
91 C1 **Novhorod-Sivers'kyy** Ukr.
110 B2 **Novi Iskŭr** Bulg.
66 D1 **Novikovo** Rus. Fed.
108 A2 **Novi Ligure** Italy
109 D2 **Novi Pazar** Serbia
109 C1 **Novi Sad** Serbia
Novoalekseyevka Kazakh. *see* **Khobda**
87 D3 **Novoanninskiy** Rus. Fed.
150 C3 **Novo Aripuanã** Brazil
91 D2 **Novoazovs'k** Ukr.
91 E2 **Novocherkassk** Rus. Fed.
89 D2 **Novodugino** Rus. Fed.
86 D2 **Novodvinsk** Rus. Fed.
Novoekonomicheskoye Ukr. *see* **Dymytrov**
152 C2 **Novo Hamburgo** Brazil
154 C2 **Novo Horizonte** Brazil
90 B1 **Novohrad-Volyns'kyy** Ukr.
Novokazalinsk Kazakh. *see* **Ayteke Bi**
91 E1 **Novokhopersk** Rus. Fed.
68 B1 **Novokuznetsk** Rus. Fed.
109 C1 **Novo Mesto** Slovenia
91 D3 **Novomikhaylovskiy** Rus. Fed.
89 E3 **Novomoskovsk** Rus. Fed.
91 D2 **Novomoskovs'k** Ukr.
91 C2 **Novomyrhorod** Ukr.
Novonikolayevsk Rus. Fed. *see* **Novosibirsk**
91 C2 **Novooleksiyivka** Ukr.
91 E2 **Novopokrovskaya** Rus. Fed.
91 D2 **Novopskov** Ukr.
Novo Redondo Angola *see* **Sumbe**
91 D3 **Novorossiysk** Rus. Fed.
88 C2 **Novorzhev** Rus. Fed.
87 E3 **Novosergiyevka** Rus. Fed.
91 D2 **Novoshakhtinsk** Rus. Fed.
82 G3 **Novosibirsk** Rus. Fed.
Novosibirskiye Ostrova *is* Rus. Fed. *see* **New Siberia Islands**
89 E3 **Novosil'** Rus. Fed.
89 D2 **Novosokol'niki** Rus. Fed.
91 C2 **Novotroyits'ke** Ukr.
91 C2 **Novoukrayinka** Ukr.
90 A1 **Novovolyns'k** Ukr.
89 E3 **Novovoronezh** Rus. Fed.
Novovoronezhskiy Rus. Fed. *see* **Novovoronezh**
89 D3 **Novozybkov** Rus. Fed.
103 D2 **Nový Jičín** Czech Rep.
86 E2 **Novyy Bor** Rus. Fed.
91 C2 **Novyy Buh** Ukr.
Novyy Donbass Ukr. *see* **Dymytrov**
Novyye Petushki Rus. Fed. *see* **Petushki**
Novyy Margelan Uzbek. *see* **Farg'ona**
89 E2 **Novyy Nekouz** Rus. Fed.
91 D1 **Novyy Oskol** Rus. Fed.
86 G2 **Novyy Port** Rus. Fed.
86 G2 **Novyy Urengoy** Rus. Fed.
69 E1 **Novyy Urgal** Rus. Fed.
Novyy Uzen' Kazakh. *see* **Zhanaozen**
103 D1 **Nowogard** Pol.
Noworadomsk Pol. *see* **Radomsko**
53 D2 **Nowra** Austr.
81 D2 **Nowshahr** Iran
74 B1 **Nowshera** Pak.
103 E2 **Nowy Sącz** Pol.
103 E2 **Nowy Targ** Pol.
82 G2 **Noyabr'sk** Rus. Fed.
105 C2 **Noyon** France
68 C2 **Noyon** Mongolia
121 C2 **Nsanje** Malawi
121 B2 **Nsombo** Zambia
118 B3 **Ntandembele** Dem. Rep. Congo
123 C2 **Ntha** S. Africa
111 B3 **Ntoro, Kavo** *pt* Greece
118 A2 **Ntoum** Gabon
119 D3 **Ntungamo** Uganda
Nuanetsi *r.* Zimbabwe *see* **Mwenezi**
79 C2 **Nu'aym** *reg.* Oman
116 B2 **Nubian Desert** Sudan
150 B4 **Nudo Coropuna** *mt.* Peru
143 D3 **Nueces** *r.* U.S.A.
129 E1 **Nueltin Lake** Can.
150 B2 **Nueva Loja** Ecuador
153 A4 **Nueva Lubecka** Arg.
145 B2 **Nueva Rosita** Mex.
144 B1 **Nuevo Casas Grandes** Mex.
144 B2 **Nuevo Ideal** Mex.
145 C2 **Nuevo Laredo** Mex.
117 C4 **Nugaal** *watercourse* Somalia
105 C2 **Nuits-St-Georges** France
Nu Jiang *r.* China/Myanmar *see* **Salween**
Nukha Azer. *see* **Şäki**
49 J6 **Nuku'alofa** Tonga
49 M4 **Nuku Hiva** *i.* Fr. Polynesia
48 G4 **Nukumanu Islands** P.N.G.
76 B2 **Nukus** Uzbek.
50 B2 **Nullagine** Austr.
50 C3 **Nullarbor** Austr.
50 B3 **Nullarbor Plain** Austr.
115 D4 **Numan** Nigeria
67 C3 **Numazu** Japan
51 C1 **Numbulwar** Austr.
93 E3 **Numedal** *val.* Norway
59 C3 **Numfoor** *i.* Indon.
53 C3 **Numurkah** Austr.
Nunap Isua *c.* Greenland *see* **Farewell, Cape**
127 G2 **Nunavik** *reg.* Can.
129 E1 **Nunavut** *admin. div.* Can.
99 C3 **Nuneaton** U.K.
126 A3 **Nunivak Island** U.S.A.
106 B1 **Nuñomoral** Spain
108 A2 **Nuoro** Italy
78 B2 **Nuqrah** Saudi Arabia
77 C1 **Nura** *r.* Kazakh.
101 E3 **Nuremberg** Ger.
74 B1 **Nūrestān** Afgh.
52 A2 **Nuriootpa** Austr.
92 I3 **Nurmes** Fin.
Nürnberg Ger. *see* **Nuremberg**
53 C2 **Nurri, Mount** *h.* Austr.
62 A1 **Nu Shan** *mts* China
74 A2 **Nushki** Pak.
127 I2 **Nuuk** Greenland
127 I2 **Nuussuaq** Greenland
127 I2 **Nuussuaq** *pen.* Greenland
80 B3 **Nuwaybi' al Muzayyinah** Egypt
122 A3 **Nuwerus** S. Africa
122 B3 **Nuweveldberge** *mts* S. Africa
86 F2 **Nyagan'** Rus. Fed.
75 D1 **Nyainqêntanglha Feng** *mt.* China
75 D2 **Nyainqêntanglha Shan** *mts* China
Nyakh Rus. Fed. *see* **Nyagan'**
117 A3 **Nyala** Sudan
119 D4 **Nyamtumbo** Tanz.
Nyande Zimbabwe *see* **Masvingo**
86 D2 **Nyandoma** Rus. Fed.
118 B3 **Nyanga** Congo
118 B3 **Nyanga** *r.* Gabon
121 C2 **Nyanga** Zimbabwe
121 C1 **Nyasa, Lake** Africa
Nyasaland *country* Africa *see* **Malawi**
88 C3 **Nyasvizh** Belarus
62 A2 **Nyaunglebin** Myanmar
93 F4 **Nyborg** Denmark
92 I1 **Nyborg** Norway
93 G4 **Nybro** Sweden
Nyenchen Tanglha Range *mts* China *see* **Nyainqêntanglha Shan**
119 D3 **Nyeri** Kenya
68 C3 **Nyingchi** China
103 E2 **Nyíregyháza** Hungary
93 F5 **Nykøbing** Denmark
93 G4 **Nyköping** Sweden
53 C2 **Nymagee** Austr.
93 G4 **Nynäshamn** Sweden
53 C2 **Nyngan** Austr.
88 B3 **Nyoman** *r.* Belarus/Lith.
105 D3 **Nyons** France
86 E2 **Nyrob** Rus. Fed.
103 D1 **Nysa** Pol.
134 C2 **Nyssa** U.S.A.
119 C3 **Nyunzu** Dem. Rep. Congo
83 I2 **Nyurba** Rus. Fed.
91 C2 **Nyzhni Sirohozy** Ukr.
91 C2 **Nyzhn'ohirs'kyy** Ukr.
118 B3 **Nzambi** Congo
119 D3 **Nzega** Tanz.
114 B4 **Nzérékoré** Guinea
120 A1 **N'zeto** Angola

O

136 C2 **Oahe, Lake** U.S.A.
49 L1 **O'ahu** *i.* U.S.A.
52 B2 **Oakbank** Austr.
140 B2 **Oakdale** U.S.A.
53 D1 **Oakey** Austr.
138 B3 **Oak Grove** U.S.A.
99 C3 **Oakham** U.K.
134 B1 **Oak Harbor** U.S.A.
138 C3 **Oak Hill** U.S.A.
135 B3 **Oakland** *CA* U.S.A.
139 D3 **Oakland** *MD* U.S.A.
138 B2 **Oak Lawn** U.S.A.
136 C3 **Oakley** U.S.A.
50 B2 **Oakover** *r.* Austr.
134 B2 **Oakridge** U.S.A.
141 D1 **Oak Ridge** U.S.A.
54 B3 **Oamaru** N.Z.
64 B2 **Oas** Phil.
145 C3 **Oaxaca** Mex.
86 F2 **Ob'** *r.* Rus. Fed.
Ob, Gulf of *sea chan.* Rus. Fed. *see* **Obskaya Guba**
88 C2 **Obal'** Belarus
118 B2 **Obala** Cameroon
96 B2 **Oban** U.K.
106 B1 **O Barco** Spain
Obbia Somalia *see* **Hobyo**
136 C3 **Oberlin** U.S.A.
53 C2 **Oberon** Austr.
101 F3 **Oberviechtach** Ger.
59 C3 **Obi** *i.* Indon.
151 D3 **Óbidos** Brazil
66 D2 **Obihiro** Japan
69 E1 **Obluch'ye** Rus. Fed.
89 E2 **Obninsk** Rus. Fed.
119 C2 **Obo** C.A.R.
117 C3 **Obock** Djibouti
103 D1 **Oborniki** Pol.
118 B3 **Obouya** Congo
89 E3 **Oboyan'** Rus. Fed.
86 D2 **Obozerskiy** Rus. Fed.
144 B2 **Obregón, Presa** *resr* Mex.
109 D2 **Obrenovac** Serbia
134 B2 **O'Brien** U.S.A.
87 E3 **Obshchiy Syrt** *hills* Kazakh./Rus. Fed.
86 G2 **Obskaya Guba** *sea chan.* Rus. Fed.
114 B4 **Obuasi** Ghana
90 C1 **Obukhiv** Ukr.
86 D2 **Ob''yachevo** Rus. Fed.
141 D3 **Ocala** U.S.A.
144 B2 **Ocampo** Mex.
106 C2 **Ocaña** Spain
150 B2 **Occidental, Cordillera** *mts* Col.
150 B4 **Occidental, Cordillera** *mts* Peru
139 D3 **Ocean City** *MD* U.S.A.
139 E3 **Ocean City** *NJ* U.S.A.
128 B2 **Ocean Falls** Can.
135 C4 **Oceanside** U.S.A.

91 C2 Ochakiv Ukr.
86 E3 Ocher Rus. Fed.
101 E3 Ochsenfurt Ger.
110 B1 Ocna Mureș Romania
90 B2 Ocnița Moldova
141 D2 Oconee r. U.S.A.
145 C3 Ocosingo Mex.
141 E1 Ocracoke Island U.S.A.
October Revolution Island i. Rus. Fed. see Oktyabr'skoy Revolyutsii, Ostrov
59 C3 Ocussi enclave East Timor
116 B2 Oda, Jebel mt. Sudan
66 D2 Ōdate Japan
67 C3 Odawara Japan
93 E3 Odda Norway
106 B2 Odemira Port.
111 C3 Ödemiș Turkey
93 F4 Odense Denmark
101 D3 Odenwald reg. Ger.
102 C1 Oder r. Ger./Pol.
102 C1 Oderbucht b. Ger.
Odesa Ukr. see Odessa
90 C2 Odessa Ukr.
143 C2 Odessa U.S.A.
114 B4 Odienné Côte d'Ivoire
89 E3 Odoyev Rus. Fed.
103 D1 Odra r. Ger./Pol.
151 E3 Oeiras Brazil
101 D2 Oelde Ger.
136 C2 Oelrichs U.S.A.
101 F2 Oelsnitz Ger.
100 B1 Oenkerk Neth.
137 E3 O'Fallon U.S.A.
109 C2 Ofanto r. Italy
101 D2 Offenbach am Main Ger.
102 B2 Offenburg Ger.
66 C3 Oga Japan
117 C4 Ogadēn reg. Eth.
66 C3 Oga-hantō pen. Japan
67 C3 Ōgaki Japan
136 C2 Ogallala U.S.A.
Ogasawara-shotō is Japan see Bonin Islands
115 C4 Ogbomosho Nigeria
134 D2 Ogden U.S.A.
139 D2 Ogdensburg U.S.A.
126 C2 Ogilvie r. Can.
126 C2 Ogilvie Mountains Can.
141 D2 Oglethorpe, Mount U.S.A.
130 B2 Ogoki r. Can.
130 B2 Ogoki Reservoir Can.
88 B2 Ogre Latvia
109 C1 Ogulin Croatia
81 D2 Ogurjaly Adasy i. Turkm.
115 C2 Ohanet Alg.
138 B3 Ohio r. U.S.A.
138 C2 Ohio state U.S.A.
101 E2 Ohrdruf Ger.
101 F2 Ohře r. Czech Rep.
111 B2 Ohrid Macedonia
151 D2 Oiapoque Brazil
139 D2 Oil City U.S.A.
100 A3 Oise r. France
67 B4 Ōita Japan
144 B2 Ojinaga Mex.
152 B2 Ojos del Salado, Nevado mt. Arg./Chile
89 F2 Oka r. Rus. Fed.
120 A3 Okahandja Namibia
120 A3 Okakarara Namibia
128 C3 Okanagan Falls Can.
128 C3 Okanagan Lake Can.
134 C1 Okanogan U.S.A.
134 C1 Okanogan r. U.S.A.
74 B1 Okara Pak.
120 B2 Okavango r. Africa
120 B2 Okavango Delta swamp Botswana
67 C3 Okaya Japan
67 B4 Okayama Japan
67 C4 Okazaki Japan
141 D3 Okeechobee U.S.A.
141 D3 Okeechobee, Lake U.S.A.
141 D2 Okefenokee Swamp U.S.A.
99 A4 Okehampton U.K.
115 C4 Okene Nigeria
101 E1 Oker r. Ger.
74 A2 Okha India
83 K3 Okha Rus. Fed.
75 C2 Okhaldhunga Nepal
83 K3 Okhotka r. Rus. Fed.
83 K3 Okhotsk Rus. Fed.
83 K3 Okhotsk, Sea of Japan/Rus. Fed.
Okhotskoye More sea Japan/Rus. Fed. see Okhotsk, Sea of
91 C1 Okhtyrka Ukr.
69 E3 Okinawa i. Japan
67 B3 Oki-shotō is Japan
143 D1 Oklahoma state U.S.A.
143 D1 Oklahoma City U.S.A.
143 D1 Okmulgee U.S.A.
Oknitsa Moldova see Ocnița
78 A2 Oko, Wadi watercourse Sudan
118 B3 Okondja Gabon
128 C2 Okotoks Can.
89 D3 Okovskiy Les for. Rus. Fed.
118 B3 Okoyo Congo
92 H1 Øksfjord Norway
62 A2 Oktwin Myanmar
Oktyabr' Kazakh. see Kandyagash
Oktyabr'sk Kazakh. see Kandyagash
86 D2 Oktyabr'skiy Rus. Fed.
83 L3 Oktyabr'skiy Rus. Fed.
87 E3 Oktyabr'skiy Rus. Fed.
86 F2 Oktyabr'skoye Rus. Fed.
83 H1 Oktyabr'skoy Revolyutsii, Ostrov i. Rus. Fed.
89 D2 Okulovka Rus. Fed.
66 C2 Okushiri-tō i. Japan
92 □B2 Ólafsfjörður Iceland
92 □A3 Ólafsvík Iceland
88 B2 Olaine Latvia
93 G4 Öland i. Sweden
52 B2 Olary Austr.
136 B3 Olathe CO U.S.A.
137 E3 Olathe KS U.S.A.
153 B3 Olavarría Arg.
103 D1 Oława Pol.
108 A2 Olbia Italy
126 C2 Old Crow Can.
101 D1 Oldenburg Ger.
102 C1 Oldenburg in Holstein Ger.
100 C1 Oldenzaal Neth.
98 B3 Oldham U.K.
97 B3 Old Head of Kinsale hd Ireland
96 C2 Oldmeldrum U.K.
128 C2 Olds Can.
129 D2 Old Wives Lake Can.
139 D2 Olean U.S.A.
103 E1 Olecko Pol.
83 J2 Olekminsk Rus. Fed.
91 C2 Oleksandrivka Ukr.
Oleksandrivs'k Ukr. see Zaporizhzhya
91 C2 Oleksandriya Ukr.
86 C2 Olenegorsk Rus. Fed.
83 I2 Olenek Rus. Fed.
83 I2 Olenek r. Rus. Fed.
89 D2 Olenino Rus. Fed.
Olenivs'ki Kar"yery Ukr. see Dokuchayevs'k
Olenya Rus. Fed. see Olenegorsk
Oleshky Ukr. see Tsyurupyns'k
103 D1 Olesno Pol.
90 B1 Olevs'k Ukr.
106 B2 Olhão Port.
123 D1 Olifants r. Moz./S. Africa
122 A2 Olifants watercourse Namibia
123 D1 Olifants S. Africa
122 A3 Olifants r. S. Africa
122 B2 Olifantshoek S. Africa
154 C2 Olímpia Brazil
151 F3 Olinda Brazil
123 C1 Oliphants Drift Botswana
107 C2 Oliva Spain
155 D2 Oliveira Brazil
Olivença Moz. see Lupilichi
106 B2 Olivenza Spain
140 B2 Olla U.S.A.
152 B2 Ollagüe Chile
77 C2 Olmaliq Uzbek.
106 C1 Olmedo Spain
105 D3 Olmeto France
150 B3 Olmos Peru
138 B3 Olney U.S.A.
103 D2 Olomouc Czech Rep.
86 C2 Olonets Rus. Fed.
64 B2 Olongapo Phil.
104 B3 Oloron-Ste-Marie France
107 D1 Olot Spain
69 D1 Olovyannaya Rus. Fed.
83 L2 Oloy r. Rus. Fed.
100 C2 Olpe Ger.
103 E1 Olsztyn Pol.
110 B2 Olt r. Romania
110 C2 Oltenița Romania
143 C2 Olton U.S.A.
81 C1 Oltu Turkey
Ol'viopol' Ukr. see Pervomays'k
111 B3 Olympia tourist site Greece
134 B1 Olympia U.S.A.
Olympus, Mount mt. Greece see Mount Olympus
134 B1 Olympus, Mount U.S.A.
83 M2 Olyutorskiy Rus. Fed.
83 M3 Olyutorskiy, Mys c. Rus. Fed.
66 D2 Ōma Japan
97 C1 Omagh U.K.
137 D2 Omaha U.S.A.
79 C2 Oman country Asia
79 C2 Oman, Gulf of Asia
54 A2 Omarama N.Z.
120 A3 Omaruru Namibia
120 B2 Omatako watercourse Namibia
122 B2 Omaweneno Botswana
116 B3 Omdurman Sudan
53 C3 Omeo Austr.
145 C3 Ometepec Mex.
78 A3 Om Hajēr Eritrea
81 C2 Omīdīyeh Iran
128 B2 Omineca Mountains Can.
120 A3 Omitara Namibia
100 C1 Ommen Neth.
83 L2 Omolon r. Rus. Fed.
100 B3 Omont France
82 F3 Omsk Rus. Fed.
83 L2 Omsukchan Rus. Fed.
110 C1 Omu, Vârful mt. Romania
67 A4 Ōmura Japan
138 A2 Onalaska U.S.A.
139 D3 Onancock U.S.A.
138 C1 Onaping Lake Can.
131 C3 Onatchiway, Lac l. Can.
63 A2 Onbingwin Myanmar
120 A2 Oncócua Angola
122 B3 Onderstedorings S. Africa
120 A2 Ondjiva Angola
69 D1 Öndörhaan Mongolia
122 B1 One Botswana
86 C2 Onega Rus. Fed.
86 C2 Onega r. Rus. Fed.
86 C2 Onega, Lake Rus. Fed.
139 D2 Oneida Lake U.S.A.
137 D2 O'Neill U.S.A.
139 D2 Oneonta U.S.A.
110 C1 Onești Romania
Onezhskoye Ozero l. Rus. Fed. see Onega, Lake
122 B2 Ongers watercourse S. Africa
65 B2 Ongjin N. Korea
73 C3 Ongole India
121 □D3 Onilahy r. Madag.
115 C4 Onitsha Nigeria
120 A3 Onjati Mountain Namibia
67 C3 Ōno Japan
156 D6 Onotoa atoll Kiribati
122 A2 Onseepkans S. Africa
50 A2 Onslow Austr.
141 E2 Onslow Bay U.S.A.
130 A2 Ontario prov. Can.
134 C2 Ontario U.S.A.
139 D2 Ontario, Lake Can./U.S.A.
107 C2 Ontinyent Spain
51 C2 Oodnadatta Austr.
Oostende Belgium see Ostend
100 B2 Oosterhout Neth.
100 A2 Oosterschelde est. Neth.
100 B1 Oost-Vlieland Neth.
128 B2 Ootsa Lake Can.
128 B2 Ootsa Lake l. Can.
118 C3 Opala Dem. Rep. Congo
130 C2 Opataca, Lac l. Can.
103 D2 Opava Czech Rep.
141 C2 Opelika U.S.A.
140 B2 Opelousas U.S.A.
117 A4 Opienge Dem. Rep. Congo
130 C2 Opinaca, Réservoir resr Can.
131 D2 Opiscotéo, Lac l. Can.
88 C2 Opochka Rus. Fed.
144 A2 Opodepe Mex.
103 D1 Opole Pol.
106 B1 Oporto Port.
54 C1 Opotiki N.Z.
93 E3 Oppdal Norway
134 C1 Opportunity U.S.A.
54 B1 Opunake N.Z.
120 A2 Opuwo Namibia
110 B1 Oradea Romania
Orahovac Kosovo see Rahovec
114 B1 Oran Alg.
152 B2 Orán Arg.
65 B1 Ŏrang N. Korea
53 C2 Orange Austr.
105 C3 Orange France
122 A2 Orange r. Namibia/S. Africa
143 E2 Orange U.S.A.
141 D2 Orangeburg U.S.A.
Orange Free State prov. S. Africa see Free State
141 D2 Orange Park U.S.A.
138 C2 Orangeville Can.
145 D3 Orange Walk Belize
101 F1 Oranienburg Ger.
122 A2 Oranjemund Namibia
147 C3 Oranjestad Aruba
120 B3 Orapa Botswana
110 B1 Orăștie Romania
Orașul Stalin Romania see Brașov
108 B2 Orbetello Italy
53 C3 Orbost Austr.
141 D3 Orchid Island U.S.A.
111 B3 Orchomenos Greece
50 B1 Ord, Mount h. Austr.
106 B1 Ordes Spain
70 B2 Ordos China
80 B1 Ordu Turkey
Ordzhonikidze Rus. Fed. see Vladikavkaz
91 C2 Ordzhonikidze Ukr.
93 G4 Örebro Sweden
134 B2 Oregon state U.S.A.
134 B1 Oregon City U.S.A.
141 E1 Oregon Inlet U.S.A.
87 C3 Orekhovo-Zuyevo Rus. Fed.
89 E3 Orel Rus. Fed.
83 K3 Orel', Ozero l. Rus. Fed.
135 D2 Orem U.S.A.
111 C3 Ören Turkey
87 E3 Orenburg Rus. Fed.
54 A3 Orepuki N.Z.
111 C2 Orestiada Greece
93 F4 Öresund str. Denmark/Sweden
Oretana, Cordillera mts Spain see Toledo, Montes de
99 D3 Orford Ness hd U.K.
89 F2 Orgtrud Rus. Fed.
74 A1 Orgūn Afgh.
111 C3 Orhaneli Turkey
111 C2 Orhangazi Turkey
68 D1 Orhon Gol r. Mongolia
152 B1 Oriental, Cordillera mts Bol.
150 B2 Oriental, Cordillera mts Col.
150 B4 Oriental, Cordillera mts Peru
107 C2 Orihuela Spain
91 D2 Orikhiv Ukr.
130 C3 Orillia Can.
93 I3 Orimattila Fin.
150 C2 Orinoco r. Col./Venez.
150 C2 Orinoco Delta Venez.
75 C2 Orissa state India
88 B2 Orissaare Estonia
108 A3 Oristano Italy
93 I3 Orivesi l. Fin.
151 D3 Oriximiná Brazil
145 C3 Orizaba Mex.
145 C3 Orizaba, Pico de vol. Mex.
154 C1 Orizona Brazil
92 E3 Orkanger Norway
93 F4 Örkelljunga Sweden
93 E3 Orkla r. Norway
96 C1 Orkney Islands U.K.
154 C2 Orlândia Brazil
141 D3 Orlando U.S.A.
104 C2 Orléans France
139 F2 Orleans U.S.A.
139 E1 Orléans, Île d' i. Can.
Orléansville Alg. see Chlef
74 A2 Ormara Pak.
64 B2 Ormoc Phil.
141 D3 Ormond Beach U.S.A.
98 B3 Ormskirk U.K.
104 B2 Orne r. France
92 F2 Ørnes Norway
92 G3 Örnsköldsvik Sweden
114 B3 Orodara Burkina
134 C1 Orofino U.S.A.
139 F2 Orono U.S.A.
Oroqen Zizhiqi China see Alihe
64 B3 Oroquieta Phil.
108 A2 Orosei Italy
108 A2 Orosei, Golfo di b. Italy
103 E2 Orosháza Hungary
135 B3 Oroville U.S.A.
52 A2 Orroroo Austr.
93 F3 Orsa Sweden
89 D3 Orsha Belarus
87 E3 Orsk Rus. Fed.
110 B2 Orșova Romania
93 E3 Ørsta Norway
106 B1 Ortegal, Cabo c. Spain
104 B3 Orthez France
106 B1 Ortigueira Spain
108 B1 Ortles mt. Italy
108 B2 Ortona Italy
137 D1 Ortonville U.S.A.
83 J2 Orulgan, Khrebet mts Rus. Fed.
Orūmīyeh Iran see Urmia
Orūmīyeh, Daryācheh-ye salt l. Iran see Urmia, Lake
152 B1 Oruro Bol.
104 B2 Orvault France
108 B2 Orvieto Italy
93 F3 Os Norway
146 B4 Osa, Península de pen. Costa Rica
137 E3 Osage r. U.S.A.
137 D3 Osage City U.S.A.
67 C4 Ōsaka Japan
77 D1 Osakarovka Kazakh.
101 E1 Oschersleben (Bode) Ger.
108 A2 Oschiri Italy
138 C2 Oscoda U.S.A.
89 E3 Osetr r. Rus. Fed.
139 D1 Osgoode Can.
77 D2 Osh Kyrg.
120 A2 Oshakati Namibia
130 C3 Oshawa Can.
120 A2 Oshikango Namibia
66 C2 Ō-shima i. Japan
67 C4 Ō-shima i. Japan
138 B2 Oshkosh U.S.A.
81 C2 Oshnovīyeh Iran
115 C4 Oshogbo Nigeria
118 B3 Oshwe Dem. Rep. Congo
109 C1 Osijek Croatia
128 B2 Osilinka r. Can.
108 B2 Osimo Italy
Osipenko Ukr. see Berdyans'k
123 D2 Osizweni S. Africa
137 E2 Oskaloosa U.S.A.
93 G4 Oskarshamn Sweden
89 E3 Oskol r. Rus. Fed.
93 F4 Oslo Norway
93 F4 Oslofjorden sea chan. Norway
80 B1 Osmancık Turkey
111 C2 Osmaneli Turkey
80 B2 Osmaniye Turkey
88 C2 Os'mino Rus. Fed.
101 D1 Osnabrück Ger.
153 A4 Osorno Chile
106 C1 Osorno Spain
128 C3 Osoyoos Can.
100 B2 Oss Neth.
51 D4 Ossa, Mount Austr.
83 L3 Ossora Rus. Fed.
89 D2 Ostashkov Rus. Fed.
101 D1 Oste r. Ger.
100 A2 Ostend Belgium
101 E1 Osterburg (Altmark) Ger.
93 F3 Österdalälven r. Sweden
101 D1 Osterholz-Scharmbeck Ger.
101 E2 Osterode am Harz Ger.
92 F3 Östersund Sweden
Ostfriesische Inseln is Ger. see East Frisian Islands
100 C1 Ostfriesland reg. Ger.
93 G3 Östhammar Sweden
103 D2 Ostrava Czech Rep.
103 D1 Ostróda Pol.
89 E3 Ostrogozhsk Rus. Fed.
90 B1 Ostroh Ukr.
103 E1 Ostrołęka Pol.
101 F2 Ostrov Czech Rep.
88 C2 Ostrov Rus. Fed.
Ostrovets Pol. see Ostrowiec Świętokrzyski
89 F2 Ostrovskoye Rus. Fed.

103 E1 **Ostrowiec Świętokrzyski** Pol.
103 E1 **Ostrów Mazowiecka** Pol.
Ostrowo Pol. *see* **Ostrów Wielkopolski**
103 D1 **Ostrów Wielkopolski** Pol.
109 C2 **Ostuni** Italy
110 B2 **Osŭm** *r.* Bulg.
67 B4 **Ōsumi-kaikyō** *sea chan.* Japan
67 B4 **Ōsumi-shotō** *is* Japan
106 B2 **Osuna** Spain
139 D2 **Oswego** U.S.A.
99 B3 **Oswestry** U.K.
67 C3 **Ōta** Japan
54 B3 **Otago Peninsula** N.Z.
54 C2 **Otaki** N.Z.
77 D2 **Otar** Kazakh.
66 D2 **Otaru** Japan
120 A2 **Otavi** Namibia
67 D3 **Ōtawara** Japan
92 G2 **Oteren** Norway
134 C1 **Othello** U.S.A.
120 A3 **Otjiwarongo** Namibia
109 C2 **Otočac** Croatia
Otog Qi China *see* **Ulan**
117 B3 **Otoro, Jebel** *mt.* Sudan
Otpor Rus. Fed. *see* **Zabaykal'sk**
93 E4 **Otra** *r.* Norway
109 C2 **Otranto, Strait of** Albania/Italy
67 C3 **Ōtsu** Japan
93 E3 **Otta** Norway
130 C3 **Ottawa** Can.
130 C3 **Ottawa** *r.* Can.
138 B2 **Ottawa** *IL* U.S.A.
137 D3 **Ottawa** *KS* U.S.A.
130 B2 **Ottawa Islands** Can.
98 B2 **Otterburn** U.K.
130 B2 **Otter Rapids** Can.
100 B2 **Ottignies** Belgium
137 E2 **Ottumwa** U.S.A.
150 B3 **Otuzco** Peru
52 B3 **Otway, Cape** Austr.
140 B2 **Ouachita** *r.* U.S.A.
140 B2 **Ouachita, Lake** U.S.A.
140 B2 **Ouachita Mountains** U.S.A.
110 [illegible] **Ouadda** C.A.R.
115 D3 **Ouaddaï** *reg.* Chad
114 B3 **Ouagadougou** Burkina
114 B3 **Ouahigouya** Burkina
114 B3 **Oualâta** Maur.
118 C2 **Ouanda-Djailé** C.A.R.
114 B2 **Ouarâne** *reg.* Maur.
115 C1 **Ouargla** Alg.
114 B1 **Ouarzazate** Morocco
100 A2 **Oudenaarde** Belgium
122 B3 **Oudtshoorn** S. Africa
107 C2 **Oued Tlélat** Alg.
114 B1 **Oued Zem** Morocco
104 A2 **Ouessant, Île d'** *i.* France
118 B2 **Ouesso** Congo
97 B2 **Oughterard** Ireland
118 B2 **Ouham** *r.* C.A.R./Chad
114 B1 **Oujda** Morocco
92 H3 **Oulainen** Fin.
107 D2 **Ouled Farès** Alg.
92 I2 **Oulu** Fin.
92 I3 **Oulujärvi** *l.* Fin.
108 A1 **Oulx** Italy
115 E3 **Oum-Chalouba** Chad
115 D3 **Oum-Hadjer** Chad
115 E3 **Ounianga Kébir** Chad
100 B2 **Oupeye** Belgium
100 C3 **Our** *r.* Ger./Lux.
106 B1 **Ourense** Spain
142 A1 **Ouricurí** Brazil
154 C2 **Ourinhos** Brazil
155 D2 **Ouro Preto** Brazil
100 B2 **Ourthe** *r.* Belgium
98 C3 **Ouse** *r.* U.K.
Outaouais, Rivière des *r.* Can. *see* **Ottawa**
131 D3 **Outardes, Rivière aux** *r.* Can.
131 D2 **Outardes Quatre, Réservoir** *resr* Can.
96 A2 **Outer Hebrides** *is* U.K.
Outer Mongolia *country* Asia *see* **Mongolia**
120 A3 **Outjo** Namibia
129 D2 **Outlook** Can.
92 I3 **Outokumpu** Fin.
52 B3 **Ouyen** Austr.
108 A2 **Ovace, Punta d'** *mt.* France
152 A3 **Ovalle** Chile
106 B1 **Ovar** Port.
92 H2 **Överkalix** Sweden
137 E3 **Overland Park** U.S.A.
135 D3 **Overton** U.S.A.
92 H2 **Övertorneå** Sweden
106 B1 **Oviedo** Spain
141 D3 **Oviedo** U.S.A.
88 B2 **Ovišrags** *hd* Latvia
93 E3 **Øvre Årdal** Norway
93 F3 **Øvre Rendal** Norway
90 B1 **Ovruch** Ukr.
118 B3 **Owando** Congo
67 C4 **Owase** Japan
143 D1 **Owasso** U.S.A.
137 E2 **Owatonna** U.S.A.
139 D2 **Owego** U.S.A.
138 B3 **Owensboro** U.S.A.
135 C3 **Owens Lake** U.S.A.
130 B3 **Owen Sound** Can.
51 D1 **Owen Stanley Range** *mts* P.N.G.
115 C4 **Owerri** Nigeria
115 C4 **Owo** Nigeria
138 C2 **Owosso** U.S.A.
134 C2 **Owyhee** U.S.A.
134 C2 **Owyhee** *r.* U.S.A.
129 D3 **Oxbow** Can.
54 B2 **Oxford** N.Z.
99 C4 **Oxford** U.K.
140 C2 **Oxford** U.S.A.
129 E2 **Oxford Lake** Can.
145 D2 **Oxkutzcab** Mex.
52 B2 **Oxley** Austr.
97 B1 **Ox Mountains** *hills* Ireland
135 C4 **Oxnard** U.S.A.
67 C3 **Oyama** Japan
118 B2 **Oyem** Gabon
129 C2 **Oyen** Can.
105 D2 **Oyonnax** France
77 C2 **Oyoqquduq** Uzbek.
64 B3 **Ozamiz** Phil.
140 C2 **Ozark** *AL* U.S.A.
137 E3 **Ozark** *MO* U.S.A.
137 E3 **Ozark Plateau** U.S.A.
137 E3 **Ozarks, Lake of the** U.S.A.
83 L3 **Ozernovskiy** Rus. Fed.
88 B3 **Ozersk** Rus. Fed.
89 E3 **Ozery** Rus. Fed.
87 D3 **Ozinki** Rus. Fed.

P

127 I2 **Paamiut** Greenland
122 A3 **Paarl** S. Africa
103 D1 **Pabianice** Pol.
75 C2 **Pabna** Bangl.
88 C3 **Pabradė** Lith.
74 A2 **Pab Range** *mts* Pak.
150 B3 **Pacasmayo** Peru
142 B2 **Pacheco** Mex.
109 C3 **Pachino** Italy
145 C2 **Pachuca** Mex.
135 B3 **Pacifica** U.S.A.
157 E9 **Pacific-Antarctic Ridge** S. Pacific Ocean
156 **Pacific Ocean**
61 C2 **Pacitan** Indon.
52 B2 **Packsaddle** Austr.
103 D1 **Paczków** Pol.
60 B2 **Padang** Indon.
60 B1 **Padang Endau** Malaysia
60 B2 **Padangpanjang** Indon.
60 A1 **Padangsidimpuan** Indon.
101 D2 **Paderborn** Ger.
Padova Italy *see* **Padua**
143 D3 **Padre Island** U.S.A.
99 A4 **Padstow** U.K.
52 B3 **Padthaway** Austr.
108 B1 **Padua** Italy
138 B3 **Paducah** U.S.A.
143 C2 **Paducah** U.S.A.
65 B1 **Paegam** N. Korea
Paektu-san *mt.* China/N. Korea *see* **Baitou Shan**
65 A2 **Paengnyŏng-do** *i.* S. Korea
54 C1 **Paeroa** N.Z.
Pafos Cyprus *see* **Paphos**
109 C2 **Pag** Croatia
109 B2 **Pag** *i.* Croatia
64 B3 **Pagadian** Phil.
60 A2 **Pagai Selatan** *i.* Indon.
60 B2 **Pagai Utara** *i.* Indon.
59 D1 **Pagan** *i.* N. Mariana Is
61 C2 **Pagatan** Indon.
142 A1 **Page** U.S.A.
88 B2 **Pagėgiai** Lith.
153 E5 **Paget, Mount** S. Georgia
136 B3 **Pagosa Springs** U.S.A.
88 C2 **Paide** Estonia
99 B4 **Paignton** U.K.
93 I3 **Päijänne** *l.* Fin.
75 C2 **Paikü Co** *l.* China
60 B2 **Painan** Indon.
138 C2 **Painesville** U.S.A.
142 A1 **Painted Desert** U.S.A.
Paint Hills Can. *see* **Wemindji**
96 B3 **Paisley** U.K.
92 H2 **Pajala** Sweden
150 A3 **Paján** Ecuador
150 C2 **Pakaraima Mountains** *mts* S. America
150 D2 **Pakaraima Mountains** S. America
74 A2 **Pakistan** *country* Asia
62 A1 **Pakokku** Myanmar
88 B2 **Pakruojis** Lith.
103 D2 **Paks** Hungary
130 A2 **Pakwash Lake** Can.
62 B2 **Pakxan** Laos
63 B2 **Pakxé** Laos
115 D4 **Pala** Chad
60 B2 **Palabuhanratu, Teluk** *b.* Indon.
111 C3 **Palaikastro** Greece
111 B3 **Palaiochora** Greece
73 B3 **Palakkat** India
122 B1 **Palamakoloi** Botswana
107 D1 **Palamós** Spain
83 L3 **Palana** Rus. Fed.
64 B2 **Palanan** Phil.
61 C2 **Palangkaraya** Indon.
74 B2 **Palanpur** India
123 C1 **Palapye** Botswana
83 L2 **Palatka** Rus. Fed.
141 D3 **Palatka** U.S.A.
59 C2 **Palau** *country* N. Pacific Ocean
63 A2 **Palaw** Myanmar
64 A3 **Palawan** *i.* Phil.
64 A3 **Palawan Passage** *str.* Phil.
88 B2 **Paldiski** Estonia
89 F2 **Palekh** Rus. Fed.
60 B2 **Palembang** Indon.
106 C1 **Palencia** Spain
145 C3 **Palenque** Mex.
108 B3 **Palermo** Italy
143 D2 **Palestine** U.S.A.
62 A1 **Paletwa** Myanmar
Palghat India *see* **Palakkat**
74 B2 **Pali** India
48 G4 **Palikir** Micronesia
109 C2 **Palinuro, Capo** *c.* Italy
111 B3 **Paliouri, Akrotirio** *pt* Greece
100 B3 **Paliseul** Belgium
92 I3 **Paljakka** *h.* Fin.
88 C2 **Palkino** Rus. Fed.
73 B4 **Palk Strait** India/Sri Lanka
Palla Bianca *mt.* Austria/Italy *see* **Weißkugel**
54 C2 **Palliser, Cape** N.Z.
157 F7 **Palliser, Îles** *is* Fr. Polynesia
106 B2 **Palma del Río** Spain
107 D2 **Palma de Mallorca** Spain
154 D3 **Palmas** Brazil
151 E4 **Palmas** Brazil
154 B3 **Palmas, Campos de** *hills* Brazil
114 B4 **Palmas, Cape** Liberia
141 D3 **Palm Bay** U.S.A.
135 C4 **Palmdale** U.S.A.
154 C3 **Palmeira** Brazil
151 E3 **Palmeirais** Brazil
126 C2 **Palmer** U.S.A.
55 A2 **Palmer Land** *reg.* Antarctica
49 K5 **Palmerston** *atoll* Cook Is
54 C2 **Palmerston North** N.Z.
109 C3 **Palmi** Italy
145 C2 **Palmillas** Mex.
150 B2 **Palmira** Col.
154 B2 **Palmital** Brazil
135 C4 **Palm Springs** U.S.A.
Palmyra Syria *see* **Tadmur**
49 K3 **Palmyra Atoll** N. Pacific Ocean
135 B3 **Palo Alto** U.S.A.
117 B3 **Paloich** Sudan
[illegible] C3 [illegible] Mex.
61 D2 **Palopo** Indon.
107 C2 **Palos, Cabo de** *c.* Spain
92 I3 **Paltamo** Fin.
61 C2 **Palu** Indon.
83 M2 **Palyavaam** *r.* Rus. Fed.
150 B3 **Pamar** Col.
121 C3 **Pambarra** Moz.
104 C3 **Pamiers** France
77 D3 **Pamir** *mts* Asia
141 E1 **Pamlico Sound** *sea chan.* U.S.A.
152 B1 **Pampa Grande** Bol.
153 B3 **Pampas** *reg.* Arg.
150 B2 **Pamplona** Col.
107 C1 **Pamplona** Spain
111 D2 **Pamukova** Turkey
60 B2 **Panaitan** *i.* Indon.
73 B3 **Panaji** India
146 B4 **Panama** *country* Central America
Panamá Panama *see* **Panama City**
146 C4 **Panamá, Canal de** *canal* Panama
Panamá, Golfo de *g.* Panama *see* **Panama, Gulf of**
146 C4 **Panama, Gulf of** *g.* Panama
Panama Canal *canal* Panama *see* **Panamá, Canal de**
146 C4 **Panama City** Panama
140 C2 **Panama City** U.S.A.
135 C3 **Panamint Range** *mts* U.S.A.
60 B1 **Panarik** Indon.
64 B2 **Panay** *i.* Phil.
109 D2 **Pančevo** Serbia
64 B2 **Pandan** Phil.
64 B2 **Pandan** Phil.
75 C2 **Pandaria** India
73 B3 **Pandharpur** India
88 B2 **Panevėžys** Lith.
Panfilov Kazakh. *see* **Zharkent**
61 C2 **Pangkalanbuun** Indon.
60 A1 **Pangkalansusu** Indon.
60 B2 **Pangkalpinang** Indon.
61 D2 **Pangkalsiang, Tanjung** *pt* Indon.
127 H2 **Pangnirtung** Can.
86 G2 **Pangody** Rus. Fed.
89 F3 **Panino** Rus. Fed.
74 B2 **Panipat** India
74 A2 **Panjgur** Pak.
Panjim India *see* **Panaji**
118 A2 **Pankshin** Nigeria
65 C1 **Pan Ling** *mts* China
75 C2 **Panna** India
50 A2 **Pannawonica** Austr.
154 B2 **Panorama** Brazil
65 B1 **Panshi** China
152 C1 **Pantanal** *reg.* Brazil
145 C2 **Pánuco** Mex.
145 C2 **Pánuco** *r.* Mex.
71 A3 **Panxian** China
62 B1 **Panzhihua** China
109 C3 **Paola** Italy
118 B2 **Paoua** C.A.R.
63 B2 **Paôy Pêt** Cambodia
103 D2 **Pápa** Hungary
54 B1 **Papakura** N.Z.
145 C2 **Papantla** Mex.
96 □ **Papa Stour** *i.* U.K.
54 B1 **Papatoetoe** N.Z.
49 M5 **Papeete** Fr. Polynesia
100 C1 **Papenburg** Ger.
80 B2 **Paphos** Cyprus
137 D2 **Papillion** U.S.A.
59 D3 **Papua** *reg.* Indon.
59 D3 **Papua, Gulf of** P.N.G.
59 D3 **Papua New Guinea** *country* Oceania
89 F3 **Para** *r.* Rus. Fed.
50 A2 **Paraburdoo** Austr.
154 C1 **Paracatu** Brazil
155 C1 **Paracatu** *r.* Brazil
52 A2 **Parachilna** Austr.
109 D2 **Paraćin** Serbia
155 D1 **Pará de Minas** Brazil
151 D2 **Paradise** Guyana
135 B3 **Paradise** U.S.A.
140 B1 **Paragould** U.S.A.
151 D3 **Paraguai** *r.* Brazil
147 D3 **Paraguaná, Península de** *pen.* Venez.
152 C2 **Paraguay** *r.* Arg./Para.
152 C2 **Paraguay** *country* S. America
155 D2 **Paraíba do Sul** *r.* Brazil
154 B1 **Paraíso** Brazil
145 C3 **Paraíso** Mex.
114 C4 **Parakou** Benin
52 A2 **Parakylia** Austr.
151 D2 **Paramaribo** Suriname
83 L3 **Paramushir, Ostrov** *i.* Rus. Fed.
152 B3 **Paraná** Arg.
154 B2 **Paraná** *state* Brazil
154 A3 **Paraná** *r.* S. America
154 C1 **Paranã, Serra do** *hills* Brazil
154 C3 **Paranaguá** Brazil
154 B1 **Paranaíba** Brazil
154 B2 **Paranaíba** *r.* Brazil
154 B2 **Paranapanema** *r.* Brazil
154 B2 **Paranapiacaba, Serra** *mts* Brazil
154 B2 **Paranavaí** Brazil
90 A2 **Parângul Mare, Vârful** *mt.* Romania
54 B2 **Paraparaumu** N.Z.
155 D2 **Parati** Brazil
52 A2 **Paratoo** Austr.
151 D3 **Parauaquara, Serra** *h.* Brazil
154 B1 **Paraúna** Brazil
105 C2 **Paray-le-Monial** France
74 B2 **Parbati** *r.* India
74 B3 **Parbhani** India
101 C1 **Parchim** Ger.
103 E1 **Parczew** Pol.
155 E1 **Pardo** *r. Bahia* Brazil
154 B2 **Pardo** *r. Mato Grosso do Sul* Brazil
154 C2 **Pardo** *r. São Paulo* Brazil
103 D1 **Pardubice** Czech Rep.
152 C1 **Parecis, Serra dos** *hills* Brazil
130 [illegible] **Parent** Can.
130 C3 **Parent, Lac** *l.* Can.
61 C2 **Parepare** Indon.
89 D2 **Parfino** Rus. Fed.
111 B3 **Parga** Greece
109 C3 **Parghelia** Italy
147 D3 **Paria, Gulf of** Trin. and Tob./Venez.
150 C2 **Parima, Serra** *mts* Brazil
151 D3 **Parintins** Brazil
104 C2 **Paris** France
140 C1 **Paris** *TN* U.S.A.
143 D2 **Paris** *TX* U.S.A.
93 H3 **Parkano** Fin.
142 A2 **Parker** U.S.A.
138 C3 **Parkersburg** U.S.A.
53 C2 **Parkes** Austr.
138 A1 **Park Falls** U.S.A.
134 B1 **Parkland** U.S.A.
137 D1 **Park Rapids** U.S.A.
106 C1 **Parla** Spain
108 B2 **Parma** Italy
134 C2 **Parma** U.S.A.
151 E3 **Parnaíba** Brazil
151 E3 **Parnaíba** *r.* Brazil
Parnassus, Mount *mt.* Greece *see* **Parnassos**
54 B2 **Parnassus** N.Z.
111 B3 **Parnonas** *mts* Greece
88 B2 **Pärnu** Estonia
65 B2 **P'aro-ho** *l.* S. Korea
52 B2 **Paroo** *watercourse* Austr.
Paropamisus *mts* Afgh. *see* **Safīd Kūh**
111 C3 **Paros** *i.* Greece
135 D3 **Parowan** U.S.A.
153 A3 **Parral** Chile
53 D2 **Parramatta** Austr.
144 B2 **Parras** Mex.
126 D2 **Parry, Cape** Can.
126 E1 **Parry Islands** Can.
130 B3 **Parry Sound** Can.
137 D3 **Parsons** U.S.A.
108 B3 **Partanna** Italy
101 D2 **Partenstein** Ger.
104 B2 **Parthenay** France
108 B3 **Partinico** Italy
66 B2 **Partizansk** Rus. Fed.
97 B2 **Partry Mountains** *hills* Ireland
151 D3 **Paru** *r.* Brazil
131 E3 **Pasadena** Can.
135 C4 **Pasadena** *CA* U.S.A.
143 D3 **Pasadena** *TX* U.S.A.
62 A2 **Pasawng** Myanmar
140 C2 **Pascagoula** U.S.A.
110 C1 **Paşcani** Romania
134 C1 **Pasco** U.S.A.
155 E1 **Pascoal, Monte** *h.* Brazil
Pascua, Isla de *i.* S. Pacific Ocean *see* **Easter Island**
Pas de Calais *str.* France/U.K. *see* **Dover, Strait of**
102 C1 **Pasewalk** Ger.

129 D2 Pasfield Lake Can.
89 D1 Pasha Rus. Fed.
64 B2 Pasig Phil.
60 B1 Pasir Putih Malaysia
103 D1 Pasłęk Pol.
74 A2 Pasni Pak.
153 A4 Paso Río Mayo Arg.
135 B3 Paso Robles U.S.A.
97 B3 Passage West Ireland
155 D2 Passa Tempo Brazil
102 C2 Passau Ger.
152 C2 Passo Fundo Brazil
155 C2 Passos Brazil
88 C2 Pastavy Belarus
150 B3 Pastaza r. Peru
150 B2 Pasto Col.
74 B1 Pasu Pak.
61 C2 Pasuruan Indon.
88 B2 Pasvalys Lith.
103 D2 Pásztó Hungary
153 A5 Patagonia reg. Arg.
75 C2 Patan Nepal
54 B1 Patea N.Z.
139 E2 Paterson U.S.A.
74 B1 Pathankot India
Pathein Myanmar see Bassein
136 B2 Pathfinder Reservoir U.S.A.
61 C2 Pati Indon.
74 B1 Patiala India
62 A1 Patkai Bum mts India/Myanmar
111 C3 Patmos i. Greece
75 C2 Patna India
81 C2 Patnos Turkey
154 B3 Pato Branco Brazil
152 C3 Patos, Lagoa dos l. Brazil
155 C1 Patos de Minas Brazil
152 B3 Patquía Arg.
Patra Greece see Patras
111 B3 Patras Greece
75 C2 Patratu India
154 C1 Patrocínio Brazil
63 B3 Pattani Thai.
63 B2 Pattaya Thai.
128 B2 Pattullo, Mount Can.
129 D2 Patuanak Can.
146 B3 Patuca r. Hond.
144 B3 Pátzcuaro Mex.
104 B3 Pau France
104 B3 Pau, Gave de r. France
104 B2 Pauillac France
150 C3 Pauini Brazil
62 A1 Pauk Myanmar
126 D2 Paulatuk Can.
Paulis Dem. Rep. Congo see Isiro
151 E3 Paulistana Brazil
151 F3 Paulo Afonso Brazil
123 D2 Paulpietersburg S. Africa
143 D2 Pauls Valley U.S.A.
62 A2 Paungde Myanmar
155 D1 Pavão Brazil
108 A1 Pavia Italy
88 B2 Pāvilosta Latvia
110 C2 Pavlikeni Bulg.
77 D1 Pavlodar Kazakh.
91 D2 Pavlohrad Ukr.
91 E1 Pavlovsk Rus. Fed.
91 D2 Pavlovskaya Rus. Fed.
139 E2 Pawtucket U.S.A.
111 B3 Paxoi i. Greece
60 B2 Payakumbuh Indon.
134 C2 Payette U.S.A.
134 C2 Payette r. U.S.A.
86 F2 Pay-Khoy, Khrebet hills Rus. Fed.
Payne Can. see Kangirsuk
130 C2 Payne, Lac l. Can.
152 C3 Paysandú Uru.
81 C1 Pazar Turkey
110 B2 Pazardzhik Bulg.
111 C3 Pazarköy Turkey
108 B1 Pazin Croatia
63 A2 Pe Myanmar
128 C2 Peace r. Can.
128 C2 Peace River Can.
53 C2 Peak Hill N.S.W. Austr.
50 A2 Peak Hill W.A. Austr.
135 E3 Peale, Mount U.S.A.
140 C2 Pearl r. U.S.A.
71 B3 Pearl River r. China
143 D3 Pearsall U.S.A.
126 F1 Peary Channel Can.
121 C2 Pebane Moz.
Peć Kosovo see Pejë
155 D1 Peçanha Brazil
154 C3 Peças, Ilha das i. Brazil
92 J2 Pechenga Rus. Fed.
86 E2 Pechora Rus. Fed.
86 E2 Pechora r. Rus. Fed.
Pechora Sea sea Rus. Fed. see Pechorskoye More
86 E2 Pechorskoye More sea Rus. Fed.
88 C2 Pechory Rus. Fed.
142 B1 Pecos NM U.S.A.
143 C2 Pecos TX U.S.A.
143 C3 Pecos r. U.S.A.
103 D2 Pécs Hungary
142 B3 Pedernales Mex.
155 D1 Pedra Azul Brazil
154 C2 Pedregulho Brazil
151 E3 Pedreiras Brazil
73 C4 Pedro, Point Sri Lanka
151 E3 Pedro Afonso Brazil
152 B2 Pedro de Valdivia Chile
154 B1 Pedro Gomes Brazil
152 C2 Pedro Juan Caballero Para.
106 B1 Pedroso Port.
96 C3 Peebles U.K.
141 E2 Pee Dee r. U.S.A.
126 D2 Peel r. Can.
98 A2 Peel Isle of Man
128 C2 Peerless Lake Can.
54 B2 Pegasus Bay N.Z.
101 E3 Pegnitz Ger.
62 A2 Pegu Myanmar
62 A2 Pegu Yoma mts Myanmar
153 B3 Pehuajó Arg.
101 E1 Peine Ger.
88 C2 Peipus, Lake Estonia/Rus. Fed.
Peiraias Greece see Piraeus
154 B2 Peixe r. Brazil
155 C2 Peixoto, Represa resr Brazil
151 D4 Peixoto de Azevedo Brazil
109 D2 Pejë Kosovo
123 C2 Peka Lesotho
60 B2 Pekalongan Indon.
60 B1 Pekan Malaysia
60 B1 Pekanbaru Indon.
Peking China see Beijing
130 B3 Pelee Island Can.
61 D2 Peleng i. Indon.
103 D2 Pelhřimov Czech Rep.
92 I2 Pelkosenniemi Fin.
122 A2 Pella S. Africa
137 E2 Pella U.S.A.
59 D3 Pelleluhu Islands P.N.G.
92 H2 Pello Fin.
128 A1 Pelly r. Can.
Pelly Bay Can. see Kugaaruk
128 A1 Pelly Mountains Can.
152 C3 Pelotas Brazil
152 C2 Pelotas, Rio das r. Brazil
139 F1 Pemadumcook Lake U.S.A.
60 B1 Pemangkat Indon.
60 A1 Pematangsiantar Indon.
121 D2 Pemba Moz.
120 B2 Pemba Zambia
119 D3 Pemba Island Tanz.
128 B2 Pemberton Can.
137 D1 Pembina r. Can.
137 D1 Pembina r. Can./U.S.A.
130 C3 Pembroke Can.
99 A4 Pembroke U.K.
141 D3 Pembroke Pines U.S.A.
106 C1 Peñalara mt. Spain
154 B2 Penápolis Brazil
106 B1 Peñaranda de Bracamonte Spain
107 C1 Peñarroya mt. Spain
106 B2 Peñarroya-Pueblonuevo Spain
106 B1 Peñas, Cabo de c. Spain
153 A4 Penas, Golfo de g. Chile
111 C2 Pendik Turkey
134 C1 Pendleton U.S.A.
128 B2 Pendleton Bay Can.
134 C1 Pend Oreille Lake U.S.A.
Penfro U.K. see Pembroke
74 B3 Penganga r. India
118 C3 Penge Dem. Rep. Congo
123 D1 Penge S. Africa
70 C2 Penglai China
71 A3 Pengshui China
106 B2 Peniche Port.
96 C3 Penicuik U.K.
60 B1 Peninsular Malaysia pen. Malaysia
108 B2 Penne Italy
52 A3 Penneshaw Austr.
98 B2 Pennines hills U.K.
139 D2 Pennsylvania state U.S.A.
127 H2 Penny Icecap Can.
89 D2 Peno Rus. Fed.
139 F2 Penobscot r. U.S.A.
52 B3 Penola Austr.
50 C3 Penong Austr.
157 E6 Penrhyn Basin S. Pacific Ocean
53 D2 Penrith Austr.
98 B2 Penrith U.K.
140 C2 Pensacola U.S.A.
55 B1 Pensacola Mountains Antarctica
61 C1 Pensiangan Malaysia
128 C3 Penticton Can.
96 C1 Pentland Firth sea chan. U.K.
99 B3 Penygadair h. U.K.
87 D3 Penza Rus. Fed.
99 A4 Penzance U.K.
83 L2 Penzhinskaya Guba b. Rus. Fed.
142 A2 Peoria AZ U.S.A.
138 B2 Peoria IL U.S.A.
107 C1 Perales del Alfambra Spain
111 B3 Perama Greece
131 D3 Percé Can.
50 B2 Percival Lakes imp. l. Austr.
51 E2 Percy Isles Austr.
107 D1 Perdido, Monte mt. Spain
154 C1 Perdizes Brazil
86 F2 Peregrebnoye Rus. Fed.
150 B2 Pereira Col.
154 B2 Pereira Barreto Brazil
Pereira de Eça Angola see Ondjiva
90 A2 Peremyshlyany Ukr.
89 E2 Pereslavl'-Zalesskiy Rus. Fed.
91 C1 Pereyaslav-Khmel'nyts'kyy Ukr.
153 B3 Pergamino Arg.
92 H3 Perhonjoki r. Fin.
131 C2 Péribonka, Lac l. Can.
152 B2 Perico Arg.
144 B2 Pericos Mex.
104 C2 Périgueux France
150 B2 Perija, Sierra de mts Venez.
111 B3 Peristeri Greece
153 A4 Perito Moreno Arg.
101 E1 Perleberg Ger.
86 E3 Perm' Rus. Fed.
109 D2 Përmet Albania
Pernambuco Brazil see Recife
52 A2 Pernatty Lagoon imp. l. Austr.
110 B2 Pernik Bulg.
Pernov Estonia see Pärnu
105 C2 Péronne France
145 C3 Perote Mex.
105 C3 Perpignan France
99 A4 Perranporth U.K.
Perrégaux Alg. see Mohammadia
141 D2 Perry FL U.S.A.
141 D2 Perry GA U.S.A.
137 E2 Perry IA U.S.A.
143 D1 Perry OK U.S.A.
138 C2 Perrysburg U.S.A.
143 C1 Perryton U.S.A.
137 F3 Perryville U.S.A.
Pershnotravnevoye Ukr. see Pershotravens'k
99 B3 Pershore U.K.
91 D2 Pershotravens'k Ukr.
Persia country Asia see Iran
Persian Gulf g. Asia see The Gulf
50 A3 Perth Austr.
96 C2 Perth U.K.
159 F5 Perth Basin Indian Ocean
86 C2 Pertominsk Rus. Fed.
105 D3 Pertuis France
108 A2 Pertusato, Capo c. France
150 B3 Peru country S. America
138 B2 Peru U.S.A.
157 H6 Peru Basin S. Pacific Ocean
157 H7 Peru-Chile Trench S. Pacific Ocean
108 B2 Perugia Italy
154 C2 Peruíbe Brazil
100 A2 Péruwelz Belgium
90 C2 Pervomays'k Ukr.
91 C2 Pervomays'ke Ukr.
Pervomayskiy Rus. Fed. see Novodvinsk
89 F3 Pervomayskiy Rus. Fed.
91 D2 Pervomays'kyy Ukr.
108 B2 Pesaro Italy
108 B2 Pescara Italy
108 B2 Pescara r. Italy
74 B1 Peshawar Pak.
109 D2 Peshkopi Albania
109 C1 Pesnica Slovenia
104 B3 Pessac France
89 E2 Pestovo Rus. Fed.
140 C2 Petal U.S.A.
100 B3 Pétange Lux.
147 D3 Petare Venez.
144 B3 Petatlán Mex.
121 C2 Petauke Zambia
130 C3 Petawawa Can.
138 B2 Petenwell Lake U.S.A.
52 A2 Peterborough Austr.
130 C3 Peterborough Can.
99 C3 Peterborough U.K.
96 D2 Peterhead U.K.
55 R3 Peter I Island Antarctica
129 E1 Peter Lake Can.
50 B2 Petermann Ranges mts Austr.
129 D2 Peter Pond Lake Can.
128 A2 Petersburg AK U.S.A.
139 D3 Petersburg VA U.S.A.
101 D1 Petershagen Ger.
Peter the Great Bay b. Rus. Fed. see Petra Velikogo, Zaliv
Petitjean Morocco see Sidi Kacem
131 E2 Petit Mécatina r. Can.
145 D2 Peto Mex.
138 C1 Petoskey U.S.A.
80 B2 Petra tourist site Jordan
66 B2 Petra Velikogo, Zaliv b. Rus. Fed.
111 B2 Petrich Bulg.
Petroaleksandrovsk Uzbek. see To'rtko'l
88 C2 Petrodvorets Rus. Fed.
Petrokov Pol. see Piotrków Trybunalski
151 E3 Petrolina Brazil
77 C1 Petropavlovsk Kazakh.
83 L3 Petropavlovsk-Kamchatskiy Rus. Fed.
110 B1 Petroşani Romania
Petrovskoye Rus. Fed. see Svetlograd
89 F3 Petrovskoye Rus. Fed.
89 E2 Petrovskoye Rus. Fed.
69 D1 Petrovsk-Zabaykal'skiy Rus. Fed.
86 C2 Petrozavodsk Rus. Fed.
123 C2 Petrusburg S. Africa
123 C2 Petrus Steyn S. Africa
122 B3 Petrusville S. Africa
Petsamo Rus. Fed. see Pechenga
87 F3 Petukhovo Rus. Fed.
89 E2 Petushki Rus. Fed.
60 A1 Peureula Indon.
83 M2 Pevek Rus. Fed.
102 B2 Pforzheim Ger.
102 C2 Pfunds Austria
101 D3 Pfungstadt Ger.
123 C1 Phagameng S. Africa
123 C2 Phahameng S. Africa
123 D1 Phalaborwa S. Africa
74 B2 Phalodi India
63 A3 Phangnga Thai.
62 B1 Phăng Xi Păng mt. Vietnam
63 B2 Phan Rang-Thap Cham Vietnam
63 B2 Phan Thiêt Vietnam
63 B3 Phatthalung Thai.
62 A2 Phayao Thai.
129 D2 Phelps Lake Can.
141 C2 Phenix City U.S.A.
63 A2 Phet Buri Thai.
63 B2 Phetchabun Thai.
63 B2 Phichit Thai.
139 D3 Philadelphia U.S.A.
136 C2 Philip U.S.A.
Philip Atoll atoll Micronesia see Sorol
Philippeville Alg. see Skikda
100 B2 Philippeville Belgium
51 C2 Philippi, Lake imp. l. Austr.
100 A2 Philippine Neth.
156 C4 Philippine Basin N. Pacific Ocean
64 B2 Philippines country Asia
64 B2 Philippine Sea N. Pacific Ocean
126 C2 Philip Smith Mountains U.S.A.
122 B3 Philipstown S. Africa
53 C3 Phillip Island Austr.
137 D3 Phillipsburg U.S.A.
63 B2 Phimun Mangsahan Thai.
123 C2 Phiritona S. Africa
63 B2 Phitsanulok Thai.
63 B2 Phnom Penh Cambodia
Phnum Pénh Cambodia see Phnom Penh
142 A2 Phoenix U.S.A.
49 J4 Phoenix Islands Kiribati
63 B2 Phon Thai.
62 B2 Phong Nha Vietnam
62 B1 Phôngsali Laos
62 B1 Phong Thô Vietnam
62 B2 Phônsavan Laos
62 B2 Phrae Thai.
Phu Cuong Vietnam see Thu Dâu Môt
120 B3 Phuduhudu Botswana
63 A3 Phuket Thai.
63 B2 Phumĭ Kâmpóng Trâlach Cambodia
62 A2 Phumiphon, Khuan Thai.
63 B2 Phumĭ Sâmraông Cambodia
63 B2 Phu Quôc, Đao i. Vietnam
123 C2 Phuthaditjhaba S. Africa
Phu Vinh Vietnam see Tra Vinh
62 A2 Phyu Myanmar
108 A1 Piacenza Italy
108 B2 Pianosa, Isola i. Italy
110 C1 Piatra Neamţ Romania
151 E3 Piauí r. Brazil
108 B1 Piave r. Italy
117 B4 Pibor r. Sudan
117 B4 Pibor Post Sudan
Picardie reg. France see Picardy
104 C2 Picardy reg. France
140 C2 Picayune U.S.A.
152 B2 Pichanal Arg.
144 A2 Pichilingue Mex.
98 C2 Pickering U.K.
130 A2 Pickle Lake Can.
151 E3 Picos Brazil
153 B4 Pico Truncado Arg.
53 D2 Picton Austr.
54 B2 Picton N.Z.
73 C4 Pidurutalagala mt. Sri Lanka
154 C2 Piedade Brazil
145 C3 Piedras Negras Guat.
145 B2 Piedras Negras Mex.
93 I3 Pieksämäki Fin.
92 I3 Pielinen l. Fin.
136 C2 Pierre U.S.A.
105 C3 Pierrelatte France
123 D2 Pietermaritzburg S. Africa
Pietersaari Fin. see Jakobstad
Pietersburg S. Africa see Polokwane
123 D2 Piet Retief S. Africa
110 B1 Pietrosa mt. Romania
110 C1 Pietrosu, Vârful mt. Romania
128 C2 Pigeon Lake Can.
137 F1 Pigeon River U.S.A.
153 B3 Pigüé Arg.
93 I3 Pihlajavesi l. Fin.
92 I3 Pihtipudas Fin.
145 C3 Pijijiapan Mex.
89 D2 Pikalevo Rus. Fed.
130 A2 Pikangikum Can.
136 C3 Pikes Peak U.S.A.
122 A3 Piketberg S. Africa
138 C3 Pikeville U.S.A.
103 D1 Piła Pol.
153 C3 Pilar Arg.
152 C2 Pilar Para.
75 B2 Pilibhit India
53 C2 Pilliga Austr.
154 C1 Pilões, Serra dos mts Brazil
150 C4 Pimenta Bueno Brazil
88 C3 Pina r. Belarus
153 C3 Pinamar Arg.
60 B1 Pinang i. Malaysia
80 B2 Pınarbaşı Turkey
146 B2 Pinar del Río Cuba
64 B2 Pinatubo, Mount vol. Phil.
103 E1 Pińczów Pol.
151 E3 Pindaré r. Brazil
Pindos mts Greece see Pindus Mountains
111 B2 Pindus Mountains mts Greece
140 B2 Pine Bluff U.S.A.
136 C2 Pine Bluffs U.S.A.
50 C1 Pine Creek Austr.
136 B2 Pinedale U.S.A.
86 D2 Pinega Rus. Fed.
129 D2 Pinehouse Lake Can.
111 B3 Pineios r. Greece

141 D3 **Pine Islands** *FL* U.S.A.
141 D4 **Pine Islands** *FL* U.S.A.
128 C1 **Pine Point (abandoned)** Can.
136 C2 **Pine Ridge** U.S.A.
108 A2 **Pinerolo** Italy
Pines, Isle of *i.* Cuba *see* **Juventud, Isla de la**
123 D2 **Pinetown** S. Africa
140 B2 **Pineville** U.S.A.
70 B2 **Pingdingshan** China
70 B2 **Pingdu** China
62 B1 **Pingguo** China
71 B3 **Pingjiang** China
70 A2 **Pingliang** China
70 B1 **Pingquan** China
71 C3 **P'ingtung** Taiwan
Pingxi China *see* **Yuping**
71 A3 **Pingxiang** *Guangxi* China
71 B3 **Pingxiang** *Jiangxi* China
70 B2 **Pingyin** China
155 C2 **Pinhal** Brazil
151 E3 **Pinheiro** Brazil
52 B3 **Pinnaroo** Austr.
101 D1 **Pinneberg** Ger.
Pinos, Isla de *i.* Cuba *see* **Juventud, Isla de la**
145 C3 **Pinotepa Nacional** Mex.
48 H6 **Pins, Île des** *i.* New Caledonia
88 C3 **Pinsk** Belarus
152 B2 **Pinto** Arg.
135 D3 **Pioche** U.S.A.
119 C3 **Piodi** Dem. Rep. Congo
108 B2 **Piombino** Italy
86 F2 **Pionerskiy** Rus. Fed.
103 E1 **Pionki** Pol.
103 D1 **Piotrków Trybunalski** Pol.
137 D2 **Pipestone** U.S.A.
131 C3 **Pipmuacan, Réservoir** *resr* Can.
154 B2 **Piquiri** *r.* Brazil
154 C1 **Piracanjuba** Brazil
154 C2 **Piracicaba** Brazil
155 D1 **Piracicaba** *r.* Brazil
154 C2 **Piraçununga** Brazil
111 B3 **Piraeus** Greece
154 C2 **Piraí do Sul** Brazil
154 C2 **Piraju** Brazil
154 C2 **Pirajuí** Brazil
154 B1 **Piranhas** Brazil
151 F3 **Piranhas** *r.* Brazil
155 D1 **Pirapora** Brazil
154 C1 **Pirenópolis** Brazil
154 C1 **Pires do Rio** Brazil
Pirineos *mts* Europe *see* **Pyrenees**
151 E3 **Piripiri** Brazil
109 D2 **Pirot** Serbia
59 C3 **Piru** Indon.
108 B2 **Pisa** Italy
152 A1 **Pisagua** Chile
150 B4 **Pisco** Peru
102 C2 **Písek** Czech Rep.
79 D2 **Pīshīn** Iran
74 A1 **Pishin** Pak.
145 D2 **Pisté** Mex.
109 C2 **Pisticci** Italy
108 B2 **Pistoia** Italy
106 C1 **Pisuerga** *r.* Spain
134 B2 **Pit** *r.* U.S.A.
114 A3 **Pita** Guinea
154 B2 **Pitanga** Brazil
155 D1 **Pitangui** Brazil
49 O6 **Pitcairn Island** Pitcairn Is
49 O6 **Pitcairn Islands** *terr.* S. Pacific Ocean
92 H2 **Piteå** Sweden
92 H2 **Piteälven** *r.* Sweden
110 B2 **Pitești** Romania
75 C2 **Pithoragarh** India
142 A2 **Pitiquito** Mex.
86 C2 **Pitkyaranta** Rus. Fed.
96 C2 **Pitlochry** U.K.
128 B2 **Pitt Island** Can.
137 E3 **Pittsburg** U.S.A.
138 D2 **Pittsburgh** U.S.A.
139 E2 **Pittsfield** U.S.A.
53 D1 **Pittsworth** Austr.
155 C2 **Piumhí** Brazil
150 A3 **Piura** Peru
90 C2 **Pivdennyy Buh** *r.* Ukr.
131 E3 **Placentia** Can.
135 B3 **Placerville** U.S.A.
146 C2 **Placetas** Cuba
143 C2 **Plains** U.S.A.
143 C2 **Plainview** U.S.A.
60 B2 **Plaju** Indon.
61 C2 **Plampang** Indon.
154 C1 **Planaltina** Brazil
137 D2 **Plankinton** U.S.A.
143 D2 **Plano** U.S.A.
154 C2 **Planura** Brazil
140 B2 **Plaquemine** U.S.A.
106 B1 **Plasencia** Spain
109 C1 **Plaški** Croatia
147 C4 **Plato** Col.
137 D2 **Platte** *r.* U.S.A.
138 A2 **Platteville** U.S.A.
139 E2 **Plattsburgh** U.S.A.
101 F1 **Plau** Ger.
101 F2 **Plauen** Ger.
101 F1 **Plauer See** *l.* Ger.
89 E3 **Plavsk** Rus. Fed.
106 B2 **Playa de Castilla** *coastal area* Spain
129 E2 **Playgreen Lake** Can.
63 B2 **Plây Ku** Vietnam
153 B3 **Plaza Huincul** Arg.
143 D3 **Pleasanton** U.S.A.
54 B2 **Pleasant Point** N.Z.
138 B3 **Pleasure Ridge Park** U.S.A.
104 C2 **Pleaux** France
130 B2 **Pledger Lake** Can.
54 C1 **Plenty, Bay of** *g.* N.Z.
136 C1 **Plentywood** U.S.A.
86 D2 **Plesetsk** Rus. Fed.
131 C2 **Plétipi, Lac** *l.* Can.
100 C2 **Plettenberg** Ger.
122 B3 **Plettenberg Bay** S. Africa
110 B2 **Pleven** Bulg.
Plevna Bulg. *see* **Pleven**
109 C2 **Pljevlja** Montenegro
108 A2 **Ploaghe** Italy
109 C2 **Ploče** Croatia
103 D1 **Płock** Pol.
109 C2 **Pločno** *mt.* Bos.-Herz.
104 B2 **Ploemeur** France
Ploești Romania *see* **Ploiești**
110 C2 **Ploiești** Romania
89 F2 **Ploskoye** Rus. Fed.
104 B2 **Plouzané** France
110 B2 **Plovdiv** Bulg.
Plozk Pol. *see* **Płock**
121 B3 **Plumtree** Zimbabwe
88 B2 **Plungė** Lith.
144 B2 **Plutarco Elías Calles, Presa** *resr* Mex.
88 C3 **Plyeshchanitsy** Belarus
99 A4 **Plymouth** U.K.
138 B2 **Plymouth** U.S.A.
147 D3 **Plymouth (abandoned)** Montserrat
99 B3 **Plynlimon** *h.* U.K.
88 C2 **Plyussa** Rus. Fed.
102 C2 **Plzeň** Czech Rep.
114 B3 **Pô** Burkina
108 B1 **Po** *r.* Italy
61 C1 **Po, Tanjung** *pt* Malaysia
77 E2 **Pobeda Peak** China/Kyrg.
Pobedy, Pik *mt* China/Kyrg. *see* **Pobeda Peak**
140 B1 **Pocahontas** U.S.A.
134 D2 **Pocatello** U.S.A.
90 B1 **Pochayiv** Ukr.
89 D3 **Pochep** Rus. Fed.
89 D3 **Pochinok** Rus. Fed.
145 C3 **Pochutla** Mex.
139 D3 **Pocomoke City** U.S.A.
155 C2 **Poços de Caldas** Brazil
89 D2 **Poddor'ye** Rus. Fed.
91 D1 **Podgorenskiy** Rus. Fed.
109 C2 **Podgorica** Montenegro
82 G3 **Podgornoye** Rus. Fed.
83 H2 **Podkamennaya Tunguska** *r.* Rus. Fed.
89 E2 **Podol'sk** Rus. Fed.
109 D2 **Podujevë** Kosovo
Podujevo Kosovo *see* **Podujevë**
122 A2 **Pofadder** S. Africa
89 D3 **Pogar** Rus. Fed.
105 E3 **Poggibonsi** Italy
109 D2 **Pogradec** Albania
66 B2 **Pogranichnyy** Rus. Fed.
Po Hai *g.* China *see* **Bo Hai**
65 B2 **P'ohang** S. Korea
48 G3 **Pohnpei** *atoll* Micronesia
90 B2 **Pohrebyshche** Ukr.
110 B2 **Poiana Mare** Romania
118 C3 **Poie** Dem. Rep. Congo
118 B3 **Pointe-Noire** Congo
126 A2 **Point Hope** U.S.A.
128 C1 **Point Lake** Can.
138 C3 **Point Pleasant** U.S.A.
104 C2 **Poitiers** France
104 C2 **Poitou, Plaines et Seuil du** *plain* France
74 B2 **Pokaran** India
53 C1 **Pokataroo** Austr.
75 C2 **Pokhara** Nepal
119 C2 **Poko** Dem. Rep. Congo
83 J2 **Pokrovsk** Rus. Fed.
91 D2 **Pokrovskoye** Rus. Fed.
Pola Croatia *see* **Pula**
142 A1 **Polacca** U.S.A.
106 B1 **Pola de Lena** Spain
106 B1 **Pola de Siero** Spain
103 D1 **Poland** *country* Europe
55 C1 **Polar Plateau** Antarctica
80 B2 **Polatlı** Turkey
88 C2 **Polatsk** Belarus
77 C3 **Pol-e Khomrī** Afgh.
61 C2 **Polewali** Indon.
118 B2 **Poli** Cameroon
102 C1 **Police** Pol.
109 C2 **Policoro** Italy
105 D2 **Poligny** France
64 B2 **Polillo Islands** Phil.
80 B2 **Polis** Cyprus
90 B1 **Polis'ke** Ukr.
109 C3 **Polistena** Italy
103 D1 **Polkowice** Pol.
107 D2 **Pollença** Spain
109 C3 **Pollino, Monte** *mt.* Italy
86 F2 **Polnovat** Rus. Fed.
91 D2 **Polohy** Ukr.
123 C1 **Polokwane** S. Africa
90 B1 **Polonne** Ukr.
134 D1 **Polson** U.S.A.
91 C2 **Poltava** Ukr.
66 B2 **Poltavka** Rus. Fed.
91 D2 **Poltavskaya** Rus. Fed.
88 C2 **Põltsamaa** Estonia
88 C2 **Põlva** Estonia
Polyanovgrad Bulg. *see* **Karnobat**
92 J2 **Polyarnyy** Rus. Fed.
86 C2 **Polyarnyye Zori** Rus. Fed.
111 B2 **Polygyros** Greece
111 B2 **Polykastro** Greece
156 E6 **Polynesia** *is* Pacific Ocean
106 B2 **Pombal** Port.
102 C1 **Pomeranian Bay** *b.* Ger./Pol.
108 B2 **Pomezia** Italy
92 I2 **Pomokaira** *reg.* Fin.
110 C2 **Pomorie** Bulg.
Pomorska, Zatoka *b.* Ger./Pol. *see* **Pomeranian Bay**
155 D1 **Pompéu** Brazil
143 D1 **Ponca City** U.S.A.
147 D3 **Ponce** Puerto Rico
73 B3 **Pondicherry** India
127 G2 **Pond Inlet** Can.
Ponds Bay Can. *see* **Pond Inlet**
106 B1 **Ponferrada** Spain
117 A4 **Pongo** *watercourse* Sudan
123 D2 **Pongola** *r.* S. Africa
123 D2 **Pongolapoort Dam** *dam* S. Africa
128 C2 **Ponoka** Can.
154 B3 **Ponta Grossa** Brazil
154 C1 **Pontalina** Brazil
105 D2 **Pont-à-Mousson** France
154 A2 **Ponta Porã** Brazil
105 D2 **Pontarlier** France
102 B2 **Pontcharra** France
140 B2 **Pontchartrain, Lake** U.S.A.
154 B1 **Ponte de Pedra** Brazil
106 B2 **Ponte de Sor** Port.
154 B1 **Ponte do Rio Verde** Brazil
98 C3 **Pontefract** U.K.
129 D3 **Ponteix** Can.
155 D2 **Ponte Nova** Brazil
150 D4 **Pontes-e-Lacerda** Brazil
106 B1 **Pontevedra** Spain
Ponthierville Dem. Rep. Congo *see* **Ubundu**
138 B2 **Pontiac** *IL* U.S.A.
138 C2 **Pontiac** *MI* U.S.A.
60 B2 **Pontianak** Indon.
Pontine Islands *is* Italy *see* **Ponziane, Isole**
104 B2 **Pontivy** France
151 D2 **Pontoetoe** Suriname
104 C2 **Pontoise** France
129 E2 **Ponton** Can.
99 B4 **Pontypool** U.K.
99 B4 **Pontypridd** U.K.
108 B2 **Ponziane, Isole** *is* Italy
99 C4 **Poole** U.K.
Poona India *see* **Pune**
52 B2 **Pooncarie** Austr.
152 B1 **Poopó, Lago de** *l.* Bol.
150 B2 **Popayán** Col.
83 I2 **Popigay** *r.* Rus. Fed.
52 B2 **Popiltah** Austr.
129 E2 **Poplar** *r.* Can.
137 E3 **Poplar Bluff** U.S.A.
118 B3 **Popokabaka** Dem. Rep. Congo
Popovichskaya Rus. Fed. *see* **Kalininskaya**
110 C2 **Popovo** Bulg.
103 E2 **Poprad** Slovakia
151 E4 **Porangatu** Brazil
74 A2 **Porbandar** India
126 C2 **Porcupine** *r.* Can./U.S.A.
108 B1 **Pordenone** Italy
108 B1 **Poreč** Croatia
154 B2 **Porecatu** Brazil
114 C3 **Porga** Benin
93 H3 **Pori** Fin.
54 B2 **Porirua** N.Z.
88 C2 **Porkhov** Rus. Fed.
104 B2 **Pornic** France
83 K3 **Poronaysk** Rus. Fed.
75 D1 **Porong** China
111 B3 **Poros** Greece
92 I1 **Porsangerfjorden** *sea chan.* Norway
93 E4 **Porsgrunn** Norway
111 D3 **Porsuk** *r.* Turkey
97 C1 **Portadown** U.K.
97 D1 **Portaferry** U.K.
138 B2 **Portage** U.S.A.
129 E3 **Portage la Prairie** Can.
128 B3 **Port Alberni** Can.
106 B2 **Portalegre** Port.
143 C2 **Portales** U.S.A.
128 A2 **Port Alexander** U.S.A.
128 B2 **Port Alice** Can.
140 B2 **Port Allen** U.S.A.
134 B1 **Port Angeles** U.S.A.
97 C2 **Portarlington** Ireland
51 D4 **Port Arthur** Austr.
Port Arthur China *see* **Lüshunkou**
143 E3 **Port Arthur** U.S.A.
96 A3 **Port Askaig** U.K.
52 A2 **Port Augusta** Austr.
147 C3 **Port-au-Prince** Haiti
131 E2 **Port aux Choix** Can.
122 B3 **Port Beaufort** S. Africa
73 D3 **Port Blair** India
52 B3 **Port Campbell** Austr.
131 D2 **Port-Cartier** Can.
54 B3 **Port Chalmers** N.Z.
141 D3 **Port Charlotte** U.S.A.
147 C3 **Port-de-Paix** Haiti
128 A2 **Port Edward** Can.
155 D1 **Porteirinha** Brazil
151 D3 **Portel** Brazil
130 B3 **Port Elgin** Can.
123 C3 **Port Elizabeth** S. Africa
96 A3 **Port Ellen** U.K.
98 A2 **Port Erin** Isle of Man
122 A3 **Porterville** S. Africa
135 C3 **Porterville** U.S.A.
Port Étienne Maur. *see* **Nouâdhibou**
52 B3 **Port Fairy** Austr.
54 C1 **Port Fitzroy** N.Z.
Port Francqui Dem. Rep. Congo *see* **Ilebo**
118 A3 **Port-Gentil** Gabon
115 C4 **Port Harcourt** Nigeria
128 B2 **Port Hardy** Can.
Port Harrison Can. *see* **Inukjuak**
131 D3 **Port Hawkesbury** Can.
99 B4 **Porthcawl** U.K.
50 A2 **Port Hedland** Austr.
Port Herald Malawi *see* **Nsanje**
99 A3 **Porthmadog** U.K.
131 E2 **Port Hope Simpson** Can.
138 C2 **Port Huron** U.S.A.
106 B2 **Portimão** Port.
Port Keats Austr. *see* **Wadeye**
Port Láirge Ireland *see* **Waterford**
53 C2 **Portland** *N.S.W.* Austr.
52 B3 **Portland** *Vic.* Austr.
139 E2 **Portland** *ME* U.S.A.
134 B1 **Portland** *OR* U.S.A.
143 D3 **Portland** *TX* U.S.A.
99 B4 **Portland, Isle of** *pen.* U.K.
128 A2 **Portland Canal** *inlet* Can.
97 C2 **Portlaoise** Ireland
143 D3 **Port Lavaca** U.S.A.
52 A2 **Port Lincoln** Austr.
114 A4 **Port Loko** Sierra Leone
113 I8 **Port Louis** Mauritius
Port-Lyautrey Morocco *see* **Kenitra**
52 B3 **Port MacDonnell** Austr.
53 D2 **Port Macquarie** Austr.
Portmadoc U.K. *see* **Porthmadog**
128 B2 **Port McNeill** Can.
131 D3 **Port-Menier** Can.
59 D3 **Port Moresby** P.N.G.
96 A3 **Portnahaven** U.K.
Port Nis U.K. *see* **Port of Ness**
122 A2 **Port Nolloth** S. Africa
Port-Nouveau-Québec Can. *see* **Kangiqsualujjuaq**
Porto Port. *see* **Oporto**
150 C3 **Porto Acre** Brazil
154 B2 **Porto Alegre** Brazil
152 C3 **Porto Alegre** Brazil
Porto Alexandre Angola *see* **Tombua**
Porto Amélia Moz. *see* **Pemba**
151 D4 **Porto Artur** Brazil
154 B2 **Porto Camargo** Brazil
151 D4 **Porto dos Gaúchos Óbidos** Brazil
150 D4 **Porto Esperidião** Brazil
108 B2 **Portoferraio** Italy
96 A1 **Port of Ness** U.K.
151 E3 **Porto Franco** Brazil
147 D3 **Port of Spain** Trin. and Tob.
108 B1 **Portogruaro** Italy
108 B2 **Portomaggiore** Italy
154 B2 **Porto Mendes** Brazil
152 C2 **Porto Murtinho** Brazil
151 E4 **Porto Nacional** Brazil
114 C4 **Porto-Novo** Benin
154 B2 **Porto Primavera, Represa** *resr* Brazil
134 B2 **Port Orford** U.S.A.
151 D3 **Porto Santana** Brazil
154 B2 **Porto São José** Brazil
108 A3 **Portoscuso** Italy
155 E1 **Porto Seguro** Brazil
108 B2 **Porto Tolle** Italy
108 A2 **Porto Torres** Italy
154 B3 **Porto União** Brazil
105 D3 **Porto-Vecchio** France
150 C3 **Porto Velho** Brazil
150 A3 **Portoviejo** Ecuador
96 B3 **Portpatrick** U.K.
52 B3 **Port Phillip Bay** Austr.
52 A2 **Port Pirie** Austr.
96 A2 **Portree** U.K.
128 B3 **Port Renfrew** Can.
97 C1 **Portrush** U.K.
116 B1 **Port Said** Egypt
141 C3 **Port St Joe** U.S.A.
123 C3 **Port St Johns** S. Africa
141 D3 **Port St Lucie City** U.S.A.
123 D3 **Port Shepstone** S. Africa
99 C4 **Portsmouth** U.K.
139 E2 **Portsmouth** *NH* U.S.A.
138 C3 **Portsmouth** *OH* U.S.A.
139 D3 **Portsmouth** *VA* U.S.A.
153 B5 **Port Stephens** Falkland Is
97 C1 **Portstewart** U.K.
116 B3 **Port Sudan** Sudan
140 C3 **Port Sulphur** U.S.A.
99 B4 **Port Talbot** U.K.
134 B1 **Port Townsend** U.S.A.
106 B2 **Portugal** *country* Europe
Portugália Angola *see* **Chitato**
Portuguese Guinea *country* Africa *see* **Guinea-Bissau**
Portuguese Timor *country* Asia *see* **East Timor**
Portuguese West Africa *country* Africa *see* **Angola**
97 B2 **Portumna** Ireland
105 C3 **Port-Vendres** France

48 H5 **Port Vila** Vanuatu
52 A2 **Port Wakefield** Austr.
50 B1 **Port Warrender** Austr.
153 A5 **Porvenir** Chile
93 I3 **Porvoo** Fin.
65 B2 **Poryŏng** S. Korea
152 C2 **Posadas** Arg.
89 E2 **Poshekhon'ye** Rus. Fed.
Poshekon'ye-Volodarsk Rus. Fed. *see* **Poshekhon'ye**
92 I2 **Posio** Fin.
61 D2 **Poso** Indon.
151 E4 **Posse** Brazil
101 E2 **Pößneck** Ger.
143 C2 **Post** U.S.A.
Poste-de-la-Baleine Can. *see* **Kuujjuarapik**
114 C2 **Poste Weygand** Alg.
122 B2 **Postmasburg** S. Africa
108 B1 **Postojna** Slovenia
Postysheve Ukr. *see* **Krasnoarmiys'k**
109 C2 **Posušje** Bos.-Herz.
123 C2 **Potchefstroom** S. Africa
143 E1 **Poteau** U.S.A.
109 C2 **Potenza** Italy
108 B2 **Potenza** *r.* Italy
151 E3 **Poti** *r.* Brazil
81 C1 **P'ot'i** Georgia
155 E1 **Potiraguá** Brazil
115 D3 **Potiskum** Nigeria
139 D3 **Potomac, South Branch** *r.* U.S.A.
152 B1 **Potosí** Bol.
64 B2 **Pototan** Phil.
142 C3 **Potrero del Llano** Mex.
101 F1 **Potsdam** Ger.
139 E2 **Potsdam** U.S.A.
139 D2 **Pottstown** U.S.A.
139 D2 **Pottsville** U.S.A.
131 E3 **Pouch Cove** Can.
139 E2 **Poughkeepsie** U.S.A.
98 B3 **Poulton-le-Fylde** U.K.
155 C2 **Pouso Alegre** Brazil
63 B2 **Poŭthĭsăt** Cambodia
103 D2 **Považská Bystrica** Slovakia
109 C2 **Povlen** *mt.* Serbia
106 B1 **Póvoa de Varzim** Port.
136 B2 **Powell** U.S.A.
135 D3 **Powell, Lake** *resr* U.S.A.
128 B3 **Powell River** Can.
154 B1 **Poxoréu** Brazil
71 B3 **Poyang** China
71 B3 **Poyang Hu** *l.* China
109 D2 **Požarevac** Serbia
145 C2 **Poza Rica** Mex.
109 C1 **Požega** Croatia
109 D2 **Požega** Serbia
79 D2 **Pozm Tīāb** Iran
103 D1 **Poznań** Pol.
106 C2 **Pozoblanco** Spain
152 C2 **Pozo Colorado** Para.
109 B3 **Pozzallo** Italy
108 B2 **Pozzuoli** Italy
60 B2 **Prabumulih** Indon.
102 C2 **Prachatice** Czech Rep.
63 A2 **Prachuap Khiri Khan** Thai.
103 D1 **Praděd** *mt.* Czech Rep.
104 C3 **Prades** France
155 E1 **Prado** Brazil
102 C1 **Prague** Czech Rep.
Praha Czech Rep. *see* **Prague**
143 C2 **Prairie Dog Town Fork** *r.* U.S.A.
138 A2 **Prairie du Chien** U.S.A.
60 A1 **Prapat** Indon.
154 C1 **Prata** Brazil
108 B2 **Prato** Italy
137 D3 **Pratt** U.S.A.
140 C2 **Prattville** U.S.A.
61 C2 **Praya** Indon.
63 B2 **Preăh Vihéar** Cambodia
89 F2 **Prechistoye** Rus. Fed.
129 D2 **Preeceville** Can.
88 C2 **Preiļi** Latvia
53 C2 **Premer** Austr.
105 C2 **Prémery** France
101 F1 **Premnitz** Ger.
102 C1 **Prenzlau** Ger.
66 B2 **Preobrazheniye** Rus. Fed.
63 A2 **Preparis Island** Cocos Is
63 A2 **Preparis North Channel** Cocos Is
63 A2 **Preparis South Channel** Cocos Is
103 D2 **Přerov** Czech Rep.
142 A2 **Prescott** U.S.A.
142 A2 **Prescott Valley** U.S.A.
109 D2 **Preševo** Serbia
152 B2 **Presidencia Roque Sáenz Peña** Arg.
151 E3 **Presidente Dutra** Brazil
154 B2 **Presidente Epitácio** Brazil
154 B1 **Presidente Murtinho** Brazil
155 C1 **Presidente Olegário** Brazil
154 B2 **Presidente Prudente** Brazil
142 C3 **Presidio** U.S.A.
103 E2 **Prešov** Slovakia
111 B2 **Prespa, Lake** Europe
139 F1 **Presque Isle** U.S.A.
Pressburg Slovakia *see* **Bratislava**
101 F2 **Pressel** Ger.
98 B3 **Preston** U.K.
134 D2 **Preston** U.S.A.
96 B3 **Prestwick** U.K.
155 C1 **Preto** *r.* Brazil
123 C2 **Pretoria** S. Africa
Pretoria-Witwatersrand-Vereeniging *prov.* S. Africa *see* **Gauteng**
111 B3 **Preveza** Greece
63 B2 **Prey Vêng** Cambodia
124 A4 **Pribilof Islands** U.S.A.
109 C2 **Priboj** Serbia
135 D3 **Price** U.S.A.
140 C2 **Prichard** U.S.A.
106 C2 **Priego de Córdoba** Spain
88 B3 **Prienai** Lith.
122 B2 **Prieska** S. Africa
103 D2 **Prievidza** Slovakia
109 C2 **Prijedor** Bos.-Herz.
109 C2 **Prijepolje** Serbia
Prikaspiyskaya Nizmennost' *lowland* Kazakh./Rus. Fed. *see* **Caspian Lowland**
111 B2 **Prilep** Macedonia
101 F3 **Přimda** Czech Rep.
91 D2 **Primorsko-Akhtarsk** Rus. Fed.
129 D2 **Primrose Lake** Can.
129 D2 **Prince Albert** Can.
122 B3 **Prince Albert** S. Africa
126 E2 **Prince Albert Peninsula** Can.
122 B3 **Prince Albert Road** S. Africa
126 D2 **Prince Alfred, Cape** Can.
122 A3 **Prince Alfred Hamlet** S. Africa
127 G2 **Prince Charles Island** Can.
55 H2 **Prince Charles Mountains** Antarctica
131 D3 **Prince Edward Island** *prov.* Can.
128 B2 **Prince George** Can.
51 D1 **Prince of Wales Island** Austr.
126 F2 **Prince of Wales Island** Can.
128 A2 **Prince of Wales Island** U.S.A.
126 E2 **Prince of Wales Strait** Can.
126 E1 **Prince Patrick Island** Can.
126 F2 **Prince Regent Inlet** *sea chan.* Can.
128 A2 **Prince Rupert** Can.
51 D1 **Princess Charlotte Bay** Austr.
55 H2 **Princess Elizabeth Land** *reg.* Antarctica
128 B2 **Princess Royal Island** Can.
128 B3 **Princeton** Can.
138 B3 **Princeton** *IN* U.S.A.
137 E2 **Princeton** *MO* U.S.A.
134 B2 **Prineville** U.S.A.
86 C2 **Priozersk** Rus. Fed.
Pripet *r.* Belarus *see* **Prypyats'**
90 A1 **Pripet Marshes** Belarus/Ukr.
109 D2 **Prishtinë** Kosovo
Priština Kosovo *see* **Prishtinë**
101 F1 **Pritzwalk** Ger.
105 C3 **Privas** France
109 C2 **Privlaka** Croatia
89 F2 **Privolzhsk** Rus. Fed.
110 D2 **Prizren** Kosovo
151 D2 **Professor van Blommestein Meer** *resr* Suriname
145 D2 **Progreso** Mex.
81 C1 **Prokhladnyy** Rus. Fed.
109 D2 **Prokuplje** Serbia
Prome Myanmar *see* **Pyè**
154 C2 **Promissão** Brazil
154 C2 **Promissão, Represa** *resr* Brazil
126 D3 **Prophet** *r.* Can.
128 B2 **Prophet River** Can.
51 D2 **Proserpine** Austr.
Proskurov Ukr. *see* **Khmel'nyts'kyy**
103 D2 **Prostějov** Czech Rep.
89 E3 **Protvino** Rus. Fed.
110 C2 **Provadiya** Bulg.
105 D3 **Provence** *reg.* France
139 E2 **Providence** U.S.A.
146 B3 **Providencia, Isla de** *i.* Caribbean Sea
83 N2 **Provideniya** Rus. Fed.
105 C2 **Provins** France
135 D2 **Provo** U.S.A.
129 C2 **Provost** Can.
91 C2 **Prubiynyy, Mys** *pt* Ukr.
154 B3 **Prudentópolis** Brazil
126 C2 **Prudhoe Bay** U.S.A.
100 C2 **Prüm** Ger.
105 D3 **Prunelli-di-Fiumorbo** France
103 D1 **Pruszcz Gdański** Pol.
103 E1 **Pruszków** Pol.
110 C1 **Prut** *r.* Europe
88 B3 **Pruzhany** Belarus
91 D2 **Pryazovs'ke** Ukr.
91 C1 **Pryluky** Ukr.
91 D2 **Prymors'k** Ukr.
91 D2 **Prymors'kyy** Ukr.
143 D1 **Pryor** U.S.A.
90 B1 **Prypyats'** *r.* Belarus/Ukr.
103 E2 **Przemyśl** Pol.
103 E1 **Przeworsk** Pol.
Przheval'sk Kyrg. *see* **Karakol**
111 C3 **Psara** *i.* Greece
81 C1 **Psebay** Rus. Fed.
91 D3 **Pshekha** *r.* Rus. Fed.
88 C2 **Pskov** Rus. Fed.
88 C2 **Pskov, Lake** Estonia/Rus. Fed.
111 B2 **Ptolemaïda** Greece
109 C1 **Ptuj** Slovenia
150 B3 **Pucallpa** Peru
71 B3 **Pucheng** China
65 B2 **Puch'ŏn** S. Korea
103 D1 **Puck** Pol.
92 I2 **Pudasjärvi** Fin.
70 C2 **Pudong** China
86 C2 **Pudozh** Rus. Fed.
Puduchcheri India *see* **Pondicherry**
Puducherry India *see* **Pondicherry**
145 C3 **Puebla** Mex.
136 C3 **Pueblo** U.S.A.
153 B3 **Puelén** Arg.
153 A3 **Puente Alto** Chile
106 C2 **Puente-Genil** Spain
153 A4 **Puerto Aisén** Chile
152 B1 **Puerto Alegre** Bol.
145 C3 **Puerto Ángel** Mex.
146 B4 **Puerto Armuelles** Panama
150 C2 **Puerto Ayacucho** Venez.
146 B3 **Puerto Barrios** Guat.
146 B3 **Puerto Cabezas** Nic.
153 A4 **Puerto Cisnes** Chile
144 A2 **Puerto Cortés** Mex.
145 C3 **Puerto Escondido** Mex.
152 B1 **Puerto Frey** Bol.
150 C2 **Puerto Inírida** Col.
152 C1 **Puerto Isabel** Bol.
150 B3 **Puerto Leguízamo** Col.
146 B3 **Puerto Lempira** Hond.
144 A2 **Puerto Libertad** Mex.
146 B3 **Puerto Limón** Costa Rica
106 C2 **Puertollano** Spain
153 B4 **Puerto Madryn** Arg.
150 C4 **Puerto Maldonado** Peru
Puerto México Mex. *see* **Coatzacoalcos**
147 D4 **Puerto Miranda** Venez.
153 A4 **Puerto Montt** Chile
153 A5 **Puerto Natales** Chile
150 C2 **Puerto Nuevo** Col.
150 C2 **Puerto Páez** Venez.
144 A1 **Puerto Peñasco** Mex.
152 C2 **Puerto Pinasco** Para.
147 C3 **Puerto Plata** Dom. Rep.
150 B3 **Puerto Portillo** Peru
Puerto Presidente Stroessner Para. *see* **Ciudad del Este**
64 A3 **Puerto Princesa** Phil.
154 A3 **Puerto Rico** Arg.
147 D3 **Puerto Rico** *terr.* West Indies
158 C3 **Puerto Rico Trench** Caribbean Sea
146 A3 **Puerto San José** Guat.
153 B5 **Puerto Santa Cruz** Arg.
152 C2 **Puerto Sastre** Para.
144 B2 **Puerto Vallarta** Mex.
87 D3 **Pugachev** Rus. Fed.
74 B2 **Pugal** India
54 B2 **Pukaki, Lake** N.Z.
49 K5 **Pukapuka** *atoll* Cook Is
129 D2 **Pukatawagan** Can.
65 B1 **Pukchin** N. Korea
65 B1 **Pukch'ŏng** N. Korea
109 C2 **Pukë** Albania
54 B1 **Pukekohe** N.Z.
65 B1 **Puksubaek-san** *mt.* N. Korea
Pula China *see* **Nyingchi**
108 B2 **Pula** Croatia
108 A3 **Pula** Italy
152 B2 **Pulacayo** Bol.
103 E1 **Puławy** Pol.
92 I3 **Pulkkila** Fin.
134 C1 **Pullman** U.S.A.
64 B2 **Pulog, Mount** Phil.
64 B3 **Pulutan** Indon.
150 A3 **Puná, Isla** *i.* Ecuador
54 B2 **Punakaiki** N.Z.
123 D1 **Punda Maria** S. Africa
73 B3 **Pune** India
65 B1 **P'ungsan** N. Korea
121 C2 **Púnguè** *r.* Moz.
119 C3 **Punia** Dem. Rep. Congo
74 B1 **Punjab** *state* India
153 B3 **Punta Alta** Arg.
153 A5 **Punta Arenas** Chile
153 C3 **Punta del Este** Uru.
146 B3 **Punta Gorda** Belize
146 B3 **Puntarenas** Costa Rica
150 B1 **Punto Fijo** Venez.
92 I3 **Puolanka** Fin.
Puqi China *see* **Chibi**
82 G2 **Pur** *r.* Rus. Fed.
75 C3 **Puri** India
100 B1 **Purmerend** Neth.
Purnea India *see* **Purnia**
75 C2 **Purnia** India
75 C2 **Puruliya** India
150 C3 **Purus** *r.* Brazil/Peru
61 B2 **Purwakarta** Indon.
61 C2 **Purwodadi** Indon.
65 B1 **Puryŏng** N. Korea
74 B3 **Pusad** India
65 B2 **Pusan** S. Korea
89 E3 **Pushchino** Rus. Fed.
Pushkino Azer. *see* **Biläsuvar**
89 E2 **Pushkino** Rus. Fed.
88 C2 **Pushkinskiye Gory** Rus. Fed.
88 C2 **Pustoshka** Rus. Fed.
62 A1 **Putao** Myanmar
71 B3 **Putian** China
Puting China *see* **De'an**
61 C2 **Puting, Tanjung** *pt* Indon.
101 F1 **Putlitz** Ger.
60 B1 **Putrajaya** Malaysia
122 B2 **Putsonderwater** S. Africa
102 C1 **Puttgarden** Ger.
150 B3 **Putumayo** *r.* Col.
61 C1 **Putusibau** Indon.
90 B2 **Putyla** Ukr.
91 C1 **Putyvl'** Ukr.
93 I3 **Puula** *l.* Fin.
130 C1 **Puvirnituq** Can.
70 B2 **Puyang** China
104 C3 **Puylaurens** France
119 C3 **Pweto** Dem. Rep. Congo
99 A3 **Pwllheli** U.K.
92 J2 **Pyaozerskiy** Rus. Fed.
63 A2 **Pyapon** Myanmar
83 G2 **Pyasina** *r.* Rus. Fed.
87 D4 **Pyatigorsk** Rus. Fed.
91 C2 **P"yatykhatky** Ukr.
62 A2 **Pyè** Myanmar
88 C3 **Pyetrykaw** Belarus
93 H3 **Pyhäjärvi** *l.* Fin.
92 H3 **Pyhäjoki** *r.* Fin.
92 I3 **Pyhäsalmi** Fin.
62 A1 **Pyingaing** Myanmar
62 A2 **Pyinmana** Myanmar
62 A1 **Pyin-U-Lwin** Myanmar
65 B2 **Pyŏksŏng** N. Korea
65 B2 **P'yŏnggang** N. Korea
65 B2 **P'yŏngsan** N. Korea
65 B2 **P'yŏngsong** N. Korea
65 B2 **P'yŏngt'aek** S. Korea
65 B2 **P'yŏngyang** N. Korea
135 C2 **Pyramid Lake** U.S.A.
80 B3 **Pyramids of Giza** *tourist site* Egypt
107 D1 **Pyrenees** *mts* Europe
111 B3 **Pyrgetos** Greece
111 C3 **Pyrgi** Greece
111 B3 **Pyrgos** Greece
91 C1 **Pyryatyn** Ukr.
103 C1 **Pyrzyce** Pol.
88 C2 **Pytalovo** Rus. Fed.
111 B3 **Pyxaria** *mt.* Greece

Q

Qaanaaq Greenland *see* **Thule**
Qabqa China *see* **Gonghe**
123 C3 **Qacha's Nek** Lesotho
69 D2 **Qagan Nur** China
Qahremānshahr Iran *see* **Kermānshāh**
68 C2 **Qaidam Pendi** *basin* China
79 C2 **Qalamat Abū Shafrah** Saudi Arabia
78 A2 **Qal'at al Aẓlam** Saudi Arabia
78 A2 **Qal'at al Mu'aẓẓam** Saudi Arabia
78 B2 **Qal'at Bīshah** Saudi Arabia
76 C3 **Qal'eh-ye Now** Afgh.
129 E1 **Qamanirjuaq Lake** Can.
Qamanittuaq Can. *see* **Baker Lake**
78 C3 **Qamar, Ghubbat al** *b.* Yemen
79 C3 **Qamar, Ghubbat al** *b.* Yemen
68 C2 **Qamdo** China
78 B3 **Qam Hadīl** Saudi Arabia
127 I2 **Qaqortoq** Greenland
80 A3 **Qārah** Egypt
Qarkilik China *see* **Ruoqiang**
Qarqan China *see* **Qiemo**
77 C3 **Qarshi** Uzbek.
78 B2 **Qaryat al Ulyā** Saudi Arabia
127 I2 **Qasigiannguit** Greenland
116 A2 **Qaşr al Farāfirah** Egypt
79 D2 **Qaşr-e Qand** Iran
81 C2 **Qaşr-e Shīrīn** Iran
127 I2 **Qassimiut** Greenland
78 B3 **Qa'tabah** Yemen
79 C2 **Qatar** *country* Asia
116 A2 **Qattâra Depression** Egypt
Qausuittuq Can. *see* **Resolute**
76 B3 **Qāyen** Iran
81 C1 **Qazax** Azer.
81 C1 **Qazımämmäd** Azer.
81 C2 **Qazvīn** Iran
Qena Egypt *see* **Qinā**
127 I2 **Qeqertarsuaq** Greenland
127 I2 **Qeqertarsuaq** *i.* Greenland
127 I2 **Qeqertarsuatsiaat** Greenland
127 I2 **Qeqertarsuup Tunua** *b.* Greenland
79 C2 **Qeshm** Iran
74 A1 **Qeyşār, Kūh-e** *mt.* Afgh.
70 B3 **Qiandao Hu** *resr* China
70 A3 **Qianjiang** China
70 B2 **Qianjiang** China
69 E1 **Qianjin** China
65 A1 **Qian Shan** *mts* China
71 A3 **Qianxi** China
70 C2 **Qidong** China
77 E3 **Qiemo** China
71 A3 **Qijiang** China
68 C2 **Qijiaojing** China
127 H2 **Qikiqtarjuaq** Can.
74 A2 **Qila Ladgasht** Pak.
68 C2 **Qilian Shan** *mts* China
127 J2 **Qillak** *i.* Greenland
70 B3 **Qimen** China
127 H1 **Qimusseriarsuaq** *b.* Greenland
116 B2 **Qinā** Egypt
Qincheng China *see* **Nanfeng**
70 A2 **Qingcheng** China
70 C2 **Qingdao** China
68 C2 **Qinghai Hu** *salt l.* China
68 C2 **Qinghai Nanshan** *mts* China
Qingjiang China *see* **Huai'an**
Qingjiang China *see* **Zhangshu**
70 B2 **Qingshuihe** China
70 A2 **Qingtongxia** China
70 A2 **Qingyang** China
Qingyuan China *see* **Yizhou**
71 B3 **Qingyuan** *Guangdong* China
65 A1 **Qingyuan** *Liaoning* China
Qingzang Gaoyuan *plat.* China *see* **Tibet, Plateau of**
70 B2 **Qingzhou** China
70 B2 **Qinhuangdao** China
Qinjiang China *see* **Shicheng**

70 A2 **Qin Ling** *mts* China
Qinting China *see* **Lianhua**
70 B2 **Qinyang** China
71 A3 **Qinzhou** China
71 B4 **Qionghai** China
70 A2 **Qionglai Shan** *mts* China
71 B4 **Qiongshan** China
71 A4 **Qiongzhong** China
69 E1 **Qiqihar** China
81 D3 **Qīr** Iran
Qishan China *see* **Qimen**
79 C3 **Qishn** Yemen
66 B1 **Qitaihe** China
70 B2 **Qixian** *Henan* China
70 B2 **Qixian** *Shanxi* China
Qogir Feng *mt.* China/Pakistan *see* **K2**
81 D2 **Qom** Iran
Qomishēh Iran *see* **Shāhrezā**
Qomolangma Feng *mt.* China/Nepal *see* **Everest, Mount**
76 B2 **Qo'ng'irot** Uzbek.
Qoqek China *see* **Tacheng**
77 D2 **Qo'qon** Uzbek.
76 B2 **Qoraqalpog'iston** Uzbek.
80 B2 **Qornet es Saouda** *mt.* Lebanon
81 C2 **Qorveh** Iran
79 C2 **Qoṭbābād** Iran
101 C1 **Quakenbrück** Ger.
53 C2 **Quambone** Austr.
63 B2 **Quang Ngai** Vietnam
63 B2 **Quang Tri** Vietnam
62 B1 **Quan Hoa** Vietnam
Quan Long Vietnam *see* **Ca Mau**
Quan Phu Quoc *i.* Vietnam *see* **Phu Quôc, Dao**
71 B3 **Quanzhou** *Fujian* China
71 B3 **Quanzhou** *Guangxi* China
108 A3 **Quartu Sant'Elena** Italy
142 A2 **Quartzsite** U.S.A.
81 C1 **Quba** Azer.
76 B3 **Quchan** Iran
53 C3 **Queanbeyan** Austr.
131 C3 **Québec** Can.
131 C2 **Québec** *prov.* Can.
101 E2 **Quedlinburg** Ger.
Queen Adelaide Islands *is* Chile *see* **Reina Adelaida, Archipiélago de la**
128 A2 **Queen Charlotte** Can.
128 A2 **Queen Charlotte Islands** Can.
128 B2 **Queen Charlotte Sound** *sea chan.* Can.
128 B2 **Queen Charlotte Strait** Can.
126 E1 **Queen Elizabeth Islands** Can.
55 I2 **Queen Mary Land** *reg.* Antarctica
126 F2 **Queen Maud Gulf** Can.
55 F2 **Queen Maud Land** *reg.* Antarctica
55 P1 **Queen Maud Mountains** Antarctica
52 B3 **Queenscliff** Austr.
52 B1 **Queensland** *state* Austr.
51 D4 **Queenstown** Austr.
54 A3 **Queenstown** N.Z.
Queenstown Ireland *see* **Cobh**
123 C3 **Queenstown** S. Africa
121 C2 **Quelimane** Moz.
153 A4 **Quellón** Chile
Quelpart Island *i.* S. Korea *see* **Cheju-do**
142 B2 **Quemado** U.S.A.
Que Que Zimbabwe *see* **Kwekwe**
154 B2 **Querência do Norte** Brazil
145 B2 **Querétaro** Mex.
101 E2 **Querfurt** Ger.
128 B2 **Quesnel** Can.
128 B2 **Quesnel Lake** Can.
74 A1 **Quetta** Pak.
146 A3 **Quetzaltenango** Guat.
64 A3 **Quezon** Phil.
64 B2 **Quezon City** Phil.
120 A2 **Quibala** Angola
150 B2 **Quibdó** Col.
104 B2 **Quiberon** France
120 A2 **Quilengues** Angola
104 C3 **Quillan** France
153 C3 **Quilmes** Arg.
Quilon India *see* **Kollam**
51 D2 **Quilpie** Austr.
153 A3 **Quilpué** Chile
120 A1 **Quimbele** Angola
152 B2 **Quimilí** Arg.
104 B2 **Quimper** France
104 B2 **Quimperlé** France
135 B3 **Quincy** *CA* U.S.A.
141 D2 **Quincy** *FL* U.S.A.
137 E3 **Quincy** *IL* U.S.A.
139 E2 **Quincy** *MA* U.S.A.
107 C1 **Quinto** Spain
121 D2 **Quionga** Moz.
120 A2 **Quirima** Angola
53 D2 **Quirindi** Austr.
154 B1 **Quirinópolis** Brazil
131 D3 **Quispamsis** Can.
121 C3 **Quissico** Moz.
120 A2 **Quitapa** Angola
150 B3 **Quito** Ecuador
151 F3 **Quixadá** Brazil
71 A3 **Qujing** China
75 D1 **Qumar He** *r.* China
123 C3 **Qumrha** S. Africa
115 E1 **Qunayyin, Sabkhat al** *salt marsh* Libya
129 E1 **Quoich** *r.* Can.
52 A2 **Quorn** Austr.
79 C2 **Qurayat** Oman
77 C3 **Qŭrghonteppa** Tajik.
Quxar China *see* **Lhazê**
Quyang China *see* **Jingzhou**
63 B2 **Quy Nhơn** Vietnam
71 B3 **Quzhou** China
Qyteti Stalin Albania *see* **Kuçovë**
Qyzyltü Kazakh. *see* **Kishkenekol'**

R

103 D2 **Raab** *r.* Austria
92 H3 **Raahe** Fin.
100 C1 **Raalte** Neth.
61 C2 **Raas** *i.* Indon.
61 C2 **Raba** Indon.
114 B1 **Rabat** Morocco
59 E3 **Rabaul** P.N.G.
50 C2 **Rabbit Flat** Austr.
78 A2 **Rābigh** Saudi Arabia
103 D2 **Rabka** Pol.
Râbniţa Moldova *see* **Rîbniţa**
Rabyānah, Ramlat *des.* Libya *see* **Rebiana Sand Sea**
131 E3 **Race, Cape** Can.
140 B3 **Raceland** U.S.A.
139 E2 **Race Point** U.S.A.
63 B3 **Rach Gia** Vietnam
103 D1 **Racibórz** Pol.
138 B2 **Racine** U.S.A.
78 B3 **Radā'** Yemen
110 C1 **Rădăuţi** Romania
138 B3 **Radcliff** U.S.A.
74 B2 **Radhanpur** India
130 C2 **Radisson** Can.
103 E1 **Radom** Pol.
103 D1 **Radomsko** Pol.
90 B1 **Radomyshl'** Ukr.
111 B2 **Radoviš** Macedonia
88 B2 **Radviliškis** Lith.
78 A2 **Raḑwa, Jabal** *mt.* Saudi Arabia
90 B1 **Radyvyliv** Ukr.
75 C2 **Rae Bareli** India
100 C2 **Raeren** Belgium
54 C1 **Raetihi** N.Z.
78 A2 **Rāf** *h.* Saudi Arabia
152 B3 **Rafaela** Arg.
118 C2 **Rafaï** C.A.R.
78 B2 **Rafḩā'** Saudi Arabia
79 C1 **Rafsanjān** Iran
119 C2 **Raga** Sudan
64 B3 **Ragang, Mount** *vol.* Phil.
109 B3 **Ragusa** Italy
61 D2 **Raha** Indon.
88 D3 **Rahachow** Belarus
78 A3 **Rahad** *r.* Sudan
74 B2 **Rahimyar Khan** Pak.
110 D2 **Rahovec** Kosovo
73 B3 **Raichur** India
75 C2 **Raigarh** India
128 C3 **Rainbow Lake** Can.
134 B1 **Rainier, Mount** *vol.* U.S.A.
130 A3 **Rainy Lake** Can./U.S.A.
129 E3 **Rainy River** Can.
75 C2 **Raipur** India
93 H3 **Raisio** Fin.
88 C2 **Raja** Estonia
73 C3 **Rajahmundry** India
61 C1 **Rajang** *r.* Malaysia
74 B2 **Rajanpur** Pak.
73 B4 **Rajapalaiyam** India
74 B2 **Rajasthan** *state* India
74 B2 **Rajasthan Canal** *canal* India
74 B2 **Rajgarh** India
60 B2 **Rajik** Indon.
74 B2 **Rajkot** India
75 C2 **Raj Nandgaon** India
74 B2 **Rajpur** India
75 C2 **Rajshahi** Bangl.
54 B2 **Rakaia** *r.* N.Z.
74 B1 **Rakaposhi** *mt.* Pak.
90 A2 **Rakhiv** Ukr.
91 D1 **Rakitnoye** Rus. Fed.
88 C2 **Rakke** Estonia
88 C2 **Rakvere** Estonia
141 E1 **Raleigh** U.S.A.
141 E2 **Raleigh Bay** U.S.A.
48 H3 **Ralik Chain** *is* Marshall Is
75 C2 **Ramanuj Ganj** India
123 C2 **Ramatlabama** S. Africa
104 C2 **Rambouillet** France
99 A4 **Rame Head** *hd* U.K.
97 C1 **Ramelton** Ireland
89 E2 **Rameshki** Rus. Fed.
74 B2 **Ramgarh** India
81 C2 **Rāmhormoz** Iran
110 C1 **Râmnicu Sărat** Romania
110 B1 **Râmnicu Vâlcea** Romania
89 E3 **Ramon'** Rus. Fed.
135 C4 **Ramona** U.S.A.
123 C1 **Ramotswa** Botswana
75 B2 **Rampur** India
62 A1 **Ramree Island** Myanmar
98 A2 **Ramsey** Isle of Man
130 B3 **Ramsey Lake** Can.
99 D4 **Ramsgate** U.K.
81 C2 **Rāmshir** Iran
62 A1 **Ramsing** India
75 C2 **Ranaghat** India
61 C1 **Ranau** Malaysia
153 A3 **Rancagua** Chile
154 B2 **Rancharia** Brazil
75 C2 **Ranchi** India
93 F4 **Randers** Denmark
63 B3 **Rangae** Thai.
75 D2 **Rangapara** India
54 B2 **Rangiora** N.Z.
49 M5 **Rangiroa** *atoll* Fr. Polynesia
54 C1 **Rangitaiki** *r.* N.Z.
60 B2 **Rangkasbitung** Indon.
63 A2 **Rangoon** Myanmar
75 C2 **Rangpur** Bangl.
129 E1 **Rankin Inlet** Can.
53 C2 **Rankin's Springs** Austr.
Rankovićevo Serbia *see* **Kraljevo**
96 B2 **Rannoch Moor** *moorland* U.K.
63 A3 **Ranong** Thai.
59 C3 **Ransiki** Indon.
61 C2 **Rantaupanjang** Indon.
60 A1 **Rantauprapat** Indon.
61 C2 **Rantepao** Indon.
92 I2 **Ranua** Fin.
93 E4 **Ranum** Denmark
78 B2 **Ranyah, Wādī** *watercourse* Saudi Arabia
49 J6 **Raoul Island** Kermadec Is
49 M6 **Rapa** *i.* Fr. Polynesia
108 A2 **Rapallo** Italy
136 C2 **Rapid City** U.S.A.
88 B2 **Rapla** Estonia
74 A2 **Rapur** India
49 L6 **Rarotonga** *i.* Cook Is
153 B4 **Rasa, Punta** *pt* Arg.
Ras al Khaimah U.A.E. *see* **Ra's al Khaymah**
79 C2 **Ra's al Khaymah** U.A.E.
116 B3 **Ras Dejen** *mt.* Eth.
88 B2 **Raseiniai** Lith.
116 B2 **Ra's Ghārib** Egypt
81 C2 **Rasht** Iran
74 A2 **Ras Koh** *mt.* Pak.
110 C1 **Râşnov** Romania
88 C2 **Rasony** Belarus
79 C2 **Ra's Şirāb** Oman
108 B3 **Rass Jebel** Tunisia
87 D3 **Rasskazovo** Rus. Fed.
79 C2 **Ras Tannūrah** Saudi Arabia
101 D1 **Rastede** Ger.
48 I2 **Ratak Chain** *is* Marshall Is
93 F3 **Rätan** Sweden
123 C2 **Ratanda** S. Africa
74 B2 **Ratangarh** India
63 A2 **Rat Buri** Thai.
62 A1 **Rathedaung** Myanmar
101 F1 **Rathenow** Ger.
97 C1 **Rathfriland** U.K.
97 C1 **Rathlin Island** U.K.
Rathluirc Ireland *see* **Charleville**
100 C2 **Ratingen** Ger.
74 B2 **Ratlam** India
73 B3 **Ratnagiri** India
73 C4 **Ratnapura** Sri Lanka
90 A1 **Ratne** Ukr.
142 C1 **Raton** U.S.A.
96 D2 **Rattray Head** *hd* U.K.
93 G3 **Rättvik** Sweden
101 E1 **Ratzeburg** Ger.
78 B2 **Raudhatain** Kuwait
92 □B2 **Raufarhöfn** Iceland
54 C1 **Raukumara Range** *mts* N.Z.
93 H3 **Rauma** Fin.
88 C2 **Rauna** Latvia
61 C2 **Raung, Gunung** *vol.* Indon.
75 C2 **Raurkela** India
66 D2 **Rausu** Japan
90 B2 **Răut** *r.* Moldova
134 D1 **Ravalli** U.S.A.
81 C2 **Ravānsar** Iran
108 B2 **Ravenna** Italy
102 B2 **Ravensburg** Ger.
50 B3 **Ravensthorpe** Austr.
74 B1 **Ravi** *r.* Pak.
74 B1 **Rawalpindi** Pak.
103 D1 **Rawicz** Pol.
50 B3 **Rawlinna** Austr.
136 B2 **Rawlins** U.S.A.
153 B4 **Rawson** Arg.
75 C3 **Rayagada** India
69 E1 **Raychikhinsk** Rus. Fed.
78 B3 **Raydah** Yemen
87 E3 **Rayevskiy** Rus. Fed.
134 B1 **Raymond** U.S.A.
53 D2 **Raymond Terrace** Austr.
143 D3 **Raymondville** U.S.A.
129 D2 **Raymore** Can.
145 C2 **Rayón** Mex.
63 B2 **Rayong** Thai.
78 A2 **Rayyis** Saudi Arabia
104 B2 **Raz, Pointe du** *pt* France
81 C2 **Razāzah, Buḩayrat ar** *l.* Iraq
110 C2 **Razgrad** Bulg.
110 C2 **Razim, Lacul** *lag.* Romania
111 B2 **Razlog** Bulg.
Raz"yezd 3km Rus. Fed. *see* **Novyy Urgal**
104 B2 **Ré, Île de** *i.* France
99 C4 **Reading** U.K.
138 C3 **Reading** U.S.A.
139 D2 **Reading** U.S.A.
123 C2 **Reagile** S. Africa
115 E2 **Rebiana Sand Sea** *des.* Libya
66 D1 **Rebun-tō** *i.* Japan
50 B3 **Recherche, Archipelago of the** *is* Austr.
89 D3 **Rechytsa** Belarus
151 F3 **Recife** Brazil
123 C3 **Recife, Cape** S. Africa
100 C2 **Recklinghausen** Ger.
152 C2 **Reconquista** Arg.
137 D1 **Red** *r.* Can./U.S.A.
140 B2 **Red** *r.* U.S.A.
100 B3 **Redange** Lux.
141 C1 **Red Bank** U.S.A.
Red Basin *basin* China *see* **Sichuan Pendi**
131 E2 **Red Bay** Can.
135 B2 **Red Bluff** U.S.A.
98 C2 **Redcar** U.K.
129 C2 **Redcliff** Can.
121 B2 **Redcliff** Zimbabwe
52 B2 **Red Cliffs** Austr.
128 C2 **Red Deer** Can.
126 E3 **Red Deer** *r.* Can.
129 D2 **Red Deer Lake** Can.
135 B2 **Redding** U.S.A.
99 C3 **Redditch** U.K.
137 D2 **Redfield** U.S.A.
137 D3 **Red Hills** U.S.A.
130 A2 **Red Lake** Can.
130 A2 **Red Lake** *l.* Can.
137 E1 **Red Lakes** U.S.A.
134 E1 **Red Lodge** U.S.A.
134 B2 **Redmond** U.S.A.
137 D2 **Red Oak** U.S.A.
104 B2 **Redon** France
106 B1 **Redondela** Spain
106 B2 **Redondo** Port.
78 A2 **Red Sea** Africa/Asia
128 B1 **Redstone** *r.* Can.
100 B1 **Reduzum** Neth.
128 C2 **Redwater** Can.
137 E2 **Red Wing** U.S.A.
137 D2 **Redwood Falls** U.S.A.
97 C2 **Ree, Lough** *l.* Ireland
134 B2 **Reedsport** U.S.A.
54 B2 **Reefton** N.Z.
143 D3 **Refugio** U.S.A.
102 C2 **Regen** Ger.
155 E1 **Regência** Brazil
102 C2 **Regensburg** Ger.
114 C2 **Reggane** Alg.
109 C3 **Reggio di Calabria** Italy
108 B2 **Reggio nell'Emilia** Italy
110 B1 **Reghin** Romania
129 D2 **Regina** Can.
154 C2 **Registro** Brazil
122 A1 **Rehoboth** Namibia
80 B2 **Rehovot** Israel
101 F2 **Reichenbach** Ger.
141 E1 **Reidsville** U.S.A.
99 C4 **Reigate** U.K.
105 C2 **Reims** France
153 A5 **Reina Adelaida, Archipiélago de la** *is* Chile
101 E1 **Reinbek** Ger.
129 D2 **Reindeer** *r.* Can.
129 E2 **Reindeer Island** Can.
129 D2 **Reindeer Lake** Can.
92 F2 **Reine** Norway
106 C1 **Reinosa** Spain
100 C3 **Reinsfeld** Ger.
123 C2 **Reitz** S. Africa
122 B2 **Reivilo** S. Africa
129 D1 **Reliance** Can.
107 D2 **Relizane** Alg.
52 A2 **Remarkable, Mount** *h.* Austr.
79 C2 **Remeshk** Iran
105 D2 **Remiremont** France
100 C2 **Remscheid** Ger.
102 B1 **Rendsburg** Ger.
139 D1 **Renfrew** Can.
60 B2 **Rengat** Indon.
90 B2 **Reni** Ukr.
52 B2 **Renmark** Austr.
48 H5 **Rennell** *i.* Solomon Is
101 D2 **Rennerod** Ger.
104 B2 **Rennes** France
129 D1 **Rennie Lake** Can.
108 B2 **Reno** *r.* Italy
135 C3 **Reno** U.S.A.
70 A3 **Renshou** China
138 B2 **Rensselaer** U.S.A.
75 C2 **Renukut** India
54 B2 **Renwick** N.Z.
61 D2 **Reo** Indon.
136 D3 **Republican** *r.* U.S.A.
127 G2 **Repulse Bay** Can.
150 B3 **Requena** Peru
107 C2 **Requena** Spain
60 B2 **Resag, Gunung** *mt.* Indon.
111 B2 **Resen** Macedonia
154 B2 **Reserva** Brazil
91 C2 **Reshetylivka** Ukr.
152 C2 **Resistencia** Arg.
110 B1 **Reşiţa** Romania
126 F2 **Resolute** Can.
127 H2 **Resolution Island** Can.
155 D1 **Resplendor** Brazil
145 C3 **Retalhuleu** Guat.
98 C3 **Retford** U.K.
105 C2 **Rethel** France
111 B3 **Rethymno** Greece
113 I8 **Réunion** *terr.* Indian Ocean
107 D1 **Reus** Spain
Reut *r.* Moldova *see* **Răut**
102 B2 **Reutlingen** Ger.
86 C2 **Revda** Rus. Fed.
128 C2 **Revelstoke** Can.
144 A3 **Revillagigedo, Islas** *is* Mex.
128 A2 **Revillagigedo Island** U.S.A.
75 C2 **Rewa** India

134 D2 **Rexburg** U.S.A.
135 B3 **Reyes, Point** U.S.A.
160 M4 **Reykjanes Ridge** N. Atlantic Ocean
92 □A3 **Reykjanestá** *pt* Iceland
92 □A3 **Reykjavík** Iceland
145 C2 **Reynosa** Mex.
Reẓā'īyeh Iran *see* **Urmia**
Reẓā'īyeh, Daryācheh-ye *salt l.* Iran *see* **Urmia, Lake**
88 C2 **Rēzekne** Latvia
Rheims France *see* **Reims**
Rhein *r.* Ger. *see* **Rhine**
100 C1 **Rheine** Ger.
101 F1 **Rheinsberg** Ger.
Rhin *r.* France *see* **Rhine**
100 C2 **Rhine** *r.* Europe
138 B1 **Rhinelander** U.S.A.
101 F1 **Rhinluch** *marsh* Ger.
101 F1 **Rhinow** Ger.
108 A1 **Rho** Italy
139 E2 **Rhode Island** *state* U.S.A.
111 C3 **Rhodes** Greece
111 C3 **Rhodes** *i.* Greece
Rhodesia *country* Africa *see* **Zimbabwe**
111 B2 **Rhodope Mountains** Bulg./Greece
105 C3 **Rhône** *r.* France/Switz.
Rhum *i.* U.K. *see* **Rum**
Rhuthun U.K. *see* **Ruthin**
98 B3 **Rhyl** U.K.
155 D1 **Riacho dos Machados** Brazil
154 C1 **Rialma** Brazil
154 C1 **Rianópolis** Brazil
60 B1 **Riau, Kepulauan** *is* Indon.
106 B1 **Ribadeo** Spain
106 B1 **Ribadesella** Spain
154 B2 **Ribas do Rio Pardo** Brazil
121 C2 **Ribáuè** Moz.
98 B3 **Ribble** *r.* U.K.
93 E4 **Ribe** Denmark
154 C2 **Ribeira** *r.* Brazil
154 C2 **Ribeirão Preto** Brazil
104 C2 **Ribérac** France
152 B1 **Riberalta** Bol.
90 B2 **Rîbniţa** Moldova
102 C1 **Ribnitz-Damgarten** Ger.
138 A1 **Rice Lake** U.S.A.
123 D2 **Richards Bay** S. Africa
143 D2 **Richardson** U.S.A.
126 C2 **Richardson Mountains** Can.
135 D3 **Richfield** U.S.A.
134 C1 **Richland** U.S.A.
138 A2 **Richland Center** U.S.A.
53 D2 **Richmond** *N.S.W.* Austr.
51 D2 **Richmond** *Qld* Austr.
134 B1 **Richmond** Can.
54 B2 **Richmond** N.Z.
122 B3 **Richmond** S. Africa
98 C2 **Richmond** U.K.
138 C3 **Richmond** *IN* U.S.A.
138 C3 **Richmond** *KY* U.S.A.
139 D3 **Richmond** *VA* U.S.A.
141 D2 **Richmond Hill** U.S.A.
53 D1 **Richmond Range** *hills* Austr.
77 E1 **Ridder** Kazakh.
130 C3 **Rideau Lakes** Can.
135 C3 **Ridgecrest** U.S.A.
140 B2 **Ridgeland** U.S.A.
102 C1 **Riesa** Ger.
101 D1 **Rieste** Ger.
123 B2 **Riet** *r.* S. Africa
101 D2 **Rietberg** Ger.
122 B2 **Rietfontein** S. Africa
108 B2 **Rieti** Italy
136 B3 **Rifle** U.S.A.
88 B2 **Rīga** Latvia
88 B2 **Riga, Gulf of** Estonia/Latvia
79 C2 **Rīgān** Iran
134 D2 **Rigby** U.S.A.
131 E2 **Rigolet** Can.
93 H3 **Riihimäki** Fin.
55 D2 **Riiser-Larsen Ice Shelf** Antarctica
108 B1 **Rijeka** Croatia
134 C2 **Riley** U.S.A.
105 C2 **Rillieux-la-Pape** France
78 B2 **Rimah, Wādī al** *watercourse* Saudi Arabia
103 E2 **Rimavská Sobota** Slovakia
128 C2 **Rimbey** Can.
108 B2 **Rimini** Italy
Rîmnicu Sărat Romania *see* **Râmnicu Sărat**
Rîmnicu Vîlcea Romania *see* **Râmnicu Vâlcea**
131 D3 **Rimouski** Can.
144 B2 **Rincón de Romos** Mex.
93 F3 **Ringebu** Norway
93 E4 **Ringkøbing** Denmark
92 G2 **Ringvassøya** *i.* Norway
99 C4 **Ringwood** U.K.
101 D1 **Rinteln** Ger.
154 B3 **Rio Azul** Brazil
150 B3 **Riobamba** Ecuador
155 D2 **Rio Bonito** Brazil
150 C4 **Rio Branco** Brazil
154 C3 **Rio Branco do Sul** Brazil
154 B2 **Rio Brilhante** Brazil
155 D2 **Rio Casca** Brazil
154 C2 **Rio Claro** Brazil
153 B3 **Río Colorado** Arg.
153 B3 **Río Cuarto** Arg.
155 D2 **Rio de Janeiro** Brazil
155 D2 **Rio de Janeiro** *state* Brazil
153 B5 **Río Gallegos** Arg.
153 B5 **Río Grande** Arg.
152 C3 **Rio Grande** Brazil
144 B2 **Río Grande** Mex.
143 D3 **Rio Grande** *r.* Mex./U.S.A.
143 D3 **Rio Grande City** U.S.A.
150 B1 **Ríohacha** Col.
150 B3 **Rioja** Peru
145 D2 **Río Lagartos** Mex.
151 F3 **Rio Largo** Brazil
105 C2 **Riom** France
152 B1 **Río Mulatos** Bol.
154 C3 **Rio Negro** Brazil
155 D1 **Rio Pardo de Minas** Brazil
154 C1 **Rio Preto, Serra do** *hills* Brazil
142 B1 **Rio Rancho** U.S.A.
150 B3 **Río Tigre** Ecuador
64 A3 **Rio Tuba** Phil.
154 B1 **Rio Verde** Brazil
145 C2 **Río Verde** Mex.
154 B1 **Rio Verde de Mato Grosso** Brazil
90 C1 **Ripky** Ukr.
99 C3 **Ripley** U.K.
107 D1 **Ripoll** Spain
98 C2 **Ripon** U.K.
66 D1 **Rishiri-tō** *i.* Japan
Rîşnov Romania *see* **Râşnov**
93 E4 **Risør** Norway
122 B2 **Ritchie** S. Africa
73 D3 **Ritchie's Archipelago** *is* India
134 C1 **Ritzville** U.S.A.
152 B2 **Rivadavia** Arg.
108 B1 **Riva del Garda** Italy
146 B3 **Rivas** Nic.
152 C3 **Rivera** Uru.
114 B4 **River Cess** Liberia
129 D2 **Riverhurst** Can.
52 C2 **Riverina** *reg.* Austr.
122 B3 **Riversdale** S. Africa
135 C4 **Riverside** U.S.A.
136 B2 **Riverton** U.S.A.
131 D3 **Riverview** Can.
105 C3 **Rivesaltes** France
131 D3 **Rivière-au-Renard** Can.
131 D3 **Rivière-du-Loup** Can.
139 F1 **Rivière-Ouelle** Can.
90 B1 **Rivne** Ukr.
108 A1 **Rivoli** Italy
120 B2 **Rivungo** Angola
54 B2 **Riwaka** N.Z.
78 B2 **Riyadh** Saudi Arabia
81 C1 **Rize** Turkey
70 B2 **Rizhao** China
105 C2 **Roanne** France
138 D3 **Roanoke** U.S.A.
141 E1 **Roanoke** *r.* U.S.A.
141 E1 **Roanoke Rapids** U.S.A.
135 E3 **Roan Plateau** U.S.A.
146 B3 **Roatán** Hond.
52 A3 **Robe** Austr.
52 B2 **Robe, Mount** *h.* Austr.
101 F1 **Röbel** Ger.
130 C2 **Robert-Bourassa, Réservoir** *resr* Can.
53 D1 **Roberts, Mount** Austr.
92 H3 **Robertsfors** Sweden
122 A3 **Robertson** S. Africa
114 A4 **Robertsport** Liberia
Robert Williams Angola *see* **Caála**
130 C3 **Roberval** Can.
50 A2 **Robinson Range** *hills* Austr.
52 B2 **Robinvale** Austr.
129 D2 **Roblin** Can.
128 C2 **Robson, Mount** Can.
143 D3 **Robstown** U.S.A.
Roçadas Angola *see* **Xangongo**
108 B3 **Rocca Busambra** *mt.* Italy
153 C3 **Rocha** Uru.
98 B3 **Rochdale** U.K.
154 B1 **Rochedo** Brazil
100 B2 **Rochefort** Belgium
104 B2 **Rochefort** France
52 B3 **Rochester** Austr.
137 E2 **Rochester** *MN* U.S.A.
139 E2 **Rochester** *NH* U.S.A.
139 D2 **Rochester** *NY* U.S.A.
94 A2 **Rockall** *i.* N. Atlantic Ocean
160 L4 **Rockall Bank** N. Atlantic Ocean
138 B2 **Rockford** U.S.A.
51 E2 **Rockhampton** Austr.
141 D2 **Rock Hill** U.S.A.
50 A3 **Rockingham** Austr.
138 A2 **Rock Island** U.S.A.
143 C3 **Rocksprings** U.S.A.
136 B1 **Rock Springs** *MT* U.S.A.
136 B2 **Rock Springs** *WY* U.S.A.
141 D1 **Rockwood** U.S.A.
136 C3 **Rocky Ford** U.S.A.
141 E1 **Rocky Mount** U.S.A.
128 C2 **Rocky Mountain House** Can.
124 F4 **Rocky Mountains** Can./U.S.A.
100 B3 **Rocroi** France
102 C1 **Rødbyhavn** Denmark
131 E2 **Roddickton** Can.
104 C3 **Rodez** France
Rodi *i.* Greece *see* **Rhodes**
89 F2 **Rodniki** Rus. Fed.
Rodos Greece *see* **Rhodes**
Rodos *i.* Greece *see* **Rhodes**
Rodosto Turkey *see* **Tekirdağ**
50 A2 **Roebourne** Austr.
50 B1 **Roebuck Bay** Austr.
123 C1 **Roedtan** S. Africa
100 B2 **Roermond** Neth.
100 A2 **Roeselare** Belgium
127 G2 **Roes Welcome Sound** *sea chan.* Can.
128 C2 **Rogers** Can.
140 B1 **Rogers** U.S.A.
138 C3 **Rogers, Mount** U.S.A.
138 C1 **Rogers City** U.S.A.
157 G8 **Roggeveen Basin** S. Pacific Ocean
122 B3 **Roggeveldberge** *esc.* S. Africa
92 G2 **Rognan** Norway
134 B2 **Rogue** *r.* U.S.A.
74 B2 **Rohtak** India
49 M5 **Roi Georges, Îles du** *is* Fr. Polynesia
88 B2 **Roja** Latvia
60 B1 **Rokan** *r.* Indon.
88 C2 **Rokiškis** Lith.
90 B1 **Rokytne** Ukr.
154 B2 **Rolândia** Brazil
137 E3 **Rolla** U.S.A.
143 C2 **Rolling Prairies** *reg.* U.S.A.
51 D2 **Roma** Austr.
Roma Italy *see* **Rome**
123 C2 **Roma** Lesotho
143 D3 **Roma** U.S.A.
141 E2 **Romain, Cape** U.S.A.
110 C1 **Roman** Romania
158 E5 **Romanche Gap** *sea feature* S. Atlantic Ocean
59 C3 **Romang, Pulau** *i.* Indon.
110 B1 **Romania** *country* Europe
91 C3 **Roman-Kosh** *mt.* Ukr.
69 D1 **Romanovka** Rus. Fed.
105 D2 **Romans-sur-Isère** France
105 D2 **Rombas** France
64 B2 **Romblon** Phil.
108 B2 **Rome** Italy
141 C2 **Rome** *GA* U.S.A.
139 D2 **Rome** *NY* U.S.A.
99 D4 **Romford** U.K.
105 C2 **Romilly-sur-Seine** France
91 C1 **Romny** Ukr.
104 C2 **Romorantin-Lanthenay** France
99 C4 **Romsey** U.K.
134 D1 **Ronan** U.S.A.
96 □ **Ronas Hill** U.K.
151 D4 **Roncador, Serra do** *hills* Brazil
106 B2 **Ronda** Spain
154 B2 **Rondon** Brazil
154 B1 **Rondonópolis** Brazil
74 B1 **Rondu** Pak.
71 A3 **Rong'an** China
Rongcheng China *see* **Rongxian**
Rongcheng China *see* **Jianli**
71 A3 **Rongjiang** China
62 A1 **Rongklang Range** *mts* Myanmar
Rongmei China *see* **Hefeng**
71 B3 **Rongxian** China
93 F4 **Rønne** Denmark
93 G4 **Ronneby** Sweden
55 A2 **Ronne Ice Shelf** Antarctica
101 D1 **Ronnenberg** Ger.
100 A2 **Ronse** Belgium
Rooke Island *i.* P.N.G. *see* **Umboi**
74 B2 **Roorkee** India
100 B2 **Roosendaal** Neth.
135 E2 **Roosevelt** U.S.A.
128 B2 **Roosevelt, Mount** Can.
55 N2 **Roosevelt Island** Antarctica
104 B3 **Roquefort** France
150 C2 **Roraima, Mount** Guyana
93 F3 **Røros** Norway
90 C2 **Ros'** *r.* Ukr.
142 B3 **Rosa, Punta** *pt* Mex.
106 B2 **Rosal de la Frontera** Spain
153 B3 **Rosario** Arg.
144 A1 **Rosario** *Baja California* Mex.
144 B2 **Rosario** *Sinaloa* Mex.
144 B2 **Rosario** *Sonora* Mex.
147 C3 **Rosario** Venez.
152 B2 **Rosario de la Frontera** Arg.
151 D4 **Rosário Oeste** Brazil
144 A1 **Rosarito** *Baja California* Mex.
144 A2 **Rosarito** *Baja California Sur* Mex.
142 A3 **Rosarito** *Baja California Sur* Mex.
109 C3 **Rosarno** Italy
143 C2 **Roscoe** U.S.A.
104 B2 **Roscoff** France
97 B2 **Roscommon** Ireland
97 C2 **Roscrea** Ireland
147 D3 **Roseau** Dominica
137 D1 **Roseau** U.S.A.
134 B2 **Roseburg** U.S.A.
96 C2 **Rosehearty** U.K.
143 D3 **Rosenberg** U.S.A.
101 D1 **Rosengarten** Ger.
102 C2 **Rosenheim** Ger.
129 D2 **Rosetown** Can.
122 A2 **Rosh Pinah** Namibia
110 C2 **Roşiori de Vede** Romania
93 F4 **Roskilde** Denmark
89 D3 **Roslavl'** Rus. Fed.
134 B1 **Roslyn** U.S.A.
109 C3 **Rossano** Italy
97 B1 **Rossan Point** Ireland
51 E1 **Rossel Island** P.N.G.
55 N1 **Ross Ice Shelf** Antarctica
131 D3 **Rossignol, Lake** Can.
128 C3 **Rossland** Can.
97 C2 **Rosslare** Ireland
97 C2 **Rosslare Harbour** Ireland
101 F2 **Roßlau** Ger.
101 E2 **Roßleben** Ger.
114 A3 **Rosso** Maur.
105 D3 **Rosso, Capo** *c.* France
99 B4 **Ross-on-Wye** U.K.
91 D1 **Rossosh'** Rus. Fed.
128 A1 **Ross River** Can.
55 N2 **Ross Sea** Antarctica
92 F2 **Røssvatnet** *l.* Norway
81 D3 **Rostāq** Iran
129 D2 **Rosthern** Can.
102 C1 **Rostock** Ger.
89 E2 **Rostov** Rus. Fed.
91 D2 **Rostov-na-Donu** Rus. Fed.
Rostov-on-Don Rus. Fed. *see* **Rostov-na-Donu**
104 B2 **Rostrenen** France
92 G2 **Røsvik** Norway
92 H2 **Rosvik** Sweden
142 C2 **Roswell** U.S.A.
59 D2 **Rota** *i.* N. Mariana Is
59 C3 **Rote** *i.* Indon.
101 D1 **Rotenburg (Wümme)** Ger.
101 E3 **Roth** Ger.
98 C2 **Rothbury** U.K.
101 E3 **Rothenburg ob der Tauber** Ger.
98 C3 **Rotherham** U.K.
96 C2 **Rothes** U.K.
96 B3 **Rothesay** U.K.
53 C2 **Roto** Austr.
105 D3 **Rotondo, Monte** *mt.* France
54 C1 **Rotorua** N.Z.
54 C1 **Rotorua, Lake** N.Z.
101 E2 **Rottenbach** Ger.
102 C2 **Rottenmann** Austria
100 B2 **Rotterdam** Neth.
102 B2 **Rottweil** Ger.
49 I5 **Rotuma** *i.* Fiji
105 C1 **Roubaix** France
104 C2 **Rouen** France
Roulers Belgium *see* **Roeselare**
53 D2 **Round Mountain** Austr.
131 E3 **Round Pond** *l.* Can.
143 D2 **Round Rock** U.S.A.
134 E1 **Roundup** U.S.A.
96 C1 **Rousay** *i.* U.K.
130 C3 **Rouyn-Noranda** Can.
Rouyuanchengzi China *see* **Huachi**
92 I2 **Rovaniemi** Fin.
91 D2 **Roven'ki** Rus. Fed.
91 D2 **Roven'ky** Ukr.
108 B1 **Rovereto** Italy
63 B2 **Rôviĕng Tbong** Cambodia
108 B1 **Rovigo** Italy
108 B1 **Rovinj** Croatia
53 C1 **Rowena** Austr.
Równe Ukr. *see* **Rivne**
64 B3 **Roxas** *Mindanao* Phil.
64 B2 **Roxas** *Mindoro* Phil.
64 A2 **Roxas** *Palawan* Phil.
64 B2 **Roxas** *Panay* Phil.
52 A2 **Roxby Downs** Austr.
142 C1 **Roy** *NM* U.S.A.
134 D2 **Roy** *UT* U.S.A.
138 B1 **Royale, Isle** *i.* U.S.A.
104 B2 **Royan** France
99 C3 **Royston** U.K.
90 C2 **Rozdil'na** Ukr.
91 C2 **Rozdol'ne** Ukr.
103 E2 **Rožňava** Slovakia
100 B3 **Rozoy-sur-Serre** France
87 D3 **Rtishchevo** Rus. Fed.
Ruanda *country* Africa *see* **Rwanda**
54 C1 **Ruapehu, Mount** *vol.* N.Z.
54 A3 **Ruapuke Island** N.Z.
89 D2 **Ruba** Belarus
79 B3 **Rub' al Khālī** *des.* Saudi Arabia
119 D3 **Rubeho Mountains** Tanz.
91 D2 **Rubizhne** Ukr.
77 E1 **Rubtsovsk** Rus. Fed.
126 B2 **Ruby** U.S.A.
135 C2 **Ruby Mountains** U.S.A.
76 C3 **Rudbar** Afgh.
66 C2 **Rudnaya Pristan'** Rus. Fed.
89 D3 **Rudnya** Rus. Fed.
76 C1 **Rudnyy** Kazakh.
Rudolf, Lake *salt l.* Eth./Kenya *see* **Turkana, Lake**
82 E1 **Rudol'fa, Ostrov** *i.* Rus. Fed.
Rudolph Island *i.* Rus. Fed. *see* **Rudol'fa, Ostrov**
101 E2 **Rudolstadt** Ger.
116 B3 **Rufa'a** Sudan
119 D3 **Rufiji** *r.* Tanz.
153 B3 **Rufino** Arg.
121 B2 **Rufunsa** Zambia
70 C2 **Rugao** China
99 C3 **Rugby** U.K.
136 C1 **Rugby** U.S.A.
102 C1 **Rügen** *i.* Ger.
119 C3 **Ruhengeri** Rwanda
101 E2 **Ruhla** Ger.
88 B2 **Ruhnu** *i.* Estonia
100 C2 **Ruhr** *r.* Ger.
71 C3 **Rui'an** China
142 B2 **Ruidoso** U.S.A.
144 B2 **Ruiz** Mex.
119 D3 **Rukwa, Lake** Tanz.
96 A2 **Rum** *i.* U.K.
109 C1 **Ruma** Serbia
78 B2 **Rumāh** Saudi Arabia
117 A4 **Rumbek** Sudan
147 C2 **Rum Cay** *i.* Bahamas
139 E2 **Rumford** U.S.A.
103 D1 **Rumia** Pol.
105 D2 **Rumilly** France
50 C1 **Rum Jungle** Austr.
66 D2 **Rumoi** Japan
121 C2 **Rumphi** Malawi
54 B2 **Runanga** N.Z.
98 B3 **Runcorn** U.K.

120 A2 **Rundu** Namibia
119 C2 **Rungu** Dem. Rep. Congo
119 D3 **Rungwa** Tanz.
68 B2 **Ruoqiang** China
130 C2 **Rupert** *r.* Can.
134 D2 **Rupert** U.S.A.
130 C2 **Rupert Bay** Can.
Rusaddir N. Africa *see* **Melilla**
121 C2 **Rusape** Zimbabwe
110 C2 **Ruse** Bulg.
137 E1 **Rush City** U.S.A.
121 C2 **Rushinga** Zimbabwe
77 D3 **Rushon** Tajik.
136 C2 **Rushville** U.S.A.
53 C3 **Rushworth** Austr.
129 D2 **Russell** Can.
54 B1 **Russell** N.Z.
137 D3 **Russell** U.S.A.
140 C2 **Russellville** *AL* U.S.A.
140 B1 **Russellville** *AR* U.S.A.
138 B3 **Russellville** *KY* U.S.A.
101 D2 **Rüsselsheim** Ger.
82 F2 **Russian Federation** *country* Asia/Europe
81 C1 **Rust'avi** Georgia
123 C2 **Rustenburg** S. Africa
140 D2 **Ruston** U.S.A.
61 D2 **Ruteng** Indon.
98 B3 **Ruthin** U.K.
139 E2 **Rutland** U.S.A.
Rutog China *see* **Dêrub**
119 C3 **Rutshuru** Dem. Rep. Congo
119 E4 **Ruvuma** *r.* Moz./Tanz.
79 C2 **Ruweis** U.A.E.
89 E2 **Ruza** Rus. Fed.
77 C1 **Ruzayevka** Kazakh.
87 D3 **Ruzayevka** Rus. Fed.
119 C3 **Rwanda** *country* Africa
89 E3 **Ryazan'** Rus. Fed.
89 F3 **Ryazhsk** Rus. Fed.
86 C2 **Rybachiy, Poluostrov** *pen.* Rus. Fed.
Rybach'ye Kyrg. *see* **Balykchy**
89 E2 **Rybinsk** Rus. Fed.
89 E2 **Rybinskoye Vodokhranilishche** *resr* Rus. Fed.
103 D1 **Rybnik** Pol.
Rybnitsa Moldova *see* **Rîbniţa**
89 E3 **Rybnoye** Rus. Fed.
99 D4 **Rye** U.K.
Rykovo Ukr. *see* **Yenakiyeve**
89 D3 **Ryl'sk** Rus. Fed.
Ryojun China *see* **Lüshunkou**
67 C3 **Ryotsu** Japan
69 E3 **Ryukyu Islands** *is* Japan
89 D3 **Ryzhikovo** Rus. Fed.
103 E1 **Rzeszów** Pol.
91 E1 **Rzhaksa** Rus. Fed.
89 D2 **Rzhev** Rus. Fed.

S

79 C2 **Sa'ādatābād** Iran
101 E2 **Saale** *r.* Ger.
101 E2 **Saalfeld** Ger.
134 B1 **Saanich** Can.
100 C3 **Saar** *r.* Ger.
102 B2 **Saarbrücken** Ger.
88 B2 **Sääre** Estonia
88 B2 **Saaremaa** *i.* Estonia
92 I2 **Saarenkylä** Fin.
93 I3 **Saarijärvi** Fin.
100 C3 **Saarlouis** Ger.
80 B2 **Sab' Ābār** Syria
107 D1 **Sabadell** Spain
67 C3 **Sabae** Japan
61 C1 **Sabah** *state* Malaysia
61 C2 **Sabalana** *i.* Indon.
146 B2 **Sabana, Archipiélago de** *is* Cuba
150 B1 **Sabanalarga** Col.
60 A1 **Sabang** Indon.
155 D1 **Sabará** Brazil
108 B2 **Sabaudia** Italy
122 B3 **Sabelo** S. Africa
119 D2 **Sabena Desert** Kenya
115 D2 **Sabhā** Libya
123 D2 **Sabie** *r.* Moz./S. Africa
123 D2 **Sabie** S. Africa
145 B2 **Sabinas** Mex.
145 B2 **Sabinas Hidalgo** Mex.
143 E3 **Sabine** *r.* U.S.A.
131 D3 **Sable, Cape** Can.
141 D3 **Sable, Cape** U.S.A.
131 E3 **Sable Island** Can.
106 B1 **Sabugal** Port.
78 B3 **Şabyā** Saudi Arabia
76 B3 **Sabzevār** Iran
137 D2 **Sac City** U.S.A.
120 A2 **Sachanga** Angola
130 A2 **Sachigo Lake** Can.
65 B3 **Sach'on** S. Korea
126 D2 **Sachs Harbour** Can.
154 C1 **Sacramento** Brazil
135 B3 **Sacramento** U.S.A.
135 B3 **Sacramento** *r.* U.S.A.
142 B2 **Sacramento Mountains** U.S.A.
135 B2 **Sacramento Valley** U.S.A.
110 B1 **Săcueni** Romania
123 C3 **Sada** S. Africa
107 C1 **Sádaba** Spain
Sá da Bandeira Angola *see* **Lubango**
78 B3 **Şa'dah** Yemen
63 B3 **Sadao** Thai.
79 B3 **Şadārah** Yemen
63 B2 **Sa Đec** Vietnam
74 B2 **Sadiqabad** Pak.
72 D2 **Sadiya** India
67 C3 **Sadoga-shima** *i.* Japan
107 D2 **Sa Dragonera** *i.* Spain
81 D2 **Safāshahr** Iran
93 F4 **Säffle** Sweden
142 B2 **Safford** U.S.A.
99 D3 **Saffron Walden** U.K.
114 B1 **Safi** Morocco
76 C3 **Safīd Kūh** *mts* Afgh.
155 D1 **Safiras, Serra das** *mts* Brazil
86 D2 **Safonovo** Rus. Fed.
89 D2 **Safonovo** Rus. Fed.
78 B2 **Safrā' as Sark** *esc.* Saudi Arabia
75 C2 **Saga** China
67 B4 **Saga** Japan
62 A1 **Sagaing** Myanmar
67 C3 **Sagamihara** Japan
74 B2 **Sagar** India
Sagarmatha *mt.* China/Nepal *see* **Everest, Mount**
138 C2 **Saginaw** U.S.A.
138 C2 **Saginaw Bay** U.S.A.
Saglouc Can. *see* **Salluit**
106 B2 **Sagres** Port.
146 B2 **Sagua la Grande** Cuba
139 F1 **Saguenay** *r.* Can.
107 C2 **Sagunto** Spain
76 B2 **Sagyndyk, Mys** *pt* Kazakh.
106 B1 **Sahagún** Spain
114 C3 **Sahara** *des.* Africa
Şaḩara el Gharbîya *des.* Egypt *see* **Western Desert**
Şaḩara el Sharqîya *des.* Egypt *see* **Eastern Desert**
Saharan Atlas *mts* Alg. *see* **Atlas Saharien**
74 B2 **Saharanpur** India
75 C2 **Saharsa** India
114 B3 **Sahel** *reg.* Africa
74 B1 **Sahiwal** Pak.
144 B2 **Sahuayo** Mex.
78 B2 **Şāḩūq** *reg.* Saudi Arabia
114 C1 **Saïda** Alg.
Saïda Lebanon *see* **Sidon**
75 C2 **Saidpur** Bangl.
67 B3 **Saigō** Japan
Saigon Vietnam *see* **Ho Chi Minh City**
75 D2 **Saiha** India
70 B1 **Saihan Tal** China
67 B4 **Saiki** Japan
93 I3 **Saimaa** *l.* Fin.
144 B2 **Sain Alto** Mex.
96 C3 **St Abb's Head** *hd* U.K.
131 E3 **St Alban's** Can.
99 C4 **St Albans** U.K.
138 C3 **St Albans** U.S.A.
St Alban's Head *hd* U.K. *see* **St Aldhelm's Head**
99 B4 **St Aldhelm's Head** *hd* U.K.
St-André, Cap *c.* Madag. *see* **Vilanandro, Tanjona**
96 C2 **St Andrews** U.K.
131 E2 **St Anthony** Can.
134 D2 **St Anthony** U.S.A.
52 B3 **St Arnaud** Austr.
131 E2 **St-Augustin** Can.
131 E2 **St Augustin** *r.* Can.
141 D3 **St Augustine** U.S.A.
99 A4 **St Austell** U.K.
104 C2 **St-Avertin** France
147 D3 **St-Barthélemy** *terr.* West Indies
98 B2 **St Bees Head** *hd* U.K.
105 D3 **St-Bonnet-en-Champsaur** France
99 A4 **St Bride's Bay** U.K.
104 B2 **St-Brieuc** France
130 C3 **St Catharines** Can.
141 D2 **St Catherines Island** U.S.A.
99 C4 **St Catherine's Point** U.K.
137 E3 **St Charles** U.S.A.
138 C2 **St Clair, Lake** Can./U.S.A.
105 D2 **St-Claude** France
99 A4 **St Clears** U.K.
137 E1 **St Cloud** U.S.A.
138 A1 **St Croix** *r.* U.S.A.
147 D3 **St Croix** Virgin Is (U.S.A.)
99 A4 **St David's** U.K.
99 A4 **St David's Head** *hd* U.K.
113 I8 **St-Denis** Can.
104 C2 **St-Denis** France
St-Denis-du-Sig Alg. *see* **Sig**
105 D2 **St-Dié** France
105 C2 **St-Dizier** France
130 C3 **Ste-Adèle** Can.
131 D3 **Ste-Anne-des-Monts** Can.
139 E1 **Ste-Foy** Can.
105 D2 **St-Égrève** France
128 A1 **St Elias Mountains** Can.
131 D2 **Ste-Marguerite** *r.* Can.
139 E1 **Ste-Marie** Can.
Ste-Marie, Cap *c.* Madag. *see* **Vohimena, Tanjona**
Sainte-Marie, Île *i.* Madag. *see* **Boraha, Nosy**
Ste-Rose-du-Dégelé Can. *see* **Dégelis**
129 E2 **Sainte Rose du Lac** Can.
104 B2 **Saintes** France
105 C2 **St-Étienne** France
104 C2 **St-Étienne-du-Rouvray** France
130 C3 **St-Félicien** Can.
97 D1 **Saintfield** U.K.
105 D3 **St-Florent** France
105 C2 **St-Flour** France
136 C3 **St Francis** U.S.A.
104 C3 **St-Gaudens** France
53 C1 **St George** Austr.
135 D3 **St George** U.S.A.
141 D3 **St George Island** U.S.A.
131 C3 **St-Georges** Can.
147 D3 **St George's** Grenada
131 E3 **St George's Bay** Can.
97 C3 **St George's Channel** Ireland/U.K.
105 D2 **St Gotthard Pass** *pass* Switz.
113 C7 **St Helena** *i.* S. Atlantic Ocean
113 C7 **St Helena, Ascension and Tristan da Cunha** *terr.* S. Atlantic Ocean
122 A3 **St Helena Bay** S. Africa
122 A3 **St Helena Bay** *b.* S. Africa
98 B3 **St Helens** U.K.
134 B1 **St Helens, Mount** *vol.* U.S.A.
95 C4 **St Helier** Channel Is
100 B2 **St-Hubert** Belgium
139 E1 **St-Hyacinthe** Can.
138 C1 **St Ignace** U.S.A.
130 B3 **St Ignace Island** Can.
99 A4 **St Ives** U.K.
St Jacques, Cap Vietnam *see* **Vung Tau**
128 A2 **St James, Cape** Can.
130 C3 **St-Jean, Lac** *l.* Can.
104 B2 **St-Jean-d'Angély** France
104 B3 **St-Jean-de-Luz** France
104 B2 **St-Jean-de-Monts** France
130 C3 **St-Jean-sur-Richelieu** Can.
139 E1 **St-Jérôme** Can.
134 C1 **St Joe** *r.* U.S.A.
131 D3 **Saint John** Can.
137 D3 **St John** U.S.A.
139 F1 **St John** *r.* U.S.A.
147 D3 **St John's** Antigua
131 E3 **St John's** Can.
142 B2 **St Johns** U.S.A.
141 D2 **St Johns** *r.* U.S.A.
139 E2 **St Johnsbury** U.S.A.
137 E3 **St Joseph** U.S.A.
130 A2 **St Joseph, Lake** Can.
St-Joseph-d'Alma Can. *see* **Alma**
130 B3 **St Joseph Island** Can.
139 E1 **St-Jovité** Can.
104 C2 **St-Junien** France
94 B2 **St Kilda** *is* U.K.
147 D3 **St Kitts and Nevis** *country* West Indies
151 D2 **St-Laurent-du-Maroni** Fr. Guiana
131 E3 **St Lawrence** Can.
131 D3 **St Lawrence** *inlet* Can.
131 D3 **St Lawrence, Gulf of** Can.
126 A2 **St Lawrence Island** U.S.A.
104 B2 **St-Lô** France
114 A3 **St-Louis** Senegal
137 E3 **St Louis** U.S.A.
137 E1 **St Louis** *r.* U.S.A.
147 D3 **St Lucia** *country* West Indies
147 D3 **St Lucia Channel** Martinique/St Lucia
123 D2 **St Lucia Estuary** S. Africa
96 [illegible] **St Magnus Bay** U.K.
104 B2 **St-Malo** France
104 B2 **St-Malo, Golfe de** *g.* France
147 C3 **St-Marc** Haiti
St Mark's S. Africa *see* **Cofimvaba**
147 D3 **St-Martin** *terr.* West Indies
122 A3 **St Martin, Cape** S. Africa
129 E2 **St Martin, Lake** Can.
139 D2 **St Marys** U.S.A.
124 A3 **St Matthew Island** U.S.A.
59 D3 **St Matthias Group** *is* P.N.G.
130 C3 **St-Maurice** *r.* Can.
130 C3 **St-Michel-des-Saints** Can.
104 B2 **St-Nazaire** France
104 C1 **St-Omer** France
129 C2 **St Paul** Can.
137 E2 **St Paul** U.S.A.
156 A8 **St-Paul, Île** *i.* Indian Ocean
137 E2 **St Peter** U.S.A.
95 C4 **St Peter Port** Channel Is
89 D2 **St Petersburg** Rus. Fed.
141 D3 **St Petersburg** U.S.A.
131 E3 **St-Pierre** St Pierre and Miquelon
139 E1 **St-Pierre, Lac** *l.* Can.
131 E3 **St Pierre and Miquelon** *terr.* N. America
104 B2 **St-Pierre-d'Oléron** France
105 C2 **St-Pourçain-sur-Sioule** France
131 D3 **St Quentin** Can.
105 C2 **St-Quentin** France
105 D3 **St-Raphaël** France
122 B3 **St Sebastian Bay** S. Africa
104 B2 **St-Sébastien-sur-Loire** France
131 D3 **St-Siméon** Can.
129 E2 **St Theresa Point** Can.
130 B3 **St Thomas** Can.
105 D3 **St-Tropez** France
105 D3 **St-Tropez, Cap de** *c.* France
St Vincent, Cape *c.* Port. *see* **São Vicente, Cabo de**
52 A3 **St Vincent, Gulf** Austr.
147 D3 **St Vincent and the Grenadines** *country* West Indies
147 D3 **St Vincent Passage** St Lucia/St Vincent
100 C2 **St-Vith** Belgium
129 D2 **St Walburg** Can.
104 C2 **St-Yrieix-la-Perche** France
59 D1 **Saipan** *i.* N. Mariana Is
67 C3 **Saitama** Japan
152 B1 **Sajama, Nevado** *mt.* Bol.
122 B2 **Sak** *watercourse* S. Africa
67 C4 **Sakai** Japan
67 B4 **Sakaide** Japan
78 B2 **Sakākah** Saudi Arabia
136 C1 **Sakakawea, Lake** U.S.A.
Sakarya Turkey *see* **Adapazarı**
111 D2 **Sakarya** *r.* Turkey
66 C3 **Sakata** Japan
65 B1 **Sakchu** N. Korea
66 D1 **Sakhalin** *i.* Rus. Fed.
123 C2 **Sakhile** S. Africa
81 C1 **Şäki** Azer.
88 B3 **Šakiai** Lith.
69 E3 **Sakishima-shotō** *is* Japan
62 B2 **Sakon Nakhon** Thai.
74 A2 **Sakrand** Pak.
122 B3 **Sakrivier** S. Africa
67 D3 **Sakura** Japan
91 C2 **Saky** Ukr.
93 G4 **Sala** Sweden
130 C3 **Salaberry-de-Valleyfield** Can.
88 B2 **Salacgrīva** Latvia
109 C2 **Sala Consilina** Italy
133 C4 **Salada, Laguna** *salt l.* Mex.
152 C2 **Saladas** Arg.
152 B3 **Salado** *r.* Arg.
153 B3 **Salado** *r.* Arg.
145 C2 **Salado** *r.* Mex.
114 B4 **Salaga** Ghana
122 B1 **Salajwe** Botswana
79 C2 **Salakh, Jabal** *mt.* Oman
115 D3 **Salal** Chad
78 A2 **Salâla** Sudan
79 C3 **Şalālah** Oman
145 B2 **Salamanca** Mex.
106 B1 **Salamanca** Spain
139 D2 **Salamanca** U.S.A.
106 B1 **Salas** Spain
63 B2 **Salavan** Laos
59 C3 **Salawati** *i.* Indon.
61 D2 **Salayar** *i.* Indon.
157 G7 **Sala y Gómez, Isla** *i.* S. Pacific Ocean
Salazar Angola *see* **N'dalatando**
104 C2 **Salbris** France
88 C3 **Šalčininkai** Lith.
106 C1 **Saldaña** Spain
122 A3 **Saldanha** S. Africa
88 B2 **Saldus** Latvia
53 C3 **Sale** Austr.
86 F2 **Salekhard** Rus. Fed.
73 B3 **Salem** India
138 B3 **Salem** *IL* U.S.A.
137 E3 **Salem** *MO* U.S.A.
134 B2 **Salem** *OR* U.S.A.
137 D2 **Salem** *SD* U.S.A.
96 B2 **Salen** U.K.
109 B2 **Salerno** Italy
108 B2 **Salerno, Golfo di** *g.* Italy
98 B3 **Salford** U.K.
151 E2 **Salgado** *r.* Brazil
103 D2 **Salgótarján** Hungary
151 F3 **Salgueiro** Brazil
136 B3 **Salida** U.S.A.
111 C3 **Salihli** Turkey
88 C3 **Salihorsk** Belarus
121 C2 **Salima** Malawi
121 C2 **Salimo** Moz.
137 D3 **Salina** *KS* U.S.A.
135 D3 **Salina** *UT* U.S.A.
109 B3 **Salina, Isola** *i.* Italy
145 C3 **Salina Cruz** Mex.
155 D1 **Salinas** Brazil
144 B2 **Salinas** Mex.
135 B3 **Salinas** U.S.A.
135 B3 **Salinas** *r.* U.S.A.
107 D2 **Salines, Cap de ses** *c.* Spain
151 E3 **Salinópolis** Brazil
99 C4 **Salisbury** U.K.
139 D3 **Salisbury** *MD* U.S.A.
141 D1 **Salisbury** *NC* U.S.A.
Salisbury Zimbabwe *see* **Harare**
99 B4 **Salisbury Plain** U.K.
151 E3 **Salitre** *r.* Brazil
92 I2 **Salla** Fin.
143 E1 **Sallisaw** U.S.A.
127 G2 **Salluit** Can.
75 C2 **Sallyana** Nepal
81 C2 **Salmās** Iran
128 C3 **Salmo** Can.
134 D1 **Salmon** U.S.A.
134 C1 **Salmon** *r.* U.S.A.
128 C2 **Salmon Arm** Can.
134 C2 **Salmon River Mountains** U.S.A.
100 C3 **Salmtal** Ger.
118 B2 **Salo** C.A.R.
93 H3 **Salo** Fin.
105 D3 **Salon-de-Provence** France
Salonica Greece *see* **Thessaloniki**
110 B1 **Salonta** Romania
87 D4 **Sal'sk** Rus. Fed.
122 B3 **Salt** *watercourse* S. Africa
107 D1 **Salt** Spain
142 A2 **Salt** *r.* U.S.A.
152 B2 **Salta** Arg.
99 A4 **Saltash** U.K.
96 B3 **Saltcoats** U.K.
145 B2 **Saltillo** Mex.
134 D2 **Salt Lake City** U.S.A.
154 C2 **Salto** Brazil
152 C3 **Salto** Uru.
155 E1 **Salto da Divisa** Brazil
154 B2 **Salto del Guairá** Para.

135 C4 **Salton Sea** *salt l.* U.S.A.
154 B3 **Salto Osório, Represa** *resr* Brazil
154 B3 **Salto Santiago, Represa de** *resr* Brazil
141 D2 **Saluda** U.S.A.
76 B3 **Saluq, Kūh-e** *mt.* Iran
108 A2 **Saluzzo** Italy
151 F4 **Salvador** Brazil
79 C2 **Salwah** Saudi Arabia
62 A2 **Salween** *r.* China/Myanmar
81 C2 **Salyan** Azer.
138 C3 **Salyersville** U.S.A.
122 A1 **Salzbrunn** Namibia
102 C2 **Salzburg** Austria
101 E1 **Salzgitter** Ger.
101 D2 **Salzkotten** Ger.
101 E1 **Salzwedel** Ger.
144 B1 **Samalayuca** Mex.
66 D2 **Samani** Japan
64 B2 **Samar** *i.* Phil.
87 E3 **Samara** Rus. Fed.
Samarahan Malaysia *see* **Sri Aman**
59 E3 **Samarai** P.N.G.
61 C2 **Samarinda** Indon.
77 C3 **Samarqand** Uzbek.
81 C2 **Sāmarrā'** Iraq
81 C1 **Şamaxı** Azer.
119 C3 **Samba** Dem. Rep. Congo
61 C1 **Sambaliung** *mts* Indon.
75 C2 **Sambalpur** India
60 C2 **Sambar, Tanjung** *pt* Indon.
60 B1 **Sambas** Indon.
121 □E2 **Sambava** Madag.
74 B2 **Sambhar** India
90 A2 **Sambir** Ukr.
61 C2 **Sambo** Indon.
61 C2 **Samboja** Indon.
153 C3 **Samborombón, Bahía** *b.* Arg.
65 B2 **Samch'ŏk** S. Korea
Samch'ŏnp'o S. Korea *see* **Sach'on**
81 C2 **Samdi Dag** *mt.* Turkey
119 D3 **Same** Tanz.
121 B2 **Samfya** Zambia
78 B2 **Samīrah** Saudi Arabia
65 B1 **Samjiyŏn** N. Korea
Sam Neua Laos *see* **Xam Nua**
48 J5 **Samoa** *country* S. Pacific Ocean
156 E6 **Samoa Basin** S. Pacific Ocean
Samoa i Sisifo *country* S. Pacific Ocean *see* **Samoa**
109 C1 **Samobor** Croatia
110 B2 **Samokov** Bulg.
111 C3 **Samos** *i.* Greece
Samothrace *i.* Greece *see* **Samothraki**
111 C2 **Samothraki** Greece
111 C2 **Samothraki** *i.* Greece
61 C2 **Sampit** Indon.
119 C3 **Sampwe** Dem. Rep. Congo
143 E2 **Sam Rayburn Reservoir** U.S.A.
62 B2 **Sâm Sơn** Vietnam
80 B1 **Samsun** Turkey
81 C1 **Samtredia** Georgia
63 B3 **Samui, Ko** *i.* Thai.
63 B2 **Samut Songkhram** Thai.
114 B3 **San** Mali
78 B3 **Şan'ā'** Yemen
118 A2 **Sanaga** *r.* Cameroon
81 C2 **Sanandaj** Iran
146 B3 **San Andrés, Isla de** *i.* Caribbean Sea
106 B1 **San Andrés del Rabanedo** Spain
142 B2 **San Andres Mountains** U.S.A.
145 C3 **San Andrés Tuxtla** Mex.
143 C2 **San Angelo** U.S.A.
143 D3 **San Antonio** U.S.A.
135 C4 **San Antonio, Mount** U.S.A.
152 B2 **San Antonio de los Cobres** Arg.
153 B4 **San Antonio Oeste** Arg.
108 B2 **San Benedetto del Tronto** Italy
144 A3 **San Benedicto, Isla** *i.* Mex.
135 C4 **San Bernardino** U.S.A.
135 C4 **San Bernardino Mountains** U.S.A.
142 B3 **San Blas** Mex.
141 C3 **San Blas, Cape** U.S.A.
146 C4 **San Blas, Punta** *pt* Panama
152 B1 **San Borja** Bol.
144 B2 **San Buenaventura** Mex.
64 B2 **San Carlos** Phil.
147 D4 **San Carlos** Venez.
153 A4 **San Carlos de Bariloche** Arg.
147 C4 **San Carlos del Zulia** Venez.
104 C2 **Sancerrois, Collines du** *hills* France
135 C4 **San Clemente** U.S.A.
135 C4 **San Clemente Island** U.S.A.
105 C2 **Sancoins** France
48 H5 **San Cristobal** *i.* Solomon Is
150 B2 **San Cristóbal** Venez.
145 C3 **San Cristóbal de las Casas** Mex.
146 C2 **Sancti Spíritus** Cuba
123 D1 **Sand** *r.* S. Africa
61 C1 **Sandakan** Malaysia
93 E3 **Sandane** Norway
111 B2 **Sandanski** Bulg.
114 A3 **Sandaré** Mali
96 C1 **Sanday** *i.* U.K.
143 C2 **Sanderson** U.S.A.
150 C4 **Sandia** Peru
135 C4 **San Diego** U.S.A.
111 D3 **Sandıklı** Turkey
93 E4 **Sandnes** Norway
92 F2 **Sandnessjøen** Norway
118 C3 **Sandoa** Dem. Rep. Congo
103 E1 **Sandomierz** Pol.
89 E2 **Sandovo** Rus. Fed.
94 B1 **Sandoy** *i.* Faroe Is
134 C1 **Sandpoint** U.S.A.
71 B3 **Sandu** China
94 B1 **Sandur** Faroe Is
138 C2 **Sandusky** U.S.A.
122 A3 **Sandveld** *mts* S. Africa
122 A2 **Sandverhaar** Namibia
93 F4 **Sandvika** Norway
93 G3 **Sandviken** Sweden
131 E2 **Sandwich Bay** Can.
135 D2 **Sandy** U.S.A.
129 D2 **Sandy Bay** Can.
51 E2 **Sandy Cape** Austr.
130 A2 **Sandy Lake** Can.
130 A2 **Sandy Lake** *l.* Can.
141 D2 **Sandy Springs** U.S.A.
144 A1 **San Felipe** Mex.
145 B2 **San Felipe** Mex.
150 C1 **San Felipe** Venez.
144 A2 **San Fernando** Mex.
145 C2 **San Fernando** Mex.
64 B2 **San Fernando** *Luzon* Phil.
64 B2 **San Fernando** *Luzon* Phil.
106 B2 **San Fernando** Spain
147 D3 **San Fernando** Trin. and Tob.
150 C2 **San Fernando de Apure** Venez.
141 D3 **Sanford** *FL* U.S.A.
139 E2 **Sanford** *ME* U.S.A.
141 E1 **Sanford** *NC* U.S.A.
152 B3 **San Francisco** Arg.
135 B3 **San Francisco** U.S.A.
107 D2 **San Francisco Javier** Spain
74 B3 **Sangamner** India
83 J2 **Sangar** Rus. Fed.
108 A3 **San Gavino Monreale** Italy
101 E2 **Sangerhausen** Ger.
61 C2 **Sanggau** Indon.
118 B3 **Sangha** *r.* Congo
109 C3 **San Giovanni in Fiore** Italy
59 C2 **Sangir** *i.* Indon.
59 C2 **Sangir, Kepulauan** *is* Indon.
65 B2 **Sangju** S. Korea
63 A2 **Sangkhla Buri** Thai.
61 C1 **Sangkulirang** Indon.
73 B3 **Sangli** India
118 B2 **Sangmélima** Cameroon
121 C3 **Sango** Zimbabwe
San Gottardo, Passo del *pass* Switz. *see* **St Gotthard Pass**
136 B3 **Sangre de Cristo Range** *mts* U.S.A.
75 C2 **Sangsang** China
144 A2 **San Hipólito, Punta** *pt* Mex.
145 D3 **San Ignacio** Belize
152 B1 **San Ignacio** Bol.
144 A2 **San Ignacio** Mex.
130 C2 **Sanikiluaq** Can.
71 A3 **Sanjiang** China
Sanjiang China *see* **Jinping**
67 C3 **Sanjō** Japan
135 B3 **San Joaquin** *r.* U.S.A.
153 B4 **San Jorge, Golfo de** *g.* Arg.
146 B4 **San José** Costa Rica
64 B2 **San Jose** Phil.
64 B2 **San Jose** Phil.
135 B3 **San Jose** U.S.A.
144 A2 **San José, Isla** *i.* Mex.
144 B2 **San José de Bavicora** Mex.
64 B2 **San Jose de Buenavista** Phil.
144 A2 **San José de Comondú** Mex.
144 B2 **San José del Cabo** Mex.
150 B2 **San José del Guaviare** Col.
152 B3 **San Juan** Arg.
146 B3 **San Juan** *r.* Costa Rica/Nic.
147 C3 **San Juan** Dom. Rep.
147 D3 **San Juan** Puerto Rico
135 D3 **San Juan** *r.* U.S.A.
152 C2 **San Juan Bautista** Para.
145 C3 **San Juan Bautista Tuxtepec** Mex.
147 D4 **San Juan de los Morros** Venez.
145 C2 **San Juan del Río** Mex.
134 B1 **San Juan Islands** U.S.A.
144 B2 **San Juanito** Mex.
136 B3 **San Juan Mountains** U.S.A.
153 B4 **San Julián** Arg.
75 C2 **Sankh** *r.* India
63 B2 **San Khao Phang Hoei** *mts* Thai.
100 C2 **Sankt Augustin** Ger.
105 D2 **Sankt Gallen** Switz.
105 D2 **Sankt Moritz** Switz.
Sankt-Peterburg Rus. Fed. *see* **St Petersburg**
102 C2 **Sankt Veit an der Glan** Austria
100 C3 **Sankt Wendel** Ger.
80 B2 **Şanlıurfa** Turkey
142 B3 **San Lorenzo** Mex.
106 B2 **Sanlúcar de Barrameda** Spain
144 B2 **San Lucas** Mex.
153 B3 **San Luis** Arg.
145 B2 **San Luis de la Paz** Mex.
142 A2 **San Luisito** Mex.
135 B3 **San Luis Obispo** U.S.A.
135 B3 **San Luis Obispo Bay** U.S.A.
145 B2 **San Luis Potosí** Mex.
144 A1 **San Luis Río Colorado** Mex.
143 D3 **San Marcos** U.S.A.
108 B2 **San Marino** *country* Europe
108 B2 **San Marino** San Marino
144 B2 **San Martín de Bolaños** Mex.
153 A4 **San Martín de los Andes** Arg.
135 B3 **San Mateo** U.S.A.
153 B4 **San Matías, Golfo** *g.* Arg.
70 B2 **Sanmenxia** China
146 B3 **San Miguel** El Salvador
152 B2 **San Miguel de Tucumán** Arg.
135 B4 **San Miguel Island** U.S.A.
145 C3 **San Miguel Sola de Vega** Mex.
71 B3 **Sanming** China
153 B3 **San Nicolás de los Arroyos** Arg.
135 C4 **San Nicolas Island** U.S.A.
110 B1 **Sânnicolau Mare** Romania
123 C2 **Sannieshof** S. Africa
114 B4 **Sanniquellie** Liberia
103 E2 **Sanok** Pol.
64 B2 **San Pablo** Phil.
144 B2 **San Pablo Balleza** Mex.
152 B2 **San Pedro** Arg.
152 B1 **San Pedro** Bol.
114 B4 **San-Pédro** Côte d'Ivoire
144 A2 **San Pedro** Mex.
142 A2 **San Pedro** *watercourse* U.S.A.
106 B2 **San Pedro, Sierra de** *mts* Spain
144 B2 **San Pedro de las Colonias** Mex.
152 C2 **San Pedro de Ycuamandyyú** Para.
142 A3 **San Pedro el Saucito** Mex.
146 B3 **San Pedro Sula** Hond.
108 A3 **San Pietro, Isola di** *i.* Italy
96 C3 **Sanquhar** U.K.
144 A1 **San Quintín, Cabo** *c.* Mex.
153 B3 **San Rafael** Arg.
108 A2 **San Remo** Italy
143 D2 **San Saba** U.S.A.
147 C2 **San Salvador** *i.* Bahamas
146 B3 **San Salvador** El Salvador
152 B2 **San Salvador de Jujuy** Arg.
108 B2 **Sansepolcro** Italy
109 C2 **San Severo** Italy
109 C2 **Sanski Most** Bos.-Herz.
152 B1 **Santa Ana** Bol.
146 B3 **Santa Ana** El Salvador
144 A1 **Santa Ana** Mex.
135 C4 **Santa Ana** U.S.A.
152 B1 **Santa Ana de Yacuma** Bol.
144 B2 **Santa Bárbara** Mex.
135 C4 **Santa Barbara** U.S.A.
154 B2 **Santa Bárbara, Serra de** *hills* Brazil
152 B2 **Santa Catalina** Chile
135 C4 **Santa Catalina Island** U.S.A.
154 B3 **Santa Catarina** *state* Brazil
150 C3 **Santa Clara** Col.
146 C2 **Santa Clara** Cuba
135 B3 **Santa Clara** U.S.A.
135 C4 **Santa Clarita** U.S.A.
107 D1 **Santa Coloma de Gramanet** Spain
Santa Comba Angola *see* **Waku-Kungo**
109 C3 **Santa Croce, Capo** *c.* Italy
153 B5 **Santa Cruz** *r.* Arg.
152 B1 **Santa Cruz** Bol.
64 B2 **Santa Cruz** Phil.
135 B3 **Santa Cruz** U.S.A.
145 C3 **Santa Cruz Barillas** Guat.
155 E1 **Santa Cruz Cabrália** Brazil
107 C2 **Santa Cruz de Moya** Spain
114 A2 **Santa Cruz de Tenerife** Islas Canarias
152 C2 **Santa Cruz do Sul** Brazil
135 C4 **Santa Cruz Island** U.S.A.
48 H5 **Santa Cruz Islands** Solomon Is
107 D2 **Santa Eulalia del Río** Spain
152 B3 **Santa Fé** Arg.
142 B1 **Santa Fe** U.S.A.
154 B2 **Santa Fé do Sul** Brazil
154 B1 **Santa Helena de Goiás** Brazil
153 B3 **Santa Isabel** Arg.
Santa Isabel Equat. Guinea *see* **Malabo**
48 G4 **Santa Isabel** *i.* Solomon Is
154 B1 **Santa Luisa, Serra de** *hills* Brazil
151 E3 **Santa Luzia** Brazil
144 A2 **Santa Margarita, Isla** *i.* Mex.
152 C2 **Santa Maria** Brazil
144 B1 **Santa María** *r.* Mex.
135 B4 **Santa Maria** U.S.A.
123 D2 **Santa Maria, Cabo de** *c.* Moz.
106 B2 **Santa Maria, Cabo de** *c.* Port.
155 C1 **Santa Maria, Chapadão de** *hills* Brazil
151 E3 **Santa Maria das Barreiras** Brazil
109 C3 **Santa Maria di Leuca, Capo** *c.* Italy
155 D1 **Santa Maria do Suaçuí** Brazil
150 B1 **Santa Marta** Col.
135 C4 **Santa Monica** U.S.A.
151 E4 **Santana** Brazil
110 B1 **Sântana** Romania
106 C1 **Santander** Spain
108 A3 **Sant'Antioco** Italy
108 A3 **Sant'Antioco, Isola di** *i.* Italy
107 D2 **Sant Antoni de Portmany** Spain
151 D3 **Santarém** Brazil
106 B2 **Santarém** Port.
154 B1 **Santa Rita do Araguaia** Brazil
153 B3 **Santa Rosa** Arg.
152 C2 **Santa Rosa** Brazil
135 B3 **Santa Rosa** *CA* U.S.A.
142 C2 **Santa Rosa** *NM* U.S.A.
146 B3 **Santa Rosa de Copán** Hond.
135 B4 **Santa Rosa Island** *CA* U.S.A.
140 C2 **Santa Rosa Island** *FL* U.S.A.
144 A2 **Santa Rosalía** Mex.
134 C2 **Santa Rosa Range** *mts* U.S.A.
106 B1 **Santa Uxía de Ribeira** Spain
154 B1 **Santa Vitória** Brazil
107 D1 **Sant Carles de la Ràpita** Spain
135 C4 **Santee** U.S.A.
152 C2 **Santiago** Brazil
153 A3 **Santiago** Chile
147 C3 **Santiago** Dom. Rep.
144 B2 **Santiago** Mex.
146 B4 **Santiago** Panama
64 B2 **Santiago** Phil.
106 B1 **Santiago de Compostela** Spain
146 C2 **Santiago de Cuba** Cuba
144 B2 **Santiago Ixcuintla** Mex.
144 B2 **Santiago Papasquiaro** Mex.
106 C1 **Santillana** Spain
107 D2 **Sant Joan de Labritja** Spain
107 D1 **Sant Jordi, Golf de** *g.* Spain
155 D2 **Santo Amaro de Campos** Brazil
154 B2 **Santo Anastácio** Brazil
155 C2 **Santo André** Brazil
152 C2 **Santo Angelo** Brazil
154 B2 **Santo Antônio da Platina** Brazil
151 F4 **Santo Antônio de Jesus** Brazil
150 C3 **Santo Antônio do Içá** Brazil
155 C2 **Santo Antônio do Monte** Brazil
147 D3 **Santo Domingo** Dom. Rep.
144 A2 **Santo Domingo** Mex.
142 B1 **Santo Domingo Pueblo** U.S.A.
111 C3 **Santorini** *i.* Greece
155 C2 **Santos** Brazil
155 D2 **Santos Dumont** Brazil
157 I7 **Santos Plateau** S. Atlantic Ocean
152 C2 **Santo Tomé** Arg.
153 A4 **San Valentín, Cerro** *mt.* Chile
146 B3 **San Vicente** El Salvador
144 A1 **San Vicente** Mex.
64 B2 **San Vicente** Phil.
150 B4 **San Vicente de Cañete** Peru
108 B2 **San Vincenzo** Italy
108 B3 **San Vito, Capo** *c.* Italy
71 A4 **Sanya** China
155 C2 **São Bernardo do Campo** Brazil
152 C2 **São Borja** Brazil
154 C2 **São Carlos** Brazil
155 D1 **São Felipe, Serra de** *hills* Brazil
151 D4 **São Félix** Brazil
151 D3 **São Félix** Brazil
155 D2 **São Fidélis** Brazil
155 D1 **São Francisco** Brazil
151 F4 **São Francisco** *r.* Brazil
154 C3 **São Francisco, Ilha de** *i.* Brazil
154 C3 **São Francisco do Sul** Brazil
152 C3 **São Gabriel** Brazil
155 D2 **São Gonçalo** Brazil
155 C1 **São Gonçalo do Abaeté** Brazil
155 C1 **São Gotardo** Brazil
154 B1 **São Jerônimo, Serra de** *hills* Brazil
155 D2 **São João da Barra** Brazil
155 C2 **São João da Boa Vista** Brazil
106 B1 **São João da Madeira** Port.
155 D1 **São João da Ponte** Brazil
155 D2 **São João del Rei** Brazil
155 D1 **São João do Paraíso** Brazil
155 D1 **São João Evangelista** Brazil
155 D2 **São João Nepomuceno** Brazil
154 C2 **São Joaquim da Barra** Brazil
152 D2 **São José** Brazil
154 C2 **São José do Rio Preto** Brazil
155 C2 **São José dos Campos** Brazil
154 C3 **São José dos Pinhais** Brazil
154 A1 **São Lourenço** Brazil
155 C2 **São Lourenço** Brazil
151 E3 **São Luís** Brazil
154 C2 **São Manuel** Brazil
154 C1 **São Marcos** *r.* Brazil
151 E3 **São Marcos, Baía de** *b.* Brazil
155 E1 **São Mateus** Brazil
154 B3 **São Mateus do Sul** Brazil
105 C2 **Saône** *r.* France
155 C2 **São Paulo** Brazil
154 C1 **São Paulo** *state* Brazil
155 D2 **São Pedro da Aldeia** Brazil
151 E3 **São Raimundo Nonato** Brazil
155 C1 **São Romão** Brazil
São Salvador Angola *see* **M'banza Congo**
São Salvador do Congo Angola *see* **M'banza Congo**
155 C2 **São Sebastião, Ilha do** *i.* Brazil
154 C2 **São Sebastião do Paraíso** Brazil
154 B1 **São Simão** Brazil
154 B1 **São Simão, Barragem de** *resr* Brazil
59 C2 **Sao-Siu** Indon.
113 D5 **São Tomé** São Tomé and Príncipe
113 D5 **São Tomé** *i.* São Tomé and Príncipe
155 D2 **São Tomé, Cabo de** *c.* Brazil
113 D5 **São Tomé and Príncipe** *country* Africa
155 C2 **São Vicente** Brazil
106 B2 **São Vicente, Cabo de** *c.* Port.
59 C3 **Saparua** Indon.
107 D2 **Sa Pobla** Spain
89 F3 **Sapozhok** Rus. Fed.
66 D2 **Sapporo** Japan
109 C2 **Sapri** Italy
143 D1 **Sapulpa** U.S.A.
81 C2 **Saqqez** Iran
81 C2 **Sarāb** Iran
63 B2 **Sara Buri** Thai.
Saragossa Spain *see* **Zaragoza**
89 F3 **Sarai** Rus. Fed.
109 C2 **Sarajevo** Bos.-Herz.
87 E3 **Saraktash** Rus. Fed.
62 A1 **Saramati** *mt.* India/Myanmar
139 E2 **Saranac Lake** U.S.A.
109 D3 **Sarandë** Albania
64 B3 **Sarangani Islands** Phil.
87 D3 **Saransk** Rus. Fed.
87 E3 **Sarapul** Rus. Fed.
141 D3 **Sarasota** U.S.A.
90 B2 **Sarata** Ukr.
136 B2 **Saratoga** U.S.A.

139 E2 **Saratoga Springs** U.S.A.
61 C1 **Saratok** Malaysia
87 D3 **Saratov** Rus. Fed.
79 D2 **Saravan** Iran
61 C1 **Sarawak** *state* Malaysia
111 C2 **Saray** Turkey
111 C3 **Sarayköy** Turkey
79 D2 **Sarbāz** Iran
76 B3 **Sarbīsheh** Iran
74 B2 **Sardarshahr** India
Sardegna *i.* Italy *see* **Sardinia**
108 A2 **Sardinia** *i.* Italy
92 G2 **Sarektjåkkå** *mt.* Sweden
77 C3 **Sar-e Pol** Afgh.
158 C3 **Sargasso Sea** *sea* N. Atlantic Ocean
74 B1 **Sargodha** Pak.
115 D4 **Sarh** Chad
79 D2 **Sarhad** *reg.* Iran
81 D2 **Sārī** Iran
111 C3 **Sarıgöl** Turkey
81 C1 **Sarıkamış** Turkey
61 C1 **Sarikei** Malaysia
51 D2 **Sarina** Austr.
115 D2 **Sarīr Tibesti** *des.* Libya
65 B2 **Sariwŏn** N. Korea
111 C2 **Sarıyer** Turkey
77 D2 **Sarkand** Kazakh.
111 C2 **Şarköy** Turkey
104 C3 **Sarlat-la-Canéda** France
59 D3 **Sarmi** Indon.
153 B4 **Sarmiento** Arg.
130 C2 **Sarnia** Can.
90 B1 **Sarny** Ukr.
60 B2 **Sarolangun** Indon.
111 B3 **Saronikos Kolpos** *g.* Greece
111 C2 **Saros Körfezi** *b.* Turkey
103 E2 **Sárospatak** Hungary
87 D3 **Sarova** Rus. Fed.
Sarpan *i.* N. Mariana Is *see* **Rota**
105 D2 **Sarrebourg** France
106 B1 **Sarria** Spain
107 C1 **Sarrión** Spain
105 D3 **Sartène** France
Sartu China *see* **Daqing**
111 C3 **Saruhanlı** Turkey
103 D2 **Sárvár** Hungary
81 D3 **Sarvestān** Iran
76 B2 **Sarykamyshskoye Ozero** *salt l.* Turkm./Uzbek.
77 D2 **Saryozek** Kazakh.
77 D2 **Saryshagan** Kazakh.
77 C2 **Sarysu** *watercourse* Kazakh.
77 D3 **Sary-Tash** Kyrg.
75 C2 **Sasaram** India
67 A4 **Sasebo** Japan
129 D2 **Saskatchewan** *prov.* Can.
129 D2 **Saskatchewan** *r.* Can.
129 D2 **Saskatoon** Can.
83 I2 **Saskylakh** Rus. Fed.
123 C2 **Sasolburg** S. Africa
87 D3 **Sasovo** Rus. Fed.
114 B4 **Sassandra** Côte d'Ivoire
108 A2 **Sassari** Italy
102 C1 **Sassnitz** Ger.
114 A3 **Satadougou** Mali
136 C3 **Satanta** U.S.A.
73 B3 **Satara** India
123 D1 **Satara** S. Africa
87 E3 **Satka** Rus. Fed.
75 C2 **Satna** India
77 C2 **Satpayev** Kazakh.
74 B2 **Satpura Range** *mts* India
63 B2 **Sattahip** Thai.
110 B1 **Satu Mare** Romania
63 B3 **Satun** Thai.
144 B2 **Saucillo** Mex.
93 E4 **Sauda** Norway
92 □B2 **Sauðárkrókur** Iceland
78 D2 **Saudi Arabia** *country* Asia
105 C3 **Saugues** France
137 E1 **Sauk Center** U.S.A.
105 C2 **Saulieu** France
88 B2 **Saulkrasti** Latvia
130 B3 **Sault Sainte Marie** Can.
138 C1 **Sault Sainte Marie** U.S.A.
77 C1 **Saumalkol'** Kazakh.
59 C3 **Saumlakki** Indon.
104 B2 **Saumur** France
120 B1 **Saurimo** Angola
109 D2 **Sava** *r.* Europe
49 J5 **Savai'i** *i.* Samoa
91 E1 **Savala** *r.* Rus. Fed.
114 C4 **Savalou** Benin
141 D2 **Savannah** *GA* U.S.A.
140 C1 **Savannah** *TN* U.S.A.
141 D2 **Savannah** *r.* U.S.A.
63 B2 **Savannakhét** Laos
130 A2 **Savant Lake** Can.
111 C3 **Savaştepe** Turkey
114 C4 **Savè** Benin
105 D2 **Saverne** France
89 F2 **Savino** Rus. Fed.
86 D2 **Savinskiy** Rus. Fed.
Savoie *reg.* France *see* **Savoy**
108 A2 **Savona** Italy
93 I3 **Savonlinna** Fin.
105 D2 **Savoy** *reg.* France
93 F4 **Sävsjö** Sweden
59 C3 **Savu** *i.* Indon.
92 I2 **Savukoski** Fin.
Savu Sea *sea* Indon. *see* **Laut Sawu**
74 B2 **Sawai Madhopur** India
62 A1 **Sawan** Myanmar
62 A2 **Sawankhalok** Thai.
136 B3 **Sawatch Range** *mts* U.S.A.
Sawhāj Egypt *see* **Sūhāj**
121 B2 **Sawmills** Zimbabwe
79 C3 **Şawqirah, Dawḩat** *b.* Oman
Şawqirah Bay *b.* Oman *see* **Şawqirah, Dawḩat**
53 D2 **Sawtell** Austr.
134 C2 **Sawtooth Range** *mts* U.S.A.
68 C1 **Sayano-Shushenskoye Vodokhranilishche** *resr* Rus. Fed.
76 C3 **Saýat** Turkm.
79 C3 **Sayḩūt** Yemen
93 I3 **Säynätsalo** Fin.
69 D2 **Saynshand** Mongolia
139 D2 **Sayre** U.S.A.
144 B3 **Sayula** Mex.
145 C3 **Sayula** Mex.
128 B2 **Sayward** Can.
Sayyod Turkm. *see* **Saýat**
89 E2 **Sazonovo** Rus. Fed.
114 B2 **Sbaa** Alg.
98 B2 **Scafell Pike** *h.* U.K.
109 C3 **Scalea** Italy
96 □ **Scalloway** U.K.
108 B2 **Scandicci** Italy
96 C1 **Scapa Flow** *inlet* U.K.
96 B2 **Scarba** *i.* U.K.
130 C3 **Scarborough** Can.
147 D3 **Scarborough** Trin. and Tob.
98 C2 **Scarborough** U.K.
64 A2 **Scarborough Shoal** *sea feature* S. China Sea
96 A2 **Scarinish** U.K.
Scarpanto *i.* Greece *see* **Karpathos**
100 B2 **Schaerbeek** Belgium
105 D2 **Schaffhausen** Switz.
100 B1 **Schagen** Neth.
102 C2 **Schärding** Austria
100 A2 **Scharendijke** Neth.
101 D1 **Scharhörn** *i.* Ger.
101 D1 **Scheeßel** Ger.
131 D2 **Schefferville** Can.
135 D3 **Schell Creek Range** *mts* U.S.A.
139 E2 **Schenectady** U.S.A.
143 D3 **Schertz** U.S.A.
101 E3 **Scheßlitz** Ger.
100 C1 **Schiermonnikoog** *i.* Neth.
100 B2 **Schilde** Belgium
108 B1 **Schio** Italy
101 F2 **Schkeuditz** Ger.
101 E1 **Schladen** Ger.
102 C2 **Schladming** Austria
101 E2 **Schleiz** Ger.
102 B1 **Schleswig** Ger.
101 D2 **Schloss Holte-Stukenbrock** Ger.
101 D2 **Schlüchtern** Ger.
101 E3 **Schlüsselfeld** Ger.
101 F2 **Schmalkalden, Kurort** Ger.
101 D2 **Schmallenberg** Ger.
Schmidt Island *i.* Rus. Fed. *see* **Shmidta, Ostrov**
101 F2 **Schmölln** Ger.
101 D1 **Schneverdingen** Ger.
101 E1 **Schönebeck (Elbe)** Ger.
101 E1 **Schöningen** Ger.
100 B2 **Schoonhoven** Neth.
59 D3 **Schouten Islands** P.N.G.
97 B3 **Schull** Ireland
101 E3 **Schwabach** Ger.
102 B2 **Schwäbische Alb** *mts* Ger.
101 F3 **Schwandorf** Ger.
61 C2 **Schwaner, Pegunungan** *mts* Indon.
101 E1 **Schwarzenbek** Ger.
101 F2 **Schwarzenberg** Ger.
122 A2 **Schwarzrand** *mts* Namibia
Schwarzwald *mts* Ger. *see* **Black Forest**
102 C2 **Schwaz** Austria
102 C1 **Schwedt an der Oder** Ger.
101 E2 **Schweinfurt** Ger.
101 E1 **Schwerin** Ger.
101 E1 **Schweriner See** *l.* Ger.
105 D2 **Schwyz** Switz.
108 B3 **Sciacca** Italy
95 B4 **Scilly, Isles of** U.K.
138 C3 **Scioto** *r.* U.S.A.
136 B1 **Scobey** U.S.A.
53 D2 **Scone** Austr.
110 B2 **Scornicești** Romania
55 C3 **Scotia Ridge** S. Atlantic Ocean
149 F8 **Scotia Sea** S. Atlantic Ocean
96 C2 **Scotland** *admin. div.* U.K.
128 B2 **Scott, Cape** Can.
123 D3 **Scottburgh** S. Africa
136 C3 **Scott City** U.S.A.
136 C2 **Scottsbluff** U.S.A.
140 C2 **Scottsboro** U.S.A.
96 B1 **Scourie** U.K.
139 D2 **Scranton** U.S.A.
98 C3 **Scunthorpe** U.K.
105 E2 **Scuol** Switz.
Scutari Albania *see* **Shkodër**
99 D4 **Seaford** U.K.
98 C2 **Seaham** U.K.
129 E2 **Seal** *r.* Can.
122 B3 **Seal, Cape** S. Africa
52 B3 **Sea Lake** Austr.
143 D3 **Sealy** U.S.A.
140 B1 **Searcy** U.S.A.
98 B2 **Seascale** U.K.
134 B1 **Seattle** U.S.A.
139 E2 **Sebago Lake** U.S.A.
144 A2 **Sebastián Vizcaíno, Bahía** *b.* Mex.
Sebastopol Ukr. *see* **Sevastopol'**
Sebenico Croatia *see* **Šibenik**
110 B1 **Sebeş** Romania
60 B2 **Sebesi** *i.* Indon.
88 C2 **Sebezh** Rus. Fed.
80 B1 **Şebinkarahisar** Turkey
141 D3 **Sebring** U.S.A.
61 C2 **Sebuku** *i.* Indon.
128 B3 **Sechelt** Can.
150 A3 **Sechura** Peru
73 B3 **Secunderabad** India
137 E3 **Sedalia** U.S.A.
105 C2 **Sedan** France
54 B2 **Seddon** N.Z.
114 A3 **Sédhiou** Senegal
142 A2 **Sedona** U.S.A.
101 E2 **Seeburg** Ger.
101 E1 **Seehausen (Altmark)** Ger.
122 A2 **Seeheim** Namibia
104 C2 **Sées** France
101 E2 **Seesen** Ger.
101 E1 **Seevetal** Ger.
114 A4 **Sefadu** Sierra Leone
123 C1 **Sefare** Botswana
93 F3 **Segalstad** Norway
60 B1 **Segamat** Malaysia
86 C2 **Segezha** Rus. Fed.
114 B3 **Ségou** Mali
106 C1 **Segovia** Spain
86 C2 **Segozerskoye, Ozero** *resr* Rus. Fed.
115 D2 **Séguédine** Niger
114 B4 **Séguéla** Côte d'Ivoire
143 D3 **Seguin** U.S.A.
107 C2 **Segura** *r.* Spain
106 C2 **Segura, Sierra de** *mts* Spain
120 B3 **Sehithwa** Botswana
93 H3 **Seinäjoki** Fin.
104 C2 **Seine** *r.* France
104 B2 **Seine, Baie de** *b.* France
105 C2 **Seine, Val de** *val.* France
103 E1 **Sejny** Pol.
60 B2 **Sekayu** Indon.
114 B4 **Sekondi** Ghana
134 B1 **Selah** U.S.A.
59 C3 **Selaru** *i.* Indon.
61 C2 **Selatan, Tanjung** *pt* Indon.
126 B2 **Selawik** U.S.A.
98 C3 **Selby** U.K.
136 C1 **Selby** U.S.A.
111 C3 **Selçuk** Turkey
120 B3 **Selebi-Phikwe** Botswana
Selebi-Pikwe Botswana *see* **Selebi-Phikwe**
105 D2 **Sélestat** France
Seletyteniz, Oz. *salt l.* Kazakh. *see* **Siletiteniz, Ozero**
92 □A3 **Selfoss** Iceland
114 A3 **Sélibabi** Maur.
142 A1 **Seligman** U.S.A.
116 A2 **Selîma Oasis** Sudan
111 C3 **Selimiye** Turkey
114 B3 **Sélingué, Lac de** *l.* Mali
89 D2 **Selizharovo** Rus. Fed.
93 E4 **Seljord** Norway
129 E2 **Selkirk** Can.
96 C3 **Selkirk** U.K.
128 C2 **Selkirk Mountains** Can.
142 A2 **Sells** U.S.A.
140 C2 **Selma** *AL* U.S.A.
135 C3 **Selma** *CA* U.S.A.
105 D2 **Selongey** France
99 C4 **Selsey Bill** *hd* U.K.
89 D3 **Sel'tso** Rus. Fed.
Selukwe Zimbabwe *see* **Shurugwi**
150 B3 **Selvas** *reg.* Brazil
134 C1 **Selway** *r.* U.S.A.
129 D1 **Selwyn Lake** Can.
128 A1 **Selwyn Mountains** Can.
51 C2 **Selwyn Range** *hills* Austr.
60 B2 **Semangka, Teluk** *b.* Indon.
61 C2 **Semarang** Indon.
60 B1 **Sematan** Malaysia
118 B2 **Sembé** Congo
81 C2 **Şemdinli** Turkey
91 C1 **Semenivka** Ukr.
87 D3 **Semenov** Rus. Fed.
61 C2 **Semeru, Gunung** *vol.* Indon.
91 E2 **Semikarakorsk** Rus. Fed.
89 E3 **Semiluki** Rus. Fed.
136 B2 **Seminoe Reservoir** U.S.A.
143 C2 **Seminole** U.S.A.
141 D2 **Seminole, Lake** U.S.A.
77 E1 **Semipalatinsk** Kazakh.
61 C1 **Semitau** Indon.
Sem Kolodezey Ukr. *see* **Lenine**
81 D2 **Semnān** Iran
61 C1 **Semporna** Malaysia
105 C2 **Semur-en-Auxois** France
Semyonovskoye Rus. Fed. *see* **Bereznik**
Semyonovskoye Rus. Fed. *see* **Ostrovskoye**
150 C3 **Sena Madureira** Brazil
120 B2 **Senanga** Zambia
67 B4 **Sendai** Japan
67 D3 **Sendai** Japan
141 D2 **Seneca** U.S.A.
114 A3 **Senegal** *country* Africa
114 A3 **Sénégal** *r.* Maur./Senegal
102 C1 **Senftenberg** Ger.
119 D3 **Sengerema** Tanz.
151 E4 **Senhor do Bonfim** Brazil
103 D2 **Senica** Slovakia
108 B2 **Senigallia** Italy
109 B2 **Senj** Croatia
92 G2 **Senja** *i.* Norway
122 B2 **Senlac** S. Africa
105 C2 **Senlis** France
63 B2 **Senmonorom** Cambodia
116 B3 **Sennar** Sudan
130 C3 **Senneterre** Can.
123 C3 **Senqu** *r.* Lesotho
105 C2 **Sens** France
109 D1 **Senta** Serbia
128 B2 **Sentinel Peak** Can.
123 C1 **Senwabarwana** S. Africa
75 B2 **Seoni** India
65 B2 **Seoul** S. Korea
155 D2 **Sepetiba, Baía de** *b.* Brazil
59 D3 **Sepik** *r.* P.N.G.
61 C1 **Sepinang** Indon.
131 D2 **Sept-Îles** Can.
87 D4 **Serafimovich** Rus. Fed.
100 B2 **Seraing** Belgium
59 C3 **Seram** *i.* Indon.
60 B2 **Serang** Indon.
60 B1 **Serasan, Selat** *sea chan.* Indon.
109 D2 **Serbia** *country* Europe
76 D3 **Serdar** Turkm.
117 C3 **Serdo** Eth.
89 E3 **Serebryanyye Prudy** Rus. Fed.
60 B1 **Seremban** Malaysia
119 D3 **Serengeti Plain** Tanz.
121 C2 **Serenje** Zambia
90 B2 **Seret** *r.* Ukr.
87 D3 **Sergach** Rus. Fed.
86 F2 **Sergino** Rus. Fed.
89 E2 **Sergiyev Posad** Rus. Fed.
Sergo Ukr. *see* **Stakhanov**
74 A1 **Serhetabat** Turkm.
61 C1 **Seria** Brunei
61 C1 **Serian** Malaysia
111 B3 **Serifos** *i.* Greece
80 B2 **Serik** Turkey
59 C3 **Sermata, Kepulauan** *is* Indon.
Sernyy Zavod Turkm. *see* **Kükürtli**
86 F3 **Serov** Rus. Fed.
120 B3 **Serowe** Botswana
106 B2 **Serpa** Port.
Serpa Pinto Angola *see* **Menongue**
89 E3 **Serpukhov** Rus. Fed.
155 D2 **Serra** Brazil
155 C1 **Serra das Araras** Brazil
108 A3 **Serramanna** Italy
154 B1 **Serranópolis** Brazil
100 A3 **Serre** *r.* France
111 B2 **Serres** Greece
151 F4 **Serrinha** Brazil
155 D1 **Sêrro** Brazil
154 C2 **Sertãozinho** Brazil
59 D3 **Serui** Indon.
120 B3 **Serule** Botswana
61 C2 **Seruyan** *r.* Indon.
68 C2 **Sêrxü** China
120 A2 **Sesfontein** Namibia
108 B2 **Sessa Aurunca** Italy
108 A2 **Sestri Levante** Italy
105 C3 **Sète** France
155 D1 **Sete Lagoas** Brazil
92 G2 **Setermoen** Norway
93 E4 **Setesdal** *val.* Norway
115 C1 **Sétif** Alg.
67 B4 **Seto-naikai** *sea* Japan
114 B1 **Settat** Morocco
98 B2 **Settle** U.K.
106 B2 **Setúbal** Port.
106 B2 **Setúbal, Baía de** *b.* Port.
130 A2 **Seul, Lac** *l.* Can.
81 C1 **Sevan** Armenia
76 A2 **Sevan, Lake** Armenia
Sevana Lich *l.* Armenia *see* **Sevan, Lake**
91 C3 **Sevastopol'** Ukr.
Seven Islands Can. *see* **Sept-Îles**
131 D2 **Seven Islands Bay** Can.
99 D4 **Sevenoaks** U.K.
105 C3 **Sévérac-le-Château** France
130 B2 **Severn** *r.* Can.
122 B2 **Severn** S. Africa
99 B4 **Severn** *r.* U.K.
86 D2 **Severnaya Dvina** *r.* Rus. Fed.
83 H1 **Severnaya Zemlya** *is* Rus. Fed.
86 D2 **Severnyy** Rus. Fed.
86 F2 **Severnyy** Rus. Fed.
83 I3 **Severobaykal'sk** Rus. Fed.
86 C2 **Severodvinsk** Rus. Fed.
83 L3 **Severo-Kuril'sk** Rus. Fed.
92 J2 **Severomorsk** Rus. Fed.
86 C2 **Severoonezhsk** Rus. Fed.
83 H2 **Severo-Yeniseyskiy** Rus. Fed.
91 D3 **Severskaya** Rus. Fed.
135 D3 **Sevier** *r.* U.S.A.
135 D3 **Sevier Lake** U.S.A.
Sevilla Spain *see* **Seville**
106 B2 **Seville** Spain
Sevlyush Ukr. *see* **Vynohradiv**
89 D3 **Sevsk** Rus. Fed.
126 C2 **Seward** U.S.A.
126 B2 **Seward Peninsula** U.S.A.
128 A2 **Sewell Inlet** Can.
128 C2 **Sexsmith** Can.
144 B2 **Sextín** *r.* Mex.
86 G1 **Seyakha** Rus. Fed.
113 I6 **Seychelles** *country* Indian Ocean
92 □C2 **Seyðisfjörður** Iceland
Seyhan Turkey *see* **Adana**
80 B2 **Seyhan** *r.* Turkey
91 C1 **Seym** *r.* Rus. Fed./Ukr.

83 L2 **Seymchan** Rus. Fed.
53 C3 **Seymour** Austr.
123 C3 **Seymour** S. Africa
138 B3 **Seymour** *IN* U.S.A.
143 D2 **Seymour** *TX* U.S.A.
105 C2 **Sézanne** France
108 B2 **Sezze** Italy
110 C1 **Sfântu Gheorghe** Romania
115 D1 **Sfax** Tunisia
Sfîntu Gheorghe Romania *see* **Sfântu Gheorghe**
's-Gravenhage Neth. *see* **The Hague**
96 A2 **Sgurr Alasdair** *h.* U.K.
70 A2 **Shaanxi** *prov.* China
Shabani Zimbabwe *see* **Zvishavane**
91 D2 **Shabel'sk** Rus. Fed.
77 D3 **Shache** China
55 C1 **Shackleton Range** *mts* Antarctica
86 F3 **Shadrinsk** Rus. Fed.
99 B4 **Shaftesbury** U.K.
126 B2 **Shageluk** U.S.A.
Shāhābād Iran *see* **Eslāmābād-e Gharb**
74 A2 **Shahdad Kot** Pak.
75 C2 **Shahdol** India
77 C3 **Shah Fuladi** *mt.* Afgh.
75 B2 **Shahjahanpur** India
76 B3 **Shāh Kūh** *mt.* Iran
81 D2 **Shahr-e Bābak** Iran
81 D2 **Shahr-e Kord** Iran
81 D2 **Shāhrezā** Iran
77 C3 **Shahrisabz** Uzbek.
Shāhrūd Iran *see* **Emāmrūd**
79 B2 **Shaj'ah, Jabal** *h.* Saudi Arabia
89 E2 **Shakhovskaya** Rus. Fed.
Shakhterskoye Ukr. *see* **Pershotravens'k**
Shakhty Rus. Fed. *see* **Gusinoozersk**
91 E2 **Shakhty** Rus. Fed.
Shakhtyorskoye Ukr. *see* **Pershotravens'k**
86 D3 **Shakhun'ya** Rus. Fed.
114 C4 **Shaki** Nigeria
66 D2 **Shakotan-hantō** *pen.* Japan
66 D2 **Shakotan-misaki** *c.* Japan
76 B2 **Shalkar** Kazakh.
76 C2 **Shalkarteniz, Solonchak** *salt marsh* Kazakh.
68 C2 **Shaluli Shan** *mts* China
129 E2 **Shamattawa** Can.
143 C1 **Shamrock** U.S.A.
70 A2 **Shandan** China
70 B2 **Shandong** *prov.* China
70 C2 **Shandong Bandao** *pen.* China
121 B2 **Shangani** Zimbabwe
121 B2 **Shangani** *r.* Zimbabwe
70 B1 **Shangdu** China
70 C2 **Shanghai** China
70 C2 **Shanghai** *mun.* China
71 B3 **Shanghang** China
70 A2 **Shangluo** China
70 B2 **Shangnan** China
71 B3 **Shangrao** China
70 B2 **Shangshui** China
77 E2 **Shangyou Shuiku** *resr* China
70 C2 **Shangyu** China
69 E1 **Shangzhi** China
Shangzhou China *see* **Shangluo**
134 B1 **Shaniko** U.S.A.
97 B2 **Shannon** *r.* Ireland
97 B2 **Shannon, Mouth of the** Ireland
62 A1 **Shan Plateau** Myanmar
Shansi *prov.* China *see* **Shanxi**
71 B3 **Shantou** China
Shantung *prov.* China *see* **Shandong**
70 B2 **Shanxi** *prov.* China
71 B3 **Shaoguan** China
71 B3 **Shaowu** China
70 C2 **Shaoxing** China
71 B3 **Shaoyang** China
96 C1 **Shapinsay** *i.* U.K.
116 C2 **Shaqrā'** Saudi Arabia
74 A1 **Sharan** Afgh.
90 B2 **Sharhorod** Ukr.
79 C2 **Sharjah** U.A.E.
88 C2 **Sharkawshchyna** Belarus
50 A2 **Shark Bay** Austr.
78 A2 **Sharm ash Shaykh** Egypt
138 C2 **Sharon** U.S.A.
86 D3 **Shar'ya** Rus. Fed.
121 B3 **Shashe** *r.* Botswana/Zimbabwe
117 B4 **Shashemenē** Eth.
Shashi China *see* **Jingzhou**
134 B2 **Shasta, Mount** *vol.* U.S.A.
134 B2 **Shasta Lake** U.S.A.
115 D2 **Shāţi', Wādī ash** *watercourse* Libya
Shatilki Belarus *see* **Svyetlahorsk**
89 E2 **Shatura** Rus. Fed.
129 D3 **Shaunavon** Can.
138 B2 **Shawano** U.S.A.
130 C3 **Shawinigan** Can.
143 D1 **Shawnee** U.S.A.
83 M2 **Shayboveyem** *r.* Rus. Fed.
50 B2 **Shay Gap (abandoned)** Austr.
89 E3 **Shchekino** Rus. Fed.
89 E2 **Shchelkovo** Rus. Fed.
Shcherbakov Rus. Fed. *see* **Rybinsk**
Shcherbinovka Ukr. *see* **Dzerzhyns'k**
89 E3 **Shchigry** Rus. Fed.
91 C1 **Shchors** Ukr.
88 B3 **Shchuchyn** Belarus
91 D1 **Shebekino** Rus. Fed.
117 C4 **Shebelē Wenz, Wabē** *r.* Ethiopia/Somalia
77 C3 **Sheberghān** Afgh.
138 B2 **Sheboygan** U.S.A.
91 D3 **Shebsh** *r.* Rus. Fed.
97 C2 **Sheelin, Lough** *l.* Ireland
136 B3 **Sheep Mountain** U.S.A.
99 D4 **Sheerness** U.K.
98 C3 **Sheffield** U.K.
143 C2 **Sheffield** U.S.A.
Sheikh Othman Yemen *see* **Ash Shaykh 'Uthman**
Shekhem West Bank *see* **Nāblus**
89 E2 **Sheksna** Rus. Fed.
89 E2 **Sheksninskoye Vodokhranilishche** *resr* Rus. Fed.
83 M2 **Shelagskiy, Mys** *pt* Rus. Fed.
131 D3 **Shelburne** Can.
138 B2 **Shelby** *MI* U.S.A.
134 D1 **Shelby** *MT* U.S.A.
141 D1 **Shelby** *NC* U.S.A.
138 B3 **Shelbyville** *IN* U.S.A.
140 C1 **Shelbyville** *TN* U.S.A.
83 L2 **Shelikhova, Zaliv** *g.* Rus. Fed.
126 B3 **Shelikof Strait** U.S.A.
129 D2 **Shellbrook** Can.
Shelter Bay Can. *see* **Port-Cartier**
134 B1 **Shelton** U.S.A.
137 D2 **Shenandoah** U.S.A.
139 D3 **Shenandoah** *r.* U.S.A.
139 D3 **Shenandoah Mountains** U.S.A.
118 A2 **Shendam** Nigeria
Shengli Feng *mt.* China/Kyrg. *see* **Pobeda Peak**
86 D2 **Shenkursk** Rus. Fed.
70 B2 **Shenmu** China
Shensi *prov.* China *see* **Shaanxi**
70 C1 **Shenyang** China
71 B3 **Shenzhen** China
90 B1 **Shepetivka** Ukr.
53 C3 **Shepparton** Austr.
99 D4 **Sheppey, Isle of** *i.* U.K.
131 D3 **Sherbrooke** *N.S.* Can.
130 C3 **Sherbrooke** *Que.* Can.
97 C2 **Shercock** Ireland
116 B3 **Shereiq** Sudan
136 B2 **Sheridan** U.S.A.
52 A2 **Sheringa** Austr.
86 F2 **Sherkaly** Rus. Fed.
143 D2 **Sherman** U.S.A.
100 B2 **'s-Hertogenbosch** Neth.
96 □ **Shetland Islands** U.K.
76 B2 **Shetpe** Kazakh.
Shevchenko Kazakh. *see* **Aktau**
91 D2 **Shevchenkove** Ukr.
137 D1 **Sheyenne** *r.* U.S.A.
79 B3 **Shibām** Yemen
67 C3 **Shibata** Japan
66 D2 **Shibetsu** Japan
71 B3 **Shicheng** China
70 C2 **Shidao** China
96 B2 **Shiel, Loch** *l.* U.K.
Shigatse China *see* **Xigazê**
77 E2 **Shihezi** China
Shihkiachwang China *see* **Shijiazhuang**
Shijiao China *see* **Fogang**
70 B2 **Shijiazhuang** China
Shijiusuo China *see* **Rizhao**
74 A2 **Shikarpur** Pak.
67 B4 **Shikoku** *i.* Japan
66 D2 **Shikotsu-ko** *l.* Japan
86 D2 **Shilega** Rus. Fed.
75 C2 **Shiliguri** India
97 C2 **Shillelagh** Ireland
75 D2 **Shillong** India
89 F3 **Shilovo** Rus. Fed.
69 E1 **Shimanovsk** Rus. Fed.
117 C3 **Shimbiris** *mt.* Somalia
67 C3 **Shimizu** Japan
74 B1 **Shimla** India
67 C4 **Shimoda** Japan
73 B3 **Shimoga** India
66 D2 **Shimokita-hantō** *pen.* Japan
67 B4 **Shimonoseki** Japan
89 D2 **Shimsk** Rus. Fed.
96 B1 **Shin, Loch** *l.* U.K.
62 A1 **Shingbwiyang** Myanmar
67 C4 **Shingū** Japan
123 D1 **Shingwedzi** S. Africa
123 D1 **Shingwedzi** *r.* S. Africa
66 D3 **Shinjō** Japan
119 D3 **Shinyanga** Tanz.
67 D3 **Shiogama** Japan
67 C4 **Shiono-misaki** *c.* Japan
71 A3 **Shiping** China
98 C3 **Shipley** U.K.
142 B1 **Shiprock** U.S.A.
71 A3 **Shiqian** China
Shiqizhen China *see* **Zhongshan**
70 A2 **Shiquan** China
78 B2 **Shi'r, Jabal** *h.* Saudi Arabia
67 C3 **Shirane-san** *mt.* Japan
67 C3 **Shirane-san** *vol.* Japan
81 D3 **Shīrāz** Iran
66 D2 **Shiretoko-misaki** *c.* Japan
66 D2 **Shiriya-zaki** *c.* Japan
76 B3 **Shīrvān** Iran
74 B2 **Shiv** India
74 B2 **Shivpuri** India
70 B2 **Shiyan** China
70 A2 **Shizuishan** China
67 C4 **Shizuoka** Japan
89 D3 **Shklow** Belarus
109 C2 **Shkodër** Albania
83 H1 **Shmidta, Ostrov** *i.* Rus. Fed.
67 B4 **Shōbara** Japan
Sholapur India *see* **Solapur**
158 F8 **Shona Ridge** S. Atlantic Ocean
77 C3 **Sho'rchi** Uzbek.
74 B1 **Shorkot** Pak.
135 C3 **Shoshone** *CA* U.S.A.
134 D2 **Shoshone** *ID* U.S.A.
135 C3 **Shoshone Mountains** U.S.A.
123 C1 **Shoshong** Botswana
91 C1 **Shostka** Ukr.
70 B2 **Shouxian** China
78 A3 **Showak** Sudan
142 A2 **Show Low** U.S.A.
91 C2 **Shpola** Ukr.
140 B2 **Shreveport** U.S.A.
99 B3 **Shrewsbury** U.K.
77 D2 **Shu** Kazakh.
Shuangjiang China *see* **Tongdao**
62 A1 **Shuangjiang** China
Shuangxi China *see* **Shunchang**
66 B1 **Shuangyashan** China
87 E4 **Shubarkuduk** Kazakh.
116 B1 **Shubrā al Khaymah** Egypt
89 D2 **Shugozero** Rus. Fed.
Shuidong China *see* **Dianbai**
120 B2 **Shumba** Zimbabwe
110 C2 **Shumen** Bulg.
87 F3 **Shumikha** Rus. Fed.
88 C2 **Shumilina** Belarus
143 C3 **Shumla** U.S.A.
89 D3 **Shumyachi** Rus. Fed.
71 B3 **Shunchang** China
126 B2 **Shungnak** U.S.A.
78 B3 **Shuqrah** Yemen
121 C2 **Shurugwi** Zimbabwe
89 F2 **Shushkodom** Rus. Fed.
81 C2 **Shushtar** Iran
128 C2 **Shuswap Lake** Can.
89 F2 **Shuya** Rus. Fed.
89 F2 **Shuyskoye** Rus. Fed.
62 A1 **Shwebo** Myanmar
62 A1 **Shwedwin** Myanmar
62 A2 **Shwegun** Myanmar
62 A2 **Shwegyin** Myanmar
62 A1 **Shweli** *r.* Myanmar
77 C2 **Shymkent** Kazakh.
74 B1 **Shyok** *r.* India/Pak.
91 C2 **Shyroke** Ukr.
90 C2 **Shyryayeve** Ukr.
59 C3 **Sia** Indon.
74 A2 **Siahan Range** *mts* Pak.
74 B1 **Sialkot** Pak.
Siam *country* Asia *see* **Thailand**
Sian China *see* **Xi'an**
64 B3 **Siargao** *i.* Phil.
64 B3 **Siasi** Phil.
88 B2 **Šiauliai** Lith.
123 D1 **Sibasa** S. Africa
109 C2 **Šibenik** Croatia
83 G2 **Siberia** *reg.* Rus. Fed.
60 A2 **Siberut** *i.* Indon.
74 A2 **Sibi** Pak.
Sibir' *reg.* Rus. Fed. *see* **Siberia**
118 B3 **Sibiti** Congo
110 B1 **Sibiu** Romania
60 A1 **Sibolga** Indon.
62 A1 **Sibsagar** India
61 C1 **Sibu** Malaysia
118 B2 **Sibut** C.A.R.
64 A3 **Sibutu** *i.* Phil.
64 B2 **Sibuyan** *i.* Phil.
64 B2 **Sibuyan Sea** Phil.
128 C2 **Sicamous** Can.
63 A3 **Sichon** Thai.
70 A2 **Sichuan** *prov.* China
70 A3 **Sichuan Pendi** *basin* China
105 D3 **Sicié, Cap** *c.* France
Sicilia *i.* Italy *see* **Sicily**
108 B3 **Sicilian Channel** Italy/Tunisia
108 B3 **Sicily** *i.* Italy
150 B4 **Sicuani** Peru
111 C3 **Sideros, Akrotirio** *pt* Greece
122 B3 **Sidesaviwa** S. Africa
75 C2 **Sidhi** India
74 B2 **Sidhpur** India
107 D2 **Sidi Aïssa** Alg.
107 D2 **Sidi Ali** Alg.
114 B1 **Sidi Bel Abbès** Alg.
114 A2 **Sidi Ifni** Morocco
114 B1 **Sidi Kacem** Morocco
60 A1 **Sidikalang** Indon.
111 B2 **Sidirokastro** Greece
96 C2 **Sidlaw Hills** U.K.
99 B4 **Sidmouth** U.K.
134 B1 **Sidney** Can.
136 C1 **Sidney** *MT* U.S.A.
136 C2 **Sidney** *NE* U.S.A.
138 C2 **Sidney** *OH* U.S.A.
141 D2 **Sidney Lanier, Lake** U.S.A.
61 D1 **Sidoan** Indon.
80 B2 **Sidon** Lebanon
154 B2 **Sidrolândia** Brazil
103 E1 **Siedlce** Pol.
100 C2 **Sieg** *r.* Ger.
101 D2 **Siegen** Ger.
63 B2 **Siĕmréab** Cambodia
Siem Reap Cambodia *see* **Siĕmréab**
108 B2 **Siena** Italy
103 D1 **Sieradz** Pol.
142 B2 **Sierra Blanca** U.S.A.
153 B4 **Sierra Grande** Arg.
114 A4 **Sierra Leone** *country* Africa
158 E4 **Sierra Leone Basin** N. Atlantic Ocean
158 E4 **Sierra Leone Rise** N. Atlantic Ocean
144 B2 **Sierra Mojada** Mex.
142 A2 **Sierra Vista** U.S.A.
105 D2 **Sierre** Switz.
116 C3 **Sīfenī** Eth.
111 B3 **Sifnos** *i.* Greece
107 C2 **Sig** Alg.
127 I2 **Sigguup Nunaa** *pen.* Greenland
110 B1 **Sighetu Marmaţiei** Romania
110 B1 **Sighişoara** Romania
60 A1 **Sigli** Indon.
92 □B2 **Siglufjörður** Iceland
102 B2 **Sigmaringen** Ger.
100 B3 **Signy-l'Abbaye** France
106 C1 **Sigüenza** Spain
114 B3 **Siguiri** Guinea
88 B2 **Sigulda** Latvia
63 B2 **Sihanoukville** Cambodia
92 I3 **Siilinjärvi** Fin.
81 C2 **Siirt** Turkey
60 B2 **Sijunjung** Indon.
74 B2 **Sikar** India
74 A1 **Sikaram** *mt.* Afgh.
114 B3 **Sikasso** Mali
137 F3 **Sikeston** U.S.A.
66 B2 **Sikhote-Alin'** *mts* Rus. Fed.
111 C3 **Sikinos** *i.* Greece
103 D2 **Siklós** Hungary
65 A2 **Sikuaishi** China
88 B2 **Šilalė** Lith.
144 B2 **Silao** Mex.
101 D1 **Silberberg** *h.* Ger.
75 D2 **Silchar** India
77 D1 **Siletiteniz, Ozero** *salt l.* Kazakh.
75 C2 **Silgarhi** Nepal
80 B2 **Silifke** Turkey
75 C1 **Siling Co** *salt l.* China
110 C2 **Silistra** Bulg.
111 C2 **Silivri** Turkey
93 F3 **Siljan** *l.* Sweden
93 E4 **Silkeborg** Denmark
88 C2 **Sillamäe** Estonia
98 B2 **Silloth** U.K.
140 B1 **Siloam Springs** U.S.A.
123 D2 **Silobela** S. Africa
60 B1 **Siluas** Indon.
88 B2 **Šilutė** Lith.
81 C2 **Silvan** Turkey
154 C1 **Silvânia** Brazil
74 B2 **Silvassa** India
137 E1 **Silver Bay** U.S.A.
142 B2 **Silver City** U.S.A.
136 B3 **Silverton** U.S.A.
62 B1 **Simao** China
130 C3 **Simard, Lac** *l.* Can.
111 C3 **Simav** Turkey
111 C3 **Simav Dağları** *mts* Turkey
118 C2 **Simba** Dem. Rep. Congo
138 C2 **Simcoe** Can.
139 D2 **Simcoe, Lake** Can.
78 A3 **Simēn** Eth.
60 A1 **Simeulue** *i.* Indon.
91 C3 **Simferopol'** Ukr.
75 C2 **Simikot** Nepal
135 C4 **Simi Valley** U.S.A.
Simla India *see* **Shimla**
110 B1 **Şimleu Silvaniei** Romania
100 C3 **Simmern (Hunsrück)** Ger.
92 I2 **Simo** Fin.
129 D2 **Simonhouse** Can.
60 B2 **Simpang** Indon.
51 C2 **Simpson Desert** Austr.
93 F4 **Simrishamn** Sweden
60 A1 **Sinabang** Indon.
116 B2 **Sinai** *pen.* Egypt
105 E3 **Sinalunga** Italy
71 A3 **Sinan** China
65 B2 **Sinanju** N. Korea
62 A1 **Sinbo** Myanmar
62 A1 **Sinbyugyun** Myanmar
150 B2 **Sincelejo** Col.
60 B2 **Sindangbarang** Indon.
111 C3 **Sındırgı** Turkey
86 E2 **Sindor** Rus. Fed.
111 C2 **Sinekçi** Turkey
106 B2 **Sines** Port.
106 B2 **Sines, Cabo de** *c.* Port.
116 B3 **Singa** Sudan
75 C2 **Singahi** India
60 B1 **Singapore** *country* Asia
61 C2 **Singaraja** Indon.
63 B2 **Sing Buri** Thai.
119 D3 **Singida** Tanz.
62 A1 **Singkaling Hkamti** Myanmar
61 D2 **Singkang** Indon.
60 B1 **Singkawang** Indon.
60 B2 **Singkep** *i.* Indon.
60 A1 **Singkil** Indon.
53 D2 **Singleton** Austr.
Sin'gosan N. Korea *see* **Kosan**
62 A1 **Singu** Myanmar
Sining China *see* **Xining**
108 A2 **Siniscola** Italy
109 C2 **Sinj** Croatia
61 D2 **Sinjai** Indon.
116 B3 **Sinkat** Sudan
151 D2 **Sinnamary** Fr. Guiana
Sînnicolau Mare Romania *see* **Sânnicolau Mare**
Sinoia Zimbabwe *see* **Chinhoyi**
80 B1 **Sinop** Turkey
65 B1 **Sinp'o** N. Korea
61 C1 **Sintang** Indon.
100 B2 **Sint Anthonis** Neth.

100 A2 **Sint-Laureins** Belgium
147 D3 **Sint Maarten** *i.* Neth. Antilles
100 B2 **Sint-Niklaas** Belgium
143 D3 **Sinton** U.S.A.
65 A1 **Sinŭiju** N. Korea
64 B3 **Siocon** Phil.
103 D2 **Siófok** Hungary
105 D2 **Sion** Switz.
137 D2 **Sioux Center** U.S.A.
137 D2 **Sioux City** U.S.A.
137 D2 **Sioux Falls** U.S.A.
130 A2 **Sioux Lookout** Can.
65 A1 **Siping** China
129 E2 **Sipiwesk Lake** Can.
55 P2 **Siple, Mount** Antarctica
55 P2 **Siple Island** Antarctica
Sipolilo Zimbabwe *see* **Guruve**
60 A2 **Sipura** *i.* Indon.
64 B3 **Siquijor** Phil.
93 E4 **Sira** *r.* Norway
Siracusa Italy *see* **Syracuse**
51 C1 **Sir Edward Pellew Group** *is* Austr.
110 C1 **Siret** Romania
110 C1 **Siret** *r.* Romania
78 A1 **Sirhān, Wādī an** *watercourse* Saudi Arabia
79 C2 **Sīrīk** Iran
61 C1 **Sirik, Tanjung** *pt* Malaysia
62 B2 **Siri Kit, Khuan** Thai.
128 B1 **Sir James MacBrien, Mount** Can.
79 C2 **Sīrjān** Iran
81 C2 **Şırnak** Turkey
74 B2 **Sirohi** India
60 A1 **Sirombu** Indon.
74 B2 **Sirsa** India
115 D1 **Sirte** Libya
115 D1 **Sirte, Gulf of** Libya
88 B2 **Širvintos** Lith.
109 C1 **Sisak** Croatia
63 B2 **Sisaket** Thai.
145 C2 **Sisal** Mex.
122 B2 **Sishen** S. Africa
81 C2 **Sisian** Armenia
127 I2 **Sisimiut** Greenland
129 D2 **Sisipuk Lake** Can.
63 B2 **Sisŏphŏn** Cambodia
105 D3 **Sisteron** France
Sitang China *see* **Sinan**
[illegible] **Sitapur** India
111 C3 **Siteia** Greece
123 D2 **Siteki** Swaziland
128 A2 **Sitka** U.S.A.
100 B2 **Sittard** Neth.
62 A1 **Sittaung** Myanmar
62 A2 **Sittaung** *r.* Myanmar
62 A1 **Sittwe** Myanmar
61 C2 **Situbondo** Indon.
80 B2 **Sivas** Turkey
111 C3 **Sivaslı** Turkey
80 B2 **Siverek** Turkey
88 D2 **Siverskiy** Rus. Fed.
80 B2 **Sivrihisar** Turkey
116 A2 **Sīwah** Egypt
75 B1 **Siwalik Range** *mts* India/Nepal
Siwa Oasis *oasis* Egypt *see* **Wāḥāt Sīwah**
105 D3 **Six-Fours-les-Plages** France
70 B2 **Sixian** China
123 C2 **Siyabuswa** S. Africa
Sjælland *i.* Denmark *see* **Zealand**
109 D2 **Sjenica** Serbia
92 G2 **Sjøvegan** Norway
91 C2 **Skadovs'k** Ukr.
93 F4 **Skagen** Denmark
93 E4 **Skagerrak** *str.* Denmark/Norway
134 B1 **Skagit** *r.* U.S.A.
128 A2 **Skagway** U.S.A.
92 G2 **Skaland** Norway
93 F4 **Skara** Sweden
74 B1 **Skardu** Pak.
103 E1 **Skarżysko-Kamienna** Pol.
103 D2 **Skawina** Pol.
114 A2 **Skaymat** Western Sahara
128 B2 **Skeena** *r.* Can.
128 B2 **Skeena Mountains** Can.
98 D3 **Skegness** U.K.
92 H3 **Skellefteå** Sweden
92 H3 **Skellefteälven** *r.* Sweden
97 C2 **Skerries** Ireland
93 F4 **Ski** Norway
111 B3 **Skiathos** *i.* Greece
97 B3 **Skibbereen** Ireland
92 □B2 **Skíðadals-jökull** *glacier* Iceland
98 B2 **Skiddaw** *h.* U.K.
93 E4 **Skien** Norway
103 E1 **Skierniewice** Pol.
115 C1 **Skikda** Alg.
52 B3 **Skipton** Austr.
98 B3 **Skipton** U.K.
93 E4 **Skive** Denmark
92 H1 **Skjervøy** Norway
Skobelev Uzbek. *see* **Farg'ona**
111 B3 **Skopelos** *i.* Greece
89 E3 **Skopin** Rus. Fed.
111 B2 **Skopje** Macedonia
111 C3 **Skoutaros** Greece
93 F4 **Skövde** Sweden
83 J3 **Skovorodino** Rus. Fed.
139 F2 **Skowhegan** U.S.A.
92 H2 **Skröven** Sweden
88 B2 **Skrunda** Latvia
128 A1 **Skukum, Mount** Can.
123 D1 **Skukuza** S. Africa
88 B2 **Skuodas** Lith.
90 B2 **Skvyra** Ukr.
96 A2 **Skye** *i.* U.K.
111 B3 **Skyros** Greece
111 B3 **Skyros** *i.* Greece
93 F4 **Slagelse** Denmark
60 B2 **Slamet, Gunung** *vol.* Indon.
97 C2 **Slaney** *r.* Ireland
88 C2 **Slantsy** Rus. Fed.
109 C1 **Slatina** Croatia
110 B2 **Slatina** Romania
143 C2 **Slaton** U.S.A.
129 C1 **Slave** *r.* Can.
114 C4 **Slave Coast** Africa
128 C2 **Slave Lake** Can.
77 D1 **Slavgorod** Rus. Fed.
88 C2 **Slavkovichi** Rus. Fed.
Slavonska Požega Croatia *see* **Požega**
109 C1 **Slavonski Brod** Croatia
90 B1 **Slavuta** Ukr.
90 C1 **Slavutych** Ukr.
66 B2 **Slavyanka** Rus. Fed.
Slavyanskaya Rus. Fed. *see* **Slavyansk-na-Kubani**
91 D2 **Slavyansk-na-Kubani** Rus. Fed.
89 D3 **Slawharad** Belarus
103 D1 **Sławno** Pol.
99 C3 **Sleaford** U.K.
97 A2 **Slea Head** *hd* Ireland
130 C2 **Sleeper Islands** Can.
97 D1 **Slieve Donard** *h.* U.K.
96 A2 **Sligachan** U.K.
Slieve Gamph *hills* Ireland *see* **Ox Mountains**
Sligeach Ireland *see* **Sligo**
97 B1 **Sligo** Ireland
97 B1 **Sligo Bay** Ireland
93 G4 **Slite** Sweden
110 C2 **Sliven** Bulg.
Sloboda Rus. Fed. *see* **Ezhva**
110 C2 **Slobozia** Romania
128 C3 **Slocan** Can.
88 C3 **Slonim** Belarus
100 B1 **Sloten** Neth.
99 C4 **Slough** U.K.
103 D2 **Slovakia** *country* Europe
108 B1 **Slovenia** *country* Europe
91 D2 **Slov''yans'k** Ukr.
102 C1 **Słubice** Pol.
90 B1 **Sluch** *r.* Ukr.
100 A2 **Sluis** Neth.
103 D1 **Słupsk** Pol.
88 C3 **Slutsk** Belarus
97 A2 **Slyne Head** *hd* Ireland
68 C1 **Slyudyanka** Rus. Fed.
131 D2 **Smallwood Reservoir** Can.
88 C3 **Smalyavichy** Belarus
88 C3 **Smarhon'** Belarus
129 D2 **Smeaton** Can.
109 D2 **Smederevo** Serbia
109 D2 **Smederevska Palanka** Serbia
91 C2 **Smila** Ukr.
88 C3 **Smilavichy** Belarus
88 C2 **Smiltene** Latvia
137 D3 **Smith Center** U.S.A.
128 B2 **Smithers** Can.
141 E1 **Smithfield** *NC* U.S.A.
134 D2 **Smithfield** *UT* U.S.A.
139 D3 **Smith Mountain Lake** U.S.A.
130 C3 **Smiths Falls** Can.
53 D2 **Smithtown** Austr.
53 D2 **Smoky Cape** Austr.
137 D3 **Smoky Hills** U.S.A.
92 E3 **Smøla** *i.* Norway
89 D3 **Smolensk** Rus. Fed.
89 D3 **Smolensko-Moskovskaya Vozvyshennost'** *hills* Belarus/Rus. Fed.
111 B2 **Smolyan** Bulg.
66 B2 **Smolyoninovo** Rus. Fed.
130 B3 **Smooth Rock Falls** Can.
Smyrna Turkey *see* **İzmir**
91 D2 **Smyrnove** Ukr.
92 □B3 **Snæfell** *mt.* Iceland
98 A2 **Snaefell** *h.* Isle of Man
128 A1 **Snag (abandoned)** Can.
134 C1 **Snake** *r.* U.S.A.
134 D2 **Snake River Plain** U.S.A.
Snare Lakes Can. *see* **Wekweêtì**
92 F3 **Snåsvatn** *l.* Norway
100 B1 **Sneek** Neth.
97 B3 **Sneem** Ireland
122 B3 **Sneeuberge** *mts* S. Africa
Snegurovka Ukr. *see* **Tetiyiv**
103 D1 **Sněžka** *mt.* Czech Rep.
108 B1 **Snežnik** *mt.* Slovenia
103 E1 **Śniardwy, Jezioro** *l.* Pol.
Sniečkus Lith. *see* **Visaginas**
91 C2 **Snihurivka** Ukr.
93 E3 **Snøhetta** *mt.* Norway
Snovsk Ukr. *see* **Shchors**
129 D1 **Snowbird Lake** Can.
99 A3 **Snowdon** *mt.* U.K.
Snowdrift Can. *see* **Łutselk'e**
129 C1 **Snowdrift** *r.* Can.
142 A2 **Snowflake** U.S.A.
129 D2 **Snow Lake** Can.
134 C1 **Snowshoe Peak** U.S.A.
52 A2 **Snowtown** Austr.
53 C3 **Snowy** *r.* Austr.
53 C3 **Snowy Mountains** Austr.
143 C2 **Snyder** U.S.A.
121 □D2 **Soalala** Madag.
121 □D2 **Soanierana-Ivongo** Madag.
90 B2 **Sob** *r.* Ukr.
65 B2 **Sobaek-sanmaek** *mts* S. Korea
117 B4 **Sobat** *r.* Sudan
89 F2 **Sobinka** Rus. Fed.
151 E4 **Sobradinho, Barragem de** *resr* Brazil
151 E3 **Sobral** Brazil
91 D3 **Sochi** Rus. Fed.
65 B2 **Sŏch'ŏn** S. Korea
49 L5 **Society Islands** Fr. Polynesia
150 B2 **Socorro** Col.
142 B2 **Socorro** *NM* U.S.A.
142 B2 **Socorro** *TX* U.S.A.
144 A3 **Socorro, Isla** *i.* Mex.
56 B4 **Socotra** *i.* Yemen
63 B3 **Soc Trăng** Vietnam
106 C2 **Socuéllamos** Spain
92 I2 **Sodankylä** Fin.
134 D2 **Soda Springs** U.S.A.
93 G3 **Söderhamn** Sweden
93 G4 **Södertälje** Sweden
116 A3 **Sodiri** Sudan
117 B4 **Sodo** Eth.
93 G3 **Södra Kvarken** *str.* Fin./Sweden
123 C1 **Soekmekaar** S. Africa
Soerabaia Indon. *see* **Surabaya**
101 D2 **Soest** Ger.
53 C2 **Sofala** Austr.
110 B2 **Sofia** Bulg.
121 □D2 **Sofia** *r.* Madag.
Sofiya Bulg. *see* **Sofia**
Sofiyevka Ukr. *see* **Vil'nyans'k**
75 D1 **Sog** China
93 E3 **Sognefjorden** *inlet* Norway
111 D2 **Söğüt** Turkey
Sohâg Egypt *see* **Sūhāj**
Sohar Oman *see* **Şuḩār**
100 B2 **Soignies** Belgium
105 C2 **Soissons** France
90 A1 **Sokal'** Ukr.
65 B2 **Sokch'o** S. Korea
111 C3 **Söke** Turkey
81 C1 **Sokhumi** Georgia
114 C4 **Sokodé** Togo
89 F2 **Sokol** Rus. Fed.
101 F2 **Sokolov** Czech Rep.
115 C3 **Sokoto** Nigeria
115 C3 **Sokoto** *r.* Nigeria
90 B2 **Sokyryany** Ukr.
73 B3 **Solapur** India
135 B3 **Soledad** U.S.A.
89 F2 **Soligalich** Rus. Fed.
99 C3 **Solihull** U.K.
86 E3 **Solikamsk** Rus. Fed.
87 E3 **Sol'-Iletsk** Rus. Fed.
100 C2 **Solingen** Ger.
122 A1 **Solitaire** Namibia
92 G3 **Sollefteå** Sweden
93 G4 **Sollentuna** Sweden
107 D2 **Sóller** Spain
101 D2 **Solling** *hills* Ger.
89 E2 **Solnechnogorsk** Rus. Fed.
60 B2 **Solok** Indon.
48 H4 **Solomon Islands** *country* S. Pacific Ocean
48 G4 **Solomon Sea** S. Pacific Ocean
61 D2 **Solor, Kepulauan** *is* Indon.
105 D2 **Solothurn** Switz.
81 D2 **Solṭānābād** Iran
101 D1 **Soltau** Ger.
89 D2 **Sol'tsy** Rus. Fed.
96 C3 **Solway Firth** *est.* U.K.
120 B2 **Solwezi** Zambia
111 C3 **Soma** Turkey
117 C4 **Somalia** *country* Africa
120 B1 **Sombo** Angola
109 C1 **Sombor** Serbia
144 B2 **Sombrerete** Mex.
138 C3 **Somerset** U.S.A.
123 C3 **Somerset East** S. Africa
126 F2 **Somerset Island** Can.
122 A3 **Somerset West** S. Africa
110 B1 **Someş** *r.* Romania
101 E2 **Sömmerda** Ger.
146 B3 **Somoto** Nic.
75 C2 **Son** *r.* India
65 C1 **Sŏnbong** N. Korea
93 E5 **Sønderborg** Denmark
101 E2 **Sondershausen** Ger.
Søndre Strømfjord *inlet* Greenland *see* **Kangerlussuaq**
108 A1 **Sondrio** Italy
63 B2 **Sông Câu** Vietnam
62 B1 **Sông Đa, Hô** *resr* Vietnam
119 D4 **Songea** Tanz.
65 B1 **Sŏnggan** N. Korea
65 B1 **Songhua Hu** *resr* China
65 B1 **Songjianghe** China
Sŏngjin N. Korea *see* **Kimch'aek**
63 B3 **Songkhla** Thai.
65 B2 **Sŏngnam** S. Korea
65 B2 **Songnim** N. Korea
120 A1 **Songo** Angola
121 C2 **Songo** Moz.
Songololo Dem. Rep. Congo *see* **Mbanza-Ngungu**
69 E1 **Songyuan** China
Sonid Youqi China *see* **Saihan Tal**
74 B2 **Sonipat** India
89 E2 **Sonkovo** Rus. Fed.
62 B1 **Sơn La** Vietnam
74 A2 **Sonmiani** Pak.
74 A2 **Sonmiani Bay** Pak.
101 E2 **Sonneberg** Ger.
142 A2 **Sonoita** Mex.
144 A2 **Sonora** *r.* Mex.
135 B3 **Sonora** *CA* U.S.A.
143 C2 **Sonora** *TX* U.S.A.
146 B3 **Sonsonate** El Salvador
Soochow China *see* **Suzhou**
117 A4 **Sopo** *watercourse* Sudan
103 D2 **Sopron** Hungary
74 B1 **Sopur** India
108 B2 **Sora** Italy
130 C3 **Sorel** Can.
51 D4 **Sorell** Austr.
106 C1 **Soria** Spain
90 B2 **Soroca** Moldova
154 C2 **Sorocaba** Brazil
87 E3 **Sorochinsk** Rus. Fed.
Soroki Moldova *see* **Soroca**
59 D2 **Sorol** *atoll* Micronesia
59 C3 **Sorong** Indon.
119 D2 **Soroti** Uganda
92 H1 **Sørøya** *i.* Norway
108 B2 **Sorrento** Italy
92 G2 **Sorsele** Sweden
64 B2 **Sorsogon** Phil.
86 C2 **Sortavala** Rus. Fed.
92 G2 **Sortland** Norway
65 B2 **Sŏsan** S. Korea
123 C2 **Soshanguve** S. Africa
89 E3 **Sosna** *r.* Rus. Fed.
153 B3 **Sosneado** *mt.* Arg.
86 E2 **Sosnogorsk** Rus. Fed.
86 D2 **Sosnovka** Rus. Fed.
88 C2 **Sosnovyy Bor** Rus. Fed.
103 D1 **Sosnowiec** Pol.
91 C1 **Sosnytsya** Ukr.
86 F3 **Sos'va** Rus. Fed.
91 D2 **Sosyka** *r.* Rus. Fed.
145 C2 **Soto la Marina** Mex.
118 B2 **Souanké** Congo
111 B3 **Souda** Greece
104 C3 **Souillac** France
Sŏul S. Korea *see* **Seoul**
104 B2 **Soulac-sur-Mer** France
104 D3 **Soulom** France
Soûr Lebanon *see* **Tyre**
107 D2 **Sour el Ghozlane** Alg.
129 D3 **Souris** Man. Can.
131 D3 **Souris** P.E.I. Can.
129 E3 **Souris** *r.* Can.
151 F3 **Sousa** Brazil
115 D1 **Sousse** Tunisia
104 B3 **Soustons** France
122 B3 **South Africa, Republic of** *country* Africa
99 C4 **Southampton** U.K.
129 F1 **Southampton, Cape** Can.
129 F1 **Southampton Island** Can.
73 D3 **South Andaman** *i.* India
52 A1 **South Australia** *state* Austr.
140 B2 **Southaven** U.S.A.
142 B2 **South Baldy** *mt.* U.S.A.
130 B3 **South Baymouth** Can.
138 B2 **South Bend** U.S.A.
141 D2 **South Carolina** *state* U.S.A.
58 B2 **South China Sea** N. Pacific Ocean
South Coast Town Austr. *see* **Gold Coast**
136 C2 **South Dakota** *state* U.S.A.
99 C4 **South Downs** *hills* U.K.
159 E6 **Southeast Indian Ridge** Indian Ocean
55 O2 **Southeast Pacific Basin** S. Pacific Ocean
129 D2 **Southend** Can.
99 D4 **Southend-on-Sea** U.K.
54 B2 **Southern Alps** *mts* N.Z.
50 A3 **Southern Cross** Austr.
129 E2 **Southern Indian Lake** Can.
159 D7 **Southern Ocean**
141 E1 **Southern Pines** U.S.A.
Southern Rhodesia *country* Africa *see* **Zimbabwe**
96 B3 **Southern Uplands** *hills* U.K.
55 J2 **South Geomagnetic Pole (2008)** Antarctica
149 G8 **South Georgia** *terr.* S. Atlantic Ocean
149 G8 **South Georgia and the South Sandwich Islands** *terr.* S. Atlantic Ocean
138 B2 **South Haven** U.S.A.
129 E1 **South Henik Lake** Can.
119 D2 **South Horr** Kenya
54 B2 **South Island** N.Z.
65 B2 **South Korea** *country* Asia
135 B3 **South Lake Tahoe** U.S.A.
55 L3 **South Magnetic Pole (2008)** Antarctica
149 F9 **South Orkney Islands** S. Atlantic Ocean
136 C2 **South Platte** *r.* U.S.A.
98 B3 **Southport** U.K.
141 E2 **Southport** U.S.A.
130 C3 **South River** Can.
96 C1 **South Ronaldsay** *i.* U.K.
123 D3 **South Sand Bluff** *pt* S. Africa
149 H8 **South Sandwich Islands** S. Atlantic Ocean
55 C4 **South Sandwich Trench** S. Atlantic Ocean
129 D2 **South Saskatchewan** *r.* Can.
129 E2 **South Seal** *r.* Can.
149 E9 **South Shetland Islands** Antarctica
98 C2 **South Shields** U.K.
54 B1 **South Taranaki Bight** *b.* N.Z.
156 C8 **South Tasman Rise** Southern Ocean

130 C2 **South Twin Island** Can.
96 A2 **South Uist** *i.* U.K.
South-West Africa *country* Africa *see* **Namibia**
Southwest Peru Ridge S. Pacific Ocean *see* **Nazca Ridge**
53 D2 **South West Rocks** Austr.
99 D3 **Southwold** U.K.
109 C3 **Soverato** Italy
88 B2 **Sovetsk** Rus. Fed.
86 F2 **Sovetskiy** Rus. Fed.
91 C2 **Sovyets'kyy** Ukr.
123 C2 **Soweto** S. Africa
66 D1 **Sōya-misaki** *c.* Japan
65 B2 **Soyang-ho** *l.* S. Korea
104 C2 **Soyaux** France
90 C1 **Sozh** *r.* Europe
110 C2 **Sozopol** Bulg.
100 B2 **Spa** Belgium
106 C1 **Spain** *country* Europe
Spalato Croatia *see* **Split**
99 C3 **Spalding** U.K.
135 D2 **Spanish Fork** U.S.A.
Spanish Guinea *country* Africa *see* **Equatorial Guinea**
97 B2 **Spanish Point** Ireland
Spanish Sahara *terr.* Africa *see* **Western Sahara**
146 C3 **Spanish Town** Jamaica
108 B3 **Sparagio, Monte** *mt.* Italy
135 C3 **Sparks** U.S.A.
138 A2 **Sparta** U.S.A.
141 D2 **Spartanburg** U.S.A.
111 B3 **Sparti** Greece
109 C3 **Spartivento, Capo** *c.* Italy
89 D3 **Spas-Demensk** Rus. Fed.
89 F2 **Spas-Klepiki** Rus. Fed.
66 B2 **Spassk-Dal'niy** Rus. Fed.
89 F3 **Spassk-Ryazanskiy** Rus. Fed.
111 B3 **Spatha, Akrotirio** *pt* Greece
96 B2 **Spean Bridge** U.K.
136 C2 **Spearfish** U.S.A.
143 C1 **Spearman** U.S.A.
Spence Bay Can. *see* **Taloyoak**
137 D2 **Spencer** *IA* U.S.A.
134 D2 **Spencer** *ID* U.S.A.
52 A2 **Spencer Gulf** *est.* Austr.
98 C2 **Spennymoor** U.K.
54 B2 **Spenser Mountains** N.Z.
101 D3 **Spessart** *reg.* Ger.
96 C2 **Spey** *r.* U.K.
101 D3 **Speyer** Ger.
100 C1 **Spiekeroog** *i.* Ger.
100 B2 **Spijkenisse** Neth.
100 B3 **Spincourt** France
128 C2 **Spirit River** Can.
103 E2 **Spišská Nová Ves** Slovakia
82 C1 **Spitsbergen** *i.* Svalbard
102 C2 **Spittal an der Drau** Austria
93 E3 **Spjelkavik** Norway
109 C2 **Split** Croatia
129 E2 **Split Lake** Can.
129 E2 **Split Lake** *l.* Can.
134 C1 **Spokane** U.S.A.
138 A1 **Spooner** U.S.A.
102 C1 **Spree** *r.* Ger.
122 A2 **Springbok** S. Africa
131 E3 **Springdale** Can.
140 B1 **Springdale** U.S.A.
101 D1 **Springe** Ger.
142 C1 **Springer** U.S.A.
142 B2 **Springerville** U.S.A.
136 C3 **Springfield** *CO* U.S.A.
138 B3 **Springfield** *IL* U.S.A.
139 E2 **Springfield** *MA* U.S.A.
137 E3 **Springfield** *MO* U.S.A.
138 C3 **Springfield** *OH* U.S.A.
134 B2 **Springfield** *OR* U.S.A.
140 C1 **Springfield** *TN* U.S.A.
123 C3 **Springfontein** S. Africa
131 D3 **Springhill** Can.
141 D3 **Spring Hill** U.S.A.
54 B2 **Springs Junction** N.Z.
51 D2 **Springsure** Austr.
135 D2 **Springville** U.S.A.
98 D3 **Spurn Head** *hd* U.K.
128 B3 **Squamish** Can.
109 C3 **Squillace, Golfo di** *g.* Italy
Srbija *country* Europe *see* **Serbia**
108 C2 **Srebrenica** Bos.-Herz.
110 C2 **Sredets** Bulg.
83 L3 **Sredinnyy Khrebet** *mts* Rus. Fed.
83 L2 **Srednekolymsk** Rus. Fed.
Sredne-Russkaya Vozvyshennost' *hills* Rus. Fed. *see* **Central Russian Upland**
Sredne-Sibirskoye Ploskogor'ye *plat.* Rus. Fed. *see* **Central Siberian Plateau**
110 B2 **Srednogorie** Bulg.
69 D1 **Sretensk** Rus. Fed.
61 C1 **Sri Aman** Malaysia
73 B4 **Sri Jayewardenepura Kotte** Sri Lanka
73 C3 **Srikakulam** India
73 C4 **Sri Lanka** *country* Asia
74 B1 **Srinagar** India
73 B3 **Srivardhan** India
101 D1 **Stade** Ger.
101 E1 **Stadensen** Ger.
100 C1 **Stadskanaal** Neth.
101 D2 **Stadtallendorf** Ger.
101 D1 **Stadthagen** Ger.
101 E2 **Staffelstein** Ger.
99 B3 **Stafford** U.K.
99 C4 **Staines** U.K.
91 D2 **Stakhanov** Ukr.
Stakhanovo Rus. Fed. *see* **Zhukovskiy**
Stalin Bulg. *see* **Varna**
Stalinabad Tajik. *see* **Dushanbe**
Stalingrad Rus. Fed. *see* **Volgograd**
Staliniri Georgia *see* **Ts'khinvali**
Stalino Ukr. *see* **Donets'k**
Stalinogorsk Rus. Fed. *see* **Novomoskovsk**
Stalinogród Pol. *see* **Katowice**
Stalinsk Rus. Fed. *see* **Novokuznetsk**
103 E1 **Stalowa Wola** Pol.
138 B1 **Stambaugh** U.S.A.
99 C3 **Stamford** U.K.
139 E2 **Stamford** *CT* U.S.A.
143 D2 **Stamford** *TX* U.S.A.
Stampalia *i.* Greece *see* **Astypalaia**
122 A1 **Stampriet** Namibia
92 F2 **Stamsund** Norway
123 C2 **Standerton** S. Africa
138 C2 **Standish** U.S.A.
123 D2 **Stanger** S. Africa
Stanislav Ukr. *see* **Ivano-Frankivs'k**
Stanke Dimitrov Bulg. *see* **Dupnitsa**
153 C5 **Stanley** Falkland Is
136 C1 **Stanley** U.S.A.
Stanleyville Dem. Rep. Congo *see* **Kisangani**
Stann Creek Belize *see* **Dangriga**
111 B3 **Stanos** Greece
83 I3 **Stanovoye Nagor'ye** *mts* Rus. Fed.
83 J3 **Stanovoy Khrebet** *mts* Rus. Fed.
53 D1 **Stanthorpe** Austr.
137 E1 **Staples** U.S.A.
103 E1 **Starachowice** Pol.
Stara Planina *mts* Bulg./Serbia *see* **Balkan Mountains**
89 D2 **Staraya Russa** Rus. Fed.
89 D2 **Staraya Toropa** Rus. Fed.
110 C2 **Stara Zagora** Bulg.
49 L4 **Starbuck Island** Kiribati
103 D1 **Stargard Szczeciński** Pol.
89 D2 **Staritsa** Rus. Fed.
141 D3 **Starke** U.S.A.
140 C2 **Starkville** U.S.A.
102 C2 **Starnberg** Ger.
91 D2 **Starobil's'k** Ukr.
89 D3 **Starodub** Rus. Fed.
103 D1 **Starogard Gdański** Pol.
90 B2 **Starokostyantyniv** Ukr.
91 D2 **Starominskaya** Rus. Fed.
91 D2 **Staroshcherbinovskaya** Rus. Fed.
91 D2 **Starotitarovskaya** Rus. Fed.
89 F3 **Staroyur'yevo** Rus. Fed.
89 E3 **Starozhilovo** Rus. Fed.
99 B4 **Start Point** U.K.
88 C3 **Staryya Darohi** Belarus
86 G2 **Staryy Nadym** Rus. Fed.
89 E3 **Staryy Oskol** Rus. Fed.
101 E2 **Staßfurt** Ger.
103 E1 **Staszów** Pol.
139 D2 **State College** U.S.A.
141 D2 **Statesboro** U.S.A.
141 D1 **Statesville** U.S.A.
160 L1 **Station Nord** Greenland
139 D3 **Staunton** U.S.A.
93 E4 **Stavanger** Norway
87 D4 **Stavropol'** Rus. Fed.
Stavropol'-na-Volge Rus. Fed. *see* **Tol'yatti**
87 D4 **Stavropol'skaya Vozvyshennost'** *hills* Rus. Fed.
52 B3 **Stawell** Austr.
123 C2 **Steadville** S. Africa
136 B2 **Steamboat Springs** U.S.A.
101 E2 **Stedten** Ger.
128 C2 **Steen River** Can.
134 C2 **Steens Mountain** U.S.A.
100 C1 **Steenwijk** Neth.
126 E2 **Stefansson Island** Can.
Stegi Swaziland *see* **Siteki**
110 B1 **Ştei** Romania
101 E3 **Steigerwald** *mts* Ger.
100 B2 **Stein** Neth.
129 E3 **Steinbach** Can.
100 C1 **Steinfurt** Ger.
120 A3 **Steinhausen** Namibia
92 F3 **Steinkjer** Norway
122 A2 **Steinkopf** S. Africa
122 B2 **Stella** S. Africa
122 A3 **Stellenbosch** S. Africa
105 D3 **Stello, Monte** *mt.* France
105 D2 **Stenay** France
101 E1 **Stendal** Ger.
Steornabhagh U.K. *see* **Stornoway**
Stepanakert Azer. *see* **Xankändi**
52 B2 **Stephens Creek** Austr.
129 E2 **Stephens Lake** Can.
131 E3 **Stephenville** Can.
143 D2 **Stephenville** U.S.A.
Stepnoy Rus. Fed. *see* **Elista**
122 B3 **Sterling** S. Africa
136 C2 **Sterling** *CO* U.S.A.
138 B2 **Sterling** *IL* U.S.A.
136 C1 **Sterling** *ND* U.S.A.
138 C2 **Sterling Heights** U.S.A.
87 E3 **Sterlitamak** Rus. Fed.
101 E1 **Sternberg** Ger.
128 C2 **Stettler** Can.
138 C2 **Steubenville** U.S.A.
99 C4 **Stevenage** U.K.
129 E2 **Stevenson Lake** Can.
138 B2 **Stevens Point** U.S.A.
126 C2 **Stevens Village** U.S.A.
134 D1 **Stevensville** U.S.A.
128 B2 **Stewart** Can.
128 A1 **Stewart** *r.* Can.
54 A3 **Stewart Island** N.Z.
127 G2 **Stewart Lake** Can.
123 C3 **Steynsburg** S. Africa
102 C2 **Steyr** Austria
122 B3 **Steytlerville** S. Africa
128 A2 **Stikine** *r.* Can.
128 A2 **Stikine Plateau** Can.
122 B3 **Stilbaai** S. Africa
137 E1 **Stillwater** *MN* U.S.A.
143 D1 **Stillwater** *OK* U.S.A.
135 C3 **Stillwater Range** *mts* U.S.A.
109 D2 **Štip** Macedonia
96 C2 **Stirling** U.K.
52 A2 **Stirling North** Austr.
92 F3 **Stjørdalshalsen** Norway
103 D2 **Stockerau** Austria
93 G4 **Stockholm** Sweden
98 B3 **Stockport** U.K.
135 B3 **Stockton** U.S.A.
98 C2 **Stockton-on-Tees** U.K.
143 C2 **Stockton Plateau** U.S.A.
63 B2 **Stœng Trêng** Cambodia
96 B1 **Stoer, Point of** U.K.
99 B3 **Stoke-on-Trent** U.K.
98 C2 **Stokesley** U.K.
92 F2 **Stokmarknes** Norway
110 B2 **Stol** *mt.* Serbia
109 C2 **Stolac** Bos.-Herz.
100 C2 **Stolberg (Rheinland)** Ger.
82 E2 **Stolbovoy** Rus. Fed.
88 C3 **Stolin** Belarus
101 F2 **Stollberg** Ger.
101 D1 **Stolzenau** Ger.
96 C2 **Stonehaven** U.K.
99 C4 **Stonehenge** *tourist site* U.K.
129 E2 **Stonewall** Can.
129 D2 **Stony Rapids** Can.
92 G2 **Storavan** *l.* Sweden
Store Bælt *sea chan.* Denmark *see* **Great Belt**
92 F3 **Støren** Norway
92 I1 **Storfjordbotn** Norway
92 F2 **Storforshei** Norway
126 E2 **Storkerson Peninsula** Can.
137 D2 **Storm Lake** U.S.A.
93 E3 **Stornosa** *mt.* Norway
96 A1 **Stornoway** U.K.
86 E2 **Storozhevsk** Rus. Fed.
90 B2 **Storozhynets'** Ukr.
92 F3 **Storsjön** *l.* Sweden
92 H2 **Storslett** Norway
92 G2 **Storuman** Sweden
92 G2 **Storuman** *l.* Sweden
99 C4 **Stour** *r. England* U.K.
99 D4 **Stour** *r. England* U.K.
130 A2 **Stout Lake** Can.
88 C3 **Stowbtsy** Belarus
99 D3 **Stowmarket** U.K.
97 C1 **Strabane** U.K.
102 C2 **Strakonice** Czech Rep.
102 C1 **Stralsund** Ger.
122 A3 **Strand** S. Africa
93 E3 **Stranda** Norway
97 D1 **Strangford Lough** *inlet* U.K.
96 B3 **Stranraer** U.K.
105 D2 **Strasbourg** France
130 B3 **Stratford** Can.
54 B1 **Stratford** N.Z.
143 C1 **Stratford** U.S.A.
99 C3 **Stratford-upon-Avon** U.K.
128 C2 **Strathmore** Can.
96 C2 **Strathspey** *val.* U.K.
102 C2 **Straubing** Ger.
134 C2 **Strawberry Mountain** U.S.A.
51 C3 **Streaky Bay** Austr.
138 B2 **Streator** U.S.A.
99 B4 **Street** U.K.
110 B2 **Strehaia** Romania
94 B1 **Streymoy** *i.* Faroe Is
82 G2 **Strezhevoy** Rus. Fed.
101 F3 **Stříbro** Czech Rep.
153 B4 **Stroeder** Arg.
101 D1 **Ströhen** Ger.
109 C3 **Stromboli, Isola** *i.* Italy
96 B2 **Stromeferry** U.K.
96 C1 **Stromness** U.K.
92 G3 **Strömsund** Sweden
96 C1 **Stronsay** *i.* U.K.
53 D2 **Stroud** Austr.
99 B4 **Stroud** U.K.
100 C1 **Strücklingen (Saterland)** Ger.
111 B2 **Struga** Macedonia
88 C2 **Strugi-Krasnyye** Rus. Fed.
122 B3 **Struis Bay** S. Africa
111 B2 **Struma** *r.* Bulg.
99 A3 **Strumble Head** *hd* U.K.
111 B2 **Strumica** Macedonia
122 B2 **Strydenburg** S. Africa
111 B2 **Strymonas** *r.* Greece
93 E3 **Stryn** Norway
90 A2 **Stryy** Ukr.
90 A2 **Stryy** *r.* Ukr.
128 B2 **Stuart Lake** Can.
53 C2 **Stuart Town** Austr.
Stuchka Latvia *see* **Aizkraukle**
Stučka Latvia *see* **Aizkraukle**
130 A2 **Stull Lake** Can.
89 E3 **Stupino** Rus. Fed.
55 M3 **Sturge Island** Antarctica
138 B2 **Sturgeon Bay** U.S.A.
130 C3 **Sturgeon Falls** Can.
130 A3 **Sturgeon Lake** Can.
138 B2 **Sturgis** *MI* U.S.A.
136 C2 **Sturgis** *SD* U.S.A.
52 B1 **Sturt, Mount** *h.* Austr.
50 B1 **Sturt Creek** *watercourse* Austr.
50 C1 **Sturt Plain** Austr.
52 B1 **Sturt Stony Desert** Austr.
123 C3 **Stutterheim** S. Africa
102 B2 **Stuttgart** Ger.
140 B2 **Stuttgart** U.S.A.
92 □A2 **Stykkishólmur** Iceland
90 B1 **Styr** *r.* Belarus/Ukr.
155 D1 **Suaçuí Grande** *r.* Brazil
116 B3 **Suakin** Sudan
71 C3 **Suao** Taiwan
78 A3 **Suara** Eritrea
60 B1 **Subi Besar** *i.* Indon.
109 C1 **Subotica** Serbia
110 C1 **Suceava** Romania
Suchan Rus. Fed. *see* **Partizansk**
97 B2 **Suck** *r.* Ireland
152 B1 **Sucre** Bol.
154 B2 **Sucuriú** *r.* Brazil
Suczawa Romania *see* **Suceava**
89 E2 **Suda** Rus. Fed.
91 C3 **Sudak** Ukr.
116 A3 **Sudan** *country* Africa
130 B3 **Sudbury** Can.
99 D3 **Sudbury** U.K.
117 A4 **Sudd** *swamp* Sudan
89 F2 **Sudislavl'** Rus. Fed.
89 F2 **Sudogda** Rus. Fed.
94 B1 **Suðuroy** *i.* Faroe Is
89 E3 **Sudzha** Rus. Fed.
107 C2 **Sueca** Spain
116 B2 **Suez** Egypt
116 B2 **Suez, Gulf of** Egypt
80 B2 **Suez Canal** *canal* Egypt
139 D3 **Suffolk** U.S.A.
140 A3 **Sugar Land** U.S.A.
139 E1 **Sugarloaf Mountain** U.S.A.
53 D2 **Sugarloaf Point** Austr.
70 A2 **Suhait** China
116 B2 **Sūhāj** Egypt
79 C2 **Şuḩār** Oman
68 D1 **Sühbaatar** Mongolia
101 E2 **Suhl** Ger.
109 C1 **Suhopolje** Croatia
70 B2 **Suide** China
66 B2 **Suifenhe** China
69 E1 **Suihua** China
71 B3 **Sui Jiang** *r.* China
70 A2 **Suining** China
70 B2 **Suiping** China
97 C2 **Suir** *r.* Ireland
Suixian China *see* **Suizhou**
70 B2 **Suiyang** China
70 B2 **Suizhou** China
74 B2 **Sujangarh** India
74 B1 **Sujanpur** India
74 A2 **Sujawal** Pak.
60 B2 **Sukabumi** Indon.
60 B2 **Sukadana** Indon.
67 D3 **Sukagawa** Japan
60 C2 **Sukaraja** Indon.
Sukarnapura Indon. *see* **Jayapura**
Sukarno, Puntjak *mt.* Indon. *see* **Jaya, Puncak**
89 E3 **Sukhinichi** Rus. Fed.
89 F2 **Sukhona** *r.* Rus. Fed.
62 A2 **Sukhothai** Thai.
74 A2 **Sukkur** Pak.
89 E2 **Sukromny** Rus. Fed.
59 C3 **Sula, Kepulauan** *is* Indon.
74 A1 **Sulaiman Range** *mts* Pak.
Sulawesi *i.* Indon. *see* **Celebes**
101 D1 **Sulingen** Ger.
150 A3 **Sullana** Peru
138 B3 **Sullivan** *IN* U.S.A.
137 E3 **Sullivan** *MO* U.S.A.
140 B2 **Sulphur** U.S.A.
143 D2 **Sulphur Springs** U.S.A.
138 C1 **Sultan** Can.
Sultanabad Iran *see* **Arāk**
64 B3 **Sulu Archipelago** *is* Phil.
64 A3 **Sulu Sea** N. Pacific Ocean
101 E3 **Sulzbach-Rosenberg** Ger.
79 C2 **Sumāil** Oman
Sumatera *i.* Indon. *see* **Sumatra**
60 A1 **Sumatra** *i.* Indon.
61 D2 **Sumba** *i.* Indon.
61 C2 **Sumba, Selat** *sea chan.* Indon.
61 C2 **Sumbawa** *i.* Indon.
61 C2 **Sumbawabesar** Indon.
119 D3 **Sumbawanga** Tanz.
120 A2 **Sumbe** Angola
96 □ **Sumburgh** U.K.
96 □ **Sumburgh Head** *hd* U.K.
119 C2 **Sumeih** Sudan
61 C2 **Sumenep** Indon.
67 D4 **Sumisu-jima** *i.* Japan
131 D3 **Summerside** Can.
138 C3 **Summersville** U.S.A.
141 D2 **Summerville** U.S.A.
137 D1 **Summit** U.S.A.
128 B2 **Summit Lake** Can.
103 D2 **Šumperk** Czech Rep.
81 C1 **Sumqayıt** Azer.
141 D2 **Sumter** U.S.A.
91 C1 **Sumy** Ukr.
75 D2 **Sunamganj** Bangl.
65 B2 **Sunan** N. Korea
79 C2 **Şunaynah** Oman

52 B3 **Sunbury** Austr.
139 D2 **Sunbury** U.S.A.
65 B2 **Sunch'ŏn** N. Korea
65 B3 **Sunch'ŏn** S. Korea
123 C2 **Sun City** S. Africa
93 H3 **Sund** Fin.
60 B2 **Sunda, Selat** *str.* Indon.
136 C2 **Sundance** U.S.A.
75 C2 **Sundarbans** *coastal area* Bangl./India
74 B1 **Sundarnagar** India
Sunda Strait *str.* Indon. *see* **Sunda, Selat**
Sunda Trench Indian Ocean *see* **Java Trench**
98 C2 **Sunderland** U.K.
128 C2 **Sundre** Can.
93 G3 **Sundsvall** Sweden
123 D2 **Sundumbili** S. Africa
60 B2 **Sungailiat** Indon.
60 B2 **Sungaipenuh** Indon.
60 B1 **Sungai Petani** Malaysia
80 B1 **Sungurlu** Turkey
75 C2 **Sun Kosi** *r.* Nepal
93 E3 **Sunndalsøra** Norway
134 C1 **Sunnyside** U.S.A.
135 B3 **Sunnyvale** U.S.A.
141 D3 **Sunrise** U.S.A.
83 I2 **Suntar** Rus. Fed.
74 A2 **Suntsar** Pak.
114 B4 **Sunyani** Ghana
92 I3 **Suomussalmi** Fin.
67 B4 **Suō-nada** *b.* Japan
86 C2 **Suoyarvi** Rus. Fed.
142 A2 **Superior** *AZ* U.S.A.
137 D2 **Superior** *NE* U.S.A.
138 A1 **Superior** *WI* U.S.A.
138 B1 **Superior, Lake** Can./U.S.A.
63 B2 **Suphan Buri** Thai.
81 C2 **Süphan Dağı** *mt.* Turkey
89 D3 **Suponevo** Rus. Fed.
81 C2 **Sūq ash Shuyūkh** Iraq
70 B2 **Suqian** China
78 A2 **Sūq Suwayq** Saudi Arabia
Suquṭrā *i.* Yemen *see* **Socotra**
79 C2 **Ṣūr** Oman
74 A2 **Surab** Pak.
61 C2 **Surabaya** Indon.
61 C2 **Surakarta** Indon.
74 B2 **Surat** India
74 B2 **Suratgarh** India
63 A3 **Surat Thani** Thai.
89 D3 **Surazh** Rus. Fed.
109 D2 **Surdulica** Serbia
100 C3 **Sûre** *r.* Lux.
74 B2 **Surendranagar** India
82 F2 **Surgut** Rus. Fed.
64 B3 **Surigao** Phil.
63 B2 **Surin** Thai.
151 D2 **Suriname** *country* S. America
75 C2 **Surkhet** Nepal
Surt Libya *see* **Sirte**
Surt, Khalīj *g.* Libya *see* **Sirte, Gulf of**
60 B2 **Surulangun** Indon.
81 C2 **Süsangerd** Iran
89 F2 **Susanino** Rus. Fed.
135 B2 **Susanville** U.S.A.
80 B1 **Suşehri** Turkey
139 D3 **Susquehanna** *r.* U.S.A.
131 D3 **Sussex** Can.
101 D1 **Süstedt** Ger.
100 C1 **Sustrum** Ger.
83 K2 **Susuman** Rus. Fed.
111 C3 **Susurluk** Turkey
74 B1 **Sutak** India
53 D2 **Sutherland** Austr.
122 B3 **Sutherland** S. Africa
136 C2 **Sutherland** U.S.A.
134 B2 **Sutherlin** U.S.A.
74 B2 **Sutlej** *r.* India/Pak.
138 C3 **Sutton** U.S.A.
99 C3 **Sutton Coldfield** U.K.
98 C3 **Sutton in Ashfield** U.K.
66 D2 **Suttsu** Japan
49 I5 **Suva** Fiji
Suvalki Pol. *see* **Suwałki**
89 E3 **Suvorov** Rus. Fed.
90 B2 **Suvorove** Ukr.
103 E1 **Suwałki** Pol.
141 D3 **Suwanee Sound** *b.* U.S.A.
63 B2 **Suwannaphum** Thai.
141 D3 **Suwannee** *r.* U.S.A.
Suways, Qanāt as *canal* Egypt *see* **Suez Canal**
Suweis, Qanâ el *canal* Egypt *see* **Suez Canal**
65 B2 **Suwŏn** S. Korea
79 C2 **Sūzā** Iran
89 F2 **Suzdal'** Rus. Fed.
89 D3 **Suzemka** Rus. Fed.
70 B2 **Suzhou** *Anhui* China
70 C2 **Suzhou** *Jiangsu* China
67 C3 **Suzu** Japan
67 C3 **Suzu-misaki** *pt* Japan
82 B1 **Svalbard** *terr.* Arctic Ocean
90 A2 **Svalyava** Ukr.
92 H2 **Svappavaara** Sweden
91 D2 **Svatove** Ukr.
63 B2 **Svay Riĕng** Cambodia
93 F3 **Sveg** Sweden
88 C2 **Švenčionys** Lith.
93 F4 **Svendborg** Denmark
Sverdlovsk Rus. Fed. *see* **Yekaterinburg**
111 B2 **Sveti Nikole** Macedonia
66 C1 **Svetlaya** Rus. Fed.
88 B3 **Svetlogorsk** Rus. Fed.
87 D4 **Svetlograd** Rus. Fed.
88 B3 **Svetlyy** Rus. Fed.
93 I3 **Svetogorsk** Rus. Fed.
103 E2 **Svidník** Slovakia
111 C2 **Svilengrad** Bulg.
110 B2 **Svinecea Mare, Vârful** *mt.* Romania
110 C2 **Svishtov** Bulg.
88 B3 **Svislach** Belarus
103 D2 **Svitavy** Czech Rep.
91 C2 **Svitlovods'k** Ukr.
69 E1 **Svobodnyy** Rus. Fed.
110 B2 **Svoge** Bulg.
92 F2 **Svolvær** Norway
88 C3 **Svyetlahorsk** Belarus
141 D2 **Swainsboro** U.S.A.
120 A3 **Swakopmund** Namibia
52 B3 **Swan Hill** Austr.
128 C2 **Swan Hills** Can.
129 D2 **Swan Lake** Can.
97 C1 **Swanlinbar** Ireland
129 D2 **Swan River** Can.
53 D2 **Swansea** Austr.
99 B4 **Swansea** U.K.
122 B3 **Swartkolkvloer** *salt pan* S. Africa
123 C2 **Swartruggens** S. Africa
Swatow China *see* **Shantou**
123 D2 **Swaziland** *country* Africa
93 G3 **Sweden** *country* Europe
143 C2 **Sweetwater** U.S.A.
136 B2 **Sweetwater** *r.* U.S.A.
122 B3 **Swellendam** S. Africa
103 D1 **Świdnica** Pol.
103 D1 **Świdwin** Pol.
103 D1 **Świebodzin** Pol.
103 D1 **Świecie** Pol.
129 D2 **Swift Current** Can.
97 C1 **Swilly, Lough** *inlet* Ireland
99 C4 **Swindon** U.K.
102 C1 **Świnoujście** Pol.
105 D2 **Switzerland** *country* Europe
97 C2 **Swords** Ireland
88 C3 **Syanno** Belarus
89 D1 **Syas'troy** Rus. Fed.
89 D2 **Sychevka** Rus. Fed.
53 D2 **Sydney** Austr.
131 D3 **Sydney** Can.
131 D3 **Sydney Mines** Can.
91 D2 **Syeverodonets'k** Ukr.
111 B2 **Sykia** Greece
86 E2 **Syktyvkar** Rus. Fed.
140 C2 **Sylacauga** U.S.A.
75 D2 **Sylhet** Bangl.
102 B1 **Sylt** *i.* Ger.
138 C2 **Sylvania** U.S.A.
51 C1 **Sylvester, Lake** *imp. l.* Austr.
111 C3 **Symi** *i.* Greece
91 D2 **Synel'nykove** Ukr.
90 C2 **Synyukha** *r.* Ukr.
109 C3 **Syracuse** Italy
136 C3 **Syracuse** *KS* U.S.A.
139 D2 **Syracuse** *NY* U.S.A.
77 C2 **Syrdar'ya** *r.* Asia
80 B2 **Syria** *country* Asia
80 B2 **Syrian Desert** Asia
111 B3 **Syros** *i.* Greece
91 D2 **Syvash, Zatoka** *lag.* Ukr.
91 C2 **Syvas'ke** Ukr.
87 D3 **Syzran'** Rus. Fed.
102 C1 **Szczecin** Pol.
103 D1 **Szczecinek** Pol.
103 E1 **Szczytno** Pol.
Szechwan *prov.* China *see* **Sichuan**
103 E2 **Szeged** Hungary
103 D2 **Székesfehérvár** Hungary
103 D2 **Szekszárd** Hungary
103 E2 **Szentes** Hungary
103 D2 **Szentgotthárd** Hungary
103 E2 **Szerencs** Hungary
103 D2 **Szigetvár** Hungary
103 E2 **Szolnok** Hungary
103 D2 **Szombathely** Hungary
Sztálinváros Hungary *see* **Dunaújváros**

T

117 C4 **Taagga Duudka** *reg.* Somalia
64 B2 **Tabaco** Phil.
78 B2 **Tābah** Saudi Arabia
108 A3 **Tabarka** Tunisia
76 B3 **Ṭabas** Iran
79 C1 **Tabāsin** Iran
81 D3 **Tābask, Kūh-e** *mt.* Iran
150 C3 **Tabatinga** *Amazonas* Brazil
154 C2 **Tabatinga** *São Paulo* Brazil
114 B2 **Tabelbala** Alg.
128 C3 **Taber** Can.
64 B2 **Tablas** *i.* Phil.
102 C2 **Tábor** Czech Rep.
119 D3 **Tabora** Tanz.
114 B4 **Tabou** Côte d'Ivoire
81 C2 **Tabrīz** Iran
48 L3 **Tabuaeran** *atoll* Kiribati
78 A2 **Tabūk** Saudi Arabia
93 G4 **Täby** Sweden
77 E2 **Tacheng** China
102 C2 **Tachov** Czech Rep.
64 B2 **Tacloban** Phil.
150 B4 **Tacna** Peru
134 B1 **Tacoma** U.S.A.
152 C3 **Tacuarembó** Uru.
142 B3 **Tacupeto** Mex.
114 C2 **Tademaït, Plateau du** Alg.
Tadjikistan *country* Asia *see* **Tajikistan**
117 C3 **Tadjourah** Djibouti
80 B2 **Tadmur** Syria
129 E2 **Tadoule Lake** Can.
Tadzhikskaya S.S.R. *country* Asia *see* **Tajikistan**
65 B2 **T'aebaek-sanmaek** *mts* N. Korea/S. Korea
Taech'ŏn S. Korea *see* **Poryŏng**
65 B2 **Taegu** S. Korea
65 B2 **Taejŏn** S. Korea
65 B3 **Taejŏng** S. Korea
65 B2 **T'aepaek** S. Korea
107 C1 **Tafalla** Spain
152 B2 **Tafi Viejo** Arg.
79 D2 **Taftān, Kūh-e** *mt.* Iran
91 D2 **Taganrog** Rus. Fed.
91 D2 **Taganrog, Gulf of** Rus. Fed./Ukr.
62 A1 **Tagaung** Myanmar
64 B2 **Tagaytay City** Phil.
64 B3 **Tagbilaran** Phil.
64 B2 **Tagudin** Phil.
51 E1 **Tagula Island** P.N.G.
64 B3 **Tagum** Phil.
106 B2 **Tagus** *r.* Port./Spain
60 B1 **Tahan, Gunung** *mt.* Malaysia
115 C2 **Tahat, Mont** *mt.* Alg.
69 E1 **Tahe** China
49 M5 **Tahiti** *i.* Fr. Polynesia
143 E1 **Tahlequah** U.S.A.
135 B3 **Tahoe, Lake** U.S.A.
135 B3 **Tahoe City** U.S.A.
126 E2 **Tahoe Lake** Can.
115 C3 **Tahoua** Niger
79 C2 **Tahrūd** Iran
128 B3 **Tahsis** Can.
116 B2 **Ṭahṭā** Egypt
64 B3 **Tahuna** Indon.
70 B2 **Tai'an** China
70 A2 **Taibai Shan** *mt.* China
Taibus Qi China *see* **Baochang**
71 C3 **T'aichung** Taiwan
70 B2 **Taihang Shan** *mts* China
54 C1 **Taihape** N.Z.
71 B3 **Taihe** China
70 C2 **Tai Hu** *l.* China
52 A3 **Tailem Bend** Austr.
71 C3 **T'ainan** Taiwan
111 B3 **Tainaro, Akra** *c.* Greece
155 D1 **Taiobeiras** Brazil
71 C3 **T'aipei** Taiwan
Taiping China *see* **Chongzuo**
60 B1 **Taiping** Malaysia
Tairbeart U.K. *see* **Tarbert**
71 B3 **Taishan** China
70 B2 **Tai Shan** *hills* China
119 D3 **Taita Hills** Kenya
153 A4 **Taitao, Península de** *pen.* Chile
71 C3 **T'aitung** Taiwan
92 I2 **Taivalkoski** Fin.
92 H2 **Taivaskero** *h.* Fin.
71 C3 **Taiwan** *country* Asia
Taiwan Shan *mts* Taiwan *see* **Chungyang Shanmo**
71 B3 **Taiwan Strait** China/Taiwan
77 C1 **Taiynsha** Kazakh.
70 B2 **Taiyuan** China
70 B2 **Taizhou** *Jiangsu* China
71 C3 **Taizhou** *Zhejiang* China
78 B3 **Ta'izz** Yemen
145 C3 **Tajamulco, Volcán de** *vol.* Guat.
77 D3 **Tajikistan** *country* Asia
74 B2 **Taj Mahal** *tourist site* India
Tajo *r.* Spain *see* **Tagus**
63 A2 **Tak** Thai.
54 B2 **Takaka** N.Z.
115 C2 **Takalous, Oued** *watercourse* Alg.
67 B4 **Takamatsu** Japan
67 C3 **Takaoka** Japan
54 B1 **Takapuna** N.Z.
67 C3 **Takasaki** Japan
122 B1 **Takatokwane** Botswana
122 B1 **Takatshwaane** Botswana
67 C3 **Takayama** Japan
67 C3 **Takefu** Japan
60 A1 **Takengon** Indon.
63 B2 **Takêv** Cambodia
Takhiatash Uzbek. *see* **Taxiatosh**
63 B2 **Ta Khmau** Cambodia
74 B1 **Takht-i-Sulaiman** *mt.* Pak.
66 D2 **Takikawa** Japan
128 B2 **Takla Lake** Can.
128 B2 **Takla Landing** Can.
Takla Makan *des.* China *see* **Taklimakan Desert**
77 E3 **Taklimakan Desert** *des.* China
Taklimakan Shamo *des.* China *see* **Taklimakan Desert**
128 A2 **Taku** *r.* Can./U.S.A.
63 A3 **Takua Pa** Thai.
115 C4 **Takum** Nigeria
88 C3 **Talachyn** Belarus
74 B1 **Talagang** Pak.
146 B4 **Talamanca, Cordillera de** *mts* Costa Rica
150 A3 **Talara** Peru
59 C2 **Talaud, Kepulauan** *is* Indon.
106 C2 **Talavera de la Reina** Spain
153 A3 **Talca** Chile
153 A3 **Talcahuano** Chile
89 E2 **Taldom** Rus. Fed.
77 D2 **Taldykorgan** Kazakh.
Taldy-Kurgan Kazakh. *see* **Taldykorgan**
59 C3 **Taliabu** *i.* Indon.
64 B2 **Talisay** Phil.
61 C2 **Taliwang** Indon.
81 C2 **Tall 'Afar** Iraq
141 D2 **Tallahassee** U.S.A.
53 C3 **Tallangatta** Austr.
88 B2 **Tallinn** Estonia
140 B2 **Tallulah** U.S.A.
104 B2 **Talmont-St-Hilaire** France
90 C2 **Tal'ne** Ukr.
117 B3 **Talodi** Sudan
74 A1 **Tāloqān** Afgh.
91 E1 **Talovaya** Rus. Fed.
126 F2 **Taloyoak** Can.
88 B2 **Talsi** Latvia
152 A2 **Taltal** Chile
129 C1 **Taltson** *r.* Can.
60 A1 **Talu** Indon.
53 C1 **Talwood** Austr.
114 B4 **Tamale** Ghana
115 C2 **Tamanrasset** Alg.
99 A4 **Tamar** *r.* U.K.
Tamatave Madag. *see* **Toamasina**
144 B2 **Tamazula** Mex.
145 C2 **Tamazunchale** Mex.
114 A3 **Tambacounda** Senegal
60 B1 **Tambelan, Kepulauan** *is* Indon.
86 G1 **Tambey** Rus. Fed.
61 C1 **Tambisan** Malaysia
61 C2 **Tambora, Gunung** *vol.* Indon.
91 E1 **Tambov** Rus. Fed.
119 C2 **Tambura** Sudan
62 A1 **Tamenglong** India
145 C2 **Tamiahua, Laguna de** *lag.* Mex.
Tammerfors Fin. *see* **Tampere**
141 D3 **Tampa** U.S.A.
141 D3 **Tampa Bay** U.S.A.
93 H3 **Tampere** Fin.
145 C2 **Tampico** Mex.
69 D1 **Tamsagbulag** Mongolia
102 C2 **Tamsweg** Austria
53 D2 **Tamworth** Austr.
99 C3 **Tamworth** U.K.
119 E3 **Tana** *r.* Kenya
Tana, Lake *l.* Eth. *see* **Lake Tana**
67 C4 **Tanabe** Japan
92 I1 **Tana Bru** Norway
60 A2 **Tanahbala** *i.* Indon.
61 C2 **Tanahgrogot** Indon.
61 D2 **Tanahjampea** *i.* Indon.
60 A2 **Tanahmasa** *i.* Indon.
50 C1 **Tanami Desert** Austr.
63 B2 **Tân An** Vietnam
126 B2 **Tanana** U.S.A.
Tananarive Madag. *see* **Antananarivo**
108 A1 **Tanaro** *r.* Italy
65 B1 **Tanch'ŏn** N. Korea
64 B3 **Tandag** Phil.
110 C2 **Țăndărei** Romania
153 C3 **Tandil** Arg.
74 A2 **Tando Adam** Pak.
74 A2 **Tando Muhammad Khan** Pak.
52 B2 **Tandou Lake** *imp. l.* Austr.
67 B4 **Tanega-shima** *i.* Japan
114 B2 **Tanezrouft** *reg.* Alg./Mali
119 D3 **Tanga** Tanz.
75 C2 **Tangail** Bangl.
Tanganyika *country* Africa *see* **Tanzania**
119 C3 **Tanganyika, Lake** Africa
55 F3 **Tange Promontory** *hd* Antarctica
114 B1 **Tanger** Morocco
101 E1 **Tangermünde** Ger.
75 D1 **Tanggulashan** China
75 C1 **Tanggula Shan** *mts* China
Tangier Morocco *see* **Tanger**
75 C1 **Tangra Yumco** *salt l.* China
70 B2 **Tangshan** China
68 C2 **Taniantaweng Shan** *mts* China
59 C3 **Tanimbar, Kepulauan** *is* Indon.
64 B3 **Tanjay** Phil.
61 C2 **Tanjung** Indon.
60 A1 **Tanjungbalai** Indon.
Tanjungkarang-Telukbetung Indon. *see* **Bandar Lampung**
60 B2 **Tanjungpandan** Indon.
60 B1 **Tanjungpinang** Indon.
61 C1 **Tanjungredeb** Indon.
61 C1 **Tanjungselor** Indon.
74 B1 **Tank** Pak.
48 H5 **Tanna** *i.* Vanuatu
115 C3 **Tanout** Niger
75 C2 **Tansen** Nepal
116 B1 **Ṭanṭā** Egypt
114 A2 **Tan-Tan** Morocco
145 C2 **Tantoyuca** Mex.
119 D3 **Tanzania** *country* Africa
Tao'an China *see* **Taonan**
Taocheng China *see* **Yongchun**
Taolanaro Madag. *see* **Tôlañaro**
69 E1 **Taonan** China
109 C3 **Taormina** Italy
142 B1 **Taos** U.S.A.
114 B2 **Taoudenni** Mali
114 B1 **Taounate** Morocco
114 B1 **Taourirt** Morocco
88 C2 **Tapa** Estonia
145 C3 **Tapachula** Mex.
151 D3 **Tapajós** *r.* Brazil
60 A1 **Tapaktuan** Indon.

145 C3 **Tapanatepec** Mex.
150 C3 **Tapauá** Brazil
152 C2 **Tapera** Brazil
114 B4 **Tapeta** Liberia
74 B2 **Tapi** *r.* India
139 D3 **Tappahannock** U.S.A.
54 B2 **Tapuaenuku** *mt.* N.Z.
150 C3 **Tapurucuara** Brazil
154 B1 **Taquaral, Serra do** *hills* Brazil
154 A1 **Taquarí** *r.* Brazil
154 B1 **Taquari, Serra do** *hills* Brazil
154 C2 **Taquaritinga** Brazil
53 D1 **Tara** Austr.
115 D4 **Taraba** *r.* Nigeria
Ţarābulus Libya *see* **Tripoli**
54 C1 **Taradale** N.Z.
61 C1 **Tarakan** Indon.
111 D2 **Taraklı** Turkey
88 A3 **Taran, Mys** *pt* Rus. Fed.
54 B1 **Taranaki, Mount** *vol.* N.Z.
106 C1 **Tarancón** Spain
109 C2 **Taranto** Italy
109 C2 **Taranto, Golfo di** *g.* Italy
150 B3 **Tarapoto** Peru
90 C2 **Tarashcha** Ukr.
91 E2 **Tarasovskiy** Rus. Fed.
150 B3 **Tarauacá** Brazil
150 C3 **Tarauacá** *r.* Brazil
48 I3 **Tarawa** *atoll* Kiribati
54 C1 **Tarawera** N.Z.
77 D2 **Taraz** Kazakh.
107 C1 **Tarazona** Spain
77 E2 **Tarbagatay, Khrebet** *mts* Kazakh.
96 C2 **Tarbat Ness** *pt* U.K.
97 B2 **Tarbert** Ireland
96 A2 **Tarbert** *Scotland* U.K.
96 B3 **Tarbert** *Scotland* U.K.
104 C3 **Tarbes** France
96 B2 **Tarbet** U.K.
141 E1 **Tarboro** U.S.A.
51 C3 **Tarcoola** Austr.
53 D2 **Taree** Austr.
110 C2 **Târgovişte** Romania
110 C1 **Târgu Frumos** Romania
110 B1 **Târgu Jiu** Romania
110 B1 **Târgu Lăpuş** Romania
110 B1 **Târgu Mureş** Romania
110 C1 **Târgu Neamţ** Romania
110 C1 **Târgu Ocna** Romania
79 C2 **Tarif** U.A.E.
152 B2 **Tarija** Bol.
79 B3 **Tarīm** Yemen
77 E3 **Tarim Basin** *basin* China
119 D3 **Tarime** Tanz.
77 E2 **Tarim He** *r.* China
Tarim Pendi *basin* China *see* **Tarim Basin**
77 C3 **Tarīn Kowt** Afgh.
59 D3 **Taritatu** *r.* Indon.
123 C3 **Tarkastad** S. Africa
82 G2 **Tarko-Sale** Rus. Fed.
114 B4 **Tarkwa** Ghana
64 B2 **Tarlac** Phil.
105 C3 **Tarn** *r.* France
92 G2 **Tärnaby** Sweden
77 C3 **Tarnak** *r.* Afgh.
110 B1 **Târnăveni** Romania
103 E1 **Tarnobrzeg** Pol.
Tarnopol Ukr. *see* **Ternopil'**
103 E1 **Tarnów** Pol.
51 D2 **Taroom** Austr.
114 B1 **Taroudannt** Morocco
141 D3 **Tarpon Springs** U.S.A.
69 E1 **Tarqi** China
108 B2 **Tarquinia** Italy
107 D1 **Tarragona** Spain
107 D1 **Tàrrega** Spain
80 B2 **Tarsus** Turkey
152 B2 **Tartagal** Arg.
104 B3 **Tartas** France
88 C2 **Tartu** Estonia
80 B2 **Ţarţūs** Syria
155 D1 **Tarumirim** Brazil
89 E3 **Tarusa** Rus. Fed.
90 B2 **Tarutyne** Ukr.
108 B1 **Tarvisio** Italy
Tashauz Turkm. *see* **Daşoguz**
Tashauz Turkm. *see* **Dashkhovuz**
75 D2 **Tashigang** Bhutan
81 D3 **Tashk, Daryācheh-ye** *l.* Iran
Tashkent Uzbek. *see* **Toshkent**
130 C2 **Tasialujjuaq, Lac** *l.* Can.
130 C2 **Tasiat, Lac** *l.* Can.
131 D2 **Tasiujaq** Can.
77 E2 **Taskesken** Kazakh.
54 B2 **Tasman Bay** N.Z.
51 D4 **Tasmania** *state* Austr.
54 B2 **Tasman Mountains** N.Z.
156 D8 **Tasman Sea** S. Pacific Ocean
115 C2 **Tassili du Hoggar** *plat.* Alg.
115 C2 **Tassili n'Ajjer** *plat.* Alg.
61 D2 **Tataba** Indon.
103 D2 **Tatabánya** Hungary
90 B2 **Tatarbunary** Ukr.
83 K3 **Tatarskiy Proliv** *str.* Rus. Fed.
Tatar Strait *str.* Rus. Fed. *see* **Tatarskiy Proliv**
67 C4 **Tateyama** Japan
128 C1 **Tathlina Lake** Can.
78 B3 **Tathlīth** Saudi Arabia
78 B2 **Tathlīth, Wādī** *watercourse* Saudi Arabia
53 C3 **Tathra** Austr.
62 A1 **Tatkon** Myanmar
128 B2 **Tatla Lake** Can.
Tatra Mountains *mts* Pol./Slovakia *see* **Tatry**
103 D2 **Tatry** Pol./Slovakia
154 C2 **Tatuí** Brazil
143 C2 **Tatum** U.S.A.
81 C2 **Tatvan** Turkey
151 E3 **Taua** Brazil
155 C2 **Taubaté** Brazil
101 D3 **Tauberbischofsheim** Ger.
54 C1 **Taumarunui** N.Z.
122 B2 **Taung** S. Africa
62 A1 **Taunggyi** Myanmar
62 A2 **Taung-ngu** Myanmar
62 A2 **Taungup** Myanmar
74 B1 **Taunsa** Pak.
99 B4 **Taunton** U.K.
101 C2 **Taunus** *hills* Ger.
54 C1 **Taupo** N.Z.
54 C1 **Taupo, Lake** N.Z.
88 B2 **Tauragė** Lith.
54 C1 **Tauranga** N.Z.
139 E1 **Taureau, Réservoir** *resr* Can.
80 B2 **Taurus Mountains** *mts* Turkey
111 C3 **Tavas** Turkey
86 F3 **Tavda** Rus. Fed.
106 B2 **Tavira** Port.
99 A4 **Tavistock** U.K.
63 A2 **Tavoy** Myanmar
111 C3 **Tavşanlı** Turkey
99 A4 **Taw** *r.* U.K.
138 C2 **Tawas City** U.S.A.
61 C1 **Tawau** Malaysia
64 A3 **Tawi-Tawi** *i.* Phil.
71 C3 **Tawu** Taiwan
145 C3 **Taxco** Mex.
76 B2 **Taxiatosh** Uzbek.
77 D3 **Taxkorgan** China
96 C2 **Tay** *r.* U.K.
96 C2 **Tay, Firth of** *est.* U.K.
96 B2 **Tay, Loch** *l.* U.K.
128 B2 **Taylor** Can.
138 C2 **Taylor** *MI* U.S.A.
143 D2 **Taylor** *TX* U.S.A.
138 B3 **Taylorville** U.S.A.
78 A2 **Taymā'** Saudi Arabia
83 H2 **Taymura** *r.* Rus. Fed.
83 H2 **Taymyr, Ozero** *l.* Rus. Fed.
Taymyr, Poluostrov *pen.* Rus. Fed. *see* **Taymyr Peninsula**
83 G2 **Taymyr Peninsula** *pen.* Rus. Fed.
63 B2 **Tây Ninh** Vietnam
96 C2 **Tayport** U.K.
64 A2 **Taytay** Phil.
76 C3 **Tayyebād** Iran
82 G2 **Taz** *r.* Rus. Fed.
114 B1 **Taza** Morocco
129 D2 **Tazin Lake** Can.
86 G2 **Tazovskaya Guba** *sea chan.* Rus. Fed.
81 C1 **T'bilisi** Georgia
91 E2 **Tbilisskaya** Rus. Fed.
118 B3 **Tchibanga** Gabon
115 C3 **Tchin-Tabaradene** Niger
118 B2 **Tcholliré** Cameroon
103 D1 **Tczew** Pol.
144 B2 **Teacapán** Mex.
54 A3 **Te Anau** N.Z.
54 A3 **Te Anau, Lake** N.Z.
145 C3 **Teapa** Mex.
54 C1 **Te Awamutu** N.Z.
115 C1 **Tébessa** Alg.
60 B2 **Tebingtinggi** Indon.
60 A1 **Tebingtinggi** Indon.
144 A1 **Tecate** Mex.
114 B4 **Techiman** Ghana
144 B3 **Tecomán** Mex.
144 B2 **Tecoripa** Mex.
145 B3 **Técpan** Mex.
144 B2 **Tecuala** Mex.
110 C1 **Tecuci** Romania
68 C1 **Teeli** Rus. Fed.
98 C2 **Tees** *r.* U.K.
111 C3 **Tefenni** Turkey
60 B2 **Tegal** Indon.
146 B3 **Tegucigalpa** Hond.
115 C3 **Teguidda-n-Tessoumt** Niger
129 E1 **Tehek Lake** Can.
Teheran Iran *see* **Tehrān**
114 B4 **Téhini** Côte d'Ivoire
81 D2 **Tehrān** Iran
145 C3 **Tehuacán** Mex.
Tehuantepec, Golfo de *g.* Mex. *see* **Tehuantepec, Gulf of**
145 C3 **Tehuantepec, Gulf of** *g.* Mex.
145 C3 **Tehuantepec, Istmo de** *isth.* Mex.
114 A2 **Teide, Pico del** *vol.* Islas Canarias
99 A3 **Teifi** *r.* U.K.
Teixeira de Sousa Angola *see* **Luau**
76 C3 **Tejen** Turkm.
76 C3 **Tejen** *r.* Turkm.
Tejo *r.* Port. *see* **Tagus**
145 B3 **Tejupilco** Mex.
54 B2 **Tekapo, Lake** N.Z.
145 D2 **Tekax** Mex.
116 B3 **Tekezē Wenz** *r.* Eritrea/Eth.
111 C2 **Tekirdağ** Turkey
54 C1 **Te Kuiti** N.Z.
75 C2 **Tel** *r.* India
81 C1 **T'elavi** Georgia
80 B2 **Tel Aviv-Yafo** Israel
145 D2 **Telchac Puerto** Mex.
128 A2 **Telegraph Creek** Can.
154 B2 **Telêmaco Borba** Brazil
61 C1 **Telen** *r.* Indon.
50 B2 **Telfer Mining Centre** Austr.
99 B3 **Telford** U.K.
128 B2 **Telkwa** Can.
60 A2 **Telo** Indon.
86 E2 **Telpoziz, Gora** *mt.* Rus. Fed.
88 B2 **Telšiai** Lith.
60 B2 **Telukbatang** Indon.
60 A1 **Telukdalam** Indon.
60 B1 **Teluk Intan** Malaysia
114 C4 **Tema** Ghana
130 C3 **Temagami Lake** Can.
60 C2 **Temanggung** Indon.
123 C2 **Temba** S. Africa
83 H2 **Tembenchi** *r.* Rus. Fed.
60 B2 **Tembilahan** Indon.
123 C2 **Tembisa** S. Africa
120 A1 **Tembo Aluma** Angola
Tembué Moz. *see* **Chifunde**
99 B3 **Teme** *r.* U.K.
135 C4 **Temecula** U.S.A.
63 B3 **Temengor, Tasik** *resr* Malaysia
60 B1 **Temerluh** Malaysia
77 D1 **Temirtau** Kazakh.
139 D1 **Témiscamingue, Lac** *l.* Can.
53 C2 **Temora** Austr.
142 A2 **Tempe** U.S.A.
143 D2 **Temple** U.S.A.
97 C2 **Templemore** Ireland
102 C1 **Templin** Ger.
145 C2 **Tempoal** Mex.
120 A2 **Tempué** Angola
91 D2 **Temryuk** Rus. Fed.
91 D2 **Temryukskiy Zaliv** *b.* Rus. Fed.
153 A3 **Temuco** Chile
54 B2 **Temuka** N.Z.
145 C2 **Tenabo** Mex.
143 E2 **Tenaha** U.S.A.
73 C3 **Tenali** India
63 A2 **Tenasserim** Myanmar
99 A4 **Tenby** U.K.
117 C3 **Tendaho** Eth.
105 D3 **Tende** France
105 D3 **Tende, Col de** *pass* France/Italy
73 D4 **Ten Degree Channel** India
114 A3 **Te-n-Dghâmcha, Sebkhet** *salt marsh* Maur.
67 D3 **Tendō** Japan
114 B3 **Ténenkou** Mali
115 C2 **Ténéré** *reg.* Niger
115 D3 **Ténéré, Erg du** *des.* Niger
115 D2 **Ténéré du Tafassâsset** *des.* Niger
114 A2 **Tenerife** *i.* Islas Canarias
107 D2 **Ténès** Alg.
61 C2 **Tengah, Kepulauan** *is* Indon.
Tengcheng China *see* **Tengxian**
62 A1 **Tengchong** China
61 C2 **Tenggarong** Indon.
70 A2 **Tengger Shamo** *des.* China
77 C1 **Tengiz, Ozero** *salt l.* Kazakh.
71 B3 **Tengxian** China
119 C4 **Tenke** Dem. Rep. Congo
114 B3 **Tenkodogo** Burkina
51 C1 **Tennant Creek** Austr.
140 C1 **Tennessee** *r.* U.S.A.
140 C1 **Tennessee** *state* U.S.A.
61 C1 **Tenom** Malaysia
145 C3 **Tenosique** Mex.
61 D2 **Tenteno** Indon.
53 D1 **Tenterfield** Austr.
141 D3 **Ten Thousand Islands** U.S.A.
154 B2 **Teodoro Sampaio** Brazil
155 D1 **Teófilo Otôni** Brazil
145 C3 **Teopisca** Mex.
59 C3 **Tepa** Indon.
144 B2 **Tepache** Mex.
54 B1 **Te Paki** N.Z.
144 B3 **Tepalcatepec** Mex.
144 B2 **Tepatitlán** Mex.
144 B2 **Tepehuanes** Mex.
109 D2 **Tepelenë** Albania
144 B2 **Tepic** Mex.
102 C1 **Teplice** Czech Rep.
89 E3 **Teploye** Rus. Fed.
90 B2 **Teplyk** Ukr.
54 C1 **Te Puke** N.Z.
144 B2 **Tequila** Mex.
49 K3 **Teraina** *i.* Kiribati
108 B2 **Teramo** Italy
52 B3 **Terang** Austr.
89 E3 **Terbuny** Rus. Fed.
90 B2 **Terebovlya** Ukr.
87 D4 **Terek** *r.* Rus. Fed.
154 B2 **Terenos** Brazil
151 E3 **Teresina** Brazil
155 D2 **Teresópolis** Brazil
63 A3 **Teressa Island** India
100 A3 **Tergnier** France
80 B1 **Terme** Turkey
108 B3 **Termini Imerese** Italy
145 C3 **Términos, Laguna de** *lag.* Mex.
77 C3 **Termiz** Uzbek.
109 B2 **Termoli** Italy
59 C2 **Ternate** Indon.
100 A2 **Terneuzen** Neth.
66 C1 **Terney** Rus. Fed.
108 B2 **Terni** Italy
90 B2 **Ternopil'** Ukr.
52 A2 **Terowie** Austr.
69 F1 **Terpeniya, Mys** *c.* Rus. Fed.
69 F1 **Terpeniya, Zaliv** *g.* Rus. Fed.
128 B2 **Terrace** Can.
130 B3 **Terrace Bay** Can.
122 B2 **Terra Firma** S. Africa
140 B3 **Terrebonne Bay** U.S.A.
138 B3 **Terre Haute** U.S.A.
131 E3 **Terrenceville** Can.
100 B1 **Terschelling** *i.* Neth.
108 A3 **Tertenia** Italy
107 C1 **Teruel** Spain
92 H2 **Tervola** Fin.
109 C2 **Tešanj** Bos.-Herz.
116 B3 **Teseney** Eritrea
66 D2 **Teshio** Japan
66 D2 **Teshio-gawa** *r.* Japan
128 A1 **Teslin** Can.
128 A1 **Teslin Lake** Can.
154 B1 **Tesouro** Brazil
115 C3 **Tessaoua** Niger
99 C4 **Test** *r.* U.K.
121 C2 **Tete** Moz.
90 C1 **Teteriv** *r.* Ukr.
101 F1 **Teterow** Ger.
90 B2 **Tetiyiv** Ukr.
114 B1 **Tétouan** Morocco
110 B2 **Tetovo** Macedonia
Tetyukhe Rus. Fed. *see* **Dal'negorsk**
Teuchezhsk Rus. Fed. *see* **Adygeysk**
152 B2 **Teuco** *r.* Arg.
144 B2 **Teul de González Ortega** Mex.
101 D1 **Teutoburger Wald** *hills* Ger.
Tevere *r.* Italy *see* **Tiber**
54 A3 **Teviot** N.Z.
96 C3 **Teviot** *r.* U.K.
96 C3 **Teviothead** U.K.
61 C2 **Tewah** Indon.
51 E2 **Tewantin** Austr.
54 C2 **Te Wharau** N.Z.
99 B4 **Tewkesbury** U.K.
143 E2 **Texarkana** U.S.A.
53 D1 **Texas** Austr.
143 D2 **Texas** *state* U.S.A.
143 E3 **Texas City** U.S.A.
145 C3 **Texcoco** Mex.
100 B1 **Texel** *i.* Neth.
143 D2 **Texoma, Lake** U.S.A.
123 C2 **Teyateyaneng** Lesotho
89 F2 **Teykovo** Rus. Fed.
89 F2 **Teza** *r.* Rus. Fed.
75 D2 **Tezpur** India
72 D2 **Tezu** India
129 E1 **Tha-anne** *r.* Can.
123 C2 **Thabana-Ntlenyana** *mt.* Lesotho
123 C2 **Thaba Nchu** S. Africa
123 C2 **Thaba Putsoa** *mt.* Lesotho
123 C2 **Thaba-Tseka** Lesotho
123 C1 **Thabazimbi** S. Africa
123 C2 **Thabong** S. Africa
63 A2 **Thagyettaw** Myanmar
62 B1 **Thai Binh** Vietnam
63 B2 **Thailand** *country* Asia
63 B2 **Thailand, Gulf of** Asia
62 B1 **Thai Nguyên** Vietnam
62 B2 **Thakèk** Laos
74 B1 **Thal** Pak.
63 A3 **Thalang** Thai.
74 B1 **Thal Desert** Pak.
101 E2 **Thale (Harz)** Ger.
62 B2 **Tha Li** Thai.
53 C1 **Thallon** Austr.
123 C1 **Thamaga** Botswana
78 B3 **Thamar, Jabal** *mt.* Yemen
79 C3 **Thamarīt** Oman
130 B3 **Thames** *r.* Can.
54 C1 **Thames** N.Z.
99 D4 **Thames** *est.* U.K.
99 D4 **Thames** *r.* U.K.
79 B3 **Thamūd** Yemen
Thana India *see* **Thane**
63 A2 **Thanbyuzayat** Myanmar
62 A2 **Thandwè** Myanmar
74 B3 **Thane** India
62 B2 **Thanh Hoa** Vietnam
73 B3 **Thanjavur** India
63 A2 **Thanlyin** Myanmar
74 A2 **Thano Bula Khan** Pak.
62 B1 **Than Uyên** Vietnam
74 A2 **Thar Desert** India/Pak.
52 B1 **Thargomindah** Austr.
81 C2 **Tharthār, Buḩayrat ath** *l.* Iraq
111 B2 **Thasos** Greece
111 B2 **Thasos** *i.* Greece
62 B1 **Thât Khê** Vietnam
62 A2 **Thaton** Myanmar
74 A2 **Thatta** Pak.
62 A1 **Thaungdut** Myanmar
62 A2 **Thayawadi** Myanmar
63 A2 **Thayetchaung** Myanmar
62 A2 **Thayetmyo** Myanmar
62 A1 **Thazi** Myanmar
146 C2 **The Bahamas** *country* West Indies
98 B2 **The Cheviot** *h.* U.K.
134 B1 **The Dalles** U.S.A.
136 C2 **Thedford** U.S.A.
53 D2 **The Entrance** Austr.
99 C3 **The Fens** *reg.* U.K.
114 A3 **The Gambia** *country* Africa
52 B3 **The Grampians** *mts* Austr.
The Great Oasis *oasis* Egypt *see* **Wāḩāt al Khārijah**
79 C2 **The Gulf** Asia
100 B1 **The Hague** Neth.
129 E1 **Thelon** *r.* Can.
101 E2 **Themar** Ger.
123 C2 **Thembalihle** S. Africa
96 A1 **The Minch** *sea chan.* U.K.
97 A1 **The Mullet** *b.* Ireland
99 C4 **The Needles** *stack* U.K.
150 C3 **Theodore Roosevelt** *r.* Brazil

129 D2 **The Pas** Can.
111 B2 **Thermaïkos Kolpos** *g.* Greece
136 B2 **Thermopolis** U.S.A.
53 C3 **The Rock** Austr.
The Skaw *spit* Denmark *see* **Grenen**
99 C4 **The Solent** *str.* U.K.
130 B3 **Thessalon** Can.
111 B2 **Thessaloniki** Greece
99 D3 **Thetford** U.K.
131 C3 **Thetford Mines** Can.
62 A1 **The Triangle** *mts* Myanmar
147 D3 **The Valley** Anguilla
131 D2 **Thévenet, Lac** *l.* Can.
99 D3 **The Wash** *b.* U.K.
99 D4 **The Weald** *reg.* U.K.
143 D2 **The Woodlands** U.S.A.
140 B3 **Thibodaux** U.S.A.
129 E2 **Thicket Portage** Can.
137 D1 **Thief River Falls** U.S.A.
Thiel Neth. *see* **Tiel**
105 C2 **Thiers** France
114 A3 **Thiès** Senegal
119 D3 **Thika** Kenya
73 B4 **Thiladhunmathi Atoll** Maldives
75 C2 **Thimphu** Bhutan
105 D2 **Thionville** France
Thira *i.* Greece *see* **Santorini**
98 C2 **Thirsk** U.K.
73 B4 **Thiruvananthapuram** India
93 E4 **Thisted** Denmark
129 E1 **Thlewiaza** *r.* Can.
63 B3 **Thô Chu, Đao** *i.* Vietnam
62 A2 **Thoen** Thai.
123 D1 **Thohoyandou** S. Africa
101 E1 **Thomasburg** Ger.
97 C2 **Thomastown** Ireland
140 C2 **Thomasville** *AL* U.S.A.
141 D2 **Thomasville** *GA* U.S.A.
100 C2 **Thommen** Belgium
129 E2 **Thompson** Can.
128 E3 **Thompson** *r.* U.S.A.
134 C1 **Thompson Falls** U.S.A.
128 B2 **Thompson Sound** Can.
51 D2 **Thomson** *watercourse* Austr.
141 D2 **Thomson** U.S.A.
63 B2 **Thon Buri** Thai.
63 A2 **Thongwa** Myanmar
142 B1 **Thoreau** U.S.A.
98 C3 **Thornhill** U.K.
136 C3 **Thornton** U.S.A.
55 F2 **Thorshavnheiane** *reg.* Antarctica
123 C2 **Thota-ea-Moli** Lesotho
104 B2 **Thouars** France
62 A1 **Thoubal** India
134 D1 **Three Forks** U.S.A.
128 C2 **Three Hills** Can.
63 A2 **Three Pagodas Pass** Myanmar/Thai.
114 B4 **Three Points, Cape** Ghana
138 B2 **Three Rivers** *MI* U.S.A.
143 D3 **Three Rivers** *TX* U.S.A.
73 B3 **Thrissur** India
63 B2 **Thu Dâu Môt** Vietnam
100 B2 **Thuin** Belgium
127 H1 **Thule** Greenland
121 B3 **Thuli** Zimbabwe
102 B2 **Thun** Switz.
130 B3 **Thunder Bay** Can.
130 B3 **Thunder Bay** *b.* Can.
63 A3 **Thung Song** Thai.
101 E2 **Thüringer Becken** *reg.* Ger.
101 F2 **Thüringer Wald** *mts* Ger.
Thuringian Forest *mts* Ger. *see* **Thüringer Wald**
97 C2 **Thurles** Ireland
59 D3 **Thursday Island** Austr.
96 C1 **Thurso** U.K.
96 C1 **Thurso** *r.* U.K.
55 R2 **Thurston Island** Antarctica
101 D1 **Thüster Berg** *h.* Ger.
121 C2 **Thyolo** Malawi
Thysville Dem. Rep. Congo *see* **Mbanza-Ngungu**
79 C2 **Tīāb** Iran
151 E3 **Tianguá** Brazil
70 B2 **Tianjin** China
70 B2 **Tianjin** *mun.* China
71 A3 **Tianlin** China
70 B2 **Tianmen** China
69 E2 **Tianshan** China
70 A2 **Tianshui** China
70 A2 **Tianzhu** China
107 D2 **Tiaret** Alg.
114 B4 **Tiassalé** Côte d'Ivoire
154 B2 **Tibagi** Brazil
154 B2 **Tibagi** *r.* Brazil
118 B2 **Tibati** Cameroon
108 B2 **Tiber** *r.* Italy
Tiberias, Lake *l.* Israel *see* **Galilee, Sea of**
115 D2 **Tibesti** *mts* Chad
75 C1 **Tibet** *aut. reg.* China
68 B2 **Tibet, Plateau of** China
52 B1 **Tibooburra** Austr.
144 A2 **Tiburón, Isla** *i.* Mex.
114 B3 **Tîchît** Maur.
114 A2 **Tichla** Western Sahara
105 D2 **Ticino** *r.* Italy/Switz.
139 E2 **Ticonderoga** U.S.A.
145 D2 **Ticul** Mex.
114 A3 **Tidjikja** Maur.
100 B2 **Tiel** Neth.
70 C1 **Tieling** China
75 B1 **Tielongtan** China
100 A2 **Tielt** Belgium
100 B2 **Tienen** Belgium
68 B2 **Tien Shan** *mts* China/Kyrg.
Tientsin China *see* **Tianjin**
Tientsin *mun.* China *see* **Tianjin**
93 G3 **Tierp** Sweden
145 C3 **Tierra Blanca** Mex.
145 C3 **Tierra Colorada** Mex.
153 B5 **Tierra del Fuego, Isla Grande de** *i.* Arg./Chile
106 B1 **Tiétar, Valle de** *val.* Spain
154 C2 **Tietê** Brazil
154 B2 **Tietê** *r.* Brazil
138 C2 **Tiffin** U.S.A.
Tiflis Georgia *see* **T'bilisi**
141 D2 **Tifton** U.S.A.
90 B2 **Tighina** Moldova
75 C2 **Tigiria** India
118 B2 **Tignère** Cameroon
131 D3 **Tignish** Can.
150 B3 **Tigre** *r.* Ecuador/Peru
81 C2 **Tigris** *r.* Asia
114 A3 **Tiguent** Maur.
114 B2 **Tiguesmat** *hills* Maur.
115 D3 **Tigui** Chad
145 C2 **Tihuatlán** Mex.
144 A1 **Tijuana** Mex.
91 E2 **Tikhoretsk** Rus. Fed.
89 D2 **Tikhvin** Rus. Fed.
89 D2 **Tikhvinskaya Gryada** *ridge* Rus. Fed.
157 F7 **Tiki Basin** S. Pacific Ocean
54 C1 **Tikokino** N.Z.
81 C2 **Tikrīt** Iraq
83 J2 **Tiksi** Rus. Fed.
100 B2 **Tilburg** Neth.
152 B2 **Tilcara** Arg.
52 B1 **Tilcha (abandoned)** Austr.
114 C3 **Tîlemsi, Vallée du** *watercourse* Mali
Tilimsen Alg. *see* **Tlemcen**
114 C3 **Tillabéri** Niger
134 B1 **Tillamook** U.S.A.
63 A3 **Tillanchong Island** India
111 C3 **Tilos** *i.* Greece
52 B2 **Tilpa** Austr.
86 F2 **Til'tim** Rus. Fed.
89 E3 **Tim** Rus. Fed.
86 D2 **Timanskiy Kryazh** *ridge* Rus. Fed.
54 B2 **Timaru** N.Z.
91 D2 **Timashevsk** Rus. Fed.
Timashevskaya Rus. Fed. *see* **Timashevsk**
114 B3 **Timbedgha** Maur.
50 C1 **Timber Creek** Austr.
114 B3 **Timbuktu** Mali
115 C3 **Timia** Niger
114 C2 **Timimoun** Alg.
111 B2 **Timiou Prodromou, Akrotirio** *pt* Greece
110 B1 **Timiş** *r.* Romania
110 B1 **Timişoara** Romania
130 B3 **Timmins** Can.
89 E2 **Timokhino** Rus. Fed.
151 E3 **Timon** Brazil
59 C3 **Timor** *i.* East Timor/Indonesia
59 C3 **Timor Sea** Austr./Indon.
Timor Timur *country* Asia *see* **East Timor**
93 G3 **Timrå** Sweden
78 B2 **Tīn, Jabal** *mt.* Saudi Arabia
114 B2 **Tindouf** Alg.
53 D1 **Tingha** Austr.
75 C2 **Tingri** China
93 F4 **Tingsryd** Sweden
92 E3 **Tingvoll** Norway
Tingzhou China *see* **Changting**
59 D2 **Tinian** *i.* N. Mariana Is
Tinnelvelly India *see* **Tirunelveli**
152 B2 **Tinogasta** Arg.
111 C3 **Tinos** Greece
111 C3 **Tinos** *i.* Greece
100 A3 **Tinqueux** France
115 C2 **Tinrhert, Hamada de** Alg.
62 A1 **Tinsukia** India
52 B3 **Tintinara** Austr.
136 C1 **Tioga** U.S.A.
107 D2 **Tipasa** Alg.
97 B2 **Tipperary** Ireland
151 E3 **Tiracambu, Serra do** *hills* Brazil
109 C2 **Tirana** Albania
Tiranë Albania *see* **Tirana**
108 B1 **Tirano** Italy
52 A1 **Tirari Desert** Austr.
90 B2 **Tiraspol** Moldova
122 A2 **Tiraz Mountains** Namibia
111 C3 **Tire** Turkey
96 A2 **Tiree** *i.* U.K.
Tîrgovişte Romania *see* **Târgovişte**
Tîrgu Frumos Romania *see* **Târgu Frumos**
Tîrgu Jiu Romania *see* **Târgu Jiu**
Tîrgu Lăpuş Romania *see* **Târgu Lăpuş**
Tîrgu Mureş Romania *see* **Târgu Mureş**
Tîrgu Neamţ Romania *see* **Târgu Neamţ**
Tîrgu Ocna Romania *see* **Târgu Ocna**
74 B1 **Tirich Mir** *mt.* Pak.
Tîrnăveni Romania *see* **Târnăveni**
155 C1 **Tiros** Brazil
118 C2 **Tiroungoulou** C.A.R.
73 B3 **Tiruchchirappalli** India
73 B4 **Tirunelveli** India
73 B3 **Tirupati** India
73 B3 **Tiruppattur** India
73 B3 **Tiruppur** India
Tisa *r.* Hungary *see* **Tisza**
109 D1 **Tisa** *r.* Serbia
129 D2 **Tisdale** Can.
107 D2 **Tissemsilt** Alg.
75 C2 **Tista** *r.* India
103 E2 **Tisza** *r.* Hungary
55 L1 **Titan Dome** Antarctica
Titicaca, Lago *l.* Bol./Peru *see* **Titicaca, Lake**
152 B1 **Titicaca, Lake** *l.* Bol./Peru
75 C2 **Titlagarh** India
Titograd Montenegro *see* **Podgorica**
Titova Mitrovica Kosovo *see* **Mitrovicë**
Titovo Užice Serbia *see* **Užice**
Titovo Velenje Slovenia *see* **Velenje**
Titov Veles Macedonia *see* **Veles**
Titov Vrbas Serbia *see* **Vrbas**
110 C2 **Titu** Romania
141 D3 **Titusville** U.S.A.
99 B4 **Tiverton** U.K.
108 B2 **Tivoli** Italy
79 C2 **Ţīwī** Oman
63 A2 **Ti-ywa** Myanmar
145 D2 **Tizimín** Mex.
107 D2 **Tizi Ouzou** Alg.
114 B2 **Tiznit** Morocco
92 G2 **Tjaktjajaure** *l.* Sweden
Tjirebon Indon. *see* **Cirebon**
145 C3 **Tlacotalpán** Mex.
144 B2 **Tlahualilo** Mex.
145 C3 **Tlalnepantla** Mex.
145 C3 **Tlapa** Mex.
145 C3 **Tlaxcala** Mex.
145 C3 **Tlaxiaco** Mex.
114 B1 **Tlemcen** Alg.
123 C1 **Tlokweng** Botswana
128 B2 **Toad River** Can.
121 □D2 **Toamasina** Madag.
60 A1 **Toba, Danau** *l.* Indon.
Toba, Lake *l.* Indon. *see* **Toba, Danau**
74 A1 **Toba and Kakar Ranges** *mts* Pak.
147 D3 **Tobago** *i.* Trin. and Tob.
59 C2 **Tobelo** Indon.
130 B3 **Tobermory** Can.
96 A2 **Tobermory** U.K.
129 D2 **Tobin Lake** Can.
60 B2 **Toboali** Indon.
76 C1 **Tobol** *r.* Kazakh./Rus. Fed.
86 F3 **Tobol'sk** Rus. Fed.
Tobruk Libya *see* **Tubruq**
151 E3 **Tocantinópolis** Brazil
151 E3 **Tocantins** *r.* Brazil
141 D2 **Toccoa** U.S.A.
108 A1 **Toce** *r.* Italy
152 A2 **Tocopilla** Chile
53 C3 **Tocumwal** Austr.
59 C3 **Todeli** Indon.
108 B2 **Todi** Italy
144 A2 **Todos Santos** Mex.
128 B3 **Tofino** Can.
96 □ **Toft** U.K.
61 D2 **Togian** *i.* Indon.
61 D2 **Togian, Kepulauan** *is* Indon.
Togliatti Rus. Fed. *see* **Tol'yatti**
114 C4 **Togo** *country* Africa
74 B2 **Tohana** India
141 D3 **Tohopekaliga, Lake** U.S.A.
126 C2 **Tok** U.S.A.
116 B3 **Tokar** Sudan
69 E3 **Tokara-rettō** *is* Japan
91 F1 **Tokarevka** Rus. Fed.
80 B1 **Tokat** Turkey
49 J4 **Tokelau** *terr.* S. Pacific Ocean
91 D2 **Tokmak** Ukr.
77 D2 **Tokmok** Kyrg.
54 C1 **Tokoroa** N.Z.
68 B2 **Toksun** China
67 B4 **Tokushima** Japan
67 C3 **Tōkyō** Japan
121 □D3 **Tôlañaro** Madag.
Tolbukhin Bulg. *see* **Dobrich**
154 B2 **Toledo** Brazil
106 C2 **Toledo** Spain
138 C2 **Toledo** U.S.A.
106 C2 **Toledo, Montes de** *mts* Spain
140 B2 **Toledo Bend Reservoir** U.S.A.
121 □D3 **Toliara** Madag.
Toling China *see* **Zanda**
61 D1 **Tolitoli** Indon.
108 B1 **Tolmezzo** Italy
108 B1 **Tolmin** Slovenia
103 D2 **Tolna** Hungary
104 B3 **Tolosa** Spain
145 C3 **Toluca** Mex.
87 D3 **Tol'yatti** Rus. Fed.
138 A2 **Tomah** U.S.A.
138 B1 **Tomahawk** U.S.A.
66 D2 **Tomakomai** Japan
61 D2 **Tomali** Indon.
61 C1 **Tomani** Malaysia
106 B2 **Tomar** Port.
103 E1 **Tomaszów Lubelski** Pol.
103 E1 **Tomaszów Mazowiecki** Pol.
144 B3 **Tomatlán** Mex.
154 C2 **Tomazina** Brazil
140 C2 **Tombigbee** *r.* U.S.A.
120 A1 **Tomboco** Angola
155 D2 **Tombos** Brazil
Tombouctou Mali *see* **Timbuktu**
142 A2 **Tombstone** U.S.A.
120 A2 **Tombua** Angola
123 C1 **Tom Burke** S. Africa
106 C2 **Tomelloso** Spain
53 C2 **Tomingley** Austr.
61 D2 **Tomini, Teluk** *g.* Indon.
109 C2 **Tomislavgrad** Bos.-Herz.
103 D2 **Tompa** Hungary
50 A2 **Tom Price** Austr.
82 G3 **Tomsk** Rus. Fed.
93 F4 **Tomtabacken** *h.* Sweden
83 K2 **Tomtor** Rus. Fed.
145 C3 **Tonalá** Mex.
150 C3 **Tonantins** Brazil
99 D4 **Tonbridge** U.K.
59 C2 **Tondano** Indon.
49 J5 **Tonga** *country* S. Pacific Ocean
123 D2 **Tongaat** S. Africa
49 J6 **Tongatapu Group** *is* Tonga
71 B3 **Tongcheng** China
70 A2 **Tongchuan** China
71 A3 **Tongdao** China
65 B2 **Tongduch'ŏn** S. Korea
100 B2 **Tongeren** Belgium
65 B2 **Tonghae** S. Korea
71 A3 **Tonghai** China
65 B1 **Tonghua** China
65 B2 **Tongjosŏn-man** *b.* N. Korea
62 B1 **Tongking, Gulf of** China/Vietnam
69 E2 **Tongliao** China
70 B2 **Tongling** China
52 B2 **Tongo** Austr.
Tongquan China *see* **Malong**
71 A3 **Tongren** China
75 D2 **Tongsa** Bhutan
Tongshi China *see* **Wuzhishan**
Tongtian He *r.* China *see* **Yangtze**
96 B1 **Tongue** U.K.
Tongxian China *see* **Tongzhou**
65 B3 **T'ongyŏng** S. Korea
69 E2 **Tongyu** China
65 A1 **Tongyuanpu** China
70 B2 **Tongzhou** China
71 A3 **Tongzi** China
119 C2 **Tonj** Sudan
74 B2 **Tonk** India
81 D2 **Tonkabon** Iran
Tônlé Sab *l.* Cambodia *see* **Tonle Sap**
63 B2 **Tonle Sap** *l.* Cambodia
135 C3 **Tonopah** U.S.A.
93 F4 **Tønsberg** Norway
135 D2 **Tooele** U.S.A.
52 B3 **Tooleybuc** Austr.
53 D1 **Toowoomba** Austr.
137 D3 **Topeka** U.S.A.
144 B2 **Topia** Mex.
144 B2 **Topolobampo** Mex.
86 C2 **Topozero, Ozero** *l.* Rus. Fed.
134 B1 **Toppenish** U.S.A.
111 C3 **Torbalı** Turkey
76 B3 **Torbat-e Heydarīyeh** Iran
76 C3 **Torbat-e Jām** Iran
131 E3 **Torbay** Can.
106 C1 **Tordesillas** Spain
107 C1 **Tordesilos** Spain
92 H2 **Töre** Sweden
107 D1 **Torelló** Spain
100 B1 **Torenberg** *h.* Neth.
Toretam Kazakh. *see* **Baykonyr**
101 F2 **Torgau** Ger.
100 A2 **Torhout** Belgium
Torino Italy *see* **Turin**
67 D4 **Tori-shima** *i.* Japan
117 B4 **Torit** Sudan
154 B1 **Torixoréu** Brazil
89 D2 **Torkovichi** Rus. Fed.
106 B1 **Tormes** *r.* Spain
92 H2 **Torneälven** *r.* Sweden
131 D2 **Torngat Mountains** Can.
92 H2 **Tornio** Fin.
106 B1 **Toro** Spain
130 C3 **Toronto** Can.
89 D2 **Toropets** Rus. Fed.
119 D2 **Tororo** Uganda
Toros Dağları *mts* Turkey *see* **Taurus Mountains**
52 B3 **Torquay** Austr.
99 B4 **Torquay** U.K.
135 C4 **Torrance** U.S.A.
106 B2 **Torrão** Port.
106 B1 **Torre** *mt.* Port.
107 D1 **Torreblanca** Spain
106 C1 **Torrecerredo** *mt.* Spain
106 B1 **Torre de Moncorvo** Port.
106 C1 **Torrelavega** Spain
106 C2 **Torremolinos** Spain
52 A2 **Torrens, Lake** *imp. l.* Austr.
107 C2 **Torrent** Spain
144 B2 **Torreón** Mex.
106 B2 **Torres Novas** Port.
156 C6 **Torres Strait** Austr.
106 B2 **Torres Vedras** Port.
107 C2 **Torrevieja** Spain
96 B2 **Torridon** U.K.
96 B2 **Torridon, Loch** *b.* U.K.
106 C2 **Torrijos** Spain
139 E2 **Torrington** *CT* U.S.A.
136 C2 **Torrington** *WY* U.S.A.
107 D1 **Torroella de Montgrí** Spain
94 B1 **Tórshavn** Faroe Is
76 C2 **To'rtko'l** Uzbek.
108 A3 **Tortolì** Italy
108 A2 **Tortona** Italy
107 D1 **Tortosa** Spain
81 D2 **Ţorūd** Iran
103 D1 **Toruń** Pol.

97 B1 **Tory Island** Ireland
97 B1 **Tory Sound** *sea chan.* Ireland
89 D2 **Torzhok** Rus. Fed.
67 B4 **Tosashimizu** Japan
122 B2 **Tosca** S. Africa
108 A2 **Toscano, Arcipelago** *is* Italy
77 C2 **Toshkent** Uzbek.
89 D2 **Tosno** Rus. Fed.
68 C1 **Tosontsengel** Mongolia
152 B2 **Tostado** Arg.
101 D1 **Tostedt** Ger.
80 B1 **Tosya** Turkey
86 D3 **Tot'ma** Rus. Fed.
151 D2 **Totness** Suriname
67 B3 **Tottori** Japan
114 B4 **Touba** Côte d'Ivoire
114 B1 **Toubkal, Jbel** *mt.* Morocco
118 B2 **Touboro** Cameroon
114 B3 **Tougan** Burkina
115 C1 **Touggourt** Alg.
105 D2 **Toul** France
71 C3 **Touliu** Taiwan
105 D3 **Toulon** France
104 C3 **Toulouse** France
Tourane Vietnam *see* **Đa Năng**
104 B2 **Tourlaville** France
100 A2 **Tournai** Belgium
115 D2 **Tourndo, Oued** *watercourse* Alg./Niger
105 C2 **Tournus** France
151 F3 **Touros** Brazil
104 C2 **Tours** France
115 D2 **Toussidé, Pic** *mt.* Chad
122 B3 **Touwsrivier** S. Africa
150 B2 **Tovar** Venez.
66 D2 **Towada** Japan
134 D1 **Townsend** U.S.A.
51 D1 **Townsville** Austr.
61 D2 **Towori, Teluk** *b.* Indon.
77 E2 **Toxkan He** *r.* China
66 D2 **Tōya-ko** *l.* Japan
67 C3 **Toyama** Japan
67 C4 **Toyohashi** Japan
67 C3 **Toyota** Japan
115 C1 **Tozeur** Tunisia
81 C1 **Tqvarch'eli** Georgia
Trâblous Lebanon *see* **Tripoli**
80 B1 **Trabzon** Turkey
106 B2 **Trafalgar, Cabo** *c.* Spain
128 C3 **Trail** Can.
88 B3 **Trakai** Lith.
97 B2 **Tralee** Ireland
Trá Li Ireland *see* **Tralee**
97 C2 **Tramore** Ireland
93 F4 **Tranås** Sweden
63 A3 **Trang** Thai.
59 C3 **Trangan** *i.* Indon.
55 L2 **Transantarctic Mountains** Antarctica
110 B1 **Transylvanian Alps** *mts* Romania
108 B3 **Trapani** Italy
53 C3 **Traralgon** Austr.
63 B2 **Trat** Thai.
102 C2 **Traunstein** Ger.
54 B2 **Travers, Mount** N.Z.
138 B2 **Traverse City** U.S.A.
63 B3 **Tra Vinh** Vietnam
103 D2 **Třebíč** Czech Rep.
109 C2 **Trebinje** Bos.-Herz.
103 E2 **Trebišov** Slovakia
Trebizond Turkey *see* **Trabzon**
109 C1 **Trebnje** Slovenia
Trefynwy U.K. *see* **Monmouth**
153 C3 **Treinta y Tres** Uru.
153 B4 **Trelew** Arg.
93 F4 **Trelleborg** Sweden
130 C3 **Tremblant, Mont** *h.* Can.
109 C2 **Tremiti, Isole** *is* Italy
134 D2 **Tremonton** U.S.A.
107 D1 **Tremp** Spain
103 D2 **Trenčín** Slovakia
153 B3 **Trenque Lauquén** Arg.
Trent Italy *see* **Trento**
98 C3 **Trent** *r.* U.K.
108 B1 **Trento** Italy
139 D2 **Trenton** Can.
137 E2 **Trenton** *MO* U.S.A.
139 E2 **Trenton** *NJ* U.S.A.
131 E3 **Trepassey** Can.
153 B3 **Tres Arroyos** Arg.
155 C2 **Três Corações** Brazil
154 B2 **Três Irmãos, Represa** *resr* Brazil
154 B2 **Três Lagoas** Brazil
153 A4 **Tres Lagos** Arg.
155 C1 **Três Marias, Represa** *resr* Brazil
155 C2 **Três Pontas** Brazil
153 B4 **Tres Puntas, Cabo** *c.* Arg.
155 D2 **Três Rios** Brazil
101 F1 **Treuenbrietzen** Ger.
Treves Ger. *see* **Trier**
108 A1 **Treviglio** Italy
108 B1 **Treviso** Italy
99 A4 **Trevose Head** *hd* U.K.
109 C3 **Tricase** Italy
Trichinopoly India *see* **Tiruchchirappalli**
Trichur India *see* **Thrissur**
53 C2 **Trida** Austr.
100 C3 **Trier** Ger.
108 B1 **Trieste** Italy
108 B1 **Triglav** *mt.* Slovenia
111 B3 **Trikala** Greece
59 D3 **Trikora, Puncak** *mt.* Indon.
97 C2 **Trim** Ireland
73 C4 **Trincomalee** Sri Lanka
154 C1 **Trindade** Brazil
148 H5 **Trindade, Ilha da** *i.* S. Atlantic Ocean
152 B1 **Trinidad** Bol.
147 D3 **Trinidad** *i.* Trin. and Tob.
136 C3 **Trinidad** U.S.A.
147 D3 **Trinidad and Tobago** *country* West Indies
143 E3 **Trinity** *r.* U.S.A.
131 E3 **Trinity Bay** Can.
111 B3 **Tripoli** Greece
80 B2 **Tripoli** Lebanon
115 D1 **Tripoli** Libya
75 D2 **Tripura** *state* India
113 B9 **Tristan da Cunha** *i.* S. Atlantic Ocean
Trivandrum India *see* **Thiruvananthapuram**
108 B2 **Trivento** Italy
103 D2 **Trnava** Slovakia
59 E3 **Trobriand Islands** P.N.G.
92 F2 **Trofors** Norway
109 C2 **Trogir** Croatia
109 C2 **Troia** Italy
100 C2 **Troisdorf** Ger.
106 C2 **Trois Fourches, Cap des** *c.* Morocco
130 C3 **Trois-Rivières** Can.
87 F3 **Troitsk** Rus. Fed.
86 E2 **Troitsko-Pechorsk** Rus. Fed.
151 D3 **Trombetas** *r.* Brazil
Tromelin Island *i.* Micronesia *see* **Fais**
123 C3 **Trompsburg** S. Africa
92 G2 **Tromsø** Norway
92 F3 **Trondheim** Norway
96 B3 **Troon** U.K.
89 E3 **Trosna** Rus. Fed.
97 C1 **Trostan** *h.* U.K.
128 C2 **Trout Lake** *Alta* Can.
128 B1 **Trout Lake** *l. N.W.T.* Can.
130 A2 **Trout Lake** *l. Ont.* Can.
99 B4 **Trowbridge** U.K.
140 C2 **Troy** *AL* U.S.A.
139 E2 **Troy** *NY* U.S.A.
105 C2 **Troyes** France
135 C3 **Troy Peak** U.S.A.
109 D2 **Trstenik** Serbia
89 D3 **Trubchevsk** Rus. Fed.
Truc Giang Vietnam *see* **Bên Tre**
106 B1 **Truchas** Spain
Trucial Coast *country* Asia *see* **United Arab Emirates**
79 C2 **Trucial Coast** U.A.E.
Trucial States *country* Asia *see* **United Arab Emirates**
146 B3 **Trujillo** Hond.
150 B3 **Trujillo** Peru
106 B2 **Trujillo** Spain
147 C4 **Trujillo** Venez.
Trujillo, Monte *mt.* Dom. Rep. *see* **Duarte, Pico**
140 B1 **Trumann** U.S.A.
131 D3 **Truro** Can.
99 A4 **Truro** U.K.
61 C1 **Trus Madi, Gunung** *mt.* Malaysia
142 B2 **Truth or Consequences** U.S.A.
103 D1 **Trutnov** Czech Rep.
93 F3 **Trysil** Norway
103 D1 **Trzebiatów** Pol.
103 D1 **Trzebnica** Pol.
68 B1 **Tsagaannuur** Mongolia
Tsaidam Basin *basin* China *see* **Qaidam Pendi**
121 □D2 **Tsaratanana, Massif du** *mts* Madag.
110 C2 **Tsarevo** Bulg.
122 A2 **Tsaukaib** Namibia
Tselinograd Kazakh. *see* **Astana**
Tsementnyy Rus. Fed. *see* **Fokino**
122 A2 **Tses** Namibia
122 B1 **Tsetseng** Botswana
68 C1 **Tsetserleg** *Arhangay* Mongolia
68 C1 **Tsetserleg** *Hövsgöl* Mongolia
122 B2 **Tshabong** Botswana
122 B1 **Tshane** Botswana
91 D2 **Tshchikskoye Vodokhranilishche** *resr* Rus. Fed.
118 B3 **Tshela** Dem. Rep. Congo
118 C3 **Tshikapa** Dem. Rep. Congo
118 C3 **Tshikapa** *r.* Dem. Rep. Congo
123 C2 **Tshing** S. Africa
123 D1 **Tshipise** S. Africa
118 C3 **Tshitanzu** Dem. Rep. Congo
120 B3 **Tshootsha** Botswana
118 C3 **Tshuapa** *r.* Dem. Rep. Congo
Tshwane S. Africa *see* **Pretoria**
87 D4 **Tsimlyanskoye Vodokhranilishche** *resr* Rus. Fed.
Tsinan China *see* **Jinan**
Tsingtao China *see* **Qingdao**
Tsining China *see* **Jining**
121 □D2 **Tsiroanomandidy** Madag.
Tsitsihar China *see* **Qiqihar**
76 A2 **Ts'khinvali** Georgia
123 C3 **Tsomo** S. Africa
67 C4 **Tsu** Japan
67 D3 **Tsuchiura** Japan
66 D2 **Tsugarū-kaikyō** *str.* Japan
Tsugaru Strait *str.* Japan *see* **Tsugarū-kaikyō**
120 A2 **Tsumeb** Namibia
122 A1 **Tsumis Park** Namibia
120 B2 **Tsumkwe** Namibia
67 C3 **Tsuruga** Japan
66 C3 **Tsuruoka** Japan
67 A4 **Tsushima** *is* Japan
67 B3 **Tsuyama** Japan
123 C2 **Tswelelang** S. Africa
88 C3 **Tsyelyakhany** Belarus
91 C2 **Tsyurupyns'k** Ukr.
Tthenaagoo Can. *see* **Nahanni Butte**
59 C3 **Tual** Indon.
97 B2 **Tuam** Ireland
54 A3 **Tuapeka Mouth** N.Z.
91 D3 **Tuapse** Rus. Fed.
54 A3 **Tuatapere** N.Z.
96 A1 **Tuath, Loch a'** U.K.
142 A1 **Tuba City** U.S.A.
61 C2 **Tuban** Indon.
152 D2 **Tubarão** Brazil
102 B2 **Tübingen** Ger.
115 E1 **Tubruq** Libya
49 L6 **Tubuai Islands** *is* Fr. Polynesia
144 A1 **Tubutama** Mex.
152 C1 **Tucavaca** Bol.
128 B1 **Tuchitua** Can.
142 A2 **Tucson** U.S.A.
143 C1 **Tucumcari** U.S.A.
150 C2 **Tucupita** Venez.
151 E3 **Tucuruí** Brazil
151 E3 **Tucuruí, Represa** *resr* Brazil
107 C1 **Tudela** Spain
118 A1 **Tudun-Wada** Nigeria
106 B1 **Tuela** *r.* Port.
157 F2 **Tufts Abyssal Plain** N. Pacific Ocean
123 D2 **Tugela** *r.* S. Africa
64 B2 **Tuguegarao** Phil.
106 B1 **Tui** Spain
59 C3 **Tukangbesi, Kepulauan** *is* Indon.
126 D2 **Tuktoyaktuk** Can.
88 B2 **Tukums** Latvia
119 D3 **Tukuyu** Tanz.
145 C2 **Tula** Mex.
89 E3 **Tula** Rus. Fed.
Tulach Mhór Ireland *see* **Tullamore**
145 C2 **Tulancingo** Mex.
135 C3 **Tulare** U.S.A.
142 B2 **Tularosa** U.S.A.
110 C1 **Tulcea** Romania
90 B2 **Tul'chyn** Ukr.
Tuléar Madag. *see* **Toliara**
129 E1 **Tulemalu Lake** Can.
143 C2 **Tulia** U.S.A.
128 B1 **Tulita** Can.
140 C1 **Tullahoma** U.S.A.
53 C2 **Tullamore** Austr.
97 C2 **Tullamore** Ireland
104 C2 **Tulle** France
97 C2 **Tullow** Ireland
51 D1 **Tully** Austr.
143 D1 **Tulsa** U.S.A.
126 B2 **Tuluksak** U.S.A.
83 H3 **Tulun** Rus. Fed.
150 B2 **Tumaco** Col.
123 C2 **Tumahole** S. Africa
93 G4 **Tumba** Sweden
118 B3 **Tumba, Lac** *l.* Dem. Rep. Congo
61 C2 **Tumbangtiti** Indon.
53 C3 **Tumbarumba** Austr.
150 A3 **Tumbes** Peru
128 B2 **Tumbler Ridge** Can.
52 A2 **Tumby Bay** Austr.
65 B1 **Tumen** China
150 C2 **Tumereng** Guyana
64 A3 **Tumindao** *i.* Phil.
74 A2 **Tump** Pak.
151 D2 **Tumucumaque, Serra** *hills* Brazil
53 C3 **Tumut** Austr.
99 D4 **Tunbridge Wells, Royal** U.K.
80 B2 **Tunceli** Turkey
53 D2 **Tuncurry** Austr.
119 D4 **Tunduru** Tanz.
110 C2 **Tundzha** *r.* Bulg.
128 B1 **Tungsten (abandoned)** Can.
115 D1 **Tunis** Tunisia
108 B3 **Tunis, Golfe de** *g.* Tunisia
115 C1 **Tunisia** *country* Africa
150 B2 **Tunja** Col.
92 F3 **Tunnsjøen** *l.* Norway
Tunxi China *see* **Huangshan**
154 B2 **Tupã** Brazil
154 C1 **Tupaciguara** Brazil
140 C2 **Tupelo** U.S.A.
152 B2 **Tupiza** Bol.
83 H2 **Tura** Rus. Fed.
86 F3 **Tura** *r.* Rus. Fed.
78 B2 **Turabah** Saudi Arabia
83 J3 **Turana, Khrebet** *mts* Rus. Fed.
54 C1 **Turangi** N.Z.
76 B2 **Turan Lowland** Asia
77 D2 **Turar Ryskulov** Kazakh.
78 A1 **Ţurayf** Saudi Arabia
88 B2 **Turba** Estonia
74 A2 **Turbat** Pak.
150 B2 **Turbo** Col.
110 B1 **Turda** Romania
Turfan China *see* **Turpan**
76 C2 **Turgay** Kazakh.
76 C1 **Turgayskaya Stolovaya Strana** *reg.* Kazakh.
110 C2 **Tŭrgovishte** Bulg.
111 C3 **Turgutlu** Turkey
80 B1 **Turhal** Turkey
107 C2 **Turia** *r.* Spain
108 A1 **Turin** Italy
86 F3 **Turinsk** Rus. Fed.
90 A1 **Turiya** *r.* Ukr.
90 A1 **Turiys'k** Ukr.
90 A2 **Turka** Ukr.
119 D2 **Turkana, Lake** *salt l.* Eth./Kenya
77 C2 **Turkestan** Kazakh.
103 E2 **Túrkeve** Hungary
80 B2 **Turkey** *country* Asia/Europe
50 B1 **Turkey Creek** Austr.
76 C3 **Türkmenabat** Turkm.
76 B2 **Türkmenbaşy** Turkm.
76 B2 **Turkmenistan** *country* Asia
Turkmeniya *country* Asia *see* **Turkmenistan**
Turkmenskaya S.S.R. *country* Asia *see* **Turkmenistan**
147 C2 **Turks and Caicos Islands** *terr.* West Indies
147 C2 **Turks Islands** Turks and Caicos Is
93 H3 **Turku** Fin.
119 D2 **Turkwel** *watercourse* Kenya
135 B3 **Turlock** U.S.A.
155 D1 **Turmalina** Brazil
54 C2 **Turnagain, Cape** N.Z.
146 B3 **Turneffe Islands** Belize
100 B2 **Turnhout** Belgium
129 D2 **Turnor Lake** Can.
Tŭrnovo Bulg. *see* **Veliko Tŭrnovo**
110 B2 **Turnu Măgurele** Romania
68 B2 **Turpan** China
96 C2 **Turriff** U.K.
64 A3 **Turtle Islands** Malaysia/Phil.
77 D2 **Turugart Pass** China/Kyrg.
82 G2 **Turukhansk** Rus. Fed.
140 C2 **Tuscaloosa** U.S.A.
140 C2 **Tuskegee** U.S.A.
81 C2 **Tutak** Turkey
89 E2 **Tutayev** Rus. Fed.
73 B4 **Tuticorin** India
121 C1 **Tutubu** Tanz.
49 J5 **Tutuila** *i.* American Samoa
120 B3 **Tutume** Botswana
93 H3 **Tuusula** Fin.
49 I4 **Tuvalu** *country* S. Pacific Ocean
78 B2 **Tuwayq, Jabal** *hills* Saudi Arabia
78 B2 **Tuwayq, Jabal** *mts* Saudi Arabia
78 A2 **Tuwwal** Saudi Arabia
144 B2 **Tuxpan** Mex.
145 C2 **Tuxpan** Mex.
145 C3 **Tuxtla Gutiérrez** Mex.
62 B1 **Tuyên Quang** Vietnam
63 B2 **Tuy Hoa** Vietnam
80 B2 **Tuz, Lake** *salt l.* Turkey
Tuz Gölü *salt l.* Turkey *see* **Tuz, Lake**
81 C2 **Tuz Khurmātū** Iraq
109 C2 **Tuzla** Bos.-Herz.
91 E2 **Tuzlov** *r.* Rus. Fed.
89 E2 **Tver'** Rus. Fed.
98 B2 **Tweed** *r.* U.K.
53 D1 **Tweed Heads** Austr.
122 A2 **Twee Rivier** Namibia
135 C4 **Twentynine Palms** U.S.A.
131 E3 **Twillingate** Can.
134 D2 **Twin Falls** U.S.A.
54 B2 **Twizel** N.Z.
137 E1 **Two Harbors** U.S.A.
128 C2 **Two Hills** Can.
Tyddewi U.K. *see* **St David's**
143 D2 **Tyler** U.S.A.
83 J3 **Tynda** Rus. Fed.
Tyndinskiy Rus. Fed. *see* **Tynda**
96 B2 **Tyndrum** U.K.
98 C2 **Tyne** *r. England* U.K.
95 C2 **Tyne** *r. Scotland* U.K.
93 F3 **Tynset** Norway
80 B2 **Tyre** Lebanon
69 E1 **Tyrma** Rus. Fed.
111 B3 **Tyrnavos** Greece
52 B3 **Tyrrell, Lake** *dry lake* Austr.
108 B2 **Tyrrhenian Sea** France/Italy
76 B2 **Tyub-Karagan, Mys** *pt* Kazakh.
87 E3 **Tyul'gan** Rus. Fed.
86 F3 **Tyumen'** Rus. Fed.
83 J2 **Tyung** *r.* Rus. Fed.
Tyuratam Kazakh. *see* **Baykonyr**
99 A4 **Tywi** *r.* U.K.
123 D1 **Tzaneen** S. Africa

U

Uaco Congo Angola *see* **Waku-Kungo**
120 B2 **Uamanda** Angola
150 C3 **Uarini** Brazil
150 C3 **Uaupés** Brazil
155 D2 **Ubá** Brazil
155 D1 **Ubaí** Brazil
151 F4 **Ubaitaba** Brazil
118 B3 **Ubangi** *r.* C.A.R./Dem. Rep. Congo
Ubangi-Shari *country* Africa *see* **Central African Republic**
67 B4 **Ube** Japan
106 C2 **Úbeda** Spain
154 C1 **Uberaba** Brazil
154 C1 **Uberlândia** Brazil
106 B1 **Ubiña, Peña** *mt.* Spain
123 D2 **Ubombo** S. Africa
63 B2 **Ubon Ratchathani** Thai.
119 C3 **Ubundu** Dem. Rep. Congo
150 B3 **Ucayali** *r.* Peru
100 B2 **Uccle** Belgium
74 B2 **Uch** Pak.
77 E2 **Ucharal** Kazakh.
66 D2 **Uchiura-wan** *b.* Japan
76 C2 **Uchquduq** Uzbek.
83 J3 **Uchur** *r.* Rus. Fed.
99 D4 **Uckfield** U.K.

128 B3 **Ucluelet** Can.
83 I2 **Udachnyy** Rus. Fed.
74 B2 **Udaipur** India
91 C1 **Uday** *r.* Ukr.
93 F4 **Uddevalla** Sweden
92 G2 **Uddjaure** *l.* Sweden
100 B2 **Uden** Neth.
74 B1 **Udhampur** India
108 B1 **Udine** Italy
89 E2 **Udomlya** Rus. Fed.
62 B2 **Udon Thani** Thai.
73 B3 **Udupi** India
83 K3 **Udyl', Ozero** *l.* Rus. Fed.
67 C3 **Ueda** Japan
61 D2 **Uekuli** Indon.
118 C2 **Uele** *r.* Dem. Rep. Congo
83 N2 **Uelen** Rus. Fed.
101 E1 **Uelzen** Ger.
119 C2 **Uere** *r.* Dem. Rep. Congo
87 E3 **Ufa** Rus. Fed.
119 D3 **Ugalla** *r.* Tanz.
119 D2 **Uganda** *country* Africa
69 F1 **Uglegorsk** Rus. Fed.
89 E2 **Uglich** Rus. Fed.
89 D2 **Uglovka** Rus. Fed.
66 B2 **Uglovoye** Rus. Fed.
89 D3 **Ugra** Rus. Fed.
103 D2 **Uherské Hradiště** Czech Rep.
Uibhist a' Deas *i.* U.K. *see* **South Uist**
Uibhist a' Tuath *i.* U.K. *see* **North Uist**
101 E2 **Uichteritz** Ger.
96 A2 **Uig** U.K.
120 A1 **Uíge** Angola
65 B2 **Ŭijŏngbu** S. Korea
65 A1 **Ŭiju** N. Korea
135 D2 **Uinta Mountains** U.S.A.
120 A3 **Uis Mine** Namibia
65 B2 **Ŭisŏng** S. Korea
123 C3 **Uitenhage** S. Africa
100 C1 **Uithuizen** Neth.
131 D2 **Uivak, Cape** Can.
Ujiyamada Japan *see* **Ise**
74 B2 **Ujjain** India
Ujung Pandang Indon. *see* **Makassar**
89 F3 **Ukholovo** Rus. Fed.
Ukhta Rus. Fed. *see* **Kalevala**
86 E2 **Ukhta** Rus. Fed.
135 B3 **Ukiah** U.S.A.
127 I2 **Ukkusissat** Greenland
88 B2 **Ukmergė** Lith.
90 C2 **Ukraine** *country* Europe
Ukrainskaya S.S.R. *country* Europe *see* **Ukraine**
Ulaanbaatar Mongolia *see* **Ulan Bator**
68 C1 **Ulaangom** Mongolia
59 E3 **Ulamona** P.N.G.
70 A2 **Ulan** China
69 D1 **Ulan Bator** Mongolia
Ulanhad China *see* **Chifeng**
69 E1 **Ulanhot** China
87 D4 **Ulan-Khol** Rus. Fed.
69 D1 **Ulan-Ude** Rus. Fed.
75 D1 **Ulan Ul Hu** *l.* China
65 B2 **Ulchin** S. Korea
Uleåborg Fin. *see* **Oulu**
88 C2 **Ülenurme** Estonia
73 B3 **Ulhasnagar** India
69 D1 **Uliastai** China
68 C1 **Uliastay** Mongolia
59 D2 **Ulithi** *atoll* Micronesia
53 D3 **Ulladulla** Austr.
96 B2 **Ullapool** U.K.
98 B2 **Ullswater** *l.* U.K.
65 C2 **Ullŭng-do** *i.* S. Korea
102 D2 **Ulm** Ger.
65 B2 **Ulsan** S. Korea
96 □ **Ulsta** U.K.
97 C1 **Ulster** *reg.* Ireland/U.K.
52 B3 **Ultima** Austr.
145 D3 **Ulúa** *r.* Hond.
111 C3 **Ulubey** Turkey
111 D3 **Uluborlu** Turkey
111 C2 **Uludağ** *mt.* Turkey
126 E2 **Ulukhaktok** Can.
123 D2 **Ulundi** S. Africa
77 E2 **Ulungur Hu** *l.* China
50 C2 **Uluru** *h.* Austr.
98 B2 **Ulverston** U.K.
90 C2 **Ul'yanovka** Ukr.
87 D3 **Ul'yanovsk** Rus. Fed.
136 C3 **Ulysses** U.S.A.
90 C2 **Uman'** Ukr.
86 C2 **Umba** Rus. Fed.
59 D3 **Umboi** *i.* P.N.G.
59 D3 **Umbukul** P.N.G.
92 H3 **Umeå** Sweden
92 H3 **Umeälven** *r.* Sweden
123 D2 **Umhlanga Rocks** S. Africa
127 J2 **Umiiviip Kangertiva** *inlet* Greenland
126 E2 **Umingmaktok (abandoned)** Can.
123 D2 **Umlazi** S. Africa
78 A2 **Umm al Birak** Saudi Arabia
79 C2 **Umm as Samīm** *salt flat* Oman
116 A3 **Umm Keddada** Sudan
78 A2 **Umm Lajj** Saudi Arabia
78 A2 **Umm Mukhbār, Jabal** *mt.* Saudi Arabia
116 B3 **Umm Ruwaba** Sudan
115 E1 **Umm Sa'ad** Libya
134 B2 **Umpqua** *r.* U.S.A.
120 A2 **Umpulo** Angola
Umtali Zimbabwe *see* **Mutare**
123 C3 **Umtata** S. Africa
123 D3 **Umtentweni** S. Africa
154 B2 **Umuarama** Brazil
123 C3 **Umzimkulu** S. Africa
109 C1 **Una** *r.* Bos.-Herz./Croatia
155 E1 **Una** Brazil
154 C1 **Unaí** Brazil
126 B2 **Unalakleet** U.S.A.
78 B2 **'Unayzah** Saudi Arabia
136 B3 **Uncompahgre Peak** U.S.A.
52 B3 **Underbool** Austr.
136 C1 **Underwood** U.S.A.
89 D3 **Unecha** Rus. Fed.
53 C2 **Ungarie** Austr.
52 A2 **Ungarra** Austr.
127 H2 **Ungava, Péninsule d'** *pen.* Can.
131 D2 **Ungava Bay** Can.
Ungeny Moldova *see* **Ungheni**
90 B2 **Ungheni** Moldova
Unguja *i.* Tanz. *see* **Zanzibar Island**
119 E3 **Ungwana Bay** Kenya
154 B3 **União da Vitória** Brazil
150 C3 **Unini** *r.* Brazil
134 C1 **Union** U.S.A.
140 C1 **Union City** U.S.A.
122 B3 **Uniondale** S. Africa
139 D3 **Uniontown** U.S.A.
79 C2 **United Arab Emirates** *country* Asia
United Arab Republic *country* Africa *see* **Egypt**
95 C3 **United Kingdom** *country* Europe
United Provinces *state* India *see* **Uttar Pradesh**
133 B3 **United States of America** *country* N. America
129 D2 **Unity** Can.
100 C2 **Unna** Ger.
96 □ **Unst** *i.* U.K.
101 E2 **Unstrut** *r.* Ger.
89 E3 **Upa** *r.* Rus. Fed.
119 C3 **Upemba, Lac** *l.* Dem. Rep. Congo
122 B2 **Upington** S. Africa
74 B2 **Upleta** India
49 J5 **'Upolu** *i.* Samoa
[illegible] B2 **Upper Alkali Lake** U.S.A.
128 C2 **Upper Arrow Lake** Can.
54 C2 **Upper Hutt** N.Z.
134 B2 **Upper Klamath Lake** U.S.A.
128 B1 **Upper Liard** Can.
97 C1 **Upper Lough Erne** *l.* U.K.
137 F1 **Upper Red Lake** U.S.A.
Upper Tunguska *r.* Rus. Fed. *see* **Angara**
Upper Volta *country* Africa *see* **Burkina**
93 G4 **Uppsala** Sweden
78 B2 **'Uqlat aş Şuqūr** Saudi Arabia
Urad Qianqi China *see* **Xishanzui**
76 B2 **Ural** *r.* Kazakh./Rus. Fed.
53 D2 **Uralla** Austr.
87 E3 **Ural Mountains** Rus. Fed.
76 B1 **Ural'sk** Kazakh.
Ural'skiy Khrebet *mts* Rus. Fed. *see* **Ural Mountains**
119 D3 **Urambo** Tanz.
53 C3 **Urana** Austr.
129 D2 **Uranium City** Can.
86 F2 **Uray** Rus. Fed.
98 C2 **Ure** *r.* U.K.
86 D3 **Uren'** Rus. Fed.
82 G2 **Urengoy** Rus. Fed.
144 A2 **Ures** Mex.
Urfa Turkey *see* **Şanlıurfa**
76 C2 **Urganch** Uzbek.
100 B1 **Urk** Neth.
111 C3 **Urla** Turkey
110 C2 **Urlați** Romania
81 C2 **Urmia** Iran
81 C2 **Urmia, Lake** *salt l.* Iran
Uroševac Kosovo *see* **Ferizaj**
144 B2 **Uruáchic** Mex.
151 E4 **Uruaçu** Brazil
144 B3 **Uruapan** Mex.
150 B4 **Urubamba** *r.* Peru
151 D3 **Urucara** Brazil
151 E3 **Uruçuí** Brazil
151 E3 **Uruçuí, Serra do** *hills* Brazil
151 D3 **Urucurituba** Brazil
152 C2 **Uruguaiana** Brazil
153 C3 **Uruguay** *country* S. America
Urumchi China *see* **Ürümqi**
68 B2 **Ürümqi** China
Urundi *country* Africa *see* **Burundi**
53 D2 **Urunga** Austr.
119 D3 **Uruwira** Tanz.
110 C2 **Urziceni** Romania
67 B4 **Usa** Japan
86 E2 **Usa** *r.* Rus. Fed.
111 C3 **Uşak** Turkey
120 A3 **Usakos** Namibia
88 C2 **Usachy** Belarus
82 G1 **Ushakova, Ostrov** *i.* Rus. Fed.
77 D2 **Ushtobe** Kazakh.
Ush-Tyube Kazakh. *see* **Ushtobe**
153 B5 **Ushuaia** Arg.
86 E2 **Usinsk** Rus. Fed.
99 B4 **Usk** *r.* U.K.
88 C3 **Uskhodni** Belarus
89 E3 **Usman'** Rus. Fed.
86 D2 **Usogorsk** Rus. Fed.
104 C2 **Ussel** France
66 C1 **Ussuri** *r.* China/Rus. Fed.
66 B2 **Ussuriysk** Rus. Fed.
Ust'-Abakanskoye Rus. Fed. *see* **Abakan**
Ust'-Balyk Rus. Fed. *see* **Nefteyugansk**
91 E2 **Ust'-Donetskiy** Rus. Fed.
108 B3 **Ustica, Isola di** *i.* Italy
83 H3 **Ust'-Ilimsk** Rus. Fed.
86 E2 **Ust'-Ilych** Rus. Fed.
102 C1 **Ústí nad Labem** Czech Rep.
Ustinov Rus. Fed. *see* **Izhevsk**
103 D1 **Ustka** Pol.
83 L3 **Ust'-Kamchatsk** Rus. Fed.
77 E2 **Ust'-Kamenogorsk** Kazakh.
86 F2 **Ust'-Kara** Rus. Fed.
86 E2 **Ust'-Kulom** Rus. Fed.
83 I3 **Ust'-Kut** Rus. Fed.
91 D2 **Ust'-Labinsk** Rus. Fed.
Ust'-Labinskaya Rus. Fed. *see* **Ust'-Labinsk**
88 C2 **Ust'-Luga** Rus. Fed.
86 E2 **Ust'-Nem** Rus. Fed.
83 K2 **Ust'-Nera** Rus. Fed.
83 I2 **Ust'-Olenek** Rus. Fed.
83 K2 **Ust'-Omchug** Rus. Fed.
83 H3 **Ust'-Ordynskiy** Rus. Fed.
103 E2 **Ustrzyki Dolne** Pol.
86 F2 **Ust'-Tsil'ma** Rus. Fed.
86 D2 **Ust'-Ura** Rus. Fed.
76 B2 **Ustyurt Plateau** Kazakh./Uzbek.
89 E2 **Ustyuzhna** Rus. Fed.
146 B3 **Usulután** El Salvador
Usumbura Burundi *see* **Bujumbura**
89 D2 **Usvyaty** Rus. Fed.
135 D3 **Utah** *state* U.S.A.
135 D2 **Utah Lake** U.S.A.
88 C2 **Utena** Lith.
119 D3 **Utete** Tanz.
63 B2 **Uthai Thani** Thai.
74 A2 **Uthal** Pak.
139 D2 **Utica** U.S.A.
107 C2 **Utiel** Spain
128 C2 **Utikuma Lake** Can.
93 G4 **Utlängan** *i.* Sweden
100 B1 **Utrecht** Neth.
123 D2 **Utrecht** S. Africa
106 B2 **Utrera** Spain
92 I2 **Utsjoki** Fin.
67 C3 **Utsunomiya** Japan
87 D4 **Utta** Rus. Fed.
62 B2 **Uttaradit** Thai.
75 B1 **Uttarakhand** *state* India
75 B2 **Uttar Pradesh** *state* India
Uummannaq Greenland *see* **Dundas**
127 I2 **Uummannaq** Greenland
127 I2 **Uummannaq Fjord** *inlet* Greenland
93 H3 **Uusikaupunki** Fin.
120 A2 **Uutapi** Namibia
143 D3 **Uvalde** U.S.A.
119 D3 **Uvinza** Tanz.
123 D3 **Uvongo** S. Africa
68 C1 **Uvs Nuur** *salt l.* Mongolia
67 D4 **Uwajima** Japan
78 A2 **'Uwayriḍ, Ḥarrat al** *lava field* Saudi Arabia
116 A2 **Uweinat, Jebel** *mt.* Sudan
83 H3 **Uyar** Rus. Fed.
115 C4 **Uyo** Nigeria
79 B2 **Uyun** Saudi Arabia
152 B2 **Uyuni** Bol.
152 B2 **Uyuni, Salar de** *salt flat* Bol.
76 C2 **Uzbekistan** *country* Asia
Uzbekskaya S.S.R. *country* Asia *see* **Uzbekistan**
Uzbek S.S.R. *country* Asia *see* **Uzbekistan**
104 C2 **Uzerche** France
105 C3 **Uzès** France
90 C1 **Uzh** *r.* Ukr.
90 A2 **Uzhhorod** Ukr.
Užhorod Ukr. *see* **Uzhhorod**
109 C2 **Užice** Serbia
89 E3 **Uzlovaya** Rus. Fed.
111 C3 **Üzümlü** Turkey
111 C2 **Uzunköprü** Turkey

V

123 B2 **Vaal** *r.* S. Africa
92 I3 **Vaala** Fin.
123 C2 **Vaal Dam** S. Africa
123 C1 **Vaalwater** S. Africa
92 H3 **Vaasa** Fin.
103 D2 **Vác** Hungary
154 C2 **Vacaria** Brazil
154 B2 **Vacaria, Serra** *hills* Brazil
135 B3 **Vacaville** U.S.A.
74 B2 **Vadodara** India
92 I1 **Vadsø** Norway
105 D2 **Vaduz** Liechtenstein
94 B1 **Vágar** *i.* Faroe Is
94 B1 **Vágur** Faroe Is
103 D2 **Váh** *r.* Slovakia
49 I4 **Vaiaku** Tuvalu
88 B2 **Vaida** Estonia
136 B3 **Vail** U.S.A.
77 C3 **Vakhsh** Tajik.
Vakhstroy Tajik. *see* **Vakhsh**
79 C2 **Vakīlābād** Iran
108 B1 **Valdagno** Italy
Valdai Hills *hills* Rus. Fed. *see* **Valdayskaya Vozvyshennost'**
89 D2 **Valday** Rus. Fed.
89 D2 **Valdayskaya Vozvyshennost'** *hills* Rus. Fed.
106 B2 **Valdecañas, Embalse de** *resr* Spain
93 G4 **Valdemarsvik** Sweden
106 C2 **Valdepeñas** Spain
153 B4 **Valdés, Península** *pen.* Arg.
126 C2 **Valdez** U.S.A.
153 A3 **Valdivia** Chile
130 C3 **Val-d'Or** Can.
141 D2 **Valdosta** U.S.A.
128 C2 **Valemount** Can.
152 E1 **Valença** Brazil
105 C3 **Valence** France
107 C2 **Valencia** Spain
107 C2 **Valencia** *reg.* Spain
150 C1 **Valencia** Venez.
107 D2 **Valencia, Golfo de** *g.* Spain
106 B1 **Valencia de Don Juan** Spain
97 A3 **Valencia Island** Ireland
105 C1 **Valenciennes** France
136 C2 **Valentine** U.S.A.
64 B2 **Valenzuela** Phil.
150 B2 **Valera** Venez.
88 C2 **Valga** Estonia
109 C2 **Valjevo** Serbia
88 C2 **Valka** Latvia
93 H3 **Valkeakoski** Fin.
100 B2 **Valkenswaard** Neth.
91 D2 **Valky** Ukr.
55 G2 **Valkyrie Dome** Antarctica
145 D2 **Valladolid** Mex.
106 C1 **Valladolid** Spain
93 E4 **Valle** Norway
145 C2 **Vallecillos** Mex.
150 C2 **Valle de la Pascua** Venez.
150 B1 **Valledupar** Col.
145 C2 **Valle Hermoso** Mex.
135 B3 **Vallejo** U.S.A.
152 A2 **Vallenar** Chile
84 F5 **Valletta** Malta
137 D1 **Valley City** U.S.A.
134 B2 **Valley Falls** U.S.A.
128 C2 **Valleyview** Can.
107 D1 **Valls** Spain
129 D3 **Val Marie** Can.
88 C2 **Valmiera** Latvia
104 B2 **Valognes** France
88 C3 **Valozhyn** Belarus
154 B2 **Valparaíso** Brazil
153 A3 **Valparaíso** Chile
105 C3 **Valréas** France
59 D3 **Vals, Tanjung** *c.* Indon.
74 B2 **Valsad** India
122 B2 **Valspan** S. Africa
91 D1 **Valuyki** Rus. Fed.
106 B2 **Valverde del Camino** Spain
81 C2 **Van** Turkey
81 C2 **Van, Lake** *salt l.* Turkey
81 C1 **Vanadzor** Armenia
83 H2 **Vanavara** Rus. Fed.
140 B1 **Van Buren** *AR* U.S.A.
139 F1 **Van Buren** *ME* U.S.A.
Van Buren U.S.A. *see* **Kettering**
128 B3 **Vancouver** Can.
134 B1 **Vancouver** U.S.A.
128 B3 **Vancouver Island** Can.
138 B3 **Vandalia** *IL* U.S.A.
138 C3 **Vandalia** *OH* U.S.A.
123 C2 **Vanderbijlpark** S. Africa
128 B2 **Vanderhoof** Can.
122 B3 **Vanderkloof Dam** *dam* S. Africa
50 C1 **Van Diemen Gulf** Austr.
88 C2 **Vändra** Estonia
Väner, Lake *l.* Sweden *see* **Vänern**
93 F4 **Vänern** *l.* Sweden
93 F4 **Vänersborg** Sweden
121 □D3 **Vangaindrano** Madag.
Van Gölü *salt l.* Turkey *see* **Van, Lake**
142 C2 **Van Horn** U.S.A.
59 D3 **Vanimo** P.N.G.
83 K3 **Vanino** Rus. Fed.
104 B2 **Vannes** France
Vannovka Kazakh. *see* **Turar Ryskulov**
59 D3 **Van Rees, Pegunungan** *mts* Indon.
122 A3 **Vanrhynsdorp** S. Africa
93 H3 **Vantaa** Fin.
49 I5 **Vanua Levu** *i.* Fiji
48 H5 **Vanuatu** *country* S. Pacific Ocean
138 C2 **Van Wert** U.S.A.
122 B3 **Vanwyksvlei** S. Africa
122 B2 **Van Zylsrus** S. Africa
75 C2 **Varanasi** India
92 I1 **Varangerfjorden** *sea chan.* Norway
92 I1 **Varangerhalvøya** *pen.* Norway
88 C2 **Varapayeva** Belarus
109 C1 **Varaždin** Croatia
93 F4 **Varberg** Sweden
111 B3 **Varda** Greece
111 B2 **Vardar** *r.* Macedonia
93 E4 **Varde** Denmark
92 J1 **Vardø** Norway
101 D1 **Varel** Ger.
88 B3 **Varėna** Lith.
139 E1 **Varennes** Can.
108 A1 **Varese** Italy
155 C2 **Varginha** Brazil
93 I3 **Varkaus** Fin.
110 C2 **Varna** Bulg.
93 F4 **Värnamo** Sweden
155 D1 **Várzea da Palma** Brazil

86 C2 Varzino Rus. Fed.
Vasa Fin. see Vaasa
88 C3 Vasilyevichy Belarus
88 C2 Vasknarva Estonia
110 C1 Vaslui Romania
93 G4 Västerås Sweden
93 G3 Västerdalälven r. Sweden
88 A2 Västerhaninge Sweden
93 G4 Västervik Sweden
108 B2 Vasto Italy
91 D2 Vasylivka Ukr.
90 C1 Vasyl'kiv Ukr.
91 D2 Vasyl'kivka Ukr.
104 C2 Vatan France
111 B3 Vatheia Greece
108 B2 Vatican City Europe
92 □B3 Vatnajökull Iceland
110 C1 Vatra Dornei Romania
Vätter, Lake l. Sweden see Vättern
93 F4 Vättern l. Sweden
142 B2 Vaughn U.S.A.
105 C3 Vauvert France
121 □D2 Vavatenina Madag.
49 J5 Vava'u Group is Tonga
88 B3 Vawkavysk Belarus
93 F4 Växjö Sweden
Vayenga Rus. Fed. see Severomorsk
86 E1 Vaygach, Ostrov i. Rus. Fed.
154 C1 Vazante Brazil
101 D1 Vechta Ger.
110 C2 Vedea r. Romania
100 C1 Veendam Neth.
100 B1 Veenendaal Neth.
92 F2 Vega i. Norway
128 C2 Vegreville Can.
106 B2 Vejer de la Frontera Spain
93 E4 Vejle Denmark
110 B2 Velbŭzhdki Prokhod pass Bulg./Macedonia
122 A3 Velddrif S. Africa
100 B2 Veldhoven Neth.
109 B2 Velebit mts Croatia
100 C2 Velen Ger.
109 C1 Velenje Slovenia
109 D2 Veles Macedonia
106 C2 Vélez-Málaga Spain
155 D1 Velhas r. Brazil
109 D2 Velika Plana Serbia
88 C2 Velikaya r. Rus. Fed.
89 D2 Velikiye Luki Rus. Fed.
89 D2 Velikiy Novgorod Rus. Fed.
86 D2 Velikiy Ustyug Rus. Fed.
110 C2 Veliko Tŭrnovo Bulg.
108 B2 Veli Lošinj Croatia
89 D2 Velizh Rus. Fed.
108 B2 Velletri Italy
73 B3 Vellore India
86 D2 Vel'sk Rus. Fed.
101 F1 Velten Ger.
91 D1 Velykyy Burluk Ukr.
Velykyy Tokmak Ukr. see Tokmak
159 E4 Vema Trench Indian Ocean
108 B2 Venafro Italy
154 C2 Venceslau Bráz Brazil
104 C2 Vendôme France
108 B1 Veneta, Laguna lag. Italy
89 E3 Venev Rus. Fed.
Venezia Italy see Venice
150 C2 Venezuela country S. America
150 B1 Venezuela, Golfo de g. Venez.
108 B1 Venice Italy
141 D3 Venice U.S.A.
108 B1 Venice, Gulf of Europe
100 C2 Venlo Neth.
93 E4 Vennesla Norway
100 B2 Venray Neth.
88 B2 Venta r. Latvia/Lith.
88 B2 Venta Lith.
123 C2 Ventersburg S. Africa
123 C3 Venterstad S. Africa
108 A2 Ventimiglia Italy
99 C4 Ventnor U.K.
88 B2 Ventspils Latvia
135 C4 Ventura U.S.A.
143 C3 Venustiano Carranza, Presa resr Mex.
107 C2 Vera Spain
154 C2 Vera Cruz Brazil
145 C3 Veracruz Mex.
74 B2 Veraval India
108 A1 Verbania Italy
108 A1 Vercelli Italy
105 D3 Vercors reg. France
92 F3 Verdalsøra Norway
154 B1 Verde r. Brazil
154 B2 Verde r. Brazil
144 B2 Verde r. Mex.
142 A2 Verde r. U.S.A.
155 D1 Verde Grande r. Brazil
101 D1 Verden (Aller) Ger.
154 B1 Verdinho, Serra do mts Brazil
105 D3 Verdon r. France
105 D2 Verdun France
123 C2 Vereeniging S. Africa
106 B1 Verín Spain
91 D3 Verkhnebakanskiy Rus. Fed.
89 D3 Verkhnedneprovskiy Rus. Fed.
92 J2 Verkhnetulomskiy Rus. Fed.
92 J2 Verkhnetulomskoye Vodokhranilishche resr Rus. Fed.
87 D4 Verkhniy Baskunchak Rus. Fed.
91 E1 Verkhniy Mamon Rus. Fed.
86 D2 Verkhnyaya Toyma Rus. Fed.
89 E3 Verkhov'ye Rus. Fed.
90 A2 Verkhovyna Ukr.
83 J2 Verkhoyanskiy Khrebet mts Rus. Fed.
129 C2 Vermilion Can.
137 D2 Vermillion U.S.A.
130 A3 Vermillion Bay Can.
139 E2 Vermont state U.S.A.
135 E2 Vernal U.S.A.
122 B2 Verneuk Pan salt pan S. Africa
128 C2 Vernon Can.
143 D2 Vernon U.S.A.
141 D3 Vero Beach U.S.A.
111 B2 Veroia Greece
108 B1 Verona Italy
138 B2 Verona U.S.A.
104 C2 Versailles France
104 B2 Vertou France
123 D2 Verulam S. Africa
100 B2 Verviers Belgium
105 C2 Vervins France
105 D3 Vescovato France
87 E3 Veselaya, Gora mt. Rus. Fed.
91 C2 Vesele Ukr.
91 E2 Veselyy Rus. Fed.
105 D2 Vesoul France
140 C2 Vestavia Hills U.S.A.
92 F2 Vesterålen is Norway
92 F2 Vestfjorden sea chan. Norway
94 B1 Vestmanna Faroe Is
92 □A3 Vestmannaeyjar Iceland
92 □A3 Vestmannaeyjar is Iceland
93 E3 Vestnes Norway
Vesuvio vol. Italy see Vesuvius
108 B2 Vesuvius vol. Italy
89 E2 Ves'yegonsk Rus. Fed.
103 D2 Veszprém Hungary
93 G4 Vetlanda Sweden
86 D3 Vetluga Rus. Fed.
86 D3 Vetluzhskiy Rus. Fed.
100 A2 Veurne Belgium
119 D2 Veveno r. Sudan
105 D2 Vevey Switz.
91 D1 Veydelevka Rus. Fed.
80 B1 Vezirköprü Turkey
Vialar Alg. see Tissemsilt
152 C3 Viamao Brazil
151 E3 Viana Brazil
106 B1 Viana do Castelo Port.
Viangchan Laos see Vientiane
62 B1 Viangphoukha Laos
111 C3 Viannos Greece
154 C1 Vianópolis Brazil
108 B2 Viareggio Italy
93 E4 Viborg Denmark
Viborg Rus. Fed. see Vyborg
109 C3 Vibo Valentia Italy
107 D1 Vic Spain
144 A1 Vicente Guerrero Mex.
108 B1 Vicenza Italy
89 F2 Vichuga Rus. Fed.
105 C2 Vichy France
140 B2 Vicksburg U.S.A.
155 D2 Viçosa Brazil
52 A3 Victor Harbor Austr.
50 C1 Victoria r. Austr.
52 B3 Victoria state Austr.
Victoria Cameroon see Limbe
128 B3 Victoria Can.
153 A3 Victoria Chile
Victoria Malaysia see Labuan
113 I6 Victoria Seychelles
143 D3 Victoria U.S.A.
119 D3 Victoria, Lake Africa
52 B2 Victoria, Lake Austr.
62 A1 Victoria, Mount Myanmar
59 D3 Victoria, Mount P.N.G.
154 B3 Victoria, Sierra de la hills Arg.
120 B2 Victoria Falls waterfall Zambia/Zimbabwe
120 B2 Victoria Falls Zimbabwe
126 E2 Victoria Island Can.
55 M2 Victoria Land coastal area Antarctica
50 C1 Victoria River Downs Austr.
139 E1 Victoriaville Can.
122 B3 Victoria West S. Africa
135 C4 Victorville U.S.A.
141 D2 Vidalia U.S.A.
110 C2 Videle Romania
92 □A2 Víðidalsá Iceland
110 B2 Vidin Bulg.
74 B2 Vidisha India
140 B2 Vidor U.S.A.
153 B4 Viedma Arg.
153 A4 Viedma, Lago l. Arg.
102 C2 Viehberg mt. Austria
107 D1 Vielha Spain
100 B2 Vielsalm Belgium
101 E2 Vienenburg Ger.
103 D2 Vienna Austria
138 C3 Vienna U.S.A.
105 C2 Vienne France
104 C2 Vienne r. France
62 B2 Vientiane Laos
100 C2 Viersen Ger.
104 C2 Vierzon France
144 B2 Viesca Mex.
109 C2 Vieste Italy
62 B2 Vietnam country Asia
62 B1 Việt Tri Vietnam
64 B2 Vigan Phil.
108 A1 Vigevano Italy
106 B1 Vigo Spain
Viipuri Rus. Fed. see Vyborg
73 C3 Vijayawada India
92 □B3 Vík Iceland
111 B2 Vikhren mt. Bulg.
128 C2 Viking Can.
92 F3 Vikna i. Norway
Vila Alferes Chamusca Moz. see Guija
Vila Arriaga Angola see Bibala
Vila Bugaço Angola see Camanongue
Vila Cabral Moz. see Lichinga
Vila da Ponte Angola see Kuvango
Vila de Aljustrel Angola see Cangamba
Vila de Almoster Angola see Chiange
Vila de João Belo Moz. see Xai-Xai
Vila de Trego Morais Moz. see Chókwé
Vila Fontes Moz. see Caia
106 B2 Vila Franca de Xira Port.
106 B1 Vilagarcía de Arousa Spain
123 D1 Vila Gomes da Costa Moz.
106 B1 Vilalba Spain
Vila Luísa Moz. see Marracuene
Vila Marechal Carmona Angola see Uíge
Vila Miranda Moz. see Macaloge
121 □D2 Vilanandro, Tanjona c. Madag.
88 C2 Viļāni Latvia
106 B1 Vila Nova de Gaia Port.
107 D1 Vilanova i la Geltrú Spain
Vila Paiva de Andrada Moz. see Gorongosa
Vila Pery Moz. see Chimoio
106 B1 Vila Real Port.
106 B1 Vilar Formoso Port.
Vila Salazar Angola see N'dalatando
Vila Salazar Zimbabwe see Sango
Vila Teixeira de Sousa Angola see Luau
155 D2 Vila Velha Brazil
150 B4 Vilcabamba, Cordillera mts Peru
82 F1 Vil'cheka, Zemlya i. Rus. Fed.
92 G3 Vilhelmina Sweden
150 C4 Vilhena Brazil
88 C2 Viljandi Estonia
123 C2 Viljoenskroon S. Africa
88 B3 Vilkaviškis Lith.
83 H1 Vil'kitskogo, Proliv str. Rus. Fed.
144 B1 Villa Ahumada Mex.
106 B1 Villablino Spain
102 C2 Villach Austria
Villa Cisneros Western Sahara see Ad Dakhla
144 B2 Villa de Cos Mex.
152 B3 Villa Dolores Arg.
145 C3 Villa Flores Mex.
153 C3 Villa Gesell Arg.
145 C2 Villagrán Mex.
145 C3 Villahermosa Mex.
144 A2 Villa Insurgentes Mex.
107 C2 Villajoyosa-La Vila Joíosa Spain
152 B3 Villa María Arg.
153 B3 Villa Mercedes Arg.
152 B2 Villa Montes Bol.
144 B2 Villanueva Mex.
106 B2 Villanueva de la Serena Spain
106 C2 Villanueva de los Infantes Spain
152 C2 Villa Ocampo Arg.
142 B3 Villa Ocampo Mex.
108 A3 Villaputzu Italy
152 C2 Villarrica Para.
106 C2 Villarrobledo Spain
Villasalazar Zimbabwe see Sango
152 B2 Villa Unión Arg.
144 B2 Villa Unión Mex.
144 B2 Villa Unión Mex.
150 B2 Villavicencio Col.
152 B2 Villazon Bol.
104 C3 Villefranche-de-Rouergue France
105 C2 Villefranche-sur-Saône France
107 C2 Villena Spain
100 A2 Villeneuve-d'Ascq France
104 C3 Villeneuve-sur-Lot France
140 B2 Ville Platte U.S.A.
100 A3 Villers-Cotterêts France
105 C2 Villeurbanne France
123 C2 Villiers S. Africa
102 B2 Villingen Ger.
137 E2 Villisca U.S.A.
88 C3 Vilnius Lith.
91 C2 Vil'nohirs'k Ukr.
91 D2 Vil'nyans'k Ukr.
100 B2 Vilvoorde Belgium
88 C3 Vilyeyka Belarus
83 J2 Vilyuy r. Rus. Fed.
93 G4 Vimmerby Sweden
153 A3 Viña del Mar Chile
107 D1 Vinaròs Spain
138 B3 Vincennes U.S.A.
55 J3 Vincennes Bay Antarctica
139 D3 Vineland U.S.A.
62 B2 Vinh Vietnam
63 B2 Vinh Long Vietnam
143 D1 Vinita U.S.A.
90 B2 Vinnytsya Ukr.
55 R2 Vinson Massif mt. Antarctica
93 E3 Vinstra Norway
105 E2 Vipiteno Italy
64 B2 Virac Phil.
74 B2 Viramgam India
80 B2 Viranşehir Turkey
129 D3 Virden Can.
104 B2 Vire France
120 A2 Virei Angola
155 D1 Virgem da Lapa Brazil
142 A1 Virgin r. U.S.A.
123 C2 Virginia S. Africa
137 E1 Virginia U.S.A.
139 D3 Virginia state U.S.A.
139 D3 Virginia Beach U.S.A.
135 C3 Virginia City U.S.A.
147 D3 Virgin Islands (U.K.) terr. West Indies
147 D3 Virgin Islands (U.S.A.) terr. West Indies
63 B2 Virôchey Cambodia
109 C1 Virovitica Croatia
100 B3 Virton Belgium
88 B2 Virtsu Estonia
73 B4 Virudhunagar India
109 C2 Vis i. Croatia
88 C2 Visaginas Lith.
135 C3 Visalia U.S.A.
74 B2 Visavadar India
64 B2 Visayan Sea Phil.
93 G4 Visby Sweden
126 E2 Viscount Melville Sound sea chan. Can.
151 E3 Viseu Brazil
106 B1 Viseu Port.
110 B1 Vişeu de Sus Romania
73 C3 Vishakhapatnam India
88 C2 Višķi Latvia
109 C2 Visoko Bos.-Herz.
103 D1 Vistula r. Pol.
Vitebsk Belarus see Vitsyebsk
108 B2 Viterbo Italy
49 I5 Viti Levu i. Fiji
83 I3 Vitim r. Rus. Fed.
155 D2 Vitória Brazil
151 E4 Vitória da Conquista Brazil
106 C1 Vitoria-Gasteiz Spain
104 B2 Vitré France
105 C2 Vitry-le-François France
89 D2 Vitsyebsk Belarus
105 D2 Vittel France
108 B3 Vittoria Italy
108 B1 Vittorio Veneto Italy
106 B1 Viveiro Spain
136 C2 Vivian U.S.A.
Vizagapatam India see Vishakhapatnam
142 A3 Vizcaíno, Desierto de des. Mex.
144 A2 Vizcaíno, Sierra mts Mex.
111 C2 Vize Turkey
73 C3 Vizianagaram India
100 B2 Vlaardingen Neth.
87 D4 Vladikavkaz Rus. Fed.
89 F2 Vladimir Rus. Fed.
66 B2 Vladivostok Rus. Fed.
109 D2 Vlasotince Serbia
100 B1 Vlieland i. Neth.
100 A2 Vlissingen Neth.
109 C2 Vlorë Albania
102 C1 Vltava r. Czech Rep.
102 C2 Vöcklabruck Austria
109 C2 Vodice Croatia
Vogelkop Peninsula pen. Indon. see Doberai, Jazirah
101 D2 Vogelsberg hills Ger.
Vohémar Madag. see Iharaña
Vohibinany Madag. see Ampasimanolotra
Vohimarina Madag. see Iharaña
121 □D3 Vohimena, Tanjona c. Madag.
121 □D3 Vohipeno Madag.
119 D3 Voi Kenya
105 D2 Voiron France
131 D2 Voisey's Bay Can.
109 C1 Vojvodina prov. Serbia
92 J3 Voknavolok Rus. Fed.
Volcano Bay b. Japan see Uchiura-wan
69 F3 Volcano Islands is Japan
Volchansk Ukr. see Vovchans'k
89 E2 Volga Rus. Fed.
89 F2 Volga r. Rus. Fed.
87 D4 Volgodonsk Rus. Fed.
87 D4 Volgograd Rus. Fed.
87 D4 Volgogradskoye Vodokhranilishche resr Rus. Fed.
89 D2 Volkhov Rus. Fed.
89 D1 Volkhov r. Rus. Fed.
101 E2 Volkstedt Ger.
91 D2 Volnovakha Ukr.
90 B2 Volochys'k Ukr.
91 D2 Volodars'ke Ukr.
Volodarskoye Kazakh. see Saumalkol'
90 B1 Volodars'k-Volyns'kyy Ukr.
90 B1 Volodymyrets' Ukr.
90 A1 Volodymyr-Volyns'kyy Ukr.
89 E2 Vologda Rus. Fed.
89 E2 Volokolamsk Rus. Fed.
91 D1 Volokonovka Rus. Fed.
111 B3 Volos Greece
88 C2 Volosovo Rus. Fed.
89 D2 Volot Rus. Fed.
89 E3 Volovo Rus. Fed.
87 D3 Vol'sk Rus. Fed.
114 C4 Volta r. Ghana
114 C4 Volta, Lake resr Ghana
155 D2 Volta Redonda Brazil
110 C2 Voluntari Romania
87 D4 Volzhskiy Rus. Fed.
92 □C2 Vopnafjörður Iceland
88 C3 Voranava Belarus

160 K3 **Voring Plateau** N. Atlantic Ocean
86 F2 **Vorkuta** Rus. Fed.
88 B2 **Vormsi** *i.* Estonia
83 G2 **Vorogovo** Rus. Fed.
89 E3 **Voronezh** Rus. Fed.
89 E3 **Voronezh** *r.* Rus. Fed.
91 E1 **Vorontsovka** Rus. Fed.
Voroshilov Rus. Fed. *see* **Ussuriysk**
Voroshilovgrad Ukr. *see* **Luhans'k**
Voroshilovsk Rus. Fed. *see* **Stavropol'**
Voroshilovsk Ukr. *see* **Alchevs'k**
91 C2 **Vorskla** *r.* Rus. Fed.
88 C2 **Võrtsjärv** *l.* Estonia
88 C2 **Võru** Estonia
122 B3 **Vosburg** S. Africa
105 D2 **Vosges** *mts* France
89 E2 **Voskresensk** Rus. Fed.
93 E3 **Voss** Norway
86 C2 **Vostochnaya Litsa** Rus. Fed.
Vostochno-Sibirskoye More *sea* Rus. Fed. *see* **East Siberian Sea**
83 H3 **Vostochnyy Sayan** *mts* Rus. Fed.
66 C1 **Vostok** Rus. Fed.
49 L5 **Vostok Island** Kiribati
86 E3 **Votkinsk** Rus. Fed.
86 E3 **Votkinskoye Vodokhranilishche** *resr* Rus. Fed.
154 C2 **Votuporanga** Brazil
105 C2 **Vouziers** France
91 D1 **Vovchans'k** Ukr.
92 J2 **Voynitsa** Rus. Fed.
86 E2 **Voyvozh** Rus. Fed.
91 C2 **Voznesens'k** Ukr.
76 B2 **Vozrozhdenya Island** *pen.* Kazakh./Uzbek.
93 E4 **Vrådal** Norway
90 C2 **Vradiyivka** Ukr.
66 B2 **Vrangel'** Rus. Fed.
Vrangelya, Ostrov *i.* Rus. Fed. *see* **Wrangel Island**
109 D2 **Vranje** Serbia
110 C2 **Vratnik** *pass* Bulg.
110 B2 **Vratsa** Bulg.
109 C1 **Vrbas** *r.* Bos.-Herz.
109 C1 **Vrbas** Serbia
122 A3 **Vredenburg** S. Africa
122 A3 **Vredendal** S. Africa
100 B3 **Vresse** Belgium
100 C1 **Vriezenveen** Neth.
109 D1 **Vršac** Serbia
122 B2 **Vryburg** S. Africa
123 D2 **Vryheid** S. Africa
89 D1 **Vsevolozhsk** Rus. Fed.
Vučitrn Kosovo *see* **Vushtrri**
109 C1 **Vukovar** Croatia
86 E2 **Vuktyl'** Rus. Fed.
123 C2 **Vukuzakhe** S. Africa
90 B2 **Vulcănești** Moldova
109 B3 **Vulcano, Isola** *i.* Italy
Vulkaneshty Moldova *see* **Vulcănești**
63 B2 **Vung Tau** Vietnam
92 H2 **Vuollerim** Sweden
92 I2 **Vuotso** Fin.
109 D2 **Vushtrri** Kosovo
74 B2 **Vyara** India
Vyarkhowye Belarus *see* **Ruba**
Vyatka Rus. Fed. *see* **Kirov**
89 D2 **Vyaz'ma** Rus. Fed.
88 C1 **Vyborg** Rus. Fed.
88 C1 **Vyborgskiy Zaliv** *b.* Rus. Fed.
86 D2 **Vychegda** *r.* Rus. Fed.
88 C2 **Vyerkhnyadzvinsk** Belarus
89 D3 **Vyetka** Belarus
89 D3 **Vygonichi** Rus. Fed.
86 C2 **Vygozero, Ozero** *l.* Rus. Fed.
87 D3 **Vyksa** Rus. Fed.
90 B2 **Vylkove** Ukr.
90 A2 **Vynohradiv** Ukr.
89 D2 **Vypolzovo** Rus. Fed.
89 D2 **Vyritsa** Rus. Fed.
91 D2 **Vyselki** Rus. Fed.
90 C1 **Vyshhorod** Ukr.
89 D2 **Vyshnevolotskaya Gryada** *ridge* Rus. Fed.
89 D2 **Vyshniy-Volochek** Rus. Fed.
103 D2 **Vyškov** Czech Rep.
89 E2 **Vysokovsk** Rus. Fed.
86 C2 **Vytegra** Rus. Fed.

W

114 B3 **Wa** Ghana
100 B2 **Waal** *r.* Neth.
100 B2 **Waalwijk** Neth.
119 D2 **Waat** Sudan
128 C2 **Wabasca** *r.* Can.
128 C2 **Wabasca-Desmarais** Can.
138 B3 **Wabash** *r.* U.S.A.
129 E2 **Wabowden** Can.
103 D1 **Wąbrzeźno** Pol.
141 D3 **Waccasassa Bay** U.S.A.
101 D2 **Wächtersbach** Ger.
143 D2 **Waco** U.S.A.
115 D2 **Waddān** Libya
Waddeneilanden *is* Neth. *see* **West Frisian Islands**
Wadden Islands *is* Neth. *see* **West Frisian Islands**
100 B1 **Waddenzee** *sea chan.* Neth.
128 B2 **Waddington, Mount** Can.
100 B1 **Waddinxveen** Neth.
129 D2 **Wadena** Can.
137 D1 **Wadena** U.S.A.
50 B1 **Wadeye** Austr.
74 A2 **Wadh** Pak.
Wadhwan India *see* **Surendranagar**
116 B2 **Wadi Halfa** Sudan
116 B3 **Wad Medani** Sudan
122 B3 **Waenhuiskrans** S. Africa
70 C2 **Wafangdian** China
100 B2 **Wageningen** Neth.
127 G2 **Wager Bay** Can.
53 C3 **Wagga Wagga** Austr.
137 D2 **Wagner** U.S.A.
74 B1 **Wah** Pak.
116 A2 **Wāḥāt ad Dākhilah** Egypt
116 A2 **Wāḥāt al Baḥrīyah** Egypt
116 A2 **Wāḥāt al Farāfirah** Egypt
116 B2 **Wāḥāt al Khārijah** Egypt
116 A2 **Wāḥāt Sīwah** Egypt
137 D2 **Wahoo** U.S.A.
137 D1 **Wahpeton** U.S.A.
54 B2 **Waiau** *r.* N.Z.
59 C3 **Waigeo** *i.* Indon.
61 C2 **Waikabubak** Indon.
54 C1 **Waikaremoana, Lake** N.Z.
52 A2 **Waikerie** Austr.
54 B2 **Waimate** N.Z.
75 B3 **Wainganga** *r.* India
61 D2 **Waingapu** Indon.
129 C2 **Wainwright** Can.
126 B2 **Wainwright** U.S.A.
54 C1 **Waiouru** N.Z.
54 B2 **Waipara** N.Z.
54 C1 **Waipawa** N.Z.
54 B2 **Wairau** *r.* N.Z.
54 C1 **Wairoa** N.Z.
54 B2 **Waitaki** *r.* N.Z.
54 B1 **Waitara** N.Z.
54 B1 **Waiuku** N.Z.
67 C3 **Wajima** Japan
119 E2 **Wajir** Kenya
67 C3 **Wakasa-wan** *b.* Japan
54 A3 **Wakatipu, Lake** N.Z.
129 D2 **Wakaw** Can.
67 C4 **Wakayama** Japan
136 [illegible] **WaKeeney** U.S.A.
54 B2 **Wakefield** N.Z.
98 C3 **Wakefield** U.K.
Wakeham Can. *see* **Kangiqsujuaq**
48 H2 **Wake Island** *terr.* N. Pacific Ocean
66 D1 **Wakkanai** Japan
123 D2 **Wakkerstroom** S. Africa
120 A2 **Waku Kungo** Angola
103 D1 **Wałbrzych** Pol.
53 D2 **Walcha** Austr.
100 C1 **Walchum** Ger.
103 D1 **Wałcz** Pol.
99 B3 **Wales** *admin. div.* U.K.
53 C2 **Walgett** Austr.
119 C3 **Walikale** Dem. Rep. Congo
135 C3 **Walker Lake** U.S.A.
134 C1 **Wallace** *ID* U.S.A.
141 E2 **Wallace** *NC* U.S.A.
52 A2 **Wallaroo** Austr.
98 B3 **Wallasey** U.K.
134 C1 **Walla Walla** U.S.A.
101 D3 **Walldürn** Ger.
122 A3 **Wallekraal** S. Africa
53 C2 **Wallendbeen** Austr.
49 J5 **Wallis, Îles** *is* Wallis and Futuna Is
49 J5 **Wallis and Futuna Islands** *terr.* S. Pacific Ocean
96 □ **Walls** U.K.
98 B2 **Walney, Isle of** *i.* U.K.
99 C3 **Walsall** U.K.
136 C3 **Walsenburg** U.S.A.
101 D1 **Walsrode** Ger.
141 D2 **Walterboro** U.S.A.
120 A3 **Walvis Bay** Namibia
158 F6 **Walvis Ridge** S. Atlantic Ocean
119 C2 **Wamba** Dem. Rep. Congo
52 B1 **Wanaaring** Austr.
54 A2 **Wanaka** N.Z.
54 A2 **Wanaka, Lake** N.Z.
71 B3 **Wan'an** China
130 B3 **Wanapitei Lake** Can.
154 B3 **Wanda** Arg.
66 B1 **Wanda Shan** *mts* China
62 A1 **Wanding** China
Wandingzhen China *see* **Wanding**
54 C1 **Wanganui** N.Z.
54 B1 **Wanganui** *r.* N.Z.
53 C3 **Wangaratta** Austr.
65 B1 **Wangqing** China
62 A1 **Wan Hsa-la** Myanmar
Wankie Zimbabwe *see* **Hwange**
71 B4 **Wanning** China
100 B2 **Wanroij** Neth.
99 C4 **Wantage** U.K.
70 A2 **Wanyuan** China
70 A2 **Wanzhou** China
117 A4 **Warab** Sudan
73 B3 **Warangal** India
101 D2 **Warburg** Ger.
50 B2 **Warburton** Austr.
52 A1 **Warburton** *watercourse* Austr.
74 B2 **Wardha** India
96 C1 **Ward Hill** U.K.
128 B2 **Ware** Can.
101 F1 **Waren** Ger.
101 C2 **Warendorf** Ger.
53 D1 **Warialda** Austr.
122 A2 **Warmbad** Namibia
135 C3 **Warm Springs** U.S.A.
134 C2 **Warner Lakes** U.S.A.
134 B2 **Warner Mountains** U.S.A.
141 D2 **Warner Robins** U.S.A.
152 B1 **Warnes** Bol.
52 B3 **Warracknabeal** Austr.
53 C3 **Warrandyte** Austr.
53 C2 **Warrego** *r.* Austr.
53 C2 **Warren** Austr.
140 B2 **Warren** *AR* U.S.A.
138 C2 **Warren** *OH* U.S.A.
139 D2 **Warren** *PA* U.S.A.
97 C1 **Warrenpoint** U.K.
137 E3 **Warrensburg** U.S.A.
122 B2 **Warrenton** S. Africa
115 C4 **Warri** Nigeria
98 B3 **Warrington** U.K.
52 B3 **Warrnambool** Austr.
103 E1 **Warsaw** Pol.
138 B2 **Warsaw** U.S.A.
Warszawa Pol. *see* **Warsaw**
103 C1 **Warta** *r.* Pol.
53 D1 **Warwick** Austr.
99 C3 **Warwick** U.K.
139 E2 **Warwick** U.S.A.
134 D3 **Wasatch Range** *mts* U.S.A.
135 C3 **Wasco** U.S.A.
136 C1 **Washburn** U.S.A.
139 D3 **Washington** *DC* U.S.A.
137 F2 **Washington** *IA* U.S.A.
138 B2 **Washington** *IL* U.S.A.
138 B3 **Washington** *IN* U.S.A.
137 E3 **Washington** *MO* U.S.A.
141 E1 **Washington** *NC* U.S.A.
138 C2 **Washington** *PA* U.S.A.
135 D3 **Washington** *UT* U.S.A.
134 B1 **Washington** *state* U.S.A.
139 E2 **Washington, Mount** U.S.A.
138 C3 **Washington Court House** U.S.A.
74 A2 **Washuk** Pak.
130 C2 **Waskaganish** Can.
129 E2 **Waskaiowaka Lake** Can.
122 A2 **Wasser** Namibia
101 D2 **Wasserkuppe** *h.* Ger.
130 C3 **Waswanipi, Lac** *l.* Can.
61 D2 **Watampone** Indon.
Watenstedt-Salzgitter Ger. *see* **Salzgitter**
139 E2 **Waterbury** U.S.A.
129 D2 **Waterbury Lake** Can.
97 C2 **Waterford** Ireland
97 C2 **Waterford Harbour** Ireland
100 B2 **Waterloo** Belgium
137 E2 **Waterloo** U.S.A.
99 C4 **Waterlooville** U.K.
123 C1 **Waterpoort** S. Africa
139 D2 **Watertown** *NY* U.S.A.
137 D2 **Watertown** *SD* U.S.A.
138 B2 **Watertown** *WI* U.S.A.
97 A3 **Waterville** Ireland
139 F2 **Waterville** U.S.A.
99 C4 **Watford** U.K.
136 C1 **Watford City** U.S.A.
129 D2 **Wathaman** *r.* Can.
Watling Island *i.* Bahamas *see* **San Salvador**
143 D1 **Watonga** U.S.A.
129 D2 **Watrous** Can.
119 C2 **Watsa** Dem. Rep. Congo
138 B2 **Watseka** U.S.A.
118 C3 **Watsi Kengo** Dem. Rep. Congo
128 B1 **Watson Lake** Can.
135 B3 **Watsonville** U.S.A.
59 C3 **Watubela, Kepulauan** *is* Indon.
59 D3 **Wau** P.N.G.
117 A4 **Wau** Sudan
53 D2 **Wauchope** Austr.
138 B2 **Waukegan** U.S.A.
138 B2 **Waukesha** U.S.A.
143 D2 **Waurika** U.S.A.
138 B2 **Wausau** U.S.A.
99 D3 **Waveney** *r.* U.K.
137 E2 **Waverly** U.S.A.
130 B3 **Wawa** Can.
141 D2 **Waycross** U.S.A.
137 D2 **Wayne** U.S.A.
141 D2 **Waynesboro** *GA* U.S.A.
139 D3 **Waynesboro** *VA* U.S.A.
137 E3 **Waynesville** *MO* U.S.A.
141 D1 **Waynesville** *NC* U.S.A.
74 B1 **Wazirabad** Pak.
60 A1 **We, Pulau** *i.* Indon.
98 C2 **Wear** *r.* U.K.
143 D1 **Weatherford** *OK* U.S.A.
143 D2 **Weatherford** *TX* U.S.A.
134 B2 **Weaverville** U.S.A.
143 D3 **Webb** U.S.A.
130 B2 **Webequie** Can.
137 D1 **Webster** U.S.A.
137 E2 **Webster City** U.S.A.
55 C3 **Weddell Abyssal Plain** Southern Ocean
55 B3 **Weddell Sea** Antarctica
123 D2 **Weenen** S. Africa
100 B2 **Weert** Neth.
53 C2 **Weethalle** Austr.
53 C2 **Wee Waa** Austr.
100 C2 **Wegberg** Ger.
103 E1 **Węgorzewo** Pol.
103 E1 **Węgrów** Pol.
70 B1 **Weichang** China
101 F3 **Weiden in der Oberpfalz** Ger.
Weidongmen China *see* **Qianjin**
70 B2 **Weifang** China
70 C2 **Weihai** China
70 B2 **Wei He** *r.* China
53 C1 **Weilmoringle** Austr.
101 E2 **Weimar** Ger.
143 D3 **Weimar** U.S.A.
70 A2 **Weinan** China
71 A3 **Weining** China
51 D1 **Weipa** Austr.
53 C1 **Weir** *r.* Austr.
138 C2 **Weirton** U.S.A.
62 B1 **Weishan** China
101 E2 **Weiße Elster** *r.* Ger.
101 E2 **Weißenfels** Ger.
102 C2 **Weißkugel** *mt.* Austria/Italy
71 A3 **Weixin** China
Weizhou China *see* **Wenchuan**
103 D1 **Wejherowo** Pol.
128 C1 **Wekweêtì** Can.
138 C3 **Welch** U.S.A.
117 B3 **Weldiya** Eth.
123 C2 **Welkom** S. Africa
99 C3 **Welland** *r.* U.K.
51 C1 **Wellesley Islands** Austr.
99 C3 **Wellingborough** U.K.
53 C2 **Wellington** Austr.
54 B2 **Wellington** N.Z.
122 A3 **Wellington** S. Africa
136 B2 **Wellington** *CO* U.S.A.
137 D3 **Wellington** *KS* U.S.A.
135 D3 **Wellington** *UT* U.S.A.
153 A4 **Wellington, Isla** *i.* Chile
53 C3 **Wellington, Lake** Austr.
128 B2 **Wells** Can.
99 B4 **Wells** U.K.
134 D2 **Wells** U.S.A.
50 B2 **Wells, Lake** *imp. l.* Austr.
54 B1 **Wellsford** N.Z.
99 D3 **Wells-next-the-Sea** U.K.
142 A2 **Wellton** U.S.A.
102 C2 **Wels** Austria
99 B3 **Welshpool** U.K.
Welwitschia Namibia *see* **Khorixas**
123 C2 **Wembesi** S. Africa
130 C2 **Wemindji** Can.
134 B1 **Wenatchee** U.S.A.
71 B4 **Wenchang** China
114 B4 **Wenchi** Ghana
Wenchow China *see* **Wenzhou**
70 A2 **Wenchuan** China
70 C2 **Wendeng** China
101 E1 **Wendisch Evern** Ger.
117 B4 **Wendo** Eth.
135 D2 **Wendover** U.S.A.
71 B3 **Wengyuan** China
Wenhua China *see* **Weishan**
Wenlan China *see* **Mengzi**
Wenlin China *see* **Renshou**
71 C3 **Wenling** China
Wenquan China *see* **Yingshan**
71 A3 **Wenshan** China
52 B2 **Wentworth** Austr.
71 C3 **Wenzhou** China
123 C2 **Wepener** S. Africa
122 B2 **Werda** Botswana
101 F2 **Werdau** Ger.
101 F1 **Werder** Ger.
101 F3 **Wernberg-Köblitz** Ger.
101 E2 **Wernigerode** Ger.
101 D2 **Werra** *r.* Ger.
52 B2 **Werrimull** Austr.
53 D2 **Werris Creek** Austr.
101 D3 **Wertheim** Ger.
100 C2 **Wesel** Ger.
101 E1 **Wesendorf** Ger.
101 D1 **Weser** *r.* Ger.
101 D1 **Weser** *sea chan.* Ger.
51 C1 **Wessel, Cape** Austr.
51 C1 **Wessel Islands** Austr.
123 C2 **Wesselton** S. Africa
55 P2 **West Antarctica** *reg.* Antarctica
156 B7 **West Australian Basin** Indian Ocean
80 B2 **West Bank** *terr.* Asia
138 B2 **West Bend** U.S.A.
75 C2 **West Bengal** *state* India
99 C3 **West Bromwich** U.K.
139 E2 **Westbrook** U.S.A.
137 E2 **West Des Moines** U.S.A.
100 C2 **Westerburg** Ger.
100 C1 **Westerholt** Ger.
139 E2 **Westerly** U.S.A.
50 B2 **Western Australia** *state* Austr.
122 B3 **Western Cape** *prov.* S. Africa
116 A2 **Western Desert** Egypt
Western Dvina *r.* Europe *see* **Zapadnaya Dvina**
73 B3 **Western Ghats** *mts* India
114 A2 **Western Sahara** *terr.* Africa
Western Samoa *country* S. Pacific Ocean *see* **Samoa**
Western Sayan Mountains *reg.* Rus. Fed. *see* **Zapadnyy Sayan**
100 A2 **Westerschelde** *est.* Neth.
100 C1 **Westerstede** Ger.
101 C2 **Westerwald** *hills* Ger.
153 B5 **West Falkland** *i.* Falkland Is
138 B3 **West Frankfort** U.S.A.
100 B1 **West Frisian Islands** Neth.
96 C2 **Westhill** U.K.
55 I3 **West Ice Shelf** Antarctica
147 D2 **West Indies** *is* Caribbean Sea
100 A2 **Westkapelle** Neth.
96 A1 **West Loch Roag** *b.* U.K.
128 C2 **Westlock** Can.

100 B2 **Westmalle** Belgium
Westman Islands *is* Iceland *see* **Vestmannaeyjar**
53 C1 **Westmar** Austr.
156 C4 **West Mariana Basin** N. Pacific Ocean
140 B1 **West Memphis** U.S.A.
138 C3 **Weston** U.S.A.
99 B4 **Weston-super-Mare** U.K.
141 D3 **West Palm Beach** U.S.A.
137 E3 **West Plains** U.S.A.
137 D2 **West Point** U.S.A.
54 B2 **Westport** N.Z.
97 B2 **Westport** Ireland
129 D2 **Westray** Can.
96 C1 **Westray** *i.* U.K.
82 G2 **West Siberian Plain** *plain* Rus. Fed.
100 B1 **West-Terschelling** Neth.
136 A2 **West Thumb** U.S.A.
West Town Ireland *see* **An Baile Thiar**
135 D2 **West Valley City** U.S.A.
138 C3 **West Virginia** *state* U.S.A.
53 C2 **West Wyalong** Austr.
134 D2 **West Yellowstone** U.S.A.
59 C3 **Wetar** *i.* Indon.
128 C2 **Wetaskiwin** Can.
119 D3 **Wete** Tanz.
101 D2 **Wetzlar** Ger.
59 D3 **Wewak** P.N.G.
97 C2 **Wexford** Ireland
97 C2 **Wexford Harbour** *b.* Ireland
129 D2 **Weyakwin** Can.
129 D3 **Weyburn** Can.
101 D1 **Weyhe** Ger.
99 B4 **Weymouth** U.K.
54 C1 **Whakatane** N.Z.
129 E1 **Whale Cove** Can.
96 □ **Whalsay** *i.* U.K.
54 B1 **Whangamomona** N.Z.
54 B1 **Whangaparaoa** N.Z.
54 B1 **Whangarei** N.Z.
98 C3 **Wharfe** *r.* U.K.
143 D3 **Wharton** U.S.A.
128 C1 **Whatî** Can.
136 B2 **Wheatland** U.S.A.
138 B2 **Wheaton** U.S.A.
140 C2 **Wheeler Lake** *resr* U.S.A.
142 B1 **Wheeler Peak** *NM* U.S.A.
135 D3 **Wheeler Peak** *NV* U.S.A.
138 C2 **Wheeling** U.S.A.
98 B2 **Whernside** *h.* U.K.
128 B2 **Whistler** Can.
98 C2 **Whitby** U.K.
128 A1 **White** *r.* Can./U.S.A.
140 B2 **White** *r. AR* U.S.A.
138 B3 **White** *r. IN* U.S.A.
50 B2 **White, Lake** *imp. l.* Austr.
131 E3 **White Bay** Can.
136 C1 **White Butte** *mt.* U.S.A.
52 B2 **White Cliffs** Austr.
128 C2 **Whitecourt** Can.
134 D1 **Whitefish** U.S.A.
98 B2 **Whitehaven** U.K.
97 D1 **Whitehead** U.K.
128 A1 **Whitehorse** Can.
140 B3 **White Lake** U.S.A.
51 D4 **Whitemark** Austr.
135 C3 **White Mountain Peak** U.S.A.
116 B3 **White Nile** *r.* Sudan/Uganda
White Russia *country* Europe *see* **Belarus**
86 C2 **White Sea** Rus. Fed.
134 D1 **White Sulphur Springs** U.S.A.
141 E2 **Whiteville** U.S.A.
114 B3 **White Volta** *r.* Burkina/Ghana
136 B3 **Whitewater** U.S.A.
142 B2 **Whitewater Baldy** *mt.* U.S.A.
130 B2 **Whitewater Lake** Can.
129 D2 **Whitewood** Can.
96 B3 **Whithorn** U.K.
54 C1 **Whitianga** N.Z.
135 C3 **Whitney, Mount** U.S.A.
99 D4 **Whitstable** U.K.
51 D2 **Whitsunday Island** Austr.
53 C3 **Whittlesea** Austr.
52 A2 **Whyalla** Austr.
62 A2 **Wiang Pa Pao** Thai.
100 A2 **Wichelen** Belgium
137 D3 **Wichita** U.S.A.
143 D2 **Wichita Falls** U.S.A.
143 D2 **Wichita Mountains** U.S.A.
96 C1 **Wick** U.K.
142 A2 **Wickenburg** U.S.A.
97 C2 **Wicklow** Ireland
97 D2 **Wicklow Head** *hd* Ireland
97 C2 **Wicklow Mountains** Ireland
98 B3 **Widnes** U.K.
101 D1 **Wiehengebirge** *hills* Ger.
100 C2 **Wiehl** Ger.
103 D1 **Wieluń** Pol.
Wien Austria *see* **Vienna**
103 D2 **Wiener Neustadt** Austria
100 B1 **Wieringerwerf** Neth.
101 D2 **Wiesbaden** Ger.
100 C1 **Wiesmoor** Ger.
103 D1 **Wieżyca** *h.* Pol.
98 B3 **Wigan** U.K.
99 C3 **Wight, Isle of** *i.* U.K.
96 B3 **Wigtown** U.K.
100 B2 **Wijchen** Neth.
130 B3 **Wikwemikong** Can.
52 B2 **Wilcannia** Austr.
Wilczek Land *i.* Rus. Fed. *see* **Vil'cheka, Zemlya**
123 C3 **Wild Coast** S. Africa
101 D1 **Wildeshausen** Ger.
136 C2 **Wild Horse Hill** *mt.* U.S.A.
123 C2 **Wilge** *r.* S. Africa
48 F4 **Wilhelm, Mount** P.N.G.
101 D1 **Wilhelmshaven** Ger.
139 D2 **Wilkes-Barre** U.S.A.
55 K3 **Wilkes Land** *reg.* Antarctica
129 D2 **Wilkie** Can.
134 B1 **Willamette** *r.* U.S.A.
134 B1 **Willapa Bay** U.S.A.
142 B2 **Willcox** U.S.A.
100 B2 **Willebroek** Belgium
147 D3 **Willemstad** Neth. Antilles
52 B3 **William, Mount** Austr.
52 A1 **William Creek** Austr.
142 A1 **Williams** U.S.A.
138 C3 **Williamsburg** *KY* U.S.A.
139 D3 **Williamsburg** *VA* U.S.A.
128 B2 **Williams Lake** Can.
138 C3 **Williamson** U.S.A.
139 D2 **Williamsport** U.S.A.
141 E1 **Williamston** U.S.A.
122 B3 **Williston** S. Africa
136 C1 **Williston** U.S.A.
128 B2 **Williston Lake** Can.
135 B3 **Willits** U.S.A.
137 D1 **Willmar** U.S.A.
122 B3 **Willowmore** S. Africa
135 B3 **Willows** U.S.A.
123 C3 **Willowvale** S. Africa
50 B2 **Wills, Lake** *imp. l.* Austr.
52 A3 **Willunga** Austr.
52 A2 **Wilmington** Austr.
139 D3 **Wilmington** *DE* U.S.A.
141 E2 **Wilmington** *NC* U.S.A.
138 C3 **Wilmington** *OH* U.S.A.
141 D2 **Wilmington Island** U.S.A.
Wilno Lith. *see* **Vilnius**
101 D2 **Wilnsdorf** Ger.
101 D1 **Wilseder Berg** *h.* Ger.
141 E1 **Wilson** U.S.A.
53 C3 **Wilson's Promontory** *pen.* Austr.
100 B3 **Wiltz** Lux.
50 B2 **Wiluna** Austr.
99 D4 **Wimereux** France
123 C2 **Winburg** S. Africa
99 B4 **Wincanton** U.K.
99 C4 **Winchester** U.K.
138 C3 **Winchester** *KY* U.S.A.
139 D3 **Winchester** *VA* U.S.A.
98 B2 **Windermere** *l.* U.K.
122 A1 **Windhoek** Namibia
137 D2 **Windom** U.S.A.
51 D2 **Windorah** Austr.
136 B2 **Wind River Range** *mts* U.S.A.
53 D2 **Windsor** Austr.
130 B3 **Windsor** Can.
147 D3 **Windward Islands** Caribbean Sea
147 C3 **Windward Passage** Cuba/Haiti
137 D3 **Winfield** U.S.A.
100 A2 **Wingene** Belgium
53 D2 **Wingham** Austr.
130 B2 **Winisk** *r.* Can.
130 B2 **Winisk (abandoned)** Can.
130 B2 **Winisk Lake** Can.
63 A2 **Winkana** Myanmar
129 E3 **Winkler** Can.
114 B4 **Winneba** Ghana
138 B2 **Winnebago, Lake** U.S.A.
134 C2 **Winnemucca** U.S.A.
136 C2 **Winner** U.S.A.
140 B2 **Winnfield** U.S.A.
137 E1 **Winnibigoshish, Lake** U.S.A.
129 E3 **Winnipeg** Can.
129 E2 **Winnipeg** *r.* Can.
129 E2 **Winnipeg, Lake** Can.
129 D2 **Winnipegosis, Lake** Can.
139 E2 **Winnipesaukee, Lake** U.S.A.
140 B2 **Winnsboro** U.S.A.
137 E2 **Winona** *MN* U.S.A.
140 C2 **Winona** *MS* U.S.A.
100 C1 **Winschoten** Neth.
101 D1 **Winsen (Aller)** Ger.
101 E1 **Winsen (Luhe)** Ger.
142 A1 **Winslow** U.S.A.
141 D1 **Winston-Salem** U.S.A.
101 D2 **Winterberg** Ger.
141 D3 **Winter Haven** U.S.A.
100 C2 **Winterswijk** Neth.
105 D2 **Winterthur** Switz.
51 D2 **Winton** Austr.
54 A3 **Winton** N.Z.
52 A2 **Wirrabara** Austr.
52 A2 **Wirraminna** Austr.
99 D3 **Wisbech** U.K.
138 A2 **Wisconsin** *r.* U.S.A.
138 B2 **Wisconsin** *state* U.S.A.
138 B2 **Wisconsin Rapids** U.S.A.
Wisła *r.* Pol. *see* **Vistula**
101 E1 **Wismar** Ger.
123 C2 **Witbank** S. Africa
122 A2 **Witbooisvlei** Namibia
98 D3 **Witham** *r.* U.K.
98 D3 **Withernsea** U.K.
100 B1 **Witmarsum** Neth.
99 C4 **Witney** U.K.
123 D2 **Witrivier** S. Africa
123 C3 **Witteberg** *mts* S. Africa
101 F2 **Wittenberg, Lutherstadt** Ger.
101 E1 **Wittenberge** Ger.
101 E1 **Wittenburg** Ger.
50 A2 **Wittenoom** Austr.
101 E1 **Wittingen** Ger.
100 C3 **Wittlich** Ger.
100 C1 **Wittmund** Ger.
101 F1 **Wittstock** Ger.
122 A1 **Witvlei** Namibia
101 D2 **Witzenhausen** Ger.
103 D1 **Władysławowo** Pol.
103 D1 **Włocławek** Pol.
53 C3 **Wodonga** Austr.
59 C3 **Wokam** *i.* Indon.
62 A1 **Wokha** India
99 C4 **Woking** U.K.
101 F2 **Wolfen** Ger.
101 E1 **Wolfenbüttel** Ger.
101 D2 **Wolfhagen** Ger.
136 B1 **Wolf Point** U.S.A.
101 E1 **Wolfsburg** Ger.
100 C3 **Wolfstein** Ger.
131 D3 **Wolfville** Can.
102 C1 **Wolgast** Ger.
102 C1 **Wolin** Pol.
129 D2 **Wollaston Lake** Can.
129 D2 **Wollaston Lake** *l.* Can.
126 E2 **Wollaston Peninsula** Can.
53 D2 **Wollongong** Austr.
101 E2 **Wolmirsleben** Ger.
101 E1 **Wolmirstedt** Ger.
100 C1 **Wolvega** Neth.
99 B3 **Wolverhampton** U.K.
65 B2 **Wŏnju** S. Korea
128 B2 **Wonowon** Can.
65 B2 **Wŏnsan** N. Korea
53 C3 **Wonthaggi** Austr.
52 A2 **Woocalla** Austr.
51 C1 **Woodah, Isle** *i.* Austr.
99 D3 **Woodbridge** U.K.
134 B1 **Woodburn** U.S.A.
136 B3 **Woodland Park** U.S.A.
138 A3 **Wood River** U.S.A.
50 C2 **Woodroffe, Mount** Austr.
51 C1 **Woods, Lake** *imp. l.* Austr.
129 E3 **Woods, Lake of the** Can./U.S.A.
53 C3 **Woods Point** Austr.
131 D3 **Woodstock** *N.B.* Can.
138 C2 **Woodstock** *Ont.* Can.
54 C2 **Woodville** N.Z.
143 D1 **Woodward** U.S.A.
98 B2 **Wooler** U.K.
53 D2 **Woolgoolga** Austr.
52 A2 **Woomera** Austr.
138 C2 **Wooster** U.S.A.
122 A3 **Worcester** S. Africa
99 B3 **Worcester** U.K.
139 E2 **Worcester** U.S.A.
102 C2 **Wörgl** Austria
98 B2 **Workington** U.K.
98 C3 **Worksop** U.K.
136 B2 **Worland** U.S.A.
101 D3 **Worms** Ger.
99 A4 **Worms Head** *hd* U.K.
122 A1 **Wortel** Namibia
99 C4 **Worthing** U.K.
137 D2 **Worthington** U.S.A.
61 D2 **Wotu** Indon.
61 D2 **Wowoni** *i.* Indon.
83 N2 **Wrangel Island** Rus. Fed.
128 A2 **Wrangell** U.S.A.
96 B1 **Wrath, Cape** U.K.
136 C2 **Wray** U.S.A.
122 A2 **Wreck Point** S. Africa
Wrecsam U.K. *see* **Wrexham**
99 B3 **Wrexham** U.K.
136 B2 **Wright** U.S.A.
63 A2 **Wrightmyo** India
142 A2 **Wrightson, Mount** U.S.A.
128 B1 **Wrigley** Can.
103 D1 **Wrocław** Pol.
103 D1 **Września** Pol.
70 B2 **Wu'an** China
Wuchow China *see* **Wuzhou**
70 A2 **Wuhai** China
70 B2 **Wuhan** China
70 B2 **Wuhu** China
71 A3 **Wu Jiang** *r.* China
Wujin China *see* **Changzhou**
115 C4 **Wukari** Nigeria
75 D1 **Wuli** China
62 B1 **Wuliang Shan** *mts* China
59 C3 **Wuliaru** *i.* Indon.
118 B2 **Wum** Cameroon
71 A3 **Wumeng Shan** *mts* China
101 D1 **Wümme** *r.* Ger.
130 B2 **Wunnummin Lake** Can.
101 F2 **Wunsiedel** Ger.
101 D1 **Wunstorf** Ger.
62 A1 **Wuntho** Myanmar
100 C2 **Wuppertal** Ger.
122 A3 **Wuppertal** S. Africa
101 E2 **Wurzbach** Ger.
101 D3 **Würzburg** Ger.
101 F2 **Wurzen** Ger.
101 D2 **Wüstegarten** *h.* Ger.
59 D3 **Wuvulu Island** P.N.G.
70 A2 **Wuwei** China
70 A2 **Wuxi** *Chongqing* China
70 C2 **Wuxi** *Jiangsu* China
Wuxing China *see* **Huzhou**
71 A3 **Wuxuan** China
Wuyang China *see* **Zhenyuan**
69 E1 **Wuyiling** China
71 B3 **Wuyishan** China
71 B3 **Wuyi Shan** *mts* China
70 A1 **Wuyuan** China
71 A4 **Wuzhishan** China
70 A2 **Wuzhong** China
71 B3 **Wuzhou** China
51 D2 **Wyandra** Austr.
53 C2 **Wyangala Reservoir** Austr.
52 B3 **Wycheproof** Austr.
99 B4 **Wye** *r.* U.K.
50 B1 **Wyndham** Austr.
52 B3 **Wyndham-Werribee** Austr.
140 B1 **Wynne** U.S.A.
129 D2 **Wynyard** Can.
138 B2 **Wyoming** U.S.A.
136 B2 **Wyoming** *state* U.S.A.
53 D2 **Wyong** Austr.
103 E1 **Wyszków** Pol.
138 C3 **Wytheville** U.S.A.

X

117 D3 **Xaafuun** Somalia
62 B2 **Xaignabouli** Laos
121 C3 **Xai-Xai** Moz.
70 A1 **Xamba** China
62 B1 **Xam Nua** Laos
120 A1 **Xá-Muteba** Angola
120 A2 **Xangongo** Angola
62 A1 **Xangyi'nyilha** China
81 C2 **Xankändi** Azer.
111 B2 **Xanthi** Greece
154 B3 **Xanxerê** Brazil
150 C4 **Xapuri** Brazil
107 C2 **Xàtiva** Spain
120 B3 **Xhumo** Botswana
Xiaguan China *see* **Dali**
71 B3 **Xiamen** China
70 A2 **Xi'an** China
70 A3 **Xianfeng** China
62 A1 **Xiangcheng** China
70 B2 **Xiangfan** China
Xianghuang Qi China *see* **Xin Bulag**
Xiangjiang China *see* **Huichang**
71 B3 **Xiang Jiang** *r.* China
71 B3 **Xiangtan** China
Xiangyang China *see* **Xiangfan**
71 B3 **Xiangyin** China
70 B3 **Xianning** China
70 B2 **Xiantao** China
70 A2 **Xianyang** China
70 B2 **Xiaogan** China
69 E1 **Xiao Hinggan Ling** *mts* China
70 C2 **Xiaoshan** China
70 B2 **Xiaowutai Shan** *mt.* China
Xiayingpan China *see* **Luzhi**
Xibu China *see* **Dongshan**
71 A3 **Xichang** China
145 C2 **Xicohténcatl** Mex.
71 A3 **Xifeng** China
Xifengzhen China *see* **Qingyang**
75 C2 **Xigazê** China
71 A3 **Xilin** China
69 D2 **Xilinhot** China
68 C2 **Ximiao** China
70 B1 **Xin Bulag** China
70 B2 **Xincai** China
Xincun China *see* **Dongchuan**
Xindi China *see* **Honghu**
71 B3 **Xing'an** China
Xingba China *see* **Lhünzê**
68 C2 **Xinghai** China
70 B2 **Xinghua** China
71 B3 **Xingning** China
70 A2 **Xingping** China
70 B2 **Xingtai** China
151 D3 **Xingu** *r.* Brazil
151 D3 **Xinguara** Brazil
71 A3 **Xingyi** China
71 B3 **Xinhua** China
70 A2 **Xining** China
75 C1 **Xinjiang** *aut. reg.* China
Xinjing China *see* **Jingxi**
69 D2 **Xinkou** China
65 A1 **Xinmin** China
71 B3 **Xinning** China
71 A3 **Xinping** China
Xinshiba China *see* **Ganluo**
70 B2 **Xintai** China
Xinxian China *see* **Xinzhou**
70 B2 **Xinxiang** China
70 B2 **Xinyang** China
70 B2 **Xinyi** China
71 A4 **Xinying** China
71 B3 **Xinyu** China
77 E2 **Xinyuan** China
70 B2 **Xinzhou** China
106 B1 **Xinzo de Limia** Spain
Xiongshan China *see* **Zhenghe**
Xiongzhou China *see* **Nanxiong**
70 A2 **Xiqing Shan** *mts* China
151 E4 **Xique Xique** Brazil
70 A1 **Xishanzui** China
71 A3 **Xiushan** China
Xiushan China *see* **Tonghai**
71 B3 **Xiushui** China
71 B3 **Xiuying** China
70 B2 **Xixia** China
76 B2 **Xo'jayli** Uzbek.
70 B2 **Xuancheng** China
70 B1 **Xuanhua** China
71 A3 **Xuanwei** China
Xuanzhou China *see* **Xuancheng**
70 B2 **Xuchang** China
Xucheng China *see* **Xuwen**
117 C4 **Xuddur** Somalia

Xuefeng China see Mingxi
Xujiang China see Guangchang
71 B3 Xun Jiang r. China
71 B3 Xunwu China
107 C2 Xúquer, Riu r. Spain
71 B3 Xuwen China
71 A3 Xuyong China
70 B2 Xuzhou China
Xuzhou China see Xuzhou
111 B3 Xylokastro Greece

Y

70 A2 Ya'an China
117 B4 Yabēlo Eth.
69 D1 Yablonovyy Khrebet mts Rus. Fed.
141 D1 Yadkin r. U.S.A.
75 C2 Yadong China
70 A1 Yagan China
55 A4 Yaghan Basin S. Atlantic Ocean
89 E2 Yagnitsa Rus. Fed.
83 K2 Yagodnoye Rus. Fed.
118 B1 Yagoua Cameroon
128 C3 Yahk Can.
91 C1 Yahotyn Ukr.
144 B2 Yahualica Mex.
80 B2 Yahyalı Turkey
67 C4 Yaizu Japan
134 B1 Yakima U.S.A.
134 C1 Yakima r. U.S.A.
74 A2 Yakmach Pak.
114 B3 Yako Burkina
66 D2 Yakumo Japan
67 B4 Yaku-shima i. Japan
126 C3 Yakutat U.S.A.
128 A2 Yakutat Bay U.S.A.
83 J2 Yakutsk Rus. Fed.
91 D2 Yakymivka Ukr.
63 B3 Yala Thai.
118 C2 Yalinga C.A.R.
53 C3 Yallourn Austr.
111 C2 Yalova Turkey
90 B2 Yalpuh, Ozero l. Ukr.
91 C3 Yalta Ukr.
65 A1 Yalu Jiang r. China/N. Korea
86 F3 Yalutorovsk Rus. Fed.
67 D3 Yamagata Japan
67 B4 Yamaguchi Japan
Yamal, Poluostrov pen. Rus. Fed. see Yamal Peninsula
86 F1 Yamal Peninsula pen. Rus. Fed.
Yamankhalinka Kazakh. see Makhambet
53 D1 Yamba Austr.
150 B2 Yambi, Mesa de hills Col.
117 A4 Yambio Sudan
110 C2 Yambol Bulg.
86 G2 Yamburg Rus. Fed.
62 A1 Yamethin Myanmar
88 C2 Yamm Rus. Fed.
51 D2 Yamma Yamma, Lake imp. l. Austr.
114 B4 Yamoussoukro Côte d'Ivoire
91 C1 Yampil' Ukr.
90 B2 Yampil' Ukr.
75 C2 Yamuna r. India
62 A1 Yamzho Yumco l. China
83 K2 Yana r. Rus. Fed.
70 A2 Yan'an China
150 B4 Yanaoca Peru
78 A2 Yanbu' al Baḥr Saudi Arabia
70 C2 Yancheng China
50 A3 Yanchep Austr.
114 B3 Yanfolila Mali
118 C2 Yangambi Dem. Rep. Congo
70 B2 Yangcheng China
71 B3 Yangchun China
65 B2 Yangdok N. Korea
71 B3 Yangjiang China
Yangôn Myanmar see Rangoon
70 B2 Yangquan China
71 B3 Yangshuo China
63 B2 Yang Sin, Chư mt. Vietnam
62 B1 Yangtouyan China
70 C23 Yangtze r. China
70 C2 Yangtze, Mouth of the China
Yangtze Kiang r. China see Yangtze
70 A2 Yangxian China
70 B2 Yangzhou China
65 B1 Yanji China
137 D2 Yankton U.S.A.
83 K2 Yano-Indigirskaya Nizmennost' lowland Rus. Fed.
70 B1 Yanqing China
71 A3 Yanshan China
83 K2 Yanskiy Zaliv g. Rus. Fed.
53 C1 Yantabulla Austr.
70 C2 Yantai China
118 B2 Yaoundé Cameroon
59 D2 Yap i. Micronesia
59 D3 Yapen i. Indon.
59 D3 Yapen, Selat sea chan. Indon.
144 A2 Yaqui r. Mex.
51 D2 Yaraka Austr.
86 D3 Yaransk Rus. Fed.
48 H4 Yaren Nauru
78 B3 Yarīm Yemen
Yarkand China see Shache
Yarkant China see Shache
77 D3 Yarkant He r. China
Yarlung Zangbo r. China see Brahmaputra
131 D3 Yarmouth Can.
142 A2 Yarnell U.S.A.
86 F2 Yarongo Rus. Fed.
89 E2 Yaroslavl' Rus. Fed.
66 B2 Yaroslavskiy Rus. Fed.
53 C3 Yarra Junction Austr.
53 C3 Yarram Austr.
89 D2 Yartsevo Rus. Fed.
89 E3 Yasnogorsk Rus. Fed.
63 B2 Yasothon Thai.
53 C2 Yass Austr.
81 D2 Yāsūj Iran
111 C3 Yatağan Turkey
119 D3 Yata Plateau Kenya
129 E1 Yathkyed Lake Can.
67 B4 Yatsushiro Japan
150 C3 Yavari r. Brazil/Peru
73 B2 Yavatmal India
90 A2 Yavoriv Ukr.
67 B4 Yawatahama Japan
62 A1 Yawng-hwe Myanmar
Yaxian China see Sanya
81 D2 Yazd Iran
140 B2 Yazoo r. U.S.A.
140 B2 Yazoo City U.S.A.
111 B3 Ydra Greece
111 B3 Ydra i. Greece
63 A2 Ye Myanmar
77 D3 Yecheng China
107 C2 Yecla Spain
144 B2 Yécora Mex.
Yedintsy Moldova see Edineț
89 E3 Yefremov Rus. Fed.
91 E2 Yegorlykskaya Rus. Fed.
89 E2 Yegor'yevsk Rus. Fed.
117 B4 Yei Sudan
86 F3 Yekaterinburg Rus. Fed.
Yekaterinodar Rus. Fed. see Krasnodar
Yekaterinoslav Ukr. see Dnipropetrovs'k
Yekaterinovskaya Rus. Fed. see Krylovskaya
Yelenovskiye Kar'yery Ukr. see Dokuchayevs'k
89 E3 Yelets Rus. Fed.
89 D2 Yeligovo Rus. Fed.
114 A3 Yélimané Mali
Yelizavetgrad Ukr. see Kirovohrad
96 □ Yell i. U.K.
128 C1 Yellowknife Can.
53 C2 Yellow Mountain h. Austr.
70 B2 Yellow River r. China
69 E2 Yellow Sea N. Pacific Ocean
136 C1 Yellowstone r. U.S.A.
136 A2 Yellowstone Lake U.S.A.
88 C3 Yel'sk Belarus
78 B3 Yemen country Asia
90 B1 Yemil'chyne Ukr.
86 F2 Yemva Rus. Fed.
91 D2 Yenakiyeve Ukr.
62 A1 Yenangyaung Myanmar
62 B1 Yên Bai Vietnam
114 B4 Yendi Ghana
111 C3 Yenice Turkey
111 C3 Yenifoça Turkey
68 C1 Yenisey r. Rus. Fed.
Yeotmal India see Yavatmal
53 C2 Yeoval Austr.
99 B4 Yeovil U.K.
51 E2 Yeppoon Austr.
Yeraliyev Kazakh. see Kuryk
83 I2 Yerbogachen Rus. Fed.
81 C1 Yerevan Armenia
77 D1 Yereymentau Kazakh.
Yermentau Kazakh. see Yereymentau
143 C3 Yermo Mex.
135 C4 Yermo U.S.A.
89 D3 Yershichi Rus. Fed.
87 D3 Yershov Rus. Fed.
150 B4 Yerupaja mt. Peru
Yerushalayim Israel/West Bank see Jerusalem
65 B2 Yesan S. Korea
77 C1 Yesil' Kazakh.
111 C3 Yeşilova Turkey
83 H2 Yessey Rus. Fed.
99 A4 Yes Tor h. U.K.
53 D1 Yetman Austr.
62 A1 Ye-U Myanmar
104 B2 Yeu, Île d' i. France
87 D4 Yevlax Azer.
91 C2 Yevpatoriya Ukr.
Yexian China see Laizhou
91 D2 Yeya r. Rus. Fed.
91 D2 Yeysk Rus. Fed.
88 C2 Yezyaryshcha Belarus
Y Fenni U.K. see Abergavenny
154 A2 Ygatimí Para.
71 A3 Yibin China
70 B2 Yichang China
69 E1 Yichun Heilong. China
71 B3 Yichun Jiangxi China
Yidu China see Qingzhou
66 A1 Yilan China
110 C2 Yıldız Dağları mts Turkey
80 B2 Yıldızeli Turkey
Yilong China see Shiping
70 A2 Yinchuan China
65 B1 Yingchengzi China
71 B3 Yingde China
70 C1 Yingkou China
70 B2 Yingshan Hubei China
70 A2 Yingshan Sichuan China
71 B3 Yingtan China
Yining China see Xiushui
77 E2 Yining China
62 A1 Yinmabin Myanmar
70 A1 Yin Shan mts China
117 B4 Yirga Alem Eth.
119 D2 Yirga Ch'efē Eth.
119 D2 Yirol Sudan
Yishan China see Yizhou
70 B2 Yishui China
62 A1 Yi Tu, Nam r. Myanmar
68 C2 Yiwu China
70 C1 Yixian China
70 B2 Yixing China
71 B3 Yiyang China
71 B3 Yizhang China
71 A3 Yizhou China
Yizhou China see Yixian
92 I2 Yli-Kitka l. Fin.
92 H2 Ylitornio Fin.
92 H3 Ylivieska Fin.
93 H3 Ylöjärvi Fin.
83 K2 Ynykchanskiy Rus. Fed.
Ynys Môn i. U.K. see Anglesey
61 C2 Yogyakarta Indon.
118 B2 Yokadouma Cameroon
118 B2 Yoko Cameroon
67 C3 Yokohama Japan
66 D3 Yokote Japan
115 D4 Yola Nigeria
67 D3 Yonezawa Japan
71 B3 Yong'an China
Yongbei China see Yongsheng
71 B3 Yongchun China
70 A2 Yongdeng China
65 B2 Yŏngdŏk S. Korea
65 B2 Yŏnghŭng N. Korea
Yongjing China see Xifeng
65 B2 Yŏngju S. Korea
71 C3 Yongkang China
Yongle China see Zhen'an
62 B1 Yongren China
62 B1 Yongsheng China
71 B3 Yongzhou China
139 E2 Yonkers U.S.A.
105 C2 Yonne r. France
150 B2 Yopal Col.
50 A3 York Austr.
98 C3 York U.K.
140 C2 York AL U.S.A.
137 D2 York NE U.S.A.
139 D3 York PA U.S.A.
51 D1 York, Cape Austr.
52 A3 Yorke Peninsula Austr.
52 A3 Yorketown Austr.
98 C3 Yorkshire Wolds hills U.K.
129 D2 Yorkton Can.
87 D3 Yoshkar-Ola Rus. Fed.
97 C3 Youghal Ireland
53 C2 Young Austr.
52 A3 Younghusband Peninsula Austr.
138 C2 Youngstown U.S.A.
114 B3 Youvarou Mali
71 A3 Youyang China
77 E2 Youyi Feng mt. China/Rus. Fed.
80 B2 Yozgat Turkey
154 A2 Ypé-Jhú Para.
134 B2 Yreka U.S.A.
Yr Wyddfa mt. U.K. see Snowdon
59 D3 Ysabel Channel P.N.G.
105 C2 Yssingeaux France
93 F4 Ystad Sweden
Ysyk-Köl Kyrg. see Balykchy
77 D2 Ysyk-Köl salt l. Kyrg.
Y Trallwng U.K. see Welshpool
92 □A3 Ytri-Rangá r. Iceland
83 J2 Ytyk-Kyuyel' Rus. Fed.
71 A3 Yuanbao Shan mt. China
71 A3 Yuanjiang China
62 B1 Yuan Jiang r. China
71 B3 Yuanling China
71 A3 Yuanmou China
70 B2 Yuanping China
135 B3 Yuba City U.S.A.
66 D2 Yūbari Japan
145 C3 Yucatán pen. Mex.
146 B2 Yucatan Channel Cuba/Mex.
Yuci China see Jinzhong
50 C2 Yuendumu Austr.
71 C3 Yueqing China
71 B3 Yueyang China
86 F2 Yugorsk Rus. Fed.
71 B3 Yujiang China
83 L2 Yukagirskoye Ploskogor'ye plat. Rus. Fed.
89 E3 Yukhnov Rus. Fed.
126 B2 Yukon r. Can./U.S.A.
143 D1 Yukon U.S.A.
128 A1 Yukon admin. div. Can.
50 C2 Yulara Austr.
71 B3 Yulin Guangxi China
70 A2 Yulin Shaanxi China
62 B1 Yulong Xueshan mt. China
142 A2 Yuma AZ U.S.A.
136 C2 Yuma CO U.S.A.
135 D4 Yuma Desert U.S.A.
Yumen China see Laojunmiao
80 B2 Yunak Turkey
70 B2 Yuncheng China
71 B3 Yunfu China
71 A3 Yungui Gaoyuan plat. China
Yunjinghong China see Jinghong
Yunling China see Yunxiao
71 A3 Yunnan prov. China
52 A2 Yunta Austr.
71 B3 Yunxiao China
70 B2 Yunyang China
71 A3 Yuping China
Yuping China see Libo
82 G3 Yurga Rus. Fed.
150 B3 Yurimaguas Peru
75 C1 Yurungkax He r. China
Yuryev Estonia see Tartu
71 C3 Yü Shan mt. Taiwan
70 B2 Yushe China
68 C2 Yushu China
Yushuwan China see Huaihua
81 C1 Yusufeli Turkey
75 C1 Yutian China
71 A3 Yuxi China
89 F2 Yuzha Rus. Fed.
83 K3 Yuzhno-Sakhalinsk Rus. Fed.
91 C2 Yuzhnoukrayins'k Ukr.
70 B2 Yuzhou China
Yuzovka Ukr. see Donets'k
105 D2 Yverdon Switz.
104 C2 Yvetot France

Z

100 B1 Zaandam Neth.
69 D1 Zabaykal'sk Rus. Fed.
119 C2 Zabia Dem. Rep. Congo
78 B3 Zabīd Yemen
79 D1 Zābol Iran
79 D2 Zābolī Iran
145 D3 Zacapa Guat.
144 B3 Zacapu Mex.
144 B2 Zacatecas Mex.
145 C3 Zacatepec Mex.
145 C3 Zacatlán Mex.
111 B3 Zacharo Greece
91 D2 Zachepylivka Ukr.
144 B2 Zacoalco Mex.
145 C2 Zacualtipán Mex.
109 C2 Zadar Croatia
63 A3 Zadetkyi Kyun i. Myanmar
89 E3 Zadonsk Rus. Fed.
80 B3 Za'farānah Egypt
106 B2 Zafra Spain
Zagazig Egypt see Az Zaqāzīq
114 B1 Zagora Morocco
Zagorsk Rus. Fed. see Sergiyev Posad
109 C1 Zagreb Croatia
Zagros, Kūhhā-ye mts Iran see Zagros Mountains
81 C2 Zagros Mountains mts Iran
79 D2 Zāhedān Iran
80 B2 Zahlé Lebanon
78 B3 Ẓahrān Saudi Arabia
Zaire country Africa see Congo, Democratic Republic of the
109 D2 Zaječar Serbia
121 C3 Zaka Zimbabwe
89 F3 Zakharovo Rus. Fed.
81 C2 Zākhō Iraq
86 C2 Zakhrebetnoye Rus. Fed.
111 B3 Zakynthos Greece
111 B3 Zakynthos i. Greece
103 D2 Zalaegerszeg Hungary
110 B1 Zalău Romania
78 B2 Ẓalim Saudi Arabia
116 A3 Zalingei Sudan
90 B2 Zalishchyky Ukr.
78 A2 Ẓalmā, Jabal aẓ mt. Saudi Arabia
128 C2 Zama City Can.
Zambeze r. Moz. see Zambezi
120 C2 Zambezi r. Africa
120 B2 Zambezi Zambia
120 B2 Zambezi Escarpment Zambia/Zimbabwe
120 B2 Zambia country Africa
64 B3 Zamboanga Phil.
64 B3 Zamboanga Peninsula Phil.
103 E1 Zambrów Pol.
106 B1 Zamora Spain
144 B3 Zamora de Hidalgo Mex.
103 E1 Zamość Pol.
Zamost'ye Pol. see Zamość
75 B1 Zanda China
100 B2 Zandvliet Belgium
100 B1 Zandvoort Neth.
138 C3 Zanesville U.S.A.
77 D3 Zangguy China
75 C1 Zangsêr Kangri mt. China
81 C2 Zanjān Iran
74 B1 Zanskar Mountains India
Zante i. Greece see Zakynthos
119 D3 Zanzibar Tanz.
119 D3 Zanzibar Island Tanz.
89 E3 Zaokskiy Rus. Fed.
115 C2 Zaouatallaz Alg.
Zaouet el Kahla Alg. see Bordj Omer Driss
70 B2 Zaoyang China
83 H3 Zaozernyy Rus. Fed.
70 B2 Zaozhuang China
89 D2 Zapadnaya Dvina r. Europe
89 D2 Zapadnaya Dvina Rus. Fed.
Zapadno-Sibirskaya Ravnina plain Rus. Fed. see West Siberian Plain
68 B1 Zapadnyy Sayan reg. Rus. Fed.
143 D3 Zapata U.S.A.
92 J2 Zapolyarnyy Rus. Fed.
91 D2 Zaporizhzhya Ukr.

101 E2 **Zappendorf** Ger.
81 C1 **Zaqatala** Azer.
Zara Croatia *see* **Zadar**
80 B2 **Zara** Turkey
145 B2 **Zaragoza** Mex.
107 C1 **Zaragoza** Spain
79 C1 **Zarand** Iran
76 C3 **Zaranj** Afgh.
88 C2 **Zarasai** Lith.
89 E3 **Zaraysk** Rus. Fed.
150 C2 **Zaraza** Venez.
115 C3 **Zaria** Nigeria
90 B1 **Zarichne** Ukr.
81 D3 **Zarqān** Iran
66 B2 **Zarubino** Rus. Fed.
103 D1 **Żary** Pol.
115 D1 **Zarzis** Tunisia
88 C3 **Zaslawye** Belarus
123 C3 **Zastron** S. Africa
Zavitaya Rus. Fed. *see* **Zavitinsk**
69 E1 **Zavitinsk** Rus. Fed.
89 F2 **Zavolzhsk** Rus. Fed.
Zavolzh'ye Rus. Fed. *see* **Zavolzhsk**
103 D1 **Zawiercie** Pol.
115 E1 **Zāwiyat Masūs** Libya
77 E2 **Zaysan** Kazakh.
77 E2 **Zaysan, Lake** *l.* Kazakh.
Zaysan, Ozero *l.* Kazakh. *see* **Zaysan, Lake**
90 B2 **Zbarazh** Ukr.
90 B1 **Zdolbuniv** Ukr.
93 F4 **Zealand** *i.* Denmark
100 A2 **Zedelgem** Belgium
100 A2 **Zeebrugge** Belgium
123 C2 **Zeerust** S. Africa
101 F1 **Zehdenick** Ger.
50 C2 **Zeil, Mount** Austr.
101 F2 **Zeitz** Ger.
109 C2 **Zelena Gora** *mt.* Bos.-Herz.
87 D3 **Zelenodol'sk** Rus. Fed.
88 C1 **Zelenogorsk** Rus. Fed.
89 E2 **Zelenograd** Rus. Fed.
88 B3 **Zelenogradsk** Rus. Fed.
88 B3 **Zel'va** Belarus
119 C2 **Zémio** C.A.R.
107 D2 **Zemmora** Alg.
145 C3 **Zempoaltépetl, Nudo de** *mt.* Mex.
109 D2 **Zemun** Serbia
65 B1 **Zengfeng Shan** *mt.* China
109 C2 **Zenica** Bos.-Herz.
107 D2 **Zenzach** Alg.
101 F2 **Zerbst** Ger.
76 C4 **Zereh, Gowd-e** *depr.* Afgh.
105 D2 **Zermatt** Switz.
91 E2 **Zernograd** Rus. Fed.
Zernovoy Rus. Fed. *see* **Zernograd**
101 E2 **Zeulenroda** Ger.
101 D1 **Zeven** Ger.
100 C2 **Zevenaar** Neth.
100 B2 **Zevenbergen** Neth.
83 J3 **Zeya** Rus. Fed.
79 C2 **Zeydābād** Iran
79 C2 **Zeynālābād** Iran
83 J3 **Zeyskoye Vodokhranilishche** *resr* Rus. Fed.
103 D1 **Zgierz** Pol.
88 B3 **Zhabinka** Belarus
Zhabye Ukr. *see* **Verkhovyna**
Zhaksy Sarysu *watercourse* Kazakh. *see* **Sarysu**
76 A2 **Zhalpaktal** Kazakh.
77 C1 **Zhaltyr** Kazakh.
Zhambyl Kazakh. *see* **Taraz**
76 B2 **Zhanaozen** Kazakh.
Zhangaqazaly Kazakh. *see* **Ayteke Bi**
Zhangde China *see* **Anyang**
Zhangdian China *see* **Zibo**
66 A1 **Zhangguangcai Ling** *mts* China
71 B3 **Zhangjiajie** China
70 B1 **Zhangjiakou** China
71 B3 **Zhangping** China
71 B3 **Zhangshu** China
65 A1 **Zhangwu** China
70 A2 **Zhangxian** China
68 C2 **Zhangye** China
71 B3 **Zhangzhou** China
76 A2 **Zhanibek** Kazakh.
71 B3 **Zhanjiang** China
71 B3 **Zhao'an** China
69 E1 **Zhaodong** China
Zhaoge China *see* **Qixian**
71 B3 **Zhaoqing** China
71 A3 **Zhaotong** China
75 C1 **Zhari Namco** *salt l.* China
77 E2 **Zharkent** Kazakh.
89 D2 **Zharkovskiy** Rus. Fed.
77 E2 **Zharma** Kazakh.
90 C2 **Zhashkiv** Ukr.
Zhaxi China *see* **Weixin**
77 D2 **Zhayrem** Kazakh.
Zhdanov Ukr. *see* **Mariupol'**
71 C3 **Zhejiang** *prov.* China
82 F1 **Zhelaniya, Mys** *c.* Rus. Fed.
Zheleznodorozhnyy Rus. Fed. *see* **Yemva**
Zheleznodorozhnyy Uzbek. *see* **Qo'ng'irot**
89 E3 **Zheleznogorsk** Rus. Fed.
Zheltyye Vody Ukr. *see* **Zhovti Vody**
70 A2 **Zhen'an** China
70 A2 **Zhenba** China
71 A3 **Zheng'an** China
71 B3 **Zhenghe** China
70 B2 **Zhengzhou** China
70 B2 **Zhenjiang** China
Zhenjiang China *see* **Zhenjiang**
71 A3 **Zhenyuan** China
91 E1 **Zherdevka** Rus. Fed.
86 D2 **Zheshart** Rus. Fed.
77 C2 **Zhezkazgan** Kazakh.
77 C2 **Zhezkazgan** Kazakh.
83 J2 **Zhigansk** Rus. Fed.
70 B2 **Zhijiang** China
76 C1 **Zhitikara** Kazakh.
89 D3 **Zhizdra** Rus. Fed.
88 D3 **Zhlobin** Belarus
90 B2 **Zhmerynka** Ukr.
74 A1 **Zhob** Pak.
88 C3 **Zhodzina** Belarus
83 L1 **Zhokhova, Ostrov** *i.* Rus. Fed.
Zholkva Ukr. *see* **Zhovkva**
Zhongba China *see* **Jiangyou**
75 C2 **Zhongba** China
Zhongduo China *see* **Youyang**
Zhonghe China *see* **Xiushan**
70 A2 **Zhongning** China
Zhongping China *see* **Huize**
71 B3 **Zhongshan** China
Zhongshan China *see* **Lupanshui**
70 A2 **Zhongwei** China
Zhongxin China *see* **Xangyi'nyilha**
70 B2 **Zhoukou** China
70 C2 **Zhoushan** China
90 A1 **Zhovkva** Ukr.
91 C2 **Zhovti Vody** Ukr.
65 A2 **Zhuanghe** China
70 B2 **Zhucheng** China
89 D3 **Zhukovka** Rus. Fed.
89 E2 **Zhukovskiy** Rus. Fed.
70 B2 **Zhumadian** China
Zhuoyang China *see* **Suiping**
71 B3 **Zhuzhou** *Hunan* China
71 B3 **Zhuzhou** *Hunan* China
90 A2 **Zhydachiv** Ukr.
88 C3 **Zhytkavichy** Belarus
90 B1 **Zhytomyr** Ukr.
103 D2 **Žiar nad Hronom** Slovakia
70 B2 **Zibo** China
103 D1 **Zielona Góra** Pol.
100 A2 **Zierikzee** Neth.
62 A1 **Zigaing** Myanmar
115 E2 **Zīghan** Libya
71 A3 **Zigong** China
Zigui China *see* **Guojiaba**
114 A3 **Ziguinchor** Senegal
144 B3 **Zihuatanejo** Mex.
103 D2 **Žilina** Slovakia
115 D2 **Zillah** Libya
83 H3 **Zima** Rus. Fed.
145 C2 **Zimapán** Mex.
121 B2 **Zimbabwe** *country* Africa
114 A4 **Zimmi** Sierra Leone
110 C2 **Zimnicea** Romania
86 C2 **Zimniy Bereg** *coastal area* Rus. Fed.
115 C3 **Zinder** Niger
78 B3 **Zinjibār** Yemen
91 C1 **Zin'kiv** Ukr.
Zinoyevsk Ukr. *see* **Kirovohrad**
150 B2 **Zipaquirá** Col.
103 D2 **Zirc** Hungary
75 D2 **Ziro** India
79 C2 **Zīr Rūd** Iran
103 D2 **Zistersdorf** Austria
145 B3 **Zitácuaro** Mex.
103 C1 **Zittau** Ger.
87 E3 **Zlatoust** Rus. Fed.
103 D2 **Zlín** Czech Rep.
115 D1 **Zlīṭan** Libya
103 D1 **Złotów** Pol.
89 D3 **Zlynka** Rus. Fed.
89 E3 **Zmiyevka** Rus. Fed.
91 D2 **Zmiyiv** Ukr.
89 E3 **Znamenka** Rus. Fed.
91 E1 **Znamenka** Rus. Fed.
91 C2 **Znam"yanka** Ukr.
103 D2 **Znojmo** Czech Rep.
122 B3 **Zoar** S. Africa
70 A2 **Zoigê** China
91 D1 **Zolochiv** Ukr.
90 A2 **Zolochiv** Ukr.
91 C2 **Zolotonosha** Ukr.
89 E3 **Zolotukhino** Rus. Fed.
121 C2 **Zomba** Malawi
118 B2 **Zongo** Dem. Rep. Congo
80 B1 **Zonguldak** Turkey
105 D3 **Zonza** France
114 B3 **Zorgho** Burkina
114 B4 **Zorzor** Liberia
115 D2 **Zouar** Chad
114 A2 **Zouérat** Maur.
109 D1 **Zrenjanin** Serbia
89 D2 **Zubtsov** Rus. Fed.
105 D2 **Zug** Switz.
81 C1 **Zugdidi** Georgia
Zuider Zee *l.* Neth. *see* **IJsselmeer**
106 B2 **Zújar** *r.* Spain
100 C2 **Zülpich** Ger.
100 A2 **Zulte** Belgium
121 C2 **Zumbo** Moz.
145 C3 **Zumpango** Mex.
142 B1 **Zuni Mountains** U.S.A.
71 A3 **Zunyi** China
109 C1 **Županja** Croatia
105 D2 **Zürich** Switz.
105 D2 **Zürichsee** *l.* Switz.
100 C1 **Zutphen** Neth.
115 D1 **Zuwārah** Libya
90 C2 **Zvenyhorodka** Ukr.
121 C3 **Zvishavane** Zimbabwe
103 D2 **Zvolen** Slovakia
109 C2 **Zvornik** Bos.-Herz.
114 B4 **Zwedru** Liberia
123 C3 **Zwelitsha** S. Africa
103 D2 **Zwettl** Austria
101 F2 **Zwickau** Ger.
100 C1 **Zwolle** Neth.
83 L2 **Zyryanka** Rus. Fed.
77 E2 **Zyryanovsk** Kazakh.

Acknowledgements

pages 36–37
Land Cover map data courtesy of
Center for Remote Sensing, Boston University, USA

pages 38–39
Population map data:
Gridded Population of the World (GPW), Version 3.
Palisades, NY: CIESN, Columbia University. Available at
http://sedac.ciesin.columbia.edu/plue/gpw

pages 40–41
Telecommunications traffic data:
TeleGeography Research, Washington D.C. USA
www.telegeography.com

Cover
Laguna Superior, Mexico
Image courtesy of the
Image Science and Analysis Laboratory,
NASA Johnson Space Center
http://eol.jsc.nasa.gov

KEY TO MAP PAGES AFRICA, NORTH AMERICA, SOUTH AMERICA

(see front endpapers for Oceania, Asia and Europe)

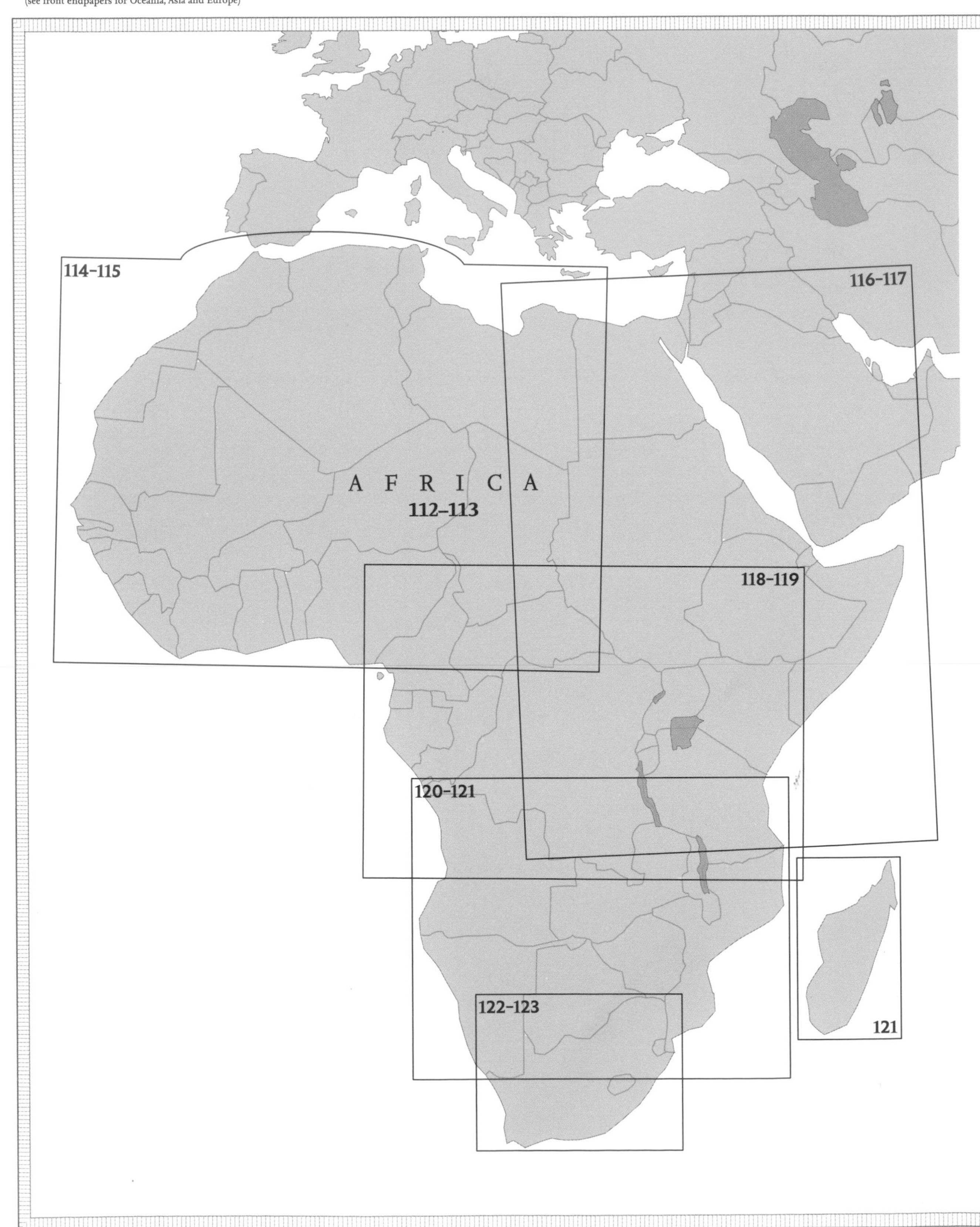